FOURTH EDITION

The Paralegal Professional

Thomas F. Goldman, JD
Professor Emeritus
Bucks County Community College

Henry R. Cheeseman, JD, LLM
Clinical Professor of Law
University of Southern California

PEARSON

Boston Columbus Indianapolis New York San Francisco Upper Saddle River
Amsterdam Cape Town Dubai London Madrid Milan Munich Paris Montreal Toronto
Delhi Mexico City Sao Paulo Sydney Hong Kong Seoul Singapore Taipei Tokyo

Editorial Director: Vernon Anthony
Acquisitions Editor: Gary Bauer
Editorial Assistant: Tanika Henderson
Director of Marketing: David Gesell
Senior Marketing Manager: Stacey Martinez
Senior Marketing Assistant: Les Roberts
Senior Managing Editor: JoEllen Gohr
Production Project Manager: Jessica H. Sykes
Senior Operations Supervisor: Pat Tonneman
Senior Art Director: Diane Ernsberger
Cover Art: Greg Kushmerek/Shutterstock.com
Editor, Digital Projects: Nichole Caldwell
Lead Media Project Manager: Karen Bretz
Full-Service Project Management: Christina Taylor/Integra Software Services
Composition: Integra Software Services
Printer/Binder: Courier/Kendallville
Cover Printer: Lehigh-Phoenix Color/Hagerstown
Text Font: 10.5/12.5, Janson Text LT Std

Library of Congress Cataloging-in-Publication Data

Goldman, Thomas F.
The paralegal professional / Thomas F. Goldman, Henry R. Cheeseman.—4th Edition.
pages cm
Includes index.
ISBN 978-0-13-295605-5
1. Legal assistants—United States—Handbooks, manuals, etc. I. Cheeseman, Henry R.
II. Title.
KF320.L4C445 2014
340.023'73—dc23

2012045167

10 9 8 7 6 5 4 3 2 1

ISBN 13: 978-0-13-295605-5
ISBN 10: 0-13-295605-5

BRIEF CONTENTS

CONTENTS

CHAPTER 6

The Court System and Alternative Dispute Resolution *194*

CHAPTER 9

CHAPTER 11

CHAPTER 12

PART IV
LEGAL SUBJECTS 471

CHAPTER 13
Torts and Product Liability 472

CHAPTER 14
Contracts and E-Commerce 514

VIDEO CASE STUDY INDEX

PART I THE PARALEGAL PROFESSION

PART II INTRODUCTION TO LAW

PART III PARALEGAL SKILLS

PART IV LEGAL SUBJECTS

FROM THE AUTHORS

Welcome to the fourth edition of *The Paralegal Professional*. In the time that has passed since the publication of the first edition, the paralegal profession has undergone a dramatic growth in its importance in the delivery of legal services. Today, the paralegal is viewed as an important member of the legal services delivery team and has the well-deserved status of a professional in the field of law. To be a member of the paralegal profession today requires developing not only conceptual knowledge, but also professional and analytical skills and a firm understanding of the ethical issues and obligations of the paralegal profession in an increasingly challenging work environment. Our goal in the fourth edition is to provide paralegal students and professionals with the foundation on which to grow and excel in this field today and in the future.

In preparing this edition, we interviewed and consulted with members of the legal profession with whom paralegals work, including hiring attorneys and human resource directors; current users of the previous editions of the text; full and adjunct instructors in paralegal studies; and numerous students across the country. Our goals are presenting a text that will enable each student to achieve his or her potential and providing a source of information for use in the workplace. The feedback of everyone we interviewed resulted in several important changes and additions to the text that help bring paralegal practice alive and illuminate the roles and tasks paralegals are asked to assume in today's legal working environment.

The fourth edition is divided into four sections that provide a logical grouping of topics and flexibility as to coverage of the most commonly practiced, substantive areas of law.

Part I: The Paralegal Profession focuses on introducing students to the paralegal profession, career opportunities, the paralegal workplace, ethics, regulation, and the use of technology on the job.
Part II: Introduction to Law provides an overview of law and the American legal system and in succession introduces students to the three areas of procedure: civil, criminal, and administrative. This treatment helps students understand, early in the course, the differences among these three legal arenas.
Part III: Paralegal Skills focuses on introducing students to interviewing, investigation, traditional and online legal research, and writing and critical thinking in the legal field.
Part IV: Legal Subjects provides an overview of the most common individual legal areas of practice. New sections in each of these chapters inform students of employment opportunities related to the field of practice.

An Essentials version of this text is also available that contains just the first three parts of this comprehensive version. It is titled ***The Paralegal Professional***: The Essentials 4th edition.

We are particularly excited about the additional Video Case Studies and exercises created as part of the **Virtual Law Office Experience** in the new **MyLegalStudiesLab** program. These Video Case Studies provide the student with a workplace context for assignments and make it easy to bring the world of the practicing paralegal into the classroom. Videos cover topics such as résumé writing and interviewing for a job, working in a law firm, the courtroom players and their roles, and paralegals performing various procedures and duties. Many of the segments present scenarios dealing with common ethical situations that paralegals will encounter on the job, making it easy to integrate ethics education throughout the course. Portfolio assignments requiring written documents are provided to allow students to demonstrate their mastery of the chapter learning objectives.

Our book has been carefully and thoroughly designed to meet the requirements set forth by the American Bar Association (ABA) and the American Association for Paralegal Education (AAFPE) regarding coverage of paralegal topics, ethical issues, professional skill development, and the other educational requirements of an introductory paralegal education course.

Thomas Goldman
Henry Cheeseman

ABOUT THE AUTHORS

Thomas F. Goldman, JD, is Professor Emeritus of Bucks County Community College, where he was a professor of Law and Management and Director of the Center for Legal Studies and the Paralegal Studies Program. He was a member of the Paralegal Studies Advisory Board and mentor at Thomas Edison State College, where he developed an Advanced Litigation Support and Technology Certificate Program in the School of Professional Studies, and implemented the online paralegal studies program for the *New York Times* knowledge network.

He is an author of textbooks in paralegal studies and technology, including *Technology in the Law Office*, *Accounting and Taxation for Paralegals*, *Civil Litigation: Process and Procedures*, *Litigation Practice: E Discovery and Technology*, *Abacus Law: A Hands-on Tutorial and Guide*, *Real Estate Fundamentals*, and *SmartDraw Tutorial and Guide.*

An accounting and economics graduate of Boston University and a graduate of Temple University School of Law, Professor Goldman has an active international law, technology law, and litigation practice. He has worked extensively with paralegals and received the award of the Legal Support Staff Guild. He was elected the Legal Secretaries Association Boss of the Year for his contribution to cooperative education of encouraging the use of paralegals and legal assistants in law offices. He also received the Bucks County Community College Alumni Association Professional Achievement Award. He has been an educational consultant on technology to educational institutions and major corporations and is a frequent speaker and lecturer on educational, legal, and technology issues.

Henry R. Cheeseman is an award-winning author of several business law textbooks published by Prentice Hall, including the definitive and highly regarded *Business Law.* Other textbooks by Professor Cheeseman published by Prentice Hall are *Contemporary Business and Online Commerce Law*, *The Legal Environment of Business and Online Commerce*, *Essentials of Business and Online Commerce*, and *Introduction to Law.* He has earned six degrees, including a Juris Doctor degree from the UCLA School of Law, an LLM degree from Boston University, and an MBA degree from the University of Chicago. Professor Cheeseman is a Clinical Professor of Law and the Director of Legal Studies at the Marshall School of Business, University of Southern California. Students there voted him the best teacher of the year on many occasions, earning him the "Golden Apple" Teacher Award. He has also served at the Center for Excellence in Teaching at the university. Professor Cheeseman recognizes the importance of the paralegal to the practice of law, and has co-authored this new and exciting edition of *The Paralegal Professional.*

BUILD A SOLID FOUNDATION FOR YOUR PARALEGAL CAREER!

Written by an award-winning team, *The Paralegal Professional* 4e builds the foundation in substantive and procedural legal knowledge and real-world skills that you will need throughout your course of study. The book emphasizes the following:

DEVELOP CRITICAL THINKING AND PROCEDURAL SKILLS!

End-of-chapter material in this edition focuses on developing critical thinking and hands-on skills including the following exercises and assignments:

- Web research exercises
- Critical thinking and writing questions
- Video Case Studies
- Ethics analysis and discussion questions
- Collaborative skill-building exercises
- Legal analysis and writing cases
- Paralegal portfolio building exercises
- Cases for briefing
- Working with the Language of the Court
- New MyLegalStudiesLab Virtual Law Office Experience assignments

LEARN ABOUT TECHNOLOGY APPLICATIONS IN THE LAW OFFICE

To be effective on the job, you will need to become comfortable using computers and common legal office software. A revised and updated Chapter 4, Technology and the Paralegal, introduces you to the types of application programs and their uses commonly found in law offices today.

UNDERSTAND HOW TO HANDLE ETHICAL SITUATIONS IN THE WORKPLACE

The Paralegal Professional 4e text and package are designed to build a strong foundational understanding of ethical principles for paralegals in the introductory course. Resources include Chapter 2, Ethics and Professional Responsibility; new Ethical Perspective boxes integrated throughout the textbook; and an expanded set of ethics-related video segments from the Paralegal Professional Classroom Video Series Segments.

NEW FOR THE FOURTH EDITION

- *The Paralegal Professional* text has been re-edited to ensure consistency in coverage, use of terminology, and improved readability.
- New *MyLegalStudiesLab Virtual Law Office Experience* assignments have been added to the end of each chapter and identify the resources available in the lab and the portfolio items students will develop as they complete Virtual Law Office assignments.
- Information on current and future opportunities in the paralegal profession, including certification requirements, has been updated in Chapter 1, The Paralegal Profession.
- Changes in the practice of e-filing and the ethical issues resulting from these changes are discussed in Chapter 2, Ethics and Professional Responsibility.
- Learning Objectives and the content in Chapter 3, The Paralegal Workplace, have been revised to improve the flow of topics.
- Technology tools and usage have been updated to reflect the most current hardware and software used in practice in Chapter 4, Technology and the Paralegal.
- The role of the paralegal in the litigation process has been revised to reflect contemporary practice in Chapter 7, Civil Litigation. Coverage of time limits and pleadings has been revised. Samples of state fact pleading and federal notice pleading complaints are now provided, along with a sample answer for the state fact pleading complaint. Each of these is tied to the end-of-chapter Video Case Studies and used as pleading in the related Virtual Law Office Experience.
- New Chapter 8 now covers criminal law and procedure in one chapter. Content from the crimes chapter, Chapter 19 in the third edition, is now combined with procedures in this chapter.
- New Chapter 9 covers administrative law
- New exhibits on fee and client engagement and non-engagement documents have been added to Chapter 11, Legal Writing and Critical Legal Thinking, and the chart comparing *ALWD* 4 and *Bluebook* 19 is updated.
- Changes in electronic legal research engines and search options are covered in Chapter 12, Legal Research.
- Case law and applications have been updated in all of the substantive law chapters.
- Content from the crimes Chapter 19 in the third edition is now combined with procedures in Chapter 8.

KEY FEATURES OF THE TEXTBOOK

PARALEGALS AT WORK CHAPTER OPENER

These opening scenarios offer a hypothetical fact situation that a professional paralegal might encounter on the job. They are designed to stimulate a student's interest in the material to be covered in the chapter.

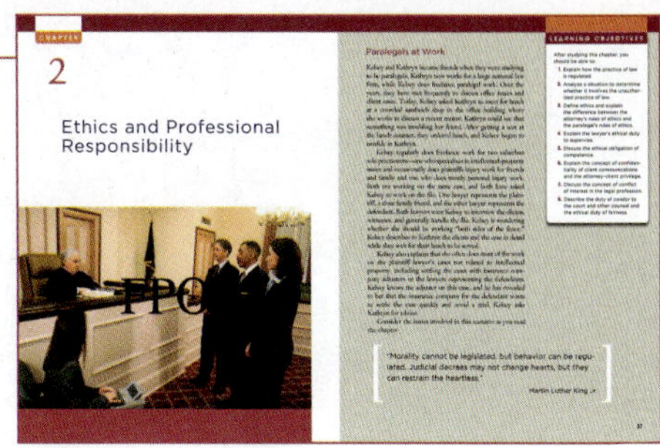

ETHICAL PERSPECTIVE BOXES

These boxes concern hypothetical fact situations and ethical dilemmas that paralegals might face in their professional careers.

ETHICAL PERSPECTIVE

Arkansas Rules of Professional Conduct

RULE 1.7. CONFLICT OF INTEREST: CURRENT CLIENTS

(a) Except as provided in paragraph (b), a lawyer shall not represent a client if the representation involves a concurrent conflict of interest. A concurrent conflict of interest exists if:

(1) the representation of one client will be directly adverse to another client; or

(2) there is a significant risk that the representation of one or more clients will be materially limited by the lawyer's responsibilities to another client, a former client or a third person or by a personal interest of the lawyer.

(b) Notwithstanding the existence of a concurrent conflict of interest under paragraph (a), a lawyer may represent a client if:

SIDEBAR BOXES

These boxes provide additional information and commentary on chapter topics.

WISCONSIN RULES OF PROFESSIONAL CONDUCT FOR ATTORNEYS

Contrast and compare the Wisconsin Rules of Professional Conduct for Attorneys at http://www.legis.wisconsin.gov/rsb/scr/5200.pdf, with the American Bar Association Model Rules of

SIDEBAR

PARALEGALS IN PRACTICE BOXES

In the fourth edition, we include profiles of paralegals practicing in a variety of practices. Their commentary provides students with insight into the world of practicing paralegals.

Paralegals *in* Practice

PARALEGAL PROFILE

Vicki Voisin

Vicki Voisin, an Advanced Certified Paralegal, is nationally recognized as an author and speaker on ethical issues related to the paralegal profession. She is the creator and presenter of EthicsBasics, a program designed to raise awareness of ethical concerns by legal professionals and corporate employees. She also publishes an e-magazine titled Strategies for Paralegals Seeking Excellence *(www.paralegalmentor.com). Vicki is a past president of the National Association of Legal Assistants (NALA), and presently serves on NALA's Advanced Certification Board. She has over 20 years of paralegal experience and is currently employed by*

The most important paralegal skills needed in the law office where I work are a familiarity with court rules and ethical issues, the ability to communicate clearly with clients, excellent organizational skills, and an attentiveness to detail and accuracy.

I also believe that technology plays an important role in the legal profession. Although technology allows attorneys and paralegals to work faster, it does not necessarily guarantee that all of the work results are accurate. Paralegals should be aware of the potential ethical hazards that technology can introduce, especially in the areas of confidentiality and conflicts of interest. For example, unless done properly, redaction (editing) on electronically filed documents can be un-covered, resulting in the disclosure of confidential and/or privileged information to third parties.

All paralegals should be aware of their ethical obligations and those of an attorney. My advice is to familiarize yourself with the American Bar Association's Model Rules of Professional Conduct, as well as its Guidelines for the Utilization of Paralegal Services. Then, become acquainted with the related Model Rules and Guidelines for your particular state, if available. Also, join professional associations to keep abreast of trends, and

ADVICE FROM THE FIELD ARTICLES

These articles feature professional advice straight from the experts on interviewing skills, developing your portfolio, professional development, handling clients, and more.

Advice *from the* Field

TECHNOLOGY IS A TOOL, NOT A CASE STRATEGY IN THE COURTROOM

Michael E. Cobo

The latest legal technology products such as animations and courtroom presentation systems can be very alluring to lawyers. After learning about these products, you may be anxious to use them. But you should keep in mind that technology products are only tools to implement a solution and are not solutions in themselves. The key issue is: What is your case strategy and what do you need to present?

An expensive, ill-planned use of technology to be larger and hold more visual or textual information. Strategically, some exhibits need to be used in conjunction with others or need to be in the view of the jury more often than not.

ASSESS YOURSELF

Before you spend a dime to develop the visual strategy, create a presentation or invest in any technol-

IN THE WORDS OF THE COURT BOXES

Excerpts from key court cases are presented to familiarize students with important legal decisions.

IN THE WORDS OF THE COURT . . .

***TRAMMELL V. UNITED STATES*, 445 U.S. 40 (1980)**

BURGER C. J.

The privileges between priest and penitent, attorney and client, and physician and patient limit protection to private communication. These privileges are rooted in the imperative need for confidence and trust. The priest-penitent privilege recognizes the

MYLEGALSTUDIESLAB VIRTUAL LAW OFFICE EXPERIENCE FOR *THE PARALEGAL PROFESSIONAL* 4E

The MyLegalStudiesLab Virtual Law Office Experience for *The Paralegal Professional* is a multimedia course program including an integrated e-book designed to provide students with the tools they need to confirm their mastery of legal concepts and applications and then apply their knowledge and skills in a workplace context. Students watch realistic video scenarios, work with case files and documents, and use the technology tools they will find in the law office to do the work paralegals are asked to do in practice. Throughout the course, students build a portfolio of work demonstrating that they have the training and experience employers are looking for.

- Students engage in a workplace experience as law office interns.

- Students see technology being used in the law office and develop an understanding of how best to deploy technology in practice.

- Students build a comprehensive portfolio of workplace products to show potential employers.

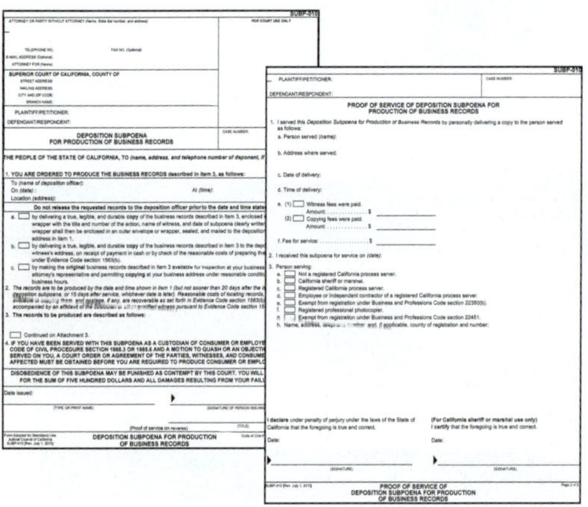

SUBP-010

ATTORNEY OR PARTY WITHOUT ATTORNEY (Name, State Bar number, and address) FOR COURT USE ONLY

TELEPHONE NO.: FAX NO. (Optional):
E-MAIL ADDRESS (Optional):
ATTORNEY FOR (Name):

SUPERIOR COURT OF CALIFORNIA, COUNTY OF
STREET ADDRESS:
MAILING ADDRESS:
CITY AND ZIP CODE:
BRANCH NAME:

PLAINTIFF/PETITIONER:
DEFENDANT/RESPONDENT:

DEPOSITION SUBPOENA
FOR PRODUCTION OF BUSINESS RECORDS — CASE NUMBER:

THE PEOPLE OF THE STATE OF CALIFORNIA, TO (name, address, and telephone number of deponent, if

1. YOU ARE ORDERED TO PRODUCE THE BUSINESS RECORDS described in item 3, as follows:
To (name of deposition officer):
On (date): At (time):
Location (address):
Do not release the requested records to the deposition officer prior to the date and time state
a. ☐ by delivering a true, legible, and durable copy of the business records described in item 3, enclosed
wrapper with the title and number of the action, name of witness, and date of subpoena clearly writte
wrapper shall then be enclosed in an outer envelope or wrapper, sealed, and mailed to the deposition
address in item 1.
b. ☐ by delivering a true, legible, and durable copy of the business records described in item 3 to the depo
witness's address, on receipt of payment in cash or by check of the reasonable costs of preparing the
under Evidence Code section 1563(b).
c. ☐ by making the original business records described in item 3 available for inspection at your business
attorney's representative and permitting copying at your business address under reasonable conditio
business hours.
2. The records are to be produced by the date and time shown in item 1 (but not sooner than 20 days after the i
deposition subpoena, or 15 days after service, whichever date is later). Reasonable costs of locating records,
accompanied by an affidavit of the custodian or other qualified witness pursuant to Evidence Code section 15
3. The records to be produced are described as follows:

☐ Continued on Attachment 3.

4. IF YOU HAVE BEEN SERVED WITH THIS SUBPOENA AS A CUSTODIAN OF CONSUMER OR EMPLOYE
CODE OF CIVIL PROCEDURE SECTION 1985.3 OR 1985.6 AND A MOTION TO QUASH OR AN OBJECTI
SERVED ON YOU, A COURT ORDER OR AGREEMENT OF THE PARTIES, WITNESSES, AND CONSUME
AFFECTED MUST BE OBTAINED BEFORE YOU ARE REQUIRED TO PRODUCE CONSUMER OR EMPLO

DISOBEDIENCE OF THIS SUBPOENA MAY BE PUNISHED AS CONTEMPT BY THIS COURT. YOU WILL
FOR THE SUM OF FIVE HUNDRED DOLLARS AND ALL DAMAGES RESULTING FROM YOUR FAIL

Date issued:
(TYPE OR PRINT NAME) (SIGNATURE OF PERSON ISSUING)
(Proof of service on reverse) (TITLE)

DEPOSITION SUBPOENA FOR PRODUCTION OF BUSINESS RECORDS

SUBP-010

PLAINTIFF/PETITIONER: CASE NUMBER:
DEFENDANT/RESPONDENT:

PROOF OF SERVICE OF DEPOSITION SUBPOENA FOR PRODUCTION OF BUSINESS RECORDS

1. I served this *Deposition Subpoena for Production of Business Records* by personally delivering a copy to the person served as follows:
a. Person served (name):
b. Address where served:
c. Date of delivery:
d. Time of delivery:
e. (1) ☐ Witness fees were paid.
Amount: . . . . $ ______
(2) ☐ Copying fees were paid.
Amount: . . . . $ ______
f. Fee for service: . . . . $ ______
2. I received this subpoena for service on (date):
3. Person serving:
a. ☐ Not a registered California process server.
b. ☐ California sheriff or marshal.
c. ☐ Registered California process server.
d. ☐ Employee or independent contractor of a registered California process server.
e. ☐ Exempt from registration under Business and Professions Code section 22350(b).
f. ☐ Registered professional photocopier.
g. ☐ Exempt from registration under Business and Professions Code section 22451.
h. Name, address, telephone number, and, if applicable, county of registration and number:

I declare under penalty of perjury under the laws of the State of California that the foregoing is true and correct.
Date:
(SIGNATURE)

(For California sheriff or marshal use only)
I certify that the foregoing is true and correct.
Date:
(SIGNATURE)

PROOF OF SERVICE OF DEPOSITION SUBPOENA FOR PRODUCTION OF BUSINESS RECORDS

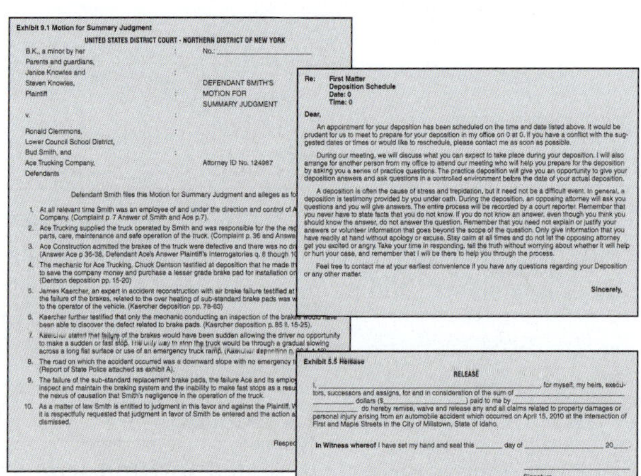

Exhibit 9.1 Motion for Summary Judgment

UNITED STATES DISTRICT COURT - NORTHERN DISTRICT OF NEW YORK

B.K., a minor by her Parents and guardians, Janice Knowles and Steven Knowles, Plaintiff : No.: ______

v. : DEFENDANT SMITH'S MOTION FOR SUMMARY JUDGMENT

Ronald Clemmons, Lower Council School District, Bud Smith, and Ace Trucking Company, Defendants : Attorney ID No. 124987

Defendant Smith files this Motion for Summary Judgment and alleges as fo

1. At all relevant time Smith was an employee of and under the direction and control of A Company. (Complaint p. 7 Answer of Smith and Ace p.7).
2. Ace Trucking supplied the truck operated by Smith and was responsible for the the re parts, care, maintenance and safe operation of the truck. (Complaint p. 36 and Answe
3. Ace Construction admitted the brakes of the truck were defective and there was no dr (Answer Ace p 36-38, Defendant Ace's Answer Plaintiff's Interrogatories q. 8 though 1
4. The mechanic for Ace Trucking, Chuck Dentson testified at deposition that he made th to save the company money and purchase a lesser grade brake pad for installation o (Dentson deposition pp. 15-20)
5. James Kaercher, an expert in accident reconstruction with air brake failure testified at the failure of the brakes, related to the over heating of sub-standard brake pads was to the operator of the vehicle. (Kaercher deposition pp. 78-83)
6. Kaercher further testified that only the mechanic conducting an inspection of the brakes would have been able to discover the defect related to brake pads. (Kaercher deposition p. 85 ll. 15-25).
7. Kaercher stated that failure of the brakes would have been sudden allowing the driver no opportunity to make a sudden or fast stop. The only way to stop the truck would be through a gradual slowing across a long flat surface or use of an emergency truck ramp.
8. The road on which the accident occurred was a downward slope with no emergency (Report of State Police attached as exhibit A).
9. The failure of the sub-standard replacement brake pads, the failure Ace and its emplo inspect and maintain the braking system and the inability to make fast stops as a resu the nexus of causation that Smith's negligence in the operation of the truck.
10. As a matter of law Smith is entitled to judgment in this favor and against the Plaintiff. It is respectfully requested that judgment in favor of Smith be entered and the action a dismissed.

Respec

Re: **First Matter**
Deposition Schedule
Date: 0
Time: 0

Dear,

An appointment for your deposition has been scheduled on the time and date listed above. It would be prudent for us to meet to prepare for your deposition in my office on 0 at 0. If you have a conflict with the suggested dates or times or would like to reschedule, please contact me as soon as possible.

During our meeting, we will discuss what you can expect to take place during your deposition. I will also arrange for another person from my office to attend our meeting who will help you prepare for the deposition by asking you a series of practice questions. The practice deposition will give you an opportunity to give your deposition answers and ask questions in a controlled environment before the date of your actual deposition.

A deposition is often the cause of stress and trepidation, but it need not be a difficult event. In general, a deposition is testimony provided by you under oath. During the deposition, an opposing attorney will ask you questions and you will give answers. The entire process will be recorded by a court reporter. Remember that you never have to state facts that you do not know. If you do not know an answer, even though you think you should know the answer, do not answer the question. Remember that you need not explain or justify your answers or volunteer information that goes beyond the scope of the question. Only give information that you have readily at hand without apology or excuse. Stay calm at all times and do not let the opposing attorney get you excited or angry. Take your time in responding, tell the truth without worrying about whether it will help or hurt your case, and remember that I will be there to help you through the process.

Feel free to contact me at your earliest convenience if you have any questions regarding your Deposition or any other matter.

Sincerely,

Exhibit 5.5 Release

RELEASE

I, ______________________, for myself, my heirs, executors, successors and assigns, for and in consideration of the sum of ______________ dollars ($______________) paid to me by ______________ do hereby remise, waive and release any and all claims related to property damages or personal injury arising from an automobile accident which occurred on April 15, 2010 at the intersection of First and Maple Streets in the City of Millstown, State of Idaho.

In Witness whereof I have set my hand and seal this ______ day of ______________ 20____.

____
Signature

- Students can test their mastery of concepts and concept applications by taking quizzes and receiving feedback and a link to e-book content.

Within the MyLegalStudiesLab, students can access a wealth of resources to complete assignments, including:

- *Ask the Law Librarian Instructional Videos* answer students' research and writing questions.

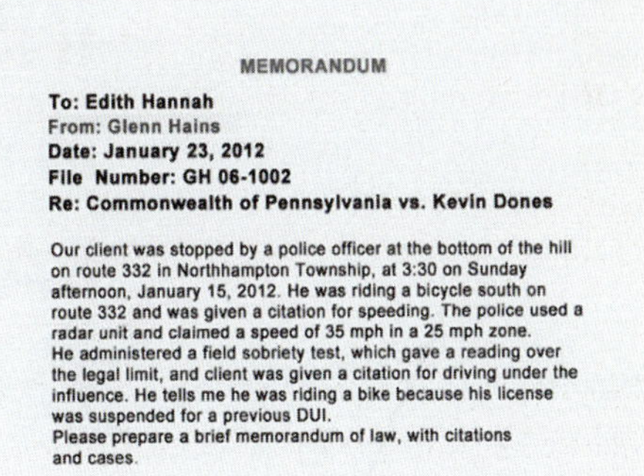

MEMORANDUM

To: Edith Hannah
From: Glenn Hains
Date: January 23, 2012
File Number: GH 06-1002
Re: Commonwealth of Pennsylvania vs. Kevin Dones

Our client was stopped by a police officer at the bottom of the hill on route 332 in Northhampton Township, at 3:30 on Sunday afternoon, January 15, 2012. He was riding a bicycle south on route 332 and was given a citation for speeding. The police used a radar unit and claimed a speed of 35 mph in a 25 mph zone. He administered a field sobriety test, which gave a reading over the legal limit, and client was given a citation for driving under the influence. He tells me he was riding a bike because his license was suspended for a previous DUI.
Please prepare a brief memorandum of law, with citations and cases.

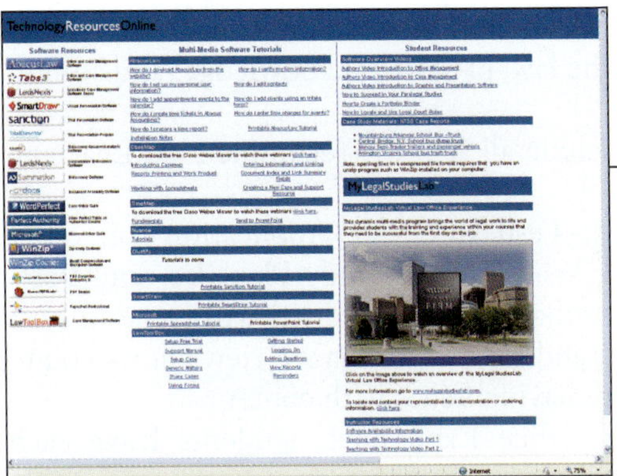

- *Ask Technical Support* links to the Technology Resources Website for technology and legal software support.
  AbacusLaw Tutorials
  LexisNexis CaseMap Tutorials
  SmartDraw Tutorials
  Sanction Tutorials
  Microsoft Office Tutorials

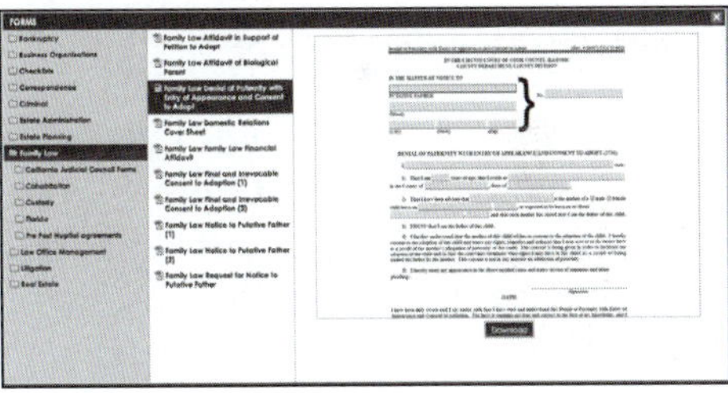

- *Forms File* contains hundreds of examples of commonly used legal documents for the major legal specialties.

- *Case Materials* contains all of the case information and documents needed to complete assignments.

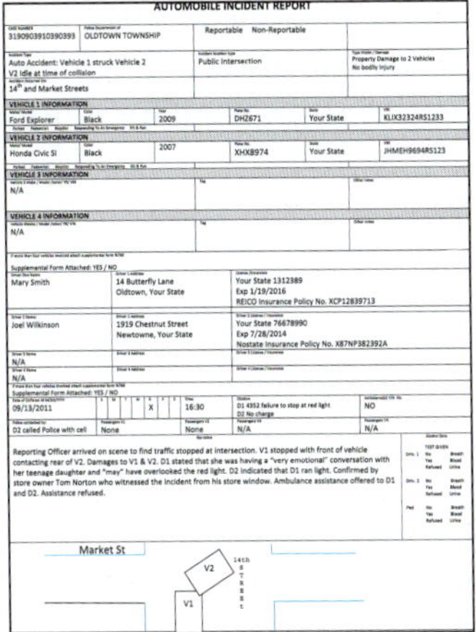

AUTOMOBILE INCIDENT REPORT

3190903910390393 | OLDTOWN TOWNSHIP | Reportable Non-Reportable
Auto Accident: Vehicle 1 struck Vehicle 2
V2 Idle at time of collision | Public Intersection | Property Damage to 2 Vehicles
No bodily injury
14th and Market Streets

VEHICLE 1 INFORMATION
Ford Explorer | Black | 2009 | DHZ671 | Your State | KLIX32324RS1233

VEHICLE 2 INFORMATION
Honda Civic SI | Black | 2007 | XHX8974 | Your State | JHMEH9694RS123

VEHICLE 3 INFORMATION
N/A

VEHICLE 4 INFORMATION
N/A

Supplemental Form Attached: YES / NO
Mary Smith | 14 Butterfly Lane
Oldtown, Your State | Your State 1312389
Exp 1/19/2016
REICO Insurance Policy No. XCP12839713
Joel Wilkinson | 1919 Chestnut Street
Newtowne, Your State | Your State 76678990
Exp 7/28/2014
Nostate Insurance Policy No. X87NP382392A
N/A
N/A
Supplemental Form Attached: YES / NO
09/13/2011 | X | 16:30 | D1 4352 failure to stop at red light
D2 No charge | NO
D2 called Police with cell | None | None | N/A | N/A

Reporting Officer arrived on scene to find traffic stopped at intersection. V1 stopped with front of vehicle contacting rear of V2. Damages to V1 & V2. D1 stated that she was having a "very emotional" conversation with her teenage daughter and "may" have overlooked the red light. D2 indicated that D1 ran light. Confirmed by store owner Tom Norton who witnessed the incident from his store window. Ambulance assistance offered to D1 and D2. Assistance refused.

Market St
14th Street
V2
V1

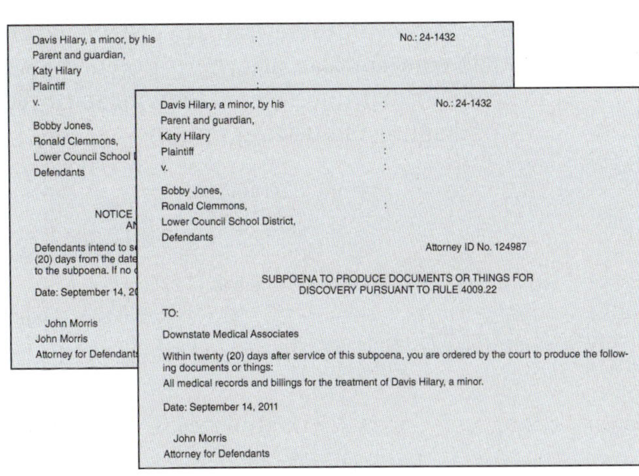

Davis Hilary, a minor, by his Parent and guardian,
Katy Hilary
Plaintiff
v.
Bobby Jones,
Ronald Clemmons,
Lower Council School District,
Defendants

No.: 24-1432

Attorney ID No. 124987

SUBPOENA TO PRODUCE DOCUMENTS OR THINGS FOR DISCOVERY PURSUANT TO RULE 4009.22

TO:

Downstate Medical Associates

Within twenty (20) days after service of this subpoena, you are ordered by the court to produce the following documents or things:

All medical records and billings for the treatment of Davis Hilary, a minor.

Date: September 14, 2011

John Morris
Attorney for Defendants

PROGRAM BENEFITS AND INSTRUCTOR RESOURCES FOR MYLEGALSTUDIESLAB VIRTUAL LAW OFFICE EXPERIENCE FOR *THE PARALEGAL PROFESSIONAL* 4E

- MyLegalStudiesLab content is book-specific, with an integrated e-book built into the program, making it a self-contained study and experiential learning environment.
- MyLegalStudiesLab makes it easy for you to confirm that students are achieving measurable outcomes for knowledge of the law, procedural knowledge, and administrative workplace skills.
- All course outcomes are assessed and include all AAFPE-recommended Learning Objectives.
- Legal Concept Study Plan Pre- and Post-Tests and Legal Application quiz questions feed into an instructor gradebook. Assigning the Study Plan Pre- and Post-Tests before class greatly increases the probability that students will come to class having read the assignment. The student and class performance view allows you to see, before class starts, where students are having issues with content.
- Upon completion of the Virtual Law Office Experience, students leave each course with a print and e-portfolio of workplace documents ready-made to present to potential employers, greatly increasing placement potential.
- For selected assignments, use of legal software is integrated into the Virtual Law Office Experience, to be assigned at the instructor's option.
- Instructor supplements, including the Instructor's Manual, PowerPoint Lecture Screens, and Test Generator, have been upgraded and include the Virtual Law Office Assignment teaching notes and rubrics.
- Once a MyLegalStudiesLab course is set up, you can copy the course and share it with other instructors and adjuncts, ensuring consistency in course coverage and course outcomes across your program.

A MyLegalStudiesLab access code, with or without the Pearson *Paralegal Professional* 4e eText, can be packaged with the print textbook at a value price.

Access to MyLegalStudiesLab can also be purchased directly online at www.mylegalstudieslab.com and can also be ordered through the bookstore in printed, standalone code format. Please contact your local representative to arrange for a preview or for packaging and pricing options.

INTEGRATE ETHICS INSTRUCTION INTO THE INTRODUCTORY COURSE!

Many paralegal programs struggle with the question of how to integrate dedicated ethics instruction into a paralegal curriculum already packed with coursework. *The Paralegal Professional* 4e text and package are designed to build a strong foundational understanding of ethical principles for paralegals in the introductory course. Resources include:

Chapter 2: Ethics and Professional Responsibility

The fundamental ethics issues and principles are presented in Chapter 2.

Ethical Perspective Boxes Integrated throughout the Textbook

These boxes present hypothetical fact situations and ethical dilemmas that highlight situations paralegals might face in their professional careers.

> **ETHICAL PERSPECTIVE**
>
> *Proposed Michigan Standards for Imposing Lawyer Sanctions [Without Commentary] (Submitted in June 2002 by the Attorney Discipline Board)*
>
> **Preface**
>
> These Michigan Standards for Imposing Lawyer Sanctions were adopted by the State of Michigan Attorney Discipline Board (ADB or Board) on [date] under the authority granted by the Michigan Supreme Court in its order dated [date], and are intended for use by the Attorney Discipline Board and its hearing panels in impos-

Paralegal Practice and Ethics-Related Video Case Study Segments

These videos are located in the MyLegalStudiesLab. Many of the segments present situations involving paralegal ethics and illustrate common UPL, Confidentiality, Conflict of Interest, Billing, and Zealous Representation issues.

Need More Coverage of Ethics in a Handy Supplemental Guide?

ETHICS FOR THE PARALEGAL PROFESSIONAL
by Deborah Orlik

If more depth in dealing with ethical issues is desired, this handy guide can be packaged with the textbook at low cost. (ISBN: 0-13-310929-1)

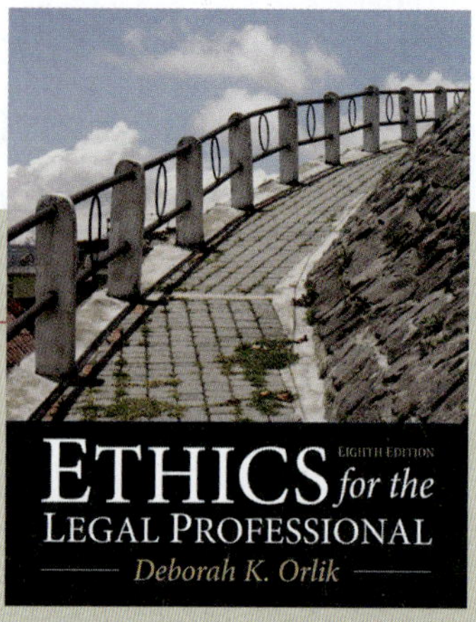

ETHICS FOR THE PARALEGAL PROFESSIONAL

by Deborah Orlik

If more depth in dealing with ethical issues is desired, this handy guide can be packaged with the textbook at low cost. (ISBN: 0-13-310929-1)

MOVIE GUIDE FOR LEGAL STUDIES

by Kent Kauffman

This supplemental movie guide to 33 of the most popular movies that deal with legal issues can be packaged with *Paralegal Professional* 4e. It includes a synopsis of each movie with notes on key scenes and discussion questions that can be assigned or discussed in class. Teaching notes are included in the 4e Instructor's Manual. (ISBN: 0-13-506375-2)

PEARSON ENGLISH/SPANISH LEGAL DICTIONARY

by Antonio Figueroa, Norma C. Connolly

2004, 464 pp., Paper; The approximately 1,200 terms presented in this book are up-to-date in their use and interpretation. They are easy to find, use, and correlate in both languages. (ISBN: 0-13-113738-7)

INSTRUCTOR'S MANUAL WITH TOOLKIT

FOR NEW INSTRUCTORS

The Instructor's Manual, Test Generator, and PPT Package can be downloaded from our Instructor's Resource Center. To access supplementary materials online, instructors need to request an instructor access code. Go to www.pearsonhighered.com/irc, where you can register for an instructor access code. Within 48 hours of registering you will receive a confirming e-mail including an instructor access code. Once you have received your code, locate your text in the online catalog and click on the Instructor Resources button on the left side of the catalog product page. Select a supplement and a log-in page will appear. Once you have logged in, you can access instructor material for all Pearson textbooks.

The Instructor's Manual has been dramatically expanded to accommodate the needs of instructors with any level of experience. Whether you are a first-time instructor or an experienced hand, this tool contains a wealth of teaching materials including the following:

- Teaching Suggestions
- Students: How the textbook and Instructor's Manual will help you
- Preparing for Class
- Your First Day of Class
- Model Course Syllabi and Outline
    - One-Semester Course
    - Two-Quarter Course
- Use of Computer Technology
- Content Comparison: Miller, *Paralegal Today* 6e

- **Each chapter includes:**
    - Teacher to Teacher Notes
    - Pre-Chapter Warm-up
    - Learning Objectives
    - Paralegals at Work
    - Chapter Outline

- **Answers to: (includes the questions and the answers)**
    - Working the Web
    - Critical Thinking and Writing Questions
    - Ethical Analysis and Discussion Questions
    - Developing Your Collaboration Skills
    - Video Case Studies
    - Paralegal Portfolio Exercises

TESTGEN TEST GENERATOR

This computerized test generation system gives you maximum flexibility in preparing tests. It can create custom tests and print scrambled versions of a test at one time, as well as build tests randomly by chapter, level of difficulty, or question type. The software also allows online testing and record-keeping and the ability to add problems to the database.

POWERPOINT LECTURE PRESENTATION PACKAGE

Lecture Presentation screens for each chapter are available.

COMPLETE INTERACTIVE ONLINE COURSES: COURSECONNECT!

COURSECONNECT INTRODUCTION TO PARALEGAL STUDIES ONLINE COURSES

CourseConnect courses contain customizable modules of content mapped to major learning outcomes. Each learning objective contains interactive tutorials, rich media, discussion questions, MP3-downloadable lectures, assessments, and interactive activities that address different learning styles. CourseConnect courses follow a consistent 21-step instructional design process, yet each course is developed individually by instructional designers and instructors who have taught the course online. Test questions, created by assessment professionals, were developed at all levels of Blooms Taxonomy. When you buy a CourseConnect course, you purchase a complete package that provides you with detailed documentation that you can use for your accreditation reviews. **CourseConnect courses can be delivered in any commercial platform such as WebCT, BlackBoard, Angel, or eCollege platforms.**

TWO CHOICES IN COURSECONNECT COURSES

Introduction to Paralegal Studies (covers the first 3 parts of the textbook)
Introduction to Paralegal Studies and the Law (covers all 4 parts of the textbook)

For more information regarding which course and platform application are right for your school, please contact your representative or call 800-635-1579.

ACKNOWLEDGMENTS

A round of applause to those whose insights contributed to the learning aspects of the fourth edition. Special thanks to:

Michael Fitch, for his guidance and encouragement early in the development of the project.

Kathryn Myers, for her generosity and kindness in allowing the use of material on portfolios and for the guidance she unknowingly gave by her example of enthusiasm, dedication, and hard work in support of paralegal education.

Lilian Harris, for her constant encouragement and help in developing materials on family law and the needs of tireless paralegal program directors and faculty to teach students the real-world approach.

Richard Opie, for sharing his ideas and materials.

Joy Smucker, for her encouragement in developing soft skills materials.

Deborah Orlik, for her help in really understanding the ethics of the paralegal profession.

Bill Mulkeen, for his encouragement and insights into the educational needs of students.

Don Swanson, an independent paralegal, for his expertise in the role of the paralegal in e-discovery and his total dedication to helping paralegal students by volunteering endless hours to help paralegal educators and authors and sharing real-life experiences and paralegal educational needs.

Members of the AAFPE board, including Pamela Bailey, Marissa Campbell, Christine Lissitzyn, Bob LeClair, Ed Husted, and Carolyn Smoot, for sharing ideas and materials and offering guidance in developing materials for this book that meet the needs of the paralegal student and faculty.

The inspiring panelists and speakers at the AAFPE annual and regional meetings over the past 14 years, for providing insights, guidance, suggestions, and encouragement.

The officers and members of the local and national professional associations, including NALA, NFPA, NALS, and ALA, for allowing the use of materials but mostly for suggesting topics and real-life issues to be covered.

Paralegal Edie Hannah of Tom Goldman's law office, for her tireless reviews, detail checking, encouragement and support, countless hours on the phone getting materials, and networking with other paralegal professionals to obtain comments and input to make this textbook relevant to working paralegals as well as to students preparing for the profession.

The students in Tom Goldman's classes, for testing the text and online materials in a class setting and graciously providing suggestions and feedback.

Vivi Wang, Tiffany Lee, and Ashley Anderson, Professor Henry Cheeseman's research assistants at the Marshall School of Business at the University of Southern California, for their excellent assistance in conducting legal and paralegal research for this book.

Much gratitude to the reviewers of the fourth edition:

Laura Alfano, Virginia College
Laura Barnard, Lakeland Community College
Carol Brady, Milwaukee Area Technical College
Kelly Collinsworth, Morehead State University

Jennifer Cote, Madonna University
Steven Dayton, Fullerton College
Warren Hodges, Forsyth Technical Community College
Dario Hunter, Mohave Community College
Joy Kastanias, Florida Atlantic University
Diana Lamphiere, Davenport College of Business
Sondi Lee, Camden County College
Carol Linker, University of Toledo
Ted Major, Shelton State Community College
Dianna Murphy, Morehead State University
Anne Oestreicher, Northeast Wisconsin Technical College
Beth Pless, Northeast Wisconsin Technical College
Christy Powers, St. Petersburg Junior College
Judi Quinby, Kennesaw State University
Anne Schacherl, Madison Area Technical College
John Whitehead, Kilgore College

AND TO REVIEWERS OF THE PAST EDITIONS

Hakim Ben Adjoua, Columbus State Community College
Mercedes P. Alonso-Knapp, Florida International University
Sue Armstrong, Central Washington University
Laura C. Barnard, Lakeland Community College
Karen Betancourt, University of Texas at Brownsville and Texas Southmost College
Carol Brady, Milwaukee Area Tech—Milwaukee
Linda Cabral Marrero, Mercy College
Chelsea Campbell, Lehman College CUNY
Anderson Castro, Florida International University
Mark A. Ciccarelli, Kent State University, OH
Belinda Clifton, IIA College
Karen Cook, Anne Arundel Community College
Subrina Cooper, University of Southern Mississippi
Jennifer Cote, Madonna University
Brian Craig, Minnesota School of Business—Richfield
Ernest Davila, San Jacinto College North, Texas
Steven A. Dayton, Fullerton College
Stephanie Delaney, Highline Community College
Robert Donley, Central Pennsylvania College
Tara L. Duncan, Everest College, Phoenix, AZ
Jameka Ellison, Florida Metro University—Lakeland
Linda Gassaway, McLennan Community College
Katherine Greenwood, Loyola University
Louise B. Gussin, University of Maryland University College
Laura J. Hansen-Brown, Kaplan University, Florida
P. Darrel Harrison, Miramar College, San Diego, CA
Linda Hornsby, Florida International University
Dee Janssen Lammers, Pima Community College, Tucson, AZ
Jennifer Jenkins, South College—Knoxville
Alan Katz, Cape Fear Community College
Pierre A. Kleff, Jr., The University of Texas at Brownsville
Nance Kriscenski, Manchester Community College
Elaine Lerner, Kaplan College—Online
Victoria H. Lopez, Southwestern College, California

Margaret Lovig, Coastline Community College, California
Robert McDonald, Franciscan University
Alan Mege, LeHigh Valley College
Hillary Michaud, Stevenson University
Sharla Miller-Fowler, Amarillo College
Leslie Miron, Mercy College
R. Eileen Mitchell, University of New Orleans
Anne Murphy Brown, J.D., Ursuline College
Kathryn L. Myers, Saint Mary-of-the-Woods College
Lisa Newman, Brown Mackie College—Atlanta
Mary People, Arapahoe Community College, Colorado
Deborah Periman, University of Alaska—Anchorage
Anthony Piazza, Dan N. Myers University
Beth Pless, Northeast Wisconsin Technical College
Pat Roberson, New Mexico Junior College
Robin Rossenfeld, Community College of Aurora, Colorado
Wesley K. Sasano, Everest College—Rancho Cucamonga, California
Labron Shuman, Delaware County Community College
Kathy Smith, Community College of Philadelphia
Deborah Vinecour, SUNY Rockland Community College
Alex A. Yarborough, Virginia College at Birmingham

Thomas F. Goldman
Henry R. Cheeseman

PART

I

The Paralegal Profession

Since the late 1960s, the importance of the paralegal profession has grown significantly in importance in the legal community. It has evolved into a profession that demands strong professional skills, a firm foundation in ethics, and increasingly higher levels of knowledge, especially of technology. Career opportunities and career choices for the paralegal have never been better. Potential employers are as diverse as the duties paralegals are asked to perform. Today's paralegals need specialized skills in many areas. Formal programs of study and continuing education programs have developed to help individuals obtain the necessary skills. As with other professions, ethical rules and regulations have evolved to help paralegals avoid conflicts and possible malpractice. These topics will be discussed in Part I.

CHAPTER

1

The Paralegal Profession

Paralegals at Work

On the Friday before Thanksgiving, Ariel sits in the bleachers watching her high school alma mater, Lincoln High, take on Council Rock High. Ariel's brother, Ethan, is a senior on the football team, and this is his last high school football game.

Ariel graduated from Lincoln in 2010 and went on to get her bachelor's degree with a major in English and a minor in Languages. She spots Mr. Marshall, her high school guidance counselor, and goes over to greet him.

After briefly catching up, Ariel asks Mr. Marshall about the career advice he's given to her brother. Ethan is thinking about a legal career but isn't interested in criminal justice or law enforcement. He's also not sure about the time and dedication it takes to get through law school. Mr. Marshall tells her that he gave Ethan information on local paralegal programs.

Ariel has been working as an editorial assistant for a small publisher of medical books. Although she always has plenty of work to do, she's not challenged in her job. She wants to use the language and writing skills she's developed, as well as have more autonomy and control over her work. Ariel asks Mr. Marshall whether a paralegal career makes sense for her.

Consider these issues as you read the chapter.

LEARNING OBJECTIVES

After studying this chapter, you should be able to:

1. Describe the role of the paralegal in the delivery of legal services.
2. Explain the importance of professional skills in career advancement.
3. Explain why education and training are necessary to be recognized as a member of the paralegal profession.
4. Describe the different approaches to the certification and regulation of the paralegal profession.
5. Discuss the job opportunities for the paralegal.

> "The great can protect themselves, but the poor and humble require the arm and shield of the law."
>
> *Andrew Jackson*

Learning Objective 1
Describe the role of the paralegal in the delivery of legal services.

INTRODUCTION TO THE PARALEGAL PROFESSION

Prior to the late 1960s, many of the functions of today's paralegals were performed by legal staff members with titles such as "legal secretary" and "lay assistant." Much of the work was also performed by law clerks—recent law school graduates who had not yet passed the bar exam. Now, members of the legal community are accustomed to working with paralegals as members of the legal team. As the educational level of paralegals increases, so will the responsibility given to them. In many areas of law, the cost of legal services has increased, and the use of paralegals in many cases permits the delivery of quality legal services at a reduced cost to the client.

Career opportunities for the paralegal have never been better. Paralegals are employed in every area of legal services. They interview clients, conduct factual investigations, do legal research, prepare legal documents, assist at the counsel table in trials, and even represent clients in some administrative hearings. As the use of computer technology has become more commonplace in law offices and courts, paralegals with the necessary skills and training are being used in litigation support and handling electronic discovery issues. They are employed in government, corporations, and law firms of all sizes.

What Is a Paralegal?

Paralegal (legal assistant) A person qualified by education, training, or work experience who is employed or retained by a lawyer, law office, corporation, governmental agency or other entity and who performs specifically delegated substantive legal work for which a lawyer is responsible; the equivalent term is *legal assistant*.

American Bar Association (ABA) The largest professional legal organization in the United States.

National Federation of Paralegal Associations (NFPA) A professional organization of state and local paralegal associations, founded in 1974.

National Association of Legal Assistants (NALA) A professional organization for legal assistants that provides continuing education and professional certification for paralegals, incorporated in 1975.

A great deal of confusion has arisen as to what the professional in this field should be called or what the professionals should call themselves. The terms **paralegal** and **legal assistant** have been used most frequently in the United States. They are used interchangeably by the **American Bar Association (ABA)**, the **National Federation of Paralegal Associations (NFPA)**, and the **National Association of Legal Assistants (NALA)**. The confusion stems in part from the shift away from the titles of "secretary" or "administrative assistant" or, in some organizations, "law office assistant."

The exact definition of *legal assistant* has been the subject of discussions by national organizations including the ABA, NFPA, and NALA, as well as many state legislatures, supreme courts, and bar associations. The trend is toward the use of the term *paralegal* and away from the term *legal assistant*. In recognition of this trend, the American Bar Association changed the name of its Standing Committee on Legal Assistants to the Standing Committee on Paralegals.

The American Bar Association's 1997 definition of a paralegal or legal assistant, which also has been adopted by the National Association of Legal Assistants, is:

> A legal assistant or paralegal is a person qualified by education, training, or work experience who is employed or retained by a lawyer, law office, corporation, governmental agency or other entity and who performs specifically delegated substantive legal work for which a lawyer is responsible.

The National Federation of Paralegal Associations adopted a resolution in 2002 eliminating the term *legal assistant* from its definition of *paralegal* because that term now is being used to refer to positions outside the paralegal profession. Accordingly, the NFPA defines a paralegal as:

> A paralegal is a person qualified through education, training or work experience to perform substantive legal work that requires knowledge of legal concepts as customarily, but not exclusively performed by a lawyer. This person may be retained or employed by a lawyer, law office, governmental agency or other entity or may be authorized by administrative, statutory or court authority to perform this work.

Web Exploration
Check the current definition approved by the American Bar Association at **www.abanet.org**.

Web Exploration
Review the full NFPA resolution at **www.paralegals.org**.

What Do Paralegals Do?

The primary function of paralegals is to assist attorneys in preparing for hearings, trials, meetings, and real estate closings. In many cases, paralegals do the preparatory work, assisting in the creation of documents and forms, coordinating

Paralegals *in* Practice

PARALEGAL PROFILE

Vicki L. Karayan

During her 12-year paralegal career, Vicki L. Karayan has worked for both law firms and business corporations. She is currently employed at WellPoint, Inc., in Camarillo, California, the nation's second largest company in the healthcare industry. As an Advanced Certified Paralegal, her present position of Business Change Advisor focuses on compliance reporting and legal research for the company's consumer marketing department.

I became inspired to pursue a paralegal career after going through a difficult, personal legal battle. After graduating with an associate's degree in Applied Science with a Legal Studies emphasis, I worked in a general practice firm. Later, I worked for a bankruptcy law firm where I eventually became the trainer/staff manager of seven offices. A family move led to a new job in a nationwide bankruptcy firm where I learned to track federal and state regulatory requirements.

In order to work closer to home, I took an Administrative Assistant position in the Medicaid Marketing department for a corporate healthcare company. What started as an entry level job grew into a whole new position, as I offered better ways to tackle the company's market compliance reporting and legal research, and also helped improve office efficiency and staff training. Three promotions later, I believe I owe much of my career success to actively looking for opportunities to apply knowledge and skills learned from previous jobs and experiences, and from learning how to network with people, building strong working relationships based on ethical practices.

My advice is: try not to limit yourself to traditional paralegal job descriptions. Some of the best opportunities are found by looking "outside the box" and obtaining as many business and technology skills as possible. Finally, find what you love to do, and then network by making new business connections through individuals you already know and others you meet. These contacts can help your work go more smoothly and provide invaluable information in the future.

procedures and other activities, and in many offices maintaining the financial records of the firm.

People tend to think of paralegals as working in private law offices directly under the supervision of attorneys. Actually, employers of paralegals are just as diverse as the duties paralegals are asked to perform. Many paralegals are employed by the state, federal, and local government, including their regulatory bodies. The paralegal's activities might include analyzing legal material for internal use, collecting and analyzing data, as well as preparing information and explanatory material for use by the general public.

More and more paralegals are coming to the paralegal profession from other professions. For example, they may come from nursing, bringing with them specialized knowledge that they can combine with the legal skills learned in a paralegal program. Their knowledge of medicine, combined with their legal knowledge, gives them a unique ability to analyze specialized material. For example, they are frequently hired to analyze medical materials for trial attorneys, both plaintiff and defense, or are employed as case analysts and claims representatives for health insurance companies. Those with other specialties can take a similar path. For example, those with engineering and other science degrees can find jobs in specialized areas of the law, such as patents and intellectual property. A paralegal with a criminal justice or a forensic science background, for example, may be uniquely qualified to work with criminal defense attorneys and prosecutors.

Prior to the recognition of paralegals as a separate profession, individuals typically acquired specialized knowledge of a narrow legal field through on-the-job training. Someone working with a lawyer—usually a secretary—learned the daily routine tasks and became knowledgeable about that lawyer's specific area of law. Many of these individuals became important sources of information, such as what documents are required for a real estate closing, the steps in preparing and filing estate and trust accountings, or the procedures in preparing and filing pleadings. These were the first

Web Exploration

Review the Model Standards and Guidelines of the National Association of Legal Assistants at **http://www.nala.org/model.aspx**.

Advice *from the* Field

PEOPLE SKILLS CRITICAL TO PROFESSIONAL SUCCESS

Kathleen Call, Executive Director, Robert Half Legal

Kathleen Call is executive director of Robert Half Legal, a leading staffing service specializing in the placement of legal professionals, ranging from project attorneys and paralegals to administrators, legal secretaries, and other support staff. Robert Half Legal, which works with law firms and corporate legal departments, has offices throughout the United States and Canada.

When you think of which skills will be most important to your career advancement over the next five years, chances are "proficiency with technology" ranks high on your list. Knowledge of key software applications has become a critical success factor in the legal profession. However, to be considered for the best job opportunities in the future, you'll not only need technical competency, but also solid interpersonal skills and problem-solving abilities.

Audio- and video-conferencing, email, corporate Intranets and, of course, the Internet have increased exponentially the amount—and speed—of day-to-day professional communication. The expanded use of technology will make it more important for legal professionals to be able to communicate effectively and articulately.

Another significant development driving the need for strong soft skills is the trend toward a more collaborative workplace. In a team-based office environment, diplomacy, flexibility, persuasiveness and management skills are critical. In a survey we commissioned among executives at the nation's 1,000 largest companies, 79 percent of respondents said self-managed employee work teams will increase productivity for U.S. companies. These productivity gains will only be realized, however, if team members can work together effectively. As a result, firms are placing a premium on excellent interpersonal skills.

WHAT ARE PEOPLE SKILLS?

Since soft skills are intangible and therefore hard to quantify, how do you determine whether you have what it takes to succeed? Our firm has identified a composite of key interpersonal traits represented by the acronym "PEOPLE":

Problem-solving abilities (organization, judgment, logic, creativity, conflict resolution)

Ethics (diplomacy, courtesy, honesty, professionalism)

Open-mindedness (flexibility, open to new business ideas, positive outlook)

Persuasiveness (excellent communication and listening skills)

Leadership (accountability, management and motivational skills)

Educational interests (continuous thirst for knowledge and skills development)

A deficiency in these skills can seriously limit your career prospects, whether you're applying for a new job as a legal assistant or seeking to move upward as an attorney within your current firm. Just as workers who failed to enhance their technical skills were left behind by the digital revolution, those who dismiss the significance of PEOPLE skills can find themselves stagnating in dead-end jobs.

ASSESS YOUR STRENGTHS AND WEAKNESSES

While it's relatively easy to measure the development of your proficiency with technology, it's much more challenging to gauge your progress in enhancing your PEOPLE skills. Again, this is primarily because these qualities are more subjective in nature. Since there are no classes on "flexibility" or "positive outlook" at the typical college or university, how do you acquire and upgrade your interpersonal abilities?

The following steps will help you take an accurate inventory of your strengths and weaknesses:

Honestly evaluate your aptitude in each of the PEOPLE skills. Which seem to come naturally? Is there room for improvement in any area?

Ask trusted friends, family members and coworkers for their opinions. How would they rate your PEOPLE skills?

COMMIT TO LEARNING

It takes time and experience to fully develop interpersonal skills, so don't expect to see improvement overnight. Here are some effective strategies to help you continue your progress:

Develop a list of the characteristics you'd most like to develop in yourself. Then brainstorm specific activities that will boost your abilities in your selected areas. For example, if you'd like to refine your leadership skills, volunteer to work on cases that provide the opportunity to supervise others or manage a project from start to finish.

Observe those who demonstrate strong PEOPLE skills in the areas you'd like to improve. How do they apply their abilities in various situations? How are their responses different than what yours would be?

Select a mentor. The best candidate is someone in the legal field whom you admire. Ask your prospective mentor if he or she would advise you, particularly in those PEOPLE skills that you've determined require enhancement. Since it's difficult to see yourself objectively, a mentor's ongoing support and feedback can be invaluable.

Enhance your listening skills. Concentrate on paying close attention to what others are saying. In general, avoid interrupting but ask for clarification when necessary. To prevent misunderstandings, paraphrase information in your own words when you are given complex instructions.

Become a better writer. Read books on effective writing so that you can develop a more concise style, or consider taking a journalism or business writing course. Proofread everything you write, especially e-mail. Because electronic messages are prepared and sent quickly, they can be inadvertently filled with typographical and grammatical errors. In addition, it's important to employ PEOPLE skills in your writing, explaining yourself diplomatically and courteously.

Refine your verbal communication. Know what you want to say before you speak, and use a tone and style appropriate to the audience. When leaving a voice-mail message, organize your thoughts in advance to avoid being vague or rambling. If you're presenting a report to an attorney or client, rehearse a few times so your delivery will be smooth and your message clear.

Become a volunteer. You can acquire stronger leadership and organizational skills through volunteer work. Whether it's becoming involved in a trade association or helping your favorite charity, the skills you develop can be used on the job in a variety of situations.

Seek growth opportunities outside the workplace. Hobbies and leisure-time activities are an enjoyable way to enrich your PEOPLE skills. By coaching your child's soccer team, for example, you'll develop motivational and managerial skills, and become better at dealing with diverse personalities. If you'd like to enhance your creativity, consider taking an art or music class.

paralegals. Today, many of the skills and procedures formerly acquired on the job are taught at institutions specializing in the education of paralegals or legal assistants. These programs may offer a certificate, a two-year associate degree, or a four-year bachelor's degree.

In 1968, the American Bar Association (ABA) formed the Standing Committee on Legal Assistants (later changed to the Standing Committee on Paralegals). The purpose of this committee was originally to investigate the use of lay assistants in the law office. The ABA gave this committee jurisdiction over standards for the education and training of legal assistants. The committee monitors trends in the field and recommends to the House of Delegates (the policymaking body of the ABA) training programs that meet its standards for quality education.

Professional Skills

The skills needed by a paralegal are varied and often depend on the nature of the legal specialty in which one works. Common to all paralegals are certain skills (also known as "soft skills") such as communication, initiative, resourcefulness, problem solving, perseverance, teamwork, leadership, and self-motivation.

Everyone has goals in life. An experienced runner may strive to finish a marathon, or a skilled writer may have a vision of writing a great novel. Achieving a specific goal requires a certain set of skills. If the goal is to be a successful paralegal, certain basic skills are needed. You may already have some of the necessary basic skills, such as

- the ability to read English (unless someone is reading this book to you);
- the ability to communicate at some level in writing or speaking; and
- initiative (you demonstrated this by signing up for this course or picking up this book to learn about the paralegal profession).

In addition, you may have other basic skills, such as

- facility with computers and the Internet;
- the ability to speak a second or third language; and
- a background in medicine, engineering, business, or some other academic or occupational area.

Some other skills are less obvious, such as resourcefulness, perseverance, analytical skills, and interpersonal skills, including cultural sensitivity. These will be explored in greater depth as they are applied to the paralegal profession. We cannot all run a marathon or write a novel, but we all can acquire most of the basic skills by making an effort to improve ourselves and attain the knowledge base to achieve most, if not all, of our goals.

Through hard work and commitment, many people achieve much more than they believed they were capable of. If one is willing to work hard enough, most personal and professional goals can be attained. A good starting point in achieving goals is to understand one's strengths and weaknesses, capitalize on strengths, and work on overcoming weaknesses.

NATIONAL ASSOCIATION OF LEGAL ASSISTANTS MODEL STANDARDS AND GUIDELINES FOR UTILIZATION OF LEGAL ASSISTANTS-PARALEGALS

Preamble

Proper utilization of the services of legal assistants contributes to the delivery of cost effective, high-quality legal services. Legal assistants and the legal profession should be assured that measures exist for identifying legal assistants and their role in assisting attorneys in the delivery of legal services. Therefore, the National Association of Legal Assistants, Inc., hereby adopts these Standards and Guidelines as an educational document for the benefit of legal assistants and the legal profession....

III Standards

A legal assistant should meet certain minimum qualifications. The following standards may be used to determine an individual's qualifications as a legal assistant:

(1) Successful completion of the Certified Legal Assistant (CLA)/Certified Paralegal (CP) certifying examination of the National Association of Legal Assistants, Inc.;

(2) Graduation from an ABA approved program of study for legal assistants;

(3) Graduation from a course of study for legal assistants which is institutionally accredited but not ABA approved, and which requires not less than the equivalent of 60 semester hours of classroom study;

(4) Graduation from a course of study for legal assistants, other than those set forth in (2) and (3) above, plus not less than six months of in-house training as a legal assistant;

(5) A baccalaureate degree in any field, plus not less than six months in-house training as a legal assistant;

(6) A minimum of three years of law-related experience under the supervision of an attorney, including at least six months of in-house training as a legal assistant; or

(7) Two years of in-house training as a legal assistant.

For purposes of these Standards, "in-house training as a legal assistant" means attorney education of the employee concerning legal assistant duties and these Guidelines. In addition to review and analysis of assignments, the legal assistant should receive a reasonable amount of instruction directly related to the duties and obligations of the legal assistant.

Source: Copyright 2007; Adopted 1984; Revised 1994, 1997, 2005. NALA, Inc. Reprinted with permission of the National Association of Legal Assistants, www.nala.org, 1516 S. Boston, #200, Tulsa, OK 74119.

CHECKLIST Strengths and Weaknesses

My strengths:

- ☐ How can I capitalize on my strengths?

My weaknesses:

- ☐ How can I overcome my weaknesses?

Resourcefulness

Resourcefulness is the ability to meet and handle situations by finding solutions to problems. It is one of the most valuable skills anyone can have—and one that is not easily taught. A resourceful person in the office is sometimes referred to as the "can-do" person. This is the person who usually finds a creative way to accomplish something everyone else has given up on. Creativity is used to solve the problem by "thinking outside the box" and not limiting the solution to tried-and-true methods. When everyone else says, "I can't find this witness," the resourceful person tries a new approach and finds the witness. When others use only an Internet search engine, the resourceful person uses social media websites to locate the witness.

In the legal workplace, the person who gets noticed is the one who finds a way to get the job done in time for the hearing, meeting, or arbitration. He or she is willing to use unconventional ways to get the job finished when the power goes out or the computer crashes just before a deadline. Lawyers need resourceful people and reward them to keep them on the team.

Commitment

Commitment means finishing what one starts. In the old story of the tortoise (turtle) and the hare (rabbit), the tortoise wins the race by being "slow and steady." He wins because of his commitment—putting everything into the race and not stopping until the job is done. Many people start jobs and don't finish them. Others start what seems to be an insurmountable task and—to everyone's amazement—finish, and finish well. Taking on an assignment in a law office requires commitment. Team members are expected to finish the task, whether it is researching a case, writing a brief, filing a pleading, or organizing a file.

As a professional, you are expected to finish tasks within the assigned time frame. There is no excuse for not completing certain tasks, such as filing a complaint with the court before the **statute of limitations** expires, or getting the brief to the court by the court-imposed deadline. Even a simple thing like getting to court on time requires commitment.

Not everyone has the commitment necessary to be an effective professional. You have to decide whether you are willing to make the commitment. Others will be depending on you, and if you do not want to commit, admit it to yourself and to the others who are depending on you, and then choose some other activity or profession. Choosing a profession, whether it is the legal profession, the paralegal profession, the medical profession, or the accounting profession, requires a commitment to serve others. As a paralegal professional, you are making a commitment to your clients that you will provide the best professional advice, skill, and effort, and they will depend on your professionalism.

Analytical Skills

Analytical skills involve using a step-by-step process to solve a problem. For example, analytical skills may be used to find a missing witness by analyzing the person's background. The analysis may reveal that the person is part of a group, such as a professional society, that publishes a membership directory. Or, analytical skills may be used to find out what made a bottle explode, injuring a client. Determining the actual cause requires a step-by-step analysis of the potential reasons, and then narrowing down the possible causes.

One of the basic skills that both law students and paralegal students are taught is legal analysis, or the ability to identify the key facts and legal issues of a case and compare and contrast them to the law and to other cases. This is a skill that develops with time. As you study the law and learn about specific crimes, torts, and other areas of law, you will learn the individual elements of each. You will then be able to determine

SIDEBAR

CREATING AN IMPRESSION

To create a positive impression, try to:

- have a positive attitude
- be diplomatic
- be flexible
- establish a good rapport with others
- be a team player
- be resourceful
- be adaptable
- be thorough

whether these elements exist in actual cases. For example, in contract law, you will learn what conduct is a valid acceptance of a contract offer, and in tort law, what constitutes reasonable conduct under the circumstances.

Interpersonal Skills

The ability to communicate and work with others is vital to success as a paralegal, as well as to success in other endeavors. To categorize people, coworkers, colleagues, and employers might be unfair, but we all do it. We think—and sometimes say—things like, "He's a pleasure to work with" or "She has clients eating out of her hand." Conversely, we might say things like, "She's the most negative person I know" or "He's only out for himself." These comments reflect the other person's interpersonal skills (or the lack of), the ability to communicate and work with others.

How we relate to others can make the job easier or harder. This includes not just other members of the legal team, but also clients, witnesses, and opposing parties. Obviously, everyone on the team must have a certain level of trust and confidence in the others on the team. People who have a good working relationship accomplish more, and enjoy doing it. By contrast, conflict and tension make the job harder and can cause people to take shortcuts or avoid contact, which can result in poor performance and potential malpractice.

Not everyone has the personality to deal with every type of situation and every type of personality. For example, some may have trouble dealing with difficult clients. But everyone on the legal team has to develop the skills to work with other people, or recognize when they may have to have someone else handle certain aspects of a case, or a certain client. The skill is in recognizing these situations and making the appropriate adjustments. Some might call this "sensitivity"—to other people's needs, desires, wants, likes, and dislikes.

Cultural differences are discussed later, but in the American culture, for example, people tend to be sensitive to odors—breath, body, environmental. We do not want to offend. Our use of language is another area of sensitivity. We try to avoid using words that we believe will offend the other person in a specific circumstance, such as telling off-color jokes in a religious setting in front of a person of the cloth Some refer to interpersonal skills as "sensitivity" to other people's needs, desires, wants, likes, and dislikes. The starting point in working with attorneys, paralegals, and support staff, clients and opposing counsel, court personnel, and others is to be sensitive to these issues. What offends you probably offends others. Being sensitive to how others react to your words, conduct, and actions can provide good clues as to what is acceptable and what is not.

In the past, interpersonal skills were used primarily in face-to-face contact, telephone conversations, and written communications. Today these skills are also necessary in other forms of communication, such as emails and other electronic communications. For example, the "happy face" and "frowning face" icons [" :-) " and " :-("] in an email could be interpreted as overfamiliarity. THE USE OF ALL CAPITAL LETTERS might be interpreted as shouting or anger. Poor spelling and bad grammar in emails are likely to be seen as sloppiness or carelessness. In the past, letters were dictated, typed, proofread, and then signed. Today we often dash off an email without much thought—and sometimes the email reflects just that. How we respond by email affects how our clients view our capabilities and skill.

Communication Skills

Good communication means expressing ideas effectively. The practice of law requires effective communication, both oral and written. The lawyer and paralegal who work together must be able to communicate assignments and information with clarity—and frequently, with brevity. Over time, communication will improve as each person comes to understand how the other communicates.

Communication is made more complex by subtleties, nuances, and expressions that may require interpretation or explanation. For example, an attorney who is accustomed to using traditional book methods of research may ask a new paralegal (who has a deep understanding of computer research methods and little traditional book experience) to "check the pocket parts." This means checking for the latest updates or changes to a statute or case law. A paralegal who is accustomed to doing computer research may not understand what this expression means. Or asking a paralegal to "Shepardize" a case may have no meaning to someone who has learned only the Westlaw system, in which the method for checking other cases is called "KeyCiting," or the Loislaw system, which refers to this checking as "GlobalCiting."

Communication can be a major problem in a fast-paced office where information moves very quickly. In the middle of a court hearing, the litigation attorney may send a text message from court to the support paralegal at the office to ask for information about an unexpected case the other side has brought up. Nowadays, we rarely have the time to develop a common written and oral language base for communication among attorneys, paralegals, clients, opposing attorneys, and court personnel. And yet letters, pleadings, contracts, and other written documents must be clear and accurate. In many situations, an idea, request, or demand must be carefully communicated in only one document.

Oral communication must also be clear and precise, and first impressions matter. If a first discussion in person or by telephone is filled with slang or poor grammar, it may create a poor impression of the firm's professionalism, ability, and legal skill. It can influence a client's decision to retain the firm, the inclination of a judge to grant a request, or a court clerk's willingness to give you the help you need.

SIDEBAR

COMMUNICATION SKILLS

Do I:

- read with comprehension?
- listen effectively and accurately and interpret nonverbal communication?
- write in clear, concise, and grammatically correct English?
- speak in clear, concise, and grammatically correct English?
- use language to persuade?
- tailor the nature of the communication to maximize understanding in the intended audience, including people with different levels of education and different cultural backgrounds?

Source: American Association for Paralegal Education

Career Planning

Learning Objective 2

Explain the importance of professional skills in career advancement.

Career planning should include planning for education and perfecting professional skills. A sound educational plan is built on a foundation of general education courses that will be useful in any occupation and meet basic core requirements for an associate's or bachelor's degree. Occupation-related courses, such as paralegal specialty courses, should be selected with an eye toward transferability and suitability at a higher education level.

This is not to say that all courses must be transferable from one school to another, or from an associate-degree program to a bachelor's- or master's-degree program. Something can be learned from every course you take, even if it is only the realization that you do not wish to pursue a particular area of study. Think of the people you know who have pursued a career only to discover later that they are not interested in this line of work One of your early educational goals should be to explore areas of your actual or potential interest. Many students find a new career path after taking a required class they thought they would not like.

It is also clearer today than ever that successful paralegals must have a solid foundation in computer skills. As a paralegal advances in the profession, he or she must maintain and build upon these skills as computers and software become more sophisticated.

CHECKLIST My Career Roadmap

- ☐ Skills I need to acquire:
- ☐ Skills I need to strengthen:
- ☐ Courses I should take:
- ☐ Extracurricular activities for the résumé:
- ☐ Interim work experience I should seek:
- ☐ Volunteer activities:
- ☐ Short-term career goals:
- ☐ Long-term career goals:

Paralegal Education in the United States

> According to the Department of Labor, jobs requiring a master's degree are expected to grow the fastest, while those requiring a high school diploma will experience the slowest growth over the 2010–20 timeframe. Employment of paralegals and legal assistants is expected to grow by 18 percent from 2010 to 2020, about as fast as the average for all occupations. This occupation attracts many applicants, and competition for jobs will be strong. Experienced, formally trained paralegals should have the best job prospects.
>
> ***Source:*** U.S. Department of Labor, *Occupational Outlook Handbook*, 2012–13 Edition, Paralegals and Legal Assistants.

The best-trained, most highly skilled individual is the one most likely to land a job. Given the choice, a prospective employer is more likely to hire an applicant with an associate's degree or a bachelor's degree in paralegal studies, rather than an applicant with only a high school diploma and a paralegal certificate.

An estimated 1,000 paralegal education programs are available in the United States. These programs offer on-site or online instruction, or a hybrid format combining online and on-site instruction. Some of these programs have obtained ABA approval, and many are members of the **American Association for Paralegal Education (AAfPE),** which requires substantial compliance with ABA guidelines as a condition of membership.

What are the qualifications that allow someone to call him- or herself a "paralegal" or a "legal assistant" and to be billed as a paralegal? This question is not easy to answer. Just as the practice of law falls to the individual states for regulation, so does regulation of the paralegal profession. Regulations for paralegals lack uniformity in both the state statutes and court rules. Few states have laws such as the California statute shown in Exhibit 1.2 on page 21. Perhaps the most consistent and universal requirements are those established by the ABA's Standing Committee on Paralegals and the American Association for Paralegal Education (AAfPE), a national association of paralegal educators. These requirements have become the de facto standard for the minimum qualifications necessary for a person to call him- or herself a paralegal or legal assistant.

The ABA Standing Committee Guidelines require that instruction be at the post-secondary level and contain at least 60 semester hours, including general educational and legal specialty courses. Of these 60 hours, at least 18 must be general education courses and at least 18 must be legal specialty courses.

For purposes of the Guidelines, a "legal specialty course" is interpreted in Guideline G-303(c)d as a course (1) in a specific area of law, procedure, or legal process, (2) which has been developed for legal assistants and emphasizes legal assistant skills, forms, documents, procedures, and legal principles and theories, and (3) which is pertinent to the legal assistants' performance of a job.

Compliance with the ABA and the AAfPE guidelines is voluntary. As stated by the ABA,

> "Seeking approval from the American Bar Association is a voluntary process initiated by the institution offering the program. Therefore, the lack of approval does not necessarily mean a paralegal program is not of good quality and reputable." Source: http://www.americanbar.org/groups/paralegals/resources/career_information.html

A majority of programs have chosen not to incur the cost of undergoing the process for approval by the ABA. Many programs may offer a majority of courses in online or hybrid format that do not meet ABA guidelines, which limit the number of such courses that may be offered as part of the program of study.

Types of Educational Programs

The ultimate goals of the paralegal's education are to obtain a good job and to perform at a professional level. The demands on paralegals today require more advanced skills and abilities than in the past. Whereas basic typing, office, and business communications

Web Exploration

Check the available resources for paralegal students at the different national paralegal organizations:

National Federation of Paralegal Associations
http://www.paralegals.org

National Association of Legal Assistants
http://www.nala.org

Association of Legal Administrators
http://www.alanet.org

International Paralegal Management Association
http://www.paralegalmanagement.org/ipma/

NALS, the association for legal professionals
http://www.nals.org

Web Exploration

See the complete Occupational Outlook Handbook of the Bureau of Labor Statistics at http://www.bls.gov/ooh/legal/paralegals-and-legal-assistants.htm

American Association for Paralegal Education (AAfPE) A national organization of paralegal educators and institutions offering paralegal education programs.

Learning Objective 3

Explain why education and training are necessary to be recognized as a member of the paralegal profession.

RELEVANT PARALEGAL SKILLS

Skill Development

- Critical thinking skills
- Organizational skills
- General communication skills
- Interpersonal skills
- Legal research skills
- Legal writing skills
- Computer skills
- Interviewing and investigation skills

Acquisition of Knowledge

- Organization and operation of the legal system
- Organization and operation of law offices
- The paralegal profession and ethical obligations
- Contracts
- Torts
- Business organizations
- Litigation procedures

skills might have been acceptable for a starting position in a law firm twenty years ago, greater skills are demanded of those looking for a paralegal position today.

More employers today are also asking for transcripts showing the courses taken and the minimum number of hours of study as spelled out in the ABA guidelines, even for graduates of non-ABA-accredited institutions. However, the reality is that many attorneys do not know what educational requirements are needed to obtain a paralegal degree or certificate. And in many cases, they do not know the elements of the ABA, NFPA, or NALA definitions of "paralegal" or "legal assistant."

Paralegal educational programs generally fall into two categories: those offering a certificate, and those offering a degree—either an **associate's degree** or a **bachelor's degree.** These programs may be offered by a two-year community or junior college or a four-year college or university. A number of business and private **proprietary schools** also offer paralegal programs.

Associate's degree A college degree in science (AS), arts (AA), or applied arts (AAS), generally requiring two years of full-time study.

Bachelor's degree A college degree generally requiring four years of full-time study.

Proprietary school A private, as opposed to public, institution, generally for profit, offering training and education.

A student's prior educational and professional background will determine, in many cases, which of the programs to select. Those who already have a bachelor's or other higher academic degree may need only the legal specialty courses. Those who come from a specialty background, such as nursing or another science-related field, may want to broaden their education by taking courses of a general nature in addition to the legal specialty courses.

Certificate Programs

Most educational institutions with paralegal or legal assistant programs offer a **certificate** that recognizes completion of a program of study that requires less than what is required to receive a degree. Some certificates award college credits; others do not. For students who already possess a baccalaureate degree, obtaining additional college credits probably isn't an issue. However, for students without an undergraduate degree, programs that do not offer college credit still can be valuable but should be considered carefully. At the very least, the actual time spent in the classroom should be equivalent to the minimums of college credit courses.

Certificate A recognition of the completion of a program of study that requires less than that needed for a degree.

Those planning to transfer should consider whether their credits may be carried over to another institution. Even if they have no immediate intent to continue in school, it would be wise to plan ahead and not lose the hours and credits they have earned in the event they later decide to go on to obtain a degree.

Students should also consider what is acceptable in the community in which they intend to work. Many professional paralegal organizations are reporting that a bachelor's degree is becoming necessary to obtain many paralegal positions. The U.S. Attorney's Office, for example, is requiring at least a four-year degree for a paralegal position.

Associate Degree Programs

Many community colleges and junior colleges offer an associate's degree in science (AS), arts (AA), or applied arts (AAS) in paralegal or legal assistant studies. For many students these programs offer a community-based transition into higher education. For others it is a way of getting back into higher education while working at a full-time job or another occupation. Associate degree programs also tend to be a cost-effective educational environments for trying different areas of study before finding an area of concentration.

Support services are often available for returning students or students who need additional help. Many of these schools offer English courses for those for whom English is a second language. Assistance is also provided for those who need a refresher course or help with study skills after years away from school.

Web Exploration

The IPMA Position Paper is available at **www.paralegalmanagement.org/management-resources/resources-for-paralegal-managers/ipma-position-papers**.

Baccalaureate Programs

Some of the earliest paralegal programs were built on a model in which a bachelor's degree was the prerequisite for entering a paralegal program of study. A number of programs now offer a bachelor's degree in paralegal studies. One national organization, the International Paralegal Management Association (IPMA), has recommended the bachelor's degree as the minimum qualification to enter the profession:

> A baccalaureate degree should be the minimum requirement for employment as a paralegal. Paralegals have assumed many responsibilities previously handled by lawyers. These responsibilities include complex legal issues; clear writing, researching, and critical thinking skills; and a strong academic background. The IPMA believes this accepted professional standard of academic achievement lends greater credibility and respect to increasing paralegal participation in the legal profession.
>
> *Source:* International Paralegal Management Association (IPMA) http://www.paralegalmanagement.org/images/stories/documents/education-position-paper.pdf

The increase in the professional recognition of paralegals has resulted in their gaining more responsibility, as well as greater expectations regarding their skills and education. As the standing of the paralegal on the legal team rises, so will the demand for those with a broad-based education to serve in those positions. Four-year programs of study are attempting to meet that demand by merging traditional four-year core requirements with legal specialty courses.

The paralegal serving in a family law practice provides a good example of this demand. In the highly charged emotional environment of custody and divorce cases, knowledge of family and child psychology is essential. For those in an intellectual property practice, an understanding of science and engineering is a basic requirement. The four-year time frame allows more flexibility to explore and build skills and knowledge, as well as to meet the increasing demand for broader education.

Graduate Programs

A few colleges and universities now offer graduate degrees in legal studies. Others offer advanced degrees in related areas such as legal administration.

Specialty Certificates

Specialty certificates, such as the legal nurse consultant certificate, offer an excellent entry point into a paralegal career. Specialty certificates combined with degrees in other fields of study, such as nursing, journalism, and computer science, are like a capstone program preparing a person for entry into a new career. One of the greatest demands has been for those with a background in nursing combined with a paralegal education. A growing number of colleges are offering a certificate in Legal Nurse Consulting.

Paralegal Advance Competency Exam (PACE) The National Federation of Paralegal Associations' certification exam. Candidates must have two years of experience and a bachelor's degree and have completed a paralegal course at an accredited school.

Paralegal Certification

The National Federation of Paralegal Associations (NFPA) administers the **Paralegal Advance Competency Exam (PACE)** to test the competency level of experienced paralegals. In order to sit for this exam, the candidate must meet the following requirements:

- The paralegal cannot have been convicted of a felony nor be under suspension, termination, or revocation of a certificate, registration, or license by any entity.
- An associate's degree in paralegal studies obtained from an institutionally accredited and/or ABA-approved paralegal education program; and six (6) years' substantive paralegal experience; OR
- A bachelor's degree in any course of study obtained from an institutionally accredited school and three (3) years of substantive paralegal experience; OR
- A bachelor's degree and completion of a paralegal program with an institutionally accredited school; said paralegal program may be embodied in a bachelor's degree; and two (2) years' substantive paralegal experience; OR
- Four (4) years' substantive paralegal experience on or before December 31, 2000.

Web Exploration

Detailed information on PACE can be obtained at **www.paralegals.org/displaycommon.cfm?an=1&subarticlenbr=888**

Learning Objective 4

Describe the different approaches to the certification and regulation of the paralegal profession.

Those who successfully pass the exam may use the designation "PACE-Registered Paralegal" or "RP." Continued use of the designation requires 12 additional hours of continuing legal or specialty education every 2 years, with at least one hour of legal ethics.

Since 1976, the National Association of Legal Assistants has conferred the **Certified Legal Assistant (CLA)** designation upon those who pass its two-day comprehensive examination. In 2004, NALA registered the certification mark "CP" with the U.S. Patent and Trademark Office for those who prefer the term "Certified Paralegal." To be eligible to take the exam for this certificate, the following requirements must be met:

Certified Legal Assistant (CLA) A designation by the National Association of Legal Assistants for those who take and pass NALA's two-day comprehensive examination.

1. Graduation from a legal assistant program that is:
   - approved by the American Bar Association; or
   - an associate-degree program; or
   - a post-baccalaureate certificate program in legal assistant studies; or
   - a bachelor's-degree program in legal assistant studies; or
   - a legal-assistant program which consists of a minimum of 60 semester hours (900 clock hours or 90 quarter hours) of which at least 15 semester hours (225 clock hours or 22.5 quarter hours) are substantive legal courses.
2. A bachelor's degree in any field plus one year's experience as a legal assistant. Successful completion of at least 15 semester hours (or 22.5 quarter hours or 225 clock hours) of substantive legal assistant courses will be considered equivalent to one year's experience as a legal assistant.
3. A high school diploma or equivalent plus seven (7) years' experience as a legal assistant under the supervision of a member of the Bar, plus evidence of a minimum of twenty (20) hours of continuing legal education credit to have been completed within a two (2) year period prior to the examination date.

Web Exploration

General information about paralegal certification, including requirements, exam subjects, and testing schedule, can be found at **www.nala.org/Certification.aspx**.

To maintain the CLA designation, 50 hours of continuing legal assistant education must be completed every five years. For those who have achieved the initial designation, NALA also offers specialist credentials for those practicing in a specific area of law, such as bankruptcy, intellectual property, civil litigation, probate, and estate planning. Successful completion of these examinations permits the additional designation Certified Legal Assistant–Specialty (CLAS).

NALS offers members and nonmembers the opportunity to sit for three unique certifications dedicated to the legal services profession—ALS, PLS, and PP. The exams are of varying levels and are developed by professionals in the industry.

1. **ALS**—the basic certification for legal professionals exam—covers:
   Part 1: Written Communications
   Part 2: Office Procedures and Legal Knowledge
   Part 3: Ethics, Human Relations, and Judgment

ALS (Accredited Legal Secretary) The basic certification for legal professionals from NALS.

PLS (Professional Legal Secretary) The advanced certification for legal professionals from NALS.

PP (Professional Paralegal) Certification from NALS for those performing paralegal duties.

2. **PLS**—the advanced certification for legal professionals exam—covers:
   Part 1: Written Communications
   Part 2: Office Procedures and Technology
   Part 3: Ethics and Judgment
   Part 4: Legal Knowledge and Skills
3. **PP**—professionals performing paralegal duties. Eligibility requires five years' experience performing paralegal or legal assistant duties. A candidate may receive a partial waiver of one year if he or she has a postsecondary degree, other certification, or a paralegal certificate. A candidate with a paralegal degree may receive a two-year partial waiver. The exam covers:
   Part 1: Written Communications
   Part 2: Legal Knowledge and Skills
   Part 3: Ethics and Judgment Skills
   Part 4: Substantive Law

A comparison of the various exams—NALS, NALA, and NFPA—is presented in Exhibit 1.1.

Exhibit 1.1 Legal certification comparison chart

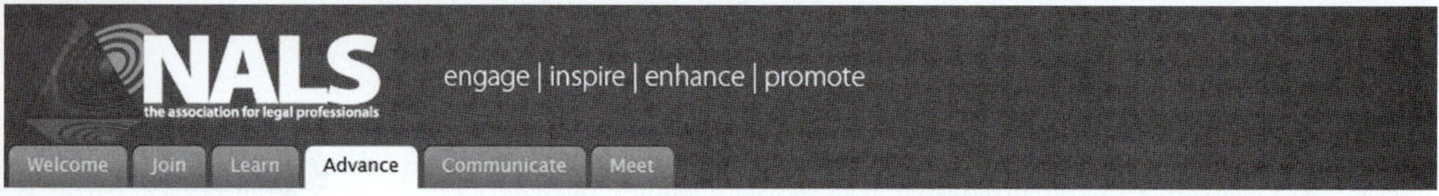

Comparison Chart

THIS CHART COMPARES THE CERTIFICATION EXAMS OFFERED BY:

NALS...the association for legal professionals
National Association for Legal Assistants (NALA)
National Federation of Paralegal Associations, Inc. (NFPA)

Please Note: The content of the chart below is verified only as to the information about the NALS Professional Paralegal (PP) exam and the NALS Professional Legal Secretary...the advanced certification for legal professionals (PLS) exam. The information regarding NALA and NFPA® exams is unverified, and provided for informational and comparison purposes only. The NALA and NFPA information below was obtained from publicly available sources.

	NALS Professional Paralegal (PP) – NALS	**NALS** Professional Legal Secretary... the advanced certification for legal professionals (PLS)	**NALA** Certified Paralegal (CP); Certified Legal Assistant (CLA)	**NFPA®** Paralegal Advanced Competency Exam (PACE)
Organization Established	1929, incorporated in 1949	1929, incorporated in 1949	1975	1974
Certification Established	2004	1960	1976	1996
Membership Information	4,000 individual members $108 new member (7) ($98/yr after) $53 associate (8) $19 student	4,000 individual members $108 new member (7) ($98/yr after) $53 associate (8) $19 student	6,000 individual members $99 new member – active (2) $84 associate (3) $40 student $50 sustaining (4)	15,000 (includes affiliate organizations, no information is available on individual member) $70 new member (paralegal or paralegal supervisor) $60 associate (5) $50 student $120 sustaining (6)

(continued)

Exhibit 1.1 Legal certification comparison chart *(continued)*

Number Certified	522 (eff 03/12)	5,674 (eff 03/12)	16,900 (eff 03/12)	824 (eff 02/12)
Eligibility to Test Education and/or Employment	Five years' experience performing paralegal duties.Partial waivers: (1) A maximum two-year waiver may be granted for completion of a paralegal degree. (2) A maximum one-year waiver may be granted for post-secondary degrees, successful completion of the PLS exam, or other certifications.	Three years' experience in the legal field.Partial Waiver: (1) A maximum one year waiver may be granted for post-secondary degrees, successful completion of the ALS exam, or other certifications.	(1) Graduation from paralegal program that is: (a) Approved by the American Bar Association; or (b) An associate degree program; or (c) A post-baccalaureate certificate program in paralegal studies; or (d) A bachelor's degree program in paralegal studies; or (e) A paralegal program which consists of a minimum of 60 semester hours of which at least 15 semester hours are substantive legal courses. (2) Bachelor's degree in any field plus one year's experience as a paralegal. Successful completion of at least 15 hours of substantive legal courses will be considered equivalent to one year's experience as a paralegal. (3) High school diploma or equivalent plus seven years' experience as a paralegal under supervision of a member of the bar, plus evidence of a minimum of 20 hours of CLE within two-year period prior to exam date.	(1) An associates degree in paralegal studies obtained from an institutionally accredited and/or ABA approved paralegal education program; and six years substantive paralegal experience; OR (2) Bachelor's degree in any course of study obtained from an institutionally accredited school and three years of substantive paralegal experience; OR (3) Bachelor's degree and completion of a paralegal program within an institutionally accredited school (which may be embodied in the bachelor's degree) and two years substantive paralegal experience; OR (4) Four years substantive paralegal experience completed on or before December 31, 2000.
Examination Topics	Part 1 – Written Communications: Grammar and word usage, spelling, punctuation, number usage, capitalization, composition and expression Part 2 – Legal Knowledge and Skills: Legal research, citations, legal terminology, the court system and ADR, and the legal skills of interviewing clients and witnesses, planning and conducting investigations, and docketing Part 3 – Ethics and Judgment: Ethical situations involving contact with clients, the public, coworkers, and subordinates; other ethical considerations for the legal profession; decisionmaking and analytical ability; and ability to recognize priorities Part 4 – All areas of substantive law, including administrative; business organizations and contracts; civil procedure and litigation; criminal; family; real property; torts; wills, trusts, and estates; admiralty and maritime; antitrust; bankruptcy; environmental; federal civil rights and employment discrimination; immigration; intellectual property; labor; oil and gas; pension and profit sharing; taxation; water; workers' compensation	Part 1- Written Communications: Grammar and word usage, punctuation, number usage, capitalization, spelling, and composition and expression Part 2 – Office Procedures and Technology: records management, computer information systems, equipment/ information services, office procedures and practices, office accounting Part 3 – Ethics and Judgment: Ethical situations involving contact with clients, the public, coworkers; ethical considerations for legal profession; decisionmaking and analytical ability; ability to recognize priorities Part 4 – Legal Knowledge and Skills: Legal Knowledge: citations, legal research, and the ability to prepare legal documents based on oral instructions and materials; all areas of substantive law	Federal law and procedure, major subject areas include communications, ethics, legal research, human relations and interviewing techniques, judgment and analytical ability, legal terminology. Section on Substantive Law includes five miniexaminations covering the American Legal System and four of the following areas: administrative law, bankruptcy, business, organizations/ corporations, contracts, family law, criminal law and procedure, litigation, probate and estate planning, real estate.	Domain I – Administration of client legal matters: conflict checks; develop, organize and maintain client files; develop and maintain calendar/tickler systems; develop/maintain databases; coordinate client services. Domain II – Development of client legal matters: client interviews; analyze information; collaborate with counsel; prepare, file, and serve legal documents/exhibits; prepare clients/witnesses for legal proceedings. Domain III – Factual/legal research: obtain factual/legal information; investigate/compile facts; inspect/evaluate evidence; ascertain/analyze legal authority. Domain IV – Factual/legal writing: communicate with client/counsel; draft legal analytical documents. Domain V – Office Administration: personnel management; acquire technology; coordinate and utilize vendor services; create and maintain library of legal resources; develop/maintain billing system. (Ethics imbedded throughout)

(continued)

Exhibit 1.1 Legal certification comparison chart *(continued)*

Length of Exam	one day	one day	two days	four hours – 200 questions
Testing Sites	nationally/most major cities	nationally/most major cities	nationally/mostmajor cities	200+ Sylvan Learning Centers
Frequency of Exam	First Saturday in March Last Saturday in September (no waiting period to retest)	First Saturday in March Last Saturday in September (no waiting period to retest)	March April July December	Within 90 days of approval of application (six month waiting period to retest)
Cost of Exam Member Nonmember	$200 (retake $50/section) $250 (retake $60/section) PLS Members Part 4: $150 (retake $50) PLS Nonmember Part 4: $200 (retake $60)	$150 (retake $40/section) $200 (retake $50/section)	$250 (retake $60/section) $275 (retake $60/section)	Exam Fee: $225; Application Fee:$25 (retake $250) Exam Fee: $250; Application Fee: $75 (retake $350)
Recertification Frequency CLE Required Topics	Every five years 75 hours (five hours legal ethics) Minimum of 50 hours on substantive areas, minimum of 5 hours on ethics, and maximum of 20 hours on other areas. Substantive areas should include those that reflect the substantive nature of a paralegal's work, enhance a paralegal's knowledge of the profession, update knowledge of the law, or relate to the Professional Paralegal examination; including, but not limited to, procedural and communications skills, legal research and citations, and procedural and substantive law.	Every five years 75 hours Education on PLS exam topics or teaching, lecturing, writing, earning college credit, earning other certifications	Every five years 50 hours Legal assistant topics or teaching	Every two years 12 hours (one hour legal ethics) Substantive law; specific nature of paralegal profession, i.e., computer skills, research techniques, management skills, etc.; ethics
Recertification Costs	$75	$75	$50	$25 (if a topic is not pre-approved by NFPA, individual or speaker may request approval – $25 for a speaker or non-member; $10 for individual member)

1. 200,000 paralegals nationwide per U.S. Department of Labor, Bureau of Labor Statistics, http://stats.bls.gov (3/21/04)
2. Anyone who completed CLA exam; graduated from ABA program for legal assistants; graduated from legal assistant accredited course not ABA approved/not less than 60 semester hours of study; graduated from legal assistant course/not less than six months of in-house training as legal assistant whose attorney-employer attests individual is qualified as legal assistant ("attorney attests"); or earned baccalaureate degree in any field plus at least six months in-house training as legal assistant whose attorney attests; person with at least three years of law-related experience and at least six months in-house training as a legal assistant whose attorney attests; or person who has a minimum of two years in-house training as a legal assistant whose attorney attests.
3. Attorneys, educators, legal assistant supervisors.
4. Individuals, law firms, corporations and legal assistant program representatives who endorse or promote the legal assistant concept or promote the legal assistant profession.
5. Nonvoting; former paralegal or legal professional other than paralegal
6. Nonvoting; persons, partnerships, corporations, associations supporting purposes and activities of NFPA.
7. Members include those who work for attorneys, e.g., paralegals/legal assistants, secretaries, office managers. court personnel. This fee does not include state or local chapter dues.
8. Educators, judges, attorneys

Legal Certification Comparison Chart prepared by Kathleen L. McRae, PLS, RP and Lyn M. Hurlbutt, PP, PLS, CLA, RP, CPS.

Originally published on www.nals.org. Used by permission of NALS.

Minimum Education

The **International Paralegal Management Association (IPMA)** is an organization for paralegal management professionals. In its position paper on paralegal education, the IPMA states:

International Paralegal Management Association (IPMA) A North American association for legal assistant managers.

> [N]early 80% of IPMA member organizations require the bachelor's degree when hiring, and many require specific paralegal education and/or give credit for professional certifications.

Legal assistants have assumed many responsibilities formerly handled by lawyers. Working with complex legal issues requires that a legal assistant possess clear writing, researching, and critical thinking abilities.

Making a Personal Assessment and Setting Goals

If you are reading this book, you probably have made at least a tentative goal to enter the paralegal profession. The job you ultimately choose should be more than a way to earn an income and should also be work that gives you satisfaction and fulfillment. The paralegal field offers a variety of specialties. An early goal should be to take courses that will help you identify the specialty you would enjoy most. Perhaps you are already experienced in a field that will lead to a specialty, such as nursing, engineering, or law enforcement.

One of the first steps is to assess your own skills and personal qualities. What are your abilities? What are your personality traits? Do you like working under deadlines? Do you enjoy working with certain groups of people, such as the elderly or those with disabilities? As you will find out, the paralegal profession offers opportunities in many types of working environments. Understanding your interests, skills, and preferred working conditions will help you select the best path toward achieving your professional goals.

Selecting a Specialty

It is never too early to set career goals. After you start your first job, you will learn more about the various areas of practice that are available to you. Your ultimate specialty might stem from your educational background, such as journalism or medicine, or from an area of special interest, such as environmental issues. It may also result simply from a preference to work with certain types of clients, such as the elderly people with disabilities.

A career may take many twists and turns, and it is never too late to make a career adjustment or choose a new path. Many successful individuals begin a career later in life, and schools are full of nontraditional students seeking a career change. For example, there are many former nurses in the paralegal profession who, after working in the medical field for many years, made a change to the paralegal field.

Your decision should be based on a self-evaluation of your likes and dislikes, interests, passions, and any physical or geographic limitations. If you hate to fly, you probably will not want a job that requires travel. If you are not comfortable with strangers, you probably will not want a job as a paralegal investigator for a litigation firm. If you like books and research, you may be interested in working as a firm's librarian or researcher.

CHECKLIST Career Planning

- ☐ My current paralegal job-related skills are:
- ☐ My special interests are:
- ☐ My passions are:
- ☐ My personality traits are:
- ☐ My geographical work and living desires are:
- ☐ My willingness to accept responsibility is:
- ☐ My level of self-motivation is:

Assessing Your Background

As the law has become more specialized, so has the demand for paralegals with more than just paralegal skills. Law firms specializing in medical malpractice frequently look for paralegals who also have a medical background, such as nursing. Firms with large, complex cases often look for someone with computer database skills to manage the files. Paralegals with journalism experience are sought out for their interviewing and writing skills.

Your personal background can be an asset when added to your paralegal certificate or degree. As you begin your professional training, take stock of your entire educational background, special skills, and talents, as well as personal areas of interest. A self-assessment early in your studies helps you recognize your strengths and acknowledge weaknesses that you need to work on.

Assessing Your Skills

You may well have a number of personal skills that will benefit you in the future as a paralegal. You might have great interpersonal skills, communicate well orally and in writing, and be a highly motivated person—all qualities of a good paralegal.

Individuals with language skills are particularly in demand in international law, as well as in working with clients who lack English-language skills. The paralegal who understands a second language or the cultural nuances among clients can be invaluable.

Assessing Your Interests

What are your personal interests? Do you enjoy the outdoors in your free time? If so, working on environmental issues may give you satisfaction. Do you find yourself drawn to volunteering or working in your free time with shut-ins and elderly people?

Selecting Your Electives

Becoming aware of your interests and background knowledge enables you to select the elective courses that can qualify you for work in a specialty field. Taking electives is a good way to explore an area in which you think you might be interested, without committing to more than one semester or a few credits of study. Many students find new interests and a potential career direction after taking courses in areas they had not considered previously.

For example, you may find high-technology industries to be exciting, and wonder how a paralegal might fit into this growth area. One of the fastest-growing fields is that of intellectual property law. In the age of computers and the Internet, with its global technology marketplace, protection of intellectual property has become a critical concern for individuals and companies alike. Taking a three-credit course in intellectual property may introduce the paralegal student to a new area of interest in a potential growth area of the paralegal profession. This is also true for other emerging areas, such as environmental law and legal nurse consulting.

Regulating the Practice of Law

To protect the public, certain professions, such as law, require state licensure as a method of regulating who can practice. Once they are licensed, lawyers must follow the rules found in their state's code of ethics. The ethical code of most states substantially follows the Model Rules of Professional Conduct created by the American Bar Association. A serious violation of these rules can result in the loss of one's license to practice law.

Paralegals, with a few exceptions, have no state license requirement to enter the profession, and no unified code of ethics. State regulations and ethics opinions concerning paralegals are neither uniform nor mandatory. Various paralegal organizations have established their own sets of ethical rules, and violations of these rules can result in a loss of membership in the organization. However, one of the worst ethical pitfalls for a paralegal is the risk of unauthorized practice of law, which can subject a paralegal to prosecution under a state's criminal code. This issue will be discussed in more detail in Chapter 2.

Regulating the Paralegal Profession

Regulation and licensing of the paralegal profession have been some of the hottest topics in the legal and paralegal communities. Each state, through its legislature and court system, regulates and licenses the practice of law. With the development of the paralegal profession has come a new set of concerns and controversies surrounding what constitutes the **unauthorized practice of law (UPL),** such as who should be permitted to render legal services, and under what conditions.

Unauthorized Practice of Law (UPL) Giving legal advice, where legal rights may be affected, by anyone not licensed to practice law.

There is a continuing debate between bar organizations and paralegal professional organizations over regulation of the paralegal profession. Generally, the bar organizations, such as the American Bar Association, do not see the need for expending the additional time, effort, and cost for certification of paralegals. Their position is broadly based on the argument that the public is protected by the attorney's obligation to supervise the paralegal and the attorney's responsibility to the public. For the most part, the paralegal profession has sought some level of regulation, certification, or licensure. Somewhere in the middle are increasing numbers of employers of paralegals who want some level of assurance that those they hire are qualified to serve as paralegals. As the responsibilities undertaken by paralegals have increased, so have the educational requirements. Within the legal profession has come a concern as whether those who hold themselves out as paralegals are truly qualified. Members of the paralegal profession see this as no different from the organized bar monitoring the activities of those holding themselves out as lawyers.

State Licensing

Some states have attempted to set up licensing systems or define who may use the title "paralegal." A case in point is the proposal rejected in 1999 by the New Jersey Supreme Court to license paralegals, which had been developed after five years of study by that court's committee on paralegal education and regulation. If it had been approved, this proposal would have made New Jersey the first state to license paralegals. The approaches of two other states are as follows:

- California leads the nation in setting stringent educational requirements that may become a model for other states. In 2000, California amended its Business and Professional Code requiring minimum educational standards for paralegals. See Exhibit 1.2.

Exhibit 1.2 California regulation of paralegals

While other state legislatures and courts wrestle with the minimum standards, California addressed the requirements in a 2000 amendment to the Business and Professional Code that requires a paralegal to possess at least one of the following:

(1) A certificate of completion of a paralegal program approved by the American Bar Association.
(2) A certificate of completion of a paralegal program at an institution that requires a minimum of 24 semester, or equivalent, units in law-related courses, accredited by a national or regional accreditation organization or approved by the Bureau for Private Postsecondary and Vocational Education.
(3) A baccalaureate or advanced degree and minimum of one year of law-related experience under an attorney who is an active member of the State Bar of California.
(4) A high school diploma or general equivalency diploma and a minimum of three years' law-related experience under the supervision of a California attorney, with this training being completed before December 31, 2003.

Other states might look to the California statute in deciding the question of who is qualified by education, training, or work experience.

- After a number of efforts, a Hawaii State Bar Association task force on paralegal certification developed a voluntary certification proposal for consideration by the Hawaii Supreme Court. This proposal was a compromise that recognized the opposition from some segments of the bar.

To some observers it is obvious that the organized bar is fearful of the incursion of the paralegal profession into the practice of law. For some attorneys, the issue is the possible loss of business. Others are concerned that the quality of legal services will be degraded by those who hold themselves out as members of the legal profession.

Florida and Ohio are among the states that have addressed the issue of certification of paralegals.

Florida Registered Paralegal

> A Florida Registered Paralegal is a person with education, training, or work experience, who works under the direction and supervision of a member of The Florida Bar and who performs specifically delegated substantive legal work for which a member of The Florida Bar is responsible and who has met the requirements of registration as set forth in Chapter 20 of the Rules Regulating The Florida Bar. A Florida Registered Paralegal is not a member of The Florida Bar and may not give legal advice or practice law. Florida Registered Paralegal and FRP are trademarks of The Florida Bar.
>
> *Source:* www.floridabar.org

Ohio State Bar Association Certified Paralegal

> The Ohio State Bar Association offers a voluntary credentialing program for paralegals. Individuals meeting the OSBA definition of "paralegal," meeting the eligibility requirements and passing a written examination will be designated as an "OSBA Certified Paralegal." This credential, along with a logo provided for the purpose may be used by the paralegal to the extent permitted by the Supreme Court of Ohio's Rules for the Government of the Bar and Rules of Professional Conduct.
>
> OSBA Paralegal Certification provides a valuable credential for paralegals in Ohio through the use of objective standards which measure the training, knowledge, experience and skill of paralegals. It requires a commitment to excellence and will assist lawyers and law firms in identifying the highly qualified paralegal professionals.
>
> *Source:* http://www.ohiobar.org/pub/?articleid=785

For the paralegal, it is a question of status as well as expanding job opportunities. With the establishment of minimum standards comes a certain status that members of a profession are entitled to enjoy. For those who have worked hard to develop their paralegal skills through education and experience, these standards eliminate unqualified individuals from the pool of job applicants. The stated goals of lawyer and paralegal groups are not that far apart: both groups are interested in the delivery of quality legal services at affordable prices, and in creating a reasonable standard of living for practitioners.

The traditional role of the attorney in advising and representing clients is limited to those who are admitted to practice as lawyers under the applicable state law. Some exemptions do exist under state law that allow nonlawyers to perform certain services, such as document preparation, which, subject to certain limitations, is permitted under California law.

Federal Practice

Under federal regulations, nonlawyers may represent parties before the Social Security Administration, the Patent Office, and other agencies. However, a conflict may arise between the federal law and state laws that limits this activity. For example, Florida sought unsuccessfully to enjoin a practitioner authorized to practice before the Patent Office, alleging UPL. *Sperry v. Florida*, 373 U.S. 379 (1963).

Advice *from the* Field

NORTH CAROLINA STATE BAR PARALEGAL CERTIFICATION PROGRAM

I recommend a visit to the North Carolina State Bar's Paralegal website (http://www.nccertifiedparalegal.org) for information on the benefits of paralegal certification. The first page is shown below.

PLAN FOR CERTIFICATION OF PARALEGALS

The State Bar's interest in the paralegal profession promotes proper utilization of paralegals and assures that legal services are professionally and ethically offered to the public. The Plan for Certification of Paralegals approved by the NC State Bar and adopted by the NC Supreme Court in 2004 will assist in the development of paralegal standards, raise the profile of the paralegal profession, and standardize the expectations of the public and other legal professionals.

The State Bar has worked diligently with attorneys and paralegals across our state to establish a voluntary North Carolina certification program with requirements that are properly defined and that will ensure the credential has value. Through education and experience, the North Carolina certification plan will assist lawyers and administrators in distinguishing paralegals that meet or exceed the skills required for certification. As multi-skilled professionals, paralegals have a diverse knowledge base and must practice effective interpersonal communication skills to maintain collaborative relationships within the legal team. Paralegals, like attorneys, will continue to be held accountable to the highest of ethical and professional standards.

Paralegals certified by the State Bar may use the following designations:

- North Carolina Certified Paralegal
- North Carolina State Bar Certified Paralegal
- Paralegal Certified by the North Carolina State Bar Board of Paralegal Certification
- NCCP

This site has two brochures that may be downloaded,

NC Certified Paralegal—A Primer for Paralegals

NC Certified Paralegal—A Primer for Attorneys

Both brochures review the benefits to the public, to the profession, to attorneys, and to paralegals. I think that they give a great overall response to the question of whether to become certified. North Carolina began their certification program July 1, 2005. As of February 2006, the Board had received 1,489 applications and had certified 762. The applicants qualified under the grandfather clause, which ended June 30, 2007.

Under federal regulation, a paralegal can, without supervision, represent individuals before the Social Security Administration, including appearing before administrative law judges on behalf of clients. Paralegals may appear as representatives of claimants for disability claims; claims regarding Medicare Parts A, B, and C; and cases of overpayment and underpayment of benefits.

As a representative of a claimant before the Social Security Administration, a paralegal may obtain information, submit evidence, and make statements and arguments. The difference between the paralegal and the attorney is only in the matter of direct versus indirect payment for services. The Social Security Administration pays the attorney directly, whereas the paralegal must bill the client for services rendered. Within the Social Security Administration, paralegals are employed as decision writers and case technicians.

Opportunities for Paralegals

The U.S. Bureau of Labor Statistics, in its 2010–2020 projection, indicated a continued demand for legal services from government, individuals, and businesses alike. It further stated that paralegals and legal assistants are expected to account for 46,900 new jobs as legal establishments attempt to reduce costs by assigning these workers more tasks that were once performed by lawyers. This encompasses additional growth

Web Exploration

Check the latest paralegal statistics in the *Occupational Outlook Handbook* from the Department of Labor, Bureau of Labor Statistics at **http://www.bls.gov/oco/home.htm**.

Learning Objective 5

Discuss the job opportunities for the paralegal.

of the occupation as well as the need for individuals to replace existing employees. The Labor Department estimates might be increased further by the de facto requirement found in the court opinions that more paralegals be used to perform services instead of attorneys, who bill at higher rates.

Projections Data from the National Employment Matrix

Occupational title	SOC Code	Employment, 2010	Projected employment, 2020	Change, 2010-2020	
				Number	Percent
Paralegals and legal assistants	23-2011	256,000	302,900	46,900	8

Source: *Occupational Outlook Handbook,* 2012-13 Edition, U.S. Department of Labor, Bureau of Labor Statistics, Employment Projections program.

Paralegals held about 263,800 jobs in 2008, according to the Bureau of Labor Statistics, U.S. Department of Labor, *Occupational Outlook Handbook*, 2012–13 Edition. In 2010, full-time wage-and-salary paralegals and legal assistants had a median annual earnings, including bonuses, of $46,680. The middle 50 percent earned between $36,080 and $59,310. The top 10 percent earned more than $74,870, and the bottom 10 percent earned less than $29,460. Annual mean in the industries with the highest levels of employment of paralegals as of May 2011 were:

Legal Services	$47,790
Federal Executive Branch	$64,750
Local Government	$50,980
State Government	$44,850
Management of Companies and Enterprises	$59,390

Source: *Occupational Outlook Handbook,* 2012-13 Edition, U.S. Department of Labor, Bureau of Labor Statistics.

Top-paying states for this occupation:

State	Employment (1)	Hourly mean wage	Annual mean wage (2)
District of Columbia	6,950	$32.75	$ 68,120
California	26,030	$28.38	$59,030
New Jersey	6,790	$27.10	$ 56,370
New York	22,340	$26.36	$54,840
Illinois	9,820	$25.79	$53,640

(1) Estimates for detailed occupations do not sum to the totals because the totals include occupations not shown separately. Estimates do not include self-employed workers.

(2) Annual wages have been calculated by multiplying the hourly mean wage by a "year-round, full-time" hours figure of 2,080 hours; for those occupations where there is not an hourly mean wage published, the annual wage has been directly calculated from the reported survey data.

Source: U.S. Bureau of Labor Statistics | Division of Occupational Employment Statistics

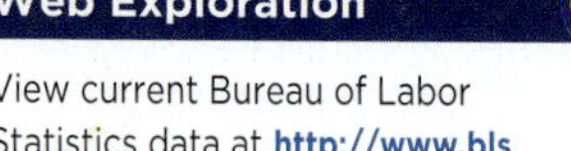

View current Bureau of Labor Statistics data at **http://www.bls.gov/oes/home.htm**

Compensation for paralegals varies according to working environment and geographic location. As with most jobs and professions, salaries tend to be higher in large metropolitan areas and lower in small and rural areas. Large firms tend to pay more, and small firms tend to pay less. At times, these variations in compensation can be justified by the costs of working in certain locations, such as higher taxation and the cost of commuting.

The Future

The future of the paralegal profession may be determined by clients who are unwilling or unable to pay what they see as inflated fees for lawyers. The future could also be dictated, to some extent, by the courts. When fee petitions are submitted to courts for approval, important billing issues arise that affect paralegals. This is one of the areas in which the definition of "paralegal" has come into play. For example, certain secretarial or clerical tasks are considered overhead (part of the cost of running the office) and should be performed at no additional cost to the client. However, in some cases, these tasks are charged to the client as paralegal fees. Courts allow charges for paralegal fees but not for secretarial fees. In other cases, higher attorney rates are charged for performing tasks that could have been delegated to a paralegal. Courts have reduced claims for legal fees where using a paralegal for these tasks would have resulted in lower charges.

For instance, summarizing depositions traditionally has been a task delegated to paralegals. Assume that the paralegal takes two hours to complete the task and the paralegal's time is billed to the client at $75 per hour. (Don't get excited—that doesn't necessarily have any bearing on what you may be paid). The client would be charged $150. For a lawyer to do the same work, if billed out at $175 per hour, the client would be charged $350. Unless there is a good reason for the lawyer to do the work, the decision to delegate the work to a lawyer is unfair to the client. A number of court decisions are beginning to focus on the fairness and propriety of attorney billing for certain services. As other federal and state courts weigh in on this line of decisions, law firms may have to hire more paralegals.

Web Exploration

The Kathryn Myers student portfolio article and other information for students can be found on the American Association for Paralegal Education website at **www.aafpe.org**.

National Association of Legal Secretaries (NALS) Since 1999, an association for legal professionals. It was originally formed in 1949 as an association for legal secretaries.

Getting Started

As you start your legal studies and paralegal career, consider the suggestions and advice in the following *Advice from the Field* by a leading paralegal educator.

Advice *from the* Field

THE STUDENT PORTFOLIO

Kathryn Myers, Coordinator, Paralegal Studies, Saint Mary-of-the-Woods College, Paralegal Studies Program

A portfolio is a purposeful collection of student work that is accumulated over time. The material reveals the extent of student learning, achievement, and development. The "portfolio system" is intended to specify knowledge and competence in areas considered necessary to successfully work as a paralegal/legal assistant while leaving the selection of means of documentation of competency to the individual student. Documentation of knowledge and skill acquisition can take a variety of forms, including, but not limited to,

letters of support
diaries
videotapes and audiotapes of work
pleadings
memoranda
course projects
registration receipts from continuing education and other conferences attended
proof of membership in professional organizations
subscriptions to legal publications

Typically, much of the material can be compiled from projects and activities required within courses.

(continued)

PROCEDURE

The portfolio shall contain documentation of knowledge and skill acquisition based on the Core Competencies established by the American Association for Paralegal Education. Those core competencies are divided into two areas—skill development and acquisition of knowledge. Within those areas are competencies based on:

Skill Development

- critical thinking skills
- organizational skills
- general communication skills
- interpersonal skills
- legal research skills
- legal writing skills
- computer skills
- interviewing and investigation skills

Acquisition of Knowledge

- organization and operation of the legal system
- organization and operation of law offices
- the paralegal profession and ethical obligations
- contracts
- torts
- business organizations
- litigation procedures

It is understood that the areas may overlap somewhat and that these areas do not cover all competencies associated with the program, student growth, or professional success. However, students who perfect these competencies and who perform from this educational base have a foundation for success.

It is suggested that the student purchase a secure container to collect and organize the material, [such as] a hanging file folder or file box. This portfolio may be maintained on computer disk; however, you will not have any graded materials if this is the only method of collection you use.

Students should keep a log of all materials completed. When completing each assignment, [they should] enter the document in the log, with a column to check for inclusion in the campus portfolio and another to check for inclusion in the professional portfolio. Some documents may, of course, overlap in their application.

Students are responsible for the contents of their portfolios. The student should periodically review the contents of the portfolio and add or remove materials based on decisions as to the extent to which the contents adequately represent knowledge and skill acquisition in each of the areas outlined below. This portfolio is not intended to be a compilation of senior level work; rather, it is useful to provide work of varying levels of efficiency to show, among other things, growth and improvement.

CONTENT

To be a successful paralegal/legal assistant, the student must possess a common core of legal knowledge as well as acquire vital critical thinking, organizational, communication, and interpersonal skills. Courses in a student's program should provide the student with the means to develop the competencies, which have been divided into the following sections:

- Area 1 Understanding the Profession and Its Ethical Obligations
- Area 2 Research
- Area 3 Legal Writing
- Area 4 Basic Skills
- Area 5 Acquisition of Legal Knowledge
- Area 6 Professional Commitment Beyond Coursework
- Area 7 Evaluation of Professional Growth/ Evaluation of Program
- Appendix

GUIDELINES FOR SELECTING ENTRIES

When selecting entries, students should bear in mind that each piece is part of a much larger whole and that, together, the artifacts and rationale make a powerful statement about individual professional development. Asking the following questions may help with decision making.

1. What do I want my portfolio to show about me as a paralegal? What are my attributes as a paralegal?
2. What do I want my portfolio to demonstrate about me as a learner? How and what have I learned?
3. What directions for my future growth and development does my self-evaluation suggest? How can I show them in my portfolio?
4. What points have been made by others about me as a paralegal and learner? How can I show them in my portfolio?
5. What effect does my professionalism have upon my peers? How can I show this in my portfolio?
6. What overall impression do I want my portfolio to give a reviewer about me as a learner and as a paralegal?

When decision making about what to include becomes a challenge, it may be helpful to look at each artifact and ask yourself, "What would including this item add that has not already been said or shown?" Remember that portfolios create representative records of your professional development; they are not intended to be comprehensive.

VALUES AND ATTITUDES

Values and attitudes determine the choices we make in our lives. They cross the boundaries of subject-matter areas. Thus, in this final section of your portfolio, you are asked to look at your own values and attitudes and then write a one- to three-page paper in which you reflect upon your own values. Identify one or more values that are important to you. Explain how they influence your choices as a person, parent, future paralegal, voter, and/or citizen of the global community. Include specific examples.

The following questions may help you choose a topic for your essay: What does it mean to be honest? fair? tolerant? open to new ideas and experiences? respect evidence? Which is more important—decreasing the production of greenhouse gases or preserving jobs?

The right to choose how many children we want or controlling world population growth? Freedom to produce pornographic art or the right of children to be sheltered from such experiences? Spending more time with your children or getting a second job so you can buy things you want?

There are no easy answers to these questions. Have fun thinking about your own values. Remember to include specific examples from your own life!

TRANSCRIPTS

Include copies of unofficial transcripts from all colleges and universities that you have attended.

Degree evaluation

Graduation evaluation

Awards or recognitions

Include a copy of your degree evaluation, if you received one.

Include a copy of your graduation evaluation.

Include copies of awards or recognitions you have received.

PROFESSIONAL PORTFOLIO

Modify this inclusive portfolio into a professional portfolio. This professional portfolio will be representative, not comprehensive. Each artifact chosen for inclusion should represent at least one significant aspect of you and/or your accomplishments that can be translated into employability. Use these guidelines to prepare your professional portfolio:

1. Prepare your portfolio as a showcase of your best work—your highest achievements. This will involve selecting from artifacts in your portfolio and adding new ones.
2. Do not send your portfolio when you apply for a job. Rather, include in your cover letter a statement concerning your portfolio. For example: "Throughout my paralegal studies program at ____________ College, I developed a professional portfolio that clearly and concisely exhibits my attributes as a paralegal. I would be pleased to share this portfolio with you during an interview."
3. If granted an interview, take your portfolio with you. Be prepared to present the highlights. Practice presenting it effectively. In some instances, you might be asked to present it at the beginning of the interview, and in other instances, you might use it as a source of evidence or enhancement of a point you make in the interview. Interviewing practices vary widely from employer to employer. Portfolios are most likely to be reviewed in situations where the employer is familiar with the abilities of a paralegal.
4. If the interviewer(s) is particularly interested and would like to examine your portfolio more closely, offer to leave it if at all possible. You should make explicit arrangements for collecting it and, of course, follow through as planned. It could be that your portfolio will create the impression that tips the scales in your favor.
5. Remember—it is likely that some people in a position to hire are not familiar with professional portfolios as you know them. Take time to concisely explain that developing your portfolio has been a process of reflection and evaluation that has helped you to know yourself as a paralegal and to establish a foundation for career-long professional development. To some extent, presenting your portfolio will inform the interviewer about both you and the portfolio concept and process.
6. Keep your portfolio up to date. As you continue to gain experience and to grow professionally, alter it to reflect your development. It is not only your first job application that may be enhanced by a well-prepared and presented portfolio but developing your portfolio is an excellent foundation for meeting any expectation of continuing legal education.

CONCLUSION

It is my hope and intention that by your creating this portfolio, you have an opportunity to reflect upon your education and to emphasize to yourself and others that you are capable and qualified to perform as a paralegal. It is time to believe in you. Good luck!

Concept Review *and* Reinforcement

LEGAL TERMINOLOGY

ALS (Accredited Legal Secretary) 15
American Association for Paralegal Education (AAfPE) 12
American Bar Association (ABA) 4
Associate's degree 13
Bachelor's degree 13
Certificate 13
Certified Legal Assistant (CLA) 15
International Paralegal Management Association (IPMA) 19
Legal assistant 4
National Association of Legal Assistants (NALA) 4
National Association of Legal Secretaries (NALS) 25
National Federation of Paralegal Associations (NFPA) 4
Paralegal 4
Paralegal Advance Competency Exam (PACE) 14
PLS (Professional Legal Secretary) 16
PP (Professional Paralegal) 16
Proprietary school 13
Unauthorized Practice of Law (UPL) 21

SUMMARY OF KEY CONCEPTS

What Is a Paralegal?

Definition	A paralegal, or legal assistant, is "a person qualified by education, training, or work experience who is employed or retained by a lawyer, law office, corporation, governmental agency or other entity who performs specifically delegated substantive legal work for which a lawyer is responsible." (American Bar Association, 1997)

What Do Paralegals Do?

Function of Paralegals	The primary function of paralegals is to assist attorneys in preparing for hearings, trials, meetings, and closings.

Professional Skills

Definition	Some professional skills are called "soft skills." These include communication skills, initiative, resourcefulness, problem solving, commitment, teamwork, leadership, and self-motivation.
Resourcefulness	The ability to meet and handle a situation and find solutions to problems.
Commitment	The ability to complete what one starts out to do.
Analytical Skills	Analytical skills involve following a step-by-step process to solve a problem.
Interpersonal Skills	The ability to work with people.
Communication Skills	Good communication means expressing ideas effectively—both orally and in writing.

Career Planning

Career Planning	Career planning includes educational planning and a plan for perfecting professional skills.
Paralegal Education in the United States	An estimated 1,000 paralegal education programs are available in the United States. These programs are offered in on-site, online, and hybrid formats combining online and on-site instruction. Some of these programs have ABA accreditation.

Qualifications of a Paralegal	Qualification guidelines have been established by the American Bar Association's Standing Committee on Paralegals and the American Association for Paralegal Education.
Types of Educational Programs	1. Certificate programs 2. Associate degree programs 3. Baccalaureate programs 4. Graduate programs 5. Specialty certificates
Paralegal Certification	PACE (Paralegal Advance Competency Exam) of the National Federation of Paralegal Associations CLA (Certified Legal Assistant) title given by the National Association of Legal Assistants ALS (the basic certification for legal professionals of NALS) PLS (the advanced certification for legal professionals of NALS) PP (Professional Paralegal certification of NALS)
Making a Personal Assessment and Setting Goals	1. What are your other job skills? 2. What are your personality traits? 3. Do you like working under deadlines? 4. Do you like working with certain groups of people? 5. What are your personal interests? 6. Recognize your strengths. 7. Acknowledge weaknesses.
Selecting a Specialty	Your decision should be based on a self-evaluation of your likes and dislikes, interests, passions, and any physical or geographic limitations.
Assessing Your Background	Doing a self-assessment early in your studies offers you an opportunity to recognize your strengths and develop them, and to acknowledge weaknesses that you need to address.
Regulating the Practice of Law	
Reasons for Regulating the Practice of Law	The practice of law is regulated by state government and court rule to protect the public from incompetent and unscrupulous practitioners.
Regulating the Paralegal Profession	The traditional role of the attorney in advising and representing clients is limited to those who are admitted to practice as lawyers under the applicable state law. Some exemptions do exist that allow nonlawyers to perform certain services under state law.
State Licensing	To address the issue of the unauthorized practice of law, some states have enacted legislation requiring a license to perform certain paralegal functions.
Federal Practice	Under federal regulations, nonlawyers may represent parties before the Social Security Administration, the Patent Office, and other agencies.
Opportunities for Paralegals	
Compensation Issues for the Paralegal	In 2010, the median annual salary for full-time paralegals was $46,680. Income level will vary by specialty, size of firm, and geographical area. The U.S. Department of Labor projects that this profession will continue to grow at 18% per year through the year 2020.
The Future	
Career Planning	As courts require the use of paralegals to reduce legal costs, law firms may have to hire more paralegals and delegate more work to them.

WORKING THE WEB

1. Review the latest information on standards for paralegals of the ABA Standing Committee on Paralegals website at http://www.americanbar.org/groups/paralegals.html.
2. Review the latest "blawg" postings on Paralegals at http://www.abajournal.com/blawgs/topic/paralegals/.
3. The Bureau of Labor Statistics' publication *Occupational Outlook Handbook* is updated regularly. Download a copy of the current version on Paralegals and Legal Assistants and compare the salary ranges with those in this text. Have they changed? www.bls.gov/oco/ocos114.htm
4. One of the significant issues for paralegals over the past years has been whether paralegals are classified as exempt with respect to overtime under the U.S. Department of Labor regulations. Download a copy of the current presentation on executive, administrative, and professional exemption at http://www.dol.gov/whd/flsa/index.htm.
5. Print out a copy of the mission statement or homepage of each of the major national paralegal associations:
   a. International Paralegal Management Association: www.paralegalmanagement.org
   b. NALS, the association for legal professionals: http://www.nals.org
   c. National Federation of Paralegal Associations: www.paralegals.org
   d. National Association of Legal Assistants: www.nala.org
   e. Association of Legal Administrators: www.alanet.org
6. Compare your skills with the list of knowledge or competencies required of principal legal administrators at http://www.alanet.org/about/knowledgelist.aspx.

CRITICAL THINKING & WRITING QUESTIONS

1. How does the American Bar Association define the term "paralegal"?
2. What are the minimum qualifications that a paralegal should meet?
3. What is the role of the paralegal in the legal system?
4. Why should those planning to become paralegals or legal assistants get a well-grounded education and develop the necessary skills before seeking employment?
5. How can one satisfy the court that he or she is qualified as a paralegal and not as merely a legal secretary?
6. What is the advantage to the paralegal in obtaining the PACE or CLA designations?
7. What educational plan makes the most sense for you? Why?
8. How can a candidate for a paralegal position demonstrate that he or she has the qualifications for employment as a paralegal?
9. Why would an employer, such as the U.S. Attorney's office, require a four-year degree for those seeking a paralegal position?
10. Complete the Career Planning checklist on page 19 and assess your personal skills and professional goals. Based on your answers, how well prepared are you for a career as a paralegal? What skills need development?
11. How does assessing your interests and skills help in choosing a career path?
12. What skills are required to be a paralegal and why are they important?
13. Complete the Strengths and Weaknesses checklist on page 8 of this chapter.
14. Why are good English writing and speaking skills important for the paralegal?
15. Complete the My Career Roadmap checklist on page 11 of this chapter.
16. How can you use the Strengths and Weaknesses checklist in preparing your personal career roadmap?
17. What advantages might a person have in entering the paralegal profession later in life?
18. What actions have you observed in other people that demonstrated their resourcefulness? What qualities have others recognized in you that would be considered "resourceful"?
19. How can you demonstrate the characteristic of "commitment"?
20. Start to network by setting up a meeting with a working paralegal and preparing a list of questions to ask at that meeting.

Building Paralegal Skills

VIDEO CASE STUDIES

When Friends Ask for Legal Advice

Dante, a paralegal, is approached by a friend for legal advice about his apartment lease. His landlord is refusing to allow him to have a dog in his apartment.

After viewing the video case study in MyLegalStudiesLab, answer the following:

1. Would a paralegal working in a real estate office be able to give advice as an incidental activity?
2. Is advising the person that you are a paralegal enough to avoid UPL in this situation?
3. What is the law in your state on UPL? How would it address this situation?

Résumé Writing Do's and Don'ts

Two human resource directors in a law office review some of the résumés they have received and discuss the errors people often make in submitting job applications.

After viewing the video case study in MyLegalStudiesLab, answer the following:

1. Why are a good résumé and cover letter so important in getting a paralegal position?
2. What are some of the skills human resource directors look for in new hires?
3. Make a list of skills you need to acquire and courses you should take in pursuing your paralegal studies.

Independent Paralegal

Don Swanson, President of Five Star Legal, an independent paralegal service, discusses the pros and cons of being an independent paralegal.

After viewing the video case study in MyLegalStudiesLab, answer the following:

1. What are the advantages and disadvantages of working as an independent paralegal?
2. Are there any regulatory issues in your jurisdiction on working as an independent paralegal?

ETHICS ANALYSIS & DISCUSSION QUESTIONS

1. Does your state, whether by statute, regulation, code, guideline, or court rule, define "Paralegal" or "Legal Assistant"? If it does, what is that definition and where is it defined? If not, should it formally define the term? Explain why or why not.
2. Does your state have a statute or court rule on the regulation of paralegal or legal assistant practice? What are the requirements to practice as a paralegal or legal assistant? Does the law define the practice in some other terminology?
3. Does your state have minimum educational requirements for paralegals? Should there be a set of minimum qualifications? Explain why or why not.
4. Does having a set of minimum educational requirements eliminate the need for a set of ethical guidelines? Explain.

DEVELOPING YOUR COLLABORATION SKILLS

Working on your own or with a group of other students, review the scenario at the beginning of the chapter, and discuss the employment options and educational issues involved.

1. Discuss why Ethan and Ariel should or should not consider a paralegal career. What are the advantages or disadvantages? What strengths or skills can Ethan and Ariel bring to this career?
2. Working individually or in a group, complete the following:
   a. Summarize, in writing, your career advice to Ethan and Ariel.
   b. Share your advice with other students or groups. Does your group have any additional advice or recommendations?
   c. Take on the role of Ethan or Ariel. Might they have any other questions for Mr. Marshall about the paralegal profession? Make a list of additional questions. Where might Ethan and Ariel get additional information about the paralegal profession?
3. Select a spokesperson who can summarize and present your group's recommendations to the class.

PARALEGAL PORTFOLIO EXERCISE

Using a three-ring binder, start a portfolio of your work and accomplishments in this course. Include any work you are doing in other courses that best represents your growing "skill set." Prepare binder tabs with the following headings, and insert them in your binder:

A. Understanding the Profession and Its Ethical Obligations
B. Research
C. Legal Writing
D. Basic Skills
E. Acquisition of Legal Knowledge
F. Professional Commitment Beyond Coursework
G. Evaluation of Professional Growth/Evaluation of Program
H. Appendix

LEGAL ANALYSIS & WRITING CASES

Doe v. Condon 341 S.C. 22, 532 S.E.2d 879 (2000)

The Unauthorized Practice of Law and the Paralegal

A paralegal asked the court if he could conduct unsupervised "wills and trusts" seminars for the public, "emphasizing" living trusts during the course of his presentation and answering estate-planning questions from the audience. He proposed a fee-splitting arrangement with his attorney–employer.

The South Carolina Supreme Court ruled: The activities of a paralegal do not constitute the practice of law as long as they are limited to work of a preparatory nature, such as legal research, investigation, or the composition of legal documents, which enables licensed attorney–employer to carry a given matter to a conclusion through his own examination, approval, or additional effort. . . .

. . . The paralegal plays a supporting role to the supervising attorney. Here the roles are reversed. The attorney would support the paralegal. Petitioner would play the lead role, with no meaningful attorney supervision and the attorney's presence and involvement only surfaces on the back end. Meaningful attorney supervision must be present throughout the process. The line between what is and what is not permissible conduct by a non-attorney is sometimes unclear as a potential trap for the unsuspecting client. . . . It is well settled the paralegal may not give legal advice, consult, offer legal explanations, or make legal recommendations.

Questions

1. Why is the practice of law limited to licensed attorneys?
2. What tasks may a paralegal perform?
3. What tasks may a paralegal not perform?
4. Why does the answering of legal questions about the need for a will or a trust constitute the unauthorized practice of law (UPL)?
5. Why is a fee-splitting arrangement between a lawyer and a paralegal prohibited?

Note: If in South Carolina, include the parallel citation: 341 S.C. 22. The Lexis citation for this case is 2000 S.C. LEXIS 125.

Sperry v. Florida 373 U.S. 379 (1963)

Petitioner, not a lawyer and not admitted to practice in Florida as a lawyer, was nevertheless authorized to practice before the U.S. Patent Office pursuant to federal statute (35 U.S.C. § 31). The Florida Bar sued to prevent him from representing patent applicants, preparing and prosecuting the patent claims, and advising applicants in the State of Florida.

The Supreme Court, in holding that the Petitioner was permitted to perform tasks incident to prosecuting of patent claims, said,

> by virtue of the Supremacy Clause, Florida may not deny to those failing to meet its own qualifications the right to perform the functions within the scope of the federal authority.

The Court further stated,

> since patent practitioners are authorized to practice before the Patent Office, the State maintains control over the practice of law within its borders except to the limited extent for the accomplishment of the federal objective.

Questions

1. Does this decision allow anyone to practice before any federal agency without being licensed?
2. What are the prerequisites for nonlawyers to act on behalf of others before federal agencies?
3. What steps would a paralegal have to take to prosecute patent claims?

WORKING WITH THE LANGUAGE OF THE COURT CASE

Missouri v. Jenkins

491 U.S. 274 (1989)
Supreme Court of the United States

Read the following case excerpts. Information on preparing a briefing is provided in Appendix A: How to Brief a Case. In your brief, prepare a written answer to each of the following questions.

1. What is the difference between "market rates" for paralegals and the cost to the attorney for paralegal services?
2. Does billing for paralegal services at market rates unfairly benefit the law firm?
3. According to this court, how is a reasonable attorney's fee calculated?
4. How does the public benefit from allowing paralegals to be billed at market rates?
5. Does this court believe that a reasonable attorney's fee should include paralegal fees?

Brennan, J., delivered the opinion of the Court.

This is the attorney's fee aftermath of major school desegregation litigation in Kansas City, Missouri. We [are hearing this case to decide] should the fee award compensate the work of paralegals and law clerks by applying the market rate for their work?

I

This litigation began in 1977 as a suit by the Kansas City Missouri School District (KCMSD), the school board, and the children of two school board members, against the State of Missouri and other defendants. The plaintiffs alleged that the State, surrounding school districts, and various federal agencies had caused and perpetuated a system of racial segregation in the schools of the Kansas City metropolitan area.... After lengthy proceedings, including a trial that lasted 7½ months during 1983 and 1984, the District Court found the State of Missouri and KCMSD liable.... It ordered various intradistrict remedies, to be paid for by the State and KCMSD, including $260 million in capital improvements and a magnet-school plan costing over $200 million.

The plaintiff class has been represented, since 1979, by Kansas City lawyer Arthur Benson and, since 1982, by the NAACP Legal Defense and Educational Fund, Inc. (LDF). Benson and the LDF requested

(continued)

attorney's fees under the Civil Rights Attorney's Fees Awards Act of 1976, 42 U.S.C. § 1988. Benson and his associates had devoted 10,875 attorney hours to the litigation, as well as 8,108 hours of paralegal and law clerk time. For the LDF, the corresponding figures were 10,854 hours for attorneys and 15,517 hours for paralegals and law clerks. Their fee applications deleted from these totals 3,628 attorney hours and 7,046 paralegal hours allocable to unsuccessful claims against the suburban school districts. With additions for postjudgment monitoring and for preparation of the fee application, the District Court awarded Benson a total of approximately $1.7 million and the LDF $2.3 million....

Both Benson and the LDF employed numerous paralegals, law clerks (generally law students working part-time), and recent law graduates in this litigation. The court awarded fees for their work based on Kansas City market rates for those categories. As in the case of the attorneys, it used current rather than historic market rates in order to compensate for the delay in payment. It therefore awarded fees based on hourly rates of $35 for law clerks, $40 for paralegals, and $50 for recent law graduates. [....]

III

Missouri's second contention is that the District Court erred in compensating the work of law clerks and paralegals (hereinafter collectively "paralegals") at the market rates for their services, rather than at their cost to the attorney. While Missouri agrees that compensation for the cost of these personnel should be included in the fee award, it suggests that an hourly rate of $15—which it argued below corresponded to their salaries, benefits, and overhead—would be appropriate, rather than the market rates of $35 to $50. According to Missouri, § 1988 does not authorize billing paralegals' hours at market rates, and doing so produces a "windfall" for the attorney.

We begin with the statutory language, which provides simply for "a reasonable attorney's fee as part of the costs." Clearly, a "reasonable attorney's fee" cannot have been meant to compensate only work performed personally by members of the bar. Rather, the term must refer to a reasonable fee for the work product of an attorney.

Thus, the fee must take into account the work not only of attorneys but also of secretaries, messengers, librarians, janitors, and others whose labor contributes to the work product for which an attorney bills her client; and it also must take account of other expenses and profit. The parties have suggested no reason why the work of paralegals should not be similarly compensated, nor can we think of any. We thus take as our starting point the self-evident proposition that the "reasonable attorney's fee" provided for by statute should compensate the work of paralegals, as well as that of attorneys.

The more difficult question is how the work of paralegals is to be valuated in calculating the overall attorney's fee.

The statute specifies a "reasonable" fee for the attorney's work product. In determining how other elements of the attorney's fee are to be calculated, we have consistently looked to the marketplace as our guide to what is "reasonable." In *Blum v. Stenson*, 465 U.S. 886 (1984), for example, we rejected an argument that attorney's fees for nonprofit legal service organizations should be based on cost. We said: "The statute and legislative history establish that 'reasonable fees' under § 1988 are to be calculated according to the prevailing market rates in the relevant community...." A reasonable attorney's fee under § 1988 is one calculated on the basis of rates and practices prevailing in the relevant market, i.e., "in line with those [rates] prevailing in the community for similar services by lawyers of reasonably comparable skill, experience, and reputation," and one that grants the successful civil rights plaintiff a "fully compensatory fee," comparable to what "is traditional with attorneys compensated by a fee-paying client."

If an attorney's fee awarded under § 1988 is to yield the same level of compensation that would be available from the market, the "increasingly widespread custom of separately billing for the services of paralegals and law students who serve as clerks," all else being equal, the hourly fee charged by an attorney whose rates include paralegal work in her hourly fee, or who bills separately for the work of paralegals at cost, will be higher than the hourly fee charged by an attorney competing in the same market who bills separately for the work of paralegals at "market rates." In other words, the prevailing "market rate" for attorney time is not independent of the manner in which paralegal time is accounted for. Thus, if the prevailing practice in a given community were to bill paralegal time separately at market rates, fees awarded the attorney at market rates for attorney time would not be fully compensatory if the court refused to compensate hours billed by paralegals or did so only at "cost." Similarly, the fee awarded would be too high if the court accepted separate billing for paralegal hours in a market where that was not the custom.

We reject the argument that compensation for paralegals at rates above "cost" would yield a "windfall" for the prevailing attorney. Neither petitioners nor anyone else, to our knowledge, has ever suggested that the hourly rate applied to the work of an associate attorney in a law firm creates a windfall for the firm's partners or is otherwise improper under § 1988, merely because it exceeds the cost of the attorney's services. If the fees are consistent with market rates and practices, the "windfall" argument has no more force with regard to paralegals than it does for associates. And it would hardly accord with Congress' intent to provide a "fully compensatory fee" if the prevailing plaintiff's attorney in a civil rights lawsuit were not permitted to bill separately for paralegals, while the defense attorney in the same litigation was able to take advantage of the prevailing practice and obtain market rates for such work. Yet that is precisely the result sought in this case by the State of Missouri, which appears to have paid its own outside counsel for the work of paralegals at the hourly rate of $35.

Nothing in § 1988 requires that the work of paralegals invariably be billed separately. If it is the practice in the relevant market not to do so, or to bill the work of paralegals only at cost, that is all that § 1988 requires. Where, however, the prevailing practice is to bill paralegal work at market rates, treating civil rights lawyers' fee requests in the same way is not only permitted by § 1988, but also makes economic sense. By encouraging the use of lower cost paralegals rather than attorneys wherever possible, permitting market-rate billing of paralegal hours "encourages cost-effective delivery of legal services and, by reducing the spiraling cost of civil rights litigation, furthers the policies underlying civil rights statutes."

Such separate billing appears to be the practice in most communities today. In the present case, Missouri concedes that "the local market typically bills separately for paralegal services," and the District Court found that the requested hourly rates of $35 for law clerks, $40 for paralegals, and $50 for recent law graduates were the prevailing rates for such services in the Kansas City area. Under these circumstances, the court's decision to award separate compensation at these rates was fully in accord with § 1988.

IV

The courts correctly granted a fee enhancement to compensate for delay in payment and approved compensation of paralegals and law clerks at market rates. The judgment of the Court of Appeals is therefore Affirmed.

MYLEGALSTUDIESLAB

MyLegalStudiesLab Virtual Law Office Experience Assignments

Complete the pre-test, study plan, and post-test for this chapter and answer the Legal Applications questions as assigned. These will help you confirm your mastery of the concepts and their application to legal scenarios. Then complete the Virtual Law Office assignments as assigned by your instructor. These assignments are designed to develop your workplace skills. Completing the assignments for this chapter will result in producing the following documents for inclusion in your portfolio:

VLOE 1.1	Skills and Tasks Self-Assessment Form
VLOE 1.2	Personal calendar for the next four months

CHAPTER

2

Ethics and Professional Responsibility

Paralegals at Work

Kelsey and Kathryn became friends when they were studying to be paralegals. Kathryn now works for a large national law firm, while Kelsey does freelance paralegal work. Over the years, they have met frequently to discuss office issues and client cases. Today, Kelsey asked Kathryn to meet for lunch at a crowded sandwich shop in the office building where she works to discuss a recent matter. Kathryn could see that something was troubling her friend. After getting a seat at the lunch counter, they ordered lunch, and Kelsey began to confide in Kathryn.

Kelsey regularly does freelance work for two suburban sole practioners—one who specializes in intellectual-property issues and occasionally does plaintiffs injury work for friends and family and one who does mostly personal injury work. Both are working on the same case, and both have asked Kelsey to work on the file. One lawyer represents the plaintiff, a close family friend, and the other lawyer represents the defendant. Both lawyers want Kelsey to interview the clients, witnesses, and generally handle the file. Kelsey is wondering whether she should be working "both sides of the fence." Kelsey describes to Kathryn the clients and the case in detail while they wait for their lunch to be served.

Kelsey also explains that she often does most of the work on the plaintiff lawyer's cases not related to intellectual property, including settling the cases with insurance company adjusters or the lawyers representing the defendants. Kelsey knows the adjuster on this case, and he has revealed to her that the insurance company for the defendant wants to settle the case quickly and avoid a trial. Kelsey asks Kathryn for advice.

Consider the issues involved in this scenario as you read the chapter.

LEARNING OBJECTIVES

After studying this chapter, you should be able to:

1. Explain how the practice of law is regulated.
2. Analyze a situation to determine whether it involves the unauthorized practice of law.
3. Define ethics and explain the difference between the attorney's rules of ethics and the paralegal's rules of ethics.
4. Explain the lawyer's ethical duty to supervise.
5. Discuss the ethical obligation of competence.
6. Explain the concept of confidentiality of client communications and the attorney–client privilege.
7. Discuss the concept of conflict of interest in the legal profession.
8. Describe the duty of candor to the court and other counsel and the ethical duty of fairness.

> "Morality cannot be legislated, but behavior can be regulated. Judicial decrees may not change hearts, but they can restrain the heartless."
>
> Martin Luther King Jr.

INTRODUCTION TO ETHICS

Every profession has a set of rules that members of that profession are expected to follow. These rules typically set forth the minimum in ethical behavior—the very least each professional should do. In the field of law, these rules are referred to as "the rules of ethics" or "the rules of professional responsibility."

Each state regulates the right to practice law, and therefore each state has adopted its own rules of **ethics**. The Supreme Court or legislature of each state has created a committee or board that is authorized to enforce these rules of professional responsibility. States typically have a bar association to receive and investigate complaints against lawyers. With a few exceptions, most states have adopted some form of the American Bar Association **Model Rules of Professional Conduct**. This provides a high degree of consistency in the **ethical guidelines** for the legal profession across the country. Exhibit 2.1 shows the links and resources provided by the American Bar Association (ABA) regarding ethics. The ABA monitors the status of state ethical rules and issues a report on the status of state reviews. A portion of this report is shown in Exhibit 2.2.

National paralegal associations, such as the National Association of Legal Assistants (NALA) and the National Federation of Paralegal Associations (NFPA), also have ethics

Ethics Minimally acceptable standards of conduct in a profession.

ABA Model Rules of Professional Conduct A recommended set of ethics and professional conduct guidelines for lawyers, prepared by the American Bar Association, and originally released in 1983.

Ethical guidelines Rules of minimally acceptable professional conduct.

Web Exploration

The links to state ethics resources on the ABA website may be found at http://www.americanbar.org/groups/professional_responsibility/resources/links_of_interest.html

Web Exploration

Check the latest version of the ABA Model Rules of Professional Conduct at http://www.abanet.org/cpr/mrpc/model_rules.htm.

Web Exploration

The American Bar Association Center for Professional Responsibility website has links to other national, state, and international ethics resources. One of the resources available online is its report on the status of individual state review of Professional Conduct Rules. The full report may be viewed at http://www.abanet.org/cpr/jclr/ethics_2000_status_chart.pdf.

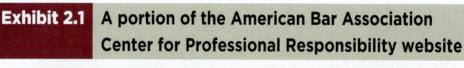

Exhibit 2.1 A portion of the American Bar Association Center for Professional Responsibility website

Home Contact Sitemap fax: 918-582-6772 Search: GO

ABOUT PARALEGALS
THE ASSOCIATION OF LEGAL ASSISTANTS • PARALEGALS

About NALA & Join | About Paralegals | Certification | Continuing Education | Facts & Findings | Affiliated Associations | Members' Area

About Paralegals

According to the U.S. Bureau of Labor Statistics, employment of paralegals and legal assistants is projected to grow 22 percent between 2006 and 2016, much faster than the average for all occupations. Review this area and the links below to learn more about the paralegal profession and NALA's role in leading the field.

Click here to read about the Paralegal Profession in the Bureau of Labor Statistics Occupational Outlook Handbook, 2010-2011

This section sponsored by:

GO THE DISTANCE FROM A DISTANCE
THE GEORGE WASHINGTON UNIVERSITY MASTER'S IN PARALEGAL STUDIES ONLINE
LEARN MORE NOW ›

A legal assistant or paralegal is a person qualified by education, training or work experience who is employed or retained by a lawyer, law office, corporation, governmental agency or other entity who performs specifically delegated substantive legal work for which a lawyer is responsible. (Adopted by the ABA in 1997)

NALA Code of Ethics and Professional Responsibility

Copyright 2007; Adopted 1975; Revised 1979, 1988; 1995; 2007.
National Association of Legal Assistants, Inc.

Each NALA member agrees to follow the canons of the NALA Code of Ethics and Professional Responsibility Violations of the Code may result in cancellation of membership. First adopted by the NALA membership in May of 1975, the Code of Ethics and Professional Responsibility is the foundation of ethical practices of paralegals in the legal community.

A paralegal must adhere strictly to the accepted standards of legal ethics and to the general principles of proper conduct. The performance of the duties of the paralegal shall be governed by specific canons as defined herein so that justice will be served and goals of the profession attained. (See Model Standards and Guidelines for Utilization of Legal Assistants, Section II.)

The canons of ethics set forth hereafter are adopted by the National Association of Legal Assistants, Inc., as a general guide intended to aid paralegals and attorneys. The enumeration of these rules does not mean there are not others of equal importance although not specifically mentioned. Court rules, agency rules and statutes must be taken into consideration when interpreting the canons.

Definition: Legal assistants, also known as paralegals, are a distinguishable group of persons who assist attorneys in the delivery of legal services. Through formal education, training and experience, legal assistants have knowledge and expertise regarding the legal system and substantive and procedural law which qualify them to do work of a legal nature under the supervision of an attorney.

In **2001**, NALA members also adopted the ABA definition of a legal assistant/paralegal, as follows:

A legal assistant or paralegal is a person qualified by education, training or work experience who is employed or retained by a lawyer, law office, corporation, governmental agency or other entity who performs specifically delegated substantive legal work for which a lawyer is responsible. (Adopted by the ABA in 1997)

Canon 1.
A paralegal must not perform any of the duties that attorneys only may perform nor take any actions that attorneys may not take.

Reprinted with permission of NALA, The Association for Paralegals-Legal Assistants. Inquiries should be directed to NALA, 516 S. Boston, #200, Tulsa, OK 74119, www.nala.org

Exhibit 2.2 **Portion of the ABA Status of State Review of Professional Conduct Rules as of September 14, 2011**

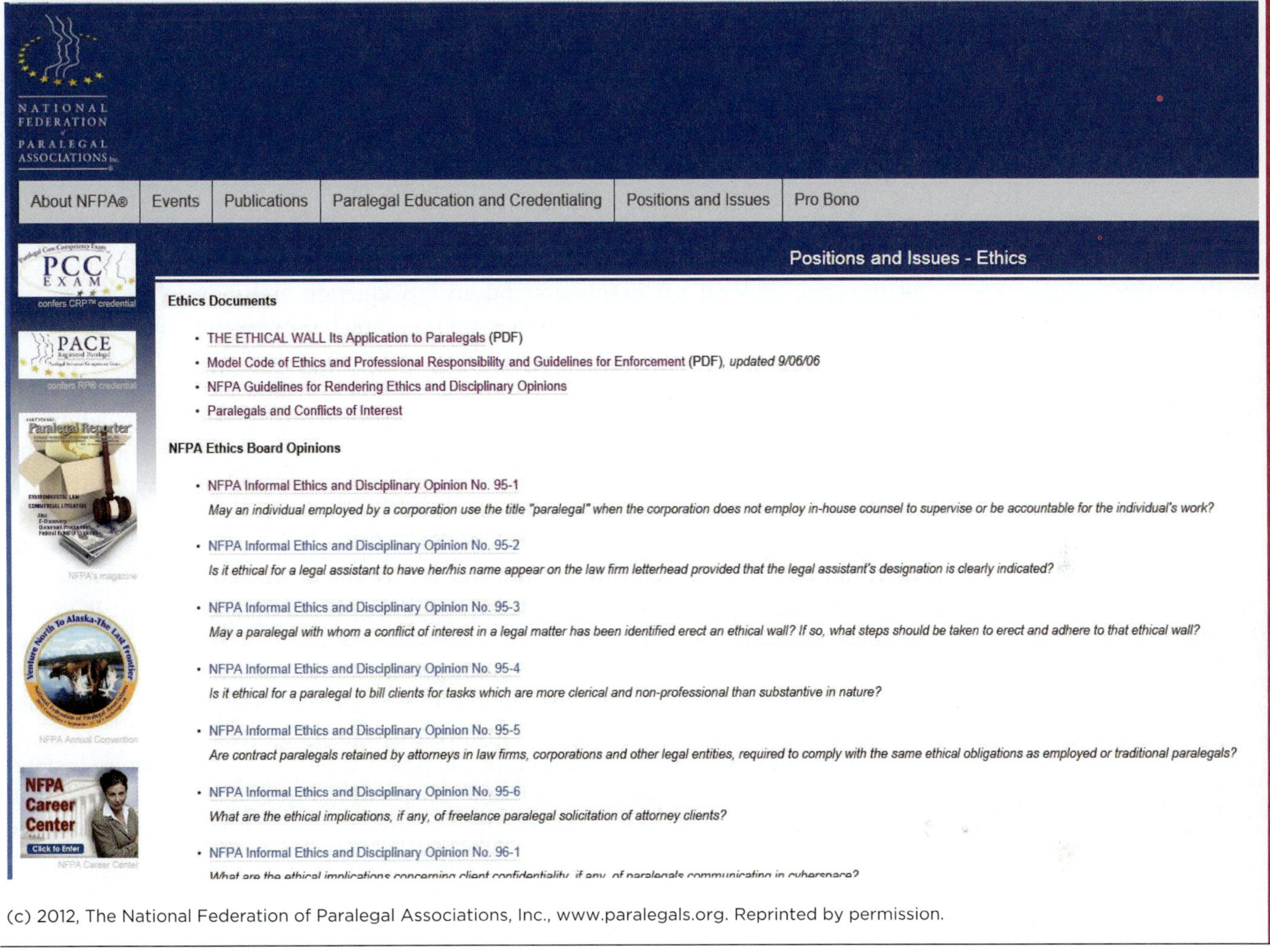

guidelines. These organizations require members to conduct themselves in accordance with these guidelines as a condition of continued membership in the organization.

Regulation of the Practice of Law

Learning Objective 1
Explain how the practice of law is regulated.

Just as the practice of medicine and other professions is regulated, the practice of law is regulated in an attempt to protect the public from incompetent and unscrupulous practitioners. The purpose of regulating and monitoring those who practice law can be found in the Preamble to the Illinois Supreme Court Rules of Professional Conduct:

> The practice of law is a public trust. Lawyers are the trustees of the system by which citizens resolve disputes among themselves, punish and deter crime, and determine their relative rights and responsibilities toward each other and their government. Lawyers therefore are responsible for the character, competence and integrity of the persons whom they assist in joining their profession; for assuring access to that system through the availability of competent legal counsel; for maintaining public confidence in the system of justice by acting competently and with loyalty to the best interests of their clients; by working to improve that system to meet the challenges of a rapidly changing society; and by defending the integrity of the judicial system against those who would corrupt, abuse or defraud it.

For certain occupations and professions, such as law, a license is required in order to offer services to the public. In some professions, obtaining a license may be as simple as completing a form and providing proof that the requirements for education and experience have been satisfied. But for the profession of law, a qualifying examination is required after proving that the necessary legal education has been obtained.

The examination is generally referred to as the "bar exam." The word *bar* is derived from an old custom in courtrooms of using a physical railing to separate the public, who observe court proceedings from a rear seating area, from the front area of the court where the judge, jury, witness stand, and counsel tables are located. Only attorneys are permitted to "pass the bar" and enter this front area.

The bar examination tests the applicant's basic legal knowledge and attempts to ensure a minimum standard of competency. Passing the exam is the first step in getting "admitted to practice." Candidates are admitted upon the recommendation of the state or local bar examiners and an introduction and motion by an existing member of the bar of that court. Admission is completed by a ceremony where attorneys are sworn in by the court to which they are admitted to practice.

Admission to practice before one court does not automatically authorize practice before other courts. Each state has its own rules and standards. Generally, admission to the highest court of the state confers admission to all of the lower courts of that state. The right to practice before the various federal courts requires a separate application and admission to practice. Admission to federal court is generally granted upon motion of an existing member of the court bar upon submission of proof of good character and proof of admission to practice before the highest court of the state.

In some states, prior admission in one state for a required period of time is sufficient for admission to another state without taking the exam. However, today's rules have generally eliminated these alternative methods of admission to the practice of law. Even seasoned attorneys seeking admission to states such as California and Florida must retake the examination for that state in order to be admitted.

The rules that must be followed in the practice of law are found in each state's code of professional responsibility or canons of ethics. Most states have adopted the Model Rules of Professional Conduct approved by the ABA, with some variation. The rules of conduct are enforced by state disciplinary committees, and sanctions may be imposed against offending attorneys. Complaints about breaches of ethical behavior are referred to a committee for investigation, or a committee may act upon the recommendation of a court. Minor infractions may subject the lawyer to reprimand or censure. Serious cases may result in temporary or permanent loss of the license to practice law, called *disbarment*.

Unauthorized Practice of Law (UPL) Giving legal advice, if legal rights may be affected, by anyone not licensed to practice law.

The **Unauthorized Practice of Law (UPL)** is a statutory criminal violation, and complaints of UPL are generally referred to the state's attorney for prosecution. It should be noted that some other ethical breaches may also be violations of a criminal statute. For example, attorneys who breach a client's trust by taking money out of the client's fund are guilty of violating both an ethical rule and the criminal law against theft.

The Paralegal and Licensing

There are, with a few exceptions, no state licensing requirements for working as a paralegal. Some states, such as California, Maine, and North Carolina, have enacted legislation establishing licensure of paralegals to perform some of the functions often performed by lawyers,. Generally, these rules are an attempt to regulate unsupervised freelance or independent paralegals who provide document preparation services. At best, these laws carve out a small part of law practice that may be performed by nonlawyers without their being charged with the unlawful practice of law. But no jurisdiction allows anyone other than a licensed attorney to give legal advice or opinions. Even the selection of the correct form is considered a lawyer's function, as specified in the California Business Code.

There is a fine line between lawful activity and the unlawful practice of law. Recommending or selecting a form could impact a person's legal rights, and may subject the unlicensed person to a charge of UPL. The issue for the paralegal is knowing when explaining information or helping someone fill in a blank form is UPL.

Although each state is free to define the practice of law differently, the statutes have certain elements in common. A typical definition of the "practice of law" is that of Rule 31of the Rules of the Supreme Court of Arizona:

> A. "Practice of law" means providing legal advice or services to or for another by:
>
> (1) preparing any document in any medium intended to affect or secure legal rights for a specific person or entity;
> (2) preparing or expressing legal opinions;
> (3) representing another in a judicial, quasi-judicial, or administrative proceeding, or other formal dispute resolution process such as arbitration and mediation;
> (4) preparing any document through any medium for filing in any court, administrative agency or tribunal for a specific person or entity; or
> (5) negotiating legal rights or responsibilities for a specific person or entity....

Penalties for the Unauthorized Practice of Law

Some states have specifically addressed the issue of the unauthorized practice of law by paralegals and legal assistants. For example, Pennsylvania has enacted a statute that makes it a misdemeanor for "any person, including, but not limited to, a paralegal or legal assistant who within this Commonwealth, shall practice law..." 42 Pa. C.S.A. § 2524.

The drafters of these statutes were concerned that the title of paralegal or legal assistant would be misinterpreted as meaning that a person has been admitted to practice law. However, an unresolved question in Pennsylvania and other states is what specific conduct constitutes the "practice of law." Because that interpretation will vary from state to state, paralegals must be aware of how courts have defined the unauthorized practice of law in each jurisdiction they work in.

In those states that have enacted legislation to regulate paralegal activity, some guidance is offered by definitions within the statutes. For example, California defines activities permitted by an "Unlawful Detainer Assistant" or a "Legal Document Assistant":

Chapter 5.5. Legal Document Assistants and Unlawful Detainer Assistants

Article 1. General Provisions

> 6400(a) "Unlawful detainer assistant" means any individual who for compensation renders assistance or advice in the prosecution or defense of an unlawful detainer claim or action, including any bankruptcy petition that may affect the unlawful detainer claim or action.
> (b) "Unlawful detainer claim" means a proceeding, filing, or action affecting rights or liabilities of any person that arises under Chapter 4 (commencing with Section 1159) of Title 3 of Part 3 of the Code of Civil Procedure and that contemplates an adjudication by a court.
> (c) "Legal document assistant" means:
> (1) Any person who is not exempted under Section 6401 and who provides, or assists in providing, or offers to provide, or offers to assist in providing, for compensation, any self-help service to a member of the public who is representing himself or herself in a legal matter, or who holds himself or herself out as someone who offers that service or has that authority. This paragraph does not apply to any individual whose assistance consists merely of secretarial or receptionist services.

Avoiding UPL

Learning Objective 2
Analyze a situation to determine whether it involves the unauthorized practice of law.

Every paralegal must carefully consider the question of how to avoid UPL. Although there is much uncertainty about what constitutes UPL, some general guidelines are provided.

Avoiding UPL: Holding Oneself Out

A common thread in the law of UPL is the prohibition against "holding oneself out" as a lawyer when not admitted to practice law. Florida defines UPL as follows:

> Any person not licensed or otherwise authorized to practice law in this state who practices law in this state or holds himself or herself out to the public as qualified to practice law in this state, or who willfully pretends to be, or willfully takes or uses any name, title, addition, or description implying that he or she is qualified, or recognized by law as qualified, to practice law in this state, commits a felony of the third degree....
>
> Chapter *2004-287*, Senate Bill 1776.

For paralegals, one of the most basic rules in avoiding UPL is to inform the parties with whom they are dealing that they are not lawyers. Paralegals must not hold themselves out as being anything other than a paralegal, and parties who have contact with the paralegal must know the limited role a paralegal has on the legal team.

Making sure clients understand the role of the paralegal can be a challenge. For some clients, the paralegal is their main contact with the law firm, and is the one through whom all documents and information are communicated. Some may believe that because a paralegal is a person with advanced training and knowledge, he or she can perform some of the functions normally performed by lawyers, such as giving legal advice and opinions.

Some clients may come from backgrounds where the distinctions between lawyers and other staff members are not clear. For example, some may come from countries with legal systems where legal professionals play different roles, or where different terms are used for those who perform legal-type functions, such as notaries. For persons for whom English is a second language, problems in translation may contribute to the misunderstanding.

Paralegals must immediately make it clear that they are paralegals and not lawyers. In a first meeting with anyone, whether that person is a client, witness, opposing attorney, or a courthouse staff member, the wisest course of action is to advise him or her of one's position as a paralegal. A short statement such as, "I am the paralegal for attorney [name of attorney]" may be sufficient to put the other party on notice. Business cards and letterheads, where permitted, should clearly state the title of paralegal. Correspondence should always include the title of paralegal as part of the signature block. In its Business Code, California has attempted to protect the public by requiring the following statement to be made to prospective clients:

> (4) The statement: "I am not an attorney" and, if the person offering legal document assistant or unlawful detainer assistant services is a partnership or a corporation, or uses a fictitious business name, "(name) is not a law firm. I/we cannot represent you in court, advise you about your legal rights or the law, or select legal forms for you."

This provision tries to avoid the problem of a paralegal misleading the public into thinking he or she is a lawyer when limited services are provided, such as document preparation.

Never allow the other party to think you are anything other than what you are—a professional who is a paralegal. For those who are not familiar with the role of the paralegal, you may have to clarify what the paralegal can and cannot do in your jurisdiction.

Avoiding UPL: Giving Advice

Every state prohibits anyone other than a licensed attorney from expressing legal opinions. A paralegal cannot give legal opinions or advice. This rule sounds simple, but actually following it can be complicated. Paralegals must carefully monitor their communications to avoid giving legal advice or rendering a legal opinion. Certain clients and those seeking "a little free advice" may not respect the limitations on the paralegal's role in the legal system.

Certain statements addressed to a paralegal should send up a red flag. A request from a client to prepare a power of attorney or some other document "without bothering the lawyer" should give the paralegal pause. Even in a social setting, legal advice may be casually requested, and the statement, "I am not an attorney" or "I cannot represent you in court, advise you about your legal rights or the law, or select legal forms for you" may need to be repeated.

If legal rights may be affected, it probably is legal advice. However, this is not always easy to determine. Consider the seemingly innocent question, "How should I sign my name?" If a person is signing a document in a representative capacity as the officer of a corporation or on behalf of another person under a power of attorney, she must indicate that capacity when signing. Telling the client to simply sign her name without also telling her to indicate her representative capacity might be considered giving legal advice because the client's legal rights could be affected if he or she does not indicate representative capacity.

Avoiding UPL: Filling Out Forms

Filling out forms for clients also can be a source of trouble. In some jurisdictions, paralegals are permitted to assist clients in preparing certain documents. Other courts, however, view this assistance as rendering legal advice. As one Tennessee court has stated,

> As a general matter, other courts have held that the sale of self-help legal kits or printed legal forms does not constitute the unauthorized practice of law as long as the seller provides the buyer no advice regarding which forms to use or how the forms should be filled out.
>
> *Fifteenth Judicial District Unified Bar Association v. Glasgow*, No. M1996-00020-COA-R3-CV, 1999 Tenn. App. LEXIS 815 (Tenn. Ct. of App., Dec. 10, 1999)

A Florida court considering this issue held that UPL consists of

> a nonlawyer who has direct contact with individuals in the nature of consultation, explanation, recommendations, advice, and assistance in the provision, selection, and completion of legal forms engages in the unlicensed practice of law.... [W]hile a nonlawyer may sell certain legal forms and type up instruments completed by clients, a nonlawyer "must not engage in personal legal assistance in conjunction with her business activities, including the correction of errors and omissions...."
>
> *The Florida Bar v. We The People Forms and Service Center of Sarasota, Inc.*, 883 So.2d 1280 (Fla. 2004)

Avoiding UPL: Representing Clients

Nonlawyers are sometimes permitted to represent another person before a judicial or quasi-judicial board, such as an administrative agency. However, it is often difficult to know under what circumstances this is acceptable. Some jurisdictions and administrative agencies do permit those who are not licensed or admitted to practice to appear in court or before administrative law judges or referees on behalf of clients. Under limited circumstances, law students may represent clients under the guidance and supervision of an attorney, depending on the jurisdiction, the nature of the action, and the level of the court.

Acting as a legal representative has traditionally been the role of lawyers. But even lawyers are not always permitted to represent certain parties. A lawyer admitted to practice in one state may not necessarily be permitted to represent the same client in another state. Lawyers admitted to practice in one jurisdiction, however, may ask the court of another jurisdiction for permission to appear and try a specific case. This is a courtesy usually granted for a single case, and the trial attorney is usually required to retain a local attorney to act as co-counsel and advise as to local rules and procedures. The complexity of the situation is raised in a portion of a report on the Unauthorized Practice of Law prepared by the Nevada Assistant Bar Counsel:

> The Bar has received complaints of out-of-state counsel participating in the pre-litigation mediation procedures. Writing notification letters, engaging in discovery, and appearing at pre-litigation mediations in a representative capacity is generally the practice of law. In Nevada there is no mechanism to obtain authority from the Supreme Court to appear in pre-litigation cases. Therefore, engaging in legal activities involving Nevada disputes and Nevada parties requires a licensed Nevada attorney....
>
> (Unauthorized Practice of Law, David A. Clark, Assistant Bar Counsel, September 20, 2001)

If the rules regarding representation of clients are unclear for members of the bar, they are certainly not clear for members of the paralegal profession. Generally, only duly admitted lawyers in the jurisdiction may represent parties. But this rule has been modified to allow law students in some states to represent parties in certain situations, under appropriate supervision. In some states, a nonlawyer employee may represent a business in some proceedings before administrative agencies or before the minor judiciary, such as small claims courts. There is no uniformity among the rules concerning when nonlawyers may represent parties or before which agencies or courts. Any appearance before a court must be approached carefully. Even something very minor, such as the presentation of a request for continuance of a case, may be considered the practice of law by some courts.

The rules for appearing before federal and state administrative agencies also lack uniformity. Some federal agencies specifically permit nonlawyers to appear. The Social Security Administration allows representation by nonlawyers to nearly the same extent as lawyers. The U.S. Patent Office also permits nonlawyer practice. Some state agencies, by specific legislation or administrative rule, also permit representation by nonlawyers.

Avoiding UPL: Guidelines

The Model Standards and Guidelines for the Utilization of Legal Assistants written by the National Association of Legal Assistants (NALA) provide guidelines for avoiding UPL:

Guideline 1

Legal Assistants Should:

1. Disclose their status as legal assistants at the outset of any professional relationship with a client, other attorneys, a court or administrative agency or personnel thereof, or members of the general public.

Guideline 2

Legal Assistants Should Not:

1. Establish attorney–client relationships; set legal fees; give legal opinions or advice; or represent a client before a court, unless authorized to do so by said court; nor
2. Engage in, encourage, or contribute to any act that could constitute the unauthorized practice of law.

Guideline 3

Legal Assistants May Perform Services for an Attorney in the Representation of a Client, Provided:

1. The services performed by the legal assistant do not require the exercise of independent professional legal judgment;
2. The attorney maintains a direct relationship with the client and maintains control of all client matters;
3. The attorney supervises the legal assistant;
4. The attorney remains professionally responsible for all work on behalf of the client, including any actions taken or not taken by the legal assistant in connection therewith; and
5. The services performed supplement, merge with, and become the attorney's work product.

Learning Objective 3

Define ethics and explain the difference between the attorney's rules of ethics and the paralegal's rules of ethics.

Ethical Duties and Obligations

Ethics are the minimally acceptable standards of behavior in a profession. Ethical conduct is expected and required of every member of the legal team, including attorneys, paralegals, litigation support staff, information technologists, and outside consultants.

All members of the legal team, including nonlawyer members, must understand their ethical obligations and how the ethics rules are to be followed and enforced.

Ethical guidelines are enforced by the court in the jurisdiction where the attorney is practicing or where a case is being tried. These rules are as much a part of the administration of justice as the rules of civil or criminal procedure and the rules of evidence. The supervising attorney of every legal team must follow the ethics rules and ensure that the members of the legal team follow the same rules. As law firms utilize more outside consultants and experts, they must carefully consider who has the responsibility to instruct the nonlawyer members of the team and who is responsible for ensuring their compliance. While it is ultimately the responsibility of the lawyer to supervise these nonlawyers, in many cases this obligation falls to the paralegal or litigation manager.

Among the ethical obligations of the attorney, and the legal team acting as agent of the attorney, are:

- Competency (Model Rules of Professional Conduct, Rule 1.1),
- Confidentiality (Model Rules of Professional Conduct, Rule 1.6(A)),
- Conflicts of Interest (Model Rules of Professional Conduct, Rule 1.7),
- Candor (Model Rules of Professional Conduct, Rule 3.3),
- Fairness to Opposing Party and Counsel (Model Rules of Professional Conduct, Rule 3.4), and
- Duty to Supervise (Model Rules of Professional Conduct, Rules 5.1 and 5.3).

Related to the ethical duty of confidentiality is the rule of attorney–client privilege and the **work product** doctrine under **Federal Rules of Evidence** Rule 501. These rules of evidence bar the legal team from having to testify, and protect from disclosure work that the legal team has prepared for trial.

Federal Rules of Evidence The rules governing the admissibility of evidence in federal court.

Ethical Guidelines and Rules

Lawyers generally need to follow only one set of ethics rules. These rules are enacted by the state legislature and are adopted by the supreme court of the state in which lawyers practice.

Most states have adopted the Model Rules of Professional Conduct (MRPC), prepared by the ABA and originally released in 1983. Each state reviews the MRPC and adopts either the entire set, or portions of it as it thinks appropriate for its jurisdiction.

Unlike the MRPC for lawyers, no single source of ethical rules exists for the legal assistant. Legal assistants must follow state statutes and conduct themselves in conformity with the rules of professional conduct and ethics opinions applicable to attorneys. The two major legal assistant organizations, the National Federation of Paralegal Associations (NFPA) and the National Association of Legal Assistants (NALA), provide ethical codes for their members.

Although legal assistants are not governed directly by the ethical rules for attorneys, there is an intertwined relationship between the lawyer, the client, and the paralegal. Under the MRPC, the lawyer ultimately is responsible for the actions of the paralegal. What the paralegal does or does not do can have a real impact on the lawyer's duties and obligations to the client.

ABA Model Guidelines for the Utilization of Paralegal Services

In 1991, the ABA's policymaking body, the House of Delegates, initially adopted a set of guidelines intended to govern the conduct of lawyers when utilizing paralegals or legal assistants. These guidelines were updated in 2002 to reflect the legal and policy developments that had taken place since 1991.

Model Guidelines for the Utilization of Legal Assistant Services A set of guidelines by the ABA policymaking body, the House of Delegates, intended to govern the conduct of lawyers when they are utilizing paralegals or legal assistants.

Paralegals *in* Practice

PARALEGAL PROFILE

Vicki Voisin

Vicki Voisin, an Advanced Certified Paralegal, is nationally recognized as an author and speaker on ethical issues related to the paralegal profession. She is the creator and presenter of EthicsBasics, a program designed to raise awareness of ethical concerns by legal professionals and corporate employees. She also publishes an e-magazine titled Strategies for Paralegals Seeking Excellence *(www.paralegalmentor.com). Vicki is a past president of the National Association of Legal Assistants (NALA), and presently serves on NALA's Advanced Certification Board. She has over 20 years of paralegal experience and is currently employed by Running, Wise & Ford in Charlevoix, Michigan.*

The most important paralegal skills needed in the law office where I work are a familiarity with court rules and ethical issues, the ability to communicate clearly with clients, excellent organizational skills, and an attentiveness to detail and accuracy.

I also believe that technology plays an important role in the legal profession. Although technology allows attorneys and paralegals to work faster, it does not necessarily guarantee that all of the work results are accurate. Paralegals should be aware of the potential ethical hazards that technology can introduce, especially in the areas of confidentiality and conflicts of interest. For example, unless done properly, redaction (editing) on electronically filed documents can be un-covered, resulting in the disclosure of confidential and/or privileged information to third parties.

All paralegals should be aware of their ethical obligations and those of an attorney. My advice is to familiarize yourself with the American Bar Association's Model Rules of Professional Conduct, as well as its Guidelines for the Utilization of Paralegal Services. Then, become acquainted with the related Model Rules and Guidelines for your particular state, if available. Also, join professional associations to keep abreast of trends, and attend continuing education programs as often as possible.

Attorneys are bound by the ethical code adopted by the state in which they practice. As a general rule, whatever the ethical rules forbid the attorney from doing, they also forbid the paralegal from doing. Paralegals, therefore, can look to their state's adopted set of rules, or code of professional responsibility, for guidance in deciding what is appropriate or inappropriate from an ethical perspective.

By the rule of agency, the paralegal, as an agent of the supervising attorney, also becomes an agent of the client. The attorney is an agent of the client, and the paralegal is a subagent. As a subagent, the same duties that are owed to the law firm are also owed to the client.

A question that arises in firms engaged in corporate and securities practice is whether the paralegal can purchase securities (stock) in a client corporation. Some firms have written policies prohibiting members of the firm, including paralegals, from purchasing the securities of client corporations. A more complex issue is that of the propriety of using information obtained from the client to purchase or sell the client's securities. The use of inside information to trade stocks is generally a violation of federal securities laws. If a purchase or sale was made based upon material inside information, or information not generally available to the public, the trade may be illegal.

For the attorney, guidance is available under Model Rule 1.7 and the comments to the Rule, which provide that an attorney must refuse employment when personal interests, including financial interests, might sway professional judgment. To the extent that this rule applies to the attorney, good judgment would dictate that it applies to the paralegal as well.

Web Exploration

The National Associations' Ethics Codes and ethical guidelines can be reviewed at:

National Federation of Paralegal Associations
http://www.paralegals.org/displaycommon.cfm?an=1&subarticlenbr=330

National Association of Legal Assistants
http://www.nala.org

NALS, the Association for Legal Professionals
http://www.nals.org

Association of Legal Administrators
www.alanet.org

Ethics Codes of Paralegal Associations

The paralegal profession has no unified code of ethics. State regulations and ethics opinions applicable to paralegals are not uniform. However, national organizations such as the National Association of Legal Assistants and the National Federation of Paralegal Associations each provide a uniform code of ethical conduct for their members.

National Federation of Paralegal Associations

The National Federation of Paralegal Associations, Inc. (NFPA) is a professional organization composed of paralegal associations and individual paralegals throughout the United States and Canada. Members of NFPA reflect the diversity of the paralegal profession and vary widely in background, experience, and education. NFPA promotes the growth, development, and recognition of the paralegal profession as an integral partner in the delivery of legal services.

In April 1997, the NFPA adopted its Model Disciplinary Rules to enforce the NFPA Model Code. However, unlike the sanctions for violations by an attorney of the state-adopted rules of ethics, such as loss of the right to practice (disbarment), no such sanctions exist for the breach of association rules by a paralegal, except loss of membership.

National Association of Legal Assistants

The National Association of Legal Assistants (NALA), formed in 1975, is a leading professional association for legal assistants. NALA provides continuing professional education, development, and certification, and is best known in the profession for its Certified Legal Assistant (CLA) examination. The ABA Standing Committee on Paralegals has recognized the CLA designation as a mark of high professional achievement.

Supervision

Learning Objective 4

Explain the lawyer's ethical duty to supervise.

Under Rules 5.1 and 5.3 of the Model Rules of Professional Conduct, the **supervising attorney** has the ethical obligation to supervise all who work on a case, including their ethical conduct. Each person supervised by the attorney is the **agent** of the attorney. Under agency law, the agent and the **principal**—the attorney—have a **fiduciary relationship** to each other. The agent must obey the reasonable instructions of the principal, and the principal is presumed to know everything the agent learns in the ordinary course of working for the attorney on the case. The attorney is ultimately responsible for the ethical conduct of the agent.

Supervising attorney The member of the legal team to whom all others on the team report and who has the ultimate responsibility for the actions of the legal team.

Agent A party who acts on behalf of another.

Principal A party who employs another person to act on his or her behalf.

Fiduciary relationship A relationship under which one party has a duty to act for the interest and benefit of another while acting within the scope of the relationship.

ARTICLE VIII. ILLINOIS RULES OF PROFESSIONAL CONDUCT OF 2010

RULE 5.1: RESPONSIBILITIES OF PARTNERS, MANAGERS, AND SUPERVISORY LAWYERS

(a) A partner in a law firm, and a lawyer who individually or together with other lawyers possesses comparable managerial authority in a law firm, shall make reasonable efforts to ensure that the firm has in effect measures giving reasonable assurance that all lawyers in the firm conform to the Rules of Professional Conduct.

(b) A lawyer having direct supervisory authority over another lawyer shall make reasonable efforts to ensure that the other lawyer conforms to the Rules of Professional Conduct.

(c) A lawyer shall be responsible for another lawyer's violation of the Rules of Professional Conduct if:

   (1) the lawyer orders or, with knowledge of the specific conduct, ratifies the conduct involved; or

   (2) the lawyer is a partner or has comparable managerial authority in the law firm in which the other lawyer practices, or has direct supervisory authority over the other lawyer, and knows of the conduct at a time when its consequences can be avoided or mitigated but fails to take reasonable remedial action

Under Rule 5.1, partners and lawyers with managerial authority in the firm must ensure that other lawyers' conduct conforms to the ethical code. Under Rule 5.3(b), supervising attorneys with direct authority over nonlawyers have an ethical obligation to ensure that the conduct of those persons is compatible with the obligations of the lawyer. Under Rule 5.3(b), what happens in the handling and processing of a case by the legal team is ultimately the responsibility of the supervising attorney, including any ethical breaches.

The attorney is the one to whom the client looks for professional advice and/or resolution of a case. The attorney will suffer any sanctions that result from a failure by members of the legal team to follow and enforce the ethical rules. These sanctions can come from two sources: the court hearing the underlying action and the attorney disciplinary agency. The court typically punishes this type of misbehavior with monetary sanctions, to compensate the other side for the time and effort they expended or will expend because of the abuse. The attorney disciplinary agency's punishment can include, in extreme cases, disbarment or suspension from practice before the court for a period of time, or in less extreme cases, public or private censure. In addition, under some circumstances "unfair" litigation tactics may result in a suit for malpractice by the client against the attorney and the law firm.

Web Exploration

A list of commissions and committees may be seen at **http://www.americanbar.org/groups.html**.

RULES GOVERNING THE MISSOURI BAR AND THE JUDICIARY RULES OF PROFESSIONAL CONDUCT

RULE 4-5.3: RESPONSIBILITIES REGARDING NONLAWYER ASSISTANTS

With respect to a nonlawyer employed or retained by or associated with a lawyer:

a. a partner, and a lawyer who individually or together with other lawyers possesses comparable managerial authority in a law firm, shall make reasonable efforts to ensure that the firm has in effect measures giving reasonable assurance that the person's conduct is compatible with the professional obligations of the lawyer;

b. a lawyer having direct supervisory authority over the nonlawyer shall make reasonable efforts to ensure that the person's conduct is compatible with the professional obligations of the lawyer; and

c. a lawyer shall be responsible for conduct of such a person that would be a violation of the Rules of Professional Conduct if engaged in by a lawyer if:
   (1) the lawyer orders or, with the knowledge of the specific conduct, ratifies the conduct involved; or
   (2) the lawyer is a partner, or has comparable managerial authority in the law firm in which the person is employed, or has direct supervisory authority over the person and knows of the conduct at a time when its consequences can be avoided or mitigated but fails to take reasonable remedial action.

Source: http://www.courts.mo.gov/courts/ClerkHandbooksP2RulesOnly.nsf/c0c6ffa99df4993f86256ba50057dcb8/f264eb01f0599e3186256ca6005211e3?OpenDocument

Learning Objective 5

Discuss the ethical obligation of competence.

Competence

Competence/competent The minimum level of knowledge and skill required of a professional.

Rules of court A court's rules for the processing and presentation of cases.

ABA Model Rule of Professional Conduct 1.1 requires that lawyers provide competent representation to a client. **Competent** representation requires the legal knowledge, skill, thoroughness, and preparation that are reasonably necessary for the representation. The standards require, at minimum, an understanding of the **rules of court.** These rules continue to grow in number and complexity, especially those regarding electronic discovery. New rules require greater levels of knowledge in order to competently represent clients. Further, lawyers must be able to communicate with clients in the language of technology about methods of creation and sources of

ETHICAL PERSPECTIVE

The Association of the Bar of the City of New York Formal Opinion 1995-12 Committee on Professional and Judicial Ethics July 6, 1995 Action: Formal Opinion

...DR 6-101(A)(2) mandates that "[a] lawyer shall not...[h]andle a legal matter without preparation adequate in the circumstances." Adequate preparation requires, not only that a lawyer conduct necessary legal research, but also that he or she gather information material to the claims or defenses of the client. See *Mason v. Balcom,* 531 F.2d 717, 724 (5th Cir. 1976). The lawyer's inability, because of a language barrier, to understand fully what the client is telling him or her may unnecessarily impede the lawyer's ability to gather the information from the client needed to familiarize the lawyer with the circumstances of the case. This makes communication via the interpreter vital since it may be the only practical way that a free-flowing dialogue can be maintained with the client, and the only means by which the lawyer can actually and substantially assist the client.

The duty to represent a client competently, embodied in DR 6-101(A)(1), requires a lawyer confronted with a legal matter calling for legal skills or knowledge outside the lawyer's experience or ability, to associate with lawyers with skills or knowledge necessary to handle the legal matter. When a lawyer is confronted with a legal matter requiring non-legal skills or knowledge outside the lawyer's experience or ability and these skills or knowledge are necessary for the proper preparation of the legal matter, DR 6-101(A)(2) appears to require that the lawyer associate with professionals in other disciplines who possess the requisite skills or knowledge needed by the lawyer to prepare the legal matter. The interpreter appears to be the type of professional envisioned by EC 6-3's observation that "[p] roper preparation and representation may require the association by the lawyer of professionals in other disciplines." When the need for an interpreter is apparent or it is reasonable to conclude that an interpreter is required for effective communication, failure to take steps with the client to secure an interpreter may be a breach of the duty to represent the client competently....

electronic documents and the methods for retrieving them and processing them for submission to opposing counsel and the court about highly technical issues involved in the case. This may require an attorney to retain outside consultants or to associate with attorneys who are familiar with the issues. As explained in the Formal Opinion of the Association of the Bar of the City of New York in the Ethical Perspective above, the use of interpreters of the language of technology is similar to the use of foreign language interpreters.

WISCONSIN RULES OF PROFESSIONAL CONDUCT FOR ATTORNEYS

SCR 20:1.1 Competence

A lawyer shall provide competent representation to a client. Competent representation requires the legal knowledge, skill, thoroughness and preparation reasonably necessary for the representation.

SIDEBAR

WISCONSIN RULES OF PROFESSIONAL CONDUCT FOR ATTORNEYS

Contrast and compare the Wisconsin Rules of Professional Conduct for Attorneys at http://www.legis.wisconsin.gov/rsb/scr/5200.pdf, with the American Bar Association Model Rules of Professional Responsibility at http://www.abanet.org/cpr/mrpc/mrpc_toc.html, and the ethical rules in your jurisdiction.

Learning Objective 6

Explain the concept of confidentiality of client communications and the attorney-client privilege.

Confidentiality and Privilege

All members of the legal team must understand their obligations with regard to the duty of confidentiality and attorney–client privilege. The differences in these related concepts can be confusing. There are two sets of rules: ethical rules and rules of evidence. Confidentiality is an ethical obligation. **Privilege** is a rule of evidence.

Privilege A rule of evidence that protects certain forms of communication from disclosure at trial. The attorney-client privilege provides that communication between the attorney and client in obtaining legal advice may not be required to be revealed in court.

Confidentiality A duty imposed on the attorney to keep communications from clients secret. The rule enables clients to obtain legal advice by allowing the client to freely and openly give the attorney all the relevant facts.

Confidentiality

The ethical obligation to keep client information confidential is founded on the belief that clients should be able to tell their attorneys everything about their case so the attorney can give proper legal advice. **Confidentiality** is an ethical obligation. Rule 1.6 of the ABA's Model Rules requires that lawyers "not reveal information relating to representation of a client" until the client gives informed consent to the disclosure after being advised of the consequences of disclosure, except for disclosures that are "impliedly authorized." Everything the lawyer or the members of the legal team learn about the case from every possible source is to be kept confidential. For example, if the client's case is written up in the local daily newspaper and that sets out details of the case, the legal team is not free to discuss them, even though the details have been made public.

Web Exploration

Review the most current version of Rule 1.6 on Confidentiality in your jurisdiction with the American Bar Association Model Rules of Professional Conduct at the American Bar Association website at **www.abanet.org/cpr/mrcp/rule1.6.html**.

Attorney–client privilege A rule of evidence permitting an attorney to refuse to testify as to confidential client information.

Privilege

All communication between the client and the lawyer for the purpose of obtaining legal advice is protected by **attorney–client privilege.** This rule of evidence protects the client by preventing the attorney from being required to reveal information communicated by the client. Note that the information is also confidential, but privilege is different from the duty of confidentiality. The privilege only applies when the lawyer is questioned under oath. At that point, the attorney must invoke the privilege, saying, "I refuse to answer because that is confidential information covered by the attorney–client privilege." This could happen any time the attorney is under oath. Some examples are responses to interrogatories or requests for production of documents, testimony in court, in a deposition, or before a grand jury. Only the client can waive the privilege and allow the attorney to reveal protected information. The privilege may not be waived by the attorney. It is the client's right to preserve the privilege except in limited circumstances, such as when the information is about a crime of violence that the client is about to commit.

> The attorney–client privilege is founded on the assumption that encouraging clients to make the fullest disclosure to their attorneys enables the latter to act more effectively. We have recognized that an attorney's effectiveness depends upon his ability to rely on the assistance of various aides, be they secretaries, file clerks, telephone operators, messengers, clerks not yet admitted to the bar, and aids of other sorts. The privilege must include all the persons who act as the attorney's agents.
>
> *Von Bulow v. Von Bulow*, 811 F. 2d 136 (2d Cir. 1987)

For the privilege to apply, the client must keep the information secret. If the client reveals the same information to someone other than the attorney or legal staff, the

IMPLIED ATTORNEY-CLIENT RELATIONSHIP

An implied attorney-client relationship may result when a prospective client divulges confidential information during a consultation with an attorney for the purpose of retaining the attorney, even if actual employment does not result.

Pro-Hand Sers. Trust v., Monthei, 49 P.3d 56, 59 (Mont. 2002).

IN THE WORDS OF THE COURT . . .

***TRAMMELL V. UNITED STATES,* 445 U.S. 40 (1980)**

BURGER C. J.

The privileges between priest and penitent, attorney and client, and physician and patient limit protection to private communication. These privileges are rooted in the imperative need for confidence and trust. The priest-penitent privilege recognizes the human need to disclose to a spiritual counselor, in total and absolute confidence, what are believed to be flawed acts or thoughts and to receive priestly consolation and guidance in return. The lawyer-client privilege rests on the need for the advocate and counselor to know all that relates to the client's reasons for seeking representation if the professional mission is to be carried out. Similarly, the physician must know all that a patient can articulate in order to identify and to treat disease; barriers to full disclosure would impair diagnosis and treatment.

privilege is lost. The concept of privilege also extends to persons while acting within certain roles, such as:

1. Spouse
2. Clergy–penitent
3. Doctor–patient
4. Psychotherapist–patient
5. Participants in settlement negotiations

In the following case, the court confirmed that the principle of privileged communications extends not just to the attorney, but also to legal support staff who work on the team.

Claim of Privilege

The attorney–client privilege is not automatically invoked. The person claiming the privilege (usually the client) has the burden to establish its existence, called a **claim of privilege.**

Claim of privilege Preventing the disclosure of confidential communications as evidence based on a recognized privilege.

> To sustain a claim of privilege, the party invoking it must demonstrate that the information at issue was a communication between client and counsel or his employee, that it was intended to be and was in fact kept confidential, and that it was made in order to assist in obtaining or providing legal advice or services to the client
>
> SR Int'l Bus. Ins. Co. v. World Trade Ctr. Prop. No. 01 Civ 9291 (S.D.N.Y. July 3, 2002), quoting *Browne of New York City, Inc. v. Ambase Corp.* 150 F.R.D. 465 (S.D.N.Y. 1993)

Extension of Attorney–Client Privilege to Others

It is now accepted that the efficient administration of justice requires lawyers to engage others, such as legal assistants, accountants, and other experts. This would not be possible if the privilege did not extend to these agents of the attorney including, most recently, public relations firms. The U.S. District Court for the Southern District of New York summarized the law, stating:

> the privilege in appropriate circumstances extends to otherwise privileged communications that involve persons assisting the lawyer in the rendition of legal services. This principle has been applied universally to cover office personnel, such as secretaries and law clerks, who assist lawyers in performing their tasks. But it has been applied more broadly as well. For example, in *United States v. Kovel,* the Second Circuit held that a client's communication with an accountant employed by his attorney were privileged

where made for the purpose of enabling the attorney to understand the client situation in order to provide legal advice.

IN RE Grand Jury Subpoenas dated March 24, 2003 directed to (A) Grand Jury Witness Firm and (B) Grand Jury Witness, M11-188 (USDC, S.D.N.Y.) (June 2, 2003)

In the modern practice of law, the attorney must rely on others, such as paralegals, legal secretaries, investigators, and law clerks, to assist in the vigorous representation of the client. These agents must also be covered by the attorney–client privilege; to do otherwise would obligate the attorney to guard every document, exhibit, and pretrial memorandum from the eyes of everyone on the legal team and perform every task personally, including interviews of clients and witnesses, the typing of reports and memoranda, fact and legal research, and the preparation of trial exhibits and documents. This is clearly not desirable or cost effective for the client or the administration of justice.

The Self-Defense Exception

Due process An established course of judicial proceedings or other activity designed to ensure the legal rights of an individual.

Self-defense exception The right to reveal a client confidence when necessary to defend oneself against a claim of wrongful conduct.

The rules concerning the duty of confidentiality and attorney–client privilege are not absolute. Lawyers who are accused of wrongdoing (either intentional or negligent) by their clients must be able to defend themselves. This defense may require the use of confidential privileged information. Therefore, lawyers will not be bound by the rules of confidentiality and privilege in this situation because of an inherent right to **due process.** This is frequently referred to as the "**self-defense exception.**"

One of the most significant cases involving the self-defense exception is *Qualcomm, Inc. v. Broadcom Corp.* In this case, substantial sanctions were assessed against the client. In response, the client made accusations of wrongdoing by outside counsel as part of its attempt to exonerate itself.

THE PENNSYLVANIA RULES OF PROFESSIONAL CONDUCT RULE 1.6(C)(4) PROVIDES

(c) A lawyer may reveal such information to the extent that the lawyer reasonably believes necessary:

...(4) to establish a claim or defense on behalf of the lawyer in a controversy between the lawyer and the client, to establish a defense to a criminal charge or civil claim or disciplinary proceeding against the lawyer based upon conduct in which the client was involved, or to respond to allegations in any proceeding concerning the lawyer's representation of the client;

IN THE WORDS OF THE COURT . . .

UNITED STATES DISTRICT COURT SOUTHERN DISTRICT OF CALIFORNIA CASE NO. 05CV1958-RMB (BLM)

Qualcomm, Inc, Plaintiff

v.

Broadcom Corp, Defendant

ORDER REMANDING PART OF ORDER OF MAGISTRATE COURT RE MOTIONS FOR SANCTIONS DATED 1/07/08

. . . Qualcomm filed four declarations of employees, in spite of the fact it had maintained its position of invoking attorney-client privilege. All four declarations were exonerative of Qualcomm and critical of the services and advice of their retained counsel. None were filed under seal.

This introduction of accusatory adversity between Qualcomm and its retained counsel regarding the issue of assessing responsibility for the failure of discovery changes the factual basis which supported the court's earlier order denying the self-defense exception to Qualcomm's attorney-client privilege. *Meyerhofer v. Empire Fire & Marine Ins. Co.,* 497 F.2d 1190, 1194-95 (2d Cir. 1974); *Hearn v. Rhay,* 68 F.R.D. 574, 581 (E.D. Wash. 1975); *First Fed. Sav. & Loan Ass'n v. Oppenheim, Appel, Dixon & Co.,* 110 F.R.D. 557, 560-68 (S.D.N.Y. 1986); A.B.A. Model Rules of Prof. Conduct 1.6(b)(5) & comment 10.

Accordingly, the court's order denying the self-defense exception to the attorney-client privilege is vacated. The attorneys have a due process right to defend themselves under the totality of circumstances presented in this sanctions hearing where their alleged conduct regarding discovery is in conflict with that alleged by Qualcomm concerning performance of discovery responsibilities. See, e.g., *Miranda v. So. Pac. Transp. Co.,* 710 F.2d 516, 522-23 (9th Cir. 1983). . . .

The full opinion of the court may be viewed at www.ediscoverylaw.com/Brewster.pdf

Work Product Doctrine

The **work product doctrine** provides a limited protection for material prepared by the attorney, or those working for the attorney, in anticipation of litigation or for trial. The work product doctrine is different from both the attorney–client privilege and the duty of confidentiality. The attorney–client privilege and the duty of confidentiality relate to any information provided by the clients regardless of whether it involves potential litigation. The work product doctrine applies only to work created in anticipation of litigation, or for trial.

Work product doctrine A qualified immunity from discovery for "work product of the lawyer" except on a substantial showing of "necessity or justification" of certain written statements and memoranda prepared by counsel in representation of a client, generally in preparation for trial.

Exceptions and Limitations to the Work Product Doctrine

The work product doctrine does not cover documents prepared in the normal operation of the client's business, such as sales reports, data analysis, or summaries of business operations:

> The work product doctrine does not extend to documents in an attorney's possession that were prepared by a third party in the ordinary course of business and that would have been created in essentially similar form irrespective of any litigation anticipated by counsel.
>
> *In Re Grand Jury Subpoenas,* 318 F.3d 379 (2nd Cir. 2002)

In other words, the client cannot obtain protection for internal business documents by giving them to the attorney. Giving them to the attorney does not make them work product; they are not protected from discovery by the other side simply because they are in the possession of the attorney.

IN THE WORDS OF THE COURT . . .

Work Product Doctrine

ELECTRONIC DATA SYSTEMS CORPORATION V. STEINGRABER
4:02 CV 225 USDC, E.D. TEXAS, 2003.

The work product doctrine is narrower than the attorney-client privilege in that it only protects materials prepared "in anticipation of litigation [Fed. R. Civ. P. 26(b) (3)], whereas the attorney-client privilege protects confidential legal communications between an attorney and client regardless of whether they involve possible litigation."

IN THE WORDS OF THE COURT...

Work Product Doctrine

***HICKMAN V. TAYLOR* 329 U.S. 496 (1947)**

The U.S. Supreme Court recognized the work product doctrine and its importance, saying:

> Proper preparation of a client's case demands that he assemble information, sift what he considers to be the relevant from the irrelevant facts, prepare his legal theories and plan his strategy without undue and needless interference. That is the historical and the necessary way in which lawyers act within the framework of our system of jurisprudence to promote justice and to protect their clients' interests.
>
> This work is reflected, of course, in interviews, statements, memoranda, correspondence, briefs, mental impressions, personal beliefs, and countless other tangible and intangible ways—aptly though roughly termed by the Circuit Court of Appeals in this case as the "work product of the lawyer." Were such materials open to opposing counsel on mere demand, much of what is now put down in writing would remain unwritten.
>
> An attorney's thoughts, heretofore inviolate, would not be his own. Inefficiency, unfairness and sharp practices would inevitably develop in the giving of legal advice and in the preparation of cases for trial. The effect on the legal profession would be demoralizing. And the interests of the clients and the cause of justice would be poorly served...
>
> ...where relevant and non-privileged facts remain hidden in an attorney's file and where production of those facts is essential to the preparation of one's case, discovery may be properly had.

Inadvertent Disclosure of Confidential Information

In the practice of law, confidential or privileged information is sometimes disclosed inadvertently. An email may be sent to the wrong address, the wrong number may be speed dialed on a fax machine, or a letter may be sent in the incorrect envelope. The admissibility of the inadvertently disclosed documents will depend on the individual jurisdiction, and courts follow no single policy.

Judicial Views

There are three judicial views on handling the inadvertent disclosure of confidential and privileged information: (1) automatic waiver; (2) no waiver; and (3) balancing test.

> ***Automatic waiver***—These cases hold that once confidentiality is breached, the privilege is automatically waived. There is nothing that will redeem the privilege, and therefore the documents may be used by the party that received them by accident.
>
> ***No waiver***—Under this theory, the privilege is only destroyed when a client makes a knowing, voluntary waiver of the privilege. Therefore, the attorney's inadvertent disclosure does not constitute a waiver.
>
> ***Balancing test***—The courts using the balancing test look to several factors: (1) the nature of the methods taken to protect the information, (2) efforts made to correct the error, (3) the extent of the disclosure, and (4) fairness. Remedies under this test may include unlimited use of the disclosed materials, the court-ordered return of documents, or disqualification of attorneys who have reviewed inadvertently disclosed documents.

ABA Ethics Opinion

The ABA's long-standing view on inadvertent disclosure was contained in its opinion 92-368, which advocated for confidentiality of privileged materials to protect the client, and imposed a burden upon receiving attorneys to not review privileged material and to return it following instructions given to them by the disclosing attorney. The ABA has issued a formal opinion modifying 92-368, which states:

> A lawyer who receives a document from opposing parties or their lawyers and knows or reasonably should know that the document was inadvertently sent should promptly notify the sender in order to permit the sender to take protective measures. To the extent that Formal Opinion 92-368 opined otherwise, it is hereby withdrawn.

However, the ABA has not given direction as to what should happen to the attorney who reads the inadvertently disclosed document, and whether the information can be used by the other side. Each jurisdiction may have a different rule. The California courts have addressed these questions in *Rico v. Mitsubishi Motors Corp.*

Web Exploration

The complete version of the Formal Opinion can be found at: **http://www.nycbar.org/ethics/ethics-opinions-local/1995-opinions/1134-formal-opinion-1995-12**

IN THE WORDS OF THE COURT . . .

Rico v. Mitsubishi Motors Corp., 42 Cal.4th 807 (2007), 171 P.3d 1092, 68 Cal.Rptr.3d 758

Here we consider what action is required of an attorney who receives privileged documents through inadvertence and whether the remedy of disqualification is appropriate. We conclude that, under the authority of *State Comp. Ins. Fund v. WPS, Inc.* (1999) 70 Cal. App. 4th 644 (State Fund), an attorney in these circumstances may not read a document any more closely than is necessary to ascertain that it is privileged. Once it becomes apparent that the content is privileged, counsel must immediately notify opposing counsel and try to resolve the situation....

Moreover, we agree with the Court of Appeal that, "when a writing is protected under the absolute attorney work product privilege, courts do not invade upon the attorney's thought processes by evaluating the content of the writing. Once [it is apparent] that the writing contains an attorney's impressions, conclusions, opinions, legal research or theories, the reading stops and the contents of the document for all practical purposes are off limits. In the same way, once the court determines that the writing is absolutely privileged, the inquiry ends. Courts do not make exceptions based on the content of the writing." Thus, "regardless of its potential impeachment value, Yukevich's personal notes should never have been subject to opposing counsel's scrutiny and use."

ETHICAL PERSPECTIVE

Arizona Ethics Rules

ER 1.6. CONFIDENTIALITY OF INFORMATION

(a) A lawyer shall not reveal information relating to the representation of a client unless the client gives informed consent, the disclosure is impliedly authorized in order to carry out the representation or the disclosure is permitted or required by paragraphs (b), (c) or (d), or ER 3.3(a)(3).

(b) A lawyer shall reveal such information to the extent the lawyer reasonably believes necessary to prevent the client from committing a criminal act that the lawyer believes is likely to result in death or substantial bodily harm.

(c) A lawyer may reveal the intention of the lawyer's client to commit a crime and the information necessary to prevent the crime.

(continued)

(d) A lawyer may reveal such information relating to the representation of a client to the extent the lawyer reasonably believes necessary:
  (1) to prevent the client from committing a crime or fraud that is reasonably certain to result in substantial injury to the financial interests or property of another and in furtherance of which the client has used or is using the lawyer's services;
  (2) to mitigate or rectify substantial injury to the financial interests or property of another that is reasonably certain to result or has resulted from the client's commission of a crime or fraud in furtherance of which the client has used the lawyer's services;
  (3) to secure legal advice about the lawyer's compliance with these Rules;
  (4) to establish a claim or defense on behalf of the lawyer in a controversy between the lawyer and the client, to establish a defense to a criminal charge or civil claim against the lawyer based upon conduct in which the client was involved, or to respond to allegations in any proceeding concerning the lawyer's representation of the client; or
  (5) to comply with other law or a final order of a court or tribunal of competent jurisdiction directing the lawyer to disclose such information.

Learning Objective 7
Discuss the concept of conflict of interest in the legal profession.

Conflict of interest A situation where the interest of one client is directly adverse to the interest of another client.

Conflict of Interest

The basis of the **conflict of interest** rule is the belief that a person cannot be loyal to two clients whose interests are adverse to one another. Lawyers cannot represent two clients with actual or potentially conflicting interests, such as a husband and wife in a domestic relations case. An attorney also may not represent a client when the attorney has a financial interest in the subject matter of the case, such as when the attorney is a partner in a real estate transaction. Nonlawyer members of the legal team must also avoid conflicts of interest. For example, both sides of a case may not use the same paralegal. However, in many cases, the lines are not as clear.

Rule 1.7 of the Model Rules of Professional Conduct addresses conflicts of interest. A lawyer should not represent another client if "representation of one client will be directly adverse to another client" unless both clients give their informed

Learning Objective 8
Describe the duty of candor to the court and other counsel and the ethical duty of fairness.

ETHICAL PERSPECTIVE

Arkansas Rules of Professional Conduct

RULE 1.7. CONFLICT OF INTEREST: CURRENT CLIENTS

(a) Except as provided in paragraph (b), a lawyer shall not represent a client if the representation involves a concurrent conflict of interest. A concurrent conflict of interest exists if:
  (1) the representation of one client will be directly adverse to another client; or
  (2) there is a significant risk that the representation of one or more clients will be materially limited by the lawyer's responsibilities to another client, a former client or a third person or by a personal interest of the lawyer.

(b) Notwithstanding the existence of a concurrent conflict of interest under paragraph (a), a lawyer may represent a client if:
  (1) the lawyer reasonably believes that the lawyer will be able to provide competent and diligent representation to each affected client;
  (2) the representation is not prohibited by law;
  (3) the representation does not involve the assertion of a claim by one client against another client represented by the lawyer in the same litigation or other proceeding before a tribunal; and
  (4) each affected client gives informed consent, confirmed in writing.

consent to the dual representation, and the consent is confirmed in writing. The lawyer's personal interests or those of third parties who are not clients, such as family members, may also create a risk of a conflict that must be avoided.

Clearly, a lawyer should not accept an engagement if the lawyer's personal interests or desires will, or with reasonable probability will, adversely affect the advice to be given or services to be rendered to the prospective client. The client is entitled to independent advice from members of the legal team, meaning that the advice is not influenced by any concern for personal gain on the part of the lawyer. The information that creates a conflict of interest is not limited solely to that of the attorney representing a client. It also includes the information held by another member of the legal team, including the legal assistant.

Candor A duty of honesty to the court.

CANDOR AND FAIRNESS IN LITIGATION

Litigation is the practice of advocacy, which involves advocating a legal position to the court or persuade a trier of facts to accept a set of facts. Although an attorney must be an aggressive advocate for the client, it is also the duty of the attorney to avoid any conduct that undermines the integrity of the process. The duty to the client to persuasively present the case is qualified by the ethical obligation of **candor,** meaning that the lawyer must not mislead the court or opposing counsel with false statements of law or of facts that the lawyer knows to be false. Without mutual respect, honesty, and fairness, the system cannot function properly.

The duty of candor may simply mean that the attorney presents the current case and statutory law, even when the most current version is not favorable to the position taken. This duty requires making a complete search for *all* the law, statutory enactments and case law, and not just the law that favors the client's position. In an age of digital information, huge numbers of electronic cases may need to be searched, and it is easy to overlook a few, or not run the search as thoroughly as possible. Not making the proper inquiry of the client's staff, or not thoroughly searching all of the law, may lead to sanctions, and potentially worse, disbarment.

ETHICAL PERSPECTIVE

Proposed Michigan Standards for Imposing Lawyer Sanctions [Without Commentary] (Submitted in June 2002 by the Attorney Discipline Board)

Preface

These Michigan Standards for Imposing Lawyer Sanctions were adopted by the State of Michigan Attorney Discipline Board (ADB or Board) on [date] under the authority granted by the Michigan Supreme Court in its order dated [date], and are intended for use by the Attorney Discipline Board and its hearing panels in imposing discipline following a finding or acknowledgment of professional misconduct. Pursuant to the Court's order, these standards may be amended by the Board from time to time. The Court may at any time modify these standards or direct the Board to modify them.

(6.0) Violations of Duties Owed to the Legal System

(6.1) False Statements, Fraud, and Misrepresentation to a Tribunal. The following sanctions are generally appropriate in cases involving conduct that is prejudicial to the administration of justice or that involves dishonesty, fraud, deceit, or misrepresentation to a tribunal:

(continued)

(6.11) Disbarment is generally appropriate when a lawyer, with the intent to deceive the tribunal, makes a false statement, submits a false document, or improperly withholds material information, and causes serious or potentially serious injury.

(6.12) Suspension is generally appropriate when a lawyer knows that false statements or documents are being submitted to the tribunal or that material information is improperly being withheld, and takes no remedial action, and causes injury or potential injury.

(6.13) Reprimand is generally appropriate when a lawyer is negligent either in determining whether statements or documents submitted to a tribunal are false or in taking remedial action when material information is being withheld and causes injury or potential injury.

RHODE ISLAND RULES OF PROFESSIONAL CONDUCT

RULE 3.3 CANDOR TOWARD THE TRIBUNAL

(a) A lawyer shall not knowingly:
   (1) make a false statement of fact or law to a tribunal or fail to correct a false statement of material fact or law previously made to the tribunal by the lawyer;
   (2) fail to disclose to the tribunal legal authority in the controlling jurisdiction known to the lawyer to be directly adverse to the position of the client and not disclosed by opposing counsel; or
   (3) offer evidence that the lawyer knows to be false. If a lawyer, the lawyer's client, or a witness called by the lawyer, has offered material evidence and the lawyer comes to know of its falsity, the lawyer shall take reasonable remedial measures, including, if necessary, disclosure to the tribunal. A lawyer may refuse to offer evidence, other than the testimony of a defendant in a criminal matter, that the lawyer reasonably believes is false.

(b) A lawyer who represents a client in an adjudicative proceeding and who knows that a person intends to engage, is engaging or has engaged in criminal or fraudulent conduct related to the proceeding shall take reasonable remedial measures, including, if necessary, disclosure to the tribunal.

(c) The duties stated in paragraphs (a) and (b) continue to the conclusion of the proceeding, and apply even if compliance requires disclosure of information otherwise protected by Rule 1.6.

(d) In an ex parte proceeding, a lawyer shall inform the tribunal of all material facts known to the lawyer that will enable the tribunal to make an informed decision, whether or not the facts are adverse.

Fairness to Opposing Party and Counsel

Fairness in the practice of law has probably been an issue for as long as there has been an adversarial justice system. A number of states have established professionalism centers such as that of the Pennsylvania Bar Association shown in Exhibit 2.3. Attorneys are advocates for their clients and occasionally forget that the purpose of the legal system is justice for all. The ethical rule of fairness to opposing counsel and parties is an attempt to ensure justice is done even if one's client loses the case. Each side is expected to use its best knowledge and skills to present its position fairly and provide evidence for the **trier of fact** to determine where the truth lies. Destroying, falsifying, or tampering with evidence destroys the fabric of the system, and society loses confidence in it. The most familiar example occurs in criminal cases where the prosecutor does not turn over, as required, **exculpatory evidence** that might show that the defendant is innocent.

Trier of fact The trier of fact decides what facts are to be accepted and used in making the decision. It is usually a jury, but may be a judge who hears a case without a jury and decides the facts and applies the law

Exculpatory evidence Evidence that tends to prove the innocence of the accused or prove the facts of the defendant's case.

Exhibit 2.3 Pennsylvania Bar Association Professionalism Committee website

PENNSYLVANIA BAR ASSOCIATION

Your Other Partner

HOME
MEMBER LOGIN
EVENTS CALENDAR
SEARCH PBA SITE
JOIN PBA NOW
RENEW PBA MEMBERSHIP

Professionalism Committee - Welcome

PUBLIC RESOURCES

Professionalism Our Lifeline

Dear Colleague:

As members of the bar, we must all take responsibility to promote the integrity of the legal profession and to improve the public's perception of lawyers. As the first step, we must respect the professional obligations we have to one another.

To that end, in May 1988, the Pennsylvania Bar Association House of Delegates authorized the PBA Professionalism Committee to develop a program to enhance the professionalism of lawyers in Pennsylvania. Following a thorough review, the committee drafted its Working Rules for Professionalism. At the 1992 PBA Annual Meeting, the House of Delegates set a goal of having all lawyers in Pennsylvania endorse these rules in writing. The Ultimate goal is that, through written endorsement, we be reminded constantly that we all must practice law with civility. This will not only benefit the profession, but also clients and all others with whom we come in daily contact.

Please join this effort by endorsing the rules and return your signed endorsement today.

Hon. Abraham J. Gafni, Chair, PBA Professionalism Committee

PBA Working Rules for Professionalism

The practice of law is a profession, a genuine calling inspirited with service to the system of justice, not a common business enterprise. The quality of the profession is only as worthy as the character of the people who practice it.

Self esteem, shared respect for each other, the clients we serve, the judges and the officers with whom we work, are essential to it.

Civility is a virtue, not a shortcoming. Willingness to temper zeal with respect for society's interest in preserving responsible judicial process will help to reserve it.

USI AFFINITY
The PBA's endorsed insurance administrator
www.usiaffinity.com/pabar

Click here for more information.

PBA InCite Enter Here

MONITORED BACKUPS BY CERTIFIED ENGINEERS
CoreVault

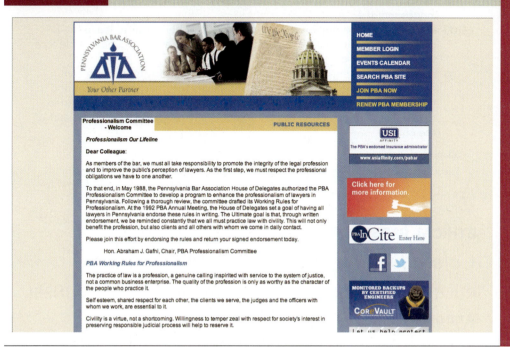

OREGON RULES OF PROFESSIONAL CONDUCT (12/01/06)

RULE 3.4 FAIRNESS TO OPPOSING PARTY AND COUNSEL

A lawyer shall not:

(a) knowingly and unlawfully obstruct another party's access to evidence or unlawfully alter, destroy or conceal a document or other material having potential evidentiary value. A lawyer shall not counsel or assist another person to do any such act;

(b) falsify evidence; counsel or assist a witness to testify falsely; offer an inducement to a witness that is prohibited by law; or pay, offer to pay, or acquiesce in payment of compensation to a witness contingent upon the content of the witness's testimony or the outcome of the case; except that a lawyer may advance, guarantee or acquiesce in the payment of:

  (1) expenses reasonably incurred by a witness in attending or testifying;

  (2) reasonable compensation to a witness for the witness's loss of time in attending or testifying; or

  (3) a reasonable fee for the professional services of an expert witness.

(c) knowingly disobey an obligation under the rules of a tribunal, except for an open refusal based on an assertion that no valid obligation exists;

(d) in pretrial procedure, knowingly make a frivolous discovery request or fail to make reasonably diligent effort to comply with a legally proper discovery request by an opposing party;

(e) in trial, allude to any matter that the lawyer does not reasonably believe is relevant or that will not be supported by admissible

(continued)

Web Resources

The Pennsylvania Bar Association Professionalism website may be viewed at: http://www.pabar.org/public/committees/proflism/about/welcome.asp

evidence, assert personal knowledge of facts in issue except when testifying as a witness, or state a personal opinion as to the justness of a cause, the credibility of a witness, the culpability of a civil litigant or the guilt or innocence of an accused;

(f) advise or cause a person to secrete himself or herself or to leave the jurisdiction of a tribunal for purposes of making the person unavailable as a witness therein; or

(g) threaten to present criminal charges to obtain an advantage in a civil matter unless the lawyer reasonably believes the charge to be true and if the purpose of the lawyer is to compel or induce the person threatened to take reasonable action to make good the wrong which is the subject of the charge.

Adopted 01/01/05

Source: http://www.osbar.org/_docs/rulesregs/orpc.pdf

ETHICAL PERSPECTIVE

Colorado Supreme Court

RULE 3.4. FAIRNESS TO OPPOSING PARTY AND COUNSEL

Annotations

Comment

(1) The procedure of the adversary system contemplates that the evidence in a case is to be marshaled competitively by the contending parties. Fair competition in the adversary system is secured by prohibitions against destruction or concealment of evidence, improperly influencing witnesses, obstructive tactics in discovery procedure, and the like.

(2) Documents and other items of evidence are often essential to establish a claim or defense. Subject to evidentiary privileges, the right of an opposing party, including the government, to obtain evidence through discovery or subpoena is an important procedural right. The exercise of that right can be frustrated if relevant material is altered, concealed or destroyed. Applicable law in many jurisdictions makes it an offense to destroy material for [the] purpose of impairing its availability in a pending proceeding or one whose commencement can be foreseen. Falsifying evidence is also generally a criminal offense. Paragraph (a) applies to evidentiary material generally, including computerized information.

Source: http://www.coloradosupremecourt.com/Regulation/Rules/appendix20/statdspp88f6.html

IN THE WORDS OF THE COURT . . .

UNITED STATES DISTRICT COURT SOUTHERN DISTRICT OF CALIFORNIA
***QUALCOMM INC. V. BROADCOM CORP.*, CASE NO. 05CV1958-B (BLM)**

ORDER GRANTING IN PART AND DENYING IN PART DEFENDANT'S MOTION FOR SANCTIONS AND SANCTIONING QUALCOMM, INCORPORATED AND INDIVIDUAL LAWYERS

b. Referral to the California State Bar

As set forth above, the Sanctioned Attorneys assisted Qualcomm in committing this incredible discovery violation by intentionally hiding or recklessly ignoring relevant documents, ignoring or rejecting numerous warning signs that Qualcomm's document search was inadequate, and blindly accepting Qualcomm's unsupported assurances that its document search was adequate. The Sanctioned Attorneys then used the lack of evidence to repeatedly and forcefully make false statements and arguments to the court and jury. As such, the Sanctioned Attorneys violated their discovery obligations and also may have violated their ethical duties. See e.g., The State Bar of California, Rules of Professional Conduct, Rule 5-200 (a lawyer shall not seek to mislead the judge or jury by a false statement of fact or law), Rule 5-220 (a lawyer shall not suppress evidence that the lawyer or the lawyer's client has a legal obligation to reveal or to produce)

Web Exploration

Contrast and compare Rule 1.6(c)(4) of the Pennsylvania Rules at **http://www.padisciplinaryboard.org/documents/RulesOfProfessionalConduct.pdf** with the American Bar Association Model Rules of Professional Responsibility at **http://www.abanet.org/cpr/mrpc/mrpc_toc.html** and the ethical rule in your jurisdiction.

ETHICAL PERSPECTIVE

Review the most current version and comments to Rule 1.6 on Confidentiality of Information of the American Bar Association Model Rules of Professional Conduct at the American Bar Association website: http://www.abanet.org/cpr/mrpc/rule_1_6.html

Concept Review *and* Reinforcement

LEGAL TERMINOLOGY

ABA Model Rules of Professional Conduct 38
Agent 47
Attorney–client privilege 50
Candor 57
Claim of privilege 51
Competence/competent 48
Confidentiality 50
Conflict of interest 56
Due process 52
Ethical guidelines 38
Ethics 38
Exculpatory evidence 58
Federal Rules of Evidence 45
Fiduciary relationship 47
Model Guidelines for the Utilization of Legal Assistant Services 45
Principal 47
Privilege 50
Rules of court 48
Self-defense exception 52
Supervising attorney 47
Trier of fact 58
Unauthorized Practice of Law (UPL) 40
Work product doctrine 53

SUMMARY OF KEY CONCEPTS

Regulation of the Practice of Law

Purpose of Regulation	The practice of law is regulated by state government and court rule in an attempt to protect the public from incompetent and unscrupulous practitioners.
The Paralegal and Licensing	With a few exceptions, there are no state licensing requirements for one to work as a paralegal—unlike the procedures that lawyers must follow to practice law.
Penalties for the Unauthorized Practice of Law	States such as Pennsylvania have specifically addressed the issue of unauthorized practice of law by paralegals and legal assistants. The Pennsylvania statute on the unauthorized practice of law makes it a misdemeanor for "any person, including, but not limited to, a paralegal or legal assistant who within this Commonwealth, shall practice law."

Avoiding UPL

Avoiding UPL: Holding Oneself Out	Parties with whom the paralegal has contact must know the limited role the paralegal plays on the legal team.
Avoiding UPL: Giving Advice	A paralegal cannot give a legal opinion or legal advice. If legal rights may be affected, it is probably legal advice.
Avoiding UPL: Filling Out Forms	A nonlawyer who explains, recommends, advises, or assists in the selection, completion, and corrections of errors and omissions of legal forms may be guilty of UPL.
Avoiding UPL: Representing Clients	1. Some jurisdictions and administrative agencies do permit those who are not licensed or admitted to practice to appear in court or before administrative law judges or referees on behalf of clients. 2. There is no uniformity among the rules outlining when nonlawyers may represent parties or what specific agencies or courts nonlawyers can appear before. Any appearance before a court must be approved carefully. 3. Even a minor activity, such as a request for continuance of a case, may be considered by some courts to be the practice of law. 4. Some federal agencies specifically permit nonlawyers to appear, such as the Social Security Administration and the U.S. Patent Office.
Avoiding UPL: Guidelines	**Guideline 1** Legal assistants should disclose their status as legal assistants at the outset of any professional relationship with a client, other attorneys, a court or administrative agency or personnel thereof, or members of the general public. **Guideline 2** Legal assistants should not: 1. establish attorney–client relationships, set legal fees, give legal opinions or advice, or represent a client before a court, unless authorized to do so by said court; nor 2. engage in, encourage, or contribute to any act that could constitute the unauthorized practice of law. **Guideline 3** Legal assistants may perform services for an attorney in the representation of a client, provided that: 1. the services performed by the legal assistant do not require the exercise of independent professional legal judgment; 2. the attorney maintains a direct relationship with the client and maintains control of all client matters; 3. the attorney supervises the legal assistant; 4. the attorney remains professionally responsible for all work on behalf of the client, including any actions taken or not taken by the legal assistant in connection therewith.

Ethical Duties and Obligations

Expected Behavior	Ethical behavior is expected and required of every member of the legal team: attorney, paralegal, litigation support, information technologist, and outside consultant.
	Ethical obligations of lawyers are enforced by the court in the jurisdiction where the attorney is practicing or where the case is being tried.

Ethical Guidelines and Rules

	Every profession develops a set of guidelines for those in the profession to follow. These may be codes of conduct or ethical guidelines. These codes typically set forth the minimum in ethical behavior—the very least each professional should do.

ABA Model Guidelines for the Utilization of Paralegal Services	A set of guidelines intended to govern the conduct of lawyers when utilizing paralegals or legal assistants.
Uniformity of Paralegal Ethics	No single source of ethical rules is set out for the paralegal. At present, unlike a violation by an attorney of the state-adopted rules that can result in loss of the right to practice (disbarment), no such sanction exists for a paralegal's breach of association rules, except loss of membership.
Ethics Codes of Paralegal Associations	1. National Federation of Paralegal Associations, Inc. 2. National Association of Legal Assistants
Supervision	
Duty to Supervise	The obligation to ensure ethical conduct is that of the supervising attorney under the ethical obligation to supervise all who work on the case for the attorney.
Competence	Competent representation requires the legal knowledge, skill, thoroughness, and preparation reasonably necessary for the representation.
The Duty of Confidentiality, Attorney–Client Privilege, and the Work Product Doctrine	
Attorney–Client Privilege	1. This privilege is a rule of evidence that applies in cases where the Rules of Evidence apply: a court of law, a deposition, or other places where a witness is under oath, such as interrogatories, responses to requests for documents, or grand jury hearings. 2. The "privilege" belongs to the client, not to the attorney. 3. The person claiming the privilege, usually the client, has the burden to establish the existence of the privilege.
Confidentiality	This is a duty imposed on the attorney and each member of the legal team working under the supervision of the attorney to enable clients to obtain legal advice by allowing the client to freely and openly give the members of the legal team all the relevant facts without fear of disclosure of these facts, except in limited situations, such as to prevent commission of a crime or to defend against a client's suit.
Claim of Privilege	The person claiming the privilege, usually the client, has the burden to establish the existence of the privilege.
Extension of Attorney–Client Privilege to Others	The efficient administration of justice requires the privilege to extend to agents of the attorney.
Work Product Doctrine	1. The work product doctrine provides a limited protection for material prepared by the attorney or those working for the attorney in anticipation of litigation or for trial. 2. The work product doctrine is different from both the attorney–client privilege and the duty of confidentiality. The attorney–client privilege and the duty of confidentiality relate to the information provided by the clients regardless of whether the information involves potential litigation.
Exceptions and Limitations to the Work Product Doctrine	The work product doctrine does not cover documents prepared in the normal operation of the client's business, such as sales reports, data analyses, or summaries of business operations.
Exception to the Third-Party Document Exception	Courts have made an exception when a lawyer is trying to find out the other party's strategy by asking about documents already in his/her possession.
Inadvertent Disclosure of Confidential Information	The treatment will depend on the individual jurisdiction. The courts follow no single policy.

Judicial Views	The three judicial views on handling the inadvertent disclosure under the attorney–client privilege are: 1. automatic waiver 2. no waiver 3. balancing test

Candor and Fairness in Litigation

	It is the duty of the advocate to avoid any conduct that undermines the integrity of the process. The duty to the client to persuasively present the case is a duty qualified by the ethical obligation (candor) to not mislead the court or opposing counsel with false statements of law or of facts that the lawyer knows to be false.
Fairness to Opposing Party and Counsel	The ethical rule of fairness to opposing counsel and parties is an attempt to ensure justice is done even if one's client loses the case.

WORKING THE WEB

1. Download the latest ethics opinions and guidelines from the NALA website at www.NALA.org.
2. Download any ethics updates from the NFPA website at www.paralegal.org.
3. Download a personal reference copy of the Model Rules of Professional Conduct from the ABA Center for Professional Responsibility at www.abanet.org/cpr.
4. Use a web browser or search engine to find the URL (web address) for your state or local bar association website that provides guidance or opinions on legal ethics.
5. Use the Internet to locate the most current version of the ethical rules as used in your jurisdiction. Save the Internet address for future reference.
6. Use the Internet to find ethics opinions or sources of information on ethics in your jurisdiction.

CRITICAL THINKING & WRITING QUESTIONS

1. What is the general theory or rationale for regulating the practice of law? How is this applied?
2. Why is "just giving advice" potentially the unauthorized practice of law?
3. How would regulation of the paralegal profession assure the public of quality legal services?
4. When may nonlawyers represent clients?
5. How can the paralegal avoid UPL?
6. How do unauthorized-practice-of-law statutes protect the public?
7. Why should the paralegal be familiar with the ABA Model Rules of Professional Conduct?
8. How do the ABA Model Guidelines for the Utilization of Legal Assistant Services define the role of the paralegal in the law office?
9. Does a paralegal's violation of the ethics rules of the national paralegal associations have the same impact as attorneys violating the ethical rules on the right to practice?
10. Would a paralegal dating a client have a conflict of interest? How could such a relationship create compromising influences and loyalties?
11. What are the reasons for protecting privileged communications?
12. Under what circumstances might a paralegal have a conflict of interest when taking a new job at a different law firm?
13. What are the potential dangers in paralegals moonlighting?
14. What is a conflict of interest under the Model Rules of Professional Conduct?
15. Does a client have an attorney–client privilege regarding information given to a paralegal during the preparation of a case? Explain.
16. What duty does a paralegal owe to the supervising attorney?
17. How is a paralegal an agent of the client?
18. In a possible conflict of interest, with whom does the ultimate decision rest?
19. Under what circumstance must a lawyer or a paralegal refuse employment?
20. What is required to invoke the attorney–client privilege?
21. What information is covered under the work product doctrine?
22. What is the duty of the trier of fact?
23. What is exculpatory evidence?
24. What is the purpose of ethics?

25. What is the purpose of the confidentiality rule in the legal setting?
26. What is the difference between the duty of confidentiality and the attorney–client privilege?
27. Can the confidentiality between attorney and client be lost? Explain.
28. Can the attorney–client privilege be lost? Explain.
29. What are the judicial approaches to the inadvertent disclosure of confidential information?
30. What ethical guidelines, if any, does your state follow?
31. What is the ethical obligation of a paralegal to the firm's client?
32. What is the ethical obligation of the paralegal to the court?
33. What is the ethical obligation of a litigation support staff member to the client? To the court? Of a litigation support person from an outside firm or consultant? Explain.
34. In addition to the attorney–client relationship, are there other relationships where there is a privilege? Why would it apply to others not in an attorney–client relationship?
35. How is a claim of privilege made?
36. Why is the attorney–client privilege extended to others working for the attorney?
37. What is the purpose of the self-defense exception to the confidentiality rule?
38. Why is conflict of interest an issue for the legal team?
39. What is required to invoke the attorney–client privilege? Explain sufficiently for a non-legal team member to be able to understand.
40. What information is protected by the work product doctrine?
41. Do the ethical rules of "fairness" prevent lawyers from aggressively advocating their client's position?
42. Why would a partner in a law firm be required to supervise the other lawyers in the firm?
43. How can members of the legal team demonstrate that they have been adequately supervised?

Building Paralegal Skills

VIDEO CASE STUDIES

Disclosure of Status

A client is meeting with his new attorney and the attorney's paralegal. He expresses some concerns about confidentiality of information given to the paralegal.

After viewing the video case study in MyLegalStudiesLab, answer the following:

1. Does the paralegal have a duty to reveal his or her status as a paralegal? Does the supervising attorney have the duty?
2. Is the paralegal bound by the same rules of confidentiality as the lawyer?
3. Is the paralegal covered under the attorney–client privilege?

Confidentiality Issue: Family Exception?

Paralegal Judy meets with her mother in a public coffee shop and tells her mother details of the case she is working on that has her "stressed out."

After viewing the video case study in MyLegalStudiesLab, answer the following:

1. Does being "stressed out" change the rules of confidentiality?
2. Is there a privilege that permits discussing the facts of a case with a family member?
3. Can the facts be discussed if names are left out?

Confidentiality Issue: Public Information

A law firm has a case that has received coverage in the local newspaper. Two of the paralegals from the same law firm are having coffee in a public coffee shop. One of the paralegals, who is not assigned to the case, reads an article about the client and asks her friend, who is working on the case, about the accuracy of the article.

After viewing the video case study in MyLegalStudiesLab, answer the following:

1. How does public disclosure of information about a client or a case change the paralegal's responsibility to maintain confidentiality?
2. Are there any ethical issues in discussing cases in a public area?
3. Is the paralegal who is not working on the case under any duty of confidentiality?

ETHICS ANALYSIS & DISCUSSION QUESTIONS

1. Are paralegals held to the same standard as attorneys when there is no supervising attorney?
2. What is the paralegal's duty to the client when the paralegal's employer breaches its duty to the client?
3. Who is responsible for the quality of the legal work performed for a client—the attorney or the paralegal?
4. Assume you have graduated from a paralegal program at a local college. While you are looking for a job where your talents can be properly utilized, a friend asks you to help him fill out a set of bankruptcy forms using a computer program he purchased at the local office supply megawarehouse. The program is designed to pick out the exemptions after the requested information has been plugged in. See *In Re Kaitangian*, Calif. 218 BR 102 (1998). Is this the unauthorized practice of law?

Paralegal Ethics in Practice

5. Assume you are offered the opportunity to work with a local law firm providing living trust services to the public. Your responsibility would be to make presentations to community groups on the advantages of living trusts. After each session, any interested person would be able to meet with you, and you would fill out the forms, collect the fee, and send the completed form and half the fee collected to the law firm for review and transmittal to the client. You would retain half the amount collected as your fee. See *Cincinnati Bar Assn. v. Kathman*, 92 Ohio St. 3d 92, 748 N.E.2d 1091 (2001). What ethical issues are involved? Explain.

DEVELOPING YOUR COLLABORATION SKILLS

Working on your own or with a group of other students assigned by your instructor, review the scenario at the beginning of the chapter.

1. In a group or individually, identify all the potential ethical issues involved in this scenario.
2. Imagine that a local lawyer who knows both Kathryn and Kelsey is sitting next to them and overhears their conversation. The lawyer then sends a letter to the local Ethics Board. Have one group represent the Ethics Board, one group represent Kathryn's employer, and another group represent Kelsey's employers.
   a. How should the Ethics Board respond?
   b. How should the lawyers Kelsey works for respond?
3. Summarize the advice the group would give to Kathryn and Kelsey, and to the law firms that employ them.

PARALEGAL PORTFOLIO EXERCISE

Prepare a memorandum of law for submission to a potential employer, outlining the existing regulations in your state for paralegals, and the application of any unauthorized practice of law statutes. Include complete citations to any cases, statutes, or regulations, and the Internet addresses of any state or local ethics sites for lawyers and/or paralegals.

LEGAL ANALYSIS & WRITING CASES

In re Aretakis, 791 N.Y.S.2d 687 (App. Div. 2005)

An attorney made certain statements public that were taken from a complaint filed against him with the state committee on disciplinary standards, in violation of the rules on confidentiality of proceeding on complaints against attorneys.

The court stated:

> The Court of Appeals has observed that Judiciary Law § 90 and its counterparts reflect a policy of keeping disciplinary proceedings involving licensed professionals

confidential until they are finally determined. The policy serves the purpose of safeguarding information that a potential complainant may regard as private or confidential and thereby removes a possible disincentive to the filing of complaints of professional misconduct. The State's policy also evinces a sensitivity to the possibility of irreparable harm to a professional's reputation resulting from unfounded accusations—a possibility which is enhanced by the more relaxed nature of the [proceedings]. Indeed, professional reputation "once lost, is not easily restored."

Questions

1. Can the reputation of a professional be tarnished by disclosure of unsubstantiated claims of ethical breaches?
2. Once tarnished, can a professional's integrity be reestablished?
3. Is the greater good served by allowing all disciplinary complaints to be made public?

WORKING WITH THE LANGUAGE OF THE COURT CASE

Tegman v. Accident and Medical Investigations

107 Wash App. 868, 30 P.3d 1092, 68 Cal.Rptr. 758 (Wash Ct. App. 2001)
Court of Appeals of Washington, Division One

Read the following case excerpted from the Court of Appeals opinion. Review and brief the case. In your brief, answer the following questions:

1. How does this court define "the practice of law"?
2. What is the standard or duty of care that this court imposes on a paralegal who does not have a supervising attorney?
3. What action does this court suggest that a paralegal take when it becomes clear that there is no supervising attorney?
4. Why should a paralegal contact the supervising attorney immediately upon being given a case to handle?
5. Based on this case, should a paralegal advise the client that he or she is a paralegal? If so, when? Why?

Becker, Mary K., A.C.J.

Between 1989 and 1991, plaintiffs Maria Tegman, Linda Leszynski, and Daina Calixto were each injured in separate and unrelated automobile accidents. After their accidents, each plaintiff retained G. Richard McClellan and Accident & Medical Investigations, Inc. (AMI) for legal counsel and assistance in handling their personal injury claims. Each plaintiff signed a contingency fee agreement with AMI, believing that McClellan was an attorney and AMI a law firm. McClellan has never been an attorney in any jurisdiction. McClellan and AMI employed Camille Jescavage, [a] licensed attorney.

Jescavage learned that McClellan entered into contingency fee agreements with AMI's clients and that McClellan was not an attorney. [Attorneys for AMI] settled a number of cases for AMI, and learned that McClellan processed settlements of AMI cases through his own bank account.

In July 1991, McClellan hired Deloris Mullen as a paralegal. Mullen considered Jescavage to be her supervising attorney, though Jescavage provided little supervision. Jescavage resigned from AMI in the first week of September 1991. McClellan told Mullen that her new supervising attorney would be James Bailey. Mullen did not immediately contact Bailey to confirm that he was her supervising attorney. [He] later told Mullen he was not.

While at AMI, Mullen worked on approximately 50–60 cases, including those of [the] plaintiffs. Mullen was aware of some of McClellan's questionable practices and knew that there were substantial improprieties involved with his operation. Mullen stopped working at AMI on December 6, 1991, when the situation became personally intolerable to her and

(continued)

she obtained direct knowledge that she was without a supervising attorney.

When she left, she did not advise any of the plaintiffs about the problems at AMI. After Mullen left, McClellan settled each plaintiff's case for various amounts without their knowledge or consent, and deposited the funds in his general account by forging their names on the settlement checks.

The "practice of law" clearly does not just mean appearing in court. In a larger sense, it includes "legal advice and counsel, and the preparation of legal instruments and contracts by which legal rights are secured." Mullen contends that her status as a paralegal precludes a finding that she was engaged in the practice of law. She argues that a paralegal is, by definition, someone who works under the supervision of an attorney, and that it is necessarily the attorney, not the paralegal, who is practicing law and owes a duty to the clients. Her argument assumes that she had a supervising attorney.

The trial court's determination that Mullen was negligent was dependent on the court's finding that Mullen knew, or should have known, that she did not have a supervising attorney over a period of several months while she was at AMI. The label "paralegal" is not in itself a shield from liability. A factual evaluation is necessary to distinguish a paralegal who is working under an attorney's supervision from one who is actually practicing law. A finding that a paralegal is practicing law will not be supported merely by evidence of infrequent contact with the supervising attorney.

As long as the paralegal does in fact have a supervising attorney who is responsible for the case, any deficiency in the quality of the supervision or in the quality of the paralegal's work goes to the attorney's negligence, not the paralegal's.

In this case, Mullen testified that she believed James Bailey was her supervising attorney after Jescavage left. The court found Mullen was not justified in that belief. Mullen testified that she had started to distrust McClellan before he informed her that Bailey would be her supervising attorney. Mullen also testified that she did not contact Bailey to confirm that he was supervising her. Bailey testified at a deposition that he did not share Mullen's clients and she did not consult him regarding any of her ongoing cases. He also said that one of the only conversations he remembers having with Mullen with respect to AMI is one where he told her that he was not her supervising attorney after she raised the issue with him. This testimony amply supports the trial court's finding that Mullen was unjustified in her belief that Bailey was her supervising attorney.

[Mullen] continued to send out demand and representation letters after Jescavage left AMI. Letters written by Mullen before Jescavage's departure identify Mullen as a paralegal after her signature, whereas letters she wrote after Jescavage's departure lacked such identification. Even after Mullen discovered, in late November 1991, that Bailey was not her supervising attorney, she wrote letters identifying "this office" as representing the plaintiffs, neglecting to mention that she was a paralegal and that no attorney was responsible for the case. This evidence substantially supports the finding that Mullen engaged in the practice of law.

Accordingly, we conclude the trial court did not err in following Bowers and holding Mullen to the duty of an attorney. The duty of care owed by an attorney is that degree of care, skill, diligence, and knowledge commonly possessed and exercised by a reasonable, careful, and prudent lawyer in the practice of law in Washington.

The court found that the standard of care owed by an attorney, and therefore also by Mullen, required her to notify the plaintiffs of: (1) the serious problems concerning the accessibility of their files to persons who had no right to see them, (2) the fact that client settlements were not processed through an attorney's trust account but, rather, McClellan's own account, (3) the fact that McClellan and AMI, as nonlawyers, had no right to enter into contingent fee agreements with clients and receive contingent fees, (4) the fact that McClellan was, in fact, engaged in the unlawful practice of law, and that, generally, (5) the clients of McClellan and AMI were at substantial risk of financial harm as a result of their association with AMI. Mullen breached her duty to her clients in all of these particulars.

We conclude the finding is supported by substantial evidence. Accordingly, the trial court did not err in concluding that Mullen was negligent.

Although Mullen was a paralegal, she is held to an attorney's standard of care because she worked on the plaintiffs' cases during a period of several months when she had no supervising attorney. The fact that she did not render legal advice directly does not excuse her; in fact, her failure to advise the plaintiffs of the

(continued)

improper arrangements at AMI is the very omission that breached her duty. Under these circumstances it is not unjust to hold her accountable as a legal cause of the plaintiffs' injuries. As all the elements of negligence have been established, we affirm the judgment against Mullen.
Affirmed.

WE CONCUR: AGID, J., COLEMAN, J.

This case also was scheduled to be published in the Washington Appellate Reports, and if cited in the courts of Washington, would require that citation as well. This case has a Lexis number of 2001 Wash. App. LEXIS 1890.

Rubin v. Enns

23 S.W.3d 382 (Texs. App.-Amarillo 2000)
Texas Court of Appeals, Seventh District

1. Does the court's "rebuttable presumption" test work? Would any other test work better?
2. Using the court's "rebuttable presumption" test, would there be some temptation on the part of the second law firm to obtain confidential information that the paralegal learned at the first law firm?
3. Do the ethics standards of the American Bar Association and paralegal associations adequately address the ethical conflicts that paralegals face? Discuss.

FACTS

Inda Crawford was employed as a legal assistant by the law firm of Hicks, Thomas & Lilienstern (HTL) for a number of years prior to May 1999. During her employment with the HTL law firm, HTL represented Michael Rubin and other real estate agents in a lawsuit against Westgate Petroleum and other defendants. Crawford worked on this case as a legal assistant for HTL and billed 170 hours of work on the case.

In May 1999, Crawford left her employment at HTL and went to work for the law firm Templeton, Smithee, Hayes, Fields, Young & Heinrich (Templeton). Templeton represented Westgate Petroleum and the other defendants in the previously mentioned lawsuit. Rubin and the other real estate agents in this case filed a writ of mandamus with trial court judge the Honorable Ron Enns to have the Templeton firm disqualified as counsel for Westgate et al. because Crawford had now switched firms.

Rubin argued that because Crawford had previously worked on the case for the HTL firm, the opposing counsel she now worked for should be disqualified from representing the opposing side in the lawsuit. The trial court judge denied the petitioners' writ of mandamus. The petitioners appealed.

ISSUE

Should the writ of mandamus be approved disqualifying a law firm that represents one side of a lawsuit because a legal assistant who worked for the law firm that represented the other side of the lawsuit has now switched firms and works for the law firm sought to be disqualified?

Boyd, Chief Justice

In *Phoenix Founders, Inc. v. Marshall*, 887 S.W.2d 831, 835 (Tex. 1994), the court had occasion to discuss at some length circumstances such as the one before us in which a paralegal has changed employment from a law firm on one side of a case to a law firm on the other side of the case. In doing so, it recognized the countervailing interests involved and noted with approval the ABA suggestion that any restrictions on the nonlawyer's employment should be held to the minimum standard necessary to protect confidentiality of client information. In the course of its discussion, the court held that a paralegal or legal assistant who changes employment and who has worked on a case is subject to a conclusive presumption that confidences and secrets were imparted. While the presumption that a legal assistant obtained confidential information is not rebuttable, the presumption that the information was shared with a new employer is rebuttable.

Such distinction was created to ensure that a nonlawyer's mobility would not be unduly restricted. However, the court emphasized that the only way the rebuttable presumption could be overcome would be

(continued)

(1) to instruct the legal assistant not to work on any matter on which the paralegal worked during the prior employment, or regarding which the paralegal had information relating to the former employer's representation; and (2) "to take other reasonable steps to ensure that the paralegal does not work in connection with the matters on which the paralegal worked during the prior employment, absent client consent."

The trial court also had before it copies of a May 17, 1999, memo from Joe Hayes, managing partner of the Templeton firm, addressed to all the lawyers and staff of the Templeton firm. In the memo, Hayes designated two cases (one of which underlies this proceeding) as those about which Crawford might possess confidential information. In the memo, the recipients were instructed that Texas Disciplinary Rules 1.05(b)(1) and 5.03(a) prohibited them, as Crawford's supervising employers, "from revealing any confidential information she might have regarding the cases." The memo also advised that to satisfy the requirements of the Disciplinary Rules, as well as those set forth by the supreme court in the In Re American Home Products Corporation case, the firm was implementing the following six policies and procedures, effective immediately:

1. Inda shall not perform any work or take any action in connection with the Westgate case or the Seger case [the second, unrelated, case].
2. Inda shall not discuss the Westgate case or the Seger case, or disclose any information she has concerning these cases, with anyone.
3. No lawyer or staff member shall discuss the Westgate case or the Seger case with Inda, or in her presence.
4. All computer information relating to the Westgate case and the Seger case shall be removed from the firm's computer system. No future information concerning either the Westgate case or the Seger case shall be stored in any electronic medium but, rather, kept solely in hard copy form with the files in the respective case.
5. The files in the Westgate case and the Seger case shall be kept in locked files under my supervision. No one shall have access to those files other than me, and those to whom I have given specific authority to access these files. Inda shall not have access to these files or the area where the files are to be maintained. At the close of each business day, all documents relating to these cases shall be placed in their respective files, which shall be returned to their storage places, which shall then be locked.
6. Inda shall not be given access to any of the files pertaining to the Westgate case or the Seger case, or their contents. None of the documents pertaining to either of these cases shall be disclosed to Inda, discussed with her, or discussed in her presence.

Our review of the record before the trial court convinces us that we cannot say he abused his discretion in arriving at his decision to deny the motion to disqualify the Templeton law firm. Accordingly, realtors' petition seeking mandamus relief must be, and is, denied.

DECISION AND REMEDY

The court of appeals affirmed the trial court's denial of the writ of mandamus, thus permitting Crawford to work for the second law firm, which had imposed sufficient safeguards to assure that confidential information obtained at the first law firm was not disclosed to the second law firm.

The court also may find that the lower court has made an error that can be corrected, by sending the case back to the lower court, and remand the case to the lower court, to take additional action or conduct further proceedings. For example, the lower court may be directed to hold further proceedings in which a jury hears testimony related to the issue of damages and makes an award of monetary damages.

An appellate court will reverse a lower court decision if it finds an error of law [in] the record. An error of law occurs if the jury was improperly instructed by the trial court judge, prejudicial evidence was admitted at trial when it should have been excluded, prejudicial evidence was obtained through an unconstitutional search and seizure, and the like. An appellate court will not reverse a finding of fact unless such finding is unsupported by the evidence or is contradicted by the evidence.

MYLEGALSTUDIESLAB

MyLegalStudiesLab Virtual Law Office Experience Assignments

Complete the pre-test, study plan, and post-test for this chapter and answer the Legal Applications questions as assigned. These will help you confirm your mastery of the concepts and their application to legal scenarios. Then complete the Virtual Law Office assignments as assigned by your instructor. These assignments are designed to develop your workplace skills. Completing the assignments for this chapter will result in producing the following documents for inclusion in your portfolio:

VLOE 2.1	Office memo on the ethical obligation of confidentiality and the rules of attorney-client privilege
VLOE 2.2	Checklist of guide to avoiding UPL, including how a paralegal or secretary should answer questions from clients and potential clients

CHAPTER

3

The Paralegal Workplace

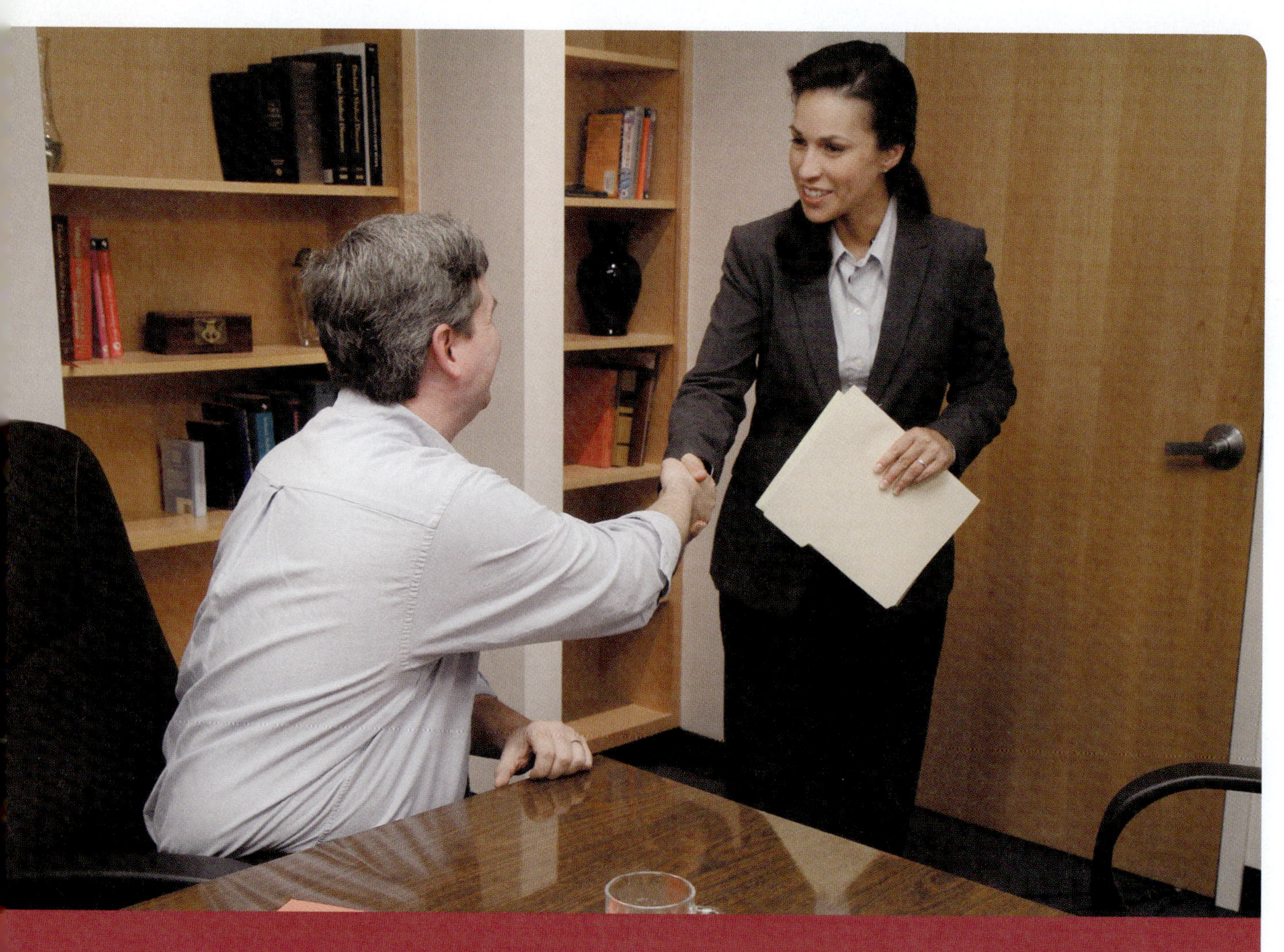

LEARNING OBJECTIVES

After studying this chapter, you should be able to:

1. Describe the different types of practice arrangements of lawyers and law firms.
2. Explain the organizational structure of law offices.
3. Describe the administrative procedures found in most law offices.
4. Prepare a traditional résumé and an electronic résumé.
5. Plan for a successful job interview.

Paralegals at Work

Law Offices
Goldenberg, Craigie, and Luria

INTEROFFICE MEMO

TO: Natasha Weiser
FROM: Cary Moritz, Office Manager
SUBJECT: Mentoring for New Hires

All of us at Goldenberg, Craigie, and Luria welcome you to our firm. We know you had other job opportunities but believe you will be professionally satisfied and challenged by working here.

The paralegal profession has changed dramatically since I first started in this field, and the one thing we can count on is more change. Please know that you can call on me at any time for advice and guidance. No question is too big or too small.

After all these years, I have seen a number of major changes in the profession. When I started out, we were hired based on keyboarding skills and basically operated as secretaries. Today, more and more lawyers treat us as a part of the legal team and demand of us as much, if not more, than they do new law graduates.

In your new job as a paralegal for Goldenberg, Craigie, and Luria, you frequently will represent our firm as the client's first point of contact and be responsible for conducting initial interviews with clients. As you prepare your interview strategies, please use me as a sounding board. It is important to build rapport so clients will feel comfortable sharing sensitive and personal information with someone who is, at first, a complete stranger. As time goes on, clients often become most comfortable with the paralegal assigned to their case.

As a paralegal, you will be expected to follow a case and do much of the administrative work, such as keeping track of the time and costs associated with each case. Bookkeeping and accounting skills can be a real plus! When I first started, I did only litigation work. When the lawyers in my firm found out that I had been a bookkeeper and had taken accounting classes, I was asked not only to work in the estates area but also was given responsibility for some of the

> "A lawyer's time and advice are his stock in trade."
>
> *Abraham Lincoln*

in-office accounting. This is something to think about as you develop your professional skill set. Getting a bachelor's degree eventually led to my job as an office manager. Additional education is always a plus!

Please know that you can count on me to help you succeed in the present and also to plan and prepare for future endeavors here at Goldenberg, Craigie, and Luria.

Consider the issues involved in this scenario as you read the chapter.

INTRODUCTION TO THE PARALEGAL WORKPLACE

As the paralegal profession has evolved, so too have the duties and roles of the paralegal within the legal system and elsewhere. The earliest legal assistants were probably legal secretaries who developed specialized skills while working for an attorney in one of the legal specialties. As the need for specialized skills became more obvious, legal assistant programs and paralegal programs were created to teach the requisite skills.

In the classic sense, a paralegal performs those tasks and activities that assist the supervising attorney in representing clients. In the broader view, the paralegal performs many of the same functions that attorneys perform, under the supervision of an attorney but limited by laws and regulations on the unauthorized practice of law (UPL). The paralegal's actual tasks and functions vary according to the type of practice, size of the firm or organization, and skill of the individual paralegal.

Learning Objective 1
Describe the different types of practice arrangements of lawyers and law firms.

Arrangements and Organization of Law Offices and Firms

The classic image of the law firm was of the sole practitioner working alone in a small office in a small town. The more modern view portrayed in movies and on TV is that of a large national or global law firm. In between are small partnerships and other types of organizations in which paralegals work—corporations, insurance companies, government agencies, and consulting firms composed of accountants, lawyers, and management consultants.

Solo Practice

Solo practice One lawyer practicing alone without the assistance of other attorneys.

A **solo practice** is one lawyer practicing alone without the assistance of other attorneys. Solo practitioners still exist, not only in small towns but in large metropolitan areas as well. The solo practitioner may be the type of employer who depends most on the skills of the paralegal in running the office, working with clients, and assisting at trial. A solo practice offers perhaps the greatest challenge and opportunity for the paralegal who wishes to be involved in every aspect of a law practice. Tasks that otherwise might be assigned to an associate will fall to the paralegal to perform.

In a litigation practice or a practice in which the attorney is frequently out of the office to attend meetings, the paralegal becomes the main point of contact and thc coordinator between clients and the attorney. In solo practices, jobs that might be done in larger firms by an accounting staff, such as preparation of payroll and maintenance of client escrow accounts, frequently are done by the paralegal. Many solo practitioners consider their paralegal to be a key resource in the practice of law.

Small Offices

Small offices Small-office arrangements ranging from individual practitioners sharing space to partnerships.

Small offices may consist of individual practitioners sharing space, or partnerships. For the small practitioner, the cost of maintaining an adequate law library, conference room, office space, and office equipment can be significant. Therefore, small firms frequently share these common services while separating client practices. The lawyers may work in similar fields, such as criminal law or family law, or they may have practices that are very different, such as estate law and insurance defense work. Depending upon the arrangement, the practitioners might refer clients to one another, but each attorney is personally responsible for the client and the client relationship.

Depending upon the arrangement, personnel such as a receptionist, secretary, or paralegal might be shared. In these situations the paralegal must be certain which of the attorneys is the supervising attorney with regard to each client. The paralegal who is working for more than one attorney in a sharing arrangement might be privy to confidential information that may not be shared with the other attorneys in the office unless they are working on the same case. In some respects, this can be thought of as an "ethical wall" environment. At the very least, the paralegal and the attorneys must clearly understand the ethical issues involved.

Partnerships

A **partnership** may consist of two or more persons who have joined together to share ownership of a business and any profit or loss from that business. Each of the partners has responsibility for the other partner and the practice. Partnerships in small-office arrangements may be "true" partnerships, sharing all aspects of the practice, or they may be partnerships in name only. In the latter case, the paralegal must consider the same ethical issues as in other office-sharing arrangements.

Partnership Two or more persons or corporations that have joined together to share ownership and profit or loss.

Within a partnership, a paralegal may work for more than one of the partners, and in effect, the partners share the paralegal's services. This can be difficult for the paralegal when two or more of the partners demand something at the same time, with the same sense of urgency. The fact that each of the partners will consider him- or herself to be "the boss" can create a delicate situation for the paralegal.

A common solution in many offices is for one of the partners to be the primary supervising attorney for the paralegal, through whom the other partners funnel work requests. From an ethical point of view, this delineates which attorney is the supervising attorney for the clients and files the paralegal concentrates on, and at the same time clarifies the lawyers' responsibilities under the rules of professional conduct.

Large Offices

Many of the **large law offices** that exist today grew from smaller, more traditional law offices. These firms expanded over the years, adding partners and associates along the way. At one time, these larger law firms were regional, confined to major cities such as New York, Chicago, Philadelphia, and Los Angeles. As the national economy grew and corporate clients expanded around the country, many firms established offices in other large cities, giving them a presence in different regions. The growth of the global economy has taken large firms one step further, with some establishing offices in foreign countries. As a result, the large law firms have taken on the characteristics of large corporations, with some firms merging to add to their specialty areas of the law and expand the availability of legal services.

Large law offices Large law offices are an outgrowth of traditional law offices that have expanded over the years, adding partners and associates along the way.

For the paralegal, the large office can be an exciting and dynamic area of practice. The paralegal might work with clients who have diverse backgrounds or are located in other regions or countries; some cases may require paralegals to travel on their own or with other members of the legal team. For clients, one of the values of a large law firm is the availability of a number of legal specialties within one legal services provider. For the paralegal, this offers the opportunity to work in different legal fields.

Working in a large law firm also has some disadvantages. There may be fewer opportunities to form personal relationships with clients and other members of the legal team. In some firms, just as in any large organization, "playing politics" also becomes an issue. A paralegal's status, as well as some of the perks and benefits of the job, may depend on the status of the individual's supervising attorney. At the same time, the opportunities for advancement in a large firm might outweigh the disadvantages.

ETHICAL PERSPECTIVE

Lawyers Who Share Offices

It is "impermissible for unaffiliated attorneys to have unrestricted access to each other's electronic files (including email and word-processing documents) and other client records. If separate computer systems are not utilized, each attorney's confidential client information should be protected in a way that guards against unauthorized access and preserves client confidences and secrets."

Source: District of Columbia Ethics Opinion 303.

Unlike the small office, in which the paralegal might serve as bookkeeper, office manager, receptionist, and second chair in litigation, a large firm typically hires support staff for each of these functions. Bookkeeping or accounting departments usually handle payroll, check requests, and other financial issues. In the larger firms, even the job of making copies takes place in a duplicating department, and the firm might have a mailroom for handling incoming and outgoing mail.

The large law firm also has specialized components to provide different types of services. Law firms in the United States frequently have litigation specialists who spend their time in the actual litigation of cases, while other attorneys within the same firm rarely, if ever, go to court. The role of the latter is to work with clients and, when the need arises, prepare materials for the litigation department. In some ways this is similar to the structure of the English legal system, in which one type of lawyer, called a "solicitor," deals directly with clients, and a different type of lawyer, called a "barrister," litigates the cases.

Just as the law has become more complex, lawyers also have come to specialize in narrow areas of practice such as environmental law, intellectual property law, health care law, insurance law, tort law, and family law. This means that paralegals in large law firms also become specialists within their supervising attorney's primary field. Large firms encourage clients to use the firm for all of their legal needs, so a lawyer in the firm frequently refers clients to other specialists within the firm, while remaining the primary contact with those clients. Some firms have lawyers whose expertise is in getting new clients. These lawyers, often former politicians and government officials, frequently are referred to as the "rainmakers." They use their network of contacts to obtain clients and then refer the clients to the specialists within the firm.

Compensation for attorneys within large firms is generally based on how much new business the attorney has brought in, as well as how many billable hours the supervising attorneys and their paralegals have been able to bill. In this kind of environment, the paralegal who is able to maintain strong relationships with clients is an invaluable asset to the firm.

General Practice

General law practice A practice that handles all types of cases.

A **general law practice** is one that handles all types of cases. This is the type of practice many people think of as the small-town lawyer—the generalist to whom everyone in town goes for advice. The reality is that generalists practice in cities as well as in small towns throughout the country. Their practices are as diverse as the law itself, handling everything from adoptions to zoning appeals. As general practitioners, they serve a function in law similar to that of the general family practice doctor in medicine.

Lawyers in this type of practice often work in several areas of law within the same day—attending a hearing in small-claims court in the morning, preparing a will before lunch, having a lunch meeting with an opposing attorney to discuss settlement of an accident case, helping someone who is forming a corporation, and in the evening, appearing at a municipal government meeting to seek a zoning approval. For many, the general practice is the most exciting type of practice, with a continually changing clientele offering all sorts of legal challenges. The paralegal in this environment has the opportunity to work with many different types of clients on many different types of legal matters. The challenge in this type of practice is to stay current in each of the areas the attorney practices.

Specialty Practice

Specialty practice A specialty practice is involved in practice in one area of law.

A **specialty practice** is involved in one area of law. Lawyers with specialty backgrounds, such as engineering, might choose to work in patent or intellectual property law. Those coming into the legal profession with accounting backgrounds might specialize in tax matters. Others have special interests and passions, such as working with senior citizens in an elder law practice or protecting the interests of children as child advocates or practicing criminal law.

Paralegals *in* Practice

PARALEGAL PROFILE

Ann W. Price

Ann W. Price, RP, has been a paralegal for over 25 years, working in different-sized law firms in diverse practice areas. Ann is currently employed as a Litigation Paralegal Specialist in the U.S. Department of Justice's Environment and Natural Resources Division in Washington, D.C. She is a PACE™ Registered Paralegal, which means she has passed the Paralegal Advance Competency Exam, a certification test developed by the National Federation of Paralegal Associations (NFPA).

In my first few paralegal positions, I was either the only paralegal in the office, or one of two paralegals supporting several attorneys. Because these were small law firms, I was given a large degree of responsibility right from the start. I routinely prepared client correspondence, assisted with discovery (gathering and managing evidence), interviewed clients, and attended trials.

Next, I worked in larger law firms, specializing in food and drug law and environmental law. As a food and drug law paralegal, I researched congressional reports, the Federal Register, and other news and legal databases to summarize findings that might be of interest to the firm's clients. As an environmental law paralegal, I worked on all phases of discovery, trial preparation, and arbitration proceedings in Superfund cases that mostly involved municipal landfill clean-ups.

My next two jobs were both related to paralegal management for large law firms with hundreds of attorneys. In one of these positions, I was an active paralegal in addition to my management duties. Eventually, I became a paralegal manager where my duties were entirely managerial. I currently work for the U.S. Department of Justice's Environment and Natural Resources Division where I provide litigation support to approximately 60 attorneys.

There are pros and cons in every type of legal work setting. Paralegals in large law firms are usually paid a larger salary, but the work they perform is often far less substantive than the work performed by paralegals in smaller firms. Large firms often give the most substantive work to the associate attorneys, particularly those right out of law school. In smaller firms, every person is expected to be able to meet any need the case requires. Also, in larger firms, there is often pressure to meet a specified number of client billable hours; many smaller law firms do not even set a minimum.

In my various jobs, the basic skills used and the work performed did not change significantly from practice area to practice area. However, the terminology and legal resources varied considerably. Continuing legal education opportunities are more prevalent in larger law firms than smaller ones. In smaller firms, education is generally limited to on-the-job training. Most law firms in the metro D.C. area, particularly the large ones, require a four-year degree, and many want a paralegal certificate as well. Individuals with two-year degrees are more likely to find employment at smaller firms, at least for their first paralegal job.

Because of the increasing complexity of the law, legal specialists frequently receive referrals from attorneys in general practice, or in other specialties. The paralegal working for a specialist often acquires such a high level of knowledge in a specific area that it may rival that of many general practitioners. One of the dangers for the paralegal with this extent of specialty knowledge is that other attorneys could ask the paralegal for answers to questions in that specialty where the answers border on, or actually result in, the unauthorized practice of law.

Because specialty law practices are often dependent on referrals from other firms, there is a natural tendency for paralegals in these specialties to accommodate referring attorneys by trying to answer questions of a legal nature. To avoid a potential claim of unauthorized practice of law, the paralegal must diplomatically avoid giving legal advice, even to an attorney from another firm.

A primary job function for the paralegal in a specialty practice is maintaining relationships with other law firms and their paralegals and secretaries. The paralegal obtains referrals for the supervising attorney and the firm as a result of relationships developed in professional associations with paralegals at other firms. For example, another paralegal may recommend his or her friend who works for a lawyer specializing in the area sought.

In many areas of specialty, the paralegal becomes a vital team member. Paralegals with skills in specific substantive areas perform services that allow the attorney to concentrate on other matters. In addition, the paralegal may handle office management tasks and other functions such as coordinating between members of the professional team and the client.

Legal Nurse Consultants and Nurse Paralegals

Nurse paralegals or legal nurse consultants Nurses who have gained medical work experience and combine it with paralegal skills.

Nurse paralegals or legal nurse consultants are nurses who combine prior medical work experience with paralegal skills. Becoming a legal nurse consultant or a nurse paralegal is an ideal career opportunity for nurses with clinical nursing experience who want to work in the legal environment. Entry to most nurse paralegal education programs requires a current license as a registered nurse and 2,000 to 6,000 hours (usually one to three years) of clinical nursing experience. Some programs are open to those with an associate degree in nursing, but usually a bachelor's degree in nursing is desired.

Nurse paralegals draw upon their knowledge of medical terminology, medical procedures, and nursing practice to decipher medical records for the legal community. The most obvious advantage is their ability to analyze medical records from both medical and legal standpoints. Their experience also enables them to conduct more effective interviews with clients, fact witnesses, and expert witnesses in cases of medical malpractice or personal injury. Graduates of these programs often work as independent nurse consultants for law firms and insurance companies. Others find in-house positions with insurance companies and law firms specializing in medical malpractice and personal injury.

Although the ABA considers the nurse paralegal and legal nurse consultant to be part of the paralegal profession, the American Association of Legal Nurse Consultants (AALNC) views this role as a subspecialty of nursing. In March 1998, the Standing Committee on Legal Assistants (now named the Standing Committee on Paralegals) of the American Bar Association decided that "legal nurses and legal nurse consultants fall squarely within the ABA definition of 'paralegal/legal assistant.'" By contrast, the AALNC has defined the legal nurse consultant as a specialty practitioner of nursing whose education should be developed and presented as specialty nursing curricula by nurse educators in partnership with legal educators. The ethical code and regulations that must be followed may depend on which professional organization legal nurse consultants are associated with.

Web Exploration

Further information on Legal Nurse Consulting can be obtained at **www.aalnc.org**.

Real Estate

Paralegals with real estate sales or title insurance backgrounds can perform many of the tasks associated with a real estate practice, such as communicating between buyers and sellers, coordinating the documentation for settlements, and preparing documents for recording purposes. Completing a course of study for becoming a licensed salesperson or a real estate broker provides a paralegal with knowledge in the practices and procedures of real estate transactions. In addition, familiarity with real estate terminology facilitates effective communication with attorneys and clients.

Complex Litigation

Complex litigation Cases involving many parties, as in a class action, or a case involving multiple or complex legal issues.

Complex litigation takes many forms, from class-action lawsuits to complex product-liability cases. Paralegals working in complex litigation typically oversee the requests for document production and maintain indexes, usually on computer databases, of the paperwork generated from the litigation. In large cases, the paralegal might supervise a staff of other paralegals or law students in summarizing discovery documents. At trial, these paralegals frequently coordinate the production of exhibits.

Environmental Law

Environmental law An area of the law dealing with the protection of the environment.

Environmental law covers everything from the cleanup of toxic waste dumps to protection of wildlife and the environment. A challenge for the environmental paralegal is in locating and obtaining public records and other documents necessary to establish environmental claims. Some of this documentation may predate computer records, such as those documenting toxic waste dumps created during World War II and the early 1950s.

Intellectual Property

In a survey by The Affiliates, a company providing temporary and full-time legal personnel, 48 percent of the attorneys surveyed indicated **intellectual property** as the fastest-growing field in law. The intellectual property paralegal assists with the formalities of protecting intellectual property, including patents, trade secrets, copyrights, and trademarks. The two main areas in this field are (a) prosecution, which involves establishing the priority of the claims that will result in the granting of the patent or copyright, and (b) litigation, which protects those rights against claims by others, such as in patent infringement cases.

Intellectual property Protection of intellectual property interests, such as patents, trademarks, and copyrights.

Elder Law

With the aging of the population has come an increased need to protect the rights of the elderly and help them obtain all the benefits to which they are entitled. This includes simple tasks such as helping individuals apply for Social Security, Medicare, or Medicaid benefits. It also entails working with the elderly to create estate plan documents, powers of attorney, and health care directives. The paralegal or legal assistant is increasingly becoming an advocate for the elderly, in many cases working in a pro bono capacity or through social service agencies. **Elder law** has also come to include the additional services of helping the elderly work through the maze of health insurance and government benefits.

Elder law Advocacy for the elderly.

Paralegal Managers

As paralegal staffs have grown, so has the need for someone to manage these personnel. Higher turnover rates and increased specialization have increased the need for someone to hire, supervise, train, and evaluate paralegals. The largest firms appoint a managing partner to handle these management and human resources tasks. But in many smaller firms, these duties fall to the individual with the title of **paralegal manager.** In many firms this person not only manages the paralegals, but also serves as a liaison between the paralegals and the attorneys. An attorney usually does not have the time to handle the nonlegal tasks required of a manager, so a paralegal manager fulfills this role. The paralegal manager acts as a leader, mentor, employee advocate, supervisor, trainer, evaluator, problem solver, and resource manager for those he or she manages. This new specialty is well recognized, and is supported by its own organization, the International Paralegal Management Association.

Paralegal manager Someone who hires, supervises, trains, and evaluates paralegals.

Check the latest IPMA News at the IPMA website, www.ipma.org.

Pro Bono Paralegals

Pro bono means working without compensation on behalf of individuals and organizations that otherwise could not afford legal assistance. Much of this work is performed by legal aid offices and community legal service programs. As members of professional associations, paralegals participate in pro bono activities at varying levels and time commitments. For example, the Massachusetts Paralegal Association supports a number of pro bono projects. In one of these, the Family Law Project, paralegals partner with attorneys to help handle domestic violence cases without compensation. Pro bono work is seen as part of an ethical obligation of the legal profession.

Pro bono Working without compensation on behalf of individuals and organizations that otherwise could not afford legal assistance.

Government Employment

Federal, state, and local governments are large employers of paralegals, and they are expected to be utilized even further in **government employment** at every level in the future. Many of these positions are found in administrative agencies such as the Social Security Administration, where paralegals work as decision writers, case schedulers, and case specialists. Just as the private law firm has discovered the value of the paralegal on the legal team, so have government law offices such as the U.S. Attorney's Office and the Office of the Solicitor General. These offices are involved

Government employment Working for federal, state, and local government agencies and authorities.

with both criminal prosecutions and civil litigation where the government is a party. Many other agencies that conduct administrative hearings utilize paralegals at all levels.

Legal Departments of Corporations

Many people think of a corporate legal department as a relaxed but conservative environment, where there is little activity other than drafting minutes of meetings and filing corporate records with federal and state governments. In reality, these departments can be very busy, dynamic environments to work in.

In the global economy, many corporations are engaged in international trade. There is a large body of law that relates to compliance with trade regulations, and international trade creates a host of unique issues related to the laws of the countries with which the domestic corporation may be doing business. For example, the transfer and sale of certain high-tech equipment must have prior government approval. Sales involving shipments to other countries require letters of credit and currency conversions. The paralegal is in the middle of these transactions, juggling the requirements from both the legal and sales or marketing perspectives. Paralegals with foreign language skills find themselves in even greater demand in handling communication issues. Those with cultural ties to the countries with which the corporation is doing business may be very useful in avoiding mistakes resulting from miscommunications or cultural misunderstandings.

DuPont, one of the largest corporations in the United States, provides a great example in the utilization of paralegals. In an effort to reduce costs, DuPont created a legal model that many companies have adopted.

"Since 1992, the DuPont Legal Model has continued to adapt and change to meet the challenges in today's corporate law. That's because the Legal Model remains a dynamic process that undergoes almost continuous re-engineering and refinement in order for us to remain competitive.... DuPont created the Paralegal Utilization Program to capture the knowledge and enthusiasm of paralegals and help case managers use all of their legal personnel more cost-effectively." *Source:* http://www.dupontlegalmodel.com/initiatives/

Self-Employment

Self-employment Working independently either as a freelance paralegal for different lawyers or, when authorized by state or federal law, performing services for the public.

Paralegals also have some opportunities to work independently, although state regulations may limit some of the opportunities for paralegal **self-employment.** Where authorized by federal law, the paralegal may actively represent clients without the supervision of an attorney, such as before the U.S. Patent Office or Social Security Administration. Many paralegals work as freelancers for different attorneys, usually on a case-by-case basis. In addition to the normal ethical obligations regarding confidentiality and conflict of interest, the freelance paralegal must observe the ethical guidelines on advertising in the local jurisdiction and avoid the appearance of being available to render legal advice.

Networking

Networking The establishment of contact with others with whom questions and information are shared.

Networking is important for every paralegal, regardless of the size or type of working environment. It is essential to establish contacts with others to share questions and information. Many paralegals develop a referral list of other paralegals they can call to get a quick answer to a new problem. Most paralegals are not too proud to call their contacts for help in meeting deadlines or getting necessary forms—whether those contacts are across the street, across the state, or across the country. During interviews, hiring attorneys sometimes ask about the paralegal's networking activity.

For the paralegal, networking may also be the key to obtaining a job. Success in finding employment often depends not only on what you know, but also whom you know. Knowing the right person, or someone who can refer you to the right person, can lead to new opportunities.

Paralegal Tasks and Functions

The actual tasks and functions the paralegal performs vary according to the type of practice, the size of the firm or organization, and the skill of the individual paralegal. Some of the more general tasks include:

- conducting interviews
- maintaining written and verbal contacts with clients and counsel
- setting up, organizing, and maintaining client files
- preparing pleadings and documents
- reviewing, analyzing, summarizing, and indexing documents and transcripts
- assisting in preparing witnesses and clients for trial
- maintaining calendar and "tickler" (reminder) systems
- conducting research, both factual and legal
- performing office administrative functions including maintaining time and billing records

Learning Objective 2

Describe the tasks and functions performed by paralegals.

SIDEBAR

DOCUMENT SPECIALIST OR PARALEGAL?

Under the definition enacted by the Maine legislature, anyone calling himself or herself a paralegal or legal assistant must work under the supervision of an attorney. Independent paralegals no longer can use the title "paralegal" or "legal assistant." This has resulted in some of them changing the name of their freelance business to "document specialist" (*Bangor Daily News,* August 16, 1999).

The California legislature has enacted a law prohibiting self-help legal document service providers from receiving compensation unless the legal document assistant is registered in the county where the service is provided and provides a bond of $25,000.

Client Interviews

Paralegals are often the first line of contact with clients. Although paralegals may not ethically or legally give legal advice or set legal fees, they frequently conduct the initial interview with the client. This might involve taking the initial client information and preparing a client data sheet (see Exhibit 3.1), or conducting a more in-depth interview to determine the facts of the matter for the attorney's review. Frequently, the paralegal continues to function as the contact point between the client and the supervising attorney or law firm. In this role, paralegals must establish rapport with clients and earn their confidence.

The paralegal must always be keenly aware of the ethical limitations in dealing with clients. This is especially true when the client develops a high level of confidence in dealing with the paralegal. When clients have confidence in a paralegal, they might have a tendency to ask the paralegal for advice and recommendations instead of "bothering" the attorney. Providing such advice or recommendations may be in violation of laws against the unauthorized practice of law.

For example, to the client, the question, "Should I make my son my power of attorney?" seems simple. However, the answer to this question is actually complex and involves many legal consequences, so it must be referred to the supervising attorney. Another example of the unauthorized practice of law might be helping the client complete blank legal forms, such as bankruptcy forms or will forms purchased at a retail store.

Investigations

The paralegal may be asked to act as the direct representative of the supervising attorney in conducting an investigation of a pending case. A paralegal trained in a specific area of law understands the facts that must be developed for a case in that area, as well as the available sources for that information. A paralegal who has had the opportunity to observe an attorney presenting evidence at trial will have a good sense of what makes good demonstrative evidence, such as models and photographs. For example, an understanding of how photographs will be used at trial, and what questions will be asked about the photographs in direct examination and cross-examination, will enable the paralegal to be certain that the photographs are taken from the correct angles, with the correct landmarks or measurements included.

Interviews conducted by the paralegal in preparation for trial could qualify for protection under attorney–client privilege, just as they do when conducted by attorneys. The paralegal must be aware of how interview material may be used and potentially obtained by opposing parties and act to protect clients' privileged communication.

Exhibit 3.1 Client data sheet

CLIENT DATA SHEET

	ACTION TAKEN/REQUIRED
1. Client Name:	
2. Client/Matter Number:	
3. Client Address:	
4. Phone: Work:	
Home:	
Fax:	
5. Email address:	
6. Social Security No.:	
7. Date of Birth:	
8. Marital Status:	
9. Client Contact:	
10. Matter:	
(a) Adverse Party:	
(b) Date of Incident:	
(c) Statute of Limitations Period:	
(d) Statute of Limitations Date:	
11. Opposing Counsel:	
12. Opposing Counsel Address:	
13. Opposing Counsel Phone:	

Legal Writing

Paralegals frequently are called upon to maintain written communications with clients, opposing attorneys, and the court. These may be in the form of correspondence, memoranda of law, or briefs for the court. Many paralegals become extremely adept at drafting complaints and supporting briefs and memoranda. Although the content is the ultimate responsibility of the supervising attorney, a paralegal with good writing skills is an invaluable asset. Well-written and well-reasoned documentation prepared by the paralegal can be easily reviewed, signed, and transmitted by the attorney, saving valuable time.

Legal Research

In the modern law office, legal research is conducted with both books and the Internet. Legal research today requires the ability to use online legal services such as Lexis, Westlaw, VersusLaw, and Loislaw, as well as government websites. The ability to conduct research of case law, statutes, and regulatory rules and procedures gives the paralegal a major advantage, and can lead to job opportunities and advancement in many firms.

What Paralegals in Legal Specialties Do

In addition to the various general tasks that most paralegals or legal assistants perform, those working in specialty areas may also perform more specialized tasks that require special knowledge, education, or skill beyond the basic skills and knowledge required of all paralegals. The following are some of the tasks that paralegals in specialty practice perform.

General business practice:

- Draft lease agreements
- Draft partnership agreements
- Draft noncompetition agreements
- Prepare real estate sales agreements and attend real estate closings
- Draft contracts for business arrangements and new ventures
- Draft employee agreements

Debtor and creditor rights:

- Draft correspondence complying with state and federal regulations concerning debt collection
- Prepare documentation to support garnishment proceedings
- Arrange for execution of judgments, including publication of notice of sales and levies on personal property
- Transfer judgments to other jurisdictions
- Prepare, file, and terminate Uniform Commercial Code financing statements
- Assist clients in filing bankruptcy petitions, including the preparation of schedules and proofs of claim
- Prepare Chapter 11 debtor's financial statements
- Attend Chapter 13 confirmation hearings

Corporate practice:

- Determine availability of, and reserve, corporate and fictitious names
- Prepare and file fictitious name registrations
- Prepare articles of incorporation, minutes, and bylaws for the corporation
- Prepare, issue, and transfer stock certificates
- Prepare shareholder agreements
- Prepare applications and file for employer identification numbers and tax registration numbers
- Prepare and file annual reports
- Prepare and file articles of dissolution
- Prepare and file securities registrations and required filings with state regulatory agencies and the Securities & Exchange Commission

Environmental law:

- Track information with regard to Superfund sites
- Determine applicability of brown fields laws to client property
- Research history of properties to determine environmental activity
- Obtain the appropriate information about sites from state and federal environmental agencies
- Obtain documentation and assist in the preparation of environmental audits

Family law:

- Collect information from clients with regard to current or prior marital status
- Interview client and collect information with regard to child support (see Exhibit 3.2)

Exhibit 3.2 Child support data form

_______________ v. _______________ No. _______________

THIS FORM MUST BE FILLED OUT

(If you are self-employed or if you are salaried by a business of which you are owner in whole or in part, you must also fill out the Supplemental Income Statement which appears on the last page of this Income and Expense Statement.)

INCOME AND EXPENSE STATEMENT OF

____

I verify that the statements made in this Income and Expense Statement are true and correct. I understand that false statements herein are made subject to the penalties of 18 Pa.C.S. §4904 relating to unsworn falsification to authorities.

Date: _______________ Plaintiff or Defendant: _______________

INCOME

Employer: _______________

Address: _______________

Type of Work: _______________

Payroll Number: _______________

Pay Period (weekly, biweekly, etc.): _______________

Gross Pay per Pay Period: $ _______________

Itemized Payroll Deductions:		
	Federal Withholding	$ ________
	Social Security	________
	Local Wage Tax	________
	State Income Tax	________
	Retirement	________
	Savings Bonds	________
	Credit Union	________
	Life Insurance	________
	Health Insurance	________
	Other (specify)	________
	________	________
	Net Pay per Pay Period	$ ________

OTHER INCOME: (Fill in Appropriate Column)

	Weekly	*Monthly*	*Yearly*
Interest	$ ________	$ ________	$ ________
Dividends	________	________	________
Pension	________	________	________
Annuity	________	________	________
Social Security	________	________	________
Rents	________	________	________
Royalties	________	________	________
Expense Account	________	________	________
Gifts	________	________	________
Unemployment Comp.	________	________	________
Workmen's Comp.	________	________	________
________	________	________	________
Total	________	________	________
TOTAL INCOME			$ ________

- Draft prenuptial agreements
- Draft divorce complaints and responsive pleadings
- Prepare motions for support
- Prepare motions for custody and visitation
- Prepare property settlement agreements
- Prepare protection-from-abuse petitions

- Prepare petitions for termination of parental rights
- Prepare adoption petitions

Immigration law:

- Prepare applications and petitions for filing with the Immigration and Naturalization Service (INS) (see Exhibit 3.3)
- Coordinate translation of foreign documents

Exhibit 3.3 Sample Immigration and Naturalization Service form

U.S. Department of Justice
Immigration and Naturalization Service

Notice of Entry of Appearance as Attorney or Representative

Appearances - An appearance shall be filed on this form by the attorney or representative appearing in each case. Thereafter, substitution may be permitted upon the written withdrawal of the attorney or representative of record or upon notification of the new attorney or representative. When an appearance is made by a person acting in a representative capacity, his personal appearance or signature shall constitute a representation that under the provisions of this chapter he is authorized and qualified to represent. Further proof of authority to act in a representative capacity may be required. **Availability of Records** - During the time a case is pending, and except as otherwise provided in 8 CFR 103.2(b), a party to a proceeding or his attorney or representative shall be permitted to examine the record of proceeding in a Service office. He may, in conformity with 8 CFR 103.10, obtain copies of Service records or information therefrom and copies of documents or transcripts of evidence furnished by him. Upon request, he/she may, in addition, be loaned a copy of the testimony and exhibits contained in the record of proceeding upon giving his/her receipt for such copies and pledging that it will be surrendered upon final disposition of the case or upon demand. If extra copies of exhibits do not exist, they shall not be furnished free on loan; however, they shall be made available for copying or purchase of copies as provided in 8 CFR 103.10.

In re: Lim Chi	Date: 09-15-2002 File No. A1357

I hereby enter my appearance as attorney for (or representative of), and at the request of the following named person(s):

Name: Lim chi	☑ Petitioner ☐ Applicant ☐ Beneficiary
Address: (Apt. No.) (Number & Street) (City) (State) (Zip Code) 275 Swamp Road Newtown Pa 18940	
Name:	☐ Petitioner ☐ Applicant ☐ Beneficiary
Address: (Apt. No.) (Number & Street) (City) (State) (Zip Code)	

Check Applicable Item(s) below:

☑ 1. I am an attorney and a member in good standing of the bar of the Supreme Court of the United States or of the highest court of the following State, territory, insular possession, or District of Columbia
Pennsylvania Supreme Court (Name of Court) and am not under a court or administrative agency order suspending, enjoining, restraining, disbarring, or otherwise restricting me in practicing law.

☐ 2. I am an accredited representative of the following named religious, charitable, social service, or similar organization established in the United States and which is so recognized by the Board:

☐ 3. I am associated with ______ the attorney of record previously filed a notice of appearance in this case and my appearance is at his request. (*If you check this item, also check item 1 or 2 whichever is appropriate.*)

☐ 4. Others (Explain Fully.)

SIGNATURE	COMPLETE ADDRESS 138 North State Street Newtown, pa 18940
NAME (Type or Print) Thomas F. Goldman	TELEPHONE NUMBER 215 555 4321

PURSUANT TO THE PRIVACY ACT OF 1974, I HEREBY CONSENT TO THE DISCLOSURE TO THE FOLLOWING NAMED ATTORNEY OR REPRESENTATIVE OF ANY RECORD PERTAINING TO ME WHICH APPEARS IN ANY IMMIGRATION AND NATURALIZATION SERVICE SYSTEM OF RECORDS:

Thomas F. Goldman
(Name of Attorney or Representative)

THE ABOVE CONSENT TO DISCLOSURE IS IN CONNECTION WITH THE FOLLOWING MATTER:

Name of Person Consenting	Signature of Person Consenting	Date
Lim Chi	Lim Chi	

(NOTE: Execution of this box is required under the Privacy Act of 1974 where the person being represented is a citizen of the United States or an alien lawfully admitted for permanent residence.)

This form may not be used to request records under the Freedom of Information Act or the Privacy Act. The manner of requesting such records is contained in 8CFR 103.10 and 103.20 Et.SEQ.

Form G-28 (09/26/00)Y

- Prepare immigration and nonimmigration visa applications
- Coordinate activities with clients in foreign jurisdictions seeking entry into the United States
- Assist clients in obtaining work visas for working in foreign countries
- Assist clients in the preparation of documentation to prove claim of marital status for submission to INS

Intellectual property:

- Conduct patent and trademark searches
- Prepare applications for patents, trademarks, or copyrights (see Exhibit 3.4)
- Assist in the preparation of documentation for proceedings regarding opposition, interference, infringement, and similar issues
- Coordinate activities and filings with foreign patent, trademark, and copyright attorneys and agents
- Work with engineers in preparation of applications and defense of patents and trade secrets
- Draft licensing agreements for intellectual property

Human resources law:

- Draft documents for tax-sheltered employee benefit plans
- Draft deferred compensation plans
- Prepare and file for Internal Revenue Service determination letters for plans
- Prepare and file annual reports such as 5500 series Internal Revenue Service forms
- Calculate employer and employee contribution levels and limitations
- Draft, review, and distribute summary plan descriptions

Litigation:

- Investigate factual allegations of cases
- Assist in locating witnesses and physical evidence
- Draft summonses, complaints, answers, and other responsive pleadings
- Organize and maintain litigation files
- Assist in the preparation of trial notebooks
- Gather, review, summarize, and index documents for trial
- Locate and arrange for interviews with expert witnesses
- Prepare written interrogatories
- Assist in preparing for and conducting depositions including videotape depositions
- Prepare or obtain subpoenas (see sample in Exhibit 3.5) and arrange for service
- Coordinate, assist, and arrange for trial exhibits
- Obtain jury pool information and assist in the selection of jury members
- Attend trial and assist in the handling of witnesses, exhibits, and evidence
- Prepare contemporaneous summaries of witness statements during trial

Learning Objective 3
Describe the administrative procedures found in most law offices.

Administrative Procedures in Law Offices and Firms

Certain administrative procedures, such as conflict checking and time keeping, are common to most, if not all, law offices. Depending on the size of the law firm and the nature of the practice, a paralegal also may be called upon to perform certain financial activities, such as preparing invoices, maintaining client escrow accounts, maintaining trust accounts, preparing payroll records, preparing court-required accounting, and completing real estate settlement forms.

Exhibit 3.4 Copyright form

FEE CHANGES
Fees are effective through June 30, 2002. After that date, check the Copyright Office Website at www.loc.gov/copyright or call (202) 707-3000 for current fee information.

FORM TX
For a Nondramatic Literary Work
UNITED STATES COPYRIGHT OFFICE

REGISTRATION NUMBER

TX TXU

EFFECTIVE DATE OF REGISTRATION

Month Day Year

DO NOT WRITE ABOVE THIS LINE. IF YOU NEED MORE SPACE, USE A SEPARATE CONTINUATION SHEET.

1

TITLE OF THIS WORK ▼

PREVIOUS OR ALTERNATIVE TITLES ▼

PUBLICATION AS A CONTRIBUTION If this work was published as a contribution to a periodical, serial, or collection, give information about the collective work in which the contribution appeared. Title of Collective Work ▼

If published in a periodical or serial give: Volume ▼ Number ▼ Issue Date ▼ On Pages ▼

2

a NAME OF AUTHOR ▼

DATES OF BIRTH AND DEATH
Year Born ▼ Year Died ▼

Was this contribution to the work a "work made for hire"?
☐ Yes
☐ No

AUTHOR'S NATIONALITY OR DOMICILE
Name of Country
OR { Citizen of ▶ USA
Domiciled in ▶

WAS THIS AUTHOR'S CONTRIBUTION TO THE WORK
Anonymous? ☐ Yes ☐ No
Pseudonymous? ☐ Yes ☐ No
If the answer to either of these questions is "Yes," see detailed instructions.

NATURE OF AUTHORSHIP Briefly describe nature of material created by this author in which copyright is claimed. ▼
Sole Author

b NAME OF AUTHOR ▼

DATES OF BIRTH AND DEATH
Year Born ▼ Year Died ▼

Was this contribution to the work a "work made for hire"?
☐ Yes
☐ No

AUTHOR'S NATIONALITY OR DOMICILE
Name of Country
OR { Citizen of ▶
Domiciled in ▶

WAS THIS AUTHOR'S CONTRIBUTION TO THE WORK
Anonymous? ☐ Yes ☐ No
Pseudonymous? ☐ Yes ☐ No
If the answer to either of these questions is "Yes," see detailed instructions.

NATURE OF AUTHORSHIP Briefly describe nature of material created by this author in which copyright is claimed. ▼

c NAME OF AUTHOR ▼

DATES OF BIRTH AND DEATH
Year Born ▼ Year Died ▼

Was this contribution to the work a "work made for hire"?
☐ Yes
☐ No

AUTHOR'S NATIONALITY OR DOMICILE
Name of Country
OR { Citizen of ▶
Domiciled in ▶

WAS THIS AUTHOR'S CONTRIBUTION TO THE WORK
Anonymous? ☐ Yes ☐ No
Pseudonymous? ☐ Yes ☐ No
If the answer to either of these questions is "Yes," see detailed instructions.

NATURE OF AUTHORSHIP Briefly describe nature of material created by this author in which copyright is claimed. ▼

NOTE
Under the law, the "author" of a "work made for hire" is generally the employer, not the employee (see instructions). For any part of this work that was "made for hire" check "Yes" in the space provided, give the employer (or other person for whom the work was prepared) as "Author" of that part, and leave the space for dates of birth and death blank.

3

a YEAR IN WHICH CREATION OF THIS WORK WAS COMPLETED
◀ Year
This information must be given in all cases.

b DATE AND NATION OF FIRST PUBLICATION OF THIS PARTICULAR WORK
Complete this information ONLY if this work has been published.
Month ▶ Day ▶ Year ▶
USA ◀ Nation

4

See instructions before completing this space.

COPYRIGHT CLAIMANT(S) Name and address must be given even if the claimant is the same as the author given in space 2. ▼

TRANSFER If the claimant(s) named here in space 4 is (are) different from the author(s) named in space 2, give a brief statement of how the claimant(s) obtained ownership of the copyright. ▼
By written agreement.

DO NOT WRITE HERE
OFFICE USE ONLY

APPLICATION RECEIVED

ONE DEPOSIT RECEIVED

TWO DEPOSITS RECEIVED

FUNDS RECEIVED

MORE ON BACK ▶ • Complete all applicable spaces (numbers 5-9) on the reverse side of this page.
• See detailed instructions. • Sign the form at line 8.

DO NOT WRITE HERE

Page 1 of ____ pages

(continued)

Exhibit 3.4 Copyright form *(continued)*

EXAMINED BY

FORM TX

CHECKED BY

☐ CORRESPONDENCE Yes

FOR COPYRIGHT OFFICE USE ONLY

DO NOT WRITE ABOVE THIS LINE. IF YOU NEED MORE SPACE, USE A SEPARATE CONTINUATION SHEET.

5

PREVIOUS REGISTRATION Has registration for this work, or for an earlier version of this work, already been made in the Copyright Office?

☐ Yes ☐ No If your answer is "Yes," why is another registration being sought? (Check appropriate box.) ▼

a. ☐ This is the first published edition of a work previously registered in unpublished form.

b. ☐ This is the first application submitted by this author as copyright claimant.

c. ☐ This is a changed version of the work, as shown by space 6 on this application.

If your answer is "Yes," give: **Previous Registration Number** ▶ **Year of Registration** ▶

6

DERIVATIVE WORK OR COMPILATION

a **Preexisting Material** Identify any preexisting work or works that this work is based on or incorporates. ▼

See instructions before completing this space.

b **Material Added to This Work** Give a brief, general statement of the material that has been added to this work and in which copyright is claimed. ▼

7

a **DEPOSIT ACCOUNT** If the registration fee is to be charged to a Deposit Account established in the Copyright Office, give name and number of Account.
Name ▼ Account Number ▼

b **CORRESPONDENCE** Give name and address to which correspondence about this application should be sent. Name/Address/Apt/City/State/ZIP ▼

Area code and daytime telephone number ▶ 480-991-7881 Fax number ▶

Email ▶

8

CERTIFICATION* I, the undersigned, hereby certify that I am the
Check only one ▶
☐ author
☐ other copyright claimant
☐ owner of exclusive right(s)
☑ authorized agent of ____________________
Name of author or other copyright claimant, or owner of exclusive right(s) ▲

of the work identified in this application and that the statements made by me in this application are correct to the best of my knowledge.

Typed or printed name and date ▼ If this application gives a date of publication in space 3, do not sign and submit it before that date.

Date ▶

Handwritten signature (X) ▼

X ______________________________

9

Certificate will be mailed in window envelope to this address:

Name ▼

Number/Street/Apt ▼

City/State/ZIP ▼

YOU MUST:
- Complete all necessary spaces
- Sign your application in space 8

SEND ALL 3 ELEMENTS IN THE SAME PACKAGE:
1. Application form
2. Nonrefundable filing fee in check or money order payable to *Register of Copyrights*
3. Deposit material

MAIL TO:
Library of Congress
Copyright Office
101 Independence Avenue, S.E.
Washington, D.C. 20559-6000

As of July 1, 1999, the filing fee for Form TX is $30.

*17 U.S.C. § 506(e): Any person who knowingly makes a false representation of a material fact in the application for copyright registration provided for by section 409, or in any written statement filed in connection with the application, shall be fined not more than $2,500.

June 1999—200,000
WEB REV: June 1999

PRINTED ON RECYCLED PAPER

☆U.S. GOVERNMENT PRINTING OFFICE: 1999-454-879/49

Exhibit 3.5 Subpoena

Commonwealth of Pennsylvania
County of Philadelphia

In the matter of: COURT OF COMMON PLEAS

Henry Thomas
(Plaintiff) (Demandante)

October Term, Yr. 2007

vs.

No. 68-96874

Thomas Cheese
(Defendant) (Demandado)

Subpoena

To: Elizabeth Rhodes
(Name of Witness) (Nombre del Testigo)

1. YOU ARE ORDERED BY THE COURT TO COME TO *(El tribunal le ordena que venga a)* Court room 654, AT PHILADELPHIA, PENNSYLVANIA ON *(en Filadelfia, Pennsylvania el)* November 4, 2007, AT *(a las)* 10 O'CLOCK A.M., TO TESTIFY ON BEHALF OF *(para atestiguar a favor de)* Henry Thomas IN THE ABOVE CASE, AND TO REMAIN UNTIL EXCUSED *(en el caso arriba mencionado y permanecer hasta que le autoricen irse).*

2. AND BRING WITH YOU THE FOLLOWING *(Y traer con usted lo siguiente)*:

NOTICE

If you fail to attend or to produce the documents or things required by this subpoena, you may be subject to the sanctions authorized by Rule 234.5 of the Pennsylvania Rules of Civil Procedure, including but not limited to costs, attorney fees and imprisonment.

AVISO

Si usted falla en comparecer o producir los documentos o cosas requeridas por esta cita, usted estara sujeto a las sanciones autorizadas por la regla 234.5 de las reglas de procedimiento civil de Pensilvania, incluyendo pero no limitado a los costos, remuneracion de abogados y encarcelamiento.

INQUIRIES CONCERNING THIS SUBPOENA SHOULD BE ADDRESSED TO *(Las preguntas que tenga acerca de esta Citacion deben ser dirigidas a)*:
ISSUED BY:

Edith Hannah
(Attorney) *(Abogado/Abogada)*

ADDRESS *(Direccion)* 8 North Broad Street, Philadelphia, PA

TELEPHONE NO. *(No. de Telefono)* 215 555 9999

ATTORNEY *(Abogado ID #)* A5B6

BY THE COURT *(Por El Tribunal)*
JOSEPH H. EVERS
PROTHONOTARY *(Protonotario)*

PRO
(Clerk) *(Escribano)*

10-200 (Rev. 7/99) Completed Subpoena must be signed and sealed by the Prothonotary (Room 266 City Hall) before service.

Conflict Checking

Conflict checking is necessary to verify that current and prior parties or matters handled by the firm will not result in a conflict of interest when accepting a new client or matter. Checking for conflicts of interest is essential to complying with ethical rules against representing competing interests. Some firms still rely on manual systems of

Conflict checking Verifying that the attorneys in the firm do not have a personal conflict and have not previously represented and are not currently representing any party with an adverse interest or conflict with the potential client.

paper lists and index cards containing the names of clients, opposing parties, and opposing attorneys in every case handled by the firm. But now, many offices use computer database software for conflict checking, and the names of clients, opposing parties, counsel, and law firms can be quickly searched electronically. However, determining conflicts is difficult where there has been only indirect representation.

Attorneys and paralegals who change firms may have to undergo a preliminary conflict check before they can accept or start employment. The conflict arises when the former firm and the new firm are, or were, on opposite sides of a case. It may be a conflict for someone who has had access to information about a case to switch to the firm representing the opposing party. Before starting employment, confidential disclosure for the limited purpose of conflict checking could prevent a serious ethical violation. In some cases, the conflict of interest may result from a financial interest such as stock ownership or investments. Making full disclosure of these potential conflict situations to the supervising attorney or to the appropriate conflict checker with the firm is important.

In many cases, the conflict can be resolved by isolating the individual from information about the case—sometimes called building an "ethical wall." An ethical wall, also known as a Chinese wall, is an attempt to shield a paralegal or lawyer from access to information about a case when there is the possibility of a conflict of interest. Most courts permit the establishment of an ethical wall to protect the parties from the conflict of interest or breach of confidentiality. As commented by a Connecticut trial court in an unpublished opinion:

> ...The court does not subscribe to the argument that, as a matter of law, screening would be ineffective when a nonlawyer switches employment to "the other side." The ABA opinions indicate that a law firm can set up appropriate screening and administrative procedures to prevent nonlawyers from working on the other side of those common cases and disclosing confidential information....
>
> *Devine v. Beinfield*, No. CV930121721 S, 1997 Conn Super Lexis 1966 (Ct. Sup. Jul. 1, 1997)

The Nevada Supreme Court specifically addresses the issue of conflicts of interest as it relates to paralegals in the *Leibowitz* case.

IN THE WORDS OF THE COURT...

LEIBOWITZ V. EIGHTH JUDICIAL DISTRICT COURT, 119 NEV. 523, 78 P.3D 515 (2003)

The Nevada Supreme Court overturned a 1994 ethics opinion, *Ciaffone v. District Court,* 113 Nev. 1165 945 P.2d 950 (1997), that prohibited paralegals from working for a firm that represents any client that had an adversarial relationship to any client of the former employer law firm. The court summarized the rationale for the ethical wall and provided an instructive guide.

> As pointed out by the amici's brief, the majority of professional legal ethics commentators, ethics tribunals, and courts have concluded that nonlawyer screening is a permissible method to protect confidences held by nonlawyer employees who change employment. Nevada is in a minority of jurisdictions that do not allow screening for nonlawyers moving from private firm to private firm.
>
> Imputed disqualification is considered a harsh remedy that "should be invoked if, and only if, the [c]ourt is satisfied that real harm is likely to result from failing to invoke it."
>
> This stringent standard is based on a client's right to counsel of the client's choosing and the likelihood of prejudice and economic harm to the client when severance of the attorney-client relationship is ordered. It is for this reason that the ABA opined in 1988 that screening is permitted for nonlawyer employees,

(continued)

while conversely concluding, through the Model Rules of Professional Conduct, that screening is not permitted for lawyers. The ABA explained that "additional considerations" exist justifying application of screening to nonlawyer employees (*i.e.,* mobility in employment opportunities which function to serve both legal clients and the legal profession) versus the Model Rule's proscription against screening where lawyers move from private firm to private firm. In essence, a lawyer may always practice his or her profession regardless of an affiliation to a law firm. Paralegals, legal secretaries, and other employees of attorneys do not have that option.

We are persuaded that *Ciaffone* misapprehended the state of the law regarding nonlawyer imputed disqualification. We therefore overrule *Ciaffone* to the extent it prohibits screening of nonlawyer employees.

When a law firm hires a nonlawyer employee, the firm has an affirmative duty to determine whether the employee previously had access to adversarial client files. If the hiring law firm determines that the employee had such access, the hiring law firm has an absolute duty to screen the nonlawyer employee from the adversarial cases irrespective of the nonlawyer employee's actual knowledge of privileged or confidential information.

Although we decline to mandate an exhaustive list of screening requirements, the following provides an instructive minimum:

(1) *"The newly hired nonlawyer [employee] must be cautioned not to disclose any information relating to the representation of a client of the former employer."*
(2) *"The nonlawyer [employee] must be instructed not to work on any matter on which [he or] she worked during the prior employment, or regarding which [he or] she has information relating to the former employer's representation."*
(3) *"The new firm should take... reasonable steps to ensure that the nonlawyer [employee] does not work in connection with matters on which [he or] she worked during the prior employment, absent client consent [i.e., unconditional waiver] after consultation."*

In addition, the hiring law firm must inform the adversarial party, or their counsel, regarding the hiring of the nonlawyer employee and the screening mechanisms utilized. The adversarial party may then: (1) make a conditional waiver (*i.e.,* agree to the screening mechanisms); (2) make an unconditional waiver (eliminate the screening mechanisms); or (3) file a motion to disqualify counsel.

However, even if the new employer uses a screening process, disqualification will always be required—absent unconditional waiver by the affected client—under the following circumstances:

(1) *"[W]hen information relating to the representation of an adverse client has in fact been disclosed [to the new employer]"; or, in the absence of disclosure to the new employer,*
(2) *"[W]hen screening would be ineffective or the nonlawyer [employee] necessarily would be required to work on the other side of a matter that is the same as or substantially related to a matter on which the nonlawyer [employee] has previously worked."*

Once a district court determines that a nonlawyer employee acquired confidential information about a former client, the district court should grant a motion for disqualification unless the district court determines that the screening is sufficient to safeguard the former client from disclosure of the confidential information. The district court is faced with the delicate task of balancing competing interests, including: (1) "the individual right to be represented by counsel of one's choice," (2) "each party's right to be free from the risk of even inadvertent disclosure of confidential information," (3) "the public's interest in the scrupulous administration of justice," and (4) "the prejudices that will inure to the parties as a result of the [district court's] decision."

Time Keeping and Billing

Keeping track of billable time is critical in ensuring that the law firm will be compensated properly for its advice and efforts on behalf of clients. Time records are the basis for most law firm billings, and without accurate time records, billings cannot be made. Responsibility for tracking time extends beyond just the attorneys and includes paralegals, and in some cases, secretaries and clerks.

Billing is one of the most important functions in a law firm. Without billing, there is no revenue to pay expenses and salaries. Although it is so essential, in many offices, billing is not treated with enough care.

The propriety of fees is addressed in Rule 1.5 of the Model Rules of Professional Conduct and is addressed by the ethical rules in most jurisdictions. The Utah Rules of Professional Conduct provide as follows.

Rule 1.5 Fees

(a) A lawyer shall not make an agreement for, charge or collect an unreasonable fee or an unreasonable amount for expenses. The factors to be considered in determining the reasonableness of a fee include the following:

(a)(1) the time and labor required, the novelty and difficulty of the questions involved and the skill requisite to perform the legal service properly;

(a)(2) the likelihood, if apparent to the client, that the acceptance of the particular employment will preclude other employment by the lawyer;

(a)(3) the fee customarily charged in the locality for similar legal services;

(a)(4) the amount involved and the results obtained;

(a)(5) the time limitations imposed by the client or by the circumstances;

(a)(6) the nature and length of the professional relationship with the client;

(a)(7) the experience, reputation and ability of the lawyer or lawyers performing the services; and

(a)(8) whether the fee is fixed or contingent.

(b) The scope of the representation and the basis or rate of the fee and expenses for which the client will be responsible shall be communicated to the client, preferably in writing, before or within a reasonable time after commencing the representation, except when the lawyer will charge a regularly represented client on the same basis or rate. Any changes in the basis or rate of the fee or expenses shall also be communicated to the client.

(c) A fee may be contingent on the outcome of the matter for which the service is rendered, except in a matter in which a contingent fee is prohibited by paragraph (d) or other law. A contingent fee agreement shall be in a writing signed by the client and shall state the method by which the fee is to be determined, including the percentage or percentages that shall accrue to the lawyer in the event of settlement, trial or appeal; litigation and other expenses to be deducted from the recovery; and whether such expenses are to be deducted before or after the contingent fee is calculated. The agreement must clearly notify the client of any expenses for which the client will be liable whether or not the client is the prevailing party. Upon conclusion of a contingent fee matter, the lawyer shall provide the client with a written statement stating the outcome of the matter and, if there is a recovery, showing the remittance to the client and the method of its determination.

(d) A lawyer shall not enter into an arrangement for, charge or collect:

(d)(1) any fee in a domestic relations matter, the payment or amount of which is contingent upon the securing of a divorce or upon the amount of alimony or support, or property settlement in lieu thereof; or

(d)(2) a contingent fee for representing a defendant in a criminal case.

(e A division of a fee between lawyers who are not in the same firm may be made only if:

(e)(1) the division is in proportion to the services performed by each lawyer or each lawyer assumes joint responsibility for the representation;

(e)(2) the client agrees to the arrangement, including the share each lawyer will receive, and the agreement is confirmed in writing; and

(e)(3) the total fee is reasonable.

View the comments to the Utah rules at **http://www.utcourts.gov/resources/rules/ucja/ch13/1_5.htm**.

The billing of clients is not limited to the time of lawyers but may include that of paralegals. As the 11th Circuit Court of Appeals has stated:

> We have held that paralegal time is recoverable as part of a prevailing party's award for attorney's fees and expenses, [but] only to the extent that the paralegal performs work traditionally done by an attorney. Quoting from *Allen v. United States Steel Corp.*, 665 F.2d 689, 697 (5th Cir. 1982): "To hold otherwise would be counterproductive because excluding reimbursement for such work might encourage attorneys to handle entire cases themselves, thereby achieving the same results at a higher overall cost."
>
> *Jean v. Nelson*, 863 F. 2d 759 (11th Cir. 1988)

Client expense records, by contrast, are usually well maintained because a check is usually written, which provides a documented record for billing purposes. But for billable time, a record must be kept by the attorney, paralegal, or other legal team member. This information frequently is recorded manually on pieces of paper called time slips or time records. Client bills are prepared manually from these records.

More offices are now using time and billing software, such as AbacusLaw. Most of these programs allow for random entry of individual time record information, which is then automatically sorted by client and project or case. These programs also allow for the entry of fees and costs expended and application of retainers, which may be included in the final billing report.

Accounting in the Law Office

In the law office working environment, your ability to understand basic financial issues makes you a more valuable member of the law office team. Unlike retail, wholesale, or manufacturing businesses that trade in goods or commodities, a law firm is a business that, as Abraham Lincoln once said, deals in "time and advice."

A major function of the legal support staff is to keep track of the time the lawyers and support staff spend on a case and then bill the client for the time expended. Financial records must be kept accurately for matters related to specific clients or for internal office activities that are part of the overall cost of running the office. If accurate records are not kept, the law office may fail or close.

When funds belong to clients, errors in internal documentation, court documents, and tax returns may result in malpractice claims. At worst, errors may result in a loss or misappropriation of client funds, which can lead to sanctions, disbarment, or criminal prosecution.

In addition to understanding the internal accounting needs of a law firm, it is useful to understand the accounting and financial affairs of clients. Understanding accounting and financial reports and documents is essential in many areas of law today.

Family Law

Domestic relations cases may have concerns related to property settlement, support, and alimony. In prenuptial agreements today, there is an increasing demand for full financial disclosure. A basic understanding of the nature and the sources of a family's financial information will enable the paralegal to prepare the necessary documents. As an example, Exhibit 3.6 shows selected pages from the New Jersey Family Part Case Information form.

Commercial Litigation

Commercial litigation typically involves actions resulting from claims of breach of contract or disputes over interpretations of provisions of a contract. This field is often very complex because of the financial implications of contract breaches and remedies. The tasks of finding, analyzing, and presenting financial information increasingly fall on litigation paralegals.

Litigation

Even in the simplest of litigation matters, a measure of damages has to be computed. Calculations of wages lost, projection of future losses, and the current or present value of a case may have to be computed or reviewed for accuracy.

Exhibit 3.6 New Jersey family case information

PART D - MONTHLY EXPENSES (computed at 4.3 wks/mo.)

Joint Marital Life Style should reflect standard of living established during marriage. Current expenses should reflect the current life style. Do not repeat those income deductions listed in Part C–3.

	Joint Marital Life Style Family, including ______ children	Current Life Style Yours and ______ children
SCHEDULE A: SHELTER		
If Tenant:		
Rent	$______	$______
Heat (if not furnished)	$______	$______
Electric & Gas (if not furnished)	$______	$______
Renter's Insurance	$______	$______
Parking (at Apartment)	$______	$______
Other Charges (Itemize)	$______	$______
If Homeowner:		
Mortgage	$______	$______
Real Estate Taxes (if not included w/mortgage payment)	$______	$______
Homeowners Ins. (if not included w/mortgage payment)	$______	$______
Other Mortgages or Home Equity Loans	$______	$______
Heat (unless Electric or Gas)	$______	$______
Electric & Gas	$______	$______
Water & Sewer	$______	$______
Garbage Removal	$______	$______
Snow Removal	$______	$______
Lawn Care	$______	$______
Maintenance	$______	$______
Repairs	$______	$______
Other Charges (Itemize)	$______	$______
Tenant or Homeowner:		
Telephone	$______	$______
Mobile/Cellular Telephone	$______	$______
Service Contracts on Equipment	$______	$______
Cable TV	$______	$______
Plumber/Electrician	$______	$______
Equipment & Furnishings	$______	$______
Internet Charges	$______	$______
Other (Itemize)	$______	$______
TOTAL	$______	$______
SCHEDULE B: TRANSPORTATION		
Auto Payment	$______	$______
Auto Insurance (number of vehicles)	$______	$______
Registration, License	$______	$______
Maintenance	$______	$______
Fuel and Oil	$______	$______
Commuting Expenses	$______	$______
Other Charges (Itemize)	$______	$______
TOTAL	$______	$______

(continued)

Exhibit 3.6 New Jersey family case information *(continued)*

PART E - BALANCE SHEET OF ALL FAMILY ASSETS AND LIABILITIES STATEMENT OF ASSETS

Description	Title to Property (H, W, J)	Date of purchase/acquisition. If claim that asset is exempt, state reason and value of what is claimed to be exempt	Value $ Put * after exempt	Date of Evaluation Mo./Day/Yr.
1. Real Property				
______	______	______	______	______
______	______	______	______	______
2. Bank Accounts, CDs				
______	______	______	______	______
______	______	______	______	______
______	______	______	______	______
3. Vehicles				
______	______	______	______	______
______	______	______	______	______
______	______	______	______	______
4. Tangible Personal Property				
______	______	______	______	______
______	______	______	______	______
______	______	______	______	______
5. Stocks and Bonds				
______	______	______	______	______
______	______	______	______	______
______	______	______	______	______
6. Pension, Profit Sharing, Retirement Plan(s) 401(k)s, etc. [list each employer]				
______	______	______	______	______
7. IRAs				
______	______	______	______	______
______	______	______	______	______
8. Businesses, Partnerships, Professional Practices				
______	______	______	______	______
______	______	______	______	______
9. Life Insurance (cash surrender value)				
______	______	______	______	______
______	______	______	______	______
10. Loans Receivable				
______	______	______	______	______
______	______	______	______	______
11. Other (specify)				
______	______	______	______	______
______	______	______	______	______

TOTAL GROSS ASSETS: $______
TOTAL SUBJECT TO EQUITABLE DISTRIBUTION: $______
TOTAL NOT SUBJECT TO EQUITABLE DISTRIBUTION: $______

Maintaining Law Firm Financial Information

Law firms, like any other business, have numerous financial obligations. Utility bills and employees must be paid on a regular basis, and accurate records must be maintained to determine which costs are chargeable to individual clients. Firms must also keep records of client funds in separate escrow accounts.

Records of the various receipts and disbursements are used to prepare the firm's tax documents. These may include filings of quarterly and annual employee withholding, income tax returns, and reports for independent contractors such as freelance paralegals, court reporters, and investigators.

Regular use of a consistent system will simplify the completion of financial reports. By using a standard system of accounting, lawyers, bookkeepers, paralegals, and secretarial personnel can easily communicate information about charges and revenues that can be used by anyone who needs the information, including outside accountants and auditors.

Reconstructing or organizing a client's financial information is a common task in many law offices. In many cases, clients deliver piles of financial documents and expect the law office personnel to sort, classify, and organize these seemingly unrelated pieces of paper for use in income tax returns, estate tax returns, settlements, and other instances where financial information is needed. Knowing how to attack the piles of paper can save time, stress, and frustration.

Safekeeping of client property and segregation of client funds from those of the law firm are important ethical obligations imposed under Rule 1.15 of the Model Rules of Professional Conduct and the ethical rules of most jurisdictions. For example, the rule in South Dakota provides in part:

Rule 1.15 Safekeeping Property

(a) A lawyer shall hold property of clients or third persons that is in a lawyer's possession in connection with a representation separate from the lawyer's own property. Funds shall be kept in a separate account maintained in the state where the lawyer's office is situated, or elsewhere with the consent of the client or third person. Other property shall be identified as such and appropriately safeguarded. Complete records of such account funds and other property shall be kept by the lawyer and shall be preserved for a period of five years after termination of the representation. A lawyer may deposit the lawyer's own funds in a client trust account for the sole purpose of paying bank service charges on that account, but only in an amount necessary for that purpose. A lawyer shall deposit into a client trust account legal fees and expenses that have been paid in advance, to be withdrawn by the lawyer only as fees are earned or expenses incurred.

(b) Upon receiving funds or other property in which a client or third person has an interest, a lawyer shall promptly notify the client or third person. Except as stated in this Rule or otherwise permitted by law or by agreement with the client, a lawyer shall promptly deliver to the client or third person any funds or other property that the client or third person is entitled to receive and, upon request by the client or third person, shall promptly render a full accounting regarding such property.

(c) When in the course of representation a lawyer is in possession of property in which two or more persons (one of whom may be the lawyer) claim interests, the property shall be kept separate by the lawyer until the dispute is resolved. The lawyer shall promptly distribute all portions of the property as to which the interests are not in dispute.

(d) Preserving Identity of Funds and Property of Client.

(1) All funds of clients paid to a lawyer or law firm, including advances for costs and expenses, shall be deposited in one or more identifiable bank accounts maintained in the state in which the law office is situated and no funds belonging to the lawyer or law firm shall be deposited therein except as follows:

(i) Funds reasonably sufficient to pay bank charges may be deposited therein.

(ii) Funds belonging in part to a client and in part presently or potentially to the lawyer or law firm must be deposited therein, but the portion belonging to the lawyer or law firm may be withdrawn when due unless the right of the lawyer or law firm to receive it is disputed by the client, in which event the disputed portion shall not be withdrawn until the dispute is finally resolved.

(2) A lawyer shall:
  (i) Promptly notify a client of the receipt of his funds, securities, or other properties.
  (ii) Identify and label securities and properties of a client promptly upon receipt and place them in a safe deposit box or other place of safekeeping as soon as practicable.
  (iii) Maintain complete records of all funds, securities, and other properties of a client coming into the possession of the lawyer and render appropriate accountings to his client regarding them.
  (iv) Promptly pay or deliver to the client as requested by a client the funds, securities, or other properties in the possession of the lawyer which the client is entitled to receive....

Web Exploration

The complete rule may be viewed at **http://www.sdbar.org/Rules/Rules/PC_Rules.htm**.

Accounting for Client Retainers and Costs

Law firms frequently request a **retainer**—a payment from a client at the beginning of a new matter. This amount may be used to offset the fees for services rendered or costs advanced on behalf of the client. Unless there is some other legally permissible arrangement, these funds do not belong to the law firm until they have been earned by rendering a service, or actual costs have been expended. Unused amounts may have to be returned to the client and those expended accounted for to the client. A sample retainer agreement under Maine Bar Rule 3.4(I) is shown in Exhibit 3.7.

Retainer A payment at the beginning of the handling of a new matter for a client. This amount may be used to offset the fees for services rendered or costs advanced on behalf of the client.

Under the rules of professional conduct in many states, a written fee agreement is required in contingency fee cases, whereas in other types of cases, it is preferred but not required.

A new approach to providing legal services is sometimes called "unbundled" legal services, or "discrete task representation." This refers to a broad range of discrete tasks that an attorney might undertake, such as advice, negotiation, document review, document preparation, and limited representation.

A lawyer may also request a nonrefundable retainer. This is a common practice when the client does not want the law firm to be able to represent the opposing party in a pending legal action, and is seen most commonly in family law or divorce actions. Legal ethics prohibit taking on a client when there is a conflict of interest. In cases of nonrefundable retainers, a statement of application of the funds should be made as a matter of financial accounting practice.

Costs Advanced

Law firms typically pay directly to the court any fees for filing documents for the client. In some cases, the costs of stenographers, expert witnesses, duplication of records, travel, phone, and copying will also be advanced. The firm must keep proper accounting for these items to be able to bill a client properly or charge the amounts expended against prepaid costs or retainers. Good practice is to include in the initial client fee letter the nature and amount of costs that will be charged for these various items.

Civil Practice: Fee and Cost Billing

In a civil litigation practice, fees may be calculated on an hourly rate, as a contingent fee, or as a combination of the two. The time records for each member of the firm must be obtained, either from the hard copies of time records or the computer printout of hours spent working on the case. The actual time may be reported to the client chronologically, with all activity by each person who worked on the file integrated with all the others, or it may be listed separately for each individual.

One of the difficulties in billing is calculating the correct amount for each person at his or her respective hourly rate. Senior partners, junior partners, associates, and paralegals may bill at different rates. It is thus good practice to calculate the total for each billable person separately, and then collectively. The totals of the individuals, of course, must equal the grand total. A comparison should be made to check mathematical accuracy.

Exhibit 3.7 Limited representation agreement

Date:__________, 20__________

1. The client, __________, retains the attorney, __________, to perform limited legal services in the following matter: __________ v. __________.

2. The client seeks the following services from the attorney (indicate by writing "yes" or "no"):

a. ______ Legal advice: office visits, telephone calls, fax, mail, e-mail;
b. ______ Advice about availability of alternative means to resolving the dispute, including mediation and arbitration;
c. ______ Evaluation of client self-diagnosis of the case and advising client about legal rights and responsibilities;
d. ______ Guidance and procedural information for filing or serving documents;
e. ______ Review pleadings and other documents prepared by client;
f. ______ Suggest documents to be prepared;
g. ______ Draft pleadings, motions, and other documents;
h. ______ Factual investigation: contacting witnesses, public record searches, in-depth interview of client;
i. ______ Assistance with computer support programs;
j. ______ Legal research and analysis;
k. ______ Evaluate settlement options;
l. ______ Discovery: interrogatories, depositions, requests for document production;
m. ______ Planning for negotiations;
n. ______ Planning for court appearances;
o. ______ Standby telephone assistance during negotiations or settlement conferences;
p. ______ Referring client to expert witnesses, special masters, or other counsel;
q. ______ Counseling client about an appeal;
r. ______ Procedural assistance with an appeal and assisting with substantive legal argument in an appeal;
s. ______ Provide preventive planning and/or schedule legal checkups;
t. ______ Other:

____

____

3. The client shall pay the attorney for those limited services as follows:

a. Hourly Fee:

The current hourly fee charged by the attorney or the attorney's law firm for services under this agreement are as follows:

i. Attorney: $__________
ii. Associate: $__________
iii. Paralegal: $__________
iv. Law Clerk: $__________

Unless a different fee arrangement is established in clause b. of this paragraph, the hourly fee shall be payable at the time of the service. Time will be charged in increments of one-tenth of an hour, rounded off for each particular activity to the nearest one-tenth of an hour.

b. Payment from Deposit:

For a continuing consulting role, client will pay to attorney a deposit of $__________, to be received by attorney on or before __________, and to be applied against attorney fees and costs incurred by client. This amount will be deposited by attorney in attorney trust account. Client authorizes attorney to withdraw funds from the trust account to pay attorney fees and costs as they are incurred by client. The deposit is refundable. If, at the termination of services under this agreement, the total amount incurred by client for attorney fees and costs is less than the amount of the deposit, the difference will be refunded to client. Any balance due shall be paid within thirty days of the termination of services.

(continued)

Exhibit 3.7 Limited representation agreement *(continued)*

c. Costs:

Client shall pay attorney out-of-pocket costs incurred in connection with this agreement, including long distance telephone and fax costs, photocopy expense and postage. All costs payable to third parties in connection with client case, including filing fees, investigation fees, deposition fees, and the like shall be paid directly by client. Attorney shall not advance costs to third parties on client behalf.

4. The client understands that the attorney will exercise his or her best judgment while performing the limited legal services set out above, but also recognizes:

a. the attorney is not promising any particular outcome,
b. the attorney has not made any independent investigation of the facts and is relying entirely on the client limited disclosure of the facts given the duration of the limited services provided, and
c. the attorney has no further obligation to the client after completing the above described limited legal services unless and until both attorney and client enter into another written representation agreement.

5. If any dispute between client and attorney arises under this agreement concerning the payment of fees, the client and attorney shall submit the dispute for fee arbitration in accordance with Rule 9(e)-(k) of the Maine Bar Rules. This arbitration shall be binding upon both parties to this agreement.

WE HAVE EACH READ THE ABOVE AGREEMENT BEFORE SIGNING IT.
Signature of client ______________________________
Signature of attorney ____________________________

At one time, firms prepared client bills manually from paper copies of time records or other office documents. Now, many firms prepare the client billing using a computer program. Most of these programs allow input of the individual time records in a random order, which can then be sorted automatically by client and project. In addition to time billing, these programs allow the entry of costs expended for inclusion in the final billing.

Timely Disbursements

As part of the settlement of a case for a client, the opposing side may pay the amount of the cash settlement to the lawyer. These funds must be retained in a separate escrow account until they are disbursed to the client, and may not be commingled with the lawyer's own funds. Records of the receipt and disbursement of these funds must be maintained properly to avoid charges of misuse of client funds.

A lawyer is not required to make disbursements until the draft or check has cleared. A check or draft is deemed cleared when the funds are available for disbursement. However, lawyers may not retain the amount for an unreasonable time. The client is entitled to earn the potential interest on the amount to be disbursed. The lawyer is not entitled to keep the amount and earn interest for his or her own account.

Trust Accounts

Trust account A separate account where the funds of the client must be held.

A **trust account** or fiduciary account contains the client's funds and should never be commingled with those of the firm or the individual attorney. A clear record of all trust transactions must be maintained. In many cases, such as trusts, estates, or cases involving children, detailed reports must be filed with the court following the court-imposed rules (as shown in Exhibit 3.8). When a checking account has been established, the check register is a primary source for creating any necessary reports. With some larger accounts, checking accounts may not have been set up. Many trust and estate accounts are invested in money market funds, stocks, bonds, and mutual funds.

Keeping a clear record is made more difficult by the potential for periodic increases and decreases in value that are not actually realized—referred to as "paper gains and

Exhibit 3.8 Selected provisions of the rules of practice and procedure in the probate courts of the state of New Hampshire

RULE 108. FIDUCIARY ACCOUNTING STANDARDS

The following standards shall be applicable to all interim and final accountings of Administrators, trustees, guardians and conservators, required or permitted to be filed with the Court.

A. Accounts shall be stated in a manner that is understandable by Persons who are not familiar with practices and terminology peculiar to the administration of estates, trusts, guardianships and conservatorships. . . .

B. A Fiduciary account shall begin with a concise summary of its purpose and content. The account shall begin with a brief statement identifying the Fiduciary, the subject matter, the relationship of Parties interested in the account to the account, and, if applicable, appropriate notice of any limitations on or requirements for action by Parties interested in the account. . . .

C. A Fiduciary account shall contain sufficient information to put parties interested in the account on notice as to all significant transactions affecting administration during the accounting period. . . .

losses." They exist on paper but have not been realized by the actual sale or transfer of the assets. Any investments by the attorney of assets held in trust must be authorized by the client or by state law. Separate records should be maintained showing the activity in each of the trust accounts, including all deposits, interest, disbursements, and bank charges.

IOLTA Accounts

IOLTA account Where the amount is too small to earn interest, court rules require the funds be deposited into a special interest-bearing account, and the interest is generally paid to support legal aid projects (Interest on Lawyers Trust Account).

When the amount of a client's funds is too small to earn interest, many states, by court rule, impose an obligation to deposit these funds into a special interest-bearing account called an **IOLTA account** (Interest on Lawyers Trust Account). Interest generated from these small accounts is paid to a court-designated agency, usually a local legal aid agency, to fund their activities. Because the cost of setting up small individual accounts is greater than the interest earned, or the amount deposited is so small that no interest would accrue to the client, everyone wins by having these funds generate some income for the public good. Reconciliation of this account is simpler because no accounting has to be made for interest accruing to the client.

Interest-Bearing Escrow Accounts

Lawyers frequently are asked to act as escrow agents or to retain client funds for future disbursements. In some cases, the amounts may be significant. As a fiduciary, the lawyer must treat these funds in the same manner as would any prudent investor. If the amount is sufficient to earn interest, the amount earned belongs to the client, not to the attorney, and must be accounted for to the client.

If client funds are earning interest, attorneys are expected to open up separate accounts for each client. In opening these accounts, the client's Social Security number or other employer identification number should be used. If the law firm maintains the account under its tax identification number, it will have to report interest annually to the client and to federal and state governments.

A significant body of law has emerged to avoid money laundering. In a law firm this may require reporting when significant amounts of cash are received. The problem is balancing the money-laundering rules and the attorney–client privilege. When amounts in excess of $10,000 are received in cash from a client, current legislation and regulation must be consulted.

To open an account with a financial institution requires a federal tax identification number. This identification number may be that of the client, the trust, the estate, or another legal entity. In some cases, the financial institution may require copies of any documentation that created the client entity, such as the trust documents, death certificate, or decedent's will. The financial institution needs this documentation to comply with existing regulations on federal withholding, money laundering, or large-deposit-reporting obligations.

Court Accounting

In addition to the preparation of filing federal and state estate tax returns, the fiduciary often has to file an accounting with the local court that administers or supervises trust and estate matters. These **court accounting** reports are designed to show that the fiduciary has administered the estate or trust properly.

Court accounting An accounting with the local court that administers or supervises trust and estate matters. These reports are designed to show that the fiduciary has properly administered the estate or trust.

In many jurisdictions, reports are also required in civil cases involving minors. Tort settlements that are negotiated between the insurance company or defendant and the minor's parent or guardian are subject to the approval of the court. This usually requires submitting a brief accounting of the expenses, including counsel fees, the proposed disbursements to compensate for out-of-pocket expenses, and the proposed investments of the proceeds until the minor reaches a certain age. In cases involving minors, all of the parties are considered as fiduciaries who must act in the best interest of the minor.

Local practice and court rules will dictate the form and methods of fiduciary accounting, called the "uniform system of accounts." The basic objective of the uniform system of accounts is to present the financial information in a consistent manner that is understandable to the court and all interested parties. The parties are entitled to full disclosure, clarity, and, when appropriate, supplemental information. Exhibit 3.9 is a sample of a model executor's account template using the uniform system of accounts. The uniform system of accounts has been accepted by some jurisdictions without formal court rule, but in others has been included in the local court rules.

Preparing Your Résumé

Learning Objective 4

Prepare a traditional résumé and an electronic résumé.

Getting a job requires presenting your credentials in a persuasive manner. A well-prepared résumé is usually the first impression you will make on a prospective employer.

A **résumé** is a short description of a person's education, a summary of work experience, and other supporting information that potential employers use in evaluating a person's qualifications for a position in a firm or other organization. Exhibits 3.10 and 3.11 provide examples. You should prepare a résumé as you see yourself today, and then look at your résumé from the perspective of a future employer. What areas do you need to strengthen to demonstrate your ability to perform the type of job you would like to have?

Résumé A short description of a person's education, a summary of work experience, and other related and supporting information that potential employers use in evaluating a person's qualifications for a position in a firm or an organization.

You should look at your résumé as a continuing work-in-progress. Constantly update your résumé to include any new job responsibilities, part-time employment skills and qualifications, and special achievements. Add meaningful items to your résumé such as courses, skills, and outside interests that will set you apart from other applicants and land you that first paralegal job after you complete your training.

After you have gathered all of the necessary information, put it into a proper résumé form, then review it. Does the résumé reflect the information you want to communicate to a prospective employer? Try to look at it with an open, objective mind. Employers are looking for individuals who demonstrate a good work ethic, a willingness to accept responsibility and take direction, and the skills necessary for the job for which they are applying.

Set your roadmap for the job you wish to obtain. What additional education, training, or skills are required? This should determine your future course of study. Work-study programs and cooperative education are good ways to demonstrate on-the-job training. Depending upon your goals, resources, and time frame, a specialized certificate such as a paralegal certificate, a degree in paralegal studies, or a bachelor's degree in paralegal studies will certainly demonstrate your level of interest and ability to achieve the minimum level of education for the job.

Résumé Formats

Many formats may be used in preparing a résumé. These are sometimes referred to as functional, chronological, reverse chronological, combination, technical, and electronic formats. There are no hard-and-fast rules for choosing a résumé format, except perhaps putting your name and contact information at the top. Always remember that the main purpose of the résumé is to get a job interview and, you hope, employment.

Exhibit 3.9 Model executor's account template sample—Pennsylvania Orphans' Court

ORPHANS' COURT RULES

MODEL EXECUTOR'S ACCOUNT

First and Final Account

FIRST AND FINAL ACCOUNT OF

William C. Doe, Executor

For

ESTATE OF John Doe, Deceased

Date of Death:	November 14, 1978
Date of Executor's Appointment:	November 24, 1978
Accounting for the Period:	November 24, 1978 to November 30, 1979

Purpose of Account: William C. Doe, Executor, offers this account to acquaint interested parties with the transactions that have occurred during his administration.

The account also indicates the proposed distribution of the estate.[1]
It is important that the account be carefully examined. Requests for additional information or questions or objections can be discussed with:

[Name of Executor, Counsel or other appropriate person]
[address and telephone number]

[*Note:* See discussion under Fiduciary Accounting Principle II with respect to presentation of collateral material needed by beneficiaries.]

Note

In Pennsylvania the date of first advertisement of the grant of letters should be shown after the date of the personal representative's appointment.

[1] Optional—for use if applicable.

SUMMARY OF ACCOUNT

	Page	*Current Value*	*Fiduciary Acquisition Value*
Proposed Distribution to Beneficiaries[1]	645	$102,974.56	$ 90,813.96
Principal			
Receipts	636		$160,488.76
			2,662.00
Net Gain (or Loss) on Sales or Other Disposition	638		$163,150.76
Less Disbursements:			
Debts of Decedent	639	$ 485.82	
Funeral Expenses	639	1,375.00	
Administration Expenses	639	194.25	
Federal and State Taxes	639	5,962.09	
Fees and Commissions	639	11,689.64	19,706.80
Balance before Distributions			$143,443.96

(continued)

Exhibit 3.9 Model executor's account template sample—Pennsylvania Orphans' Court *(continued)*

FIDUCIARY ACCOUNTING STANDARDS

Distributions to Beneficiaries	641	52,630.00
Principal Balance on Hand	641	$ 90,813.96
For Information:		
Investments Made	642	
Changes in Investment Holdings	642	
Income		
Receipts	643	$ 2,513.40
Less Disbursements	643	178.67
Balance Before Distributions		$ 2,334.73
Distributions to Beneficiaries	644	2,334.73
Income Balance on Hand		-0-
Combined Balance on Hand		$ 90,813.96

[1]Optional—for use if applicable.

Receipts of Principal

Assets Listed in Inventory (Valued as of Date of Death)			*Fiduciary Acquisition Value*
Cash:			
First National Bank—checking account		$ 516.93	
Prudent Saving Fund Society—savings account		2,518.16	
Cash in possession of decedent		42.54	$ 3,077.63
Tangible Personal Property:			
Jewelry—			
1 pearl necklace			515.00
Furniture—			
1 antique highboy		$ 2,000.00	
1 antique side table		60.00	
1 antique chair		55.00	2,115.00
Stocks:			
200 shs.	Home Telephone & Telegraph Co., common	$ 25,000.00	
50 shs.	Best Oil Co., common	5,000.00	
1,000 shs.	Central Trust Co., capital	50,850.00	
151 shs.	Electric Data Corp., common	1,887.50	
50 shs.	Fabulous Mutual Fund	1,833.33	
200 shs.	XYZ Corporation, common	6,000.00	90,570.83
Realty:			
Residence—	86 Norwood Road West Hartford, CT		$ 50,000.00
	Total Inventory		$146,278.46
Receipts Subsequent to Inventory (Valued When Received)			
2/22/79	Proceeds of Sale—Best Oil Co., rights to subscribe received 2/15/79	$ 50.00[1]	
3/12/79	Fabulous Mutual Fund, capital gains dividend received in cash	32.50	
5/11/79	Refund of overpayment of 1978 U.S. individual income tax	127.80	
9/25/79	From Richard Roe, Ancillary Administrator, net proceeds on sale of oil and gas leases in Jefferson Parish, Louisiana	10,000.00	$ 10,210.30

[1]Proceeds of sale of rights may be treated as an additional receipt, as illustrated here, or may be applied in reduction of carrying value as illustrated on page 646 of the Model Trustee's Account. Either method, consistently applied, is acceptable.

Exhibit 3.10 Sample functional résumé

SARA MARKS

2222 Market Way
Brooklyn, NY 11223
(212) 555-8634 (Home)
(212) 555-9234 (Office)

EDUCATION
Reading College, Brooklyn, NY, 2008
Associate of Science degree, GPA 4.0
Paralegal Major—ABA-approved program
Dean's List, Vice President of the Honor Society

EMPLOYMENT HISTORY
Paralegal field work, Brooklyn, NY, 2006 to 2008
Advisor, Small Claims Court and the Brooklyn Department of Consumer Affairs
- Assisted claimants with small claims forms
- Counseled individuals on consumer affairs issues

Registration and admissions clerk, Brooklyn, NY, 2004 to 2006
Reading College
- Registered incoming and returning students
- In charge of organizing the filing system, creating more efficiency in the office

Cosmetologist and Barber, Brooklyn, NY, 2000 to 2004
- Self-employed
- Handled all phases of business, including purchasing, bookkeeping, and payroll

SPECIAL SKILLS
- WordPerfect, Microsoft Office Suite
- Excellent ability to communicate with general public

PROFESSIONAL AFFILIATIONS
Manhattan Paralegal Association

Excellent references available upon request

Chronological résumé format Presents education and job history in chronological order with the most recent experience listed first.

Functional résumé format Lists a summary of the individual's qualifications with current experience and education without any emphasis on dates of employment.

The **chronological résumé format** presents education and job history in a time sequence with the most recent experience listed first. An alternative format is the reverse chronological résumé format, with the latest job listed last. Some suggest that the chronological résumé is the form used most commonly in the legal field. The **functional résumé format** usually gives a summary of the individual's qualifications and current experience and education without emphasizing dates of employment. The combination résumé format combines the chronological and functional résumé formats.

If responding to an ad in the paper, tailor your résumé to the job description or to the job listing of the individual employer. You may have to develop résumés in more than one format if the job openings require different skill sets. For example, the résumé sent to an employer looking for someone with specific computer skills should show these skills first. A job description looking for depth of experience probably should use the chronological approach.

Common elements of most résumés include:

- Heading, with your name and contact information.
- Career objective, concise and to the point, geared to the job description of the position you seek.
- Education, generally at the beginning of the résumé if you are a recent graduate, including specific academic honors and awards if applicable to the job.

Exhibit 3.11 Sample chronological résumé

MICHAEL C. SMITH

2345 Oregon Street, #A
Portland, OR 98765
(363) 282-7890

EDUCATION
Paralegal Certificate, General Litigation, 2008
University of Portland (ABA approved)
Curriculum included:

Family Law	Paralegal Practices and Procedures
Criminal Law	Legal Research and Writing
Civil Litigation	Estates, Trusts, and Wills

Bachelor of Science Degree
Transportation and Distribution Management
Golden Gate University, San Francisco, CA

EXPERIENCE
Paralegal Practice
- Drafted memos to clients
- Prepared notice of summons
- Conducted research for misdemeanor appeal cases
- Prepared points and authorities for motions
- Observed bankruptcy and family law court proceedings
- Completed necessary documents for probate
- Wrote legal memoranda

Administration and Management
- Participated in new division startup
- Dispatched and routed for the transportation of 80 to 120 special education students daily
- Supervised between 20 and 25 drivers
- Designed and implemented daily operation logs
- Liaison between drivers and school officials or parents
- Evaluated various conditions when assigning routes and equipment

EMPLOYMENT HISTORY

Susan Hildebrand, Attorney, Portland, OR Paralegal Intern	2008
Laidlaw Transit, Inc., San Francisco, CA Dispatch Manager	2002 to 2008
Hayward Unified School District Teaching Assistant	2001 to 2002
San Mateo Union High School District Office Clerk	2000 to 2001

- Experience, including paid and unpaid activities showing the employer the skills you have to offer.
- Activities, listed briefly, unless directly related to the job description, including professional organizations and educational and volunteer activities.

Cover Letters

Always include a **cover letter** with your résumé. This applies to email applications as well. The cover letter creates the first impression and demonstrates your ability to communicate in writing. Take the time to be sure it properly reflects who you are and what skills you have. The cover letter should be brief, as your qualifications will be covered in the accompanying résumé.

Cover letter A brief letter sent with a document identifying the intended recipient and the purpose of the attachment.

The cover letter should describe the job you are seeking, summarize your qualifications, request an interview, and express a desire for the job. If possible, address the cover letter directly to the person who is responsible for the hiring decision. Be sure to spell the person's name correctly and include the correct job title.

Just as you may need different résumés for different jobs, you should personalize each letter for each job application.

References

References may be requested in advertisements. Even if they are not, you may wish to add them to your résumé. Select your references carefully—they are frequently called or contacted for comment as part of the hiring process. Those you select must be contacted, and their permission obtained, before you use their names as references. Faculty members and former employers are frequently asked to be used as references. In some schools and workplaces, there are policies that limit the information that may be given about employment dates or attendance. An employer following up on one of these references may make a negative inference from the limited information given.

Keep in touch with those who do agree to give a reference and who will say good things about you to a potential employer. Keep them informed on your latest work and other extracurricular activities like charity or pro bono work so that they may speak knowledgeably about you if contacted.

Creating an Electronic Résumé

A growing number of employers are using computers to search the Internet for job applicants and to sort electronically through the résumés they receive. Human resources managers search through résumés received online or through Internet sites by entering a few words or phrases that describe the required skills and qualifications for the position they are trying to fill. Only the résumés in the computer system that match these electronic sorting terms and phrases are considered for the job. To have your résumé considered, you will need an electronic résumé in addition to the conventional printed résumé.

Computer programs that are used to search résumés generally look for certain descriptive words, similar to the key words used to conduct legal research. For example, to highlight your initiative, words such as "initiated," "started," "created," or "introduced" should be used. For leadership skills, use words such as "directed," "guided," or "organized." To attract interest in your problem-solving skills, use words such as "evaluated," "reorganized," "simplified," "solved," or "eliminated." Be sure to use these types of key words in your electronic résumé where appropriate to make your résumé stand out from the other résumés. A good starting point is to gather all the information highlighted in the Résumé Checklist.

Electronic Résumé Submission

Many potential employers and employment agencies will request that applicants submit résumés and writing samples electronically, usually as an attachment to an email. If you plan to send your résumé as an attachment to an email, be sure it will look presentable on the receiver's screen and can be printed out if desired.

You cannot be certain that the recipient has the same version of the word processing program you used to create the documents. In some cases the recipient will not have a compatible document viewer and may not be able to open or read your documents. One solution is to convert the documents to PDFs. Most word processing programs allow documents to be saved in the PDF or PDF/A format, which preserves the visual image of the document. There is almost universal access to software for reading PDFs, and a number of companies, such as Nuance and Adobe, provide free PDF readers. After you create your résumé, save a copy in the PDF format for electronic distribution. If you have writing samples that you may need to submit, save those in PDF format as well.

The first line of your résumé should contain only your full name. Type your street address, phone and fax numbers, and email address on separate lines below your name.

CHECKLIST Résumé

PERSONAL INFORMATION

- ☐ Name
- ☐ Address

EDUCATION

- ☐ High school
  - ☐ Year of graduation
- ☐ College
  - ☐ Year of graduation
  - ☐ Degree
  - ☐ Grade point average or class rank

WORK EXPERIENCE

- ☐ Current or last employer
  - ☐ Position(s) held
- ☐ Prior employer
  - ☐ Position held and dates

SPECIFIC SKILLS

- ☐ Office skills
- ☐ Computer skills
- ☐ Language skills
- ☐ Other job-related skills

OTHER

- ☐ Organizational memberships
- ☐ Licenses/certifications

Because many human resource managers search by key words, you should include a key word section near the top of your résumé. List nouns that describe your job-related skills and abilities. If you have work experience with specific job titles such as "paralegal," list these key words as well. Also include language proficiency or other specialty qualifications such as "nurse–paralegal" or "fluent in Spanish."

After you have created your résumé, save it again as a PDF file. Email the résumé to yourself or to a friend to confirm that it transmits correctly and has the desired appearance.

Think of getting a job as a process that starts with the résumé, continues through the interview, and ends with the follow-up to the interview as shown in the checklist for interview strategies.

CHECKLIST Interview Strategies

GETTING READY

- ☐ Write résumé.
- ☐ Make contacts.
- ☐ Network.
- ☐ Make appointments from mass mailings, telephone solicitations, and network contacts.

BEFORE THE INTERVIEW

- ☐ Know your résumé.
- ☐ Be familiar with a typical application form.
- ☐ Know something about the company or firm. Check the Martindale-Hubbell or Standard and Poor's directories.
- ☐ Have a list of good questions to ask the interviewer and know when to ask them.
- ☐ Rehearse your answers to possible interview questions, then rehearse again.
- ☐ Plan a "thumbnail" sketch of yourself.
- ☐ Know the location of the interview site and where to park, or become familiar with the public transportation schedule.
- ☐ Be at least 10 minutes early.
- ☐ Go alone.
- ☐ Bring copies of your résumé, list of references, and writing samples in a briefcase or portfolio.
- ☐ Check local salary ranges for the position.
- ☐ Be prepared to answer questions regarding your salary expectations.

(continued)

- ☐ Try to anticipate problem areas, such as inexperience or gaps in your work history.
- ☐ Be prepared to handle difficult questions, and know how to overcome objections.

THE INTRODUCTION

- ☐ Dress the part.
- ☐ Do not smoke, eat, chew gum, or drink coffee prior to or during the interview.
- ☐ Maintain good eye contact and good posture.
- ☐ Shake hands firmly.
- ☐ Establish rapport and be cordial without being overly familiar.
- ☐ Be positive—convert negatives to positives.
- ☐ Keep in mind that the first impressions are lasting impressions.

THE INTERVIEW

- ☐ Provide all important information about yourself.
- ☐ Sell yourself—no one else will.
- ☐ Use correct grammar.
- ☐ Do not be afraid to say, "I don't know."
- ☐ Ask questions of the interviewer.
- ☐ Do not answer questions about age, religion, marital status, or children unless you wish to. Try to address the perceived concern.
- ☐ Find out about the next interview or contact.
- ☐ Find out when a decision will be made.
- ☐ Shake hands at the end of the interview.

AFTER THE INTERVIEW

- ☐ Immediately document the interview in your placement file.
- ☐ Send personalized thank-you letters to each person who interviewed you.
- ☐ Call to follow up.

Source: Andrea Wagner, *How to Land Your First Paralegal Job* (Upper Saddle River, NJ: Prentice Hall, 2001), pp. 163–164.

Learning Objective 5
Plan for a successful job interview.

Interviewing for a Job

Most students today work at part-time or full-time jobs while pursuing their education. These might be summer jobs, holiday fill-in positions, or full-time jobs. The interviews for these positions provide opportunities to perfect your interviewing skills. Interviewing for a job can be highly stressful, but careful preparation can reduce the stress and help you put your best foot forward so you can get the job you are seeking.

After the interview, you should review what happened and the results of the interview in order to improve your interviewing skills. Even if you obtain the job, you'll want to learn what you did correctly that helped you to get the job, as well as what you could have done better, to prepare for future interviews.

The Interview

An interview for a job need not be intimidating. With a little preparation and research you can appear confident and make a good impression. Preparation starts with carefully reading the job description and the requested qualifications. Be sure that you can answer questions related to these qualifications, such as your experience in the particular area of law or special training in the use of legal specialty software. Research the firm by looking at its website, or by finding articles about the firm or its lawyers online. Prepare a list of questions that demonstrate your interest in the firm and the particular job, as shown in the checklist of interview questions. After you leave the interview, analyze your performance in the interview by reviewing the post-interview checklist. Then prepare and send a thank-you note to the person with whom you interviewed to make a positive, lasting impression.

Advice *from the* Field

THE PARALEGAL'S PORTFOLIO

Kathryn Myers, Coordinator, Paralegal Studies, Saint Mary-of-the-Woods College, Paralegal Studies Program

INTERVIEW

Q: How did the practice of assembling a portfolio come about?

A: This portfolio is actually based on the old concept of the "artist's portfolio." Anyone who is involved in a "hands-on" profession has utilized this concept for years.

Q: Instead of pictures, what do you mean when you speak of a portfolio for paralegal students?

A: A portfolio for paralegal students consists of two parts. One part is for my use in the program. The students have growth papers for each class, plus a series of other papers. I look at the collection of work to determine whether the paralegal program is doing what it says it will and whether it needs to be changed. I have modified a number of classes based on the material in this portfolio.

The other part is a professional portfolio. The students pull material from the above portfolio and create their own professional portfolio to take on interviews. This contains a copy or copies of their résumé, transcripts, selected writing samples, projects, or any other document they believe would be useful at the interview. Employers have been very impressed with this presentation.

Q: Do potential employers ever balk at seeing something that bulky? If so, how would you suggest handling it?

A: This has not been a problem for my students. As indicated earlier, we "create" two portfolios—one program-related and the other for professional purposes. I think this eliminates any problems at the interview.

Q: What is the most important thing about a portfolio?

A: The most important thing in the professional portfolio appears to be that the employer has another tool to assess the quality of the potential employee. Grades do not mean that much anymore. An "A" at [our college] may well come from a more demanding curriculum than an "A" at another institution. There is no basis for comparison unless the employer knows the grading scales/demands of the different programs. However, having a portfolio of material allows the employer to see what an interviewee can do.

Q: With that in mind, what should a paralegal student keep in mind when putting together the portfolio?

A: How a student puts a portfolio together says a lot about the student. I encourage students to incorporate both good and "not so good" work. That shows the employer that the interviewee can learn and can improve. Students collect material as they go through the program rather than waiting until the end.

Students should highlight their growth, their abilities, and their determination. They need to provide documentation that can show abilities that counter any poor grades that might appear on the transcript. This shows potential employers that test-taking is not necessarily the be-all, end-all to grades.

Most of all, the students need to let themselves shine through within the portfolio materials. Each student is unique, and each has different talents to highlight. That is the value of the portfolio.

Kathryn Myers is Coordinator, Paralegal Studies, Saint Mary-of-the-Woods College, Paralegal Studies Program. Used by permission.

CHECKLIST Questions to Ask at the Interview

- ☐ How does the firm evaluate paralegals?
- ☐ What is the growth potential for a paralegal in the firm?
- ☐ Why did the prior paralegal leave?
- ☐ How is work assigned?
- ☐ What support services are available to paralegals?
- ☐ What consideration is given for membership in paralegal associations?
- ☐ Does the firm provide any assistance for continuing education for paralegals?

CHECKLIST Analyzing How I Handled the Interview

- ☐ I arrived early for the interview.
- ☐ I greeted the interviewer warmly, with a smile and a firm handshake.
- ☐ I maintained good posture.
- ☐ I did not smoke or chew gum during the interview.
- ☐ I spoke clearly, using good grammar.
- ☐ I demonstrated enthusiasm and interest.
- ☐ I was able to answer questions asked of me.
- ☐ I sent a thank-you note within 24 hours after the interview.

Concept Review *and* Reinforcement

LEGAL TERMINOLOGY

Chronological résumé format 104
Complex litigation 78
Conflict checking 89
Court accounting 101
Cover letter 105
Elder law 79
Environmental law 78
Functional résumé format 104
General law practice 76
Government employment 79
Intellectual property 79
IOLTA account 100
Large law offices 75
Networking 80
Nurse paralegals or legal nurse consultants 78
Paralegal manager 79
Partnership 75
Pro bono 79
Résumé 101
Retainer 97
Self-employment 80
Small offices 74
Solo practice 74
Specialty practice 76
Trust account 99

SUMMARY OF KEY CONCEPTS

Arrangements and Organization of Law Offices and Firms

Solo Practice	In a solo practice, one lawyer practices alone without the assistance of other attorneys.
Small Offices	Small offices range from individual practitioners sharing space to partnerships.
Partnerships	Partnerships consist of two or more persons or corporations that have joined together to share ownership of a business and profit or loss from that business.
Large Offices	Large offices are an outgrowth of traditional law offices that have expanded over the years, adding partners and associates along the way.
General Practice	Generalists handle all types of cases.

Specialty Practice

Legal Nurse Consultants and Nurse Paralegals	Nurses who have gained medical work experience and combine it with paralegal skills.
Real Estate	Paralegals in this field can benefit from experience in real estate sales or from title insurance agencies.
Complex Litigation	Complex litigation requires document production and maintaining indexes, usually on computer databases, of the paperwork generated from litigation.

Environmental Law	Environmental law covers everything from toxic waste dumps to protection of wildlife.
Intellectual Property	Intellectual property is concerned with the formalities of protecting intellectual property interests, including patent rights, trade secrets, and copyrights and trademarks.
Elder Law	Elder law is concerned with protecting the rights of the elderly and obtaining all the benefits to which they are entitled.
Paralegal Managers	Paralegal managers hire, supervise, train, and evaluate paralegals.
Pro Bono Paralegals	Pro bono paralegals work without compensation on behalf of individuals and organizations that otherwise could not afford legal assistance.
Government Employment	Paralegals are found in administrative agencies and federal offices involved with both criminal prosecutions and civil litigation.
Legal Departments of Corporations	Paralegals handle documents, technology, and investigations, juggling legal, sales, and marketing perspectives.
Self-Employment	State regulation may limit the opportunities or restrict paralegal self-employment. Where authorized by federal law, the paralegal may actively represent clients without the supervision of an attorney.
Networking	Networking involves establishing contact with others to exchange questions and information.

Paralegal Tasks and Functions

1. Conducting interviews
2. Maintaining written and verbal contacts with clients and counsel
3. Setting up, organizing, and maintaining client files
4. Preparing pleadings and documents
5. Reviewing, analyzing, summarizing, and indexing documents and transcripts
6. Assisting in preparing witnesses and clients for trial
7. Maintaining calendar and tickler systems
8. Conducting research, both factual and legal
9. Performing office administrative functions including maintaining time and billing records

Administrative Procedures in Law Offices and Firms

Conflict Checking	The purpose of conflict checking is to verify that current and prior representations of parties and matters handled will not present a conflict of interest for the firm in accepting a new client or legal matter.
Time Keeping and Billing	In any law firm, it is essential to carefully keep track of expenses and billable time.

Accounting in the Law Office

Maintaining Law Firm Financial Information	A paralegal needs to understand the internal accounting needs of the firm and to understand and prepare client financial information.
Accounting for Client Retainers and Costs	A retainer is a payment at the beginning of the handling of a new matter for a client. This amount may be used to offset the fees for services rendered or costs advanced on behalf of the client.
Civil Practice: Fee and Cost Billing	Fees may be calculated on an hourly rate, as a contingent fee, or as a combination of the two.
Timely Disbursements	Lawyers cannot retain settlement funds for an unreasonable time.

Trust Accounts	Trust accounts are used for holding the client's funds separately.
IOLTA Accounts	Where the amount is too small to earn interest, court rules require that the funds be deposited into a special interest-bearing account, and the interest generally paid to support legal aid projects (Interest on Lawyers Trust Account).
Interest-Bearing Escrow Accounts	If the amount held for a client is sufficient to earn substantial interest, it should be deposited into an interest-bearing account for the benefit of the client.
Court Accounting	A court accounting is an accounting with the local court that administers or supervises trust and estate matters. These reports are designed to show that the fiduciary has properly administered the estate or trust.
Preparing Your Résumé	
Résumé Formats	A résumé is a brief description of a person's education, a summary of work experience, and other related and supporting information that potential employers use in evaluating a person's qualifications for a position in a firm or an organization. Chronological Résumé Format 1. Presents education and job history in chronological order with the most recent experience listed first. Functional Résumé Format 2. Gives a summary of the individual's qualifications with current experience and education without emphasizing dates of employment.
Cover Letters	The cover letter creates the first impression and is a sample of your writing skills.
Creating an Electronic Résumé	A growing number of employers use computers to search the Internet for job applicants, sorting résumés electronically.
Converting a Traditional Résumé into an Electronic Résumé	Traditional word processing documents may not be readable in electronic form and need to be converted to a readable format.
Interviewing for a Job	
The Interview	Careful interview preparation can help to eliminate some of the stress and help you put your best foot forward.

WORKING THE WEB

1. Download the Tips for Networking Success from the NALS website at http://www.nals.org/students/reading/networkingsuccess.html.
2. Review some of the job opportunities posted on the American Alliance of Paralegals website. What are the common qualifications? http://aapipara.org/Jobbank.htm
3. Check and download from the websites of the various paralegal professional associations information on paralegal occupational opportunities:
   a. National Association of Legal Assistants at www.nala.org
   b. National Federation of Paralegal Associations at www.paralegals.org
   c. International Paralegal Management Association at www.paralegalmanagement.org
   d. American Association of Legal Nurse Consultants at www.aalnc.org
   e. The American Association of Nurse Attorneys at www.taana.org
4. What paralegal opportunities are posted at www.monster.com?
5. What online resources are available to help in creating résumés?
6. What online career sources are available at:
   a. Career Resource Library at www.labor.state.ny.us
   b. America's Job Bank at www.ajb.dni.us/index.html
   c. Wall Street Journal at www.careers.wsj.com
   d. CareerWEB at www.employmentguide.com
7. What law firms in your area have a website that offers employment opportunities? Use the Martindale-Hubbell Legal Directory to find the law firms.

CRITICAL THINKING & WRITING QUESTIONS

1. What are the different forms of practice arrangements that lawyers use?
2. What are the advantages and disadvantages of working for a lawyer in solo practice?
3. What are the advantages and disadvantages of working in a small multi-lawyer office or partnership?
4. What are the advantages and disadvantages of working in large law offices or firms?
5. Would working in a specialty practice be less stressful than working in a general practice?
6. What are the advantages and disadvantages of working in a corporate legal department?
7. Why would a law firm want to hire a nurse paralegal?
8. What additional costs might a paralegal incur in working in a large-city practice in contrast to a small-town office?
9. Why would a paralegal who specializes in one legal field be at greater risk for the unauthorized practice of law?
10. Other than revealing potential employment opportunities, what advantages does networking have for a paralegal?
11. Are interviews conducted by paralegals considered privileged?
12. Why is doing a conflict check important?
13. Is it necessary to do a conflict check before starting employment at a new law firm? Why?
14. When is an ethical wall required?
15. What steps should be taken to ensure that a proper ethical screen is in place?
16. Why is accurate time keeping important to the paralegal and the law firm?
17. What is a retainer?
18. What is an IOLTA account, and what is the reason behind maintaining one?
19. What is the purpose of filing a court accounting?
20. What is the objective of a uniform system of accounts?
21. Prepare the résumé you would like to have five years from now. How would this résumé help you in selecting courses, extracurricular activities, and interim employment?
22. Prepare your current résumé in print form. What format did you use? Why?
23. Convert your print résumé to an electronic résumé. Email a copy to your instructor if requested.
24. How does assessing your interests and skills help in preparing your personal résumé?

Building Paralegal Skills

VIDEO CASE STUDIES

Preparing for a Job Interview: Résumé Advice

Paralegal student Reed meets with a college counselor for advice about preparing his résumé and obtains some suggestions for enhancing his résumé and preparing a cover letter.

After viewing the video case study in MyLegalStudiesLab, complete the following:

1. Prepare an outline of your résumé with the appropriate sections, and save it as a template for future use.
2. Complete the résumé using the template by adding your current qualifications and experience.
3. Prepare and print out a copy of the résumé using the paper you would use for submitting a résumé to a potential employer.
4. Prepare the résumé for electronic submission with an email. Prepare and send the email to yourself as if you were the potential employer.

Preparing for a Job Interview: Interviewing Advice

Paralegal student Reed meets with his college counselor to obtain advice about interviewing for a job. His counselor helps him with some of the questions he may be asked that trouble him.

After viewing the video case study in MyLegalStudiesLab, answer the following:

1. Pair up with another student and role-play with one of you acting as the human resource director and the other the applicant.
2. Make a list of questions you would ask as the interviewer.
3. Make a list of questions you would ask as the applicant.
4. Conduct the interview in front of the class or another person who can offer comments and critiques of the interview.
5. Prepare a follow-up note to the interviewer.
6. What are questions that cannot be asked? If they are asked, how will you respond to them?

Interviewing: The Good, the Bad, and the Ugly

Three paralegals are applying for a job at a prestigious law firm. Each presents him- or herself in a different manner and with a distinctive style.

After viewing the video case study at www.pearsonhighered.com/goldman, answer the following:

1. Make a list of suggestions for each of the three applicants on what they should have done or can do in their next interview to make the most positive impression.
2. What interviewing rules did each applicant follow? What rules did they violate?
3. How important is the way you dress for an interview? Explain.

ETHICS ANALYSIS & DISCUSSION QUESTIONS

1. In changing jobs from one firm to another, how does the paralegal avoid a conflict of interest?
2. What ethical and UPL problems do freelance paralegals face that those working in a single firm do not?
3. What ethical issues might arise in determining the paralegal's supervising attorney when the paralegal is working in a small firm of three attorneys?
4. Say you are working as a paralegal in a small law office shared by three attorneys, each of whom is a solo practitioner. To save money, they share a law library and a fax machine, and they use a common computer network with separate workstations but with a common file server to save files because it has an automatic backup system. You work for each of the lawyers as the need arises, answering phones and generally performing paralegal services. See District of Columbia Ethics Opinion 303. What issues of confidentiality should be considered? As the office paralegal, are there any conflict of interest problems?

Paralegal Ethics in Practice

5. You hold a bachelor's degree in paralegal studies from a prestigious college. You want to work as an independent paralegal. May you advertise in the local newspaper and put a sign on the door of your office that uses the term "paralegal," according to your state law?

DEVELOPING YOUR COLLABORATION SKILLS

Working on your own or with a group of other students, review the scenario at the beginning of the chapter discussing the changes and the opportunities in the paralegal profession.

1. Divide the class into groups of three. One person will play the role of Cary Moritz and another the role of Natasha Weiser. The third person will act as recorder and presenter.
2. Role-play Natasha's first day on the job. She receives the memo from Cary and goes to her office to offer her thanks.
   a. What additional questions could Natasha ask Cary?
   b. What additional advice could Cary offer?
3. The recorder keeps detailed notes of the conversation.
4. Once the role-play is completed, the group summarizes the expectations that Natasha and Cary would have of the other in their working relationship.
5. Repeat the activity, with students exchanging roles.

PARALEGAL PORTFOLIO EXERCISE

Develop your résumé, using the functional format to prepare the résumé you would like to have when you finish your education as a paralegal. List the skills you expect to develop or learn before you apply for your desired paralegal position.

LEGAL ANALYSIS &WRITING CASES

Jean v. Nelson, 863 F.2d 759 (11th Cir. 1988)

Reimbursement for Paralegal Time under Federal Statute

The district court awarded, and the 11th Circuit Court of Appeals upheld, reimbursement for time spent by paralegals and law clerks where the work normally was done by an attorney. The hourly rate awarded was $40, the rate at which the law firm whose paralegals and clerks were involved bills its clients.

The government challenges the rate awarded, and contends that paralegal time is compensational only at the actual cost to the plaintiff's counsel. In the context of a Title VII case, [the court] held that paralegal time is recoverable as "part of a prevailing party's award for attorney's fees and expenses, [but] only to the extent that the paralegal performs work traditionally done by an attorney. To hold otherwise would be counterproductive because excluding reimbursement for such work might encourage attorneys to handle entire cases themselves, thereby achieving the same results at a higher overall cost."

Questions

1. Does this rationale encourage lawyers to use paralegals?
2. Does this decision facilitate the availability of lower-cost quality legal services?
3. Should an attorney be allowed to charge more than out-of-pocket costs for paralegal services?

In Re Busy Beaver Bldg. Centers, Inc., 19 F.3d 833 (3rd Cir. 1994)

Paralegal Fees Based on Skill Level

In deciding the propriety of awarding paralegal fees in bankruptcy cases, the court held:

As is true with recently graduated attorneys, entry-level paralegals perform the more mundane tasks in the paralegal work spectrum, some of which may resemble those tasks generally deemed "clerical" in nature. Yet, even with these tasks, paralegals may have to bring their training or experience to bear, thereby relieving attorneys of the burden of extensive supervision and ensuring the proper completion of tasks involving the exercise, or potential exercise, of some paraprofessional judgment. Of course, the appropriate rate the attorney will command for paralegal services will ordinarily parallel the paralegal's credentials and the degree of experience, knowledge, and skill the task at hand calls for.... [P]urely clerical or secretarial tasks should not be billed at a paralegal rate, regardless of who performs them.

The short of it is that the market-driven approach of the [bankruptcy act] § 330 permits compensation for relatively low-level paralegal services if and only if analogous non-bankruptcy clients agree to pay for the same, and then only at that rate. [T]hose services not requiring the exercise of professional legal judgment...must be included in "overhead."

We cannot agree that in all cases the general ability of a legal secretary to perform some particular task determines whether a paralegal or a legal secretary is the appropriate, most efficient, employee to perform it at any given instant. At times, temporal constraints may foreclose the delegation option. At other times, a paralegal—or, for that matter, an attorney—can more productively complete a clerical task, such as photocopying documents, than can a legal secretary.

Questions

1. How can the attorney prove the skill level of paralegals when seeking compensation for paralegal services?
2. Will this kind of reasoning by the court force attorneys to hire more skilled paralegals?
3. Would the existence of a certificate or degree in paralegal studies be useful in proving that the person who worked on a case was a paralegal?

WORKING WITH THE LANGUAGE OF THE COURT CASE

Phoenix Founders Inc. v. Marshall, 887 S.W.2d 831 (1994)

Supreme Court of Texas

Read the following case, excerpted from the state supreme court's opinion. Review and brief the case. In your brief, answer the following questions.

1. What is the danger in hiring a paralegal who has worked at a competing law firm when handling a case on appeal?
2. What is the supervising attorney's responsibility in hiring a paralegal who has worked at another law firm?
3. What steps must be taken when hiring a paralegal who worked at another law firm that represents an opposing party?
4. What instructions should the paralegal who worked at another firm be given when hired?
5. Under what general circumstances will a law firm be disqualified after hiring a paralegal?

(continued)

Spector, Justice, delivered the opinion of the Court, in which Hillips, Chief Justice, and Gonzalez, Hightower, Hecht, Doggett, Cornyn, and Gammage, Justices join.

In this original proceeding, we consider whether a law firm must be disqualified from ongoing litigation because it rehired a legal assistant who had worked for opposing counsel for three weeks. We hold that disqualification is not required if the rehiring firm is able to establish that it has effectively screened the paralegal from any contact with the underlying suit. Because this standard had not been adopted in Texas prior to the trial court's disqualification order, we deny mandamus relief without prejudice to allow the trial court to reconsider its ruling in light of today's opinion.

The present dispute arises from a suit brought by Phoenix Founders, Inc. and others ("Phoenix") to collect a federal-court judgment against Ronald and Jane Beneke and others. The law firm of Thompson & Knight represented Phoenix in the original federal-court suit, which began in 1990 and ended in 1991, and has also represented them in the collection suit since its commencement in 1992. The Benekes have been represented in the latter suit by the firm of David & Goodman.

In July of 1993, Denise Hargrove, a legal assistant at Thompson & Knight, left her position at that firm to begin working for David & Goodman as a paralegal. While at David & Goodman, Hargrove billed six-tenths of an hour on the collection suit for locating a pleading. She also discussed the case generally with Mark Goodman, the Benekes' lead counsel. After three weeks at David & Goodman, Hargrove returned to Thompson & Knight to resume work as a paralegal. At the time of the rehiring, Thompson & Knight made no effort to question Hargrove in regard to potential conflicts of interest resulting from her employment at David & Goodman.

Three weeks after Hargrove had returned, counsel for the Benekes wrote to Thompson & Knight asserting that its renewed employment of Hargrove created a conflict of interest. The letter demanded that the firm withdraw from its representation of Phoenix. Hargrove resigned from Thompson & Knight the next week, after having been given the option of either resigning with severance pay or being terminated. The firm itself, however, refused to withdraw from the case. The Benekes then filed a motion to disqualify.

This Court has not previously addressed the standards governing a disqualification motion based on the hiring of a nonlawyer employee. With respect to lawyers, however, this Court has adopted a standard requiring disqualification whenever counsel undertakes representation of an interest that is adverse to that of a former client, as long as the matters embraced in the pending suit are "substantially related" to the factual matters involved in the previous suit. This strict rule is based on a conclusive presumption that confidences and secrets were imparted to the attorney during the prior representation [Coker, 765 S.W.2d at 400].

We agree that a paralegal who has actually worked on a case must be subject to the presumption set out in Coker; that is, a conclusive presumption that confidences and secrets were imparted during the course of the paralegal's work on the case. We disagree, however, with the argument that paralegals should be conclusively presumed to share confidential information with members of their firms. The Disciplinary Rules require a lawyer having direct supervisory authority over a nonlawyer to make reasonable efforts to ensure that the nonlawyer's conduct is compatible with the professional obligations of the lawyer.

The Texas Committee on Professional Ethics has considered the application of these rules in the context of a "right hand" legal secretary or legal assistant leaving one small firm and joining another that represents an adverse party. The Committee concluded that the Rules do not require disqualification of the new law firm, provided that the supervising lawyer at that firm complies with the Rules so as to ensure that the nonlawyer's conduct is compatible with the professional obligations of a lawyer. This view is consistent with the weight of authority in other jurisdictions.

The American Bar Association's Committee on Professional Ethics, after surveying case law and ethics opinions from a number of jurisdictions, concluded that the new firm need not be disqualified, as long as the firm and the paralegal strictly adhere to the screening process set forth in the opinion, and as long as the paralegal does not reveal any information relating to the former employer's clients to any person in the employing firm. A number of courts have since relied on the ABA's opinion to allow continued representation under similar conditions.

Underlying these decisions is a concern regarding the mobility of paralegals and other nonlawyers. A potential employer might well be reluctant to hire a particular nonlawyer if doing so would automatically disqualify the entire firm from ongoing litigation. This problem would be especially acute in the context of massive firms and extensive, complex litigation. Recognizing this danger, the ABA concluded "any restrictions on the nonlawyer's employment should be held to the minimum necessary to protect confidentiality of client information" [ABA Op. 1526].

We share the concerns expressed by the ABA, and agree that client confidences may be adequately safeguarded if a firm hiring a paralegal from another firm takes appropriate steps in compliance with the Disciplinary Rules. Specifically, the newly hired paralegal should be cautioned not to disclose any information relating to the representation of a client of the former employer. The paralegal should also be instructed not to work on any matter on which the paralegal worked during the prior employment, or regarding which the paralegal has information relating to the former employer's representation. Additionally, the firm should take other reasonable steps to ensure that the paralegal does not work in connection with matters on which the paralegal worked during the prior employment, absent client consent after consultation. Each of these precautions would tend to reduce the danger that the paralegal might share confidential information with members of the new firm. Thus, while a court must ordinarily presume that some sharing will take place, the challenged firm may rebut this presumption by showing that sufficient precautions have been taken to guard against any disclosure of confidences.

Absent consent of the former employer's client, disqualification will always be required under some circumstances, such as (1) when information relating to the representation of an adverse client has in fact been disclosed, or (2) when screening would be ineffective or the nonlawyer necessarily would be required to work on the other side of a matter that is the same as or substantially related to a matter on which the nonlawyer has previously worked. Ordinarily, however, disqualification is not required as long as "the practical effect of formal screening has been achieved."

In reconsidering the disqualification motion, the trial court should examine the circumstances of Hargrove's employment at Thompson & Knight to determine whether the practical effect of formal screening has been achieved. The factors bearing on such a determination will generally include the substantiality of the relationship between the former and current matters; the time elapsing between the matters; the size of the firm; the number of individuals presumed to have confidential information; the nature of their involvement in the former matter; and the timing and features of any measures taken to reduce the danger of disclosure. The fact that the present case involves representation of adverse parties in the same proceeding, rather than two separate proceedings, increases the danger that some improper disclosure may have occurred. Evidence regarding the other factors, however, may tend to rebut the presumption of shared confidences.

The ultimate question in weighing these factors is whether Thompson & Knight has taken measures sufficient to reduce the potential for misuse of confidences to an acceptable level. Because we have modified the controlling legal standard, the writ of mandamus is denied without prejudice to allow the trial court to reconsider the disqualification motion in light of today's opinion. The stay order previously issued by this Court remains in effect only so long as necessary to allow the trial court to act.

Ramirez v. Plough, Inc., 12 Cal. Rptr. 2d 423 (Ct. App. 1992)*, Court of Appeals of California

Read, and if assigned, brief this case. Prepare a written answer to each of the following questions. Note the words of the California Supreme Court on appeal.

1. How does this case illustrate the clients' cultural differences?
2. Are the views of the parent in this case the same as your own? Would you have conducted yourself in the same way as the parent?
3. What ethical obligation does the paralegal have to be sure the client who does not speak the same language understands the advice given? Does it matter if it is medical directions, as in this case, or legal advice?
4. Does a law firm have a higher duty to a non-English-speaking client than a drug company, such as the defendant in this case, does in selling a product?
5. Does the law firm have a duty to explain cultural differences in the American legal system and its procedures to non-English-speaking, non-native-born clients?

* *If citing in a California court, add "15 Cal. App. 4th 1110" after the case name and before the citation from the California Reporter, set off by commas. Ramirez v. Plough, Inc., 15 Cal. App. 4th 1110, 12 Cal. Rptr. 2d 423 (1992)*

(continued)

Thaxter, Judge

Jorge Ramirez, a minor, by his guardian ad litem Rosa Rivera, appeals from a summary judgment in favor of Plough, Inc. Appellant sued Plough alleging negligence, product liability, and fraud. The action sought damages for injuries sustained in March of 1986 when Jorge, who was then four months old, contracted Reye's Syndrome after ingesting St. Joseph Aspirin for Children (SJAC). Plough marketed and distributed SJAC.

Reye's Syndrome is a serious disease of unknown cause characterized by severe vomiting, lethargy, or irritability, which may progress to delirium or coma.

In December 1985, the Food and Drug Administration (FDA) requested that aspirin manufacturers voluntarily place a label on aspirin products warning consumers of the possible association between aspirin and Reye's Syndrome. Plough voluntarily complied and began including a warning and insert in SJAC packaging. On June 5, 1986, the Reye's Syndrome warning became mandatory.

In March 1986, SJAC labeling bore the following warning: "Warning: Reye's Syndrome is a rare but serious disease which can follow flu or chicken pox in children and teenagers. While the cause of Reye's Syndrome is unknown, some reports claim aspirin may increase the risk of developing this disease. Consult a doctor before use in children or teenagers with flu or chicken pox." In addition, the SJAC package insert included the following statement: "The symptoms of Reye's Syndrome can include persistent vomiting, sleepiness and lethargy, violent headaches, unusual behavior, including disorientation, combativeness, and delirium. If any of these symptoms occur, especially following chicken pox or flu, call your doctor immediately, even if your child has not taken any medication. Reye's Syndrome is serious, so early detection and treatment are vital."

Rosa Rivera purchased SJAC on March 12, 1986, and administered it to appellant, who was suffering from what appeared to be a cold or upper respiratory infection. She gave appellant the aspirin without reading the directions or warnings appearing on the SJAC packaging. The packaging was in English and Ms. Rivera can speak and understand only Spanish. She did not seek to have the directions or warnings translated from English to Spanish, even though members of her household spoke English.

The trial court granted Plough's motion for summary judgment on the grounds that "there is no duty to warn in a foreign language and there is no causal relationship between plaintiff's injury and defendant's activities."

It is undisputed that SJAC was marketed and intended for the treatment of minor aches and pains associated with colds, flu, and minor viral illnesses. The SJAC box promised "fast, effective relief of fever and minor aches and pains of colds."...In March 1986, federal regulations requiring a Reye's Syndrome warning had been promulgated and were final, although not yet effective....The scientific community had already confirmed and documented the relationship between Reye's Syndrome and the use of aspirin after a viral illness. There is no doubt Plough had a duty to warn of the Reye's Syndrome risk.

The question thus is whether the warning given only in English was adequate under the circumstances. Respondent argues that, as a matter of law, it has no duty to place foreign-language warnings on products manufactured to be sold in the United States and that holding manufacturers liable for failing to do so would violate public policy.

While the constitutional, statutory, regulatory, and judicial authorities relied on by respondent may reflect a public policy recognizing the status of English as an official language, nothing compels the conclusion that a manufacturer of a dangerous or defective product is immunized from liability when an English-only warning does not adequately inform non-English literate persons likely to use the product.

Plough's evidence showed that over 148 foreign languages are spoken in the United States and over 23 million Americans speak a language other than English in their homes. That evidence plainly does not prove that Plough used reasonable care in giving an English-only warning. Plough, then, resorts to arguing that the burden on manufacturers and society of requiring additional warnings is so "staggering" that the courts should preclude liability as a matter of law. We are not persuaded.

Certainly the burden and costs of giving foreign-language warnings is one factor for consideration in determining whether a manufacturer acted reasonably in using only English. The importance of that factor may vary from case to case depending upon other circumstances, such as the nature of the product, marketing efforts directed to segments of the population unlikely to be English-literate, and the actual and relative size of the consumer market which could reasonably be expected to speak or read only a certain foreign language. Plough presented no evidence from which we can gauge the extent of the burden under the facts of this case.

Ramirez submitted evidence that Plough knew Hispanics were an important part of the market for SJAC and that Hispanics often maintain their first language rather than learn English. SJAC was advertised in the Spanish media, both radio and television. That evidence raises material questions of fact concerning the foreseeability of purchase by a Hispanic not literate in English and the reasonableness of not giving a Spanish-language warning. If Plough has evidence conclusively showing that it would have been unreasonable to give its label warning in Spanish because of the burden, it did not present that evidence below.

...[I]f we accepted Plough's arguments in this case, in effect we would be holding that failure to warn in a foreign language is not negligence, regardless of the circumstances. Such a sweeping grant of immunity should come from the legislative branch of government, not the judicial. In deciding that Plough did not establish its right to judgment as a matter of law, we do not hold that manufacturers are required to warn in languages other than English simply because it may be foreseeable that non-English-literate persons are likely to use their products. Our decision merely recognizes that under some circumstances the standard of due care may require such warning.

Because the evidence shows triable issues of material fact and because Plough did not establish its immunity from liability as a matter of law, its motion for summary judgment should have been denied.

Ramirez v. Plough, Inc., 6 Cal.4th 539, 863 P.2d 167, 25 Cal. Rptr.2d 97 (1993)

California Supreme Court on Appeal—Opinion

Kennard, J.

IV

...We recognize that if a Spanish language warning had accompanied defendant's product, and if plaintiff's mother had read and heeded the warning, the tragic blighting of a young and innocent life that occurred in this case might not have occurred. Yet, as one court has aptly commented, "The extent to which special consideration should be given to persons who have difficulty with the English language is a matter of public policy for consideration by the appropriate legislative bodies and not by the Courts." (*Carmona v. Sheffield* (N.D.Cal. 1971) 325 F. Supp. 1341, 1342, affd. *per curiam* (9th Cir. 1973) 475 F.2d 738.) (**4b**) We hold only that, given the inherent limitations of the judicial process, manufacturers of nonprescription drugs have no presently existing legal duty, within the tort law system, to include foreign-language warnings with their packaging materials....

Mosk, J.

I concur. I write separately to emphasize the majority's caveat that "We do not...foreclose the possibility of tort liability premised upon the *content* of foreign-language advertising. For example, we do not decide whether a manufacturer would be liable to a consumer who detrimentally relied upon foreign-language advertising that was materially misleading as to product risks and who was unable to read English language package warnings that accurately described the risks. No such issue is presented here...."

...Evidence of the content, timing, duration, and scope of distribution of foreign-language advertising bears substantially on the question whether a non-English-literate consumer has been materially misled about product risks, and a trial court must consider that evidence if properly presented.

The majority do not define "materially misleading as to product risks," leaving that issue for another day—a day likely to arrive soon, given the high probability that foreign-language media will continue to expand in California.

MYLEGALSTUDIESLAB

MyLegalStudiesLab Virtual Law Office Experience Assignments

Complete the pre-test, study plan, and post-test for this chapter and answer the Legal Applications questions as assigned. These will help you confirm your mastery of the concepts and their application to legal scenarios. Then complete the Virtual Law Office assignments as assigned by your instructor. These assignments are designed to develop your workplace skills.

Completing the assignments for this chapter will result in producing the following documents for inclusion in your portfolio:

VLOE 3.1	Personal resumés and a cover letter in paper and electronic format
VLOE 3.3	1. Critique of each applicant, including suggestions for improvement for the next time they interview. 2. A thank-you letter for each interview.

CHAPTER

4

Technology and the Paralegal

LEARNING OBJECTIVES

After studying this chapter, you should be able to:

1. Explain why computer skills are essential in law offices and court systems.
2. Discuss the impact of the Federal Rules of Civil Procedure on the use of electronic documents and other technology in the law.
3. Explain the use of technology in the law.
4. Explain the functions of the components of a computer system in a law office.
5. Describe the types of software used in a law office and the functions they perform.
6. Describe the types of specialty applications software used in a law office.
7. Describe the features of the electronic courtroom and the paperless office.
8. Explain the features and functions of a computer network in a law office.
9. Discuss the future trends in law office technology.

Paralegals at Work

Attorneys Edith Hannah and Alice Hart have decided to combine their practices to form the Hannah Hart Law Office. Ms. Hannah has had a thriving practice for 35 years, but Ms. Hart has been in practice for only 5 years. The Hannah law firm is located across the street from the county courthouse, and the Hart office a block from the federal courthouse and government complex in a neighboring city 20 miles away. Both attorneys rely heavily on their paralegal staff to run their businesses. Elma Quinn has worked for Ms. Hannah for 25 years, and Cary Moritz has been with Ms. Hart for only 3 years.

When Elma first visited the Hart office, she was surprised to see how small Ms. Hart's library was compared to Ms. Hannah's library. She also noticed that the Hart office had fewer filing cabinets and boxes, and no large ledger books.

Elma sat down next to Cary's workstation and asked, "Where do you store all of your files? We have at least a dozen heavy fireproof file cabinets and a rented warehouse room full of boxes of closed files. I've heard of the paperless office, but you must have records somewhere. And how do you do legal research without a decent law library?" Cary explained that they are able to access almost everything they need for research online, and use their Internet subscriptions to find all of the latest cases, statutes, and regulations. He further explained that all the client files and records are kept on the computer system.

Elma expressed her real concern to Cary: "I come from the 'old school.' We use paper files and ledger books. How much will I have to learn if they decide to use your computer system?" She was also concerned about interactions between the offices. "It takes an hour to travel between the offices. I don't want to be the one to drive back and forth to exchange documents. I also know the attorneys spend most of their time in court. I just don't see how they will be able to find the time to work together."

When these firms combine their offices, do you think they will have any problems combining files, clients, and office procedures? Consider the issues involved in this scenario as you read this chapter.

> "Laws too gentle are seldom obeyed; too severe, seldom executed."
>
> Benjamin Franklin,
> *Poor Richard's Almanack* (1756)

INTRODUCTION TO TECHNOLOGY AND THE PARALEGAL

Technology has changed the way many procedures are performed in the law office and the court system. Paper-laden files in boxes and file cabinets are being replaced by electronic documents that reside on computer servers in the office and in remote locations. The computer and the Internet are increasingly used not just for document preparation, but also for client databases, accounting records, electronic communications, research, filing with the court, presenting cases at trial, and attracting new clients through firm websites.

Computer technology is used in the following ways in the law office:

word processing—preparing documents

electronic spreadsheets—performing financial calculations and financial presentations

time and billing programs—recording billable time accurately and invoicing clients

accounting programs—managing firm financial records, payroll, and client escrow accounts

calendaring—tracking deadlines, appointments, and hearing dates

graphic presentation software—preparing persuasive presentations

trial presentation software—organizing trial presentations

Internet search engines—searching for current and accurate legal and factual information to support a case

databases—maintaining records and documents

document scanning—converting documents to electronic format

document search features—locating relevant material in documents and exhibits

email and document delivery—communicating electronically

e-discovery—finding and reviewing discoverable electronic data

online collaboration—using the Internet to work collaboratively

online electronic document repositories—storing and accessing documents remotely

Web Exploration

Compare the results of the latest survey information with the data listed to the right. The full survey may be viewed at the International Paralegal Management Association website at **http://www.paralegalmanagement.org**.

The Need For Computer Skills

Learning Objective 1

Explain why computer skills are essential in law offices and court systems.

Computers are being used with greater frequency to communicate and share information in **digital format** between remote offices, courthouses, government agencies, and clients. In the past, paper had to be physically copied and sent, frequently by a costly messenger or express mail service. Now electronic files are often shared as **attachments** to emails and filed electronically with courts and government agencies. Large files can be exchanged almost instantaneously anywhere in the world, without any **hard copy.** In many ways, electronic files do not have the same issues with physical safety as paper documents. However, electronic files do have their own issues with security and confidentiality.

Digital format A computerized format utilizing a series of 0's and 1's.

Attachment A popular method of transmitting text files and graphic images by attaching the file to an email.

Hard copy A paper copy of a document.

The legal team is increasingly using the Internet for more than just legal research. Most government information can be obtained through the Internet. Finding businesses and individuals through private service providers, such as the yellow pages and white pages, is now handled more efficiently through web search engines, such as Google and Yahoo! More legal firms are also building websites for developing their own businesses, as shown in Exhibit 4.1. However, only the best of these sites are designed in a way that is truly effective in helping to attract and retain clients.

Exhibit 4.1 A typical law firm website, the new yellow pages

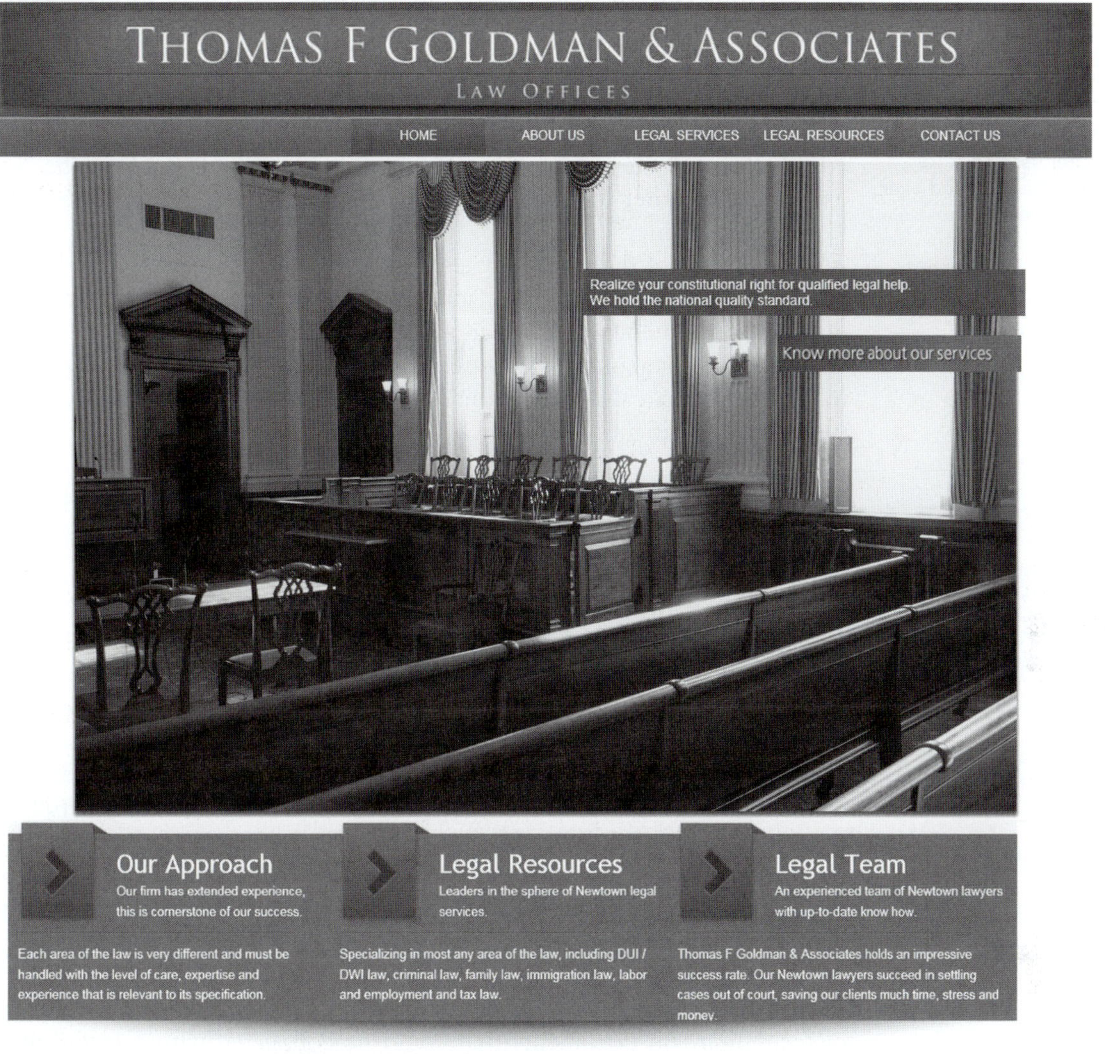

Source: Reprinted with permission from Mellon, Webster, & Shelly Law Offices.

The rise in the use of electronic documents in litigation, and new federal and state rules and case law on electronic discovery is increasing the demand for skills and knowledge in the use of technology in this area. Everyone on the legal team must now have a working familiarity with computers and the types of computer programs used in the law office. In many cases, the legal team must work with technology professionals to use computers and electronic data effectively.

At one time, the equipment of the average law office consisted of a typewriter, an adding machine, and a basic duplicating machine. Paper was king, with every document needing to be typed, edited, retyped—and frequently retyped again. In each instance, a paper copy was produced and delivered to the supervising attorney for review and additional changes. It was then returned for retyping and eventually sent to the client, sent to the opposing counsel, or filed with the court. File cabinets abounded in the law office, and numerous boxes of paper files were stored in back rooms, warehouses, and other storage locations.

But now, the trend is toward eliminating paper in the law office through the use of computer technology and software. In most law offices today, there are no typewriters, and computers are used to prepare documents using word processor software. The typical duplicating machine is now a multifunction device that can scan, print, copy, and fax documents.

Members of the legal team frequently work from locations outside the firm's main office, such as a home office, satellite office, or another firm. In some cases, they may be working in a different part of the country or world. Each member of the team may need access to electronic files or data about a case. One solution is to have all of the files stored electronically in an **electronic repository** on a secure, protected file server that authorized users may access over the Internet. The use of the Internet to store electronic files on remote servers is frequently called "cloud computing."

Electronic repository An off-site computer used to store records that may be accessed over secure Internet connections.

Online collaboration Using the Internet to conduct meetings and share documents.

Members of the team may also use the Internet to work together using **online collaboration** software. This software allows several persons to see the same document simultaneously, and in some cases, make on-screen notes and comments. A number of companies provide services and software for converting case documents to electronic form and storing the documents on a secure server. Exhibit 4.2 shows a typical remote litigation network.

Learning Objective 2
Discuss the impact of the Federal Rules of Civil Procedure on the use of electronic documents and other technology in the law.

The Impact of the Federal Rules of Civil Procedure

The December 2006 revision to the Federal Rules of Civil Procedure has had a major impact on our thinking about technology in the practice of law. The new federal rules organized and formalized what had once been a patchwork of court rules and case law on electronic discovery. There are also many new rules on electronic discovery in the state courts.

The new rules specifically address the increased use of electronic documentation in all aspects of business and personal life. Where people formerly used a pen or a typewriter to write a letter, today the communication method of choice is more likely an email or text message. The federal courts have, through the new rules of civil procedure, acknowledged the role of electronically stored information and the impact it has on litigation. The state courts are also looking at the issue, and many have implemented their own rules, which are often fashioned after the federal rules.

The legal team must always consider the impact of technology on documents connected with current or pending litigation. But they must also address the impact of technology on documents that could be connected with *potential* litigation. One

Exhibit 4.2 Secure remote access for the legal profession

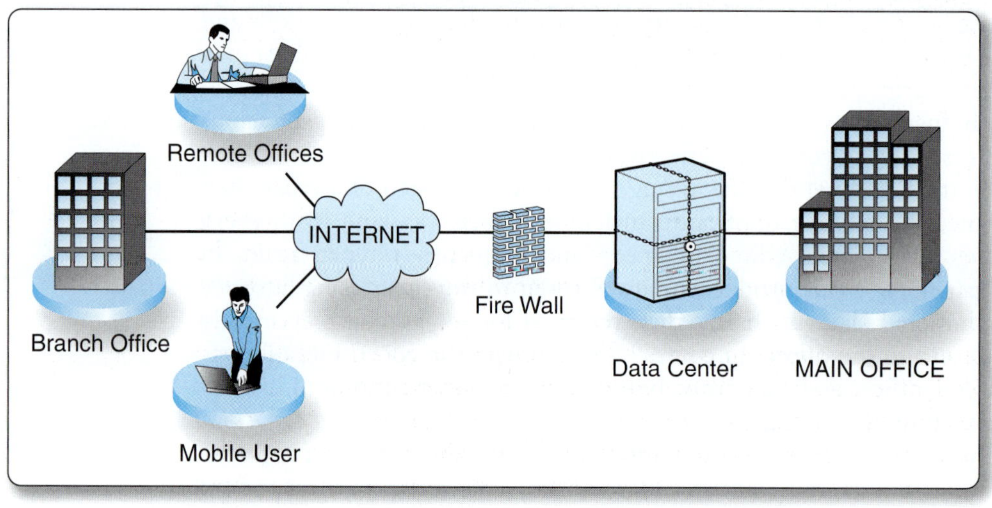

important consideration is document retention. The ability to retain documents is limited mainly by available storage space. The more space available, the greater the number of documents that can be stored, and the longer they can be retained. With electronic files, the ability to retain documents is virtually limitless. It is therefore necessary for a legal team to carefully consider rules and procedures for retaining and storing potentially sensitive documents.

Technology has had a significant impact not only on the ability to retain documents, but also on the ability to find and access them. For a litigator, stored documents can be a source of a potential "smoking gun"—a document on which the case hinges, and which may be introduced into evidence. For example, a document may admit a certain course of conduct, such as removing a safety feature for the sake of saving money. In some classic product liability or antitrust cases, tractor-trailer loads of documents have been produced, and a document may be "hiding" in a maze of possibly thousands of pieces of paper, waiting for other parties to find it. For example, in a well-known product liability case, Ford was alleged to have sold a dangerous product despite knowing that it was defective. The smoking gun was an internal company report stating that the potential monetary damages from lawsuits would be less costly than changing the design. The plaintiff team's serendipitous discovery of this document was like finding a needle in a haystack.

With technology and a big enough budget, all of the paper documents in a case can be scanned electronically in a form that allows an electronic search for the smoking gun. The search can be made easier if the documents are delivered by the opponent in a searchable electronic format pursuant to a proper discovery request.

The potentially massive delivery of documents in electronic form also raises concerns that these electronic documents may contain privileged or confidential information. These documents may need to be delivered to the opposing side in compliance with a discovery request without the opportunity to check each document for privileged or confidential material.

No longer can the legal team ignore the role of technology in law practice, whether the team is a sole practitioner with a legal secretary, or a large international law firm with in-house technical support. Everyone on the team must understand the role of various technologies in counseling and representing clients.

Technology Support in the Law Office

Larger law offices, corporate legal departments, and government offices usually have a technical support staff, frequently called the **"IT,"** or information technology, department. The IT staff handles questions and issues about the use and implementation of technology in general, and computers and software in particular. Smaller offices may have a person who is unofficially responsible for the same type of support. This person is usually the most tech-savvy member of the staff—a lawyer, paralegal, secretary, "friend" of the office, or a relative—who is sometimes referred to affectionately as the office "geek."

Technology Usage In The Law

Learning Objective 3
Explain the use of technology in the law.

The role of technology in the law has evolved in a few years from a minor role, such as that of the stand-alone word processor or copy machine, to a ubiquitous element in the management of law offices of all sizes. Computers are now being used for everything from word processing to accounting functions, such as computerized time keeping, payroll, or tax return preparation. In some offices, telephone systems even use a computerized attendant to answer the phone without human intervention.

The use of technology in litigation was once limited to large law firms working on big cases for wealthy clients who could afford to pay for the technology. Today, even the smallest law firm and litigator must use technology. Some courts and government agencies, such as the Internal Revenue Service, are demanding computerized filing. Records previously available only in paper form, such as medical records, are now provided electronically. The result is that offices of all sizes need to have computer or technology support.

Working with In-House Technology Support Staff

In the past, technology support was limited to assisting with on-site computer systems and software. Because of advances in portable computers and wireless technologies, IT departments must now support the legal team outside the office. Members of the legal team who are working from remote locations on their wireless laptops or devices may need access to files on office file servers or in remote electronic repositories. In addition, services must be provided for technology beyond computers and software. Litigation teams may require support for videotaping depositions at out-of-office or out-of-town locations, and trials may require the use of sophisticated presentation equipment.

The IT department may not have the resources in people, hardware, or software to support every demand. If the IT staff is frequently called in at the last moment, they may not have the time to gear up to support the immediate needs of the legal team. But when the support staff has time to prepare, they can usually provide many types of assistance, whether they are helping with **remote access** issues or graphic-intense litigation needs. The IT staff can offer the best support to the legal team if they are involved early in the process, and if it is clear what the legal team needs to accomplish.

For instance, if a computer simulation is considered for presenting a case at trial, calling in the IT staff at an early stage of the litigation may save time and money. The IT staff may need time to consider whether the courthouse has the necessary equipment to show the simulation, whether specialty equipment must be obtained or used, or whether the graphics must be delivered in a format compatible with the law firm's trial presentation software.

Issues in Working with Outside Technology Consultants

There are many types of technology consultants who can provide services related to computer, software, and multimedia technology. Selecting the correct consultant is a matter of understanding what type of service is needed. Many outside companies are retained on a maintenance contract to provide coverage for a period of time and at a fixed rate. Others are hired as needed at an hourly rate.

Media consultants are also frequently called to assist in a variety of situations where attorneys are presenting information to an audience. Some are called upon to prepare graphic presentations ranging from individual exhibits to multimedia simulations. Others are asked simply to operate equipment or assist in trial presentations.

To obtain the best service from a consultant, the legal team and the consultant must speak the same language in order to reach a common understanding regarding the scope of service and the desired results. Hiring a consultant who uses a system that is incompatible with the system used by the legal team can be a costly mistake, or even a disaster—sometimes not discovered until the day of trial. For example, if the legal team is using PC-based hardware and software and the consultant is using Mac OS (the operating system used by Apple computers), the consultant might produce a version that works only on an Apple computer. Although such a gross oversight might seem unlikely, it has been known to happen.

The ownership of the consultant's work product must also be addressed. Is it "work for hire" that will be owned by the law firm or client, or is it a creative work that is owned by the consultant and may be used in any way he or she wishes?

Outsourcing

Outsourcing Use of persons or services outside of the immediate office staff.

Outsourcing has become a buzzword for sending work out of the office or overseas to save money. Some of the services that can be performed in-house are better outsourced. For years, it has been a common practice for law firms to outsource the payroll function instead of preparing payroll checks and tax returns in-house. The confidentiality of information about salaries may dictate that an outside firm handles the payroll process so that only a few people in the office have access to this information. Other accounting functions may also be outsourced to an outside bookkeeping or accounting firm.

IT support is another service that may be outsourced. For example, using an outside computer consultant to provide support for hardware and software is a form of outsourcing. Such support may simply involve a help desk in a foreign location to answer questions.

Computer Hardware

Learning Objective 4
Explain the functions of the components of a computer system in a law office.

Computer hardware is the tangible or physical parts of a computer system. Every **computer system** includes at least one input device, a computer processor, and at least one output device. A system may be as small and portable as a digital watch or as large as a **mainframe** computer requiring a large room to house it.

Older models of computers, many of which are still found in many law offices, are large, ugly metal boxes connected to large, bulky, and heavy video monitors, sometimes taking up half of a desktop. Newer models are smaller and less obtrusive. In some offices, the computer system consists of a portable laptop computer, weighing as little as three to four pounds, with a docking station to connect it to a flat-screen monitor, an external keyboard and mouse, an Internet connection, and the office network.

Computers have not only become smaller, but they have also increased in speed and functionality. On older models, opening more than one document would use most of the computer system's resources, slowing it down, or even "freezing" or stopping the processing of data. Newer models will run well even while multiple documents are open or multiple applications are running at the same time, such as Word documents, Excel spreadsheets, calendaring programs, and timekeeping applications. Exhibit 4.3 shows a monitor displaying four programs that are running at the same time.

The ability to perform multiple functions simultaneously is in part the result of the increase in processing speed of newer **central processing units (CPUs),** and the availability of inexpensive dynamic or volatile computer memory, called **random access memory (RAM).** A CPU is the computer "chip" that interprets computer instructions and processes data, and RAM is the temporary computer memory that stores work in progress.

Hardware of all sizes requires software instructions to run and perform desired functions. Software is basically the instructions that tell the system how to perform each function. **Operating system** software provides the basic instructions for starting up the computer and processing the basic input and output activity. The processing of data requires additional applications software, such as that used for word processing and financial data processing.

Just as an automobile depends on fuel to operate, so the computer is dependent on a power source. All computer components must have a power source, such as an electrical outlet or battery, to operate the CPU, RAM, and output devices, such as the computer monitor and printer. After the power is turned off, computers cannot remember data or information that was on the screen unless it was saved to a permanent memory device. Power is also required to write the information on devices such as hard disk drives, USB memory devices, removable memory (SD) cards, CDs, or DVDs. These permanent memory devices do not require power to retain data—they only write or read the data to or from a computer.

Uninterruptible power supply (UPS) battery backup systems are frequently used to guard against loss of "work-in-process" when there is a temporary power loss or outage. A UPS is a battery system that can supply power to a computer or computer peripheral for a short period of time. The length of time the computer will continue to work after loss of its permanent power supply depends on the

Computer hardware A term encompassing all of the tangible or physical items of a computer system, including computers, monitors, printers, fax machines, duplicators, and similar items that usually have either an electrical connection or use batteries as a power source.

Computer system A combination of an input device, a processor, and an output device.

Mainframe A large computer system used primarily for bulk processing of data and financial information.

Central processing unit (CPU) The computer chip and memory module that perform the basic computer functions.

Random access memory (RAM) Temporary computer memory that stores work-in-process.

Operating system A basic set of instructions to the computer on how to handle basic functions, such as how to process input from "input devices" like the keyboard and mouse, the order in which to process information, and what to show on the computer monitor.

Uninterruptable power supply (UPS) A battery system that can supply power to a computer or computer peripheral for a short period of time.

Exhibit 4.3 4-page display in Microsoft Office suite

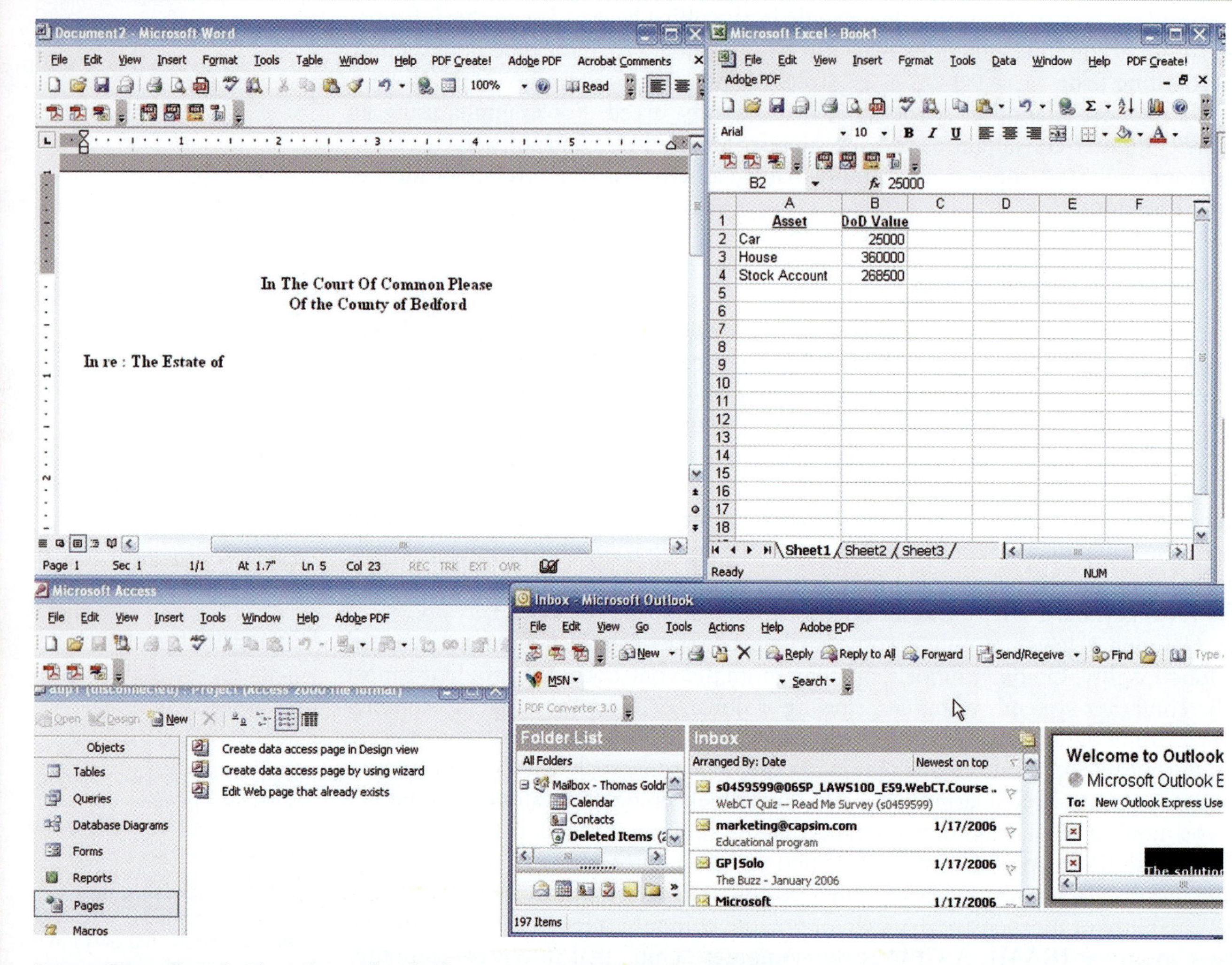

Source: *Microsoft product box shot reprinted with permission from Microsoft Corporation.*

size of the battery in the UPS, which may be as short as a few minutes or as long as an hour or more. The UPS is only designed to allow time to save the current work-in-process files and shut down the computer normally in the event of a major power outage.

Learning Objective 5

Describe the types of software used in a law office and the functions they perform.

Operating Systems

The two most popular computer systems are the PC ("personal computer") and the Apple. The original designs of these two systems were built around different central processor chips manufactured by different companies—Intel in the case of the PC, and Motorola for Apple. Each computer system requires its own unique operating system.

Although both computer systems have their advocates, the PC has a dominant position in the legal and business communities, where computers are mainly used for writing text and performing mathematical computations. The Apple system achieved a dominant position in the graphic and artistic communities.

Software Programs containing sets of instructions that tell the computer and the other computer-based electronic devices what to do and how to do it.

In 2006, Apple started to utilize the same CPU manufacturer as the PC manufacturers, allowing the new Apple computers to use software for both systems on its computers. Microsoft Windows™ is the most commonly used computer operating system for the personal computer. The latest versions, such as Windows XP, Vista, and Windows 8, are designed to take advantage of increased computer operating

Exhibit 4.4 Microsoft Word Track Changes

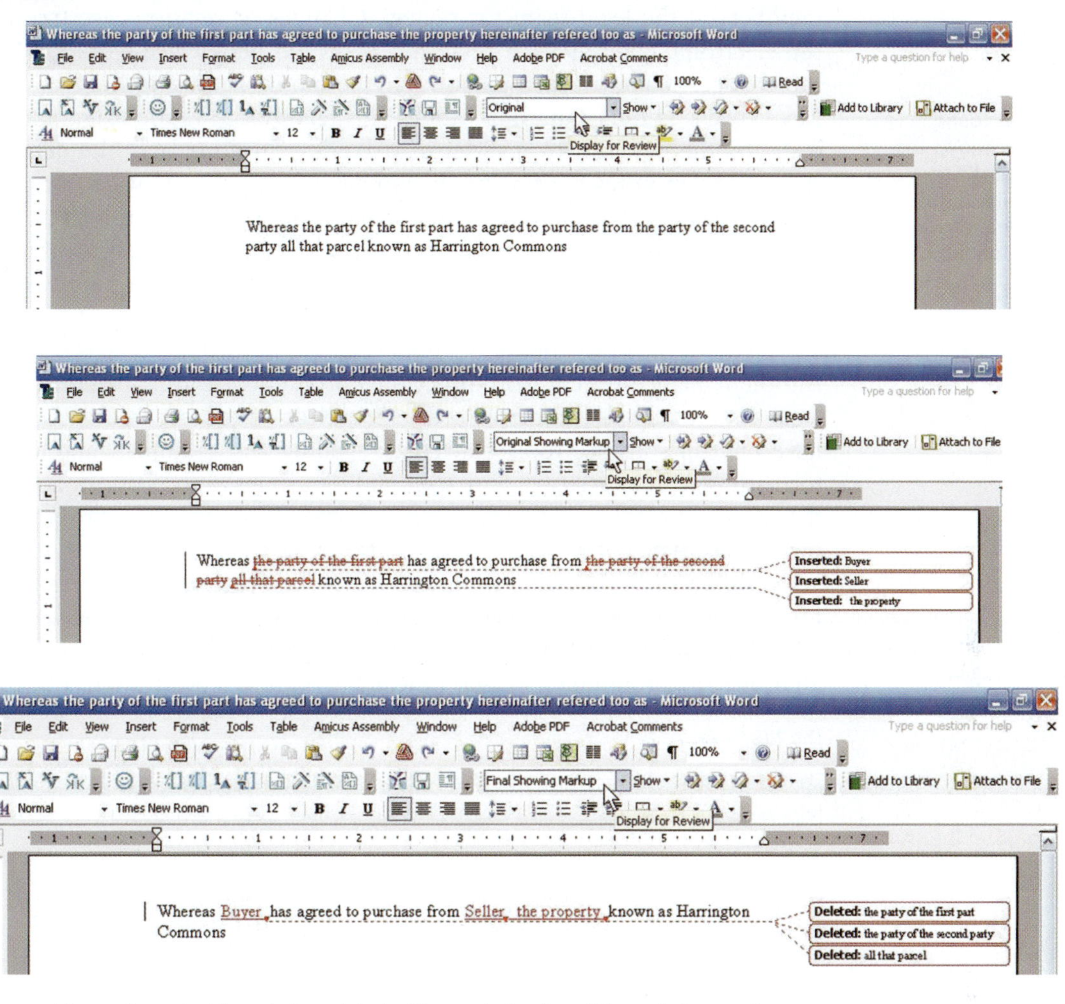

Source: *Microsoft product box shot reprinted with permission from Microsoft Corporation.*

speeds and better graphics. However, different versions of the Windows operating system may be found in the workplace.

Among the newer operating systems gaining followers is the Linux operating system. It is offered as an alternative to Microsoft operating systems and is provided without a license or royalty fee, but with the agreement that any improvements will be made available without a fee to anyone using the system.

Applications Software

Applications software programs perform specific tasks, such as preparing documents, sorting information, performing computations, and creating and presenting graphic displays. These are the programs used in the management of the law office and the management of client cases.

Applications software
Programs that perform specific tasks such as word processing.

Word Processing

Written communication and document preparation are at the heart of every law office. This writing may include letters to clients, other counsel, or the court, as well as contracts and pleadings. Achieving clarity and accuracy in writing frequently means writing, rewriting, and correcting the same document, sometimes multiple times by different members of the legal team. Computerized word processing makes it possible for other team members to easily make or suggest changes to a document before it reaches its final form. Word processing files are sent electronically to the appropriate members of the legal team for review. Changes or revisions are frequently made to the electronic copy by each reviewer. If several people are working on a document, the changes made by each person may be monitored using built-in features such as MS Word's "**Track Changes**" tool. This feature shows the original text, the deleted text, and the new text by a series of strikethrough lines over the deleted text. It also shows margin notes within the document. Exhibit 4.4 shows an original Word file, the changes inserted, old text with a strikethrough line, and the final version with the changes still showing in the margin of the document. When the final document is completed, it may be sent by email, fax (directly from the computer without printing), and in many jurisdictions, filed electronically with the court.

Track Changes As found in MS Word, a feature that shows the original text, the deleted text, and the new text, as well as a strike-through line for deleted text, the underlining or highlighting of new text, as well as margin notes in the document.

Today, the most commonly used program in the law office is the word processor. Although many different word processing programs are available, most members of the legal community use either WordPerfect™ or Microsoft Word™. These programs have built-in software tools that check spelling and grammar, and allow customized formatting with a variety of type sizes and font styles in the same document—functions that were not possible with a typewriter. Some offices use other programs, each with its own file format.

Most word processing programs allow the opening and saving of files in the file formats of other word processing programs. When a file is saved, a **file extension** (a period followed by a series of characters) is added to the end of the file name that identifies the program or format in which the file has been saved. For example:

File extension A period followed by three characters, added to the end of the file name, to identify the program or format in which the file has been saved.

the file type:	**the extension:**
Microsoft Word 2003	filename.doc
Microsoft Word 2010	filename.docx
WordPerfect	filename.wpd
Microsoft Works	filename.wps
Web documents	filename.htm
Rich text file word processing format	filename.rtf
Text file word processing format	filename.txt

WordPerfect has many other features that increase productivity. The newer versions have a feature that simulates the Microsoft Word workspace. Files are saved with the document properties, such as type font and type size, and document formatting details. The saved files also include instructions to the computer on how to display the document, security features, and hidden information, such as the "Track Changes" information. WordPerfect also has built-in viewers that allow it to open and read almost every Word document format used over the past 30 years, and permitting them to be saved in different formats.

ETHICAL PERSPECTIVE

Document Comparison Software

The history of changes and other information about a document is called *metadata*. When using Track Changes or similar comparison features, be sure to remove the metadata before sending it to the opposing counsel, the client, or the court.

The history of the changes made to a document may offer the reader insight into the strategy of the case. For example, the final price the client is willing to pay may have appeared in the original draft and not the offer letter that was sent to the opposing party. Word Help offers instructions on how to remove this information. WordPerfect has the option, "Save without Metadata," making it easy to quickly remove private or sensitive data from within office documents.

Spreadsheet Programs

Many areas of legal practice require the calculation and presentation of financial information. For example, in a family law practice, family and personal balance sheets and income and expense reports are routinely prepared for support and equitable distribution hearings. Estate lawyers must submit an "accounting" to the court for approval, showing details of how the fiduciary handled the financial affairs of the estate or trust. Litigation firms must at some point prepare documentation showing the receipts and disbursements for cases, for court approval.

As shown in Exhibit 4.5, a calculation involved in the handling of an estate may be as simple as multiplying the number of shares owned by a decedent by the value on the date of death ("D of D"), and then calculating the profit or loss when the stock was sold. Without a **spreadsheet program,** all of the calculations would have to be done manually, using a multicolumn form known as "a spreadsheet or accountant's working papers." The information would then have to be typed in a report for submission to the court, the beneficiaries, or the taxing authorities.

Spreadsheet programs Programs that permit the calculation and presentation of financial information in a grid format of rows and columns.

Using a computerized spreadsheet, such as Microsoft Excel or Corel Quattro Pro, the numbers are entered in cells, as shown in Exhibit 4.5. A formula is assigned to the cell in which the result is to be displayed. For example, a formula might direct the application to "multiply column c by column d," and then display the result in column e. The computerized spreadsheet may be laid out in the format acceptable to the court, and then printed without reentering the data, or copied into Word documents using simple "Cut" and "Paste" operations.

The use of computer spreadsheets reduces the errors that would result from manual calculations or retyping information. However, care must be taken to make sure that the formula is accurate and performs the desired calculation. Even expert spreadsheet users will enter a set of sample numbers to test the formulas they have entered.

Many offices use spreadsheet templates much like forms are used in word processing. For example, a real estate settlement spreadsheet with formulas and headings may be saved without any data. Because the formulas do not change and the form has proven accurate, it may be used as a template for other clients' real estate settlements.

Database Programs

A **database program** is a repository of information that can be sorted and presented in a meaningful manner. Before electronic databases became available, law offices used a manual card system to keep track of the names of clients and opposing parties. These cards would be searched to determine any possible conflicts of interest in representing new clients. For a small office, this system may work. But for the larger

Database program An electronic repository of information of all types that can be sorted and presented in a meaningful manner.

Exhibit 4.5 Excel spreadsheet

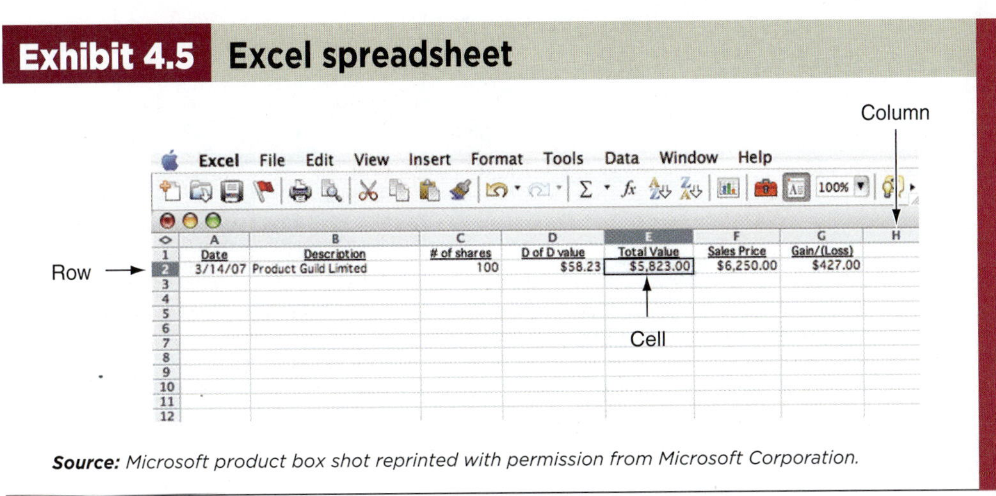

Source: *Microsoft product box shot reprinted with permission from Microsoft Corporation.*

office with many attorneys, using a card system for entering and searching large amounts of information is not realistic.

Computerized database software, such as Microsoft Access and Corel DB, will allow timely, accurate access to information by every authorized member of the legal team. For example, information may be stored in a database that includes the names, contact information, and personal data, such as birthdates, of every client, opposing party, witness, or opposing counsel that any member of the firm has ever had contact with. With a few keystrokes, a list can be prepared for checking for conflicts of interest, or a computer search can be performed for any matter in which a particular name appears.

An electronic database may also be used in maintaining client relations. Many firms use client information to send birthday and anniversary greetings or to provide updates on specific changes in the law for which the client has consulted the firm previously.

Presentation Graphics Programs

It has been said that a picture is worth a thousand words. Presentation graphics software, such as WordPerfect Presentation (see Exhibit 4.6) and Microsoft PowerPoint, are often used by attorneys to create high-quality slide shows and drawings. These graphic presentations can include text, data charts, and images.

One of the advantages of these programs is their flexibility. They can be used to prepare and display the presentation using a computer, with or without a projector, and to print out paper copies for distribution. Presentation programs typically provide stock templates of graphics, artwork, and layout as a sample that the user can easily modify. More advanced users can add sound clips, still photos, video clips, and custom graphics from other programs.

Office software suites Software consisting of commonly used office programs that manage data, manipulate financial or numeric information, or display images and presentations.

Office Software Suites

Office software suites are sets of commonly used office programs. They manage data, manipulate financial or numeric information, or display images and graphics

Exhibit 4.6 WordPerfect Presentation X4

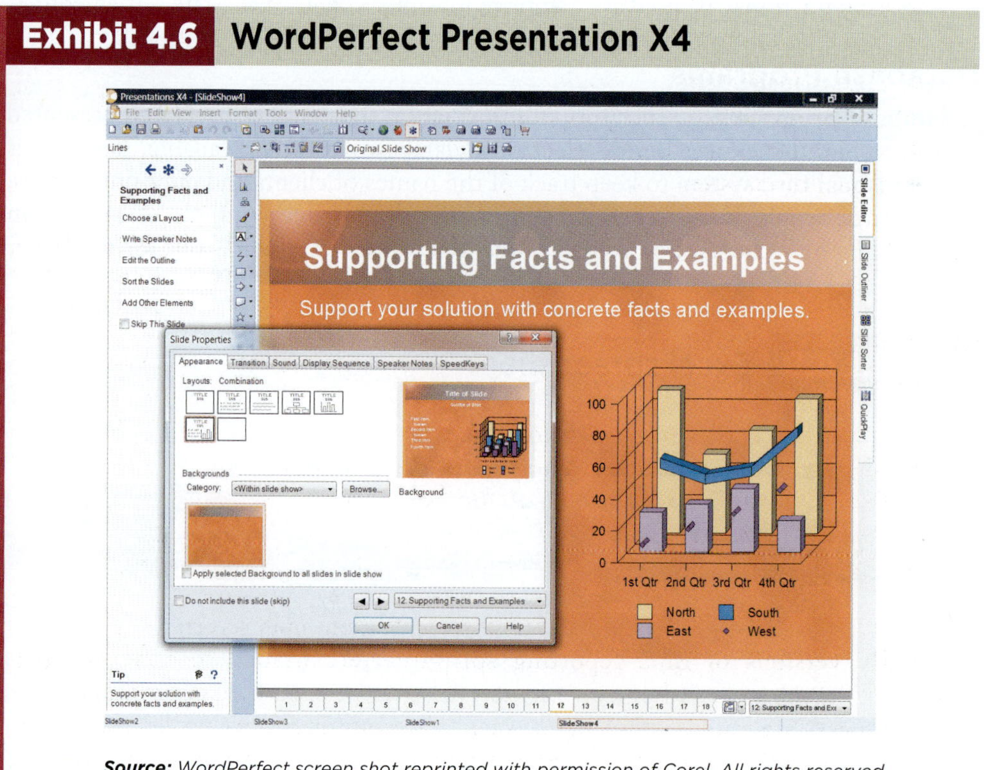

Source: WordPerfect screen shot reprinted with permission of Corel. All rights reserved.

presentations. Some of the tools in the two most common program suites, Microsoft Office and Corel WordPerfect, are shown below.

	Microsoft Office	Corel WordPerfect Office
Word processor	Word	WordPerfect
Spreadsheet	Excel	Quattro Pro
Database	Access	Paradox
Presentation graphics	PowerPoint	Presentation
Graphics	Visio	Presentation Graphics

Software suites are usually delivered on one CD, enabling all the programs to be loaded at one time, which simplifies and saves installation time. With common features and appearance, it is easier to switch between programs and copy information between the programs. For example, part of a spreadsheet may be copied into a word processing document.

Specialty Application Programs

Learning Objective 6

Describe the types of specialty applications software used in a law office.

Every year, computers become faster and more powerful, with more storage memory. Software is also becoming more powerful and capable of performing more complex functions with larger amounts of data. Whereas older models of computers could perform only basic word processing and data management tasks, newer, more powerful computers can perform complex functions seamlessly, thereby improving the management of cases and other law office functions.

Specialty application programs combine many of the basic functions found in software suites, word processing, database, spreadsheet, and graphic presentation programs, and are tailored for law office case and litigation management. They simplify the management of a law office with the use of customized input screens and preset report generators.

Specialty application programs Programs that combine many of the basic functions found in software suites, such as word processing, database management, spreadsheets, and graphic presentations, to perform law office, case, and litigation management.

Most legal specialty software falls into the following categories:

- Office management
- Case management
- Litigation support
- Transcript management
- Trial presentation

The most basic legal specialty programs are the time and billing applications. These programs provide a standard input screen to record and store the time spent on a client's case. Upon request, the program can automatically sort the data, apply the billing rates, and print out an invoice.

Among the most popular programs in this group are:

- Tabs3 from Software Technology, Inc.
- AbacusLaw from Abacus Data Systems Inc.
- ProLaw from Thomson Elite
- PCLaw from LexisNexis
- Timeslips from Sage

Web Exploration

For a self-running video demo of Tabs3, go to http://www.tabs3.com/products/videos.html.

Web Exploration

Information on the features of AbacusLaw may be found at http://www.abacuslaw.com.

Exhibit 4.7 is an example of a time and billing application input screen.

Early versions of time reporting software were limited to time keeping. With faster computers and greater memory capacity, most of these programs have other features integrated within them, such as accounting functions to track costs and expenses, and practice management functions such as calendar and contact management.

Web Exploration

Details and additional sample screen graphics about PCLaw are available at http://www.pclaw.com/.

Exhibit 4.7 **Tabs3 time and billing screens**

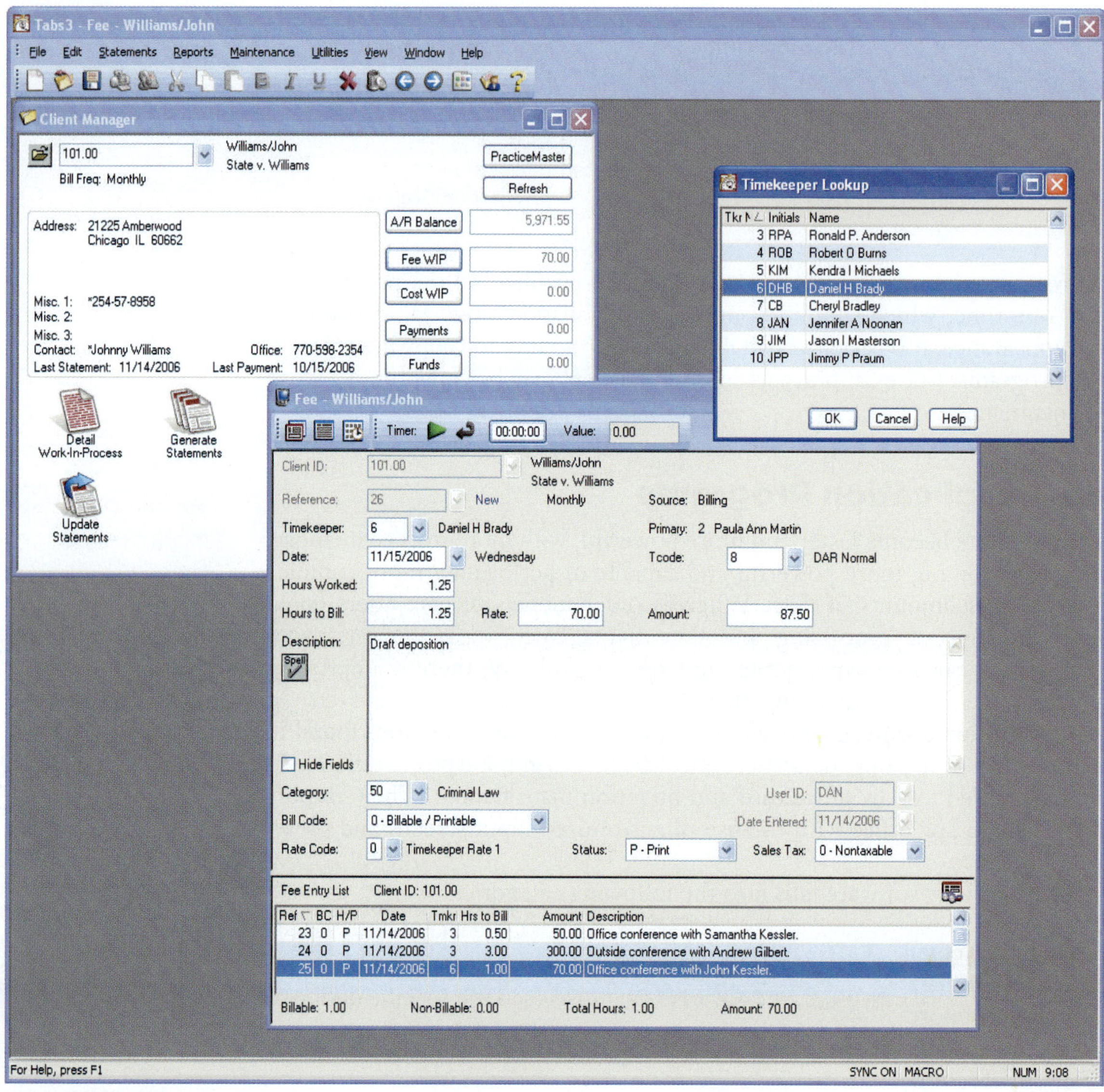

Source: Reprinted with permission from Tabs3/Practice Master.

Exhibit 4.8 shows the multiple functions integrated in AbacusLaw Accounting.

Case and Litigation Management Software

Paper has long been the bane of the litigation attorney. Even simple cases can involve hundreds of pages of documents. Complex litigation may involve millions of documents, hundreds of witnesses, and, in class-action litigation, potentially millions of clients. Keeping track of all of the documentation and parties is an overwhelming task, even with a large staff of assistants to handle the rows of file cabinets and file boxes.

Before the availability of fast computers and litigation management software, most case management work was done manually, usually by a team of paralegals and junior associate attorneys. One of the most notable product liability cases—the Ford Pinto negligence suit—provides a historic example of such an effort. The Pinto automobile was alleged to have a defective design that would cause a deadly fire that engulfed the Pinto when it was struck by another car. Teams of law students were hired to read through thousands of documents, manually index them, and look for a

Exhibit 4.8 **Abacus Accounting input screens**

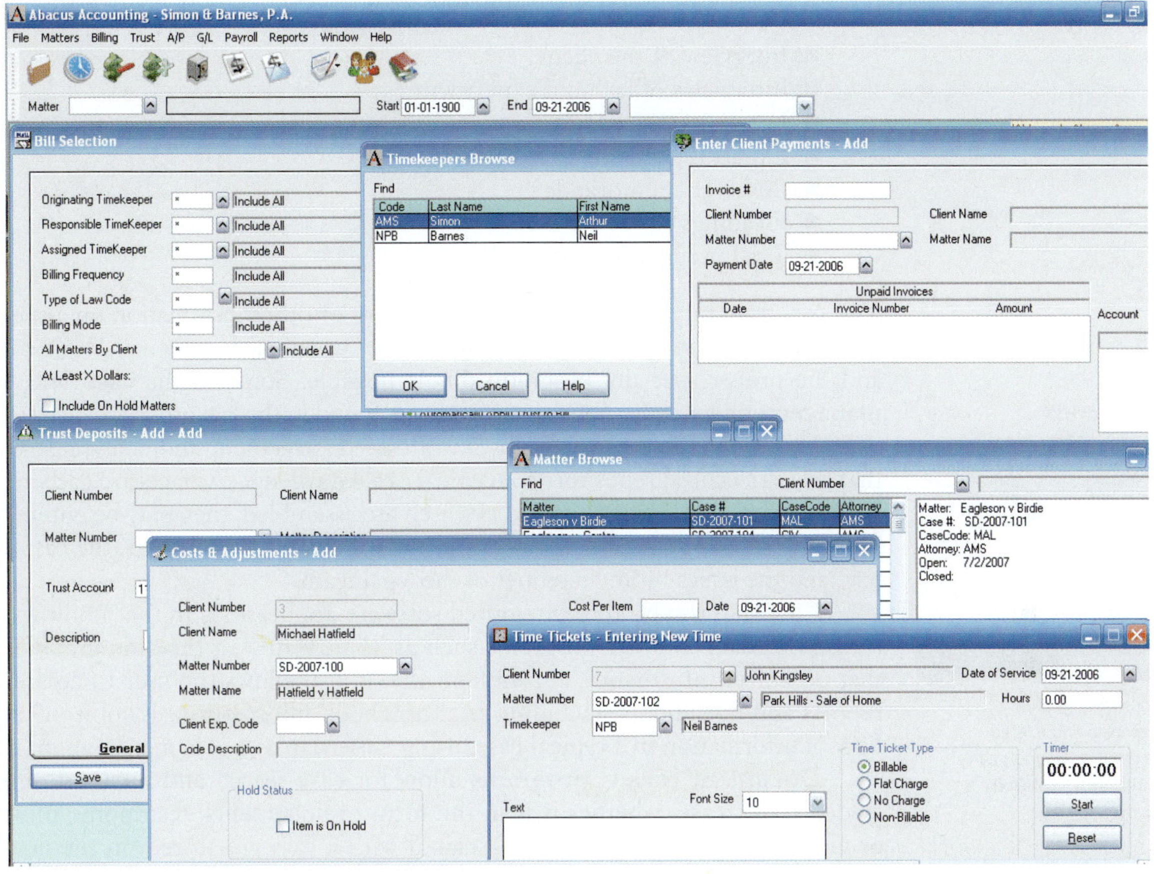

Source: *Reprinted with permission from Abacus Data Systems.*

document that would win the case. In a serendipitous discovery, this "smoking gun" document was found. It was an internal document that discussed the specific design at issue and detailed the engineering cost savings and the inherent risk by eliminating a specific part that led to the fire that engulfed the Pinto when it was struck by another car from the rear.

The use of computers by business and government for email and document storage has caused a massive increase in the number of potential documents that may have to be reviewed, tracked, and made available to opposing counsel in litigation. Managing cases with massive amounts of data has become increasingly difficult. As the number of documents has increased and cases have become more complex, the number of members of the legal team working on a given case also has increased. These factors have led to a greater need for computers to manage the documents.

Before computers, attorneys often concentrated on one case at a time with little backup or support, personally working on all of the details, documentation, pleadings, and discovery in anticipation of trial. The "team approach" to case management and litigation has allowed, in some ways, for specialization among the members of the team. Some members may specialize in discovery of documents. Others may focus on locating, interviewing, and preparing witnesses, or on investigations and legal research. All of these team members may need to share information, or access case information simultaneously.

Effective case management requires a central repository of the information gathered by all of the team members, as well as the ability for each member to access the case information stored by the others. Computer systems today permit members of the legal team to access the same information from remote locations across town, across the country, and sometimes around the world.

A typical case file contains the following documentation:

- Interview of the client
- Interviews of fact and expert witnesses
- Investigation reports
- Expert reports
- Research memoranda
- Pleadings
- Trial preparation material

The trial team must be able to find a document or other information on a specific issue quickly, from among potentially thousands of pages of documents. With a computer and the proper specialty program, this is possible. Some of the **case and litigation management specialty software programs** found in the law office are discussed below.

Case and litigation management software Case and litigation management programs are used to manage documents and the facts and issues of cases.

CaseMap™ from LexisNexis® is a case management and analysis software tool that acts as a central repository for critical case knowledge. As facts are gathered, parties are identified, and documents and research are assembled, they may be entered into the program, allowing for easy organization and exploration of the facts, the cast of characters, and the issues by any member of the legal team.

CaseMap is typical of integrated software applications in that it allows seamless transfer of data to other programs such as TimeMap™, a timeline graphic program that organizes information chronologically. It also allows the user to create specialty reports and documents, including trial notebook information. Exhibit 4.9 shows the flow of information in a typical case, using CaseMap as a case management tool.

Web Exploration

Demonstration versions of LexisNexis CaseMap and related products and webinar tutorials can be found at **http://www.casesoft.com/student.asp**.

Document review programs allow for easy search and retrieval of all of the evidence in a case, whether it is in the form of documents, testimony, photographs, or electronic files. Documents associated with a case are stored on the computer in electronic folders. These folders may be set up to store transcripts, pleadings, text files (from OCR or otherwise), casts of characters, and core databases. Some versions of these programs are designed to work on stand-alone systems such as a laptop carried into court. Others permit concurrent use by many users over a network, and some permit remote access over the Internet.

Concordance

LexisNexis Concordance is a litigation support program designed for document management. Early versions of Concordance were limited to storing and handling only four gigabytes of data, or approximately 280,000 documents. The newer version allows the management of 128 times that amount, or more than 35 million documents.

Web Exploration

Learn more about Concordance at **http://law.lexisnexis.com/concordance**

Like other document support tools, Concordance has a powerful search engine that allows searches by word, phrase, date, email address, or document type, as well as Boolean, "fuzzy," or "wild card" searches. A Boolean search uses connectors between words, such as AND, OR, or NOT, to narrow the search. A "fuzzy" or "fuzzy string" search looks for strings of letters or characters that approximately match some given pattern. A "wild card" search allows the use of a "wild" character, such as the "*" symbol, to replace a certain letter in the search word. This allows you to search for plurals or variations of words using the wild card character. For example: *Book** will find strings that have the words *Booking* and *Books*. It is also a good way to search if you do not know the spelling of a word.

Web Exploration

An interactive demo of TrialDirector, showing how trial presentation software can be used in litigation, can be viewed at **http://support.indatacorp.com/tutorials/tutorials.aspx**.

Sanction and TrialDirector

These multifaceted trial presentation programs offer a comprehensive approach to presenting all types of exhibits in the courtroom, including documents, photographs, graphic images, video presentations, and recorded depositions.

Exhibit 4.9 Managing case information using CaseMap case management and analysis software

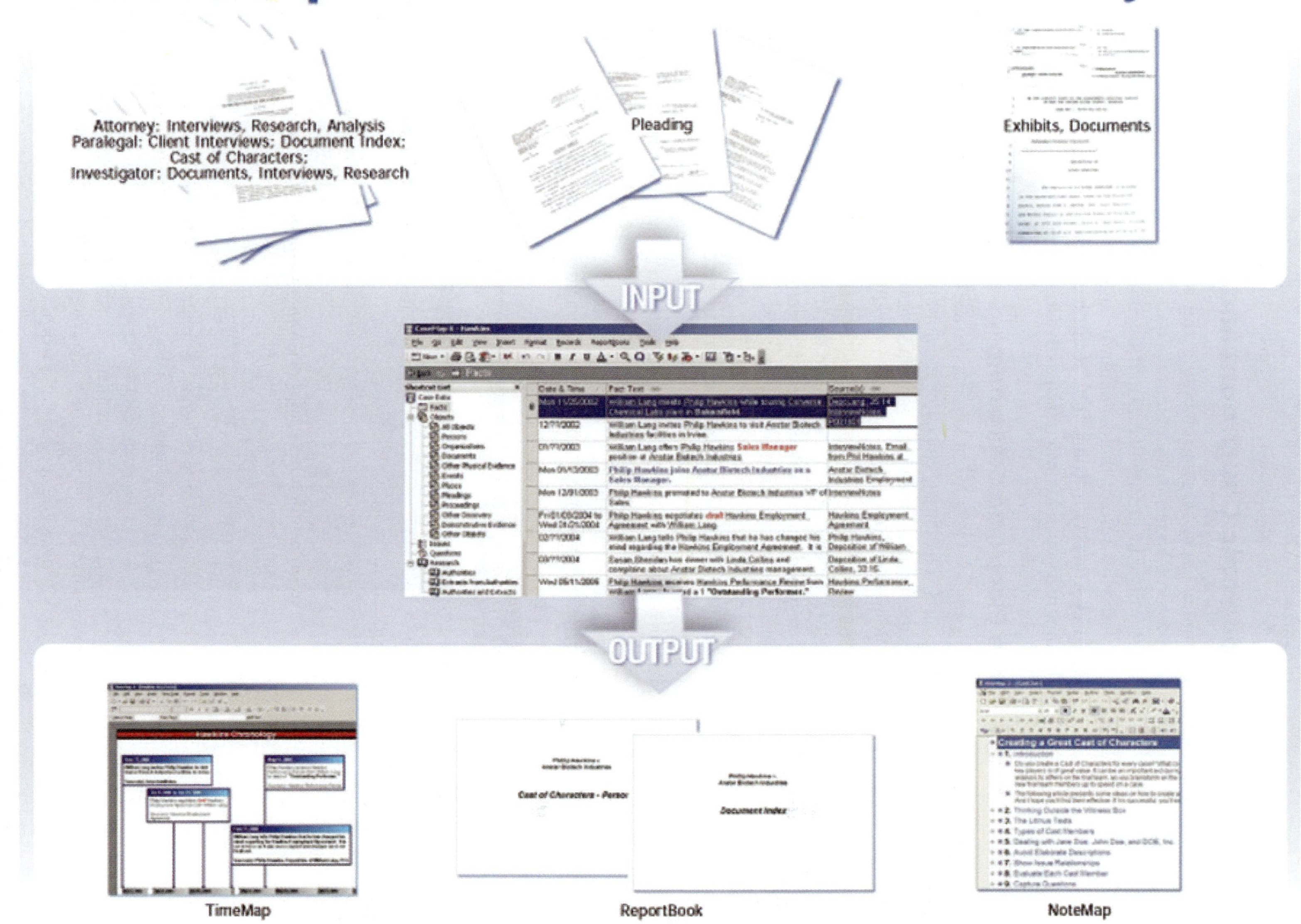

Unlike PowerPoint, which requires the creation of individual slides, these programs allow existing documents and files to be presented without any more effort than copying them into the program data file and making a selection for presentation. Trial presentation programs like Sanction are also databases of the documents organized in a case file.

Learning Objective 7
Describe the features of the electronic courtroom and the paperless office.

Electronic Courtroom and Paperless Office

Computer technology is changing the way law offices and court systems operate. The ease of creating documents such as letters, contracts, and emails has resulted in an explosion in the quantity of documents. At the same time, cases are going to trial faster because of the demand for "quicker justice," allowing less time to prepare and present a case in court. The result has been rapid growth in the use of electronic documentation and computerized case management.

The Electronic Courtroom

Increasingly, judges are embracing the use of electronics and computer-based systems in the courts. The initial reluctance to adopt new technology is giving way to acceptance of tools that enhance the speedy administration of justice.

One of the earliest uses of technology in the courtroom was the playing of videotaped depositions of expert witnesses on TV monitors in court. Getting experts to testify in person is difficult when the trial schedule is uncertain. Many professionals, such as noted surgeons and medical forensics experts, have active, lucrative practices, and demand compensation for time lost while waiting to testify. This compensation can range in the thousands of dollars per hour, and the average litigant can rarely afford this cost. A videotape or electronic recording of a deposition can be used during trial as a cost-effective method of presenting expert witnesses, or witnesses who for reasons of health or distance would not otherwise be available to testify personally.

Courtrooms are now being outfitted with computers and audiovisual presentation systems, as judicial budgets allow. Exhibit 4.10 shows the U.S. Tax Court's electronic courtroom in Virginia. Computerized courtrooms are often seen in televised trials, with

Exhibit 4.10 U.S. Tax Court's electronic courtroom

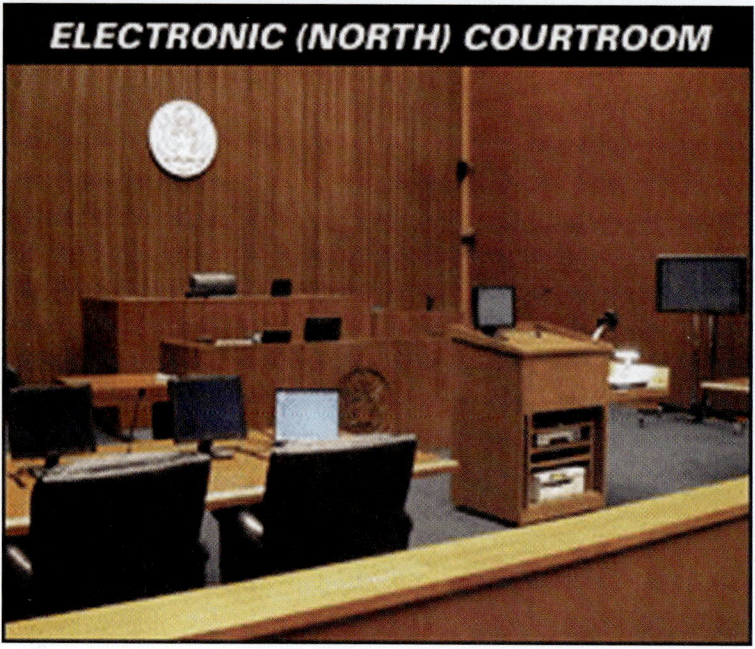

computer monitors at the counsel tables, the judge's bench, the jury, and for each of the court support personnel.

Litigation support software is used in trial to display documentary evidence, graphic presentations, and simulations of accident cases. As a witness identifies documents during testimony, relevant portions of the documents can be displayed for everyone to see at the same time, without having to pass paper copies to everyone. Lawyers can rapidly search depositions and documents on their laptop computers to find pertinent material for examination or cross-examination of the witness.

The electronic courtroom is also used in many jurisdictions for preliminary matters in criminal cases in which the judge is at a central location and the defendants are located at various lock-up facilities. Video cameras and monitors are used so that the parties can see each other during the proceeding.

The Paperless Office

To some, the ideal office has no paper documents, or "hard copies." An office where all documents are created and stored electronically is sometimes referred to as the "**paperless office,**" or "electronic office." Although it is difficult to imagine for those who have grown up in the world of paper documents, the paperless office is rapidly becoming reality.

Paperless office The paperless office is one in which most documents are created and stored electronically.

In the traditional office, documents that are created electronically with word processing software, or received by fax or email, are then printed for distribution and review. In the paperless office, documents created with word processor programs are sent electronically to the attorney for review. Paper documents are converted into electronic files using scanners and related software. One of the advantages of the paperless office is portability. This requires inexpensive portable computer memory, a computer to store and transport the documents, and small, lightweight computers to display them.

With the help of modern scanning technology, secure methods for transmitting documents, protocols for the use of electronic documents, and rules of court permitting electronic submissions, the paperless law office is now becoming the norm.

Portable Document Format (PDF)

One of the basic requirements of a system of electronic documentation is the ability to save documents in a format that cannot be easily changed. Anyone who has received a word processing document knows that it may be changed, saved, and presented as an original. The graphic image format (gif) and portable document format (PDF) are formats that the recipient cannot easily change.

Web Exploration

Acrobat tutorials "Introduction to PDFs," "Acrobat 101," and "Acrobat 201" may be found at **www.casesoft.com/student.asp**.

Anyone can view PDF documents by downloading a free PDF reader from Nuance or Adobe. However, creating documents in PDF format requires specialty software such as Adobe Acrobat or Nuance PDF Creator. As this format has become more widely accepted, attorneys have become more willing to scan and store documents in the PDF format, eliminating the need to return the original paper copies to the client.

Web Exploration

Samples of PDF files can be downloaded from the Internal Revenue Service at **www.irs.gov**.

The PDF/A format is a variation of the PDF format, which is now required by the federal courts for electronic filing, and by many state courts and government agencies. The Library of Commerce created this open universal standard for electronic documents that contains archival features allowing use into the future without additional softweare.

Scanning

The hardware originally used for scanning (converting paper documents to electronic form) was costly and frequently unreliable. Today, scanning has become a common feature in office printers and copy machines. Modern scanners provide double-sided (front and back) scanning of documents with a high degree of accuracy and at a relatively low cost. Double-sided scanning is found today in multifunction devices featuring printing, scanning, copying, and faxing, at prices under $100. These devices, when coupled with application software, allow virtually anyone to create electronic documents.

Scanning and storing of paper documents has become easier with the development of software such as PaperPort by Nuance. This software provides easy-to-use, high-speed scanning and document capture. As a document management application, it allows for organizing, finding, and sharing of both paper and digital documents.

OCR

Sometimes, documents have to be converted from a graphic image to a format that allows for editing in a word processor or other office suite of applications. The software used for this conversion has come to be referred to as optical character recognition (OCR). Products such as OmniPage, by Nuance, permit any scanned page, PDF file, or other image or document file to be converted quickly and accurately into one of a number of different editable formats, including Microsoft Word or Corel WordPerfect.

Learning Objective 8

Explain the features and functions of a computer network in a law office.

Networks

In the contemporary law office, a **workstation** generally consists of a single personal computer, a monitor, and a printer. A **computer network** is a group of workstations connected together. A network may be as little as two workstations. In large law firms, a network may link hundreds of workstations and other devices such as shared printers and fax machines, all connected through a network file server. Exhibit 4.11 is a typical computer network in a law office.

A **network file server** is a separate computer that acts as the "traffic cop" for the system, controlling the flow of information between workstations, the file server, and other peripheral devices. It also handles requests to use the resources of the system, or to access data stored there. The server requires network operating software that tells it how to communicate with the connected workstations and peripheral devices. These computers and devices are referred to as "connections."

Workstation A computer connected to a network that is used for access consisting of a monitor, input device, and a computer.

Computer network A set of workstations connected together.

Network file server A separate computer in a network that acts as the "traffic cop" of the system, controlling the flow of data.

Network Rights and Privileges

Network software has security protocols that limit access to the file server, peripheral devices such as printers, or other workstations. These rights to access the server and the other devices are sometimes called "**network rights and privileges.**" The rights or privileges determine who has access to the server, the data stored on the server, and the flow of information between connections.

Network rights and privileges Rights or privileges determine who has access to the server, the data stored on the server, and the flow of information between connections.

Exhibit 4.11 Typical network system

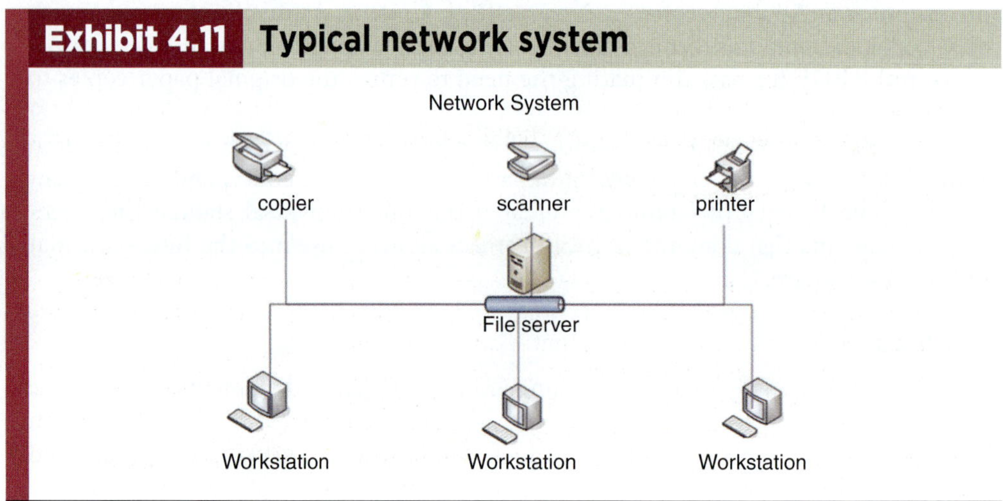

Network Administrator

Law offices that use network servers generally use them as the central repository for all electronic files. Although an individual workstation can store documents or data, it is usually stored centrally as well. Maintaining files in a central location offers a level of protection by limiting access to those who have the proper authorization, most often requiring a password for access. The person with the highest level of access to the network server is called the **network administrator.**

Network administrator The network administrator usually is the person with the highest level of access to the network file server.

Limiting access to files on a file server is one method to ensure confidentiality in a large office. File access can be limited by assigning passwords to files and granting password access only to those with a need to view and work on those specific files. Because each file or folder can be password-protected separately, ethical walls can be established by restricting access to only those who are working on a case.

Backing Up Data

The regular **backup of data** is an essential function to prevent loss of critical files and office data in the event of a disaster such as a flood, fire, earthquake, or tornado. When files are stored only on a workstation, they are backed up only if the workstation user remembers to do so. With everything on one central file server, backups can be automated to make copies of everyone's files regularly.

Backup of data Making a copy of critical files and programs in case of a loss of the original files.

It is a good policy to back up the file server daily and store the duplicate copy in a safe location away from the server location, such as a fireproof safe or a bank safe

Advice *from the* Field

TECHNOLOGY IS A TOOL, NOT A CASE STRATEGY IN THE COURTROOM

Michael E. Cobo

The latest legal technology products such as animations and courtroom presentation systems can be very alluring to lawyers. After learning about these products, you may be anxious to use them. But you should keep in mind that technology products are only tools to implement a solution and are not solutions in themselves. The key issue is: What is your case strategy and what do you need to present?

An expensive, ill-planned use of technology may result in losses at trial. These losses, or even an uncomfortable implementation of a technology product, may ultimately cause some to feel the experiment was unsuccessful and abandon future use of courtroom technology.

On the other hand, such potentially devastating results can be avoided by carefully planning a case strategy with the same care as you would plan a general trial strategy. The pitfalls will be avoided and you will present a more effective case to the trier of fact.

The trial team must remember that it is the message, not the medium, that wins at trial. Take this opportunity to vary the presentation media and develop some exhibit boards or utilize an overhead. Certain exhibits are displayed best as foamcore boards. Timelines or chronologies generally lend themselves to a board, as do other exhibits that need to be larger and hold more visual or textual information. Strategically, some exhibits need to be used in conjunction with others or need to be in the view of the jury more often than not.

ASSESS YOURSELF

Before you spend a dime to develop the visual strategy, create a presentation or invest in any technology, make a critical self-assessment. Will you be comfortable with the strategy and the technological tools that will be developed for the trial? The most effective visual communication strategy will never be effective if it is never implemented or is delivered without conviction because you are not comfortable using the tools.

The effective use of technology involves (1) creating an inventory of the visual requirements, (2) selecting the proper technologies, medium and tools, and (3) being prepared to properly use the products to implement your case strategy.

deposit box. It can be disastrous to have to reconstruct files, court-filed documents, and other essential information after a devastating storm, flood, or fire destroys a law firm's records.

Wide Area Networks

Time can be saved by sharing information electronically instead of by personal delivery or courier, even within a city, building, or floor. Many firms—even some as small as two people—maintain multiple office sites, such as a downtown and a suburban location, or a main office and a satellite office across from the courthouse. Each of these offices may have a separate computer network.

Wide area network A network of networks. Each network is treated as if it were a connection on the network.

With high-speed communication lines, these separate networks may be connected to form a **wide area network**, or "network of networks." Access to a workstation on one of the networks allows access to the other networks in the system and the peripherals attached to the network, such as network printers. This allows a person in one office to print documents on a printer in another office. Files may be shared among all the members of the legal team regardless of the office where they are physically located.

The Internet

Internet A group of computers worldwide, linked together with the added ability to search all the connections for information.

The **Internet** may be thought of as simply a very large group of computers linked together, with the ability to search all the connections for information. An office in which all of the computers are networked together is much like a small version of the Internet. Each person's computer is connected to other people's computers, generally with a main computer where the shared data files and the software reside. The network operating system controls the connections and how the requests from each computer are handled and directed. This main control computer usually is referred to as the file server (see Exhibit 4.12).

Local area network (LAN) A network of computers at one location.

The **local area network (LAN)** search tool is usually a program such as Microsoft Windows Explorer (not to be confused with the Internet browser Internet Explorer) that locates files on the local computer or the other computers that have shared access. Exhibit 4.13 shows the Explorer screen, and Exhibit 4.14 shows Search companion.

Internet service provider (ISP) The company providing the connection between the user and the Internet.

Modem A device that translates electronic signals to allow computers to communicate with each other.

Internet service providers (ISPs) provide local or toll-free access numbers that most people use to connect to their service. A **modem** is used to translate the electrical signals for transmission so the computers can "talk" to each other. The modem converts (modulates) the information from the keyboard and computer into a form that can be transferred electronically over telephone lines, cable connections, and radio waves.

At the receiving end of the signal is another modem that reconverts (demodulates) the signal into a form usable by the computer. Speeds of transmission vary

Exhibit 4.12 Network system

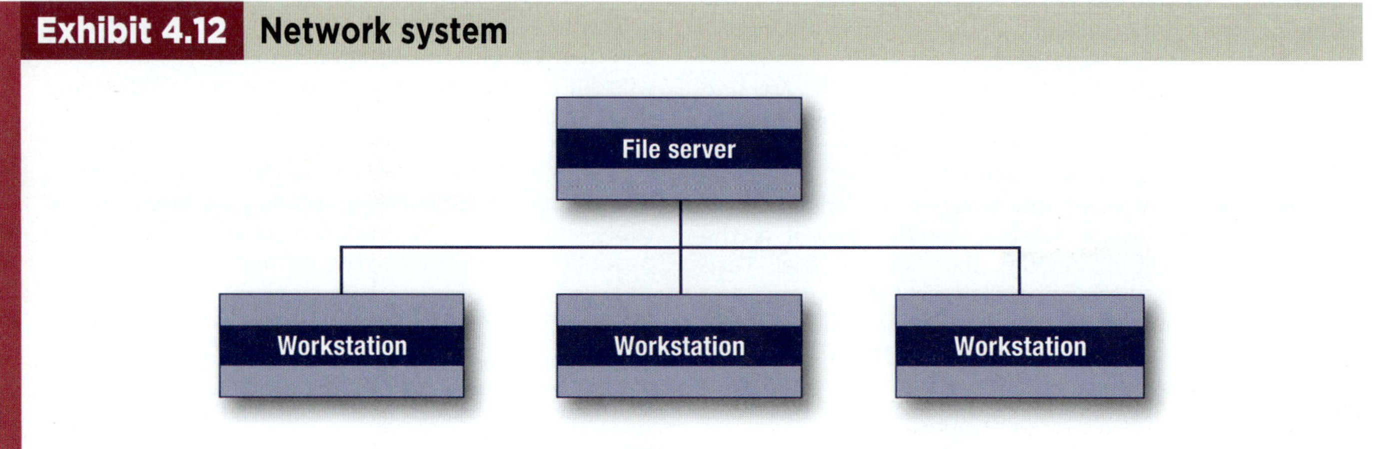

Exhibit 4.13 Explorer screen

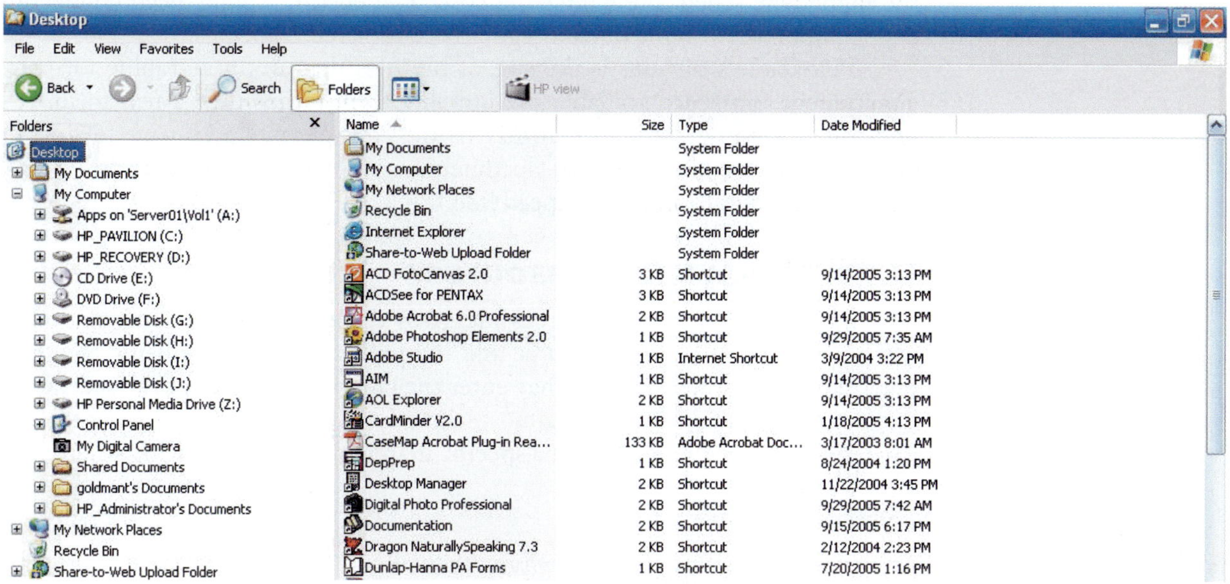

Desktop

File Edit View Favorites Tools Help

Back Search Folders HP view

Folders

- Desktop
  - My Documents
  - My Computer
    - Apps on 'Server01\Vol1' (A:)
    - HP_PAVILION (C:)
    - HP_RECOVERY (D:)
    - CD Drive (E:)
    - DVD Drive (F:)
    - Removable Disk (G:)
    - Removable Disk (H:)
    - Removable Disk (I:)
    - Removable Disk (J:)
    - HP Personal Media Drive (Z:)
    - Control Panel
    - My Digital Camera
    - Shared Documents
    - goldmant's Documents
    - HP_Administrator's Documents
  - My Network Places
  - Recycle Bin
  - Share-to-Web Upload Folder

Name	Size	Type	Date Modified
My Documents		System Folder	
My Computer		System Folder	
My Network Places		System Folder	
Recycle Bin		System Folder	
Internet Explorer		System Folder	
Share-to-Web Upload Folder		System Folder	
ACD FotoCanvas 2.0	3 KB	Shortcut	9/14/2005 3:13 PM
ACDSee for PENTAX	3 KB	Shortcut	9/14/2005 3:13 PM
Adobe Acrobat 6.0 Professional	2 KB	Shortcut	9/14/2005 3:13 PM
Adobe Photoshop Elements 2.0	1 KB	Shortcut	9/29/2005 7:35 AM
Adobe Studio	1 KB	Internet Shortcut	3/9/2004 3:22 PM
AIM	1 KB	Shortcut	9/14/2005 3:13 PM
AOL Explorer	2 KB	Shortcut	9/14/2005 3:13 PM
CardMinder V2.0	1 KB	Shortcut	1/18/2005 4:13 PM
CaseMap Acrobat Plug-in Rea...	133 KB	Adobe Acrobat Doc...	3/17/2003 8:01 AM
DepPrep	1 KB	Shortcut	8/24/2004 1:20 PM
Desktop Manager	2 KB	Shortcut	11/22/2004 3:45 PM
Digital Photo Professional	2 KB	Shortcut	9/29/2005 7:42 AM
Documentation	2 KB	Shortcut	9/15/2005 6:17 PM
Dragon NaturallySpeaking 7.3	2 KB	Shortcut	2/12/2004 2:23 PM
Dunlap-Hanna PA Forms	1 KB	Shortcut	7/20/2005 1:16 PM

Source: *Microsoft product box shot reprinted with permission from Microsoft Corporation.*

Exhibit 4.14 Search companion

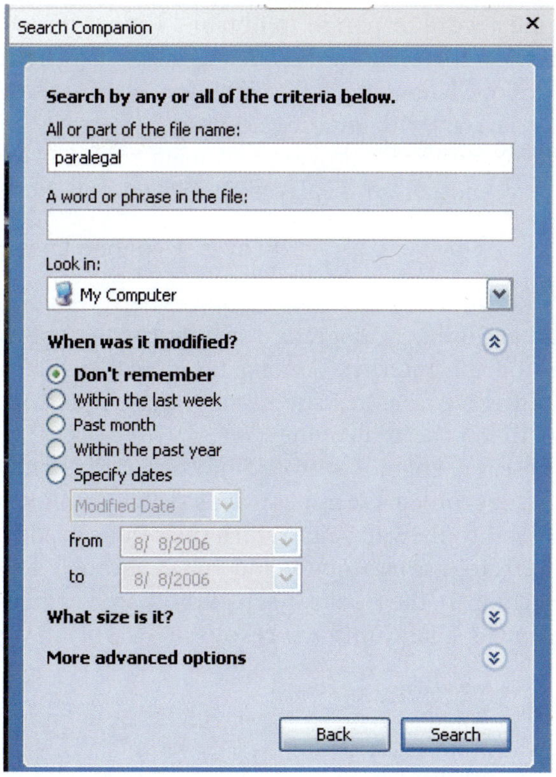

Search Companion

Search by any or all of the criteria below.

All or part of the file name:

paralegal

A word or phrase in the file:

Look in:

My Computer

When was it modified?

- **Don't remember**
- Within the last week
- Past month
- Within the past year
- Specify dates

Modified Date

from 8/ 8/2006

to 8/ 8/2006

What size is it?

More advanced options

Back Search

Source: *Microsoft product box shot reprinted with permission from Microsoft Corporation.*

widely, depending on the modem and the ISP service. A multipage document will take longer to transmit or receive than a single-page document. As with most services, the higher the speed, the higher the cost. The cost of a high-speed connection will depend upon the volume of data regularly sent or received.

Perhaps less obvious is the size of the files that are in a graphic format. Most government forms are available in a graphic form rather than a text form. A single one-page form in graphic format may be the equivalent of a 10-page text document. If such forms or other graphic documents are transmitted frequently, it might be advisable to upgrade to a high-speed line.

Online Computer Resources

The number of Internet resources increases daily. But finding information is easy when you know the specific source and the precise information being sought. If the exact source is known, the user may enter the computer address of the specific page or document and obtain the result almost instantly. However, in many cases the user will have to locate information about a specific item without first knowing where to find it.

Internet Browsers

Internet browser A program that allows a person to use a computer to access the Internet. Two of the most popular web browsers are Microsoft Internet Explorer and Firefox.

An **Internet browser** is a program that allows a person to access the Internet. Unless the computer has a direct connection to a computer database, a browser is needed. Two of the most popular web browsers are Microsoft Internet Explorer and Firefox. These browsers typically are used with Internet service providers that do not themselves provide any content, but rather act as an intermediary between the user and the World Wide Web. Some services, such as AOL and MSN, provide content such as news and weather and specialty sections for sharing information, along with Internet connections and email.

Web Exploration

Obtain a copy of the current AOL browser at www.daol.aol.com/software.

Internet browsers such as Firefox and Internet Explorer provide search features that allow a search of available web resources. These searches require only inputting into the search engine a word or phrase to obtain a listing of potentially relevant information. Also useful are specialized search engines, such as Google and Yahoo!, which use highly developed algorithms to search for relevant information and return a listing in order of relevancy with amazing accuracy.

All of the browsers basically provide two main screens—one to display email (see Exhibit 4.15) and another to display content and Internet search results (see Exhibit 4.16.)

Search Engines

Internet search engine An Internet search engine is a program designed to take a word or set of words and locate websites on the Internet.

An **Internet search engine** is a program designed to take a word, or set of words, and search websites on the Internet. Among the available Internet search engines, each searches in a different fashion. The same search request may generate totally different results on different search engines.

The number of search engines is expanding constantly. Some search engines are more suitable than others for legal searches. Many search engines are designed for use by children and families, so they may not return the results needed.

Uniform resource locator (URL) The address of a site on the Internet.

It is useful to create a search query and run it through a number of different search engines, then compare the results. Each of the search engines shown below may be accessed by entering its **URL (uniform resource locator)** in your web browser:

AltaVista	www.altavista.com
Ask.com	www.ask.com
Dogpile	www.dogpile.com
Excite	www.excite.com
Google	www.google.com
MetaCrawler	www.metacrawler.com
Yahoo!	www.yahoo.com

Exhibit 4.15 Email display

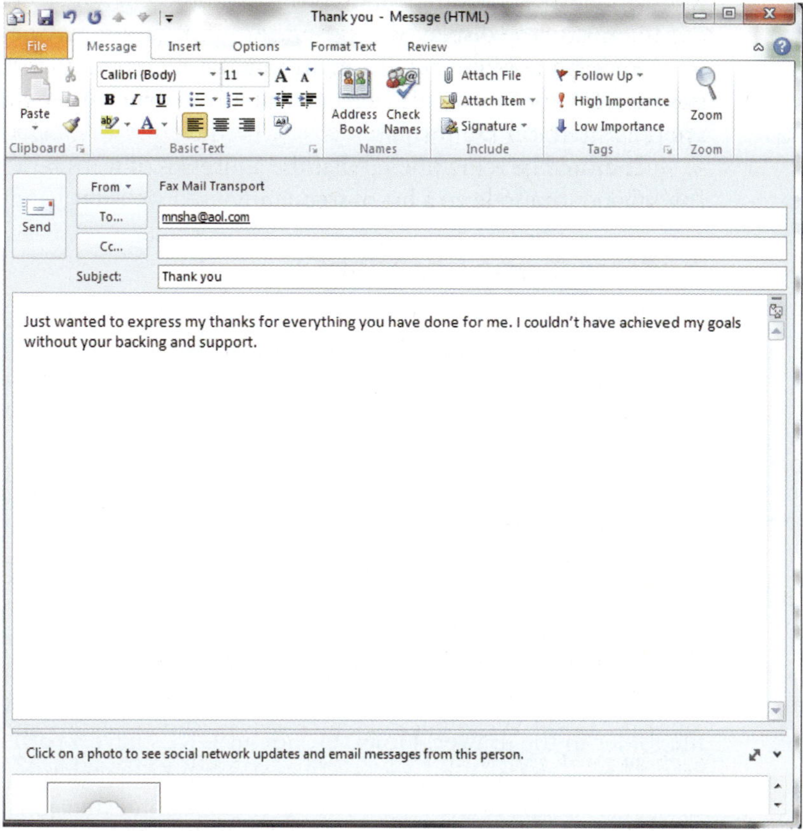

Used by permission of Microsoft.

Exhibit 4.16 Internet browser

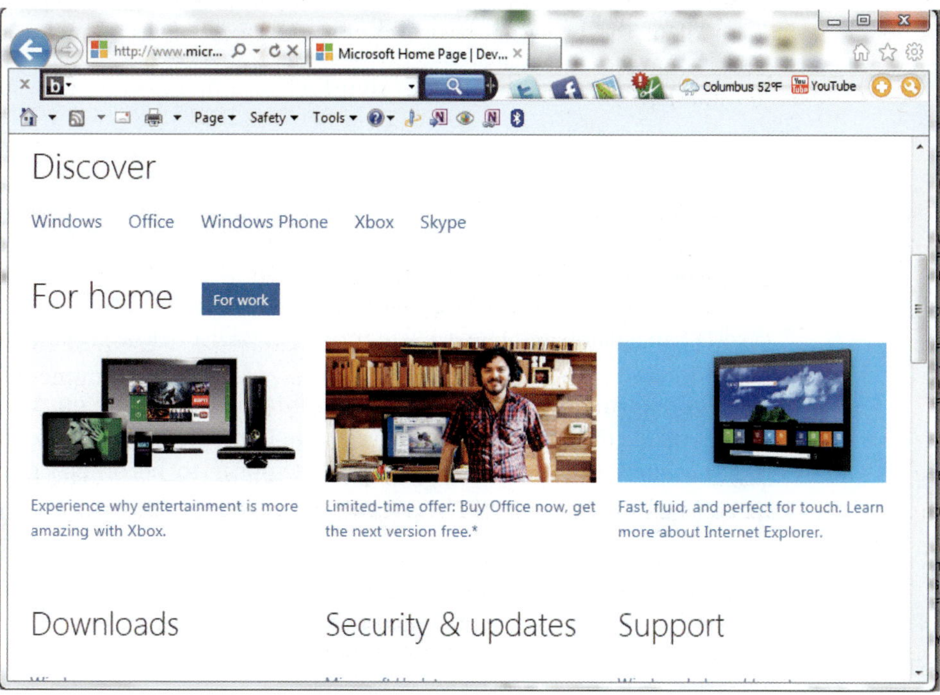

Used by permission of Microsoft.

Web Exploration

Obtain copies of tax forms from the Internal Revenue Service at **www.irs.gov**.

Upon executing the search, some of the information will be shown immediately on the screen and will not require any more searching. The data—such as a phone number, address, or other limited information—may be copied manually or printed out to capture the displayed page. Other information may be in the form of large text or graphic files. These may be many pages long or in the form of graphic image files, such as PDFs. For example, the tax forms available from the Internal Revenue Service are presented in PDF format.

It should be remembered that the addresses of websites tend to change frequently. It is a good idea to keep a list of frequently used websites handy and update it regularly.

Addresses and Locations

Computer address and location The modern equivalent of a person's telephone number is the email address. Pages on the Internet also have addresses known as the Uniform Resource Locator (URL), made up of three parts: protocol, computer, and path.

Protocol In a URL, the required format of the web address.

It is usually easier to find something when the user already has some information about its location. We find people by looking for their home or business address or their telephone number. The modern equivalent of a telephone number is the **computer address and location.** Web pages also have addresses, known as uniform resource locators, or URLs.

The URL is made up of three parts:

Protocol://Computer/Path

The **protocol** is usually "http" (hypertext transfer protocol). The "Computer" above is the name assigned to the computer on the Internet, such as www.bucks.edu. The "Path" is the directory or subdirectory on the computer where the information can be found.

The URL may be thought of as a file cabinet in which the protocol is the name of the file cabinet, the computer is the drawer in the file cabinet, and the path is the file folder in the drawer. However, not all URLs have a path as part of the address.

Part of the naming protocol is a domain nomenclature, with three-letter extensions that designate the type of website. Common extensions are:

.org	organizations
.edu	educational institutions
.com	commercial operations
.gov	government agencies
.bus	business
.mil	military

In addition, there are two-letter extensions assigned to countries, such as

.jp	Japan
.fr	France
.uk	United Kingdom

These designations refer to the country where the computer is located.

Many people save information about websites for future use, either as a copy, on cards, or in a database. The website profile checklist below provides suggested headings for such lists.

In determining the authenticity of information found on the Internet, knowing whether the computer is a commercial site (.com or .bus) or a government site (.gov) is sometimes useful. Some websites may appear to be official government websites

CHECKLIST Website Profile

- ☐ Address (URL):
- ☐ Name of organization or site:
- ☐ Key subject:
- ☐ Secondary subject:
- ☐ Cost:
- ☐ Comments:

containing official information, but actually are private sites. For example, the official URL for the Internal Revenue Service is www.irs.gov. This is not to be confused with the unofficial private website www.irs.com. To obtain the official Internal Revenue Service forms and information, you must use the official site, www.irs.gov.

Potentially one of the biggest time savers for the paralegal is the ready availability of legal forms, files, and other information on the Internet. Public information that at one time would have required a trip to the courthouse or other government office is now instantly available without leaving the law office. This information may come from public or private sources. Government information typically is available without cost, or at minimal cost. Private information may be free to all, or provided at a cost per use, per page, or per time period (such as a month).

Legal Research

In the law office, one of the most important uses of the Internet is to perform research, both factual and legal. Using powerful search engines, such as Google, Yahoo!, and Ask.com, can help the paralegal locate almost any information that is available on the Internet. More legal research is being conducted on the Internet as law offices reduce the size of paper-based law libraries in favor of online resources. A number of companies provide access to case law, statutory material, and other secondary legal sources for a fee. Among the most widely used of these are Westlaw, LexisNexis, Loislaw, and VersusLaw. Although some websites offer information without charge, most do not have the depth of information that the paid sites offer. The Cornell University Law school site is among the most popular of the free sites.

Web Exploration

Check the free resources of the Cornell Law School website at **http://www.law.cornell.edu/**.

Formats of Available Information

Most of the items that are displayed can be printed using a printer attached to a computer. At the top of most web browsers is a printer icon or a Print command within the FILE menu at the top of the page. Clicking on the icon or word PRINT in the FILE pull-down menu will initiate the print process. Patience may be necessary, as the computer may have to take some time to access the original source of the information. Clicking several times will not speed up the process and actually may result in several copies of the same information being printed.

File Attachments

A popular method for transmitting text files and graphic images is by **attachment** of the file to an email. This is much easier than it sounds. Today, almost everyone has an email address, whether at home, at work, or both. To send or receive emails requires the use of an Internet service provider and a browser, such as Internet Explorer, or an email program. In a typical email, text is entered on the keyboard and transmitted to the email account of a recipient, who reads it online. Virtually any file can be attached and sent with an email. The receiver need only click the mouse on the attachment, which may appear as an icon at the bottom of the email. In most cases, the file will open using the same program from which it was created, such as Microsoft Word, Corel WordPerfect, or Adobe Acrobat. Occasionally, a file may be in a format that the receiver does not have the software to open. This is particularly true with regard to graphic images, pictures, and drawings.

File attachment The attachment is a popular method for transmitting text files, and occasionally graphic images, by attaching the file to an email.

Receiving and Downloading Files and Attachments

The method for downloading files and attachments is the same. Users should first determine the directory (folder) into which they will be downloading these files. In Windows, this usually is a folder called My Download Files or My Files. If there is no existing folder, Windows Explorer can be used to create a file with a name assigned to it. Windows Explorer may be found in the Start directory under Programs.

CHECKLIST To Retrieve and Download a Form

- ☐ Select a file format.
- ☐ Select the file(s) you wish to receive. To select multiple items, hold down the Control button while selecting.
- ☐ Click the Review Selected Files button. A Results page will be displayed with links to the file(s) you requested.
- ☐ Select the file title to retrieve.

Most of the files attached to an email will be word processing files created and saved as either Word or WordPerfect documents. The user may want to save these files directly into the Word or WordPerfect directory. Attachments may also be opened immediately instead of saving for later use. Alternative file formats may be offered, such as MS Word, WordPerfect, or PDF, so it is important to be sure you have the appropriate program on your computer that can open and view the file.

Normally, text files and graphic images are static files; by themselves, they do not perform any function, but must be used with another program such as a word processor or graphic image viewer. It has become common, however, to send attachments that have within them mini-programs called "macros" that perform functions when activated, such as calculating sums in spreadsheets. Others are self-contained programs containing animations, such as screensavers.

Some program files have an extension of either ".exe" or ".com." Files with these extensions may run automatically after downloading. Therefore, greater caution must be taken in downloading files with these or other unknown file extensions, which may contain macros (mini programs) with formulas that run automatically and may contain computer viruses, as discussed below. Remember that it is not enough to depend on the sender being a reliable source, as even the most reliable source can have a security breach that allows a virus to be attached to a file, or the source may be forwarding files from other, less reliable sources without checking the files before sending them to you.

Sending Files

Some Internet Service Providers (ISPs) limit the amount of information that may be sent at one time, depending on the speed of the connection and how busy the system is at different times of the day. This may limit the number of pages that may be sent at one time. With increased transmission speed, or bandwidth, comes the ability to transmit much larger files and more pages at the same time.

Increasingly, large-size graphics files and images such as photographs are sent or attached to emails. The amount of time required to send a file depends on the size of the file and the bandwidth it is traveling across. Bandwidth may be thought of as a pipeline through which only a limited amount of product can be transmitted at any

ETHICAL PERSPECTIVE

Arizona Law Firm Domain Names Opinion No. 2001-05 (March 2001) Summary.

A law firm domain name does not have to be identical to the firm's actual name, but it must comply with the Rules of Professional Conduct, including refraining from being false or misleading. And it may not imply any special competence or unique affiliation unless this is factually true. A for-profit law firm domain name should not use the domain suffix ".org" nor should it use a domain name that implies that the law firm is affiliated with a given nonprofit organization or governmental entity. [ERs 7.1, 7.4, 7.5]

one time. The larger files require more bandwidth to avoid slowing down the system. To more equitably share the limited bandwidth available, ISPs and network operators limit the number of files or the size of files that one user may transmit, either permanently or temporarily during peak usage times. In some offices, the same limitations may be imposed to overcome the bandwidth limitation. Files may be transmitted in a compressed format, frequently referred to as zip files. Large files are run through a program that compresses them before being sent. The recipient of the compressed file then must uncompress the file before being able to read it.

A number of programs are available to compress and decompress files. Some of these are operated manually through several steps, and other programs perform the task automatically. For occasional use, the manual method is acceptable, but with the increasing number of compressed files, it may be more efficient to purchase one of the automatic programs. Trial versions of some of these decompression programs may be downloaded from the Internet without charge from software companies who will then encourage the user to buy the full version after the trial period expires.

ETHICAL PERSPECTIVE

Ohio Rule on Commercial Law-Related Websites

Ohio lawyers may not participate in a commercial law-related website that provides them with clients if the arrangement entails prohibited payment for referrals or if the business is engaged in the unauthorized practice of law. (Ohio Supreme Court Board of Commissioners on Grievances and Discipline opinion 2001-2)

Electronic Filing

A number of courts have established procedures for filing pleadings electronically. Each court is free to set up its own rules and procedures, which must be consulted before one attempts to use their service. The Internal Revenue Service and some states have combined in a joint effort to allow electronic filing of both the federal and state individual income tax returns in one step. The local or state tax authority retrieves the information from the Internal Revenue Service. A feature of this service, known as IRS e-file, is the return receipt when the federal and state governments receive the form.

Types of Image Formats

With increasing frequency, the Internet is being used to obtain needed forms, such as government agency forms, tax forms, or court forms. Even the best-equipped office will require one form or another that is not in the office files. It may be an unusual federal tax form or a form from another state. Most federal government forms use the PDF format, and many state agencies use it as well.

Computer and Network Security

As law offices, courts, and clients become more dependent upon the use of computers and the Internet, security has become a critical issue. Within a computer network, a virus or malicious program introduced into one workstation could adversely impact every workstation on the network and the network file server itself. Any workstation is a potential access point for programs that could corrupt the files stored on the system. In rare cases, employees have introduced annoying or potentially harmful programs as a way to get even with an employer. Part of the solution to these types of issues is to limit access to the network, such as by restricting the ability to access the file server from workstations, limiting the ability to make changes to operating systems, or limiting activity to saving documents.

Hacking Unauthorized access to a computer or computer network.

The use of the Internet from workstations has also introduced the potential for unauthorized parties gaining access to the computer network—referred to as **"hacking."** In some instances, the person wants to gain access to information in files stored on the network. In other cases, the intent is to undermine the integrity of the system by modifying files and programs or introducing computer viruses that can delete files, programs, or operating systems.

Firewalls

Firewalls Programs designed to limit access to authorized users and applications.

A **firewall** is a program designed to limit access to a computer or a network. Depending upon the complexity of the program, it may totally restrict access or limit access to certain kinds of programs or sources. For example, many parents use a form of a firewall designed to limit their children's access to certain kinds of programs and websites that are deemed to be unacceptable.

A firewall can be a two-edged sword for the paralegal: it prevents unauthorized access to the network, but it may also prevent the paralegal from accessing the firm's files from an off-site location, such as a courthouse, a client's office, or opposing counsel's offices. It is important to check a connection to be sure it will allow data to be accessed from a remote location before it is needed for a trial, deposition, or presentation. With enough time, almost any issue may be resolved with the local system administrator.

Encryption Technology

Encryption Encryption is technology that allows computer users to put a "lock" around information to prevent discovery by others.

Encryption technology basically permits a computer user to put a lock on information to protect it from being accessed by others. Encryption technology is like a lock on a house. Without the lock in place, unwanted persons can easily enter the house and steal its contents; with the lock in place, it is more difficult to enter and take the house's contents. Encryption software lets computer users scramble information so that only those who have the encryption code can enter the database and use the information.

Encryption

Confidential or privileged information sent over the Internet is frequently encrypted by the sender and unencrypted by the receiver because of the concern that it will be intercepted when transmitted over the Internet. Encryption programs use algorithms (mathematical formulas) to scramble documents. Without the proper password or encryption key, unauthorized persons are not able to read the files and determine their content.

The levels of protection offered by the different encryption programs are much like different types of combination locks. The least security is provided by a two-number combination lock frequently found on inexpensive luggage. As the numbers required for opening the lock increase to two, three, four, or more numbers, the security also increases. It is not hard to see how the two-digit combination lock can be quickly opened, while the four-digit lock requires more time and effort. For an amateur computer hacker with simple encryption-breaking software, a basic

ETHICAL PERSPECTIVE

Interception of Electronic Communications

Interception or monitoring of email communications for purposes other than assuring quality of service or maintenance is illegal under the Electronic Communications Privacy Act of 1986, as amended in 1994. [18 U.S.C. B2511(2)(a)(i)]

encryption program might be thought of as equivalent to a two- or three-number combination lock. The higher-level program, with tougher algorithms designed to thwart a professional code-breaker, would be like a lock with four or more digits. As computers become faster, more sophisticated methods will be required.

Computer Viruses

Unfortunately, some people take sadistic pleasure in developing and disseminating programs that attack and destroy computer programs, internal operating systems, and occasionally entire hard drives. These programs are known as **computer viruses.** Viruses range from those that create only a minor inconvenience to those that can destroy data and cause shutdowns.

Computer viruses Viruses are programs that attack and destroy computer programs, internal computer operating systems, and occasionally the hard drives of computers.

Some simple precautions can prevent disaster. Virus-protection programs, such as those sold by Norton, McAfee, and others, are as important to have on a computer as the computer operating system itself. This should be the first program loaded onto a new computer.

Anti-virus programs scan the computer to identify the presence of viruses, and the better programs eliminate the virus entirely. Every disk should be scanned with an anti-virus program before being used. Files that are downloaded from other computers or over the Internet should also be checked. As good as these programs are, they quickly go out-of-date as new viruses are unleashed. Therefore, these virus checking programs should be updated regularly.

Future Trends in Law Office Technology

Learning Objective 9
Discuss the future trends in law office technology.

Law offices are constantly under pressure to be more productive. Increased costs have led law office managers to look for new ways to use technology to increase productivity. Clients and the courts are not willing to approve some fees and expenses if more cost-effective methods are available. In addition, the demand for speedy justice in the courts has resulted in less time to prepare and present cases. The legal team must therefore work faster and become more productive. Advances in computer technology are providing solutions to these issues.

Looking ahead to what's on the technological horizon is imperative to the smooth and profitable functioning of the law office. Anticipating and incorporating new technology requires IT knowledge and savvy, whether it comes from in-house staff or external technology consultants. A chief information officer or chief technology officer at a corporate firm must anticipate change and plan for it in concrete and innovative ways. Those responsible for IT at smaller firms must also be well informed of technology trends. They must assess when a new tool should be added to their technology repertoire—and when it should be avoided.

The legal team is an increasingly mobile workforce, and working outside of the office is a fact of life for trial attorneys and their support staff. The litigation team may spend much of their time in courthouses or taking depositions at other offices. These tasks may be located across the street, across the country, or around the globe. Increasingly, the support staff must also work outside the office. In some cases, this work is outsourced to other firms or companies in remote locations. In addition, some lawyers, paralegals, and litigation support staff may work from home. With advances in technology, it is possible for these team members to connect with the main office and access all the needed files and electronic resources on their computers at home. These workers are sometimes referred to as **teleworkers.**

Teleworker People who work from remote locations, typically home.

Technology is developing much faster than we could have expected even a few years ago. As Raymond Kurzweil writes in his essay "The Law of Accelerating Returns" (2001),

> An analysis of the history of technology shows that technological change is exponential, contrary to the common-sense "intuitive linear" view. So we won't experience 100 years of progress in the 21st century—it will be more like 20,000 years of progress (at today's rate). The "returns," such as chip speed and cost-effectiveness, also increase exponentially. There's even exponential growth in the rate of exponential growth.

The following section describes some of the emerging technology that is available now. Some of this technology is currently in use at some law firms, while some is still under development. The list is not exhaustive but gives an idea of what businesses might expect in the near and distant future.

Emerging Technology

Videoconferencing

Videoconferencing Conferencing from multiple locations using high-speed Internet connections to transmit sound and images.

Videoconferencing is the use of the Internet, telephone lines, or special satellite systems to transmit and receive video and audio signals in real time. This technology allows parties in several locations to see and hear each other during a conference. Many law firms and their clients currently use videoconferencing on a regular basis as a method of "face-to-face" communication when parties are at remote sites, such as depositions, hearings, and conferences.

Videoconferencing is also used in many courts at various stages of court proceedings, most often at the early stages of a criminal case. This technology is now being recognized by some court rules. For example, Section 885.52(3) of the Wisconsin Supreme Court Rules defines videoconferencing as

> interactive technology that sends video, voice, and data signals over a transmission circuit so that two or more individuals or groups can communicate with each other simultaneously using video monitors.

The Wisconsin rules further establish the requirements under which videoconferencing can be used in court proceedings. They are some of the most advanced rules on videoconferencing in the country, permitting the use of this technology in all aspects of criminal and civil litigation. Rules such as these are designed to make emerging web-based technologies available to litigants, as long as certain requirements are met. With the Wisconsin courts leading the way, videoconferencing and other technologies can be expected to become important tools in a litigation practice.

VoIP

VoIP Voice over Internet Protocol is a computer Internet replacement for traditional telephone connections.

Voice over Internet Protocol **(VoIP)** is a method for transmitting voice communication over the Internet rather than through traditional telephone company services. A computer with a microphone and headset or speaker is used to complete a call to another computer or telephone over the Internet. The communication operates through software installed on a computer, and may include both voice and images. At first, VoIP was limited by the inability to connect calls to or from a conventional telephone. But services like Yahoo! Messenger now provide options that permit calling conventional phones at a very nominal rate, sometimes as low as one cent per minute.

At one time, conducting a videoconference required going to a special location and paying a substantial fee. Now, the relatively low cost and ease of use of VoIP make teleconferencing, including videoconferencing, an option for those who previously could not afford such services. Anyone with a laptop, a built-in microphone and speakers, and an inexpensive video camera can set up a videoconference from almost anywhere an Internet connection is available.

Voice Recognition

Voice recognition Computer programs for converting speech into text or commands without the use of other in/out devices such as keyboards.

Voice recognition software offers an alternative to typing by converting spoken words to text on the screen. Earlier versions of speech recognition programs were lacking in accuracy. But improved technology has brought this software to a level of accuracy approaching that of typing. Speech-enabled devices include smartphones, pad devices, and GPS devices. With programs like Dragon Naturally Speaking (Legal Version), it is now possible to dictate working drafts of legal documents directly into almost any other program, including word processors, spreadsheets, and databases, without touching a computer keyboard. The document may then be sent to another member of the legal team electronically. Software has become so advanced that portable dictation devices can be used out of the office and later connected to the office computer to transcribe documents without the intervention of a typist. The benefits to the legal team in productivity and efficiency are significant. Transcribing speech at up to 160 words per minute, voice recognition software far outpaces the speed of the average typist.

The underlying technology found in voice recognition software is now being used in automated response systems that replace live operators and receptionists at some firms. It is also used in products that help those who cannot use a keyboard because of physical disabilities.

Miniaturization and Portability

The trend in computers and related devices has been toward lightweight, portability, and extended battery life. Some laptops now weigh less than 3 pounds and are more powerful than some older desktop systems. They may include all of the capabilities of desktop systems, including built-in web cameras for videoconferencing. Similarly, cell phones such as the Apple iPhone and Google Android are now capable of taking and displaying photos and video, preparing documents, sending emails, and accessing the Internet—functions that formerly required large, hard-wired computer devices.

Wireless Technology

Only a few years ago, wires or cables were necessary to access networks or to set up network connections. Today, networks may be set up among workstations, servers, and peripherals using wireless technology. Remote access is also possible by the use of a wireless Internet connection using laptops and cell phones with built-in Internet access.

Many offices today are equipped with wireless telephones and wireless Internet networks. In addition, the worldwide availability of inexpensive high-speed Internet connections, or "hotspots," has expanded the use of wireless technologies. Wireless devices allow constant communication and enable work to be performed virtually anywhere, such as at home, the courthouse, an airport lounge, or a coffee shop. Staff members may connect to their office's wireless network through the Internet or cellular network using wireless hardware built into the computer, or through an external adapter card.

Remote Access

Remote access allows members of the legal team working on cases out of the office to connect with the office file server to retrieve documents, work on them, and send them to other members of the team anywhere in the world. If a hard copy is needed, documents may be printed on any printer accessible over the Internet, including printers in remote office locations, clients' offices, and at courthouses.

Remote collaboration

Remote collaboration means members of the team working together from multiple locations as if they were in the same physical location. Software conferencing programs allow team members to share files while seeing each other on the same screen using small cameras built into their computers. The same remote access technology also allows the taking of witness statements from remote locations while the parties can see each other or view exhibits on the computer screen.

Remote collaboration Working on a common document utilizing remote access by two or more parties.

With high-speed Internet connections, true real-time videoconferencing has become a reality. Formerly, slower connections restricted how much information could be transmitted and increased the time needed to send a document. Slower speeds also prevented full-motion, full-screen video. High-speed Internet connections now allow users to simultaneously transmit both sound and images. With the introduction of fiber optic and cable Internet services, videoconferencing from multiple locations is now available at many offices.

Wireless Computer Networks

Wireless computer networks A wireless network uses wireless technology in place of wires for connecting to the network.

Wireless computer networks are like cell phone networks in that both use radio waves to transmit signals to a receiver. Cell phone systems use cell towers, located at strategic points all over the world, to receive the signals from cellular devices. Similarly, wireless networks use wireless access points, which are essentially receivers of radio signals that convert them so they can be transmitted to a computer or to the Internet.

Hotspot A wireless access point, generally in a public area.

Unlike cell phone towers, these access points have a more limited range of only a few hundred feet. Many of these access points, or "**hotspots,**" are provided in coffee shops, airport lounges, hotels, libraries, bookstores, and other locations. Businesses often offer wireless access without charge, or at a nominal fee, as an incentive to customers to patronize the business.

With the growth of wireless hotspots, lawyers and paralegals may be connected anywhere in the world and send documents electronically back and forth as if they were in the same building. And with cellular connections provided through internal or plug-in accessories, computers can access the Internet over wide geographical areas.

Wireless Laptop Connections

Laptops may be used wirelessly to connect to the Internet without needing a hotspot by using USB plug-in devices. Subscriptions to data services are provided by most major cellular providers, such as AT&T, Verizon, and Sprint. They can provide access virtually anywhere there is cellular coverage. The popularity of these wireless services has resulted in many newer-generation laptops having the feature built-in, eliminating the need for external cards.

Thin client A computer system where programs and files are maintained on a centralized server.

"Cloud computing," often called the "**thin client,**" is now emerging in which all programs and files are maintained on a centralized server. Each user has access to the server through a "dumb terminal" (one without programs or data). The thin client model offers some additional level of control and prevents the loss of information that would occur if someone's computer were lost or damaged. Another example of cloud computing is Software as a Service (SaaS), such as Office 365 from Microsoft. The service charges a monthly fee for use of its software when needed.

CHECKLIST

Use the following checklist as a tool to assess how your firm uses technology, and to discover areas you might want to address in the future.

- ☐ Which functions are automated now? Which additional functions do you wish to automate?
- ☐ Are existing pieces of equipment mutually compatible?
- ☐ Does everyone in the office use the same software?
- ☐ Are word processing procedures standardized?
- ☐ Is the billing system interfaced with the accounting system?
- ☐ Are checks drawn on law firm accounts computer-generated or prepared manually?
- ☐ Are you using software to keep track of client expenses, such as copies, faxes, long-distance calls, and postage?
- ☐ Are telephone messages delivered accurately and in a timely manner?
- ☐ Does the office get flooded with paper interoffice memoranda?
- ☐ Is the payroll prepared in-house? Is payroll handled manually, or with software?
- ☐ Do the attorneys often carry boxes of documents to the courthouse?
- ☐ Do the paralegals spend hours preparing manual document index systems?
- ☐ How does the firm check for conflicts of interest?
- ☐ What type of calendaring system do you use for docket control and scheduling?

Source: http://www.texasbar.com/lomp/links.htm

Concept Review *and* Reinforcement

LEGAL TERMINOLOGY

Applications software 147
Backup of data 141
Case and litigation management software 136
Central processing unit (CPU) 127
Computer address and location 146
Computer hardware 127
Computer network 140
Computer system 127
Computer viruses 151
Database program 131
Digital format 122
Electronic repository 124
Encryption 150
File attachment 147
File extension 130
Firewalls 150
Hacking 150
Hard copy 122
Hotspot 154
Internet 142
Internet browser 144
Internet search engine 144
Internet service provider (ISP) 142
Local area network (LAN) 142
Mainframe 127
Modem 142
Network administrator 141
Network file server 140
Network rights and privileges 140
Office software suites 132
Online collaboration 124
Operating system 127
Outsourcing 126
Paperless office 139
Protocol 146
Random access memory (RAM) 127
Remote collaboration 126
Software 128
Specialty application programs 133
Spreadsheet programs 131
Teleworker 151
Thin client 154
Track Changes 130
Uniform resource locator (URL) 144
Uninterruptible power supply (UPS) 127
Videoconferencing 152
Voice recognition 152
VoIP 152
Wide area network 142
Wireless computer networks 154
Workstation 140

SUMMARY OF KEY CONCEPTS

The Need for Computer Skills

Why Are They Needed?	Computers are increasingly used to share information between remote offices, courthouses, government agencies, and clients.
Technology Usage in the Law	Computers are now being used for everything from word processing to computerized time keeping, payroll productions and tax return preparation. Today, even the smallest law firm and litigator must use technology. Some courts are demanding computerized filing.
Outsourcing	Outsourcing has become a buzzword for shipping work out of the office or overseas to save money. Using an outside computer consultant to help with support for the hardware and software is a form of outsourcing and may simply involve a help desk located in a foreign location to answer questions.
How Much Do I Really Need to Know?	No one can be an expert in everything. What is important is to know enough to know what you do not know and be able to find someone who does.

Understanding the Language of Technology

Why Do I Need to Know It?	An understanding of the terminology of technology is a prerequisite to understanding the technology found in the law office, the courthouse, and the clients' business.

Computer Hardware

Computer Hardware	Hardware is the term that encompasses all of the tangible or physical items, including computers, monitors, printers, fax machines, duplicators, and similar items, that usually have either an electrical connection or use batteries as a power source.

Operating Systems	
What Is an Operating System?	The operating system is a basic set of instructions to the computer on how to handle basic functions, such as how to process input from "input devices" like the keyboard and mouse, the order in which to process information, and what to show on the computer monitor.
Applications Software	
Applications Software	Applications are software that perform generic tasks such as word processing.
Word Processing Programs	Word processors are programs for creating written documents.
Track Changes	Track Changes, as used in MS Word, shows the original text, the deleted text, and the new text, as well as a strikethrough line for deleted text. New text is underlined or highlighted, and margin notes may be made within the document.
File Extensions	When a file is saved, a file extension (a period followed by three characters) is added to the end of the file name to identify the program or format in which the file has been saved.
Spreadsheet Programs	Spreadsheets are programs that permit the calculation and presentation of financial information in a grid format of rows and columns.
Database Programs	A database program is an electronic repository of information of all types that can be sorted and presented in a meaningful manner.
Presentation Graphic Programs	
	Presentation software is used to create high-quality slide shows and drawings.
Specialty Application Programs	
	Specialty application programs combine many of the basic functions found in software suites, such as word processing, database management, spreadsheets, and graphic presentations, to perform law office, case, and litigation management.
Case and Litigation Management Software	Case and litigation management programs are used to manage documents and the facts and issues of cases.
Electronic Courtroom and Paperless Office	
The Electronic Courtroom	Electronics and computer-based systems are used in the electronic courtroom.
The Paperless Office	The paperless office is one in which most documents are created and stored electronically.
Networks	
Workstation	A workstation generally consists of a computer, a monitor, and a printer.
Computer Network	A network is a set of workstations connected together.
Network Server	The network file server is a separate computer that acts as the "traffic cop" of the system, controlling the flow of information. It requests to use the resources of the system or data transferred between the connected workstations and other peripherals that are part of the network. These servers usually are the central repository for all electronic files.
Network Rights and Privileges	Rights or privileges determine who has access to the server, the data stored on the server, and the flow of information between connections.
Network Administrator	The network administrator usually is the person with the highest level of access to the network file server.

Backing Up Data	Backing up data (making copies of files) regularly is an essential function to prevent loss of critical files and office data in the event of a disaster.
Wide Area Network	A wide area network is a network of networks. Each network is treated as if it were a connection on the network.
Wireless Network	A wireless network uses wireless technology instead of wires for connecting to the network.
The Internet	
What Is It?	The Internet or the World Wide Web is a group of computers linked together with the added ability to search all the connections for information.
Online Computer Resources	
Internet Browsers	An Internet or web browser is a program that allows a person to use a computer to access the Internet. The two most popular web browsers are Microsoft Internet Explorer and Firefox.
Search Engines	An Internet search engine is a program designed to locate information on websites across the Internet.
Addresses and Locations	The email address is the modern equivalent of a person's telephone number. Pages on the Internet also have addresses known as the Uniform Resource Locator (URL), made up of three parts: protocol, computer, and path.
Formats of Available Information	
File Attachments	The attachment is a popular method for transmitting text files, and occasionally graphic images, by attaching the file to an email.
Receiving and Downloading Files and Attachments	The method for downloading files and attachments is the same. They are downloaded into a directory (a folder). If there is no existing folder, Windows Explorer can be used to create a file with a name.
Electronic Filing	
Courts	Many courts have established procedures for the electronic filing of pleadings. Each court is free to set up its own rules and procedures, which must be consulted before one attempts to use this service.
IRS	The Internal Revenue Service and some states have combined in a joint effort to allow the filing of both the federal and state individual income tax returns.
Types of Image Formats	The most popular format for computerized forms is PDF.
Computer and Network Security	
Security	Security is a critical issue in law offices and for the court as they become more and more dependent on computers and the Internet.
Firewalls	A firewall is a program designed to limit access to a computer network.
Encryption	Encryption is technology that allows computer users to put a "lock" around information to prevent discovery by others.
Computer Viruses	Viruses are programs that attack and destroy programs, internal operating systems, and occasionally hard drives.
Precautions	Virus-protection programs such as Norton or McAfee should be updated regularly.

Future Trends in Law Office Technology

	Looking ahead to what's on the technological horizon is imperative to the smooth and profitable functioning of the law office. Anticipating change and incorporating it requires IT knowledge and savvy, whether it comes in the form of in-house staff or external technology consultants.
Videoconferencing	Videoconferencing is the use of the Internet, or in some cases, telephone lines or special satellite systems, to transmit and receive video and audio signals in real time to allow parties to see and hear each other.
VoIP	Voice over Internet Protocol (VoIP) is a protocol for using the Internet as a method of communication instead of conventional telephone company services. A computer with a microphone and headset is used to complete a call to another computer or telephone over the Internet. It may be a voice connection or both voice and image.
Voice Recognition	Improved technology has brought this software to a higher level of accuracy, approaching the accuracy of typing.
Miniaturization and Portability	Smaller devices are becoming more powerful than some of the older desktop systems and laptops. Even the telephone has been reduced to a pocket-sized wireless communication device.
Wireless Technology	Hardware in many offices today includes the wireless telephone and the laptop computer with built-in wireless Internet capability. The worldwide availability of inexpensive high-speed Internet connections has expanded the availability and use of new technologies.
Remote Access	Remote access allows members of the legal team working on cases while out of the office to connect with the office file server to retrieve documents, work on them, and send them to other members of the team anywhere in the world.
Remote Collaboration	Remote collaboration means that members of the team can work collaboratively from multiple locations as if in the same physical location. This is possible through software conferencing programs that allow the sharing of files while communicating and seeing each other on the same screen.
Wireless Computer Networks	Wireless networks are similar to cell phone networks, and use radio waves to transmit signals to a receiver over a smaller area.
Wireless Laptop Connections	Laptops may be used wirelessly through plug-in devices to connect to the Internet without the limitation or use of a "hotspot."
Thin Client	A trend in "thin client" or "cloud" computing is emerging where programs and files are maintained on a centralized server and each user has access through a "dumb terminal" (one without programs or data).

WORKING THE WEB

1. Download the latest 1040 tax form and instructions from the Internal Revenue Service website at www.irs.gov.
2. Use one of the search engines listed below to find information on your school or local government:
   a. AltaVista: http://www.altavista.com
   b. Ask.com: http://www.ask.com
   c. Dogpile: http://www.dogpile.com
   d. Excite: http://www.excite.com
   e. Google: http://www.google.com
   f. MetaCrawler: http://www.metacrawler.com
   g. Yahoo!: www.yahoo.com
3. Use the Google search engine to find information on how firewalls work, and print out the first page of the

results. Using one of the results, print out a copy of the information that is most responsive to the search, and write a short summary describing what a firewall does. http://www.google.com

4. Use a search engine of your choice to run a search for legal research resources. Print a copy of the first 10 results. Mark each result that you think will be useful for you as a paralegal and explain why.
5. Prepare a step-by-step list of how to find the Code of Federal Regulations on the Government Printing Office website. http://www.access.gpo.gov
6. Prepare a list of the legislative information available online from the Library of Congress. http://www.LOC.gov
7. Use any search engine or browser search tool to find the document "How Our Laws Are Made," as revised and updated by the parliamentarian Charles W. Johnson, on a federal government website. Hint: Use quotation marks around the names. Print out the specific query you used and the URL of the source where the document was found.
8. Print out a copy of the results of the search for "firewall" using Yahoo! and compare the results to the results from Google. How many of the first 20 listings are the same?

CRITICAL THINKING & WRITING QUESTIONS

1. How can the computer and the Internet increase a paralegal's productivity?
2. What is meant by the term "computer hardware"?
3. What is the danger in using the word processing feature "Track Changes"?
4. What are applications? Give an example.
5. What are the advantages of using office suite programs?
6. How can database programs be used to avoid ethical issues?
7. How can legal office management programs help prevent malpractice?
8. What is meant by the "paperless office"? What changes in law office administration have encouraged this?
9. What is the function of a network server?
10. Why is making a backup essential in a law office?
11. What is the advantage to the legal team in having a wide area network or wireless network?
12. How has the availability of high-speed Internet impacted the use of the Internet in the law office?
13. What is an Internet browser? How is this different from Windows Explorer?
14. How reliable are the forms and documents obtained over the Internet?
15. What advantages does the Internet provide the paralegal in the law office?
16. What are the limitations of using a website to attract new clients in your state?
17. Do cross-jurisdictional-boundary websites present any problems for the law firm using the Internet? Why or why not?
18. What are some of the ways in which using an Internet browser can assist the paralegal working on a file or a case? How are URLs used in conducting Internet searches?
19. What copyright issues must a paralegal consider in using the Internet to prepare written documents and reports?
20. How can the authenticity of information obtained on the Internet be validated? Explain the issues in downloading information from websites.
21. What is the purpose of a firewall? What are the implications to the law office of not using firewalls?
22. What is a computer virus, and what should a paralegal do to protect the firm against computer viruses?
23. Should encryption software be used regularly in transmitting files electronically? Why?
24. Why would the legal team want to use encryption when transmitting a document?
25. What is a wireless access point? How could this be used in a law firm?
26. What ethical issues arise in the use of "hotspots" or public access points?

Building Paralegal Skills

VIDEO CASE STUDIES

Attorney Meet and Confer

Opposing counsel are meeting to discuss discovery issues in the case, as required under the Federal Rules of Civil Procedure. Defense counsel has recently taken over the file from another attorney and is not familiar with its contents. The attorney asks for additional time to complete discovery.

After viewing the video case study in MyLegalStudiesLab, answer the following:

1. What is the purpose of the "meet and confer" under the Federal Rules of Civil Procedure?
2. If the lawyers are not familiar with some of the electronic discovery issues, do they have an ethical obligation to have someone there who is more knowledgeable?
3. How important is it for the lawyers and paralegals to be aware of the issues in electronic discovery?

Remote Videoconference Taking Witness Video Deposition

The parent of an accident victim is not available locally for a deposition. To save time and costs, his deposition is being taken using videoconferencing.

After viewing the video case study in MyLegalStudiesLab, answer the following:

1. What arrangements must be made to take a deposition using videoconferencing?
2. What are the advantages and disadvantages of using videoconferencing for taking depositions of fact witnesses?
3. What is the role of the court reporter in a videoconference deposition?

Privilege Issue: Misdirected Email

The paralegal working on a confidential memo for a client has accidentally sent it to opposing counsel. The supervising attorney, visibly upset, gives instructions on how to handle the situation.

After viewing the video case study in MyLegalStudiesLab, answer the following:

1. What is the potential effect of the email and the confidential information for the opposing party?
2. What steps should be taken in your jurisdiction when email is inadvertently sent to the wrong party?
3. Who is ultimately responsible, and what are the penalties, for inadvertent disclosure of confidential information sent by email?

ETHICS ANALYSIS & DISCUSSION QUESTIONS

1. What are the ethical issues related to a law firm website that is available around the world when the firm is licensed to practice only in one jurisdiction?
2. Explain the ethical implication of the following: "In today's society, with the advent of the information superhighway, federal and state legislation and regulations, as well as information regarding industry trends, are easily accessed."
3. What are the ethical issues of erroneously sending or receiving by email or fax a confidential trial strategy memorandum?
4. What ethical issues arise for the law firm when it does not maintain an off-premises copy of files and client records? Does a major catastrophe, such as the flooding caused by Hurricane Katrina in New Orleans in 2005, excuse not having backup files and records?
5. What role do security protocols have in ethical compliance?
6. What ethical issues are involved in combining law practices as discussed in the opening scenario? What specific steps should be taken? Explain how these steps will prevent ethical breaches.
7. You are working in a sophisticated law firm that has the latest computers and software. You have not been trained in the use of the firm's computer encryption software for transmitting email and other electronic documents to clients and other offices of the firm. You live a few blocks from the office and consent to stay late on Friday night before a major holiday weekend when everyone has left early to avoid the rush-hour traffic.

   A client calls and asks for a copy of the trial strategy memorandum for a major case to take with him for review over the weekend. He advises that he is getting ready to get on a plane but has a computer with him that has reverse encryption software the firm gave him and tells you that he wants to read the memo while he is on the plane for the next 14 hours on his way to Tokyo. He hangs up, and you do not have his cell phone number. You send the email without using the encryption software. [*U.S. v. Thomas*, 74 F.3d. 701 6th Cir. 1996, ABA Ethics Opinion, Utah Ethics Opinion 00-01.] Have you breached any rules on client confidentiality by sending an unencrypted email containing confidential client information?

DEVELOPING YOUR COLLABORATION SKILLS

Working on your own or with a group of other students assigned by your instructor, review the scenario at the beginning of the chapter that deals with combining a paper-based office and an electronic office.

1. Divide into two teams, one team playing the role of the junior paralegal and the other the senior paralegal. Put yourself in each person's place, and make a list of the benefits of the type of office system (electronic or paper) that each is accustomed to working in.
2. Share your list with the other team. As a group, decide what systems or practices you think will be most efficient and effective to use in the combined office for performing the following activities:
   - Managing conflicts of interest
   - Performing legal research
   - Managing cases
   - Handling client files
   - Communicating with clients
   - Managing financial accounts
3. As a group, identify areas of ethical concern in a merger, and discuss how to best handle these issues.

PARALEGAL PORTFOLIO EXERCISE

Prepare a memo for a potential law office manager, outlining the advantages and disadvantages of the paperless office. What security and confidentiality issues must be considered? What potential solutions or office procedures should be put in place? Reference and cite any applicable ethical rules or opinions from your local or state court or bar association.

LEGAL ANALYSIS & WRITING CASES

Issue: Are Images Displayed on the Internet as a Result of a Search Protected by Copyright?

The defendant operates a "visual search engine" on the Internet that allows a user to obtain a list of related web content in response to a search query entered by the user. Unlike other Internet search engines, the defendant's search engine, the "Ditto Crawler," retrieves images instead of descriptive text. It produces a list of reduced, "thumbnail" pictures related to the user's query. By clicking on the desired thumbnail, a user can view the "image attributes" window displaying the full-size version of the image, a description of its dimensions, and an address for the website where it originated. By clicking on the address, the user can link to the originating website for the image. The search engine works by maintaining an indexed database of approximately two million thumbnail images obtained through a "crawler"—a computer program that travels the web in search of images to be converted into thumbnails and added to the index.

Kelly, the plaintiff, is a photographer specializing in photographs of the California Gold Rush country and photographs related to the works of Laura Ingalls Wilder. He does not sell the photographs independently, but his photographs have appeared in several books. Plaintiff also maintains two websites, one of which (www.goldrush1849.com) provides a "virtual tour" of California's Gold Rush country and promotes plaintiff's book on the subject. The other (www.showmethegold.com) markets corporate retreats in California's Gold Rush country.

Thirty-five of plaintiff's images were indexed by the Ditto Crawler and put in the defendant's image database. As a result, these images were made available in thumbnail form to users of defendant's visual search engine. After being notified of plaintiff's objections, Ditto removed the images from its database.

The plaintiff filed a copyright infringement action. One of the questions of first impression is whether the display of copyrighted images by a "visual search engine" on the Internet constitutes fair use under the Copyright Act. The court found that defendant never held out plaintiff's work as its own, or even engaged in conduct specifically directed at plaintiff's work. The plaintiff's images were swept up along with two million others available on the Internet, as part of defendant's efforts to provide its users with a better way to find images on the Internet. The defendant's purposes were, and are, inherently transformative, even if its realization of those purposes was at times imperfect. Where, as here, a new use and new technology are evolving, the broad transformative purpose of the use weighs more heavily than the inevitable flaws in its early stages of development.

Questions

1. As the use of the Internet matures, will courts view use of information from the web differently?
2. What are the implications of taking material off the Internet and including it in reports, memos, and briefs?
3. Would the decision have been different if the items were copyrighted legal forms also located by a "crawler" and displayed as a visual image, such as a PDF file?

WORKING WITH THE LANGUAGE OF THE COURT CASE

CoStar Group Inc. v. LoopNet, Inc. 164 F.Supp.2d 688 (D.C. Md. 2001)

United States District Court, Maryland

Read this case, and if assigned, brief it. In your brief, include answers to the following questions.

1. What is a "contributory infringer" under the Digital Millennium Copyright Act?
2. Who is an online service provider as defined by the Digital Millennium Copyright Act (DMCA)?
3. When does a service provider lose its immunity under the DMCA?
4. What is a "safe harbor" under the DMCA?
5. What conduct takes a service provider out of the safe harbor?

Deborah K. Chasanow

I. BACKGROUND

Plaintiffs CoStar Group, Inc. and CoStar Realty Information, Inc. (collectively CoStar) filed suit against LoopNet, Inc. (LoopNet) alleging copyright infringement. CoStar is a national provider of commercial real estate information services…which includes photographs….

LoopNet is an Internet-based company offering a service through which a user…may post a listing of commercial real estate available for lease….To include a photograph,…it is uploaded into a separate "folder,"…where it is reviewed by a LoopNet employee to determine that it is…a photograph of commercial property and that there is no obvious…violation of LoopNet's terms and conditions. If the photograph meets LoopNet's criteria…it is automatically posted….CoStar claims that over 300 of its copyrighted photographs have appeared on LoopNet's site (the number has increased over time)….

Application of copyright law in cyberspace is elusive and perplexing. The World Wide Web has progressed far faster than the law and, as a result, courts are struggling to catch up. Legislatures and courts endeavor in this growing area to maintain the free flow of information over the Internet while still protecting intellectual property rights….

Contributory Copyright Infringement

1. OVERVIEW

It is, today, a given that: one who, with knowledge of the infringing activity, induces, causes, or materially contributes to the infringing conduct of another, may be held liable as a "contributory" infringer….Put differently, liability exists if the defendant engages in "personal conduct that encourages or assists the infringement."…

CoStar does not claim that LoopNet had knowledge of its users' infringements prior to its giving notice….Given the nature of the infringements in this case, it was impossible for LoopNet to have knowledge of the alleged infringement before receiving notice from CoStar. CoStar does not attach a copyright notice to its photos and even CoStar's own expert could not identify a CoStar photo simply by reviewing it….Thus, LoopNet cannot be charged with…knowledge before receiving claims of infringement from CoStar….CoStar does not claim that LoopNet had knowledge of infringement prior to receiving notice from CoStar. [T]here remain...disputes about [its] knowledge...after receiving the claims of infringement. CoStar alleges that once it gave LoopNet notice that its photographs were being infringed, LoopNet can be charged with knowledge of continuing infringements....

The DMCA was enacted both to preserve copyright enforcement in the Internet and to provide immunity to service providers from copyright infringement liability for "passive," "automatic" actions in which a service provider's system engages through a technological process initiated by another without the knowledge of the service provider....The DMCA's protection of an innocent service provider disappears at the moment the service provider loses its innocence, i.e., at the moment it becomes aware that a third party is using its system to infringe. At that point, the Act shifts responsibility to the service provider to disable the infringing matter, "preserving the strong incentives for service providers and copyright owners to cooperate to detect and deal with copyright infringements that take place in the digital networked environment."

The DMCA seeks to strike a balance by shielding online service providers from liability in damages as long as they remove or prevent access to infringing material....The initial inquiry is whether LoopNet can be considered a service provider for the purposes of the DMCA.

a. Service Provider

In order to qualify for the safe harbor in the DMCA, LoopNet must meet the definition of "online service provider." Under § 512 (k)(1)(A), a service provider is "an entity offering the transmission, routing, or providing of connections for digital online communications, between or among points specified by a user, of material of the user's choosing, without modification to the content of the material as sent or received." 17 U.S.C. § 512(k)(1)(A)(1998)....For the other safe harbor provisions, including (c), which is at issue here, the definition is broader: "a provider of online services or network access, or the operator of facilities therefore."...

"Online services" is surely broad enough to encompass the type of service provided by LoopNet that is at issue here. The term is, of course, only a threshold to the protections of the Act. Even if LoopNet qualifies as a service provider, it must meet the other criteria.

b. Stored at the Instance of the User

A service provider is only protected from liability by the DMCA, "for infringement of copyright by reason of its storage at the direction of user of material." 17 U.S.C. § 512(c)(1)...[The photographs at issue] are uploaded at the volition of the user and are subject...to a mere screening to assess whether they are commercial property and to catch any obvious infringements....Although humans are involved rather than mere technology, they serve only as a gateway and are not involved in a selection process....Therefore, this threshold requirement is met and LoopNet is not disqualified from the safe harbor on these grounds.

c. Knowledge

The safe harbor protects service providers from liability unless they have knowledge of copyright infringement. There are three types of knowledge of infringement that can take a service provider out of the safe harbor: (1) the service provider can have actual knowledge of infringement; (2) it can be aware of facts which raise a "red flag" that its users are infringing; or (3) the copyright owner can notify the service provider in a manner "substantially" conforming with § 512 (c)(3) that its works are being infringed....The service provider does not automatically lose its liability shield upon receiving notice, but "the Act shifts responsibility to the service provider to disable the infringing matter...."

...LoopNet received notification of claimed infringement...so the adequacy of LoopNet's removal policy must be assessed to determine whether LoopNet is protected by the safe harbor.

d. Adequacy of Termination and "Take Down" Policy

Once a service provider has received notification of a claimed infringement as described in [the Act]...the service provider can remain in the safe harbor if it "responds expeditiously to remove, or disable access to, the material that is claimed to be infringing or to be the subject of infringing activity." 17 U.S.C. § 512 (c)(1)(C) (1998)....

There are several material factual disputes remaining as to whether the removal of allegedly infringing photographs was satisfactorily expeditious and whether LoopNet's termination policy was reasonable and effective. CoStar's infringement claims are based on the posting of specific photographs. Additionally, LoopNet's knowledge of the alleged infringements and its "take down" and termination policies have changed over time in fairly significant ways. In order to resolve this issue, the fact finder will have to focus on each photo and the policy in effect prior to the posting of each photo. Hence, neither party is entitled to summary judgment on this issue....

(*continued*)

3. LIABILITY FOR CONTRIBUTORY INFRINGEMENT

With regard to the photographs that were infringed before the safe harbor applied...and in case LoopNet's termination policy and take down of infringing photographs is found to be inadequate so as to remove it from the safe harbor, the analysis shifts from the DMCA back to contributory infringement. The determination of contributory infringement liability turns on a different issue of knowledge than the standard used to determine LoopNet's eligibility for the safe harbor. Here, the question is whether CoStar's notice of claimed infringement was sufficient to satisfy the knowledge prong of the test for contributory infringement either by providing actual knowledge, a "red flag" that infringement was occurring, or constructive knowledge.

...[T]he fact finder must determine along a continuum the adequacy of the policy in place prior to the posting of each specific photograph. Therefore, neither party is entitled to summary judgment on this issue.

e. Preemption of Non-Copyright Claims

...The Copyright Act preempts state law that is "equivalent to any of the exclusive rights within the general scope of copyright as specified by section 106." 17 U.S.C. § 301(a) (1996)..."To determine whether a state claim is preempted by the Act, courts must make a two-part inquiry: (1) the work must be within the scope of the subject matter of copyright, and (2) the state law rights must be equivalent to any exclusive rights within the scope of federal copyright." *Fischer v. Viacom Intern Corp.*, 115 F. Supp. 2d 535. 540 (D.Md. 2000)....The critical question, then, is whether CoStar's unfair competition claim contains an additional element or whether it is based solely on the alleged copying.

...Essentially, CoStar's claim is that LoopNet is exhibiting as its own photographs on its website that CoStar has an exclusive right to exhibit or license for exhibition. This type of reverse passing off is, in effect, a "disguised copyright infringement claim."...Therefore, this claim does not satisfy the "extra-element" test and so is equivalent to CoStar's claim under the Copyright Act. Accordingly, it is preempted....

V. CONCLUSION

For the foregoing reasons; by separate order, both motions concerning the safe harbor defense of the DMCA will be denied,...both motions concerning contributory infringement will be denied,...summary judgment will be granted in favor of LoopNet on the...preemption of the state law claims.

MYLEGALSTUDIESLAB

MyLegalStudiesLab Virtual Law Office Experience Assignments

Complete the pre-test, study plan, and post-test for this chapter and answer the Legal Applications questions as assigned. These will help you confirm your mastery of the concepts and their application to legal scenarios. Then complete the Virtual Law Office assignments as assigned by your instructor. These assignments are designed to develop your workplace skills. Completing the assignments for this chapter will result in producing the following documents for inclusion in your portfolio:

VLOE 4.1

1. Your personal calendar information for the next four months if you did not already do so in a previous lesson.
2. Summary of the time you have spent in the internship to this point.

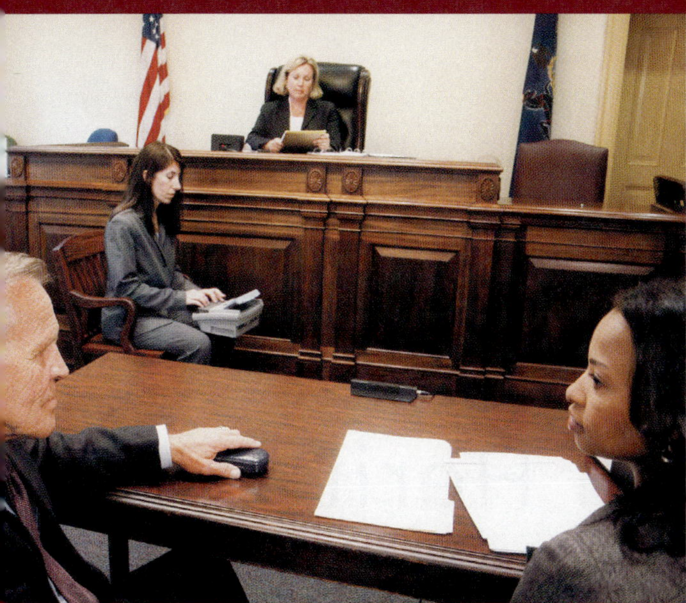

PART

Introduction to Law

The aspiring paralegal professional must become familiar with American legal heritage and how the law developed in this country over the centuries. This includes learning the historical and current sources of federal law and state law. In addition, a professional paralegal should have knowledge of the Constitution of the United States of America and how it structures the federal government, delegates powers to the federal government, reserves powers to the states, and protects us from unwelcome government intrusion into our lives. A paralegal professional must have knowledge of the American court system and the process of judicial and nonjudicial dispute resolution. A working knowledge of the civil litigation process, criminal litigation and procedure, and administrative law is also a necessary part of a paralegal professional's education. Part II, "Introduction to Law," provides the paralegal professional student with this knowledge.

CHAPTER

5

American Legal Heritage and Constitutional Law

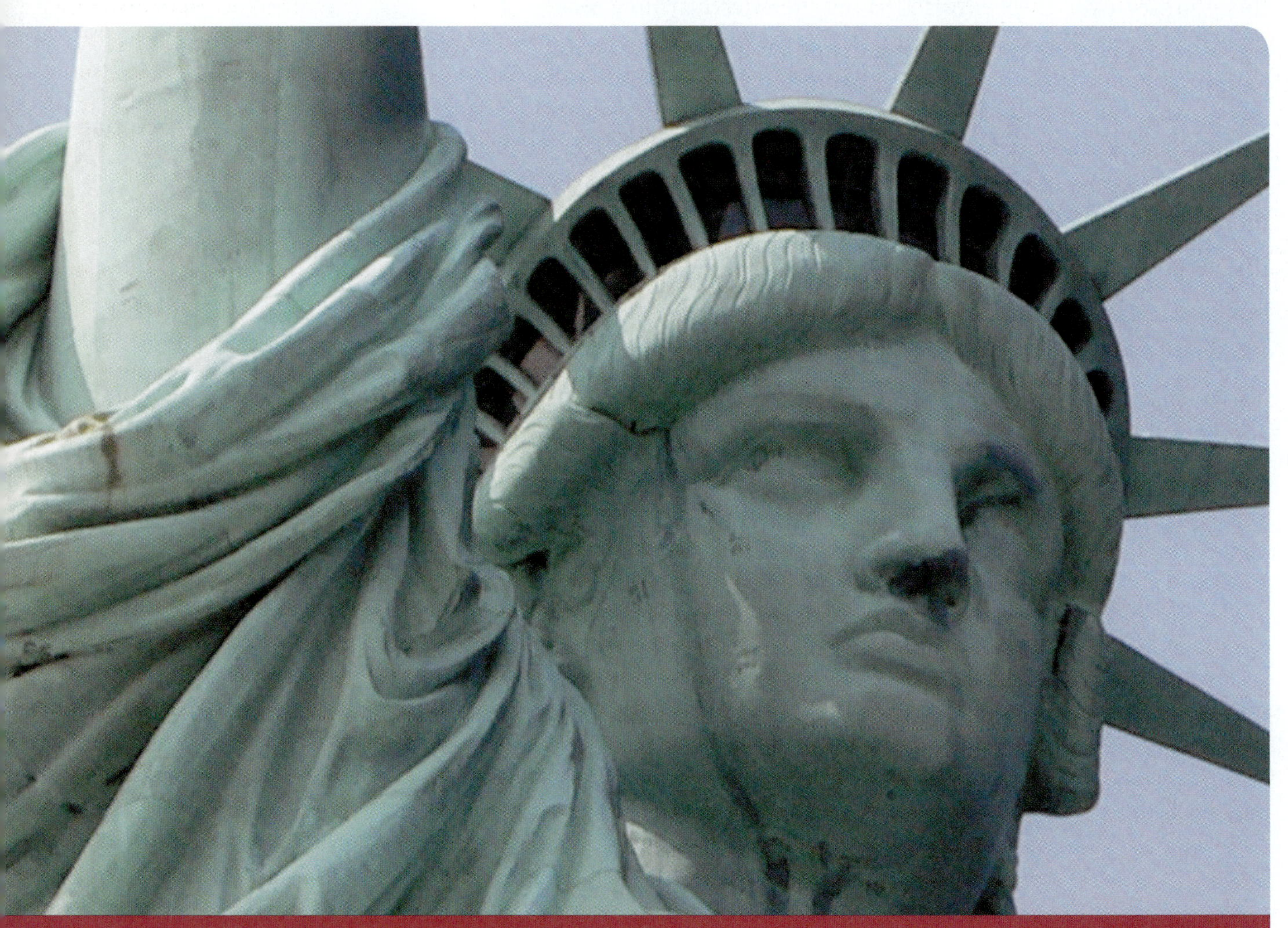

LEARNING OBJECTIVES

After studying this chapter, you should be able to:

1. Recognize the professional opportunities for paralegals in the area of constitutional law.
2. Define *law* and describe the functions of law.
3. Explain the fairness and flexibility of the law.
4. List and describe the sources of law in the United States.
5. Explain the doctrine of separation of powers and describe the checks and balances built into the U.S. Constitution.
6. Describe the Supremacy Clause of the U.S. Constitution and the preemption doctrine.
7. Describe the Commerce Clause of the U.S. Constitution.
8. Describe freedom of speech and other protections guaranteed by the Bill of Rights.
9. Describe the Equal Protection Clause and the tests used to determine whether it has been violated.
10. Explain a paralegal's duty to avoid conflicts of interest.

Paralegals at Work

You are a paralegal at a large law firm that specializes in handling issues in constitutional law. You work for Vivian Kang, a senior partner of the firm. One day Ms. Kang calls you into her office and tells you that a new client, Mr. Hayward Storm, has retained the law firm. Ms. Kang asks you to sit in with her during an interview with Mr. Storm.

Mr. Storm tells the following story: For more than twenty years he has been on radio and television, primarily as a disc jockey and talk show host. Mr. Storm most recently hosted television shows where he behaved outlandishly, using vulgar language, having guests appear on the show nude, telling disgusting jokes, and doing other things that offend many people. Mr. Storm also hosted a radio show in which he used profanity and offensive language. The Federal Communications Commission (FCC), a federal government agency, is responsible for regulating radio and television. The FCC has fined Mr. Storm and his employer for engaging in such conduct over the television and radio airwaves.

In addition, Mr. Storm explains that he will be leaving regular radio and television and has been hired to be a disc jockey for satellite radio broadcasts. He is making this change because satellite radio currently is not regulated by the FCC. Mr. Storm plans to continue his usual offensive programming on satellite radio and says he will increase his extreme language and conduct because of satellite radio's lack of FCC regulation. However, he is concerned that Congress will enact a federal statute granting the FCC the power to regulate satellite radio.

Consider the issues involved in this scenario as you read this chapter.

> "We the People of the United States, in Order to form a more perfect Union, establish Justice, insure domestic Tranquility, provide for the common defense, promote the general Welfare, and secure the Blessings of Liberty to ourselves and our Posterity, do ordain and establish this Constitution for the United States of America."
>
> *Preamble to the Constitution of the United States of America*

INTRODUCTION FOR THE PARALEGAL

A paralegal must have a foundation in the basic sources of the law of the United States. Our society makes and enforces laws that govern the conduct of the individuals, businesses, and other organizations that function within it. In the words of Judge Learned Hand, "Without law we cannot live; only with it can we insure the future which by right is ours. The best of men's hopes are enmeshed in its success" (*The Spirit of Liberty*, 1960).

Human beings do not ever make laws; it is the accidents and catastrophes of all kinds happening in every conceivable way that make law for us.

Plato, *Laws IV*, 709

Although U.S. law is based primarily on English common law, other legal systems, such as Spanish and French civil law, also influenced it. The other main sources of law in this country are the U.S. Constitution, state constitutions, federal and state statutes, ordinances, administrative agency rules and regulations, executive orders, and judicial decisions by federal and state courts.

Paralegals should be well-rounded professionals who have an understanding of this country's founding, its constitutional protections, and the current debates concerning the application of constitutional language in these modern times. To that end, this chapter provides an overview of the nature and definition of law, the history and sources of law, and the U.S. Constitution.

Learning Objective 1
Recognize the professional opportunities for paralegals in the area of constitutional law.

The following section discusses the career opportunities for paralegal professionals in the area of constitutional law.

Learning Objective 2
Define *law* and describe the functions of law.

What Is Law?

The word *law* is used in many different contexts, and its definition is very broad. *Black's Law Dictionary*, 5th edition, defines *law* as follows:

> Law, in its generic sense, is a body of rules of action or conduct prescribed by controlling authority, and having binding legal force. That which must be obeyed and followed by citizens subject to sanctions or legal consequences is a law.

CAREER OPPORTUNITIES FOR PARALEGALS IN CONSTITUTIONAL LAW

The Constitution of the United States of America is one of the most important documents ever drafted. The U.S. Constitution created a new country, one that was not ruled by kings, queens, monarchs, or dictators. The country was one of the world's first democracies—a crucial development in the history of the world.

The Constitution is considered a "living document" that has continually been applied by the United States Supreme Court and other courts to an ever-changing society. As a result, the interpretation of the Constitution has constantly evolved since its ratification more than two centuries ago.

Some members of the paralegal profession will work in practice areas that frequently involve issues in constitutional law. This is an exciting field to participate in. Paralegals who work in this area will be called upon to conduct legal research relating to constitutional provisions and amendments, find relevant cases that interpret constitutional language, and assist lawyers who present cases to the courts regarding constitutional issues. Some members of the paralegal profession will be fortunate to work on cases that will be heard and decided by the U.S. Supreme Court.

All paralegals should be familiar with several major provisions and protections of the U.S. Constitution and its amendments:

- The Supremacy Clause
- The Commerce Clause
- Freedom of speech
- Freedom of religion
- The Due Process Clause
- The Equal Protection Clause

In addition to the above provisions, paralegals should understand how the Constitution structures the federal government with its built-in checks and balances, how it grants powers to the government, and how it establishes protections against certain intrusions by the government into our lives. The Constitution of the United States of America is set forth in its entirety in Appendix F to this book.

Law consists of rules that regulate the conduct of individuals, businesses, and other organizations within society. Laws are intended to protect persons and their property from unwanted interference from others and forbid persons from engaging in certain undesirable activities.

Law That which must be obeyed and followed by citizens subject to sanctions or legal consequences. A body of rules of action or conduct prescribed by controlling authority, and having binding legal force.

Fairness of the Law

Learning Objective 3
Explain the fairness and flexibility of the law.

On the whole, the American legal system is one of the most comprehensive, fair, and democratic systems of law ever developed. Nevertheless, that system often produces errors and unjust results. These include mistakes and abuses of discretion by judges and juries, unequal applications of the law, and procedural mishaps, which sometimes allow guilty parties to go unpunished.

In *Standefer v. United States*, 447 U.S.10, 100 S.Ct.1999 (1980), the Supreme Court *affirmed* (let stand) the criminal conviction of a Gulf Oil Corporation executive for aiding and abetting the bribery of an Internal Revenue Service agent. The agent had been acquitted in a separate trial. In writing the opinion of the Court, Chief Justice Warren Burger stated, "This case does no more than manifest the simple, if discomforting, reality that different juries may reach different results under any criminal statute. That is one of the consequences we accept under our jury system."

Flexibility of the Law

Paralegals new to the profession may be surprised to find that American law is quite flexible. The law is generally responsive to cultural, technological, economic, and social changes.

Example Laws that are no longer viable—such as those that restricted the property rights of women—are often repealed.

This flexibility in the law leads to some uncertainty in predicting results of lawsuits. However, laws cannot be written in advance to anticipate every dispute that could arise in the future. Therefore, general principles are developed to be applied by courts and juries to individual disputes. The following quote from Judge Jerome Frank addresses the value of the adaptability of law (*Law and the Modern Mind*, 1930):

> The law always has been, is now, and will ever continue to be, largely vague and variable. And how could this be otherwise? The law deals with human relations in their most complicated aspects. The whole confused, shifting helter-skelter of life parades before it—more confused than ever, in our kaleidoscopic age.

The nation's armour of defence against the passions of men is the Constitution. Take that away, and the nation goes down into the field of its conflicts like a warrior without armour.
Henry Ward Beecher
Proverbs from Plymouth Pulpit, 1887

The continuing potential for unexpected problems in our society requires a legal system capable of fluidity and pliancy. Our society needs a court system that, with the able assistance of lawyers, can constantly adapt the law to the realities of ever-changing social, industrial, and political conditions. Although changes to the law should not be considered lightly, rules must be somewhat impermanent and flexible.

The legal system may appear to be flawed in its uncertainty, but the ability of the law to be flexible and adaptable is of immense social value.

Sometimes it takes years for the law to reflect the norms of society. Other times, society is led by the law. The major functions served by law are listed and described in Exhibit 5.1.

Exhibit 5.1 Functions of the law

1. Keeping the peace (such as by punishing certain activities or making them crimes).
2. Shaping moral standards (for example, by enacting laws that discourage drug and alcohol abuse).
3. Promoting social justice (for example, by enacting statutes that prohibit discrimination in employment).
4. Maintaining the status quo (such as bypassing laws that prevent the forceful overthrow of the government).
5. Facilitating orderly change (such as bypassing statutes only after considerable study, debate, and public input).
6. Facilitating planning (for example, by designing laws to allow businesses to plan their activities, allocate their productive resources, and assess the risks they take).
7. Providing a basis for compromise (as in systems where more than 90 percent of all lawsuits are settled without the need for a trial).
8. Maximizing individual freedom (for example, the rights of freedom of speech, religion, and association granted by the First Amendment to the U.S. Constitution).

Schools of Jurisprudential Thought

Jurisprudence The philosophy or science of law.

The philosophy or science of the law is referred to as **jurisprudence**. Scholars of jurisprudence attempt to explain the nature of law and how legal systems and institutions develop. These philosophers can be grouped into the following major categories:

- The **natural law school** postulates that the law is based on what is "correct." Natural law philosophers emphasize a *moral* theory of law—that is, law should be based on morality and ethics. People "discover" natural law through reasoning and by choosing between good and evil. Documents such as the U.S. Constitution, the Magna Carta, and the United Nations Charter reflect this theory.
- The **historical school** believes that the law is an aggregate of social traditions and customs that have developed over the centuries. The law is an evolutionary process, and the law gradually reflects changes in the norms of society. Thus, historical legal scholars look to past legal decisions, or precedent, to solve contemporary problems.

The law is not a series of calculating machines where definitions and answers come tumbling out when the right levers are pushed.

William O. Douglas
The Dissent, A Safeguard of Democracy, 1948

- The **analytical school** maintains that the law is shaped by logic. Analytical philosophers believe that results are reached by applying principles of logic to the specific facts of the case. The emphasis is on the logic of the result rather than on how the result is reached.
- The **sociological school** asserts that the law is a means of achieving and advancing certain sociological goals. Followers of this philosophy, known as *realists*, believe that the purpose of law is to shape social behavior. Sociological philosophers are unlikely to adhere to past law as precedent.
- The philosophers of the **command school** believe that the law is a set of rules developed, communicated, and enforced by the ruling class, and that the law does not truly reflect society's morality, history, logic, or sociology. This school maintains that the law changes when the ruling class changes.
- The **critical legal studies school** proposes that legal rules are unnecessary and are used as an obstacle by the powerful to maintain the status quo. Critical legal theorists (sometimes referred to as "Crits") argue that legal disputes should be solved by applying arbitrary rules based on broad notions of what is "fair" in each circumstance. Under this theory, subjective decision making by judges would be permitted.

- The **law and economics school** proposes that promoting market and economic efficiency should be the central goal of legal decision making. This school is called the "Chicago School" of jurisprudence because it had its roots at the University of Chicago. This school proposes, for example, that free-market principles, cost–benefit analysis, and supply-and-demand theories should be used to determine the passage of legislation and the outcome of lawsuits.

Web Exploration

Read the opinion of Chief Justice Warren of the U.S. Supreme Court in *Brown v. Board of Education* at **http://www.nationalcenter.org/brown.html**.

History of American Law

Every person in the United States should have a basic knowledge of this country's legal history. Paralegals in particular need to know the history of the law in the United States and how the law developed to become what it is today.

When the American colonies were first settled, the English system of common law was generally adopted as the system of jurisprudence. English common law became the source of much of the law of the American colonies and eventually of the United States of America. This was the foundation from which American judges developed a common law in the United States.

English Common Law

English **common law** was law developed by judges who issued written opinions when deciding cases. The principles announced in these cases became precedent for later judges deciding similar cases. The English common law can be divided into cases decided by the following courts:

Common law Law developed by judges who issue their opinions when deciding cases. The principles announced in these cases become precedent for judges to later decide similar cases.

- **Law courts**. After 1066, William the Conqueror and his successors to the throne of England replaced various local laws with one uniform system of law. The king or queen appointed loyal followers as judges in each area of the kingdom. These judges were charged with administering the law in a uniform manner in what were called **law courts**. Law at this time tended to emphasize form (legal procedure) over the substance (merits) of the case. The only relief available in law courts was a monetary award for damages.
- **Chancery (equity) courts.** Because of the sometimes unfair results and the limited relief available in the law courts, a second set of courts—the **Court of Chancery** (or **equity court**)—was established, under the authority of the Lord Chancellor. Those who believed that the decision of a law court was unfair, or that the law court could not grant an appropriate remedy, could seek relief in this court. The Chancery Court inquired into the merits of the case and was less concerned with legal procedure. The Chancellor's remedies were called *equitable remedies* because they were shaped to fit each situation. Equitable orders and remedies of the Court of Chancery took precedence over the legal decisions and remedies of the law courts.
- **Merchant courts**. As trade developed in the Middle Ages, the merchants who traveled around Europe developed certain rules to solve their commercial disputes. These rules, known as the "law of merchants" or the *law merchant*, were based upon common trade practices and usage. Eventually, a separate set of courts, called the **merchant courts**, was established to administer these rules. In the early 1900s, the merchant court was absorbed into the regular law court system of England.

Two things most people should never see made: sausages and laws.

An old saying

Adoption of the English Common Law in America

All the states of the United States of America (except Louisiana) base their legal systems primarily on the English common law. The law, equity, and merchant courts have been merged so that most U.S. courts permit aggrieved parties to seek both law and equitable orders and remedies.

The importance of common law to the American legal system is described in the following excerpt from Justice William Douglas's opinion in the 1841 case of *Penny v. Little*, 4 Ill. 301, 1841 Ill. Lexis 98 (Ill. 1841):

> The common law is a beautiful system, containing the wisdom and experiences of ages. Like the people it ruled and protected, it was simple and crude in its infancy, and became enlarged, improved, and polished as the nation advanced in civilization, virtue, and intelligence. Adapting itself to the conditions and circumstances of the people and relying upon them for its administration, it necessarily improved as the condition of the people was elevated. The inhabitants of this country always claimed the common law as their birthright, and at an early period established it as the basis of their jurisprudence.

Civil Law System

Another important legal system that has developed in the western world is the Romano-Germanic **civil law system**. This legal system, commonly called the *civil law*, dates to 450 B.C., when Rome adopted a code of laws for its citizens. A compilation of this Roman law, called the *Corpus Juris Civilis* (the Body of Civil Law), was completed in A.D. 534. Later, two national codes—the French Civil Code of 1804 (the Napoleonic Code) and the German Civil Code of 1896—became models for countries that adopted civil codes.

In contrast to Anglo-American common law, in which laws are created by both judges and legislatures, the Civil Code and the statutes that expand and interpret it are the sole sources of the law in most civil law countries. Thus, cases are adjudicated by simply applying the code provisions or statutes to a specific set of facts. In some civil law countries, court decisions do not have the force of law.

Some states in America—particularly states that have a French or Spanish heritage, such as Louisiana and the southwestern states—have incorporated civil law into their legal systems.

Learning Objective 4
List and describe the sources of law in the United States.

Sources of Law in the United States

In the more than 230 years since the founding of this country, U.S. lawmakers have developed a substantial body of law. The laws of the United States are extremely complex.

U.S. Congress, Washington, DC. The U.S. Congress, which is a bicameral system made up of the U.S. Senate and the U.S. House of Representatives, creates federal law by enacting statutes. Each state has two senators and is allocated a certain number of representatives, based on population.

Paralegals often are called upon to conduct legal research to find relevant laws and judicial decisions that affect the cases or projects to which they are assigned. It is therefore important for them to know the sources of these laws. The sources of modern law in the United States are discussed in the following sections.

Constitutions

The **Constitution of the United States of America** is the supreme law of the land. This means that any law—federal, state, or local—that conflicts with the U.S. Constitution is unconstitutional and, therefore, unenforceable.

Constitution of the United States of America The supreme law of the United States. The Constitution of the United States of America establishes the structure of the federal government, delegates powers to the federal government, and guarantees certain fundamental rights.

The principles enumerated in the Constitution are extremely broad, because the founding fathers intended them to be applied to evolving social, technological, and economic conditions. The U.S. Constitution is often referred to as a "living document" because it is so adaptable.

States also have their own constitutions, often patterned after the U.S. Constitution, though many are more detailed. Provisions of state constitutions are valid unless they conflict with the U.S. Constitution or any federal law.

Treaties

The U.S. Constitution provides that the president, with the advice and consent of the U.S. Senate, may enter into **treaties** with foreign governments. Treaties become part of the supreme law of the land. With increasing international economic relations among nations, treaties will become an even more important source of law affecting business in the future.

Treaty A compact made between two or more nations.

Codified Law

Statutes are written laws enacted by legislatures. The U.S. Congress is empowered by the Commerce Clause and other provisions of the U.S. Constitution to enact **federal statutes** to regulate foreign and interstate commerce.

Statute Written law enacted by the legislative branch of the federal and state governments that establishes certain courses of conduct.

Examples Federal statutes include laws that cover antitrust, securities, bankruptcy, labor, equal employment opportunity, environmental protection, and consumer protection.

State legislatures enact **state statutes**.

Examples State statutes include state corporation laws, partnership laws, workers' compensation laws, and the Uniform Commercial Code.

The statutes enacted by the legislative branches of federal and state governments are organized by topic in code books. Law that has been recorded and organized in this way is referred to as **codified law**. Paralegals are often called upon to conduct research to find codified law that may apply to cases they are assigned to.

State legislatures often delegate lawmaking authority to local government bodies, such as cities and municipalities, counties, school districts, and water districts. These governmental units are empowered to adopt laws called **ordinances**.

Ordinance Law enacted by local government bodies, such as cities and municipalities, counties, school districts, and water districts.

Examples Traffic laws, local building codes, and zoning laws are types of ordinances. Ordinances are also codified.

Administrative Law

The legislative and executive branches of federal and state governments are empowered to establish **administrative agencies** to enforce and interpret statutes enacted by Congress and state legislatures. Many of these agencies regulate business.

Examples Congress has created numerous agencies such as the Securities and Exchange Commission (SEC) and the Federal Trade Commission (FTC).

The U.S. Congress or state legislatures usually empower these agencies to adopt administrative rules and regulations to interpret the statutes that the agencies are authorized to enforce. These rules and regulations have the force of law. Administrative agencies usually also have the power to hear and decide disputes. Their decisions are called *orders*. Because of their power, administrative agencies often are informally called the "fourth branch" of government.

Executive Orders

Executive order An order issued by a member of the executive branch of the government.

The executive branch of the federal government is headed by the president of the United States. In each state, the governor is the head of the executive branch. The executive branch is empowered to issue **executive orders**. This power is expressly delegated by the legislative branch and is implied from the U.S. Constitution and state constitutions.

> **Example** On October 8, 2001, President George W. Bush, by executive order, established within the Executive Office of the President an Office of Homeland Security to be headed by the Assistant to the President for Homeland Security.

Judicial Decisions

Judicial decision A ruling about an individual lawsuit issued by federal and state courts.

When deciding individual lawsuits, federal and state courts issue **judicial decisions**. In these written opinions, the judge or justice usually explains the legal reasoning used to decide each case. An opinion often includes interpretations of statutes, ordinances, administrative regulations, and legal principles applied to the case. Many court decisions are reported in books available in law libraries.

Priority of Law in the United States

The U.S. Constitution and treaties take precedence over all other laws. Federal statutes take precedence over federal regulations, and federal law takes precedence over any conflicting state or local law. State constitutions rank as the highest state law, and state statutes take precedence over state regulations. State law takes precedence over local laws.

The Doctrine of *Stare Decisis*

Based on the common law tradition, past court decisions become precedents for deciding future cases. Lower courts must follow the precedents established by higher courts. That is why all federal and state courts in the United States must follow the precedents established by U.S. Supreme Court decisions.

The courts of one jurisdiction are not bound by the precedents established by the courts of another jurisdiction, although they may look to each other for guidance. Thus, state courts of one state are not required to follow the legal precedents established by the courts of another state.

Stare decisis Latin phrase meaning "to stand by the decision." Adherence to precedent.

Adherence to precedents is called ***stare decisis*** ("to stand by the decision"). The doctrine of *stare decisis* promotes uniformity of law within a jurisdiction, makes the court system more efficient, and makes the law more predictable for individuals and businesses. A court may change or reverse its legal reasoning later if a new case is presented to it and a change is warranted.

The doctrine of *stare decisis* is discussed in the following excerpt from Justice Musmanno's decision in *Flagiello v. Pennsylvania*, 417 Pa. 486, 208 A.2d 193 (1965):

> Without *stare decisis*, there would be no stability in our system of jurisprudence. Stare decisis channels the law. It erects lighthouses and flies the signals of safety. The ships of jurisprudence must follow that well-defined channel which, over the years, has been proved to be secure and worthy.

Constitution of the United States of America

Learning Objective 5
Explain the doctrine of separation of powers and describe the checks and balances built into the U.S. Constitution.

Prior to the American Revolution, each of the thirteen original colonies was a separate sovereignty under the rule of England. In September 1774, representatives of the colonies formed the Continental Congress. In 1776, the colonies declared their independence from England, and the American Revolution ensued.

The Constitutional Convention was convened in Philadelphia in May 1787 with the primary purpose of strengthening the federal government. After substantial debate, the delegates agreed to a new U.S. Constitution, which was reported to Congress in September 1787. State ratification of the Constitution was completed in 1788. Since that time, many amendments, including the Bill of Rights, have been added to the Constitution.

The U.S. Constitution serves several major functions:

1. It creates the three branches of the federal government (executive, legislative, and judicial) and allocates powers to these branches.
2. It grants the federal government certain authority to enact laws and enforce those laws.
3. It protects individual rights by limiting the government's ability to restrict those rights.

The Constitution of the United States is not a mere lawyers' document: it is a vehicle of life, and its spirit is always the spirit of the age.
Woodrow Wilson
Constitutional Government in the United States, 1927

The Constitution itself permits amendments to address social and economic changes.

The first page of the Constitution of the United States of America is shown in Exhibit 5.2.

Federalism and Delegated Powers

The U.S. form of government is referred to as **federalism**, which means that the federal government and the 50 state governments share powers. When the states

Federalism The U.S. form of government in which the federal government and the fifty state governments share powers.

Exhibit 5.2 The Constitution of the United States

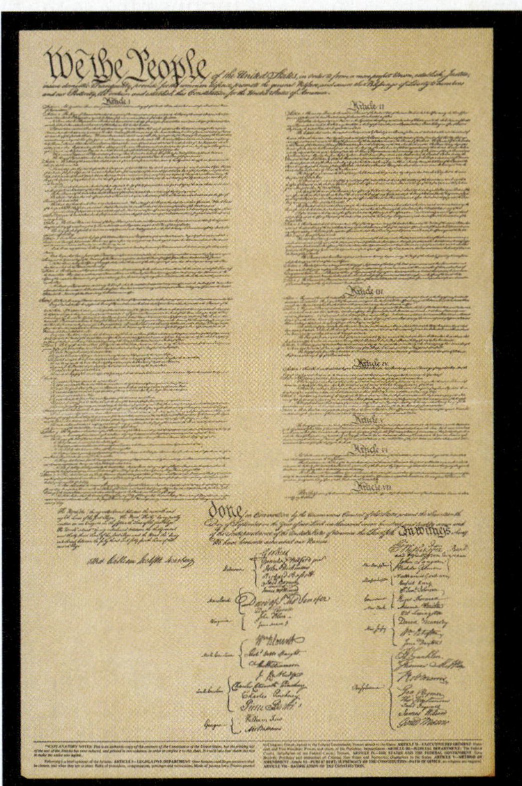

ratified the Constitution, they delegated certain powers to the federal government. These **delegated powers**, also called **enumerated powers**, authorize the federal government to deal with certain national and international affairs. State governments have powers that are not specifically delegated to the federal government by the Constitution and are empowered to deal with local affairs.

Legislative branch The part of the U.S. government that makes federal laws. It is known as Congress, and consists of the Senate and the House of Representatives.

Executive branch The part of the U.S. government that enforces the federal law; it is headed by the president.

Judicial branch The part of the U.S. government that interprets the law. It consists of the Supreme Court and other federal courts.

Checks and balances A system built into the U.S. Constitution to prevent any one of the three branches of the government from becoming too powerful.

Supremacy Clause A clause of the U.S. Constitution that establishes that the federal Constitution, treaties, federal laws, and federal regulations are the supreme law of the land.

Doctrine of Separation of Powers

The first three Articles of the Constitution divide the federal government into three branches:

1. **Article I** of the Constitution establishes the **legislative branch**. This branch is bicameral, consisting of the Senate and the House of Representatives, and is collectively referred to as *Congress*. Each state is allocated two senators. The number of representatives to the House of Representatives is determined by the population of each state. The current number of representatives is determined by the 2010 census.
2. **Article II** of the Constitution establishes the **executive branch** by providing for the election of the president and vice president. The president is not elected by popular vote, but instead by the Electoral College, whose representatives are appointed by state delegations.
3. **Article III** establishes the **judicial branch** by creating the Supreme Court and authorizing the creation of other federal courts by Congress.

Checks and Balances

Certain **checks and balances** are built into the Constitution to ensure that no one branch of the federal government becomes too powerful. Some of the checks and balances in our system of government are as follows:

1. The judicial branch has authority to examine the acts of the other two branches of government and determine whether these acts are constitutional.
2. The executive branch can enter into treaties with foreign governments only with the advice and consent of the Senate.
3. The legislative branch is authorized to create federal courts and determine their jurisdiction and to enact statutes that change judicially made law.
4. The president has veto power over bills passed by Congress. The bill goes back to Congress, where a vote of two-thirds of the members in each chamber is required to override the president's veto.
5. The president nominates persons to be U.S. Supreme Court justices, and many other federal judges, but the U.S. Senate must confirm the candidate before he or she becomes a judge.
6. The House of Representatives has the power to impeach the president for certain activities, such as treason, bribery, and other crimes. The Senate has the power to try the impeachment case, which requires a two-thirds vote of the Senate to impeach the president.

Web Exploration

Visit the website http://www.senate.gov/. Click on the word "Senators." Who are the two senators who represent your state in the U.S. Senate? Go to each senator's website and email the senator, expressing your view on a legal issue in which you are interested.

Web Exploration

Visit the website http://www.house.gov/. Who is the person who represents your home district? Go to that representative's website and read about his or her position on a current legal issue. What is the issue, and what is your representative's view on it?

Learning Objective 6

Describe the Supremacy Clause of the U.S. Constitution and the preemption doctrine.

Supremacy Clause

The **Supremacy Clause** establishes that the federal Constitution, treaties, federal laws, and federal regulations are the supreme law of the land (U.S. Const. Art. VI, § 2). State and local laws that conflict with valid federal law are unconstitutional. The concept that federal law takes precedence over state or local law is called the **preemption doctrine**.

Congress may expressly provide that a specific federal statute exclusively regulates a specific area or activity. No state or local law regulating the area or activity is valid if there is such a statute. More often, though, federal statutes do not expressly provide for exclusive jurisdiction. In these instances, state and local governments have concurrent jurisdiction to regulate the area or activity. But any state or local law that "directly and substantially" conflicts with valid federal law is preempted under the Supremacy Clause.

Example The United States government entered into treaties with other countries that established the size and length of oil tanker ships. Thus, oil tankers can transport oil between different countries using the same oil tankers. The state of Washington enacted a law that permitted only smaller oil tankers to enter its Puget Sound watercourse, which flows from waters of the Pacific Ocean. Oil tanker companies sued the state of Washington, arguing that the state law was unconstitutional. The U.S. Supreme Court held that the state law conflicted with federal law and was therefore preempted by the Supremacy Clause. *Ray v. Atlantic Richfield Co.*, 435 U.S. 151 (1978).

Commerce Clause

Learning Objective 7

Describe the Commerce Clause of the U.S. Constitution.

The **Commerce Clause** of the U.S. Constitution grants Congress the power "to regulate commerce with foreign nations, and among the several states, and with Indian tribes" (U.S. Const. Art. I, § 8, cl. 3). Because this clause authorizes the federal government to regulate commerce, it has a greater impact on business than any other provision in the Constitution. Among other things, this clause is intended to foster the development of a national market and free trade among the states.

Commerce Clause A clause of the U.S. Constitution that grants Congress the power "to regulate commerce with foreign nations, and among the several states, and with Indian tribes."

The U.S. Constitution grants the federal government the power to regulate three types of commerce. These are:

1. Commerce with Indian tribes
2. Commerce with foreign nations
3. Interstate commerce

Native Americans

Before Europeans arrived in the "New World," the land had been occupied for thousands of years by those we now refer to as Native Americans. When the United States was first founded over two centuries ago, it consisted of the original thirteen colonies, all located in the east, and primarily on the Atlantic Ocean. At that time, the U.S. Constitution delegated to the federal government the authority to regulate commerce "with the Indian tribes" (U.S. Const. Art. I, § 8, cl. 3). This included the original thirteen states as well as the territory that was to eventually become the United States of America.

Web Exploration

Visit the website of the National Museum of the American Indian at **www.nmai.si.edu**.

Example The federal government enacted the Indian Gaming Regulatory Act,[1] wherein the federal government authorized Native American tribes to operate gaming facilities. This act sets the terms of casino gambling and other gaming activities on tribal land. Today, casinos operated by Native Americans can be found in many states. Profits from the casinos have become an important source of income for members of certain tribes.

Foreign Commerce

The Commerce Clause gives the federal government the exclusive power to regulate commerce with foreign nations. Direct or indirect regulation of **foreign commerce** by state or local governments violates the Commerce Clause and is therefore unconstitutional.

Foreign commerce Commerce with foreign nations. The Commerce Clause grants the federal government the authority to regulate foreign commerce.

[1] 25 U.S.C. §§ 2701–2721.

Example Suppose the state of Michigan imposes a 20 percent sales tax on foreign automobiles sold in Michigan, but only a 6 percent tax on domestic automobiles sold in Michigan. This state act violates the Commerce Clause because Michigan has regulated foreign commerce differently than state commerce. If Michigan placed a 20 percent sales tax on all automobiles sold in Michigan, this would not violate the Commerce Clause. Under its foreign Commerce Clause power, the federal government could enact a federal law that places a 20 percent tax on foreign automobiles sold in the United States.

Interstate Commerce

Interstate commerce Commerce that moves between states or that affects commerce between states.

The Commerce Clause gives the federal government the authority to regulate **interstate commerce**. Originally, the courts interpreted this clause to mean that the federal government could regulate only the commerce that moved *in* interstate commerce between states. The modern interpretation, however, allows the federal government to regulate activities that *affect* interstate commerce.

Under the "effects on interstate commerce" test, the regulated activity does not itself have to be in interstate commerce. Thus, any **intrastate commerce** (commerce within the state) that has an effect on interstate commerce is subject to federal regulation. Theoretically, this test subjects a substantial amount of business activity in the United States to federal regulation.

Example In the famous case of *Wickard, Secretary of Agriculture v. Filburn*, 317 U.S. 111, 63 S.Ct. 82, 87 L.Ed. 122, 1942 U.S. Lexis 1046 (U.S.), a federal statute limited the amount of wheat a farmer could plant and harvest for home consumption. Filburn, a farmer, violated the law. The U.S. Supreme Court upheld the statute on the grounds that it prevented nationwide surpluses and shortages of wheat. The Court reasoned that wheat grown for home consumption would affect the supply of wheat available in interstate commerce.

State Police Power

Police power Power that permits states and local governments to enact laws to protect or promote the public health, safety, morals, and general welfare.

The states did not delegate all power to regulate business to the federal government. They retained the power to regulate much intrastate and interstate business activity that occurs within their borders. This is commonly referred to as the states' **police power**.

Police power permits states (and, by delegation, local governments) to enact laws to protect or promote the public health, safety, morals, and general welfare. This includes the authority to enact laws that regulate the conduct of business.

Examples State environmental laws, corporation and partnership laws, property laws, and local zoning ordinances and building codes are enacted under state police power.

Dormant Commerce Clause

Unduly burdening interstate commerce To unlawfully restrict or limit commerce among states. Laws may be enacted by a state to protect or promote the public health, safety, morals, and general welfare, as long as the laws do not unduly burden interstate commerce.

If the federal government has chosen not to regulate an area of interstate commerce that it would otherwise have the power to regulate under its Commerce Clause powers, this area of commerce is subject to what is referred to as the **Dormant Commerce Clause**. A state, under its police power, can enact laws to regulate that area of commerce. However, if a state enacts laws to regulate commerce that the federal government has the power to regulate but has chosen not to regulate, the Dormant Commerce Clause prohibits the state's regulation from **unduly burdening interstate commerce**.

Example Under its interstate commerce powers, the federal government could, if it wanted to, regulate corporations. However, the federal government has chosen not to. Thus, states regulate corporations. Assume that one state's corporation code permits only corporations from that state but from no other state to conduct business in that state. That state's law would unduly burden interstate commerce and would be unconstitutional.

Exhibit 5.3 Bill of Rights

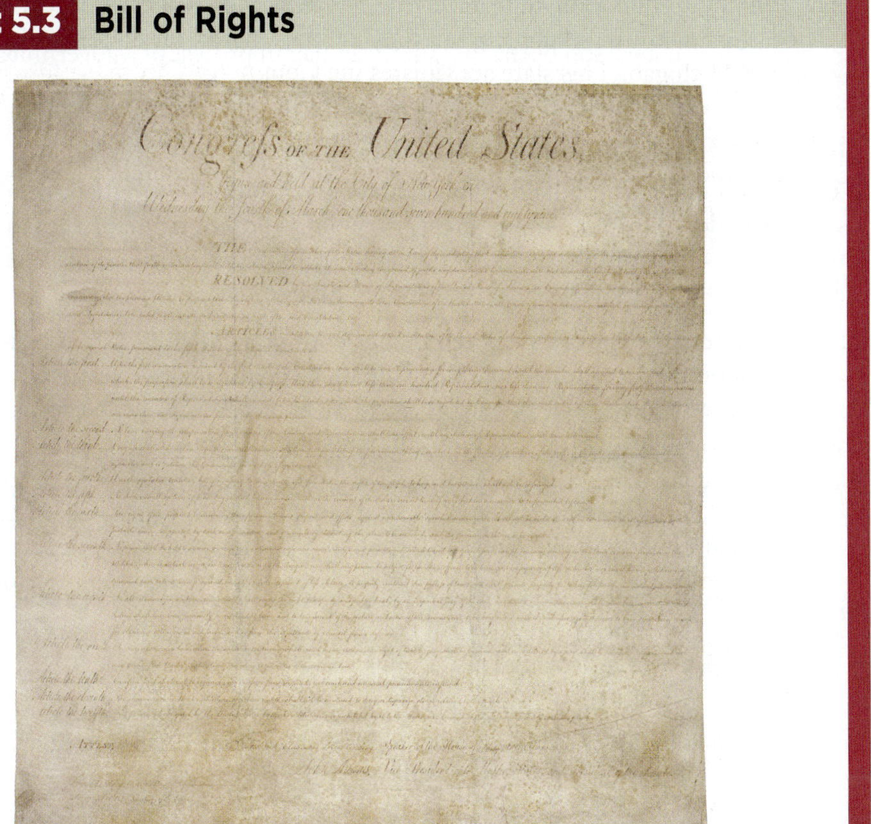

Bill of Rights and Other Amendments

In 1791, the states approved the ten amendments commonly referred to as the **Bill of Rights**, and they became part of the U.S. Constitution (see Exhibit 5.3). The Bill of Rights guarantees certain fundamental rights to natural persons and protects these rights from intrusive government action. Most of these rights, or "freedoms," also have been found applicable to so-called artificial persons, such as corporations.

The First Amendment to the Constitution guarantees the rights of free speech, assembly, and religion. In addition to the Bill of Rights, seventeen amendments have been added to the Constitution. Two important clauses from these amendments are the Due Process Clause and the Equal Protection Clause. These amendments are continually litigated and are frequent subjects of U.S. Supreme Court opinions.

Learning Objective 8
Describe freedom of speech and other protections guaranteed by the Bill of Rights.

I disapprove of what you say, but I will defend to the death your right to say it.
Voltaire

Bill of Rights The first ten amendments to the Constitution. They were added to the U.S. Constitution in 1791.

Freedom of Speech

One of the most important freedoms guaranteed by the Bill of Rights is the **freedom of speech**. Many other constitutional freedoms would be meaningless without it. It should be noted, however, that the First Amendment's Freedom of Speech Clause protects speech only, not conduct. The U.S. Supreme Court places speech into three categories: (1) fully protected speech, (2) speech with limited protection, and (3) unprotected speech.

Freedom of speech The right to engage in oral, written, and symbolic speech protected by the First Amendment.

Fully Protected Speech

Fully protected speech is speech that the government cannot prohibit or regulate. Political speech is an example of such speech.

Example The government could not enact a law that forbids citizens from criticizing the current president.

Fully protected speech Speech that cannot be prohibited or regulated by the government.

The First Amendment protects oral, written, and symbolic speech.

Example If a person burns the American flag in protest of a government policy, this is symbolic speech that is protected by the First Amendment.

Limited Protected Speech

Limited protected speech Speech that the government may not prohibit but that is subject to time, place, and manner restrictions.

The Supreme Court has held that certain types of speech are only **limited protected speech** under the First Amendment. Although the government cannot forbid this type of speech, it can subject this speech to restrictions of time, place, and manner. The following types of speech are accorded limited protection:

- **Offensive speech** is speech that offends many members of society. The Supreme Court has held that offensive speech may be restricted by the government under time, place, and manner restrictions. Note, however, that "offensive" speech is not the same as "obscene" speech.

  Example The Federal Communications Commission (FCC) can regulate the use of offensive language on television by limiting such language to times when children would be unlikely to be watching, such as late at night.

- **Commercial speech** is speech such as advertising and business solicitation. The Supreme Court has held that commercial speech is subject to proper time, place, and manner restrictions.

  Example A city could prohibit billboards along its highways for safety and aesthetic reasons as long as other forms of advertising (such as print media) are available to the commercial advertiser.

Unprotected Speech

Unprotected speech Speech that is not protected by the First Amendment and may be forbidden by the government.

There are certain types of speech that the U.S. Supreme Court has held have no protection under the Freedom of Speech Clause. These types of speech may be entirely prohibited by the government. The Supreme Court has held that the following types of speech are **unprotected speech** under the First Amendment and may be totally forbidden by the government:

- dangerous speech (including such speech as yelling "fire" in a crowded theater when there is no fire);
- fighting words that are likely to provoke a hostile or violent response from an average person;
- speech that incites the violent or revolutionary overthrow of the government (however, the mere abstract teaching of the morality and consequences of such action is protected);
- defamatory language;
- child pornography; and
- obscene speech.

Definition of Obscene Speech

The definition of **obscene speech** is quite subjective. As Justice Stewart stated, "I know it when I see it." *Facobellis v. Ohio*, 378 U.S. 184, (84 S.Ct. 1676 12 L.Ed.2d 793, 1964) U.S. Lexis 822 (U.S.) In *Miller v. California*, the Supreme Court determined that speech is obscene under these circumstances:

1. the average person, applying contemporary community standards, would find that the work, taken as a whole, appeals to the prurient interest;
2. the work depicts or describes, in a patently offensive way, sexual conduct specifically defined by the applicable state law; and
3. the work, taken as a whole, lacks serious literary, artistic, political, or scientific value. 413 U.S. 15, 93 S.Ct. 2607, 37 L.Ed.2d 419, (1973). U.S. Lexis 149 (U.S.).

States are free to define what constitutes obscene speech. Movie theaters, magazine publishers, web operators, and other media producers are often subject to challenges that the materials they display or sell are obscene, and therefore are not protected by the First Amendment.

Free Speech in Cyberspace

In our digital age, constitutional provisions drafted centuries ago must often be applied to new technologies. Once or twice in a century, a new medium comes along that presents redundancy problems in applying freedom-of-speech rights. Recently this has been true of the Internet.

The U.S. Congress enacted the Computer Decency Act to regulate the Internet. This statute made it a felony to knowingly make "indecent" or "patently offensive" materials available on computer systems, including the Internet, to persons under 18 years of age. Penalties such as fines, prison terms, and loss of licenses were imposed for those convicted of violating the Act.

Immediately, cyberspace providers and users filed lawsuits challenging the provisions of the Act as violating their free speech rights granted under the First Amendment. Proponents of the Act countered that these provisions were necessary to protect children from indecent materials.

The American Constitution is, so far as I can see, the most wonderful work ever struck off at a given time by the brain and purpose of man.
W. E. Gladstone
Kin Beyond Sea, 1878

The U.S. Supreme Court decided to hear this issue and came down on the plaintiffs' side, overturning certain provisions of the Computer Decency Act. The Court found that the terms "indecent" and "patently offensive" were too vague to define and criminally enforce. The Court reasoned that limiting the content on the Internet to what is suitable for a child would result in an unconstitutional limiting of adult speech. It further pointed out that parents can regulate their children's access to the Internet and can install blocking and filtering software programs to protect their children from seeing adult materials.

The Supreme Court declared emphatically that the Internet must be given the highest possible level of First Amendment free speech protection. The Supreme Court stated,

> As the most participatory form of mass speech yet developed, the Internet deserves the highest protection from government intrusion.

Protest, Los Angeles, California. The Freedom of Speech Clause of the First Amendment to the U.S. Constitution protects the right to engage in political speech. Freedom of speech is one of Americans' most highly prized rights.

The Court also reasoned that because the Internet is a global medium, there would be no way to prevent indecent material from flowing over the Internet from abroad.[2]

Freedom of Religion

The U.S. Constitution requires federal, state, and local governments to be neutral toward religion. The First Amendment actually contains two separate clauses regarding religion:

Establishment Clause A clause in the First Amendment that prohibits the government from either establishing a state religion or promoting one religion over others.

1. The **Establishment Clause** prohibits the government from either establishing a state religion or promoting one religion over another.

   Example An Alabama statute authorized a one-minute period of silence in school for "meditation or voluntary prayer." The U.S. Supreme Court held that the statute endorsed religion, and therefore was invalid.[3]

   Example Copies of the Ten Commandments were prominently displayed in large gold frames and hung alone in two county courthouses in Kentucky so that visitors could see them. The U.S. Supreme Court held that this violated the Establishment Clause.[4]

Free Exercise Clause A clause in the First Amendment that prohibits the government from interfering with the free exercise of religion in the United States.

2. The **Free Exercise Clause** prohibits the government from interfering with the free exercise of religion in the United States. Generally, this clause prevents the government from enacting laws that prevent individuals from practicing their chosen religion.

   Example The federal, state, or local governments could not enact a law that prohibits all religions or that prohibits churches, synagogues, mosques, or temples. The government could not prohibit religious practitioners from celebrating their major holidays and high holy days. Of course, this right to be free from government intervention in the practice of religion is not absolute.

   Example Human sacrifices are unlawful and are not protected by the First Amendment.

On the following page, a paralegal professional shares her experience of working on a constitutional law case.

Due Process Clause

Due Process Clause A clause that provides that no person shall be deprived of "life, liberty, or property" without due process of the law.

The **Due Process Clause** provides that no person shall be deprived of "life, liberty, or property" without due process of the law. This means that although the government is not prohibited from taking a person's life, liberty, or property, the government must follow a certain process to do so. The Due Process Clause is contained in both the Fifth and the Fourteenth Amendments. In the Fifth Amendment, the Due Process Clause applies to federal government action. In the Fourteenth Amendment, the Due Process Clause applies to state and local government action. There are two categories of due process: *substantive* and *procedural.*

Substantive Due Process

Substantive due process requires that government statutes, ordinances, regulations, and other laws be clear on their face and not overly broad in scope. The test of whether substantive due process is met is whether a "reasonable person" could understand the law well enough to be able to comply with it. Laws that do not meet this test are declared *void for vagueness.*

---

[2] *Reno v. American Civil Liberties Union,* 521 U.S. 844, 117 S.Ct. 2329, 138 L.Ed.2d 874, **Web**(1997) U.S. Lexis 4037 (Supreme Court of the United States).

[3] *Wallace v. Jaffree,* 472 U.S. 38, (105 S.Ct. 2479, 86 L.Ed.2d 29, **Web**1985). U.S. Lexis 91 (Supreme Court of the United States).

[4] *McCreary County, Kentucky v. American Civil Liberties Union of KY,* 545 U.S. 844, (125 S.Ct. 2722, 162 L.Ed.2d 729, **Web**2005). U.S. Lexis 5211 (Supreme Court of the United States).

Example A city ordinance that makes it illegal for persons to wear "clothes of the opposite sex" would be held unconstitutional as void for vagueness because a reasonable person would not be able to clearly determine whether his or her clothing violates the law.

Paralegals *in* Practice

PARALEGAL PROFILE

Charlotte A. Sheraden-Baker

Charlotte A. Sheraden-Baker started her legal career as a legal secretary after graduating from high school. After taking time out to raise a family, she resumed work as a legal secretary while attending night school to obtain her paralegal degree. In 2000, she graduated as Paralegal of the Year with an Associate of Applied Science degree, the oldest person in her class. After convincing her firm they needed another paralegal, Charlotte was promoted and continued evening classes to obtain her Bachelor of Arts degree. She currently works for the law firm of Warner, Smith & Harris in Fort Smith, Arkansas, where she has been employed for the last 14 years.

I work for a general practice that has 13 partners and 3 associates. I recently assisted in a constitutional law case that was appealed to the Arkansas Supreme Court over a First Amendment issue. Our client was a party to a lawsuit between two groups of a local temple. Both thought they were entitled to make governing rules for the temple, and maintain its original assets and location. Since the matter could not be resolved between the opposing parties, the state court judge was asked to rule, and he determined that an election should be held, whereby the temple members would decide.

In the process, my firm's attorneys contended that the judge overstepped his duties by overriding the already-established governing documents of the temple and assigning a different definition as to who was a member of the congregation and entitled to vote. It was argued that the judge had prohibited the free exercise of religion, as guaranteed by the First Amendment of both the federal and state constitutions. Our case was lost on appeal because it was determined the judge did not intrude into anyone's religious rights. Nonetheless, the case was a great learning experience in my legal career.

At the state court level, some of my pretrial duties included preparing, gathering, and duplicating exhibits; copying and keeping up to date on important documents; making lists of witnesses and exhibits; and more. At trial, my primary job was to ensure that the judge, court clerk, and court reporter had all the necessary documents; monitor exhibits offered, admitted, or rejected; organize witnesses and keep track of their appearances and testimony; and take notes of testimony to help with the attorney's upcoming examinations.

My duties at the state Supreme Court level were slightly different. For any case that is appealed, each party prepares a brief and responds to the other party's brief within a short time. Then, the case is set for oral argument before the state Supreme Court. Preparation of appellate briefs is complicated and precise, as the Supreme Courts require specific style, format, and content. I was asked to monitor filing deadlines, obtain the local trial transcripts and submit them to the Supreme Court, prepare an extensive summary of the pertinent trial testimony for the appeal brief, and verify or "Shepardize" all cases cited in the brief itself.

Procedural Due Process

Procedural due process requires that the government give a person proper notice and a hearing of the legal action before that person is deprived of his or her life, liberty, or property. The government action must be fair.

Procedural due process A category of due process that requires that the government give a person proper notice and hearing of the legal action before that person is deprived of his or her life, liberty, or property.

Example If federal or state government brings a criminal action against a defendant for an alleged crime, the government must notify the person of its intent (by charging the defendant with a crime) and provide the defendant with a proper hearing (a trial).

Example If the government wants to exercise its power of eminent domain and demolish a person's home to build a highway, the government must (1) give the homeowner sufficient notice of its intention, and (2) provide a hearing. Under the **Just Compensation Clause** of the Fifth Amendment, the government must pay the owner just compensation for taking the property.

Web Exploration

How does Louisiana law differ from that of the other 49 states? Go to **http://www.la-legal.com/history_louisiana_law.htm**.

Learning Objective 9

Describe the Equal Protection Clause and the tests used to determine whether it has been violated.

Equal Protection Clause A clause that provides that state, local, and federal governments cannot deny to any person the "equal protection of the laws."

Equal Protection Clause

The **Equal Protection Clause** of the Fourteenth Amendment, as interpreted by the U.S. Supreme Court, provides that state, local, and federal governments cannot deny to any person the "equal protection of the laws." The clause is designed to prohibit invidious government discrimination, and prohibits governments from enacting laws that classify and treat similarly situated persons differently. Both natural persons and businesses are protected.

The Equal Protection Clause has not been interpreted literally by the U.S. Supreme Court. The Court has held that some government laws that treat people or businesses differently are constitutional. It has established three different standards for determining whether such government action is lawful:

Strict scrutiny test A test that is applied to classifications based on a *suspect class* (such as race, national origin, citizenship) or that involves *fundamental rights* (such as voting).

1. ***Strict scrutiny test.*** Any government activity or regulation that classifies persons based on a "suspect class" (such as race) is reviewed using a strict scrutiny test. Under this standard, most government classifications of persons based on race are found to be unconstitutional.

   Example A government rule that permitted persons of one race, but not of others, to receive government benefits such as Medicaid would violate this test. But affirmative action programs that give racial minorities a "plus factor" when considered for public university admission is lawful, as long as it does not constitute a quota system.

Intermediate scrutiny test A test that is applied to classifications based on a *protected class* (such as gender or age).

2. ***Intermediate scrutiny test.*** The lawfulness of government classifications based on *protected classes* other than race (such as sex or age) is examined using an intermediate scrutiny test. Under this standard, the courts determine whether the government classification is "reasonably related" to a legitimate government purpose.

   Example A rule prohibiting persons over a certain age from military combat would be lawful, but a rule prohibiting persons over a certain age from acting as government engineers would not be. With regard to a person's gender, the U.S. Supreme Court has held that the federal government can require males, but not females, to register with the military for a possible draft.

Rational basis test A test that is applied to classifications not involving a suspect or protected class.

3. ***Rational basis test.*** The lawfulness of all government classifications that do not involve suspect or protected classes is examined using a rational basis test. Under this test, the courts will uphold government regulation as long as there is a justifiable reason for the law. This standard permits much of the government regulation of business.

   Example Providing government subsidies to farmers but not to those in other occupations is permissible.

The ethical duty and social responsibility of a paralegal professional to avoid conflicts of interest is discussed in the following feature.

Learning Objective 10

Explain a paralegal's duty to avoid conflicts of interest.

ETHICAL PERSPECTIVE

Paralegal's Duty to Avoid Conflicts of Interest

Ms. Jennifer Adams is hired as a paralegal at a law firm with expertise in real estate development law. She recently left a paralegal position at another law firm to take this new position.

At the new firm, Ms. Adams is assigned to work for Mr. Humberto Cruz, a senior partner. He is an expert in complex real estate transactions, representing clients in the purchase, development, and leasing of large shopping malls. One client

Mr. Cruz represents is Modern Properties L.P., a limited partnership that constructs and operates retail shopping malls across the country.

One day Mr. Cruz asks Ms. Adams to attend a meeting with him and the president of Modern Properties L.P. At the meeting, the president discloses a dispute that the partnership has with a tenant, Third National Bank, concerning its lease at a mall constructed and operated by Modern Properties L.P. The president explains that Third National Bank has filed a lawsuit against Modern Properties L.P. The president further explains that the partnership wants Mr. Cruz to represent the partnership in this lawsuit.

Ms. Adams realizes that her prior law firm represented Third National Bank in many lawsuits, and that she had worked on several of those cases. During the course of this work, she became privy to confidential information about Third National Bank, including its financial condition, operations, and legal strategy. Does Ms. Adams have a conflict of interest? If so, what should she do?

PARALEGAL'S ETHICAL DECISION

Model and state paralegal codes of ethics and professional responsibility provide that a paralegal is under a duty to avoid conflicts of interest. Thus, a paralegal cannot conduct work on any matter where there would be a conflict of interest with a present or past employer or with a client.

Thus, Ms. Adams must immediately disclose the fact that she previously worked on cases involving Third National Bank at the prior law firm where she was employed, and that because of that employment she possesses confidential information about Third National Bank. Because of this conflict of interest, Ms. Adams must excuse herself from working on the *Third National Bank v. Modern Properties L.P.* case.

Concept Review *and* Reinforcement

LEGAL TERMINOLOGY

SUMMARY OF KEY CONCEPTS

What Is Law?

Definition of *Law*	Law consists of a body of rules of action or conduct prescribed by a controlling authority and having binding legal force.
Functions of Law	The main functions of the law are to: • keep the peace; • shape moral standards; • promote social justice; • maintain the status quo; • facilitate orderly change; • facilitate planning; • provide a basis for compromise; and • maximize individual freedom.
Fairness	Although the American legal system is one of the fairest and most democratic systems of law, abuses and mistakes in the application of the law still occur.
Flexibility	The law must be flexible to meet social, technological, and economic changes.

Schools of Jurisprudential Thought

Natural Law	This school postulates that law is based on what is "correct"; it emphasizes a moral theory of law—that is, law should be based on morality and ethics.
Historical	These scholars believe that law is an aggregate of social traditions and customs.
Analytical	Students of this school maintain that law is shaped by logic.
Sociological	These thinkers assert that the law is a means of achieving and advancing certain sociological goals.
Command	Philosophers of this school believe that the law is a set of rules developed, communicated, and enforced by the ruling class.
Critical Legal Studies	This school maintains that legal rules are unnecessary and that legal disputes should be solved based on a general concept of fairness.
Law and Economics	Scholars of this school believe that promoting market efficiency should be the central concern of legal decision making.

History of American Law

English Common Law	English common law (or judge-made law) forms the basis of the legal systems of most states in this country. Louisiana bases its law on the French civil code.

Sources of Law in the United States

Constitutions	The U.S. Constitution establishes the federal government and enumerates its powers. Powers not given to the federal government are reserved to the states. State constitutions establish state governments and enumerate their powers.
Treaties	The president, with the advice and consent of the Senate, may enter into treaties with foreign countries.

Codified Law	• Statutes are enacted by Congress and state legislatures. • Ordinances and statutes are passed by municipalities and local government bodies to establish courses of conduct that must be followed by covered parties.
Administrative Agencies	Administrative agencies are created by the legislative and executive branches of government. They may adopt rules and regulations that govern conduct.
Executive Orders	Executive orders are issued by the president and state governors.
Judicial Decisions	Courts decide controversies by issuing decisions that state the holding of each case and the rationale the court used to reach that decision.

Doctrine of Stare Decisis

Definition	*Stare decisis* means "to stand by the decision." This doctrine requires adherence to precedent.

Constitution of the United States of America

Scope	The Constitution consists of seven articles and 27 amendments. It establishes the three branches of the federal government, enumerates their powers, and provides important guarantees of individual freedom. The Constitution was ratified by the states in 1788.
Basic Constitutional Concepts	*Federalism:* The Constitution created the federal government, which shares power with the state governments. *Delegated powers:* When the states ratified the Constitution, they delegated certain powers, called *enumerated powers*, to the federal government. *Reserved powers:* Those powers not granted to the federal government by the Constitution are reserved to the states. *Separation of powers:* Each branch of the federal government has separate powers: • the legislative branch has the power to make the law; • the executive branch has the power to enforce the law; and • the judicial branch has the power to interpret the law. *Checks and balances:* Certain checks and balances are built into the Constitution to ensure that no one branch of the federal government becomes too powerful.

Supremacy Clause

The Supremacy Clause stipulates that the U.S. Constitution, treaties, and federal law (including both statutes and regulations) are the supreme law of the land. State or local laws that conflict with federal law are unconstitutional. This is called the *preemption doctrine.*

Commerce Clause

- The Commerce Clause authorizes the federal government to regulate commerce with foreign nations, among the states, and with Native American tribes.
- The federal government has broad power to regulate any activity (including intrastate commerce) that affects interstate commerce.
- Police powers are powers reserved to the states to regulate commerce.

Bill of Rights and Other Amendments

- The Bill of Rights consists of the first ten amendments to the Constitution. They establish basic individual rights. The Bill of Rights was ratified in 1791.
- In addition to the ten amendments of the Bill of Rights, there are seventeen other amendments to the U.S. Constitution.

Freedom of Speech

The Freedom of Speech Clause of the First Amendment guarantees that the government shall not infringe on a person's right to speak. It protects oral, written, and symbolic speech. This right is not absolute—that is, some speech is not protected and other speech is granted only limited protection. The U.S. Supreme Court has placed speech in the following three categories:

1. *Fully protected speech* Speech that cannot be prohibited or regulated by the government
2. *Limited protected speech* Types of speech that are granted only limited protection under the Freedom of Speech Clause—that is, they are subject to governmental *time, place, and manner restrictions:*
   - offensive speech
   - commercial speech
3. *Unprotected speech* Speech that is not protected by the Freedom of Speech Clause:
   - dangerous speech
   - fighting words
   - speech that advocates the violent overthrow of the government
   - defamatory language
   - child pornography
   - obscene speech

Freedom of Religion

There are two religion clauses in the First Amendment. They are:

1. *Establishment Clause.* Prohibits the government from establishing a state religion or promoting religion.
2. *Free Exercise Clause.* Prohibits the government from interfering with the free exercise of religion. This right is not absolute; for example, human sacrifices are forbidden.

Due Process Clause

The Due Process Clause provides that no person shall be deprived of "life, liberty, or property" without due process. There are two categories of due process:

1. *Substantive due process:* Requires that laws be clear on their face and not overly broad in scope. Laws that do not meet this test are *void for vagueness.*
2. *Procedural due process:* Requires that the government give a person proper *notice* and *hearing* before that person is deprived of his or her life, liberty, or property. An owner must be paid *just compensation* if the government takes his or her property.

Equal Protection Clause

The Equal Protection Clause prohibits the government from enacting laws that classify and treat "similarly situated" persons differently. This standard is not absolute and the government can treat persons differently in certain situations. The U.S. Supreme Court has applied the following tests to determine if the Equal Protection Clause has been violated:

1. *strict scrutiny test* This test applies to *suspect classes* (such as race or national origin).
2. *intermediate scrutiny test* This test applies to other *protected classes* (such as sex or age).
3. *rational basis test* This test applies to government classifications that do not involve a suspect or protected class.

WORKING THE WEB

1. Go to the website http://www.usconstitution.net/const.html. Scroll down to "Amendment 7." When was this amendment ratified? What does this amendment provide? Explain.
2. Visit the website http://www.archives.gov/exhibits/charters/charters.html. A page entitled "The Charters of Freedom—A New World is at Hand" will appear on your computer screen. Do the following exercises:
   a. On the page shown, click on the third icon from the left. Read the article entitled, "The Spirit of the Revolution—The Declaration of Independence." What did the Declaration of Independence do? Explain.
   b. On the page shown, click on the sixth icon from the left. Read the article "The Constitutional Convention—Creation of the Constitution." How many states were required to ratify the Constitution?
   c. At the top of the page shown, click on the second-to-the-last icon from the right. Read the article "Expansion of Rights and Liberties—The Right of Suffrage." What amendment to the U.S. Constitution gave women the right to vote? What year was this amendment ratified?
3. Go to www.nps.gov/archive/stli/prod02.htm to read a history of the Statue of Liberty. Visit the World Heritage website describing the Statue of Liberty at www.unesco.org/en/list/307.

CRITICAL THINKING & WRITING QUESTIONS

1. Define the term "law." Is this an easy concept to define? Why?
2. Should the language of the U.S. Constitution be applied according to its original meaning, or should it be applied in a more expansive sense? Explain.
3. What is the power of the legislative branch of government? What is a statute?
4. Do you think the U.S. Supreme Court makes law when it interprets the U.S. Constitution? Explain.
5. What is the doctrine of *stare decisis*? Why is this doctrine important?
6. What does the doctrine of separation of powers provide? Can you give any examples where the separation of the powers of the three branches of government is blurred?
7. What is the purpose of the doctrine of checks and balances? Can you give any examples where one branch of the government limits the power of another branch of the government?
8. What does the Supremacy Clause provide? What would be the consequences if the Supremacy Clause did not exist? Explain.
9. What does the Commerce Clause of the U.S. Constitution do? Explain.
10. The First Amendment to the U.S. Constitution contains the Freedom of Speech Clause. Explain the differences between fully protected speech, partially protected speech, and unprotected speech.
11. The U.S. Constitution guarantees freedom of religion. Explain the difference between the Establishment Clause and the Free Exercise Clause. Can you give a possible example of a legitimate government restriction of a religious practice?
12. What does the Equal Protection Clause provide? Explain the differences between the strict scrutiny test, intermediate scrutiny test, and rational basis test.

Building Paralegal Skills

VIDEO CASE STUDIES

Difference Between a Criminal and a Civil Trial

An interview with Judge Kenney, a trial court judge, who discusses the difference between a civil and a criminal trial.

After viewing the video case study in MyLegalStudiesLab, answer the following:

1. What are the differences in the burdens of proof in a criminal and a civil matter?
2. What protections does the U.S. Constitution afford those accused of criminal acts?

A School Principal Reacts: Student Rights versus the School's Duty

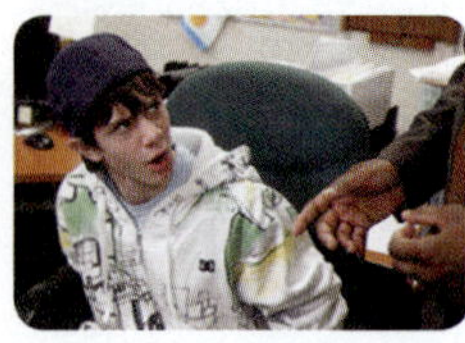

In an altercation on a school bus, it is claimed that the student involved had a contraband knife on his person. As a result, the principal has ordered that the student be searched for the knife.

After viewing the video case study in MyLegalStudiesLab, answer the following:

1. Does a student have a constitutional right of privacy?
2. Does the school have a right to search a student?
3. Are the school district and those working for it immune from suit for the actions taken?

Confidentiality Issue: Attorney–Client Privilege

Paralegal Alicia Jackson meets with a client to review answers to documents that must be sent to opposing counsel. While reviewing the answers, the client tells her about a potentially fraudulent claim.

After viewing the video case study in MyLegalStudiesLab, answer the following:

1. Does the attorney–client privilege apply to information given to a paralegal?
2. To whom does the privilege belong?
3. How is the attorney–client privilege different from the duty of confidentiality?

ETHICS ANALYSIS & DISCUSSION QUESTIONS

1. Are there any ethical issues in expressing one's personal feelings while working on a case? What if you have strong feelings against the client's position?
2. Does the American system of law depend on members of the legal team to put aside their personal beliefs and work diligently on unpopular cases or issues? How does this ensure equal justice and allow for change in the system?
3. You are working in a law firm for an attorney who has had a series of strokes that have caused a permanent reading disability and a memory impairment. Do you have any ethical obligation to the attorney's clients? Do you have any ethical obligation to the firm and to the attorney? See Philadelphia Ethics Opinion 2002–12 (2000). See also Texas Ethics Opinion 522 (1997).

DEVELOPING YOUR COLLABORATION SKILLS

With a group of students, review the facts of the following case. Then as a group, discuss the following questions.

1. What does the Interstate Commerce Clause provide?
2. Can states regulate interstate commerce that the federal government could have regulated, but has chosen not to regulate?
3. What does "unduly burdening interstate commerce" mean?
4. Does the Michigan law violate the Commerce Clause of the U.S. Constitution?

Granholm, Governor of Michigan v. Heald

The state of Michigan regulates the sale of wine within its boundaries. Michigan law permits in-state wineries to sell wine directly to consumers, including by mail or the Internet. However, Michigan law prohibits out-of-state wineries from selling wine directly to Michigan consumers, including over the Internet. Instead, Michigan requires out-of-state wineries to sell their wine to Michigan wholesalers, who then sell the wine to Michigan retailers, who then sell the wine to Michigan consumers. Many small wineries across the country rely on the Internet to sell wine to residents in other states. Out-of-state wineries, which are required by law to sell wine to Michigan wholesalers, incur a cost that in-state wineries do not incur, thus making it more costly and often unprofitable for out-of-state wineries to sell to Michigan consumers. Domaine Alfred, a small winery located in San Luis Obispo, California, and several other out-of-state wineries sued the State of Michigan. The plaintiff wineries alleged that the Michigan law caused an undue burden on interstate e-commerce, in violation of the Commerce Clause of the U.S. Constitution.

Source: Granholm, Governor of Michigan v. Heald, 554 U.S. 460, 125 S.Ct. 1885, 161 L.Ed.2d 796, (2005) U.S. Lexis 4174 (Supreme Court of the United States).

PARALEGAL PORTFOLIO EXERCISE

Research and find an article that discusses a Federal Communications Commission (FCC) clash with a radio, cable, or television station regarding the subject matter that it may broadcast. Write a memorandum, no longer than two pages, that discusses this dispute and the outcome of the case.

LEGAL ANALYSIS & WRITING CASES

Snyder v. Phelps, 131 S.Ct. 1207, (2011) U.S. Lexis 1903

Fred Phelps founded the Westboro Baptist Church in Topeka, Kansas. The church's congregation believes that God hates and punishes the United States for its tolerance of homosexuality, particularly in the U.S. military. The church frequently communicates its views by picketing at military funerals. Lance Corporal Matthew Snyder, a member of the U.S. Marines, was killed in Iraq in the line of duty. Phelps, along with six other Westboro Baptist parishioners (two of his daughters and four of his grandchildren), picketed at Lance Corporal Snyder's funeral service in Maryland. The Westboro congregation members picketed while standing on public land adjacent to a public street approximately 1,000 feet from the church. They carried placards that read, "God Hates the USA/Thank God for 9/11," "America is Doomed," "Don't Pray for the USA," "Thank God for Dead Soldiers," and "You're Going to Hell." The picketers sang hymns and recited Bible verses. The funeral procession passed within 200 to 300 feet of the picket site.

Lance Corporal Snyder's father, Albert Snyder, filed a lawsuit against Phelps, Phelps's daughters, and the Westboro Baptist Church (collectively referred to as "Westboro") in federal court, alleging intentional infliction of emotional distress and other state law tort claims. Westboro argued that their speech was protected by the First Amendment.

Question

1. Which side should prevail in this case?

Bruesewitz v. Wyeth LLC, 131 S.Ct. 1068, 2011 131 S. Ct. 1068 (2011) U.S. Lexis 1085

Vaccines are biological preparations, usually administered by needle, to improve immunity to a particular disease. The elimination of communicable diseases through vaccination was one of the greatest public health achievements of the twentieth century. Vaccines are subject to federal premarket approval by the Food and Drug Administration (FDA), a federal administrative agency.

Some vaccines have side effects, ranging from minor to serious health problems, and in rare cases, fatalities. This led to a massive increase in vaccine-related tort litigation against the manufacturers of vaccines. One group of manufacturers that was subject to such lawsuits was the manufacturers who made vaccines against diphtheria, tetanus, and pertussis (DTP). This destabilized the vaccine market, causing two of the three domestic manufacturers of DTP to withdraw from the market.

In response, the U.S. Congress enacted the National Childhood Vaccine Injury Act of 1986 (NCVIA). One of the provisions of the NCVIA stated:

> No vaccine manufacturer shall be liable in a civil action for damages arising from a vaccine-related injury or death associated with the administration of a vaccine after October 1, 1988, if the injury or death resulted from side effects that were unavoidable even though the vaccine was properly prepared and was accompanied by proper directions and warnings.

Hanna Bruesewitz was born in 1991. In 1992, her pediatrician administered doses of DTP vaccine manufactured by Lederle Laboratories (later purchased by Wyeth LLC). Hanna immediately started to experience seizures, and she has suffered seizures since being vaccinated. Hanna's parents filed a lawsuit against Lederle, alleging that the company was liable for strict liability and negligent design of the vaccine. Wyeth denied her claims, asserting that Bruesewitz's causes of action were preempted by the NCVIA.

Question

1. Does the preemption provision in the federal NCVIA bar state law product liability claims against vaccine manufacturers for alleged design defects?

WORKING WITH THE LANGUAGE OF THE COURT CASE

Brown v. Entertainment Merchants Association, 131 S. Ct. 2729 (2011)

Read the following excerpt from the U.S. Supreme Court's opinion. Review and brief the case. In your brief, answer the following questions.

1. What does the freedom of speech clause of the First Amendment provide?
2. Is there any speech that is not protected by the freedom of speech clause?
3. What decision did the U.S. Supreme Court reach?
4. What reasoning did the Supreme Court use in reaching its decision?

Scalia, Justice (joined by Kennedy, Ginsburg, Sotomayor, and Kagan)

We consider whether a California law imposing restrictions on violent video games comports with the First Amendment. California Assembly Bill 1179 (2005), Cal. Civ. Code Ann. §§ 1746-1746.5 (West 2009) (Act), prohibits the sale or rental of "violent video games" to minors, and requires their packaging to be labeled "18." The Act covers games "in which the range of options available to a player includes killing, maiming, dismembering, or sexually assaulting an image of a human being, if those acts are depicted" in a manner that "[a] reasonable person, considering the game as a whole, would find appeals to a deviant or morbid interest of minors," that is "patently offensive to prevailing standards in the community as to what is suitable for minors," and that "causes the game, as a whole, to lack serious literary, artistic, political, or scientific value for minors." § 1746(d)(1)(A). Violation of the Act is punishable by a civil fine of up to $1,000. § 1746.3.

Respondents, representing the video-game and software industries, brought a preenforcement challenge to the Act in the United States District Court for the Northern District of California. That court concluded that the Act violated the First Amendment and permanently enjoined its enforcement. The Court of Appeals affirmed, and we granted certiorari.

California correctly acknowledges that video games qualify for First Amendment protection. Like the protected books, plays, and movies that preceded them, video games communicate ideas—and even social messages—through many familiar literary devices (such as characters, dialogue, plot, and music) and through features distinctive to the medium (such as the player's interaction with the virtual world). That suffices to confer First Amendment protection. And whatever the challenges of applying the Constitution to ever-advancing technology, "the basic principles of freedom of speech and the press, like the First Amendment's command, do not vary" when a new and different medium for communication appears.

California's argument would fare better if there were a longstanding tradition in this country of specially restricting children's access to depictions of violence, but there is none. Certainly the *books* we give children to read—or read to them when they are younger—contain no shortage of gore. Grimm's Fairy Tales, for example, are grim indeed. As her just des[s]erts for trying to poison Snow White, the wicked queen is made to dance in red hot slippers "till she fell dead on the floor, a sad example of envy and jealousy." Cinderella's evil stepsisters have their eyes pecked out by doves. And Hansel and Gretel (children!) kill their captor by baking her in an oven.

High-school reading lists are full of similar fare. Homer's Odysseus blinds Polyphemus the Cyclops by grinding out his eye with a heated stake. In the Inferno, Dante and Virgil watch corrupt politicians struggle to stay submerged beneath a lake of boiling pitch, lest they be skewered by devils above the surface. And Golding's *Lord of the Flies* recounts how a schoolboy called Piggy is savagely murdered *by other children* while marooned on an island.

California's legislation straddles the fence between (1) addressing a serious social problem and (2) helping concerned parents control their children. Both ends are legitimate, but when they affect First Amendment rights they must be pursued by means that are neither seriously underinclusive nor seriously overinclusive. As a means of protecting children from portrayals of violence, the legislation is seriously underinclusive, not only because it excludes portrayals other than video games, but also because it permits a parental or avuncular veto. And as a means of assisting concerned parents it is seriously overinclusive because it abridges the First Amendment rights of young people whose parents (and aunts and uncles) think violent video games are a harmless pastime. Legislation such as this, which is neither fish nor fowl, cannot survive strict scrutiny.

We affirm the judgment below.

It is so ordered.

MYLEGALSTUDIESLAB

MyLegalStudiesLab Virtual Law Office Experience Assignments

Complete the pre-test, study plan, and post-test for this chapter and answer the Legal Applications questions as assigned. These will help you confirm your mastery of the concepts and their application to legal scenarios. Then complete the Virtual Law Office assignments as assigned by your instructor. These assignments are designed to develop your workplace skills. Completing the assignments for this chapter will result in producing the following documents for inclusion in your portfolio:

VLOE 5.1 Memo on the school's right to censor student newspaper and electronic deliveries

CHAPTER

6

The Court System and Alternative Dispute Resolution

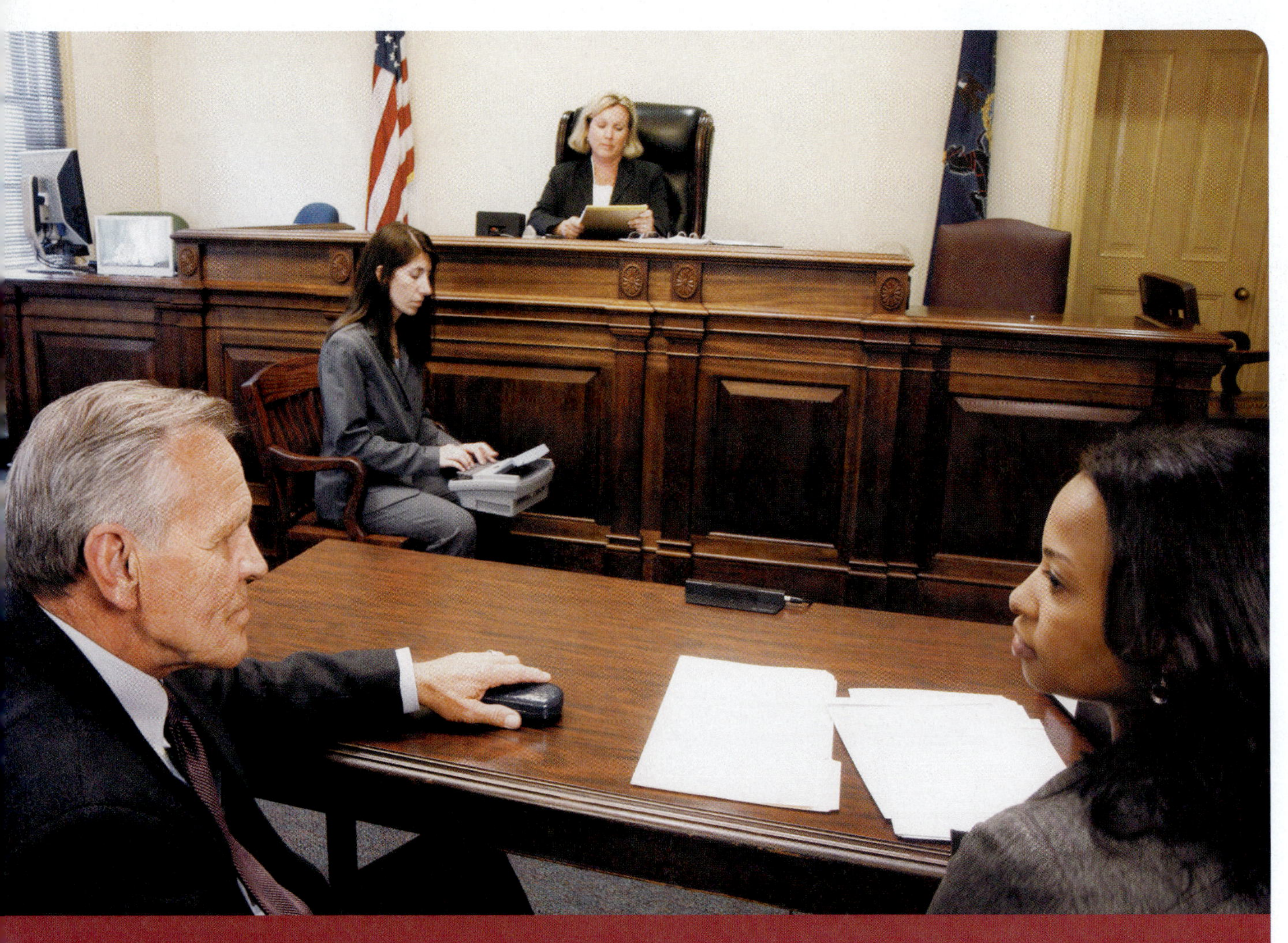

Paralegals at Work

You have applied for a position as a paralegal at a law firm that specializes in litigation. Most of the law firm's practice is in the area of torts, particularly representing plaintiffs in negligence cases. The firm has scheduled an interview with you. On the day you arrive for the interview, you are called into the office of Ms. Harriet Green, a senior partner in the firm. Ms. Green wants to assess your knowledge of judicial and nonjudicial dispute resolution. Ms. Green informs you that she will tell you the facts of a case and will ask you several questions about the case.

Ms. Green explains that Ms. Heather Andersen has retained the law firm to represent her as the plaintiff in an accident case. Ms. Green explains that Ms. Andersen was driving her automobile on the main road of your city when Mr. Joseph Burton, driving another automobile, ran a red light and hit Ms. Andersen's vehicle, causing her severe physical injuries, as well as pain and suffering. The law firm plans to file a lawsuit for negligence against Mr. Burton. Ms. Andersen is a resident of your state. Mr. Burton is a resident of another state who was visiting your state when the accident occurred.

Ms. Green asks you the following questions: What is a complaint? In what court or courts can our law firm file the complaint on behalf of Ms. Andersen? If we lose the case at trial, to what court can Ms. Andersen appeal the trial court's decision? After the case is filed in the court, is there any way of resolving the case in favor of Ms. Andersen before the case goes to trial?

Consider these issues as you read the chapter.

LEARNING OBJECTIVES

After studying this chapter, you should be able to:

1. Recognize the professional opportunities for paralegals in litigation.
2. Describe the state court systems.
3. Describe the federal court system.
4. Describe the U.S. Supreme Court and how cases reach the Court.
5. Explain subject matter jurisdiction of federal and state courts.
6. Describe *in personam* jurisdiction of courts.
7. Recognize the professional opportunities for paralegals in alternative dispute resolution.
8. Explain the use of arbitration.
9. Explain the use of mediation and other forms of alternative dispute resolution.
10. Explain a paralegal's duty to provide pro bono services to the public.

> "I was never ruined but twice; once when I lost a lawsuit, and once when I won one."
>
> *Voltaire*

Learning Objective 1

Recognize the professional opportunities for paralegals in litigation.

INTRODUCTION FOR THE PARALEGAL

The court systems and the procedures to bring and defend lawsuits are complex. To be a valuable member of the legal team, a paralegal should be knowledgeable of court systems, how a lawsuit proceeds to trial, and how it is decided in court.

Some parties to a dispute will choose to settle a case without a trial, or have the case reviewed or decided by a private party rather than by the courts. Thus, a paralegal should also be knowledgeable in the procedures for having disputes resolved outside of the court system.

The glorious uncertainty of law.

Thomas Wilbraham
A toast at a dinner of judges and counsel at Serjeants' Inn Hall

Litigation The process of bringing, maintaining, and defending a lawsuit. A court that hears matters of a specialized or limited nature.

The two major court systems in the United States are: (1) the federal court system, and (2) the court systems of the 50 states and the District of Columbia. Each of these systems has **jurisdiction** to hear different types of lawsuits. The process of bringing, maintaining, and defending a lawsuit is called **litigation**. Litigation is a difficult, time-consuming, and costly process that must comply with complex procedural rules. Although not required, most parties employ a lawyer to represent them when they are involved in a lawsuit.

Several forms of nonjudicial dispute resolution have been developed in response to the expense and difficulty of bringing a lawsuit. These methods, collectively called alternative dispute resolution (ADR), are being used more and more often to resolve disputes.

Paralegals are especially valuable in providing support to lawyers who are engaged in litigation and alternative dispute resolution. Paralegals interview clients, prepare documents submitted to courts, conduct legal research, and assist lawyers during the proceedings.

This chapter focuses on the various court systems, the jurisdiction of courts to hear and decide cases, the litigation process, and alternative dispute resolution. The following feature discusses the career opportunities for paralegal professionals in courts and litigation.

Learning Objective 2

Describe the state court systems.

State Court Systems

Paralegal professionals should be familiar with the **state court system** in which he or she will be assisting attorneys. Each state and the District of Columbia has a separate court system. Most state court systems include:

- Limited jurisdiction trial courts
- General jurisdiction trial courts
- Intermediate appellate courts
- A supreme court (or highest state court)

CAREER OPPORTUNITIES FOR PARALEGALS IN COURTS AND LITIGATION

Many paralegals are fortunate to have the opportunity to work in a special environment—the court system. Paralegals are often hired by state and federal courts to assist judges in the preparation of cases for trial. They may also assist a judge or justice by conducting research, briefing arguments, preparing documents, and completing other duties.

In addition to working for the courts directly, many more paralegals are employed by attorneys who represent clients who are involved in litigation. These paralegals may work for either plaintiffs' or defendants' attorneys in civil lawsuits involving breach of contract, negligence, product liability, business litigation, and other civil matters. These lawsuits may be in either state or federal courts.

Paralegals are also hired to work for prosecutors and defense attorneys in the area of criminal law. These paralegals assist the attorneys to prepare for and assist during trial. Criminal cases are brought in either state or federal courts, depending on whether the crimes alleged are under state or federal statutes.

A paralegal who works for the courts or litigation attorneys must have a detailed knowledge of the court systems that serve the jurisdiction that he or she works in. However, even paralegals who work in positions that are not directly involved in litigation should have knowledge of the country's court systems.

Limited Jurisdiction Trial Court

State **limited jurisdiction trial courts,** which sometimes are referred to as *inferior trial courts*, hear matters of a specialized or limited nature.

Limited jurisdiction trial court A court that hears matters of a specialized or limited nature.

Examples Some limited jurisdiction trial courts are traffic courts, juvenile courts, justice-of-the-peace courts, probate courts, family law courts, courts that hear misdemeanor criminal law cases, and civil cases involving lawsuits of less than a certain dollar amount. Because these courts are trial courts, evidence is introduced and testimony is given. Most limited jurisdiction courts keep a record of their proceedings. Their decisions usually can be appealed to a general jurisdiction court or an appellate court.

Web Exploration

Use **www.google.com** to find out if your state has a small claims court. If so, what is the dollar limit for cases to qualify for the small claims court?

Many states also have **small claims courts** to hear civil cases involving small dollar amounts (such as $5,000 or less). Generally, the parties must appear individually and cannot have a lawyer represent them. The decisions of small claims courts are often appealable to general jurisdiction trial courts or appellate courts.

General Jurisdiction Trial Court

Every state has a **general jurisdiction trial court**. These courts often are called **courts of record** because the testimony and evidence at trial are recorded and stored for future use. These courts hear cases that are not within the jurisdiction of limited jurisdiction trial courts, such as felonies, civil cases above a certain dollar amount, and other categories. Some states divide their general jurisdiction courts into two divisions: criminal cases and civil cases.

General jurisdiction trial court (court of record) A court that hears cases of a general nature that are not within the jurisdiction of limited jurisdiction trial courts.

General jurisdiction trial courts hear evidence and testimony. The decisions these courts hand down are appealable to an intermediate appellate court or the state supreme court, depending on the circumstances.

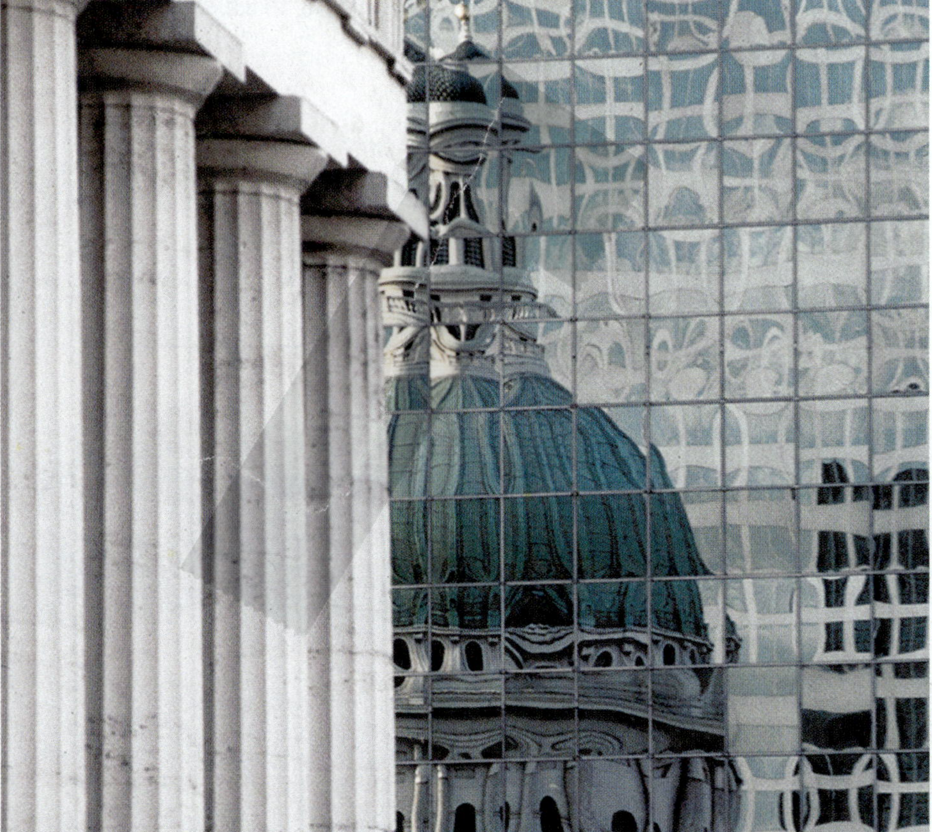

Courthouse, St. Louis, Missouri. State courts hear and decide the majority of cases in the United States.

Intermediate appellate court An intermediate court that hears appeals from trial courts.

Intermediate Appellate Court

In many states, **intermediate appellate courts** (also called *appellate courts* or *courts of appeal*) hear appeals from trial courts. These courts review the trial court record to determine any errors at trial that would require reversal or modification of the trial court's decision. Thus, the appellate court reviews either pertinent parts of the trial record or the entire record from the lower court. No new evidence or testimony is permitted. The parties usually file legal briefs with the appellate court that state the law and the facts that support their positions. Appellate courts usually grant the parties a short oral hearing.

Appellate court decisions are appealable to the state's highest court. In less populated states that do not have an intermediate appellate court, trial court decisions can be appealed directly to the state's highest court.

Highest state court The top court in a state court system. It hears appeals from intermediate state courts and certain trial courts.

Highest State Court

Each state has a **highest state court** in its court system. Most states call this highest court the *supreme court*. The function of a state supreme court is to hear appeals from intermediate state courts and certain trial courts. The highest court hears no new evidence or testimony. The parties usually submit parts of the lower court record or the entire lower court record for review. The parties also submit legal briefs to the court and typically are granted a brief oral hearing. Decisions of state supreme courts are final, unless a question of law is involved that is appealable to the U.S. Supreme Court.

Exhibit 6.1 shows a typical state court system. Exhibit 6.2 lists the websites for the court systems of the 50 states and the jurisdictions in the United States.

Web Exploration

Go to Exhibit 6.2. Find the website for your state or district or territory and go to this website. What is the name of the highest court? In what city is the highest court located?

Exhibit 6.1 A typical state court system

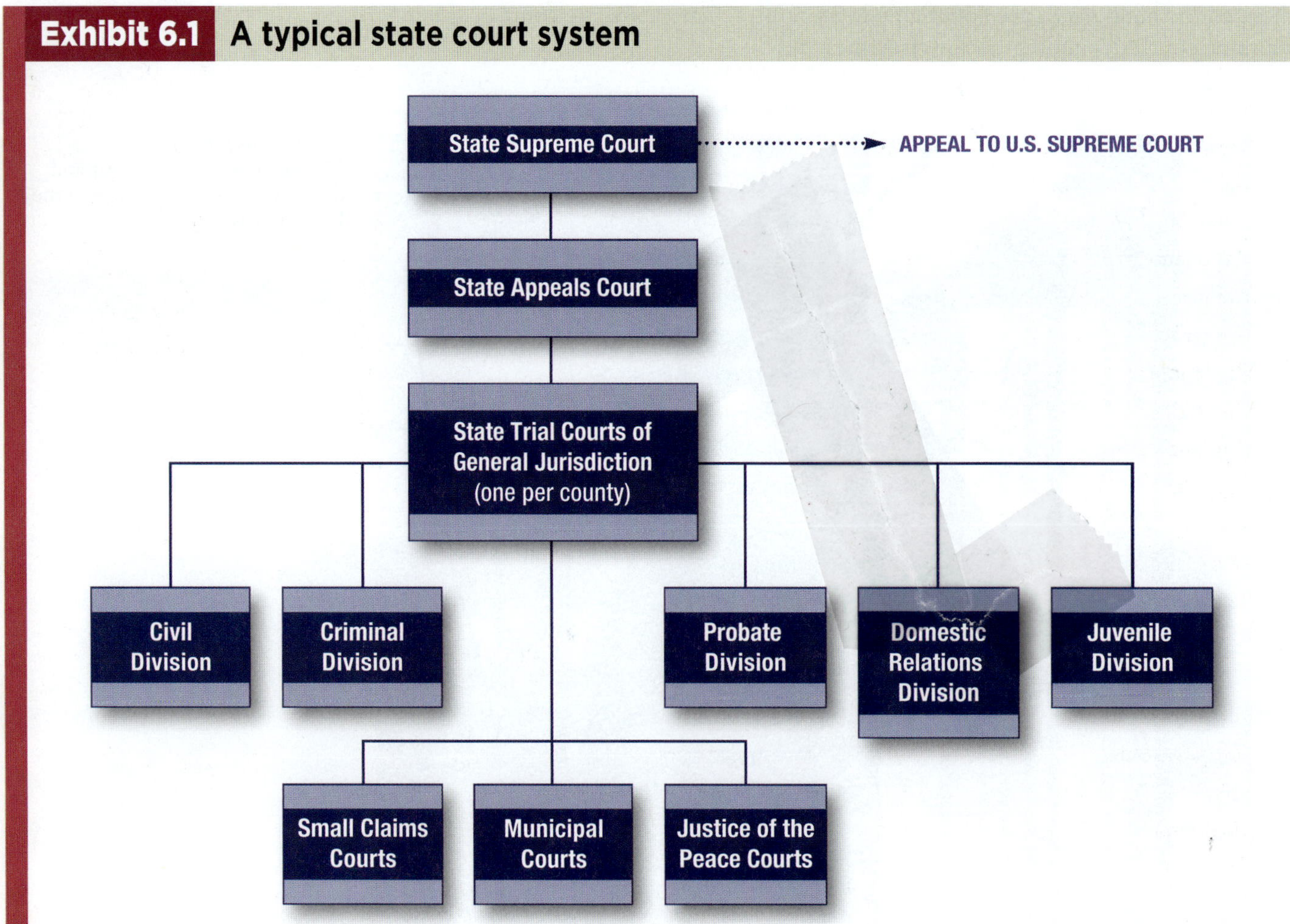

Exhibit 6.2 **Websites for state court systems and jurisdictions**

State	Website
Alabama	www.judicial.state.al.us
Alaska	www.state.ak.us/courts
Arizona	www.supreme.state.az.us
Arkansas	www.courts.state.ar.us
California	www.courtinfo.ca.gov/courts
Colorado	www.courts.state.co.us
Connecticut	www.jud.state.ct.us
Delaware	www.courts.state.de.us
District of Columbia	www.dccourts.gov
Florida	www.flcourts.org
Georgia	georgiacourts.org
Guam	www.guamsupremecourt.com
Hawaii	www.courts.state.hi.us
Idaho	www.isc.idaho.gov
Illinois	www.state.il.us/court
Indiana	www.in.gov/judiciary
Iowa	www.judicial.state.ia.us
Kansas	www.kscourts.org
Kentucky	www.courts.ky.gov
Louisiana	www.lasc.org
Maine	www.courts.state.me.us
Maryland	www.courts.state.md.us
Massachusetts	www.mass.gov/courts
Michigan	www.courts.michigan.gov
Minnesota	www.courts.state.mn.us
Mississippi	www.mssc.state.ms.us
Missouri	www.courts.mo.gov
Montana	www.montanacourts.org
Nebraska	court.nol.org
Nevada	www.nvsupremecourt.us
New Hampshire	www.courts.state.nh.us
New Jersey	www.judiciary.state.nj.us
New Mexico	www.nmcourts.com
New York	www.courts.state.ny.us
North Carolina	www.nccourts.org
North Dakota	www.ndcourts.com
Ohio	www.sconet.state.oh.us
Oklahoma	www.oscn.net/oscn/schome
Oregon	www.ojd.state.or.us

(continued)

Exhibit 6.2 Websites for state court systems and jurisdictions *(continued)*

State	Website
Pennsylvania	www.courts.state.pa.us
Puerto Rico	www.tribunalpr.org
Rhode Island	www.courts.state.ri.us
South Carolina	www.judicial.state.sc.us
South Dakota	www.sdjudicial.com
Tennessee	www.tsc.state.tn.us
Texas	www.courts.state.tx.us
Utah	www.utcourts.gov
Vermont	www.vermontjudiciary.org
Virginia	www.courts.state.va.us
Virgin Islands	www.visuperiorcourt.org
Washington	www.courts.wa.gov
West Virginia	www.wv.gov
Wisconsin	www.wicourts.gov
Wyoming	www.courts.state.wy.us

Learning Objective 3
Describe the federal court system.

Federal Court System

Paralegal professionals are sometimes involved in assisting attorneys who practice before one of the many federal courts. Article III of the U.S. Constitution provides that the federal government's judicial power is vested in the Supreme Court. The Constitution also authorizes Congress to establish "inferior" federal courts in the **federal court system**. Pursuant to this power, Congress has established special federal courts, the U.S. district courts, and the U.S. courts of appeal. Federal judges are appointed for life by the president with the advice and consent of the Senate (except bankruptcy court judges, who are appointed for 14-year terms, and U.S. Magistrate Judges, who are appointed for 8-year terms).

Special Federal Courts

Special federal courts Federal courts that hear matters of specialized or limited jurisdiction.

The **special federal courts** established by Congress have limited jurisdiction. They include:

- **U.S. Tax Court:** Hears cases involving federal tax laws
- **U.S. Court of Federal Claims:** Hears cases brought against the United States
- **U.S. Court of International Trade:** Hears cases involving tariffs and international commercial disputes
- **U.S. Bankruptcy Court:** Hears cases involving federal bankruptcy laws

U.S. District Courts

U.S. District Courts The federal court system's trial courts of general jurisdiction.

The **U.S. District Courts** are the federal court system's trial courts of general jurisdiction. The District of Columbia and each state has at least one federal district court;

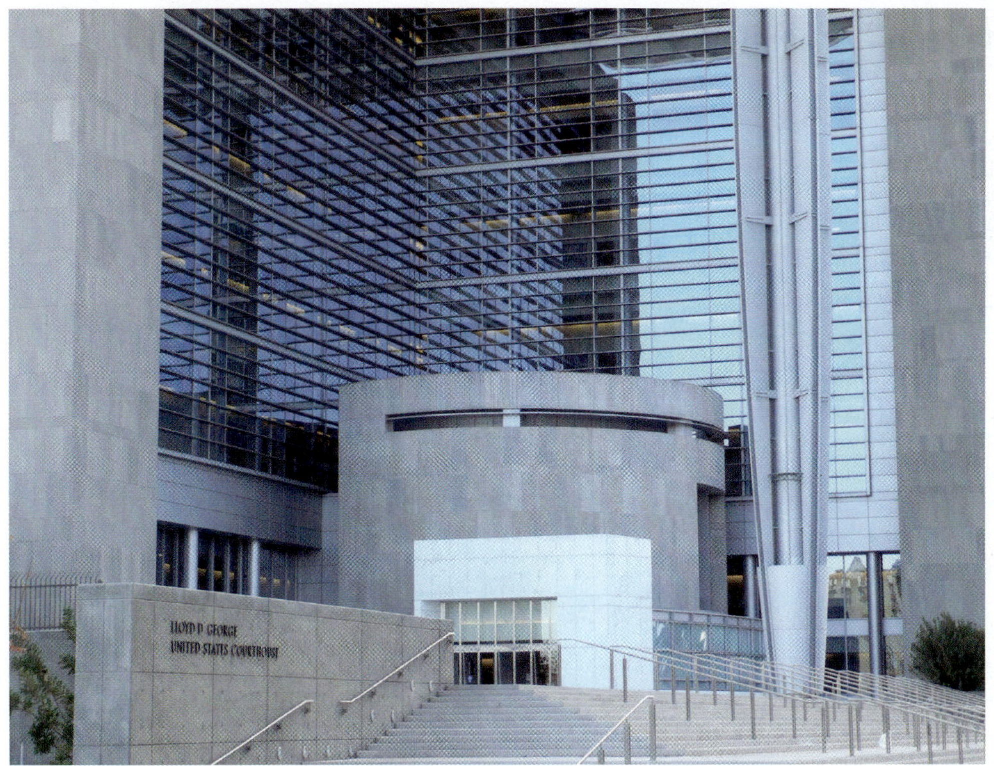

U.S. District Court, Las Vegas, Nevada This is the Lloyd D. George United States District Court for the District of Nevada, which is located in Las Vegas, Nevada. This is a federal trial court. This court, along with the other U.S. district courts located throughout the country, hears and decides lawsuits concerning matters over which it has jurisdiction. State, Washington, DC, and U.S. territory courts hear and decide matters over which they have jurisdiction. The process of bringing and defending lawsuits, preparing for court, and the trial itself is complicated, time-consuming, and expensive.

the more populated states have more than one. The geographical area that each court serves is referred to as a *district*. At present, there are 94 federal district courts. These courts are empowered to impanel juries, receive evidence, hear testimony, and decide cases. Most federal cases originate in federal district courts.

Web Exploration

Go to **http://www.uscourts.gov/courtlinks/**. Click on "District Court." Click on your state. What is the location of the U.S. District Court closest to you?

U.S. Courts of Appeals

The **U.S. Courts of Appeals** are the federal court system's intermediate appellate courts. The federal court system has 13 circuits. **"Circuit"** refers to the geographical area served by a court. Eleven are designated by a number, such as the "First Circuit," the "Second Circuit," and so on. The twelfth circuit is located in Washington, DC, and is called the District of Columbia Circuit.

U.S. Courts of Appeals The federal court system's intermediate appellate courts.

As appellate courts, these circuit courts hear appeals from the district courts located in their circuit, as well as from certain special courts and federal administrative agencies. The courts review the record of the lower court or administrative agency proceedings to determine whether any error would warrant reversal or modification of the lower court decision. No new evidence or testimony is heard. The parties file legal briefs with the court and are given a short oral hearing. Appeals usually are heard by a three-judge panel. After the panel renders a decision, a petitioner can request a review *en banc* by the full court.

Web Exploration

Go to **http://www.uscourts.gov/courtlinks/**. Click on "Court of Appeals." Click on your state. What is the location of the U.S. Court of Appeals closest to you?

A thirteenth circuit court of appeals was created by Congress in 1982, called the **Court of Appeals for the Federal Circuit**. Located in Washington, DC, this court has special appellate jurisdiction to review the decisions of the Court of Federal Claims, the Patent and Trademark Office, and the Court of International Trade. This court of appeals was created to provide uniformity in the application of federal law in certain areas, particularly patent law.

The map in Exhibit 6.3 shows the 13 federal circuit courts of appeals. Exhibit 6.4 lists the websites of the 13 U.S. courts of appeals.

Exhibit 6.3 Map of the federal circuit courts

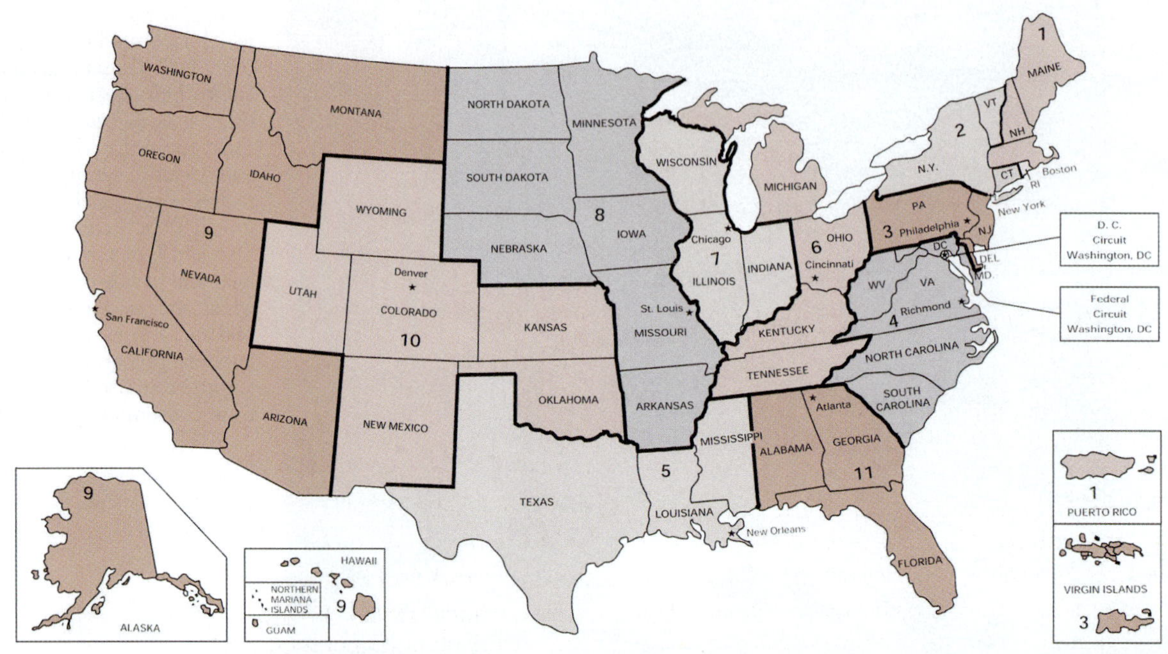

Exhibit 6.4 Websites for federal courts of appeal

United States Court of Appeals	Main Office	Website
First Circuit	Boston, Massachusetts	www.ca1.uscourts.gov
Second Circuit	New York, New York	www.ca2.uscourts.gov
Third Circuit	Philadelphia, Pennsylvania	www.ca3.uscourts.gov
Fourth Circuit	Richmond, Virginia	www.ca4.uscourts.gov
Fifth Circuit	Houston, Texas	www.ca5.uscourts.gov
Sixth Circuit	Cincinnati, Ohio	www.ca6.uscourts.gov
Seventh Circuit	Chicago, Illinois	www.ca7.uscourts.gov
Eighth Circuit	St. Paul, Minnesota	www.ca8.uscourts.gov
Ninth Circuit	San Francisco, California	www.ca9.uscourts.gov
Tenth Circuit	Denver, Colorado	www.ca10.uscourts.gov
Eleventh Circuit	Atlanta, Georgia	www.ca11.uscourts.gov
District of Columbia	Washington, DC	www.dcd.uscourts.gov
Court of Appeals for the Federal Circuit	Washington, DC	www.cafc.uscourts.gov

Supreme Court of the United States The highest court in the United States, located in Washington, DC. The Supreme Court was created by Article III of the U.S. Constitution.

Learning Objective 4

Describe the U.S. Supreme Court and how cases reach the Court.

Supreme Court of the United States

The highest court in the land is the **Supreme Court of the United States,** located in Washington, DC Paralegals should be familiar with the role of the Supreme Court, its jurisdiction, the types of cases it hears, and how it decides cases. This court is composed of nine justices who are nominated by the president and confirmed by the Senate. The president appoints one justice as **chief justice,** who is

Supreme Court of the United States, Washington, DC. The highest court in the land is the Supreme Court of the United States, located in Washington, DC. The U.S. Supreme Court decides the most important constitutional law cases and other important issues it deems ripe for review and decision. The Supreme Court's unanimous and majority decisions are precedent for all the other courts in the country.

responsible for the administration of the Supreme Court. The other eight justices are **associate justices**.

The **U.S. Supreme Court** is an appellate court, that hears appeals from federal circuit courts of appeal and, under certain circumstances, from federal district courts, special federal courts, and the highest state courts. The Supreme Court hears no evidence or testimony. As with other appellate courts, the lower court record is reviewed to determine whether an error has been committed that warrants a reversal or modification of the lower court's decision. Legal briefs are filed, and the parties are granted a brief oral hearing. The Supreme Court's decision is final and cannot be appealed.

Exhibit 6.5 illustrates the federal court system.

Exhibit 6.5 Federal court system

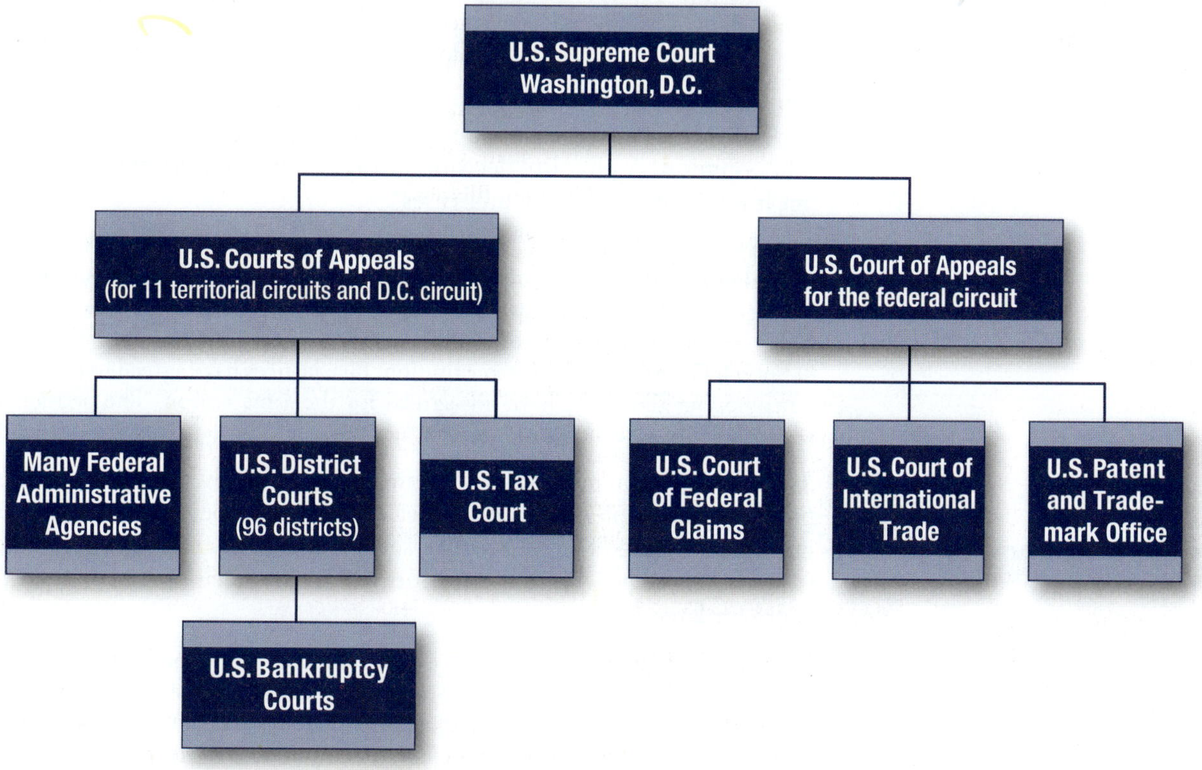

- U.S. Supreme Court Washington, D.C.
  - U.S. Courts of Appeals (for 11 territorial circuits and D.C. circuit)
    - Many Federal Administrative Agencies
    - U.S. District Courts (96 districts)
      - U.S. Bankruptcy Courts
    - U.S. Tax Court
  - U.S. Court of Appeals for the federal circuit
    - U.S. Court of Federal Claims
    - U.S. Court of International Trade
    - U.S. Patent and Trade-mark Office

Petition for *Certiorari*

Petition for *certiorari* A petition asking the Supreme Court to hear one's case.

Writ of certiorari An official notice that the Supreme Court will review one's case.

A party wishing to bring a case before the Supreme Court must file a **petition for *certiorari*** asking the Court to hear the case. If the Court decides to review a case, it will issue a ***writ of certiorari.*** Because the Court issues only about 100 opinions each year, *writs* are usually granted only in cases involving very important issues.

The justices meet once a week to discuss what cases merit review. The votes of four justices are necessary to grant an appeal and schedule an oral argument before the Court (the "rule of four"). Written opinions by the justices are usually issued many months later.

The U.S. Constitution gives Congress the authority to establish rules for the appellate review of cases by the Supreme Court, except in the rare case where mandatory review is required. However, Congress has given the Supreme Court discretion to decide what cases it will hear.

Exhibit 6.6 shows a petition for *certiorari* to the U.S. Supreme Court.

Vote of the U.S. Supreme Court

Each justice of the Supreme Court, including the Chief Justice, has an equal vote. The Supreme Court can issue the following types of decisions:

- **Unanimous decision**. If all of the justices voting agree as to the outcome and reasoning used to decide the case, it is a unanimous opinion. Unanimous decisions are precedent for later cases.

  Example If all nine justices hear a case, and all nine agree to the outcome (the petitioner wins) and the reason why (such as that the Equal Protection Clause of the U.S. Constitution had been violated), this is a unanimous decision.

- **Majority decision**. If a majority of the justices agree to the outcome and reasoning used to decide the case, it is a majority opinion. Majority decisions are precedent for later cases.

  Example If all nine justices hear a case, and five of them agree as to the outcome (the petitioner wins) and all five of those justices also agree to the same reason why (the Equal Protection Clause of the U.S. Constitution has been violated), it is a majority opinion.

- **Plurality decision**. If a majority of the justices agree to the outcome of the case, but not to the reasoning for reaching the outcome, it is a plurality opinion. A plurality decision resolves the case as to those parties, but it is not precedent for later cases.

  Example If all nine justices hear a case, and five of them agree as to the outcome, but not all of these five agree to the reason why, this is a plurality decision. For example, the petitioner wins, but three base their vote on a violation of the Equal Protection Clause and two base their vote on a violation of the Freedom of Speech Clause of the U.S. Constitution. Five justices have agreed to the same outcome, but those five have not agreed for the same reason. The petitioner wins his or her case, but the decision is not precedent for later cases.

- **Tie decision**. Sometimes the Supreme Court sits without all nine justices present because of illness or conflict of interest or because a justice has not been confirmed to fill a vacant seat on the court. In the case of a tie vote, the lower court decision is affirmed. These decisions are not precedent for later cases.

  Example A petitioner won her case at the court of appeals. At the U.S. Supreme Court, only eight justices hear the case. Four justices vote for the petitioner, and four justices vote for the respondent. This is a tie vote. The petitioner remains the winner because she won at the court of appeals. The decision of the Supreme Court sets no precedent for later cases.

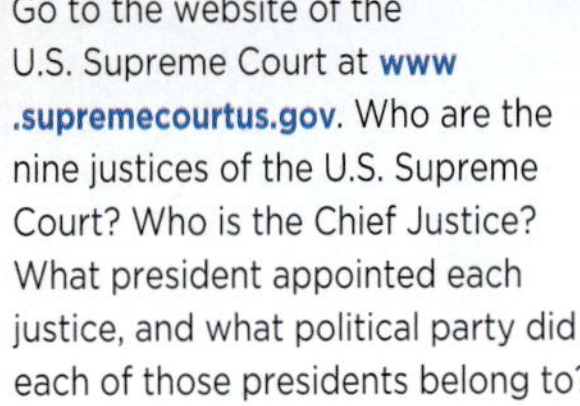

Web Exploration

Go to the website of the U.S. Supreme Court at **www.supremecourtus.gov**. Who are the nine justices of the U.S. Supreme Court? Who is the Chief Justice? What president appointed each justice, and what political party did each of those presidents belong to?

Exhibit 6.6 **Petition for *certiorari* for the case *Fisher v. The University of Texas***

No. 11-

IN THE

Supreme Court of the United States

ABIGAIL NOEL FISHER,

Petitioner,

v.

UNIVERSITY OF TEXAS AT AUSTIN et al.,

Respondents.

ON PETITION FOR A WRIT OF CERTIORARI TO THE UNITED STATES COURT OF APPEALS FOR THE FIFTH CIRCUIT

PETITION FOR A WRIT OF CERTIORARI

BERT W. REIN
Counsel of Record
WILLIAM S. CONSOVOY
THOMAS R. MCCARTHY
CLAIRE J. EVANS
WILEY REIN LLP
1776 K Street, N.W.
Washington, DC 20006
(202) 719-7000
brein@wileyrein.com

Attorneys for Petitioner

September 15, 2011

238053

COUNSEL PRESS

(800) 274-3321 • (800) 359-6859

(continued)

Exhibit 6.6 Petition for *certiorari* for the case *Fisher v. The University of Texas* (continued)

i

QUESTION PRESENTED

Whether this Court's decisions interpreting the Equal Protection Clause of the Fourteenth Amendment, including *Grutter v. Bollinger*, 539 U.S. 306 (2003), permit the University of Texas at Austin's use of race in undergraduate admissions decisions.

ii

PARTIES TO THE PROCEEDING AND RULE 29.6 STATEMENT

Petitioner in this case is Abigail Noel Fisher.

Respondents are the University of Texas at Austin; David B. Pryor, Executive Vice Chancellor for Academic Affairs in His Official Capacity; Barry D. Burgdorf, Vice Chancellor and General Counsel in His Official Capacity; William Powers, Jr., President of the University of Texas at Austin in His Official Capacity; Board of Regents of the University of Texas System; R. Steven Hicks, as Member of the Board of Regents in His Official Capacity; William Eugene Powell, as Member of the Board of Regents in His Official Capacity; James R. Huffines, as Member of the Board of Regents in His Official Capacity; Janiece Longoria, as Member of the Board of Regents in Her Official Capacity; Colleen McHugh, as Chair of the Board of Regents in Her Official Capacity; Robert L. Stillwell, as Member of the Board of Regents in His Official Capacity; James D. Dannenbaum, as Member of the Board of Regents in His Official Capacity; Paul Foster, as Member of the Board of Regents in His Official Capacity; Printice L. Gary, as Member of the Board of Regents in His Official Capacity; Kedra Ishop, Vice Provost and Director of Undergraduate Admissions in Her Official Capacity; Francisco G. Cigarroa, M.D., Interim Chancellor of the University of Texas System in His Official Capacity.

Plaintiff-Appellant below Rachel Multer Michalewicz is being served as a respondent herein.

Exhibit 6.6 **Petition for *certiorari* for the case *Fisher v. The University of Texas*** (continued)

iii

TABLE OF CONTENTS

Page

(continued)

Exhibit 6.6 **Petition for *certiorari* for the case *Fisher v. The University of Texas* (continued)**

iv

Table of Contents

A justice who agrees with the outcome of a case but not the reason proffered by other justices can issue a **concurring opinion,** setting forth his or her reasons for deciding the case. A justice who does not agree with a decision can file a **dissenting opinion** that sets forth the reasons for his or her dissent.

Exhibit 6.7 illustrates an opinion by the U.S. Supreme Court.

The Process of Choosing a U.S. Supreme Court Justice

In an effort to strike a balance of power between the executive and legislative branches of government, Article II, Section 2 of the U.S. Constitution gives the president the power to appoint Supreme Court justices "with the advice and consent of the Senate." This means that the majority of the one hundred senators must approve the president's nominee in order for that nominee to become a justice of the U.S. Supreme Court.

A president who is elected to one or two four-year terms in office may have the opportunity to nominate justices to the U.S. Supreme Court who, if confirmed, may serve many years after the president leaves office. President Barack Obama was inaugurated in January 2009, and within months after taking office, had the opportunity to nominate a justice for the Supreme Court when a justice retired. President Obama

Exhibit 6.7 Opinion of the U.S. Supreme Court: *Brown v. Board of Education*

SUPREME COURT OF THE UNITED STATES

NOS. 1, 2, 4 AND 10.—OCTOBER TERM, 1953.

1	Oliver Brown, et al., Appellants, *v.* Board of Education of Topeka, Shawnee County, Kansas, et al.	On Appeal From the United States District Court for the District of Kansas.
2	Harry Briggs, Jr., et al., Appellants, *v.* R. W. Elliott, et al.	On Appeal From the United States District Court for the Eastern District of South Carolina.
4	Dorothy E. Davis, et al., Appellants, *v.* County School Board of Prince Edward County, Virginia, et al.	On Appeal From the United States District Court for the Eastern District of Virginia.
10	Francis B. Gebhart, et al., Petitioners, *v.* Ethel Louise Belton, et al.	On Writ of Certiorari to the Supreme Court of Delaware.

[May 17, 1954.]

MR. CHIEF JUSTICE WARREN delivered the opinion of the Court.

These cases come to us from the States of Kansas, South Carolina, Virginia, and Delaware. They are premised on different facts and different local conditions,

(continued)

Exhibit 6.7 **Opinion of the U.S. Supreme Court: *Brown v. Board of Education*** (continued)

Supreme Court of the United States

No. 1 ---- *, October Term, 19* 54

Oliver Brown, Mrs. Richard Lawton, Mrs. Sadie Emmanuel et al.,
Appellants,

vs.

Board of Education of Topeka, Shawnee County, Kansas, et al.

Appeal from *the United States District Court for the* ---------------------- *District of* Kansas.

This cause *came on to be heard on the transcript of the record from the United States District Court for the* ------------ *District of* Kansas, ------------- *and was argued by counsel.*

On consideration whereof, *It is ordered and adjudged by this Court that the judgment of the said* District ---------------- *Court in this cause be, and the same is hereby,* reversed with costs; and that this cause be, and the same is hereby, remanded to the said District Court to take such proceedings and enter such orders and decrees consistent with the opinions of this Court as are necessary and proper to admit to public schools on a racially nondiscriminatory basis with all deliberate speed the parties to this case.

Per Mr. Chief Justice Warren,

May 31, 1955.

nominated Sonia Sotomayor for the seat. Sotomayor was confirmed to the Supreme Court by a majority vote of the U.S. Senate, becoming the first Hispanic person to be a justice of the U.S. Supreme Court and the third female appointed to the Court. In 2010, President Obama had a second opportunity to nominate a justice when another justice retired from the Court. The president nominated Elena Kagan, formerly the U.S. solicitor general. Kagan was confirmed by a majority vote of the U.S. Senate.

Jurisdiction of Federal and State Courts

Learning Objective 5
Explain subject matter jurisdiction of federal and state courts.

A federal or state court must have **subject matter jurisdiction** to hear a case. Article III, Section 2 of the U.S. Constitution sets forth the jurisdiction of federal courts. These courts have *limited jurisdiction* to hear cases involving federal questions and cases involving diversity of citizenship. State courts also have jurisdiction to hear various types of cases that cannot be handled by federal courts. The jurisdiction of federal and state courts to hear cases is discussed in the following paragraphs.

Subject matter jurisdiction Jurisdiction over the subject matter of a lawsuit.

Subject Matter Jurisdiction of Federal Courts

Federal courts have jurisdiction to hear cases based on the subject matter of the case. They have jurisdiction to hear cases involving "federal questions." **Federal question** cases are cases arising under the U.S. Constitution, treaties, and federal statutes and regulations. There is no dollar amount limit on federal question cases that can be brought in federal court.

Federal question A case arising under the U.S. Constitution, treaties, or federal statutes and regulations.

Example A lawsuit involving federal securities law concerns a federal question (a federal statute) and will be heard by a U.S. district court.

Subject Matter Jurisdiction of State Courts

State courts have jurisdiction to hear cases involving subject matters that federal courts do not have jurisdiction to hear. These usually involve state laws.

Examples State courts may have jurisdiction to hear cases involving the subjects of real estate law, corporation law, partnership law, limited liability company law, contract law, sales and lease contracts, and negotiable instruments.

Diversity of Citizenship

A case involving a state court subject matter may be brought in federal court if there is **diversity of citizenship**. Diversity of citizenship occurs if the lawsuit involves (a) citizens of different states, (b) a citizen of a state and a citizen or subject of a foreign country, and (c) a citizen of a state and a foreign country as plaintiff. A corporation is considered a citizen of the state in which it is incorporated and in which it has its principal place of business. The reason for giving federal courts diversity jurisdiction was to avoid the bias against nonresidents that might occur in state courts. The federal court must apply the appropriate state's law in deciding the case. The dollar amount of the controversy must exceed $75,000 to be brought under diversity jurisdiction. If this requirement is not met, the action must be brought in the appropriate state court.

Diversity of citizenship A case between (1) citizens of different states, (2) a citizen of a state and a citizen or subject of a foreign country, and (3) a citizen of a state and a foreign country where a foreign country is the plaintiff.

Example Henry, a resident of the state of Idaho, is driving his automobile in the state of Idaho when he negligently hits Mary, a pedestrian. Mary is a resident of the state of New York. There is no federal question involved in this case; it is an automobile accident that involves state negligence law. However, there is diversity of citizenship: Henry is from Idaho, while Mary is from New York. Usually the case must be brought in the state in which the automobile accident occurred because this is where most of the witnesses and evidence will be from. But in this case, Mary may bring her lawsuit in federal court in Idaho. If she does so, the case will remain in federal court. If Mary brings the case in Idaho state court, it will remain in Idaho state court if Henry agrees; however, Henry can move the case to federal court.

Exclusive and Concurrent Jurisdiction

Federal courts have **exclusive jurisdiction** to hear cases involving federal crimes, antitrust, bankruptcy, patent and copyright cases, suits against the United States, and most admiralty cases. State courts cannot hear these cases.

State and federal courts have **concurrent jurisdiction** to hear cases involving diversity of citizenship and federal questions over which federal courts do not have exclusive jurisdiction (such as cases involving federal securities laws). If a plaintiff brings a case involving concurrent jurisdiction in state court, the defendant can remove the case to federal court. If a case does not qualify to be brought in federal court, it must be brought in the appropriate state court.

Learning Objective 6
Describe *in personam* jurisdiction of courts.

Personal Jurisdiction and Other Issues

A court does not have the authority to hear all cases within its subject matter jurisdiction. To bring a lawsuit in a court, the plaintiff must have *standing to sue*. In addition, the court must have *jurisdiction* to hear the case, and the case must be brought in the proper *venue*. These topics are discussed in the following paragraphs.

Standing to Sue

To bring a lawsuit, a plaintiff must have **standing to sue**. This means the plaintiff must have some stake in the outcome of the lawsuit.

> **Example** Linda's friend Jon is injured in an accident caused by Emily. Jon refuses to sue. Linda cannot sue Emily on Jon's behalf because she does not have an interest in the result of the case.

In Personam Jurisdiction

***In personam* (personal) jurisdiction** Jurisdiction over the parties to a lawsuit.

Service of process A summons being served on a defendant to obtain personal jurisdiction over him or her.

Jurisdiction over a person is called ***in personam* jurisdiction**, or **personal jurisdiction**. A *plaintiff*, by filing a lawsuit with a court, gives the court *in personam* jurisdiction over him or her. The court must also have *in personam* jurisdiction over the *defendant*, which is usually obtained by having a summons served to that person within the territorial boundaries of the state. Serving a summons is referred to as **service of process** and is usually accomplished by personally hand-delivering the summons and complaint to the defendant.

If personal service is not possible, alternative forms of notice, such as mailing the summons or publishing a notice in a newspaper, may be permitted. A corporation is subject to personal jurisdiction in the state in which it is incorporated, has its principal office, and is doing business.

A party who disputes the jurisdiction of a court can make a *special appearance* in that court to argue against imposition of jurisdiction. Service of process is not permitted during such an appearance.

In Rem Jurisdiction

***In rem* jurisdiction** Jurisdiction to hear a case because of jurisdiction over the property at issue in the lawsuit.

A court may have jurisdiction to hear and decide a case because it has jurisdiction over the property of the lawsuit. This is called ***in rem* jurisdiction** ("jurisdiction over the thing").

> **Example** A state court would have jurisdiction to hear a dispute over the ownership of a piece of real estate located within the state. This is so even if one or more of the disputing parties lives in another state or states.

Quasi in Rem Jurisdiction

***Quasi in rem* (attachment) jurisdiction** Jurisdiction allowed a plaintiff who obtains a judgment in one state to try to collect the judgment by attaching property of a defendant located in another state.

Sometimes a plaintiff who obtains a judgment against a defendant in one state will try to collect the judgment by attaching property of the defendant that is located in another state. This is permitted under ***quasi in rem* jurisdiction**, or **attachment jurisdiction**.

Example If a plaintiff wins a monetary judgment against a defendant in a Florida state court, but the defendant's only property is located in Idaho, the Idaho state court has *quasi in rem* jurisdiction to order the attachment of the defendant's property in Idaho to satisfy the Florida court judgment.

Long-Arm Statutes

In most states, a state court can obtain jurisdiction over persons and businesses located in another state or country through the state's **long-arm statute**. These statutes extend a state's jurisdiction to nonresidents who were not served a summons within the state. The nonresident must have had some *minimum contact* with the state, as held in the leading case of *International Shoe Co. v. Washington*, 326 U.S. 310, 66 S.Ct. 154, 90 L.Ed. 95, 1945 U.S. Lexis 1447 (1945). In addition, maintenance of the suit in a particular jurisdiction must uphold the traditional notions of fair play and substantial justice.

Long-arm statute A statute that extends a state's jurisdiction to nonresidents who were not served a summons within the state.

The exercise of long-arm jurisdiction is generally permitted over nonresidents who have (1) committed torts within the state (as where a plaintiff is alleged to have caused an automobile accident in the state), (2) entered into a contract either in the state or that affects the state (and the party allegedly breached the contract), or (3) transacted other business in the state that allegedly caused injury to another person.

Venue

Venue requires lawsuits to be heard by the court with jurisdiction nearest the location in which the incident occurred or where the parties reside.

Venue A requirement that lawsuits be heard by the court with jurisdiction that is nearest the location in which the incident occurred or where the parties reside.

Example Harry, a Georgia resident, commits a felony in Los Angeles County, California. The California Superior Court, located in Los Angeles, is the proper venue because the crime was committed in Los Angeles County and the witnesses are probably from that area.

Occasionally, pretrial publicity may bias jurors located in an otherwise proper venue. In these cases, a **change of venue** may be requested so that a more impartial jury can be found. However, courts generally frown upon *forum shopping*, in which a party looks for a favorable court without a valid reason for changing venue.

Jurisdiction in Cyberspace

Obtaining personal jurisdiction over a defendant in another state has always been difficult for courts. Today, with the Internet's allowing persons and businesses to reach millions of people in other states electronically, particularly through websites, new issues have arisen as to whether courts have jurisdiction in cyberspace. For example, if a person in one state uses the website of an Internet seller located in another state, can the user sue the Internet seller in his or her state under that state's long-arm statute?

A seminal case that addresses jurisdiction in cyberspace is *Zippo Manufacturing Company v. Zippo Dot Com, Inc.*[10] In addressing jurisdiction of Internet users, the court created a "sliding scale" in order to measure the nature and quality of the commercial activity effectuated in a forum state through a website. The court stated:

> At one end of the spectrum are situations where a defendant clearly does business over the Internet. If the defendant enters into contracts with residents of a foreign jurisdiction that involve the knowing and repeated transmission of computer files over the Internet, personal jurisdiction is proper. At the opposite end are situations where a defendant has simply posted information on an Internet Web site which is accessible to users in foreign jurisdictions. A passive Web site that does little more than make information available to those who are interested in it is not grounds for the exercise of personal jurisdiction. The middle ground is occupied by interactive Web sites where

[10]952 F.Supp. 1119 Web 1997 U.S. Dist. Lexis 1701 (W.D. Pa. 1997).

a user can exchange information with the host computer. In these cases, the exercise of jurisdiction is determined by examining the level of interactivity and commercial nature of the exchange of information that occurs on the Web site.

Forum selection clause A contract provision that designates a certain court to hear disputes concerning the nonperformance of a contract.

Choice-of-law clause A contract provision that designates a certain state's or country's law to be applied to disputes concerning the nonperformance of a contract.

Applying this standard is often difficult and depends on the circumstances of the case.

Forum Selection and Choice-of-Law Clauses

In a contract, parties sometimes agree as to what courts will have jurisdiction to hear a legal dispute. Such clauses are called **forum selection clauses**.

In addition to agreeing to a forum, the parties also often agree as to what state's or country's law will apply in resolving a dispute. These clauses are called **choice-of-law clauses**.

E-Courts

In a conventional court system, litigation can be a cumbersome process. The clients, lawyers, and judges involved in the case are usually buried in documents. These documents include pleadings, interrogatories, motions, research, depositions, evidence, briefs, memorandums, and numerous other documents. By the time a case is over, reams of paper are stored in dozens, if not hundreds, of boxes. In addition, court appearances for even very small matters must be made in person, and are usually time consuming.

Example Lawyers often wait hours for a 10-minute scheduling conference or another conference with a judge. The time it takes to drive to and from court also has to be taken into account, which in some areas may amount to hours.

e-court A court that either mandates or permits the electronic filing of pleadings, briefs, and other documents related to a lawsuit. Also called a *virtual courthouse*.

The Internet has radically changed how lawyers and courts operate. It has enabled many communications between lawyers and courts to be conducted electronically. Today, the Internet and other technologies have enabled the use of **electronic courts,** or **e-courts,** also referred to as **virtual courthouses**. Technology also allows for the **electronic filing,** or **e-filing,** of pleadings, briefs, and other documents related to a lawsuit. In addition, technology allows for the scanning of evidence and documents into a computer for storage and retrieval and for emailing correspondence and documents to the court, the opposing counsel, and clients. Scheduling and other conferences with the judge or opposing counsel are held via telephone conferences and email.

Many courts have instituted electronic document filing and tracking. In some courts, e-filing of pleadings and other documents is now mandatory. Companies such as Microsoft and LexisNexis have developed systems to manage e-filings of court documents.

Learning Objective 7

Recognize the professional opportunities for paralegals in alternative dispute resolution.

Alternative dispute resolution (ADR) Methods of resolving disputes other than litigation.

Negotiation A procedure in which the parties to a dispute engage in negotiations to try to reach a voluntary settlement of their dispute.

Alternative Dispute Resolution (ADR)

The use of the court system to resolve major disputes can take years and cost thousands, if not millions, of dollars in legal fees and expenses. In commercial litigation, the normal business operations of the parties are often disrupted. To avoid or lessen these problems, businesses are increasingly turning to methods of **alternative dispute resolution (ADR)** to resolve disputes. The most common form of ADR is *arbitration*. Other forms of ADR are *negotiation*, *mediation*, *conciliation*, *minitrial*, *fact-finding*, and using a *judicial referee*.

The following feature discusses the career opportunities for paralegal professionals in alternative dispute resolution.

Negotiation

The simplest form of alternative dispute resolution is engaging in negotiation between the parties to try to settle a dispute. **Negotiation** is a procedure whereby the parties to a dispute engage in discussions to try to reach a voluntary settlement of their dispute.

CAREER OPPORTUNITIES FOR PARALEGALS IN ALTERNATIVE DISPUTE RESOLUTION

The growth in the use of alternative dispute resolution to resolve disputes has been phenomenal. Alternative dispute resolution is just that—an alternative to using the litigation process and court systems to resolve disputes.

The most common form of alternative dispute resolution is arbitration. The United States Supreme Court has upheld the use of arbitration in many types of disputes. Arbitration is used particularly in contract disputes, because many contracts contain arbitration clauses; that is, the parties to the contract have agreed not to use the court systems to resolve their disputes. Instead, they have expressly agreed that an arbitrator, and not a jury, will decide the matter. Most major companies have placed arbitration agreements in their contracts.

Examples Arbitration clauses appear in contracts to purchase goods, lease automobiles, employ services, and other types of contracts. Also, arbitration clauses are included in many employment contracts. Thus, if an employee has a dispute with his or her employer, the dispute goes to arbitration for resolution because the employee has given up his or her right to use the court system by agreeing to the arbitration clause.

Mediation also has become an indispensable method of helping to resolve disputes. In mediation, the mediator does not act as a decision maker, but instead acts as a facilitator to try to help the disputing parties reach a settlement. Mediation is often used in family law matters, particularly in settling divorce cases.

Paralegals who work on business-related matters, contract disputes, and family law matters should have a thorough understanding of alternative dispute resolution. These paralegals are often called upon to help attorneys prepare for arbitration, mediation, and other forms of alternative dispute resolution. The following sections address the major forms of alternative dispute resolution.

Negotiation may take place before a lawsuit is filed, after a lawsuit is filed, or before other forms of alternative dispute resolution are pursued.

In a negotiation, the parties are often represented by attorneys. During the proceedings, the parties usually make offers and counteroffers to one another. The parties or their attorneys also may provide information to the other side that would assist the other side in reaching an amicable settlement.

Many courts require that the parties to a lawsuit engage in settlement discussions prior to trial. The judge must be assured that a settlement of the case is not possible before he or she permits the case to go to trial. Judges often convince the parties to engage in further negotiations if they determine that the parties are not too far apart in their positions.

If a settlement of the dispute is reached through negotiation, a settlement agreement is drafted that contains the terms of the agreement. A **settlement agreement** is voluntarily entered into by the parties and resolves the dispute. Each side must sign the settlement agreement for it to become effective. The settlement agreement usually is submitted to the court, and the case is dismissed based on execution of the agreement.

Settlement agreement An agreement voluntarily entered into by the parties to a dispute that settles the dispute.

Arbitration

Learning Objective 8
Explain the use of arbitration.

Paralegals working in many areas of the law—litigation, contract law, business law, and such—will encounter arbitration clauses in some of the cases that they are working on. In **arbitration,** the parties choose an impartial third party to hear and decide the dispute, called the **arbitrator**. Arbitrators usually are selected from members of the American Arbitration Association (AAA) or another arbitration association.

Arbitration A form of ADR in which the parties choose an impartial third party to hear and decide the dispute.

Labor union agreements, franchise agreements, leases, and other commercial contracts often contain **arbitration clauses** that require disputes arising out of the contract to be submitted to arbitration. If there is no arbitration clause, the parties can enter into a **submission agreement,** whereby they agree to submit a dispute to arbitration after the dispute arises.

Arbitration clause A clause in a contract that requires disputes arising out of the contract to be submitted to arbitration.

Arbitration often has many benefits over litigation. It is less expensive, is completed faster, and is decided by a person who is knowledgeable in the area of law that is in dispute. However, some consumers and employees who are subject to arbitration agreements argue that arbitration unfairly favors businesses and employers.

In the past, some courts were reluctant to permit arbitration of a dispute or found that arbitration agreements were illegal. However, in a series of cases, the U.S. Supreme Court upheld the validity of many types of arbitration clauses or agreements.

Exhibit 6.8 is a form for a Demand for Arbitration.

Exhibit 6.8 Demand for arbitration

American Arbitration Association
Dispute Resolution Services Worldwide

_______________ **ARBITRATION RULES**
(ENTER THE NAME OF THE APPLICABLE RULES)

Demand for Arbitration

MEDIATION: *If you would like the AAA to contact the other parties and attempt to arrange mediation, please check this box.* ☐ *There is no additional administrative fee for this service.*					
Name of Respondent			Name of Representative (if known)		
Address:			Name of Firm (if applicable):		
			Representative's Address		
City	State	Zip Code	City	State	Zip Code
Phone No.		Fax No.	Phone No.		Fax No.
Email Address:			Email Address:		
The named claimant, a party to an arbitration agreement dated ______________, which provides for arbitration under the ______________ Arbitration Rules of the American Arbitration Association, hereby demands arbitration.					
THE NATURE OF THE DISPUTE					
Dollar Amount of Claim $			Other Relief Sought: ☐ Attorneys Fees ☐ Interest ☐ Arbitration Costs ☐ Punitive/ Exemplary ☐ Other __________		
AMOUNT OF FILING FEE ENCLOSED WITH THIS DEMAND (please refer to the fee schedule in the rules for the appropriate fee) $					
PLEASE DESCRIBE APPROPRIATE QUALIFICATIONS FOR ARBITRATOR(S) TO BE APPOINTED TO HEAR THIS DISPUTE:					
Hearing locale______________ (check one) ☐ Requested by Claimant ☐ Locale provision included in the contract					
Estimated time needed for hearings overall: ________hours or ________days			Type of Business: Claimant ______________ Respondent______________		
Is this a dispute between a business and a consumer? ☐Yes ☐ No Does this dispute arise out of an employment relationship? ☐Yes ☐ No If this dispute arises out of an employment relationship, what was/is the employee's annual wage range? Note: This question is required by California law. ☐Less than $100,000 ☐ $100,000 - $250,000 ☐ Over $250,000					
You are hereby notified that copies of our arbitration agreement and this demand are being filed with the American Arbitration Association's Case Management Center, located in (check one) ☐ Atlanta, GA ☐ Dallas, TX ☐ East Providence, RI ☐ Fresno, CA ☐ International Centre, NY, with a request that it commence administration of the arbitration. Under the rules, you may file an answering statement within the timeframe specified in the rules, after notice from the AAA.					
Signature (may be signed by a representative) Date:			Name of Representative		
Name of Claimant			Name of Firm (if applicable)		
Address (to be used in connection with this case):			Representative's Address:		
City	State	Zip Code	City	State	Zip Code
Phone No.		Fax No.	Phone No.		Fax No.
Email Address:			Email Address:		
To begin proceedings, please send two copies of this Demand and the Arbitration Agreement, along with the filing fee as provided for in the Rules, to the AAA. Send the original Demand to the Respondent.					
Please visit our website at www.adr.org if you would like to file this case online. AAA Customer Service can be reached at 800-778-7879					

Source: Reprinted with permission of American Arbitration Association

Federal Arbitration Act

The **Federal Arbitration Act (FAA)** was originally enacted by Congress in 1925 to reverse the longstanding judicial hostility to arbitration agreements in English common law and American courts [9 U.S.C. Sections 1 et. seq.]. The Act provides that arbitration agreements involving commerce are valid, irrevocable, and enforceable contracts, unless some grounds exist at law or equity to revoke them (such as fraud or duress). The FAA permits one party to obtain a court order to compel arbitration if the other party has failed, neglected, or refused to comply with an arbitration agreement.

Federal Arbitration Act (FAA) A federal statute that provides for the enforcement of most commercial arbitration agreements.

About half of the states have adopted the **Uniform Arbitration Act,** which promotes the arbitration of disputes at the state level. Many federal and state courts have instituted programs to refer legal disputes to arbitration or another form of alternative dispute resolution.

ADR Providers

ADR services are usually provided by private organizations or individuals who are qualified to hear and decide certain disputes. For example, the **American Arbitration Association (AAA)** is the largest private provider of ADR services. The AAA employs persons who are qualified in special areas of the law to provide mediation and arbitration services in those areas. These persons are called **neutrals**.

For example, if parties have a contract dispute involving an employment, construction, or Internet contract, or other commercial contract or business dispute, the AAA has a special group of neutrals that can hear and decide these cases. Other mediation and arbitration associations are located throughout the United States and internationally.

ADR Procedure

An arbitration agreement often describes the specific procedures that must be followed for a case to proceed through arbitration. If one party seeks to enforce an arbitration clause, that party must give notice to the other party. The parties then select an arbitration association or arbitrator as provided in the agreement. The parties usually agree on the date, time, and place of the arbitration. This can be at the arbitrator's office, a law office, or any other agreed-upon location.

At the arbitration, the parties may call witnesses to give testimony, and introduce other evidence to support their case or refute the other side's case. Rules similar to those followed by federal courts are usually adhered to at the arbitration. Often, each party pays a filing fee and other fees for the arbitration. Sometimes the agreement provides that one party will pay all of the costs of the arbitration. Arbitrators are paid by the hour or day, or another agreed-upon method of compensation.

Decision and Award

After the hearing is complete, the arbitrator reaches a decision and issues an **award**. The parties often agree in advance to be bound by the arbitrator's decision. This is called **binding arbitration**. In this situation, the decision and award of the arbitrator cannot be appealed to the courts. In **non-binding arbitration,** the decision and award of the arbitrator can be appealed to the courts. However, courts usually give great deference to an arbitrator's decision and award.

If a decision and award have been rendered by an arbitrator, but a party refuses to abide by the arbitrator's decision, the other party may file an action in court to have the arbitrator's decision enforced.

Example A contract dispute between Northwest Corporation and Southeast Corporation goes to binding arbitration. The arbitrator issues a decision that awards Southeast Corporation $5 million against Northwest Corporation. If Northwest

Paralegals *in* Practice

PARALEGAL PROFILE
Kathleen A. Stradle

Kathleen A. Stradley is a Certified Arbitrator and Certified Mediator with 26 years of paralegal experience. She also is an Advanced Certified Paralegal and Civil Litigation Specialist. Since 1998, Kathleen has worked as an independent contractor of litigation support and consulting services in North Dakota and Minnesota. She assists trial attorneys and corporations with case management and trial preparation. She also serves as a private arbitrator and mediator in legal disputes.

Becoming involved in alternative dispute resolution (ADR) has been an interesting process. Before starting my own business, I worked for several law firms and a corporation in Ohio and North Dakota. During that time, I was aware that ADR could save a lot of time and money. However, I did not know much about putting ADR into practice. So, I enrolled in an intense course that allowed me to obtain my mediator certification after 40 hours of training.

A short time later, I trained for a new binding arbitration program for the North Dakota Workers' Compensation Bureau. This program provided employees and employers with the option of binding arbitration rather than a formal administrative hearing or judicial solution. Instead, a hearing was held in front of three arbitrators, one from each of three societal areas: labor, industry, and the public. For about a year, I served as a public sector arbitrator and chairperson for the panel. After the panel was reduced to one person, I continued to serve as an arbitrator for Workers' Compensation hearings.

Later, I served as an arbitrator and mediator through the American Arbitration Association (AAA) for family, commercial, personal injury, employment/workplace, and construction industry claims. In 1997, after a terrible flood destroyed my hometown of Grand Forks, North Dakota, I mediated in many disaster-related commercial and construction disputes, as well as family law cases. In more recent years, I spoke with a number of disaster victims who experienced an ADR process. Most of them agreed that ADR was a valuable course of action that helped them rebuild their homes and lives.

Due to mandatory arbitration provisions in most contracts, and the trend of court ordered dispute resolution proceedings, I think there will be fewer trials in the future. Instead, I believe more and more lawsuits will be resolved with alternative methods. Cases using ADR proceedings typically involve fewer documents. However, these documents need to be prepared much earlier, and in greater detail, than cases that are tried in court with a jury. In mediation, each party submits their statement of the case and its value to the mediator in advance of the mediation. In arbitration, the evidence is submitted to the arbitrator in advance of the arbitration. ADR proceedings usually occur after discovery is completed and well in advance of the scheduled trial.

Source: Stradley, Kathleen A., "ADR: Changing Ground." *Facts & Findings, the Journal for Legal Assistants* XXXI.4 (January 2005): 16–17. Career Chronicle Edition 2004, NALA.

Corporation fails to pay the award, Southeast Corporation can file an action in court to have the award enforced by the court.

In the feature above, a paralegal professional discusses her experience in alternative dispute resolution.

Learning Objective 9
Explain the use of mediation and other forms of alternative dispute resolution.

Other Forms of ADR

In addition to arbitration and negotiation, other forms of ADR are available, such as *mediation*, *conciliation*, *minitrial*, *fact-finding*, and using a *judicial referee*. These forms of ADR are discussed in the following paragraphs.

Mediation

Mediation A form of negotiation in which a neutral third party assists the disputing parties in reaching a settlement of their dispute.

Mediator A neutral third party who assists the disputing parties in reaching a settlement of their dispute. The mediator cannot make a decision or an award.

Mediation is a form of negotiation in which a neutral third party assists the disputing parties in reaching a settlement of their dispute. The neutral third party is called a **mediator**. The mediator usually is a person who is an expert in the area of the dispute, or a lawyer or retired judge. The mediator is selected by the parties by agreement. Unlike an arbitrator, however, a mediator does not make a decision or an award.

A mediator's role is to assist the parties in reaching a settlement, usually as an intermediary between the parties. In many cases the mediator will meet with the parties at an agreed-upon location. The mediator will then meet with both parties, usually separately, to discuss each side of the case.

After discussing the facts of the case with each side, the mediator will encourage settlement of the dispute and will transmit settlement offers from one side to the other. In doing so, the mediator points out the strengths and weaknesses of each party's case and gives his or her opinion to each side as to why they should decrease or increase their settlement offers.

Then, the mediator gives his or her opinion to the parties as to what he or she believes to be a reasonable settlement of the case, and usually proposes settlement of the dispute. The parties are free to accept or reject the proposal. If the parties agree to a settlement, a settlement agreement is drafted, and execution of the settlement agreement ends the dispute. The parties, of course, must then perform their duties under the settlement agreement.

Example Parties to a divorce action often use mediation to try to help resolve the issues involved in the divorce, such as division of property, payment of alimony and child support, custody of children, and visitation rights.

Exhibit 6.9 is a form for a request for mediation.

Conciliation

Conciliation is often used when the parties refuse to face each other in an adversarial setting. A person named a **conciliator** helps the parties reach a resolution of their dispute. The conciliator schedules meetings and appointments during which information can be transferred between the parties. A conciliator usually carries offers and counteroffers for a settlement back and forth between the disputing parties. A conciliator cannot make a decision or an award.

Although the role of a conciliator is not to propose a settlement of the case, many often do. In many cases, conciliators are neutral third parties, although in some circumstances the parties may select an interested third party to act as the conciliator. If a settlement is reached through conciliation, a settlement agreement is drafted and executed by the parties.

Conciliation A form of dispute resolution in which a conciliator transmits offers and counteroffers between the disputing parties in helping to reach a settlement of their dispute.

Conciliator A third party in a conciliation proceeding who assists the disputing parties in reaching a settlement of their dispute. The conciliator cannot make a decision or an award.

Minitrial

A **minitrial** is a voluntary private proceeding in which the lawyers for each side present a shortened version of their case. Representatives of each side attend the minitrial and have the authority to settle the dispute. In many cases, the parties also hire a neutral third party, often someone who is an expert in the field concerning the disputed matter who presides over the minitrial. After hearing the case, the neutral third party renders an opinion as to how a court would most likely decide the case.

During a minitrial, the parties get to see the strengths and weaknesses of their own position and that of the opposing side. Once the strengths and weaknesses of both sides are exposed, the parties usually are more realistic regarding the merits of their positions, and the parties often settle the case. The parties also often settle based on the opinion rendered by the neutral third party. If the parties settle their dispute after a minitrial, they will enter into a settlement agreement.

Minitrials serve a useful purpose in that they act as a substitute for the real trial, but are much shorter, less complex, and less expensive to prepare for. Resolving a dispute through a minitrial is often preferable to an expensive and more risky trial in court.

Minitrial A voluntary private proceeding in which the lawyers for each side present a shortened version of their case to representatives of the other side, and usually to a neutral third party, in an attempt to reach a settlement of the dispute.

How many a dispute could have been deflated into a single paragraph if the disputants had dared to define their terms.

Aristotle

Fact-Finding

In fact-finding, the parties to a dispute will employ a neutral third party to investigate the dispute. The fact-finder is authorized to gather real evidence, prepare demonstrative evidence, and prepare reports of his or her findings.

A fact-finder is not authorized to make a decision or award. In some cases, a fact-finder will recommend settlement of the case. The fact-finder presents the evidence

Exhibit 6.9 Request for mediation

American Arbitration Association
Dispute Resolution Services Worldwide

REQUEST FOR MEDIATION

Name of Responding Party			Name of Representative (if known)		
Address:			Name of Firm (if applicable)		
			Representative's Address:		
City	State	Zip Code	City	State	Zip Code
Phone No.		Fax No.	Phone No.		Fax No.
Email Address:			Email Address:		

The undersigned party to an agreement contained in a written contract dated ________________, providing for mediation under the ________________________________ Mediation Procedures of the American Arbitration Association, hereby requests mediation

THE NATURE OF THE DISPUTE

CLAIM OR RELIEF SOUGHT (amount, if any):

AMOUNT OF FILING FEE ENCLOSED WITH THIS REQUEST: $

Mediation locale______________________ (check one) ☐ Requested by Filing Party ☐ Locale provision included in the contract

Type of Business: Filing Party ______________________ Responding Party______________________

You are hereby notified that copies of our mediation agreement and this request are being filed with the American Arbitration Association's Case Management Center, located in (check one) ☐ Atlanta, GA ☐ Dallas, TX ☐ East Providence, RI ☐ Fresno, CA ☐ International Centre, NY, with a request that it commence administration of this mediation.

Signature (may be signed by a representative) Date:			Name of Representative		
Name of Filling Party			Name of Firm (if applicable)		
Address (to be used in connection with this case):			Representative's Address:		
City	State	Zip Code	City	State	Zip Code
Phone No.		Fax No.	Phone No.		Fax No.
Email Address:			Email Address:		

To begin proceedings, please send two copies of this Request and the Mediation Agreement, along with the filing fee as provided for in the Rules, to the AAA. Send the original Request to the responding party.

Please visit our website at www.adr.org if you would like to file this case online. AAA Customer Service can be reached at 800-778-7879

Source: Reprinted with permission of American Arbitration Association.

and findings to the parties, who may then use such information in negotiating a settlement if they wish.

Judicial Referee

If the parties agree, the court may appoint a **judicial referee** to conduct a private trial and render a judgment. Referees, who are often retired judges, have most of the powers of a trial judge, and their decisions stand as a judgment of the court. The parties usually reserve the right to appeal.

Online ADR

Several services now offer **online arbitration**. A party may register the dispute with the service and then notify the other party by email of the registration. Most online arbitration requires the registering party to submit an amount that the party is willing to accept or pay to the other party in the online arbitration. The other party is afforded the opportunity to accept the offer. If that party accepts the offer, a settlement has been reached. The other party, however, may return a **counteroffer**. The process continues until a settlement is reached or one or both of the parties remove themselves from the online ADR process.

Online dispute resolution The use of online alternative dispute resolution services to resolve a dispute.

Online arbitration The arbitration of a dispute using online arbitration services.

Several websites also offer **online mediation** services. In an online mediation, the parties sit before their computers and sign onto the site. Two chat rooms are assigned to each party. One chat room is used for private conversations with the online mediator, and the other chat room is for conversations with both parties and the mediator.

Online mediation The mediation of a dispute using online mediation services.

Online arbitration and mediation services charge fees for their services, but the fees are usually reasonable. In an online arbitration or mediation, a settlement can be reached rather quickly without paying lawyers' fees and court costs. The parties are also acting through a more detached process rather than meeting face-to-face or negotiating over the telephone, either of which could result in verbal arguments.

The ethical duty and social responsibility of a paralegal professional to provide pro bono services to the public is discussed in the following feature.

Learning Objective 10
Explain a paralegal's duty to provide pro bono services to the public.

ETHICAL PERSPECTIVE

A Paralegal's Duty to Provide Pro Bono Services to the Public

Mr. Alvarez is a paralegal who works directly with Ms. Dawson, a partner at their law firm. In addition to her practice with the law firm, Ms. Dawson volunteers to work one evening per week at a domestic abuse center that serves women and children.

At the center, Ms. Dawson interviews domestic abuse victims and pursues whatever legal actions can be taken to assist the victims and their families. This often includes obtaining restraining orders, government assistance, and spousal and child support. All of Ms. Dawson's services at the domestic abuse center are provided pro bono. The term *pro bono* is short for the Latin phrase *pro bono publico,* which means "for the public good." Pro bono work is provided free of charge.

One day, Ms. Dawson asks Mr. Alvarez whether he would be interested in volunteering to help her one night each month at the domestic abuse shelter. Ms. Dawson explains that she could use his assistance as a paralegal to help conduct interviews, prepare documents, and obtain government and other assistance for the domestic abuse victims and their families. Mr. Alvarez would be under the supervision of Ms. Dawson while working at the center. Does a paralegal owe an ethical duty to provide pro bono services to the public?

Model and state paralegal codes of ethics do state that a paralegal has an ethical duty to provide pro bono services. Thus, a paralegal should strive to provide pro bono services under the supervision of an attorney or as authorized by a court. It is best if these services are provided to assist the poor, persons with limited education, and charitable programs, or to protect civil rights.

PARALEGAL'S ETHICAL DECISION

Because a paralegal owes an ethical duty to provide pro bono services to the public, Mr. Alvarez should agree to assist Ms. Dawson at the domestic abuse shelter one evening each month in order to fulfill his duty to the public. This would be an excellent way for Mr. Alvarez to satisfy his ethical duty as a paralegal professional.

Concept Review *and* Reinforcement

LEGAL TERMINOLOGY

Alternative dispute resolution (ADR) 214
American Arbitration Association (AAA) 217
Arbitration 215
Arbitration clauses 215
Arbitrator 215
Associate justices 203
Attachment jurisdiction 212
Award 217
Binding arbitration 217
Change of venue 213
Chief justice 202
Choice-of-law clause 214
Circuit 201
Conciliation 219
Conciliator 219
Concurrent jurisdiction 212
Concurring opinion 208
Counteroffer 221
Court of Appeals for the Federal Circuit 201
Courts of record 197
Dissenting opinion 208
Diversity of citizenship 211
E-courts 214
Exclusive jurisdiction 212
Federal Arbitration Act (FAA) 217
Federal court system 200
Federal question 211
Forum selection clause 214
General jurisdiction trial court 197
Highest state court 198
In personam jurisdiction 212
In rem jurisdiction 212
Intermediate appellate courts 198
Judicial referee 220
Jurisdiction 196
Limited jurisdiction trial courts 197
Litigation 196
Long-arm statute 213
Majority decision 204
Mediation 218
Mediator 218
Minitrial 219
Negotiation 214
Neutrals 217
Non-binding arbitration 217
Online arbitration 221
Online mediation 221
Personal jurisdiction 212
Petition for *certiorari* 204
Plurality decision 204
Quasi in rem jurisdiction 212
Service of process 212
Settlement agreement 215
Small claims courts 197
Special federal courts 200
Standing to sue 212
State court system 196
Subject matter jurisdiction 211
Submission agreement 215
Supreme Court of the United States 202
Tie decision 204
Unanimous decision 204
Uniform Arbitration Act 217
U.S. Bankruptcy Court 200
U.S. Courts of Appeals 201
U.S. Court of Federal Claims 200
U.S. Court of International Trade 200
U.S. District Courts 200
U.S. Supreme Court 203
U.S. Tax Court 200
Venue 213
Virtual courthouses 214
Writ of certiorari 204

SUMMARY OF KEY CONCEPTS

State Court Systems

Limited Jurisdiction Trial Court	This state court hears matters of a specialized or limited nature (such as misdemeanor criminal matters, traffic tickets, or civil matters under a certain dollar amount). Many states have created small claims courts that hear civil cases involving small dollar amounts (under $5,000, for example) in which parties cannot be represented by lawyers.
General Jurisdiction Trial Court	This state court hears cases of a general nature that are not within the jurisdiction of limited jurisdiction trial courts.
Intermediate Appellate Court	This state court hears appeals from state trial courts. The appellate court reviews the trial court record in making its decision. No new evidence is introduced at this level.
Highest State Court	Each state has a highest court in its court system. This court hears appeals from appellate courts and, where appropriate, trial courts. It reviews the record in making its decision, and no new evidence is introduced. Most states call this court the *supreme court.*

Federal Court System	
Special Federal Courts	Specialized federal courts have specialized or limited jurisdiction. They include: *U.S. Tax Court:* hears cases involving federal tax laws *U.S. Court of Federal Claims:* hears cases brought against the United States *U.S. Court of International Trade:* hears cases involving tariffs and international commercial disputes *U.S. Bankruptcy Court:* hears cases involving bankruptcy law
U.S. District Courts	U.S. district courts are federal trial courts of general jurisdiction that hear cases that are not within the jurisdiction of specialized courts. Each state has at least one U.S. district court; more heavily populated states have several district courts. The area served by one of these courts is called a *district.*
U.S. Courts of Appeals	U.S. Courts of Appeals are intermediate federal appellate courts that hear appeals from district courts located in their circuit, and in certain instances, from special federal courts and federal administrative agencies. There are 12 geographical circuits in the United States. Eleven serve areas composed of several states, and one covers only Washington, DC. A thirteenth circuit court—the *Court of Appeals for the Federal Circuit*—is located in Washington, DC, and reviews patent, trademark, and international trade cases.
Supreme Court of the United States	
U.S. Supreme Court	The Supreme Court is the highest court of the federal court system. It hears appeals from the circuit courts and, in some instances, from special courts and U.S. district courts. The Court, located in Washington, DC, comprises nine justices, one of whom is named Chief Justice.
Decisions by the U.S. Supreme Court	*Petition for* certiorari *and* writ of certiorari: To have a case heard by the U.S. Supreme Court, a petitioner must file a petition for *certiorari* with the Court. If the Court decides to hear the case, it will issue a *writ of certiorari.*
Voting by the U.S. Supreme Court	*Unanimous decision:* All of the justices agree as to the outcome and reasoning used to decide the case. The decision becomes precedent. *Majority decision:* A majority of justices agree as to the outcome and reasoning used to decide the case. The decision becomes precedent. *Plurality decision:* A majority of the justices agree to the outcome but not to the reasoning. The decision is not precedent. *Tie decision:* If there is a tie vote, the lower court's decision stands. The decision is not precedent. *Concurring opinion:* A justice who agrees as to the outcome of the case but not the reasoning used by other justices may write a concurring opinion setting forth his or her own reasoning. *Dissenting opinion:* A justice who disagrees with the outcome of a case may write a dissenting opinion setting forth his or her own reasoning.
Jurisdiction of Federal and State Courts	
Subject Matter Jurisdiction	The court must have jurisdiction over the subject matter of the lawsuit. Each court has limited jurisdiction to hear only certain types of cases.

Limited Jurisdiction of Federal Courts	Federal courts have jurisdiction to hear the following types of cases: *Federal question:* cases arising under the U.S. Constitution, treaties, and federal statutes and regulations. There is no dollar-amount limit. *Diversity of citizenship:* cases between (a) citizens of different states, (b) a citizen of a state and a citizen or subject of a foreign country; and (c) a citizen of a state and a foreign country where the foreign country is the plaintiff. The controversy must exceed $75,000 for the federal court to hear the case.
Jurisdiction of State Courts	State courts have jurisdiction to hear cases that federal courts do not have jurisdiction to hear.
Exclusive Jurisdiction	Federal courts have exclusive jurisdiction to hear cases involving federal crimes, antitrust, and bankruptcy; patent and copyright cases; suits against the United States; and most admiralty cases. State courts may not hear these matters.
Concurrent Jurisdiction	State courts hear some cases that may be heard by federal courts. State courts have concurrent jurisdiction to hear cases involving diversity of citizenship cases and federal question cases over which the federal courts do not have exclusive jurisdiction. The defendant may have the case removed to federal court.
Personal Jurisdiction and Other Issues	
Standing to Sue	To bring a lawsuit, the plaintiff must have some stake in the outcome of the lawsuit.
In Personam Jurisdiction (or Personal Jurisdiction)	The court must have jurisdiction over the parties to a lawsuit. The plaintiff submits to the jurisdiction of the court by filing the lawsuit there. Personal jurisdiction is obtained over the defendant by *service of process*.
In Rem Jurisdiction	A court may have jurisdiction to hear and decide a case because it has jurisdiction over the property at issue in the lawsuit (such as real estate property located in the state).
Quasi in Rem Jurisdiction (or Attachment Jurisdiction)	A plaintiff who obtains a judgment against a defendant in one state may utilize the court system of another state to attach property of the defendant located in that other state.
Long-Arm Statutes	These statutes permit a state to obtain personal jurisdiction over an out-of-state defendant as long as the defendant had the requisite minimum contacts with the state. The out-of-state defendant may be served process outside the state in which the lawsuit has been brought.
Venue	A case must be heard by the court that has jurisdiction nearest to where the incident at issue occurred or where the parties reside. A *change of venue* will be granted if prejudice would occur because of pretrial publicity or some other legitimate reason.
Forum Selection Clause	This clause in a contract designates the court that will hear any dispute that arises out of the contract.
Choice-of-Law Clause	This clause in a contract designates what state's or country's law will apply in resolving a dispute.
Alternative Dispute Resolution (ADR)	
ADR	ADR consists of *nonjudicial* means of solving legal disputes. ADR usually requires less time and money than litigation.
Negotiation	Negotiation is a procedure whereby the parties engage in discussions to try to reach a voluntary settlement of their dispute.

Arbitration	In arbitration, an impartial third party, called the *arbitrator*, hears and decides the dispute. The arbitrator makes an award that is appealable to a court if the parties have not given up this right. Arbitration is designated by the parties pursuant to: *Arbitration clause:* Agreement contained in a contract stipulating that any dispute arising out of the contract will be arbitrated. *Submission agreement:* Agreement to submit a dispute to arbitration after the dispute arises.
Federal Arbitration Act (FAA)	The FAA is a federal statute establishing that arbitration agreements involving commerce are valid, irrevocable, and enforceable contracts, unless some grounds exist at law or equity to revoke them (such as fraud or duress).
Other Forms of ADR	
Mediation	In mediation, a neutral third party, called a *mediator*, assists the parties in trying to reach a settlement. The mediator does not make an award.
Conciliation	In conciliation, an interested third party, called a *conciliator*, assists the parties in trying to reach a settlement of their dispute. The conciliator does not make an award.
Minitrial	A minitrial is a short proceeding in which the lawyers present their case to representatives of each party, who have the authority to settle the dispute.
Fact-Finding	In fact-finding, the parties hire a neutral third person, called a *fact-finder*, to investigate the dispute and report his or her findings to the adversaries.
Judicial Referee	With the consent of the parties, the court can appoint a judicial referee (usually a retired judge or lawyer) to conduct a private trial and render a judgment. The judgment stands as the judgment of the court and may be appealed to the appropriate appellate court.
Online ADR	Online ADR is a form of alternative dispute resolution where the parties use an online provider of ADR services. This could be online arbitration, online mediation, or other forms of online ADR.

WORKING THE WEB

1. Visit the website http://www.clickNsettle.com. What services are offered by this website? What are the costs of using this site's services?
2. Visit the website http://www.internetneutral.com. What services are offered by this site? What are the costs of these services?
3. Visit the website http://www.law.cornell.edu/supct/index.html. Find the most recent decision of the U.S. Supreme Court. Read the case heading and the summary of the case. Who were the parties? What issue was presented to the Supreme Court? What was the decision of the Supreme Court?
4. Go to the website http://www.adr.org.overview. Read "A Brief Overview of the American Arbitration Association." Define a "neutral."
5. Find the homepage for the courts in your state. What are the names of the courts in your state? Draw a diagram of the courts in your state. Include limited jurisdiction courts, general jurisdiction trial courts, appellate courts, and the highest state court.

CRITICAL THINKING & WRITING QUESTIONS

1. Describe the difference between state limited jurisdiction courts and general jurisdiction courts.
2. What are the functions of the state intermediate courts and the highest state courts?
3. List the special federal courts, and describe the types of cases that each of these courts can hear.
4. What is the function of U.S. District Courts? How many are there?
5. What is the function of U.S. Courts of Appeals? How many U.S. Courts of Appeals are there? How does the Court of Appeals for the Federal Circuit differ from the other U.S. Courts of Appeals?

6. What is the function of the U.S. Supreme Court? How many justices does the Supreme Court have? How does the Chief Justice differ from the Associate Justices?
7. Explain the difference between a federal court's jurisdiction to hear a case based on (1) federal question jurisdiction and (2) diversity of citizenship jurisdiction.
8. What is a long-arm statute? What is the purpose of a long-arm statute?
9. What is venue? When can a change of venue be granted?
10. What is the difference between judicial dispute resolution and nonjudicial alternative dispute resolution? Why would one be preferred over the other, and who would have a preference?
11. Define arbitration. Describe how the process of arbitration works. What is an award?

Building Paralegal Skills

VIDEO CASE STUDIES

Meet the Courthouse Team

An interview with Judge Kenney, a trial judge, who introduces members of the courthouse and the roles they serve as members of the courtroom team.

After viewing the video case study in MyLegalStudiesLab, answer the following:

1. What type of relationship should the paralegal develop with the courthouse team?
2. In addition to the courtroom team, what other members of the courthouse should the paralegal know about?

Jury Selection: Potential Juror Challenged for Cause

Trial counsel for a case, which is going to be tried before a jury, are interviewing the individual potential jurors to select an appropriate jury member.

After viewing the video case study in MyLegalStudiesLab, answer the following:

1. What is the role of the jury in the justice system?
2. Why are the attorneys allowed to request that certain individuals not be allowed to serve on a jury?
3. Is everyone guaranteed a right to a jury trial in the American system of justice?

Settlement Conference with Judge

Opposing counsel are meeting with Judge Lee prior to the start of the trial. The trial judge is presenting the strengths and weaknesses of each side in an attempt to get the parties to settle the case.

After viewing the video case study in MyLegalStudiesLab, answer the following:

1. How is a settlement conference with a judge before trial like an alternative method of dispute resolution?
2. Is the judge in the settlement conference being unfair to one side or the other?
3. Why is the judge trying to settle the case before trial?

ETHICS ANALYSIS & DISCUSSION QUESTIONS

1. May a paralegal represent a client in court?
2. Are a paralegal's time records or calendar subject to the attorney–client privilege?
3. You have been appointed as a trustee of a client's children's educational trust. You need to petition the court for a release of the funds for noneducational purposes—paying the taxes on the trust income. May you appear alone as the trustee and represent the trust in the court proceedings? Would a nonlawyer or nonparalegal be permitted to appear?

See *Ziegler v. Nickel*, 64 Cal. App. 4th 545 (Cal. 2d 1998).

DEVELOPING YOUR COLLABORATION SKILLS

With a group of other students, review the facts of the following case. As a group, discuss the following questions.

1. What is a forum selection clause?
2. What is a choice-of-law clause?
3. Is the forum selection clause in eBay's user agreement enforceable?
4. Is putting a forum selection clause (or choice-of-law clause) in a contract a good practice? Explain why.

In re eBay

eBay, Inc. is an Internet company that operates the online shopping and auction website eBay.com. Individuals and businesses buy and sell products and services on eBay.com. Before using eBay's services, an individual must register with eBay and accept its user agreement. An individual's acceptance of the user agreement must be confirmed by entering a code supplied to the user through an email message. Roddy Mordecai Richards registered with eBay using this procedure. The eBay user agreement provides that "any claim or dispute you may have against eBay must be resolved exclusively by a state or federal court located in Santa Clara County, California." A choice-of-law clause in the user agreement provides that California law governs the agreement.

Richards alleged that he purchased a vehicle on the eBay website in a transaction covered by eBay's Vehicle Protection Program. Richards never received the vehicle and later discovered that the purported seller was not the registered owner of the vehicle. Richards sued eBay in the county in Texas in which he resides to recover the $18,000 purchase price he had paid. eBay requested the Texas court to enforce the forum selection clause which provided that Santa Clara County, California, was the proper forum for Richards's lawsuit.

Source: *In re eBay*, 2010 WL 2695803 (Tex. App. Ct. July 8, 2010)

PARALEGAL PORTFOLIO EXERCISE

Based on the facts of the case described in the Opening Scenario, prepare and complete the following documents from the facts of the scenario.

1. A complaint to file the case on behalf of the plaintiff against the defendant in the appropriate trial court of your state.
2. The defendant's answer to the complaint.

LEGAL ANALYSIS & WRITING CASES

Hubbert v. Dell Corp, 835 N.E.2d 113 (Ill App 5 Dist., 2005)

Appellate Court of Illinois, Fifth District

Plaintiffs Dewayne Hubbert, Elden Craft, Chris Grout, and Rhonda Byington purchased computers from Dell Computer through Dell's website. Before purchasing their computers, each of the plaintiffs configured the model and type of computer he or she wished to order from Dell's web pages. To make their purchase, each of the plaintiffs completed online order forms on five pages on Dell's website. On each of the five pages, Dell's "Terms and Conditions of Sale" were accessible by clicking on a blue hyperlink. In order to find the terms and conditions, the plaintiffs would have had to click on the blue hyperlink and read the terms and conditions of sale. On the last page of the five-page order form, the following statement appeared: "All sales are subject to Dell's Terms and Conditions of Sale."

The plaintiffs filed a lawsuit against Dell alleging that Dell misrepresented the speed of the microprocessors included in the computers they purchased. Dell made a demand for arbitration, asserting that the plaintiffs were bound by the arbitration agreement that was contained in the Terms and Conditions of Sale. The plaintiffs countered that the arbitration clause was not part of their web contract because the Terms and Conditions of Sale were not conspicuously displayed as part of their web contract.

Question

1. Is Dell's arbitration clause enforceable against the plaintiffs?

Chanel, Inc. v. Banks, 2011 WL 121700 (D.Md Jan 13, 2011)

United States District Court for the District of Maryland

Chanel, Inc. is a corporate entity duly organized under the laws of the state of New York, with its principal place of business in New York City. Chanel is engaged in the business of manufacturing and distributing various luxury goods throughout the world, including handbags, wallets, and numerous other products under the federally registered trademark "Chanel" and monogram marks. Chanel filed suit in U.S. District Court in Maryland against defendant Ladawn Banks, a resident of Florida. Chanel alleges that Banks owned and operated the interactive website www.lovenamebrands.com, through which she sold handbags and wallets bearing counterfeit trademarks identical to the registered Chanel marks. Chanel claimed that the counterfeit goods were substantially inferior in quality to Chanel's genuine goods and that defendant's actions confused consumers as to the origin of the counterfeit goods. The goods at issue in this case were sold to a resident of Maryland. Chanel sought a default judgment against the defendant, an award of damages, and a permanent injunction against the defendant's further violation of its trademarks.

Question

1. Does the court have personal jurisdiction over the defendant?

WORKING WITH THE LANGUAGE OF THE COURT CASE

Hertz Corporation v.Friend, 130 S.Ct. 1181, Web 2009 U.S. Lexis 5114 (2010)

Read the following excerpt from the opinion of the Supreme Court. Review and brief the case. In your brief, answer the following questions.

1. Who are the parties to this lawsuit?
2. What is the doctrine of diversity of citizenship?
3. In what state or states is a corporation a resident of for purposes of diversity of citizenship?
4. What decision did the U.S. Supreme Court reach in this case?

Breyer, Justice (opinion for a unanimous Court)

The federal diversity jurisdiction statute provides that "a corporation shall be deemed to be a citizen of any State by which it has been incorporated *and of the State where it has its principal place of business.*" 28 U.S.C. Section 1332(c)(1). [W]e conclude that the phrase "principal place of business" refers to the place where the corporation's high level officers direct, control, and coordinate the corporation's activities. Lower federal courts have often metaphorically called that place the corporation's "nerve center."

In September 2007, respondents Melinda Friend and John Nhieu, two California citizens, sued petitioner, the Hertz Corporation, in a California state court. They sought damages for what they claimed were violations of California's wage and hour laws. And they requested relief on behalf of a potential class composed of California citizens who had allegedly suffered similar harms. Hertz filed a notice seeking removal to a federal court. Hertz claimed that the plaintiffs and the defendant were citizens of different States. Hence, the federal court possessed diversity-of-citizenship jurisdiction. Friend and Nhieu, however, claimed that the Hertz Corporation was a California citizen, like themselves, and that, hence, diversity jurisdiction was lacking.

To support its position, Hertz submitted a declaration by an employee relations manager that sought to show that Hertz's "principal place of business" was in New Jersey, not in California. The declaration...stated that the "leadership of Hertz and its domestic subsidiaries" is located at Hertz's "corporate headquarters" in Park Ridge, New Jersey; that its "core executive and administrative functions...are carried out" there and "to a lesser extent" in Oklahoma City, Oklahoma; and that its "major administrative operations...are found" at those two locations.

The District Court of the Northern District of California...concluded that...Hertz was a citizen of

(continued)

California. Hence, Hertz's "principal place of business" was California, and diversity jurisdiction was thus lacking. The Ninth Circuit affirmed in a brief memorandum opinion. Hertz filed a petition for certiorari. And, in light of differences among the Circuits in the application of the test for corporate citizenship, we granted the writ.

In...1844...the Court...held that a corporation was to be deemed an artificial person of the State by which it had been created. In 1928 this Court made clear that the "state of incorporation" rule was virtually absolute. [I]n 1958, Congress both codified the courts' traditional place of incorporation test and also enacted into law..."principal place of business" language. A corporation was to "be deemed a citizen of any State by which it has been incorporated and of the State where it has its principal place of business."

We conclude that "principal place of business" is best read as referring to the place where a corporation's officers direct, control, and coordinate the corporation's activities. It is the place that Courts of Appeals have called the corporation's "nerve center." And in practice it should normally be the place where the corporation maintains its headquarters—provided that the headquarters is the actual center of direction, control, and coordination, *i.e.*, the "nerve center," and not simply an office where the corporation holds its board meetings (for example, attended by directors and officers who have traveled there for the occasion).

We recognize...that, under the "nerve center" test we adopt today, there will be hard cases. For example, in this era of telecommuting, some corporations may divide their command and coordinating functions among officers who work at several different locations, perhaps communicating over the Internet. That said, our test nonetheless points courts in a single direction, towards the center of overall direction, control, and coordination. Courts do not have to try to weigh corporate functions, assets, or revenues different in kind, one from the other. Our approach provides a sensible test that is relatively easier to apply, not a test that will, in all instances, automatically generate a result.

The burden of persuasion for establishing diversity jurisdiction, of course, remains on the party asserting it. Indeed, if the record reveals attempts at manipulation—for example, that the alleged "nerve center" is nothing more than a mail drop box, a bare office with a computer, or the location of an annual executive retreat—the courts should instead take as the "nerve center" the place of actual direction, control, and coordination, in the absence of such manipulation.

Petitioner's unchallenged declaration suggests that Hertz's center of direction, control, and coordination, its "nerve center," and its corporate headquarters are one and the same, and they are located in New Jersey, not in California.

It is so ordered.

MYLEGALSTUDIESLAB

MyLegalStudiesLab Virtual Law Office Experience Assignments

Complete the pre-test, study plan, and post-test for this chapter and answer the Legal Applications questions as assigned. These will help you confirm your mastery of the concepts and their application to legal scenarios. Then complete the Virtual Law Office assignments as assigned by your instructor. These assignments are designed to develop your workplace skills. Completing the assignments for this chapter will result in producing the following documents for inclusion in your portfolio:

VLOE 6.1 List of documents and information for arbitration

VLOE 6.2
1. Outline of the elements of the actionable civil wrongs of assault and battery
2. Description of any conduct by the plaintiff that supports these causes of action
3. List of people to consider calling as witnesses, and questions to ask them in arbitration

VLOE 6.4
1. Summary of the arbitration for the case file
2. Copy of local rules for appealing from an arbitration hearing
3. Procedural checklist with any forms for appealing from an arbitration in your jurisdiction

CHAPTER

7

Civil Litigation

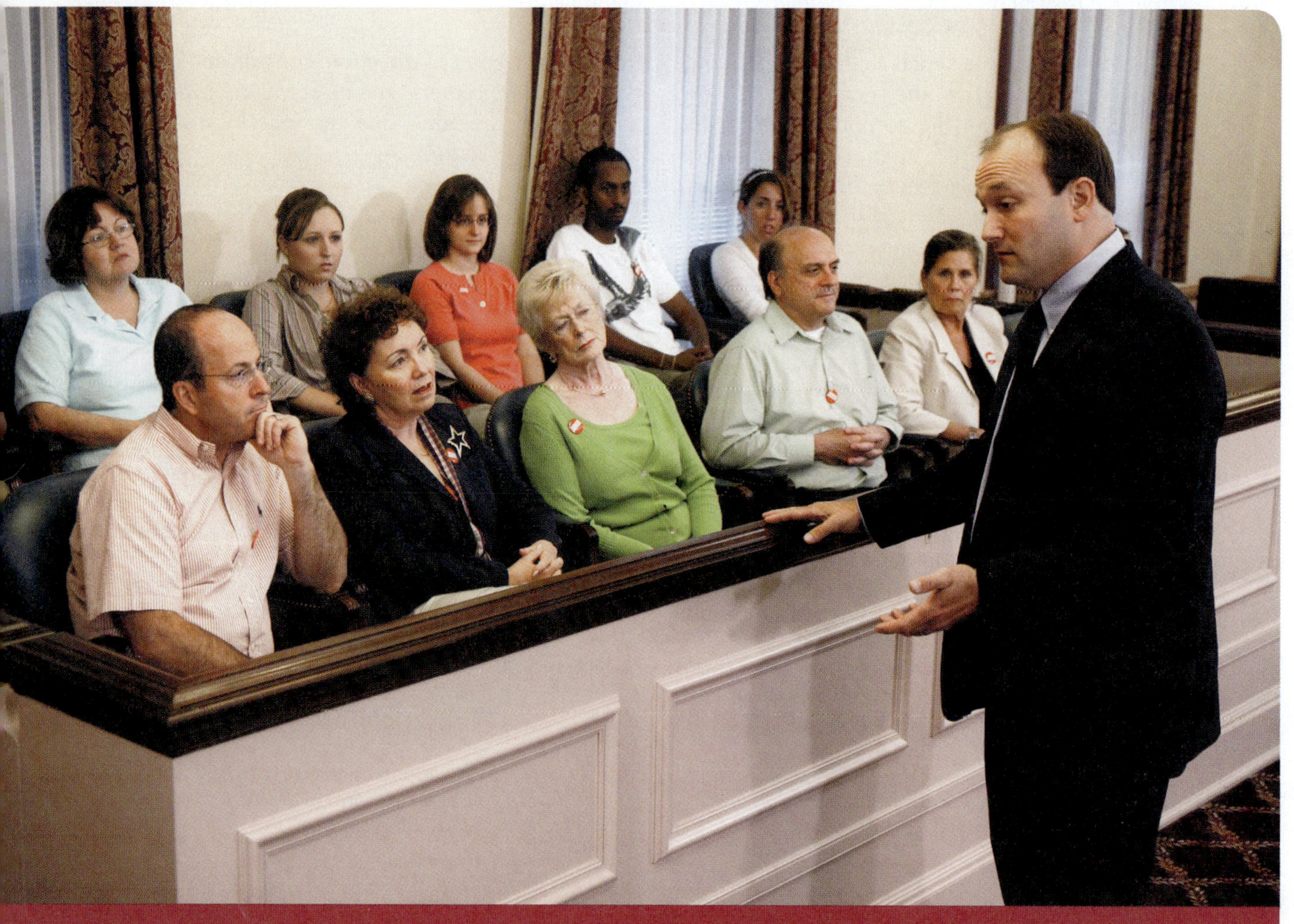

Paralegals at Work

Rowan, a middle school student, and his sister Isis, a high school student, were passengers on the last school bus of the day. They were on their way home after Rowan's basketball practice and his sister's choir practice. The bus had made its regular stops and was on a public highway when it was struck by a large commercial truck. Rowan's injuries were severe enough to prevent him from playing basketball for the rest of the season on his school team and on a local club team that was in the championship. Isis had been practicing and eagerly looking forward to traveling with the school choir on an invitational European tour, but she would miss this trip as a result of her injuries.

Their parents have retained your law firm, on a contingent fee basis, to pursue a claim for their children's injuries and their out-of-pocket expenses. A review of the medical bills shows expenses in excess of $75,000 for each child. The accident was investigated by the National Transportation Safety Board, which issued a report indicating the probable cause of the accident was the failure of the brakes on the truck. In his initial police statement, the truck driver indicated that he had had no problems with the vehicle before the accident and that he relied upon the mechanics in the maintenance facility to maintain the vehicle, especially the brakes. The trucking company has denied any liability. No initial reports or documentation were provided by the trucking company to the police because all of the truck and maintenance records are kept in electronic format at the company's corporate headquarters in another state.

Consider the issues involved in this scenario as you read the chapter.

LEARNING OBJECTIVES

After studying this chapter, you should be able to:

1. Explain the role of the paralegal in the litigation process.
2. Describe the types of civil litigation pleadings and their purposes.
3. Explain the purpose of discovery in the litigation process.
4. Explain the use of pretrial motions and settlement conferences.
5. Describe the steps in a trial.
6. Describe how a case is appealed and what decisions can be rendered by an appellate court.

> "Discourage litigation. Persuade your neighbors to compromise whenever you can. Point out to them how the nominal winner is often a real loser—in fees, and expenses, and waste of time. As a peacemaker, the lawyer has a superior opportunity of being a good man. There will still be business enough."
>
> Abraham Lincoln, *Notes on the Practice of Law* (1850)

INTRODUCTION TO CIVIL LITIGATION

Civil litigation involves legal disputes between parties seeking a remedy for a civil wrong or to enforce a contract. It differs from criminal litigation, where the government enforces a law or brings a prosecution for the breach of a law. The parties to civil litigation may be individuals, businesses, or in some cases, government agencies. Although the fundamental process is the same for most jurisdictions, the procedures may vary.

Generally, the filing of a legal dispute with a court happens after the parties have determined that they cannot resolve their differences amicably through negotiation or the use of alternative dispute resolution methods. One of the first steps in the civil litigation process is to determine which courts the case could be filed in. In the United States, cases can be filed in federal or state court. Within the state or federal court system, there may be multiple courts having the power to hear the same cause of action. The choice of a specific court may be based on geographical convenience or trial strategy.

Many lawyers specialize in civil litigation, in which a plaintiff sues a defendant to recover money damages or seek some other remedy for the alleged harm the defendant caused the plaintiff. It may be based on an automobile accident, an alleged breach of a contract, a claim of patent infringement, or any of a myriad of other civil wrongs.

In a civil case, either party can appeal the trial court's decision once a final judgment is entered. In a criminal case, only the defendant can appeal. The appeal is made to the appropriate appellate court.

Litigation The process of bringing, maintaining, and defending a lawsuit.

Paralegals often work for lawyers who specialize in civil litigation seeking monetary damages or other remedies. The litigation process, or **litigation**, is comprised of bringing, maintaining, and defending a lawsuit.

Civil litigation is an area in which a paralegal's analytical, research, writing, and other abilities are truly put to the test. Paralegals who work in the litigation field must have thorough knowledge of the litigation process, the rules of evidence, and court procedure, as well as the technology used in discovery, electronic filing, and trial presentation.

A paralegal's first introduction to a new lawsuit often begins with the scheduling of the initial conference with a client, when the law firm is first retained to represent the client as either a plaintiff or a defendant. Many times, the paralegal's first work assignment is to sit in on the initial conference between the attorney and the client and take notes. These notes are used in setting up the client or case matter file.

The paralegal usually is the one to start the new client or case file for the lawsuit. This may involve setting up the client file in the office electronic billing system and creating a case file for the specific litigation matter. Some clients have many case matters. For example, an insurance company represented by a law firm may assign many different cases to the firm, each having a separate case matter file, but there is usually only one client file for the insurance company.

Setting up a new client and case matter may include preparing client fee agreement letters for the supervising attorney's review and obtaining available evidence, documents, and other items relevant to the case. Each attorney has his or her own system for preparing a case for trial (or settlement), and the paralegal may have his or her own way of preparing the file as well. In paperless offices, this usually involves entering the information electronically into a case management system.

The paralegal is often assigned to help draft the pleadings for the case. In addition, the paralegal may contact the client for information, interview the client, draft

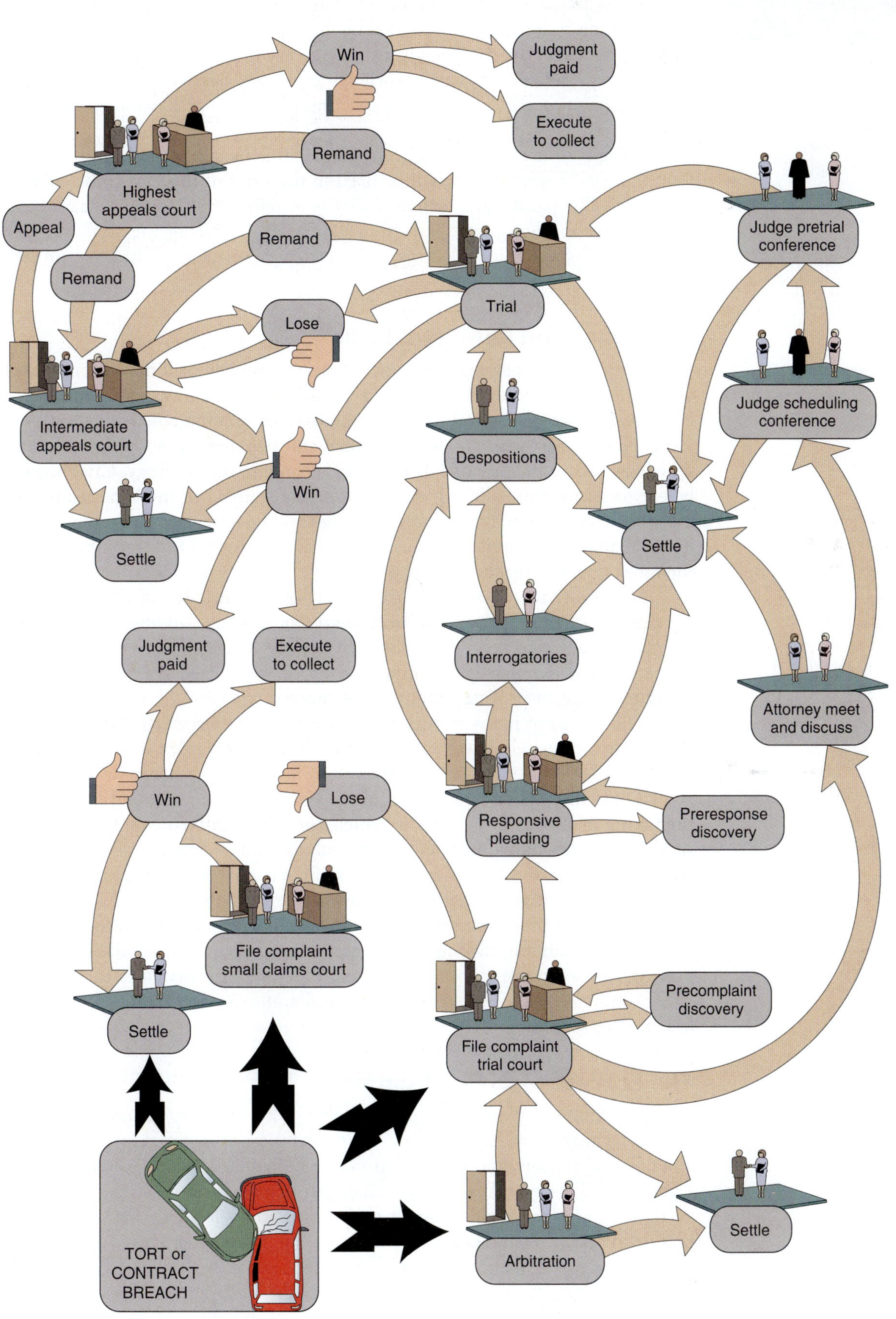

Win
Judgment paid
Execute to collect
Remand
Highest appeals court
Appeal
Remand
Remand
Judge pretrial conference
Trial
Lose
Judge scheduling conference
Intermediate appeals court
Win
Despositions
Settle
Settle
Judgment paid
Execute to collect
Interrogatories
Attorney meet and discuss
Win
Lose
Responsive pleading
Prereponse discovery
File complaint small claims court
Settle
Precomplaint discovery
File complaint trial court
TORT or CONTRACT BREACH
Settle
Arbitration

requests for production of documents and other evidence, and assist in the preparation of depositions to be taken or attended by the supervising attorney.

At this stage, the paralegal is involved in the case as much as his or her supervising attorney. Because of their knowledge of a case, paralegals can be indispensable in the preparation for lawyer–client meetings, discovery, depositions, and settlement conferences.

If the case is to go to trial, the paralegal is usually called upon to help conduct the legal research that will be used in the brief of the case to be submitted to the court. The paralegal's responsibility is to help organize the case and to use all available technology to prepare the case for trial. During the trial, the paralegal becomes indispensable in assisting the attorney to present the case on behalf of the client.

PRACTICE TIP

Continuing education courses offer the lawyer and the paralegal an opportunity to learn about new areas of law or update their knowledge of specialty areas. Many courses offer discounts for paralegals and special rates for lawyer–paralegal teams who attend together.

Civil Litigation Paralegal Skills

Learning Objective 1

Explain the role of the paralegal in the litigation process.

The civil litigation paralegal may perform any number of different tasks, including conducting legal research, typing a pleading or a court brief, making copies, interviewing witnesses, and operating audiovisual equipment. Litigation is often a fast-paced process with sudden deadlines and demands imposed by changing trial schedules, the availability of witnesses, and changing trial strategy. Civil litigation can be exciting and stimulating; it can also test the stamina of the legal team. Everyone must be willing to pitch in to meet deadlines and be fully prepared to appear in court. There may be late nights spent researching and preparing for every move or strategy the other side may make.

Obviously, the paralegal must have a basic knowledge of the law and of how the courts function. Depending on the area of practice, additional knowledge may be required in legal specialties such as intellectual property, medical malpractice, and estate law. Knowledge of unique rules in specialized courts, such as those of bankruptcy, tax, or probate, might also be necessary.

That does not mean that paralegals must know everything. But they do need to know how to research new areas of the law, locate court rules, and find other sources of information efficiently and effectively.

The skills needed by a paralegal are varied, and they depend in some cases on the nature of the legal specialty in which one works. All paralegals need certain basic skills and attributes, such as resourcefulness and dedication, as well as analytical, interpersonal, and communication skills. This is especially true for the civil litigation paralegal. Litigation attorneys come to depend on their civil litigation paralegals in the same way a surgeon depends on a nurse in the operating room. While the lawyer is thinking through the strategy and preparing mentally, the paralegal is making sure everything comes together. The paralegal manages the scheduling of clients and witnesses, prepares exhibits and audiovisual equipment, and completes last-minute research.

The Process of Civil Litigation

Civil litigation is a complex process involving the assembly of information and evidence, the analysis of facts and law, the preparation of material for trial presentation and posttrial appeals, and the execution of judgments. Typically, these tasks require a team effort. This **legal team** may include **paralegals**, investigators, information technologists, and other **legal support staff** in varying roles. Law firms have structures that define every team member's function in the litigation process. In some law firms, that structure is formalized in a written office manual with detailed job descriptions. Other law firms are less structured, with more flexibility and loosely defined roles that frequently overlap. In all of these working environments, the members of the legal team are ultimately accountable to the clients who depend on them for competent legal representation. Each member of the team shares the total responsibility, sometimes performing unassigned functions or helping others on the team when the need arises. Flexibility within the team contributes to success in the litigation process.

However, although flexibility is important, a team member's functions may be defined by the role the person is permitted to play in the courtroom. Only lawyers admitted to practice before a particular court may appear on behalf of clients in that court. Paralegals and litigation support staff sometimes may sit at a counsel table to assist the attorney, but some local rules may restrict even that activity, relegating that role to an associate attorney.

Managing Client Relationships

Clients involved in civil litigation may be individuals, small- or medium-sized businesses, or large corporate clients. When the client is a smaller business, the firm typically will communicate directly with the officers or owners of the business. But when a firm is working with larger corporations, the contact may be indirect—through **inside corporate counsel.** These in-house attorneys often select the outside law firms and monitor the handling of civil litigation.

Maintaining positive client relationships is a critical area in the practice of law. Clients want to be kept informed and have their inquiries answered promptly. Communication with inside corporate counsel may occur by sharing information electronically. With every client, minimizing the costs of litigation is important. It may be especially important to inside counsel because they must budget litigation expenditures and justify the costs of every piece of litigation to senior management.

It is important that the legal team understand the client's views and values. This is particularly important for the paralegal, who may be the person having the most direct and frequent contact with the client. Corporate or business clients frequently refer to these views and values as the "corporate culture." In some cases, clients are more concerned with the principles involved in the litigation than they are with the costs. In others, cost-consciousness dictates a very lean litigation budget and a desire to do a cost-benefit analysis for every litigation decision. In all cases, the paralegal becomes the eyes of the attorney and must keep counsel informed of the cost incurred—in effect, monitoring the litigation budget. Because it is often the paralegal who hires the outside vendors or sees the time records, the paralegal is often in the best position to monitor the budgets.

Pleadings

Learning Objective 2
Describe the types of civil litigation pleadings and their purposes.

Pleadings are the documents that are filed with a court to commence or respond to a lawsuit. In the initial pre-filing phase, it is important to be familiar with the applicable rules of the court in which the action is to be filed and tried. The form of the pleadings and the procedure for filing and serving the pleadings are dictated by the rules of the court in which the action is filed. The rules vary between federal and state courts. Within the same court system, there may also be local practice rules that amend or supplement the standard rules.

Pleadings The paperwork that is filed with the court to initiate and respond to a lawsuit.

The initial pleading filed by the plaintiff is designed to give the party being sued notice of the filing of the lawsuit. The initial responsive pleading answers the claims made by the plaintiff or adds other parties that the responding party believes are responsible for the plaintiff's losses. The initial pleadings also define the case. The complaint establishes the alleged wrong and the claims for relief. The answer filed by the defendant establishes the defenses to the plaintiff's claims.

Time Limits and Pleading Deadlines

The first time limit that must be determined in every potential civil action is when the time limit will expire for filing a particular cause of action. With the exception of

Advice *from the* Field

GETTING CASE ANALYSIS OFF TO A FAST START

by DecisionQuest

From your first conversation with a prospective client, you're learning about the dispute that led the individual or corporation to seek counsel. There are many benefits to taking a systematic approach to analyzing this knowledge. Not least of these is the favorable impression you'll make on those who retain you.

The following article presents a method for organizing and evaluating the facts about any case. And it illustrates how the early results of this dispute analysis process can be used to great effect in an initial case analysis session with your client.

When you take this approach to case analysis, you'll gain a thorough understanding of the dispute and clarify your thinking about it. And, as you sort out what you do know about the case, you'll find it easy to identify what you don't know and need to find out.

The process focuses on creating four analysis reports: a Cast of Characters, a Chronology, an Issue List, and a Question List. These reports provide a framework for organizing and evaluating critical case knowledge. If multiple people are involved in the analysis process, the reports provide a way to divide responsibility and share results. Moreover, once you standardize the analysis work product, it's easy to compare the findings in one matter to the analysis results from other similar disputes.

You should create your case analysis reports using database software, not a word-processor. Database software makes the knowledge you're organizing far easier to explore and evaluate. For example, using database software, it's easy to filter your Chronology so it displays only facts that have been evaluated as being particularly troublesome.

CAST OF CHARACTERS

Create a Cast of Characters that lists the individuals and organizations you know are involved in the dispute. This report should also catalog key documents and other important pieces of physical evidence. Capture each player's name and a description of the role the person, organization, or document plays in the case.

Also include a column in which you can indicate your evaluation of cast members. Even if you don't evaluate every player, it's essential to note the people and documents that are particularly worrisome, as well as the basis for your concerns. If you follow my recommendation that you build your dispute analysis reports using database software, you will find it easy to filter the entire cast list down to the problem players you've identified.

CHRONOLOGY

A chronology of key facts is a critical tool for analyzing any dispute. As you create the chronology, important factual disputes and areas of strength and weakness become obvious.

Begin by listing the fact and the date on which it occurred. As you enter each fact, be sure to make the important details about the fact explicit. For example, rather than simply stating "Gayle phoned David," write "Gayle phoned David, and asked him to shred the Fritz Memo." Remember that your chronology should be a memory replacement, not a memory jogger.

Since you're analyzing the case within weeks of being retained, there will be many facts for which you have only partial date information. For example, you may know that Gayle called David about the Fritz Memo sometime in June of 1993, but be unsure as to the day within June. When you run into this problem, a simple solution is to substitute a question mark for the portion of the date that's undetermined, e.g., 6/?/93.

In addition to capturing the fact and the date, be sure to list a source or sources for each fact. Now, in the early days of a case, it's likely that the sources of many of the facts you are entering in your chronology are not of a type that will pass muster come trial. However, by capturing a source such as "David Smith Interview Notes," you know to whom or what you will need to turn to develop a court-acceptable source.

The mission in early dispute analysis is to take a broad look at the potential evidence. Therefore, your chronology should be more than a list of undisputed facts. Be sure to include disputed facts and even prospective facts (i.e., facts that you suspect may turn up as the case proceeds toward trial). You'll want to distinguish the facts that are undisputed from those that are disputed or merely prospective. Include in your chronology a column that you use for this purpose.

Finally, include a column that you use to separate the critical facts from others of lesser importance. A simple solution is to have a column titled "Key" that you set up as a checkbox (checked means the fact is key, unchecked means it's not). If you're using database software, filtering the chronology down to the key items should take you about 2 seconds.

ISSUE LIST

Build a list of case issues including both legal claims and critical factual disputes. If the case has yet to be filed, list the claims and counter-claims or cross-claims you anticipate. Rather than listing just the top-level issues, consider breaking each claim down to its component parts. For example, rather than listing Fraud, list Fraud: Intent, Fraud: Reliance, and so on as separate dimensions.

In addition to listing a name for each issue, create a more detailed description of it. The description might include a brief summary of each party's position on the issue and, if it's a legal issue, the potential language of the judge's instruction.

As your case proceeds to trial, your Issue List will increase in importance. You'll use the Issue List to return to the Cast of Characters and Chronology and establish relationships between each fact, each witness, each document, and the issue or issues to which it relates. Once you've made these links, it will be easy to focus on the evidence that's being developed regarding each issue and to make decisions about case strategy based on this analysis.

QUESTION LIST

When you start case analysis early, your knowledge of the dispute is sure to be incomplete. But as you map out what is known about the case, what is unknown and must be determined becomes clear.

Each time you come up with a question about the case that you can't readily answer, get it into your Question List. You'll want your report to include a column for the question and another column where you can capture notes regarding the answer. Also include a column for evaluating the criticality of each question. Use a simple A (extremely critical), B, C, and D scale to make your assessment. Other columns to consider for your Question List are "Assigned To" and "Due Date."

The analysis reports you've begun are "living" ones. As you head toward trial, keep working on your Cast of Characters, your Chronology, your Issue List, and your Question List. These analysis reports will do far more than help you think about your case. They'll serve a myriad of concrete purposes. They'll help you keep your client up-to-date, plan for discovery, prepare to take and defend depositions, create motions for summary judgment, and make your case at settlement conferences and at trial.

the crime of murder, every wrong, whether civil or criminal, has a timeframe within which a party must bring suit or lose his right to sue. This time period is referred to as the **statute of limitations**. In some civil cases, this period may be short as thirty or sixty days. For example, under some states' laws designed to protect its primary tourist business, like the ski resort industry, the time for giving notice to the ski resort operator of a potential claim for injuries on the ski slopes is very short. More typical statutes of limitations require commencement of a cause of action for personal injuries within two or three years of the injury.

Statute of limitations A law that establishes the period during which a plaintiff must bring a lawsuit against a defendant.

In medical malpractice claims, the limitations period doesn't begin to run out until the plaintiff becomes aware or should have become aware of the injury. For example, in a claim for medical malpractice arising from a foreign object, such as a surgical sponge, being left in the person during an operation, a patient may not be aware for several years of the medical malpractice committed by the surgeon, until the cause of persistent pain is finally diagnosed. It would not be fair for the time limit to start when the injury was caused—the date of the original surgery. Fundamental fairness requires that the timeframe begin when the patient learns of the cause of the injury.

In other types of cases, the time limit may also not begin until a point in the future. Societal concepts of justice allow **minors** (children) who suffered an injury during their minority to bring a cause of action after they reach the **age of majority**, usually eighteen years of age. In these cases, the statute of limitations starts on the birthday on which the individual reaches the age of majority in the applicable jurisdiction.

In contract cases, statutes of limitations vary depending upon the particular cause of action pursued. For example, a contract dispute may involve a violation of the Uniform Commercial Code (UCC), which imposes a four-year statute of limitations. However, the same dispute, if framed as a breach of contract under the common law, may be subject to a six-year statute of limitations. It may also involve some other cause of action with a different limitations period under state law. Bringing the cause of action under the appropriate statute may give new life to a case for which the UCC limitation has expired.

Complaint

Plaintiff The party who files the complaint.

Complaint The document the plaintiff files with the court and serves on the defendant to initiate a lawsuit.

Web Exploration

Go to **www.eff.org/IP/digitalradio/XM_complaint.pdf** to view a copy of a complaint filed in U.S. district court.

Summons A court order directing the defendant to appear in court and answer the complaint.

Defendant The party who files the answer.

The **plaintiff** (the party who is suing) must file a **complaint**, in some jurisdictions called a plaintiff's original petition or summons, with the proper court. The content and form of the complaint will vary depending on each court's procedural rules. Many courts follow the federal practice of "**notice pleading**," requiring only that causes of action be stated in general terms sufficient to give the defendant notice of the allegations. Other state courts follow the traditional form, "**fact pleading**," requiring a more detailed allegations or description of the basis for the action.

A complaint must name the parties to the lawsuit, allege the ultimate facts and law violated, state the remedy requested, and recite a "prayer for relief" to be awarded by the court. The complaint can be as long as necessary, depending on the case's complexity. Exhibit 7.1 is a sample state trial court fact pleading complaint filed in New York. Exhibit 7.2 is a federal notice pleading complaint. Exhibit 7.3 is a bilingual notice to plead a complaint.

In some jurisdictions, after a complaint has been filed, the court issues a **summons**—a court order directing the **defendant** to appear in court and answer the complaint. A fundamental requirement is that notice be given to the defendant. A sheriff, another government official, or a private process server may serve on the defendant the complaint and, where required, the summons. In some cases, as when the defendant cannot be found to be served personally, the defendant may be served by other means, such as by publication.

Fact and Notice Pleading

In the federal courts and in some state courts, the complaint need only provide general allegations of the wrongful conduct, called notice pleading. The sample complaint in Exhibit 7.2 is an example of a notice pleading in federal court. Other states require fact pleading, in which the plaintiff must plead specific facts that constitute the wrong conduct. The sample state complaint in Exhibit 7.1 is an example of a fact pleading.

Court rules require an attorney to sign all documents filed. If a person is filing on his or her own behalf, called a ***pro se*** filing, an attorney's signature is not required. In federal court, Rule 11 governs the attorney's obligations and the potential penalties, as discussed in the following cases.

IN THE WORDS OF THE COURT . . .

Notice Pleading

***CONLEY V. GIBSON*, 355 U.S. 41, 47-48 (1957) 78 S.CT. 99**

. . . The respondents also argue that the complaint failed to set forth specific facts to support its general allegations of discrimination and that its dismissal is therefore proper. The decisive answer to this is that the Federal Rules of Civil Procedure do not require a claimant to set out in detail the facts upon which he bases his claim. To the contrary, all the Rules require is "a short and plain statement of the claim" that will give the defendant fair notice of what the plaintiff's claim is and the grounds upon which it rests. The illustrative forms appended to the Rules plainly demonstrate this. Such simplified "notice pleading" is made possible by the liberal opportunity for discovery and the other pretrial procedures established by the Rules to disclose more precisely the basis of both claim and defense and to define more narrowly the disputed facts and issues. Following the simple guide of Rule 8(f) that "all pleadings shall be so construed as to do substantial justice," we have no doubt that petitioners' complaint adequately set forth a claim and gave the respondents fair notice of its basis. The Federal Rules reject the approach that pleading is a game of skill in which one misstep by counsel may be decisive to the outcome and accept the principle that the purpose of pleading is to facilitate a proper decision on the merits. Cf. *Maty v. Grasselli Chemical Co., 303 U.S. 197* . . .

Exhibit 7.1 Sample State Trial Court Fact Pleading Complaint

IN THE SUPREME COURT OF NEW YORK FOR ALBANY COUNTY

B.K., a minor by her Parents and guardians, Janice Knowles and Steven Knowles, Plaintiff	: : :	No.: ______________________ Civil Action - Negligence
v.	:	
Ronald Clemmons Lower Council School District, Bud Smith, and Ace Trucking Company, Defendants	: : :	Jury Trial Demanded Attorney ID No. 124987

COMPLAINT

NOW comes the plaintiff, by her attorneys, Mason, Marshall and Benjamin and brings this complaint alleging as follows:

1. Plaintiff is B.K. a minor whose interests are represented by her parents and natural guardians, Janice and Steven Knowles, adult individuals, husband and wife, residing at 1243 Asbury Avenue, Albany, New York (hereinafter Plaintiff).
2. Defendant, Ronald Clemmons is an adult individual residing at 24 Logan Street, Albany, New York (hereinafter Defendant Clemmons).
3. Defendant Lower Council School District is a governmental unit duly authorized and existing under the laws of the State of New York with its principal place of business being 701 Wilkes Road, Albany, New York (hereinafter Defendant School).
4. Defendant Bud Smith is an adult individual residing at 332 S. Hearn Lane, Albany, New York (hereinafter Defendant Smith).
5. Defendant Ace Trucking Company is a corporation duly organized and existing under the laws of the State of New York with its principal place of business being 2501 Industrial Highway, Center Bridge, New York (hereinafter Defendant Ace).
6. At all relevant times, Defendant Clemmons, a 69 year old, duly licensed school bus driver, was employed by and under the direction, supervision and control of Defendant School.
7. At all relevant time Defendant Smith, a 46 year old, duly licensed truck driver, was employed by and under the direction, supervision and control of Defendant Ace.
8. On October 21, 2010 at approximately 7:20 a.m. Defendant Clemmons began transporting students to school on his regular morning route driving a 2005 full size school bus owned and operated by Defendant School.
9. On October 21, 2010 at approximately 8:50 a.m., after finishing his regular route, Defendant Clemmons drove to Albany City School No. 18 and loaded 44 children, ages 5 to 9 years old, and 8 adults serving as chaperons for a scheduled field trip to the Pumpkin Patch in Central Bridge, New York, about 40 miles from the school.
10. Plaintiff, born on June 12, 2003, being 7 years of age on the date in question, was one of the passengers, seated on Row 10 Seat F of the bus. A true and correct copy of the bus seating chart is attached hereto, made a part hereof and labeled as Exhibit "A".
11. Although familiar with the Central Bridge area, Defendant Clemmons had never been to the Pumpkin Patch.

(continued)

Exhibit 7.1 Sample State Trial Court Fact Pleading Complaint *(continued)*

12. Defendant School did not provide its driver, Defendant Clemmons with directions or a map to the site.
13. Defendant Clemmons asked a chaperone for directions which were obtained from a secretary in the school office.
14. Each school bus passenger seat was equipped with three color-coded lap belts, one color coded belt for each passenger in a seat. Each child was seated and restrained with a lap belt before the trip began for purposes of safety and supervision.
15. Departing the school about 9:20 a.m., Defendant Clemmons took the New York State Thruway west to exit 25A onto Interstate-88 (I-88) and then traveled west on I-88 toward exit 23, the intended exit.
16. Defendant Clemmons was confused about the directions to the Pumpkin Patch and exited at exit 24, the wrong exit. Clemmons stopped the bus on the exit 24 ramp, turned the bus around, returned to I-88, and continued traveling to exit 23, the correct exit.
17. At the end of the exit ramp for exit 23, Defendant Clemmons turned right onto State Route 30A (SR-30A) and started looking for State Route 7 (SR-7).
18. At approximately 10:30 a.m., the bus was traveling north on SR-30A between 15 and 25 mph as it approached the intersection with SR-7. The north- and southbound traffic on SR-30A were controlled by an advance warning sign that indicated a stop ahead, a stop sign, flashing red intersection control beacons, pavement markings that included the word "STOP", and a stop bar.
19. At the same time, Defendant Smith was driving a dump truck towing a utility trailer owned and operated by Defendant Ace. Defendant Smith was traveling about 45 mph westbound on SR-7. East- and westbound traffic on SR-7 at the intersection with SR-30A was controlled by flashing yellow intersection control beacons.
20. As the school bus approached the intersection, several children on board saw the sign for the Pumpkin Patch that was beyond the intersection and yelled.
21. Defendant Clemmons, who was looking for SR-7, saw the posted stop sign, slowed, but did not stop the bus, which then entered the intersection where the dump truck struck it on the right side behind the rear axle.

Count I - Plaintiff v. Defendant Clemmons

22. Plaintiff incorporates by reference the allegations contained in paragraphs 1 through 21 as though fully set forth at length herein.
23. Defendant Clemmons was negligent when he failed to stop the school bus at a stop sign breaching his duty to operate a vehicle in accordance with the rules of the road in effect in the state of New York for purposes of safety and traffic control.
24. Defendant Clemmons breached the duty of care owed to the passengers of the bus when he violated the rules of the road failing to stop at the traffic control device.
25. As a direct result of Defendant Clemmons' negligence in the operation of the school bus, Plaintiff was injured when upon impact of the dump truck with the school bus she was thrown about the interior of the school bus striking her head and shoulders on the side and roof of the bus resulting in a fractured skull and fractured vertebra at C3 and 4, contusions and abrasions.
26. As a result of the injuries sustained by Plaintiff she has suffered damages as follows:
    a. surgical treatment and repair of a fractured skull;
    b. placement of a halo brace upon her head and shoulders for stabilization and healing of vertebra fractures as C3 and 4;
    c. physical therapy to rehabilitate and restore the normal use of her head and neck;
    d. medical expenses related to the treatment and rehabilitation for the injuries sustained;

Exhibit 7.1 Sample State Trial Court Fact Pleading Complaint *(continued)*

e. time lost from school while hospitalized and unable to attend school;
f. arranging and paying for private tutors to come to her home for missed school instruction;
g. inability to participate in soccer, Daisy Scouts and other of life's pleasures, and;
h. such other damages as will be proved at trial of this matter

Wherefore plaintiff requests this Honorable court enter judgment in her favor and against the Defendants in an amount exceeding $25,000 plus interest, costs, attorneys fees and such other relief as deemed equitable.

Count II - Plaintiff v. Defendant School

27. Plaintiff incorporates by reference the allegations contained in paragraphs 1 through 21 as though fully set forth at length herein.

28. Defendant School failed to properly supervise, control and direct its employee Defendant Clemmons as follows
    a. failure to obtain proper medical certification of a bus driver known to have a heart condition, hypertension, and Type I Diabetes in violation New York Department of Motor Vehicles Article 19-A;
    b. failure to provide map and directions for driver's destination;
    c. failure to establish a policy to limit the eligibility of senior drivers known to be easily confused, distracted and unable to focus on multiple stimuli, and;
    d. such other negligence as may be discovered in preparation of the trial of this matter.

29. As a result of Defendant School negligence in employing and supervising Defendant Clemmons the collision of October 21, 2010 occurred causing plaintiff to suffer, as follows:
    a. surgical treatment and repair of a fractured skull;
    b. placement of a halo brace upon her head and shoulders for stabilization and healing of vertebra fractures as C3 and 4;
    c. physical therapy to rehabilitate and restore the normal use of her head and neck;
    d. medical expenses related to the treatment and rehabilitation for the injuries sustained;
    e. time lost from school while hospitalized and unable to attend school;
    f. arranging and paying for private tutors to come to her home for missed school instruction;
    g. inability to participate in soccer, Daisy Scouts and other of life's pleasures, and;
    h. such other damages as will be established at the trial of this matter.

Wherefore plaintiff requests this Honorable court enter judgment in her favor and against the Defendants in an amount exceeding $25,000 plus interest, costs, attorneys fees and such other relief as deemed equitable.

Count IV - Plaintiff v. Defendant Smith

30. Plaintiff incorporates by reference the allegations contained in paragraphs 1 through 21 as though fully set forth at length herein.

31. Defendant Smith was negligent in the operation and control of a dump truck driving too fast for conditions while approaching an intersection with flashing yellow lights.

32. As a direct result of Defendant Smith's negligence the dump truck he was operating struck the school bus in which Plaintiff was a passenger.

33. Plaintiff was injured when upon impact of the dump truck with the school bus she was thrown about the interior of the school bus striking her head and shoulders on the side and roof of the bus resulting in a fractured skull and vertebra at C3 and 4.

34. As a result of the injuries sustained by Plaintiff she has suffered damages as follows:
    a. surgical treatment and repair of a fractured skull;
    b. placement of a halo brace upon her head and shoulders for stabilization and healing of vertebra fractures as C3 and 4;
    c. physical therapy to rehabilitate and restore the normal use of her head and neck;
    d. medical expenses related to the treatment and rehabilitation for the injuries sustained;

(continued)

Exhibit 7.1 Sample State Trial Court Fact Pleading Complaint *(continued)*

e. time lost from school while hospitalized and unable to attend school;
f. arranging and paying for private tutors to come to her home for missed school instruction
g. inability to participate in soccer, Daisy Scouts and other of life's pleasures, and;
h. such other damages as will be established in the trial of this matter.

Wherefore plaintiff requests this Honorable court enter judgment in her favor and against the Defendants in an amount exceeding $25,000 plus interest, costs, attorneys fees and such other relief as deemed equitable.

Count V - Plaintiff v. Defendant Ace

35. Plaintiff incorporates by reference the allegations contained in paragraphs 1 through 21 as though fully set forth at length herein.

36. Defendant Ace was negligent in failing to inspect and correct mechanical deficiencies to the brake system, the air hose linking the truck and the trailer, and permitting use of a dump truck to pull a trailer.

37. Defendant Ace was negligent in allowing its driver to operate a vehicle not designed to pull a trailer and failed to properly supervise and train employee Smith concerning the rules of the road.

38. As a result of Defendant Ace's negligence the dump truck struck the school bus in which Plaintiff was a passenger.

39. Plaintiff was injured when upon impact of the dump truck with the school bus she was thrown about the interior of the school bus striking her head and shoulders on the side and roof of the bus resulting in a fractured skull and vertebra at C3 and 4.

40. As a result of the injuries sustained by Plaintiff she has suffered damages as follows:
    a. surgical treatment and repair of a fractured skull;
    b. placement of a halo brace upon her head and shoulders for stabilization and healing of vertebra fractures as C3 and 4;
    c. physical therapy to rehabilitate and restore the normal use of her head and neck;
    d. medical expenses related to the treatment and rehabilitation for the injuries sustained;
    e. time lost from school while hospitalized and unable to attend school;
    f. arranging and paying for private tutors to come to her home for missed school instruction;
    g. inability to participate in soccer, Daisy Scouts and other of life's pleasures, and;
    h. such other damages as will be established at the trial of this matter.

Wherefore plaintiff requests this Honorable court enter judgment in her favor and against the Defendants in an amount exceeding $25,000 plus interest, costs, attorneys fees and such other relief as deemed equitable

Respectfully submitted,
Mason, Marshall and Benjamin
ATTORNEYS FOR PLAINTIFF

____
Ethan Benjamin, Esquire
Attorney ID #
Mason, Marshall and Benjamin
Address
Albany, New York
Phone
Fax
Email

Exhibit 7.2 Notice Complaint Filed in Federal Court

UNITED STATES DISTRICT COURT - NORTHERN DISTRICT OF NEW YORK

B.K., a minor by her Parents and guardians, Janice Knowles and Steven Knowles, Plaintiff	: : :	No.: ______________________ COMPLAINT CIVIL ACTION - NEGLIGENCE
v. :		
Ronald Clemmons, Lower Council School District, Bud Smith, and Ace Trucking Company, Defendants :	: :	Jury Trial Demanded Attorney ID No. 124987

Plaintiff in the above captioned action alleges as follows:

JURISDICTION

1. Plaintiff and defendants are residents of different states and the amount in controversy exceeds $75,000.00, exclusive of interest and costs as specified in 28 U.S.C. §1332.

PARTIES

2. Plaintiff is B.K. a minor whose interests are represented by her parents and natural guardians, Janice and Steven Knowles, adult individuals, husband and wife, residing at 1243 Asbury Avenue, Bennington, Vermont (hereinafter Plaintiff).
3. Defendant, Ronald Clemmons is an adult individual residing at 24 Logan Street, Albany, New York (hereinafter Defendant Clemmons).
4. Defendant Lower Council School District is a governmental unit duly authorized and existing under the laws of the State of New York with its principal place of business being 701 Wilkes Road, Albany, New York (hereinafter Defendant School).
5. Defendant Bud Smith is an adult individual residing at 332 S. Hearn Lane, Pittsfield, Massachusetts (hereinafter Defendant Smith).
6. Defendant Ace Trucking Company is a corporation duly organized and existing under the laws of the State of New York with its principal place of business being 2501 Industrial Highway, Center Bridge, New York (hereinafter Defendant Ace).
7. At all relevant times, Defendant Clemmons, a 69 year old, duly licensed school bus driver, was employed by and under the direction, supervision and control of Defendant School.
8. At all relevant time Defendant Smith, a 46 year old, duly licensed truck driver, was employed by and under the direction, supervision and control of Defendant Ace.
9. On October 21, 2010, after finishing his regular route, Defendant Clemmons drove to Albany City School No. 18 and loaded 44 children, ages 5 to 9 years old, and 8 adults for a scheduled field trip.
10. Plaintiff, who was 7 old on the date in question, was a passenger on the bus, seated on Row 10 Seat F. A true and correct copy of the bus seating chart is attached hereto, made a part hereof and labeled as Exhibit "A".
11. At approximately 10:30 a.m., the bus was traveling north on SR-30A between 15 and 25 mph as it approached the intersection with SR-7. The north- and southbound traffic on SR-30A was controlled by an advance warning sign that indicated a stop ahead, a stop sign, flashing red intersection control beacons, pavement markings that included the word "STOP", and a stop bar.

(continued)

Exhibit 7.2 Notice Complaint Filed in Federal Court *(continued)*

12. Defendant Clemmons, who was looking for SR-7, saw the posted stop sign, slowed, but did not stop the bus, which then entered the intersection.

13. Upon entering the intersection, the bus was struck on the right side behind the real axel by a dump truck operated by Defendant Smith.

14. Defendant Smith was driving the dump truck with utility trailer, owned and operated by Defendant Ace. Defendant Smith was traveling about 45 mph westbound on SR-7. East- and westbound traffic on SR-7 at the intersection with SR-30A was controlled by flashing yellow intersection control beacons.

Count I - Plaintiff v. Defendant Clemmons

15. Plaintiff incorporates by reference the allegations contained in paragraphs 1 through 14 as though fully set forth at length herein.

16. Defendant Clemmons was negligent when he failed to stop the school bus at a stop sign.

17. As a result, Plaintiff was injured when the impact of the dump truck with the school bus she was thrown about the interior of the school bus striking her head and shoulders on the side and roof of the bus resulting in a fractured skull and fractured vertebra at C3 and 4, contusions and abrasions suffering damages, as follows:
    a. surgical treatment and repair of a fractured skull;
    b. placement of a halo brace upon her head and shoulders for stabilization and healing of vertebra fractures as C3 and 4;
    c. physical therapy to rehabilitate and restore the normal use of her head and neck;
    d. medical expenses related to the treatment and rehabilitation for the injuries sustained;
    e. time lost from school while hospitalized and unable to attend school;
    f. arranging and paying for private tutors to come to her home for missed school instruction;
    g. inability to participate in soccer, Daisy Scouts and other of life's pleasures, and;
    h. such other damages as will be proved at trial of this matter

Wherefore plaintiff requests this Honorable court enter judgment in her favor and against the Defendants in an amount exceeding $75,000 plus interest, costs, attorneys fees and such other relief as deemed equitable.

Count II - Plaintiff v. Defendant School

18. Plaintiff incorporates by reference the allegations contained in paragraphs 1 through 14 as though fully set forth at length herein.

19. Defendant School failed to properly supervise, control and direct its employee Defendant Clemmons

20. As a result of Defendant School negligence in employing and supervising Defendant Clemmons the collision of October 21, 2010 occurred causing plaintiff to suffer, as follows:
    a. surgical treatment and repair of a fractured skull;
    b. placement of a halo brace upon her head and shoulders for stabilization and healing of vertebra fractures as C3 and 4;
    c. physical therapy to rehabilitate and restore the normal use of her head and neck;
    d. medical expenses related to the treatment and rehabilitation for the injuries sustained;
    e. time lost from school while hospitalized and unable to attend school;
    f. arranging and paying for private tutors to come to her home for missed school instruction;
    g. inability to participate in soccer, Daisy Scouts and other of life's pleasures, and;
    h. such other damages as will be established at the trial of this matter.

Wherefore plaintiff requests this Honorable court enter judgment in her favor and against the Defendants in an amount exceeding $75,000 plus interest, costs, attorneys fees and such other relief as deemed equitable.

Exhibit 7.2 Notice Complaint Filed in Federal Court *(continued)*

Count IV - Plaintiff v. Defendant Smith

21. Plaintiff incorporates by reference the allegations contained in paragraphs 1 through 14 as though fully set forth at length herein.

22. Defendant Smith was negligent in the operation and control of a dump truck driving too fast for conditions while approaching an intersection with flashing yellow lights.

23. As a result, Plaintiff was injured upon the impact of the dump truck with the school bus she was thrown about the interior of the school bus striking her head and shoulders on the side and roof of the bus resulting in a fractured skull and vertebra at C3 and 4 and suffered damages as follows:
    a. surgical treatment and repair of a fractured skull;
    b. placement of a halo brace upon her head and shoulders for stabilization and healing of vertebra fractures as C3 and 4;
    c. physical therapy to rehabilitate and restore the normal use of her head and neck;
    d. medical expenses related to the treatment and rehabilitation for the injuries sustained;
    e. time lost from school while hospitalized and unable to attend school;
    f. arranging and paying for private tutors to come to her home for missed school instruction
    g. inability to participate in soccer, Daisy Scouts and other of life's pleasures, and;
    h. such other damages as will be established in the trial of this matter.

Wherefore plaintiff requests this Honorable court enter judgment in her favor and against the Defendants in an amount exceeding $75,000 plus interest, costs, attorneys fees and such other relief as deemed equitable.

Count V - Plaintiff v. Defendant Ace

24. Plaintiff incorporates by reference the allegations contained in paragraphs 1 through 14 as though fully set forth at length herein.

25. Defendant Ace was negligent in failing to inspect and correct mechanical deficiencies to the brake system, the air hose linking the truck and the trailer, permitting use of a dump truck to pull a trailer, allowing its driver to operate a vehicle not designed to pull a trailer, and failed to properly supervise and train employee Smith concerning the rules of the road.

26. As a result of Defendant Ace's negligence the dump truck struck the school bus in which Plaintiff was a passenger, injuring her when upon impact she was thrown about the interior of the school bus striking her head and shoulders on the side and roof of the bus resulting in a fractured skull and vertebra at C3 and 4 and suffered the following damages:
    a. surgical treatment and repair of a fractured skull;
    b. placement of a halo brace upon her head and shoulders for stabilization and healing of vertebra fractures as C3 and 4;
    c. physical therapy to rehabilitate and restore the normal use of her head and neck;
    d. medical expenses related to the treatment and rehabilitation for the injuries sustained;
    e. time lost from school while hospitalized and unable to attend school;
    f. arranging and paying for private tutors to come to her home for missed school instruction;
    g. inability to participate in soccer, Daisy Scouts and other of life's pleasures, and;
    h. such other damages as will be established at the trial of this matter.

(continued)

Exhibit 7.2 Notice Complaint Filed in Federal Court *(continued)*

Wherefore plaintiff requests this Honorable court enter judgment in her favor and against the Defendants in an amount exceeding $75,000 plus interest, costs, attorneys fees and such other relief as deemed equitable

Respectfully submitted,
Mason, Marshall and Benjamin
ATTORNEYS FOR PLAINTIFF

____
Ethan Benjamin, Esquire
Attorney ID #
Mason, Marshall and Benjamin
Address
Albany, New York
Phone
Fax
Email

VERIFICATION

I, JANICE KNOWLES, verify that I am authorized to make this verification. I verify that the Complaint is true and correct to the best of my knowledge, information and belief. I understand that false statements herein are made subject to the penalties of perjury relating to unsworn falsification to authorities.

Date: ____________________ ____________________
JANICE KNOWLES

I, STEVEN KNOWLES, verify that I am authorized to make this verification. I verify that the Complaint is true and correct to the best of my knowledge, information and belief. I understand that false statements herein are made subject to the penalties of perjury relating to unsworn falsification to authorities.

Date: ____________________ ____________________
STEVEN KNOWLES

Exhibit 7.3 Bilingual notice to plead a complaint

IN THE COURT OF COMMON PLEAS
OF PHILADELPHIA COUNTY, PENNSYLVANIA
CIVIL ACTION LAW

KATHRYN KELSEY	: NO.
vs.	: ATTORNEY I.D. NO.
KATHRYN CARROLL	: COMPLAINT IN EQUITY

COMPLAINT - CIVIL ACTION

NOTICE

You have been sued in court. If you wish to defend against the claims set forth in the following pages, you must take action within twenty (20) days after this complaint and notice are served, by entering a written appearance personally or by attorney and filing in writing with the court your defenses or objections to the claims set forth against you. You are warned that if you fail to do so the case may proceed without you and a judgment may be entered against you by the court without further notice for any money claimed in the complaint or for any other claims or relief requested by the plaintiff. You may lose money or property or other rights important to you.

You should take this paper to your lawyer at once. If you do not have a lawyer or cannot afford one, go to or telephone the office set forth below to find out where you can get legal help.

Philadelphia Bar Association
Lawyer Referral and
Information Service
One Reading Center
Philadelphia, Pennsylvania 19107
215-238-1701

AVISO

Le han demandado a usted en la corte. Si usted quiere defenderse de estas demandas expuestas en las paginas siguientes, usted tiene veinte (20) dias de plazo al partir de la fecha de la demanda y la notificacion. Hace falta asentar una compancia escrita o en persona o con un abogado y entregar a la corte en forma escrita sus defensas o sus objeciones a las demandas en contra de su persona. Sea avisado que si usted no se defiende, la corta tomara medidas y puede continuar la demanda en contra suya sin previo aviso o notificacion. Ademas, la corte puede decidir a favor del demandante y requiere que usted cumpla con todas las provisiones de esta demanda. Usted puede perer dinero o sus propiedades u oetros derechos importantes para usted.

Lieva esta demanda a un abogado immediatamente. Si no tiene abogado o si no tiene el dinero suficiente de pagartal servicio, vaya en persona o llame por telefono a la oficina cuya direccion se encuentra escrita abajo para averiguar donde se puede conseguir asistencia legal.

Asociacion de Licenciados de Filadelfia
Servicio de Referencia e
Informacion Legal
One Reading Center
Filadelfia, Pennsylvania 19107
215-238-1701

IN THE WORDS OF THE COURT . . .

Federal Rule 11

LEAHY V. EDMONDS SCHOOL DISTRICT,
NO. C07-1979 RSM, (W.D. WASH., MARCH 2, 2009).

. . . C. Rule 11 Sanctions

Defendants also argue that Plaintiff's counsel should personally be liable for attorney's fees under Rule 11. Rule 11 generally provides guidelines for attorneys to follow when submitting a pleading to the court. The rule "imposes a duty on attorneys to certify that they have conducted a reasonable inquiry and have determined that any papers filed with the court are well grounded in fact, legally tenable, and not interposed for any improper purpose." *Cooter & Gell v. Hartmarx Corp.,* 496 U.S. 384, 393 (1990). "The central purpose of Rule 11 is to deter baseless filing in district court[.]" *Id.* (internal quotations omitted). Additionally, "[s]anctions must be imposed on the signer of a paper if the paper is 'frivolous.'" *In re Keegan Mgmt. Co.,* 78 F.3d 431, 434 (9th Cir. 1996). Although the word "frivolous" does not appear in the text of the rule, it is well-established that it denotes "a filing that is *both* baseless *and* made without a reasonable and competent inquiry." *Id.* (citation omitted) (emphasis in original). The Ninth Circuit has explained that "there are basically three types of submitted papers which warrant sanctions: factually frivolous (not 'well grounded in fact'); legally frivolous (not 'warranted by existing law or a good faith argument for the extension, modification, or reversal of existing law'); and papers 'interposed for an improper purpose.'" *Business Guides, Inc. v. Chromatic Commc'ns Enterprises, Inc.,* 892 F.2d 802, 808 (9th Cir. 1989) (quoting FRCP *11*)....

CHECKLIST Preparing a Complaint

- ☐ Caption
- ☐ Body of the complaint
- ☐ Identification of parties
- ☐ Jurisdictional averments
- ☐ Background facts or those facts that apply to all causes of action
- ☐ Element of causes of action
- ☐ Negligence
- ☐ Breach of contract
- ☐ Professional malpractice
- ☐ Class actions
- ☐ Allegation of damages
- ☐ Prayer for relief (wherefore clause)
- ☐ Signature of attorney
- ☐ Affidavit or verification

Service of the Complaint

After filing the complaint and having the summons issued, the plaintiff must serve the defendant. In federal court, service must be made within 120 days. In state courts, the time period varies, but typically service must be made within 30 to 60 days after the initial filing. Failure to serve the complaint within the time limit can result in the complaint being dismissed. If it is dismissed on this basis, the plaintiff may file a motion seeking the court's permission to reinstate the complaint and reissue the summons.

The defendant also has a time limit within which to respond to the complaint by filing a responsive pleading. This time period begins to run when the complaint is actually served (not on the last day the complaint could have been served). In federal court, if served by a by a U.S. Marshall, private process server, or other authorized person, the period is 20 days. If served by notice and waiver, it is 60 days. Calculating the due date is as important for the defendant as it is for the plaintiff. Failure to respond in a timely fashion allows the plaintiff to obtain a default judgment against the defendant. Default is not automatic but a right the plaintiff may enforce. The defendant must know the rule and properly calculate the due date to avoid a **default judgment** for nonaction.

Default judgment Judgment obtained by the plaintiff against the defendant where the defendant has failed to respond in a timely fashion to the complaint.

All pleadings after the initial complaint and answer also have a response time. This includes the plaintiff's response to counterclaims or affirmative defenses asserted by the defendant, and the responses to any motions.

Responsive Pleadings

Upon receipt of the complaint, petition, or summons, the defendant and counsel have some critical decisions to make. In many instances, defendants may already have anticipated that a lawsuit would be filed against them. Being served with a complaint may not be a surprise, but the quickly approaching deadlines can be intimidating for the legal defense team, especially if the client did not promptly advise them of being served. If served personally, the defendant has a limited time in which to file a responsive pleading. In federal court, that time period is 20 days, which is probably insufficient time to thoroughly investigate and respond. Just as plaintiffs frequently wait until the last day before the statute of limitations has run, defendants frequently wait to meet with an attorney until the date the response is due. The first step may be to request from opposing counsel an **extension of time to respond**. In federal court and some state courts, the team must prepare and file a stipulation with the court if opposing counsel agrees to an extension. If the request is refused, the defense team must file a motion asking the court to grant an extension of time to respond.

Answer

The defendant is required to respond to the allegations contained in the plaintiff's complaint. This is done by preparing, filing, and serving an **answer**. Like a complaint, an answer is made up of the same sections, whether in federal or state court: a caption, numbered paragraphs, a prayer for relief, and alternative defenses.

When responding to the averments of the complaint, there are two basic choices:

1. **Admitted**—the facts of the averment in the complaint are true, or
2. **Denied**—the facts of the averment in the complaint are not true.

In some jurisdictions, simply denying averments of the complaint is not sufficient. The word "denied" with nothing more is considered a **general denial**, and the averment of the complaint is treated as if it were "admitted." In those jurisdictions, the reasons for the denial must be listed. These reasons may include the following types of responses:

1. Denied, as the facts are not as stated (and set forth specifically the alternate facts).
2. Denied, as after reasonable investigation the defendant lacks adequate knowledge to determine whether the information is true.
3. Denied, as the averment represents a conclusion of law to which no response is required.

In some instances, when the complaint is directed to multiple defendants, there may be paragraphs in the complaint that apply only to another defendant. In that event, the appropriate response would be: "No answer is required as the averments are addressed to another defendant."

Cross-Complaint and Reply

A defendant who believes that he or she has been injured by the plaintiff can file, in addition to an answer, a **cross-complaint**, or counterpetition as it is called in some jurisdictions, against the plaintiff in addition to an answer. In the cross-complaint, the defendant (now the **cross-complainant**) sues the plaintiff (now the **cross-defendant**) for damages or some other remedy. The original plaintiff must file a **reply**, or answer to the cross-complaint. Exhibit 7.4 is a sample answer. The reply—which can include affirmative defenses—must be filed with the court and served on the original defendant.

RECOGNIZING A FRIVOLOUS LAWSUIT

SIDEBAR

Although paralegals are not lawyers, they should still have some concept of whether a lawsuit has merit or not. Consider the following case: The Chungs are Korean residents who came to the United States to open a dry cleaning business. They eventually owned three dry cleaning shops in the Washington, DC, area. Roy L. Pearson was a District of Columbia administrative judge who was a customer at one of the Chungs' dry cleaning stores. Pearson walked to the Chungs' store because he did not have a car.

The Chungs had signs in the window of their store that stated "Satisfaction Guaranteed" and "Same Day Service." Pearson claimed that the Chungs lost a pair of his pants. He sued the Chungs for $67 million in damages, alleging that they had violated the DC consumer protection act. Pearson later reduced his demand to $54 million. He demanded $3 million for violation of the "Satisfaction Guaranteed" sign, $2 million for mental suffering and inconvenience, $500,000 in legal fees for representing himself, $6 million for ten years of rental car fees to drive to another cleaners, and $51 million to help similarly dissatisfied DC customers. Pearson stated that he had no choice but to take on "the awesome responsibility" for suing the Chungs on behalf of every DC resident. A website was set up to accept donations for the Chungs' legal fees of $83,000, which was eventually paid by donations.

Do you think Pearson had a legitimate legal case, or was this a frivolous lawsuit?

Cross-complaint A pleading filed by a defendant against a plaintiff to seek damages or some other remedy.

Exhibit 7.4 Sample State Answer to Fact-Pleading Complaint

IN THE SUPREME COURT OF NEW YORK FOR ALBANY COUNTY

B.K., a minor by her : No.: 2007 - 19743 - N- 11
Parents and guardians,
Janice Knowles and :
Steven Knowles,
Plaintiff : Civil Action - Negligence

v. :

Ronald Clemmons, : Jury Trial Demanded
Lower Council School District,
Bud Smith, and :
Ace Trucking Company, Attorney ID No. 097531
Defendants :

ANSWER OF DEFENDANT CLEMMONS TO PLAINTIFFS COMPLAINT
WITH AFFIRMATIVE DEFENSES

NOW comes Defendant Clemmons, by his attorneys, Li and Salva, and answers the complaint alleging as follows:

1. Admitted.
2. Admitted.
3. Admitted.
4. Admitted upon information and belief.
5. Admitted upon information and belief.
6. Admitted.
7. Admitted upon information and belief.
8. Admitted.
9. Admitted.
10. Admitted upon information and belief.
11. Admitted.
12. Admitted.
13. Denied that defendant Clemmons asked a chaperone o[r] anyone else for directions to the Pumpkin Patch. Although Clemmons had never been to the Pumpkin Patch he was familiar with the location and knew where it was and how to get there. A chaperone did provide a map and directions but it is specifically denied that this was at the request of defendant Clemmons.
14. Admitted in part and denied in part. It is admitted that each bus seat was equipped with three color coded lap belts, one for each passenger in a seat. It is specifically denied that each student on the bus was belted. After reason investigation, answering defendant lacks adequate knowledge, information or belief as the truth of the allegations concerning each child being belted or the reasons therefore. Strict proof thereof is demanded at trial.
15. Admitted.
16. Admitted in part and denied in part. It is admitted that Clemmons exited at the wrong exit, exit #24, reentered the Highway and continued to the correct exit, #23. The remaining allegations of the paragraph are denied. It is specifically denied that Clemmons was confused about the directions or the exit number. To the contrary, Clemmons was not confused when he exited at Exit 24. There was a traffic accident on the highway with police diverting thru-traffic around the

Exhibit 7.4 Sample State Answer to Fact-Pleading Complaint (*continued*)

accident by use of the exit and entrance ramps of Exit 24. It is specifically denied that Clemmons turned the bus around on the exit ramp for Exit 24. To the contrary, Clemmons was following the directions of state police diverting traffic from the highway to the ramp and back onto the highway to go around an accident blocking the lanes.

17. Admitted.
18. Admitted.
19. Admitted based upon information and belief.
20. Denied as stated. The yelling and screaming of the children was not limited to the approach of the intersection. The children were uncontrolled, jumping about and switching seats, and loudly singing, yelling, and screaming throughout the ride from Public School No. 18. After reasonable investigation, answering defendant is unable to determine whether this behavior was attributable to seeing signs for the Pumpkin Patch or simply the uncontrolled behavior of the children.
21. Denied as stated. It is true that answering defendant slowed as he approached the intersection, which was accomplished by removing his foot from the accelerator of the vehicle. Upon attempting to apply the brakes to further slow and stop the vehicle, the defendant discovered the brakes were not operating properly, thus causing the vehicle to enter the intersection without stopping. It is admitted that the vehicle was then struck by a dump truck.

Count I
Plaintiff v. Defendant Clemmons

22. No answer is required to the averments set forth in this paragraph. To the extent [an] answer is required Defendant Clemmons incorporates paragraphs 1 through 21 hereof as though fully set forth at length.
23. Denied as a conclusion of law. Further denied that Defendant Clemmons was negligent or failed to observe the rules of the road. To the contrary, Clemmons complied with all rules of the road including following the instructions of the police officers controlling traffic patterns around an accident scene. Failure to bring the vehicle to a stop was a result of mechanical failure of the brakes not the action or inaction of Clemmons.
24. Denied as a conclusion of law and for the reasons set forth in paragraph 23 which are incorporated herein by reference.
25. Denied as a conclusion of law and for reasons set forth in paragraph 23 which are incorporated herein by reference. Further denied, as after reasonable investigation, answering defendant lacks adequate knowledge as to any of the injuries suffered by the plaintiff. Strict proof thereof is demanded at the trial of this matter.
26. Denied as a conclusion of law. Further denied, as after reasonable investigation, answering defendant lacks adequate knowledge as to any of the injuries suffered by the plaintiff. Strict proof thereof is demanded at the trial of this matter.

WHEREFORE, Defendant respectfully requests that plaintiff's complaint be dismissed with prejudice.

Paragraphs 27 - 40. No answer is required as they are addressed to defendants other than Clemmons.

Affirmative Defenses

27. Defendant Clemmons incorporates by reference his answers to paragraphs 1 through 40.
28. Plaintiff's claims are barred by the statute of limitations.
29. Plaintiff's claims are barred by the doctrine of sovereign immunity.
30. Plaintiff's claims are barred by the doctrine of contributory negligence.
31. Plaintiff's claims against the answering defendant are barred by the doctrine of respondeat superior.

WHEREFORE, Defendant respectfully requests plaintiff's complaint be dismissed.

Exhibit 7.5 Pleadings process

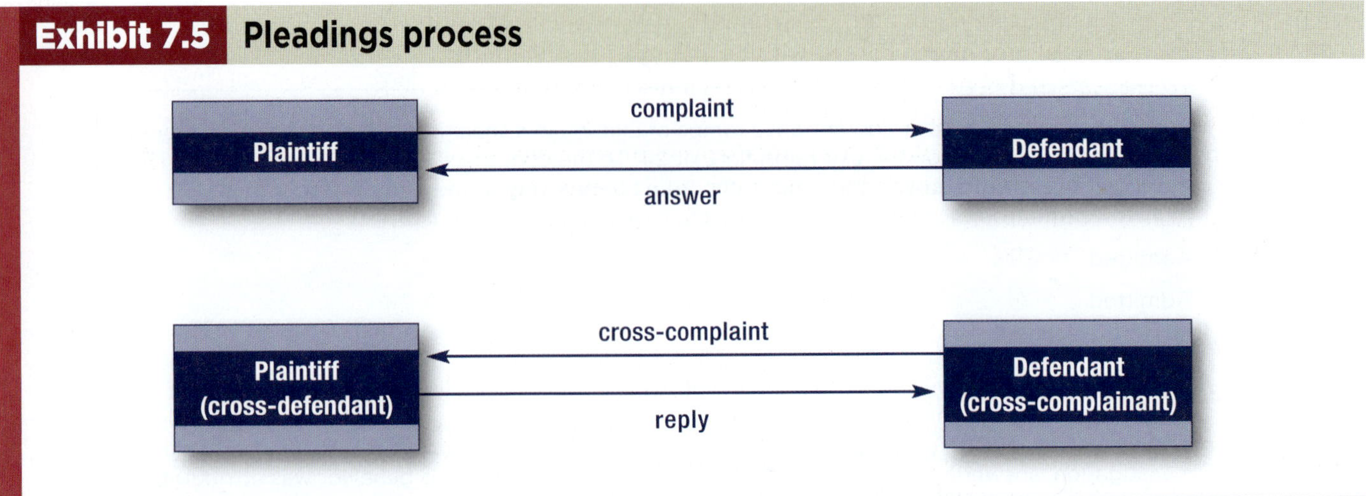

Reply A pleading filed by the original plaintiff to answer the defendant's cross-complaint.

Web Exploration

Go to http://www.statutes-of-limitations.com/state/Alabama. On the right-hand side of the page is a list of states. Click on your state to find out what the statute of limitations is for filing a negligence action in your state.

Electronic filing (e-filing) The electronic filing with the court of pleadings, briefs, and other documents related to a lawsuit.

Web Exploration

Locate the U.S. District Court that serves the county or parish in which you live. Go to that court's website and find and review the "Court Forms" for that court. http://uscourts.gov/.

Web Exploration

Visit www.abanet.org/tech/ltrc/research/efiling/ for a discussion of e-filings and the use of electronic documents in federal courts.

Learning Objective 3

Explain the purpose of discovery in the litigation process

Discovery A legal process during which both parties engage in various activities to elicit information about the case from the other party and the witnesses prior to trial.

Exhibit 7.5 illustrates the pleadings process.

Intervention and Consolidation

If other persons have an interest in the outcome of the dispute, they may step in and become parties to the lawsuit—called an **intervention**. For instance, in a lawsuit over ownership of a piece of real estate, a bank that has made a secured loan on the property can intervene because it has a stake in the outcome.

If several plaintiffs have filed separate lawsuits stemming from the same fact situation against the same defendant, the court can initiate a **consolidation** of the cases into one case if it would not cause undue prejudice to the parties. For example, if a commercial airplane crashes, killing and injuring many people, the court may consolidate all of the lawsuits against the defendant airplane company.

Electronic Filing

Increasingly, courts are implementing systems for the filing of pleadings and other documents electronically. Many of these jurisdictions permit rather than require **electronic filing (e-filing)**, but in other jurisdictions it is mandatory. Typically, the complaint, accompanied by the civil cover sheet, is the document used to create a file on the court's computer system. In some courts, a request for permission to use electronic filing must be submitted with the complaint. Others seek permission of the litigants for consent to electronic filing.

The requirements for electronic filing are not uniform or standardized. Each court has its own set of rules and requirements. The specific state or federal rules, as well as the rules for each local court, must be carefully checked, especially the format of the submitted files (such as PDF/A, or other file formats). These rules are constantly changing as technology and experience develop. The importance of checking the local rules cannot be overstated.

Discovery

Discovery is a step in the litigation process where the plaintiff and the defendant share information relevant to their dispute. Discovery serves a number of purposes: understanding and evaluating the strengths and weaknesses of the client's and the opponent's cases, preserving testimony, finding information that may be used to impeach a witness (such as showing inconsistencies in testimony), and potentially facilitating settlement.

The discovery process can be a time-consuming and sometimes frustrating phase in litigation. Paralegals are often charged with coordinating discovery requests and responses from clients and opposing parties. Successful discovery requires an organized approach, and a familiarity with the rules.

Increasingly important are the rules relating to discovery of electronic files. The methods used to locate, preserve, and produce these cyberdocuments require a new set of skills. In large or complex cases, it is often necessary for a paralegal to work with information technology experts.

Case Evaluation

Through discovery, the parties share information about the facts, documents, and statements of witnesses related to the legal dispute. By openly sharing information that may be used at trial, each side is forced to evaluate both its own case and the opponent's case and to determine whether the burdens of proof can be met. With each side fully aware of the potential evidence that can be presented, the legal team can, based on prior experience or reported similar cases, put a potential value on a trial outcome. In many cases the decision to try a case or settle a case is a business decision: Is the cost of a trial outweighed by the potential recovery? If the legal teams are well prepared, their evaluations may be surprisingly close, and settlement may be more likely than not.

Preparing for Trial

Properly completed discovery can reduce the potential for surprises in the evidence presented at trial. In fact, many of the "surprises" one sees on television trial dramas are not possible under rules that are designed to prevent the introduction of surprise witnesses and evidence.

Exhibit 7.6 Sample time deadlines using Lawyers Toolbox

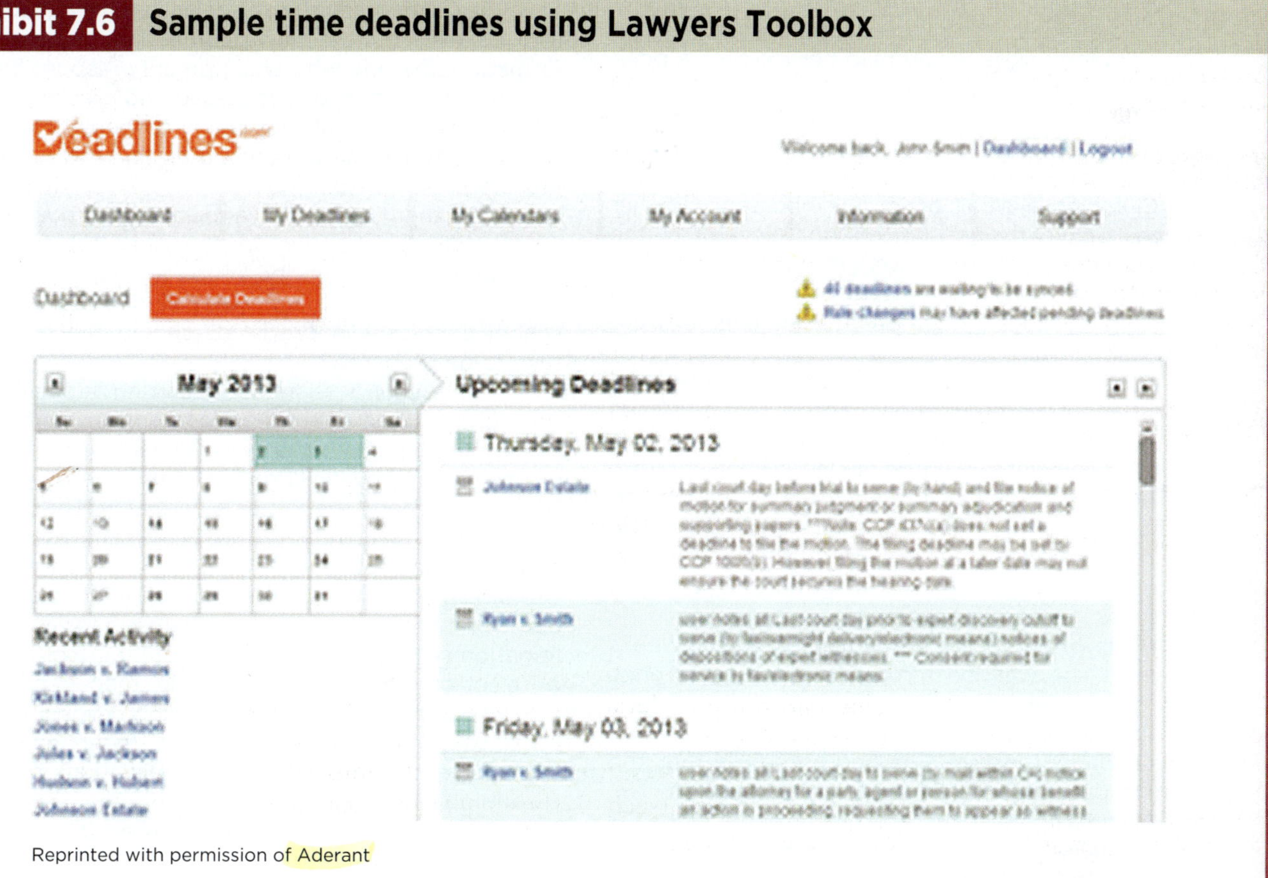

Reprinted with permission of Aderant

Preserving Oral Testimony

Discovery can also be used for preserving oral testimony. There are times when witnesses may not be available to attend trial to testify. Examples include witnesses who are gravely ill and not expected to live until trial, those who are elderly or incapacitated and physically unable to come to the courthouse, and those who are outside the geographical jurisdiction of the court. Under limited circumstances, the deposition testimony of these unavailable witnesses may be presented at trial. The deposition of witnesses is given the same treatment as if the witness were in court testifying in person.

Advice *from the* Field

THE ELECTRONIC PARALEGAL

William Mulkeen, Past President, American Association for Paralegal Education

COULD THIS BE THE FIRST DAY OF EMPLOYMENT FOR A RECENT PARALEGAL PROGRAM GRADUATE?

Maria was up before the alarm went off, ready to begin her new job and her new career. The newest paralegal at one of California's most prestigious law firms was ready to go to work. She still was amazed at how easily she had completed the interviews and had proceeded through the hiring process of the past few weeks. To be hired by such a prominent law firm was beyond her wildest dreams. She knew that her good grades, her excellent work samples and her technology skills would help her look for a position but never thought she would be so successful so quickly. The knowledge and sophisticated skill set she had acquired in her paralegal studies had paid immediate dividends.

Clutching a small portfolio embossed with her paralegal school's logo, she took the elevator to the thirty-fifth floor, got off and went through the big glass doors. Maria's legal degree and her newly acquired Certificate in Legal Information Management were about to be tested.

She knew that this potent combination of legal content and legal information management had been her key to success yet she was still very apprehensive about this new venture. Little did Maria know, but her new employers were as apprehensive as she was on her first day at the office. They had created the title of Paralegal Information Manager and that sign on the door was the first thing that caught Maria's eyes as she was showed her new office.

Maria remembered the interview a few weeks ago when she was led through a large conference room full of file boxes that she thought contained the information on the major cases she would be working on at the firm. She had asked, "Is that the Magnate case materials?" And the answer was "No, they will be accessed through the computer workstation in your new office." She remembered the senior partner telling her that the judge in the Magnate case had ordered the case to be handled electronically as much as possible. All of the documents had either been imaged or produced in native file format and a basic index of all documents had been created. The firm had chosen to optically character recognize the imaged documents for full text search capability. The trial exhibit list had to be filed electronically and the pre-trial order directed that the attorneys use all the technology available in the electronic courtroom to locate and display every document for the judge and jury.

Here she was, the Paralegal Information Manager, the gatekeeper of the management and the flow of information, the one who was primarily responsible for getting the information processed and presented. She felt overwhelmed but was ready to begin. Maria sat down and turned on the computer. She had taken the first step.

Can this happen to a paralegal school graduate? Will this happen in the near future? How can paralegal students be prepared best? What are the implications for paralegals? And what paralegal school courses and programs should the paralegal take to be prepared?

This scenario is already occurring in small ways throughout the country. Paralegals must start thinking about the training and skills necessary to work on the electronic civil litigation team emerging in the present; for many the future is here now. The process of electronic discovery; the gathering and acquisition of electronic records; the filing and preparation of this discovery; and the presentation of it in electronic courtrooms is already upon us. Demand for advanced litigation skills including an understanding of the role of electronic databases and the management of electronic documents is becoming commonplace. Paralegals must understand the technology and the ethical considerations and implications of these technological advances.

Reprinted with permission of the author.

Federal Rules of Civil Procedure—Rule 26(a) Disclosure Requirements

For many years, much of the key information in a case was disclosed only after a formal written discovery request had been issued. In many cases, no action was taken on a file until one side moved the case forward with a formal discovery request. Now, under Rule 26(a), everything the legal team intends to rely upon to prove its claims

IN THE WORDS OF THE COURT . . .

United States District Court, S.D. New York

***SECURITIES AND EXCHANGE COMMISSION V. COLLINS & AIKMAN CORP.*, NO. 07-2419 (S.D.N.Y., JANUARY 13, 2009)**

II. The Discovery Disputes

This opinion addresses four distinct but related discovery disputes. Stockman served a document request pursuant to Rule 34, asking the SEC to "produce for inspection and copying the documents and things identified" in fifty-four separate categories.[FN4] In response, the SEC produced 1.7 million documents (10.6 million pages) maintained in thirty-six separate Concordance databases—many of which use different metadata protocols.[FN5] Stockman raises the following objections. *First,* the SEC failed to identify documents responsive to requests for documents supporting particular factual allegations in the Complaint, preferring instead to "dump" 1.7 million potentially responsive documents on Stockman and then suggesting that he is capable of searching them to locate those that are relevant. *Second,* the SEC failed to perform a reasonable search for documents relating to accounting principles governing supplier rebates—both in general and with respect to the automobile industry. Instead, the SEC unilaterally limited its search to three of its divisions—and only if those divisions possessed "centralized compilations of non-privileged documents dealing specifically with rebates or accounting for rebates in the automobile industry."[FN6] *Third,* the SEC improperly asserted the deliberative process privilege with regard to certain documents. *Fourth,* the SEC failed to search its own e-mails, attachments thereto, and other records created and maintained solely in an electronic format that related to either "(i) the investigation and litigation of this matter or (ii) the handling of several large cases unrelated to C & A and the Commission's regulatory role in matters relating to rebates and rebate accounting."[FN7] The objections were raised in a series of letters rather than by formal motion.[FN8]

1. Attorney Work Product Protection Applied to Selection and Compilation

The Second Circuit has recognized that the selection and compilation of documents may fall within the protection accorded to attorney work product, despite the general availability of documents from both parties and non-parties during discovery.[FN18] However, it has labeled this protection a "narrow exception"[FN19] aimed at preventing requests with "the precise goal of learning what the opposing attorney's thinking or strategy may be."[FN20] Moreover, equity favors rejection of work product protection to a compilation of documents that are otherwise unavailable or "beyond reasonable access."[FN21] The Circuit has suggested that a court may permit *ex parte* communication of the strategy the withholding party wishes to conceal and *in camera* review of documents, so that the court may make an educated assessment whether production of the compilation will reveal a party's litigation strategy.[FN22]

C. Discussion

1. Work Product Protection

It is first necessary to determine the level of protection afforded to the *selection* of documents by an attorney to support factual allegations in a complaint. Such

(*continued*)

documents are not "core" work product. Core work product constitutes legal documents drafted by an attorney—her mental impressions, conclusions, opinions, and legal theories. This highest level of protection applies to a compilation only if it is organized by legal theory or strategy. The SEC's theory—that every document or word reviewed by an attorney is "core" attorney work product—leaves nothing to surround the core.[FN35] The first step in responding to any document request is an attorney's assessment of relevance with regard to potentially responsive documents. It would make no sense to then claim that an attorney's determination of relevance shields the selection of responsive documents from production.

With few exceptions, *Rule 26(f)* requires the parties to hold a conference and prepare a discovery plan. The Rule specifically requires that the discovery plan state the parties' views and proposals with respect to "the subject on which discovery may be needed...and whether discovery should be conducted in phases or be limited to or focused on particular issues"[FN66] and "any issues about disclosure or discovery of electronically stored information...."[FN67] Had this been accomplished, the Court might not now be required to intervene in this particular dispute. I also draw the parties' attention to the recently issued Sedona Conference Cooperation Proclamation, which urges parties to work in a cooperative rather than an adversarial manner to resolve discovery issues in order to stem the "rising monetary costs" of discovery disputes.[FN68] The Proclamation notes that courts see the discovery rules "as a mandate for counsel to act cooperatively."[FN69] Accordingly, counsel are directly to meet and confer forthwith and develop a workable search protocol that would reveal *at least some* of the information defendant seeks. If the parties cannot craft an agreement, the Court will consider the appointment of a Special Master to assist in this effort....The logic of *Rule 34* supports this limitation. When records do not result from "routine and repetitive" activity, there is no incentive to organize them in a predictable system. The purpose of the Rule is to facilitate production of records in a useful manner and to minimize discovery costs; thus it is reasonable to require litigants who do not create and/or maintain records in a "routine and repetitive" manner to organize the records in a usable[FN55] fashion prior to producing them.

...By rough analogy to *Rule 803(6)*, the option of producing documents "as they are kept in the usual course of business" under *Rule 34* requires the producing party to meet either of two tests. *First,* this option is available to commercial enterprises or entities that function in the manner of commercial enterprises. *Second,* this option may also apply to records resulting from "regularly conducted activity."[FN53] Where a producing party's activities are not "routine and repetitive" such as to require a well-organized record-keeping system—in other words when the records do not result from an "ordinary course of business"—the party must produce documents according to the sole remaining option under *Rule 34*: "organize[d] and label[ed]...to correspond to the categories in the request."[FN54]

B. Applicable Law

"A district court has wide latitude to determine the scope of discovery."[FN62] The general scope of discovery in civil litigation is defined by *Rule 26(b)(1)*.

FN62. *In re Agent Orange Product Liab. Litig.*, 517 F.3d 76, 103 (2d Cir. 2008).

Parties may obtain discovery regarding any nonprivileged matter that is relevant to any party's claim or defense....For good cause, the court may order discovery of any matter relevant to the subject matter involved in the action. Relevant information need not be admissible at the trial if the discovery appears reasonably calculated to lead to the discovery of admissible evidence.

. . . A court must limit the "frequency or extent of discovery" if one of three conditions in *Rule 26(b)(2)(C)* is present. The third limits production when "the burden or expense of the proposed discovery outweighs its likely benefit, considering the needs of the case, the amount in controversy, the parties' resources, the importance of the issues at stake in the action, and the importance of the discovery in resolving the issues."[FN63] The burden or expense may be defined in terms of time, expense, or even the "adverse consequences of the disclosure of sensitive, albeit unprivileged material."[FN64]...

VII. Conclusion

When a government agency initiates litigation, it must be prepared to follow the same discovery rules that govern private parties (albeit with the benefit of additional privileges such as deliberative process and state secrets). For the reasons set forth above, the SEC is ordered to produce or identify documents organized in response to Stockman's requests; to negotiate an appropriate search protocol to locate documents responsive to requests described above in Part IV; to submit materials allegedly covered by the deliberative process privilege to the Court for *in camera* review, together with a supporting memorandum within twenty days of the date of this Order; and to negotiate an appropriately limited search protocol with respect to agency e-mail. While the SEC has raised legitimate concerns about the burdens imposed by particular requests, it cannot unilaterally determine that those burdens outweigh defendants' need for discovery. At the very least, the SEC must engage in a good faith effort to negotiate with its adversaries and craft a search protocol designed to retrieve responsive information without incurring an unduly burdensome expense disproportionate to the size and needs of the case. The parties are therefore directed to engage in a cooperative effort to resolve the scope and design of a search with respect to the rebate issues and a search of e-mail created and maintained by the SEC. A conference is scheduled for February 13, at 5:00 pm, by which date the parties should have completed the meet and confer process in the hope of establishing an acceptable discovery program. If the parties remain at an impasse, the Court will be prepared to resolve further disputes and will consider the appointment of a Special Master to supervise the remaining discovery in this case.

SO ORDERED.

must be disclosed early in the litigation. Insufficient time to investigate the claim is not a valid excuse for failure to comply. The benefits of mandatory disclosure are twofold: (1) it provides for the early evaluation and settlement of claims; and (2) it reduces the amount, nature, and time necessary to conduct formal discovery. From a practical standpoint, the plaintiff's legal team must be prepared for disclosure at or shortly after filing the complaint.

While the new rules contemplate a specific time frame for disclosure, they do permit the attorneys to agree to some other time frame. Although the attorneys may agree to extend that time, the judge at the scheduling conference may encourage them to conclude the disclosure at a faster pace. The investigation that might have occurred under prior rules must now be completed before filing suit. For the defense team, the time to investigate and comply is very short. There is no time for procrastination in investigating and establishing the grounds to defend the claims.

Information Subject to Mandatory Disclosure

Almost anything relied upon in developing the claim must be disclosed, regardless of whether it is admissible at trial. This disclosure includes the identity of witnesses, copies of documents, a computation of damages, and a copy of any insurance policy that may be used to satisfy a judgment obtained in the litigation.

In the past, information used to compute damages represented the plaintiff attorney's thought process and was typically not released as part of discovery under the work product privilege. Under the current rule, however, the attorney's value on the case is made known within months of the complaint being filed.

From the defense standpoint, the disclosure of insurance coverage, which is not admissible at trial, is a significant change from previous discovery rules. A key element in settling most cases is the existence and limitations of insurance coverage. With both the plaintiff's calculation of damages and the defendant's insurance coverage known within months of filing the lawsuit, the chances for settlement are increased.

Experts and Witnesses

Expert witnesses expected to be called at trial must also be identified, accompanied by a copy of the expert's qualifications, a list of publications the witness has written over the preceding 10 years, a statement of compensation, and a list of other cases in which the expert has testified. The most critical element to be shared is the written report of the expert's opinion. The report states what the expert is expected to say at trial, and must include the opinion of the expert, the basis of that opinion, the information relied upon, and any assumptions made. The disclosure of the expert and his or her report must be made at least 90 days prior to trial. Some courts require the disclosure of the expert at the time of the initial disclosure, or within 30 days of receipt of the expert's report. Many lawsuits become a battle of the experts. The early disclosure of the expert and his or her opinion often leads to early resolution of the case.

Depositions

Deposition Oral testimony given by a party or witness prior to trial. The testimony is given under oath and is transcribed.

A **deposition** is oral testimony given, under oath, by a party or witness prior to trial. The person giving the deposition is called the **deponent**. The parties to the lawsuit must give their depositions if the other party requests them to do so. The deposition of a **witness** can be given voluntarily on request, or pursuant to a **subpoena** (court order). The deponent can be required to bring documents to the deposition.

Depositions are used to preserve evidence (such as when the deponent is terminally ill, ill, or otherwise not available at trial), to find out information that may lead to evidence, or to impeach testimony given by witnesses at trial. Most depositions are taken at the office of one of the attorneys. The deponent is placed under oath and then asked oral questions by the attorneys for one or more parties to the lawsuit. The questions and answers are recorded in written form by a court reporter. Depositions also can be videotaped. The deponent is given an opportunity to correct his or her answers prior to signing the deposition, depending on local practice or rules.

Interrogatories

Interrogatories Written questions submitted by one party to another. The questions must be answered in writing within a stipulated time.

Interrogatories are written questions submitted by one party to a lawsuit to another party. The questions can be highly detailed, as illustrated by the sample interrogatory in Exhibit 7.7. In some jurisdictions, certain documents must be attached to the answers. A party is required to answer the interrogatories in writing within a specified time period (typically 60 to 90 days). An attorney usually helps with the preparation of the answers, which are signed under oath.

Production of Documents

Very often, particularly in complex business cases, a substantial portion of the lawsuit is based on information contained in documents (such as memoranda,

Exhibit 7.7 Sample interrogatory

THOMAS F. GOLDMAN & ASSOCIATES
138 N. State Street
Newtown, PA 18940
(123) 555-1234

KATHRYN KELSEY	: COURT OF COMMON PLEAS
	: PHILADELPHIA COUNTY
	:
vs.	: APRIL TERM, 2011
KATHRYN CARROLL	: NO. 1234

INTERROGATORIES ADDRESSED TO KATHRYN KELSEY

You are to answer the following interrogatories under oath or verification pursuant to the Pa. R.C.P. 4005 and 4006 within thirty days from the service hereof. The answering party is under a duty to supplement responses to any questions with information discovered after these answers were given.

Also, a party or expert witness must amend prior responses if he/she obtains information upon the basis of which:

(a) he/she knows the response was incorrect when made; or

(b) he/she knows that the response, though correct when made, is no longer true.

The words "your vehicle" as used in the following interrogatories are defined as the motor vehicle you were operating at the time of the accident.

When a Standard Interrogatory uses the word: "identify", the party served with the Interrogatory must identify all documents, things and persons known to that party or to that party's attorney, and the address of all persons identified MUST be set forth.

Where a Standard Interrogatory is marked with an asterisk (*), a Request for Production may accompany the Interrogatory.

STANDARD INTERROGATORIES PURSUANT TO PHILADELPHIA RULE OF CIVIL PROCEDURE *4005

INJURIES AND DISEASES ALLEGED

1. State in detail the injuries or diseases that you allege that you suffered as a result of the accident referred to in the Complaint.

MEDICAL TREATMENT & REPORTS*

2. If you received medical treatment or examinations (including x-rays) because of injuries or diseases you suffered as a result of the accident, identify:
   (a) Each hospital at which you were treated or examined;
   (b) The dates on which each such treatment or examination at a hospital was rendered and the charges by the hospital for each;
   (c) Each doctor or practitioner by whom you were treated or examined;
   (d) The dates on which each such treatment or examination by a doctor or practitioner was rendered and the charges for each;
   (e) All reports regarding any medical treatment or examinations, setting forth the author and date of such reports.

* This document can be viewed in its entirety on the companion website.

Production of documents Request by one party to another to produce all documents relevant to the case prior to the trial.

correspondence, and company records). One party to a lawsuit may request that the other party produce all documents that are relevant to the case prior to trial. This is called **production of documents**. If the documents sought are too voluminous to be moved, are in permanent storage, or if moving the documents would disrupt ongoing business, the requesting party may be required to examine the documents at the other party's premises. Exhibit 7.8 is an example of a request for production of documents.

Physical and Mental Examination

A **physical and mental examination** (in some jurisdictions, called an **independent medical examination**, or **IME**) is permitted where the physical or mental condition of one of the parties is at issue. In a personal injury action, the physical injuries suffered, and the damages that result from those injuries, are elements of a cause of action for negligence. Thus, the defense team may obtain a physical examination of the plaintiff from a doctor of the defense team's choosing. In a guardianship proceeding, the plaintiff seeks to be appointed guardian over someone who lacks mental capacity to handle financial and other matters. Because the cause of action is dependent on the mental state of the individual, a psychiatric examination would be appropriate.

Requests for Admission

Requests for admission are written requests issued by one party to the lawsuit to the other asking that certain facts or legal issues be admitted as true. Properly used, requests for admission can narrow the focus of trial and streamline the testimony to those issues that are actually contested. Some facts are usually not in controversy, such as names, addresses, and other personal information.

Locations of accidents, time of day, and related facts may also be admitted without calling witnesses. Facts such as whether someone was speeding, not observant, or otherwise negligent are facts rarely admitted because they represent an admission of liability. However, if liability is admitted, the only issue left is damages. Where the damages are minimal, parties may admit to the facts of liability to avoid the time and cost of trial to obtain a finding of fact of something obvious. The remaining issue of how much monetary value is assigned to the wrong may be agreed upon between the parties or determined by the trier of fact in very short order with less time or expense.

> **Example** If the defendant admits as true his liability for the automobile accident, then that issue is no longer in dispute. No evidence as to the cause of the accident will be required at trial. The trial will be limited to determining damages only, resulting in a more focused and streamlined case.

E-Discovery

The use in business of email, electronic records, websites, online transactions, and other digital technologies has exploded. This technology is also used extensively in conducting personal affairs. Therefore, in many lawsuits, much of the evidence is in digital form. Winning a lawsuit may depend on the ability of a party to conduct **electronic discovery**, or **e-discovery.**

Electronic discovery (e-discovery) The discovery of emails, electronically stored data, e-contracts, and other electronic records.

Modern discovery practices permit the electronic discovery of evidence. Most federal and state courts have adopted rules that permit the e-discovery of emails, electronically stored data, e-contracts, and other electronic records. E-discovery is fast becoming a burgeoning part of the preparation of a case for trial or settlement.

The lawyer and the paralegal must have a sound understanding of permissible e-discovery. Courts have resoundingly permitted the discovery of emails and

Exhibit 7.8 Sample request for production of documents

THOMAS F. GOLDMAN & ASSOCIATES
138 N. State Street
Newtown, PA 18940
(123) 555-1234

KATHRYN KELSEY	:	COURT OF COMMON PLEAS
	:	PHILADELPHIA COUNTY
vs.	:	APRIL TERM, 2011
KATHRYN CARROLL	:	NO. 1259

REQUEST TO PRODUCE UNDER PA R.C.P. 4033 and 4009
DIRECTED TO PLAINTIFFS

Within thirty (30) days of service, please produce for inspection and copying at the office of THOMAS F. GOLDMAN & ASSOCIATES, 138 North State Street, Newtown, Pennsylvania 18940, the following:

1. All photographs and/or diagrams of the area involved in this accident or occurrence, the locale or surrounding area of the site of this accident or occurrence, or any other matter or things involved in this accident or occurrence.
2. All property damage estimates rendered for any object belonging to the Plaintiffs which was involved in this accident or occurrence.
3. All property damage estimates rendered for any object belonging to the Defendant which was involved in this accident or occurrence.
4. All statements concerning this action or its subject matter previously made by any party or witness. The statements referred to here are defined by Pa. R.C.P. 4003.4.
5. All transcriptions and summaries of all interviews conducted by anyone acting on behalf of the Plaintiff or Plaintiff's insurance carrier of any potential witness and/or person(s) who has any knowledge of the accident or its surrounding circumstances.
6. All inter-office memorandum between representative of Plaintiffs' insurance carrier or memorandum to Plaintiffs' insurance carrier's file concerning the manner in which the accident occurred.
7. All inter-office memorandum between representative of Plaintiffs' insurance carrier or memorandum to Plaintiffs' insurance carrier's file concerning the injuries sustained by the Plaintiffs.
8. A copy of any written accident report concerning this accident or occurrence signed by or prepared by Plaintiff for Plaintiffs' insurance carrier or Plaintiff's employers.
9. A copy of the face sheet of any policy of insurance providing coverage to Plaintiffs for the claim being asserted by Plaintiff in this action.
10. All bills, reports, and records from any and all physicians, hospitals, or other health care providers concerning the injuries sustained by the Defendant from this accident or occurrence.
11. All photographs and/or motion pictures of any and all surveillance of Defendant performed by anyone acting on behalf of Plaintiff, Plaintiffs' insurer and/or Plaintiffs' attorney.
12. All photographs taken of Plaintiffs' motor vehicle which depict any damage to said vehicle which was sustained as a result of this accident.
13. All photographs taken of Defendant's motor vehicle which depict any damage to said vehicle which was sustained as a result of this accident.
14. Any and all reports, writings, memorandum, Xeroxed cards and/or other writings, lists or compilations of the Defendant and others with similar names as indexed by the Metropolitan Index Bureau, Central Index Bureau or other Index Bureau in possession of the Plaintiffs or the Plaintiffs' insurance carrier.

electronic databases where relevant to a court case. A party seeking e-discovery must prepare the proper requests for such discovery as required by court rules.

In addition to discovery of email and electronic information, courts permit the use of electronic interrogatories. Some courts also permit the taking of depositions electronically. This requires that the questions by the lawyers and the answers of the deponent be communicated electronically.

Paralegals *in* Practice

PARALEGAL PROFILE
Emily A. Ewald

Emily A. Ewald is a graduate of Xavier University with a Bachelor of Science degree. She also has a Paralegal Certificate from Davenport University. Emily currently works in the area of civil/commercial and appellate litigation at the large law firm of Dickinson Wright in Grand Rapids, Michigan.

Although I have been a paralegal for six years, the first three were spent focused on one enormous case. During that period, I reviewed, organized, and managed over 450,000 documents, 1,650 deposition exhibits, a 98-page trial exhibit list, deposition designations from over 70 depositions, and other numerous assignments to assist attorneys preparing for discovery and trial. In this case, our client, the defendant, was being sued for $74 million. However, three weeks before the scheduled trial date, the case was settled for a much lower amount.

My current work duties include drafting interrogatories, interrogatory responses, motions and briefs, witness lists, juror questionnaires, and verdict forms. I also help prepare for and attend depositions, hearings, mediations, arbitrations, and trials. Additionally, I go to client meetings, expert witness meetings, and deposition preparation sessions.

More and more legal documents are being digitally produced and exchanged. For instance, we are required by all federal courts to file everything electronically through an online program called PACER (Public Access to Court Electronic Records). For e-discovery purposes, we use Summation®, a software program used to summarize case documents and search them for specific data. TrialDirector® software is used to load case exhibits, videos, and other documents onto a laptop computer, which can later be projected onto a courtroom screen for judge and jurors to see.

My main advice to new paralegals is to be flexible. You should expect to be asked to go back and forth between different case assignments, at a moment's notice. You are also likely to get some assignments in which you have little or no interest. However, always do them to the best of your ability because you will gain from the experience.

Federal and state courts have established rules of evidence that require the parties not to destroy or delete documents or other evidence that is relevant to the pending lawsuit. This prohibition is particularly important when the documents and evidence are in digital form. The destruction or deletion of e-evidence may subject the violating party to civil and criminal penalties.

In cases where digital evidence has been destroyed or deleted from electronic files, it may be possible to reconstruct the evidence. The use of computer experts will be necessary to find the missing evidence and digitally reconstruct it.

E-discovery will continue to increase as an important aspect of many lawsuits. The recovery of emails, mining of electronic databases, and reconstruction of electronic evidence will play an ever more important part of discovery in current and future lawsuits.

Learning Objective 4
Explain the use of pretrial motions and settlement conferences

Pretrial Motions

Pretrial motion A motion to try to dispose of all or part of a lawsuit prior to trial.

Paralegals employed in the civil litigation field are often called upon to prepare **pretrial motions** to try to dispose of all or part of a lawsuit prior to trial. The three major pretrial motions are the motion to dismiss, the motion for judgment on the pleadings, and the motion for summary judgment.

Motion to Dismiss

Motion to dismiss A motion that alleges that the plaintiff's complaint fails to state a claim for which relief can be granted. Also called a *demurrer*.

A defendant can file a **motion to dismiss** that may request that a plaintiff's complaint be dismissed for failure to state a claim for which relief can be granted. A motion to dismiss is sometimes called a ***demurrer***. It alleges that even if the facts as presented in the plaintiff's complaint are true, there is no reason to continue the lawsuit. For example, a motion to dismiss would be granted if the plaintiff alleges that the defendant was negligent, but the facts as alleged in the complaint do not support a claim of negligence.

A motion to dismiss can be filed with the court prior to the defendant's having filed an answer in the case. If the motion to dismiss is denied, the defendant is given further time to answer. If the court grants the motion to dismiss, the defendant does not have to file an answer. The plaintiff usually is given time to file an amended complaint. If the plaintiff fails to file an amended complaint, judgment will be entered against the plaintiff. If the plaintiff files an amended complaint, the defendant must answer the complaint or file a new motion to dismiss.

Motion for Judgment on the Pleadings

Once the pleadings are complete, either party can make a **motion for judgment on the pleadings**. This motion alleges that if all of the facts presented in the pleadings are true, the party making the motion would win the lawsuit when the law is applied to these facts. In deciding this motion, the judge cannot consider any facts outside the pleadings.

Motion for judgment on the pleadings A motion that alleges that if all the facts presented in the pleadings are taken as true, the party making the motion would win the lawsuit when the law is applied to the asserted facts.

Motion for Summary Judgment

The trier of fact (the jury, or if no jury, the judge) determines *factual issues*. A **motion for summary judgment** asserts that there are no factual disputes to be decided by the trier of fact, and that the judge should apply the law to the undisputed facts and rule in the moving party's favor. Motions for summary judgment, which can be made by either party, are supported by evidence outside the pleadings. Affidavits from the parties and witnesses, documents (such as a written contract between the parties), and depositions are common forms of evidence used to support such a motion.

If, after examining the evidence, the court finds no factual dispute, it can decide the issues raised in the summary judgment motion. This may dispense with the entire case or with part of the case. If the judge finds that a factual dispute exists, the motion will be denied and the case will go to trial.

Motion for summary judgment A motion that asserts that there are no factual disputes to be decided by a jury and that the judge can apply the law to the undisputed facts and decide the case without a jury. These motions are supported by affidavits, documents, and deposition testimony.

Settlement Conference

Federal court rules and most state court rules permit the court to direct the attorneys or parties to appear before the court for a **pretrial hearing**, or **settlement conference**. One of the major purposes of these hearings is to facilitate settlement of the case. Pretrial conferences often are held informally in the judge's chambers. If no settlement is reached, the pretrial hearing is used to identify the major trial issues and other relevant factors.

More than 90 percent of all cases are settled before they go to trial. In cases that do proceed to trial, the trial judge may advise the attorneys of his or her own rules and timetable. The judge will also advise the attorneys of any deadlines for discovery and the deadline for submitting any final motions with regard to what may be offered at the trial, called *motions in limine*.

In a number of jurisdictions, cases are referred to arbitration or other forms of alternative dispute resolution. Depending on the amount of money in controversy, some cases are required to be submitted before court-approved panels of attorneys sitting as arbitrators. In other courts, arbitration is not required, but the litigants may elect to have the case heard before an arbitration panel. Appeal rights from arbitration panel decisions vary, but cases typically may be appealed *de novo* to the trial court as if no arbitration had occurred, except possibly with the payment of an appeal fee to cover part of the cost of the arbitration.

Exhibit 7.9 shows the sequence of key events before trial.

Web Exploration

Go to **http://www.legalzoom.com/lawsuits-settlements/personal-injury/top-ten-frivolous-lawsuits**, and read the article "Top Ten Frivolous Lawsuits."

Trial

Learning Objective 5

Describe the steps in a civil trial.

Pursuant to the Seventh Amendment to the U.S. Constitution, a party to an action at law is guaranteed the right to a **jury trial** in cases in federal court. Most state constitutions contain a similar guarantee for state court actions. The trial will be by jury only if either party demands one. The right to a jury is waived if neither party files a

Exhibit 7.9 Key events before trial

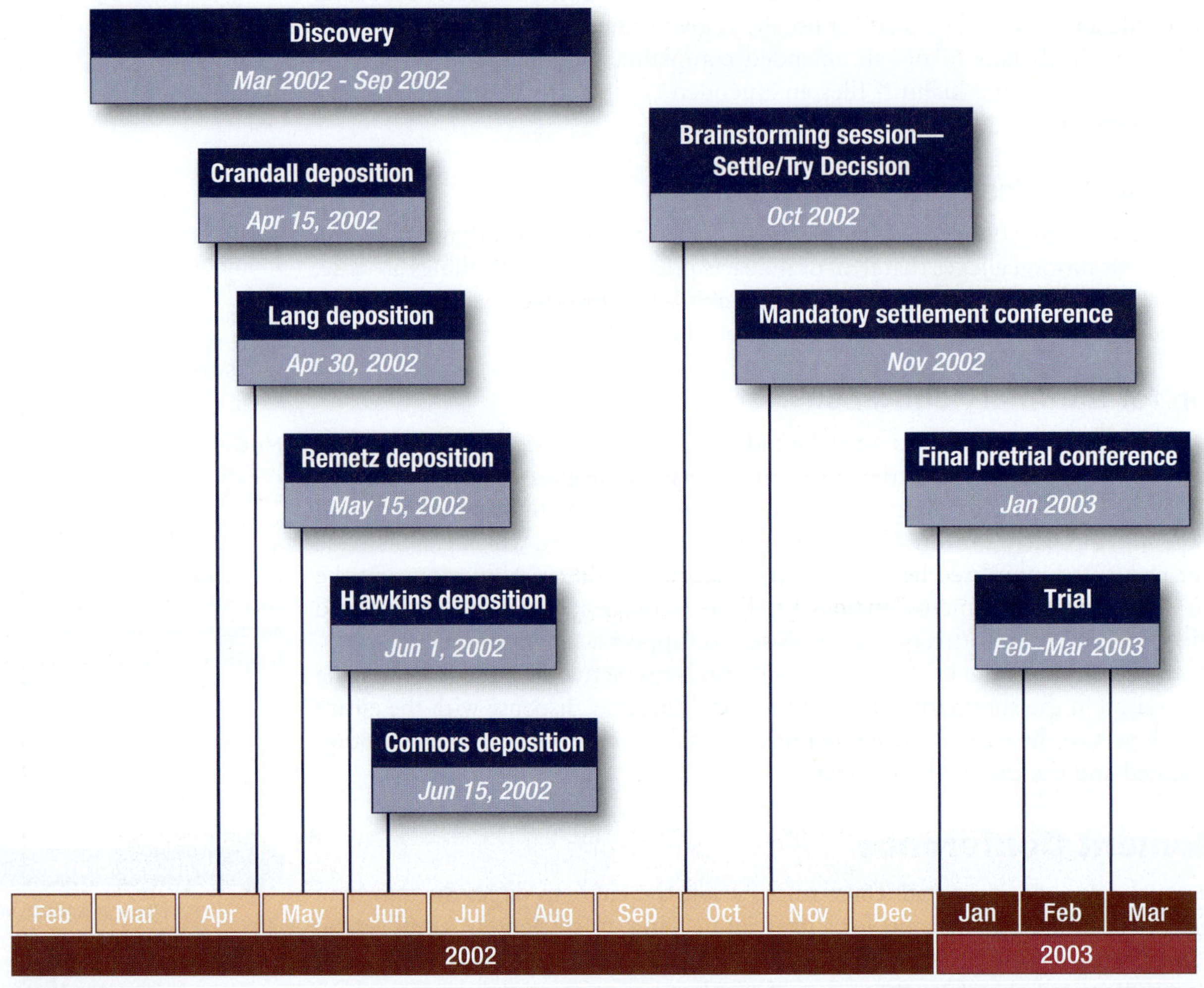

Source: Copyright 2009 LexisNexis, a division of Reed Elsevier Inc. All Rights Reserved. LexisNexis and the Knowledge Burst logo are registered trademarks of Reed Elsevier Properties Inc., and are used with permission of LexisNexis.

Trier of fact In a trial, the person or entity who decides questions of fact, as opposed to questions of law. In a jury trial, it is the jury; in a bench trial with no jury, the trier of fact is the judge.

Trial briefs Documents submitted to the judge by the parties' attorneys that contain legal support for their side of the case.

jury demand. In non-jury trials, the judge sits as the **trier of fact**. These trials also are called *waiver trials* or **bench trials**. At the time of trial, the parties usually submit to the judge **trial briefs** containing legal support for their side of the case.

Trials usually are divided into the following phases:

- Jury selection
- Opening statements
- Plaintiff's case
- Defendant's case
- Rebuttal and rejoinder
- Closing arguments
- Jury instructions
- Jury deliberation
- Entry of judgment

Voir dire The process whereby prospective jurors are asked questions by the judge and attorneys to determine whether they would be biased in their decisions.

Jury Selection

In **jury selection**, the pool of the potential jurors is usually selected from voter or automobile registration lists. Potential jurors are asked to fill out a questionnaire such as that shown in Exhibit 7.10. Individuals are then selected through a process called ***voir***

Exhibit 7.10 **Sample jury questionnaire**

JURY QUESTIONNAIRE

(Please Print)

NAME JUROR NO.

(Last) *(First)* *(Middle initial)*

SECTION OF CITY

(Currently) *(Other sections of city lived in within past ten years)*

Marital Status ☐ Married ☐ Single ☐ Divorced ☐ Separated ☐ Widowed

Occupation

(Currently) *(Other occupations within past ten years)*

Occupation of ☐ Spouse *(or deceased spouse)* ☐ Other

(Currently) *(Other occupations within past ten years)*

No. of Male Children Ages

No. of Female Children Ages

Your Level of Schooling Completed

Race ☐ White ☐ Hispanic ☐ Black ☐ Other

STOP HERE
Writing below this line is prohibited until the juror video is shown

QUESTIONS TO BE ANSWERED IN THE JURY ASSEMBLY ROOM

1. Do you have any physical or psychological disability or are you presently taking any medication? ❑ YES ❑ NO
2. (a) Have you ever been a juror before? ❑ YES ❑ NO
   (b) If so, were you ever on a hung jury? ❑ YES ❑ NO

Questions 3 through 15 apply to criminal cases only

3. Do you have any religious, moral or ethical beliefs that would prevent you from sitting in judgment in a criminal case and rendering a fair verdict? ❑ YES ❑ NO
4. Have you or anyone close to you ever been a victim of a crime? ❑ YES ❑ NO
5. Have you or anyone close to you ever been charged with or arrested for a crime, other than a traffic violation? ❑ YES ❑ NO
6. Have you or anyone close to you ever been an eyewitness to a crime, whether or not it ever came to Court? ❑ YES ❑ NO

(continued)

Exhibit 7.10 Sample jury questionnaire *(continued)*

7. Have you, or has anyone close to you, ever worked as a police officer or in other law enforcement jobs? This includes prosecutors, public defenders, private criminal defense lawyers, detectives, and security or prison guards. ❑ YES ❑ NO
8. Would you be more likely to believe the testimony of a police officer or any other law enforcement officer just because of his job? ❑ YES ❑ NO
9. Would you be less likely to believe the testimony of a police officer or any other law enforcement officer just because of his job? ❑ YES ❑ NO
10. Would you have any problem following the Court's instruction that the defendant in a criminal case is presumed to be innocent until proven guilty beyond a reasonable doubt? ❑ YES ❑ NO
11. Would you have any problem following the Court's instruction that the defendant in a criminal case does not have to take the stand or present evidence, and it cannot be held against the defendant if he or she elects to remain silent? ❑ YES ❑ NO
12. Would you have any problem following the Court's instruction in a criminal case that just because someone is arrested, it does not mean that the person is guilty of anything? ❑ YES ❑ NO
13. In general, would you have any problem following and applying the judge's instructions on the law? ❑ YES ❑ NO
14. Would you have any problem during jury deliberations in a criminal case discussing the case fully but still making up your own mind? ❑ YES ❑ NO
15. Is there any other reason you could not be a fair juror in a criminal case? ❑ YES ❑ NO

Questions 16 through 24 apply to civil cases only

16. Have you or anyone close to you ever sued someone, been sued, or been a witness? ❑ YES ❑ NO
17. Have you or anyone close to you been employed as a lawyer or in a law-related job? ❑ YES ❑ NO
18. Have you or anyone close to you been employed as a doctor or nurse or in a medical-related job? ❑ YES ❑ NO
19. In a civil case, would you have any problem following the Court's instruction that the plaintiff has the burden or proof, but unlike in a criminal case, the test is not beyond a reasonable doubt but "more likely than not"? ❑ YES ❑ NO
20. In a civil case, would you have any problem putting aside sympathy for the plaintiff and deciding the case solely on the evidence? ❑ YES ❑ NO
21. In a civil case, would you have any problem following the Court's instruction to award money for damages for things like pain and suffering, loss of life's pleasures, etc., although it is difficult to put a dollar figure on them? ❑ YES ❑ NO
22. Would you have any problem during jury deliberations in a civil case discussing the case fully but still making up your own mind? ❑ YES ❑ NO
23. Is there any reason in a civil case that you cannot follow the Court's instructions on the law? ❑ YES ❑ NO
24. Is there any reason in a civil case that you cannot otherwise be a fair juror? ❑ YES ❑ NO

dire, which means "to speak the truth." Lawyers for each party and the judge can ask questions of prospective jurors to determine whether they would be biased in their decision. Jurors can be "stricken for cause" if the court believes that the potential juror is too biased to render a fair verdict. Lawyers may also use preemptory challenges to exclude a juror from sitting on a particular case without giving any reason for the dismissal.

Once the jurors are selected (usually six to twelve jurors), they are impaneled to hear the case and are sworn in. Then the trial is ready to begin. In cases in which the Court is concerned for the safety of the jury, such as in a high-profile murder case, it can **sequester**, or separate, the jury from the outside world. Jurors are paid minimum fees for their service. Courts can hold people in contempt and fine or jail them for willful refusal to serve as jurors.

Opening Statements

Each party's attorney is allowed to make an **opening statement** to the jury. In opening statements, attorneys usually summarize the main factual and legal issues of the case and describe why they believe their client's position is valid. The information given in this statement is not considered evidence. It is the attorney's opportunity to tell the trier of fact what he or she intends to tell the jury through witnesses and evidence.

Plaintiff's Case

Plaintiffs bear the **burden of proof** to persuade the trier of fact of the merits of their case. This is called the **plaintiff's case**. The plaintiff's attorney calls witnesses to give testimony. After a witness has been sworn in, the plaintiff's attorney examines (questions) the witness. This is called **direct examination**. Documents and other evidence can be introduced through each witness.

After the plaintiff's attorney has completed his or her questions, the defendant's attorney can question the witness in **cross-examination**. The defendant's attorney can ask questions only about the subjects that were brought up during the direct examination. After the defendant's attorney completes his or her questions, the plaintiff's attorney can ask questions of the witness in **redirect examination**. The defendant's attorney then can ask questions of the witness again. This is called **recross examination**. Exhibit 7.11 illustrates this sequence for examining witnesses.

Defendant's Case

After the plaintiff has concluded his or her case, the **defendant's case** proceeds. The defendant's case must

1. rebut the plaintiff's evidence.
2. prove any affirmative defenses asserted by the defendant.
3. prove any allegations contained in the defendant's cross-complaint.

SIDEBAR: CONDUCTING A COST-BENEFIT ANALYSIS OF A LAWSUIT

A paralegal should have knowledge of how expensive and time-consuming a lawsuit is for both the client and the lawyer or law office. The choice of whether to bring or defend a lawsuit should be analyzed like any other business decision. This includes performing a **cost-benefit analysis** of the lawsuit.

The following factors should be considered in deciding whether to bring or settle a lawsuit:

- The probability of winning or losing
- The amount of money that could be won or lost
- Lawyers' fees and other costs of litigation
- Loss of time of managers and other personnel in the client's business
- The long-term effects on the relationship and reputation of the parties
- The amount of prejudgment interest provided by law
- The aggravation and psychological costs associated with a lawsuit
- The unpredictability of the legal system, and the possibility of error
- Other factors particular to the parties and claims being asserted

Exhibit 7.11 Sequence for examining witnesses

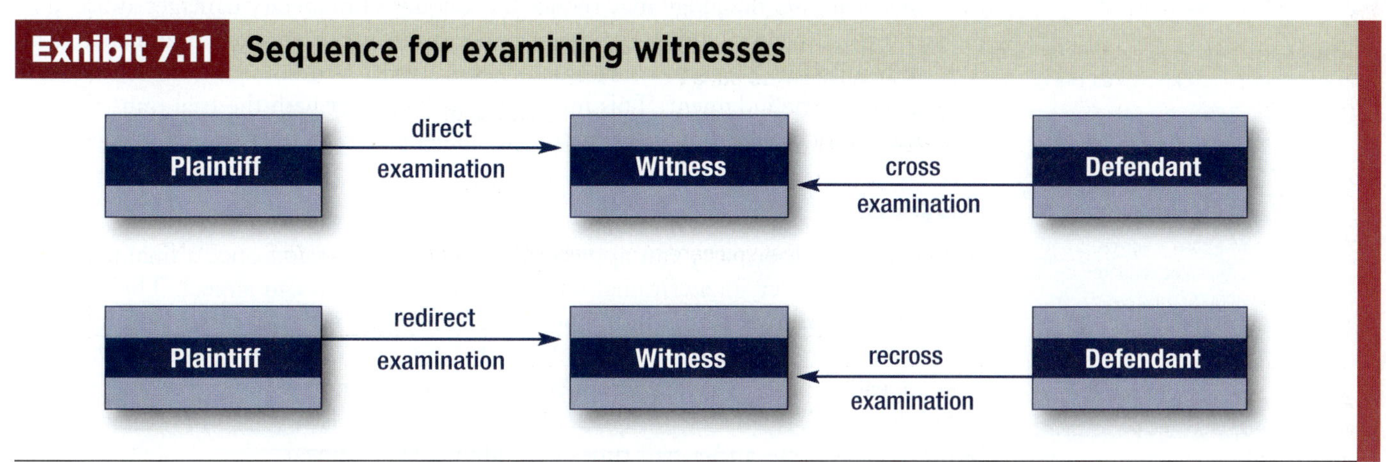

Plaintiff's case The portion of the trial in which the plaintiff calls witnesses and introduces evidence to prove the allegations contained in his or her complaint.

Defendant's case The portion of the case in which the defendant calls witnesses and introduces evidence to (1) rebut the plaintiff's evidence, (2) prove affirmative defenses, and (3) prove allegations made in a cross-complaint.

The defendant's witnesses are examined by the defendant's attorney. The plaintiff's attorney can cross-examine each witness. This is followed by redirect examination by the defendant, and recross examination by the plaintiff.

Rebuttal and Rejoinder

After the defendant's attorney has completed calling witnesses, the plaintiff's attorney can call witnesses and put forth evidence to rebut the defendant's case. This is called a **rebuttal**. The defendant's attorney can call additional witnesses and introduce other evidence to counter the rebuttal. This is called the **rejoinder**.

Closing Arguments

At the conclusion of the evidence, each party's attorney is allowed to make a **closing argument** to the jury. Each attorney tries to convince the jury to render a verdict for his or her client by pointing out the strengths in the client's case and the weaknesses in the other side's case.

Information given by the attorneys in their closing statements is not evidence. It is a chance for the attorneys to remind the jury what their opening statements said they would tell the jury through witnesses and evidence and how they had accomplished this during the trial.

Jury Instructions

Jury instructions (charges) Instructions given by the judge to the jury that informs them of the law to be applied in the case.

Once the closing arguments are completed, the judge reads the **jury instructions**, or **charges** to the jury. These instructions inform the jury about the law they must apply in deciding the case (see Exhibit 7.12). For example, in a criminal trial the judge will read the jury the statutory definition of the crime the defendant is charged with. In an accident case, the judge will read the jury the legal definition of *negligence*.

Jury Deliberation and Verdict

Verdict Decision reached by the jury.

The jury then goes into the jury room to deliberate its findings. **Jury deliberation** can take from a few minutes to many weeks. After deliberation, the jury announces its **verdict**. In civil cases, the jury also assesses damages. In criminal cases, the judge imposes penalties.

Entry of Judgment

Judgment The official decision of the court.

Appeal The process of asking an appellate court to overturn a decision after the trial court's final judgment has been entered.

Appellant The appealing party in an appeal. Also known as the *petitioner*.

In most cases, after the jury has returned its verdict, the judge enters **judgment** for the successful party, based on the verdict. This is the official decision of the court. But the court may overturn the verdict if it finds bias or jury misconduct. This is called a **judgment notwithstanding the verdict, judgment n.o.v.**, or **j.n.o.v.** (n.o.v. stands for the Latin *non obstante veredicto*.)

In a civil case, the judge may reduce the amount of monetary damages awarded by the jury if he or she finds the jury to have been biased, overly emotional, or inflamed. This is called **remittitur**. The trial court usually issues a **written memorandum** setting forth the reasons for the judgment. This memorandum, together with the trial transcript and evidence introduced at trial, constitute the permanent *record* of the trial court proceeding.

Learning Objective 6

Describe how a case is appealed and what decisions can be rendered by an appellate court.

Appeal

Appellee The responding party in an appeal. Also known as the *respondent*.

In a civil case, either party can **appeal** the trial court's decision once a final judgment is entered. However, in a criminal case, only the defendant can appeal. The appeal is made to the appropriate **appellate court** (see Exhibit 7.13). A notice of appeal must be filed within a prescribed time after judgment is entered (usually within 60 or 90 days). The appealing party is called the **appellant**, or **petitioner**. The responding party is called the **appellee**, or **respondent**. The appellant often is required to post an **appeal bond** (typically one-and-a-half times the judgment) on appeal.

Exhibit 7.12 Sample jury instructions

6.01J (Civ) PROPERTY DAMAGE

The plaintiff is entitled to be compensated for the harm done to his (her) property. If you find that the property was a total loss, damages are to be measured by either its market value or its special value to plaintiff, whichever is greater. If the property was not a total loss, damages are measured by (the difference in value before and after the harm) (the reasonable cost of repairs) and you may consider such evidence produced by defendant by way of defense to plaintiff's claim. In addition, plaintiff is entitled to be reimbursed for incidental costs or losses reasonably incurred because of the damage to the property, such as (rental of a replacement vehicle during repairs), (towing charges), (loss of use of the property), (etc.).

SUBCOMMITTEE NOTE

Damage to property is covered generally by Restatement of Torts, §§ 927 and 928. Section 927 provides for damages to be measured by the "market value" or "damages based upon its special value to [plaintiff] if that is greater than its market value." Restatement of Torts, § 927, Comment c (1934). Section 928 provides, in the case of damages not amounting to total destruction, damages measured by "the difference between the value of the chattel before the harm and the value after the harm or, at plaintiff's election, the reasonable cost of repair or restoration." This accounts for the parenthesized phrases (the difference in value before and after the harm) and (the reasonable cost of repairs).

Incidental costs will depend on the nature of the property damage. Rental of a substitute vehicle has long been recognized as one such compensable item. *Bauer v. Armour & Co.*, 84 Pa.Super. 174 (1924). Compensation for loss of use is specifically authorized by Restatement of Torts, § 928(b), in the case of less than total loss. The Subcommittee can see no logical reason why such damages should not be awarded under Section 927 in the case of total loss. *Nelson v. Johnson*, 55 D. & C. 2d 21 (Somerset C.P. 1970). Any further expense, proximately resulting from the loss or damage is recoverable under general provisions of tort law. *Nelson v. Johnson, supra*, at 33-34.

In the case of damage to automobiles, however, the appellate courts have adhered to the ancient rule requiring testimony of the one who supervised or made the repairs, prior to admission of damage estimates. *Mackiw v. Pennsylvania Threshermen & Farmers Mut. Cas. Ins. Co.*, 201 Pa.Super. 626, 193 A.2d 745 (1963). This rule has been criticized as time-consuming and "technical" by the very courts adhering to it. *Mackiw, supra*, 193 A.2d at 745. It further creates an intolerable burden on the courts, in a period when backlog has led to "compulsory" arbitration in many counties of cases valued below $10,000. E.g., *Loughery v. Barnes*, 181 Pa.Super. 352, 124 A.2d 120 (1956) (appeal after verdict of $341.30 for property damage); *Wilk v. Borough of Mt. Oliver*, 152 Pa.Super. 539, 33 A.2d 73 (1943) (new trial ordered after verdict of $175). The Subcommittee therefore adopts a rule requiring only the submission of a repair bill or estimate in proof of damages to automobiles (such bill being submitted prior to trial to defense counsel); should defendant wish to challenge such an estimate, he may do so through cross-examination and through the introduction of evidence in his own case. See *Watsontown Brick Co. v. Hercules Powder Co.*, 265 F.Supp. 268, 275 (M.D.Pa.), *aff'd*, 387 F.2d 99 (3rd Cir. 1967) (after introduction of damage evidence, burden shifts to defendant to show reduction).

Absent stipulation, the issue of reasonable compensation remains a jury issue.

6.01F (Civ) FUTURE PAIN AND SUFFERING

The plaintiff is entitled to be fairly and adequately compensated for such physical pain, mental anguish, discomfort, inconvenience and distress as you believe he (she) will endure in the future as a result of his (her) injuries. [. . .]

Briefs and Oral Argument

The parties may submit all or relevant portions of the trial record to the appellate court for review. The appellant's attorney may file an **opening brief** with the court, citing legal authority and other information to support his or her contentions on appeal. The appellee can file a **responding brief** answering the appellant's contentions.

The attorneys may make oral arguments to support their positions and clarify what they believe to be the appropriate law. But not every appellate court permits or allows oral argument in every case. In some appeals, a decision is based only upon the attorneys' written briefs. In some courts, the attorneys must, at the time of filing, make a request for oral argument or indicate a willingness to have the matter decided

Exhibit 7.13 Form 1 of appellate rules

United States District Court for the *Eastern*

District of *Pennsylvania*

File Number *US3CA 01234*

Ethan Marshall

v.) Notice of Appeal

Sara Elliott

Notice is hereby given that *Ethan Marshall* (plaintiffs) in the above named case,* hereby appeal to the United States Court of Appeals for the *Third* Circuit *from the final judgment* entered in this action on the 06 day of February, 2011.

(s) Thomas F. Goldman

(Address)

Attorney for *Plaintiff*

Address: *138 North State Street*
Newtown, Pa, 18940

* See Rule 3(c) for permissible ways of identifying appellants.

on the briefs alone. In some cases, oral argument is allowed automatically, and in other cases a reason for oral argument must be stated.

In the federal courts of appeals, oral argument is allowed unless a panel of three judges unanimously agrees, after reviewing the briefs, that the oral argument is unnecessary because the appeal is frivolous, the main issues have been correctly decided, or the facts and argument are presented adequately in the briefs and the record and their decision would not be aided by oral argument [F.R.A.P. 344].

Typically, oral arguments are made before the court without the presence of clients or witnesses. Because no additional fact-finding is permitted, it is a matter of making effective legal arguments to persuade the court to rule in favor of a legal position. Many appellate courts establish a time limit for each side. In some courts, the time limit is enforced by a warning light indicating when the time has nearly run out, and when the time has expired. The judges may waive the time limits, particularly when they have used up the attorneys' allotted time by asking questions. However, the court's treatment of the time limit is determined by local practice.

Actions by the Appellate Courts

Web Exploration

Review Rule 129 of the Court Rules of the U.S. Supreme Court at **http://supremecourtus.gov/**.

After review of the briefs, the record in the form of the trial court transcript, and oral arguments by the attorneys, an appellate court may affirm, reverse, or remand the case to the lower court. If the appellate court believes there were no errors in application of the law, it will **affirm** the decision of the lower court, and the decision will stand.

An appellate court may **reverse** a lower court decision if it finds an **error of law** in the record. Such an error may be in either the procedural law or the substantive law of the case. Examples of such errors of law include: the jury has been improperly instructed by the trial court judge, prejudicial evidence was admitted at trial even though it should have been excluded, and prejudicial evidence was obtained through an unconstitutional search and seizure. An appellate court will not reverse a finding of fact unless such finding is unsupported by the evidence or is contradicted by the evidence.

The court also may find that the lower court has made an error that can be corrected, and **remand** the case to the lower court to take additional action or conduct further proceedings. For example, the lower court may be directed to hold further proceedings in which a jury hears testimony related only to the issue of damages and makes a new award. In other cases when the court finds a reversible error, the court may **reverse and remand** the case. This means that the appellate court feels their decision cannot correct the error and the case needs to be retried. The retrial will take place in front of a new judge and a new jury.

Concept Review *and* Reinforcement

LEGAL TERMINOLOGY

Admitted 249
Affirm 270
Answer 249
Appeal 268
Appeal bond 268
Appellant (petitioner) 268
Appellate court 268
Appellee (respondent) 268
Bench trials 264
Burden of proof 267
Civil litigation 232
Closing argument 268
Complaint 238
Consolidation 252
Cost–benefit analysis 267
Cross-complainant 249
Cross-complaint 249
Cross-defendant 249
Cross-examination 267
Default judgment 248
Defendant 238
Defendant's case 267
Demurrer 262
Denied 249
Deponent 258
Deposition 258
Direct examination 267
Discovery 252
Electronic discovery (e-discovery) 260
Electronic filing (e-filing) 252
Error of law 271
Expert witnesses 258
Extension of time to respond 249
Fact pleading 238
General denial 249
Independent medical examination (IME) 260
Interrogatories 258
Intervention 252
Judgment 268
Judgment notwithstanding the verdict (j.n.o.v.) 268
Jury deliberation 268
Jury instructions (charges) 268
Jury selection 264
Jury trial 263
Litigation 232
Motion for judgment on the pleadings 263
Motion for summary judgment 263
Motion to dismiss 262
Notice pleading 238
Opening brief 269
Opening statement 267
Petitioner 268
Physical and mental examination 260
Plaintiff 238
Plaintiff's case 267
Pleadings 235
Pretrial hearing 263
Pretrial motion 262
Pro se 238
Production of documents 260
Rebuttal 268
Recross examination 267
Redirect examination 267
Rejoinder 268
Remand 271
Remittitur 268
Reply 249
Requests for admission 260
Respondent 268
Responding brief 269
Reverse 271
Reverse and remand 271
Sequester 267
Settlement conference 263
Statute of limitations 237
Subpoena 258
Summons 238
Trial briefs 264
Trier of fact 264
Verdict 268
Voir dire 264
Witness 258
Written memorandum 268

SUMMARY OF KEY CONCEPTS

Civil Litigation

What is Civil Litigation?	Civil litigation is the legal process for resolving disputes between parties. In civil litigation, the plaintiff sues a defendant to recover monetary damages or other remedy for the alleged harm the defendant caused the plaintiff.

Pleadings

What are Pleadings?	Pleadings consist of documents that initiate or respond to a lawsuit.
Complaint	A complaint (or petition) is filed by the plaintiff with the court and served, in some states, with a summons on the defendant. It sets forth the basis of the lawsuit.
Fact and Notice Pleading	Depending on the jurisdiction, the complaint must either provide a general description of the wrongful conduct alleged, which is called notice pleading, or plead specific facts alleged, which is called fact pleading.
Pleading Deadlines	Individual court rules provide a time within which the initial complaint or petition must be served, or the action will be dismissed. A responsive pleading must be filed within a certain time frame to avoid a default judgment.
Responsive Pleadings	The responding party (the defendant) must file a responsive pleading within the time allowed or request an extension of time to respond from the opposing attorney or from the court.
Answer	An answer is filed by the defendant with the court and served on the plaintiff. It usually denies most allegations of the complaint.
Cross-Complaint	A cross-complaint is filed and served by the defendant if he or she countersues the plaintiff. The defendant is the cross-complainant and the plaintiff is the cross-defendant. The cross-defendant must file and serve a reply (answer).
Intervention	In an intervention, a person who has an interest in a lawsuit becomes a party to the lawsuit.
Consolidation	Consolidation means that the court combines into one case the separate cases against the same defendant arising from the same incident, as long as doing so will not cause prejudice to the parties.
Statute of Limitations	A statute of limitations establishes the period during which a plaintiff must bring a lawsuit against a defendant. If a lawsuit is not filed within this time period, the plaintiff loses his or her right to sue.

Discovery

What is Discovery?	Discovery is the pretrial litigation process for eliciting facts of the case from the other parties and witnesses for purposes of understanding and evaluating the strengths and weaknesses of the client's case and those of opposing parties, preserving testimony, investigating information that may lead to evidence, finding information that may be used to impeach a witness, and potentially facilitating settlement.
Depositions	Depositions are oral testimony given by *deponents*, either a party or witness, and transcribed.
Interrogatories	Interrogatories are written questions submitted by one party to another party. These questions must be answered within a specified period of time.

Production of Documents	A party to a lawsuit may obtain copies of all relevant documents from the other party.
Physical and Mental Examination	Physical and mental examinations of a party are permitted upon order of the court where injuries are alleged that could be verified or disputed by such examination.
Requests for Admission	Written requests may be issued by one party in a lawsuit to another asking that certain facts or legal issues be admitted as true.
E-Discovery	In many lawsuits, much of the evidence is in digital form. Winning a lawsuit may depend on the ability of a party to conduct electronic discovery. The lawyer and the paralegal must have a sound understanding of permissible e-discovery.
Pretrial Motions	
Motion to Dismiss	A motion to dismiss alleges that even if the facts as presented in the plaintiff's complaint are true, there is no reason to continue the lawsuit. Also called a *demurrer*.
Motion for Judgment on the Pleadings	A motion for judgment on the pleadings alleges that if all facts as pleaded are true, the moving party would win the lawsuit. No facts outside the pleadings may be considered.
Motion for Summary Judgment	A motion for summary judgment alleges that there are no factual disputes, so the judge may apply the law and decide the case without a jury. Evidence outside the pleadings, however, may be considered (such as affidavits, documents, and depositions).
Settlement Conference	
Description	A settlement conference is held prior to trial between the parties in front of the judge to facilitate settlement of the case. Also called a *pretrial hearing*. If a settlement is not reached, the case proceeds to trial.
Trial	
Jury Selection	Jury selection is done through a process called *voir dire*. Biased jurors are dismissed and replaced.
Opening Statements	The parties' lawyers make opening statements to tell the jury what they intend to present at trial. These statements do not constitute evidence.
Plaintiff's Case	The plaintiff bears the burden of proof. The plaintiff calls witnesses and introduces evidence to try to prove his or her case.
Defendant's Case	The defendant calls witnesses and introduces evidence to rebut the plaintiff's case and to prove affirmative defenses and cross-complaints.
Rebuttal and Rejoinder	In rebuttal and rejoinder, the plaintiff and defendant may call additional witnesses and introduce additional evidence.
Closing Arguments	Closing arguments are made by the parties' lawyers. Their statements are not evidence.
Jury Instructions	The judge reads instructions to the jury as to what law the jurors are to apply to the case.
Jury Deliberation	The jury retires to the jury room and deliberates until it reaches a *verdict*.
Entry of Judgment	The judge may: a. enter judgment on the verdict reached by the jury. b. grant a motion of judgment n.o.v. if the judge finds that the jury was biased. This means that the jury's verdict does not stand. c. order *remittitur* (reduction) of any damages awarded if the judge finds the jury to have been biased or overly emotional.

Appeal	
Appellate Court	1. Unlike the trial court, whose main function is to make findings of facts, the appellate court's main function is to make findings of law. 2. In a civil case, unlike a criminal case, either party can appeal the trial court's decision once a final judgment is entered. In a criminal case, only the defendant can appeal. The appeal is made to the appropriate appellate court.
Briefs	In some appeals, the attorneys submit their case on "brief" only, and ask the court to make a decision based upon the written submission.
Oral Arguments	In other cases, the attorneys may, on their own request or at the request of the court, make an oral argument to support their position and clarify what they believe to be the appropriate law. Not every appellate court permits or allows oral argument in every case.
Actions by the Appellate Courts	
Affirm	The appellate court believes there have been no errors in the application of the procedural law or the substantive law and allows the prior decision to stand.
Reverse	The appellate court rules that the lower court has made a substantial error in either the procedural or the substantive law of the case.
Remand	The court finds that the lower court has made an error that can be corrected by sending the case back to the lower court for further proceedings.

WORKING THE WEB

1. Find the website for your local state trial court. Locate the local rules for filing complaints, answers, and other documents with the court.
2. Visit the website http://uscourts.gov/. Locate the U.S. District Court that serves the county or parish in which you live. Go to that court's website. Does the court require electronic filing of documents? If so, review the "user manual" on how to make electronic filings with the court.
3. Visit the U.S. Supreme Court's website: http://www.supremecourt.gov/. Click on "Case Handling Guides" and then "Guide to Filing Paid Cases" and review the requirements for filing a petition. How much detail does a paralegal need to know when assisting an attorney to file documents with the U.S. Supreme Court? Explain.
4. Visit http://www.lawtoolbox.com/. Read about the deadline calculator services available. Are these useful services?
5. Visit the website http://www.lexisone.com/. Click on "Register Here" and register for the free service to obtain court forms. Find a state form for the state court that serves the county or parish where you live. Find a federal form for the U.S. District Court that serves the county or parish where you live.

CRITICAL THINKING & WRITING QUESTIONS

1. Define "plaintiff." Define "defendant." In what procedural situations can a party be both a plaintiff and a defendant?
2. What is civil litigation? What remedy or remedies are sought by the plaintiff in civil litigation?
3. What are pleadings? Describe the following pleadings: (a) complaint, (b) answer, (c) cross-complaint, and (d) reply.
4. What is a summons? Describe service of process.
5. What is intervention? What is consolidation? Describe the purposes of these two procedures.
6. Explain statutes of limitations.
7. What is the process of discovery? What purposes does discovery serve? Explain.
8. Describe the following types of discovery: (a) deposition, (b) interrogatories, (c) production of documents, and (d) physical and mental examination.

9. Describe the differences between the following pretrial motions: (a) motion to dismiss, (b) motion for judgment on the pleadings, and (c) motion for summary judgment.
10. What is a settlement conference? What is its purpose?
11. How is a jury selected for a case? What is *voir dire*? What does *trier of fact* mean?
12. Describe the following phases of a trial: (a) opening statements, (b) plaintiff's case, (c) defendant's case, (d) rebuttal and rejoinder, and (e) closing arguments.
13. What are jury instructions? Explain. What is a verdict? What is a judgment?
14. What is an appeal? Define appellant (petitioner) and appellee (respondent).
15. Describe the following possible decisions by an appellate court: (a) affirm, (b) reverse, and (c) reverse and remand.

Building Paralegal Skills

VIDEO CASE STUDIES

Preparing for Trial: Preparing a Fact Witness

A paralegal is preparing a witness for deposition and trial and attempts to put the witness at ease by answering the witness's questions and explaining the procedures.

After viewing the video case study in MyLegalStudiesLab, answer the following:

1. Why is it necessary to prepare a person for deposition or for trial?
2. What is the most important advice the paralegal gives the witness?
3. Is preparing a witness the unauthorized practice of law?

Trial: Direct and Cross-Examination of a Witness

The attorneys in a trial ask questions of a fact witness in direct and then in cross-examination to develop the facts of a case.

After viewing the video case study in MyLegalStudiesLab, answer the following:

1. What is the purpose of direct examination?
2. What is the purpose of cross-examination?
3. Why would the attorney ask the judge whether it is acceptable to approach the witness?

ETHICS ANALYSIS & DISCUSSION QUESTIONS

1. Is there an ethical obligation not to file certain lawsuits?
2. What is meant by a "frivolous lawsuit"? Are there sanctions for filing frivolous lawsuits? Explain.
3. Should emails between lawyers and paralegals be treated as confidential and not subject to use as evidence in a case? Why or why not?
4. A former client of your firm sees you on the street at a local lunch stand and shows you a copy of a judgment rendered against him in a small claims court. He tells you he is out of work and cannot afford to hire a lawyer. Can you help the client proceed *pro se* (on his own, acting as his own lawyer)? Can you help him prepare the paperwork to appeal the judgment? Would any of this constitute the unauthorized practice of law? [See Pennsylvania comments to Ethics Rule 5.5.]
5. An ethical rule prohibits communication with an opponent who is represented by counsel. While surfing the web, you decide to see if the opposing party has a website. You locate it and check it carefully for any information that might help the investigation of the case assigned to you. You send a request to the site and receive information related to the lawsuit. Have you violated the ethical prohibition barring communications with a represented party? [See Oregon State Bar Op 2001–164.]

DEVELOPING YOUR COLLABORATION SKILLS

With a group of other students, review the Paralegals at Work at the beginning of the chapter. As a group, discuss the following questions.

1. Identify what document or documents your law firm should prepare on behalf of Rowan, Isis, and their parents to start the lawsuit. Identify what document the trucking company will file with the court to begin to defend the lawsuit.
2. What are the time limits in your jurisdiction for filing and responding to a complaint? Are there any other local requirements to commence and respond to the lawsuit?
3. Why would the state court or the federal court be more preferable in this case?

PARALEGAL & PORTFOLIO EXERCISE

Refer to the Paralegals at Work opening scenario. Find online (if possible), from a law library or a U.S. District Court, the proper form for filing a complaint for personal injuries in a U.S. district court that serves your area. Prepare as best as possible, from the facts of the case, the complaint and answer. If insufficient facts are provided to complete the complaint or answer, make up the missing information and complete these documents.

LEGAL ANALYSIS & WRITING CASES

Swierkiewicz v. Sorema N.A. 534 U.S. 506, 122 S.Ct. 992, 152 L.Ed. 1, 2002 U.S. Lexis 1374 (U.S.)

In April 1989, Akos Swierkiewicz, a native of Hungary, began working for Sorema N.A., a reinsurance company headquartered in New York. Swierkiewicz initially was employed as senior vice president and chief underwriting officer. Nearly six years later, the chief executive officer of the company demoted Swierkiewicz to a marketing position, and he was removed from his underwriting responsibilities. Swierkiewicz's underwriting responsibilities were transferred to a 32-year-old employee with less than 1 year of underwriting experience. Swierkiewicz, who was 53 years old at the time and had 26 years of experience in the insurance industry, was dismissed by Sorema.

Swierkiewicz sued Sorema to recover monetary damages for alleged age and national-origin discrimination in violation of federal antidiscrimination laws. Sorema moved to have Swierkiewicz's complaint dismissed. The District Court dismissed Swierkiewicz's complaint for not being specific enough, and the Court of Appeals affirmed. Swierkiewicz appealed to the U.S. Supreme Court.

Question

1. Under the notice pleading system, was plaintiff Swierkiewicz's complaint sufficiently stated to permit the case to go to trial? Explain why or why not.

Norgart v. The Upjohn Company 21 Cal.4th 383, 87 Cal.Rptr.2nd 453, 1999 Cal. Lexis 5308 (Cal.)

Kristi Norgart McBride lived with her husband in Santa Rosa, California. Kristi suffered from manic-depressive mental illness (now called bipolar disorder). In this disease, the person cycles between manic (very happy, expansive, extroverted) episodes and depressive episodes. The disease is often treated with prescription drugs. In April 1984, Kristi attempted suicide. A psychiatrist prescribed an antianxiety drug. In May 1985, Kristi attempted suicide again by overdosing on drugs. The doctor prescribed Halcion, a hypnotic drug, and added Darvocet-N, a mild narcotic analgesic. On October 16, 1985, after descending into a severe depression, Kristi committed suicide by overdosing on Halcion and Darvocet-N.

On October 16, 1991, exactly six years after Kristi's death, Leo and Phyllis Norgart, Kristi's parents, filed a lawsuit against the Upjohn Company, the maker of Halcion, for wrongful death based on Upjohn's alleged failure to warn of the unreasonable dangers of taking the drug. The trial court granted Upjohn's motion for summary judgment based on the fact that the one-year statute of limitations for wrongful death actions had run. The Court of Appeals reversed, and Upjohn appealed to the Supreme Court of California.

Question

1. Is the plaintiff's action for wrongful death barred by the one-year statute of limitations? Explain.

Ferlito v. Johnson & Johnson Products, Inc. 771 F.Supp. 196, 1991 U.S. Dist. Lexis 11747 (E.D.Mich.)

Susan and Frank Ferlito were invited to a Halloween party. They decided to attend as Mary (Mrs. Ferlito) and her little lamb (Mr. Ferlito). Mrs. Ferlito constructed a lamb costume for her husband by gluing cotton batting manufactured by Johnson & Johnson Products, Inc. (JJP), to a suit of long underwear. She used the same cotton batting to fashion a headpiece, complete with ears. The costume covered Mr. Ferlito from his head to his ankles, except for his face and hands, which were blackened with paint. At the party, Mr. Ferlito attempted to light a cigarette with a butane lighter. The flame passed close to his left arm, and the cotton batting ignited. He suffered burns over one-third of his body. The Ferlitos sued JJP to recover damages, alleging that the company failed to warn them of the flammability of the cotton batting. The jury returned a verdict for Mr. Ferlito in the amount of $555,000, and for Mrs. Ferlito in the amount of $70,000. JJP filed a motion for judgment notwithstanding the verdict (j.n.o.v.).

Question

1. Should defendant JJP's motion for j.n.o.v. be granted? Explain.

Pizza Hut, Inc. v. Papa John's International, Inc. 227 F.3d 489 2000 U.S. App. Lexis 23444 (5th Cir.)

Pizza Hut, Inc., the largest pizza chain in the United States, operates more than 7,000 restaurants. Papa John's International, Inc., is the third-largest pizza chain in the United States, with more than 2,050 locations. In May 1995, Papa John's adopted a new slogan, "Better Ingredients. Better Pizza," and applied for and received a federal trademark for this slogan. Papa John's spent more than $300 million building customer recognition and goodwill for this slogan. The slogan appeared on millions of signs, shirts, menus, pizza boxes, napkins, and other items and has regularly appeared as the tag line at the end of Papa John's radio and television advertisements.

On May 1, 1997, Pizza Hut launched a new advertising campaign in which it declared "war" on poor-quality pizza. The advertisements touted the "better taste" of Pizza Hut's pizza and "dared" anyone to find a better pizza. A few weeks later, Papa John's launched a comparative advertising campaign that touted the superiority of Papa John's pizza over Pizza Hut's pizza. Papa John's claimed it had sauce and dough superior to Pizza Hut's. Many of these advertisements were accompanied by Papa John's slogan, "Better Ingredients. Better Pizza."

In 1998, Pizza Hut filed a civil action in federal District Court, charging Papa John's with false advertising in violation of Section 43(a) of the federal Lanham Act. The District Court found that Papa John's slogan "Better Ingredients. Better Pizza," standing alone, was mere puffery and did not constitute false advertising. The District Court also found, however, that Papa John's claims of superior sauce and dough were misleading and that Papa John's slogan "Better Ingredients. Better Pizza" became tainted because it was associated with these misleading statements. The District Court enjoined Papa John's from using the slogan "Better Ingredients. Better Pizza." Papa John's appealed.

Question

1. Should the U.S. District Court's opinion in favor of Pizza Hut, Inc. be reversed? Explain.

Haviland & Co. v. Montgomery Ward & Co. 31 F.R.D. 578, 1962 U.S. Dist. Lexis 5964 (S.D.N.Y.)

Haviland & Company filed suit against Montgomery Ward & Company in U.S. District Court, claiming that Ward used the trademark "Haviland" on millions of dollars' worth of merchandise. As the owner of the mark, Haviland & Company sought compensation from Ward. Ward served notice to take the deposition of Haviland & Company's president, William D. Haviland. The attorneys for Haviland told the court that Haviland was 80 years old, lived in Limoges, France, and was too ill to travel to the United States for the deposition. Haviland's physician submitted an affidavit confirming these facts.

Questions

1. Must Haviland give his deposition? Explain.
2. What alternative way to take the testimony may be used? Describe these methods and their purpose.

IN RE M.C., 09-08-00465-CV (Tex.App.-Beaumont [9th Dist.] 3-5-2009)

On January 9, 2009, the court notified the parties that the appeal would be dismissed for want of prosecution unless arrangements were made for filing the record or the appellant explained why additional time was needed to file the record. It also notified the parties that the appeal would be dismissed unless the appellant remitted the filing fee for the appeal. The appellant, Blanca Carrillo, did not respond to the court's notices. The appellant did not file an affidavit of indigence and is not entitled to proceed without payment of costs. There was no satisfactory explanation for the failure to file the record, and no reasonable explanation for the failure to pay the filing fee for the appeal. The court dismissed the appeal for want of prosecution.

Questions

1. Why would a court dismiss a case for failure to meet a time deadline?
2. Why would a court dismiss a case for not paying the filing fees?
3. Is justice served by a court enforcing these time limits and filing requirements?

WORKING WITH THE LANGUAGE OF THE COURT CASE

Gnazzo v. G.D. Searle & Co., 973 F.2d 136 1992 U.S. App. Lexis 19453

United States Court of Appeals, Second Circuit

Read the following case, excerpted from the Court of Appeals opinion. Review and brief the case. In your brief, answer the following questions.

1. What is a statute of limitations? What purposes does such a statute serve?
2. What was the Connecticut statute of limitations for the injury alleged by the plaintiff?
3. What is summary judgment? Under what circumstances will it be granted?
4. What was the decision of the trial court? Of the Court of Appeals? What was the basis for each of these decisions?

Pierce, Circuit Judge

On November 11, 1974, Gnazzo had a CU-7 intrauterine device (IUD) inserted in her uterus for contraceptive purposes. The IUD was developed, marketed, and sold by G.D. Searle & Co. (Searle). When Gnazzo's deposition was taken, she stated that her doctor had informed her that "the insertion would hurt, but not for long," and that she "would have uncomfortable and probably painful periods for the first three to four months." On October 11, 1975, Gnazzo found it necessary to return to her physician due to excessive pain and cramping. During this visit she was informed by her doctor that he thought she had pelvic inflammatory disease (PID). She recalled that he stated that the infection was possibly caused by venereal disease or the use of the IUD. The PID was treated with antibiotics and cleared up shortly thereafter. Less than one year later, Gnazzo was again treated for an IUD-associated infection. This infection was also treated with antibiotics. Gnazzo continued using the IUD until it was finally removed in December of 1977.

Following a laparoscopy in March of 1989, Gnazzo was informed by a fertility specialist that she was infertile because of PID-induced adhesions resulting from her prior IUD use. Subsequent to this determination, and at the request of her then-attorneys, Gnazzo completed a questionnaire dated May 11, 1989. In response to the following question, "When and why did you first suspect that your IUD had caused you any harm?" Gnazzo responded "sometime in 1981" and explained: "I was married in April 1981, so I stopped using birth control so I could get pregnant—nothing ever happened (of course), then I started hearing and reading about how damaging IUDs could be. I figured that was the problem; however, my marriage started to crumble, so I never pursued the issue."

On May 4, 1990, Gnazzo initiated the underlying action against Searle. In an amended complaint, she alleged that she had suffered injuries as a result of her use of the IUD developed by Searle. Searle moved for summary judgment on the ground that Gnazzo's claim was time-barred by Connecticut's three-year statute of limitations for product liability actions. Searle argued, inter alia, that Gnazzo knew in 1981 that she had suffered harm caused by her IUD. Gnazzo contended that her cause of action against Searle accrued only when she learned from the fertility specialist that the IUD had caused her PID and subsequent infertility.

In a ruling dated September 18, 1991, the district court granted Searle's motion for summary judgment on the ground that Gnazzo's claim was time-barred by the applicable statute of limitations. In reaching this result, the court determined that Connecticut law provided no support for Gnazzo's contention that she should not have been expected to file her action until she was told of her infertility and the IUD's causal connection. This appeal followed.

On appeal, Gnazzo contends that the district court improperly granted Searle's motion for summary judgment because a genuine issue of material fact exists as to when she discovered, or reasonably should have discovered, her injuries and their causal connection to the defendant's alleged wrongful conduct. Summary judgment is appropriate when there is no genuine issue as to any material fact and the moving party is entitled to judgment as a matter of law. We consider the record in the light most favorable to the non-movant. However, the non-movant "may not rest upon the mere allegations of denials of her pleading, but must set forth specific facts showing that there is a genuine issue for trial."

Under Connecticut law, a product liability claim must be brought within "three years from the date when the injury is first sustained or discovered or in the exercise of reasonable care should have been discovered." In Connecticut, a cause of action accrues when a plaintiff suffers actionable harm. Actionable harm occurs when the plaintiff discovers or should discover, through the exercise of reasonable care, that he or she has been injured and that the defendant's conduct caused such injury.

Gnazzo contends that "the mere occurrence of a pelvic infection or difficulty in becoming pregnant does not necessarily result in notice to the plaintiff of a cause of action." Thus, she maintains that her cause of action did not accrue until 1989 when the fertility specialist informed her both that she was infertile and that this condition resulted from her previous use of the IUD.

Under Connecticut law, however, "the statute of limitations begins to run when the plaintiff discovers some form of actionable harm, not the fullest manifestation thereof." Therefore, as Gnazzo's responses to the questionnaire indicate[,] she suspected "sometime in 1981" that the IUD had caused her harm because she had been experiencing trouble becoming pregnant and had "started hearing and reading about how damaging IUDs could be and had figured that was the problem."

Thus, by her own admission, Gnazzo had recognized, or should have recognized, the critical link between her injury and the defendant's causal connection to it. In other words, she had "discovered, or should have discovered through the exercise of reasonable care, that she had been injured and that Searle's conduct caused such injury." However, as Gnazzo acknowledged in the questionnaire, she did not pursue the "issue" at the time because of her marital problems. Thus, even when viewed in the light most favorable to Gnazzo, the non-moving party, we are constrained to find that she knew by 1981 that she had "some form of actionable harm." Consequently, by the time she commenced her action in 1990, Gnazzo was time-barred by the Connecticut statute of limitations.

Since we have determined that Gnazzo's cause of action commenced in 1981, we need not address Searle's additional contention that Gnazzo's awareness in 1975 of her PID and her purported knowledge of its causal connection to the IUD commenced the running of the Connecticut statute of limitations at that time.

We are sympathetic to Gnazzo's situation and mindful that the unavoidable result we reach in this case is harsh. Nevertheless, we are equally aware that "it is within the Connecticut General Assembly's constitutional authority to decide when claims for injury are to be brought. Where a plaintiff has failed to comply with this requirement, a court may not entertain the suit." The judgment of the district court is affirmed.

MYLEGALSTUDIESLAB

MyLegalStudiesLab Virtual Law Office Experience Assignments

Complete the pre-test, study plan, and post-test for this chapter and answer the Legal Applications questions as assigned. These will help you confirm your mastery of the concepts and their application to legal scenarios. Then complete the Virtual Law Office assignments as assigned by your instructor. These assignments are designed to develop your workplace skills. Completing the assignments for this chapter will result in producing the following documents for inclusion in your portfolio:

VLOE 7.1

1. Completed Client Interview Form, including a short summary of the accident
2. Client summary from AbacusLaw
3. Calendar of the statute of limitations in AbacusLaw
4. A client engagement and fee letter

CHAPTER

8

Criminal Law and Procedure

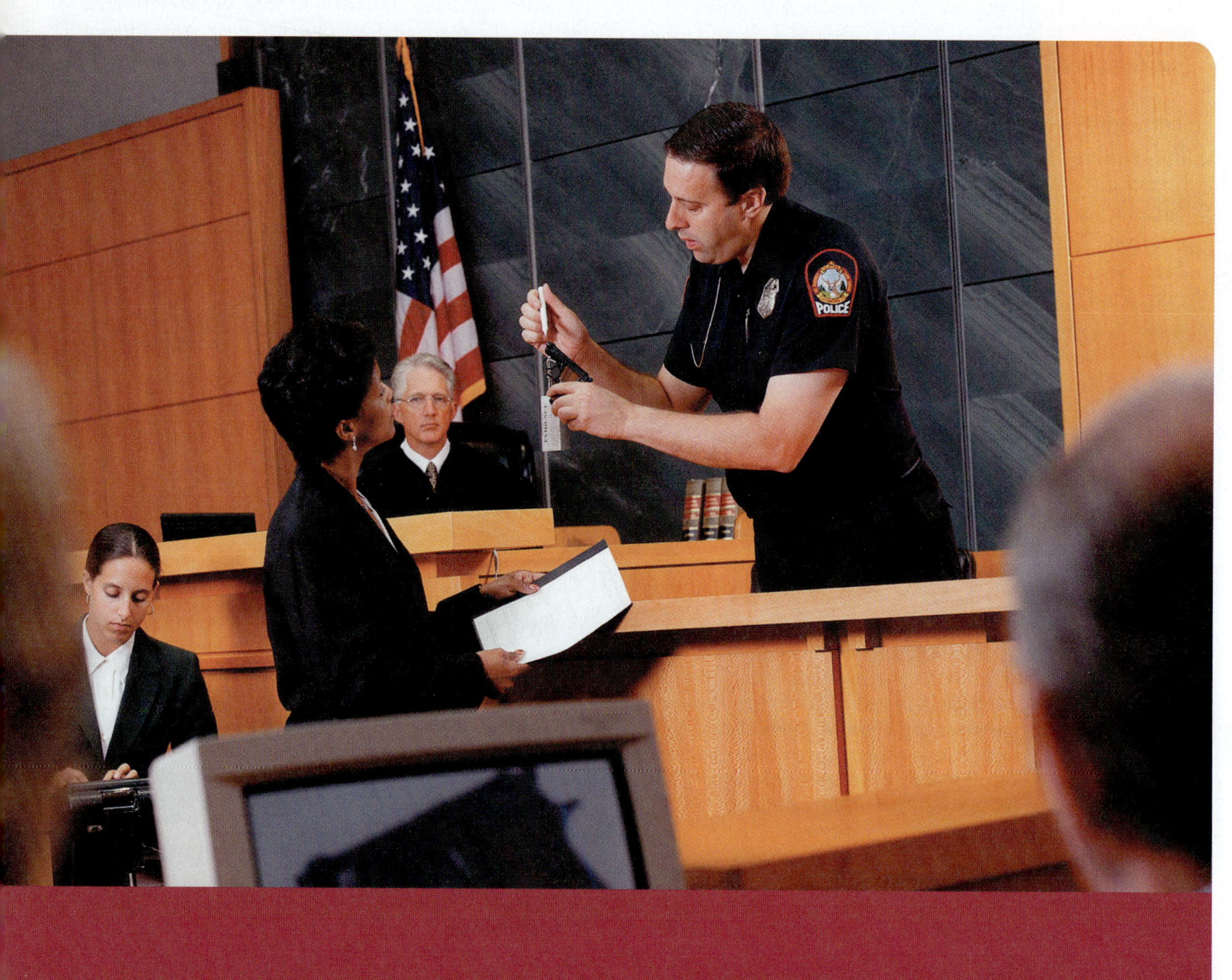

Paralegals at Work

You are a paralegal at a law firm that does criminal defense work. The law firm specializes in defending executives in white-collar criminal law matters. You work for Ms. Heather Josephson, a renowned attorney in the area of white-collar criminal defense. She informs you that the law firm has been retained to represent Mr. Keith Day, an executive now facing charges for alleged white-collar crimes. You will assist Ms. Josephson in preparing the defense of Mr. Day.

Ms. Josephson explains that Mr. Day was the founder and Chief Executive Officer (CEO) of the E-Run Corporation, one of the largest companies in the United States. Mr. Day has been served a complaint, *United States v. Day*, in which Mr. Day has been charged by the federal government with various crimes, including financial fraud.

The complaint alleges that Mr. Day, Mr. Don Scott, E-Run Corporation's Chief Financial Officer (CFO), and other corporate officers agreed to "cook the books" of the corporation to make the corporation appear to make huge profits when it was not. The complaint further alleges that the executives failed to report large debts on the company's financial statements, causing it to show a large financial profit, when in fact the corporation was losing money. When the alleged misdeeds were discovered, the E-Run Corporation failed and had to declare bankruptcy. Shareholders lost their entire investments, and the creditors of the corporation were not paid.

LEARNING OBJECTIVES

After studying this chapter, you should be able to:

1. Recognize the professional opportunities for paralegals in criminal law.
2. Identify and describe the parties and attorneys to a criminal action.
3. Describe pretrial criminal procedure.
4. Describe a criminal trial.
5. List and define the essential elements of a crime.
6. Describe the most important common crimes.
7. Explain the Fourth Amendment's protection from unreasonable search and seizure.
8. Describe the Fifth Amendment's privilege against self-incrimination, and describe *Miranda* rights.
9. Describe the Sixth Amendment's right to a public jury trial.
10. Explain a paralegal's duty to report criminal activity.

> It is better that ten guilty persons escape, than that one innocent suffer.
>
> Sir William Blackstone, *Commentaries on the Laws of England* (1809)

In addition, the complaint alleges that Mr. Day, Mr. Scott, and other officers stole money directly from the corporation and diverted corporate cash to their own personal bank accounts. Mr. Day is alleged to have used the mail, telephones, and computers to carry out the entire scheme. The complaint also alleges that Mr. Day purchased a restaurant and moved the stolen money through it to make it seem that the restaurant generated the cash.

Ms. Josephson explains that immediately after being served with the complaint, federal government agents asked Mr. Day many questions concerning his employment at E-Run Corporation and his involvement in the financial affairs of the company. Mr. Day explained to the agents how the fraud worked and his involvement in this situation. Ms. Josephson asked Mr. Day whether the federal agents had read him any rights before they questioned him, and Mr. Day answered that they had not. Mr. Day is now concerned that the information he told the federal agents "may come back to haunt him."

Ms. Josephson says that the federal government kept a wiretap on Mr. Day's telephones for twelve months, but the government failed to obtain a warrant to conduct this surveillance. Further, Mr. Day said that his spouse "knows everything," and she is willing to be a witness against him at trial. Also, the federal government has reached a plea bargain with Mr. Scott that grants Mr. Scott immunity from prosecution in return for his testimony against Mr. Day at trial.

Learning Objective 1

Recognize the professional opportunities for paralegals in criminal law.

INTRODUCTION FOR THE PARALEGAL

Paralegals who work for criminal lawyers must have knowledge of the criminal legal process. Some private lawyers specialize in representing clients accused of criminal wrongdoing. Other lawyers work for the government, either as prosecutors representing the government in criminal cases, or as government-appointed defense counsel representing defendants who cannot afford a private attorney.

For members of society to coexist peacefully and for commerce to flourish, people and their property must be protected from injury by other members of society. **Criminal laws** provide an incentive for persons to act reasonably in society and impose penalties on persons who injure others.

There can be no equal justice where the kind of trial a man gets depends on the amount of money he has.

Justice Black
Griffin v. Illinois, 351 U.S. 12 (1956)

Many common crimes involve taking or destroying property, such as arson, robbery, burglary, larceny, and other forms of theft. Other common crimes involve injury or death to other persons, such as the crimes of murder, rape, assault, and battery.

Another category of crimes is often referred to as "white-collar crimes." They are given this name because they are often committed by persons who are executives or employees of businesses. These crimes include bribery, civil fraud, and securities fraud. A business is liable for the crimes committed by its employees on behalf of the business.

A person charged with a crime in the United States is presumed innocent until proven guilty. The **burden of proof** is on the government to prove that the accused is guilty of the crime charged. The accused must be found guilty "**beyond a reasonable doubt**." Conviction requires a unanimous jury vote.

Paralegals who work in the criminal law field must have a thorough understanding of the provisions in the U.S. Constitution that protect a person charged with a

CAREER OPPORTUNITIES FOR PARALEGALS IN CRIMINAL LAW

Criminal law provides abundant job opportunities for paralegals. The criminal law system is extremely large and requires the services of thousands of lawyers, and by extension, thousands of paralegals. The job opportunities for paralegals are quite varied in this area.

Most of the crimes prosecuted in the United States involve violations of state laws. These include many violent crimes against persons and property, such as assault, battery, robbery, and rape, as well as nonviolent crimes, such as illegal drug sales, fraud, and other violations.

In each case when a defendant is charged with a violation of state law, the state files a complaint against the alleged criminal. These actions are brought by prosecutors in the local jurisdiction where the crime has been alleged to have been committed. The prosecutors are lawyers who are state government employees. The prosecutor is responsible for investigating the alleged crime and for assembling the government's case against the defendant. Paralegals have many opportunities to work for these prosecuting attorneys.

Paralegals also have opportunities to work for the attorneys who defend persons charged with criminal offenses. Many defendants in criminal cases cannot afford their own attorneys, so the government provides attorneys to represent them. These defense attorneys frequently are government employees and are referred to as public defenders. The paralegals who work for them are also state government employees. Sometimes the court will appoint an attorney in private practice to represent a defendant, and the government pays this attorney's fees.

Prosecutors and defense attorneys typically rely heavily on paralegals to conduct investigations, perform legal research, prepare documents to be filed with the court, and assist at trials. Thus, many job opportunities are available for paralegals in this area.

Many opportunities also exist in the area of prosecuting and defending matters involving white-collar crimes. These crimes involve allegations of fraud, securities violations, money laundering, racketeering, and other nonviolent activities by individuals, businesses, and other organizations. White-collar defendants may be charged with violating either state or federal criminal laws, depending on the crimes they are alleged to have committed. White-collar criminal cases are often complex. Substantial efforts are required for investigating and preparing them for trial, and paralegals are indispensable in these efforts.

In a white-collar criminal case, whether in state or federal court, the government employs lawyers to prosecute the case against the accused. In state cases, the lawyers are state employees, and in federal cases, the lawyers are federal employees. There are excellent opportunities at both the state and federal levels for paralegals to assist these prosecuting attorneys.

On the other side, white-collar defendants, who are often wealthy individuals or corporations, often have the economic ability to employ private attorneys to represent them. Many paralegals work for the law firms who represent these white-collar persons and businesses, or for the legal departments of the defendant corporations.

There will always be criminals and criminal defendants—and therefore, there will always be a need for attorneys to represent the government on one side and the defendant on the other. Consequently, there will always be a need for paralegals on both sides, and the area of criminal law will remain an important source of employment for paralegals.

crime in the United States. These include the protections against unreasonable search and seizure, against self-incrimination, against double jeopardy, and against cruel and unusual punishment, and they guarantee the right to a public jury trial.

In this important and exciting area of the law, paralegals will be called on to conduct research and assist lawyers in preparing for trial. This chapter provides the knowledge that paralegals will be expected to know regarding crimes, criminal procedure, and constitutional safeguards relating to criminal charges.

The feature above discusses the career opportunities for paralegal professionals in criminal law.

Parties and Attorneys of a Criminal Action

Learning Objective 2
Identify and describe the parties and attorneys of a criminal action.

In a criminal lawsuit, the government, rather than a private party, is the **plaintiff.** The government prosecuting a case can either be the federal government or a state or territorial government. The government is represented by a **prosecuting attorney** (or **prosecutor**). The lawyer who prosecutes criminal cases on behalf of a state is often called the state's attorney or **district attorney (DA).** The lawyer who prosecutes federal criminal cases is called the **United States Attorney**.

Exhibit 8.1 **Complaint filed by the United States government in *United States of America v. Bernard L. Madoff***

08 MAG 2735 COPY

Approved: ______________________
MARC LITT
Assistant United States Attorney

Before: HONORABLE DOUGLAS F. EATON
United States Magistrate Judge
Southern District of New York

---------------------------------------x

UNITED STATES OF AMERICA	:	**COMPLAINT**
- v. -	:	Violation of 15 U.S.C. §§ 78j(b), 78ff; 17 C.F.R. § 240.10b-5
BERNARD L. MADOFF,	:	
Defendant.	:	
	:	COUNTY OF OFFENSE: NEW YORK

---------------------------------------x

SOUTHERN DISTRICT OF NEW YORK, ss.:

THEODORE CACIOPPI, being duly sworn, deposes and says that he is a Special Agent with the Federal Bureau of Investigation, and charges as follows:

COUNT ONE
(Securities Fraud)

1. From at least in or about December 2008 through the present, in the Southern District of New York and elsewhere, BERNARD L. MADOFF, the defendant, unlawfully, wilfully and knowingly, by the use of the means and instrumentalities of interstate commerce and of the mails, directly and indirectly, in connection with the purchase and sale of securities, would and did use and employ manipulative and deceptive devices and contrivances in violation of Title 17, Code of Federal Regulations, Section 240.10b-5, by (a) employing devices, schemes, and artifices to defraud; (b) making untrue statements of material facts and omitting to state material facts necessary in order to make the statements made, in the light of the circumstances under which they were made, not misleading, and (c) engaging in acts, practices, and courses of business which operated and would operate as a fraud and deceit upon persons, to wit, MADOFF deceived investors by operating a securities business in which he traded and lost investor money, and then paid certain

Exhibit 8.1 Complaint filed by the United States government in *United States of America v. Bernard L. Madoff* (continued)

investors purported returns on investment with the principal received from other, different investors, which resulted in losses of approximately billions of dollars.

(Title 15, United States Code, Sections 78j(b) & 78ff; Title 17, Code of Federal Regulations, Section 240.10b-5; and Title 18, United States Code, Section 2.)

****

WHEREFORE, deponent prays that BERNARD L. MADOFF, the defendant, be imprisoned, or bailed, as the case may be.

DEC 11 2008

THEODORE CACIOPPI
Special Agent
Federal Bureau of Investigation

Sworn to before me this
______ day of December, 2008

/s/ Douglas F. Eaton
HONORABLE DOUGLAS F. EATON
UNITED STATES MAGISTRATE JUDGE
SOUTHERN DISTRICT OF NEW YORK

The accused, usually either an individual or a business, is the **defendant**, who is represented by a **defense attorney.** Sometimes the accused will hire a private attorney to represent him or her if he or she can afford to do so. If the accused cannot afford a lawyer, the government will provide one free of charge. This defense attorney employed by the government is often called a **public defender.**

Criminal Procedure

Learning Objective 3
Describe pretrial criminal procedure.

The court procedure for initiating and maintaining a criminal action is quite detailed, and encompasses both pretrial procedures and the actual trial. Pretrial criminal procedure consists of several distinct stages: *arrest*, *indictment* or *information*, *arraignment*, and in some cases, *plea bargaining*.

The **Federal Rules of Criminal Procedure** (FRCP) govern all criminal proceedings in the courts of the United States, as stated in FRCP Rule 1. Each state has its own rules of criminal procedure that govern criminal proceedings in its courts.

Criminal Complaint

In criminal cases, the government must file a **criminal complaint** charging the defendant with the alleged crimes. FRCP Rule 3 defines a complaint as follows:

> The complaint is a written statement of the essential facts constituting the offense charged. It must be made under oath before a magistrate judge or, if none is reasonably available, before a state or local judicial officer.

States also have their own requirements for the information to be contained in a criminal complaint.

A complaint is usually filed after the government has obtained sufficient evidence to charge the accused with a crime. This government investigation may consist of observing the accused's activities, monitoring wiretaps, obtaining information from informants or witnesses, and obtaining evidence through other means.

A copy of a criminal complaint filed by the United States government appears as Exhibit 8.1.

Arrest

Arrest warrant A document authorizing a person to be detained based upon a showing of probable cause that the person committed the crime.

Probable cause Evidence of the substantial likelihood that a person either committed or is about to commit a crime.

Before the police can arrest a person for committing a crime, they often must obtain an **arrest warrant** based upon a showing of **probable cause**—meaning there is a substantial likelihood that the person either committed or is about to commit a crime.

Example The police are tipped off by a source that a person has been involved in selling illegal drugs. If the judge finds that the information is reliable and that it constitutes probable cause, the judge will issue an arrest warrant.

If the police do not have time to obtain a warrant, they may still arrest the suspect. **Warrantless arrests** are also judged by the standard of probable cause. A warrantless arrest can be made by the police if they arrive during the commission of a crime, when a person is fleeing from the scene of a crime, or when it is likely that evidence will be destroyed.

After a person is arrested, he or she is taken to the police station for *booking*—the administrative procedure for fingerprinting and recording information about the person.

Bail

Web Exploration

Go to **www.fbi.gov** and click on "Most Wanted" and then "Ten Most Wanted Fugitives." Who is the number-one fugitive listed, and what crime is he or she wanted for?

When a person is arrested, a **bail** amount is usually set. If the arrested person "posts" the amount of the bail, he or she can be released from prison until the date of the trial. Bail will not be set if the crime is especially severe (such as murder) or if the arrestee is a flight risk who might not later show up for trial.

Most arrestees (or a relative or friend) pay a professional bail bonds person who operates a business to post the **bail bond.** Bail bonds persons usually require payment of 10 percent of the bail in order to post bond. If the bail is set at $100,000, then the amount for payment of the bail bond is $10,000. The bail bonds person keeps this $10,000 payment, and guarantees the court that he or she will pay the court $100,000 if the arrestee does not show up for trial. If this happens, the bail bonds person will attempt to recover the amount of the bond from the arrestee. Bail bonds persons often require collateral (such as the title to an automobile or a second mortgage on a house) before they issue a bail bond.

Example Susan is arrested for possession of an illegal narcotic. The court sets a bail of $100,000. Susan can pay $100,000 to the court and get out of jail until the time of her trial. At the time of her trial, she will be paid back the $100,000. If Susan cannot post bail herself, she can pay a bail bonds person $10,000 to post bail.

Indictment or Information

Accused persons must be formally charged with a crime before they can be brought to trial. This usually is done by the issuance of a **grand jury indictment** or a **magistrate's (judge's) information.** Evidence of serious crimes, such as murder, is usually presented to a **grand jury.**

FRCP Rule 6 states that a federal grand jury shall consist of between 6 and 23 citizens who are charged with evaluating the evidence presented by the government. State grand juries provide for a varying number of grand jurors. Grand jurors sit for a fixed time, such as one year.

If the grand jury determines that there is sufficient evidence to hold the accused for trial, it issues an **indictment.** Excerpts of a federal grand jury indictment appear as Exhibit 8.2. Note that the grand jury does not determine guilt. If an indictment is issued, the accused will be held until trial.

Indictment The charge of having committed a crime (usually a felony), based on the judgment of a grand jury.

> Example Dominick is arrested for first-degree murder. Usually, with this type of crime, a defendant will not be granted bail and remains in prison. Several months later, the government prosecutors will present evidence to the Grand Jury concerning Dominick's alleged crime. Dominick's lawyer will also introduce evidence claiming that Dominick did not commit the crime. After hearing this evidence, the Grand Jury issues an indictment. The Grand Jury has not made a decision that Dominick is guilty, but only decided there is enough evidence to hold him for a future trial for first-degree murder. In this case, Dominick probably will be denied bail and will remain in prison until the trial.

For lesser crimes (such as burglary or shoplifting), the accused will be brought before a **magistrate (judge),** who will decide whether there is enough evidence to hold the accused for trial. If the magistrate decides that there is enough evidence, he or she will issue an **information.** The case against the accused is dismissed if neither an indictment nor an information is issued.

Information The charge of having committed a crime (usually a misdemeanor), based on the judgment of a judge or magistrate.

Arraignment

If an indictment or information is issued, the accused is brought before a court for an **arraignment** proceeding during which the accused is (1) informed of the charges against him or her, and (2) asked to enter a *plea.* The accused may plead **guilty, not guilty,** or *nolo contendere.*

Arraignment A hearing during which the accused is brought before a court and is (1) informed of the charges against him or her and (2) asked to enter a plea.

A plea of ***nolo contendere*** means that the accused agrees to the imposition of a penalty but does not admit guilt. A *nolo contendere* plea cannot be used as evidence of liability against the accused at a subsequent civil trial. Corporate defendants often enter this plea. The government has the option of accepting a *nolo contendere* plea or requiring the defendant to plead guilty or not guilty. Depending on the nature of the crime, the accused may be released upon posting bail.

> Example The U.S. government sues a company for criminally violating federal pollution control laws. The company pleads *nolo contendere* and the government accepts the plea. The government and the company agree that the company must pay $100,000 in criminal fines but the company does not admit guilt.

Plea Bargaining

Sometimes the accused and the government enter into a **plea bargain agreement.** The government engages in plea bargaining to save costs, avoid the risks of a trial, and prevent further overcrowding of the prisons. This arrangement allows the accused to admit to a lesser crime than charged. In return, the government agrees to impose a lesser penalty or sentence than might have been obtained had the case gone to trial. In the federal system, more than 90 percent of defendants plead guilty rather than go to trial.

Plea bargain agreement An agreement in which the accused admits to a lesser crime than charged. In return, the government agrees to impose a lesser sentence than might have been obtained had the case gone to trial.

Exhibit 8.2 **Grand jury indictment of the Court of Common Pleas, County of Summit, Ohio**

COPY

DANIEL M. HORRIGAN

2008 APR -9 PM 1:28

SUMMIT COUNTY
CLERK OF COURTS

IN THE COURT OF COMMON PLEAS
COUNTY OF SUMMIT, OHIO

INDICTMENT TYPE: BINDOVER CASE NO. 2008-03-0968

INDICTMENT FOR: MURDER (1) 2903.02(B) SF; FELONIOUS ASSAULT (1) 2903.11(A)(1) F-2; ENDANGERING CHILDREN (1) 2919.22(B)(1) F-2; ENDANGERING CHILDREN (1) 2919.22(A) F-3

In the Common Pleas Court of Summit County, Ohio, of the term of MARCH in the year of our Lord, Two Thousand and Eight.

The Jurors of the Grand Jury of the State of Ohio, within and for the body of the County aforesaid, being duly impaneled and sworn and charged to inquire of and present all offenses whatever committed within the limits of said County, on their oaths, IN THE NAME AND BY THE AUTHORITY OF THE STATE OF OHIO,

COUNT ONE

DO FIND AND PRESENT That **CRAIG R. WILSON** on or about the 12th day of March, 2008, in the County of Summit and State of Ohio, aforesaid, did commit the crime of **MURDER** in that he did cause the death of C.W. (DOB: 1/1/2008) as a proximate result of **CRAIG R. WILSON** committing or attempting to commit Endangering Children and/or Felonious Assault, an offense of violence that is a felony of the first or second degree, in violation of Section 2903.02(B) of the Ohio Revised Code, A SPECIAL FELONY, contrary to the form of the statute in such case made and provided and against the peace and dignity of the State of Ohio.

COUNT TWO

And the Grand Jurors of the State of Ohio, within and for the body of the County of Summit aforesaid, on their oaths in the name and by the authority of the State of Ohio, DO FURTHER FIND AND PRESENT, that **CRAIG R. WILSON** on or about the 12th day of March, 2008, in the County of Summit aforesaid, did commit the crime of **FELONIOUS ASSAULT** in that he did knowingly cause serious physical harm to C.W. (DOB: 1/1/2008), in violation of Section 2903.11(A)(1) of the Ohio Revised Code, A FELONY OF THE SECOND DEGREE, contrary to the form of the statute in such case made and provided and against the peace and dignity of the State of Ohio.

(continued)

Exhibit 8.2 Grand jury indictment of the Court of Common Pleas, County of Summit, Ohio *(continued)*

****

Sherri Bevan Walsh /mk

SHERRI BEVAN WALSH, Prosecutor/pw

Prosecutor, County of Summit, by

Margaret Kanelli

Date: 4-8-08

Grand Jury foreperson/Deputy Foreperson

A TRUE BILL

COPY

Case No. 2008-03-0968
Page Three of Three

ORDER

TO: DREW ALEXANDER, Sheriff
County of Summit, Ohio

CRAIG R. WILSON

THAT he has been indicted by the Grand Jury of the County of Summit and that the person named in the indictment is hereby ordered to personally appear for the purpose of arraignment at 8 a.m. on the **11th** day of **April, 2008** before the Honorable Magistrate John H. Shoemaker, Judge of the Court of Common Pleas in the County of Summit Courthouse at 209 South High Street, Akron, Ohio, and THAT FAILURE TO APPEAR WILL RESULT IN A WARRANT FOR ARREST, FORFEITURE OF BOND, IF ANY, OR ADDITIONAL CRIMINAL CHARGES FOR FAILURE TO APPEAR UNDER O.R.C. SECTION 2937.99.

I certify that this is a true copy of the original indictment on file in this office.

DANIEL HORRIGAN, Clerk
Court of Common Pleas

By____________________________
Deputy

Example Harold is arrested for the crime of felony burglary, which carries a typical penalty of three years in jail if he is found guilty. The government and Harold reach a plea bargain where he will plead guilty to misdemeanor burglary and agree to a sentence of six months in jail and three years' probation.

Criminal Trial

Learning Objective 4
Describe a criminal trial.

A **criminal trial** and a civil trial have many similarities. The functions of the judge and jury are the same. The jury acts as the **trier of fact.** In cases in which the defendant exercises the right to proceed without a jury, also known as a **bench trial** or **waiver trial,** the judge acts as the trier of fact. The judge also determines questions of law. He or she acts as the arbiter of procedural rules covering the conduct of the trial, applies the law to findings of fact, and determines the sentence, fine, or other penalty if the defendant is found guilty. In some severe cases, such as murder trials, the jury may also play a role in deciding the sentence.

Trier of fact The jury is the trier of fact.

The order and presentation of evidence also are similar to those in civil cases. The prosecution goes first and puts on its case, followed by the defense's presentation of its evidence. In addition, motions for dismissal at the close of the prosecution's case are similar to those in the civil action.

Web Exploration

Go to **http://www.justice.gov/usao/nj/Press/files/pdffiles/2012/Depiro,%20Stephen%20et%20al.%20S2%20Indictment.pdf** and read a grand jury indictment of the Genovese Organized Crime Family.

A significant difference from civil litigation in many criminal cases is the concern for protecting the record (the trial transcript). Defense counsel tends to be especially concerned with making appropriate objections on the record that can be used as the basis for an appeal. Prosecutors are also very careful not to say anything on the record that the defendant can use as a basis for appeal in the event of a conviction.

Pretrial Discovery

A limited amount of **pretrial discovery** is permitted, with substantial restrictions to protect the identity of government informants and to prevent intimidation of witnesses. Defense attorneys often file motions to suppress evidence, which ask the court to exclude evidence from trial that the defendant believes the government obtained illegally. The government is also under an obligation to provide **exculpatory evidence** to the defense attorney.

Under the Federal Rules of Criminal Procedure Rule 16, upon the defendant's request, the government must disclose and make available for inspection, copying, or photographing any relevant written or recorded statements made by the defendant that are within the possession, custody, or control of the government; the existence of which is known; or where the exercise of due diligence may become known to the attorney for the government.

Determination of Guilt

At a criminal trial, unlike a civil trial, all jurors must agree *unanimously* before the accused is found guilty of the crime charged. If even one juror disagrees (he or she has reasonable doubt) about the guilt of the accused, the accused cannot be found guilty of the crime charged. If all of the jurors agree that the accused did not commit the crime, the accused is **innocent** of the crime charged.

After trial, the following rules apply:

- If the defendant is found guilty, he or she may appeal.
- If the defendant is found innocent, the government cannot appeal.
- If the jury cannot come to a unanimous decision about the defendant's guilt, the jury is considered a **hung jury.** The government may choose to retry the case before a new judge and jury.

Hung jury A jury that does not come to a unanimous decision about the defendant's guilt. The government may choose to retry the case.

Crimes

Learning Objective 5

List and define the essential elements of a crime.

A **crime** is defined as any act by an individual in violation of those duties that he or she owes to society. It is the breach of a law that requires the wrongdoer to make amends to the public. Many activities have been considered crimes throughout the ages, whereas other crimes are of recent origin.

Crime A violation of a statute for which the government imposes a punishment.

Penal Codes and Regulatory Statutes

Statutes are the primary source of criminal law. Most states have adopted comprehensive **penal codes** that define in detail the activities that are crimes within their jurisdiction, and the penalties that will be imposed for committing these crimes. Federal crimes are defined by a comprehensive federal criminal code (Title 18 of the U.S. Code). In addition, state and federal **regulatory statutes** often provide for criminal violations and penalties. The state and federal legislatures are adding to the list of crimes continually.

Penal codes Statutes that define crimes.

Regulatory statutes Statutes, such as environmental laws, securities laws, and antitrust laws, that provide for criminal violations and penalties.

The penalty for committing a crime may consist of a fine, imprisonment, or some other form of punishment (such as probation). Generally, imprisonment is imposed to (1) incapacitate the criminal so he or she will not harm others in society, (2) provide a means to rehabilitate the criminal, (3) deter others from similar conduct, and (4) inhibit personal retribution by the victim.

Classification of Crimes

Crimes are classified as *felonies*, *misdemeanors*, or *violations*.

- **Felonies** are the most serious crimes. They include crimes that are ***mala in se***—inherently evil. Most crimes against the person (such as murder or rape) and certain business-related crimes (such as embezzlement or bribery) are felonies in most jurisdictions.

  Felonies are usually punishable by imprisonment. In some jurisdictions, first-degree murder is punishable by death. Federal law and some state laws have mandatory sentencing for specified crimes. Many statutes define different degrees of crimes (such as first-, second-, and third-degree murder), with each degree earning different penalties.
- **Misdemeanors** are less serious than felonies and include many crimes against property, such as vandalism or trespassing, and violations of regulatory statutes. Many of these offenses are treated as crimes that are ***mala prohibita***—not inherently evil, but prohibited by society. Misdemeanors carry lesser penalties than felonies—they are usually punishable by fine or imprisonment for one year or less.
- **Violations** are infractions such as traffic offenses and jaywalking, which are neither felonies nor misdemeanors. These offenses are usually punishable by a fine. Occasionally, a few days of imprisonment are imposed.

Intent Crimes

For a person to be found guilty of most crimes, a *criminal act* and *criminal intent* must be proven. To commit a **criminal act,** the defendant must have actually performed the prohibited act. Under the common law, actual performance of the criminal act is called the ***actus reus*** **(guilty act).** Under the Model Penal Code, the prohibited act may be analyzed in terms of conduct, circumstances, and results.

Actus reus ("Guilty act") The actual performance of the criminal act.

Example Killing someone without legal justification is an example of *actus reus*. Sometimes the omission of an act constitutes the requisite *actus reus*.

Example A crime has been committed if a taxpayer who is under a legal duty to file a tax return fails to do so. Merely thinking about committing a crime is not a crime, because no action has been taken.

Mens rea ("Evil intent") The possession of the requisite state of mind to commit a prohibited act.

To be found guilty of a crime, the accused must also be found to have possessed the requisite subjective state of mind, or **criminal intent** (also called specific or general intent) when the act was performed. This is called the ***mens rea*** **(evil intent)** under traditional common law analysis, and *culpable mental state* under the Model Penal Code. The Model Penal Code has four levels of culpable mental state:

1. Purposefully (or intentionally)
2. Knowingly
3. Recklessly
4. Negligently (in the criminal sense)

Web Exploration

Go to **http://wings.buffalo.edu/law/bclc/web/website/allcodes2.htm** and find the penal code of the state in which your college or university is located. Find and read your state's definition of murder.

Specific intent is found where the accused purposefully, intentionally, or with knowledge commits a prohibited act. **General intent** is found where there is a showing of recklessness or a lesser degree of mental culpability. The individual criminal statutes state whether the crime requires a showing of specific or general intent. Juries may infer a defendant's intent from the facts and circumstances of the case. There is no crime if the requisite *mens rea* cannot be proven. Thus, no crime is committed if one person accidentally injures another person.

Non-Intent Crimes

Non-intent crime A crime that imposes criminal liability without a finding of *mens rea* (intent).

Most states provide for certain **non-intent crimes.** The crime of **involuntary manslaughter** is often imposed for reckless conduct.

Example If a person drives an automobile at a very high rate of speed (such as 20 miles over the speed limit) on a city street and hits and kills a pedestrian, the driver most likely will be found guilty of the crime of involuntary manslaughter and be sentenced to jail.

Criminal Acts as a Basis for Tort Actions

An injured party may bring a **civil tort action** against a wrongdoer who has caused the party injury during the commission of a criminal act. Civil lawsuits are separate from the government's criminal action against the wrongdoer. In many cases, a person injured by a criminal act will not sue the criminal to recover civil damages because the criminal is often **judgment-proof**—that is, the criminal does not have the money to pay a civil judgment.

Learning Objective 6

Describe the most important common crimes.

Common Crimes

Crimes are often categorized as crimes against persons or crimes against property. The most important types of crimes against persons or property are discussed below.

Crimes Against the Person

Crimes against the person are considered by society to be the most heinous of crimes. The most common forms of crimes against the person are:

- **Assault:** A threat of immediate harm or offensive conduct toward another person coupled with apparent present ability to carry out the attempt. Actual physical contact is not necessary.
- **Battery:** Harmful or offensive physical contact with another person without his or her consent (such as punching someone in the face without just cause).
- **Mayhem:** Depriving another person of a member of his or her body (such as cutting off a person's finger).
- **Rape:** Sexual relations with a person forcibly and against the person's will.

- **Kidnapping:** Abduction and detention of a person against his or her will.
- **False imprisonment:** Confinement or restraint of another person without authority or justification and without his or her consent.

Murder

Murder is the unlawful killing of a human being by another with intent. Murder is often categorized by degrees—such as *first degree*, *second degree*, and *third degree*—depending on the circumstances of the case. Those convicted of murder receive the harshest jail sentences.

Murder The unlawful killing of a human being by another with intent.

Sometimes a murder is committed during the commission of another crime even though the criminal did not originally intend to commit murder. Most state laws hold the perpetrator liable for the crime of murder in addition to the other crime. This is called the **felony murder rule.** The intent to commit the murder is inferred from the intent to commit the other crime. Many states also hold accomplices liable under this doctrine.

In the following feature, a paralegal professional shares her experiences as a criminal prosecution paralegal.

Robbery

At common law, **robbery** is defined as the taking of personal property from another person or business by the use of fear or force. Robbery with a deadly weapon is generally considered aggravated robbery (or armed robbery) and carries a harsher penalty.

Robbery The taking of personal property from another person by the use of fear or force.

Examples If a robber demands that the victim surrender her purse and threatens the victim with a gun, this is the crime of robbery. If a person pickpockets somebody's wallet, it is not robbery because there has been no use of force or fear. It is instead a crime of theft.

Paralegals *in* Practice

PARALEGAL PROFILE

Debra K. Jennings

Debra K. Jennings is an Advanced Certified Paralegal in Trial Practice who works for the Campbell County Attorney's Office in Gillette, Wyoming. Of her 18 years as a paralegal, the first 11 were spent in civil practice and the last seven in criminal prosecution. Debra is a member of the National Association of Legal Assistants and currently serves on its Advanced Paralegal Certification board.

I'd like to share the following case description to help illustrate the various skills and knowledge needed by a criminal prosecution paralegal: A man slammed head-on into another vehicle while driving intoxicated at three times the legal limit. At impact, he was driving over 90 mph in a 65-mph zone, on a hill in a no-passing zone, while going around a double tractor-trailer. In the other car, the female driver and her young son were severely injured, and her mother died instantly. The drunk driver also sustained serious injuries. All three survivors eventually recovered.

The man was charged with one count of Aggravated Vehicular Homicide and two counts of Driving Under the Influence with Serious Bodily Injury. As the prosecuting attorney's paralegal, I first coordinated the gathering of information, materials, documents, reports, and evidence. This included researching the defendant's criminal history and identifying applicable laws and judicial decisions as they pertained to the case facts. All relevant information was analyzed and organized.

Next, my writing and communication skills were called into play. I prepared written explanatory material on laws and recommended courses of action. I then helped the prosecutor prepare legal arguments and write pleadings, traverses, motions, and briefs. I also assisted with hearing and pre-trial groundwork. This included communicating with other agencies and law enforcement, interviewing and preparing witnesses, performing background checks of the potential jury pool, preparing exhibits and trial notebooks, as well as discussing legal issues with the prosecutor.

In the end, the evidence and arguments presented were overwhelming. The driver responsible for the crash eventually pleaded guilty. He was sentenced to 18 to 20 years on Count I and 9 to 10 years each on Counts II and III, all to run consecutively with one another. As you can see from this case, the key to any paralegal's success is being organized and able to multi-task. Educationally, the social sciences provide a great background. The bottom line: remember your real client is the attorney for whom you work.

Burglary

Burglary The taking of personal property from another's home, office, or other commercial building.

At common law, **burglary** is defined as "breaking and entering a dwelling at night" with the intent to commit a felony. Modern penal codes have broadened this definition to include daytime thefts from homes, offices, and other commercial buildings. In addition, the "breaking in" element has been abandoned by most modern definitions of burglary. Thus, unauthorized entering of a building through an unlocked door is sufficient. Aggravated burglary (or armed burglary) carries stiffer penalties.

> **Example** Harold breaks into Sharon's home and steals jewelry and other items. Harold is guilty of the crime of burglary because he entered a dwelling and committed theft.

Larceny

Larceny The taking of another's personal property other than from his or her person or building.

At common law, **larceny** is defined as the wrongful and fraudulent taking of another person's personal property that is not robbery or burglary. The taking of most kinds of personal property—including tangible property, trade secrets, computer programs, and other business property—is larceny. Neither the use of force nor the entry of a building is required. Stealing of automobiles and car stereos and pickpocketing are examples of larceny. Some states distinguish between grand larceny and petit larceny. This distinction depends on the value of the property taken.

Theft

Some states have dropped the distinction among the crimes of robbery, burglary, and larceny. Instead, these states group these crimes under the more general term **"theft."** Most of these states distinguish between grand theft and petit theft, depending on the value of the property taken.

Arson

Arson The willful or malicious burning of a building.

At common law, **arson** is defined as the malicious or willful burning of the dwelling of another person. Modern penal codes have expanded this definition to include the burning of all types of private, commercial, and public buildings.

> **Example** An owner of a motel that is not doing well financially burns down the motel to collect insurance proceeds. The owner is guilty of the crime of arson. If arson is found, the insurance company does not have to pay the proceeds of any insurance policy on the burned property.

Forgery

Forgery The fraudulent making or alteration of a written document that affects the legal liability of another person.

The crime of **forgery** occurs if a written document is fraudulently made or altered and that change affects the legal liability of another person.

> **Examples** Counterfeiting, falsifying public records, and materially altering legal documents are acts of forgery. One of the most common forms of forgery is the signing of another person's signature to a check or changing the amount of a check. Note that signing another person's signature without intent to defraud is not forgery. For instance, forgery is not committed if one spouse signs the other spouse's payroll check for deposit in a joint checking or savings account at the bank.

Extortion

Extortion Threat to expose something about another person unless that other person gives money or property. Often referred to as "blackmail."

The crime of **extortion** means obtaining property from another, with his or her consent, induced by wrongful use of actual or threatened force, violence, or fear. Extortion occurs when a person threatens to expose something about another person unless that other person gives money or property. Extortion of private persons is commonly called **blackmail.** The truth or falsity of the information is immaterial. Extortion of public officials is called extortion *"under color of official right."*

White-collar Crimes

Businesspersons are sometimes prone to commit certain types of crimes. These crimes are often referred to as **white-collar crimes,** and usually involve cunning and deceit rather than physical force. Many business and white-collar crimes are discussed in the paragraphs that follow.

White-collar crimes Crimes usually involving cunning and deceit rather than physical force.

Embezzlement

Unknown at common law, the crime of **embezzlement** is now a statutory offense. Embezzlement is the fraudulent conversion of property by a person to whom that property was entrusted. Typically, embezzlement is committed by an employer's employees, agents, or representatives (such as accountants, lawyers, trust officers, or treasurers). Embezzlers often try to cover their tracks by preparing false books, records, or entries.

Embezzlement The fraudulent conversion of property by a person to whom that property was entrusted.

The key element in embezzlement is that the stolen property was *entrusted* to the embezzler. This differs from robbery, burglary, and larceny, in which property is taken by someone not entrusted with the property.

Example A bank teller absconds with money that was deposited by customers. The employer (the bank) entrusted the teller to take deposits from its customers, and therefore the teller is guilty of embezzlement.

Criminal Fraud

Obtaining title to property through deception or trickery constitutes the crime of **criminal fraud,** also known as *false pretenses* or *deceit*. To prove fraud, the following elements must be shown:

Criminal fraud A crime that involves obtaining the title to property through deception or trickery. Also known as *"false pretenses* or *deceit."*

There are some frauds so well conducted that it would be stupidity not to be deceived by them.
C. C. Colton
Lacon, Volume 1 (1820)

1. ***The wrongdoer made a false representation of material fact.*** To be actionable as fraud, the misrepresentation must be of a past or existing material fact. Statements of opinion or predictions about the future generally do not form the basis for fraud.
2. ***The wrongdoer intended to deceive the innocent party.*** Thus, the person making the misrepresentation must either have had knowledge that the representation was false or made it without sufficient knowledge of the truth. This is called **scienter** (a "guilty mind").
3. ***The innocent party justifiably relied on the misrepresentation.*** A misrepresentation is not actionable unless the innocent party to whom the misrepresentation was directed acted upon it.
4. ***The innocent party was injured.*** To recover damages, the innocent party must prove that the fraud caused economic injury. The measure of damages is the difference between the value of the property as represented and the actual value of the property.

Example Robert Anderson, a stockbroker, promises Mary Greenberg, a prospective investor, that he will use any money she invests to purchase interests in oil wells. Based on this promise, Ms. Greenberg decides to make the investment. Mr. Anderson never intended to invest the money. Instead, he used the money for his personal needs. This is criminal fraud.

Bribery

Bribery is one of the most prevalent forms of white-collar crime. A bribe can be in the form of money, property, favors, or anything else of value. The crime of commercial bribery is the payment of bribes to private persons and businesses. This type of bribe is often called a **kickback** or a **payoff.** Intent is a necessary element of this crime. The offeror of a bribe commits the crime of bribery when the bribe is tendered. The

Bribery A crime in which one person gives another person money, property, favors, or anything else of value for a favor in return. Often referred to as a *"payoff"* or *"kickback."*

offeree is guilty of the crime of bribery when he or she accepts the bribe. The offeror can be found liable for the crime of bribery even if the person to whom the bribe is offered rejects the bribe.

Example Harriet Landers, as the purchasing agent for the ABCD Corporation, is in charge of purchasing equipment to be used by the corporation. Neal Brown, sales representative of a company that makes a type of equipment that is used by the ABCD Corporation, offers to pay her a 10 percent kickback if she buys equipment from him. She accepts the bribe and orders the equipment. Both parties are guilty of bribery.

At common law, the crime of bribery was defined as the giving or receiving of anything of value in payment for an "official act" by a public official. Public officials include legislators, judges, jurors, witnesses at trial, administrative agency personnel, and other government officials. Modern penal codes also make it a crime to bribe public officials.

Example A real estate developer who is constructing an apartment building cannot pay the building inspector to overlook a building code violation.

Criminal Conspiracy

Criminal conspiracy A crime in which two or more persons enter into an agreement to commit a crime, and an overt act is taken to further the crime.

When two or more persons enter into an *agreement* to commit a crime, it is called **criminal conspiracy.** To be liable for a criminal conspiracy, the conspirators must commit an **overt act** to further the crime. The crime itself does not have to be committed, however. The government usually brings criminal conspiracy charges if (1) the defendants have been thwarted in their efforts to commit the underlying crime, or (2) insufficient evidence is available to prove the underlying crime.

Example Two securities brokers agree by telephone to commit a securities fraud. They also obtain a list of potential victims and prepare false financial statements necessary for the fraud. Because they entered into an agreement to commit a crime and took overt action, the brokers are guilty of the crime of criminal conspiracy even if they didn't carry out the securities fraud.

New York Police Department, Times Square, New York City

Constitutional Safeguards

Suspected criminals are provided many rights and protections by both the U.S. Constitution and state constitutions. People in this country are guaranteed the right to be free from unreasonable searches and seizures, and any evidence obtained illegally is considered "tainted" evidence and cannot be used in court. People who are suspected of a criminal act may assert their right of privilege against self-incrimination and may choose not to testify at any pretrial proceedings or at trial. Parties have a right to a public trial by a jury of their peers. In addition, if convicted of a crime, the criminal cannot be subjected to cruel and unusual punishment.

When the framers drafted the U.S. Constitution, they included provisions that protect persons from unreasonable government intrusion and provide safeguards for those accused of crimes. Although these safeguards originally applied only to federal cases, the Fourteenth Amendment's Due Process Clause makes them applicable to state criminal law cases as well. The most important constitutional safeguards and privileges are discussed in the following paragraphs.

Fourth Amendment Protection Against Unreasonable Searches and Seizures

Learning Objective 7
Explain the Fourth Amendment's protection from unreasonable search and seizure.

The **Fourth Amendment** to the U.S. Constitution protects persons and corporations from overzealous investigative activities by the government. It protects the rights of the people from **unreasonable search and seizure** by the government and allows people to be secure in their persons, houses, papers, and effects.

Unreasonable search and seizure Any search and seizure by the government that violates the Fourth Amendment.

Search Warrants

Search and seizure by the government is lawful if it is "reasonable." **Search warrants** based on probable cause are necessary in most cases. If the police receive a tip from a reasonable source that someone is engaged in criminal activity, the police can present this information to a judge, who will issue a search warrant if he or she finds probable cause. These warrants specifically state the place and scope of the authorized search. General searches beyond the specified area are forbidden. A copy of a search warrant appears as Exhibit 8.3.

Search warrant A warrant issued by a court that authorizes the police to search a designated place for specified contraband, articles, items, or documents. A search warrant must be based on probable cause.

Warrantless Searches

Warrantless searches generally are permitted only (1) incident to arrest, (2) where evidence is in "plain view," or (3) when evidence will likely be destroyed. Warrantless searches are also judged by the probable-cause standard.

> **Example** The police are notified that a person of a certain description has committed a crime in a specific location. The police arrive on the scene and find a suspect nearby who meets the description. The police may conduct a warrantless search of the individual in order to protect the police from danger while making the arrest.

Search of Business Premises

Generally, the government does not have the right to search business premises without a search warrant on probable cause or pursuant to a warrantless search based on probable cause. However, businesses in certain hazardous and regulated industries are subject to warrantless searches if proper statutory procedures are met.

> **Examples** Sellers of firearms and liquor, coal mines, and automobile junkyards may be subject to warrantless searches.

A business may also give consent to search the premises, including employee desks and computers, because of the lack of an expectation of privacy in those items.

Exhibit 8.3 Search warrant of the federal U.S. district court

AO 93 (Rev. 01/09) Search and Seizure Warrant

UNITED STATES DISTRICT COURT

for the

In the Matter of the Search of)
(Briefly describe the property to be searched)
or identify the person by name and address)) Case No.
)
)
)

SEARCH AND SEIZURE WARRANT

To: Any authorized law enforcement officer

An application by a federal law enforcement officer or an attorney for the government requests the search of the following person or property located in the ______________ District of ______________________
(identify the person or describe the property to be searched and give its location):

The person or property to be searched, described above, is believed to conceal *(identify the person or describe the property to be seized)*:

I find that the affidavit(s), or any recorded testimony, establish probable cause to search and seize the person or property.

YOU ARE COMMANDED to execute this warrant on or before ______________________
(not to exceed 10 days)

❐ in the daytime 6:00 a.m. to 10 p.m. ❐ at any time in the day or night as I find reasonable cause has been established.

Unless delayed notice is authorized below, you must give a copy of the warrant and a receipt for the property taken to the person from whom, or from whose premises, the property was taken, or leave the copy and receipt at the place where the property was taken.

The officer executing this warrant, or an officer present during the execution of the warrant, must prepare an inventory as required by law and promptly return this warrant and inventory to United States Magistrate Judge

______________________________________.
(name)

❐ I find that immediate notification may have an adverse result listed in 18 U.S.C. § 2705 (except for delay of trial), and authorize the officer executing this warrant to delay notice to the person who, or whose property, will be searched or seized *(check the appropriate box)* ❐for ______ days *(not to exceed 30)*.
❐until, the facts justifying, the later specific date of ______________.

Date and time issued: ______________ ______________________________
Judge's signature

City and state: ______________ ______________________________
Printed name and title

Exhibit 8.3 Search warrant of the federal U.S. district court *(continued)*

AO 93 (Rev. 01/09) Search and Seizure Warrant (Page 2)

Return

Case No.:	Date and time warrant executed:	Copy of warrant and inventory left with:

Inventory made in the presence of :

Inventory of the property taken and name of any person(s) seized:

Certification

I declare under penalty of perjury that this inventory is correct and was returned along with the original warrant to the designated judge.

Date: ____________________

____
Executing officer's signature

____
Printed name and title

Exclusionary Rule

Exclusionary rule A rule that says evidence obtained from an unreasonable search and seizure can generally be prohibited from introduction at a trial or administrative proceeding against the person searched.

Evidence obtained from an unreasonable search and seizure is considered tainted evidence ("fruit of a poisonous tree"). Under the **exclusionary rule,** such evidence can be prohibited from introduction at a trial or administrative proceeding against the person searched. This evidence, however, is freely admissible against other persons.

The U.S. Supreme Court has created a *good-faith exception* to the exclusionary rule. This exception allows evidence otherwise obtained illegally to be introduced as evidence against the accused if the police officers who conducted the search reasonably believed they were acting pursuant to a lawful search warrant.

Learning Objective 8
Describe the Fifth Amendment's privilege against self-incrimination, and describe *Miranda* rights.

Fifth Amendment Privilege Against Self-Incrimination

The **Fifth Amendment** to the U.S. Constitution provides that no person "shall be compelled in any criminal case to be a witness against himself." Thus, a person cannot be compelled to give testimony against him- or herself. It is also improper for a jury to infer guilt from the defendant's exercise of his or her constitutional right to remain silent. A person who asserts this right is described as having "taken the Fifth." This protection applies to federal cases and is extended to state and local criminal cases through the Due Process Clause of the Fourteenth Amendment.

Self-incrimination The Fifth Amendment states that no person shall be compelled in any criminal case to be a witness against him- or herself.

The privilege against **self-incrimination** applies only to natural persons who are accused of crimes. Therefore, "artificial" persons (such as corporations and partnerships) cannot raise this protection against incriminating testimony. Thus, business records of corporations and partnerships are not protected from disclosure, even if they incriminate individuals who work for the business. But certain "private papers" of businesspersons (such as personal diaries) are protected from disclosure.

The Fifth Amendment protects only an individual from being forced to testify. It does not apply to nontestimonial evidence such as fingerprints, body fluids, and the like, which may be compelled without violating the Fifth Amendment.

Miranda Rights

Most people have not read and memorized the provisions of the U.S. Constitution. The U.S. Supreme Court recognized this fact when it decided the landmark case *Miranda v. Arizona*, 384 U.S. 436 86 S.Ct. 1602, 16 L.Ed.2d 694(1966), 1966 U.S. Lexis 2817. The Court held that the Fifth Amendment right against self-incrimination is not meaningful unless a criminal suspect has knowledge of this right. Therefore, the Supreme Court required that the following warning—colloquially referred to as the ***Miranda* rights**—be read to a criminal suspect before he or she is interrogated by the police or other government officials:

***Miranda* rights** Rights that a suspect must be informed of before being interrogated so that the suspect will not unwittingly give up his or her Fifth Amendment right.

- You have the right to remain silent.
- Anything you say can and will be used against you.
- You have the right to consult a lawyer and to have a lawyer present with you during interrogation.
- If you cannot afford a lawyer, a lawyer will be appointed to represent you free of charge.

Many police departments read a more detailed version of the *Miranda* rights that is designed to cover all issues that a detainee might encounter while in police custody. A detainee may also be asked to sign a statement acknowledging that the *Miranda* rights have been read to him or her. A copy of the *Miranda* rights appears as Exhibit 8.4. Although the holding in *Miranda* has been questioned, the U.S. Supreme Court recently upheld it in *Miranda v. Arizona*, 384 U.S. 436 86 S.Ct. 1602, 16 L.Ed.2d 694(1966),

Exhibit 8.4 ***Miranda* rights form**

MIRANDA RIGHTS

- You have the right to remain silent and refuse to answer questions. Do you understand?
- Anything you do say may be used against you in a court of law. Do you understand?
- You have the right to consult an attorney before speaking to the police and to have an attorney present during questioning now or in the future. Do you understand?
- If you cannot afford an attorney, one will be appointed for you before any questioning if you wish. Do you understand?
- If you decide to answer questions now without an attorney present you will still have the right to stop answering at any time until you talk to an attorney. Do you understand?
- Knowing and understanding your rights as I have explained them to you, are you willing to answer my questions without an attorney present?

1966 U.S. Lexis 2817, stating, "[w]e do not think there is justification for overruling *Miranda*. *Miranda* has become embedded in routine police practice to the point where the warnings have become part of our national culture."

Any statements or confessions obtained from a suspect prior to being read his or her *Miranda* rights can be excluded from evidence at trial.

The criminal is to go free because the constable has blundered.

Chief Judge Cardozo
People v. Defore (1926)

Example Margaret is arrested by the police for suspicion of using and distributing illegal narcotics. The police start asking her questions about these issues before reading Margaret her *Miranda* rights. During this questioning, Margaret admits to the offenses. Margaret's statements are inadmissible at court because she had not been read her *Miranda* rights.

Immunity from Prosecution

On occasion, the government wants to obtain information from a suspect who has asserted his or her Fifth Amendment privilege against self-incrimination. The government can try to achieve this by offering the suspect **immunity from prosecution,** in which the government agrees not to use any evidence given by a person who has been granted immunity. Once immunity is granted, the suspect loses the right to assert his or her Fifth Amendment privilege.

Immunity from prosecution The government's agreement not to use against a person any evidence given by that person.

Grants of immunity often are given when the government wants the suspect to give information that will lead to the prosecution of other, more important criminal suspects. Partial grants of immunity are also available. For example, a suspect may be granted immunity from prosecution for a serious crime but not for a lesser crime, in exchange for information. Some persons who are granted immunity are placed in witness protection programs in which they are given a new identity, are relocated, and are found new employment.

Attorney–Client Privilege

To obtain a proper defense, the accused person must be able to tell his or her attorney facts about the case without fear that the attorney will be called as a witness against the accused. The **attorney–client privilege** is protected by the Fifth Amendment. Either the client or the attorney can raise this privilege. For the privilege to apply, the information must be told to the attorney in his or her capacity as an attorney, and not as a friend, neighbor, or other similar relationship.

Attorney–client privilege A rule that says a client can tell his or her lawyer anything about the case without fear that the attorney will be called as a witness against the client.

Example Cedric is accused of murder. He employs Hillary, a renowned criminal attorney, to represent him. During the course of their discussions, Cedric confesses to the murder. Hillary cannot be a witness against Cedric at his criminal trial. Cedric is permitted to tell his lawyer the truth so that she can prepare the best defense she can for him.

Other Privileges

The following privileges have also been recognized under the Fifth Amendment, where the accused may keep the following individuals from being a witness against him or her. The reasons are stated in parentheses.

- **Psychiatrist/psychologist–patient privilege** (the accused may tell the truth in order to seek help for his or her condition)
- **Priest/rabbi/minister/imam–penitent privilege** (the accused may tell the truth in order to repent, to obtain help, and to seek forgiveness for his or her deed)
- **Spouse–spouse privilege** (the couple can be open with one another so that they will remain together)
- **Parent–child privilege** (the family can be open with one another so that they will remain together)

However, a spouse or child who is injured by a spouse or parent (as in cases of domestic abuse) may testify against the accused. In addition, if the accused discloses that he or she is planning to commit a crime in the future (such as murder), then the accused's lawyer, psychiatrist, psychologist, priest, rabbi, minister, or imam is required to report this to the police or other relevant authorities.

The U.S. Supreme Court has held that there is no accountant–client privilege under federal law. Thus, an accountant could be called as a witness in cases involving federal securities laws, federal mail or wire fraud, or other federal crimes he or she learns of while working for a client. Nevertheless, approximately 20 states have enacted special statutes that create an **accountant–client privilege.** An accountant cannot be called as a witness against a client in a court action in a state where these statutes are in effect. Federal courts do not recognize these laws, however.

Fifth Amendment Protection Against Double Jeopardy

Double Jeopardy Clause
A clause of the Fifth Amendment that protects persons from being tried twice for the same crime.

The **Double Jeopardy Clause** of the Fifth Amendment protects persons from being tried twice for the same crime. For example, if the state tries a suspect for the crime of murder and the suspect is found innocent, the state cannot bring another trial against the accused for the same crime. But if the same criminal act involves several different crimes, the accused may be tried for each of the crimes without violating the Double Jeopardy Clause. For example, if the accused is alleged to have killed two people during a robbery, the accused may be tried for each of the two murders and for the robbery.

If the same act violates the laws of two or more jurisdictions, each jurisdiction may try the accused. For instance, if an accused person kidnaps a person in one state and takes the victim across a state border into another state, the act violates the laws of two states and the federal government. Thus, three jurisdictions can prosecute the accused without violating the Double Jeopardy Clause.

If an accused is tried once and the jury reaches a hung jury—that is, the verdict is not unanimous—then the government can retry the case against the accused without violating the Double Jeopardy Clause.

Example The government tries a defendant for the crime of murder, and the jury reaches a 10 to 2 verdict—that is, 10 jurors vote guilty and two jurors vote not guilty. This is a hung jury. Since no decision was reached, the government may, if it wants, retry the case against the accused. This does not violate the Double Jeopardy Clause.

Sixth Amendment Right to a Public Trial

Learning Objective 9
Describe the Sixth Amendment's right to a public jury trial.

The **Sixth Amendment** guarantees that criminal defendants have these rights:

1. The right to be tried by an impartial jury of the state or district in which the alleged crime was committed.
2. The right to confront (cross-examine) the witnesses against the accused.
3. The right to have the assistance of a lawyer.
4. The right to have a speedy trial.

The federal **Speedy Trial Act** requires that a criminal defendant be brought to trial within 70 days after indictment. 18 U.S.C. Section 3161(c)(1). States have similar acts that require speedy trials for criminal defendants. However, courts may grant continuances to serve the "ends of justice."

Eighth Amendment Protection Against Cruel and Unusual Punishment

The **Eighth Amendment** protects criminal defendants from **cruel and unusual punishment.**

This means the government cannot use torture. The Eighth Amendment does not prohibit capital punishment, but it does limit the form of capital punishment that is imposed. For example, the U.S. Supreme Court has held that injection by lethal dosage of drugs generally is not cruel and unusual punishment, and is permitted as a means of capital punishment.

Learning Objective 10
Explain a paralegal's duty to report criminal activity.

ETHICAL PERSPECTIVE

Paralegal's Duty to Report Criminal Activity

Ms. Gutierrez is a paralegal who works at a white-collar criminal defense law firm. Ms. Gutierrez works directly for Mr. Darrow, a partner at the law firm.

One day, Mr. Darrow requests that Ms. Gutierrez sit in on a meeting with him and a client of the firm. The client, Mr. Elliot, owns Beta Corporation. Mr. Elliot explains that he and Beta Corporation are under investigation by the federal government for engaging in criminal fraud, insider trading, wire fraud, and mail fraud. Mr. Elliot has hired Mr. Darrow and his law firm to represent him and the company during the federal investigation and possible criminal lawsuit. At the meeting, Mr. Elliot discloses that he wants to get cash out of Beta Corporation before the federal government goes any further with its investigation.

Mr. Darrow, who is an expert in white-collar criminal matters, tells Mr. Elliot he can accomplish this if Mr. Elliot starts another business that is secretly owned by Mr. Elliot through a front, transfers the cash from Beta Corporation to this new business, and then transfers the cash to a bank located in the Bahamas and into a bank account in Mr. Elliot's name. Mr. Darrow explains that the Bahamas has bank secrecy laws that prevent any party, including the United States government, from discovering the owner of and the amount of money in bank accounts that are located in the Bahamas.

Mr. Elliot asks Mr. Darrow if he will help him do this, and Mr. Darrow agrees. The actions that Mr. Elliot proposes, and that Mr. Darrow has agreed to help accomplish, would constitute criminal conspiracy, criminal fraud, money laundering, and other federal crimes. Ms. Gutierrez has been a witness to this conversation and agreement.

What should Ms. Gutierrez do?

PARALEGAL'S ETHICAL DECISION

State paralegal codes of ethics and professional responsibility provide that a paralegal who possesses knowledge of future criminal activity must report this knowledge to the appropriate authorities. This is true even if the paralegal has become aware

(continued)

of the information in a situation where the attorney–client privilege or the work product rule would normally protect such information from being disclosed.

Ms. Gutierrez owes an ethical duty to report the criminal conspiracy between Mr. Elliot and attorney Mr. Darrow to the appropriate authorities. This decision is difficult for a paralegal professional to make because it would implicate her supervising attorney. Even so, Ms. Gutierrez owes an ethical duty to report the criminal conspiracy, regardless of the potential consequences to her employment.

Concept Review *and* Reinforcement

LEGAL TERMINOLOGY

SUMMARY OF KEY CONCEPTS

Parties and Attorneys of a Criminal Action

Parties to a Criminal Lawsuit	*Plaintiff:* the government. *Defendant:* the person or business accused of the crime.
Attorneys in a Criminal Lawsuit	*Prosecuting attorney:* the attorney who represents the government. These can be: • District attorney (DA), who prosecutes criminal cases on behalf of the state. • United States Attorney, who prosecutes criminal cases on behalf of the federal government. *Defense attorney:* the attorney who represents the person or party accused of the crime. These can be: • Public defender: a government attorney who represents the accused. • Private attorney: a nongovernment attorney whom the accused hires to represent him or her.

Criminal Procedure

Pretrial Criminal Procedure	*Arrest:* The person is arrested pursuant to an arrest warrant based upon a showing of probable cause, or, where permitted, by a warrantless arrest. *Indictment or information:* Grand juries issue indictments; magistrates (judges) issue informations. These formally charge the accused with specific crimes. *Arraignment:* The accused is informed of the charges against him or her and enters a plea in court. The plea may be *not guilty*, *guilty*, or *nolo contendere*. *Plea bargaining:* The government and the accused may negotiate a settlement agreement wherein the accused agrees to admit to a lesser crime than charged.

Criminal Trial

Outcomes	*Conviction:* requires unanimous vote of jury. *Innocent:* requires unanimous vote of jury. *Hung jury:* nonunanimous vote of the jury; the government may prosecute the case again.
Crimes	A crime is an act done by a person in violation of certain duties that he or she owes to society, the breach of which the law provides a penalty for.
Penal Codes and Regulatory Statutes	Penal codes are state and federal statutes that define many crimes. Criminal conduct also is defined in many regulatory statutes.
Parties to a Criminal Lawsuit	*Plaintiff:* the government, which is represented by the prosecuting attorney or prosecutor or district attorney in the state court systems. In the federal system, this attorney is called the United States Attorney. *Defendant:* the person or business accused of the crime, who is represented by a defense attorney. If the defense attorney is a government attorney, that attorney is called a public defender.
Classification of Crimes	*Felonies:* the most serious kinds of crimes; *mala in se* (inherently evil); usually punishable by imprisonment. *Misdemeanors:* less serious crimes; usually punishable by fine or imprisonment for less than one year. Many are considered *mala prohibita* (not inherently evil, but prohibited by society). *Violations:* not a felony or a misdemeanor; generally punishable by a fine.
Elements of a Crime	Intent crimes require the following elements: *Actus reus:* guilty act. *Mens rea:* evil intent.

Non-intent Crimes	Non-intent crimes do not require intent. An example is the crime of involuntary manslaughter that can be based on reckless conduct, although death of the victim was not intended.
Common Crimes	
Crimes Against the Person	Crimes against the person include: • Assault • Battery • Mayhem • Rape • Kidnapping • False imprisonment
Murder	Murder is the unlawful killing of another human being with intent.
Robbery	Robbery is the taking of personal property from another by fear or force.
Burglary	Burglary is the unauthorized entering of a building to commit a felony.
Larceny	Larceny is the wrongful taking of another's property other than from his or her person or building.
Theft	Theft is the wrongful taking of another's property, whether by robbery, burglary, or larceny.
Arson	Arson is the malicious and willful burning of a building.
Forgery	Forgery is the fraudulent making or altering of a written document that affects the legal liability of another person.
Extortion	Extortion is the threat to expose something about another person unless that person gives up money or property. Also called *blackmail*.
White-Collar Crimes	
	White-collar crimes are those that tend to be committed by businesspersons and involve cunning and trickery rather than physical force.
Embezzlement	Embezzlement is the fraudulent conversion of property by a person to whom the property was entrusted.
Criminal Fraud	Criminal fraud involves obtaining the title to another's property through deception or trickery. Also called *false pretenses* or *deceit*.
Bribery	Bribery is the offer of payment of money or property or something else of value in return for an unwarranted favor. The payer of a bribe also is guilty of the crime of bribery. *Commercial bribery* is the offer of a payment of a bribe to a private person or a business. This often is referred to as a *kickback* or *payoff*. Bribery of a public official for an "official act" is a crime.
Constitutional Safeguards	
	The U.S. Constitution includes provisions that protect persons from unreasonable government intrusion and provide safeguards for those accused of crimes.

Fourth Amendment Protection Against Unreasonable Searches and Seizures

The Fourth Amendment protects persons and corporations from unreasonable searches and seizures.
Reasonable searches and seizures: based on probable cause are lawful.
Search warrant: stipulates the place and scope of the search.
Warrantless search: permitted only.
1. incident to an arrest.
2. where evidence is in plain view.
3. where it is likely that evidence will be destroyed.

Exclusionary rule: evidence obtained from an unreasonable search and seizure is tainted evidence that may not be introduced at a government proceeding against the person searched.
Business premises: protected by the Fourth Amendment, except that certain regulated industries may be subject to warrantless searches authorized by statute.

Fifth Amendment Privilege Against Self-Incrimination

The Fifth Amendment provides that no person "shall be compelled in any criminal case to be a witness against himself." A person asserting this privilege is said to have "taken the Fifth."
Nontestimonial evidence: evidence (such as fingerprints or body fluids) that is not protected.
Businesses: a privilege that applies only to natural persons; businesses cannot assert the privilege.
Miranda *rights:* a right of a criminal suspect to be informed of his or her Fifth Amendment rights before the suspect can be interrogated by the police or government officials.
Immunity from prosecution: granted by the government to obtain otherwise privileged evidence; the government agrees not to use the evidence given against the person who gave it.
Attorney–client privilege: An accused's lawyer cannot be called as a witness against the accused.
Other privileges: The following privileges have been recognized, with some limitations:
- psychiatrist/psychologist–patient
- priest/rabbi/minister/imam–penitent
- spouse–spouse
- parent–child

Accountant–client privilege: None recognized at the federal level. Some states recognize this privilege in state law actions.

Fifth Amendment Protection Against Double Jeopardy

The Fifth Amendment protects persons from being tried twice by the same jurisdiction for the same crime. If the act violates the laws of two or more jurisdictions, each jurisdiction may try the accused.

Sixth Amendment Right to a Public Trial

The Sixth Amendment guarantees criminal defendants the following rights:
1. to be tried by an impartial jury
2. to confront the witness
3. to have the assistance of a lawyer
4. to have a speedy trial (Speedy Trial Law)

Eighth Amendment Protection Against Cruel and Unusual Punishment

The Eighth Amendment protects criminal defendants from cruel and unusual punishment. Capital punishment is permitted.

WORKING THE WEB

1. Go to the website of Crime Stoppers USA at http://www.crimestopusa.com. Read about what the organization does.
2. Go to the website of the Federal Bureau of Investigation (FBI) at http://www.fbi.gov/. Read one of the articles that appears under the section "Breaking News." What is the subject matter of this article?
3. Go to www.google.com or other Internet search engine and find the website for the prosecuting attorney's office for the county in which you are located. Read the information that is available that describes the functions of the county prosecutor.
4. Go to the website of the U.S. Attorney at http://www.justice.gov/usao/. What is the mission of the United States Attorneys? Find the address and telephone number of the U.S. Attorney's office closest to you.

CRITICAL THINKING & WRITING QUESTIONS

1. Who are the parties to a criminal action? What lawyers are involved in a criminal action?
2. Describe the function of a criminal complaint.
3. Describe a grand jury. What is the function of a grand jury? What is an indictment?
4. What is a plea? Describe the process of plea bargaining.
5. What is a trier of fact? What is its function in a criminal trial?
6. What is a penal code? Give an example of a crime defined by the penal code. What types of crimes are prohibited by regulatory statutes? Give an example of this type of crime.
7. Define *actus reus*. Define *mens rea*. What is a non-intent crime? Give an example.
8. Define the following common crimes: (a) robbery, (b) burglary, (c) larceny, (d) murder, and (e) involuntary manslaughter.
9. Describe each of the following crimes: (a) forgery, (b) extortion, (c) bribery, (d) embezzlement, and (e) criminal fraud
10. What does the Fourth Amendment's protection against unreasonable search and seizure protect persons against? What is a search warrant? What is *probable cause*? Explain the exclusionary rule.
11. What does the Fifth Amendment privilege against self-incrimination protect against? Describe *Miranda* rights. Describe the attorney–client privilege.
12. Explain the Fifth Amendment's protection against double jeopardy. What is a hung jury?
13. Explain the Sixth Amendment's right to a public jury trial.

Building Paralegal Skills

VIDEO CASE STUDIES

Attorney–Client Privilege: Confidentiality Issue

In a meeting between a paralegal and a client, the client reveals to the paralegal conduct that may be criminal in nature.

After viewing the video case study in MyLegalStudiesLab, answer the following:

1. Does the paralegal have a duty to disclose fraudulent activity?
2. Is the paralegal protected under the attorney–client privilege?
3. Is information about the commission of a crime covered under the duty of confidentiality?

ETHICS ANALYSIS & DISCUSSION QUESTIONS

1. Is the information given to a paralegal by a criminal client covered under the Fifth Amendment when he or she interviews the person?
2. What obligation does a paralegal have to make available exculpatory evidence discovered during the investigation of a case?
3. You are a paralegal who works for the state government assisting a public defender in the defense of common criminals. One defendant is accused of attempted murder of his spouse. It is obvious the defendant is guilty of this charge. Can you report this fact to the judge overseeing the case? Explain.
4. In the prior example, you are at a meeting with the public defender and the defendant says, "I may have missed killing her before, but if I get off she's dead!" Do you have a duty to report this statement to the judge overseeing the case or other government official? Explain.

DEVELOPING YOUR COLLABORATION SKILLS

With a group of other students, review the facts of the following case. As a group, discuss the following questions.

1. What does the Fourth Amendment provide regarding searches and seizures of evidence?
2. Under what circumstances are warrantless searches considered "reasonable"?
3. Is the warrantless search of Gant's automobile justified as a search incident to an arrest?

Arizona v. Gant, 556 U.S. 332 (2009)

Acting on an anonymous tip that a residence in Tucson, Arizona, was being used to sell drugs, police officers knocked on the front door of the residence. Rodney Gant opened the door, and the police asked to speak to the owner. Gant identified himself and stated that the owner was expected to return later. The police officers left the residence. Later, the police conducted a records search that revealed an outstanding warrant for Gant's arrest for driving with a suspended license.

When the police officers returned to the house that evening, Gant drove up in an automobile, parked in the driveway, got out of his car, and shut the door. One of the police officers called to Gant and he walked toward the officer. When Gant was about 10 to 12 feet from the car, the officer arrested Gant, handcuffed him, and locked him in the backseat of a patrol car.

The police officers searched Gant's car, and found a gun and a bag of cocaine. Gant was charged with possession of a narcotic drug for sale. At the criminal trial, Gant moved to suppress the evidence seized from the car on the grounds that the warrantless search violated the Fourth Amendment. The Arizona trial court held that the search was permissible as a search incident to an arrest. The jury found Gant guilty, and he was sentenced to a three-year term in prison. The Arizona Supreme Court held that the search of Gant's car was unreasonable and violated the Fourth Amendment, and that the evidence was therefore inadmissible at trial. The case was appealed to the U.S. Supreme Court.

PARALEGAL PORTFOLIO EXERCISE

Using a general web search site, Westlaw or LexisNexis legal services, or a law library, find a copy of the jury instructions for first-degree murder in your state. Write a legal memorandum discussing the elements necessary to prove first-degree murder in your state.

LEGAL ANALYSIS & WRITING CASES

State v. Wilson, No. 2004 Ohio 2838 (Ohio Ct. App. June 3, 2004) Web Ohio App. Lexis 2503

Court of Appeals of Ohio

Gregory O. Wilson, who had been arguing earlier in the day with his girlfriend, Melissa Spear, approached a parked car in which Ms. Spear was seated and poured gasoline from a beer bottle over her head. When Ms. Spear exited the car, Wilson ignited her with his cigarette lighter, setting her body on fire. As Ms. Spear became engulfed in flames, and while bystanders tried to assist her, Wilson walked away and down the street as if nothing had happened. Paramedics arrived at the scene. A witness described her after the fire as "totally black, no hair, laying there with her skin melted off of her, the flesh looked like it was melted. She was black, looking up at me saying 'help me.'"

Ms. Spear was transported from the scene to the hospital. When she arrived, she had third-degree burns on her face, neck, trunk, arms, hands, and thighs. She was put in a medically induced coma and placed on a respirator. She remained in a coma for 45 days, during which time she underwent ten surgeries that excised her burn wounds and placed synthetic skin dressing or skin grafts onto her wound sites. Ms. Spear was transferred to a rehabilitation facility. Upon her release from the rehabilitation facility, she received continual treatment and medicine for pain, infection, and depression. Nine months after the incident occurred, and five days before her 30th birthday, Ms. Spear's seven-year-old son found her lying dead in her bed. The State of Ohio brought criminal charges against Wilson. Wilson argues that the evidence is insufficient to support his conviction for aggravated murder, contending that the state failed to prove the element of causation beyond a reasonable doubt.

Question

1. Was there sufficient causation between Wilson's act of setting Ms. Spear on fire and Ms. Spear's death nine months later to warrant a conviction for murder?

Kyllo v. United States, 533 U.S. 27 , 121 S.Ct. 2038, Web 2001 U.S. Lexis 4487 (2001)

Government agents suspected that marijuana was being grown in the home of Danny Kyllo, which was part of a triplex building in Florence, Oregon. Indoor marijuana growth typically requires high-intensity lamps. In order to determine whether an amount of heat was emanating from Kyllo's home consistent with the use of such lamps, federal agents used a thermal imager to scan the triplex. Thermal imagers detect infrared radiation and produce images of the radiation. The scan of Kyllo's home, which was performed from an automobile on the street, showed that the roof over the garage and a side wall of Kyllo's home were "hot." The agents used this scanning evidence to obtain a search warrant authorizing a search of Kyllo's home. During the search, the agents found an indoor growing operation involving more than 100 marijuana plants. Kyllo was indicted for manufacturing marijuana, a violation of federal criminal law. Kyllo moved to suppress the imaging evidence and the evidence it led to, arguing that the evidence was obtained during an unreasonable search that violated the Fourth Amendment to the U.S. Constitution.

Question

1. Is the use of a thermal-imaging device aimed at a private home from a public street to detect relative amounts of heat within the home a "search" within the meaning of the Fourth Amendment?

WORKING WITH THE LANGUAGE OF THE COURT CASE

Kentucky v. King, 131 S.Ct. 1849 (2011)

Read the following case, excerpted from the U.S. Supreme Court's opinion. Review and brief the case. In your brief, answer the following questions:

1. What does the Fourth Amendment provide?
2. Must a search be conducted pursuant to a search warrant to be constitutional?
3. Are there exceptions where a search warrant need not be obtained by the police before a search may be conducted? If so, was a warrantless search permitted in this case?
4. What was the vote of the U.S. Supreme Court in this case?

Alito, Justice (joined by Roberts, Chief Justice, and Scalia, Kennedy, Thomas, Breyer, Sotomayor, and Kagan)

This case concerns the search of an apartment in Lexington, Kentucky. Police officers set up a controlled buy of crack cocaine outside an apartment complex. Undercover Officer Gibbons watched the deal take place from an unmarked car in a nearby parking lot. After the deal occurred, Gibbons radioed uniformed officers to move in on the suspect. He told the officers that the suspect was moving quickly toward the breezeway of an apartment building, and he urged them to "hurry up and get there" before the suspect entered an apartment.

In response to the radio alert, the uniformed officers drove into the nearby parking lot, left their vehicles, and ran to the breezeway. Just as they entered the breezeway, they heard a door shut and detected a very strong odor of burnt marijuana. At the end of the breezeway, the officers saw two apartments, one on the left and one on the right, and they did not know which apartment the suspect had entered. Gibbons had radioed that the suspect was running into the apartment on the right, but the officers did not hear this statement because they had already left their vehicles. Because they smelled marijuana smoke emanating from the apartment on the left, they approached the door of that apartment.

Officer Steven Cobb, one of the uniformed officers who approached the door, testified that the officers banged on the left apartment door "as loud as [they] could" and announced, "'This is the police'" or "'Police, police, police.'" Cobb said that "[a]s soon as [the officers] started banging on the door," they "could hear people inside moving," and "[i]t sounded as [though] things were being moved inside the apartment." These noises, Cobb testified, led the officers to believe that drug-related evidence was about to be destroyed.

At that point, the officers announced that they "were going to make entry inside the apartment." Cobb then kicked in the door, the officers entered the apartment, and they found three people in the front room: respondent Hollis King, respondent's girlfriend, and a guest who was smoking marijuana. The officers performed a protective sweep of the apartment during which they saw marijuana and powder cocaine in plain view. In a subsequent search, they also discovered crack cocaine, cash, and drug paraphernalia. Police eventually entered the apartment on the right. Inside, they found the suspected drug dealer who was the initial target of their investigation.

In the Fayette County Circuit Court, a grand jury charged respondent [King] with trafficking in marijuana, first-degree trafficking in a controlled substance, and second-degree persistent felony offender status. Respondent filed a motion to suppress the evidence from the warrantless search, but the Circuit Court denied the motion. The Circuit Court concluded that the officers had probable cause to investigate the marijuana odor and that the officers "properly conducted [the investigation] by initially knocking on the door of the apartment unit and awaiting the response or consensual entry." Exigent circumstances justified the warrantless entry, the court held, because "there was no response at all to the knocking," and because "Officer Cobb heard movement in the apartment which he reasonably concluded were persons in the act of destroying evidence, particularly narcotics because of the smell." Respondent then entered a conditional guilty plea, reserving his right to appeal the denial of his suppression motion. The court sentenced respondent to 11 years' imprisonment. The Kentucky Court of Appeals affirmed. The Supreme Court of Kentucky reversed. We granted certiorari.

Although the text of the Fourth Amendment does not specify when a search warrant must be obtained, this Court has inferred that a warrant must generally be secured. [T]he warrant requirement is subject to certain reasonable exceptions. One well-recognized exception applies when "'the exigencies of the situation' make the needs of law enforcement so compelling that [a] warrantless search is objectively reasonable under the Fourth Amendment."

Police officers may enter premises without a warrant when they are in hot pursuit of a fleeing suspect. And—what is relevant here—the need "to prevent the imminent destruction of evidence" has long been recognized as a sufficient justification for a warrantless search. Destruction of evidence issues probably occur most frequently in drug cases because drugs may be easily destroyed by flushing them down a toilet or rinsing them down a drain. Where, as here, the police did not create the exigency by engaging or threatening to engage in conduct that violates the Fourth Amendment, warrantless entry to prevent the destruction of evidence is reasonable and thus allowed.

Like the court below, we assume for purposes of argument that an exigency existed. Because the officers in this case did not violate or threaten to violate the Fourth Amendment prior to the exigency, we hold that the exigency justified the warrantless search of the apartment. The judgment of the Kentucky Supreme Court is reversed, and the case is remanded for further proceedings not inconsistent with this opinion.

It is so ordered.

MYLEGALSTUDIESLAB

Virtual Law Office Experience Assignments

Complete the pre-test, study plan, and post-test for this chapter and answer the Legal Applications questions as assigned. These will help you confirm your mastery of the concepts and their application to legal scenarios. Then complete the Virtual Law Office assignments as assigned by your instructor. These assignments are designed to develop your workplace skills. Completing the assignments for this chapter will result in producing the following documents for inclusion in your portfolio:

VLOE 8.1	Memo listing the criminal code sections, elements of the crimes, and conduct observed on the video indicating violation of these criminal statutes
VLOE 8.2	Office memo on ethical rules concerning disclosure of a client's admission that they have committed a crime

CHAPTER

9

Administrative Law

LEARNING OBJECTIVES

After studying this chapter, you should be able to:

1. Recognize the professional opportunities for paralegals in the administrative law area.
2. Define *administrative law*.
3. Describe the types of government regulation of business.
4. List and explain the functions of administrative agencies.
5. Explain the scope of the Administrative Procedure Act.
6. Describe the powers of administrative agencies.
7. Describe administrative searches.
8. Explain the judicial review of administrative agency decisions.
9. List and describe important federal administrative agencies.
10. Describe public disclosure of administrative agency actions.

Paralegals at Work

You are a paralegal at a law firm that specializes in representing persons who allege that they have been discriminated against at work. Your supervisor is Ms. Emilia Ortiz, a renowned attorney in the area of equal opportunity in employment. Ms. Ortiz has informed you that the law firm has been retained to represent Ms. Ester Soto, an employee of the Sof-Tech Corporation, a midsize high-tech company that produces software for financial institutions. Ms. Ortiz said that you will assist her in preparing the case for Ms. Soto.

Ms. Ortiz explained that Ms. Soto would be coming to the law office for a consultation and that you would be attending the meeting, which would be held in the law firm's conference room. At the meeting, Ms. Soto explained that she is currently employed as the controller of Sof-Tech. The company has a niche market and has been very successful.

When Ms. Ortiz asked Ms. Soto her background, she explained that her parents immigrated to the United States from Paraguay when she was 15 years old. Ms. Soto attended high school in New York City, graduated from New York University with an undergraduate degree in economics, and obtained a Masters of Business Administration (MBA) degree from the University of Chicago with a major in finance. Before being hired by Sof-Tech Corporation, Ms. Soto worked at two companies for a period of seven years. At the second of these two companies, she was promoted to Controller. Ms. Soto was hired as Controller of Sof-Tech Corporation five years ago, and has worked at that position ever since.

Ms. Soto explained that when the position of Chief Financial Officer (CFO) became available at Sof-Tech Corporation, she had applied for the job. Although she met the work and educational requirements of the CFO position, she was rejected for the job. Instead, another applicant, a Caucasian male with less experience than she, was hired for the position. Ms. Soto believes that she was

> "Good government is an empire of laws."
>
> John Adams, *Thoughts on Government* (1776)

not promoted because of her gender and her ethnicity. Ms. Soto explained more details of her case before the meeting ended.

After Ms. Soto left the meeting, Ms. Ortiz asked you to have the answers to the following questions ready when a follow-up meeting is held in a few days: What federal act has been violated, according to the facts alleged by Ms. Soto? What administrative agency has authority to hear the case? Can you go online and find a rule or regulation of the administrative agency that defines the type of discrimination being alleged by Ms. Soto? Can a complaint be filed on behalf of Ms. Soto at the administrative agency? Does the agency have the power to hear the case, and if so, who will hear the case? Are there any rules that the administrative agency must follow in hearing the case? Is the decision of the administrative agency subject to judicial review?

Learning Objective 1
Recognize the professional opportunities for paralegals in the administrative law area.

INTRODUCTION FOR THE PARALEGAL

Many paralegal professionals work in the area of administrative law. Some work for federal administrative agencies such as the Securities and Exchange Commission (SEC), the Federal Trade Commission (FTC), and other federal agencies. Paralegals also often work for state administrative agencies, including state corporations departments, environmental protection agencies, and other regulatory agencies.

Justice is the end of government. It is the end of civil society. It ever has been, and ever will be pursued, until it be obtained, or until liberty be lost in the pursuit.
James Madison
The Federalist No. 51 (1788)

In the administrative law field, paralegals may also work for attorneys who represent clients who are subject to regulation by administrative agencies. For example, if a client is prosecuted by the SEC for violation of federal securities laws, an attorney will represent the client at the proceedings. Those who seek licenses from administrative agencies to conduct business are also often represented by attorneys. For example, someone who wishes to form a national bank must obtain permission from the Office of the Comptroller of the Currency. An attorney may assist the person in dealing with that agency. Paralegals often assist attorneys in preparing for such administrative agency matters.

The following feature discusses the career opportunities for paralegal professionals in administrative law.

CAREER OPPORTUNITIES FOR PARALEGAL PROFESSIONALS IN ADMINISTRATIVE LAW

Lawyers increasingly employ paralegals in areas of law that involve practice before administrative agencies. Administrative law has become extremely important for businesses and individuals alike. Administrative agencies govern many aspects of business, and our personal lives as well.

The number of administrative agencies in this country is staggering. The federal government alone has dozens of agencies. These range from agencies that regulate specific industries to agencies whose powers apply to large segments of society and the economy. The following are only a few of the major federal administrative agencies:

- Environmental Protection Agency (EPA): regulates air, water, hazardous waste, and other types of pollution.
- Equal Employment Opportunity Commission (EEOC): enforces many antidiscrimination laws that affect businesses and their employees.
- Federal Trade Commission (FTC): enforces many consumer protection laws.
- Food and Drug Administration (FDA): regulates the safety of foods, drugs, cosmetics, and medical devices.
- Federal Communications Commission (FCC): regulates radio, television, cable, and other broadcast media.
- National Labor Relations Board (NLRB): regulates labor union formation, elections, bargaining with employers, and other labor issues.
- Securities and Exchange Commission (SEC): regulates the issuance, sale, and purchase of securities, including stocks and bonds.

- Department of Homeland Security (DHS): coordinates certain federal agencies in protecting the country against terrorism and other threats.

In addition to federal administrative agencies, there are thousands of state and local administrative agencies. These include agencies that license and regulate corporations and financial institutions, protect the environment, and perform many other functions. At the local level, cities and municipalities have administrative agencies that regulate construction, set building codes, establish zoning regulations, issue water permits, and perform other duties.

Paralegals often work for lawyers who specialize in making appearances before specific federal, state, and local administrative agencies. For example, lawyers prepare applications for submission to the Federal Communications Commission (FCC) to obtain licenses to operate radio, television, or cable companies. Lawyers are also asked to prepare applications to the federal Food and Drug Administration (FDA) to obtain approval to market a new drug.

The federal government has enacted the Administrative Procedure Act (APA), which establishes rules for legal practice before federal administrative agencies. There are similar statutes that set administrative procedures at the state level. In addition, each administrative agency has its own rules and regulations for submitting applications and appearing at hearings before it.

Paralegals who work for lawyers specializing in certain areas of administrative law must become familiar with a particular agency's rules and procedures. Paralegals often are called upon to assist in drafting documents that will be submitted to administrative agencies and preparing cases that will be decided by these agencies. Thus, paralegals often become experts in certain areas of administrative law, and therefore can be indispensable to lawyers who practice before those administrative agencies.

Administrative Law

Learning Objective 2

Define *administrative law.*

Businesses are generally free to produce goods or services, enter into contracts, and otherwise conduct business as they see fit. However, businesses are also subject to substantial federal, state, and local government regulations. Government regulation is designed to protect employees and the public from unsafe and abusive practices by businesses. Many times when a regulatory statute is enacted, an **administrative agency** (or **regulatory agency**) is created to enforce the law. Because of their importance, administrative agencies are informally referred to as the "fourth branch of government."

Administrative agency (regulatory agency) An agency that the government creates to enforce a statute.

Regulatory agencies, and the industries, businesses, and professionals they regulate, are governed by a body of **administrative law.** These laws are often referred to as **regulatory statutes.** Sometimes when the legislative branch enacts a new statute, it authorizes an existing administrative agency to administer and enforce the law (see Exhibit 9.1).

Administrative law (regulatory statute) Law that governments enact to regulate industries, businesses, and professionals.

Example When Congress enacted the **Securities Act of 1933** and the Securities Exchange Act of 1934, it created the Securities and Exchange Commission (SEC), a federal administrative agency, to administer and enforce those statutes.

General Government Regulation

Learning Objective 3

Describe the types of government regulation of business.

Many administrative agencies regulate businesses and industries collectively. This is called **general government regulation.** Most of the industries and businesses in the United States are subject to these laws. These laws do not regulate a specific industry but apply to all industries and businesses except those that are specifically exempt from certain regulations.

General government regulation Laws that regulate businesses and industries collectively.

Examples The federal National Labor Relations Board (NLRB) is empowered to regulate the formation and operation of labor unions in most industries and businesses in the United States. The federal Occupational Safety and Health Administration (OSHA) is authorized to regulate workplace safety for most industries and businesses in the country. The U.S. Equal Employment Opportunity Commission (EEOC) enforces equal opportunity in employment laws that cover most workers in the United States.

Exhibit 9.1 Administrative agency

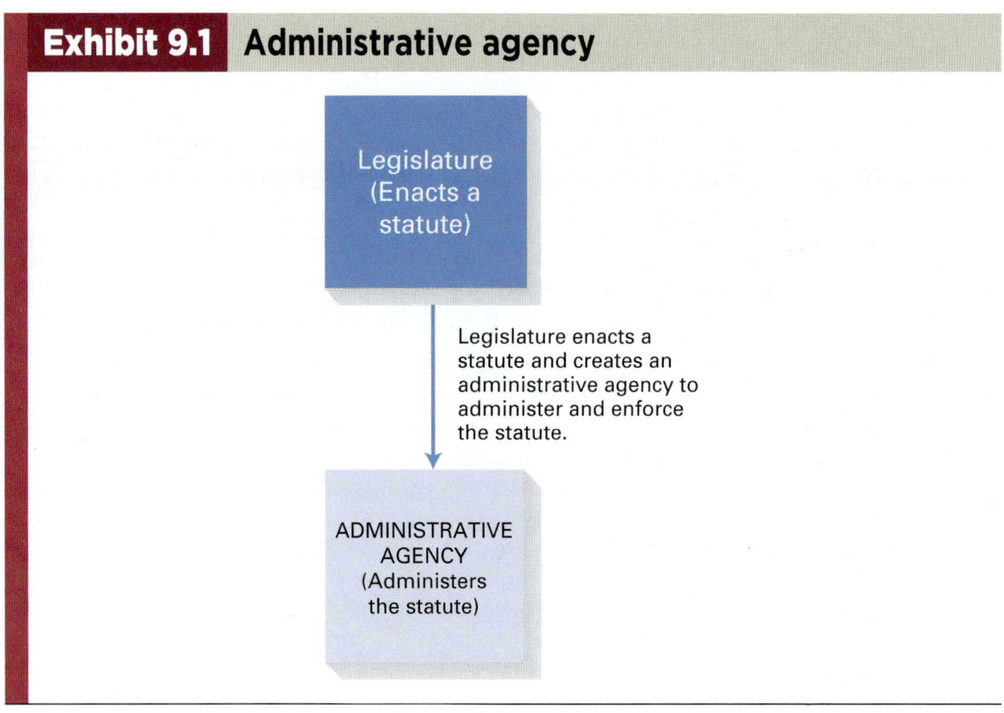
Legislature
(Enacts a
statute)
Legislature enacts a statute and creates an administrative agency to administer and enforce the statute.
ADMINISTRATIVE
AGENCY
(Administers
the statute)

Specific Government Regulation

Some administrative agencies, and the laws they enforce, are created to regulate specific industries or areas of commerce only. That is, an industry is subject to administrative laws that are specifically adopted to regulate that industry. This is called **specific government regulation** of business. Administrative agencies that are industry specific are created to administer those specific laws.

Specific government regulation Laws that regulate a specific industry or type of business.

Examples The Federal Communications Commission (FCC) regulates the operation of television and radio stations. The Federal Aviation Administration (FAA) regulates the operation of commercial airlines. The Office of the Comptroller of the Currency regulates the licensing and operation of national banks.

Federal and state governments have enacted many statutes to protect air, water, and the environment from pollution.

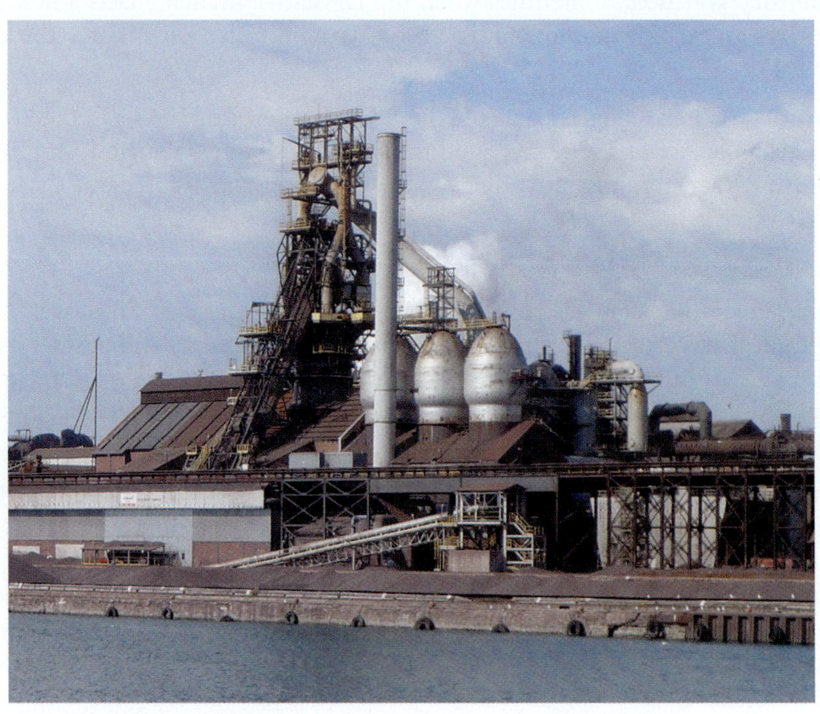

Administrative Agencies

Learning Objective 4
List and explain the functions of administrative agencies.

Administrative agencies are created by federal, state, and local governments to enforce regulatory statutes. Government agencies range from large, complex federal agencies, such as the Department of Homeland Security, to local zoning boards. There are more than one hundred federal administrative agencies. Thousands of other administrative agencies have been created by state and local governments.

Cabinet-Level Federal Departments

At the federal level, the president can create **cabinet-level federal departments** that answer directly to the president. The president appoints cabinet members subject to confirmation by a majority vote of the U.S. Senate. Cabinet-level departments advise the president and are responsible for enforcing specific laws enacted by Congress. The fifteen departments of the executive branch are:

Cabinet-level federal agencies Federal agencies that advise the president and are responsible for enforcing specific administrative statutes enacted by Congress.

Department of Agriculture
Department of Commerce
Department of Defense
Department of Education
Department of Energy
Department of Health and Human Services
Department of Homeland Security
Department of Housing and Urban Development
Department of Interior
Department of Justice
Department of Labor
Department of State
Department of Transportation
Department of the Treasury
Department of Veterans Affairs

The organizational structure of the Department of Labor is set forth in Exhibit 9.2.

Department of Homeland Security

After the terrorist attacks of September 11, 2001, President George W. Bush issued an executive order to create the Office of Homeland Security. The president called for the office to be made into a cabinet-level department. Congress responded by enacting the **Homeland Security Act (HSA)** of 2002,[1] which created the cabinet-level **U.S. Department of Homeland Security (DHS).** The creation of the DHS was the largest government reorganization in more than fifty years.

U.S. Department of Homeland Security (DHS) A cabinet-level federal administrative agency whose mission is to enforce laws to prevent terrorist attacks and related criminal activities.

The act placed twenty-two federal agencies, with approximately two hundred thousand employees, under the umbrella of the DHS. The DHS is the second-largest government agency, after the Department of Defense, and the agencies it oversees include:

- the Bureau of Customs and Border Protection
- the Bureau of Citizenship and Immigration Services
- the U.S. Secret Service
- the Federal Emergency Management Agency
- the Federal Computer Incident Response Center
- the National Domestic Preparedness Office

[1] Public Law 107–295 (2002).

Exhibit 9.2 Organizational chart of the U.S. Department of Labor

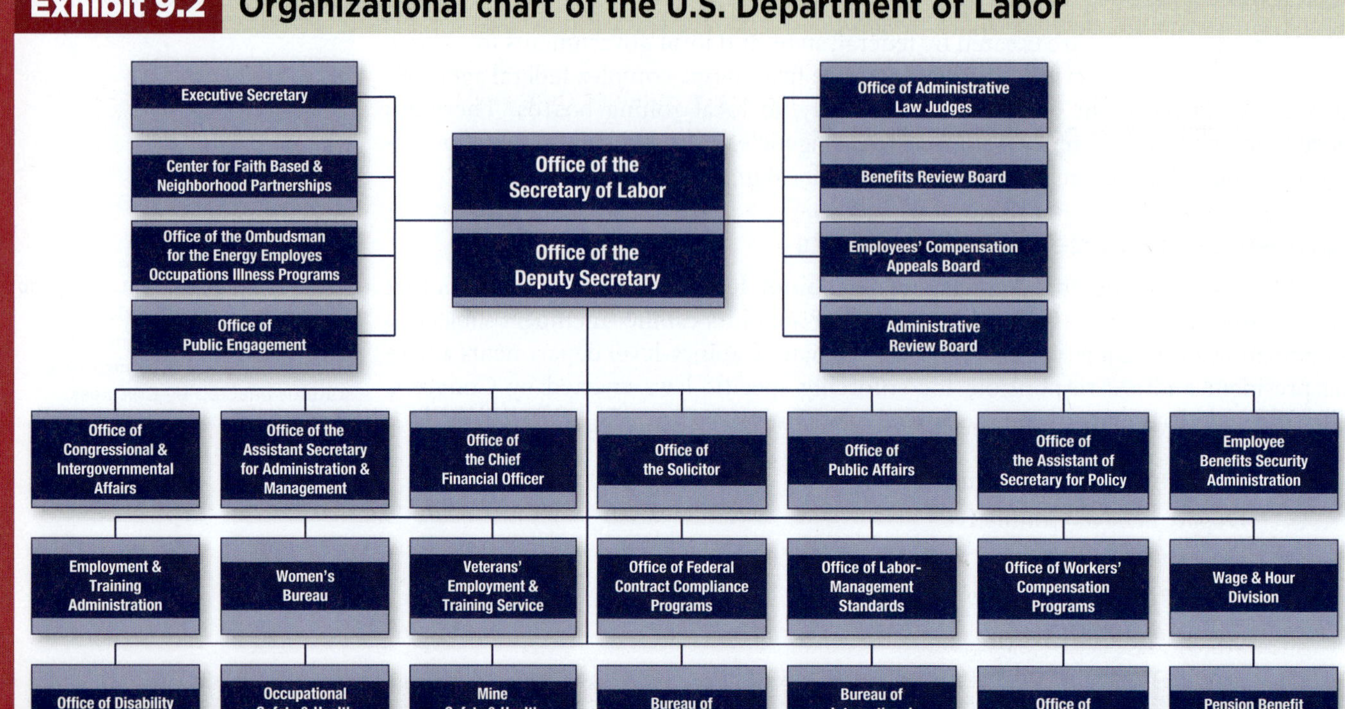

- the U.S. Coast Guard and
- portions of the Federal Bureau of Investigation, Treasury Department, Commerce Department, and Justice Department.

The mission of the DHS is to enforce laws to prevent domestic terrorist attacks, reduce vulnerability to terrorist attacks, minimize the harm caused by such attacks, and assist in recovery in the event of a terrorist attack. The DHS provides services in the following critical areas:

(1) border and transportation security, including protecting airports, seaports, and borders, and providing immigration and visa processing;
(2) chemical, biological, radiological, and nuclear countermeasures, including metering the air for biological agents and developing vaccines and treatments for biological agents;
(3) information analysis and infrastructure protection, including protecting communications systems, power grids, transportation networks, telecommunications, and cyber systems; and
(4) emergency preparedness and response to terrorist incidents, including training first responders and coordinating government disaster relief.

Independent Federal Administrative Agencies

Independent federal administrative agencies Federal agencies that have broad regulatory powers over key areas of the national economy.

At the federal level, Congress has created more than 100 administrative agencies called **independent federal administrative agencies.** These agencies have broad regulatory powers over key areas of the national economy and society.

Examples The Securities and Exchange Commission (SEC) regulates the issuance and trading of securities. The Federal Trade Commission (FTC) enforces federal antitrust and consumer protection laws. The Federal Communications Commission (FCC) regulates radio and television broadcasting and telecommunications.

State and Local Administrative Agencies

All states have created administrative agencies to enforce and interpret state regulatory law. **State administrative agencies** are empowered to enforce state statutes and have a profound effect on business. They have the power to adopt rules and regulations to interpret the statutes they are authorized to administer.

State administrative agencies Agencies created by legislative branches of states to administer state regulatory laws.

Examples Most states have a corporation department to enforce state corporation law and regulate the issuance of securities, a banking department to license and regulate the operation of banks, fish and game departments to regulate fishing and hunting within the state's boundaries, workers' compensation boards to decide workers' compensation claims for injuries that occur on the job, and environmental protection departments to regulate the land, waterways, and other environmental matters.

Local governments such as cities, municipalities, and counties create **local administrative agencies** to administer local regulatory law.

Local administrative agencies Agencies created by cities, municipalities, and counties to administer local regulatory law.

Examples Counties have numerous administrative boards to regulate county activities. Cities and towns have school boards, zoning commissions, and other administrative bodies to regulate city and town matters.

In the following feature, a paralegal professional and owner of his own business discusses his position as a non-attorney Social Security Disability Appeals Representative.

Exhibit 9.3 is an application form for an administrative hearing regarding a Social Security matter.

Paralegals *in* Practice

PARALEGAL PROFILE

Melvin E. Irvin

Since 1996, Melvin E. Irvin has worked as a non-attorney Social Security Disability Appeals Representative in the San Jose, California, area. He legally represents clients before the Social Security Administration (SSA) in appeals for Social Security disability benefits. In addition to being a Marine Corps veteran, Mel is a graduate from Santa Clara University Law School Institute for Paralegal Studies. He also earned the Certified Paralegal (CP) designation from the National Association of Legal Assistants.

As President of my own corporation, Melvin E. Irvin Disability Representative, Inc., I represent about 55-60 clients at any given time. The most important skills needed in my position are above-average communication skills and a good working knowledge of Social Security Law. There are no specific educational requirements to become a non-attorney Disability Representative except that you cannot be a disbarred attorney, or disallowed by another government administration from practicing. Naturally, a college degree and a paralegal certificate are very helpful.

Over the past 20 years, successful representation has become more difficult as the SSA has significantly reduced its claim allowance rates. SSA representation fees are paid only on a contingency basis, whether you are an attorney or non-attorney. Since the SSA is backlogged on disability cases, currently more than 700,000 nationally, it may take two or more years before a new representative sees the first paycheck. This is due to the length of time it takes for a case to be resolved. Even so, my work is very rewarding because it allows me to help people who really need assistance.

I find that many people in the U.S. today still believe that paralegals can perform work directly for the public. According to Section 6450 of the California Business and Professions Code, those who call themselves paralegals must be attorney supervised, with few exceptions. One exception is legally representing the public in administrative law settings such as the SSA. As the current President of the California Alliance of Paralegal Associations, I help educate others about the paralegal profession. Part of my role is to encourage local paralegal associations to appoint Public Information Officers who can respond to questions from the legal community, the public, and the media.

Exhibit 9.3 Application for Social Security administrative hearing

SOCIAL SECURITY ADMINISTRATION
OFFICE OF HEARINGS AND APPEALS

Form Approved
OMB No. 0960-0269

REQUEST FOR HEARING BY ADMINISTRATIVE LAW JUDGE
[Take or mail original and all copies to your local Social Security Office]

PRIVACY ACT NOTICE ON REVERSE SIDE OF FORM.

1. CLAIMANT	2. WAGE EARNER, IF DIFFERENT	3. SOC. SEC. CLAIM NUMBER	4. SPOUSE's CLAIM NUMBER

5. **I REQUEST A HEARING BEFORE AN ADMINISTRATIVE LAW JUDGE.** I disagree with the determination made on my claim because:

An Administrative Law Judge of the Office of Hearings and Appeals will be appointed to conduct the hearing or other proceedings in your case. You will receive notice of the time and place of a hearing at least 20 days before the date set for a hearing.

6. If you have additional evidence to submit check the following block and complete the statement: ☐

I have additional evidence to submit from (name and address of source): ____________

(Please submit it to the Social Security Office within 10 days. Attach an additional sheet if you need more space.)

7. Check one of the blocks:

☐ I wish to appear at a hearing.

☐ I do not wish to appear and I request that a decision be made based on the evidence in my case. (Complete Waiver Form HA-4608)

You have a right to be represented at the hearing. If you are not represented but would like to be, your Social Security Office will give you a list of legal referral and service organizations. (If you are represented and have not done so previously, complete and submit form SSA-1696 (Appointment of Representative).)

[You should complete No. 8 and your representative (if any) should complete No. 9. If you are represented and your representative is not available to complete this form, you should also print his or her name, address, etc. in No. 9.]

8. (CLAIMANT'S SIGNATURE)	9. (REPRESENTATIVE'S SIGNATURE/NAME)
ADDRESS	(ADDRESS) ☐ ATTORNEY; ☐ NON ATTORNEY;
CITY STATE ZIP CODE	CITY STATE ZIP CODE
DATE AREA CODE AND TELEPHONE NUMBER	DATE AREA CODE AND TELEPHONE NUMBER

TO BE COMPLETED BY SOCIAL SECURITY ADMINISTRATION-ACKNOWLEDGMENT OF REQUEST FOR HEARING

10. **Request for Hearing RECEIVED for the Social Security Administration on** ____________ by: ____________

(TITLE) ADDRESS

11. Was the request for hearing received within 65 days of the reconsidered determination?
☐ YES ☐ NO

If no is checked, attach claimant's explanation for delay; and attach copy of appointment notice, letter, or other pertinent material or information in the Social Security Office.

12. Claimant not represented -
☐ list of legal referral and service organizations provided

13. Interpreter needed -
☐ enter language (including sign language): ____________

14. Check one: ☐ Initial Entitlement Case
☐ Disability Cessation Case
☐ Other Postentitlement Case

15. Check claim type(s):
☐ RSI only ------------------------------ (RSI)
☐ Title II Disability-worker or child ------------------------------ (DIWC)
☐ Title II Disability-widow(er) only ------------------------------ (DIWW)
☐ SSI Aged only ------------------------------ (SSIA)
☐ SSI Blind only ------------------------------ (SSIB)
☐ SSI Disability only ------------------------------ (SSID)
☐ SSI Aged/Title II ------------------------------ (SSAC)
☐ SSI Blind/Title II ------------------------------ (SSBC)
☐ SSI Disability/Title II ------------------------------ (SSDC)
☐ HI Entitlement ------------------------------ (HIE)
☐ Other-Specify: (____________)

16. **HO COPY SENT TO:** ____________ HO on ____________
☐ CF Attached: ☐ Title II; ☐ Title XVI; or
☐ Title II CF held in FO to establish CAPS ORBIT; or
☐ CF requested ☐ Title II; ☐ Title XVI
(Copy of teletype or phone report attached)

17. **CF COPY SENT TO:** ____________ HO on ____________
☐ CF Attached: ☐ Title II; ☐ Title XVI
☐ Other Attached: ____________

FORM **HA-501-U5** (5-1996) EF (7-2000)
Issue old stock

CLAIMS FOLDER

Learning Objective 5
Explain the scope of the Administrative Procedure Act.

Administrative Procedure

Administrative law is a combination of *substantive* and *procedural law*. **Substantive administrative law** is law enacted by Congress or a state legislature that an administrative agency enforces. **Procedural administrative law** establishes the procedures that must be followed by an administrative agency while enforcing substantive laws.

Examples Congress created the federal Environmental Protection Agency (EPA) to enforce federal environmental laws to protect the environment. This is an example of substantive law—laws to protect the environment. In enforcing these laws, the EPA must follow certain established procedural rules (such as requirements to provide notice and a hearing). These are examples of procedural law.

Administrative Procedure Act

In 1946, Congress enacted the **Administrative Procedure Act (APA).**[2] This act is very important because it establishes procedures that federal administrative agencies must follow in conducting their affairs. The APA requires federal agencies to give notice of actions they plan on taking. It also requires hearings to be held in most cases, and it requires certain procedural safeguards and protocols to be followed at these proceedings.

Administrative Procedure Act (APA) A federal statute that establishes procedures to be followed by federal administrative agencies while conducting their affairs.

The APA also establishes how **rules and regulations** can be adopted by federal administrative agencies. This includes providing notice of proposed **rule making,** granting a time period for receiving comments from the public regarding proposed rule making, and holding hearings to take evidence. The APA provides a procedure for receiving evidence and hearing requests for the granting of federal licenses (such as a license to operate a national bank). The APA also establishes notice and hearing requirements, and rules for conducting agency adjudicative actions, such as actions to take away licenses from certain persons (for example, securities brokers' licenses). Most states have also enacted administrative procedural statutes that govern state administrative procedures.

Administrative Law Judges

Administrative law judges (ALJs) preside over administrative proceedings and decide questions of law and fact concerning each case. Each ALJ is an employee of the administrative agency that he or she serves. Both the administrative agency and the respondent may be represented by counsel. Witnesses may be examined and cross-examined, evidence may be introduced, and objections may be made. There is no jury, since the ALJ determines all questions of fact.

Administrative law judge (ALJ) An employee of an administrative agency who presides over an administrative proceeding and decides questions of law and fact concerning cases.

An ALJ's decision is issued in the form of an **administrative order.** The order must state the reasons for the ALJ's decision, and becomes final if it is not appealed. If appealed, the decision is reviewed by the administrative agency. Further appeal can be made to the appropriate federal court (in federal agency actions) or state court (in state agency actions).

Administrative order A decision issued by an administrative law judge.

Powers of Administrative Agencies

Learning Objective 6
Describe the powers of administrative agencies.

When an administrative agency is created, it is delegated certain powers. The agency has only the legislative, judicial, and executive powers that are delegated to it. This is called the **delegation doctrine.** Thus, an agency can adopt a rule or regulation (a legislative function), prosecute a violation of the statute or rule (an executive function), and adjudicate the dispute (a judicial function). The courts have upheld as constitutional this combined power of administrative agencies. If an administrative agency acts outside the scope of its delegated powers, it is an unconstitutional act.

Delegation doctrine A doctrine that provides that when an administrative agency is created, it is delegated certain powers, and that the agency can use only the legislative, judicial, and executive powers that are delegated to it.

The legislative powers delegated to administrative agencies consist of substantive rule making, interpretative rule making, issuing statements of policy, and granting licenses.

[2] 5 U.S.C. Sections 551–706.

Rule Making

Substantive rule A rule issued by an administrative agency that has the force of law and to which covered persons and businesses must adhere.

Many federal statutes expressly authorize an administrative agency to issue **substantive rules.** A substantive rule is much like a statute: It has the force of law, and certain persons and businesses must adhere to it. Violators may be held civilly or criminally liable, depending on the rule. All substantive rules are subject to judicial review.

> **Example** The Securities and Exchange Commission (SEC) is authorized to prohibit fraud in the purchase and sale of securities. The SEC therefore has the power to adopt rules that define what fraudulent conduct is prohibited by the federal securities laws.

A federal administrative agency that proposes to adopt a substantive rule must follow procedures set forth in the APA.[3] This means the agency must do the following:

1. It must publish a general notice of the proposed rule making in the ***Federal Register.*** The notice must include:
   a. the time, place, and nature of the rule-making proceeding;
   b. the legal authority pursuant to which the rule is proposed; and
   c. the terms or substance of the proposed rule or a description of the subject and issues involved.
2. The agency must give interested persons an opportunity to participate in the rule-making process. This may involve oral hearings.
3. It must review all written and oral comments. Then the agency announces its *final rule making* in the matter. This procedure is often referred to as *notice-and-comment rule making*, or **informal rule making.**
4. The APA may require, in some instances, **formal rule making.** Here, the agency must conduct a trial-like hearing at which the parties may present evidence, engage in cross-examination, present rebuttal evidence, and similar procedures.

Interpretive rule A rule issued by an administrative agency that interprets existing statutory language.

Statement of policy A statement issued by an administrative agency that announces a proposed course of action that the agency intends to follow in the future.

Administrative agencies can issue an **interpretive rule** that interprets existing statutory language. Such rules do not establish new laws. Administrative agencies may issue a **statement of policy.** Such a statement announces a proposed course of action that an agency intends to follow in the future. Interpretive rules and statements of policy do not have the force of law and public notice and participation are not required.

A proposed rule published in the *Federal Register* is set forth in Exhibit 9.4.

Code of Federal Regulations (CFR) A codification of the regulations that have been adopted by executive departments and administrative agencies of the federal government.

Code of Federal Regulations

Rules and regulations adopted by federal administrative agencies are published in the *Federal Register*. The **Code of Federal Regulations (CFR)** is the codification of the regulations that have been adopted by executive departments and administrative agencies of the federal government. Each rule and regulation is assigned a CFR citation, such as 29 CFR 1604.11(a). This citation would be read as "title 29, part 1604, section 11, paragraph (a)."

The CFR is divided up into fifty titles that represent general areas subject to federal regulation. These titles are listed in Exhibit 9.5.

Each title is divided into chapters that state the name of the issuing department or agency. Each chapter is subdivided into parts that cover specific regulatory areas. Most parts are further subdivided into subparts. Each title of the CFR is updated once

Web Exploration

Go to the Electronic Code of Federal Regulations (e-CFR) website at **www.ecfr.gpoaccess.gov.** Where the word "Browse" appears, select the title "Labor" and click on "Go." What regulatory entities are responsible for administering labor law?

[3] 5 U.S.C. Section 553.

Exhibit 9.4 **Proposed rule published in the *Federal Register***

12506

Proposed Rules

Federal Register
Vol. 77, No. 41
Thursday, March 1, 2012

This section of the FEDERAL REGISTER contains notices to the public of the proposed issuance of rules and regulations. The purpose of these notices is to give interested persons an opportunity to participate in the rule making prior to the adoption of the final rules.

DEPARTMENT OF TRANSPORTATION

Federal Aviation Administration

14 CFR Part 39

[Docket No. FAA–2012–0187; Directorate Identifier 2011–NM–094–AD]

RIN 2120–AA64

Airworthiness Directives; The Boeing Company Airplanes

AGENCY: Federal Aviation Administration (FAA), DOT.

ACTION: Notice of proposed rulemaking (NPRM).

SUMMARY: We propose to adopt a new airworthiness directive (AD) for certain The Boeing Company Model 757 airplanes. This proposed AD was prompted by fuel system reviews conducted by the manufacturer. This proposed AD would require modifying the fuel quantity indication system (FQIS) wiring or fuel tank systems to prevent development of an ignition source inside the center fuel tank. We are proposing this AD to prevent ignition sources inside the center fuel tank, which, in combination with flammable fuel vapors, could result in fuel tank explosions and consequent loss of the airplane.

DATES: We must receive comments on this proposed AD by April 30, 2012.

ADDRESSES: You may send comments, using the procedures found in 14 CFR 11.43 and 11.45, by any of the following methods:

- *Federal eRulemaking Portal:* Go to *http://www.regulations.gov.* Follow the instructions for submitting comments.
- *Fax:* 202–493–2251.
- *Mail:* U.S. Department of Transportation, Docket Operations, M–30, West Building Ground Floor, Room W12–140, 1200 New Jersey Avenue SE., Washington, DC 20590.
- *Hand Delivery:* Deliver to Mail address above between 9 a.m. and 5 p.m., Monday through Friday, except Federal holidays.

Examining the AD Docket

You may examine the AD docket on the Internet at *http://www.regulations.gov;* or in person at the Docket Management Facility between 9 a.m. and 5 p.m., Monday through Friday, except Federal holidays. The AD docket contains this proposed AD, the regulatory evaluation, any comments received, and other information. The street address for the Docket Office (phone: 800–647–5527) is in the **ADDRESSES** section. Comments will be available in the AD docket shortly after receipt.

FOR FURTHER INFORMATION CONTACT: Tak Kobayashi, Aerospace Engineer, Propulsion Branch, ANM–140S, FAA, Seattle Aircraft Certification Office (ACO), 1601 Lind Avenue SW., Renton, Washington 98057–3356; phone: 425–917–6499; fax: 425–917–6590; email: *takahisa.kobayashi@faa.gov.*

SUPPLEMENTARY INFORMATION:

Comments Invited

We invite you to send any written relevant data, views, or arguments about this proposal. Send your comments to an address listed under the **ADDRESSES** section. Include "Docket No. FAA–2012–0187; Directorate Identifier 2011–NM–094–AD" at the beginning of your comments. We specifically invite comments on the overall regulatory, economic, environmental, and energy aspects of this proposed AD. We will consider all comments received by the closing date and may amend this proposed AD because of those comments.

We will post all comments we receive, without change, to *http://www.regulations.gov,* including any personal information you provide. We will also post a report summarizing each substantive verbal contact we receive about this proposed AD.

Discussion

The FAA has examined the underlying safety issues involved in fuel tank explosions on several large transport airplanes, including the adequacy of existing regulations, the service history of airplanes subject to those regulations, and existing maintenance practices for fuel tank systems. As a result of those findings, we issued a regulation titled "Transport Airplane Fuel Tank System Design Review, Flammability Reduction and Maintenance and Inspection Requirements" (66 FR 23086, May 7, 2001). In addition to new airworthiness standards for transport airplanes and new maintenance requirements, this rule included Special Federal Aviation Regulation No. 88 ("SFAR 88," Amendment 21–78, and subsequent Amendments 21–82 and 21–83).

Among other actions, SFAR 88 requires certain type design (i.e., type certificate (TC) and supplemental type certificate (STC)) holders to substantiate that their fuel tank systems can prevent ignition sources in the fuel tanks. This requirement applies to type design holders for large turbine-powered transport airplanes and for subsequent modifications to those airplanes. It requires them to perform design reviews and to develop design changes and maintenance procedures if their designs do not meet the new fuel tank safety standards. As explained in the preamble to the rule, we intended to adopt airworthiness directives to mandate any changes found necessary to address unsafe conditions identified as a result of these reviews.

In evaluating these design reviews, we have established four criteria intended to define the unsafe conditions associated with fuel tank systems that require corrective actions. The percentage of operating time during which fuel tanks are exposed to flammable conditions is one of these criteria. The other three criteria address the failure types under evaluation: single failures, a combination of failures, and unacceptable service (failure) experience. For all four criteria, the evaluations included consideration of previous actions taken that may mitigate the need for further action.

We have determined that the actions identified in this proposed AD are necessary to reduce the potential of ignition sources inside the center fuel tank, which has been identified to have a high flammability exposure. Ignition sources inside the center fuel tank, in combination with flammable fuel vapors, could result in fuel tank explosions and consequent loss of the airplane.

The combination of a latent failure within the center fuel tank and a subsequent single failure of the fuel quantity indicating system (FQIS) wiring or components outside the fuel tank can cause development of an

(continued)

Exhibit 9.4 Proposed rule published in the *Federal Register* (continued)

ignition source inside the center fuel tank. Latent in-tank failures, including corrosion/deposits at wire terminals, conductive debris on fuel system probes, wires or probes contacting the tank structure, and wire faults, could create a conductive path inside the center fuel tank. Out-tank single failures including hot shorts in airplane wiring and/or the FQIS processor could result in electrical energy being transmitted into the center fuel tank via the FQIS wiring. The electrical energy, if combined with a latent in-tank failure, could be sufficient to create an ignition source inside the center fuel tank, which, combined with flammable fuel vapors could result in a catastrophic fuel tank explosion.

SFAR 88 and Fuel Tank Flammability Reduction Rule

The National Transportation Safety Board (NTSB) determined that the combination of a latent failure inside the center fuel tank and a subsequent single failure of the FQIS wiring or components outside the fuel tank was the most likely ignition source inside the center fuel tank that resulted in the TWA Flight 800 explosion. After the TWA 800 accident, we issued AD 99–03–04, Amendment 39–11018 (64 FR 4959, February 2, 1999), and AD 98–20–40, Amendment 39–10808 (63 FR 52147, September 30, 1998), mandating separation of the FQIS wiring that penetrates the fuel tank from high power wires and circuits on the classic Boeing 737 and 747 airplanes. Those ADs resulted in installation of Transient Suppression Units (TSUs), Transient Suppression Devices (TSDs), or Isolated Fuel Quantity Transmitter (IFQT) as a method of compliance with the AD requirements.

After we issued those ADs, the findings from the SFAR 88 review showed that most transport category airplanes with high flammability fuel tanks needed TSUs, TSDs, or IFQTs to prevent electrical energy from entering the fuel tanks via the FQIS wiring in the event of a latent failure in combination with a single failure.

Installation of those FQIS protection devices, however, was determined unnecessary on those airplanes that are required to comply with the "Reduction of Fuel Tank Flammability in Transport Category Airplanes" rule (73 FR 42444, July 21, 2008), referred to as the Fuel Tank Flammability Reduction (FTFR) rule. The FTFR rule requires incorporation of a flammability reduction means (FRM) that converts high flammability fuel tanks into low flammability fuel tanks for certain airplane models. Therefore, the unsafe condition identified by SFAR 88 is mitigated by incorporation of an FRM, as discussed in the FTFR rule.

This proposed AD is intended to address the unsafe condition associated with the FQIS wiring that penetrates the center fuel tank for all Boeing Model 757 airplanes that are not subject to the requirements of the FTFR rule. This proposed AD would apply to airplanes operated in all-cargo service and airplanes operated under Title 14 Code of Federal Regulations (CFR) part 91, since those airplanes are not subject to the requirements of the FTFR rule. Also, this proposed AD would apply to airplanes for which the State of Manufacture issued the original certificate of airworthiness or export airworthiness approval prior to January 1, 1992, since those airplanes are also not subject to the requirements of the FTFR rule. However, as explained in paragraph 2–5.a. of Advisory Circular 120–98, "Operator Requirements for Incorporation of Fuel Tank Flammability Reduction Requirements," dated May 7, 2009, to operate a pre-1992 airplane in passenger service after December 26, 2017, operators must incorporate an FRM that meets the requirements of § 26.33(c) before that date. For such airplanes on which an FRM is incorporated, further compliance with this proposed AD is not required.

The nitrogen generating system (NGS) being developed by Boeing to meet the FTFR rule addresses the unsafe condition of this AD, as well as providing other safety improvements. Paragraph (h) of this proposed AD provides that, for operators not required to comply with the FTFR rule, electing to comply with the FTFR rule would be an acceptable method of addressing the unsafe condition.

As discussed in the FTFR rule, the FAA recognized that separate airworthiness actions would be initiated to address the remaining fuel system safety issues for airplanes for which an FRM is not required. We have notified design approval holders that service instructions to support introduction of FQIS protection are now necessary for fuel tanks that are not required to be modified with an FRM by the FTFR rule. To date we have not received any service information from Boeing addressing this specific threat; therefore, we are proceeding with this proposal, which would require modifications using methods approved by the Manager of the Seattle Aircraft Certification Office.

We plan similar actions for those Boeing and Airbus airplanes with similar FQIS vulnerabilities that are not affected by the FTFR rule.

FAA's Determination

We are proposing this AD because we evaluated all the relevant information and determined the unsafe condition described previously is likely to exist or develop in other products of the same type design.

Proposed AD Requirements

This proposed AD would require modifying the FQIS wiring or fuel tank systems to prevent development of an ignition source inside the center fuel tank.

Costs of Compliance

We estimate that this proposed AD affects 352 airplanes of U.S. registry. We have been advised that some of those airplanes are subject to the requirements of the FTFR rule and therefore are excluded from the requirements of this AD.

Because the manufacturer has not yet developed a modification commensurate with the actions specified by this proposed AD, we cannot provide specific information regarding the required number of work hours or the cost of parts to do the proposed modification. In addition, modification costs will likely vary depending on the operator and the airplane configuration. The proposed compliance time of 60 months should provide ample time for the development, approval, and installation of an appropriate modification.

Based on similar modifications, however, we can provide some estimated costs for the proposed modification in this NPRM. The modifications mandated by AD 99–03–04, Amendment 39–11018 (64 FR 4959, February 2, 1999), and AD 98–20–40, Amendment 39–10808 (63 FR 52147, September 30, 1998), for the classic Boeing Model 737 and 747 airplanes (i.e., TSD, TSU, IFQT) are not available for Boeing Model 757 airplanes. But, based on the costs associated with those modifications, we estimate the cost of this new proposed modification to be no more than $100,000 per airplane. The Honeywell FQIS may need additional modifications, which may cost as much as $100,000 per airplane. The cost impact of the proposed AD therefore is estimated to be between $100,000 and $200,000 per airplane.

As indicated earlier in this preamble, we specifically invite the submission of comments and other data regarding the costs of this proposed AD.

Exhibit 9.4 Proposed rule published in the *Federal Register* (continued)

12508 Federal Register / Vol. 77, No. 41 / Thursday, March 1, 2012 / Proposed Rules

Authority for This Rulemaking

Title 49 of the United States Code specifies the FAA's authority to issue rules on aviation safety. Subtitle I, section 106, describes the authority of the FAA Administrator. Subtitle VII: Aviation Programs, describes in more detail the scope of the Agency's authority.

We are issuing this rulemaking under the authority described in subtitle VII, part A, subpart III, section 44701: "General requirements." Under that section, Congress charges the FAA with promoting safe flight of civil aircraft in air commerce by prescribing regulations for practices, methods, and procedures the Administrator finds necessary for safety in air commerce. This regulation is within the scope of that authority because it addresses an unsafe condition that is likely to exist or develop on products identified in this rulemaking action.

Regulatory Findings

We determined that this proposed AD would not have federalism implications under Executive Order 13132. This proposed AD would not have a substantial direct effect on the States, on the relationship between the national Government and the States, or on the distribution of power and responsibilities among the various levels of government.

For the reasons discussed above, I certify this proposed regulation:

(1) Is not a "significant regulatory action" under Executive Order 12866,

(2) Is not a "significant rule" under the DOT Regulatory Policies and Procedures (44 FR 11034, February 26, 1979),

(3) Will not affect intrastate aviation in Alaska, and

(4) Will not have a significant economic impact, positive or negative, on a substantial number of small entities under the criteria of the Regulatory Flexibility Act.

List of Subjects in 14 CFR Part 39

Air transportation, Aircraft, Aviation safety, Incorporation by reference, Safety.

The Proposed Amendment

Accordingly, under the authority delegated to me by the Administrator, the FAA proposes to amend 14 CFR part 39 as follows:

PART 39—AIRWORTHINESS DIRECTIVES

1. The authority citation for part 39 continues to read as follows:

Authority: 49 U.S.C. 106(g), 40113, 44701.

§ 39.13 [Amended]

2. The FAA amends § 39.13 by adding the following new airworthiness directive (AD):

The Boeing Company: Docket No. FAA–2012–0187; Directorate Identifier 2011–NM–094–AD.

(a) Comments Due Date

We must receive comments by April 30, 2012.

(b) Affected ADs

None.

(c) Applicability

This AD applies to The Boeing Company Model 757–200, –200PF, –200CB, and –300 series airplanes; certificated in any category; for which compliance with 14 CFR 121.1117(d), 125.509(d), or 129.117(d) is not required; regardless of the date of issuance of the original certificate of airworthiness or export airworthiness approval.

(d) Subject

Joint Aircraft System Component (JASC)/Air Transport Association (ATA) of America Code 7397: Engine fuel system wiring.

(e) Unsafe Condition

This AD was prompted by fuel system reviews conducted by the manufacturer. We are issuing this AD to prevent development of an ignition source inside the center fuel tank caused by a latent in-tank failure combined with electrical energy transmitted into the center fuel tank via the fuel quantity indicating system (FQIS) wiring due to a single out-tank failure.

(f) Compliance

Comply with this AD within the compliance times specified, unless already done.

(g) Modification

Within 60 months after the effective date of this AD, modify the FQIS wiring or fuel tank systems to prevent development of an ignition source inside the center fuel tank, in accordance with a method approved by the Manager, Seattle Aircraft Certification Office (ACO), FAA.

Note 1 to paragraph (g) of this AD: After accomplishment of the actions required by paragraph (g) of this AD, maintenance and/or preventive maintenance under 14 CFR part 43 is permitted provided the maintenance does not result in changing the AD-mandated configuration (reference 14 CFR 39.7).

(h) Optional Installation of Flammability Reduction Means

As an alternative to the requirements of paragraph (g) of this AD, operators may elect to comply with the requirements of 14 CFR 121.1117 or 14 CFR 125.509 or 14 CFR 129.117 (not including the exclusion of cargo airplanes in Sections 121.1117(j), 129.117(j), and 125.509(j)). Following this election, failure to comply with Sections 121.1117, 129.117, and 125.509 is a violation of this AD.

(i) Alternative Methods of Compliance (AMOCs)

(1) The Manager, Seattle ACO, FAA, has the authority to approve AMOCs for this AD, if requested using the procedures found in 14 CFR 39.19. In accordance with 14 CFR 39.19, send your request to your principal inspector or local Flight Standards District Office, as appropriate. If sending information directly to the manager of the ACO, send it to the attention of the person identified in the Related Information section of this AD. Information may be emailed to: *9-ANM-Seattle-ACO-AMOC-Requests@faa.gov.*

(2) Before using any approved AMOC, notify your appropriate principal inspector, or lacking a principal inspector, the manager of the local flight standards district office/certificate holding district office.

(j) Related Information

For more information about this AD, contact Tak Kobayashi, Aerospace Engineer, Propulsion Branch, ANM–140S, FAA, Seattle Aircraft Certification Office (ACO), 1601 Lind Avenue SW., Renton, Washington 98057–3356; phone: 425–917–6499; fax: 425–917–6590; email: *takahisa.kobayashi@faa.gov.*

Issued in Renton, Washington, on February 21, 2012.

Ali Bahrami,

Manager, Transport Airplane Directorate, Aircraft Certification Service.

[FR Doc. 2012–4931 Filed 2–29–12; 8:45 am]

BILLING CODE 4910–13–P

DEPARTMENT OF JUSTICE

Drug Enforcement Administration

21 CFR Part 1308

[Docket No. DEA–345]

Schedules of Controlled Substances: Placement of Five Synthetic Cannabinoids Into Schedule I

AGENCY: Drug Enforcement Administration, Department of Justice.

ACTION: Notice of proposed rulemaking.

SUMMARY: The Drug Enforcement Administration (DEA) proposes placing five synthetic cannabinoids 1-pentyl-3-(1-naphthoyl)indole (JWH–018), 1-butyl-3-(1-naphthoyl)indole (JWH–073), 1-[2-(4-morpholinyl)ethyl]-3-(1-naphthoyl)indole (JWH–200), 5-(1,1-dimethylheptyl)-2-(3-hydroxycyclohexyl)-phenol (CP–47,497), and 5-(1,1-dimethyloctyl)-2-(3-hydroxycyclohexyl)-phenol (cannabicyclohexanol, CP–47,497 C8 homologue) including their salts, isomers, and salts of isomers whenever the existence of such salts, isomers, and salts of isomers is possible, into Schedule I of the Controlled Substances Act (CSA). This proposed action is pursuant to the CSA which requires that

Exhibit 9.5 Titles of the Code of Federal Regulations

Title 1	General Provisions	Title 26	Internal Review
Title 2	Grants and Agreements	Title 27	Alcohol, Tobacco Products, and Firearms
Title 3	The President	Title 28	Judicial Administration
Title 4	Accounts	Title 29	Labor
Title 5	Administrative Personnel	Title 30	Mineral Resources
Title 6	Homeland Security	Title 31	Money and Finance: Treasury
Title 7	Agriculture	Title 32	National Defense
Title 8	Aliens and Nationality	Title 33	Navigation and Navigable Waters
Title 9	Animal and Animal Products	Title 34	Education
Title 10	Energy	Title 35	Reserved (formerly Panama Canal)
Title 11	Federal Elections	Title 36	Parks, Forests, and Public Property
Title 12	Banks and Banking	Title 37	Patents, Trademarks, and Copyrights
Title 13	Business Credit and Assistance	Title 38	Pensions, Bonuses, and Veterans' Relief
Title 14	Aeronautics and Space	Title 39	Postal Service
Title 15	Commerce and Foreign Trade	Title 40	Protection of Environment
Title 16	Commercial Practices	Title 41	Public Contracts and Property Management
Title 17	Commodity and Securities Exchanges	Title 42	Public Health
Title 18	Conservation of Power and Water Resources	Title 43	Public Lands: Interior
Title 19	Custom Duties	Title 44	Emergency Management and Assistance
Title 20	Employees' Benefits	Title 45	Public Welfare
Title 21	Food and Drugs	Title 46	Shipping
Title 22	Foreign Relations	Title 47	Telecommunication
Title 23	Highways	Title 48	Federal Acquisition Regulations System
Title 24	Housing and Urban Development	Title 49	Transportation
Title 25	Indians	Title 50	Wildlife and Fisheries

each calendar year and is available in printed form. Federal rules and regulations are also available in the **Electronic Code of Federal Regulations (e-CFR)** at www.ecfr.gpoaccess.gov.

An example of an administrative rule adopted by the federal Equal Employment Opportunity Commission (EEOC) is shown in Exhibit 9.6.

Licensing Power

License Permission that an administrative agency grants to persons or businesses to conduct certain types of commerce or professions.

Statutes often require the issuance of a government **license** before a person or business can enter certain types of industries (such as banks, television and radio stations, and commercial airlines) or professions (such as doctors, lawyers, dentists, certified public accountants, and contractors). The administrative agency that regulates the specific area is given **licensing power** to determine whether to grant a license to an applicant.

Applicants must usually submit detailed applications to the appropriate administrative agency. In addition, the agency usually accepts written comments from interested parties and holds hearings on the matter. Courts generally defer to the expertise of administrative agencies in licensing matters.

> **Example** A group of persons wants to start a new national bank. To do this, the applicants must obtain approval from the Office of the Comptroller of Currency (OCC), a federal administrative agency that charters, supervises, and regulates national banks. The group will hire lawyers, economists, accountants, and other professionals to prepare the application. After considering the application, the OCC will either approve or reject it.

Judicial Authority

Judicial authority Authority of an administrative agency to adjudicate cases in an administrative proceeding

Many administrative agencies have the **judicial authority** to decide cases through administrative proceedings. Such a proceeding is initiated when an agency serves a complaint on a party the agency believes has violated a statute or an administrative rule or order.

Exhibit 9.6 Administrative rule adopted by the Equal Employment Opportunity Commission

United States Code of Federal Regulations
Title 29-Labor

Subtitle B-Regulations Relating to Labor

Chapter XIV–Equal Employment Opportunity Commission
Part 1604–Guidelines on Discrimination Because of Sex

Section 1604.11–Sexual harassment

(a) Harassment on the basis of sex is a violation of section 703 of title VII. Unwelcome sexual advances, requests for sexual favors, and other verbal or physical conduct of a sexual nature constitute sexual harassment when (1) submission to such conduct is made either explicitly or implicitly a term or condition of an individual's employment, (2) submission to or rejection of such conduct by an individual is used as the basis for employment decisions affecting such individual, or (3) such conduct has the purpose or effect of unreasonably interfering with an individual's work performance or creating an intimidating, hostile, or offensive working environment.

(b) In determining whether alleged conduct constitutes sexual harassment, the Commission will look at the record as a whole and at the totality of the circumstances, such as the nature of the sexual advances and the context in which the alleged incidents occurred. The determination of the legality of a particular action will be made from the facts, on a case by case basis.

(c) [Reserved]

(d) With respect to conduct between fellow employees, an employer is responsible for acts of sexual harassment in the workplace where the employer (or its agents or supervisory employees) knows or should have known of the conduct, unless it can show that it took immediate and appropriate corrective action.

(e) An employer may also be responsible for the acts of non-employees, with respect to sexual harassment of employees in the workplace, where the employer (or its agents or supervisory employees) knows or should have known of the conduct and fails to take immediate and appropriate corrective action. In reviewing these cases the Commission will consider the extent of the employer's control and any other legal responsibility which the employer may have with respect to the conduct of such non-employees.

(f) Prevention is the best tool for the elimination of sexual harassment. An employer should take all steps necessary to prevent sexual harassment from occurring, such as affirmatively raising the subject, expressing strong disapproval, developing appropriate sanctions, informing employees of their right to raise and how to raise the issue of harassment under title VII, and developing methods to sensitize all concerned.

(g) Other related practices: Where employment opportunities or benefits are granted because of an individual's submission to the employer's sexual advances or requests for sexual favors, the employer may be held liable for unlawful sex discrimination against other persons who were qualified for but denied that employment opportunity or benefit.

The principles involved here continue to apply to race, color, religion or national origin.

Example The Occupational Safety and Health Administration (OSHA) is a federal administrative agency empowered to enforce worker safety rules. OSHA can bring an administrative proceeding against an employer for violating a federal worker safety rule. The agency can make a decision that the employer violated the rule and order the violator to pay a fine.

Procedural due process Due process that requires the respondent to be given proper and timely notice of the allegations or charges against him or her and an opportunity to present evidence on the matter.

In adjudicating cases, an administrative agency must comply with the Due Process Clause of the U.S. Constitution (or state constitution, if applicable). **Procedural due process** requires the respondent to be given proper and timely notice of the allegations or charges against him or her and an opportunity to present evidence on the matter.

A decision of an administrative law judge (ALJ) is set forth in Exhibit 9.7.

Exhibit 9.7 Decision of an administrative law judge

INITIAL DECISION RELEASE NO. 432

ADMINISTRATIVE PROCEEDING

FILE NO. 3-14161

UNITED STATES OF AMERICA

Before the

SECURITIES AND EXCHANGE COMMISSION

In the Matter of	:	
	:	INITIAL DECISION
GORDON A. DRIVER	:	September 22, 2011
	:	
	:	

APPEARANCES: Spencer E. Bendell and Susan F. Hannan for the Division of Enforcement, Securities and Exchange Commission. Gordon A. Driver, pro se.

BEFORE: Robert G. Mahony, Administrative Law Judge.

INTRODUCTION

The Securities and Exchange Commission (Commission) issued its Order Instituting Proceedings (OIP) on December 10, 2010, pursuant to Section 15(b) of the Securities Exchange Act of 1934 (Exchange Act). The OIP alleges that on December 14, 2009, a final judgment was entered by consent against Respondent Gordon A. Driver (Driver or Respondent) permanently enjoining him from future violations of the federal securities laws. The Commission instituted this proceeding to determine whether these allegations are true and, if so, to decide whether remedial action is appropriate in the public interest. The Division of Enforcement (Division) seeks to bar Driver from association with any broker or dealer. Additionally, the Division seeks to collaterally bar Driver under the Dodd-Frank Wall Street Reform and Consumer Protection Act of 2010 (Dodd-Frank Act) from association with any investment adviser, municipal securities dealer, municipal advisor, transfer agent, or nationally recognized statistical rating organization (NRSRO).

Exhibit 9.7 Decision of an administrative law judge *(continued)*

FINDINGS OF FACT

Driver, age fifty-one as of May 14, 2009, was a resident of Las Vegas, Nevada, and Hamilton, Ontario, Canada. From 1998 to 2007, during which Driver engaged in part of the conduct underlying the Judgment against him, Driver resided in Southern California.

From February 2006 to May 2009, Driver, acting as an unregistered broker, engaged in the misconduct underlying the Judgment against him. During this time, Driver was associated with Axcess Automation, LLC (Axcess), an entity registered as a Nevada limited liability company since October 17, 2007. Driver acted as Axcess' manager, was a signatory on the bank accounts into which investors wired funds, and had sole discretionary authority over the accounts through which he traded investor funds.

Driver raised at least $14.1 million from over 100 investors in the United States and Canada from approximately February 2006 to May 2009. Driver fraudulently misrepresented to investors that he would use their funds to trade "e-Mini S&P 500 futures" using proprietary software, and that he would provide investors with between one percent and five percent weekly return. Driver solicited friends, neighbors, and business acquaintances, and hired "finders" personally to recruit additional investors. Driver directed investors to wire transfer their funds into his personal bank account or into an account held in Axcess' name.

Driver used $3.7 million of the $14.1 million deposited into these accounts to engage in futures trading, ultimately resulting in a cumulative loss of $3.55 million. Additionally, Driver operated a "ponzi scheme" and misappropriated approximately $10.7 million of the $14.1 million by using funds received from new investors to pay existing investors. Further, over $1.1 million of the $14.1 million collected from investors was misappropriated by Driver and used by him to pay his personal expenses.

In February 2009, Driver prepared and provided a false annual statement, on Axcess letterhead, to forty-eight investors falsely showing an account balance of $9.6 million as of December 31, 2008, when, in fact, Driver only held a total of approximately $276,000 in all its bank accounts. Further, Driver fabricated and provided a trading account statement to at least one "finder" in October 2008, falsely stating an account balance of approximately $34.7 million when, in fact, the account balance was approximately $11,000.

On December 3, 2009, Driver consented to the entry of the Judgment permanently restraining and enjoining him from violating Sections 5 and 17(a) of the Securities Act of 1933, Sections 10(b) and 15(a) of the Exchange Act, and Rule 10b-5 promulgated thereunder. Additionally, Driver was ordered to pay disgorgement. On December 14, 2009, the Judgment was filed.

CONCLUSIONS OF LAW

Based on the foregoing, Driver is subject to Section 15(b)(6) of the Exchange Act, and the Administrative Law Judge has grounds to impose remedial sanctions, including a collateral bar under the Dodd-Frank Act, if such sanctions are in the public interest.

To determine whether sanctions under Section 15(b) of the Exchange Act are in the public interest, the Commission considers six factors: (1) the egregiousness of the respondent's actions; (2) whether the violations were isolated or recurrent; (3) the degree of scienter; (4) the sincerity of the respondent's assurances against future violations; (5) the respondent's recognition of the wrongful nature of his or her conduct; and (6) the likelihood that the respondent's occupation will present opportunities for future violations. No one factor is controlling. Remedial sanctions are not intended to punish a respondent, but to protect the public from future harm.

Driver's actions were egregious and recurrent. Driver engaged in a "ponzi scheme" spanning more than three years causing substantial harm to over 100 investors. He provided false and misleading information to certain of those investors and "finders." Additionally, Driver used significant investor funds for his own benefit.

Driver acted with scienter. Driver had sole discretion and authority over the bank accounts into which he directed investors to wire transfer their funds. He had actual knowledge of the trading losses he was incurring, while at the same time continuing to provide false and misleading information to investors regarding the account balances.

(continued)

Exhibit 9.7 Decision of an administrative law judge *(continued)*

Driver has not admitted the wrongful nature of his conduct. Likewise, he has made no assurances against future violations. Throughout his Deposition, Driver asserted his privilege against self-incrimination under the Fifth Amendment. Without an associational bar, the potential for Driver's future violations remains. Further, the Commission has often emphasized, the public interest determination extends to the public-at-large, the welfare of investors as a class, and standards of conduct in the securities business generally.

In view of the factors in their entirety, a collateral bar is necessary and appropriate in the public interest.

ORDER

IT IS ORDERED that, pursuant to Section 15(b)(6)(A) of the Securities Exchange Act of 1934, Gordon A. Driver is barred from association with any broker, dealer, investment adviser, municipal securities dealer, municipal advisor, transfer agent, and NRSRO, and from participating in an offering of penny stock.

The Commission will enter an order of finality unless a party files a petition for review or a motion to correct a manifest error of fact, or the Commission determines on its own initiative to review the Initial Decision as to a party. If any of these events occur, the Initial Decision shall not become final as to that party.

Robert G. Mahony
Administrative Law Judge

UNITED STATES OF AMERICA

Before the

SECURITIES AND EXCHANGE COMMISSION

SECURITIES EXCHANGE ACT OF 1934

Rel. No. 65707/November 8, 2011

Admin. Proc. File No. 3-14161

In the Matter of :
:
GORDON A. DRIVER :
:
:

NOTICE THAT INITIAL DECISION HAS BECOME FINAL

The time for filing a petition for review of the initial decision in this proceeding has expired. No such petition has been filed by Gordon A. Driver, and the Commission has not chosen to review the decision on its own initiative.

Accordingly, notice is hereby given, pursuant to Rule 360(d) of the Commission's Rules of Practice, that the initial decision of the administrative law judge has become the final decision of the Commission with respect to Gordon A. Driver. The order contained in that decision is hereby declared effective. That order barred Gordon A. Driver from association with any broker, dealer, investment adviser, municipal securities dealer, municipal advisor, transfer agent, and NRSRO, and from participating in an offering of penny stock.

For the Commission by the Office of the General Counsel, pursuant to delegated authority.

Elizabeth M. Murphy, Secretary

Executive Power

Administrative agencies are usually granted **executive powers,** such as the power to investigate and prosecute possible violations of statutes, administrative rules, and administrative orders.

Executive power Power that administrative agencies are granted, such as to investigate and prosecute possible violations of statutes, administrative rules, and administrative orders.

> **Example** The Antitrust Division of the United States Department of Justice suspects that three companies in the same line of commerce are engaged in illegal price fixing. The Department of Justice has the authority to investigate whether a criminal violation of the Sherman Antitrust Act has occurred. The Department of Justice can prosecute suspected criminal violators of criminal antitrust laws.

The legislative, judicial, and executive powers of administrative agencies are described in Exhibit 9.8.

Administrative Searches

Learning Objective 7
Describe administrative searches.

To perform its functions, an agency must often obtain information from the persons and businesses under investigation, as well as from other sources. If the required information is not supplied voluntarily, or if those being investigated do not voluntarily give permission for the inspection of their premises, the agency may issue an administrative subpoena to search the premises and obtain the necessary evidence. This is called an **administrative search.**

Exhibit 9.8 Powers of administrative agencies

Power	Description of Power
1. Legislative Power	
A. Substantive rule making	To adopt rules that advance the purpose of the statutes that the agency is empowered to enforce. These rules have the force of law. Public notice and participation are required.
B. Interpretive rule making	To adopt rules that interpret statutes. These rules do not establish new laws. Neither public notice nor participation is required.
C. Statements of policy	To announce a proposed course of action the agency plans to take in the future. These statements do not have the force of law. Public participation and notice are not required.
D. Licensing	To grant licenses to applicants (e.g., television station licenses, bank charters) and to suspend or revoke licenses.
2. Judicial Power	The power to adjudicate cases through an administrative proceeding. This includes the power to issue a complaint, hold a hearing by an administrative law judge (ALJ), and issue an order deciding the case and assessing remedies.
3. Executive Power	The power to prosecute violations of statutes and administrative rules and orders. This includes the power to investigate suspected violations, issue administrative subpoenas, and conduct administrative searches.

Administrative subpoena An order that directs the subject of the subpoena to disclose the requested information.

An administrative agency can issue an **administrative subpoena** to a business or person subject to its jurisdiction. The subpoena directs the party to disclose the requested information to the administrative agency. The administrative agency can seek judicial enforcement of the subpoena if the party does not comply.

Unreasonable search and seizure Any search and seizure by the government that violates the Fourth Amendment to the U.S. Constitution.

Most inspections by administrative agencies are considered "searches" that are subject to the **Fourth Amendment to the U.S. Constitution.** This amendment protects persons (including businesses) from **unreasonable search and seizure.** Searches by administrative agencies are generally considered to be "reasonable," within the meaning of the Fourth Amendment, if

- the party voluntarily agrees to the search;
- the search is conducted pursuant to a validly issued **search warrant**;
- a warrantless search is conducted in an emergency situation;
- the business is part of a special industry where warrantless searches are automatically considered valid (such as the sale of liquor or firearms); or
- the business is part of a hazardous industry and a statute expressly provides for non-arbitrary warrantless searches (such as coal mines).

Evidence from an unreasonable search and seizure not meeting any of these requirements is considered "tainted evidence" and is inadmissible in court.

Learning Objective 8
Explain the judicial review of administrative agency decisions.

Judicial Review of Administrative Agency Actions

Many federal statutes expressly provide for **judicial review of administrative agency actions.** Where an enabling statute does not provide for review by the agency, the APA authorizes judicial review of agency actions. The party appealing the decision of an administrative agency is called the **petitioner.**

Decisions of federal administrative agencies are appealed to the appropriate federal court. Decisions of state administrative agencies may be appealed to the proper state court. The federal appeal process is illustrated in Exhibit 9.9.

Learning Objective 9
List and describe important federal administrative agencies.

Federal Administrative Agencies

Federal administrative agencies Federal administrative agencies that are created by Congress.

The federal government has created numerous administrative agencies that have the authority to enforce federal statutes enacted by Congress. Several major **federal administrative agencies** and the areas of the law that they are empowered to regulate are discussed below.

Equal Employment Opportunity Commission (EEOC)

Equal Employment Opportunity Commission (EEOC) The federal administrative agency that is responsible for enforcing most federal antidiscrimination laws.

The **Equal Employment Opportunity Commission (EEOC)** is the federal administrative agency responsible for enforcing certain federal antidiscrimination laws. Some of the federal statutes that the EEOC is empowered to enforce are:

We hold these truths to be self-evident, that all men and women are created equal.
Elizabeth Cady Stanton (1848)

- **Title VII of the Civil Rights Act of 1964,**[4] which prohibits job discrimination based on race, color, national origin, sex, and religion.
- **Pregnancy Discrimination Act of 1978,**[5] which forbids employment discrimination because of "pregnancy, childbirth, or related medical conditions."
- **Title I of the Americans with Disabilities Act of 1990,**[6] as amended by the **Americans with Disabilities Act Amendments Act of 2008 (ADAAA),**[7] which prohibits employment discrimination against qualified

[4]42 U.S.C. Sections 2000(d) et seq.
[5]42 U.S.C. Section 2000(e)(K).
[6]42 U.S.C. Sections 12111–12117.
[7]Public Law 110–325, 122 Stat. 3553 (2008).

Exhibit 9.9 Appeal of a federal administrative agency rule, order, or decision

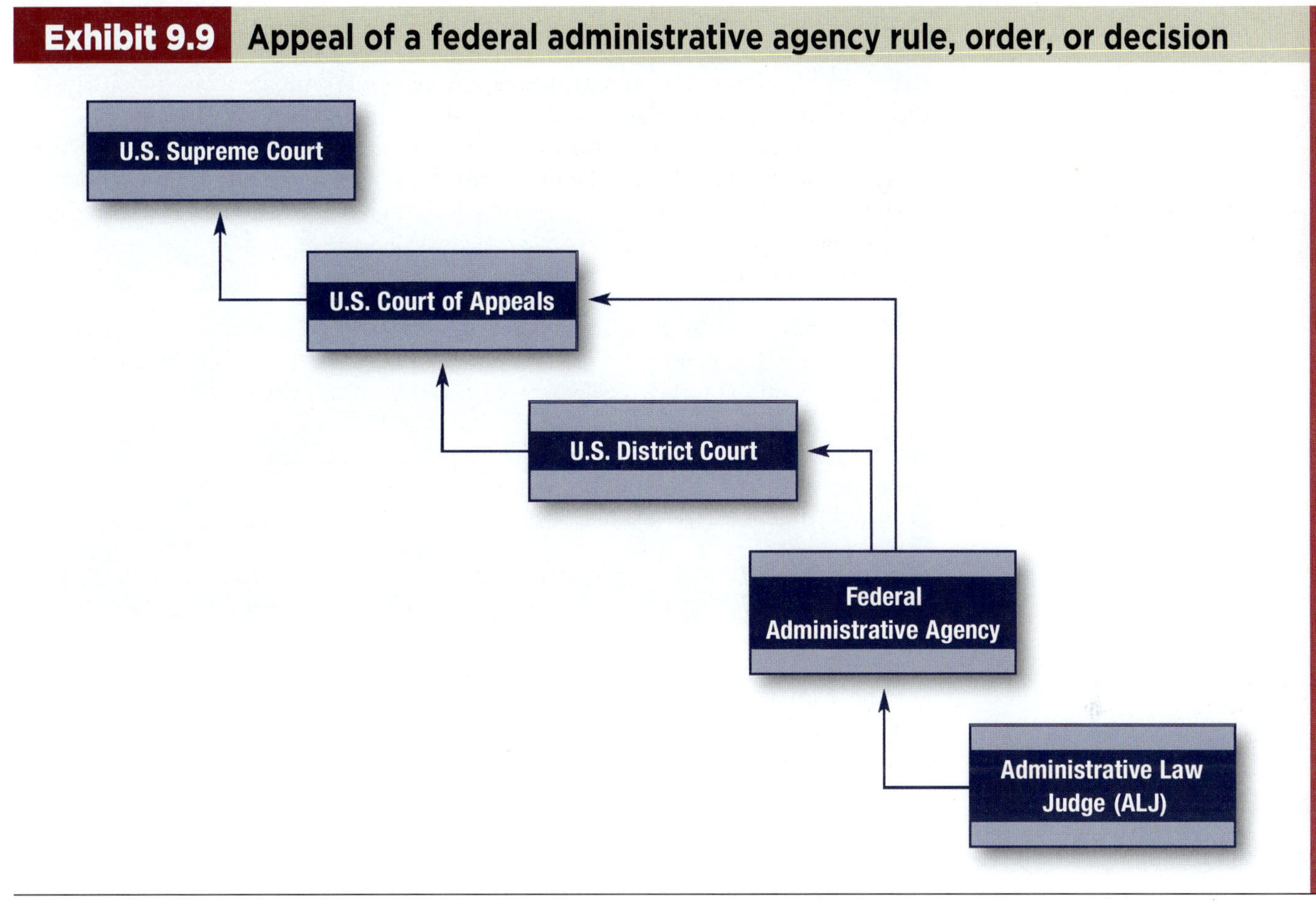

individuals with disabilities with regard to job application procedures, hiring, compensation, training, promotion, and termination.

- **Equal Pay Act of 1963,**[8] which protects both sexes from pay discrimination based on sex.
- **Age Discrimination in Employment Act of 1967 (ADEA),**[9] which protects people who are 40 or older from discrimination because of their age.
- **Genetic Information Nondiscrimination Act of 2008 (GINA),**[10] which makes it illegal for an employer to discriminate against job applicants and employees based on genetic information.

The EEOC is empowered to interpret these statutes, conduct investigations, encourage conciliation between parties, and bring suits to enforce the law. The EEOC can also seek injunctive relief.

We won't have a society if we destroy the environment.
Margaret Mead

Environmental Protection Agency (EPA)

The **Environmental Protection Agency (EPA)** is a federal administrative agency that is empowered to enforce federal environmental protection laws. The EPA has broad rule-making powers to advance the environmental laws it is empowered to administer. The agency also has adjudicative powers to hold hearings, make decisions, and order remedies for violations of federal environmental laws. In addition, the EPA can initiate judicial proceedings in court against alleged violators.

Environmental Protection Agency (EPA) A federal administrative agency created by Congress to coordinate the implementation and enforcement of the federal environmental protection laws.

[8]29 U.S.C. Section 206(d).
[9]29 U.S.C. Sections 621–634.
[10]Public Law 110–233, 122 Stat. 881.

The EPA is charged with enforcing the Clean Air Act,[11] Clean Water Act,[12] Safe Drinking Water Act,[13] Endangered Species Act,[14] Comprehensive Environmental Response, Compensation, and Liability Act (CERCLA, or "the Superfund"),[15] Insecticide, Fungicide, and Rodenticide Act,[16] and numerous other federal laws designed to protect the environment.

Food and Drug Administration (FDA)

The **Food, Drug, and Cosmetic Act (FDCA** or **FDC Act)** [17] was enacted in 1938. This federal statute regulates the testing, manufacture, distribution, and sale of foods, drugs, cosmetics, and medicinal devices in the United States. The **Food and Drug Administration (FDA)** is the federal administrative agency empowered to enforce the FDCA.

Food and Drug Administration (FDA) The federal administrative agency that administers and enforces the federal Food, Drug, and Cosmetic Act.

Before certain food additives, drugs, cosmetics, and medicinal devices can be sold to the public, they must receive FDA approval. A manufacturer must submit an application to the FDA that contains relevant information about the safety and uses of the product. The FDA, after considering the evidence, will either approve or deny the application.

The FDA can seek search warrants and conduct inspections; obtain orders for the seizure, recall, and condemnation of products; seek injunctions; and turn over suspected criminal violations to the U.S. Department of Justice for prosecution.

Securities and Exchange Commission (SEC) The federal administrative agency that is empowered to administer federal securities laws. The SEC can adopt rules and regulations to interpret and implement federal securities laws.

Securities and Exchange Commission (SEC)

The **Securities and Exchange Commission (SEC)** is a federal administrative agency that is empowered to administer federal securities laws. Two of the primary statutes enforced by the SEC are the Securities Act of 1933 and the Securities Exchange Act of

[11]Public Law 88-206.
[12]33 U.S.C. Sections 1251–1367.
[13]21 U.S.C. Section 349 and 300f–300j-25.
[14]16 U.S.C. Sections 1531–1544.
[15]42 U.S.C. Sections 9601–9675.
[16]7 U.S.C. Sections 135 et seq.
[17]21 U.S.C. Section 301.

1934. The Securities Act is a federal statute that primarily regulates the issue of securities by companies and other businesses. The **Securities Exchange Act of 1934**[18] is a federal statute primarily designed to prevent fraud in the trading of securities.

The major responsibilities of the SEC are as follows:

- The SEC can adopt rules (also called regulations) that further the purpose of the federal securities statutes. These rules have the force of law.
- It can investigate alleged securities violations and bring enforcement actions against suspected violators. This may include recommendations for criminal prosecution. Criminal prosecutions of violations of federal securities laws are brought by the U.S. Department of Justice.
- The SEC may bring a civil action to recover monetary damages from violators of securities laws.
- The SEC regulates the activities of securities brokers and advisors. This includes registering brokers and advisors and taking enforcement action against those who violate securities laws

Occupational Safety and Health Administration (OSHA)

In 1970, Congress enacted the **Occupational Safety and Health Act**[19] to promote safety in the workplace. The **Occupational Safety and Health Administration (OSHA)** is the agency empowered to adopt rules and regulations to interpret and enforce the Occupational Safety and Health Act. OSHA has established thousands of specific workplace safety standards that employers must meet. The act also imposes record-keeping and reporting requirements on employers and requires them to post notices in the workplace, informing employees of their rights under the act.

Occupational Safety and Health Administration (OSHA) A federal administrative agency that is empowered to enforce the Occupational Safety and Health Act.

OSHA is also empowered to inspect places of employment for health hazards and safety violations. If a violation is found, OSHA can issue a written citation that requires the employer to abate or correct the situation. Employers who violate the act, OSHA rules and regulations, or OSHA citations are subject to both civil and criminal penalties.

National Labor Relations Board (NLRB)

The **National Labor Relations Board (NLRB)** is a federal administrative body that oversees union elections, prevents employers and unions from engaging in illegal and unfair labor practices, and enforces and interprets certain federal labor laws. The decisions of the NLRB are enforceable in court.

National Labor Relations Board (NLRB) A federal administrative agency that oversees union elections, prevents employers and unions from engaging in illegal and unfair labor practices, and enforces and interprets certain federal labor laws.

Some of the federal statutes that the NLRB is empowered to enforce are:

- The **Norris-LaGuardia Act.** Enacted in 1932, this statute stipulates that it is legal for employees to organize.[20]
- The **National Labor Relations Act (NLRA).** Also known as the **Wagner Act,** this statute was enacted in 1935.[21] The NLRA establishes the right of employees to form and join labor organizations, to bargain collectively with employers, and to engage in concerted activity to promote these rights.
- The **Labor Management Relations Act.** Also known as the **Taft-Hartley Act,** Congress enacted this statute in 1947 to (1) expand the activities that labor unions can engage in, (2) give employers the right

[18] 15 U.S.C. Sections 78a–78mm.
[19] 29 U.S.C. Sections 553, 651–678.
[20] 29 U.S.C. Sections 101–110, 113–115.
[21] 29 U.S.C. Sections 151–169.

to engage in free speech efforts against unions prior to a union election, and (3) give the president of the United States the right to seek an injunction (for up to 80 days) against a strike that would create a national emergency.[22]

- The **Labor Management Reporting and Disclosure Act.** In 1959, Congress enacted this statute, also known as the **Landrum-Griffin Act,** to regulate internal union affairs and establish the rights of union members.[23]

Consumer Product Safety Commission (CPSC)

Consumer Product Safety Commission (CPSC) A federal administrative agency empowered to adopt rules and regulations to interpret and enforce the Consumer Product Safety Act.

In 1972, Congress enacted the **Consumer Product Safety Act (CPSA)**[24] and created the **Consumer Product Safety Commission (CPSC).** This agency is empowered to conduct research on the safety of consumer products, collect data regarding injuries caused by consumer products, and adopt rules and regulations to interpret and enforce the CPSA.

The CPSC issues product safety standards for consumer products that pose an unreasonable risk of injury. If a consumer product is found to be imminently hazardous—that is, if its use causes an unreasonable risk of death or serious injury or illness—the manufacturer can be required to recall, repair, or replace the product or take other corrective action. Alternatively, the CPSC can seek injunctions, bring actions to seize hazardous consumer products, seek civil penalties for knowing violations of the act, or seek criminal penalties for knowing and willful violations of the act or of CPSC rules. A notice of the recall of a hazardous toy by the Consumer Safety Product Commission appears as Exhibit 9.10.

Exhibit 9.10 Notice of recall of a hazardous toy by the Consumer Safety Product Commission

U.S. Consumer Product
Safety Commission
www.cpsc.gov

Health Canada
www.hc-sc.gc.ca

Firm's Recall Hotline: (855) 880-4504
CPSC Recall Hotline: (800) 638-2772
CPSC Media Contact: (301) 504-7908
HC Media Contact: (613) 957-2983

FOR IMMEDIATE RELEASE
September 8, 2011
Release #11-321

Dolls Recalled by Pottery Barn Kids Due To Strangulation Hazard

WASHINGTON, D.C.-The U.S. Consumer Product Safety Commission and Health Canada, in cooperation with the firm named below, today announced a voluntary recall of the following consumer product. Consumers should stop using recalled products immediately unless otherwise instructed. It is illegal to resell or attempt to resell a recalled consumer product.

Name of Product: Chloe, Sophie and Audrey soft dolls

Units: About 81,000 in the United States and 1,300 in Canada

Importer: Pottery Barn Kids, a division of Williams-Sonoma Inc., of San Francisco, Calif.

---

[22] 29 U.S.C. Section 141 et seq.
[24] 15 U.S.C. Section 2051.
[23] 29 U.S.C. Section 401 et seq.

Exhibit 9.10 Notice of recall of a hazardous toy by the Consumer Safety Product Commission *(continued)*

Hazard: The hair on the Chloe and Sophie dolls may contain loops that are large enough to fit around a child's head and neck, and the headband on the Audrey doll, if loosened, can form a loop that fits around a child's head and neck. These loops can pose a strangulation hazard.

Incidents/Injuries: The firm has received five reports of dolls with looped hair, including one report in which a loop of the Chloe doll's hair was found around the neck of a 21-month old child. The child was not injured.

Description: This recall involves soft dolls sold under the names Audrey, Chloe and Sophie. The dolls measure about 17 inches high and have hair made of yarn. Audrey's hair is black, Chloe's hair is dark brown and Sophie's hair is blonde. The dolls are part of Pottery Barn Kids' Girl Doll Collection. The doll's name can be found on a tag sewn onto her bottom.

Sold exclusively at: Pottery Barn Kids stores nationwide, online at www.potterybarnkids.com and through Pottery Barn Kids catalogs from July 2006 to April 2011 for about $40.

Manufactured in: China

Remedy: Consumers should take the dolls away from children immediately and cut the looped hair of the Chloe and Sophie dolls and remove the headband of the Audrey doll to eliminate the hazard. Consumers may also call Pottery Barn Kids for instructions on how to return the affected dolls for a merchandise credit.

Consumer Contact: For additional information, contact Pottery Barn Kids toll-free at (855) 880-4504 between 4 a.m. and 9 p.m. PT seven days a week or visit the firm's website at www.potterybarnkids.com

Note: Health Canada's press release is available at http://cpsr-rspc.hc-sc.gc.ca/PR-RP/recall-retrait-eng.jsp?re_id=1389

Federal Trade Commission (FTC)

The **Federal Trade Commission Act (FTC Act)** was enacted in 1914.[25] The **Federal Trade Commission (FTC)** is empowered to enforce the FTC Act as well as other federal consumer protection statutes. Section 5 of the FTC Act prohibits "unfair and deceptive practices." It has been used extensively to regulate unscrupulous business conduct. This section gives the FTC the authority to bring an administrative proceeding to end a deceptive or unfair practice, such as false and deceptive advertising.

Federal Trade Commission (FTC) A federal administrative agency empowered to enforce the Federal Trade Commission Act and other federal consumer protection statutes.

The FTC can also issue interpretive rules, general statements of policy, trade regulation rules, and guidelines that define unfair or deceptive practices, and it can conduct investigations of suspected antitrust violations. The FTC may issue cease-and-desist orders, require affirmative disclosures to consumers, order corrective advertising, or other actions. The FTC may also sue to obtain compensation on behalf of consumers.

Consumer Financial Protection Bureau (CFPB)

The **Consumer Financial Protection Bureau (CFPB),** a new federal administrative agency, began operation in 2011. This agency has the authority to prohibit unfair, deceptive, or abusive acts or practices regarding consumer financial products and services. It also acts as a watchdog over credit cards, debit cards, mortgages, payday loans, and other consumer financial products and services. The CFPB has authority

Consumer Financial Protection Bureau (CFPB) A federal administrative agency that is responsible for enforcing federal consumer financial protection statutes.

[25] 15 U.S.C. Sections 41–51.

to supervise all participants in the consumer finance and mortgage area, including depository institutions such as commercial and savings banks and non-depository businesses such as insurance companies, mortgage brokers, credit counseling firms, and debt collectors. The CFPB has authority to enforce the following statutes:

- Consumer Financial Protection Act of 2010
- Mortgage Reform and Anti-Predatory Lending Act of 2010
- Truth in Lending Act (TILA)
- Equal Credit Opportunity Act
- Fair Credit Reporting Act
- Fair Debt Collection Practices Act
- Home Mortgage Disclosure Act
- Electronic Funds Transfer Act
- Truth in Savings Act

The CFPB is authorized to adopt rules to interpret and enforce the provisions of the acts it administers. The CFPB has investigative and subpoena powers, and may refer matters to the U.S. Attorney General for criminal prosecution.

Learning Objective 10
Describe public disclosure of administrative agency actions.

Individual Rights and Disclosure of Administrative Agency Actions

Public concern over the possible secrecy of federal administrative agency actions led Congress to enact several statutes that promote public disclosure of agency activities and protect parties from overly obtrusive agency actions. These statutes are discussed in the paragraphs that follow.

Freedom of Information Act

Freedom of Information Act (FOIA) A federal act that gives the public access to documents in the possession of federal administrative agencies. There are many exceptions to disclosure.

The **Freedom of Information Act (FOIA)**[26] was enacted to give the public access to most documents in the possession of federal administrative agencies. The act requires federal administrative agencies to publish agency procedures, rules, regulations, interpretations, and other such information in the *Federal Register*. The act also requires agencies to publish quarterly indexes of certain documents. In addition, the act specifies time limits for agencies to respond to requests for information, sets limits on copying charges, and provides for disciplinary action against agency employees who refuse to honor proper requests for information.

Example If a person suspects that he or she, or someone else, was subject to the Federal Bureau of Investigation (FBI) inquiry during the anti-communist McCarthy hearings, that person may submit a Freedom of Information Act request to obtain copies of any information on this subject from the FBI.

For purposes of privacy, the following documents are exempt from disclosure: (1) documents classified by the president to be in the interests of national security; (2) documents that are statutorily prohibited from disclosure; (3) records whose disclosure would interfere with law enforcement proceedings; (4) medical, personnel, and similar files; and (5) documents containing trade secrets or other confidential or privileged information. Decisions by federal administrative agencies to not publicly disclose documents requested under the act are subject to judicial review in a U.S. district court.

A sample letter to request information from the Federal Bureau of Investigation under the Freedom of Information Act appears as Exhibit 9.11. An actual FOIA request made to multiple government entities is shown in Exhibit 9.12.

---

[26] 5 U.S.C. Section 552.

Exhibit 9.11 Sample letter requesting information pursuant to the Freedom of Information Act

Date: ___________________
Federal Bureau of Investigation

Record/Information Dissemination Section
Attn: FOIPA Request
170 Marcel Drive
Winchester, VA 22602-4843

Dear FOIA Officer,

This is a request under the Freedom of Information Act.

Date range of request: _____________________________

Description of Request:

____

____

____

Please search the FBI's indices to the Central Records System for the information responsive to this request related to:

____

____

____

I am willing to pay up to [$__] for the processing of this request. Please inform me if the estimated fees will exceed this limit before processing my request.

I am seeking information for personal use and not for commercial use.

Thank you for your consideration,

Name: ____

Title (optional): ____

Business (if applicable): ____

Street Address: ____

City/State/ZIP Code: ____

Country (if applicable): ____

Telephone (optional): ____

Email (optional): ____

Government in the Sunshine Act

The **Government in the Sunshine Act**[27] was enacted to open most federal administrative agency meetings to the public. There are some exceptions to this rule. These include meetings (1) where a person is accused of a crime, (2) concerning an agency's issuance of a subpoena, (3) where attendance of the public would significantly frustrate the implementation of a proposed agency action, and (4) concerning day-to-day operations. Decisions by federal administrative agencies to close meetings to the public are subject to judicial review in U.S. district courts.

Government in the Sunshine Act A federal act that opens most federal administrative agency meetings to the public.

[27] 5 U.S.C. Section 552(b).

Exhibit 9.12 Request for information pursuant to the Freedom of Information Act

January 13, 2009

Director, Freedom of Information and Security Review
Department of Defense
1155 Defense Pentagon, Room 2C757
Washington, D.C. 20301-1155

FOIA/PA Mail Referral Unit
Department of Justice
Room 115
LOC Building
Washington, D.C. 20530-0001

Information and Privacy Coordinator
Central Intelligence Agency
Washington, D.C. 20505

Office of Information Programs and Services
A/GIS/IPS/RL
U.S. Department of State
Washington, D.C. 20522-8100

Re: REQUEST UNDER FREEDOM OF INFORMATION ACT
Expedited Processing Requested

To Whom It May Concern:

This letter constitutes a request ("Request") pursuant to the Freedom of Information Act ("FOIA") Section 552 *et seq.*, the Department of Defense implementing regulations, 32 C.F.R. Section 286.1 *et seq.*, the Department of Justice implementing regulations, 22 C.F.R. Section 171.1 *et seq.*, the Central Intelligence Agency implementing regulations, 32 C.F.R. Section 1900.01 *et seq.*, and the President's Memorandum of January 21, 2009, 74 Fed. Reg. 4683 (Jan. 26, 2009) and the Attorney General's Memorandum of March 19, 2009, 74 Fed. Reg. 49,892 (Sep. 29, 2009). The Request is submitted by the American Civil Liberties Union Foundation and the American Civil Liberties Union (collectively, the "ACLU").

This Request seeks records pertaining to the use of unmanned aerial vehicles ("UAVs")—commonly referred to as "drones" and including the MQ-1 Predator and MQ-9 Reaper—by the CIA and the armed forces for the purpose of killing targeted individuals. In particular, we seek information about the legal basis in domestic, foreign, and international law for the use of drones to conduct targeted killings. We request information regarding the rules and standards that the Armed Forces and the CIA use to determine when and where these weapons may be used, the targets that they may be used against, and the processes in place to decide whether their use is legally permissible in particular circumstances, especially in the face of anticipated civilian casualties. We also seek information about how these rules and standards are implemented and enforced. We request information about how the consequences of drone strikes are assessed, including methods for determining the number of civilian and non-civilian casualties. Finally, we request information about the frequency of drone strikes and the number of individuals—Al Qaeda, Afghan Taliban, other targeted individuals, innocent civilians, or otherwise—who have been killed or injured in these operations....

I. Requested Records

1. All records created after September 11, 2001 pertaining to the legal basis in domestic, foreign and international law upon which unmanned aerial vehicles ("UAVs" or "drones") can be used to execute targeted killings ("drone strikes"),...

Exhibit 9.12 Request for information pursuant to the Freedom of Information Act *(continued)*

2. All records created after September 11, 2001 pertaining to agreements, understandings, cooperation or coordination between the U.S. and the governments of Afghanistan, Pakistan, or any other country regarding the use of drones to effect targeted killings in the territory of those countries,...

3. All records created after September 11, 2001 pertaining to the selection of human targets for drone strikes and any limits on who may be targeted by a drone strike.

4. All records created after September 11, 2001 pertaining to civilian casualties in drone strikes, including but not limited to measures regarding the determination of the likelihood of civilian casualties, measures to limit civilian casualties, and guidelines about when drone strikes may be carried out despite a likelihood of civilian casualties....

****

If the Request is denied in whole or in part, we ask that you justify all deletions by reference to specific exemptions to FOIA. We expect the release of all segregable portions of otherwise exempt material. We reserve the right to appeal a decision to withhold any information....

Thank you for your prompt attention to this matter. Please furnish applicable records to:

Jonathan Manes
National Security Project
American Civil Liberties Union
125 Broad Street, 18th Floor
New York, NY 10004

Example The Federal Communications Commission (FCC) is debating whether to grant an applicant permission to purchase a television station license. This meeting is not protected by any of the exceptions in the Sunshine Act. The FCC must publish a public notice of place, date, and time of the meeting so that persons may appear at the meeting.

Equal Access to Justice Act

Congress enacted the **Equal Access to Justice Act**[28] to protect persons from harassment by federal administrative agencies. Under this act, a private party who is the subject of an unjustified federal administrative agency action can sue to recover attorneys' fees and other costs. The courts have generally held that the agency's conduct must be extremely outrageous before an award will be made under the act. A number of states have similar statutes.

Equal Access to Justice Act A federal act that protects persons from harassment by federal administrative agencies.

Privacy Act

The federal **Privacy Act**[29] concerns individual privacy. It stipulates that federal administrative agencies can maintain only the information about an individual that is relevant and necessary to accomplish a legitimate agency purpose. The act affords individuals the right to access agency records concerning themselves and to correct those records. Many states have enacted similar privacy acts.

Privacy Act A federal act that states that federal administrative agencies can maintain only information about an individual that is relevant and necessary to accomplish a legitimate agency purpose.

[28] 5 U.S.C. Section 504.
[29] 5 U.S.C. Section 552(a).

Concept Review *and* Reinforcement

LEGAL TERMINOLOGY

SUMMARY OF KEY CONCEPTS

Administrative Law

Administrative Law	Administrative law is enacted by governments to regulate industries, businesses, and professionals, and to protect consumers and other members of society.
General Government Regulation	General regulations are enacted by governments to regulate businesses and industries collectively.
Specific Government Regulation	Specific regulations are enacted by governments to regulate certain industries or areas of commerce only.

Administrative Agencies

Administrative Agencies	Agencies are created by federal and state legislative and executive branches. They are staffed by professionals who have expertise in a certain area of commerce and who interpret and apply designated statutes.
Cabinet-Level Federal Departments	Cabinet-level departments are created by the president to regulate certain activities and advise the president. The president appoints cabinet members subject to confirmation by a majority vote of the U.S. Senate.
Independent Federal Administrative Agencies	Independent administrative agencies are created by Congress to regulate areas of the national economy and society.
State and Local Administrative Agencies	State administrative agencies are created by states and local cities and municipalities to regulate areas of commerce and society.

Administrative Procedure

Administrative Procedure Act (APA)	The APA establishes procedures (e.g., notice, hearing) for federal agencies to follow in conducting their affairs. States have enacted their own procedural acts to govern state agencies.
Administrative Law Judge (ALJ)	The ALJ is an employee of the administrative agency who presides over the administrative proceeding, decides questions of law and fact, and issues a decision in the form of an order.

Powers of Administrative Agencies

Delegation Doctrine	When an administrative agency is created, it is delegated certain powers. The agency has rule-making power, licensing power, judicial authority, and executive power.
Rule Making	Rule making is the power to adopt substantive rules that have the force of law and must be adhered to by covered persons and businesses.
Licensing Power	Licensing power is the authority to issue licenses before a person or business can enter certain types of industries.
Judicial Authority	Judicial authority is the authority to decide cases in an administrative proceeding.
Executive Power	Executive power is the power to prosecute violations of statutes and administrative rules and regulations.
Administrative Searches	Administrative agencies have the power to conduct administrative searches and to issue administrative subpoenas to conduct searches and to obtain information and evidence.
Judicial Review of Administrative Agency Actions	The Administrative Procedure Act (APA), many federal statutes, and many state administrative statutes and local ordinances expressly provide for judicial review by courts of administrative agency actions.

Federal Administrative Agencies	
Equal Employment Opportunity Commission (EEOC)	The EEOC enforces federal antidiscrimination laws.
Environmental Protection Agency (EPA)	The EPA enforces federal environmental protection laws.
Food and Drug Administration (FDA)	The FDA regulates the testing, manufacture, distribution, and sale of foods, drugs, cosmetics, and medical devices.
Securities and Exchange Commission (SEC)	The SEC enforces federal securities laws.
Occupational Safety and Health Administration (OSHA)	OSHA enforces workplace safety standards.
National Labor Relations Board (NLRB)	The NLRB enforces federal labor laws.
Federal Trade Commission (FTC)	The FTC regulates business conduct and practices.
Consumer Product Safety Commission (CPSC)	The CPSC regulates the safety of consumer products.
Consumer Financial Protection Bureau (CFPB)	The CFPB regulates consumer financial products and services.
Individual Rights and Disclosure of Administrative Agency Actions	
Freedom of Information Act	The FOIA is a federal law that gives the public access to most documents in the possession of federal administrative agencies. It also requires federal administrative agencies to publish agency procedures, rules, regulations, interpretations, and other information in the *Federal Register*.
Government in the Sunshine Act	This federal law opens certain federal administrative agency meetings to the public.
Equal Access to Justice Act	This federal law protects persons from harassment by federal administrative agencies and provides certain penalties for its violation.
Privacy Act	The Privacy Act (a) restricts information a federal administrative agency can maintain about an individual, and (b) gives individuals the right to access agency records concerning themselves.

WORKING THE WEB

1. Go to the website www.fda.gov. This is the website for the Federal Food and Drug Administration (FDA). Click on one of the "Hot Topic" subject matters that interests you and write a one-page report on that information.
2. Go to the website www.cpsc.gov. This is the website for the federal Consumer Product Safety Commission (CPSC). Click on "Recent Recalls" for the most current month. Find a recall of a product that interests you and write a half-page report describing the product and its recall.
3. Go to the website of the U.S. Environmental Protection Agency at www.epa.gov. Click on "Newsroom." Under the term "Regional Newsroom" select your state and click on "Go." Read a current news release and summarize it.
4. Go to the website of the Federal Trade Commission at www.ftc.gov. Click on "Consumer Protection." What is "Today's Tip"?

CRITICAL THINKING & WRITING QUESTIONS

1. What is an administrative law?
2. What is the difference between general government regulation and specific government regulation?
3. How do cabinet-level federal departments differ from independent federal administrative agencies?
4. Explain the difference between substantive administrative law and procedural administrative law.
5. What is the Administrative Procedure Act (APA)? What is its main purpose?
6. What is an administrative law judge (ALJ)? What does an ALJ do?
7. Describe the following: (1) substantive rule, (2) interpretive rule, and (3) statement of policy.
8. Describe each of the following powers of an administrative agency: (1) licensing power, (2) judicial authority, and (3) executive power.
9. What is the Freedom of Information Act (FOIA)?
10. Describe each of the following: (1) Government in the Sunshine Act, (2) Equal Access to Justice Act, and (3) Privacy Act.

Building Paralegal Skills

VIDEO CASE STUDIES

Administrative Agency Hearing: The Role of the Paralegal

A school bus driver has been injured in what he claims to be a work-related injury. His employer—the school district—has raised objections, requiring a Workers' Compensation hearing. A paralegal appears before the Workers' Compensation hearing officer representing the school bus driver.

After viewing the video case study in MyLegalStudiesLab, answer the following:

1. Why are matters of this type heard before administrative hearing officers instead of going directly to court?
2. Is the paralegal committing the unauthorized practice of law in representing the school bus driver in this matter?
3. Are paralegals in your jurisdiction permitted to represent clients before administrative agencies?

ETHICS ANALYSIS & DISCUSSION QUESTIONS

1. What ethical guidelines apply to the representation of parties before administrative agencies by a paralegal?
2. May paralegals advertise their availability to appear before administrative agencies? Explain.
3. As a recent graduate of a four-year degree program, you wish to get started in your career. At your local computer store, you purchase a copy of software that can be used to create various commonly used legal forms. You invite a group of friends and relatives to your home and offer to use the program to prepare powers of attorney and living wills (advance medical directives) for them. See *Unauthorized Practice of Law v. Parsons Tech.*, 179 F.3d 956 (5th Cir. 1999). Are there any UPL issues? Explain.

DEVELOPING YOUR COLLABORATION SKILLS

With a group of other students, review the facts of the following case. As a group, discuss the following questions.

1. What government agency was involved in this case?
2. Did the agency conduct a proper search of the business premises?
3. Did LaGrou knowingly engage in the improper storage of meat, poultry, and other food products, in violation of federal food safety laws?

United States of America v. LaGrou Distribution Systems, Incorporated 466 F.3d 585 (7th Cir. 2006)

United States Court of Appeals for the Seventh Circuit

LaGrou Distribution Systems, Incorporated, operated a cold storage warehouse and distribution center in Chicago, Illinois. The warehouse stored raw, fresh, and frozen meat, poultry, and other food products that were owned by customers who paid LaGrou to do so. More than 2 million pounds of food went into and out of the warehouse each day. The warehouse had a rat problem for a considerable period of time. LaGrou workers consistently found rodent droppings and rodent-gnawed products, and they caught rats in traps throughout the warehouse on a daily basis. The manager of the warehouse and the president of LaGrou were aware of this problem and discussed it weekly. The problem became so bad that workers were assigned to "rat patrols" to search for rats and to put out traps to catch rats. At one point, the rat patrols were trapping as many as 50 rats per day. LaGrou did not inform its customers of the rodent infestation. LaGrou would throw out product that had been gnawed by rats.

One day, a food inspector for the United States Department of Agriculture (USDA), a federal administrative agency, went to the LaGrou warehouse and discovered the rat problem. The following morning, 14 USDA inspectors and representatives of the federal Food and Drug Administration (FDA) arrived at the warehouse to begin an extensive investigation. The inspectors found the extensive rat infestation and the contaminated meat. The contaminated meat could transmit bacterial, viral, parasitic, and fungal pathogens, including *E. coli* and *Salmonella*, which could cause severe illness in human beings.

The USDA ordered the warehouse shut down. Of the 22 million pounds of meat, poultry, and other food products stored at the warehouse, 8 million pounds were found to be adulterated and were destroyed. The remaining product had to be treated with strict decontamination procedures. The U.S. government brought charges against LaGrou for violating federal food safety laws. The U.S. District Court ordered LaGrou to pay restitution of $8.2 million to customers who lost product and to pay a $2 million fine, and it sentenced LaGrou to a 5-year term of probation. LaGrou appealed to the U.S. Court of Appeals.

PARALEGAL PORTFOLIO EXERCISE

Prepare a memorandum, no longer than three pages, that discusses the general powers of a federal administrative agency, and the specific powers of the Federal Food and Drug Administration (FDA).

LEGAL ANALYSIS & WRITING CASES

Entergy Corporation v. Riverkeeper, Inc., 129 S.Ct. 1498, 173 L.Ed.2d 369 (2009)

Supreme Court of the United States

Entergy Corporation operates large power plants that generate electrical power. In the course of generating power, these plants also generate large amounts of heat. To cool its facilities, Entergy uses cooling water intake structures that extract water from nearby water sources. These structures pose various risks to the environment, particularly to aquatic organisms that live in the affected water, by squashing them against intake screens (called "impingement") or suctioning them into the cooling system (called "entrainment"). The Clean Water Act, a federal statute, mandates that a point source of pollution, such as a power plant, install the "best technology" available for minimizing adverse environmental impact.

The Environmental Protection Agency (EPA), a federal administrative agency, adopted a rule that requires new power plants to install the "most effective technology" that would reduce impingement and entrainment mortality by up to 98 percent. The EPA conducted a cost-benefit analysis and adopted a different rule for existing power plants. This EPA rule allows existing plants to deploy a mix of less expensive technology that is "commercially available and practicable." This technology would reduce impingement and entrainment by more than 80 percent. Thus, the EPA chose not to require existing plants to deploy the more expensive[,] most effective technology that it requires for new power plants.

Riverkeeper, Inc. and other environmental groups (Riverkeeper) challenged the EPA rule for existing power plants, alleging that the EPA was not empowered to use cost-benefit analysis when setting performance standards for power plants. Riverkeeper asserts that the Clean Water Act's "best technology" language required existing power plants to deploy the most effective technology equal to that required of new power plants.

Question

1. Is the EPA permitted to use cost–benefit analysis in promulgating rules for technology to be deployed by existing point sources of water pollution under the Clean Water Act?

People v. Paulson, 216 Cal.App.3d 1480, 265 Cal.Rptr. 579 (Cal. Ct. App. 1990)

Court of Appeal of California

Lee Stuart Paulson owned a liquor license for My House, a bar in San Francisco. The California Department of Alcoholic Beverage Control (Department) is the state administrative agency that regulates bars in that state. The California Business and Professions Code, which is administered by the Department, prohibit[s] "any kind of illegal activity on licensed premises." An anonymous informer tipped the Department that narcotics were being sold on the premises of My House, an establishment that sold liquor, and that the narcotics were kept in a safe behind the bar on the premises. A special department investigator entered the bar during its hours of operation, identified himself, and informed Paulson that he was conducting an inspection. The investigator, who did not have a search warrant, opened the safe without seeking Paulson's consent. Twenty-two bundles of cocaine, totaling 5.5 grams, were found in the safe. Paulson was arrested. At his criminal trial, Paulson challenged the lawfulness of the Department's search.

Question

1. Is the Department's search constitutional?

WORKING WITH THE LANGUAGE OF THE COURT CASE

R. Williams Construction Company v. Occupational Safety & Health Review Commission 464 F.3d 1060 (9th Cir. 2006)

United States Court of Appeals for the Ninth Circuit

Read the following case, excerpted from the court of appeals' opinion. Review and brief the case. In your brief, answer the following questions:

1. What administrative agency was involved in this case?
2. What administrative agency rules were alleged to have been violated in this case?
3. What were the violations found by the administrative law judge (ALJ)?
4. Was the penalty assessed sufficient based on the facts of the case?

Fletcher, Circuit Judge

Petitioner R. Williams Construction Co. ("Williams" or "the Company") petitions for review of a final order of the Federal Occupational Safety and Health Review Commission (the "Commission"), affirming violations of the Occupational Safety and Health Act ("OSHA") in the wake of a trench collapse and death of an employee at a construction site in Santa Ynez, California.

On September 19, 2002, a trench collapse at a sewer-construction project at the Chumash Casino Project in Santa Ynez, California, killed Jose Aguiniga, a Williams employee, and seriously injured Adam Palomar, another Williams employee. On the day of the collapse, the trench was ten to twelve feet deep and between three and four feet wide at the bottom. The trench was about thirteen feet wide at the top and more than forty feet long. The sides of the trench rose vertically from the bottom for approximately five feet, after which they sloped backwards at about a forty-five degree angle. An earthen slope at the west end of the trench provided the workers' only access to and egress from the bottom. Ground water seeped into the soil continuously.

Williams used a number of submersible pumps to remove the ground water that seeped into the trench. Although the pumps could be pulled up and cleaned from the top of the trench, it was the practice to do so from inside the trench. Adam Palomar and Jose Aguiniga, two Williams employees, were generally responsible for cleaning the pumps and did so as needed throughout any given workday without receiving specific instructions.

On the day before the accident, a hydraulic jack shoring system, which supported the trench wall, had been removed. On the day of the accident, Palomar and Aguiniga entered the unshored trench to clean the pumps, remaining there for about fifteen minutes. As the two were exiting the trench, the north wall

(continued)

collapsed, burying Aguiniga completely and Palomar almost completely. Aguiniga died, and Palomar was severely injured.

OSHA conducted an investigation and cited the Company for safety violations. The first citation charged the Company with failing to instruct its employees in the recognition and avoidance of unsafe conditions and in the regulations applicable to their work environment, as required by 29 C.F.R. § 1926.21(b)(2). The second citation charged the Company with failing to ensure that no worker would have to travel more than 25 feet to reach a safe point of egress, as required by 29 C.F.R. § 1926.651(c)(2). The third citation charged the Company with failing to ensure that a "competent person"—i.e., one with specific training in soil analysis and protective systems and capable of identifying dangerous conditions—performed daily inspections of excavations for evidence of hazardous conditions, as required by 29 C.F.R. §§ 1926.651(k)(1). The fourth violation charged the Company with failing to ensure that the walls of the excavation be either sloped or supported, as required by 29 C.F.R. § 1926.652(a)(1).

The Administrative Law Judge (ALJ) conducted a two-day hearing, during which several Williams employees provided testimony. Palomar testified that he worked for Williams for approximately nine months prior to the accident and had never received any training in trench safety. He testified that there was no safety meeting at the beginning of the workday on September 19, 2002. He was never told not to enter the trench and did not know who his supervisor was. He received all of his work instructions from Sergio Lopez, who acted as translator because Palomar speaks only Spanish.

John (J.P.) Williams testified that he was the supervisor at the Santa Ynez worksite and was responsible for employee safety at the site. He admitted that he never looked at the company safety manual, which was located behind the seat of his truck; he also had not been trained as an OSHA "competent person" or received any other safety training other than on the job. He was unfamiliar with OSHA sloping and trenching requirements and did not conduct any physical tests on the soil in the trench.

Based on the testimony at the hearing, the ALJ affirmed the [OSHA] citations. This resulted in a total penalty of $22,000. The ALJ's findings, based upon the witnesses' testimony regarding Williams' lack of attention to safety standards, is supported by substantial evidence.

Williams violated 29 C.F.R. § 1926.21(b)(2) for failing to instruct each employee in the recognition and avoidance of unsafe conditions and for failing to eliminate other hazards: Williams provided no training in trenching hazards to at least the two employees working in the trench; moreover, no Williams supervisor was familiar with OSHA regulations.

Williams also violated 29 C.F.R. § 1926.651(c)(2) by providing only one safe means of egress at the east end of the 45-foot trench. A violation is established so long as employees have *access* to a dangerous area more than 25 feet from a means of egress. In addition, Williams violated 29 C.F.R. § 1926.651(k)(1) for failing to designate a "competent person" with sufficient training and knowledge to identify and correct existing and predictable hazards.

The ALJ findings, and the reasonable inferences drawn from them, easily satisfy the substantial-evidence standard. Consequently, the ALJ's decision affirming the citations is affirmed.

MYLEGALSTUDIESLAB

MyLegalStudiesLab Virtual Law Office Experience Assignments

Complete the pre-test, study plan, and post-test for this chapter and answer the Legal Applications questions as assigned. These will help you confirm your mastery of the concepts and their application to legal scenarios. Then complete the Virtual Law Office assignments as assigned by your instructor. These assignments are designed to develop your workplace skills. Completing the assignments for this chapter will result in producing the following documents for inclusion in your portfolio:

VLOE 9.1 Office memo on when a paralegal may represent a client under our local state and federal rules, laws, and regulations

PART

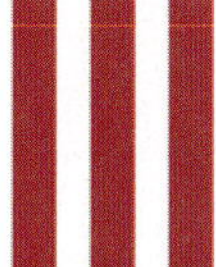

III Paralegal Skills

The aspiring paralegal professional must develop a certain set of basic skills to work as part of a legal team in the law office, the courts, administrative agencies, and in the alternative dispute resolution process. Excellent verbal and written skills are crucial for paralegals who will be interviewing clients and witnesses. Paralegals must also develop an ability to think critically and analytically when performing legal research and writing briefs, memoranda of the law, and general correspondence. Today's paralegal must be familiar with the technology used to conduct legal and factual research, such as digital libraries and Internet research services, as well as conventional sources of print information. Part III covers the basic skills needed for a paralegal professional to be successful in the job.

CHAPTER

10

Interviewing and Investigation Skills

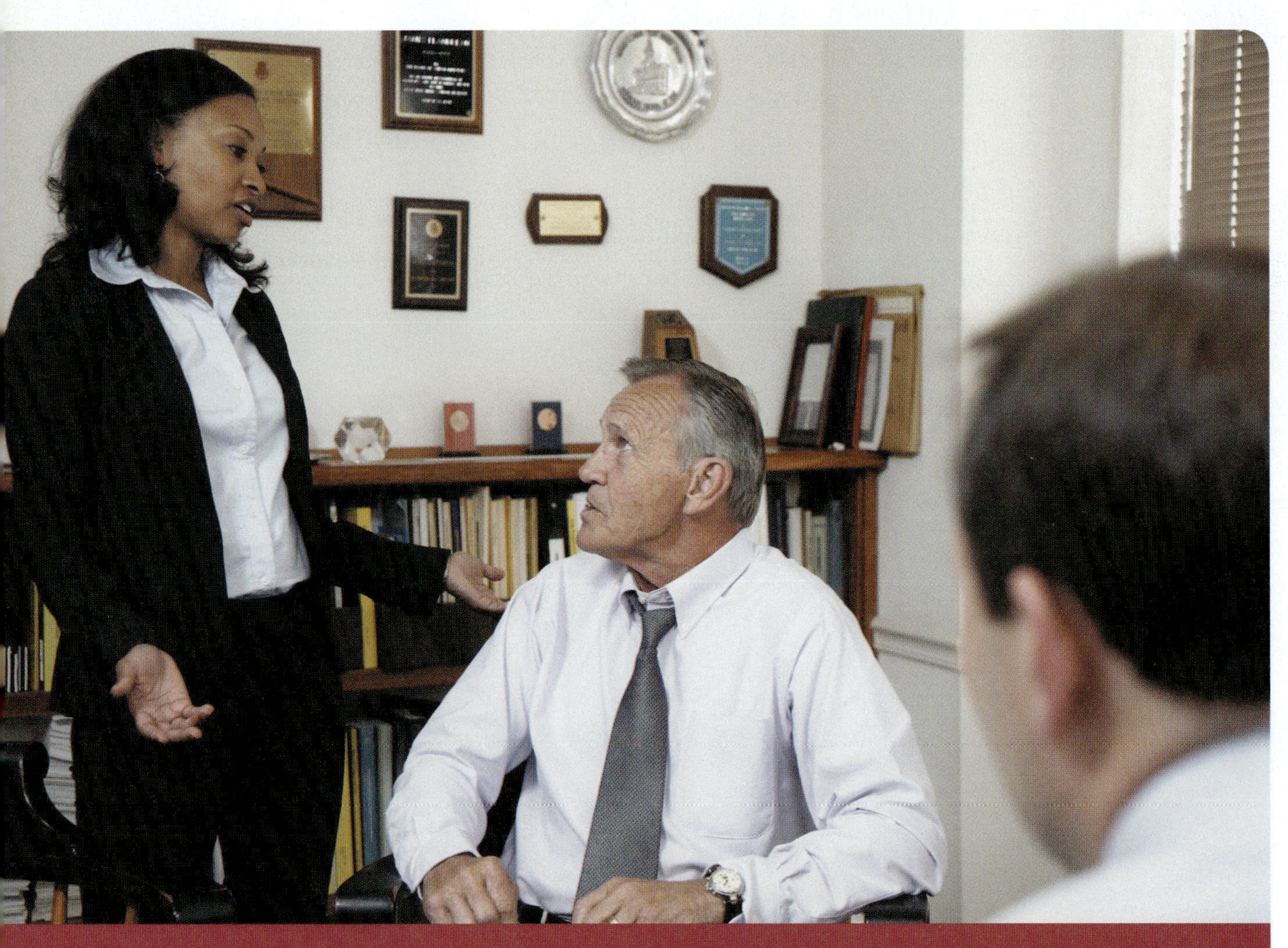

LEARNING OBJECTIVES

After studying this chapter, you should be able to:

1. Explain the importance of the initial contact with clients and witnesses.
2. Describe the issues in preparing for and conducting an interview.
3. Explain how expert witnesses are used in litigation.
4. Explain the steps and process of conducting an investigation.
5. Explain the function of the trial notebook and its relationship to case management.

Paralegals at Work

Sara had been working for only a few weeks as a paralegal intern for a small, boutique litigation firm. Mrs. Weiser, one of the two paralegals supporting the two trial attorneys, told Sara about her long-planned Alaskan cruise that she would be taking with her husband for their 25th anniversary. The reality of the situation started to set in when Sara was advised that the cruise would begin in Anchorage the next day, and Mrs. Weiser was scheduled to leave within the hour to catch a plane. Sara's concerns intensified when she and Mrs. Weiser reviewed the office calendar and it became obvious that Sara would be alone in the office during the time Mrs. Weiser was gone. The attorneys and the other full-time paralegal were involved in a major medical malpractice case in another state for at least the next two weeks. Clearly, it was expected that Sara would be in charge of the office, answering the phone and taking care of anyone who came in. Somewhat troubling was the fact that Sara would have no contact with Mrs. Weiser for the duration of the cruise or with the other paralegal or attorneys during the trial. The instructions Mrs. Weiser gave her left no doubt that she would be very busy:

"Now remember—we advertise on TV, and Mr. Elliott expects us to screen potential clients without bothering him with loser cases. I've left a couple of files for you to work on while I'm gone. The Morales case just came in. It's an accident case that happened a few years ago, and you need to get her in for an initial interview. Get all the necessary facts and see what else we have to do to move it along and whether we need to settle it or file suit. Oh, by the way, you do speak Spanish, don't you? Mrs. Morales is from Puerto Rico".

> "It is the spirit and not the form of law that keeps justice alive."
>
> *Earl Warren*

"The LaCorte case is on the trial list for next month. We don't have an expert yet who can substantiate our theory of the case. See what you can find. Oh, and you'd better get that case organized so they can start trial immediately in case the current trial lasts longer than the expected three weeks. All the material is in piles or in boxes in Mr. Martin's office. Prepare a trial notebook, or you can try that new case management software we just got that is supposed to make life easier. I'm sure, with your computer skills, that you can get it up and running and use it to get the case ready for trial".

Consider the issues involved in this scenario as you read the chapter.

INTRODUCTION TO INTERVIEWING AND INVESTIGATIONS

Communication skills are at the heart of a paralegal's ability to conduct successful interviews and investigations. The paralegal is often the firm's first point of contact with a new client or witness. The impression the paralegal makes is also the impression the firm makes. As someone once said, we have only one opportunity to make a good first impression. In some practices, the paralegal is the first one to meet with the client and conduct the initial interview before referring the client to the supervising attorney. In other practices, clients are interviewed first by the supervising attorney and then referred to the paralegal for a detailed factual interview.

The paralegal must be able to interview clients, fact witnesses, expert witnesses, investigators, and others, including public records custodians who may have access to information necessary for the preparation of a case. The skill of the interviewer or investigator can determine the accuracy and completeness of the information obtained—and ultimately, the outcome of the case.

The impressions created and the relationship developed with a new client may also be the deciding factors in whether the client stays with the firm or seeks other counsel. Professional relationships developed with public officials, public custodians of records, hospital records librarians, police investigators, and similar independent investigators can make the paralegal's job much easier and ultimately benefit the client.

Interviews

Learning Objective 1

Explain the importance of the initial contact with clients and witnesses.

Paralegals frequently conduct the initial investigation of a client's case and make the initial contact with potential witnesses. This initial contact may be a telephone call to set up a meeting or a telephone interview. The meeting may take place in the office or at the witness's home or place of business. The initial contact with a potential witness, just as with a potential client, may set the tone for the interview and can influence the willingness of the person to cooperate. Any contact that a paralegal has with a client, or a prospective client, should be treated as an interview. It may involve limited contact, such as a **screening interview**, or be an initial in-depth, fact-gathering interview. In each case, the paralegal usually is the first point of contact with the client for the firm.

Screening interview Limited first contact with a prospective new client.

A screening interview is the initial contact with the client. This usually begins with an initial telephone call to the firm, although a person may appear unexpectedly at the reception desk, looking for an attorney to determine whether the firm is interested in taking the case, and what it will cost.

Screening Interview

Many clients come to a law firm or lawyer from a referral source, such as a current or former client. This source of clients sometimes serves as a type of screening. The referral source has probably told the potential client something about the firm's practice and the perceived reputation or ability of the lawyer or firm. Other potential clients may have found the firm's name and phone number in the telephone book, on a website listing of attorneys, or from a law firm advertisement. Some simply appear at the office door and ask for an appointment or basic information about the firm's areas of practice or interest in taking a case. In smaller offices, the paralegal is often the one who handles these drop-in visits or calls, doubling as receptionist or phone operator.

The screening interview is often filled with potential landmines. If the paralegal solicits too much information or the prospective client volunteers too much information, an implied attorney–client relationship may be created. An implied attorney–client relationship has been found to exist, even if no fee is paid, if the party believes he or she is divulging confidential information for the purpose of obtaining legal advice. If too little information is obtained, the attorney will not have enough information to decide whether he or she wants to talk to the potential client. Therefore, the paralegal or receptionist has to decide how much information to take and how much information to give.

First Meeting

At the very least, it is prudent for the paralegal to advise the potential client that paralegals are not lawyers, and that only a lawyer can give legal advice. Also, the potential client should be advised that any information given to the paralegal in this initial meeting may not be subject to **attorney–client privilege**.

Attorney–client privilege A client's right to have anything told to a lawyer while seeking legal advice kept confidential in most instances.

The prospective client may want a quick answer to the question, "Do I have a case?" The answer requires a legal analysis that only the attorney can make. The attorney/employer probably does not want to be bothered with most early contacts but also does not want to lose a good case. Should the paralegal give advice or have this person speak with a lawyer? Most of these potential problems can be avoided by having a policy or strategy in place in advance. Most offices have a policy regarding the fee for an initial interview. Many offer a no-cost initial interview to determine the validity of a case and check for any potential conflicts of interest that might require the office to decline the case. In some offices, a nominal fee is charged. This may be a flat rate or an hourly rate. In many jurisdictions, referrals from the local lawyer referral office or legal aid office are charged a token fee, sometimes as little as $5, or for indigent cases, no fee as part of a local pro bono program. The paralegal should ask the firm's policy before attempting to give and receive information from potential clients.

Implied Attorney–Client Relationship

If too much information is taken, the potential client may think he or she now is represented by a lawyer. The courts have ruled on the side of the prospective client, holding that an **implied attorney–client relationship** exists, even where the attorney did

Implied attorney–client relationship An implied attorney-client relationship may result when a prospective client divulges confidential information during a consultation with an attorney for the purpose of retaining the attorney, even if actual employment does not result.

IN THE WORDS OF THE COURT . . .

Implied Attorney–Client Relationship

***PRO HAND SERVICES TRUST V. MONTHEI*, 49 P.3D 56, 59 (MONT. 2002).**

"An implied attorney–client relationship may result when a prospective client divulges confidential information during a consultation with an attorney for the purpose of retaining the attorney, even if actual employment does not result."

Web Exploration

Contrast and compare the Missouri Rule 4-1.18 at **http://www.courts.mo.gov/courts/ClerkHandbooksP2RulesOnly.nsf** with ABA Rule 1.18 at **www.abanet.org/cpr** and the rule in your jurisdiction.

Conflict of interest Representation of another with conflicting rights.

Ethical wall An artificial barrier preventing anyone who may have a conflict of interest from accessing client information.

Statute of limitations A time limit within which a case must be brought; if a case is not filed within that timeframe, the right to seek redress in court is lost.

not expressly agree to take the case. In this "implied" relationship, the client is entitled to expect the same degree of confidentiality under the attorney–client privilege. In addition, a **conflict of interest** may result if the firm is already representing another party in the same matter, which would result in disqualification of the attorney or require the establishment of an **ethical wall** to prevent access to information by members of the legal team who have a conflict.

One of the biggest sources of potential malpractice is missing a **statute of limitations** on a client's case. The statute of limitations is a time period within which a case must be filed with the court. If not filed within the required timeframe, the right to bring a cause of action is lost. The statute of limitations is set by legislation, and each state has the power to set its own statute of limitations for each type of case. For example, in many states the time limit for filing a tort action arising out of an automobile action is two years, and a contract action six years, but in some states the suit must be filed in as little as 30 days. A client seeking a lawyer may not be aware of the timeframe. But to the lawyer, the failure to act before the statute runs out may result in a claim for malpractice.

The timing of the statute of limitations deadline must always be considered when taking the initial call or during the first contact with the potential client. If a court holds that an implied attorney–client relationship exists at the time the statute of limitations has expired, the failure of the attorney to take action may be held to be malpractice. The remedy in such a malpractice claim would be for the lawyer to pay what would have been recovered if the case had gone forward and a recovery obtained. During this first point of contact with the potential client, the paralegal must be prepared to take appropriate action and refer the matter to the supervising attorney.

Good practice requires that the client be appropriately notified in writing of the decision of the law firm to accept or decline the representation. If the representation is accepted, a fee agreement should accompany the cover letter. Exhibit 10.1a

IMPLIED ATTORNEY-CLIENT RELATIONSHIP

SIDEBAR

An implied attorney-client relationship may result when a prospective client divulges confidential information during a consultation with an attorney for the purpose of retaining the attorney, even if actual employment does not result.

Pro-Hand Servs. Trust v. Monthei, 49 P.3d 56, 59 (Mont. 2002).

The attorney-client privilege applies to all confidential communications made to an attorney during preliminary discussions of the prospective professional employment, as well as those made during the course of any professional relationship resulting from such discussions.

Hooser v. Superior Court, 101 Cal. Rptr. 2d 341, 346 (Ct. App. 2000).

ETHICAL PERSPECTIVE

Missouri Bar—Rules of Professional Conduct

RULE 4-1.18: DUTIES TO PROSPECTIVE CLIENT

(a) A person who discusses with a lawyer the possibility of forming a client-lawyer relationship with respect to a matter is a prospective client.

(b) Even when no client-lawyer relationship ensues, a lawyer who has had discussions with a prospective client shall not use or reveal information learned in the consultation, except as Rule 4-1.9 would permit with respect to information of a former client.

(c) A lawyer subject to Rule 4-1.18(b) shall not represent a client with interests materially adverse to those of a prospective client in the same or a substantially related matter if the lawyer received information from the prospective client that could be significantly harmful to that person in the matter, except as provided in Rule 4-1.18(d). If a lawyer is disqualified from representation under Rule 4-1.18(c), no lawyer in a firm with which that lawyer is associated may knowingly undertake or continue representation in such a matter, except as provided in Rule 4-1.18(d).

(d) When the lawyer has received disqualifying information as defined in Rule 4-1.18(c), representation is permissible if:

   (1) both the affected client and the prospective client have given informed consent, confirmed in writing, or

   (2) the lawyer who received the information took reasonable measures to avoid exposure to more disqualifying information than was reasonably necessary to determine whether to represent the prospective client and the disqualified lawyer is timely screened from any participation in the matter.

Exhibit 10.1a Hourly fee engagement letter

January 29, 2013

Mr. and Mrs. Thomas Daniels

12 Route 189

Your town, State

RE: ***Employment of Mason, Marshall and Benjamin by Mr. and Mrs. Thomas Daniels***

Dear Mr. and Mrs. Daniels:

Thank you for selecting Mason, Marshall and Benjamin to represent you with respect to the breach of contract action against Honey Bee Pollinators, Ltd. This letter will confirm our recent discussion regarding the scope and terms of this engagement.

Our firm has agreed to represent you in this lawsuit. I personally will supervise the case. However, it is anticipated that other lawyers and legal assistants in the firm also will work on the case.

We will attempt to obtain compliance with the provisions of the contract to have fruit trees on your property pollinated as agreed or, in the alternative, to seek damages for breach of the contract.

You have agreed to pay for our services based on the time we spend working on the case. My current hourly rate is $250 per hour. The rates of our associates currently range between $125 and $225 per hour. Paralegals, who will be utilized where appropriate to avoid unnecessary attorney fees, currently are charged at $75 per hour. These rates are subject to change once a year, usually in December. Generally, you will be billed for all time spent on your matter, including telephone calls.

As discussed, our current estimate for this engagement is $5,000, not including any out-of-pocket expenses for experts, court reporter fees, or court fees. This estimate is imprecise as my knowledge of the facts at this time is limited. We will advise you if fees will be significantly higher than this estimate. At such time, you may decide to restrict the scope of our efforts or we may make other adjustments. This estimate does not include cost items.

You have paid us the sum of $3,000 as an advance against fees and costs, which we have deposited to our trust account. After your receipt of monthly statements, we will pay the amount of the statement from the trust account. If any portion of the advance is unexpended at the conclusion of the case, it will be refunded to you. If the advance is expended, you have agreed to pay subsequent monthly statements on receipt. An interest charge of one and one-half percent per month is charged on statement balances not paid within 30 days of billing.

You will appreciate we can make no guarantee of a successful conclusion in any case. However, the attorneys of this firm will make their best efforts on your behalf.

My objectives are to provide you with excellent legal services and to protect your interests in the event of my unexpected death, disability, impairment, or incapacity. To accomplish this, I have arranged with another lawyer to assist with closing my practice in the event of my death, disability, impairment, or incapacity. In such event, my office staff or the assisting lawyer will contact you and provide you with information about how to proceed.

If this letter fairly states our agreement, please so indicate by signing and returning the enclosed copy in the enclosed business reply envelope. If you have any questions or concerns, please call me to discuss them. We greatly appreciate the opportunity to represent you on this case and look forward to working with you.

Sincerely,

Owen Mason, Esq.

Mason, Marshall and Benjamin

Exhibit 10.1b Contingent fee engagement letter

RE: ***Employment of Mason, Marshall and Benjamin by Jonathan Leonard***

Dear Mr. Leonard:

Thank you for selecting our firm to represent you with respect to the personal injury action against Acme Trucking Company. This letter will confirm our recent discussion regarding the scope and terms of this engagement.

Our firm has agreed to represent you in this lawsuit. I personally will supervise the case. However, it is anticipated that other lawyers and legal assistants in the firm also will work on the case.

We will represent you in the investigation, preparation, and civil trial of your claim against Acme Trucking in the U.S. District Court or Local Trial Court to the rendering of a verdict. Our engagement at this time does not cover any appellate activity or post-trial work on your behalf.

We will be compensated on a contingent fee basis. We will receive for our services 25% of any recovery plus all out-of-pocket costs for service and filing fees, expert witness fees, court reporter fees, and charges for investigation, travel and accommodation, telephone long distance, photocopies. These out-of-pocket costs will be billed to you on a monthly basis itemizing the monies we have advanced on your behalf.

As discussed, our current estimate cost for out-of-pocket expenses for this engagement is $5,000. This estimate is imprecise as my knowledge of the facts at this time is limited.

You have paid us the sum of $1,000.00 as an advance against costs, which we have deposited to our trust account. After your receipt of monthly statements, we will pay the amount of the statement from the trust account. If any portion of the advance is unexpended at the conclusion of the case, it will be refunded to you. If the advance is expended, you have agreed to pay subsequent monthly statements on receipt.

You will appreciate we can make no guarantee of a successful conclusion in any case. However, the attorneys of this firm will use their best efforts on your behalf.

You understand that we represent other plaintiffs involved in the same case and, where possible, will prorate costs. You have agreed that our firm representing the other plaintiffs is acceptable to you.

If this letter fairly states our agreement, will you please so indicate by signing and returning the enclosed copy in the enclosed business reply envelope. If you have any questions or concerns, please call me to discuss them. We greatly appreciate the opportunity to represent you on this case and look forward to working with you.

Sincerely,

Owen Mason

Mason, Marshall and Benjamin

is a sample hourly fee engagement letter, and Exhibit 10.1b is a contingent fee engagement letter. If representation is declined, the paralegal may draft a letter summarizing the facts as related by the client and the facts as determined by the firm, and including the reason for declining the representation. A recommendation to clients concerning the next step in their cause of action should be made as soon as possible. Quick action is particularly necessary if the client is a defendant who is mandated by the court's rules to file a timely, responsive pleading to the complaint served on the client.

It is also not unusual for a law office to receive calls not only from potential clients, but also from those attempting to get information about the firm's existing clients. Particularly in family law cases, a party may call as if seeking representation, but in reality is trying to find out whether the other party has retained the firm.

Letters of Engagement and Termination of Engagement

Many causes of friction between lawyers and their clients are related to fees and costs. Thus many states require a written fee agreement that is signed by the lawyer and the client. This agreement, also called an "engagement letter," is addressed to a client and sets out the specific duties the law firm agrees to undertake for the client. In other words, the letter states what the firm will or will not do for the client. It may also spell out the specific obligations the firm will undertake, the basis of the fee (contingent fee, hourly fee, flat fee, or a combination of these), and the terms of payment. In litigation cases, the engagement letter may clarify who is responsible for the payment of costs and expenses related to the investigation, such as deposition costs.

Non-Engagement

A non-engagement letter may be more important than an engagement letter. It tells the person (the would-be client) that the firm will not represent him or her. This is important when a statute of limitations may be approaching and the engagement is declined. The potential client must be clearly advised that the firm is not representing him or her and that he or she should seek other counsel immediately. If a person believes that he or she is represented, and the lawyer does not clearly express that the firm is not accepting the representation, an implied attorney–client relationship may arise. A sample non-engagement letter is shown in Exhibit 10.2.

Web Exploration

Sample engagement, non-engagement, and termination letters are available at **http://www.abanet.org/genpractice/magazine/2007/jan-feb/sampleengageletters.html#letter-1.**

Preparing for the Interview

Learning Objective 2

Describe the issues in preparing for and conducting an interview.

The first step in preparing for an interview is to understand the purpose of the interview and the outcome desired. Understanding the goals of the interview, the background or cultural issues, and the nature of the situation of the individual will help in structuring a successful interview. The fundamental purpose of any interview is to obtain all of the relevant facts for the case. Another purpose of an initial interview with a new client is to instill confidence in the client regarding the firm and its personnel. Occasionally an interview must be conducted without time for preparation, such as when the paralegal is asked to fill in for someone else at the last moment.

Exhibit 10.2 Non-engagement letter

Dear Mr. Wilkins:

Thank you for consulting our firm about your case against the Acme Trucking Company. After reviewing the facts, we regret that we cannot represent you in this matter.

I strongly recommend that you contact another lawyer immediately. Failure to act immediately may result in the barring your ability to file suit. If you do not have another lawyer in mind, I suggest you call the Bar Association Referral service at 218-555-1000.

Thank you for contacting me. I hope to be of service to you in the future.

Very truly yours,

____

Ethan Benjamin

Mason, Marshall and Benjamin

IN THE WORDS OF THE COURT...

Identity of Clients

***HOOSER V. SUPERIOR COURT OF SAN DIEGO COUNTY*, 84 CAL.APP.4TH 997, 101 CAL.RPTR.2D 341. (CAL. APP. 2000)**

...the identity of an attorney's clients is sensitive personal information that implicates the clients' rights of privacy. "[E]very person [has the right] to freely confer with and confide in his attorney in an atmosphere of trust and serenity...." (*Willis v. Superior Court* (1980) 112 Cal.App.3d 277, 293.)

Clients routinely exercise their right to consult with counsel, seeking to obtain advice on a host of matters that they reasonably expect to remain private. A spouse who consults a divorce attorney may not want his or her spouse or other family members to know that he or she is considering divorce.

Similarly, an employee who is concerned about conduct in his workplace, an entrepreneur planning a new business endeavor, an individual with questions about the criminal or tax consequences of his or her acts, or a family member who desires to rewrite a will may consult an attorney with the expectation that the consultation itself, as well as the matters discussed therein, will remain confidential until such time as the consultation is disclosed to third parties, through the filing of a lawsuit, the open representation of the client in dealing with third parties or in some other manner.

Upon such public disclosure of the attorney–client relationship, the client's privacy concerns regarding the fact of the consultation evaporate and there is no longer a basis for preventing the attorney from identifying the client. (See *Satterlee v. Bliss* (1869) 36 Cal. 489, 501.) However, until such a public disclosure occurs, the client's identity is itself a matter of privacy, subject to the protection against involuntary disclosure through compelled discovery against the attorney.

Investigation Checklists

The investigation checklist should not be viewed as a static document, but should be supplemented to the purposes and circumstances of each interview. The checklist should start with a listing of all of the parties that should be interviewed, including initial fact witnesses. (See Exhibit 10.3) As additional parties and witnesses are interviewed, more people may be identified who need to be added to the list. Exhibit 10.4 is a witness information form that may be used to organize information received from a witness.

Investigation of locations and physical evidence may reveal other locations and evidence that should be investigated. Initial interviews may also reveal the need for one or more expert witnesses to be added to the investigation checklist.

A checklist can be a valuable tool in ensuring that all the information required for a case is obtained during the initial interview. The same checklist also offers a good foundation for developing a more detailed interview plan when there is more time for preparation.

PRACTICE TIP

Investigation checklists, such as Exhibit 10.3, are only starting points in gathering information. Be alert to additional information that may be available based on the responses of clients and witnesses. Update and modify the checklist to adapt it to each case. Do not allow yourself to become so preoccupied with filling in the blanks that you miss important clues that could lead to additional information.

Physical Surroundings

The physical surroundings in the interview location can set the tone for the interview. Depending upon the purpose of the interview and the person being interviewed, the paralegal may wish to create either a formal or an informal environment.

You probably can remember a situation in which someone interviewed you from across a desk. Didn't you feel a certain formality? Dealing with opposing counsel might be best handled in this type of meeting. However, interviewing clients or witnesses in such an environment may instill a feeling of subservience to the interviewer. By contrast, an informal setting with a low coffee table and living room-style chairs may give the meeting a more personal tone and help the interviewee feel more relaxed and on an equal footing with the interviewer. In most cases, the paralegal will want to create the impression of

Exhibit 10.3 Investigation checklist for auto accident

INVESTIGATION CHECKLIST

Client name ______

Phone (hm) ______ (wk) ______ (cell) ______

Current address ______

Prior address(es) ______

Date of birth ______ Place of birth ______

Social Security No. ______

VEHICLE CLIENT OPERATING/PASSENGER

Owner and type of motor vehicle ______

Insurance Co. ______ Policy number ______

Insurance company contact ______ Phone ______

Date of incident ______ Time of day ______ Weather conditions ______

Location of incident ______

City, State ______ County ______ Municipality ______

Opposing party ______

Address ______

Phone (hm) ______ (wk) ______ (cell) ______

Owner and type of motor vehicle ______

Insurance Co. ______ Policy number ______

FACT WITNESSES

Name ______ Address ______

Name ______ Address ______

Name ______ Address ______

Name of ambulance ______

Name of hospital ______

Police report issued ______ Copy ordered ______

Photographs of scene taken ______

Name of treating physicians ______

EXPERT WITNESSES

Name ______ Address ______

Name ______ Address ______

Summary of cause of action ______

Attach detailed accident/incident description, accident reports, and diagrams.

being a competent professional, but in some situations, creating a more relaxed atmosphere may be beneficial. Some witnesses are more cooperative and helpful when they feel as if they are the ones in charge and are in the position of helping the interviewer.

Dress and Appearance

During an interview, first impressions are very important. The impression a paralegal makes when walking into the room for the initial interview may set the stage for the entire relationship with the client or witness. Clothing, posture, and manner of greeting help create this first impression.

Exhibit 10.4 Witness information form

Witness Information

CLIENT PERSONAL DATA

Client Name | Case No. | File No.

Address | City, State, Zip | Phone

CASE DATA

File Label | Case issue | Date

Responsible Attorney(s)

WITNESS DATA

Witness Name

Aliases, if any | US Citizen ☐ Yes ☐ No

Current Address | City, State, Zip | Phone

Past Address(es)

Date & Place of Birth | Sex | Race | Age | Current Marital Status ☐ Single ☐ Divorced ☐ Married ☐ Widowed ☐ Separated

Name of Spouse | Number/Former Marriages | Number/Children

Name of Children (natural & adopted) | Age | Name | Age

Current Employer

Address | City, State, Zip | Phone

Job Title | Supervisor | From | To

Previous Employer

Address | City, State, Zip | Phone

Job Title | Supervisor | From | To

Education/Name of School	City/State	From	To	Degree
High School				
College				
Technical/Other				

Witness for ☐ Plaintiff ☐ Defendant | Type of Witness ☐ Expert ☐ Character ☐ Eye Witness | Have you ever been a party or witness in a court suit? ☐ No ☐ Yes

If yes, where & when

OTHER PERTINENT DATA

Form 8567 - 9/86 SYCOM Madison, WI Printed in U.S.A.

Clothing sends a nonverbal message about the person and the firm. The impression a person makes upon walking into the room can enhance or destroy credibility. In the practice of law, or in a corporate law department, professionals must be prepared for the unexpected. Many attorneys, male and female alike, keep a "going-to-court suit" in the office just in case it is needed at a moment's notice. When the new client comes in, attorneys can change quickly into more polished and professional dress while the receptionist or secretary buys them time.

A client may be put off by a paralegal's "casual Friday" appearance, believing that the paralegal is not taking the matter seriously. The working paralegal, however, usually doesn't have time to change when the unexpected arises, often being the one to "buy time" for the attorney. Therefore, paralegals always must be prepared to make a good impression and tailor their appearance appropriately as the situation warrants. In the case of field interviews, a casual appearance may be preferred to put the potential witness at ease. In the office, suits with jackets are appropriate for men and women. In the field, removing the jacket may give the impression of less formality.

Communication Skills in a Multicultural Society*

Clients, witnesses, and others with whom the paralegal comes in contact should never be stereotyped. At the same time, paralegals should be aware of the gender, religious, and ethnic sensitivities of people. A paralegal's skill as an interviewer depends on the ability to appreciate how and why individuals act and react differently. Paralegals must not assume that everyone in each category believes and acts the same and must be sensitive to issues that may cause a person to communicate in an unexpected way. The following discussion will point out some general differences in the way men and women communicate, followed by some cultural background considerations.

Web Exploration

Check religious holiday dates at http://www.interfaithcalendar.org/.

Gender differences

A man, in comparison to a woman, is more likely to

- have been socialized to perform more aggressively and boast of his successes;
- have learned from childhood games that winning is desirable;
- be motivated by competition;
- view conflict as impersonal, a necessary part of working relationships;
- be impressed by power, ability, and achievement;
- hear only the literal words and miss the underlying emotion;
- not express his true feelings through facial expressions;
- have a more direct communication style.

A woman is more likely to

- have been socialized to work cooperatively and to be modest about her success;
- have learned from childhood games to compromise and collaborate, and continue to be motivated by affiliation;
- compete primarily with herself—with her own expectations of what she should be able to accomplish;
- take conflict personally;
- be impressed by personal disclosure and professional courage;
- have the ability to focus on several projects at the same time;
- be proficient at decoding nonverbal meanings and likely to display her feelings through facial expression and body language;
- have an indirect style, except with other women of equal rank.

---

*This section on communication skills is adapted from *Crosstalk: Communicating in a Multicultural Workplace* by Sherron Kenton and Deborah Valentine, 1997. Reprinted with permission of the authors.

Considering the receiver's attitudes about the paralegal:

- Man-to-man: He may afford the paralegal instant credibility based on being the same gender.
- Woman-to-woman: She may expect the paralegal to be friendly, nurturing, and concerned, and may afford the paralegal instant credibility based on same-gender assumptions.
- Paralegal man-to-woman: She may expect that the paralegal will not really listen to her.
- Paralegal woman-to-man: He may expect the paralegal to be friendly and nurturing, even passive-dependent. Any aggressive behavior or deviation from his expectation could cause him discomfort and confusion, or produce negative responses. He may simply disregard the female paralegal.

Cultural Sensitivity

The culturally sensitive person is aware of how religious and ethnic backgrounds and belief systems influence behavior. As the cultural makeup of the United States has become more diverse, the need for **cultural sensitivity** in the legal and paralegal professions has grown. Just as men and women are said to be different in some ways, so are those of differing cultural backgrounds.

Interviewing a Latino male, for example, may require a different approach than interviewing an Asian female. Even subtleties of eye contact can affect an interview. Whereas Americans view eye contact as a sign of sincerity, some Asian cultures view this as aggressive. In developing communication skills, paralegals must become sensitive to how they are perceived and learn to fashion their approach to maximize accuracy of communication.

The effectiveness of paralegals also is influenced by how well they "read" the cultural backgrounds of those with whom they interact. This involves manners of speaking, dressing, and acting, and whether one is a man or a woman in that culture. What is heard may not be what was intended. What is intended to be perceived may not be what the other person actually perceives because of cultural differences that affect the interpretation of words and body language. We will briefly highlight some general characteristics of four cultural groups.

European background

Generally, the countries of Western Europe, including Scandinavia, comprise those of European background. This group is extraordinarily large and complex, which limits attempts to make cultural generalities. In terms of gender differences, men and women with roots in the European culture may have different initial reactions to the paralegal and attitudes about the topic. Male and female listeners alike tend to perceive men as having more credibility than women of equal rank, experience, and training. Men tend to be more credible to other men, and women may be more credible to other women.

Now consider the cultural implications of graphic pictures of physical injuries from car crashes. These photos are acceptable in the United States, but Germans tend to dislike the sight of blood and the British are likely to be offended by violence.

According to Kenton and Valentine, if the paralegal appears to be European–American, receivers of communication may be concerned that the paralegal will

- reject their opinions;
- take advantage of them or hold them back;
- consider them different in a negative way;
- deny them equal opportunities.

Latino background

Collectively, Latin America encompasses 51 countries generally considered to be those south of the U.S. border: Mexico and the countries of Central America, South America, and the Caribbean islands. With so vast an area, many differences can be expected from country to country and even from city to city. The languages, too, are not the same. Portuguese is spoken in Brazil, and the Spanish that is spoken in South America differs from the Spanish spoken in Puerto Rico. The Latino–American population has moved closer to becoming the largest minority group in the United States. According to Kenton and Valentine, individuals with roots in the Latino culture tend to

- value family and loyalty to family;
- honor nationalism;
- exhibit a strong sense of honor;
- have a fatalistic view of the world;
- express passion in speech, manner, and deed.

Asian background

More than 30 countries can be considered Asian—among them, China, Malaysia, Japan, the Philippines, India, and Korea. They, too, demonstrate vast differences from culture to culture. Some generalizations may be made, however. Asian cultures generally consider that being direct and to the point is rude, and relationships are considered top priority. The Japanese, for example, tend to prefer an indirect style of communication. In communicating with people who have an Asian background, then, it might be best to begin with pleasantries about the weather, sports, or inquire about the well-being of the individual and his or her family.

Roots in the African culture

African Americans represent the largest ethnic group in the United States. A distinction should be made between African Americans of recent immigration who have stronger cultural ties to the African culture and African Americans with long family ties within the United States whose cultural roots are American. According to Kenton and Valentine, some of the African core beliefs and cultural values that may influence attitudes and behavior are

- a holistic worldview;
- emotion and expressiveness;
- a keen sense of justice or fairness.

Conducting the Interview

In the first meeting, the paralegal must make clear that he or she is a paralegal and not an attorney. During the first few minutes of the interview, paralegals must build a relationship with the interviewee, explain the reason for the interview, and eliminate any barriers that would prevent the interviewee from sharing the necessary information. Sometimes the interviewee seems to be fully cooperative, when in fact he or she is not cooperating. The subject matter may be embarrassing, he or she may have a fear of authority figures, or the interviewee might be uncomfortable using certain terms that are necessary to describe the situation.

Effective interviewers learn the verbal and nonverbal cues that help them understand the reasons for the interviewee's reluctance to answer questions. In some situations, the solution is first to ask easy questions, such as the person's name and address. Once the interviewee starts speaking, he or she often has less trouble answering well thought-out questions that build logically on the previous information.

This is not always the case, though. In times of great stress, clients have been known to read the name on a nameplate in the office and state it as their own name! The interviewer must be careful to avoid embarrassing the interviewee and have questions prepared that can be answered easily, thereby helping the person gain composure, such as, "My records show that you live at 123 South Main Street. Is that correct?" or "How do you spell your name?"

Listening Skills

A good interviewer must master the skill of listening. Most of us hear the words being said but may not be listening to *what* is being said. Instead of concentrating on what is being said, the interviewer may be emotionally influenced by the speaker's message, distracted by the speaker's physical behavior, or thinking about the next question he or she wants to ask.

CHECKLIST Tips for being a good listener

- ☐ Give your full attention on the person who is speaking. Don't look out the window or at what else is going on in the room.
- ☐ Make sure your mind is focused, too. It can be easy to let your mind wander if you think you know what the person is going to say next, but you might be wrong! If you feel your mind wandering, change the position of your body and try to concentrate on the speaker's words.
- ☐ Let the speaker finish before you begin to talk. Speakers appreciate having the chance to say everything they would like to say without being interrupted. When you interrupt, it looks like you aren't listening, even if you really are.
- ☐ Let yourself finish listening before you begin to speak! You can't really listen if you are busy thinking about what you want say next.
- ☐ Listen for main ideas. The main ideas are the most important points the speaker wants to get across. They may be mentioned at the start or end of a talk, and repeated a number of times. Pay special attention to statements that begin with phrases such as "My point is..." or "The thing to remember is..."
- ☐ Ask questions. If you are not sure you understand what the speaker has said, just ask. It is a good idea to repeat in your own words what the speaker said so that you can be sure your understanding is correct. For example, you might say, "When you said that no two zebras are alike, did you mean that the stripes are different on each one?"
- ☐ Give feedback. Sit up straight and look directly at the speaker. Now and then, nod to show that you understand. At appropriate points you may also smile, frown, laugh, or be silent. These are all ways to let the speaker know that you are really listening. Remember, you listen with your face.

Interviewing clients and witnesses requires not only understanding their background, but also understanding what type of witness they are—friendly, hostile, or expert—and how that might result in a bias toward the client or the type of case for which they are being interviewed. Fact witnesses may not want to get involved in the case. A hostile witness might say either what he or she thinks you want to hear or only what will advance his or her agenda. Some fact witnesses may be influenced by religious, ethnic, or racial prejudice, and may not be as concerned for the truth as they are for someone "paying" for committing the wrongful act.

When listening, the paralegal must focus on what is said, and not on how it is said. Some people are not articulate, and the facts may be lost if the interviewer doesn't listen carefully. Others may try to shock or put off the interviewer by using words intended to cause a reaction, similar to the "trash talk" used in sports to get the listener to react emotionally and lose concentration.

Good listeners avoid distractions. They do not allow themselves to lose focus because of noise or activity in the area of the interview or a speaker's annoying physical habits, such as tapping fingers or feet. Good listeners focus on the message and block out distractions.

More importantly, good interviewers do not make assumptions about the facts of the case. Professional interviewers must listen in a nonjudgmental, impartial manner to what is really being said. They listen with an open mind. Making assumptions about people or facts can lead to attempts to make the facts fit the interviewer's preconceived notions. Sometimes the facts are not what they first seem to be. Many people have been released from jail after DNA evidence proved they did not commit a crime that everyone assumed they had committed. Even though fact witnesses were interviewed and gave different versions of the incident, it was the DNA evidence that proved the person to be innocent.

Leading Questions

Leading questions are those that suggest the desired answer. In conducting a cross-examination, lawyers in trial frequently use leading questions to force the witness to answer in a desired manner. Leading questions do not lead to open-ended answers but are directed toward a desired answer, often yes or no, such as: "You ran the red light, didn't you?" or "Have you stopped kicking your dog?"

Web Exploration

For more information on listening skills, see the Texas A&M website at **http://www.scs.tamu.edu/selfhelp/elibrary/listening_skills.asp**.

Leading question A question that suggests the answer.

Open-Ended Questions

Open-ended questions are designed to give interviewees an opportunity to tell their story, instead of limiting their response to "yes" or "no." Open-ended questions create a **narrative opportunity** for the witness. For example, the interviewer may ask: "Tell me what you did today" or "Tell me about your life since the accident."

Narrative opportunity A question that allows the witness to give a full explanation.

Open-ended question A question that usually does not have a yes or no answer.

In fact interviews, the witness should receive the opportunity for open-ended narrative answers. Asking a leading question to obtain only an answer that you desire may prevent the witness from sharing information that is important to your case. For example, if an interviewer wants to know whether the client was observed at the scene, a leading question might be, "Did you see my client at the scene of the accident?" The answer to this question may be "yes" or "no," and will not elicit very much additional information. A better question might be, "Who was present at the scene of the accident?" This kind of question may lead to information about additional witnesses who could be interviewed. Similarly, the question, "How fast were the cars going prior to the impact?" is much better than, "Were the cars speeding before the impact?" In this context, the term "speeding" may be interpreted as "exceeding the speed limit" instead of "going too fast for the conditions."

With the witness's statements in hand at the time of trial, the trial attorney might then ask a leading question such as, "My client wasn't present at the scene of the accident, was she?" or "Isn't it true that the defendant was speeding before the impact?" With knowledge of the prior statement, there should be no surprise in the answer at trial. If there is, the prior statement can be used to impeach the credibility of the witness as part of the trial strategy.

At times, the interviewer may want to focus clients or witnesses by asking questions that give them a perspective of time or place, such as, "What did you observe at noon on Saturday?" or "Tell me what happened on September 11, 2001." The tragedy of that day will haunt the memories of Americans and most of the rest of the world, so little stimulus will be needed to elicit where they were and what they observed. In the case of traumatic events in people's lives—the loss of a loved one, the birth of a child, or a serious accident in which they were injured—little stimulus will be needed to elicit where they were and what they observed. Other, less important days and times tend to blur and have to be brought to the consciousness of the witness by questions such as, "Let's think back to August 19, 2001" and "What happened to you that day?"

Discovery Limitations

Discovery is the pretrial process during which the parties try to learn everything relevant about the case. This includes the investigation phase where basic information is gathered without the formality of statements signed under oath, such as written interrogatories, or before a court reporter authorized to administer oaths such as in a formal deposition.

In discovery, the scope of the inquiry is only limited generally to that which is **relevant**. Evidence is relevant if the fact is logically connected and tends to prove or disprove a fact in issue. Under the federal rules of evidence,

Rule 26(b)

Discovery Scope and Limits.
(1) Scope in General.
Unless otherwise limited by court order, the scope of discovery is as follows: Parties may obtain discovery regarding any nonprivileged matter that is relevant to any party's claim or defense—including the existence, description, nature, custody, condition, and

> location of any documents or other tangible things and the identity and location of persons who know of any discoverable matter. For good cause, the court may order discovery of any matter relevant to the subject matter involved in the action. Relevant information need not be admissible at the trial if the discovery appears reasonably calculated to lead to the discovery of admissible evidence. All discovery is subject to the limitations imposed by Rule 26(b)(2)(C).

For the investigator or interviewer, the general rule is that information may be sought, even if it is not admissible, as long as it is relevant and may lead to relevant information that will be admissible at trial. This includes information that may be used in trial to show bias, lack of credibility, and challenges to the qualifications of an expert.

Moral Versus Ethical Considerations

Moral obligation An obligation based on one's own conscience.

Ethical obligation A minimum standard of conduct, usually within one's profession.

In the investigation of a case, it is often necessary to understand the difference between moral and ethical obligations. A **moral obligation** is one based on one's own conscience or a person's personal rules of correct conduct, which may come from within the person's own community. Some communities, for instance, may consider it to be morally improper to ask someone to give information about another person. An **ethical obligation** is a responsibility of the legal profession under the ABA Model Rules of Professional Conduct, which includes thoroughness in representing a client. Ethical obligations apply to all members of the legal team, including those acting on behalf of a supervising attorney.

Is it ethically improper to ask someone to tell the truth surrounding the facts of a case that may lead to a neighbor, relative, or friend being held liable for his or her actions? For the paralegal and the legal team, the primary ethical obligation is the duty to the client. Some members of the legal team, for example, may be offended asking a mother to testify against her child. This is a moral issue for the mother if testifying will result in financial hardship or ruin because of a verdict based on the child's negligent conduct. However, the ethical duty to the client may require the paralegal to take this course of action.

Privileged Communication

Privileged communication A communication that a person has a right to be kept confidential based on the relationship with the other person, such as attorney and client.

Certain forms of communication are considered privileged and not usable at trial unless the privilege is waived. Forms of **privileged communication** are:

1. Attorney–client communications
2. Doctor–patient communications
3. Priest–penitent communications
4. Spousal communications during marriage

Each of these privileges can be waived, but the waiver must come from the client, patient, penitent, or spouse making the statement with the belief that the information is privileged. Some rules of ethics now permit certain otherwise privileged communications to be revealed to prevent harm or injury to another. In some cases, such as when another person's life may be in danger, these people may be compelled by a court to testify even when they believe it is a violation of their moral duty to the person from whom they have received the information.

Information gathered from the client is privileged if it is part of the representation of the client and necessary for rendering competent legal advice. When the paralegal is acting on behalf of the attorney, communications between a client and the paralegal are protected by the same privilege as those between the client and the attorney. The paralegal, therefore, is in the same position as the attorney to whom the confidential information has been communicated. The paralegal must carefully guard the confidential information and not inadvertently or intentionally reveal it.

ETHICAL PERSPECTIVE

New Hampshire Rules of Professional Conduct

RULE 1.6. CONFIDENTIALITY OF INFORMATION

(a) A lawyer shall not reveal information relating to the representation of a client unless the client gives informed consent. The disclosure is impliedly authorized in order to carry out the representation or the disclosure is permitted by paragraph (B).

Web Exploration

Contrast and compare the New Hampshire Rule at **http://www.courts.state.NH.US/supreme/orders/20072507.pdf** with the ABA Model Rules at **www.abanet.org/cpr** and the analogous rule in your jurisdiction.

Expert Witnesses

Learning Objective 3

Explain how expert witnesses are used in litigation.

Expert witness A person qualified by education or experience to render an opinion based on a set of facts.

Expert witnesses are individuals whose background, education, and experience are such that courts recognize them as qualified to give opinions in a certain subject based on a set of facts. An expert witness may be a doctor certified by a board of medical experts or an engineer specializing in an area of science such as the flammability of fabrics. A report of an expert may advise, based on the facts of the potential case, whether there is sufficient evidence to support a cause of action. Without this report, the lawyers may be obligated to advise clients that they have no actionable cause of action.

There is no clear rule on whether what is revealed to an expert in the preparation of a case is protected by attorney–client privilege. The question is whether the information given to the testifying expert is protected to the same extent as that revealed to a member of the trial team, including other attorneys, paralegals, and secretarial staff working on the case. Certainly, anything revealed to an expert who is listed as an expert witness on the list of witnesses to be called at trial is discoverable.

Some law firms retain an expert to advise them but do not use that expert to testify. The advice and information provided by these experts to help in the preparation for trial may be protected under the attorney-client privilege or the work product doctrine. Although the privilege is the client's, the paralegal and others on the legal team must be careful not to divulge privileged or confidential material without authorization.

IN THE WORDS OF THE COURT . . .

FEDERAL RULES OF CIVIL PROCEDURE 26 F.R.C.P. 26(B)(4)

(4) Trial Preparation: Experts

(A) A party may depose any person who has been identified as an expert whose opinions may be presented at trial. If a report from the expert is required under subdivision (a)(2)(B), the deposition shall not be conducted until after the report is provided.

(B) A party may, through interrogatories or by deposition, discover facts known or opinions held by an expert who has been retained or specially employed by another party in anticipation of litigation or preparation for trial and who is not expected to be called as a witness at trial, only as provided in Rule 35(b) or upon a showing of exceptional circumstances under which it is impracticable for the party seeking discovery to obtain facts or opinions on the same subject by other means.

(C) Unless manifest injustice would result, (i) the court shall require that the party seeking discovery pay the expert a reasonable fee for time spent in responding to discovery under this subdivision; and (ii) with respect to discovery obtained under subdivision (b)(4)(B) of this rule the court shall require the party seeking discovery to pay the other party a fair portion of the fees and expenses reasonably incurred by the latter party in obtaining facts and opinions from the expert.

The expert retained for background trial advice must have as much confidence in the legal team as the legal team has in the expert's advice and integrity. Some experts fear that the legal team will give them only selective information. With the limited information provided, they might give an expert opinion that is not what they would have given if they had received the complete set of facts.

Exhibit 10.5 indicates factors to be considered in arranging for an expert witness.

In the deposition, verify the accuracy and currency of the expert's professional information, including all resume and curriculum vitae items. Verify the opinions are those of the expert and, if based on the work of others, who these others are and what other experts' writings were consulted. It is important to have on the record the assumptions upon which the expert has formed the opinion and the steps followed in reaching the opinion.

Exhibit 10.5 Expert witness form

EXPERT WITNESS CHECKLIST

BACKGROUND

Full name ______ Date of birth ______

Business address ______

Business telephone number ______ Business fax number ______

Business email address ______ Business website ______

Locations of prior offices ______

Home address ______

Home telephone number ______

EDUCATION

Schools attended ______ Dates of attendance ______

Degrees or honors awarded ______

Continuing education courses ______

WORK HISTORY

Place of employment ______ Dates of employment ______

Job description ______

Reasons for leaving ______

Specific area of expertise ______

Published articles and books ______

Professional affiliations ______

Professional magazines subscribed to ______

Licenses and jurisdictions ______

Litigations or disciplinary action ______

PRIOR LEGAL EXPERIENCE

Ratio of plaintiff/defense cases ______

Prior clients including date (plaintiff or defendant) ______

Types of investigations with dates ______

Deposition testimony given with dates ______

Court testimony with dates ______

Legal references ______

AVAILABILITY

Vacation plans and dates ______ Potential meeting dates ______

Investigating Claims

Learning Objective 4

Explain the steps and process of conducting an investigation.

The legal team must gather all of the relevant information about a cause of action before making a recommendation to a client to file a lawsuit or respond to a claim of wrongdoing. In most cases, the paralegal has some indication of the area of law or the nature of the claim before the first interview with the client. This may be determined from a brief telephone interview when the client calls for an appointment, or from talking to the supervising attorney when the paralegal is assigned to the investigation. If paralegals specialize in certain areas of law, they are likely to already have some understanding of the elements of the claims or rights the client wishes to assert. Those in general practice and those entering a new area of law must try to understand the rules of law as they apply to the client's issue.

Web Exploration

For more information on the changes in the revised Restatement of the Law Third, Torts, visit the American Law Institute website at **http://www.ali.org/ali/promo6081.htm**.

For example, in a product liability case, understanding the common law elements of negligence is not enough. One must also understand the law of **strict liability** for product defect cases as found in the **Restatement of the Law Third, Torts: Product Liability**. Whereas in common law negligence, a breach of duty must be proven, strict liability does not require a finding of fault. An interview considering only negligence as the basis for a legal action could result in the client being advised that he or she does not have a claim when, under the concept of no-fault liability for defective products, a claim might exist.

Strict liability Liability without requiring a finding of fault.

Restatement of the Law Third, Torts A legal treatise with suggested rules of laws relating to torts.

The first step is to determine the legal basis of a client's claim. With an understanding of the legal basis of the claim and the applicable law, an investigative plan can be prepared to obtain the necessary witness statements, locate physical evidence, and obtain photographs, reports, and other evidence for use in preparation for trial. Knowing what elements of the action must be proven dictates what evidence must be located, such as witnesses, photographs, reports, and physical evidence. Knowing the elements of the claim will also ensure that the proper questions are asked in the interview, which then will dictate the necessary investigation steps.

For example, where a claim of negligence is to be made, photographic evidence may be essential in demonstrating the hazard that gave rise to the claim. If a client has been injured in a fall at a store, photographs showing the hazardous condition should be obtained as quickly as possible. In the case of strict liability involving a product, preservation of the defective product or photographic documentation of the defect becomes essential as a matter of proof.

One of the most useful tools for gathering information about a case is the digital camera. Digital photographs may be shared on computer networks or may be transmitted via the Internet to clients, possible witnesses, and other members of the legal team. It also is useful to take pictures of potential witnesses so that other members of the legal team may recognize them at the time of depositions and trial. If the photographs are going to be used as evidence at trial, it should be kept in mind that the photographer may need to be called as a witness to authenticate them.

A Defense Perspective

Most people quite naturally think of a lawsuit from the plaintiff's perspective, in terms of the violation of rights and the resulting injury. In a perfect world, only legitimate actions would be filed and the law would provide a perfect remedy for all wrongs committed. But not every plaintiff is in the right, and frivolous or even fraudulent lawsuits are sometimes filed.

The balance in the American legal system is achieved in part by allowing a vigorous defense on behalf of the defendant. A plaintiff may claim, for example, that she slipped and was injured as a result of the negligence of a storeowner. But the defendant storeowner might be innocent of any wrongdoing or breach of any duty to the plaintiff. It is good to remember that for every plaintiff there is a defendant, and for each party there is a law firm and an attorney willing to represent him or her.

Obtaining Official Reports

Most incidents giving rise to litigation have some type of official report associated with them. In a negligence action, it may be a police accident or incident report, emergency medical services report, fire department call report, or an incident report of safety violations from a federal, state, or local authority. These reports are filed in central depositories as public records. A useful starting point in an investigation is thus to obtain any official reports associated with the case. These reports frequently indicate the time and location of the incident and the names of fact witnesses. In some cases, detailed diagrams or photographs may accompany the reports. Exhibit 10.6 is an example of a police accident report form.

Fact Analysis

Analyzing the facts begins with interviewing the client and obtaining her or his account of the time, place, circumstances, and other participants or witnesses involved. Exhibit 10.7 is a sample client interview form. A complete analysis usually requires further field investigation of the location, the objects involved (such as an automobile), and interviews of the parties and witnesses. One person's perception may not reflect reality. A client's recollection and description of the physical surroundings may not be consistent with the investigator's observations at the location. For example, what one person describes as a narrow, congested walkway may actually be a standard-width, open sidewalk.

The ultimate trier of fact will be the jury, a panel of arbitrators, or a judge acting as the trier of fact. Therefore, analysis of the facts must support the presentation of a client's claim or defense in an **arbitration** or trial.

Arbitration A form of ADR in which the parties choose an impartial third party to hear and decide the dispute.

Locations

Careful analysis of a claim includes verification of the physical aspects of the actual location where the incident occurred. Ask any group of people to describe a location, and you're likely to get a different description from each person. The direction from which the person viewed the location (from the south, north, east, or west) may affect the person's description, as will many other factors. The driver's view from behind the wheel of a large tractor-trailer might be different from the view from behind the wheel of a small sports car.

Web Exploration

Find your home on Google Earth at **http://earth.google.com**.

Investigation of a case should include a trip to the location where the incident occurred. The trier of fact will be relying upon the presentations of the attorneys to describe the location. They will also be looking at the place from a neutral point of view, usually without any prior familiarity with the location. The diagrams presented at trial are usually sterile, one-dimensional aerial views, and photographs from the points of view of all the participants can make the difference in understanding the duties and responsibilities of the litigants. Unlike diagrams of the location, the photographs typically will be from the point of view of the plaintiff, defendant, or witnesses who may have been at ground level, behind the wheel of a vehicle, or looking out of a building window.

Satellite photos are available of locations around the world. Google Earth™ offers web access to images that may be modified to add descriptions such as street names and points of interest, such as lodgings, restaurants, schools, churches, and other places.

Tangible Evidence

Tangible evidence consists of the physical objects that may have caused an injury. Examples of such objects might include a giveaway toy from a fast-food restaurant that was swallowed by a two-year-old, a bottle that exploded, or an automobile with brakes that failed or seatbelts that snapped. In some cases, the tangible evidence is essential to proving negligence or an element of strict liability.

Much has been written about the effects of a plaintiff's or defendant's failure to preserve critical tangible evidence. In some cases, the failure to preserve evidence has resulted in the plaintiff or defendant losing the case.

Exhibit 10.6 Sample police accident report form

COMMONWEALTH OF PENNSYLVANIA
POLICE ACCIDENT REPORT

(XX) REFER TO OVERLAY SHEETS

REPORTABLE ☐ NON - REPORTABLE ☐

PENNDOT USE ONLY

POLICE INFORMATION

1. INCIDENT NUMBER
2. AGENCY NAME
3. STATION/ PRECINCT | 4. PATROL ZONE
5. INVESTIGATOR | BADGE NUMBER
6. APPROVED BY | BADGE NUMBER
7. INVESTIGATION DATE | 8. ARRIVAL TIME

ACCIDENT INFORMATION

9. ACCIDENT DATE | 10. DAY OF WEEK
11. TIME OF DAY | 12. NUMBER OF UNITS
13. # KILLED | 14.# INJURED | 15. PRIV. PROP. ACCIDENT Y ☐ N ☐
16. DID VEHICLE HAVE TO BE REMOVED FROM THE SCENE? UNIT 1 Y ☐ N ☐ UNIT 2 Y ☐ N ☐
17. VEHICLE DAMAGE 0 - NONE 1 - LIGHT 2 - MODERATE 3 - SEVERE UNIT 1 ☐ UNIT 2 ☐
18. HAZARDOUS MATERIALS Y ☐ N ☐ | 19. PENNDOT PROPERTY Y ☐ N ☐

ACCIDENT LOCATION

20. COUNTY | CODE
21. MUNICIPALITY | CODE

PRINCIPAL ROADWAY INFORMATION

22. ROUTE NO. OR STREET NAME
23. SPEED LIMIT | (24) TYPE HIGHWAY | (25) ACCESS CONTROL

INTERSECTING ROAD:

26. ROUTE NO. OR STREET NAME
27. SPEED LIMIT | (28) TYPE HIGHWAY | (29) ACCESS CONTROL

IF NOT AT INTERSECTION:

30. CROSS STREET OR SEGMENT MARKER
31. DIRECTION FROM SITE N S E W | 32. DISTANCE FROM SITE FT. MI.
33. DISTANCE WAS MEASURED ☐ ESTIMATED ☐
(34) CONSTRUCTION ZONE ☐ | (35) TRAFFIC CONTROL DEVICE PRINCIPAL ☐ INTERSECTING ☐

UNIT # 1

36. LEGALLY PARKED ? Y ☐ N ☐ | 37. REG. PLATE | 38. STATE
39. PA TITLE OR OUT-OF-STATE VIN
40. OWNER
41. OWNER ADDRESS
42. CITY, STATE & ZIPCODE
43. YEAR | 44. MAKE
45. MODEL - (NOT BODY TYPE) | 46. INS. Y ☐ N ☐ UNK ☐
(47) BODY TYPE | (48) SPECIAL USAGE | (49) VEHICLE OWNERSHIP
(50) INITIAL IMPACT POINT | (51) VEHICLE STATUS | (52) TRAVEL SPEED
(53) VEHICLE GRADIENT | (54) DRIVER PRESENCE ☐ | (55) DRIVER CONDITION
56. DRIVER NUMBER | 57. STATE
58. DRIVER NAME
59. DRIVER ADDRESS
60. CITY, STATE & ZIPCODE
61. SEX | 62. DATE OF BIRTH | 63. PHONE
64. COMM. VEH. Y ☐ N ☐ | 65. DRIVER CLASS | 66. DRIVER SS #
67. CARRIER
68. CARRIER ADDRESS
69. CITY, STATE & ZIPCODE
70. USDOT # | ICC # | PUC #
(72) VEH. CONFIG. | (73) CARGO BODY TYPE | 74. GVWR
75. NO. OF AXLES | (76) HAZ ARDOUS MATERIALS | 77. RELEASE OF HAZ MAT Y ☐ N ☐ UNK ☐

UNIT # 2

36. LEGALLY PARKED ? Y ☐ N ☐ | 37. REG. PLATE | 38. STATE
39. PA TITLE OR OUT-OF-STATE VIN
40. OWNER
41. OWNER ADDRESS
42. CITY, STATE & ZIPCODE
43. YEAR | 44. MAKE
45. MODEL - (NOT BODY TYPE) | 46. INS. Y ☐ N ☐ UNK ☐
(47) BODY TYPE | (48) SPECIAL USAGE | (49) VEHICLE OWNERSHIP
(50) INITIAL IMPACT POINT | (51) VEHICLE STATUS | (52) TRAVEL SPEED
(53) VEHICLE GRADIENT | (54) DRIVER PRESENCE ☐ | (55) DRIVER CONDITION
56. DRIVER NUMBER | 57. STATE
58. DRIVER NAME
59. DRIVER ADDRESS
60. CITY, STATE & ZIPCODE
61. SEX | 62. DATE OF BIRTH | 63. PHONE
64. COMM. VEH. Y ☐ N ☐ | 65. DRIVER CLASS | 66. DRIVER SS #
67. CARRIER
68. CARRIER ADDRESS
69. CITY, STATE & ZIPCODE
70. USDOT # | ICC # | PUC #
(72) VEH. CONFIG. | (73) CARGO BODY TYPE | 74. GVWR
75. NO. OF AXLES | (76) HAZ ARDOUS MATERIALS | 77. RELEASE OF HAZ MAT Y ☐ N ☐ UNK ☐

AA-45 (1/92) PAGE: CENTER FOR HIGHWAY SAFETY

(continued)

Exhibit 10.6 Sample police accident report form *(continued)*

78. RESPONDING EMS AGENCY — INCIDENT #:

79. MEDICAL FACILITY — ACCIDENT DATE:

80. PEOPLE INFORMATION

A	B	C	D	E	F	G	NAME	ADDRESS	H	I	J	K	L	M

81. ILLUMINATION ☐ 82. WEATHER ☐

83. ROAD SURFACE ☐

84. PENNSYLVANIA SCHOOL DISTRICT (IF APPLICABLE)

85. DESCRIPTION OF DAMAGED PROPERTY

OWNER

ADDRESS

PHONE

86. DIAGRAM

87. NARRATIVE - IDENTIFY PRECIPITATING EVENTS, CAUSATION FACTORS, SEQUENCE OF EVENTS, WITNESS STATEMENTS, AND PROVIDE ADDITIONAL DETAILS. LIKE INSURANCE INFORMATION AND LOCATION OF TOWED VEHILCES, IF KNOWN.

INSURANCE INFORMATION	COMPANY	INSURANCE INFORMATION	COMPANY
UNIT 1	POLICY NO	UNIT 2	POLICY NO

88. WITNESSES	NAME	ADDRESS	PHONE
	NAME	ADDRESS	PHONE

	89. VIOLATIONS INDICATED	90. SECTION NUMBERS (ONLY IF CHARGED)	TC NTC
UNIT 1			☐ ☐
UNIT 2			☐ ☐

UNIT 1	91. PROBABLE USE	92. TYPE TEST	93. RESULTS 0.___%	☐ NO TEST ☐ REFUSE ☐ UNK	UNIT 2	91. PROBABLE USE	92. TYPE TEST	93. RESULTS 0.___%	☐ NO TEST ☐ REFUSE ☐ UNK	94. INVESTIGATION COMPLETE ? YES ☐ NO ☐

AA-45 (1/92) PAGE: CENTER FOR HIGHWAY SAFETY

Source: Pennsylvania Department of Transportation, Bureau of Highway Safety and Traffic Engineering. Used with permission.

Exhibit 10.7 Initial client interview form

CLIENT INTERVIEW CHECKLIST

CLIENT PERSONAL INFORMATION

Name ____________________

Address ____________________

City ________ State ________ Zip ________

Phone (hm) ________ (wk) ________ (cell) ________

How long at this address ____________________

Date of birth ________ Place of birth ________

Social Security No. ____________________

Prior address ____________________

City ________ State ________ Zip ________

Dates at this address ____________________

Employer ____________________

Job description ____________________

Marital status ________ Maiden name ________

Spouse's name ________ Date of birth ________

Child's name ________ Date of birth ________

Child's name ________ Date of birth ________

Child's name ________ Date of birth ________

CASE INFORMATION

Case referred by ____________________

Case type ☐ Appeal ☐ Business ☐ Corporate ☐ Estate ☐ Litigation
☐ Municipal ☐ Real Estate ☐ Tax ☐ Trust ☐ Other

Opposing party(ies) ____________________

Opposing party ____________________

Address ____________________

Opposing attorney ____________________

Address ____________________

Date of incident ________ Statute of limitation date ________

Summary of facts ____________________

It is important to understand the local rules with regard to the loss or destruction of evidence, or **spoliation of evidence**, and its effect on a cause of action. In determining the appropriate penalty for spoliation of evidence, courts are most likely to consider:

Spoliation of evidence Destruction of evidence.

1. the degree of fault of the party who altered or destroyed the evidence;
2. the degree of prejudice suffered by the opposing party; and
3. the availability of a lesser sanction that will protect the opposing party's rights and deter future similar conduct (See *Schroeder v. Department of Transportation*, 710 A2d 23 (1998).

Exhibit 10.8 Sample timeline using LexisNexis TimeMap

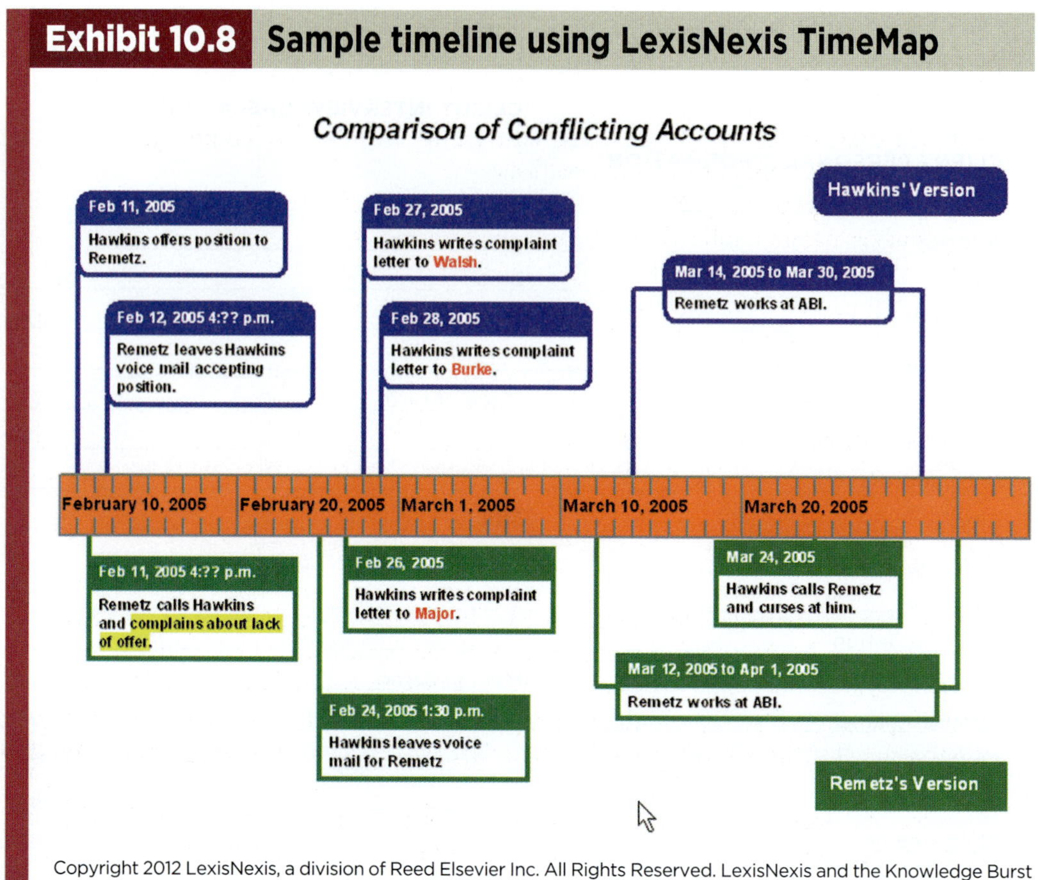

Following a Timeline

An investigation should explore not only the incident itself, but also events leading up to the incident, as well as the events and occurrences that followed it. (See Exhibit 10.8 for a comparison of conflicting accounts.) Some of the facts leading up to and following the incident may be critical. An essential question in some cases may be whether the incident could have occurred in the time period asserted by the parties. For example, could a party have taken only 20 minutes to drive 30 miles through crowded rush-hour traffic on city streets? In a food-poisoning case, could ingestion of the food at noon have caused the reaction claimed by 1:00 p.m.? Most food-poisoning cases take 6 to 12 hours from ingestion of the tainted food until the onset of symptoms. If the ingestion occurred only an hour prior, this may indicate that the claimant might have been negligent or the wrong source was identified as the cause of the illness.

The starting point for developing a timeline is the time of the alleged injury. Also important, from the standpoint of proving fault or the absence of fault, are the events that led up to the incident. From the damages standpoint, the events after the incident, including treatment and subsequent changes in the person's life or lifestyle, are important.

Freedom of Information Act (FOIA)

Freedom of Information Act (FOIA) A federal statute permitting access to federal agency records.

The **Freedom of Information Act (FOIA)** is a federal statute designed to make available to the public the information possessed by the federal government and its agencies. The federal government can be a good source of information. Many documents filed by persons or businesses are available through the government and are frequently provided online, such as corporate filings with the Securities and

Exchange Commission. Other information may be available by request. However, some limitations apply to the information available. The general exceptions in FOIA, 5 U.S.C. § 552, are:

1. classified documents concerning national defense and foreign policy;
2. internal personnel rules and practices;
3. exemptions under other laws that require information to be withheld, such as patent applications and income tax returns;
4. confidential business information and trade secrets;
5. intra-agency and inter-agency internal communications not available by law to a party in litigation;
6. protection of privacy of personnel and medical files and private lives of individuals;
7. law enforcement investigatory files;
8. examination, operation, or condition reports of agencies responsible for the regulation and supervision of financial institutions; and
9. geological and geophysical information and data, including maps concerning wells.

Many federal agencies do not require a formal FOIA request. Some federal agencies, such as the National Transportation Safety Board (NTSB), make information available online. The Consumer Product Safety Commission (CPSC) site is helpful in finding information about defective products that may be a cause of a client's injuries, but limitations are placed on the information that an agency may disclose under federal law.

Under the provisions of the Electronic Freedom of Information Act (FOIA) Amendments of 1996, all federal agencies are required to use electronic information technology to foster public availability of FOIA records. The Act requires each agency to make electronically available the documents described in 5 U.S.C. Sec. 552(a)(2) that the agency created after November 1, 1996. CPSC's electronic. Source: http://www.cpsc.gov/library/foia/foia.html

Web Exploration

Obtain a copy of the latest CPSC FOIA report at **http://www.cpsc.gov/LIBRARY/FOIA/foia.html**.

CPSC LIMITATIONS OF FOIA DISCLOSURE

SIDEBAR

15 U.S.C. § 2055. Public disclosure of information release date: 2005-08-01

(a) Disclosure requirements for manufacturers or private labelers; procedures applicable
  (1) Nothing contained in this Act shall be construed to require the release of any information described by subsection (b) of section 552 of title 5 or which is otherwise protected by law from disclosure to the public.
  (2) All information reported to or otherwise obtained by the Commission or its representative under this Act[,] which information contains or relates to a trade secret or other matter referred to in section 1905 of title 18 or subject to section 552 (b)(4) of title 5[,] shall be considered confidential and shall not be disclosed.
  (3) The Commission shall, prior to the disclosure of any information which will permit the public to ascertain readily the identity of a manufacturer or private labeler of a consumer product, offer such manufacturer or private labeler an opportunity to mark such information as confidential and therefore barred from disclosure under paragraph (2).
  (4) All information that a manufacturer or private labeler has marked to be confidential and barred from disclosure under paragraph (2), either at the time of submission or pursuant to paragraph (3), shall not be disclosed, except in accordance with the procedures established in paragraphs (5) and (6)....

Locating Witnesses

Most witnesses can be located by the use of directories. The web has also become a valuable tool for locating witnesses.

Directories

Investigators usually keep a collection of telephone books of the areas in which they work. But the use of printed telephone directories has declined in favor of online, Internet-based directories, which may be searched by phone number, address, or last name. Directories are not limited to the United States and are available online for most parts of the world. Businesses may also be located using commercial or industrial directories, both domestically and internationally.

In addition to telephone directories, directories are published by trade organizations, professional groups, and educational institutions. These directories may be limited to their memberships but can be useful in cases where the name and the association are known, but not the city, state, or country where the person can be found.

The Web

As paper is replaced by electronic media, more directories are being placed online. In addition, search engines can be used to locate individuals, businesses, and organizations on the Internet. Communications companies and other private firms offer a number of online directories. Many organizations and publishers of professional directories now offer their print directories online. These services may change or

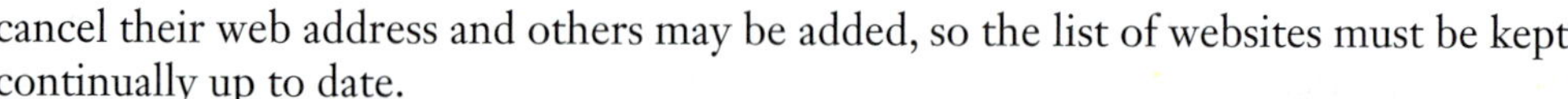

cancel their web address and others may be added, so the list of websites must be kept continually up to date.

The web is also a good source of information about both expert and lay witnesses. Social networking sites, such as Facebook, offer information on millions of people who otherwise would not be in a directory. A search of Facebook, YouTube, blogs, and other similar websites may produce information that can be used for finding people and learning about them. The sites may also provide information about a witness's good or questionable behavior that might demonstrate a credibility issue. For example, the posting of a web camera image of a high-profile athlete or celebrity at a party has resulted in a loss of endorsement contracts because of questions of improper conduct. Public postings by potential parties and witnesses may also indicate a potential bias, hostility, or in the case of a potential juror, a predisposition or prejudice about a particular party. In some cases, jurors posting to their websites, Facebook, or other social networking sites may show a violation of jury deliberation secrecy that might result in a new trial.

Web Exploration

For information or making an FOIA request to the Department of Justice is available at **http://www.justice.gov/oip/foia-resources.html**.

Web Exploration

Check frequently requested information at the NTSB website: **http://www.ntsb.gov**

Web Exploration

Experts can be located using the free LexisNexis/Martindale-Hubbell website at **http://experts.martindale.com/**.

CHECKLIST Investigation Information Sources

Information Source	Web Address	Physical Location	Comments
Police Records—Local	www.		
Police Records—State	www.		
Birth Records	www.		
Death Records	www.		
Driver's License	www.		
Vehicle Registration	www.		
Corporate Records	www.		
Real Estate—Recorder	www.		
Real Estate—Tax	www.		
Real Estate—Land Mapping	www.		
Register of Wills	www.		
Trial Court	www.		
Federal District Court—Clerk's Office	www.	Room Federal Courthouse	
Federal Bankruptcy Court	www.		
Occupational License	www.		
Weather Reports	www.		

Personalize this list by adding the local or regional office web address, mailing addresses, and room numbers for personal visits. Add comments and note any applicable contact people, costs, or hours of operation.

Learning Objective 5

Explain the function of the trial notebook and its relationship to case management.

Interviews, Investigations, and Trials

It is never too soon to start preparing for trial. Trial preparation starts with the first client contact or with gathering the first document related to a case. Good preparation for trial also includes an assessment of how well clients and witnesses will react in depositions or in court under the pressure of cross-examination and how they will be perceived by opposing counsel, the judge, or the jury. An important practical consideration in deciding whether to try a case is how the parties will appear to the jury. Will they come across as being truthful and likeable? Or will they appear dishonest, unpleasant, or untrustworthy? These observational notes may be of great interest when the legal team must decide whether to settle or try the case.

Effectively managing a case may involve reviewing, sorting, and marking for identification hundreds or even thousands of documents, photographs, and other items. Careful tracking and organizing should start at the beginning of the case management process. Good case management requires a thoughtful process for storing, handling, examining, evaluating, and indexing every page. In the computer age, case management also includes making decisions on whether to use electronic display technologies in addition to conventional paper exhibits. **Demonstrative evidence**, such as the defective products in a strict liability action or an automobile in a motor vehicle accident, may need to be obtained and preserved for examination by expert witnesses or for use at trial.

There are almost as many different approaches to setting up case files and managing cases as there are legal teams. One of the traditional approaches is the case or **trial notebook**. Summary information about the case is maintained in a notebook with tabs for each major activity, party, expert, or element of proof needed. A sample of the sections is shown in Exhibit 10.9. If a trial notebook system is used, the team must maintain and organize the case file, file boxes, or file cabinets where the hard copies of documents, exhibits, and other evidence are maintained. If only one trial or case notebook is kept for the team, someone working on the case must take responsibility for being certain that there is no duplication of effort and that the most current activities are entered. When multiple copies of the notebook are used, each trial notebook must be updated regularly so that all members of the legal team are using the same information.

Case and Practice Management Software

The legal team may work on a number of cases at the same time, and each case may be in a different stage of preparation. With the team approach to handling cases, each member of the team must be able to access case information and know what the other members of the team have done, as well as what remains to be done. In the traditional paper file approach, the physical file is the repository of everything in the case, including interview notes, pleadings, and exhibits. To work on a specific part of a case, the physical file has to be located and the needed folder pulled.

In the **"paperless" office**, everything, in theory, is available on the computer screen. Documents are scanned into an electronic format and saved on the computer. Pleadings and notes are saved as word processor files. Transcripts of depositions and court hearings are also stored in electronic form. In a case with voluminous paperwork and days or weeks of deposition transcripts, case management software can allow relevant documents or appropriate deposition notes to be accessed quickly and efficiently.

Web Exploration

The complete set of policies and procedures for the current judges in U.S. District Court for the Eastern District of Pennsylvania may be found at http://www.paed.uscourts.gov/us08001.asp.

Trial notebook A summary of the case, tabbed for each major activity, witness, or element of proof.

"Paperless" office An office with electronic documents.

VIDEO GUIDELINES

Chambers Policies and Procedures
Bruce W. Kauffman, J.

13. Videotaped Testimony
All videotape recordings should be conducted with an acute sensitivity that the videotape may be shown to a jury. Skillful organization of the testimony, elimination of unnecessary objections, and conservation of time are strongly urged. Videotaped testimony should begin with the witness being sworn. Whenever a deposition or videotape is to be used, a transcript of the testimony and all exhibits should be furnished to the Court in advance. Objections should be submitted to the Court well in advance of the tapes being offered so that the tapes may be appropriately edited.

SIDEBAR

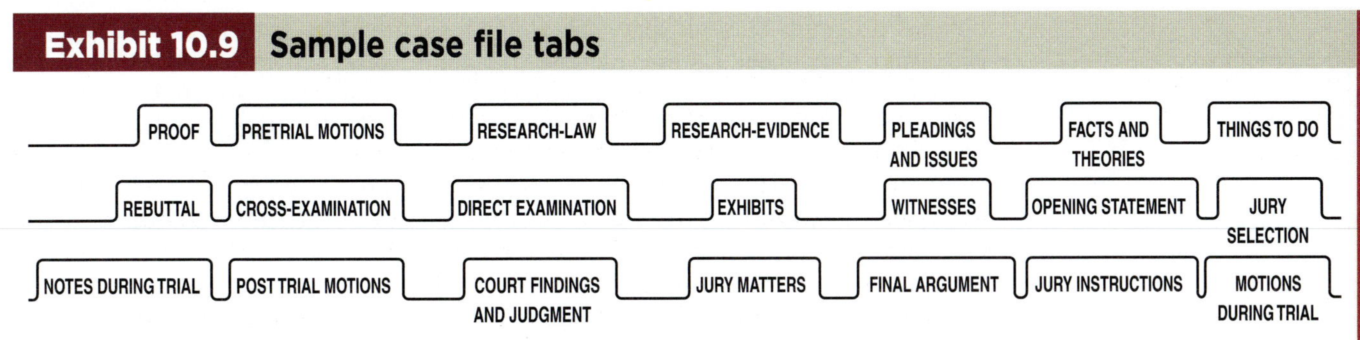

Paralegals *in* Practice

PARALEGAL PROFILE

Kevin D. Gasiewski

Kevin D. Gasiewski is a Certified Legal Assistant Specialist in Intellectual Property. After a career in law enforcement, he obtained his first paralegal job in the City Attorney's Office of Ann Arbor, Michigan. Later, he worked for Ford Global Technologies, LLC, and is now employed by Brooks Kushman P.C. Kevin is an active member of the Legal Assistants Section of the State Bar of Michigan, of which he is a past chairperson and a recipient of its 2003 Mentor Award.

My work focuses mainly on trademark prosecution, maintenance, and protection. During the initial interview with a client interested in registering a trademark, it is important to fully identify all team members, vendors, and third-party manufacturers connected to the proposed mark. I also ask questions regarding the mark itself and who designed it, as well as the goods, services, and countries for which it is intended. This data will be needed if the trademark is challenged, and for future maintenance or protection requirements.

My job also includes protecting trademarks from illegal use. When customs officials notify us that they are detaining suspected counterfeit goods, I initiate an investigation. I examine the subject trademark, determine the origin of the goods, and ascertain the final destination of the goods. The investigation results help me confirm whether or not the suspect goods are genuine.

Interview and investigation data are stored electronically, including contacts' information, specimen images showing use of the trademark, evidence showing the fame of the mark, and documents filed in support of the mark. The databases I use also contain a field for listing key phrases, words, and acronyms to make data searches easier and more efficient.

Although formal education is a definite plus in my field, it is equally important to stress your skills when applying for a paralegal position. Not only were my police investigation and interview skills attractive to employers, these abilities also provided me with the confidence to complete the wide variety of assignments typically encountered as a trademark paralegal.

Case management or practice management software can be used to manage both the law office itself and the cases within the office. This software has evolved out of earlier programs that tracked time spent on cases, sometimes with a calendar component that could be used to track deadlines and statutes of limitation. Modern programs also include practice management functions such as time and cost tracking, conflict checking, scheduling, and contact management. Others allow for management of the individual cases, including the tracking of documents, parties, issues, and events.

Software

Case management software is evolving constantly as the various vendors try to meet the demands and needs of their customers. Some nonlegal software has case or practice management-type functions. Microsoft Outlook provides a combination contact manager, calendar/scheduler, task "to do" list, and email function. More sophisticated programs, such as AbacusLaw from Abacus Data Systems and Practice Manager from Tabs3, provide the same functions, as well as outlining, billing, integrated research management, timelines, and other functions. LexisNexis CaseSoft offers individual programs that can share data, including CaseMap, TimeMap, TextMap, and NoteMap. One of the features of CaseMap is the ability to organize a case by facts, objects, or parties and create a chronology, as shown in Exhibit 10.10. CaseSoft can then seamlessly create timelines from the chronological information by using the TimeMap program (see Exhibit 10.11).

Exhibit 10.10 CaseMap features

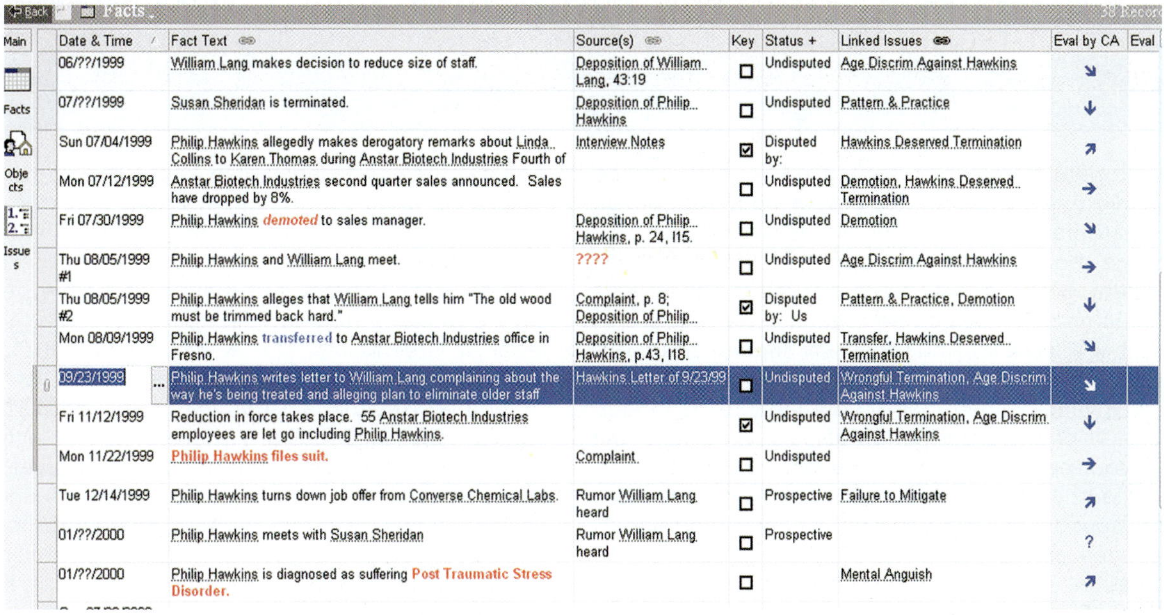

Back | Facts | 38 Records

Main | Facts | Objects | Issues

Date & Time	Fact Text	Source(s)	Key	Status +	Linked Issues	Eval by CA	Eval
06/??/1999	William Lang makes decision to reduce size of staff.	Deposition of William Lang, 43:19	☐	Undisputed	Age Discrim Against Hawkins	↘	
07/??/1999	Susan Sheridan is terminated.	Deposition of Philip Hawkins	☐	Undisputed	Pattern & Practice	↓	
Sun 07/04/1999	Philip Hawkins allegedly makes derogatory remarks about Linda Collins to Karen Thomas during Anstar Biotech Industries Fourth of	Interview Notes	☑	Disputed by:	Hawkins Deserved Termination	↗	
Mon 07/12/1999	Anstar Biotech Industries second quarter sales announced. Sales have dropped by 8%.		☐	Undisputed	Demotion, Hawkins Deserved Termination	→	
Fri 07/30/1999	Philip Hawkins *demoted* to sales manager.	Deposition of Philip Hawkins, p. 24, l15.	☐	Undisputed	Demotion	↘	
Thu 08/05/1999 #1	Philip Hawkins and William Lang meet.	????	☐	Undisputed	Age Discrim Against Hawkins	→	
Thu 08/05/1999 #2	Philip Hawkins alleges that William Lang tells him "The old wood must be trimmed back hard."	Complaint, p. 8; Deposition of Philip	☑	Disputed by: Us	Pattern & Practice, Demotion	↓	
Mon 08/09/1999	Philip Hawkins transferred to Anstar Biotech Industries office in Fresno.	Deposition of Philip Hawkins, p.43, l18.	☐	Undisputed	Transfer, Hawkins Deserved Termination	↘	
09/23/1999	Philip Hawkins writes letter to William Lang complaining about the way he's being treated and alleging plan to eliminate older staff	Hawkins Letter of 9/23/99	☐	Undisputed	Wrongful Termination, Age Discrim Against Hawkins	↘	
Fri 11/12/1999	Reduction in force takes place. 55 Anstar Biotech Industries employees are let go including Philip Hawkins.		☑	Undisputed	Wrongful Termination, Age Discrim Against Hawkins	↓	
Mon 11/22/1999	**Philip Hawkins files suit.**	Complaint	☐	Undisputed		→	
Tue 12/14/1999	Philip Hawkins turns down job offer from Converse Chemical Labs.	Rumor William Lang heard	☐	Prospective	Failure to Mitigate	↗	
01/??/2000	Philip Hawkins meets with Susan Sheridan	Rumor William Lang heard	☐	Prospective		?	
01/??/2000	Philip Hawkins is diagnosed as suffering **Post Traumatic Stress Disorder.**		☐		Mental Anguish	↗	

Exhibit 10.11 TimeMap features

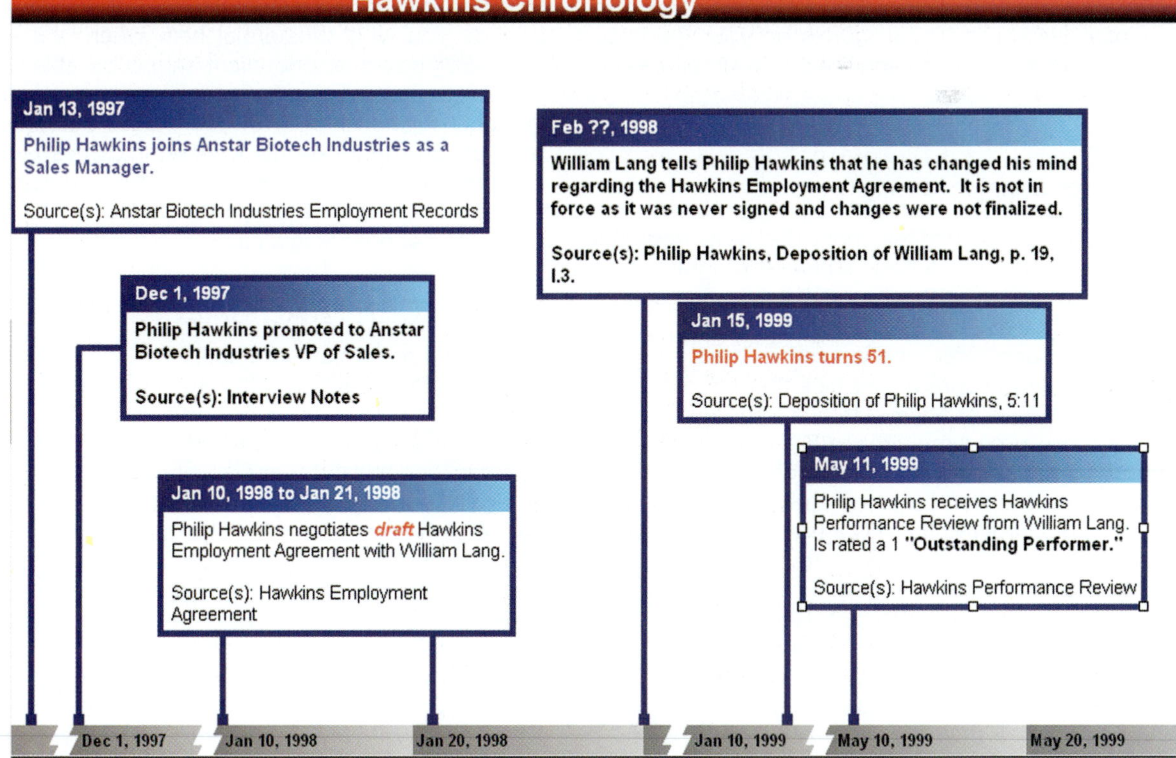

Advice *from the* Field

THE 10 AREAS OF INFORMATION YOU SHOULD ALWAYS HAVE AT YOUR FINGERTIPS

Neal R. Bevans

The ultimate paralegal resource guide is the place you save every important piece of information you have gathered in your daily work as a paralegal. This resource should contain telephone numbers, e-mails, important dates, notes about attorneys and judges and much more. The couple of hours you spend creating it will save you hundreds of hours throughout your career, give you a competitive edge and make you an invaluable member of your legal team. In fact, having all of this information at your fingertips will make you seem almost superhuman.

If putting together your own paralegal resource guide sounds unusual, it isn't. Legal professionals have been creating their own handy references for decades. When I first started out as a lawyer, a senior partner at my firm had a ragged manila file folder on his credenza containing copies of complaints he previously used in a wide variety of cases. When he needed a new complaint, he would pull out some of those old pleadings and reuse them. Your system might be a similar large file folder on your desk. Perhaps you keep everything stored in a database on your laptop, or in a network folder. Whatever method you currently use to hang on to your important information, you need to pull it all together and put it in one place. Let these 10 categories be your guide to organizing your resources and making your job easier.

1. COMPLETE CONTACT INFORMATION

Although there are a lot of telephone database programs available, including some basic software programs that came with most computers, many people find simple solutions are better.

A telephone reference is easy to create in any word processing program. The nice thing about using Corel WordPerfect or Microsoft Word to create these tables is these programs already are running on your computer, you can keep the files open while you work on other materials, you can constantly update your entries and alphabetizing them is a breeze. For instance, Janice Johnson, a paralegal for attorney Russ Becker in Morganton, N.C., said she uses a client list she originally created using WordPerfect. Her basic client list includes a chart consisting of the client's name, phone numbers, postal and e-mail addresses and notes.

Johnson said she encourages clients to contact her via e-mail. "I can check on e-mail in an extremely timely manner without having an interruption while a client is in my office," she said. "I also can respond back without getting caught on a call that ends up going entirely too long[.] Also, I have a word-for-word record of what information was given to the client through the e-mail contacts."

BlackBerry wireless devices are another great way to store contact information and have become very popular among law firms. Dana Martin, a paralegal at Greenbaum, Doll & McDonald, with offices in Ohio, Kentucky, Tennessee and the District of Columbia, likes the fact that with her BlackBerry, she can retrieve her e-mail anywhere, anytime. "We have Microsoft Outlook and [the BlackBerry] gives wireless access to that and my address book." She said she takes the BlackBerry with her wherever she goes.

The notes category is where your telephone reference really shines. You might not think having a notes section is important, but little details about your contacts really can help.

Denise Cunningham, a paralegal for attorney M. Lynne Osterholt in Louisville, K.Y., said she lists personal information for many of her contacts. "Along with the addresses, I also put in other information, like birthdays and anniversaries."

Little, personal details, such as remembering a client's birthday or the names of a client or contact's children, can help build personal relationships and provide you with substantial help when you need it most. For instance, one client might be able to help you locate another client who is missing or unavailable. Personal relationships with courthouse personnel will put you on the inside track when it comes to things as simple as when to schedule a hearing or earn you a warning phone call when your firm forgets to file appropriate paperwork in a case.

2. ONE CENTRAL CALENDAR

Everyone knows having a calendar isn't a luxury, it's an absolute necessity. With so much to do and so little time to do it, your calendar must be accurate, easy to access and contain enough information so you can understand what you need to do. "Experts all agree you should have one calendar, not different calendars for work, for play and for the holidays. You should have one calendar for everything," said Cunningham, who has been a paralegal for almost 25 years.

Cunningham said the calendar feature on her Palm is the most used feature and it often comes in handy in court, especially when scheduling court dates. "We write in our appointments or when pleadings are due. We depend on the Palm now, although we also keep a regular calendar. I like the Palm. It's wonderful and I take it everywhere."

Martin has her BlackBerry synced to her office calendar. "If I have an event on my [office] calendar that would notify me that I had an event coming up, I would get the same notification on my BlackBerry."

Whether you use a book-sized calendar, software or the latest handheld device, the important thing is to have one central calendar that is easy to access and update.

3. COURTHOUSE CONTACTS

Whether you decide to go high-tech or stick with low-tech methods to create your paralegal resource, it should contain additional information beyond just telephone contacts and important dates. It should contain plenty of information about the courthouse, including a list of the types of information that can be found in each office, as well as the names of your contact people in those offices. When you find a friendly face at the courthouse, put that person's name in your courthouse reference in as many different places as possible. The next time you call that office, ask for that person.

4. ATTORNEY PECULIARITIES

No ultimate reference would be complete without an "attorney peculiarities" section. This is a section to remind you about the various idiosyncrasies of the people with whom you must interact everyday. If the attorney has a hang up about the way pleadings are prepared (such as never staple, always use paper clips) then make a running list of these preferences. These notes can save you a lot of time, effort and frustration later. If you get new employees in the firm, you also can provide this list to them.

5. JUDGE PECULIARITIES

The basic premise about keeping track of attorney peculiarities applies to judges even more. Every judge with whom I have ever worked has had a different approach to court proceedings, pleadings, drafting orders and even when and where the attorneys should stand in the courtroom. Some judges like to be referred to as "Your Honor" in every context. Some judges have a habit of leaving work every day at 3 p.m.

Other judges think nothing of making you wait for hours outside their offices before they will sign an order. All of these characteristics should be written down for future reference. Attorneys have been doing this for years. When an attorney has a case pending before an unknown judge, he or she always will call a friend and ask about that judge's characteristics. Then the attorney adapts to that judge's approach. You should do the same thing.

One prosecutor, who preferred to remain anonymous, had a judge who would routinely appear for calendar calls in December wearing a Santa Claus cap. He would then give probation or suspended sentences to nearly every case pending. This is an important piece of information, not only for prosecutors who never wanted to have cases pending before that judge near Christmas, but also for defense attorneys who did.

6. ESSENTIAL FORMS

One of the primary reasons to create an ultimate paralegal resource is for the forms. Forms are the dirty little secret in the legal profession. Every time you come across a good form, put a copy into your paralegal reference guide. Copy the file over to your CD, store it on your flash memory card and put it someplace where you can access it again. There is another reason your forms should be stored in digital format: These days, many federal courts are requiring pleadings to be filed electronically.

"Federal courts are requiring briefs to be filed in Adobe Acrobat," Martin added. With a complete file of forms and pleadings, you will be ready to go in no time.

7. BRIEF AND MEMO BANKS

Your resource also should contain copies of briefs and memoranda used in other cases. We have all had the experience of realizing our current assignment is exactly like a brief we had to prepare last year in another case. Being able to pull up that previous brief can be a huge timesaver and be a real feather in your cap.

Although law firms often have firm-wide brief banks, keeping one of your own always is a good idea. The one time you need access to the law firm's brief bank probably will be the one time the system is down. Having your own brief bank also helps when you have to work at home and have no direct access to the firm's computer system. Your personal brief bank should contain all of the generic appellate briefs and memos you use on a daily basis. For anything more specialized than that, you always can pull it off the main network later.

8. FREQUENTLY ASKED QUESTIONS

If clients ask you the same questions repeatedly, it's time to digitize the answer and keep it available to print at a moment's notice. You might have clients who always ask how to get to the courthouse or what they should wear to court. Give them the answer in written form. It's easier for you and gives them something tangible they can review later.

Lisa Mazzonetto, a paralegal at the McDonald Law Offices in Asheville, N.C., handles domestic cases exclusively. She often gets questions about how long it takes to complete a case, what the basic rules about

(continued)

child visitation are, and what a client should do if he or she wishes to have a Temporary Restraining Order taken out against an unruly spouse. Mazzonetto has this information ready in writing, which frees up her time and gives clients a handy reference if they ever need it.

9. PRIVATE COMPUTER INFORMATION

In these days of Internet legal research and databases, it's important to have a handy reference containing all URLs, passwords and notes about how to access specific sites.

"There is an incredible amount of information out there that is key to day-to-day work in a law office. In my field of work, online tax records and register of deeds, [Department of Motor Vehicles] records, postal addresses, Web sites and people locator sites are very important," Mazzonetto said.

To keep all of your passwords confidential, yet easy to access, you can keep the list in a Word table and update it regularly. You also can password-protect the file to keep the wrong people from accessing it.

10. VENDOR AND SUPPLIER RECORDS

Your ultimate resource should contain information about all your office hardware and software, including vendor names, toll-free support numbers, license numbers and any other information you will need to get help if you have software or hardware problems. Keeping this information in your resource guide can save you a lot of time, especially when a service representative asks you for information contained on the computer or program that isn't currently working.

CREATING A DIGITIZED RESOURCE GUIDE

Now that you know the most important areas to include in your resource guide, you must decide in what format you will keep the information accessible. People have different preferences as to the format that suits them best. Some like to keep a binder with all the information printed out, while others prefer to keep a fully digitized version. Still others prefer a combination of both print and digital records for their resource guides.

There are a lot of different legal software programs available with which you can create a digital paralegal resource guide. They range from simple databases to complete law firm packages containing billing and accounting software, calendar features and complex databases. In high-tech offices, the calendar and case management system is available firm-wide and can be accessed by anyone on the network. However, not all law offices have taken this step into the 21st century. In situations where the office is filled with standalone systems, you will keep this information on your computer and on a backup CD.

David Moyer uses database programs to create lists of clients and documents in his freelance paralegal practice in Cuyahoga, O.H. "I use database programs, such as Microsoft Access and Excel. I use the databases for client conflict of interest checks, to name just one example."

Use programs that have been tried and tested in the real world or in firms similar in size and structure to your firm. Mazzonetto's firm uses Time & Chaos (www.chaossoftware.com). "It acts as our daily, weekly and monthly calendar; client address book and To-Do lists. It's very inexpensive, but an incredible asset."

Johnson's North Carolina firm uses Abacus Data Systems['] AbacusLaw (www.abacuslaw.com), which has been around for years and functions as a client database, calendar and docketing system. "We use Abacus as a database and tracking system here at our office," Johnson said. "I don't know how we survived as well as we did before we went to this system. Today, not to have some type of program for client information and management, along with a deadline system is like living in the dark ages and asking for a malpractice suit."

Martin's firm has a separate Information Technology division. "We have a very complex piece of software that keeps track of client information, accounting, billing and case management. Our whole office is really tied together. We are a regional firm and everybody can get to the same documents."

For many firms, tailor-made programs are the best way to go. Norma Schvaneveldt, a paralegal in Chattanooga, T.N., said her former firm, Eric Buchanan & Associates, relied on software created for the firm's specialty area of law. "We kept track of client information on the computer through a case management software program especially configured to handle Social Security cases. We also used it for our long-term disability cases. If you were out of town and needed to review a file, as long as you had Internet access, you could review any file."

THE POWER OF YOUR RESOURCE GUIDE

The smartest thing you can do with your ultimate paralegal resource is to organize it and keep it all in one place. Let everyone in the firm think you are superhuman, with an incredible memory for names, dates, telephone numbers and the myriad of other information law firms need on a daily basis. Your ultimate paralegal resource can be your secret weapon.

Concept Review *and* Reinforcement

LEGAL TERMINOLOGY

SUMMARY OF KEY CONCEPTS

Interviews/Interviewing

Interview	Any contact you have with a client, or prospective client, is a type of interview.
Screening Interview	The typical first contact with a client usually is a telephone call, but some people just appear at the office door, asking for an appointment or basic information about the firm's ability or interest in taking a case.
First Meeting	1. The paralegal must be careful to make clear that he or she is a paralegal and not an attorney. 2. The paralegal must build a relationship with the individual, let him or her understand the purpose of the interview, and eliminate any barriers that would prevent obtaining the necessary information.
Implied Attorney–Client Relationship	If too much information is taken, the potential client will think he or she is now represented by a lawyer. The courts have ruled on the side of the potential client, holding that an implied attorney–client relationship exists.
Cultural Sensitivity	The culturally sensitive person is aware of the reasons for differences in the way people behave based on a religious and ethnic backgrounds and belief systems.

Preparing for the Interview

Outcomes	1. The first step is to understand the outcomes desired, one of which is to instill confidence in the firm and its personnel. 2. The ideal outcome of any interview is to obtain all the necessary, relevant facts for the case.
Physical Surroundings	Depending upon the purpose of the interview and the person being interviewed, a formal or an informal environment may be desired.
Dress and Appearance	Clothing worn in an interview sends a nonverbal message about the paralegal and the firm or business, and the initial impression can enhance or destroy credibility.
Communication Skills in a Multicultural Society	Interviewers must appreciate how and why individuals act and react differently.

Listening Skills	An interviewer must learn to listen to what is actually being said and not just to the words themselves.
Leading Questions	Leading questions are questions that suggest the desired answer. Lawyers in conducting a cross-examination in trial frequently use leading questions to force the witness to answer in a desired manner.
Open-Ended Questions	Open-ended questions are designed to create a narrative opportunity for the witness.
Moral versus Ethical Considerations	
Moral Obligations	Moral obligations are based on one's own conscience or perceived rules of correct conduct, generally held by the person's own community.
Ethical Obligations	Ethical obligations are obligations of the legal professional under the ABA Model Rules of Professional Conduct. An important ethical obligation is thoroughness in representing a client.
Privileged Communications	
Forms of Privileged Communications	Attorney–client communications Doctor–patient communications Priest–penitent communications Spousal communications during marriage
Waivers	Privileges can be waived, but the waiver must come from the client, patient, penitent, or spouse making the statement with the belief that it is privileged.
Investigating Claims	
Expert Witnesses	
Definition	Expert witnesses are individuals whose background, education, and experience are such that courts will recognize them as qualified to give opinions based on a set of facts.
Freedom of Information Act (FOIA)	
Definition	FOIA is a federal statute designed to open to the public the information in the possession of the federal government and its agencies.
Locating Witnesses	
Directories	1. Phone books 2. Cross-reference directories 3. Membership directories
The Web	Search engines can help locate individuals, businesses, and organizations on the Internet. The Web is also a source of information about individuals from public sources and social networking sites.
Interviews, Investigations, and Trials	
Trial Preparation	Trial preparation starts with the first client contact and the gathering of the first document. Good preparation for trial includes an assessment of how well clients and witnesses will react in depositions or in court under the pressure of cross-examination and how they will be perceived by opposing counsel, the judge, or the jury.

Case Management	Good case management requires a thoughtful process for storing, handling, examining, evaluating, and indexing every page. In the computer age, case management involves decisions on the appropriateness and potential use of electronic display technologies, as well as conventional paper exhibits.
Traditional Case Management	The case notebook or trial notebook was one of the common traditional approaches to case management.
Case and Practice Management Software	Case management or practice management programs can be used to manage the law office and the cases within the office.

WORKING THE WEB

1. Use the Internet to find and print out a map of the local area around your school.
2. Use the Internet to obtain driving directions from your home to your school's main entrance. Print out the directions and related maps.
3. Obtain a satellite image of your school from Google Earth: http://earth.google.com. How might this be more helpful in investigating a case than other maps available on the Internet?
4. Use Findlaw to locate an accounting expert in your state: www.findlaw.com. Print out a list of experts listed.
5. Use the LexisNexis Martindale–Hubbell website to locate an expert witness for a patent intellectual property case involving an electronic device. Print out a copy of the contact information.
6. Using the search function of your computer browser, find and print out a copy of Rule 26 of the Federal Rules of Civil Procedure.
7. Download a trial copy of TimeMap from LexisNexis using the link on the Technology Resources Website: http://media.pearsoncmg.com/ph/chet/chet_goldman_techresources_1/
8. Prepare a timeline of the assignments and exams for the courses you are currently taking. Print a copy of the timeline.
9. Assume you have been asked to work on a case in which a pedestrian was struck by a car going north on the west side of the Flat Iron Building in Manhattan (New York City). Print out a satellite image of the location showing the building and the traffic flow using Google Earth: http://www.google.com/earth/index.html. Note that you will have to download the Google Earth viewer. Check with your instructor before downloading on a school computer. What is the proper direction of the vehicle traffic? Was the crosswalk visible? Were any other potential images available? Prepare a short memorandum about your findings.

CRITICAL THINKING & WRITING QUESTIONS

1. What are the legal and ethical issues involved for the paralegal when the potential client says he or she just wants a quick answer to a question such as, "Do I have a case?" Explain fully, including references to the applicable state statute.
2. What is a screening interview? What potential ethical and malpractice issues are involved?
3. How is the implied attorney–client relationship created? What are the critical issues for the law firm when this relationship is established?
4. Does the attorney have a duty to keep the names of clients confidential? Explain the ethical rules that apply.
5. What are the ethical or legal implications of not advising a party that you are a paralegal and not a lawyer?
6. What is the difference between "listening" and "hearing" during an interview? Explain.
7. How can stereotypes prevent hearing what is said in interviews?
8. What role do cultural issues play in the interview process? Explain.
9. What are the strategic reasons for using leading questions and using open-ended questions? Give an example of when each would be better used than the other type.

10. In representing a client, is it acceptable or required to ignore an ethical or moral consideration? Explain, giving an example and reason for breaching each.
11. Explain fully the reasons for conducting a thorough investigation of a case. What ethical issues dictate how an investigation is to be conducted?
12. How can the Internet be used to effectively conduct an investigation of a case? Explain, comparing with examples of conventional methods that could also be used.
13. Using the facts in the *Palsgraf* case in Appendix A, prepare a list of witnesses who might be called in that case. Prepare an interview checklist for each of the witnesses.
14. Using the facts in the *Palsgraf* case in Appendix A, prepare an investigative checklist, including a list of the evidence that should be gathered in the case and a list and description of any photographs needed.
15. In conducting an interview, when would it be appropriate to dress in "casual Friday" attire?
16. Why is it important to visit the site of the accident in a motor vehicle case being prepared for trial?
17. Under what circumstances might it be advisable for someone in the firm other than you to handle an interview with a client or witness?
18. Why would someone feel a moral obligation to not answer questions in an interview?
19. Why would a law firm hire an expert witness, but then not call that person as a witness at trial?
20. How useful is the Freedom of Information Act in obtaining state or local government documents? Explain.
21. Can a client restrict the use of information obtained as part of the investigation in preparation for trial even if doing so will have adverse consequences, in the opinion of the attorney? Why or why not?
22. What are the issues and potential problems in using a trial notebook?
23. How does the use of case management software improve the effectiveness of the legal team? Who has the ultimate responsibility for managing the case file when using case management software?

Building Paralegal Skills

VIDEO CASE STUDIES

UPL Issue: Working with a Witness

A paralegal investigating an accident case creates the impression that he is acting in an official capacity when requesting a fact witness to appear to give a formal statement. When the fact witness appears for the statement, he is offered compensation for his time.

After viewing the video case study in MyLegalStudiesLab, answer the following:

1. Does the paralegal have a duty to divulge his role as a paralegal when interviewing potential witnesses?
2. Is it appropriate to offer compensation to a fact witness?
3. Should the same rules of ethics apply to investigators as well as to paralegals?

Zealous Representation Issue: When You Are Asked to Lie

A paralegal has been instructed by his supervising attorney to do whatever is necessary to obtain information needed in a particular case.

After viewing the video case study in MyLegalStudiesLab, answer the following:

1. What is pretexting?
2. Is it ethical to lie to obtain needed information?
3. Is a paralegal bound by ethical rules when acting as an investigator?

ETHICS ANALYSIS & DISCUSSION QUESTIONS

Review the opening scenario of this chapter. What are the ethical issues involved? Prepare a suggested policy, referencing the specific ethics code sections, to present to the supervising attorney of the firm. Address the issues of how to answer the phone and what should and should not be said. Your instructor may provide you with specifics, such as the fee for an initial consultation.

DEVELOPING YOUR COLLABORATION SKILLS

Working on your own or with a group of other students, review the scenario at the beginning of the chapter and the discussion that takes place between Sara and Mrs. Weiser.

1. a. Prepare a list of questions Sara should ask before starting work. Discuss who should be asked these questions, and what actions Sara should or should not take.
   b. What are the ethical issues facing Sara?
   c. What are the potential malpractice issues facing the firm?
2. Write a summary of the advice the group would give to Sara.
3. Form groups of three. Designate one person who will act as Sara, one as a potential client, and the third as a supervising paralegal.
   a. As the paralegal interviewer of the client who has just walked into the office after being injured in an accident, use the facts of the *Palsgraf* case in the Appendix or one assigned by your instructor.
   b. As the client, be sure you understand whether you have a case and that the fee is acceptable.
   c. As the supervising paralegal, comment on the interview, what issues were raised, and what you would have done differently.

PARALEGAL PORTFOLIO EXERCISE

Using the current information for your area or jurisdiction, complete the Investigation Information Sources checklist. Print out a copy for your portfolio.

LEGAL ANALYSIS & WRITING CASES

Limitations on Obtaining Information in Criminal Cases Under the FOIA

***Department of Justice v. Landano*, 508 U.S. 165 (1993)**

The FOIA can be a good source of information in criminal cases as well as civil litigation. As with discovery-limitation exemptions in civil cases, additional exemptions exist under the Act in criminal cases. Landano was convicted in New Jersey state court for murdering a police officer during what may have been a gang-related robbery. In an effort to support his claim in subsequent state court proceedings that his rights were violated by withholding material exculpatory evidence, he filed Freedom of Information Act requests with the Federal Bureau of Investigation (FBI) for information it had compiled in connection with the murder investigation.

When the FBI redacted some documents and withheld others, Landano filed an action, seeking disclosure of the contents of the requested files. The court held that the government is not entitled to a presumption that all sources supplying information to the FBI in the course of a criminal investigation are confidential sources within the meaning of Exemption 7(D). Further, a source should be deemed "confidential" if the source furnished information with the understanding that the FBI would not divulge the communication except to the extent it thought necessary for law-enforcement purposes.

Questions

1. Does this unfairly subject an informant to potential harassment?
2. Does limiting information unfairly prevent the defendant from receiving a fair trial?
3. Does the limitation effectively limit any usefulness in making a request under the FOIA?

Spoliation of Evidence

***In Re Daimlerchrysler Ag Securities Litigation* No. 00-993-JJF (D. Del. Nov. 25, 2003)**

Defendants requested relief in the form of sanctions against the plaintiff for the spoliation of evidence[,] contending that a personal assistant to one of the Plaintiffs, Jaclyn Thode, had destroyed documents that she used to prepare a list of meetings and/or conversations prepared at the request of general counsel, who had failed to instruct her to preserve the documents used in making the list. The court in ruling on the defendant's motion concluded that sanctions were not warranted as a result of the alleged spoliation of evidence. The un-rebutted deposition testimony and affidavit of Ms. Thode establish that she discarded her handwritten notes after converting them into typewritten form, consistent with her practice in the past. Ms. Thode had no information or understanding about the substance of the litigation and no information as to the purpose of counsels' request, and thus she had no reason to alter or omit any information from the documents and that she acted unintentionally when she discarded the steno pads and pink message notes. The Court also found the Defendants did not suffer any prejudice, because they had a complete and accurate chronology of the contents of the documents that were discarded. The court cited *Son, Inc. v. Louis & Nashville R.R. Co.*, 695 F.2d 253, 259 (7th Cir.1982) (finding that destruction of evidence was not intentional where handwritten notes were discarded after being typed and person handling evidence had no reason to omit or alter necessary information).

Questions

1. Should the investigation of a case where documents include transcription also include inquiry into the source of transcripted notes? Why or why not?
2. Why would not knowing the purpose of creating the notes matter in determining the potential spoliation of evidence?
3. What advice would you give to someone who has the responsibility of transcribing or keeping minutes of meetings?

WORKING WITH THE LANGUAGE OF THE COURT CASE

Department of the Interior v. Klamath Water Users Protective Association, 532 U.S. 1 (2001)

Supreme Court of the United States

Read, and if assigned, brief this case. In your brief, answer the following questions.

1. What are the two conditions under which a document qualifies for exemption under the Freedom of Information Act, Exemption 5?
2. How is "agency" defined under the FOIA?
3. What is the "deliberative process" privilege? Does non-governmental litigation have an equivalent privilege?
4. What is the purpose of the deliberative process privilege?
5. What is the "general philosophy" behind the FOIA?

Justice Souter delivered the opinion of the Court. Documents in issue here, passing between Indian Tribes and the Department of the Interior, addressed tribal interests subject to state and federal proceedings to determine water allocations. The question is whether the documents are exempt from the disclosure requirements of the Freedom of Information Act, as "intra-agency memorandums or letters" that would normally be privileged in civil discovery [5 U.S.C. § 552(b)(5)]. We hold they are not.

I

...[T]he Department's Bureau of Indian Affairs (Bureau) filed claims on behalf of the Klamath Tribe alone in an Oregon state-court adjudication intended to allocate water rights. Since the Bureau is responsible for administering land and water held in trust for Indian tribes...it consulted with the Klamath Tribe, and the two exchanged written memorandums on the appropriate scope of the claims ultimately submitted....The Bureau does not, however, act as counsel for the Tribe, which has its own lawyers and has independently submitted claims on its own behalf.[1]

...[T]he Klamath Water Users Protective Association is a nonprofit association of water users in the Klamath River Basin, most of whom receive water from the Klamath Project, and whose interests are adverse to the tribal interests owing to scarcity of water. The Association filed a series of requests with the Bureau under the Freedom of Information Act (FOIA) [5 U.S.C. § 552] seeking access to communications between the Bureau and the Basin Tribes during the relevant time period. The Bureau turned over several

[1]The Government is "not technically acting as [the Tribes'] attorney. That is, the Tribes have their own attorneys, but the United States acts as trustee" [Tr. of Oral Arg. 5]. "The United States has also filed claims on behalf of the Project and on behalf of other Federal interests" in the Oregon adjudication [Id. At 6]. The Hoopa Valley, Karuk, and Yurok Tribes are not parties to the adjudication. [Brief for Respondent 7]

documents but withheld others as exempt under the attorney work-product and deliberative process privileges. These privileges are said to be incorporated in FOIA Exemption 5, which exempts from disclosure "inter-agency or intra-agency memorandums or letters which would not be available by law to a party other than an agency in litigation with the agency" [§ 552(b)(5)]. The Association then sued the Bureau under FOIA to compel release of the documents....

Upon request, FOIA mandates disclosure of records held by a federal agency, see 5 U.S.C. § 552, unless the documents fall within enumerated exemptions....

A

Exemption 5 protects from disclosure "inter-agency or intra-agency memorandums or letters which would not be available by law to a party other than an agency in litigation with the agency" [5 U.S.C. § 552(b)(5)]. To qualify, a document must thus satisfy two conditions: Its source must be a Government agency, and it must fall within the ambit of a privilege against discovery under judicial standards that would govern litigation against the agency that holds it.

Our prior cases on Exemption 5 have addressed the second condition, incorporating civil discovery privileges.... So far as they might matter here, those privileges include the privilege for attorney work-product and what is sometimes called the "deliberative process" privilege. Work-product protects "mental processes of the attorney" while deliberative process covers "documents reflecting advisory opinions, recommendations and deliberations comprising part of a process by which governmental decisions and policies are formulated." The deliberative process privilege rests on the obvious realization that officials will not communicate candidly among themselves if each remark is a potential item of discovery and front-page news, and its object is to enhance "the quality of agency decisions,"... by protecting open and frank discussion among those who make them within the Government....

The point is not to protect Government secrecy pure and simple, however, and the first condition of Exemption 5 is no less important than the second; the communication must be "inter-agency or intra-agency" [5 U.S.C. § 552(b)(5)].... With exceptions not relevant here, "agency" means "each authority of the Government of the United States," and "includes any executive department, military department, Government corporation, Government-controlled corporation, or other establishment in the executive branch of the Government..., or any independent regulatory agency."...

Although neither the terms of the exemption nor the statutory definitions say anything about communications with outsiders, some Courts of Appeals have held that in some circumstances a document prepared outside the Government may... qualify... under Exemption 5....

> It is... possible... to regard as an intra-agency memorandum one that has been received by an agency, to assist it in the performance of its own functions, from a person acting in a governmentally conferred capacity other than on behalf of another agency—e.g., in a capacity as... consultant to the agency.

Typically, courts taking the latter view have held that the exemption extends to communications between Government agencies and outside consultants hired by them.... In such cases, the records submitted by outside consultants played essentially the same part in an agency's process of deliberation as documents prepared by agency personnel might have done.... [T]he fact about the consultant that is constant... is that the consultant does not represent an interest of its own, or the interest of any other client, when it advises the agency that hires it. Its only obligations are to truth and its sense of what good judgment calls for, and in those respects the consultant functions just as an employee would be expected to do.

B

...The Tribes, on the contrary, necessarily communicate with the Bureau with their own, albeit entirely legitimate, interests in mind. While this fact alone distinguishes tribal communications from the consultants' examples recognized by several Courts of Appeals, the distinction is even sharper, in that the Tribes are self-advocates at the expense of others seeking benefits inadequate to satisfy everyone.

...All of this boils down to requesting that we read an "Indian trust" exemption into the statute, a reading that is out of the question for reasons already explored. There is simply no support for the exemption in the statutory text, which we have elsewhere insisted be read strictly in order to serve FOIA's

(continued)

mandate of broad disclosure, which was obviously expected and intended to affect Government operations. In FOIA, after all, a new conception of Government conduct was enacted into law, "a general philosophy of full agency disclosure." Congress had to realize that not every secret under the old law would be secret under the new.

The judgment of the Court of Appeals is affirmed. *It is so ordered.*

The differences among the various circuits on the use of unpublished opinions was clarified by the Amendment to the Federal Rules of Appellate Procedure approved by the United States Supreme Court on April 12, 2006, when it approved the citation of unpublished opinions.

The proposed new Rule 32.1 as submitted for comment to Congress provided;

> Proposed new Rule 32.1 permits the citation in briefs of opinions, orders, or other judicial dispositions that have been designated as "not for publication," "non-precedential," or the like and supersedes limitations imposed on such citation by circuit rules. New Rule 32.1 takes no position on whether unpublished opinions should have any precedential value, leaving that issue for the circuits to decide. The Judicial Conference amended the proposed rule so as to apply prospectively to unpublished opinions filed on or after January 1, 2007. A court may, by local rule, continue to permit or restrict citation to unpublished opinions filed before that date.

MYLEGALSTUDIESLAB

MyLegalStudiesLab Virtual Law Office Experience Assignments

Complete the pre-test, study plan, and post-test for this chapter and answer the Legal Applications questions as assigned. These will help you confirm your mastery of the concepts and their application to legal scenarios. Then complete the Virtual Law Office assignments as assigned by your instructor. These assignments are designed to develop your workplace skills. Completing the assignments for this chapter will result in producing the following documents for inclusion in your portfolio:

VLOE 10.1	Summary of the information from the on-site investigation
VLOE 10.2	Summary of the interview with the witness
VLOE 10.3	Memo to Mr. Saunders with opinion on using a paid fact witness
VLOE 10.4	List of additional investigation that should be undertaken

CHAPTER

11

Legal Writing and Critical Legal Thinking

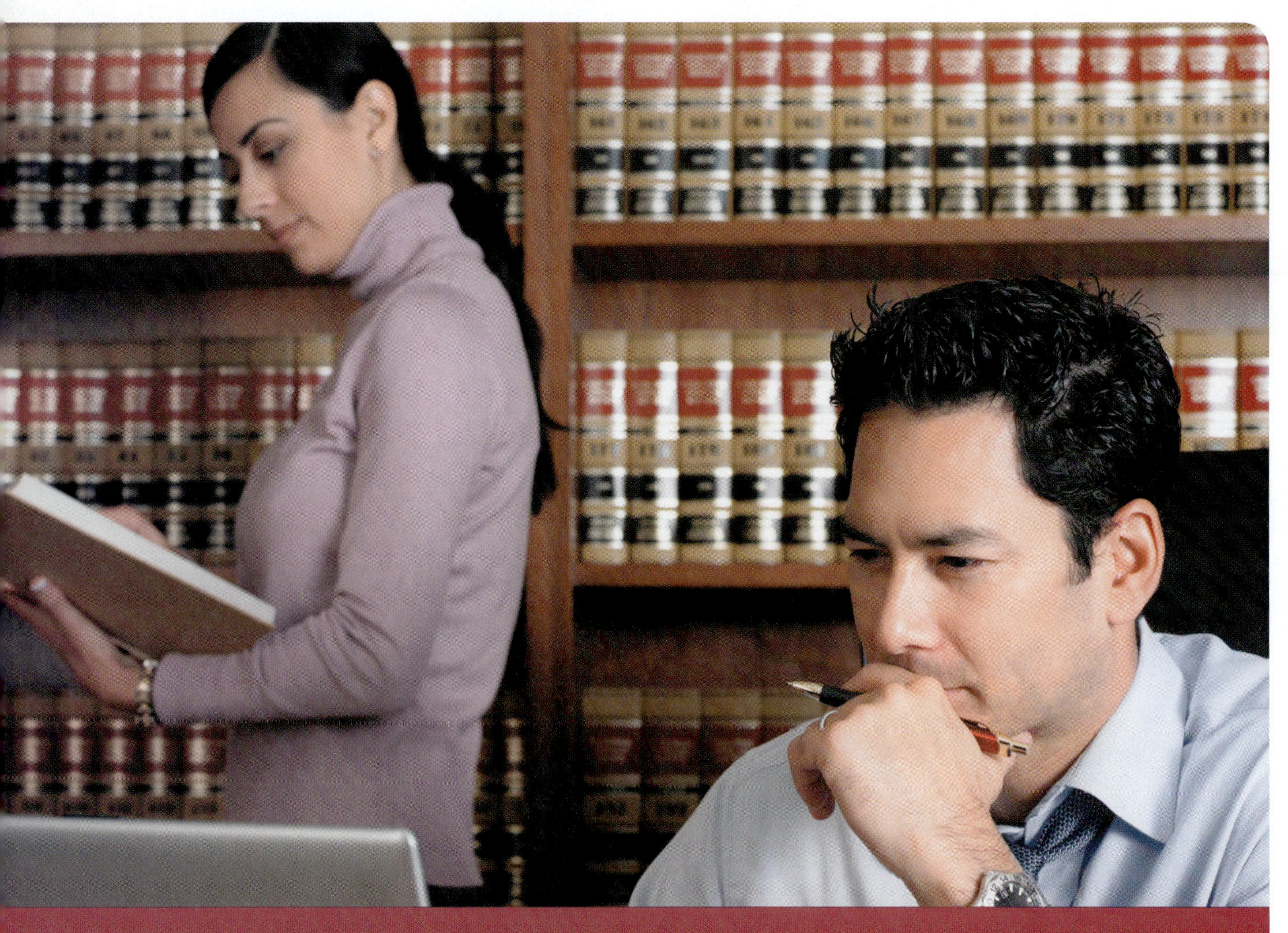

LEARNING OBJECTIVES

After studying this chapter, you should be able to:

1. Explain the process of critical legal thinking.
2. Explain the ethical duty of candor toward the tribunal.
3. Describe the similarities and differences between a memorandum of law and a court brief.
4. Explain the need for proper citation form, and describe how to use it.

Paralegals at Work

Amanda Chen had worked for the law firm of Douglas and Myers for only a few weeks when the senior partner, who specialized in mergers and acquisitions, asked her to sit in on the meeting with a long-term client, Bill Johnson, and his daughter, Tonya. One of the senior paralegals on the staff told Amanda that her role was to take notes, since the partner never took notes in meetings. He conducted the interviews, asked the questions, and didn't want anyone else to interfere.

After escorting the client and his daughter from the reception area to the partner's office, Amanda was asked to take a seat in the corner and record the meeting notes. Mr. Johnson made it clear that he expected his attorney to get the charges of driving under the influence against Tonya dropped. Tonya acknowledged that she had been drinking at a country-western bar and knew she was well over the legal drinking limit. She had tested her alcohol level on a breath analyzer that the bar made available to its patrons.

Upon leaving the bar, Tonya went out to her car, got in, started it, and then fell asleep at the wheel. A police officer found her in this condition, woke her, and took her to the hospital for a blood alcohol test. The officer cited her for operating a vehicle while under the influence of alcohol, based on her .09 percent blood alcohol level.

After the clients left, the partner told Amanda to prepare a memorandum of law that he could use to get the charges against the client's daughter dismissed.

After doing a little research, Amanda realized that the law was against getting the charges dismissed. Furthermore, in the meeting with her father and the partner, Tonya had admitted to being intoxicated. Based on advice from the other paralegals, Amanda was concerned about putting anything negative into the memo and decided to write a memo presenting a case for dismissal.

Consider the issues involved in this scenario as you read the chapter.

> "Justice is the end of government. It is the end of civil society. It ever has been, and ever will be pursued, until it be obtained, or until liberty be lost in the pursuit."
>
> *James Madison*

INTRODUCTION TO LEGAL WRITING AND CRITICAL LEGAL THINKING

Legal writing can take a number of forms: memos, letters, opinions, memoranda of law for internal purposes, and briefs for the court. The presentation formats of these documents are very different, depending on the intended audience. But all of these types of writing share the need for clarity and accuracy. Preparation of these documents starts with an understanding of the material facts of a case and identifying the legal issues. Critical legal thinking is the process by which the law is applied to the facts to answer the client's issue.

Learning Objective 1

Explain the process of critical legal thinking.

Critical Legal Thinking

Critical legal thinking The process of identifying the issue, the material facts, and the applicable law and applying the law to come to a conclusion.

Issue The legal matter in dispute.

Critical legal thinking is the process by which the law is applied to the facts to answer the client's issue. The writer must identify the **issue** presented by a case (the legal matter in dispute), the material (key or relevant) facts in the case, and the applicable law, and then apply the law to the facts to come to a conclusion that answers the issue or issues presented. Critical legal thinking puts the pieces of the legal puzzle together. The critical thinking process starts with a clear understanding of the facts of the client's case and identifying the legal issues in that case.

Before starting the research, the researcher must have a clear picture of all the material facts. An important purpose of the interview with the client is to determine those facts. However, some of the facts that the client thinks are important may actually not be relevant in deciding the legal issue. And some of the facts that seem unimportant to the client may actually be relevant or even critical to the outcome of the case. For example, it may not seem important to the client that he was struck by a driver going north. But this may turn out to be a material fact when it is determined that the street was a one-way street going south.

Identifying relevant facts can also be important in all types of claims, whether in tort, contract, or some other area of the law. For example, if a client signed an employee noncompetition agreement, state law may say that the agreement is unenforceable unless it was signed before commencing employment, or unless full and adequate consideration was given for signing the agreement after commencing employment. It may be essential to ask the client exactly when the agreement was signed.

Understanding the relevant facts enables the researcher to review the case and statutory law to determine which cases or statutes are applicable to the client's case. A difference in one key fact may make all the difference in the outcome of the case. Consider the case of the client charged with killing King Kong. According to the facts of the case, King Kong is a giant ape, and not a human being. The murder statute of the jurisdiction defines murder as the taking of the life of a human being by another human being; therefore, if King Kong is not a human being, the statute has not been violated. The client may be guilty of hunting out of season, hunting without a license, or killing an endangered species, but not of murder.

However, if the killer were sued in court for a civil cause of action, additional facts that were immaterial in the murder prosecution may become material. King Kong's owner may file a suit for damages for loss of an irreplaceable item. In that case, other facts may indicate that the killer is liable for damages. Determining which facts are relevant depends on the type of case (civil or criminal), the wrong that was alleged, or the right that was alleged to have been violated.

The American justice system is based on both statutory and case law. Just as in the criminal law case discussed above, factual analysis requires determining the elements of the crime, looking at the statute, and applying the facts to those elements. It may also be necessary to look at case law for precedent on how those facts are applied.

IN THE WORDS OF THE COURT...

WHITING V. STATE, NO. A-8755 (ALASKA APP. OCTOBER 12, 2005)

MANNHEIMER, JUDGE.

Michael T. Whiting appeals his conviction for felony driving under the influence,...the facts...: Whiting and his girlfriend and his girlfriend's six-year-old son decided to go fishing in Gastineau Channel. Whiting piloted a skiff into the channel and then turned the motor off. The three occupants of the skiff fished while the skiff drifted in the channel; Whiting sat in the rear of the skiff near the motor. While Whiting was fishing, he was also drinking alcoholic beverages.

A Coast Guard vessel approached the skiff..., discovered that he was under the influence. Whiting claimed that he had been sober when he piloted the boat into the channel, and that he did not become intoxicated until after he stopped the motor and the fishing began.

...Whiting's argument hinges on his assertion that the statutory definition of driving under the influence, AS 28.35.030(a)[,] does not include the situation where an intoxicated person is in control of a watercraft whose engine is not running. Whiting's assertion is incorrect....this Court held that "operating" a watercraft includes being in control of the watercraft, even if its engine is not running.

We addressed essentially the same argument in *Kingsley v. State,* 11 p. 3d 1001 (Alaska App. 2000). The defendant in *Kingsley* drove his car into a snow berm, where it became stuck. Kingsley turned the engine off and decided to remain in the car. According to Kingsley, it was only then that he consumed a bottle of whiskey and became intoxicated.

Kingsley argued that, under these circumstances, he was not intoxicated when he was operating the vehicle, and he was never in "control" of the vehicle after he became intoxicated. We rejected this narrow definition of "control."

As Kingsley acknowledges in his brief to this court, a person who engages the engine of a vehicle and allows it to run is not merely exercising physical control over the vehicle but is also "operating" it. Thus, if the engine of Kingsley's vehicle had been running when the police arrived, the State might have proved that Kingsley was operating the vehicle while intoxicated. But the State had to prove only that Kingsley was in actual physical control of the vehicle while intoxicated.

...A person's attempt to operate a vehicle may furnish convincing proof that the person is in actual physical control of the vehicle, but a person may exercise actual physical control over a vehicle without making active attempts to operate it.

Whiting was the one who had piloted the skiff into the channel, and Whiting remained primarily in the rear of the skiff, nearest the motor, while his girlfriend and her son sat in the front of the skiff. Under these facts, as a matter of law, Whiting was in physical control of the skiff, and he was therefore operating the skiff for purposes of the DUI statute.

For example, all states have laws prohibiting driving under the influence of alcohol. Some of these statutes use the terms "vehicle" and "operating." The researcher may need to determine how courts have defined a "vehicle" and what conduct is considered "operating." Defense counsel must examine the case law carefully to try to differentiate the client's fact pattern from decided cases. Slight variations in facts can be important in making a compelling argument.

Facts are pieces of information or details that in reality exist, or have occurred, and are not based on theory, supposition, or conjecture. Facts, in the law, are circumstances, events, actions, occurrences, or states, rather than opinions or interpretations. A statement that a car was traveling south on State Street at 60 miles per hour, as shown on a police officer's radar unit, is a statement of fact. A statement by a witness standing on the sidewalk that the car appeared to be traveling faster than 55 miles per hour is an opinion or conjecture, not fact.

Facts Information or details that are not based on theory, opinion, or conjecture.

Material facts Facts significant or essential to the issue.

Immaterial facts Facts that are not essential to the matter or issue at hand.

Facts may be divided into **material facts** and **immaterial facts.** A material fact is a fact that has some significant or essential connection with the issue or matter at hand. An immaterial fact is one that has no probative value in the matter at issue. Some facts, while not relevant because they do not prove or disprove a matter in issue, may lead to relevant material facts.

For example, the information revealed in an investigation may show that a defendant was coming from a doctor's office and driving within the speed limit when he struck another car in the rear at a red stoplight. Is the fact that he was coming from the doctor's office a relevant fact in the accident? It may be, if he was given medication at the doctor's office that caused blurred vision or drowsiness and if the doctor had told him not to drive or operate any machinery. The information that he was coming from the doctor's office was not in itself relevant to proving the allegations, but it led to the discovery of other relevant material facts.

Legal Writing

The purpose of writing is to communicate. If the writing does not communicate the subject to the reader, it has not served its purpose. But there are many types of written communication, and there are as many writing styles as there are writers. A writer of a novel may devote pages to setting the stage for the characters and many more pages to developing those characters. Readers probably come to expect this and look forward to long paragraphs that create the setting and describe the characters.

Skilled legal writers are more like the writers of short stories. They must quickly and accurately set the stage in only a few words and tell the story in a small space. Skilled legal writers are able to explain, persuade, and state facts for the record accurately, concisely, and clearly. Unlike the novelist or poet, the legal writer must follow a set of guidelines dictated by ethical and procedural rules, while at the same time clearly presenting an answer to a client, or persuading a court to adopt a certain position.

Paralegals *in* Practice

PARALEGAL PROFILE

Ann L. Atkinson

Ann L. Atkinson is a graduate of the University of Nebraska with a Bachelor of Science Degree in Education. She is also an Advanced Certified Paralegal with over 27 years of legal experience. Her professional memberships include the Nebraska Paralegal Association, the National Association of Legal Assistants, and the National Association of Bond Lawyers. Ann is currently employed by the law firm of Kutak Rock LLP in their Omaha, Nebraska, office.

I specialize in public finance law, which generally is transactional in nature—preparing, reviewing, and revising contracts or negotiated "deals" between parties. Specifically, I assist the attorneys as they work with state housing agencies or municipalities when they issue bonds for public purposes. The bonds represent a "loan" of money from bondholders. The attorneys with whom I work often act as bond counsel (where we are counsel for the bond issue itself), or we may also serve as underwriter's counsel (in which we are counsel to the underwriter of the bonds).

Since our department focuses primarily on single-family housing, we prepare all the documents that enable an issuer to issue bonds. These bonds then provide proceeds from which the issuer can offer single-family homes to first-time homebuyers at a "below market" interest rate. Our department also handles transactions for multi-family housing such as apartment buildings being constructed, acquired, and/or rehabilitated.

In my position, I coordinate all the things that need to be done in order for a bond issue to close. In order to do so, I rely heavily on writing and critical thinking skills. Tasks include preparing initial drafts of bond documents, researching statutes, proofing and reviewing offering documents and third-party opinions, and assisting with bond closings including the preparation of closing transcripts. Thus, a knowledge of correct grammar, spelling, and punctuation is essential. Critical thinking skills are very useful when preparing documents because they help you follow document processes—the flow of funds, the timing requirements for notices, and knowing when and how to obtain amendment approvals.

Legal writing is a process. It requires research, analysis, organization, writing, editing, and proofreading. Sometimes it requires starting over when the final document, viewed from the position of the ultimate reader, does not communicate the necessary information or tell the story.

In the legal working environment, time to rethink, re-research, and rewrite is a luxury the paralegal will not often have. The paralegal must develop strong research and writing skills to be able to work efficiently and minimize the time necessary to produce an acceptable document, whether it is a letter, an office memorandum, or a court brief.

Writing Styles

Two of the most common types of legal documents are the brief and the memorandum. Both address a legal issue and apply a set of facts to applicable law. However, each requires a totally different writing style. The **memorandum** is a working document that is used by the legal team in the preparation of a case. It must give an objective analysis of the case and describe any alternative interpretations of the facts and the law. The analysis should be similar to the objective analysis used by a court to decide a case. For example, the Ninth Circuit Court of Appeals used this type of analysis in determining whether consent to a search was "voluntary":

Memorandum A working document for the legal team to use in the preparation of a case.

> Fed.R.Crim.P. 12(e) states that "[w]here factual issues are involved in determining a [pretrial] motion, the court shall state its essential findings on the record." Such a record is necessary to our review.... Compliance with the rule 12(e) requirement is particularly important in a case such as this, where we examine "all the surrounding circumstances".... Factual subtleties may well affect a determination of voluntariness under this test... *U.S. v. Castrillon*, 716 F.2d 1279 (9th Cir. 1983).

A brief written by an advocate before a court will have a different style than an internal memorandum. The brief is designed to advocate the client's point of view and convince the court to adopt a position favorable to the client.

The **opinion letter** to a client requires a different style. The opinion letter must explain to a client, who is generally untrained in the law, what legal options the client has and what can and cannot be done based on the set of facts provided by the client. In some ways it is an educational document—it must be informative and provide options with sufficient detail to allow the client to make an appropriate decision.

Opinion letter A formal statement of advice to the client based on the lawyer's expert knowledge.

Duty of candor The duty of honesty to the court.

Duty of Candor

The **duty of candor** is the ethical obligation to be honest with the court. In some jurisdictions, such as Indiana, the ethical rule is titled "Candor Toward the Tribunal." The duty of candor is set forth in Rule 3.3 in the Model Rules of Professional Conduct:

Learning Objective 2
Explain the ethical duty of candor toward the tribunal.

A WORD OF CAUTION

The speed, ease of use, and widespread availability of email have created a new writing style that is more casual and uses shorthand terminology to communicate. Those in the legal profession must remember that every email could potentially become a piece of evidence in an electronic discovery request. Emails are frequently forwarded to others without the knowledge of the original writer, and hundreds of copies may be unintentionally distributed to other recipients.

In the legal setting, shortcuts should not be taken in writing emails. The same formality and care that go into writing a letter on legal stationery should be used in writing an email. Even greater care should be used when the email may contain privileged or confidential information. Such information may accidentally end up in the hands of those not covered by the ethical obligation to maintain confidentiality. In some cases, an email may be accidentally sent to opposing counsel, resulting in a breach of the attorney–client or work product privileges.

The duty of candor means that although lawyers must be zealous advocates, they also have an ethical obligation to not mislead the court. A brief that intentionally distorts or hides the truth or intentionally misleads the court can potentially destroy a legal career. Even if it doesn't result in sanctions, suspension, or disbarment, judges talk with their colleagues, and a reputation for questionable integrity is hard to correct. At the least, the court will always remember the attorney's shoddy work and may question his or her credibility in the future, even if the attorney's later cases are accurate, honest, and well prepared.

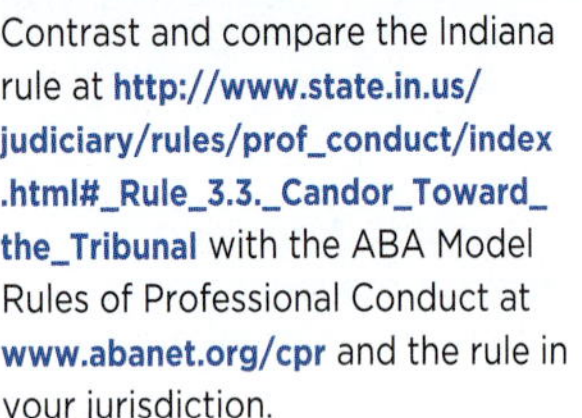

Contrast and compare the Indiana rule at **http://www.state.in.us/judiciary/rules/prof_conduct/index.html#_Rule_3.3._Candor_Toward_the_Tribunal** with the ABA Model Rules of Professional Conduct at **www.abanet.org/cpr** and the rule in your jurisdiction.

RULE 3.3. CANDOR TOWARD THE TRIBUNAL

(a) A lawyer shall not knowingly:
   (1) make a false statement of fact or law to a tribunal or fail to correct a false statement of material fact or law previously made to the tribunal by the lawyer;
   (2) fail to disclose to the tribunal legal authority in the controlling jurisdiction known to the lawyer to be directly adverse to the position of the client and not disclosed by opposing counsel; or
   (3) offer evidence that the lawyer knows to be false. If a lawyer, the lawyer's client, or a witness called by the lawyer, has offered material evidence and the lawyer comes to know of its falsity, the lawyer shall take reasonable remedial measures, including, if necessary, disclosure to the tribunal. A lawyer may refuse to offer evidence, other than the testimony of a defendant in a criminal matter, that the lawyer reasonably believes is false.

(b) A lawyer who represents a client in an adjudicative proceeding and who knows that a person intends to engage, is engaging or has engaged in criminal or fraudulent conduct related to the proceeding shall take reasonable remedial measures, including, if necessary, disclosure to the tribunal.

(c) The duties stated in paragraphs (a) and (b) continue to the conclusion of the proceeding, and apply even if compliance requires disclosure of information otherwise protected by Rule 1.6.

(d) In an ex parte proceeding, a lawyer shall inform the tribunal of all material facts known to the lawyer which will enable the tribunal to make an informed decision, whether or not the facts are adverse.

Indiana Rules of Court, Rules of Professional Conduct, including Amendments made through January 1, 2012.

CHECKLIST Memorandum of Law Template

- ☐ To:
- ☐ From:
- ☐ Date:
- ☐ Subject:
- ☐ Facts
- ☐ Issue(s)
- ☐ Discussion
- ☐ Conclusion

Learning Objective 3

Describe the similarities and differences between a memorandum of law and a court brief.

Preparing Office Memoranda

In researching and writing a memorandum of law, the paralegal must be careful to include all the relevant statutes and case law, even those that negatively impact the client's case. Some paralegals are intimidated by the gruff and even downright nasty attitude of certain lawyers, particularly trial counsel in the middle of a stressful case, and are fearful of including information that will upset them. In these situations, the paralegal is afraid the lawyer will "shoot the messenger" if the memorandum contains bad news. However, the reality is that, the attorney *must* know the weaknesses in the case, along with the strengths. Nothing is more upsetting to an attorney, whether in court or in a meeting with a client or opposing counsel, than to be surprised by a case, facts, or law that has not been covered in the office memorandum of law.

Office memoranda are frequently filed in the office for future reference and are usually indexed by subject. If another case arises that has a similar fact pattern, a previous memorandum may provide a good starting point and can be a major time saver. The facts upon which the conclusion is based must be clearly stated so that the memorandum may be indexed properly, and easily found for later use. All statutes, regulations, and cases must be cited properly so anyone reading the memorandum in the future can look them up. Listing relevant websites that were used in preparing the memorandum is also helpful.

Starting Point

The starting point for the legal researcher is to make sure the assignment is understood. What has the researcher been asked to research? For the memorandum of law, the assignment is usually to answer a question:

- "What is the current law on . . . ?"
- "What is the current law on alcohol blood level for driving under the influence?"
- "What happens if . . . ?"
- "What happens if this is a second conviction for driving under the influence?"
- "What is the procedure for . . . ?"
- "What is the procedure for appealing a small claims judgment to a trial court?"

Before starting an assignment, the paralegal must be certain what is really being asked. Any uncertainties should be resolved by asking the person for whom the assignment is being prepared. It is often useful for the paralegal to restate, in the form of a question, what he believes he is being asked to research, such as, "What are the rights of an individual who . . . ?" This will help clarify the issue in the mind of the researcher and confirm that he is researching the precise issue that the attorney is requesting.

At the outset, paralegals must also be sure to have all the relevant facts. Knowing certain facts may change the outcome—for example, the requirement in some states that a subscribing witness to a decedent's will cannot be a beneficiary. The paralegal should ascertain all the necessary facts about the case in order to prepare an accurate memorandum.

Memorandum of Law Format

The supervising attorney will usually prepare an assignment memo with a request to research and prepare an office memorandum on a specific subject or case. A sample of an assignment memo is shown in Exhibit 11.1. Frequently, the assignment is given to the

Exhibit 11.1 Assignment memo

MEMORANDUM

To: Edith Hannah
From: Glenn Hains
Date: January 23, 2006
File Number: GH 06-1002
Re: Commonwealth of Pennsylvania vs. Kevin Dones

Our client was stopped by a police officer at the bottom of the hill on route 332 in Northampton Township, at 3:30 on Sunday afternoon, January 15, 2006. He was riding a bicycle south on route 332 and was given a citation for speeding. The police used a radar unit and claimed a speed of 35 mph in a 25 mph zone. He administered a field sobriety test, which gave a reading over the legal limit, and client was given a citation for driving under the influence. He tells me he was riding a bike because his license was suspended for a previous DUI.

Please prepare a brief memorandum of law, with citations and cases.

Exhibit 11.2 Word search function

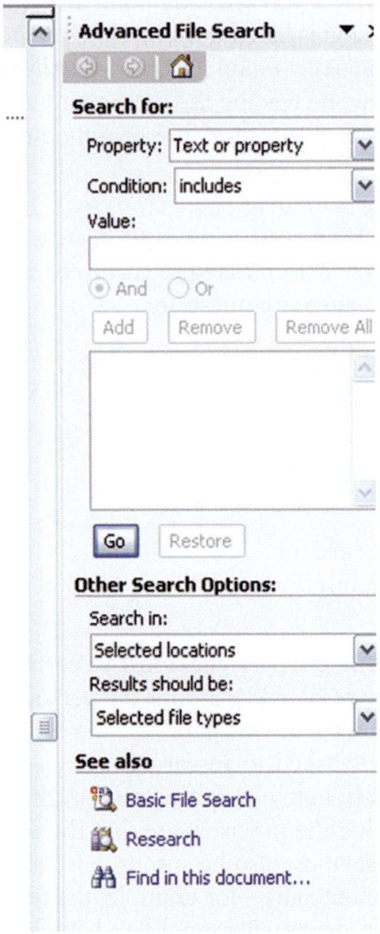

Source: Microsoft product box shots reprinted with permission from Microsoft Corporation.

paralegal in a face-to-face meeting. When the assignment is made orally, it is a good idea to confirm the specific assignment if there is any uncertainty about what is being requested.

The format or template for office memoranda is fairly standard, as shown in the memorandum of law template. Some offices may add, for identification purposes, headings such as office file numbers or client identifiers. The format in some offices includes subject matter with legal terms or areas of law so memoranda can be filed and retrieved if future cases require research on the same subject. Copies of memoranda and other documents are now often stored electronically as word processor files or templates that can be retrieved and used as samples for new projects, as shown in Exhibit 11.2.

When taking an assignment to research and write a memorandum, a few basics should be remembered. The attorney probably will not redo the research or add much content, and will refer to the material submitted with the memorandum. The memorandum must be an unbiased presentation of the law as it exists, and it must be clearly presented. If the content of the memorandum is not accurate and complete, the attorney relying on the analysis and discussion may be embarrassed before opposing counsel or the court, or caught off guard by information he or she was unaware of.

Points to remember in preparing a memorandum of law:

- **Never** rely on case law headnotes. Headnotes are not a primary source of the law.
- **Always** check the actual language of the court cases. It is the primary authority.

- **Check** the dates of the cases and statutes. Be sure they are current law.
- **Shepardize** (GlobalCite, KeyCite, V.Cite) the cases you used to be certain they have not been overruled by a later case or statute.
- **Don't** be afraid to show the cases and statutes that are against the client's position.
- **Cite all** sources used. Never plagiarize.
- **Analyze** opposing case law for any differences that may give the attorney a chance to distinguish the negative cases in some way based on the facts or the law.
- **Ask** the attorney if you don't understand the issues or questions involved. It is better to admit that you are having a problem with the research than to give the attorney incorrect, incomplete, or unintelligible information.

The format of the memorandum of law is determined by the nature of the assignment, the number of issues, and the ultimate use of the memorandum, as well as personal preferences of the person giving the assignment.

The components of a memorandum of law and the components of a court opinion (case) are similar. Exhibit 11.3 presents a comparison. Some case opinions have a brief summary or syllabus of the case that is prepared by an editor, such as the editors of West Publishing Company, or Supreme Court editors. The syllabus is not an official part of the case but is provided for the reader's convenience. Some attorneys prefer to have a short "Answer" under the "Statement of the Assignment." The Answer is generally a shortened version of the main points of the conclusion.

Samples of a traditional memorandum of law and one prepared for internal government use are shown in Exhibits 11.4 and 11.5.

If you have ever "briefed" a case, you will notice the similarity to the list of items shown in the comparison above. A sample of a case and a case brief is provided in Appendix A: How to Brief a Case.

Facts

The writer of a legal memorandum must have a clear statement of the facts from which to work. All of the facts relied upon in writing the assignment memo must be included as part of the final memorandum. Other members of the firm may read the memorandum, and they need to understand the specific facts upon which the analysis is based, particularly if the paralegal is not available to answer questions about the

Exhibit 11.3 Components of court opinions and memorandums of law

COURT OPINIONS	MEMORANDUMS OF LAW
Caption: Parties, citation, relevant dates	**Heading:** Assigning party, client, file number
Judicial history: Prior proceeding (how the case got to this court)	**Statement of the assignment:** History of what happened and why the client sought representation
Issue: Legal question before the court	**Issue:** Legal issues of clients raised in statement of assignment
Facts: Relevant facts used to decide case	**Statement of facts:** Relevant facts
Analysis and discussion: Discussion of the facts, rules of law, issues, judicial reasons for decision	**Analysis and discussion:** Discussion of each issue, how the applicable law applies, what relevant facts impact the decision
Conclusion: Holding of the Court	**Conclusion:** Restatement of the conclusion to each issue analyzed and discussed above, summarizing the main points

Exhibit 11.4 Sample memorandum of law prepared by leading legal research provider

MEMORANDUM OF LAW

TO: Ellen Holroyd, Esq.

FROM: [redacted]

DATE: January 29, 2004

RE: SEC Definitions of Terms Under the Sarbanes-Oxley Act of 2002

QUESTION PRESENTED

With regard to its regulations promulgated pursuant to the Sarbanes-Oxley Act of 2002, how does the Security and Exchange Commission define the concepts "material violation", "credible evidence", and "reasonable behavior" by an attorney?

DISCUSSION

Section 307 of the Sarbanes-Oxley Act of 2002 ("Sarbanes-Oxley") requires the Securities and Exchange Commission ("SEC") to "prescribe minimum standards of professional conduct for attorneys appearing and practicing before the Commission in any way in the representation of issuers." Implementation of Standards of Professional Conduct for Attorneys, Securities Act Release No. 33,8185, 68 Fed. Reg. 6,296 (Feb. 6, 2003.) According to the SEC, these standards "must include a rule requiring an attorney to report evidence of a material violation of securities laws or breach of fiduciary duty or similar violation by the issuer." Id., at 6,296. This memorandum discusses the definitions embraced by the SEC for "material violation," "credible evidence," and "reasonable behavior" by an attorney, three concepts found in the regulations adopted by the SEC pertaining to Sarbanes-Oxley.

Page 4 of 27

memorandum. It is often necessary to recite other facts that were not relied upon in the analysis and the reasons for not considering them. It may also be necessary to explain how a result would be different if a particular fact were different. For example, a memorandum may have a notation that the fact pattern was based upon all of the participants being over the age of majority for contracting, or over the age to purchase and consume alcoholic beverages.

Exhibit 11.4 Sample memorandum of law prepared by leading legal research provider *(continued)*

III. Definition of "Reasonable Behavior" By An Attorney

Such a definition necessarily brings up next the question of what the SEC deems to be "reasonable behavior" for attorneys with regard to their duty to report actual or suspected Sarbanes-Oxley violations. In its formulation of what constitutes "reasonable behavior" on the part of an attorney under the Sarbanes-Oxley regulations, the SEC points out that it is not a "bright line" test, and that it is dependent on the circumstances surrounding not just the alleged violation, but also the attorney involved:

> This formulation, while intended to adopt an objective standard, also recognizes that there is a range of conduct in which an attorney may engage without being unreasonable. The "circumstances" are the circumstances at the time the attorney decides whether he or she is obligated to report the information. These circumstances may include, among others, the attorney's professional skills, background and experience, the time constraints under which the attorney is acting, the attorney's previous experience and familiarity with the client, and the availability of other lawyers with whom the lawyer may consult.

Implementation of Standards of Professional Conduct for Attorneys, Securities Act Release No. 33,8185, 68 Fed. Reg. 6,296, 6,302 (Feb. 6, 2003.) Thus, what is deemed reasonable behavior for one attorney could differ significantly from that for another attorney, depending on the various factors laid out by the SEC.

CONCLUSION

While the SEC provided guidance as to the meanings of all three concepts discussed in this memo, it is clear that it intended there to be no "bright line", "one size fits all" definitions for these phrases. That said, a "material violation" for purposes of the SEC's Sarbanes-Oxley rules would appear to be a violation of such consequence that a reasonable and prudent investor would consider it important to know about when determining whether to buy, sell, or hold a particular security. "Credible evidence" would appear to be evidence of a material violation substantial enough that a prudent

Exhibit 11.5 Sample memorandum of law prepared by the U.S. Department of Justice

U.S. Department of Justice
Immigration and Naturalization Service

HQADN 70/23

Office of the Executive Associate Commissioner

425 1 Street NW
Washington, DC 20536

May 24, 2001

MEMORANDUM FOR: Michael A. Pearson
Executive Associate Commissioner
Office of Field Operations

FROM: Michael D. Cronin /s/
Acting Executive Associate Commissioner
Office of Programs

SUBJECT: Public Law 106-378, adjustment of status of certain Syrian nationals.

This memorandum provides eligibility information and adjudication policy guidance for the implementation of Public Law 106-378, which pertains to the adjustment of certain Syrian nationals who were granted asylum after arriving in the United States after December 31, 1991.

ELIGIBILITY

Public Law 106-378 provides for the adjustment of status of a principal alien as well as an alien who is the spouse, child, or unmarried son or daughter of a principal alien.

Principal alien. In order to be eligible for adjustment under this law, the principal alien must:

1. Be a Jewish national of Syria;
2. Have arrived in the United States after December 31, 1991, after being permitted by the Syrian government to depart from Syria;
3. Be physically present in the United States at the time of filing the application to adjust status;
4. Apply for adjustment of status under Public Law 106-378 no later than October 26, 2001, or, have applied for adjustment of status under another provision of law prior to October 27, 2000, and request to have the basis of that application changed to Public Law 106-378;
5. Have been physically present in the United States for at least one year after being granted asylum;
6. Not be firmly resettled in any foreign country; and Memorandum: Public Law 106-378, adjustment of status of certain Syrian nationals.

REQUIRED FIELD OFFICE ACTION

Field offices are to identify all potentially eligible Syrian asylee adjustment applications and forward them and the related A-files to NSC within 30-days of this memorandum. The appropriate code, "SY6, 7 or 8" and reference to Public Law 106-378 must be noted. A-files are to be routed to the NSC in separate batches, with individual cover sheets attached to the outside face of each file reflecting "**SYRIAN ASYLEE P. L. 106-378**". If, for whatever reason, a field office cannot accomplish this goal, they are to provide a report to their respective region identifying each case, explaining the reason(s), and advising the anticipated date of completion of the A-file transfer. Regions are requested to review the report and take appropriate action.

SERVICE CENTER ACTION ON APPROVED ASYLEE APPLICATIONS

The NSC must review all asylum adjustment cases received via Direct Mail as well as all cases forwarded to them from the field to cull out those Syrian nationals whose applications contain evidence of Syrian nationality, arrival

Exhibit 11.5 **Sample memorandum of law prepared by the U.S. Department of Justice** *(continued)*

in the United States after December 31, 1991, and a grant of asylum or asylee dependent status. The NSC must also retrieve A-files belonging to qualifying Syrian applicants inappropriately coded as "AS" adjustments, and take corrective action. A list containing the names of Syrian asylees has already been provided to the NSC to help in this regard. The NSC will also track the total number of cases approved. After the NSC approves 2,000 principal beneficiaries under this law, the NSC will stop adjudicating applications, and will notify HQ ISD and HQ ADN that the numerical limitation has been reached.

SUPPLEMENTAL FILING INSTRUCTIONS

The Form I-485 supplemental filing instructions are being modified to instruct qualified applicants to identify themselves by writing **"SYRIAN ASYLEE P. L. 106-378"** in Part 2, Block 2. Since many qualified Syrian asylees may be unaware of their special classification or the correct way to claim it, the NSC should review all newly submitted asylee adjustment applications, and, when appropriate, endorse the Form I-485 as described above. When an applicant's eligibility to adjust under Public Law 106-378 has been verified, the adjudicator will check the "other" block in the "Section of Law" portion of the FOR INS USE ONLY Section of Form I-485 and will enter the notation, **"Public Law 106-378."**

CONCLUSION

Segregating the Syrian asylum adjustments for proper adjudication is essential to preserve the use of the 10,000 visa numbers authorized annually for other asylees who are eligible to adjust their status. If you have questions regarding the adjudication of Syrian-processed asylum adjustments, please contact your center or regional representative. If needed, service center. . . .

Source: United States Department of Justice.

Analysis

Critical legal thinking is essential to the legal writing process. It involves analyzing the law to find the similarities and differences in cases that could be used to argue for or against the client's position. The memorandum the paralegal prepares may be the basis for the court brief that the attorney or someone else will prepare. To be able to meet the ethical obligation to the court, the person who presents a persuasive argument on behalf of the client must know all the relevant statutory and case law, and understand how it applies to the client's case.

A memorandum must present both sides of the issue and be a neutral, objective presentation of applicable laws as they apply to the facts of the case. Any issues that the opposing attorney or the judge may raise should be considered and presented. A good analysis will include a discussion of cases that may be used by opposing counsel, and how those cases can be distinguished from the client's case.

Editing and Rewriting

The written word is a reflection of the writer. Although the paralegal may have written the memorandum for a particular person, many others may eventually read it, and everyone who reads it will evaluate the writer's abilities. In other words, every memorandum could potentially impact the writer's reputation. Therefore, the memorandum should be carefully re-read, revised, and proofread before sending the final draft to the recipient. Certain elements should be considered when editing and revising, such as:

- Is the writing clear?
- Are words used properly?
- Is the spelling correct?
- Is the grammar correct?

Language differences may also be an important consideration. If the memorandum is being written for an audience for whom English is a second language, the writer should indicate this in the memorandum. Where there are variations in the translation of certain foreign language terms, those variations should be clarified. For example, if the facts were translated from Spanish, it may be important to note which Spanish dialect they were translated from.

Preparing Court Briefs

Amicus curia Briefs submitted by interested parties, as a "friend of the court," who do not have standing in the action.

A brief is written for the court and is designed to persuade the court to accept the client's position. Each court has rules specifying the requirements for briefs submitted by the parties and by ***amicus curia***—"friends of the court." The rules determine the format and the sections that must be included in the brief. In some courts, the format is based on the personal preferences of the judge. Before undertaking the task of writing a brief, the writer should always obtain a current copy of the court rules and contact the judge's law clerk for any additional limitations or requirements.

Sometimes the court is unable to read the brief thoroughly before the oral argument. In these situations, the brief's preliminary statement becomes a critical part of the brief because it focuses the court on the issues presented and the arguments being made. Being able to state the client's side of the case briefly is not easy, but it is worth the effort. It requires a clear, concise, and careful choice of words. An effective preliminary statement will be remembered as the hearing progresses, and later when the court is making its analysis and decision.

A table of contents, partial table of authorities, summary of the argument, and conclusion of an *amicus curia* brief submitted in a case to the United States Supreme Court is shown in Exhibit 11.6.

Learning Objective 4

Explain the need for proper citation format, and describe how to use it.

Citations

Citation A reference to the source of the information.

A legal **citation** is a reference to the source of the information that allows the reader to find that source. The citation must be sufficient for the reader to be able find the material, and the format must be one that others in the legal community generally accept and use. If a person in California submits a brief to a court, a person in New York or in Florida must be able to use the citations to locate the items referred to in the document in a traditional legal library or electronic law source such as Loislaw, VersusLaw, Lexis, or Westlaw.

Primary authority The actual law itself.

Secondary authority Writings that explain or comment on the law.

All legal authorities are either a primary authority or a secondary authority. A **primary authority** is the law itself, and includes constitutions, statutes, cases, and administrative regulations. A **secondary authority** explains and comments on the primary authority, or is used as a tool for locating primary authority (such as treatises, encyclopedias, digests, or dictionaries). With a consistent citation format, the reader can locate the primary or secondary authorities referenced in a document.

Judges and lawyers in some states are abandoning the long-standing tradition of putting citations in the body of a document and now are putting the citations at the bottom of each page of the document in the footnotes. They claim it makes reading legal opinions easier by eliminating the citations' interference with the flow of words.

Traditional Print Sources

The traditional method for publishing primary and secondary authority is in paper form, in books, or as a collection or series of books. Where a case, statute, or regulation is available in more than one series of books, the citation to both locations—known as parallel citations—is required. For example, if a case is published in both the official reporter of the state and a private publication, such as those published by West Publishing, both citations must be given. The citation form is basically the same for each:

Volume	Reporter and Series	Page
232	Atlantic 2d	44

In this example, in the citation "232 A.2d 44," "232" refers to the volume in the Atlantic 2d series of the reporter service of West Publishing Company, and "44" refers to the page on which the case may be found.

Bluebook

The most commonly used guide to citation form is the publication *The Bluebook: A Uniform System of Citation*. This is the generally accepted authority for proper citation form, unless the rules of a particular court dictate a different citation format.

Exhibit 11.6 ***Amicus curia*** **brief filed with the U.S. Supreme Court**

No. 08-479

In The
Supreme Court of the United States

SAFFORD UNIFIED SCHOOL DISTRICT #1, *et al.*,
Petitioners,

v.

APRIL REDDING,
LEGAL GUARDIAN OF MINOR CHILD,
Respondent.

On Writ of Certiorari to the
United States Court of Appeals
for the Ninth Circuit

BRIEF OF *AMICI CURIAE*
THE RUTHERFORD INSTITUTE,
GOLDWATER INSTITUTE
AND CATO INSTITUTE
IN SUPPORT OF RESPONDENT

John W. Whitehead
Counsel of Record
Douglas R. McKusick
THE RUTHERFORD INSTITUTE
1440 Sachem Place
Charlottesville, VA 22911
(434) 978-3888

Timothy Lynch
Ilya Shapiro
CATO INSTITUTE
1000 Massachusetts Ave., NW
Washington, DC 20001
(202) 218-4600

Clint Bolick
Nicholas C. Dranias
GOLDWATER INSTITUTE
SCHARF-NORTON CENTER
FOR CONSTITUTIONAL
LITIGATION
500 E. Coronado Road
Phoenix, AZ 85004
(602) 462-5000

LANTAGNE LEGAL PRINTING
801 East Main Street Suite 100 Richmond, Virginia 23219 (800) 847-0477

TABLE OF AUTHORITIES

Cases

Bell v. Wolfish, 441 U.S. 520 (1979)........................7, 9

C.B. by and through Breeding v. Driscoll, 82 F.3d 383 (11th Cir. 1996)...13

Calabretta v. Floyd, 189 F.3d 808 (9th Cir. 1991).......5

Camara v. Municipal Court, 387 U.S. 523 (1967)..6, 7

Cornfield by Lewis v. Consol. High Sch. Dist. No. 230, 991 F.2d 1316 (7th Cir. 1993)...............8, 11, 17

Doe v. Renfrow, 631 F.2d 91 (7th Cir.), *reh'g denied*, 635 F.2d 582 (7th Cir. 1980), *cert. denied*, 451 U.S. 1022 (1981).................................5

Edwards v. Aguillard, 482 U.S. 578 (1987)..............19

Illinois v. Gates, 462 U.S. 213 (1983)........................16

Leatherman v. Tarrant County Narcotics, Intelligence & Coordination Unit, 507 U.S. 163 (1993)..22

Lilly v. Virginia, 527 U.S. 116 (1999).......................12

Mary Beth G. v. City of Chicago, 723 F.2d 1263 (7th Cir. 1983)...5

Maryland v. Garrison, 480 U.S. 79 (1987)...............15

New Jersey v. T.L.O., 469 U.S. 325 (1985).......passim

O'Connor v. Ortega, 480 U.S. 709 (1987)....................6

Pearson v. Callahan, 129 S.Ct. 808 (2009).........21, 22

Phaneuf v.Fraikin, 448 F.3d 591 (2d Cir. 2006) 5, 8, 11

(continued)

Exhibit 11.6 ***Amicus curia*** **brief filed with the U.S. Supreme Court** *(continued)*

SUMMARY OF THE ARGUMENT

In *New Jersey v. T.L.O.*, 469 U.S. 325 (1985), this Court accommodated the interests of public school educators and administrators in maintaining order and discipline in public schools by easing the restrictions on searches normally imposed upon state actors by the Fourth Amendment. In ruling that in-school searches of students in the school setting need not be supported by probable cause, however, the *T.L.O.* decision made clear that the "reasonableness" of a school search largely depends on whether the search is "excessively intrusive in light of the age and sex of the student and nature of the infraction." *Id.* at 342. This Court clearly signaled that the severity of the privacy invasion must be considered when deciding whether school officials have violated a student's Fourth Amendment rights.

In light of *T.L.O.*'s direction to consider the intrusiveness of a search, the *en banc* Ninth Circuit correctly understood here that a strip search of a student will be reasonable only when school officials have clear evidence to justify it. Strip searches are unquestionably privacy invasions of a different order and higher degree than "ordinary" searches and should be undertaken rarely. Only when school officials have highly credible evidence showing (1) the student is in possession of objects posing a significant danger to the school and (2) that the student has secreted the objects in a place only a strip search will uncover is such a search reasonable.

CONCLUSION

Throughout their merits brief, Petitioners decry a regrettable consequence of the decision below: educators must now "school themselves" in Fourth Amendment jurisprudence and allows courts to second-guess their judgment. But, given the seriousness of the intrusion effected by strip searches, this consequence is unavoidable.

School officials must realize that they may conduct strip searches only in extremely limited circumstances, and only on the basis of compelling evidence. The alternative implicit in the Petitioners' suggested resolution of this case is an unblinking deference to school officials that places students' privacy and security in grave jeopardy.

For the above reasons, the Ninth Circuit properly found that the strip search of Savana Redding was not reasonable and therefore violated the Fourth Amendment. That decision should be affirmed as guidance to school officials, and to ensure that the practice of strip-searching students remains appropriately rare.

For example, the executive administrator of the Superior Court of Pennsylvania issued this notice:

> Pennsylvania Superior Court will be issuing opinions containing a Universal Citation. This citation will be as follows:
>
> Jones v. Smith, 1999 PA Super, 1.
>
> The second number is a Court-issued number on the opinion. Each opinion will also have numbered paragraphs, to be used for pinpoint citation, e.g., Jones v. Smith, 1999 PA Super, 1, 15. Citation to opinions that have not yet been issued an Atlantic 2d citation are to be in the Universal Citation number. After the official citation has been issued, citation is to be only the official citation, and not the Universal Citation.

Therefore, an attorney submitting a brief to the Superior Court of Pennsylvania must use that court's specified citation form.

ALWD Citation Format

Association of Legal Writing Directors (ALWD) A society for professors who coordinate legal writing instruction.

The **Association of Legal Writing Directors (ALWD)** is a society for professors who coordinate legal writing instruction in legal education. They have compiled a system of citation that is specified in the *ALWD Citation Manual, A Professional System of Citation*.

The *ALWD Citation Manual*, as set out in its preface, is "a set of rules that reflects a consensus in the legal profession about how citations should function." The *ALWD Manual* includes, in addition to the general citation rules, an appendix containing court citation rules for the individual states. Exhibit 11.7 shows the comparison between the *Bluebook* and the ALWD rules for citation format.

Web Exploration

Check the ALWD website for the latest updates at **www.alwd.org**.

Universal Citation Format

The *Universal Citation Guide* represents an attempt by the American Association of Law Libraries' (AALL) Committee on Citation Formats to create a set of universal citation rules for American law that is vendor (publisher) neutral and medium (print and electronic) neutral.

The various forms of electronic distribution require a system of citation that can be applied consistently to allow researchers to find the referenced authority regardless of the research tool used. Whereas traditional, book-based citations reference the page numbers of the books, the **Universal Citation Format** relies upon the courts to use numbered paragraphs in their opinions. Any publisher of the case law must then preserve the information provided by the court, including the citation references to the case and paragraph.

Universal Citation Format A system for citation relying on the courts to number the paragraphs in their opinions.

Anyone who has read and compared a case in a book with a case online is aware that the page size and the display are different. Unless the online computer display is in a photo-image format, such as PDF, locating a specific page or reference can be difficult. Librarians and courts are recognizing the need for the on-screen user to be able to pinpoint citations, and the Universal Citation Format represents an attempt to make pinpointing possible. The difficulty with some courts is the requirement that the Universal Citation Format be used only until the hard copy is published, at which time the traditional citation must be used. As a result, you may see the following citation format within documents:

Jones v. Smith, 1999 Pennsylvania Superior 1, ___Pa Super___, ___A2d___(1999)

The blank spaces are provided for the eventual insertion of the volume and page numbers in the print version when they become available. Appendix D lists court name abbreviations.

Other Citation Formats

Many states, including Pennsylvania, have adopted as their official citation format one that originally was created by publishers such as West Publishing Company. These sometimes are referred to as **vendor-specific citation formats.** The West Publishing Company format is based on the West Regional Reporter system and its publications of federal material.

Vendor-specific citation format The citation format of a legal publisher adopted by a court.

New methods of electronic information technology, such as databases, CD-ROMs, and the Internet, have created a number of problems with the traditional citation formats. Some of the vendors have claimed copyright protection for their pagination systems. In 1985, West Publishing Company, in a case against Mead Data Central, argued successfully that the wholesale use of its pagination by a competing online publisher infringed upon West's copyright interest in the arrangement of cases in its court reports. But in a 1998 case involving Matthew Bender & Company and West Publishing Company, the Second Circuit held that West's pagination was not protected by copyright. Obviously, all claims to a pagination system or citation system that is vendor specific will result in some action to protect the corporate claim for copyright, trademark, or potential patent for some electronic methodology.

Table of Authorities

A **table of authorities** is a listing of the citations or other references that are used in a document, along with the page numbers where they are mentioned. A tool for creating a Table of Authorities is included in the two most popular word processor programs used in the law office, WordPerfect and Microsoft Word. In Word, each authority is first identified and marked by opening the Table of Authorities menu (pressing ALT+SHIFT+I). The authorities are then organized by category, as

Table of authorities A listing of the citations or other references in a document and the page numbers where they are located.

Exhibit 11.7 Comparison of selected ALWD third edition rules and *The Bluebook* 18th edition rules

RULE	ALWD CITATION	BLUEBOOK CITATION	DIFFERENCES
Typeface **ALWD:** Rule 1 **BB:** B13 & Rule 2.0	Ordinary type and *italics* (or underlining). No distinctions based on type of document (law review v. court document) or placement of citation within the paper. Rule 1.1 in the third edition indicates that some journals and book publishers that do not follow ALWD require the use of large and small capital letters; Sidebar 23.2 provides examples of how to use large and small capital letters in various circumstances.	Ordinary type, *italics* (or underlining), and SMALL CAPS. Different fonts required depending on type of document and where source is cited within the paper.	ALWD has one set of conventions, not two. ALWD does not use small caps as a typeface.
Abbreviations and Spacing **ALWD:** Rule 2 **BB:** B5.1.1(v), B10.1, & Rule 6.1	F. Supp. F.3d Corp. Govt. Intl. Petr. In citations, ALWD gives the writer the flexibility to abbreviate words found in the appendices.	F. Supp. F.3d Corp. Gov't Int'l Pet'r In citations, the *Bluebook* requires that words in a case citation (as opposed to a case name used in a textual sentence) be abbreviated if the words appear in the Tables.	No substantial differences on spacing. ALWD abbreviations end with periods; some Bluebook abbreviations include apostrophes. ALWD provides flexibility regarding use of abbreviations.
Capitalization **ALWD:** Rule 3 **BB:** B10.6 & Rule 8	*Federal Civil Procedure before Trial*	*Federal Civil Procedure Before Trial*	ALWD eliminates the "and prepositions of four or fewer letters" part of the *Bluebook*, which brings legal citation closer to non-legal style.
Numbers **ALWD:** Rule 4 **BB:** Rule 6.2	Indicates that the convention in law is to use words for zero through ninety-nine in all text and notes. However, ALWD provides flexibility on whether to designate numbers with words or numerals. Ordinal contractions are presented as follows: 1st, 2d, 3d, 4th, etc.	Use words for zero through ninety-nine in all text and notes. Ordinal contractions are presented as follows: 1st, 2d, 3d, 4th, etc.	No substantial differences, other than ALWD allows for more flexibility. However, ALWD inserts a comma in some four-digit numerals: 3,000.
Page spans **ALWD:** Rule 5 **BB:** Rule 3.2(a)	125–126 **or** 125–26	125–26	ALWD gives a choice on how to present a page span; you may retain all digits or drop repetitive digits and retain two digits on the right-hand side of the span, as in Bluebook 3.2(a).

Exhibit 11.7 Comparison of selected ALWD third edition rules and *The Bluebook* 18th edition rules *(continued)*

RULE	ALWD CITATION	BLUEBOOK CITATION	DIFFERENCES
Footnotes and endnotes **ALWD:** Rule 7 **BB:** Rule 3.2(b)–(c)	n. 7 nn. 12–13	n. 7 nn. 12–13	ALWD requires a space after n. or nn. abbreviation.
Supra **and** *infra* **ALWD:** Rule 10 **BB:** Rule 3.5	*Supra* n. 45.	*Supra* note 45.	Under ALWD, abbreviate note as "n." and place a space after the period.
Id. **ALWD:** Rule 11.3 **BB:** B5.2, Rules 4.1, 10.9 & 12.9	*Id.* at 500.	*Id.* at 500.	Basically similar rules. ALWD eliminates the "5 *id.* in a row" rule found in Bluebook Rule 10.9. In the ALWD Manual, *id.* cannot be used with Practitioner and Court documents. Rule 29.6.
Cases **ALWD:** Rule 12 **BB:** B5 & Rule 10	*Brown v. Bd. of Educ.*, 349 U.S. 294, 297 (1955). *MBNA Am. Bank, N.A. v. Cardoso*, 707 N.E.2d 189 (Ill. App. 1st Dist. 1998). [required inclusion of district court information]	*Brown v. Bd. of Educ.*, 349 U.S. 294, 297 (1955). *MBNA Am. Bank, N.A. v. Cardoso*, 707 N.E.2d 189 (Ill. App. Ct. 1st Dist. 1998). [permissive inclusion of district information]	Under ALWD, case names are always italicized or underlined. Under ALWD, you do not have to abbreviate words in case names. For those who want to abbreviate, Appendix 3 provides a longer list of words that are abbreviated. ALWD requires division and district information for state appellate courts, and eliminates "Ct." from most court abbreviations. For cases cited from Westlaw or LexisNexis, ALWD does not require the docket number of the case. ALWD also requires two asterisks to identify multiple pages of a pinpoint cite.
Constitutions **ALWD:** Rule 13 **BB:** B7 & Rule 11	U.S. Const. amend. V.	U.S. Const. amend. V.	No substantial differences.

(continued)

Exhibit 11.7 **Comparison of selected ALWD third edition rules and *The Bluebook* 18th edition rules** (*continued*)

RULE	ALWD CITATION	BLUEBOOK CITATION	DIFFERENCES
Statutes **ALWD:** Rule 14 **BB:** B6.1.1, B6.1.2 & Rule 12	18 U.S.C. § 1965 (2000).	18 U.S.C § 1965 (2000).	No substantial differences.
Legislative Materials **ALWD:** Rules 15 & 16 **BB:** B6.1.6 & Rule 13	Sen. Res. 146, 109th Cong. (2005).	S. Res. 146, 109th Cong. (2005).	ALWD abbreviates Senate as "Sen." instead of "S." to avoid confusion with other abbreviations. Most forms are relatively consistent.
Court Rules **ALWD**: Rule 17 **BB:** B6.1.3 & Rule 12.8	Fed. R. Civ. P. 11.	Fed. R. Civ. P. 11.	No substantial differences.
Administrative Materials **ALWD:** Rules 19 and 20 **BB:** B6.1.4 & Rule 14.2	34 C.F.R. § 607.1 (2006). 70 Fed. Reg. 10868 (Mar. 5, 2005).	34 C.F.R. § 607.1 (2006). 70 Fed. Reg. 10868 (Mar. 5, 2005).	C.F.R. citation is the same. Both require an exact date for Fed. Reg. citations. ALWD includes guidance about how to cite C.F.R. references found on unofficial electronic databases, such as Westlaw and LexisNexis. Rule 19.1(d).
Books and Treatises **ALWD**: Rule 22 **BB:** B8 & Rule 15	Charles Alan Wright, Arthur R. Miller & Mary Kay Kane, *Federal Practice and Procedure* vol. 7A, § 1751, 10–17 (3d ed., West 2005). OR Charles Alan Wright et al., *Federal Practice and Procedure* vol. 7A, § 1751, 10–17 (3d ed., West 2005).	7A Charles Alan Wright, Arthur R. Miller & Mary Kay Kane, *Federal Practice and Procedure* § 1751, at 10–17 (3d ed. 2005). OR 7A Charles Alan Wright et al., *Federal Practice and Procedure* § 1751, at 10–17 (3d ed. 2005).	ALWD places volume information after the title, just like any other subdivisions. ALWD separates subdivisions separated with a comma, but no "at." ALWD requires that the publisher be included, no matter what type of document. ALWD uses et al. for three authors or more, compared with the *Bluebook* which uses et al. for two authors or more.
Legal Periodicals **ALWD**: Rule 23	Geoffrey P. Miller, *Bad Judges*, 83 Tex. L. Rev. 431 (2004). Margaret Graham Tebo, *Duty Calls*, 91 ABA J. 35 (Apr. 2005).	Geoffrey P. Miller, *Bad Judges*, 83 Tex. L. Rev. 431 (2004). Margaret Graham Tebo, *Duty Calls*, A.B.A. J., Apr. 2005, at 35.	ALWD eliminates most distinctions between consecutively and non-consecutively paginated articles. Include longer date for non-consecutively paginated journals, but do so within the parenthetical.

Exhibit 11.7 Comparison of selected ALWD third edition rules and *The Bluebook* 18th edition rules (*continued*)

RULE	ALWD CITATION	BLUEBOOK CITATION	DIFFERENCES
BB: B9 & Rule 16	Carrie Ann Wozniak, Student Author, *Difficult Problems Call for New Solutions: Are Guardians Proper for Viable Fetuses of Mentally Incompetent Mothers in State Custody?* 34 Stetson L. Rev. 193 (2004). Jodi Wilgoren, *Prosecution Lays out Case for Harsh Sentencing of B.T.K. Killer in Gory Detail*, 154 N.Y. Times A14 (Aug. 18, 2005).	Carrie Ann Wozniak, Comment, *Difficult Problems Call for New Solutions: Are Guardians Proper for Viable Fetuses of Mentally Incompetent Mothers in State Custody?* 34 Stetson L. Rev. 193 (2004). Jodi Wilgoren, *Prosecution Lays out Case for Harsh Sentencing of B.T.K. Killer in Gory Detail*, N.Y. Times, Aug. 18, 2005, at A14.	ALWD uses the term "Student Author" to replace Note, Comment, Recent Development, etc.
A.L.R. Annotations **ALWD**: Rule 24 **BB**: Rule 16.6.6	Carolyn Kelly MacWilliam, *Individual and Corporate Liability for Libel and Slander in Electronic Communications, Including E-mail, Internet and Websites*, 3 A.L.R.6th 153 (2005).	Carolyn Kelly MacWilliam, Annotation, *Individual and Corporate Liability for Libel and Slander in Electronic Communications, Including E-mail, Internet and Websites*, 3 A.L.R.6th 153 (2005).	ALWD eliminates the "Annotation" reference.
Legal Dictionaries **ALWD**: Rule 25 **BB**: Rule 15.8	*Black's Law Dictionary* 87 (Bryan A. Garner ed., 8th ed., West 2004).	*Black's Law Dictionary* 87 (8th ed. 2004).	ALWD treats dictionaries like books.
Legal Encyclopedias **ALWD**: Rule 26 **BB**: Rule 15.8	98 C.J.S. *Witnesses* § 397 (2002). 68 Am. Jur. 2d *Schools* §§ 20–24 (2000 & Supp. 2005).	98 C.J.S. *Witnesses* § 397 (2002). 68 Am. Jur. 2d *Schools* §§ 20–24 (2000 & Supp. 2005).	No substantial differences; however, ALWD provides expanded coverage and includes a list of many abbreviations for state encyclopedias.
Internet **ALWD**: Rule 40 **BB**: Rule 18.2.3	Fed. Jud. Ctr., *History of the Federal Judiciary*, http://www.fjc.http://www.fjc.gov/history/home.nsf (accessed Aug. 18, 2005).	Federal Judicial Center, *History of the Federal Judiciary* (visited Aug. 18, 2005), at http://www.fjc.gov/history/home.nsf.	ALWD permits the abbreviation of an organizational author's name, to save space. ALWD uses "accessed" instead of "visited" to be consistent with non-legal citation guides. The *Bluebo*c contains different formats f(material that appears only on the Web and for materia that appears on the Web ar in other media. The positioı of the date parenthetical moves depending on the type of information cited.

(*continued*)

Exhibit 11.7 Comparison of selected ALWD third edition rules and *The Bluebook* 18th edition rules (*continued*)

RULE	ALWD CITATION	BLUEBOOK CITATION	DIFFERENCES
Signals **ALWD**: Rule 44 **BB:** B4 & Rule 1.2	Signals are *e.g., accord, see, see also, cf., contra, compare . . . with, but see, but cf.*, and *see generally.*	Signals are *e.g., accord, see, see also, cf., contra, compare . . . with, but see, but cf.*, and *see generally.*	Under ALWD, all signals may be separated with semicolons. Under the *Bluebook*, a new citation sentence must start when there is a new type of signal. (Signals are categorized by type in the *Bluebook*—supportive, comparative, contradictory, or background—whereas in ALWD, the signals are ordered individually.) ALWD does not use any punctuation after a signal.
Order of Cited Authority **ALWD**: Rule 45 **BB**: B4.5 & Rule 1.4	ALWD lists federal, state, and foreign court cases first by jurisdiction, then in reverse chronological order.	Federal (appellate and trial) court cases are ordered in reverse chronological order. State court cases are first alphabetized by state, and then ranked within each state.	Minor differences in the order when looking at the list of specific sources: (1) Under ALWD, statutes (federal and state) come before rules of evidence and procedure, whereas in the *Bluebook*, federal statutes and rules of evidence and procedure come before state statutes and rules of evidence and procedure. (2) Under the ALWD, the student-authored articles are classified with all other material in law reviews, law journals, and other periodicals, whereas in the *Bluebook*, the student-authored articles are separate, and cited after the non-student-authored articles.
Quotations **ALWD**: Rule 47 **BB**: B12 & Rule 5	ALWD says to block indent passages if they contain at least fifty words OR if they exceed four lines of typed text.	The *Bluebook* says to block indent passages if they contain at least 50 words.	ALWD does not require you to count the exact number of words in long quotations.

Exhibit 11.8 Table of Authorities selection menus

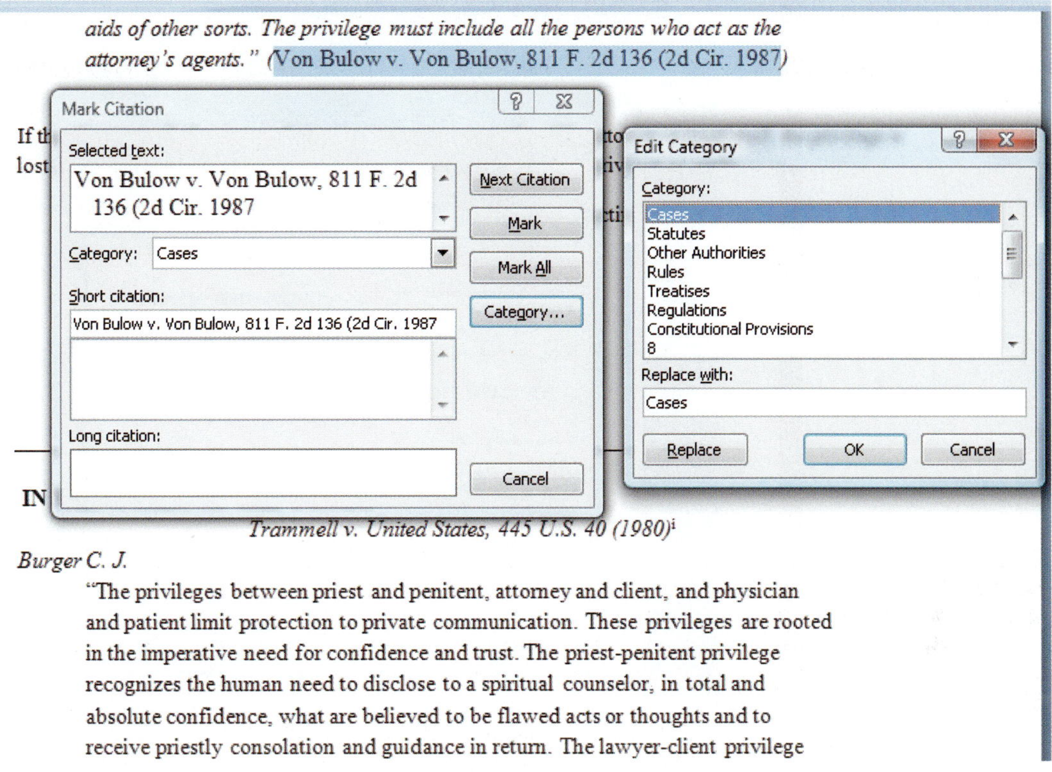

Exhibit 11.9 Table of Authorities hidden characters

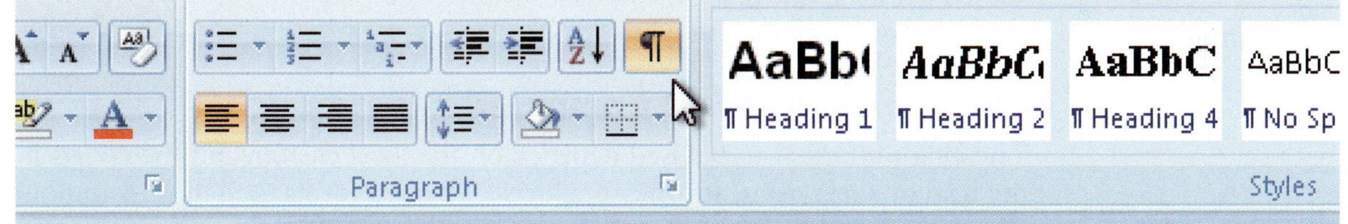

shown in Exhibit 11.8. Each authority is marked and an identifier inserted into the document called a TA or Table of Authority Entry in MS Word. These marks are visible when the Hidden Marks button is selected, as shown in Exhibit 11.9.

The table of authorities may be inserted using the Insert Table of Authorities selection in the Reference tab, as shown in Exhibit 11.10.

Cite Checking

Cite checking is the process of checking each referenced case or statute to determine that it is valid and that it has not been repealed or overturned. Cite checking also involves verifying that the proper citation format has been used for each cite. The format to be used—*Bluebook*, *ALWD Citation Manual*, or Universal Citation Format—as

Cite checking The process of verifying proper citation format in a document.

Exhibit 11.10 Table of Authorities options menu

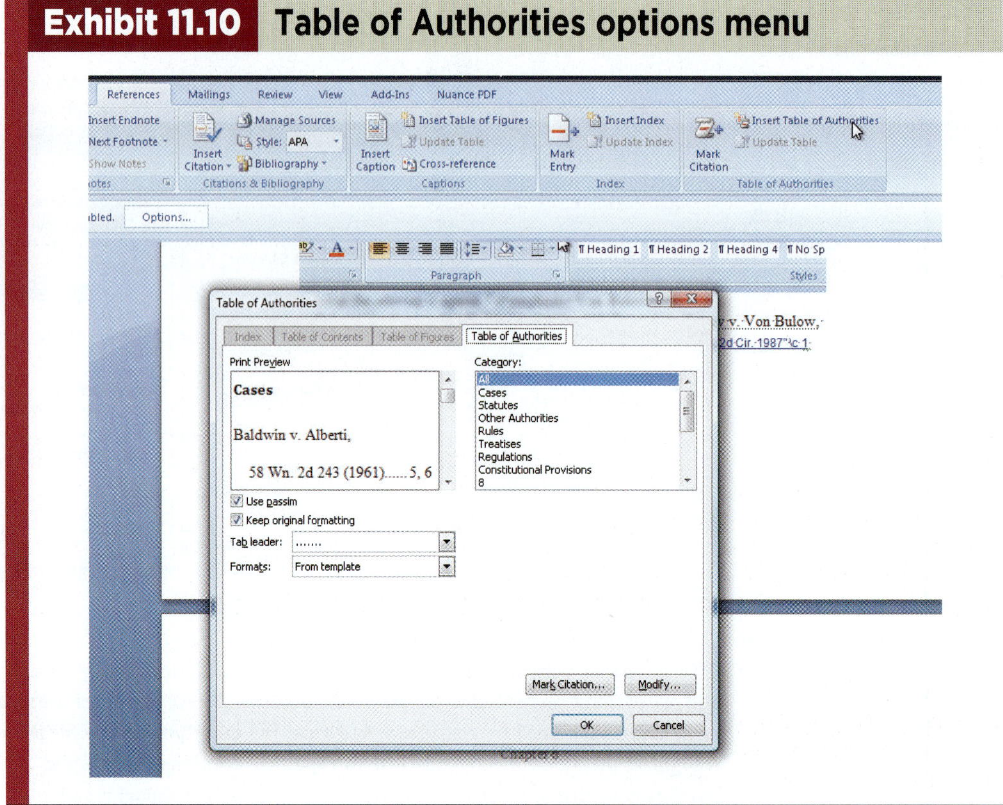

well as the rigor with which the citation rules must be applied, depend on the preferences of the attorney for whom the document is prepared, or those of the court or judge to whom it is submitted. Some courts view improper citation format with a jaundiced eye, the same way they view incorrect punctuation, spelling, and grammar. Others may be upset if the citations do not reference the paper or online legal research service available to them.

Bluebook and *ALWD* Compared

The citation format to be used depends on the local custom and the courts in which the firm or supervising attorney practices. The two forms used most commonly—the *Bluebook* and the *ALWD Manual*—have a number of similarities.

Both of these manuals are divided into parts—the *Bluebook* into three parts and the *ALWD Manual* into seven. The parts are further divided into rules. The *Bluebook* has 20 basic rules, and the *ALWD* has 50 rules. Most of the rules have a common pattern, and some rules are the same for each manual. For example, *Bluebook* Rule 12 and *ALWD* Rule 14, on the method of citing statutes, are the same. They both dictate the same format for citing the United States Code, such as 18 U.S.C. § 1965 (1994). Other rules have minor variations in presentation. For example, *Bluebook* Rule 10.2.2 states, "Do not abbreviate 'United States,'" whereas *ALWD* Rule 12.2(g) states, "United States as party: Cite as U.S. Omit 'America.'"

Sample *Bluebook* citation formats:

Rule 11 Constitutions: U.S.Const.art.I, § 9, cl.2.
Rule 10 Cases: United States v Shaffer Equip. Co., 11 F.3d 450 (4th Cir. 1993)
Rule 12 Statutes: 42 U.S.C. § 1983 (1994)

Sample *ALWD* citation formats:

Rule 13 Constitutions: U.S. Const.art. IV, § 5(b)
Rule 12 Cases: Brown v. Bd. Of Educ., 349 U.S. 294
U.S. v. Chairse, 18 F.Supp. 2d 1021
(D. Minn. 1998)
Rule 14 Statutory Codes: 18 U.S.C. § 1965 (1994)

Advice *from the* Field

PROFESSIONAL COMMUNICATION

by Kathryn L. Myers, Associate Professor and Coordinator of Paralegal Studies at Saint Mary-of-the-Woods College in Saint Mary-of-the-Woods, IN

There are countless misunderstandings, conflicts, and disagreements in every organization in the United States. Effective listening skills are almost extinct in many firms, and gossip among colleagues has become commonplace. The result is lost productivity, hurt feelings, hidden agendas, loss of innovative ideas, and mistrust among coworkers.

The importance of professional communication skills in dealing with these problems cannot be overstressed. *The Wall Street Journal* recently reported a study involving more than one hundred Fortune 500 executives who ranked interpersonal communication first, across the board, as the most valuable skill they considered in hiring or promotion decisions. Lack of interpersonal communication skills impedes professional effectiveness in influencing[,] persuading, and negotiating, all of which are crucial to success.

Professional communication may take the form of written communication, active listening, or nonverbal communication, all of which require interpersonal communication skills. All three skills work together to define professional communication, but this article focuses specifically on written communication.

Writing intimidates many people, but there are times when writing is the best way to communicate and often is the only way to get a message across. Good writers must have access to at least one quality writing guide. Some good choices are: *The Elements of Style*, by William Strunk, Jr., and E.B. White for lawyers, paralegals, and others engaged in formal writing; *The Bedford Handbook*, by Diana T. Hacker; *How 10: A Handbook for Office Professionals*, by James L. and Lyn R. Clark; and *The Associated Press Stylebook* for traditional journalists is the professional bible.

The following tips are offered as examples of what careful writers must consider.

BE CAUTIOUS

Written communication is more concrete than verbal communication and is less forgiving of errors. Once something is written and sent, it cannot be taken back; and it cannot be nuanced or explained away as readily as can be done with the spoken word.

Communicators in writing must meet the challenges of spelling, grammar, punctuation, and style in addition to the actual wording (rhetoric). Modern technology superficially makes writing seem easier by providing grammar and spelling checks, but these tools are not failsafe. They may actually contribute to egregious errors if the writer is not carefully involved with the writing and proofreading the material for sense.

REMEMBER THE ABC'S OF WRITING

Accuracy—Proof and reproof

Brevity—Keep sentences short

Clarity—Use active voice for clear meaning

BEWARE OF COMMON ERRORS

Commas—Use commas after each part of full dates (*e.g.*, "Wednesday, July 13, 2005," or "July 13, 2005," unless the year falls at the end of the sentence. No comma is used with a calendar date expressed alone (*e.g.*, "February 14.") Do not use commas where the year stands by itself (*e.g.*, "the year 2005 was special.").

Restrictive words, phrases, or clauses modify the main idea and are essential to its meaning. These are not set off by commas. Nonrestrictive words, phrases, or clauses, however, do not significantly change the meaning of the sentence and are set off by commas. Place commas inside quotation marks and parentheses.

Semicolons—Use semicolons when there are two or more independent clauses that do not have coordinating conjunctions, or when the clauses are joined by a transitional expression such as "however." Also use them to separate clauses in a series which have internal commas. Place semicolons outside quotation marks and parentheses.

Colons—Use colons after independent clauses that introduce a formal list or enumeration of items, but not if a verb of being precedes the list. Use a colon after a business salutation and to introduce formal quotations (*e.g.*, the court held: "no offense was proven...").

Dashes—Use dashes instead of commas to achieve greater pause and emphasis to what follows. Also use them in place of commas with parenthetical expressions or appositives that contain internal commas.

Ellipsis—An ellipsis is a series of three periods to indicate one or more words are missing from the middle of a sentence in the quoted text. If the missing text is at the end of a sentence, this fact is indicated with a fourth period—the sentence period—at the end of the series.

Quotation Marks—Quotation marks are used to show directly quoted speech or text as well as the titles of published articles. Quotations of 50 words or more do not use quotation marks but, rather, are written as separate paragraph(s), single spaced, and indented on the right and left margins greater than the normal text.

Apostrophe—The apostrophe is used to indicate a missing letter in a contraction (*e.g.*, "it's" for "it is" or "don't" for "do not") or to denote singular possession

(continued)

(*e.g.*, "Mary's"), or plural possession (*e.g.*, "the companies' policies.") "Its" is the correct (albeit counterintuitive) possessive form of "it." No apostrophe is used. All possessive case pronouns (my, your, yours, their, its, whose, theirs, ours) are written without apostrophes.

When there is joint ownership, the apostrophe attaches to the last noun (*e.g.*, "it was Dick and Jane's home"). With individual possession where there are two or more nouns, each noun shows ownership (*e.g.*, "it was either Dick's or Jane's").

WATCH YOUR GRAMMAR

Active Voice—Using action verbs and active voice provides clear and readable sentences.

Noun/Pronoun Agreement—A singular noun (legal assistant) must have a singular pronoun (his/her). Plural nouns (legal assistants) must have plural pronouns (their). Avoid confusion by writing in the plural form when possible.

Subjective Case—Use the subjective case of a pronoun (I, he, she, you, we, they, who, it, whoever) for the subject, for the complement of a "being" verb, and after the infinitive "to be" when this verb does not have a subject directly preceding it.

Objective Case—Use the objective case of a pronoun (me, him, her, you, us, them, whom, it, whomever) as the direct or indirect object of a verb, the object of a preposition, the subject of any infinitive, the object of the infinitive "to be" when it has a subject directly preceding it, and the object of any other infinitive.

Noun/Verb Agreement—Singular nouns take singular verbs. Know the difference among present, past, and future tenses. Do not switch verb tenses in documents unless the material requires the switch.

Identifiers (Modifiers)—Place identifiers (modifiers) (*e.g.*, adjectives and adverbs) as close as possible to the words they identify (modify).

Proper Pairs—Certain words (correlative conjunctions) must be used in pairs (*e.g.*, either/or, neither/nor, not only/but also).

Clichés, Slang, and Jargon—Avoid clichés: use them only when there is a sound reason to believe that a particular cliché will strengthen your rhetoric. Use slang and "legalese" only when it would be awkward for the reader not to do so, and only if you are sure the reader will understand the reference. A judge, for example, expects to read some amount of legalese. He or she likely would be disappointed to see none at all in a trial brief.

Spelling—Use your spelling checker, but proofread to make sure you do not have correct spelling of the wrong word (*e.g.*, "she was soaking in the tube."). Great care should be taken to spell the names of people and companies correctly.

Acronyms and Abbreviations—Except for acronyms and abbreviations in common usage and which are self-explanatory in context (*e.g.*, "the Hon. James Parker" or "she is an interpreter with NATO"), give full titles and names when the acronym or abbreviation first is mentioned. Err on the side of spelling it out if there is any doubt.

Numbers—In general, single-digit numbers should be written as words; double digit, as numerals in written materials unless the number is used to begin a sentence (*e.g.*, "I had only 10 reference books when I began five years ago.").

Source Acknowledgement—The source of borrowed material of any kind must be attributed with quotation marks if directly quoted, or by attribution if not directly quoted (*e.g.*, "I shall return," Gen. MacArthur promised, or, "General Douglas MacArthur promised he would be back"). In formal research and in legal writing, complete citations must be provided according to the legal convention or the style prescribed by the particular publication.

LETTERS

Correspondence is a primary form of communication between the law firm and the world. It is vital that correspondence be crafted well to properly reflect both the reputation of the law office and your own professionalism. Correspondence must be free of grammar and spelling errors, and the research and analysis must be absolutely correct.

There are different types of letters for different purposes: informational letters, opinion letters, and demand letters, to name a few. Although paralegals would not sign their names to opinion or demand letters, it is quite common for them to draft substantial portions of this correspondence.

There are certain parts to a letter that are necessary for successful correspondence.

Format—There are three primary formats: 1) full block, 2) modified block with blocked paragraphs, and 3) modified block with indented paragraphs.

Letterhead—Preprinted letterhead needs no additional information; but subsequent pages need to contain an identification of the letter, or a header including the name of the addressee, the date, and the page number.

Date—The full date appears below the letterhead at the left or right margin depending on the format used.

Method of Delivery—This appears at the left margin below the date if delivery other than U.S. Postal Service is used.

Recipient's Address Block—The inside address is placed at the left margin and should include:

The recipient

The recipient's title (if any)

The name of the business (if appropriate)

The address

Reference Line—Usually introduced with "Re:" the reference line identifies the subject of the letter. Depending upon office requirements, it may contain case identification.

Salutation—Legal correspondence generally is formal; and the salutation is followed with a colon, such as "Dear Ms. Myers:" You can use the first name if you know the person well, although it is a safer practice to remain formal. It is best to address the letter to a named individual. This may mean calling the recipient business and identifying a person to whom the letter should be addressed.

Body—The body of the letter should have three components:

1. Introduction: For normal business letters, your letter should start with an overall summary, showing in the first paragraph why the letter is relevant to the reader. Don't make [the] reader go past the first paragraph to find out why the letter was sent.
2. Main section: The body of the letter needs to explain the reason for the correspondence, including any relevant background and current information. Make sure the information flows logically to make your points effectively.
3. Requests/instructions: The closing of the letter is the final impression you leave with the reader. End with an action point such as, "I will call you later this week to discuss the matter."

Closing—Following the body of the letter, the closing consists of a standard statement and/or an action item.

Signature and Title—Clearly identify the writer by name and title.

Initials of Drafter—This is a reference to the author (KLM) and the typist (sbk).

Enclosure Notation—"Enc." or "Encs." notations are used to identify one or more enclosures.

Copies to Others—The traditional "cc" notation, formerly meaning "carbon copy," now means "courtesy copy" and is used universally. Some writers, however, will use only "c" or "copy to," along with the name(s), to identify others receiving copies of the document.

PROOFREADING

Even when you believe your draft is exactly what you want, read it one more time. This rule is for everything you write whether it is a memorandum, letter, proposal, or some other document. It is true no matter how many drafts you have written.

Use both the grammar and spelling checker on your computer, paying very close attention to every word highlighted. Do not place total faith in your computer. Instead, have both a printed dictionary and a thesaurus nearby to double-check everything your computer's editing tools highlight, because the computer tools are not always reliable.

Make sure your document is clear and concise. Is there anything that could be misinterpreted? Does it raise questions or fail to make the point you need to make? Can you reduce the number of words or unnecessarily long words? Do not use a long word when a short one works as well; do not use two words when one will do; and do not waste the reader's time with unnecessary words or phrases.

Is your written communication well organized? Does each idea proceed logically from one paragraph to the next? Make sure written communications are easy to read, contain the necessary information, use facts where needed, and avoid information that is not relevant. Be sure to specify the course of action you expect, such as a return call or an order.

Close appropriately, whether formally or informally, according to the nature of the communication. This may seem obvious, but it is sometimes overlooked and can make written communications look amateurish. This diminishes your chances of meeting your written communication's goals.

Communication is vital to the success of any workplace; and in the legal arena, professionals live or die by the communicated word. Well-crafted documents are a positive step toward being a successful professional.

Concept Review *and* Reinforcement

LEGAL TERMINOLOGY

SUMMARY OF KEY CONCEPTS

Critical Legal Thinking: Definitions

Critical Legal Thinking	Critical legal thinking is the process of identifying legal issues, determining relevant facts, and applying the applicable law to those facts to reach a conclusion that answers the legal questions or issues presented. The paralegal must understand the audience for whom the document is being prepared: the client, the supervising attorney, other members of the legal team, or the court.
Facts	Facts are pieces of information or details that actually exist, or have occurred, as opposed to theories, suppositions, or conjectures. In the law, facts are circumstances of an event, actions, occurrences, or states of affairs, rather than interpretations of their significance.
Material Fact	A material fact is a fact that is significant or essential to the issue or matter at hand.
Immaterial Fact	An immaterial fact is one that is not essential to the matter at issue.

Legal Writing

Standards	1. The language used must be clear to the intended reader. 2. The writer must make an honest presentation of the facts and arguments. 3. Arguments advocating a new interpretation to the existing law, as well as the current law, must be clearly stated. 4. The ethical obligation to the court must be obeyed, including the presentation of any adverse authority in the jurisdiction. 5. Any factual variation must be presented, and the sources used clearly identified by proper citation in a format acceptable to the reader.
Duty of Candor	There is an obligation to be honest with the court and not to mislead the court.

Preparing Office Memoranda

Purpose	1. The memorandum is a working document, written for the legal team, to be used in the preparation and presentation of a case. 2. The paralegal must understand the specific assignment. For the memorandum of law, the assignment is usually to answer a question. 3. Office memoranda are frequently indexed by subject and filed in the office for future reference. If a similar fact pattern requires research, a prior memorandum may be a good starting point and can be a major timesaver. 4. The facts relied upon in writing the assignment memorandum must be a part of the final memorandum; other people who read the memorandum need to understand the specific facts it is based on. 5. A memorandum must present both sides of the issue, and in that respect be a neutral, unbiased, objective presentation of the law as it applies to the facts of the case. Issues that the opposing attorney or the judge may raise should be considered and presented. A good analysis includes a discussion of how the fact pattern may differ in cases that are not on point.

Preparing Court Briefs

	Written for the court, the brief provides written advocacy of the client's position and must be written to convince the court to adopt a position favorable to the client.

Citations

Purpose	A citation should allow someone else to find the case or other material mentioned in a document. The format must be generally accepted and used by others in the legal community.
Traditional Sources: Print Citation Format	The basic paper citation form is: Volume, Book or Series, Page Number Example: 232 Atlantic 2d 44 "232" refers to the volume in the Atlantic 2d series reporter service of West Publishing Company, and "44" refers to the page on which the case may be found.
Bluebook Citation Format	The *Bluebook* has been the generally accepted authority for proper citation form, unless the rules of a particular court dictate a different citation format.
ALWD Citation Format	This citation format authority was written by the Association of Legal Writing Directors.
Universal Citation Format	Traditionally, book-based citation used information based on internal page numbers. Universal Citation Format relies upon the courts to provide numbered paragraphs in their opinions.
Table of Authorities	A table of authorities is a listing of the citations or other references in a document and the page numbers where they are located.
Cite Checking	Documents must be checked to verify that the referenced cases and statutes are valid, that the cases and statutes have not been repealed or overturned, and that they are written in the proper citation format. The strictness with which the citation rules must be applied, as well as the method used—*Bluebook*, *ALWD*, or Universal Citation Format—depend on the wishes and demands of the attorney for whom the document is being prepared, or those of the court or judge to whom it will be submitted.

WORKING THE WEB

1. Summarize in a memo the requirements for briefs submitted to the United States Supreme Court, and the citation to the applicable rule. http://www.supremecourt.gov/ctrules/ctrules.aspx or http://www.law.cornell.edu/rules/supct.
2. Use the Internet to find information on preparing an internal office memorandum or the requirements for filing briefs in your jurisdiction's highest court. For example, in California they may be found at http://www.courts.ca.gov/documents/title_3.pdf, or in Kansas at http://www.kscourts.org/Appellate-Clerk/Filing-Forms/default.asp.
3. The Legal Law Institute at Cornell Law School offers a number of sources for the legal writer, including citation information. Use the LII website to download the section from *Introduction to Basic Legal Citation* by Peter W. Martin—"Who Sets Citation Norms"—at http://www.law.cornell.edu/citation/1-600.htm.
4. Use the homepage link from the web page in question 3, and download your personal copy of the reference document.
5. If you are using the *ALWD Manual* for citation rules, download a copy of the latest updates at www.alwd.org.

CRITICAL THINKING & WRITING QUESTIONS

1. What is critical legal thinking? Explain and give an example.
2. Why is it important to have all the material facts before beginning the research to prepare a memorandum of law?
3. What is meant by "material facts"? Give an example of a material fact.
4. What is meant by an "immaterial fact"? Give an example.
5. What is the goal of legal writing?
6. Why should headnotes not be used in legal writing?
7. How important is it to Shepardize the cases in a memorandum of law or brief? When should this be done? Why?

8. How are the memorandum of law and the court brief similar? How are they different? Explain.
9. Contrast and compare the fact situation in the opening scenario and the Alaskan case of *Whiting v. State* presented in this chapter. What are the similarities, and what are the points that could be used to argue that the law does not apply?
10. How does the general duty to inform the court preserve the integrity of the judicial process? See *Hazel-Atlas Glass Co. v. Hartford-Empire Co.*, 322 U.S. 238 (1944).
11. Are sanctions against attorneys for failing to observe a duty of candor to the court an appropriate remedy? See *Beam v. IPCO Corp.*, 838 F.2d 242 (7th Cir. 1998).
12. What are the relevant facts in the *Palsgraf v. LIRR* case found in Appendix A? What facts are interesting but not relevant facts? Create a computer search query using the facts in the *Palsgraf* case, and search the case law of your jurisdiction using these relevant facts. Prepare a short brief of the latest case you find, using proper *Bluebook* and *ALWD* citation formats.
13. What questions should a paralegal ask before preparing a memorandum of law or a brief?
14. Why should both sides of a case be presented in an office memorandum of law?
15. Why would an attorney request that all parallel citations be listed for each case listed in a memorandum of law?
16. How would knowing the intended audience influence the writing of a memorandum of law or a brief?
17. What level of confidentiality should be attached to the preparation and handling of a memorandum of law? Why?

Building Paralegal Skills

VIDEO CASE STUDIES

Zealous Representation Issue: Candor to the Court

The supervising attorney is due in another courtroom and asks the paralegal to appear for him and submit a brief, which the paralegal has prepared. The lawyer does not read the petition and accepts the paralegal's statement that it includes the current law on the subject.

After viewing the video case study in MyLegalStudiesLab, answer the following:

1. What is the duty of the legal team to present up-to-date information to the court when seeking relief?
2. Can legal research from a prior case be used in an argument to the court?
3. Who is held responsible for misleading the court on the accuracy of legal authority, the paralegal or the attorney?

Zealous Representation Issue: Signing Documents

Court rules require that pleadings be signed by the attorney. With the court about to close and the statute of limitations running out that day, the paralegal signs the attorney's name and files the paperwork.

After viewing the video case study in MyLegalStudiesLab, answer the following:

1. What is the purpose of having the attorney sign all pleadings?
2. Would electronic filing have avoided this problem?
3. What are the dangers in relying upon electronic filing of documents?

ETHICS ANALYSIS & DISCUSSION QUESTIONS

1. What are the ethical issues in failing to properly cite authorities used in a document?
2. What are the ethical obligations in arguing to the court for a change in the law and not following the current law?
3. What are the ethical obligations to the client when analysis of the law indicates there is no valid claim?
4. Assume you have been working for a legal specialist in estate law for a number of years and have taken a number of advanced courses in the field. You are highly regarded in the paralegal community and seen as the person to call for help in the field. Your supervising attorney decides to take a three-week bicycle trip through the Swiss Alps and leaves you in charge of the office.

During his absence, you give a talk to a local senior citizens group on the advantages of preparing a will. You meet with most of the people in the audience after the talk and tell them that a simple will can be prepared for $25 (your office's standard fee) and proceed to take the information from them for a will. You prepare the individual wills and send copies marked DRAFT to each person, along with an invoice for the $25 fee and a note to return the fee if they wish to have the will completed. Everyone accepts and sends in the fee.

Upon his return, the attorney looks over the wills, tells you they are "letter perfect," and says, "It's just what I would have done." See *Cincinnati Bar v. Kathman*, 92 Ohio St. 92 (2001) quoting *People v. Cassidy*, 884 P.2d 309 (Colo. 1994).

What are the legal and ethical issues?

5. It is the week between Christmas and New Year's Day. You are the only one covering the office while all of the lawyers and support personnel are on vacation. A client who is traveling in Asia calls and asks you to fax to his hotel a copy of an opinion letter prepared by your supervising attorney. You helped prepare the opinion letter and know that it contains a summary of the facts, including details about the opposing parties, case strategy, and potential violations of law. May you send it? What are the ethical issues, if any?
6. You are working for the local prosecutor as a paralegal. The District Attorney asks you to prepare an office memorandum of law on the question: Is there any duty to advise the court of any changes in the law or facts after the case has been presented?
7. You prepared a memorandum of law for the firm's trial attorney, and a brief for the court that was used in the case that started today. Closing arguments will be made tomorrow. You now discover case law that is favorable to the other side and that effectively overturns the case law you used in the memorandum of law and brief. What do you do? Are there any ethical issues? Explain fully.

DEVELOPING YOUR COLLABORATION SKILLS

Working on your own or with a group of other students assigned by your instructor, review the scenario at the beginning of the chapter.

1. Divide the group into two teams.
   a. One team is to prepare a memorandum for the court in the form of a brief.
   b. One team is to prepare a memorandum of law for the partner.
   c. After the memorandums are finished, each group will compare the two documents and write a report on the differences between them.
2. As a group, prepare a memo that Amanda might prepare for the supervising paralegal or other attorney on the handling of the interview and any concerns or recommendations.
3. Discuss any ethical concerns that Amanda might have, based on the interview and the potential handling of the case.

PARALEGAL PORTFOLIO EXERCISE

Prepare a memorandum of law for the supervising attorney using the information in the memorandum assignment below. Use the statutory and case law of your local jurisdiction.

Memorandum Assignment

To: Edith Hannah
From: Richard Wasserbly
Date: January 23, 2013
File Number: GH 06-1002
Re: State of (your state) v. Kevin Dones

Our client was stopped by a police officer at the bottom of a 1-mile-long 10% grade hill on State Route 332 in Northhampton Township, at 3:30 p.m. on Sunday afternoon, January 15, 2012. He was riding a bicycle south on State Route 332. He was given a motor vehicle citation for speeding. They used a radar unit and claim a speed of 35 mph in a 25 mph zone. He also was administered a field sobriety test, which gave a reading over the legal limit, and was given a citation for driving under the influence. He tells me he was riding a bike because his license was suspended for having two previous DUIs.

Please prepare a brief memorandum of law, with citations and cases.

LEGAL ANALYSIS & WRITING CASES

The Continuing Duty to Inform the Court of Changes in the Law

***United States v. Shaffer Equipt. Co.* 11 F.3d 450 (4th Cir. 1993)**

Government counsel learned that its expert witness had lied about his credentials and that the witness had lied in other litigation. The attorney did not immediately notify the court or opposing counsel. In finding against the government, the court extended the duty of candor to include a continuing duty to inform the court of any development that may conceivably affect the outcome of litigation.

Questions

1. Is preserving the integrity of the judicial process more important than the duty to vigorously pursue a client's case?
2. Is there a duty to inform the court when an attorney suspects that a client may have committed perjury?
3. What additional burden is placed on the paralegal in preparing material for a case in light of this decision?

WORKING WITH THE LANGUAGE OF THE COURT CASE

Golden Eagle Distributing Corp. v. Burroughs, 801 F.2d. 1531 (9th Cir. 1986)

United States Court of Appeals, Ninth Circuit

Read and brief this case. In your brief, answer the following questions.

1. What is the intent of Federal Rules of Civil Procedure Rule 11?
2. What test does the court use to determine whether sanctions should be imposed under FRCP Rule 11?
3. What is meant by the "ethical duty of candor"?
4. Is there a conflict between the attorney's ethical obligations under the ABA Model Rules of Professional Conduct and the requirements of FRCP 11?
5. Do attorneys have any duty to cite cases adverse to their client's case? Explain.

Schroeder, Circuit Judge

This is an appeal from the imposition of sanctions under Rule 11 of the Federal Rules of Civil Procedure as amended in 1983. The appellant, a major national law firm, raises significant questions of first impression.

The relevant portions of the amended Rule provide: Every pleading, motion, and other paper of a party represented by an attorney shall be signed by at least one attorney.... The signature of an attorney... constitutes a certificate by him that he has read the pleading, motion, or other paper; that to the best of his knowledge, information, and belief formed after reasonable inquiry, it is well grounded in fact and is warranted by existing law or a good faith argument for the extension, modification, or reversal of existing law.... If a pleading, motion, or other paper is signed in violation of this rule, the court, upon motion or upon its own initiative, shall impose upon the person who signed it, a represented party, or both, an appropriate sanction....

In this appeal, we must decide whether the district court correctly interpreted Rule 11.

...Golden Eagle Distributing Corporation filed the underlying action in Minnesota state court for fraud, negligence, and breach of contract against Burroughs, because of an allegedly defective computer system. Burroughs removed the action to the federal district court in Minnesota. Burroughs then moved pursuant to 28 U.S.C. § 1404(a) to transfer the action to the Northern District of California.... Burroughs next filed the motion for summary judgment, which gave rise to the sanctions at issue here. It argued that the California, rather than the Minnesota, statute of limitations applied and that all of Golden Eagle's claims were time-barred under California law. It also contended that Golden Eagle's claim for economic loss arising from negligent manufacture lacked merit under California law. Golden Eagle filed a response, arguing that Minnesota law governed the statute of limitations question and that Burroughs had misinterpreted California law regarding economic loss....

After a hearing, the district judge denied Burroughs' motion and directed the Kirkland & Ellis attorney who had been responsible for the summary judgment motion to submit a memorandum explaining why sanctions should not be imposed under Rule 11.... Proper understanding of this appeal requires some comprehension of the nature of Burroughs' arguments and the faults which the district court found with them....

Kirkland & Ellis's opening memorandum argued that Golden Eagle's claims were barred by California's three-year statute of limitations. The question was whether the change of venue from Minnesota to California affected which law applied.... In imposing sanctions, the district court held that Kirkland & Ellis's argument was "misleading" because it suggested that there already exists a *forum non conveniens* exception to the general rule that the transferor's law applies.... [The case cited] raised the issue but did not decide it.... Kirkland & Ellis's corollary argument, that a Minnesota court would have dismissed the case on *forum non conveniens* grounds, was found to be "misleading" because it failed to note that one prerequisite to such a dismissal is that an alternative forum be available....

Kirkland & Ellis also argued that Golden Eagle's claim for negligent manufacture lacked merit because Golden Eagle sought damages for economic loss, and such damages are not recoverable under California law [as demonstrated in the *Seely* case].... The district court sanctioned Kirkland & Ellis for not citing three cases whose holdings it concluded were adverse to *Seely*:... The district court held that these omissions violated counsel's duty to disclose adverse authority, embodied in Model Rule 3.3, Model Rules of Professional Conduct Rule 3.3 (1983), which the court viewed as a "necessary corollary to Rule 11."

... The district court's application of Rule 11 in this case strikes a chord not otherwise heard in discussion of this Rule. The district court did not focus on whether a sound basis in law and in fact existed for the defendant's motion for summary judgment. Indeed it indicated that the motion itself was nonfrivolous.... Rather, the district court looked to the manner in which the motion was presented. The district court in this case held that Rule 11 imposes upon counsel an ethical "duty of candor." ... It said:

The duty of candor is a necessary corollary of the certification required by Rule 11. A court has a right to expect that counsel will state the controlling law fairly and fully; indeed, unless that is done the court cannot perform its task properly. A lawyer must not misstate the law, fail to disclose adverse authority (not disclosed by his opponent), or omit facts critical to the application of the rule of law relied on....

With the district court's salutary admonitions against misstatements of the law, failure to disclose directly adverse authority, or omission of critical facts, we have no quarrel. It is, however, with Rule 11 that we must deal. The district court's interpretation of Rule 11 requires district courts to judge the ethical propriety of lawyers' conduct with respect to every piece of paper filed in federal court. This gives us considerable pause....

The district court's invocation of Rule 11 has two aspects. The first, which we term "argument identification," is the holding that counsel should differentiate between an argument "warranted by existing law" and an argument for the "extension, modification, or reversal of existing law." The second is the conclusion that Rule 11 is violated when counsel fails to cite what the district court views to be directly contrary authority.

... The text of the Rule... does not require that counsel differentiate between a position which is supported by existing law and one that would extend it. The Rule on its face requires that the motion be either one or the other.... The district court's ruling appears to go even beyond the principle of Rule 3.3 of the ABA Model Rules, which proscribes "knowing" false statements of material fact or law. The district court made no finding of a knowing misstatement, and, given the well-established objective nature of the Rule 11 standard, such a requirement would be inappropriate. Both the earnest advocate exaggerating the state of the current law without knowingly misrepresenting it, and the unscrupulous lawyer knowingly deceiving the court, are within the scope of the district court's interpretation.

This gives rise to serious concerns about the effect of such a rule on advocacy. It is not always easy to decide whether an argument is based on established law or is an argument for the extension of existing law. Whether the case being litigated is... materially the same as earlier precedent is frequently the very issue which prompted the litigation in the first place. Such questions can be close.

(continued)

Sanctions under Rule 11 are mandatory.... In even a close case, we think it extremely unlikely that a judge, who has already decided that the law is not as a lawyer argued it, will also decide that the loser's position was warranted by existing law. Attorneys who adopt an aggressive posture risk more than the loss of the motion if the district court decides that their argument is for an extension of the law which it declines to make. What is at stake is often not merely the monetary sanction but the lawyer's reputation.

The "argument identification" requirement adopted by the district court therefore tends to create a conflict between the lawyer's duty zealously to represent his client, Model Code of Professional Responsibility Canon 7, and the lawyer's own interest in avoiding rebuke. The concern on the part of the bar that this type of requirement will chill advocacy is understandable....

... Were the scope of the rule to be expanded as the district court suggests, mandatory sanctions would ride on close decisions concerning whether or not one case is or is not the same as another. We think Rule 11 should not impose the risk of sanctions in the event that the court later decides that the lawyer was wrong. The burdens of research and briefing by a diligent lawyer anxious to avoid any possible rebuke would be great. And the burdens would not be merely on the lawyer. If the mandatory provisions of the Rule are to be interpreted literally, the court would have a duty to research authority beyond that provided by the parties to make sure that they have not omitted something.

The burden is illustrated in this case, where the district court based its imposition of sanctions in part upon Kirkland & Ellis's failure to cite authorities which the court concluded were directly adverse to a case it did cite. The district court charged the appellant with constructive notice of these authorities because they were identified in Shepard's as "distinguishing" the case Kirkland & Ellis relied on.

... Amended Rule 11 of the Federal Rules of Civil Procedure does not impose upon the district courts the burden of evaluating under ethical standards the accuracy of all lawyers' arguments. Rather, Rule 11 is intended to reduce the burden on district courts by sanctioning, and hence deterring, attorneys who submit motions or pleadings which cannot reasonably be supported in law or in fact. We therefore reverse the district court's imposition of sanctions for conduct which it felt fell short of the ethical responsibilities of the attorney. Reversed.

MYLEGALSTUDIESLAB

MyLegalStudiesLab Virtual Law Office Experience Assignments

Complete the pre-test, study plan, and post-test for this chapter and answer the Legal Applications questions as assigned. These will help you confirm your mastery of the concepts and their application to legal scenarios. Then complete the Virtual Law Office assignments as assigned by your instructor. These assignments are designed to develop your workplace skills. Completing the assignments for this chapter will result in producing the following documents for inclusion in your portfolio:

VLOE 11.1	Printout of the weather on the day of the accident (one year ago today in your home town)
VLOE 11.2	Aerial view of the scene (at the intersection nearest your home)

CHAPTER

12

Legal Research

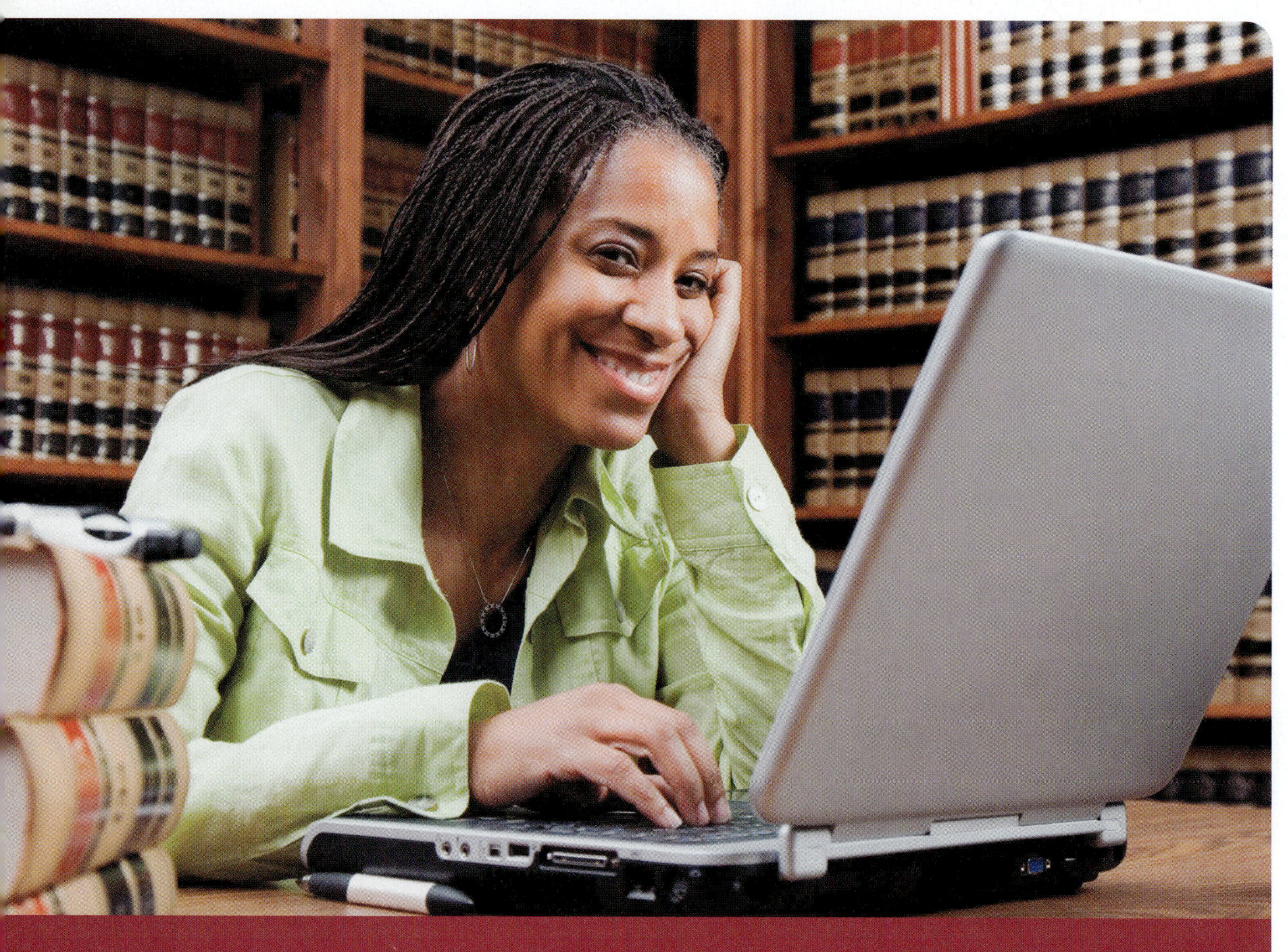

LEARNING OBJECTIVES

After studying this chapter, you should be able to:

1. Define "legal research" and create a legal research plan.
2. Explain the differences between primary resources, secondary resources, and finding tools.
3. Create a search query.
4. Explain the need for, and the methods of, updating legal research.

Paralegals at Work

Mr. Mulkeen, the managing partner of a large multinational law firm, was preparing for an executive committee meeting with the senior partners from the firm's offices around the world. The diverse group ranged from young partners on the fast track seeking direct experience to older senior partners concerned more with developing client contacts than working on cases directly. Some of the firm's newer offices specialized in specific areas of law, such as their five-person health care group in Chicago and their 20-person intellectual property office in San Francisco.

As with all law firms, reducing costs was high on the agenda. One of the major items on the firm's budget was the law library. Some partners wanted to expand the library, while others wanted to cut it. Mr. Mulkeen wanted to keep as many staff members as possible happy and reach a consensus among a cross-section of the firm's members. At the meeting, he indicated that the firm was at a crossroads in making a decision about the firm's law library. They needed to decide what to keep, what to get rid of, and what to commit resources to. The cost of the space for the library was a major issue for the firm, as was the increasing cost of law reporters and upkeep services.

Mr. Wasserbly, a senior partner who had been with the firm more than 25 years, reminded everyone that when he started with the firm, the library didn't have the same resources as it had currently, and that the law book collection was an object of pride that he frequently pointed out

> "This trial is a travesty; it's a travesty of a mockery of a sham of a mockery of a travesty of two mockeries of a sham. I move for a mistrial."
>
> *Woody Allen,* Bananas

to new clients. He said the firm could research case law in most jurisdictions back to the first volume of the case reporters, and the firm had all of the volumes of the state and federal statutes and codes. Research could be done on weekends if necessary, and pages were copied out of the books. He didn't feel comfortable eliminating any of the hardbound volumes and said that there was value in being able to thumb through the pages to find something, even if you weren't sure what you were looking for.

Kathryn, one of the senior paralegals, said that she didn't use the library that much, and that it was mostly a place for her to spread things out. She and her supervising attorney did most of their research at their desks, using computers to access online research services. She felt limited, she said, in using the hourly fee research services for research because the cost could not always be billed to the client and the bookkeeping department was critical about the office having to absorb the fees. Kathryn also pointed out that the litigation team was always in court or trying cases out of town, so the in-house library didn't really do the litigation team much good anyway.

Kevin, one of the firm's long-term secretaries, expressed concern with eliminating the current library. He explained that when working for one of the general-practice attorneys, it was often necessary to get up to speed on a new area of law, and he had to browse through some of the encyclopedias and treatises just to understand the basic issues and terminology. He said he couldn't do this using the computer—at least not until the terminology was understood.

Consider the issues involved in this scenario as you read the chapter.

INTRODUCTION TO RESEARCH FOR THE PARALEGAL

One of the most important skills a paralegal can develop is the ability to find current legal and factual information in a timely manner. Knowing where to look is just as important as knowing what to look for. Clients expect their legal counsel to use the most current law in advising them. The paralegal is expected to be able to analyze the relevant facts and find the current statutory and case law that applies to those facts.

The frequent changes in court decisions and statutes present a challenge to the legal profession. Traditional law libraries consisting of printed materials may not have the latest versions of cases, statutes, or regulations until days or weeks after they are issued because of the time required to assemble, print, and send out printed versions of the updates.

Internet and computer technology allows for more rapid access to the latest information. Many courts now issue the electronic version of court opinions as soon as the opinion is handed down. Instant availability of these decisions is necessary because the ethical duty of candor requires the most current decision to be used in court filings, even before the printed version is available.

Although the ability to obtain current case law is important, in many cases an older common law case may still be precedent. The problem is that some electronic or online services, such as VersusLaw, may not have included the older cases in their database of available cases. For example, VersusLaw only includes state appellate court cases from Illinois and Pennsylvania from 1950 and the California Court of Appeals from 1944. For that reason, being able to find the case the old-fashioned way by checking through the books is a valuable skill. When using an electronic case service, the dates of the available cases should be checked to be certain that they cover the time period needed for the search.

Legal Research

Learning Objective 1

Define "legal research" and create a legal research plan.

Legal research is the process of finding the answer to a legal question. The legal question usually involves a specific set of facts, and the answer may include federal, state, and local statutory law, administrative agency regulation, and case law.

Legal research The process of finding the answer to a legal question.

Before starting, the researcher must have a clear picture of the relevant facts, the legal question, and what information the person who assigned the research needs. With this in mind, proceeding in a systematic way will save time and ensure that all research avenues have been considered. A systematic approach begins with planning the research and knowing what issues must be addressed and covered.

Creating a Research Plan

The first step in legal research is setting up a research plan. The research plan helps the researcher focus on the issues, the sources, and the methods for finding the answer and the controlling law. A few basic questions should be considered in setting up the research plan.

1. What is the issue or legal question?
   a. a statute or regulation
   b. a legal question involving a set of facts
2. What is the appropriate search terminology?
   a. words
   b. phrases
   c. legal terms
   d. popular names of statutes or cases
3. What type of research material is available?
   a. traditional
   b. computer
4. What jurisdiction or jurisdictions are involved?
   a. federal
   b. state
   c. local
5. What is the controlling law?
   a. statutory
   b. regulatory
   c. case law
6. What are the types of resources to be used?
   a. primary
   b. secondary
   c. finding tools
7. Where is the needed research material located?
   a. in-house traditional materials
   b. fee-based legal services
   c. free web-based remote libraries

Using checklists for each search, such as the Research Plan: Words and Phrases and the Research Search Items checklists shown later in the chapter, is a good way to be sure all appropriate terms and sources have been used. When the checklist has been filled out, a record of the results is available for follow-up by the researcher or a colleague.

Paralegals *in* Practice

PARALEGAL PROFILE

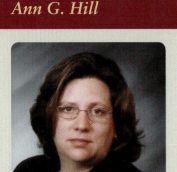

Ann G. Hill

Returning to school after spending over ten years as a legal secretary, Ann G. Hill earned a paralegal certificate at Illinois State University in 2000. She also earned the Insurance Institute of America Certificate in General Insurance in 2003, and obtained her paralegal certification through the National Association of Legal Assistants in 2004. Ann is currently a legal assistant for a major insurance company in Bloomington, Illinois. In her spare time, she serves as a pro bono paralegal providing legal assistance to Social Security clients of the local legal aid society.

I currently specialize in records/information management, legal research, and project management. Legal research is often similar to putting together a massive jigsaw puzzle. When researching a specific issue, I initially review applicable statutes and case law. Then, I look for agency rules, since agencies often have statutory authority to enact rules that carry the force of law. When researching contracts issues, I examine project funding since funds are often tied to federal and state grant programs with many stipulations. I also look at professional organizations' Web sites for legal information relevant to their particular field.

A good research paralegal must be able to "step back," view the issue from different perspectives, and analyze the data. I try to identify factors that could impact the outcome of the legal opinion. I then ask the client more questions. Since clients are not always aware of relevant factors and potential issues, you must be able to "think outside the box" in order to know what questions will prove most helpful to the case.

During the research process, I take advantage of credible research already completed. I use a variety of online search services including Westlaw®, Lexis®, and PACER. Law journal and legal news articles posted on the Internet often contain information about specific laws, regulations, and cases relevant to a particular issue. No matter what research methods are used, I always "shepardize" case law, use annotated statutes when possible, and strive to be thorough.

To be truly successful in the paralegal profession, continue to pursue a variety of learning opportunities. For example, consider helping to fill the need for legal services among low income families and senior citizens who cannot afford private attorneys. By partnering with a legal aid society, you can gain valuable experience while serving your community.

What Is the Issue or Legal Question?

Legal research is like a puzzle to be solved. To solve it, understanding the assigned question is essential. Valuable time may be wasted if the paralegal takes the wrong research path because the question was not clear or the lawyer requesting the research was not clear about the information needed. At times the question is framed with some specificity:

Find the statute...
Example: "What is the statute of limitations for filing a tort action for...?"
Get me the case of...
Example: "What is the language of the *Miranda* decision on...?"

More often, however, the question is much more vague:

How does the law address this set of facts...
Example: "How does the law address a case where our client suffered a broken leg three years ago when the car in which he was a passenger was hit...?"

In such cases, the paralegal should follow up by asking questions to determine exactly what legal issue he or she is being asked to research.

Researchers must first understand which facts are relevant and what areas of law apply to the case they are asked to research. Unlike the cases in textbooks and court opinions, in real life, the **relevant facts** and the specific area of substantive or procedural law that applies are usually not so clear. The initial interview with the client may have focused on what the client or the interviewer *thought at that time* was the applicable law. Further research may indicate that other areas of law must also be considered.

Relevant facts Facts crucial to the case and having legal significance.

For example, what may seem to be a simple rear-end automobile accident caused by negligent driving may in actuality be a case of product liability caused by a manufacturing defect on the part of the automobile manufacturer or the supplier of a defective part. To analyze a case properly, the researcher must know the factual elements of both a negligence case and a product liability case. The researcher must also understand the facts of the case at hand. Some facts are crucial to the case; others may not be important or have any legal significance.

What Is the Appropriate Search Terminology?

Knowing the legal terminology used in research materials is critical. The indexes of printed research materials use words selected by the editors of the publishing company. Different publishers do not always use the same words or legal terms to index the same rules of law. For example, one publisher may use the term "infant" to identify people under the age of majority, while another publisher uses the term "minor." If the researcher is presented with the question, "What are the contract rights of a person under the age of majority?", using "minor" to search an index in one source will not produce the desired results if that source's publisher listed the information under "infant."

Computer research is not dependent on using the terms selected by the publishers in an index. Most computer research allows for searches of words found in the documents themselves using a **search query,** in which the computer looks through the entire document for every instance of the selected words.

Search query Specific words used in a computerized search.

It is also important to keep in mind the differences in terminology used in legal and factual research. Finding cases and statutes requires the use of the legal terminology used by the courts, legal professionals, and authors of legal treatises. However, these words and phrases may not be the most useful in locating factual information on the Internet or elsewhere. For example, whereas the term "infant" is often used by legal texts to describe those under the age of majority, this term may not be useful for finding information on underage drinking in newspaper articles. Or, statutes may use the expression "driving under the influence," while newspaper articles may use the terms "drunk driving" or "driving while intoxicated."

What Type of Research Material Is Available?

Traditionally, the law library has consisted of books in paper form such as case reporters, legal encyclopedias, legal dictionaries, and a host of finding tools such as paper card indexes and digests. Increasingly, law libraries are replacing books with online computer services such as Westlaw, Lexis, and Loislaw. Others combine traditional paper-based materials with electronic research tools.

Paralegal students who have grown up in the era of online research frequently ask why they need to learn how to use a traditional "paper" law library. One reason is that in the working world, not every office has access to all the latest computer resources. Lawyers continue to be faced with situations where they are trying a case out of town or in a different courthouse and need to check an unexpected case or statute, only to find that online resources are unavailable in that location. In some cases, the available online resources may not provide much older case law that, while old, is still good law or is valid "precedent" for current cases.

Frequently, paralegals accompany the lawyer to court. During the trial, they may be asked to slip out of the courtroom and conduct a quick bit of legal research. In some courthouses, a public computer terminal is not available in the law library, laptop computers cannot be connected to outgoing phone lines for security reasons, and cell phones are held at the security desk. In these situations, the paralegal must conduct the research quickly and accurately using traditional book methods. In short, the paralegal must be able to find the information needed when the familiar resources are not available.

What Jurisdictions Are Involved?

Research may involve federal, state, or local law. Some questions point to a certain jurisdiction—for example, "What is the age of majority in Florida?" At other times, the jurisdiction is not as clear: "What law controls the situation of an unruly passenger on a flight from Los Angeles to Philadelphia?" Here the paralegal must consider jurisdictional issues related to California, Pennsylvania, and federal statutes. Or consider the case of the driver from Georgia who is driving a truck belonging to a South Carolina company and has an accident in Alabama. The legal team working on that case might want to know the law in each jurisdiction before deciding where to file suit. Determining at the outset the appropriate jurisdictions to be searched reduces the number of books that must be searched and reduces the amount of online computer search time needed.

What Is the Controlling Law?

The controlling law is found in primary sources—statutes, regulations, and case law. Knowing which set of materials to use—the statutes of the jurisdiction, the regulations of a certain administrative agency, or the courts of a specific jurisdiction—will save time when doing the research. Irrelevant sources can be eliminated from consideration, and the source of the needed material can be located onsite or online. The controlling law may be narrowed to that of a local city, county, or parish, such as the municipal zoning ordinances or local plumbing code.

What Types of Resources Should Be Used?

Primary source of law The actual law itself.

Secondary source of law Writings about the law.

Finding tools Publications used to find primary and secondary sources.

Law libraries usually have both primary and secondary sources of the law. A **primary source** is the actual law itself, which consists of the statutes and the case law that are reprinted in the text. **Secondary sources** are not the laws themselves but, instead, are writings about the law, such as legal encyclopedias and digests. A third set of resources is referred to as "finding tools"—publications, such as digests or the *Index to Legal Periodicals*, that are used to find primary and secondary sources. Frequently, sources contain both secondary sources and **finding tools** in one publication, such as the *American Law Reports*. Some services combine all three into one service or publication. Exhibit 12.1 delineates primary sources, secondary sources, and finding tools.

Ultimately, only primary sources of law are used in preparing a legal memorandum or brief. Secondary sources are useful, efficient ways to get an overview of an area of law or learn the terminology used in a certain field of law that the researcher is not familiar with. A torts specialist may suddenly be asked to research an issue related to a different area of law, such as negotiable instruments, and may be lost trying to remember the terminology and rules from courses taken long ago. Secondary sources such as legal encyclopedias can thus supply a quick review of that area and point the researcher to the appropriate primary sources, such as the commercial code of that state. Legal dictionaries frequently list cases that have defined certain legal terms and can also be a starting point for case research.

Exhibit 12.1 Research materials

Primary Sources	Secondary Sources	Finding Tools
Constitutions	Legal dictionaries	Digests
Statutes	Legal encyclopedias	Citators
Court decisions	Treatises	Indexes
Common-law cases	Law reviews	
Administrative regulations	Textbooks	
Ordinances	Legal periodicals	
Court rules		

Where Is the Needed Research Material Located?

It would be ideal to have a complete print and electronic library available onsite, such as the libraries at most law schools. However, law libraries are costly to acquire and maintain. The materials can run into the hundreds of dollars per volume, and the annual upkeep for pocket parts, supplemental volumes, and new case reporters is nearly as expensive. The availability of space is another factor. Office space is expensive, and as a library grows, more floor space must be used for books instead of people. Finally, the cost of filing the updates and keeping the space orderly must be considered. If the collection is large enough, a full-time librarian may be needed. In smaller offices, these tasks take up the time of paralegals, time that could better be spent performing billable services for clients.

These issues have spurred the adoption of electronic libraries such as the fee-based online services provided by Loislaw, Lexis, Westlaw, and VersusLaw, as well as the free online services provided by some colleges and universities such as the Cornell School of Law. Virtually all primary material is available online. Some proprietary secondary materials, such as encyclopedias, are not available from all sources. Depending on the resources needed to complete an assignment, the paralegal may have to locate the needed material at a remote library such as a bar association or a law school library.

Executing the Research Plan

After laying out a plan of action based on the preliminary questions in the assignment, the research plan can be executed. As with the execution of any plan, detours should be expected. The law is constantly evolving, as new statutes are enacted and new cases are handed down. During the research process, the researcher must look for changes or potential changes due to pending legislation and cases on appeal. Word lists and citations must be updated and new search paths followed.

The time spent initially in creating a list of search terms and phrases will save time when the research plan is executed. In looking for a statute, knowing the subject matter of the desired law, such as "blood alcohol level for driving," or the popular name of the law, such as "Sarbanes-Oxley," will save time by focusing the search on a specific statutory or popular name index.

The research plan should be executed in a systematic way using a checklist of the terms and research materials. Not every search term will result in a successful search. However, some search terms may lead to other search terms. When a circular search brings the researcher back to a previous result, this indicates a dead end, and the researcher must proceed on a more fruitful path.

The researcher must also keep a list of citations, both successful and unsuccessful, which should be continually updated as the research progresses. When the time comes to finalize the research in a written document, the researcher will have the citation references available and will not have to go back and find the material again. In the event of additional, similar research assignments, the researcher will also have a ready reference to pick up the search and proceed quickly, using relevant terms and citations.

Legislative branch The part of the government that makes law by enacting legislation. At the federal legal, the legislative branch is Congress (the Senate and the House of Representatives).

Finding the Law

Learning Objective 2

Explain the differences among primary resources, secondary resources, and finding tools.

Finding "the law" seems like it should be an easy thing to accomplish. We go to the original source and read it. But what is the original source, and how is it located in a modern law library?

Statutory law is found in the statutes and regulations passed by the **legislative branch** of government. Case law is found in court decisions of the **judicial branch.** In the United States, laws are created at the federal, state, and local levels. At the federal legislative level, laws are passed by the United States Congress, which is a **bicameral** legislative body—meaning that there are two legislative houses, the House of Representatives and the Senate. At the state government level, all of the state legislatures are bicameral except Nebraska's, which has only one legislative body. Local governing bodies include cities, towns, and boroughs. At the judicial level, both federal

Judicial branch The court system.

Bicameral In the American system, a legislature consisting of two bodies—usually a house of representatives and a senate.

CHECKLIST Research

Primary Sources	Secondary Sources
Case ☐ Name ☐ Citation	Encyclopedia—National ☐ Name ☐ Key or descriptive word
Federal statute ☐ Federal citation ☐ Popular name	Encyclopedia—State ☐ Name ☐ Key or descriptive word
State (name) ☐ State citation ☐ Popular name	Treatises ☐ Name ☐ Citation
Local jurisdiction name ☐ Local citation ☐ Popular name	Restatement of law ☐ Name ☐ Citation
Administrative regulations ☐ Federal agency name ☐ Citation	Periodicals ☐ Citation
State agency name ☐ Citation	Practice books ☐ Name ☐ Citation
Local agency name ☐ Citation	Dictionary ☐ Name
Constitution ☐ Federal citation ☐ State citation	Digest ☐ Name ☐ Citation

and state courts create case law through their court decisions. The law is also found in the regulations enacted by administrative agencies as a result of the authority granted to them by the legislative branch of government, whether federal, state, or local.

Usually, the assignment is to find the current controlling law. However, occasionally the research assignment is to find the law that was in control at a point in the past, such as what the blood alcohol limit was last year when the client was cited for driving under the influence.

When looking for the applicable law, we might start by asking:

- Is there a statute?
- Are there administrative regulations?
- Is there case law on point?

If there is a statute in the applicable jurisdiction, that statute will be controlling. Regulations enacted to enforce the statute will also be controlling, subject to compliance with the statutory authority under which they are enacted. Case law may also exist to clarify and explain the law based on the facts of the cases before the courts.

Primary Sources and Authority

Primary sources are the law. They include constitutions, both state and federal. Primary law includes statutes enacted by the legislative branch of government and the regulations of the administrative agencies established by the legislature to carry out the statutory enactments. Court rules and court decisions are sources of primary law from the judicial branch of government.

Mandatory and Persuasive Authority

Mandatory authority Court decisions that are binding on all lower courts.

Research should start with primary sources that are **mandatory authority.** Mandatory authority is legal authority that the courts must follow when making decisions. In

WHEN ARE COURT DECISIONS PRECEDENTS?

Courts issue published or unpublished opinions. A **published opinion** is a court's written explanation of its decision on a case, which is intended to be relied upon as a statement of the law based on the facts of the case. In some cases, the court will issue an informal statement of its ruling—an **unpublished opinion**—which is intended to apply only to the parties before the court and to the very narrow issue of the particular case based on the specific facts before the court. Unlike published opinions, the courts generally do not intend unpublished opinions to be used as precedent in other cases. However, it should be understood that unpublished opinions are not "secret" opinions. Many are available online, and others are available from the clerk's office.

There is some controversy with regard to the use of unpublished opinions in other court proceedings. The controversy has centered on the right of lawyers to use the unpublished opinions in arguments to the court. In reviewing the issue, the 8th Circuit Court of Appeals made the following observations:

> Before concluding, we wish to indicate what this case is not about. It is not about whether opinions should be published, whether that means printed in a book or available in some other accessible form to the public in general. Courts may decide, for one reason or another, that some of their cases are not important enough to take up pages in a printed report. Such decisions may be eminently practical and defensible, but in our view they have nothing to do with the authoritative effect of any court decision.
>
> The question presented here is not whether opinions ought to be published, but whether they ought to have precedential effect, whether published or not. We point out, in addition, that "unpublished" in this context has never meant "secret." So far as we are aware, every opinion and every order of any court in this country, at least of any appellate court, is available to the public. You may have to walk into a clerk's office and pay a per-page fee, but you can get the opinion if you want it. Indeed, most appellate courts now make their opinions, whether labeled "published" or not, available to anyone online.

Anastasoff v. U.S., 223 F. 3d 898 (8th cir. 2000).

Following the publication of the initial opinion, the court declared the issues in the case, which concerned the recovery of tax payments, as moot, since the taxpayer received her refund, stating,

> ...Here, the case having become moot, the appropriate and customary treatment is to vacate our previous opinion and judgment, remand to the District Court, and direct that Court to vacate its judgment as moot. We now take exactly that action. The constitutionality of that portion of Rule 28A(i) which says that unpublished opinions have no precedential effect remains an open question in this Circuit....

Anastasoff v. U.S., No. 99-3917EM, (8th Cir. Dec. 18, 2000).

The issue of using unpublished opinions has been resolved among federal courts with the passage of Federal Rule 32.1, Citing Judicial Dispositions, which permits the inclusion of those cases issued after January 1, 2007:

Rule 32.1. Citing Judicial Dispositions

(a) Citation Permitted. A court may not prohibit or restrict the citation of federal judicial opinions, orders, judgments, or other written dispositions that have been:

   (i) designated as "unpublished," "not for publication," "non-precedential," "not precedent," or the like; and
   (ii) issued on or after January 1, 2007.

(b) Copies Required. If a party cites a federal judicial opinion, order, judgment, or other written disposition that is not available in a publicly accessible electronic database, the party must file and serve a copy of that opinion, order, judgment, or disposition with the brief or other paper in which it is cited.

addition to statutes and administrative regulations and ordinances, mandatory authority includes case law from higher courts. The highest court in the United States is the United States Supreme Court. The decisions of the Supreme Court are mandatory for all lesser federal and state courts. The decisions of the highest appellate court of a state are mandatory authority for all lesser courts of that state.

If mandatory authority cannot be found, the researcher should search for **persuasive authority,** which is authority the courts are not required to follow, but is from a respected source and is well reasoned. Decisions of some state courts traditionally have been looked at as being so well reasoned that courts in other states have been persuaded to follow that legal reasoning in deciding cases for their own state when they did not have any previously decided cases or statutes on point.

Published opinion A court's written explanation of its decision on a case intended to be relied upon as a statement of the law based on the facts of the case.

Unpublished opinions Cases that the court does not feel have precedential effect and are limited to a specific set of facts.

Persuasive authority Court decisions the court is not required to follow but are well reasoned and from a respected court.

Web Exploration

View a high-resolution version of the original copy of the U.S. Constitution at **www.archives.gov**.

A good example of a persuasive opinion is that of Justice Cardozo in the New York Court of Appeals case of *Palsgraf v. Long Island Railroad Company*, 248 N.Y. 339, 192 N.E. 99 (N.Y. 1928) (see Appendix A, "How To Brief a Case"). Many courts, even today, find the logic and reasoning of Justice Cardozo in *Palsgraf* to be persuasive, and the case is frequently quoted by courts in other states.

Constitutions

The United States Constitution is the ultimate primary law that sets the guidelines, limits, and authority of federal and state governments. The state constitutions are the ultimate law for the individual states, and they set the guidelines, limits, and authority of the government and the local governing bodies of that state. The constitutions are primary sources—the original or primary source of law.

Finding a section of the U.S. Constitution is probably the easiest task in legal research. This document is reproduced in many publications, including many textbooks, is available in virtually every public library, and is easily available on the Internet from many sources, including the National Archives. Finding the Constitution for individual states, however, is not as easy. Although some are posted on general-interest websites, most require access to specialty legal research websites, or to the paper version, generally found in the bound volumes of the state statutes.

Statutes

Web Exploration

Read the latest U.S. Supreme Court opinion at **http://www.supremecourtus.gov**.
Visit the homepage of the Legal Information Institute at Cornell University Law School to see the information provided at **www.cornell.lii.edu**.

Statutes enacted by the legislative branch of government are primary sources of the law. The statute of the United States—the *United States Code*—is available online from a number of free sources, including the U.S. Government Printing Office. Many states currently make their state statutes available online through an official state website. Until a few years ago, this free-access source was generally limited to state legislators. However, web-based resources should be used with caution. Some unofficial sites appear to be an "official" primary source of the law, but in reality are not complete or up-to-date.

Court Decisions

Web Exploration

Search and view the full text of Supreme Court decisions issued between 1937 and 1975 at **http://supcourt.ntis.gov/**.

Court decisions are also primary authority. The U.S. Supreme Court and some federal courts provide their current opinions and decisions online. Notably, the Legal Information Institute at Cornell University provides free access to the U.S. Supreme Court opinions, as well as those of many other courts. But many court decisions generally are not available from free web sources and require the use of a paid subscription or fee-based services such as Lexis, Westlaw, Loislaw, and VersusLaw. Exhibit 12.2 shows the homepage of U.S. Courts with judiciary links.

Bench opinion The initial version of a decision issued from the bench of the court.

Slip opinion A copy of the opinion sent to the printer.

Case syllabus In a court opinion, a headnote for the convenience of the reader.

Headnotes The syllabus or summary of the points of law prepared by the editorial staff of a publisher.

Courts such as the U.S. Supreme Court issue opinions from the "bench" called **bench opinions.** A **slip opinion** is then sent for printing. This second version may contain corrections to the bench opinion. See the U.S. Supreme Court comments on the difference in Exhibit 12.3.

Within cases, the court's actual language is the primary source of the law. However, the **case syllabus,** summaries, interpretations, or abstracts of the points of law presented by the editorial staff of the publishers of the case law, usually called **headnotes,** are *not* the primary source of law. Rather, they are explanations, interpretations, or comments that help the reader understand the legal concepts. As such, they are secondary sources. Note the cautionary comment in the syllabus of the Supreme Court case in Exhibit 12.4. Contrast the syllabus of the case with the opinion of the court in Exhibit 12.5.

Legal dictionaries and encyclopedias also use headnotes—short, single-concept definitions and summaries—to provide basic information. When doing research, it should be kept in mind that these short "snippets" are taken out of the context of the case in which they were presented. None of the factual or procedural background is given in the headnote describing how the decision came about.

Taking court statements out of the context of the case in which they appeared, and relying on case headnotes or summaries, can present many problems for the

Exhibit 12.2 U.S. Courts website

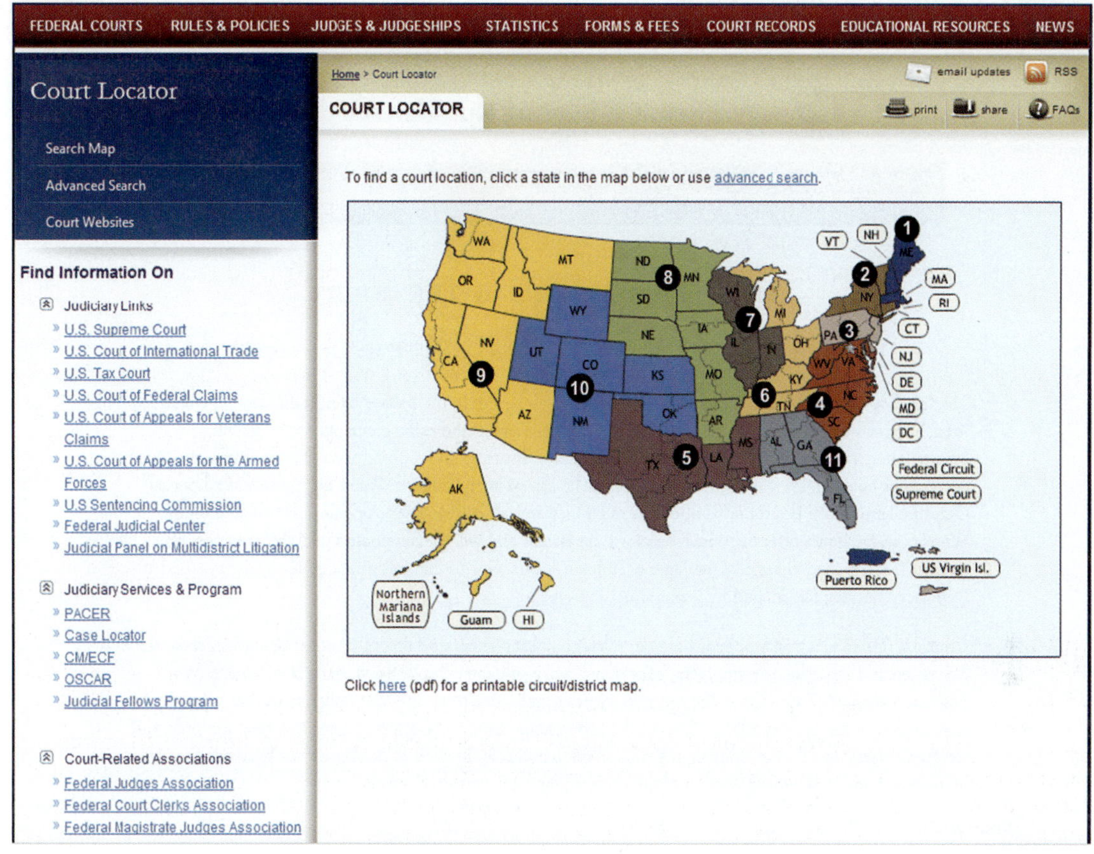

Source: Administrative Office of the U.S. Courts, Washington, D.C.

researcher—the most obvious of which is accuracy. Was the headnote or summary copied correctly from the final version of the opinion? Judges have been known to correct errors in the language of opinions. Did the editor writing the note use the final version of the opinion? More importantly—does the statement accurately reflect the majority view, or does it reflect a minority or dissenting view? Was it the actual decision on the point of law before the court, therefore having the precedential weight of a "**holding**" of the court? Or was it merely **dicta**—comments having no precedential authority because it was not related directly to the court decision? Contrast the headnote and the full court opinion in the case in Exhibit 12.6.

Holding The actual decision on the specific point of law the court was asked to decide.

Dicta Court comments on issues not directly related to the holding and therefore not having precedential effect.

Doing legal research requires finding the most current and accurate statement of the legislative enactments and of the court. Presenting editorial headnotes, judges' dicta, or a dissenting opinion as current and accurate legal authority is a potential career-ending act. The members of your legal team may rely on the potentially erroneous statements to prepare the case and their prosecution or defense strategy based on the inaccurate information. Notwithstanding the potential effect on the outcome of the case, it may result in a severe reprimand or dismissal from employment.

Presenting erroneous information to the court is also an ethical violation of the duty of candor toward the tribunal under Rule 3.3 of the Model Rules of Professional Conduct. It does not matter to the court that it was prepared by someone other than the attorney presenting the case, the brief, or the oral argument; it is treated as a breach of the duty of candor to the court by the attorney.

This is not to say that dissenting opinions and dicta may not be used when presenting an argument to the court. Although this material is not binding authority, it may have persuasive value in making an argument. Many of the finest jurists have issued

Exhibit 12.3 Supreme Court explanation on differences between bench and slip opinions

2005 TERM OPINIONS OF THE COURT

Slip Opinions, *Per Curiams* (PC), and Original Case Decrees (D)

The "slip" opinion is the second version of an opinion. It is sent to the printer later in the day on which the "bench" opinion is released by the Court. Each slip opinion has the same elements as the bench opinion--majority or plurality opinion, concurrences or dissents, and a prefatory syllabus--but may contain corrections not appearing in the bench opinion. The slip opinions collected here are those issued during October Term 2005 (October 3, 2005, through October 1, 2006). These opinions are posted on this Website within hours after the bench opinions are issued and will remain posted until the opinions are published in a bound volume of the United States Reports. For further information, see Column Header Definitions and the file entitled Information About Opinions.

Caution: These electronic opinions may contain computer-generated errors or other deviations from the official printed slip opinion pamphlets. Moreover, a slip opinion is replaced within a few months by a paginated version of the case in the preliminary print, and--one year after the issuance of that print--by the final version of the case in a U. S. Reports bound volume. In case of discrepancies between the print and electronic versions of a slip opinion, the print version controls. In case of discrepancies between the slip opinion and any later official version of the opinion, the later version controls.

Source: Supreme Court of the United States.

Exhibit 12.4 Sample of U.S. Supreme Court syllabus

Syllabus

NOTE: Where it is feasible, a syllabus (headnote) will be released, as is being done in connection with this case, at the time the opinion is issued.
The syllabus constitutes no part of the opinion of the Court but has been prepared by the Reporter of Decisions for the convenience of the reader.
See United States v. Detroit Timber & Lumber Co., 200 U.S. 321, 337.

SUPREME COURT OF THE UNITED STATES

ROPER, SUPERINTENDENT, POTOSI CORRECTIONAL CENTER v. SIMMONS

CERTIORARI TO THE SUPREME COURT OF MISSOURI

No. 03—633.Argued October 13, 2004-Decided March 1, 2005

At age 17, respondent Simmons planned and committed a capital murder. After he had turned 18, he was sentenced to death. His direct appeal and subsequent petitions for state and federal postconviction relief were rejected. This Court then held, in *Atkins* v. *Virginia*, 536 U.S. 304, that the Eighth Amendment, applicable to the States through the Fourteenth Amendment, prohibits the execution of a mentally retarded person. Simmons filed a new petition for state postconviction relief, arguing that *Atkins'* reasoning established that the Constitution prohibits the execution of a juvenile who was under 18 when he committed his crime. The Missouri Supreme Court agreed and set aside Simmons' death sentence in favor of life imprisonment without eligibility for release. It held that, although *Stanford* v. *Kentucky*, 492 U.S. 361, rejected the proposition that the Constitution bars capital punishment for juvenile offenders younger than 18, a national consensus has developed against the execution of those offenders since *Stanford*.

Held: The Eighth and Fourteenth Amendments forbid imposition of the death penalty on offenders who were under the age of 18 when their crimes were committed. Pp. 6–25.

(a) The Eighth Amendment's prohibition against "cruel and unusual punishments" must be interpreted according to its text, by considering history,

Source: Supreme Court of the United States.

Exhibit 12.5 Sample opinion of the U.S. Supreme Court

Opinion of the Court

NOTICE: This opinion is subject to formal revision before publication in the preliminary print of the United States Reports.Readers are requested to notify the Reporter of Decisions, Supreme Court of the United States, Washington, D. C. 20543, of any typographical or other formal errors, in order that corrections may be made before the preliminary print goes to press.

SUPREME COURT OF THE UNITED STATES

No. 03–633

DONALD P. ROPER, SUPERINTENDENT, POTOSI CORRECTIONAL CENTER, PETITIONER v. CHRISTOPHER SIMMONS

ON WRIT OF CERTIORARI TO THE SUPREME COURT OF MISSOURI

[March 1, 2005]

Justice Kennedy delivered the opinion of the Court.

This case requires us to address, for the second time in a decade and a half, whether it is permissible under the Eighth and Fourteenth Amendments to the Constitution of the United States to execute a juvenile offender who was older than 15 but younger than 18 when he committed a capital crime. In *Stanford* v. *Kentucky*, 492 U.S. 361 (1989), a divided Court rejected the proposition that the Constitution bars capital punishment for juvenile offenders in this age group. We reconsider the question.

I

At the age of 17, when he was still a junior in high school, Christopher Simmons, the respondent here, committed murder. About nine months later, after he had turned 18, he was tried and sentenced to death. There is little doubt that Simmons was the instigator of the crime. Before its commission Simmons said he wanted to murder someone. In chilling, callous terms he talked about his plan, discussing it for the most part with two friends, Charles Benjamin and John Tessmer, then aged 15 and 16 respectively. Simmons proposed to commit burglary and murder by breaking and entering, tying up a

Source: Supreme Court of the United States.

dissenting views that eventually became the law in future cases. And dicta in another case may well be a valid argument in the present case being decided. The researcher's duty is to make clear whether the information is binding or persuasive authority. Sometimes it is not clear whether something is binding authority, as stated by one court:

> What exactly constitutes "dicta" is hotly contested and judges often disagree about what is or is not dicta in a particular case. See *United States v. Johnson*, 256 F.3d 895, 914–16 (9th Cir. 2001) (en banc) (Kozinski, J., concurring). In Johnson, Judge Kozinski explained that, "where a panel confronts an issue germane to the eventual resolution of the case, and resolves it after reasoned consideration in a published opinion, that ruling becomes the law of the circuit, regardless of whether doing so is necessary in some strict logical sense." Id. at 914; accord *Cetacean Cmty. v. Bush*, 386 F.3d 1169,1173 (9th Cir. 2004) (quoting Johnson); *Miranda B. v. Kitzhaber*, 328 F.3d 1181, 1186 (9th Cir. 2003) (per curiam) (same).
>
> Only "[w]here it is clear that a statement is made casually and without analysis, where the statement is uttered in passing without due consideration of the alternatives, or where it is merely a prelude to another legal issue that commands the panel's full attention, it may be appropriate to re-visit the issue in a later case." Johnson, 256 F.3d at 915. Nevertheless, "any such reconsideration should be done cautiously and rarely—only where the later panel is convinced that the earlier panel did not make a deliberate decision to adopt the rule of law it announced." Id. If, however, "it is clear that a majority of the panel has focused on the legal issue presented by the case before it and made

Exhibit 12.6 Regional reporter sample page

Reference to Volume and Name of Reporter

Case Name

COM. v. ZAENGLE

Cite as 497 A.2d 1335 (Pa.Super. 1985)

Pa. 1335 ← Reporter Page Number

COMMONWEALTH of Pennsylvania
v.
John Stephen ZAENGLE, Appellant.
Superior Court of Pennsylvania.
Argued April 3, 1984.
Date of Opinion → Filed Aug. 16, 1985.

Beginning of West's Editor Summary → Defendant was convicted in the Court of Common Pleas, Criminal Division, Cumberland County, No. 886 Criminal 1982, Keller, J., of one count of driving while under the influence and three counts of homicide by vehicle, and he appealed his sentences. The Superior Court remanded for resentencing, 332 Pa.Super. 137, 480 A.2d 1224, and State appealed. The Supreme Court, 497 A.2d 1330, remanded for proceedings consistent with *Commonwealth v. Frisbie*. The Superior Court, No. 175 Harrisburg 1983, Olszewski, J., held that imposing multiple sentences upon defendant for the multiple deaths which resulted from his single violation of the homicide by vehicle statute was permissible.

End of Summary → Sentences reinstated.

West Digest Topic and Corresponding West Key Number → Criminal Law 984(7)

Legislature authorized multiple sentences for multiple deaths resulting from a single violation of homicide by vehicle statute, 75 Pa.C.S.A. § 3732.

Lawyers →

Taylor P. Andrews, Public Defender, Carlisle, for appellant.

Kevin A. Hess, Asst. Dist. Atty., Carlisle, for Commonwealth, appellee. ← Lawyers

Before WICKERSHAM, OLSZEWSKI, AND HOFFMAN, JJ. ← Judges Who Heard Case

OLSZEWSKI, Judge:

By order of the Supreme Court, 497 A.2d 1330, this case has been remanded for proceedings consistent with *Commonwealth v. Frisbie*, 506 Pa. 461, 485 A.2d 1098 (1984). *Frisbie* holds that, where legislatively authorized, the imposition of multiple sentences upon a defendant whose single unlawful act injures multiple victims is legal. In the instant case, appellee driving drunk killed three people. The test of legislative authorization under *Frisbie* looks to the language of the statute defining the offense. *See id.* at 466, 485 A.2d at 1100 (comparing the language of 18 Pa.C.S. Sec 2705 with that of 18 Pa.C.S. Sec. 2707 and 2710). The operative language in 75 Pa.C.S. Sec. 3732 penalizes "(a)ny person who unintentionally causes *the death of another person*." (Emphasis added.) Applying the *Frisbie* analysis to the facts of this case, we conclude that the legislature did authorize multiple sentences for multiple deaths resulting from a single violation of 75 Pa.C.S. Sec. 3732. Accord *Commonwealth v. Zaengle*, 332 Pa.Super. 137, 141, 480 A.2d 1224, 1228 (1984) (Olszewski J., dissenting). ← Beginning of Court's Opinion

The sentences imposed by the trial court are reinstated.

---

a deliberate decision to resolve the issue, that ruling becomes the law of the circuit and can only be overturned by an en banc court or by the Supreme Court." Id. at 916; see also Cetacean Cmty., 386 F.3d at 1173; Miranda B., 328 F.3d at 1186.

This understanding of binding circuit authority was further articulated in *Barapind v. Enomoto*, 400 F.3d 744 (9th Cir. 2005) (en banc) (per curiam), where we said that when a panel has "addressed [an] issue and decided it in an opinion joined in relevant part by a majority of the panel," the panel's decision becomes "law of the circuit." Id. at 750-51 (footnote omitted).

Padilla v. Lever, No. 03-56259 (9th Cir. November 23, 2005)

Secondary Sources

Secondary sources explain the law. Trying to understand a new area of law can be difficult, and secondary sources are useful sources about the history of an area of law, the issues involved, and in some situations the direction the law may be taking. A secondary source may also be the editorial headnotes of a case or an in-depth scholarly interpretation, such as a treatise, a law review article, or an article in a scholarly journal or other periodical.

Legal Dictionaries

Legal dictionaries, as opposed to general English or other specialized dictionaries, define words and phrases as used in the law. The "law," as with most professions, trades, and occupations, has developed its own specialized vocabulary. Each specialized area of law also develops its own specialized terminology. Lawyers in specialty fields, such as antitrust law, use terms that have developed specialized meaning through case decisions. For example, in antitrust law, the term "tying arrangement" is used to describe the situation in which one product can be purchased only with another product. This term comes from the 1947 antitrust case of *International Salt v. United States*, 332 U.S. 392 (1947), which held that a patent is presumed to give the patent holder "market power" (another legal term), making it illegal to "tie the sale of the patented product to the sale of another." Without an understanding of the basic terminology and legal concepts, it is hard to conduct proper legal research using either traditional books or computer-based services. Exhibit 12.7 is a sample page from *Black's Law Dictionary* illustrating the term "tying."

Secondary Sources—Legal Encyclopedias

Legal encyclopedias, like legal dictionaries, can provide basic background and understanding of an area in order to start research. They can provide an overview of the concepts and history of an area of law, the basic legal issues involved, and the terminology. The annotations (lists of case citations) can also provide a starting point for case law research. National encyclopedias such as *Corpus Juris Secundum* (CJS) and *American Jurisprudence* (Am Jur) provide selected cases from all jurisdictions for reference and research. Exhibit 12.8 is a sample page from *American Jurisprudence.*

State-specific encyclopedias generally limit case references or citations to that jurisdiction. Where the research is on a new area of law for the jurisdiction, the national coverage may be preferable in order to find information on persuasive authority from other jurisdictions. Exhibit 12.9 is a sample page from *Corpus Juris Secundum.*

Exhibit 12.7 ***Black's Law Dictionary,* sample page**

confesses in open court. U.S. Const. Art. IV, § 2, cl. 2.

tying, *adj. Antitrust.* Of or relating to an arrangement whereby a seller sells a product to a buyer only if the buyer purchases another product from the seller <tying agreement>.

tying arrangement. *Antitrust.* **1.** A seller's agreement to sell one product or service only if the buyer also buys a different product or service. The product or service that the buyer wants to buy is known as the *tying product* or *tying service*; the different product or service that the seller insists on selling is known as the *tied product* or *tied service*. Tying arrangements may be illegal under the Sherman or Clayton Act if their effect is too anticompetitive. **2.** A seller's refusal to sell one product or service unless the buyer also buys a different product or service. — Also termed *tying agreement; tie-in; tie-in arrangement*. Cf. RECIPROCAL DEALING.

tying product. See TYING ARRANGEMENT (1).

tyranny, *n.* Arbitrary or despotic government; the severe and autocratic exercise of sovereign power, whether vested constitutionally in one ruler or usurped by that ruler by breaking down the division and distribution of governmental powers. — **tyrannical, tyrannous**, *adj.*

tyrant, *n.* A sovereign or ruler, legitimate or not, who wields power unjustly and arbitrarily to oppress the citizenry; a despot.

Source: Black's Law Dictionary, 7e, 1995. Reprinted with permission of Thomson/West Publishing.

Exhibit 12.8 *American Jurisprudence*, sample page

is infected with a contagious disease[90] or has been dangerously exposed to such a disease.[91]

§ 317. —Children infected with the AIDS virus

Acquired Immune Deficiency Syndrome (AIDS) disables victims of the disease by collapsing their immune systems, making them unable to fight infection.[92] State education authorities, rather than local school authorities, are the appropriate parties to promulgate regulations concerning the right of AIDS-infected children to attend public school, since the state's power to regulate on the issue, inferable from its broad grant of authority to supervise the schools, pre-empts any rights of local authorities under their statutory discretion to exclude children from school to prevent the spread of contagious disease.[93]

◆ *Caution:* State statutes and local health regulations concerning contagious diseases in general, which make no specific reference to AIDS, do not apply to the decision whether AIDS-infected students should be allowed to attend public school.[94]

Procedures for determining whether AIDS-infected children should be excluded from a public school have withstood a due process challenge, one court having upheld the constitutionality of a plan which provided for an impartial decision by a medical panel, proper notice, and the opportunity to call and cross-examine witnesses.[95] However, distinguishing between students known to be infected with AIDS and students who were unidentified carriers of AIDS-related complex or asymptomatic carriers is constitutionally unacceptable since the proposed exclusion from public school of only the known AIDS-infected children constitutes an equal protection violation.[96]

◆ *Practice Guide:* Numerous organizations, both medical and educational, have formulated guidelines on when AIDS carriers should be segregated from the rest of the population. In cases concerning the right of a student with AIDS to attend school, courts have received evidence of the guidelines

90. Kenney v. Gurley, 208 Ala. 623, 95 So. 34, 26 A.L.R. 813 (1923); Nutt v. Board of Education of City of Goodland, Sherman County, 128 Kan. 507, 278 P. 1065 (1929).

As to the right to public education, generally, see §§ 242 et seq.

Forms: Answer—Defense—School district providing home teaching to student with contagious or infectious disease pending determination whether student's attendance at school would be danger to others. 22 Am Jur Pl & Pr Forms (Rev), Schools, Form 182.

91. Bright v. Beard, 132 Minn. 375, 157 N.W. 501 (1916).

92. Board of Educ. of City of Plainfield, Union County v. Cooperman, 105 N.J. 587, 523 A.2d 655, 38 Ed. Law Rep. 607, 60 A.L.R.4th 1 (1987).

Law Reviews: AIDS in public schools: Resolved issues and continuing controversy, 24 J Law and Educ 1:69 (1995).

Students with AIDS: Protecting an infected child's right to a classroom education and developing a school's AIDS policy, 40 S Dakota LR 1:72 (1995).

93. Board of Educ. of City of Plainfield, Union County v. Cooperman, 105 N.J. 587, 523 A.2d 655, 38 Ed. Law Rep. 607, 60 A.L.R.4th 1 (1987).

94. District 27 Community School Bd. by Granirer v. Board of Educ. of City of New York, 130 Misc. 2d 398, 502 N.Y.S.2d 325, 32 Ed. Law Rep. 740 (Sup. Ct. 1986).

95. Board of Educ. of City of Plainfield, Union County v. Cooperman, 105 N.J. 587, 523 A.2d 655, 38 Ed. Law Rep. 607, 60 A.L.R.4th 1 (1987).

Forms: Complaint, petition, or declaration—To enjoin expulsion of student who tested positive for AIDS virus—By guardian. 22 Am Jur Pl & Pr Forms (Rev), Schools, Form 177.

96. District 27 Community School Bd. by Granirer v. Board of Educ. of City of New York, 130 Misc. 2d 398, 502 N.Y.S.2d 325, 32 Ed. Law Rep. 740 (Sup. Ct. 1986).

537

Source: American Jurisprudence, 2e, 2000. Reprinted with permission of Thomson/West Publishing.

Exhibit 12.9 Page from *Corpus Juris Secundum,* a legal encyclopedia

§§ 58–59 SOCIAL SECURITY 81 C.J.S.

individual who died fully insured,[65] and have physical or mental impairments which, under regulations promulgated for the purpose, are deemed to be of such severity as to preclude engaging in any gainful activity.[66] The requirements for obtaining disability benefits by such persons are more restrictive than requirements for the insured individual himself.[67] The physical impairment necessary to a finding of disability is placed on a level of severity to be determined administratively,[68] and the regulations adopted to carry out the statutory provisions have been upheld.[69]

A claim for disability is judged solely by medical criteria,[70] without regard to non-medical factors[71] such as age, education, and work experience,[72] in contrast to the considerations given to an insured individual's age, education, and work experience, in determining his ability to engage in substantial gainful activity, as discussed supra § 56. An individual cannot qualify for disability insurance benefits unless suffering from an impairment listed in the appendix to the regulations applicable to disabilities, or from one or more unlisted impairments that singly or in combination are the medical equivalent of a listed impairment.[73] The benefits are to be paid only for a disabling medical impairment,[74] and not simply for the inability to obtain employment.[75]

§ 59. Benefits of Disabled Child

A disabled child of an insured individual who is, or would have been, eligible for social security benefits, may be entitled to disability insurance benefits.

Research Note

Status as child eligible for benefits under statute generally is discussed supra § 41.

Library References

Social Security and Public Welfare ⟹123, 140.5.

Under the provisions of the Social Security Act,[76] disabled children of retired or disabled insured individuals, and of insured individuals who have died, may be paid benefits if they have been disabled since before they reached twenty-two years of age, and if they meet the other conditions of eligibility.[77] The purpose of the provision is to provide a measure of income and security to those who have lost a wage-earner on whom they depended,[78] or to provide support for the dependents of a disabled wage earner,[79] and not to replace only that support enjoyed by the child prior to the onset of disability.[80] The liberal perspective of the Act applies to the award of children's disability benefits.[81]

In order to be entitled to recover benefits under this provision, the child must have been disabled,[82] as defined elsewhere in the Act,[83] prior to attaining a specified age,[84] and must be un-

65. U.S.—Sullivan v. Weinberger, C.A. Ga., 493 F.2d 855, certiorari denied 95 S.Ct. 1958, 421 U.S. 967, 44 L.Ed.2d 455.

66. U.S.—Wokojance v. Weinberger, C. A.Ohio, 513 F.2d 210, certiorari denied 96 S.Ct. 106, 423 U.S. 856, 46 L.Ed.2d 82.

Hendrix v. Finch, D.C.S.C., 310 F. Supp. 513.

Baby sitting; domestic work
U.S.—Dixon v. Weinberger, C.A.Ga., 495 F.2d 202.

Time impairment manifest
U.S.—Sullivan v. Weinberger, C.A.Ga., 493 F.2d 855, certiorari denied 95 S.Ct. 1958, 421 U.S. 967, 44 L.Ed.2d 455.

67. U.S.—Wokojance v. Weinberger, C. A.Ohio, 513 F.2d 210, certiorari denied 96 S.Ct. 106, 423 U.S. 856, 46 L.Ed.2d 82.

Solis v. U. S. Secretary of Health, Ed. and Welfare, D.C.Puerto Rico, 372 F.Supp. 1223—Truss v. Richardson, D. C.Mich., 338 F.Supp. 741—Nickles v. Richardson, D.C.S.C., 326 F.Supp. 777.

68. U.S.—Gillock v. Richardson, D.C. Kan., 322 F.Supp. 354.

69. U.S.—Sullivan v. Weinberger, C.A. Ga., 493 F.2d 855, certiorari denied 95 S.Ct. 1958, 421 U.S. 967, 44 L.Ed.2d 455.

Gunter v. Richardson, D.C.Ark., 335 F.Supp. 907—Zanoviak v. Finch, D.C. Pa., 314 F.Supp. 1152—Frasier v. Finch, D.C.Ala., 313 F.Supp. 160, affirmed, C. A., 434 F.2d 597.

70. U.S.—Wokojance v. Weinberger, C. A.Ohio, 513 F.2d 210, certiorari denied 96 S.Ct. 106, 423 U.S. 856, 46 L.Ed.2d 82.

71. U.S.—Sullivan v. Weinberger, C.A. Ga., 493 F.2d 855, certiorari denied 95 S.Ct. 1958, 421 U.S. 967, 44 L.Ed.2d 455.

72. U.S.—Gillock v. Richardson, D.C. Kan., 322 F.Supp. 354.

73. U.S.—Wokojance v. Weinberger, C. A.Ohio, 513 F.2d 210, certiorari denied 96 S.Ct. 106, 423 U.S. 856, 46 L.Ed.2d 82.

Gillock v. Richardson, D.C.Kan., 322 F.Supp. 354—Hendrix v. Finch, D.C.S. C., 310 F.Supp. 513.

74. U.S.—Sullivan v. Weinberger, C.A. Ga., 493 F.2d 855, certiorari denied 95 S.Ct. 1958, 421 U.S. 967, 44 L.Ed.2d 455.

75. U.S.—Sullivan v. Weinberger, C.A. Ga., 493 F.2d 855, certiorari denied 95 S.Ct. 1958, 421 U.S. 967, 44 L.Ed.2d 455.

76. 42 U.S.C.A. § 402(d).

77. U.S.—Lowe v. Finch, D.C.Va., 297 F.Supp. 667—Blevins v. Fleming, D.C. Ark., 180 F.Supp. 287.

78. U.S.—Ziskin v. Weinberger, D.C. Ohio, 379 F.Supp. 124.

79. U.S.—Jimenez v. Weinberger, Ill., 94 S.Ct. 2496, 417 U.S. 628, 41 L.Ed.2d 363, appeal after remand, C.A., 523 F.2d 689, certiorari denied 96 S.Ct. 3200.

80. U.S.—Jimenez v. Weinberger, Ill., 94 S.Ct. 2496, 417 U.S. 628, 41 L.Ed.2d 363, appeal after remand, C.A., 523 F.2d 689, certiorari denied 96 S.Ct. 3200.

81. U.S.—Ziskin v. Weinberger, D.C. Ohio, 379 F.Supp. 124.

82. U.S.—Ziskin v. Weinberger, D.C. Ohio, 379 F.Supp. 124.

83. 42 U.S.C.A. § 423.

84. U.S.—Ziskin v. Weinberger, D.C. Ohio, 379 F.Supp. 124—Moon v. Richardson, D.C.Va., 345 F.Supp. 1182.

Source: From *Corpus Juris Secundum,* © The West Group, a Thomson Company. Reproduced with permission.

Treatises, Law Reviews, and Legal Periodicals

Some secondary sources are considered very authoritative, and may be of sufficient scholarly value to be persuasive to the court. For example, the treatise on Torts by Prosser is frequently used in arguments and is accepted as persuasive authority by most courts. In new areas of the law such as cyber law, or emerging and changing areas such as privacy rights, courts frequently welcome a well-reasoned scholarly article from a law review or other legal journal that makes a clear and convincing argument using thorough research and well-reasoned thought. In some instances, these articles are like the ***amicus curia*** briefs submitted to the court by interested parties that have no actual standing as a party but have a clear interest in the outcome.

Amicus curia Briefs submitted by interested parties, as "friends of the court," who do not have standing in the action.

Finding Tools

Finding tools are resources that help to "find" the law. Finding the right case, statute, or regulation can be difficult, particularly if it is a challenge to find the correct term or phrase to conduct the search. For example, West Publishing might use the phrase "Bills and Notes" and another publisher might use the term "holder" to refer to the same cases and material on negotiable instruments. In these instances, a finding tool may be a helpful resource.

Indexes are valuable finding tools. Among the more useful sets of indexes and **citators** are those that cross-reference material. Some indexes use the commonly used or popular name of a case or statute to provide the citation or reference to the original source. For example, the commonly used or popular name for the statement of rights read to criminal defendants when arrested is "Miranda Rights." Using a popular name index provides the citation to the case in which the U.S. Supreme Court established the reading of these rights to defendants: *Miranda v Arizona*, 384 U.S 436 (1966).

Citator An index of cases.

Legal digests provide lists of cases in subject topic format, with cases generally in chronological order from the earliest to the latest. Digests do not, however, offer the detailed analysis found in encyclopedias. Exhibit 12.10 is a sample page from *West's Digest*.

Personal Research Strategy

Over time, each paralegal develops his or her own personal search strategy, which may be adapted based on the nature of the problem, the issue to be researched, and the resources available. When the legal issue in an assignment is well defined and focuses on a specific case or statute, it may be possible to start with the original primary source. More likely, however, the research assignment will be less well defined and may only recite a set of facts describing the client's situation. A possible area of law may be suggested, such as "driving too fast for conditions," or "personal injury from an automobile accident." But the precise legal issue may not be defined.

In this situation, the facts must be used to determine the area of law. If the paralegal is unfamiliar with the area of law, the connection may not be obvious. Secondary sources provide a good reference source to acquire a general understanding about an area of law. As the paralegal learns more about the specifics of the area of law and the essential elements of its causes of actions, the applicable law should become clearer. One of the advantages of using the traditional book form of research is the ability to flip pages back and forth and scan many items that can lead to a specific point of law. This is sometimes referred to as "the serendipity of research."

Computer search engines can also lead to specific case law and statutes. The challenge is in how to construct the search query or question. If the researcher does not know what facts to include in the query, the resulting report may not be accurate. Computers, for the most part, are limited to finding only the things the search query specifically asks for. Learning the relevant facts to create the proper question may involve using the print resources first to determine the relevant facts or the proper terminology. For example, in a case of an alleged copyright violation under the fair-use doctrine, is the status of the alleged violator as a nonprofit organization relevant?

Exhibit 12.10 ***West's Federal Digest,* sample page**

CRIMINAL LAW

SUBJECTS INCLUDED

Acts and omissions in violation of law punishable as offenses against the public

Nature and elements of crime in general

Capacity to commit crime, nature and extent of responsibility therefore in general, and responsibility of principals, accessories, etc.

Jurisdiction over and place of prosecution of crimes

Limitation of time for prosecution

Preliminary complaints, warrants, examination and commitment

Arraignment and pleas

Evidence in criminal proceedings

Trial, and acquittal or conviction

Motions in arrest of judgment and for new trial

Judgment or sentence and final commitment

Review on appeal, writ of error or certiorari

Prosecution and punishment of successive offenses or of habitual criminals

Modes of punishment and prevention of crime in general

SUBJECTS EXCLUDED AND COVERED BY OTHER TOPICS

Arrest, see ARREST

Bail, see BAIL

Constitutional rights and privileges of accused not peculiar to matters within scope of this topic, see CONSTITUTIONAL LAW, INDICTMENT AND INFORMATION, JURY, SEARCHES AND SEIZURES, WITNESSES and other specific topics

Convicts, disabilities and regulation, see CONVICTS

Costs in criminal prosecutions, see COSTS

Extradition of fugitives, see EXTRADITION AND DETAINERS

Fines in general, see FINES

Grand juries and inquisitions by them, see GRAND JURY

Habeas corpus to obtain discharge from imprisonment, see HABEAS CORPUS

Included offenses, conviction under indictment for broader offense, see INDICTMENT AND INFORMATION

Indictments or other accusations, see INDICTMENT AND INFORMATION and specific topics relating to particular offenses

Injunction against commission of crime, see INJUNCTION

Judgment of acquittal, conviction or sentence, effect as adjudication, see JUDGMENT

Jury trial, right to and waiver, and qualifications and selection of jurors, see JURY

Juvenile offenders, special rules and proceedings, see INFANTS

Source: *Federal Digest, West's Federal Digest,* 4e. Reprinted with permission of Thomson/West Publishing.

Always verify that the law to be cited in the memorandum of law is current. Look for pending cases and legislation that might change the answer to the legal question. Look in legal journals, periodicals, and legal newspapers, as well as newspapers of general circulation for cases that are on appeal that involve the same legal issues. Check the legislative services for pending legislation that may have an impact on the case. Research that is concerned with giving clients advice on future actions may depend on knowing the changes that may change the basic parameters of the law. For example, should a smoking section be installed in a new restaurant if there is not yet an ordinance that prohibits smoking? Are the tax rates for estate planning going to change next year?

A Final Word on Executing the Legal Research Plan

This final piece of advice must be emphasized: *know when to ask for help*. Everyone on the legal team who has done legal research has hit a dead end at one time or another. Sometimes taking a few minutes to ask a question will yield the "magic" word, term, or phrase that will lead to the answer.

Using Printed Legal Reference Works

Most legal references have a set of common features. They generally have a section, usually in the introduction, that explains its coverage and how to use the book or service. This section typically includes the abbreviations used throughout the work (see Exhibit 12.11), and describes the method of pagination—for example, standard page numbering or section numbers. The table of contents (see Exhibit 12.12) also provides a general list of major topics. The index at the end provides the details of the coverage. Multivolume sets might have a separate set of volumes containing this index. Each volume might also contain an index for that specific volume.

Most of these legal reference works also contain a table of the cases that are mentioned in the text. This is a useful feature when a case seems to be relevant or on point, and the paralegal wants to see other cases on the same issue. A table of statutes may also be included to help the researcher find cases or discussions of a statute.

Exhibit 12.11 Sample list of abbreviations

ABBREVIATIONS

A. *Atlantic Reporter*
A.2d *Atlantic Reporter, Second Series*
Abb. *Abbott's Circuit Court Reports, U.S.*
Abb.Adm. *Abbott's Admiralty Reports, U.S.*
Adams L.J. *Adams County Legal Journal*
Add. *Addison's Reports*
Am.Dec. *American Decisions*
Am.L.J., N.S. *American Law Journal, New Series*
Am.L.J.,O.S. *American Law Journal, Hall's*
Am.L.Reg., N.S. *American Law Register, New Series*
Am.L.Reg., O.S. *American Law Register, Old Series*
Am.Rep. *American Reports*
Am.St.Rep. *American State Reports*
Ann.Cas. *American & English Annotated Cases*
Ashm. *Ashmead's Reports*
Baldw. *Baldwin's Reports, U.S.*
Beaver *Beaver County Legal Journal*
Ben. *Benedict's Reports, U.S.*
Berks *Berks County Legal Journal*
Binn. *Binney's Reports*
Binns' Just. *Binns' Justice*
Biss. *Bissell's Reports, U.S.*
Black *Black's United States Supreme Court Reports*
Blair *Blair County Law Reports*
Blatchf.C.C. *Blatchford's Reports, U.S.*
Bond *Bond's Reports, U.S.*
B.R. *Bankruptcy reports*
Bright.E.C. *Brightly's Election Cases*
Bright.N.P. *Brightly's Nisi Prius Reports*
Browne *P.A. Browne's reports*
Brock. *Brockenbrough's Reports, U.S.*
Bucks *Bucks County Law Reporter*
C.A. *United States Court of Appeals*
C.C.A. *United States Circuit Court of Appeals*
Cambria *Cambria County Legal Journal*
Cambria C.R. *Cambria County Reports*
Camp. *Campbell's Legal Gazette Reports*
Cent. *Central Reporter*
C.C. *(see Pa.C.C.) County Court Reports*
Chest. *Chester County Reports*

Source: From *Purdon's Pennsylvania Statutes Annotated,* © 1994 by West Group, a Thomson Company. Reproduced with permission.

Exhibit 12.12 Sample table of contents

Source: From *Pennsylvania Estate Planning and Drafting, 2/E,* by Robert J. Weinberg. © George T. Bisel Company, Inc. Reproduced by permission.

Web Explorations

VersusLaw Research Manual: **https://server.iad.liveperson.net/hc/s-65442687/cmd/kbresource/kb-5427540797510340552/front_page!PAGETYPE?category=8**
Lexis: **www.lexisnexis.com/**
Westlaw: **www.westlaw.com/about/**
VersusLaw: **www.versuslaw.com**
Loislaw: **www.loislaw.com**

Pocket parts An update to a book that is a separate document that slips into a pocket in the back of the main volume.

Learning Objective 3
Create a search query.

Updates

Print material is updated in a number of ways. One of the most frequent methods is the use of **pocket parts,** so called because they are slipped into a pocket in the back of the hard-cover volume. Usually these are annual updates, but they may also be produced more or less frequently, depending on the publisher and the need for updates. Materials may also be updated by supplemental pamphlets, which are usually paperbacks. Updates may be issued monthly, quarterly, annually, or semi-annually.

It is essential that the pocket part or supplement be consulted every time a primary source is used. In statutory research, for example, the main volumes may be many years old, and sections of the law may have been amended or repealed. The pocket parts or other supplements, not the main volume, contain the latest information. For this reason, some researchers look at the pocket part before consulting the main volume. More and more frequently, additional updates are provided online. The paralegal must learn how each resource is updated and the frequency of the updates. Exhibit 12.13 is a sample pocket part supplement.

Constructing a Computer Search Query

Successful computer research requires the use of appropriate search words in a search query. In the English language, some words have different meanings in different contexts, or to different groups or professions. For example, the word "head" usually means the top of a person's body. But to a sailor, it means a bathroom. To a bartender, it means the foam at the top of a beverage.

As with any profession, the legal profession also has its own vocabulary. This includes words defined by the courts over the years to have specific meanings when used in a legal context. For example, in commercial law, the definition of the term "holder" is "a person to whom a negotiable instrument has been properly negotiated." To the layperson, the term may mean people holding something in their hands—not necessarily a negotiable instrument, or holding something with any legal formality attached to it.

People in all areas of life develop words and phrases that help them understand their fields of interest. In creating laws, legislatures use language in special ways that may not be clear to laypersons or even to legal researchers who are not accustomed to the terminology of the lawmakers. The editors who create indexes to legal reference tools also have their own vocabulary and methods of indexing material. For example, West Publishing Company editors originally created the index of 450 West Digest Topics for indexing cases published in case reporters (see Exhibit 12.14).

Finding print materials requires that the paralegal understand what items are included under each index classification. The word "holder," for example, is listed in the West Digest index under "Statutes," but the word "holder," as defined above, is also found under the West Digest Topic "Bills and Notes." *Black's Law Dictionary* defines the same word in the language of the negotiable instrument law. Using the West Topic heading "Bills and Notes" and "holder" in some computer searches of conventional Westlaw products will not return cases of negotiable instrument holders. But using the terms "negotiable instrument" and "holder" as the search words in a computer search will yield the desired result. Because paralegals cannot be sure whether the research will be done using a traditional paper library or a computer search or, if online, which particular online research service, they must understand how each resource organizes the information.

Knowing how to use both traditional and computer methods, and recognizing the strengths and weaknesses of each system, are important in conducting searches. Traditional research may be a better option when general background research is needed or when the paralegal isn't familiar with an area of law. Indexing systems are grouped by concept, and once paralegals get into the right area of law, they can browse easily. The ability to flip pages back and forth when they are generally in the right area is particularly helpful in statutory research, as many of the computer-based systems perform that task slowly, if at all—and that is assuming the paralegal can figure out how the index has been developed to create the computer search term.

ELECTRONIC SEARCHING STRATEGY

SIDEBAR

Searching is a process, not an event. . . . Searching a library is not about spending time and mental energy formulating the "golden query" that retrieves your desired information in a single stroke. In practice, good online searching involves formulating a succession of queries until you are satisfied with the results. As you view results from one search, you'll come across additional leads that you did not identify in your original search. You can incorporate these new terms into your existing query or create a new one. After each query, evaluate its success by asking:

- Did I find what I was looking for?
- What better information could still be out there?
- How can I refine my query to find better information?

Issuing multiple queries can be frustrating or rewarding, depending on how long it takes you to identify the key material you need to answer your research problem.

Source: CASELAW

Exhibit 12.13 Sample pocket part supplement

13 Pa.C.S.A. § 1105 **COMMERCIAL CODE**

DIVISION 1
GENERAL PROVISIONS

CHAPTER 11

SHORT TITLE, CONSTRUCTION, APPLICATION AND SUBJECT MATTER OF TITLE

§ 1105. Territorial application of title; power of parties to choose applicable law

Notes of Decisions

Bankruptcy 6

1. In general

In re Eagle Enterprises, Inc., Bkrtcy.E.D.Pa. 1998, 223 B.R. 290, [main volume] affirmed 237 B.R. 269.

2. Law governing

When parties agree to apply foreign law, pursuant to which their contract to "lease" goods kept in Pennsylvania will be deemed a true "lease," despite fact that contract does not permit lessor to terminate agreement but affords him an option to purchase goods for nominal consideration, Pennsylvania law will not give effect to that choice. In re Eagle Enterprises, Inc., E.D.Pa.1999, 237 B.R. 269.

4. Third parties

In re Eagle Enterprises, Inc., Bkrtcy.E.D.Pa. 1998, 223 B.R. 290, [main volume] affirmed 237 B.R. 269.

6. Bankruptcy

While Chapter 7 debtor and equipment lessor were generally free, under Pennsylvania statute, to agree what law would govern their rights and duties, debtor and equipment lessor could not impose their choice of law on Chapter 7 trustee, as party who never agreed to choice-of-law provision, in order to prevent trustee from challenging parties' characterization, as equipment "lease," of agreement which required debtor to pay alleged rent throughout full term of lease, and which then allowed debtor to acquire equipment at end of lease for nominal consideration of one dollar, merely because lease would allegedly have been recognized as true lease under law of foreign country that parties chose to govern their agreement. In re Eagle Enterprises, Inc., E.D.Pa.1999, 237 B.R. 269.

CHAPTER 12

GENERAL DEFINITIONS AND PRINCIPLES OF INTERPRETATION

§ 1201. General definitions

Notes of Decisions

11. Lease or lease intended as security

Under Pennsylvania law, "lease" transaction in which "lessee" cannot terminate "lease" during its term, but may thereafter become owner of "leased" goods for no additional or nominal additional consideration, does not create lease, but rather a security interest. In re Eagle Enterprises, Inc., E.D.Pa.1999, 237 B.R. 269.

When parties agree to apply foreign law, pursuant to which their contract to "lease" goods kept in Pennsylvania will be deemed a true "lease," despite fact that contract does not permit lessor to terminate agreement but affords him an option to purchase goods for nominal consideration, Pennsylvania law will not give effect to that choice. In re Eagle Enterprises, Inc., E.D.Pa.1999, 237 B.R. 269.

13. Security interest

Revised Pennsylvania statute defining term "security interest" seeks to correct shortcomings of its predecessor by focusing inquiry of lease/security interest analysis on economics of the transaction, rather than on intent of the parties. In re Kim, Bkrtcy.E.D.Pa.1999, 232 B.R. 324.

Whether, under Pennsylvania law, lease or security interest is created by a particular transaction is no longer within exclusive control of the parties and subject to possible manipulation through artful document drafting; rather, issue is to be determined by reference to uniform criteria set forth in revised statute defining term "security interest." In re Kim, Bkrtcy.E.D.Pa.1999, 232 B.R. 324.

In determining whether debtor's lease was a disguised security interest or a true lease under Pennsylvania law, bankruptcy court was required to consider entire "transaction" and was not constrained to look solely to documents signed by the parties which were designated "lease" or which made use of terms commonly found in leases, but could examine both parol and extrin-

4

Source: From *Purdon's Pennsylvania Consolidated Statutes Annotated, 2001 Cumulative Annual Pocket Part.*

Exhibit 12.14 West Digest Topics and their numerical designations

No.	Topic
1	Abandoned and Lost Property
2	Abatement and Revival
4	Abortion and Birth Control
5	Absentees
6	Abstracts of Title
7	Accession
8	Accord and Satisfaction
9	Account
10	Account, Action on
11	Account Stated
11a	Accountants
12	Acknowledgment
13	Action
14	Action on the Case
15	Adjoining Landowners
15a	Administrative Law and Procedure
16	Admiralty
17	Adoption
18	Adulteration
19	Adultery
20	Adverse Possession
21	Affidavits
23	Agriculture
24	Aliens
25	Alteration of Instruments
26	Ambassadors and Consuls
27	Amicus Curiae
28	Animals
29	Annuities
30	Appeal and Error
31	Appearance
33	Arbitration
34	Armed Services
35	Arrest
36	Arson
37	Assault and Battery
38	Assignments
40	Assistance, Writ of
41	Associations
42	Assumpsit, Action of
43	Asylums
44	Attachment
45	Attorney and Client
46	Attorney General
47	Auctions and Auctioneers
48	Audita Querela
48a	Automobiles
48b	Aviation
49	Bail
50	Bailment
51	Bankruptcy
52	Banks and Banking
54	Beneficial Associations
55	Bigamy
56	Bills and Notes
58	Bonds
59	Boundaries
60	Bounties
61	Breach of Marriage Promise
62	Breach of the Peace
63	Bribery
64	Bridges
65	Brokers
66	Building and Loan Associations
67	Burglary
68	Canals
69	Cancellation of Instruments
70	Carriers
71	Cemeteries
72	Census
73	Certiorari
74	Champerty and Maintenance
75	Charities
76	Chattel Mortgages
76a	Chemical Dependents
76h	Children Out-of-Wedlock
77	Citizens
78	Civil Rights
79	Clerks of Courts
80	Clubs
81	Colleges and Universities
82	Collision
83	Commerce
83h	Commodity Futures Trading Regulation
84	Common Lands
85	Common Law
88	Compounding Offenses
89	Compromise and Settlement
89a	Condominium
90	Confusion of Goods
91	Conspiracy
92	Constitutional Law
92b	Consumer Credit
92h	Consumer Protection
93	Contempt
95	Contracts
96	Contribution
97	Conversion
98	Convicts
99	Copyrights and Intellectual Property
100	Coroners
101	Corporations
102	Costs
103	Counterfeiting
104	Counties
105	Court Commissioners
106	Courts (see also Topic 170b Federal Courts)
107	Covenant, Action of
108	Covenants
108a	Credit Reporting Agencies
110	Criminal Law
111	Crops
113	Customs and Usages
114	Customs Duties
115	Damages
116	Dead Bodies
117	Death
117g	Debt, Action of
117t	Debtor and Creditor
118a	Declaratory Judgment
119	Dedication
120	Deeds
122a	Deposits and Escrows
123	Deposits in Court
124	Descent and Distribution
125	Detectives
126	Detinue
129	Disorderly Conduct
130	Disorderly House
131	District and Prosecuting Attorneys
132	District of Columbia
133	Disturbance of Public Assemblage
134	Divorce
135	Domicile
135h	Double Jeopardy
136	Dower and Curtesy
137	Drains
138	Drugs and Narcotics
141	Easements
142	Ejectment
143	Election of Remedies
144	Elections
145	Electricity
146	Embezzlement
148	Eminent Domain
148a	Employers' Liability
149	Entry, Writ of
150	Equity
151	Escape
152	Escheat
154	Estates in Property
156	Estoppel
157	Evidence
158	Exceptions, Bill of
159	Exchange of Property
160	Exchanges
161	Execution
162	Executors and Administrators
163	Exemptions
164	Explosives
165	Extortion and Threats
166	Extradition and Detainers
167	Factors
168	False Imprisonment
169	False Personation
170	False Pretenses
170a	Federal Civil Procedure
170b	Federal Courts
171	Fences
172	Ferries
174	Fines
175	Fires
176	Fish
177	Fixtures
178	Food
179	Forcible Entry and Detainer
180	Forfeitures
181	Forgery
183	Franchises
184	Fraud
185	Frauds, Statute of
186	Fraudulent Conveyances
187	Game
188	Gaming
189	Garnishment
190	Gas
191	Gifts
192	Good Will
193	Grand Jury
195	Guaranty
196	Guardian and Ward
197	Habeas Corpus
198	Hawkers and Peddlers
199	Health and Environment
200	Highways
201	Holidays
202	Homestead
203	Homicide
204	Hospitals
205	Husband and Wife
205h	Implied and Constructive Contracts
206	Improvements
207	Incest
208	Indemnity
209	Indians

Exhibit 12.14 West Digest Topics and their numerical designations *(continued)*

210 Indictment and Information
211 Infants
212 Injunction
213 Innkeepers
216 Inspection
217 Insurance
218 Insurrection and Sedition
219 Interest
220 Internal Revenue
221 International Law
222 Interpleader
223 Intoxicating Liquors
224 Joint Adventures
225 Joint-Stock Companies and Business Trusts
226 Joint Tenancy
227 Judges
228 Judgment
229 Judicial Sales
230 Jury
231 Justices of the Peace
232 Kidnapping
232a Labor Relations
233 Landlord and Tenant
234 Larceny
235 Levees and Flood Control
236 Lewdness
237 Libel and Slander
238 Licenses
239 Liens
240 Life Estates
241 Limitation of Actions
242 Lis Pendens
245 Logs and Logging
246 Lost Instruments
247 Lotteries
248 Malicious Mischief
249 Malicious Prosecution
250 Mandamus
251 Manufactures
252 Maritime Liens
253 Marriage
255 Master and Servant
256 Mayhem
257 Mechanics' Liens
257a Mental Health
258a Military Justice
259 Militia
260 Mines and Minerals
265 Monopolies
266 Mortgages
267 Motions
268 Municipal Corporations
269 Names
270 Navigable Waters
271 Ne Exeat
272 Negligence
273 Neutrality Laws
274 Newspapers
275 New Trial
276 Notaries
277 Notice
278 Novation
279 Nuisance
280 Oath
281 Obscenity
282 Obstructing Justice
283 Officers and Public Employees
284 Pardon and Parole
285 Parent and Child
286 Parliamentary Law
287 Parties
288 Partition
289 Partnership
290 Party Walls
291 Patents
292 Paupers
294 Payment
295 Penalties
296 Pensions
297 Perjury
298 Perpetuities
299 Physicians and Surgeons
300 Pilots
302 Pleading
303 Pledges
304 Poisons
305 Possessory Warrant
306 Postal Service
307 Powers
307a Pretrial Procedure
308 Principal and Agent
309 Principal and Surety
310 Prisons
311 Private Roads
313 Process
313a Products Liability
314 Prohibition
315 Property
316 Prostitution
316a Public Contracts
317 Public Lands
317a Public Utilities
318 Quieting Title
319 Quo Warranto
319h Racketeer Influenced and Corrupt Organizations
320 Railroads
321 Rape
322 Real Actions
323 Receivers
324 Receiving Stolen Goods
325 Recognizances
326 Records
327 Reference
328 Reformation of Instruments
330 Registers of Deeds
331 Release
332 Religious Societies
333 Remainders
334 Removal of Cases
335 Replevin
336 Reports
337 Rescue
338 Reversions
339 Review
340 Rewards
341 Riot
342 Robbery
343 Sales
344 Salvage
345 Schools
346 Scire Facias
347 Seals
348 Seamen
349 Searches and Seizures
349a Secured Transactions
349b Securities Regulation
350 Seduction
351 Sequestration
352 Set-Off and Counterclaim
353 Sheriffs and Constables
354 Shipping
355 Signatures
356 Slaves
356a Social Security and Public Welfare
357 Sodomy
358 Specific Performance
359 Spendthrifts
360 States
361 Statutes
362 Steam
363 Stipulations
365 Submission of Controversy
366 Subrogation
367 Subscriptions
368 Suicide
369 Sunday
370 Supersedeas
371 Taxation
372 Telecommunications
373 Tenancy in Common
374 Tender
375 Territories
376 Theaters and Shows
378 Time
379 Torts
380 Towage
381 Towns
382 Trade Regulation
384 Treason
385 Treaties
386 Trespass
387 Trespass to Try Title
388 Trial
389 Trover and Conversion
390 Trusts
391 Turnpikes and Toll Roads
392 Undertakings
393 United States
394 United States Magistrates
395 United States Marshals
396 Unlawful Assembly
396a Urban Railroads
398 Usury
399 Vagrancy
400 Vendor and Purchaser
401 Venue
402 War and National Emergency
403 Warehousemen
404 Waste
405 Waters and Water Courses
406 Weapons
407 Weights and Measures
408 Wharves
409 Wills
410 Witnesses
411 Woods and Forests
413 Workers' Compensation
414 Zoning and Planning
450 Merit Systems Protection (Merit Systems Protection Board Reporter)

Source: *West Digest Topics. Reprinted with permission of Thomson/West Publishing.*

By contrast, for a narrow, fact-based question, or if the researcher already has a citation or case name to work from, computer-based research usually is the better approach. Success in research depends on recognizing the best tools for a specific problem and using them efficiently.

Knowing the legal terminology used in the indexes of the research materials is critical. As noted previously, publishers of legal materials do not always use the same words or legal terms to index the same rules of law. One publisher may use the term "infant" to identify people under the age of majority, whereas another publisher may index that group of people under "minor." Different online services may require the use of a different set of search terms when formulating a query.

Creating a List of Research Terms

The paralegal should create one list of words for online searches and a separate list for searches of traditional print sources. The list should be updated as the paralegal performs research, adding or deleting words and phrases and annotating the list with citations for future research. The word list should be developed from the facts of the question, the parties, the locations, the case-specific goods and services, their status, or the relationships among them.

Consider the case of the off-duty police officer who had just come from a doctor's visit where he had been given a medication to reduce his blood pressure. He was involved in a rear-end collision with a van of schoolchildren returning from selling candy at a fundraiser. The driver of the van was one of the children's mothers, and was also a teacher at the school. A skateboarder darted in front of one of the vehicles, resulting in the collision. The checklist Research Plan: Words and Phrases is a good way to put together a list of the words and phrases to be searched.

What are some of the words and terms with which to start researching the issue of liability? As with most cases, each person has multiple roles or statuses that must be considered: teacher, parent, driver, police officer, student, child, principal, agent of school, agent of other parents, or patient. Further, the situation may have been caused by any of a number of factors—road conditions, weather, time of day, speed, medical issues, carelessness, and/or distractions. Also to be considered are the vehicles' braking abilities, possible manufacturing defects, and airbag deployment issues.

Obviously, not every issue comes into play in every case. Before starting the research, the researcher must identify the relevant terms that apply to the case being researched. The time spent creating the list will save time chasing dead ends or irrelevant issues. In creating the word list, the researcher should think of words, legal terms, and phrases, and consider alternatives to those words—synonyms, antonyms, and related terms. Appropriate language may be found using secondary sources and finding tools such as legal dictionaries, encyclopedias, and treatises.

Computer Research Providers

The three primary full-service online providers of computer research services—LexisNexis, Loislaw, and Westlaw—provide a broad range of legal materials, including cases, statutes, and regulations. In addition, there are limited-service search providers that specialize in providing cases and limited access to additional items, such as the *Code of Federal Regulations.*

In using a limited-service provider, it is important to check the coverage dates and content. In some cases, the same information is available from other sources, such as the *United States Code* and the *Code of Federal Regulations*, which are available online through the GPO Access website. In all cases, researchers must be certain that they have checked for all the latest update sources.

Search Method and Query

Each of the online providers uses words to find and retrieve documents. As part of the publication process, indexes are prepared of every word in the document, and

CHECKLIST Research Plan: Words and Phrases

Concepts and Issues	Generic Words and Phrases	Text-Based Research Terms	Computer-Based Research Terms
Persons Status Relationship Occupation Group Class			
Item(s) Involved			
Location(s)			
Subject Matter			
Jurisdiction Federal State City Locality			
Cause of Action Tort Contract Family Law Commercial			
Relief Sought Injunction Damages Compensatory Punitive Mandamus			
Defenses			

the words are tabulated for frequency. The query the researcher creates will be used by the service to search this index. VersusLaw uses a full-text retrieval method that searches every word except "stop words"—words that are used too commonly in documents to be used in a search, such as "the," "not," "of," and "and."

Creating the Query

When you conduct a search, you are asking the search engine to find the indexed words you have chosen. These may be legal specialty words or common English words. Single words may be in any of the Internet or legal search engines. Frequently you will be looking for more detailed information. Using combinations of words in the search can narrow the search results. Usually, the most productive search contains a combination of words, which may consist of multiple-word terms and phrases, such as "strict liability," "legal malpractice," "automobile accident," or "reckless indifference."

Using Connectors

Connectors are words that tell the search engine to look for documents containing combinations of words. Connectors may be thought of as instructions to the search engine, such as "Find me documents in which the words 'strict' AND 'liability' appear." The word AND is a connector that instructs the search engine to return only the documents in which *both* of the words are found. Exhibit 12.15 shows a Loislaw search with the AND connector.

Connectors Instructions in a search query on how to treat the words in the query.

The connector OR instructs the search engine to retrieve those documents that have *either* term—the word "strict" OR the word "liability." Exhibit 12.16 depicts a Lexis search with the OR connector.

Exhibit 12.15 Loislaw search with AND connector

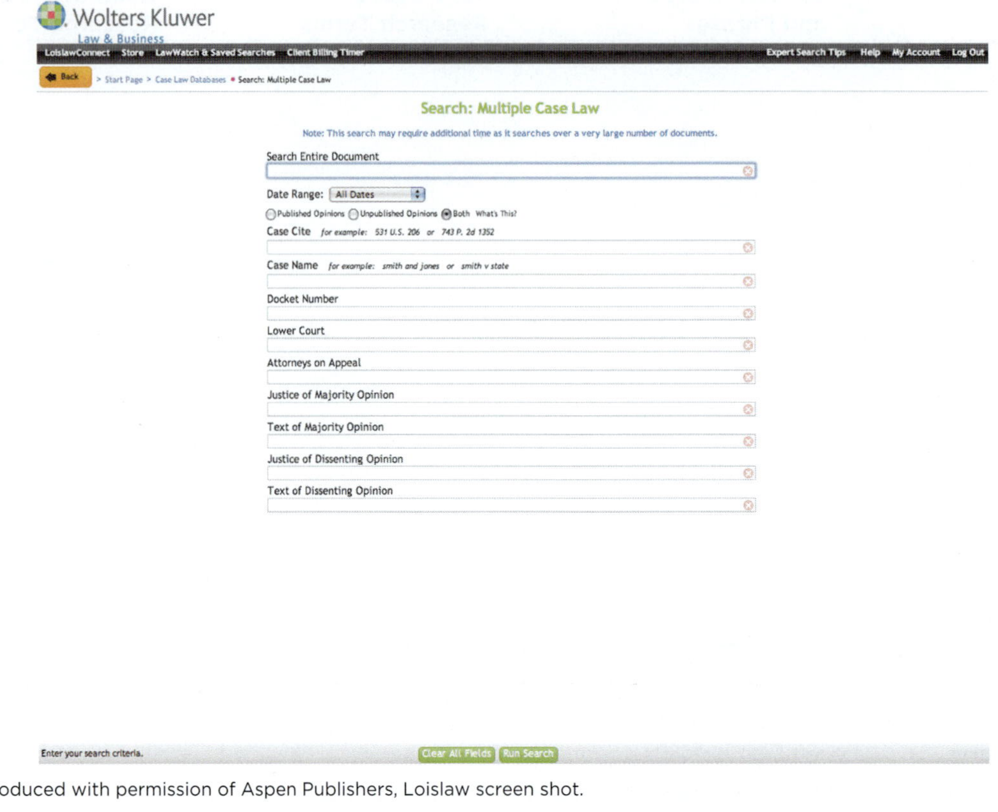

Source: Reproduced with permission of Aspen Publishers, Loislaw screen shot.

The NOT connector instructs the search to eliminate certain words. For example, you may wish to review documents in which the word "malpractice" is found, but *not* documents with the word "medical."

Exhibit 12.16 Lexis search with OR connector

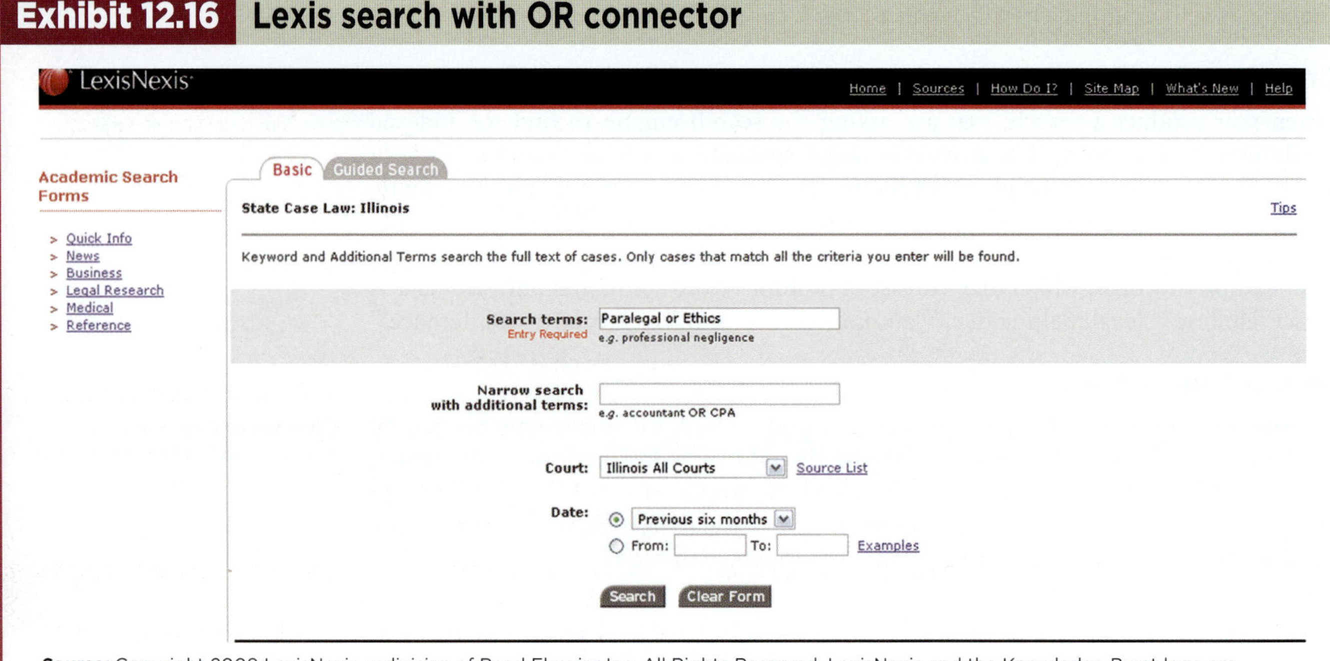

Source: Copyright 2009 LexisNexis, a division of Reed Elsevier Inc. All Rights Reserved. LexisNexis and the Knowledge Burst logo are registered trademarks of Reed Elsevier Properties Inc. and are used with the permission of LexisNexis.

Exhibit 12.17 Comparison grid from VersusLaw

VersusLaw	LEXIS	Westlaw
Connectors		
and	and	and, &
or	or	or, *space*
not	and not	but not, %
Proximity operators		
w/n	w/n	w/n, /n
w/n	pre/n	pre/n, +n
Exact phrase match		
unlawful entry	unlawful entry	"unlawful entry"
Wild Cards - end of root words		
*	!	!
Wild Cards - single character		
?	*	*
Order of operators		
proximity operators, not, and, or	or, *proximity operators*, and, and not	or, *proximity operators*, and, but not

Source: www.versuslaw.com

In some cases, it might be assumed that there will be other words between the desired terms, such as in the phrase "Paralegals are bound by the ethics of their profession." The NEAR connector helps to locate documents where the terms are near each other—for example: "Find 'paralegal' NEAR 'ethics.'" The NEAR connector allows the paralegal to search for words near each other by specifying the maximum number of words apart.

Exhibit 12.17 gives a comparison of these concepts in VersusLaw, and Exhibit 12.18 provides a guide to connectors for Westlaw.

Exhibit 12.18 Westlaw guide to connectors

USING CONNECTORS

Connector	You type	Westlaw retrieves documents
AND	&	containing both search terms: **work-place & safety**
OR	a space	containing either search term or both search terms: **landlord lessor**
Grammatical Connectors	/p	containing search terms in the same paragraph: **warrant! /p habitat!**
	/s	containing search terms in the same sentence: **danger! /s defect!**
	+s	in which the first term precedes the second within the same sentence: **capital +s gain**
Numerical Connectors	/n (where *n* is a number)	containing search terms with *n* terms of each other: **issues /5 fact**
	+n (where *n* is a number)	in which the first term precedes the second by *n* terms: **20 + 5 1080**
BUT NOT	%	not containing the term or terms following the percent symbol (%): **tax taxation % tax taxation/3 income**

Source: Reproduced with permission from West Group.

Search Engines

Great advances have been made in computer search methods. It is no longer necessary to know the exact word or phrase to be able to find the desired information in a computer database. Boolean searches with words and connectors are being supplemented with advanced search engines that can conduct searches using phrases or sentences, sometimes referred to as "natural language" searches. For example, a query may ask, "What is the statute of limitations for a person injured as a result of a defective brake part in an automobile?"

Modern search engines can also automatically substitute words that are conceptually similar. When "automobile" is used in a search query, the search engine also searches using words such as "vehicle," "motor vehicle," "truck," "bus," and other similar terms. This is referred to as a "conceptual search." Still other search engines automatically search for the singular or plural and may even search for similar terms in other languages.

Learning Objective 4

Explain the need for, and the methods of, updating legal research.

Updating Legal Research

The legal team must always use the most current statutory and case law in advising clients and arguing cases to the court. The ethical rules of the legal profession require candor to the court, which in turn demands that the latest information be provided to the court. One of the features of the American legal system is its constant change. Courts attempt to meet the needs of a changing society by reviewing prior case law and, when appropriate, overruling or modifying it as the contemporary American view of justice dictates. The American legal system's concept of ***stare decisis*** provides that we use prior case law as **precedent,** but the law may be adapted to new situations or changed as American society changes. Occasionally, existing case law may be held unconstitutional, such as in the landmark case of *Roe v. Wade*, 410 U.S. 113 (1973).

Stare decisis The legal principle that prior case law should apply unless there is a substantial change in society necessitating a change in the case law.

Precedent Prior case law that is controlling.

Knowing whether the case law being used in a legal argument is current is a vital part of the lawyer's obligation to the client and to the court. Up to the moment before the arguments are made to the court or the brief is submitted, a case that the attorney or the opponent is using as a basis for a legal argument may be overturned. The ethical obligation of candor, shown below in the Ethical Perspective, requires the use of most current case law.

For paralegals, an essential part of legal research is verifying that they have the latest case or statute. The process is complicated by the method by which changes in statutes or case law are released to the public. Ultimately, new statutes and new case law are reported in a published form, both in paper and online, but not all publications are able to disseminate the information daily. Paper versions take time to print and distribute. Not all electronic versions are posted immediately. Therefore, it becomes important to know how quickly the reporting services used by the law firm distribute new cases or changes in statutes. More and more courts have their own websites and release case opinions electronically, along with the print versions, to the public and publishing companies. For example, you can check decisions of the U.S. Supreme Court daily by accessing its website.

The greatest difficulty is in knowing whether the cases or statutes have affected the case being researched. When the court specifically mentions a case being cited in a memorandum of law or a court brief, the paralegal has to know if the new case follows, reverses, or in some way differs from the older case.

As soon as a case is entered into an electronic case law database, such as Westlaw, Lexis, Loislaw, or VersusLaw, a general search can be made for references to the case name or citation. Before the case is entered, however, the same search will not show the newest reference. Even a reference to the case will not indicate whether the case law has changed. It will only indicate that another case has referred to it. Someone must actually read the case to see how the court has used it or referred to it in the opinion.

ETHICAL PERSPECTIVE

Idaho Rules of Professional Conduct

RULE 3.3 CANDOR TOWARD THE TRIBUNAL

(a) A lawyer shall not knowingly:

(1) make a false statement of fact or law to a tribunal or fail to correct a false statement of material fact or law previously made to the tribunal by the lawyer;

(2) fail to disclose to the tribunal legal authority in the controlling jurisdiction known to the lawyer to be directly adverse to the position of the client and not disclosed by opposing counsel; or

(3) offer evidence that the lawyer knows to be false. If a lawyer, the lawyer's client, or a witness called by the lawyer, has offered material evidence and the lawyer comes to know of its falsity, the lawyer shall take reasonable remedial measures, including, if necessary, disclosure to the tribunal. A lawyer may refuse to offer evidence, other than the testimony of a defendant in a criminal matter, that the lawyer reasonably believes is false.

(b) A lawyer who represents a client in an adjudicative proceeding and who knows that a person intends to engage, is engaging or has engaged in criminal or fraudulent conduct related to the proceeding shall take reasonable remedial measures, including, if necessary, disclosure to the tribunal.

(c) The duties stated in paragraphs (a) and (b) continue to the conclusion of the proceeding, and apply even if compliance requires disclosure of information otherwise protected by Rule 1.6.

(d) In an ex parte proceeding, a lawyer shall inform the tribunal of all material facts known to the lawyer that will enable the tribunal to make an informed decision, whether or not the facts are adverse.

Web Exploration

Contrast and compare the Idaho rule at **http://isb.idaho.gov/pdf/rules/irpc.pdf** with the ABA Model Rules of Professional Conduct at **www.abanet.org/cpr** and the rule in your jurisdiction.

Shepard's

Shepard's Citations is a multivolume set of books listing cases and statutes by their respective citations and giving the citation of every other case in which the listed case was mentioned. *Shepard's* has long been a standard tool of legal research in law libraries. The listings originally were compiled by editors who physically read through every reported case to find citations. These were then reported by case citation, with every other mention of the case reported by its citation in chronological fashion, and notations indicating whether the opinion was reversed, affirmed, followed, overruled, or distinguished. The process of using *Shepard's* to check legal citations came to be called "Shepardizing"—a term that many legal assistants still use, even when using other citation-checking services such as Westlaw's KeyCite. An advantage to using the *Shepard's Citator* is the editorial symbol system, which indicates how the new case affects the case being checked, as shown in Exhibit 12.19.

The problem with the traditional paper form of *Shepard's* is the lag in time for the print version to be prepared and sent out to subscribers. *Shepard's* now provides the same service online through the Lexis service. Subscribers can obtain the latest case information, to the day, by calling a toll-free number. One of the difficulties in using the print version of *Shepard's* is the number of hardbound volumes and paperback updates required to be consulted, and finding the latest update pamphlet if someone has misfiled it in the law library. Exhibit 12.20 is an example of the print version for cases in *Shepard's*.

Many educational institutions and public libraries subscribe to the web-based LexisNexis Academic Universe. *Shepard's* citation service (shown in Exhibit 12.21) is usually available for the U.S. Supreme Court as part of the service, but other federal and state *Shepard's* citation services may not be included because of the cost of the additional license fees involved.

Exhibit 12.19 ***Shepard's* symbols showing effects of new cases**

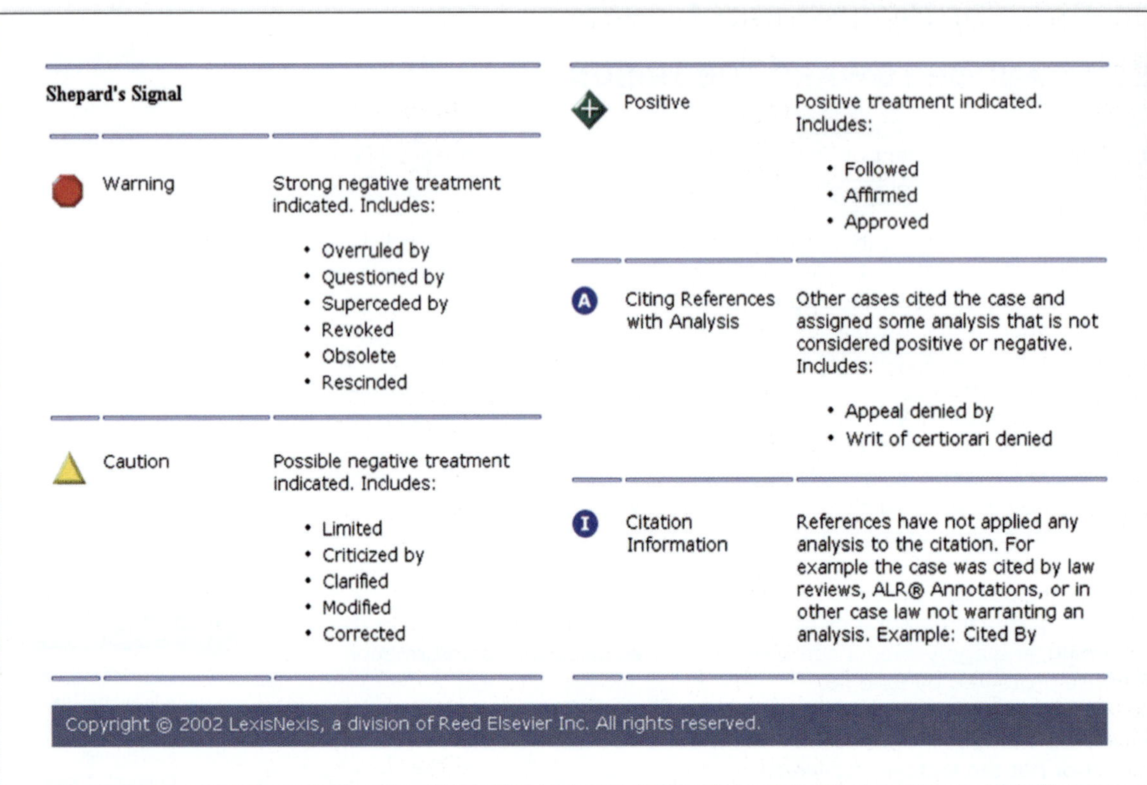

Shepard's Signal		
Warning		Strong negative treatment indicated. Includes: • Overruled by • Questioned by • Superceded by • Revoked • Obsolete • Rescinded
Caution		Possible negative treatment indicated. Includes: • Limited • Criticized by • Clarified • Modified • Corrected
Positive		Positive treatment indicated. Includes: • Followed • Affirmed • Approved
A	Citing References with Analysis	Other cases cited the case and assigned some analysis that is not considered positive or negative. Includes: • Appeal denied by • Writ of certiorari denied
I	Citation Information	References have not applied any analysis to the citation. For example the case was cited by law reviews, ALR® Annotations, or in other case law not warranting an analysis. Example: Cited By

GlobalCite™

GlobalCite Loislaw's tool for searching cases containing references to another case.

Loislaw's **GlobalCite** provides a reverse chronological list of the case law, the statutes ordered by number of citation occurrences, the regulations listed in order of relevancy, and reference to other databases in the Loislaw library. Exhibit 12.22 shows a GlobalCite screen.

KeyCite™

KeyCite Westlaw's tool for searching cases containing references to another case.

KeyCite is the Westlaw online citation update service. The Westlaw KeyCite is a combination citator and case finder. Unlike other, similar services, KeyCite uses the West Key number system and West Headnotes.

V. Cite™

V. Cite VersusLaw's tool for searching cases containing references to another case.

V. Cite, VersusLaw's citation tool, will produce a list of all cases within the selected jurisdictions that have cited the case being searched. The list that a V. Cite search produces will include cases that have cited the initial case, which most likely will discuss similar issues. An additional V. Cite feature allows the appending of a specific term to the search request. For example, including the word "damages" in the "additional query information" section of the V. Cite form will restrict the search to cases that cite the searched case and also discuss "damages."

Exhibit 12.20 Example of print version case presentation in *Shepard's*

—157—	—558—	—558—
Oregon v Plowman 1992	**Oregon v Plowman 1992**	**Oregon v Plowman 1992**
(838P2d558)	(314Ore157)	(314Ore157)
s 107OrA782	s 813P2d1114	s 813P2d1114
cc 314Ore170	cc 813P2d1115	cc 813P2d1115
e 315Ore375	cc 838P2d566	cc 838P2d566
315Ore380	840P2d1324	840P2d1324
317Ore[4]258	e 840P2d1325	e 840P2d1325
317Ore451	841P2d650	841P2d650
f 317Ore452	e 845P2d1285	e 845P2d1285
j 317Ore472	845P2d1289	845P2d1289
f 318Ore488	j 851P2d1147	j 851P2d1147
318Ore492	j 852P2d888	j 852P2d888
d 318Ore497	854P2d959	854P2d959
116OrA189	855P2d[4]625	855P2d[4]625
e 116OrA192	857P2d107	Calif
h 116OrA265	f 857P2d108	17CaR2d296
j 119OrA303	j 857P2d119	e 19CaR2d448
j 120OrA333	f 871P2d458	e 19CaR2d449
121OrA384	871P2d461	Iowa
j 128OrA14	d 871P2d463	500N W 42
71OLR689	j 874P2d1348	
22A5268n		
Shepard's Oregon Citations, *Oregon Reports division, shows citations from:* • *state reports* • Oregon Law Review • *annotations (ALR® 5th)*	Shepard's Oregon Citations, *Oregon Cases division, shows citations from Oregon as published in the* Pacific Reporter.	Shepard's Pacific Reporter Citations, *P.2d division, shows citations from all cases published in a West regional reporter.*

Source:

Parallel Citations

Most cases are reported in more than one service or set of books. A **parallel citation** is a cite to the same material, usually a case, in another source. Frequently a state has an official publication, such as the court's own publication, and a private publication, such as the *West Reporter*. In some cases, *West* was, and is, the official reporter, and there may not be a parallel print source. One of the many uses of *Shepard's* is to find the parallel citation to other locations for the same case.

Parallel citation The citation to the same case in a different publication.

Shepard's also provides update information on statutory citations. Amendments and repeals of statutory information are listed in *Shepard's*. Citations to any cases in which the statute has been cited are also listed, with information on how the case law considered the statute.

Exhibit 12.21 LexisNexis Total *Shepard's*® Table of Authorities

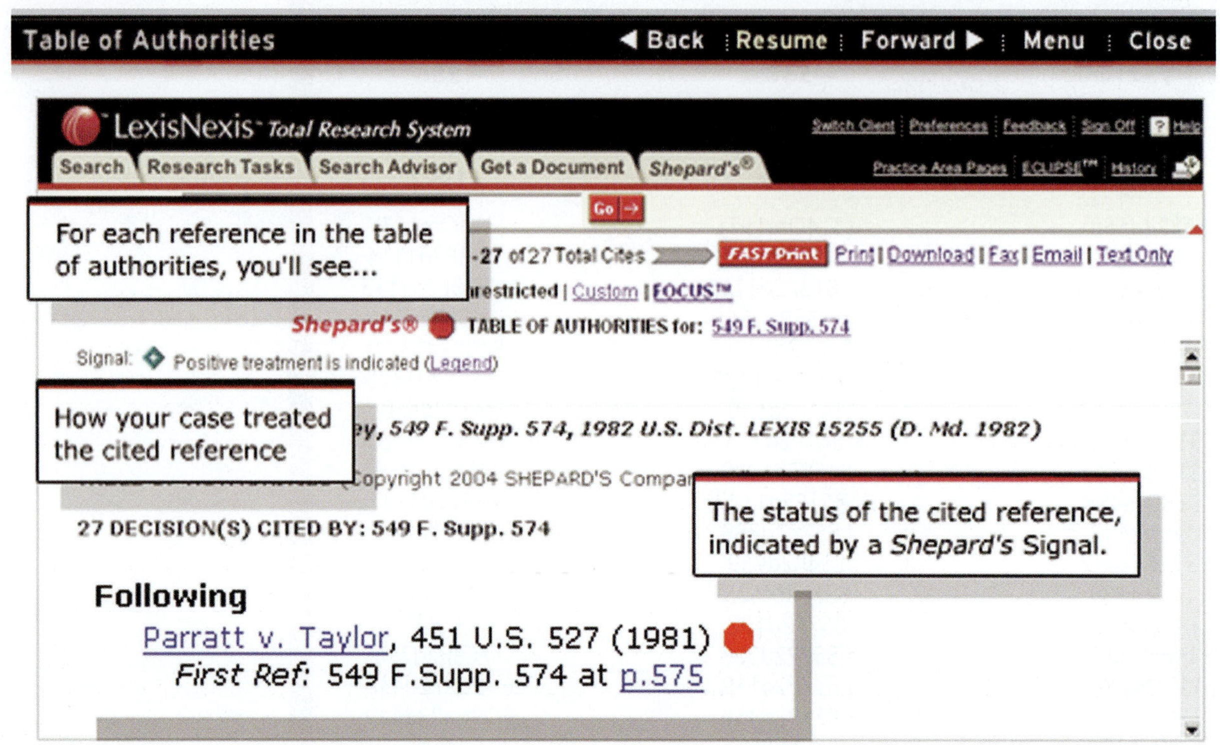

Source: Copyright 2009 LexisNexis, a division of Reed Elsevier Inc. All Rights Reserved. LexisNexis and the Knowledge Burst logo are registered trademarks of Reed Elsevier Properties, Inc. and are used with the permission of LexisNexis.

Exhibit 12.22 GlobalCite screen

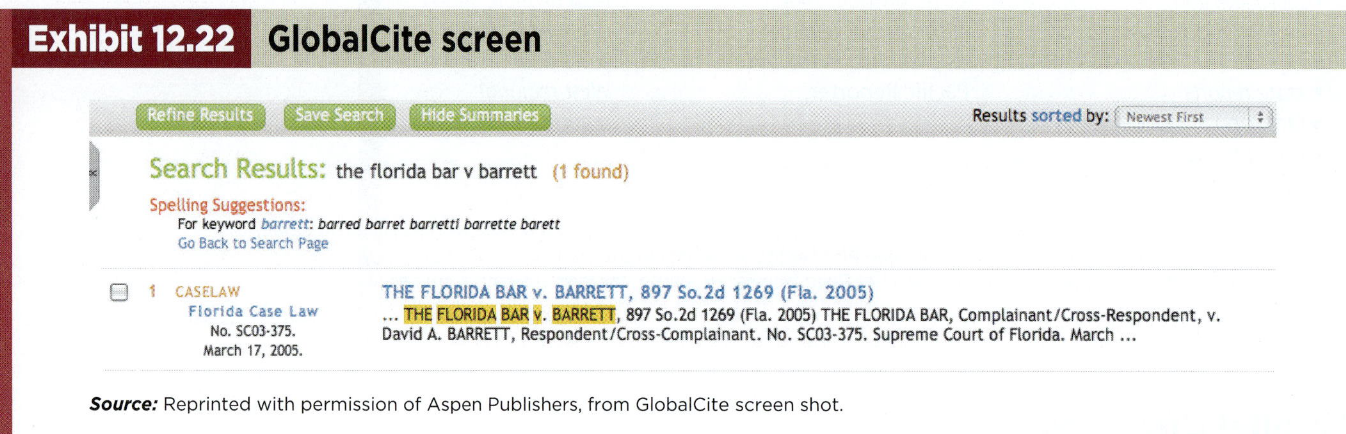

Source: Reprinted with permission of Aspen Publishers, from GlobalCite screen shot.

CHECKLIST Research Search Items

- ☐ Client:
- ☐ Issue:
- ☐ Search terms and phrases:
- ☐ Search combinations used:
- ☐ Date:

CHECKLIST Research Sources Checked

Checked Source	Citation	Update Service Checked	✓	Web Location
Primary Sources				
	State statute			www.
	USC			www.
	USCA			www.
	CFR			www.
	Local ordinance			www.
				www.
Secondary Sources				
	State digest			www.
	Federal digest			www.
	ALR			www.
				www.
	Encyclopedia			www.
	State			www.
	C.J.S.			www.
	Periodicals			www.
	Treatises			www.

Concept Review *and* Reinforcement

LEGAL TERMINOLOGY

Amicus curia 446
Bench opinion 438
Bicameral 435
Case syllabus 438
Citator 446
Connectors 455
Dicta 439
Finding tools 434
GlobalCite 460
Headnotes 438
Holding 439
Judicial branch 435
KeyCite 460
Legal research 431
Legislative branch 435
Mandatory authority 436
Parallel citation 461
Persuasive authority 437
Pocket parts 450
Precedent 458
Primary source of law 434
Published opinion 437
Relevant facts 432
Search query 433
Secondary source of law 434
Slip opinion 438
Stare decisis 458
Unpublished opinions 437
V. Cite 460

SUMMARY OF KEY CONCEPTS

Legal Research

	Legal research is the process of finding the answer to a legal question.

Creating a Research Plan

	The research plan helps to focus on the issues, sources, and methods for finding the answer to a legal question and the controlling law.
What Is the Issue or Legal Question?	After clarifying the question being asked, the next step is to determine the relevant facts based on the applicable law.
What Is the Appropriate Search Terminology?	Print research materials require finding material based on a printed index of individual words as selected by editors of the service.
	Computer research allows for searches of words found in the documents using a text search of requested words in the search query.
What Type of Research Material Is Available?	The paralegal must be able to find the information needed when the familiar resources are not available. Because paralegals cannot always be sure whether the research can be done using a traditional paper library or a computer search, they must understand how to use each system.
What Jurisdictions Are Involved?	Focusing on a single jurisdiction or a minimum number of jurisdictions reduces the number of books necessary and saves online computer search time.
What Is the Controlling Law?	Knowing which set of materials to use, the statutes of the jurisdiction, the regulation of a given administrative agency, or the courts of a given jurisdiction will save time in doing the research.
What Types of Resources Should Be Used?	1. Primary sources of law are used in preparing the legal memo or brief. 2. Secondary sources are useful, efficient ways to get an overview of an area of law or learn the terminology of a particular field that the paralegal is not familiar with. 3. Finding tools are publications for finding both primary and secondary sources.
Where Is the Needed Research Material Located?	The needed material may have to be located at a remote library such as a bar association library or a law school library.
Creating a List of Research Terms	Separate lists should be created for online searches and traditional print source searches.
Executing the Research Plan	As with the execution of any plan, detours should be expected, as the law is constantly evolving. New statutes are enacted, and new judicial opinions are handed down. During the research process, the researcher must look for changes and potential changes in pending legislation and cases on appeal.

Finding the Law

The Controlling Law	The controlling law may be found at federal, state, or local legislative or judicial levels.
Primary Sources and Authority	Primary sources include the law, constitutions, statutes, regulations, court rules, and case decisions.
Mandatory and Persuasive Authority	1. Mandatory authority is legal authority that the courts must follow. 2. Persuasive authority is legal authority the courts are not required to follow but is from a respected source and is well reasoned.
Constitutions	Constitutions are primary sources that set the guidelines, limits, and authority of the federal and state governments.
Statutes	Statutes are enacted by the legislative branch of government.

Court Decisions	The actual court language is a primary source of the law. The syllabus, summaries, interpretations, or abstracts of the points of law presented by the editorial staffs of the publishers—usually called headnotes—are *not* a primary source of law.
Secondary Sources	Secondary sources explain the law. 1. Legal dictionaries, as opposed to general English or other specialized dictionaries, define words and phrases as used in the law. 2. Legal encyclopedias provide the background to understand the area sufficiently to start the research. They provide an overview of the concepts and history of an area of law, the legal issues involved, and the terminology. 3. Treatises, law reviews, and legal periodicals are authoritative or of sufficient scholarly value to be persuasive to the court.
Finding Tools	Finding tools help to "find" the law. 1. Digests provide lists of cases in a subject topic format, with cases generally in chronological order. 2. Indexes and citators cross-reference material such as by the commonly used or popular name of a case or statute.
Personal Research Strategy	
	Over time, each paralegal develops a personal search strategy based on the nature of the problem or issue to be researched and the resources available.
	A personal research strategy includes methods of verifying that the law cited in the memorandum of law is current law, and methods for looking for pending cases and legislation that might change the answer to the legal question.
A Final Word on Executing the Legal Research Plan	
	Know when to ask for help.
Using Printed Legal Reference Works	
Common Features	• Table of abbreviations • Table of contents in the front • Index of terms in the back • Table of cases and citations
Updates	Print material is frequently updated with pocket parts, usually issued annually and slipped into the back of the volume in a pocket.
	Paperback supplements are issued annually, semi-annually, quarterly, or monthly.
	Online updates from the publishers are increasingly available for some materials.
Constructing a Computer Search Query	
Creating a List of Research Terms	A query is a combination of words, phrases, and connectors used to search for an answer.
Search Method and Query	Each online provider uses words to find and retrieve documents. As part of the publication process, indexes are prepared of every word in the document, the words are tabulated for frequency, and a word index is prepared. The query is used to search this index.
Creating the Query	The search engine is used to find the indexed words the paralegal has chosen; they may be legal specialty words or common English words. Using combinations of words in the search can narrow the search results.
Using Connectors	AND instructs the search to return documents in which both of the words are found. OR instructs the search engine to find documents that contain either term. NEAR may be used to find the occurrence of desired words within a set number of words of each other.

Updating Legal Research	
	1. *Shepard's:* A multivolume set of books listing cases and statutes by their respective citations and giving the citation of every other case in which the listed case was mentioned; checking citations is often called "Shepardizing." 2. GlobalCite (Loislaw): Provides a reverse chronological list of the case law, a list of statutes in the order of the highest number of citation occurrences, regulations in relevancy order, and reference to other databases in the Loislaw library. 3. KeyCite (Westlaw): An online citation update service. 4. V. Cite (VersusLaw): An online citation tool.
Parallel Citation	
	A citation to the same material, usually a case, in another source.
Statutory Law Updates	*Shepard's* provides updated information on amendments and repeals of statutory information. Citations to any cases in which the statute has been cited are also listed, with information on how the case law considered the statute.

WORKING THE WEB

1. Use the Government Printing Office website to find and print out the summary and purpose of 21 CFR 404, or any other section assigned by your instructor. www.gpoaccess.gov
2. Make a list of the federal primary sources available on the Government Printing Office website.
3. From the sitemap of the VersusLaw website, print out for your future computer searches the printable version of the *VersusLaw Research Manual.* http://www.versuslaw.com/features/sitemap.htm
4. Use the Legal Information Institute at the Cornell University website to find title 44 C.F.R. 201 and print out the list of key responsibilities of FEMA and state and local/tribal governments. http://www.law.cornell.edu Does this site provide direct access or a link to another source? Explain. What primary federal sources does this site offer?
5. Conduct a search for information on paralegal ethics using two different search engines, and print out a copy of the first page of each result. Are they the same? What is the difference in results and order of presentation? Possible search engines include: Google, www.google.com; Yahoo!, www.yahoo.com; Ask, www.ask.com; and Findlaw, www.findlaw.com.
6. If you have access to Loislaw, LexisNexis, Westlaw, or VersusLaw, conduct a search for paralegal ethics cases for your jurisdiction. Prepare a list of authorities cited in the search.
7. Print out the current list of opinions of the U.S. Supreme Court at http://www.supremecourt.gov.
8. Print out the complete version of Rule 3.3, Candor Toward the Tribunal, of the ABA Model Rules of Professional Conduct, at http://www.abanet.org/cpr/mrpc/mrpc_toc.html.
9. Under the theory of *stare decisis*, on which courts would the decisions of a court have a binding effect? Would a decision in a case be binding on future cases if the decision were available only in the clerk's office?
10. Would your answer be the same if the decision were available in the clerk's office at first but then available in printed form or online at a later date? When would the decision become effective as precedent?
11. Where is the "law" found?
12. Who makes the "law" under the United States legal system?
13. What is meant by a "bicameral" legislature?
14. In legal research, what is meant by "primary source"?
15. What is a "treatise"? Is it a primary source? Explain.
16. What is a headnote in legal research? Is it a primary source? Explain.
17. What is dicta? What is its effect on other courts? Explain.
18. Of what weight do courts give secondary sources? Explain fully.
19. Why are finding tools important to the legal researcher? Give an example of how a finding tool might be used.
20. Do unpublished opinions have precedential effect? Explain.

CRITICAL THINKING & WRITING QUESTIONS

1. Using the facts in the *Palsgraf* case in Appendix A, prepare a search query using connectors to locate the law or a similar case in your jurisdiction. Run the search using an online legal research service, if available.
2. Why does a paralegal have to be familiar with both traditional and electronic research tools and methods?

3. Why does the paralegal have to know how quickly changes in statutory and case law are updated by online and traditional primary and secondary sources?
4. Why is knowledge of the underlying law in an area important in constructing a question for online research?
5. How can a researcher be certain that a case that seems to be on point is still the current case law?
6. Why should secondary sources not be relied upon in citing binding authority?
7. Why would a researcher use a traditional paper resource before using an online research tool?
8. How does the use of connectors help in conducting online research? Give an example.
9. Why might an identical search query return different results?
10. Why must researchers clearly understand the question they are being asked to research? How can they be certain they do?

Building Paralegal Skills

VIDEO CASE STUDIES

Legal Research: Are Books Obsolete?

In the middle of a trial, a trial attorney sends his paralegal to the courthouse law library to find a case that has been cited as precedent by opposing counsel in oral argument. Without a valid password, the paralegal is advised to use traditional "paper" research methods.

After viewing the video case study in MyLegalStudiesLab, answer the following:

1. What are the differences between using books and using electronic legal research?
2. Are traditional paper-based reference materials as current as electronic reference sources?
3. Are there any differences in the different legal research services such as Lexis, Westlaw, Loislaw, or VersusLaw?

Fees and Billing Issue: Using Time Effectively

A paralegal has responded to the request of her supervising attorney for information on a question of law. After spending considerable time, she is helped by another paralegal, who quickly provides the information she is looking for. However, she also finds out that her supervising attorney was merely "curious," and there was no client to bill for the research time.

After viewing the video case study in MyLegalStudiesLab, answer the following:

1. What questions should a paralegal ask before commencing the research?
2. At what point should the paralegal ask for help, and from whom should the help be sought?
3. Is there any value in doing legal research when there is no specific client or case to which it will apply?

ETHICS ANALYSIS & DISCUSSION QUESTIONS

1. Is there an ethical obligation under the Model Rules to perform legal research competently? Explain.
2. What is the ethical obligation under the Model Rules to provide the court with legal authority that is not favorable to your client's legal position?
3. What is the ethical obligation to "Shepardize" cases and statutes before submitting a brief or memorandum of law to the court?

For answers, look at American Bar Association Rule 3.3, Candor Toward the Tribunal, and Rule 1.1, Competence (ABA Model Rules of Professional Conduct, 2002).

Confidentiality

There are few certainties in the area of ethics, for paralegals or in any profession. What qualifies as ethical conduct is in most cases based on state law and court interpretation applied to a set of facts. The citation listed below represents one legal opinion and is provided as a research starting point. Do not assume that the same rule applies in your jurisdiction. For the following:

- Prepare a written statement based on your state law.
- Use your state bar association website as a starting point.

You are waiting for a fax needed for a case on which you are working. While you are standing by the fax machine, a fax comes in from an attorney at an opposing firm containing a letter about settlement that was clearly intended for the attorney's client and not for opposing counsel. It was sent by your best friend, the paralegal who is working on that case at the opposing firm. She is stressed out by the case and made the mistake of dialing your fax number rather than the client's. From your reading of the letter, it appears the information would greatly help your law office win the case. See *State Compensation Insurance Fund v. The WPS, Inc.*, 70 Cal. App. 4th 644 (1999).

Do you quietly return the fax to your friend and say nothing to anyone? Do you read it carefully to be sure of the contents? Do you return it to opposing counsel? Do you tell your supervising attorney about the letter, and describe its contents?

DEVELOPING YOUR COLLABORATION SKILLS

Working on your own or with a group of other students assigned by your instructor, review the scenario at the beginning of the chapter and discuss the different views on law libraries, including traditional versus computer legal research.

1. Write a summary of the potential advantages and disadvantages of each point of view.
2. Prepare a report to the executive committee considering the different views of members of the firm with a solution that might satisfy most users of the firm's library.
3. The group should divide into two teams. One team will conduct a research assignment using traditional methods and the other will conduct the assignment using computer research tools.
   a. Each team is to complete the checklist Research Sources Checked, and prepare a copy for the members of the other team and your instructor.
   b. After you have completed the research, prepare a short memorandum of law to submit to your instructor.
4. Complete a second research project, with each team now using the other approach to research. The traditional methods team now will use computer tools, and the computer tools team will conduct the research using traditional tools. Prepare a short memorandum and complete the checklist Research Sources Checked.
5. Based on your experience doing traditional and computer research, what recommendations would you make to the managing partner in the opening scenario?

PARALEGAL PORTFOLIO EXERCISE

Complete the "Web Location" section of the checklist Research Sources Checked. When preparing the list, include alternative sources where available. Print a copy for your portfolio for future use and a copy for your instructor.

LEGAL ANALYSIS & WRITING CASES

Copying of Material for Future Research and Law Library Archives from Copyrighted Magazines and Journals

***American Geophysical Union v. Texaco Inc.* 37 F.3d 881 (2d Cir. 1994)**

Most researchers understand that misuse of copyrighted material may subject them to liability under the copyright laws. The case of *American Geophysical Union v. Texaco* illustrates the potential liability in regularly copying copyrighted articles for personal archives. Researchers at Texaco regularly made copies of articles for future reference from the works of the plaintiff and 82 other publishers of scientific and technical journals. Texaco raised the defense of "fair use" as permitted under the copyright law.

Fair use as a defense depends on four tests: (1) the purpose and character of the use—including whether for nonprofit educational purposes or commercial use; (2) the nature of copyright work—the law generally recognizes a greater need to disseminate factual works than works of fiction or fantasy; (3) amount and substantiality of portion used—was the quantity used reasonable in relation to the purpose of the copying? (4) effect on potential market or value—will the copying have an impact on the sale of the works, and is there an efficient mechanism for the licensing of the works?

Questions

1. How does copyright law apply to a student copying copyrighted materials while doing research for a class project?
2. Would the answer be the same if the student were doing the research as part of an assignment while working in a law office?
3. Does it matter whether the work copied is a court case or an article by an expert in automobile airbags liability? Why?

WORKING WITH THE LANGUAGE OF THE COURT CASE

Hart v. Massanari, 266 F.3d 1155 (9th Cir. 2001)

United States Court of Appeals, Ninth Circuit

Read and brief this case. In your brief, answer the following questions.

1. Why are unpublished decisions of courts not valid as precedent in future cases?
2. What is the difference between controlling authority and persuasive authority?
3. How might an unpublished opinion be used in this case?
4. Has the adoption of Rule 32.1 changed the effect of this case?
5. Why does this court believe it is important, in writing an opinion of the court, to recite all the relevant facts?
6. What is the effect of binding precedent on other courts?

Kozinski, Circuit Judge

Appellant's...brief cites...an unpublished disposition, not reported in the *Federal Reporter*....The full text...is marked with the following notice: "This disposition is not appropriate for publication and may not be cited to or by the courts of this circuit....Unpublished dispositions and orders of this Court are not binding precedent...[and generally] may not be cited to or by the courts of this circuit."...[9th Cir.R.36-3.]

We ordered counsel to show cause as to why he should not be disciplined for violating Ninth Circuit Rule 36-3. Counsel responds by arguing that Rule 36-3 may be unconstitutional...[relying]...on the Eighth Circuit's opinion in *Anastasoff v. United States*, [which] while vacated, continues to have persuasive force...

A. Anastasoff held that Eighth Circuit Rule 28A(i),...that unpublished dispositions are not precedential[,]*...violates Article III of the Constitution....We believe that Anastasoff overstates the case....

Anastasoff focused on one aspect of the way federal courts do business—the way they issue opinions—and held that they are subject to a constitutional limitation derived from the [constitutional] framers' conception of what it means to exercise the judicial power....We question whether the "judicial power" clause contains any limitation at all, separate from the specific limitations of Article III and other parts of the Constitution....The term "judicial power" in Article III is more likely descriptive than prescriptive....

**Our rule operates...differently from...the Eighth Circuit...Rule 28A(i) [that] says that "[u]npublished decisions are not precedent." [W]e say that unpublished dispositions are "not binding precedent."...Our rule...prohibits citation of an unpublished disposition to any of the courts of our circuit. The Eighth Circuit's rule allows citation..., but provides that the authority is persuasive rather than binding.*

B. Modern federal courts are the successors of the English courts that developed the common law....Common law judges did not make law as we understand that concept; rather, they "found" the law with the help of earlier cases that had considered similar matters. An opinion was evidence of what the law is, but it was not an independent source of law....The idea that judges declared rather than made the law remained firmly entrenched in English jurisprudence until the early nineteenth century....For centuries, the most important sources of law were not judicial opinions themselves, but treatises that restated the law....

The modern concept of binding precedent...came about only gradually over the nineteenth and early twentieth centuries. Lawyers began to believe that judges made, not found, the law. This coincided with monumental improvements in the collection and reporting of case authorities...and [as] a more comprehensive reporting system began to take hold, it became possible for judicial decisions to serve as binding authority....

II

Federal courts today do follow some common law traditions. When ruling on a novel issue of law, they will generally consider how other courts have ruled on the same issue....Law on point is the law. If a court must decide an issue governed by a prior opinion that constitutes binding authority, the later court is bound to reach the same result, even if it considers the rule unwise or incorrect. Binding authority must be followed unless and until overruled by a body competent to do so.

In determining whether it is bound by an earlier decision, a court considers not merely the "reason and

(*continued*)

spirit of cases" but also "the letter of particular precedents." ... This includes not only the rule announced, but also the facts giving rise to the dispute, other rules considered and rejected, and the views expressed in response to any dissent or concurrence. Thus, when crafting binding authority, the precise language employed is often crucial to the contours and scope of the rule announced.

... A decision of the Supreme Court will control that corner of the law unless and until the Supreme Court itself overrules or modifies it.... Thus, the first panel to consider an issue sets the law not only for all the inferior courts in the circuit, but also future panels of the court of appeals. Once a panel resolves an issue in a precedential opinion, the matter is deemed resolved, unless overruled by the court itself sitting en banc, or by the Supreme Court....

Controlling authority has much in common with persuasive authority. Using the techniques developed at common law, a court confronted with apparently controlling authority must parse the precedent in light of the facts presented and the rule announced. Insofar as there may be factual differences between the current case and the earlier one, the court must determine whether those differences are material to the application of the rule or allow the precedent to be distinguished on a principled basis.... But there are also very important differences between controlling and persuasive authority.... [I]f a controlling precedent is determined to be on point, it must be followed.... Thus, an opinion of our court is binding within our circuit, not elsewhere....

III

While we agree with Anastasoff that the principle of precedent was well established in the common law courts by the time Article III of the Constitution was written, we do not agree that it was known and applied in the strict sense in which we apply binding authority today....

In writing an opinion, the court must be careful to recite all facts that are relevant to its ruling, while omitting facts that it considers irrelevant. Omitting relevant facts will make the ruling unintelligible to those not already familiar with the case; including inconsequential facts can provide a spurious basis for distinguishing the case in the future....

While federal courts of appeals generally lack discretionary review authority, they use their authority to decide cases by unpublished—and nonprecedential—dispositions to achieve the same end.... That a case is decided without a precedential opinion does not mean it is not fully considered.... The disposition is not written in a way that makes it suitable for governing future cases.... An unpublished disposition is, more or less, a letter from the court to parties familiar with the facts, announcing the result and the essential rationale of the court's decision....

IV

We conclude that Rule 36-3 is constitutional. We also find that counsel violated the rule. Nevertheless, we are aware that Anastasoff may have cast doubt on our rule's constitutional validity. Our rules are obviously not meant to punish attorneys who, in good faith, seek to test a rule's constitutionality. We therefore conclude that the violation was not willful and exercise our discretion not to impose sanctions.

The order to show cause is DISCHARGED.

In a footnote in the case of *Cogan v. Barnhart*, USDC Mass, 03-12421-WGY, the court commented:

"Citation to unpublished opinions has been an issue of considerable debate, which continues until today. The Eighth and Ninth Circuits are on extreme ends of the debate. *Anastasoff v. US*, 223 F. 3d 898 ... (holding that unpublished opinions have precedential effect); *Hart v. Massanari*, ... (upholding its local rule prohibiting the citation of unpublished decisions as constitutional)....

MYLEGALSTUDIESLAB

MyLegalStudiesLab Virtual Law Office Experience Assignments

Complete the pre-test, study plan, and post-test for this chapter and answer the Legal Applications questions as assigned. These will help you confirm your mastery of the concepts and their application to legal scenarios. Then complete the Virtual Law Office assignments as assigned by your instructor. These assignments are designed to develop your workplace skills. Completing the assignments for this chapter will result in producing the following documents for inclusion in your portfolio:

VLOE 12.1	Electronic copies of documents to proceed with the case using the American Arbitration Association procedures
VLOE 12.2	Office memo summary of the law on product liability and strict liability in your state

PART

IV

Legal Subjects

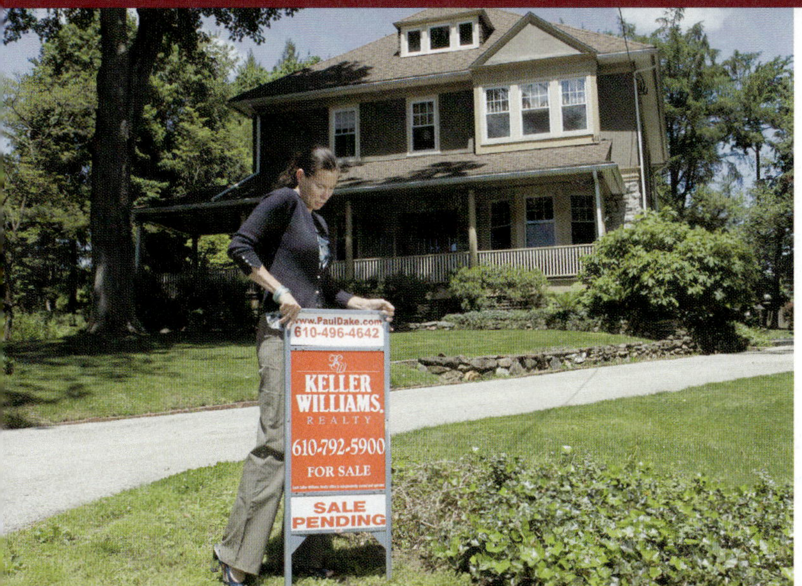

Part IV presents an overview of the basic rules of law in the most common areas of law in which paralegals may work. The principles discussed in each area are generally applicable in all jurisdictions; however, there are variations in state and local laws, and paralegals must check for these variations in the jurisdiction in which they work. By studying these areas of law, you will begin to learn the terminology of the law. Read each of the substantive law chapters with a view toward identifying those areas that stimulate an interest in taking more advanced courses or as a possible area of specialization as a paralegal.

CHAPTER

13

Torts and Product Liability

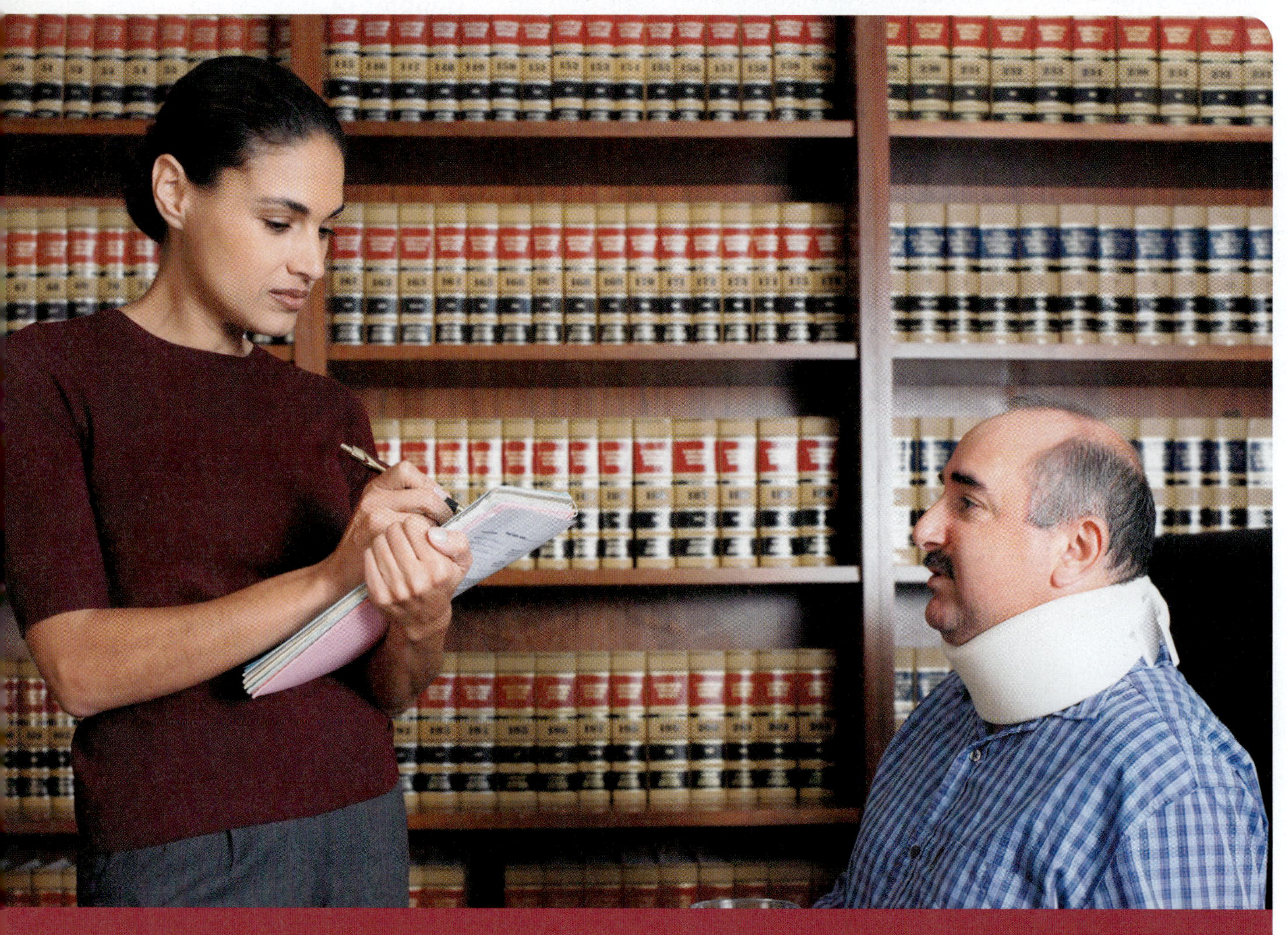

Paralegals at Work

As a paralegal, you work for a law firm that represents clients in tort actions against automobile insurance companies and other defendants. Most of the law firm's business comes from automobile accident cases. Your firm specializes in representing the injured plaintiffs in these negligence and product liability lawsuits.

You work for Mr. Joshua Berk, senior litigator for the firm. One day Mr. Berk invites you into his office. He explains that the firm has just been retained by a plaintiff, Mrs. Helen Sheen, to represent her and her daughter, Jessica, in a lawsuit. He also tells you that you will be assisting him in preparation of the case.

Mr. Berk explains the following facts of the case: Two months ago, Mrs. Sheen and her husband, Mr. Patrick Sheen, were driving on the Interstate 10 freeway to Las Vegas in their one-year-old SUV manufactured by Chrysler. When Mrs. Sheen was driving the SUV, Mr. Sheen was in the passenger's seat, and their 4-year-old daughter, Jessica, was in the back seat of the car. Mrs. Sheen, Mr. Sheen, and Jessica were wearing their seatbelts.

While in the State of Nevada, and about 20 miles from Las Vegas, Mrs. Sheen heard the steering wheel of the SUV rattle and then felt it loosen in her hands. She lost control of the vehicle, and the vehicle flipped over several times before coming to a stop upside down and 40 feet from the freeway. Mr. Sheen died in the accident.

Jessica suffered severe back injuries that will require at least $100,000 worth of surgeries over the next year. Her future injuries from the accident cannot be predicted at this time. Mrs. Sheen was not physically injured in the accident, but suffers severe emotional distress.

Investigators of the accident scene have determined that Mrs. Sheen was driving at the legal speed limit of 70 miles per hour. Investigation also has shown that one of the bolts

LEARNING OBJECTIVES

After studying this chapter, you should be able to:

1. Recognize the professional opportunities for paralegals in the tort and product liability law areas.
2. List and describe intentional torts against persons.
3. List and describe intentional torts against property.
4. List and explain the elements necessary to prove negligence.
5. List and describe special negligence doctrines.
6. Explain a paralegal's duty not to commit professional malpractice.
7. Describe and apply the doctrine of strict liability to product liability cases.
8. Describe punitive damages and explain when they are awarded.
9. Describe the type of defects to which the doctrine of strict liability applies.
10. Explain a paralegal's duty to disclose information that could cause bodily harm.

> "Negligence is not actionable unless it involves the invasion of a legally protected interest, the violation of a right. Proof of negligence in the air, so to speak, will not do."
>
> *C. J. Cardozo, Palsgraf v. Long Island Railroad Co.* (1928)

holding the steering wheel in place had broken off, causing the steering wheel to become loose and unmanageable at the time of the accident. The steering wheel and steering wheel column for the SUV was manufactured by the submanufacturer Steering Columns Corporation and installed in the Chrysler SUVs.

Consider the issues involved in this scenario as you read this chapter.

Learning Objective 1
Recognize the professional opportunities for paralegals in the tort and product liability law areas.

INTRODUCTION FOR THE PARALEGAL

Many paralegals work for lawyers who represent clients involved in intentional tort, negligence, and product liability cases. These are civil lawsuits in which the plaintiff is usually seeking to recover monetary damages from the defendant or the defendant's insurance company. In this type of case, the paralegal may be working for the plaintiff's lawyer, the defendant's lawyer, or lawyers at the defendant's insurance company.

Tort A wrong. There are three categories of torts: (1) intentional torts, (2) unintentional torts (negligence), and (3) strict liability.

Tort is the French word for a "wrong." Tort law protects a variety of injuries and provides remedies for them. Under tort law, an injured party can bring a civil lawsuit to seek compensation for a wrong done to the party or to the party's property. Many torts originate in common law. The courts and legislatures have extended tort law to reflect changes in modern society.

Tort damages are monetary damages sought from the offending party that are intended to compensate the injured party for the injury suffered. These monetary damages may consist of past and future medical expenses, loss of wages, pain and suffering, mental distress, and other damages caused by the defendant's tortious conduct. If the victim of a tort dies, his or her beneficiaries can bring a **wrongful death action** to recover damages from the defendant.

Thoughts much too deep for tears subdue the Court When I assumpsit bring, and godlike waive a tort.

J. L. Adolphus
The Circuiteers (1885)

A special type of tort—strict liability—is available primarily in product liability cases. Under strict liability, a party can be held liable even if that party was not negligent or at fault for causing the plaintiff's injuries. For example, manufacturers, sellers, and other parties in the chain of distribution of a defective product can be held strictly liable. Punitive damages, which are awarded to punish the defendant, are often recoverable in strict liability cases.

Tort and product liability lawsuits make up a substantial portion of the civil lawsuits in the United States. Therefore, a paralegal should have knowledge of the major tort principles and the elements of each tort.

This chapter covers various tort laws, including intentional torts, negligence, and strict liability.

The following feature discusses the career opportunities for paralegal professionals in tort and product liability law.

Intentional torts A category of torts that requires that the defendant possessed the intent to do the act that caused the plaintiff's injuries.

Learning Objective 2
List and describe intentional torts against persons.

Intentional Torts Against Persons

The law protects a person from unauthorized touching, restraint, or other contact. In addition, the law protects a person's reputation and privacy. Violations of these rights are actionable as **intentional torts.** Intentional torts against persons are discussed in the paragraphs that follow.

CAREER OPPORTUNITIES FOR PARALEGAL PROFESSIONALS IN TORT AND PRODUCT LIABILITY LAW

A substantial number of lawsuits in the United States involve torts. Therefore, a substantial number of paralegals work for lawyers who practice in this area of law. A tort occurs when one party violates a duty owed to another party and injures that party. The injured party often brings a civil lawsuit to recover monetary damages and other remedies.

The most familiar form of a tort is negligence, and the most common form of negligence occurs in automobile accidents. Attorneys representing clients who have been injured in automobile accidents usually handle a large number of cases. The defense law firms who represent the insurance companies also have large caseloads of negligence automobile lawsuits.

Paralegals who work for either the plaintiff lawyers or the defense lawyers in automobile injury cases are responsible for handling a large caseload. Paralegals who work for plaintiff lawyers are typically called upon to draft complaints, requests for discovery, and other documents associated with the case. Paralegals who work for defense law firms have the parallel duties of drafting answers, requests for discovery, and other documents associated with the cases. Paralegals who work on automobile tort cases become experts and often do much of the work on these cases, under the supervision of the attorney, of course.

Because 90 percent of these cases settle, there is usually not much opportunity to conduct legal research. However, more complex cases, and those that do go to trial, may require the paralegal to conduct research to help the attorney prepare the brief for the case.

Among the many other types of torts are professional malpractice (e.g., medical malpractice by doctors), defamation of character, intentional infliction of emotional distress, invasion of privacy, misappropriation of the right to publicity, malicious prosecution, negligent infliction of emotional distress, liability of landowners, and other forms of intentional and unintentional torts.

A special area of tort law is product liability law. These cases involve lawsuits by injured plaintiffs against companies who manufacture and sell products to consumers. A special tort doctrine called strict liability often applies to these types of cases, which usually are more complex and, therefore, require more expertise of the paralegals who work for the plaintiff and defense lawyers representing the clients in these cases. In product liability cases paralegals are called upon to interview persons, conduct investigations, conduct research, and draft documents.

The area of torts will remain an important one for the employment of paralegals. Therefore, paralegals should have knowledge of the various types of intentional torts, unintentional torts, and product liability.

Assault

Assault is (1) the threat of immediate harm or offensive contact, or (2) any action that arouses reasonable apprehension of imminent harm. Actual physical contact is unnecessary.

Assault (1) The threat of immediate harm or offensive contact or (2) any action that arouses reasonable apprehension of imminent harm. Actual physical contact is unnecessary for an action to be an assault.

Example Suppose a 6-foot 5-inch, 250-pound male makes a fist and threatens to punch a 5-foot, 100-pound woman. If the woman is afraid that the man will physically harm her, she can sue him for assault. If instead she is a black-belt karate champion and laughs at the threat, there is no assault because the threat does not cause any apprehension.

Battery

Battery is unauthorized and harmful or offensive physical contact with another person. Basically, the interest protected here is each person's reasonable sense of dignity and safety.

Battery Unauthorized and harmful or offensive direct or indirect physical contact with another person that causes injury.

Examples Intentionally hitting someone is considered battery because it is harmful. Throwing a rock, shooting an arrow or a bullet, knocking off a hat, pulling a chair out from under someone, and poisoning a drink are all instances of actionable battery if an injury results. The victim need not be aware of the harmful or offensive contact (it may take place while the victim is asleep). Assault and battery often occur together, but they do not have to (such as when the perpetrator hits the victim on the back of the head without any warning).

Sometimes a person acts with the intent to injure one person but actually injures another. The **doctrine of transferred intent** applies to these situations. Under this doctrine, the law transfers the perpetrator's intent from the target to the actual victim of the act. The victim can then sue the defendant.

Example Peter shoots a gun toward Mable with the intent of killing her but instead the bullet strikes Mildred, a bystander, who is injured. Mildred can recover damages from Peter for her injuries.

Web Exploration

Go to **http://www.supreme.courts.state.tx.us/historical/1998/feb/970558.pdf** and read the case *Wal-Mart Stores v. Resendez*. What issue was involved in this case? Was Wal-Mart found liable in this case? Why or why not?

False Imprisonment

The intentional confinement or restraint of another person without authority or justification and without that person's consent constitutes **false imprisonment.** The victim may be restrained or confined by physical force, barriers, threats of physical harm, or the perpetrator's false assertion of legal authority (that is, *false arrest*). A threat of future harm or moral pressure is not considered false imprisonment. Rather, the false imprisonment must be carried out.

Example Merely locking one door to a building when other exits are not locked is not false imprisonment. A person is not obliged to risk danger or an affront to his or her dignity by attempting to escape.

Merchant protection statute A state statute that allows merchants to stop, detain, and investigate suspected shoplifters without being held liable for false imprisonment if (1) there are reasonable grounds for the suspicion, (2) suspects are detained for only a reasonable time, and (3) investigations are conducted in a reasonable manner.

Shoplifting causes substantial losses to merchants each year. Almost all states have enacted **merchant protection statutes,** also known as the **shopkeeper's privilege.** These statutes allow merchants to stop, detain, and investigate suspected shoplifters without being held liable for false imprisonment if:

1. There are reasonable grounds for the suspicion;
2. Suspects are detained for only a reasonable time; and
3. Investigations are conducted in a reasonable manner.

Defamation of Character

A person's reputation is a valuable asset. Therefore, every person is protected during his or her lifetime from false statements by others. This protection ends upon a person's death. The tort of **defamation of character** requires a plaintiff to prove that (1) the defendant made an *untrue statement of fact* about the plaintiff, and (2) the statement was intentionally or accidentally published to a third party. In this context, publication simply means that a third person heard or saw the untrue statement. It does not just mean that the statement appeared in newspapers, magazines, or books.

The term for an oral defamatory statement is **slander.**

Slander Oral defamation of character.

Examples If a radio host makes an untrue statement of fact about a person over the radio waves, it would be slander. False statements that appear in a letter, newspaper, magazine, book, photograph, movies, video, and the like would be **libel.**

Libel A false statement that appears in a letter, newspaper, magazine, book, photograph, movie, video, or other medium.

Publishing an untrue statement of fact is not the same as publishing an opinion. The publication of opinions is usually not actionable.

Examples The statement "My lawyer is lousy" is an opinion and not defamation. The statement "My lawyer has been disbarred from the practice of law" when she has not been disbarred is an untrue statement of fact and is actionable as defamation.

In *New York Times Co. v. Sullivan*, 376 U.S. 254, 84 S.Ct. 710 (1964), the U.S. Supreme Court held that *public officials* cannot recover for defamation unless they can prove that the defendant acted with "actual malice." Actual malice means that the defendant made the false statement knowingly or with reckless disregard of its falsity. This requirement has since been extended to *public figure* plaintiffs such as movie stars, sports personalities, and other celebrities.

Disparagement or Trade Libel

Business firms rely on their reputations and the quality of their products and services to attract and keep customers. State unfair-competition laws protect businesses from disparaging statements made by competitors and others. A disparaging statement is an untrue statement made by one person or business about the products, services, property, or reputation of another business.

Example If a competitor of Dell Computers told a prospective customer that "Dell Computers always break down," when in fact they rarely break down, that would be product disparagement. **Disparagement** is also called *trade libel* and *product disparagement*.

Misappropriation of the Right to Publicity

Each person has the exclusive legal right to control and profit from the commercial use of his or her name and personality during his or her lifetime. This is a valuable right, particularly to well-known persons such as sports figures and movie stars. Any attempt by another person to appropriate a living person's name or identity for commercial purposes is actionable. The wrongdoer is liable for the tort of **misappropriation of the right to publicity** (also called the *tort of appropriation*).

Misappropriation of the right to publicity A tort in which one party appropriates a person's name or identity for commercial purposes.

Example If an advertising agency places the likeness of a famous actor on a billboard advertising a product without the actor's permission, it has engaged in the tort of misappropriation of the right to publicity.

In such cases, the plaintiff can (1) recover the unauthorized profits made by the offending party, and (2) obtain an injunction against further unauthorized use of his or her name or identity. Many states provide that the right to publicity survives a person's death and may be enforced by the deceased's heirs.

Invasion of the Right to Privacy

The law recognizes each person's right to live his or her life without being subjected to unwarranted and undesired publicity. Violation of this right constitutes the tort of **invasion of the right to privacy.** Examples of this tort are reading someone else's mail, wiretapping, and similar actions. In contrast to defamation, the fact does not have to be untrue. Therefore, truth is not a defense to a charge of invasion of privacy. If the fact is public information, there is no claim to privacy. But a fact that was once public (such as the commission of a crime) may become private after the passage of time.

Invasion of the right to privacy A tort that constitutes the violation of a person's right to live his or her life without being subjected to unwarranted and undesired publicity.

Examples Secretly taking photos of another person with a cell phone camera in a men's or women's locker room would constitute invasion of the right to privacy. Reading someone's mail, wiretapping someone's telephone, and reading someone's email without authorization to do so are also examples of invasion of the right to privacy.

Placing someone in a "false light" constitutes an invasion of privacy as well.

Examples Sending an objectionable telegram to a third party and signing another's name would place the purported sender in a false light in the eyes of the receiver. Falsely attributing beliefs or acts to another can also form the basis of a lawsuit.

Intentional Infliction of Emotional Distress

In some situations a victim suffers mental or emotional distress without first being physically harmed. The Restatement (Second) of Torts provides that a person whose extreme and outrageous conduct intentionally or recklessly causes severe emotional distress to another is liable for that emotional distress. This is called the tort of

Intentional infliction of emotional distress A tort that occurs when a person's extreme and outrageous conduct intentionally or recklessly causes severe emotional distress to another person. Also known as the *tort of outrage*.

intentional infliction of emotional distress, or the *tort of outrage*. The plaintiff must prove that the defendant's conduct was "so outrageous in character and so extreme in degree as to go beyond all possible bounds of decency, and to be regarded as atrocious and utterly intolerable in a civilized society." An indignity, an annoyance, rough language, or an occasional inconsiderate or unkind act does not constitute outrageous behavior. However, repeated annoyances or harassment coupled with threats are considered "outrageous."

The tort does not require any publication to a third party or physical contact between the plaintiff and the defendant.

> **Example** A credit collection agency making harassing telephone calls to a debtor every morning between 1:00 and 5:00 A.M. is outrageous conduct.

The mental distress suffered by the plaintiff must be severe. Many states require that this mental distress be manifested by some form of physical injury, discomfort, or illness such as nausea, ulcers, headaches, or miscarriage. This requirement is intended to prevent false claims of mental distress. Some states have abandoned this requirement, and their courts have held that shame, humiliation, embarrassment, anger, fear, and worry constitute severe mental distress.

Malicious Prosecution

Malicious prosecution A lawsuit in which the original defendant sues the original plaintiff for bringing a lawsuit without probable cause and with malice.

Businesses and individuals often believe they have a reason to sue someone to recover damages or other remedies. If the plaintiff has a legitimate reason to bring the lawsuit and does so, but does not win the lawsuit, he or she does not have to worry about being sued by the person whom he or she sued. But a losing plaintiff does have to worry about being sued by the defendant in a second lawsuit for **malicious prosecution** if certain elements are met. In a lawsuit for malicious prosecution, the original defendant sues the original plaintiff. In this second lawsuit, which is a *civil* action for damages, the original defendant is the plaintiff and the original plaintiff is the defendant. To succeed in a malicious prosecution lawsuit, the courts require the current plaintiff to prove all of the following:

1. The plaintiff in the original lawsuit (now the defendant) instituted or was responsible for instituting the original lawsuit.
2. There was no *probable cause* for the first lawsuit (that is, it was a frivolous lawsuit).
3. The plaintiff in the original action brought it with *malice*. (*Caution:* This is a very difficult element to prove.)
4. The original lawsuit was terminated in favor of the original defendant (now the plaintiff).
5. The current plaintiff suffered injury as a result of the original lawsuit.

> **Example** A customer purchases a dress at a women's clothing store. A button falls off the dress, so the customer brings a civil lawsuit against the store to recover $1 million for negligence and intentional infliction of emotional distress. The store spends $30,000 for legal fees in defending the lawsuit. The jury does not hold for the customer. The store can now bring a case against the customer for malicious prosecution. The store has a very good chance of proving the elements of malicious prosecution and recovering damages against the customer.

Civil Fraud

Contracting parties must be careful not to be taken by **fraud.** Basically, if a deal sounds "too good to be true," it is an indication that the situation might be fraudulent. Often frauds are difficult to detect. If there is fraud, the innocent party can get out of the contract and recover his or her losses. To prove **civil fraud,** the following elements must be shown:

He that's cheated twice by the same man, is an accomplice with the Cheater.
Thomas Fuller
Gnomologia (1732)

1. ***The wrongdoer made a false representation of material fact.*** To be actionable as fraud, the misrepresentation must be of a past or existing material fact. Statements of opinion or predictions about the future generally do not form the basis for fraud.
2. ***The wrongdoer intended to deceive the innocent party.*** Thus, the person making the misrepresentation must either have had knowledge that the representation was false or made the representation without sufficient knowledge of the truth. This is called **scienter** ("guilty mind").
3. ***The innocent party justifiably relied on the misrepresentation.*** A misrepresentation is not actionable unless the innocent party to whom the misrepresentation was directed acted upon it.
4. ***The innocent party was injured.*** To recover damages, the innocent party must prove that the fraud caused economic injury. The measure of damages is the difference between the value of the property as represented and the actual value of the property.

Where fraud has occurred, the victim of the fraud can sue the fraudulent party for fraud, and the plaintiff may recover damages from the defendant. However, in many cases of fraud, the perpetrator of the fraud has spent the money or possibly hidden the money so that it cannot be recovered. In this case, the victim loses the money or property.

Intentional Torts Against Property

There are two general categories of property: real property and personal property. *Real property* consists of land and anything permanently attached to that land. *Personal property* consists of things that are movable, such as automobiles, books, clothes, and pets. The law recognizes certain torts against real and personal property. These torts are discussed in the paragraphs that follow.

Trespass to Land

Learning Objective 3
List and describe intentional torts against property.

Interference with an owner's right to exclusive possession of land constitutes the tort of **trespass to land.** There does not have to be any interference with the owner's use or enjoyment of the land; the ownership itself is what counts. Thus, unauthorized use of another person's land is trespass even if the owner is not using it. Actual harm to the property is not necessary.

Hard cases make bad law.
Legal maxim

Examples Trespass to land includes entering another person's land without permission, remaining on the land of another after permission to do so has expired (as when a guest refuses to leave), and causing something or someone to enter another's land (as when one person builds a dam that causes another person's land to flood). A person who is pushed onto another's land or enters that land with good reason is not liable for trespass. Also, a person may enter another person's land to save a child or a pet from harm.

Trespass to and Conversion of Personal Property

The tort of **trespass to personal property** occurs whenever one person damages another person's personal property or interferes with that person's enjoyment of his or her personal property. The injured party can sue for damages.

Example Breaking another's car window is trespass to personal property.

Automobile Accident Automobile accidents are a primary cause of injury and death in the United States. Most states require owners to carry automobile insurance, but the required amount of coverage is often low. Automobile accidents comprise a large percentage of the negligence lawsuits in this country.

Depriving the true owner of the use and enjoyment of his or her personal property by taking over such property and exercising ownership rights over it constitutes the tort of **conversion of personal property.** Conversion also occurs when someone who originally is given possession of personal property fails to return it (for example, when a person fails to return a borrowed car). The rightful owner can sue to recover the property. If the property was lost or destroyed, the owner can sue to recover its value.

Learning Objective 4
List and explain the elements necessary to prove negligence.

Unintentional Torts—Negligence

Under the doctrine of **unintentional tort,** commonly referred to as **negligence,** a person is liable for harm that is the *foreseeable consequence* of his or her actions. Negligence is defined as "the omission to do something which a reasonable man would do, or doing something which a prudent and reasonable man would not do." See *Blyth v. Birmingham Waterworks Co.*, 11 Exch. 781, 784 (1856).

Unintentional tort/negligence A doctrine that says a person is liable for harm that is the foreseeable consequence of his or her actions.

Example A driver who causes an automobile accident because he or she fell asleep at the wheel is liable for any resulting injuries caused by his or her negligence.

No court has ever given, nor do we think ever can give, a definition of what constitutes a reasonable or an average man.
Lord Goddard C.J.R.
Regina v. McCarthy (1954)

To be successful in a negligence lawsuit, the plaintiff must prove that (1) the defendant owed a *duty of care* to the plaintiff, (2) the defendant *breached* this duty of care, (3) the plaintiff suffered *injury*, and (4) the defendant's negligent act *caused* the plaintiff's injury. Each of these elements is discussed in the paragraphs that follow.

Duty of Care

To determine whether a defendant is liable for negligence, it first must be ascertained whether the defendant owed a **duty of care** to the plaintiff. Duty of care refers to the obligation we all owe to each other—the duty not to cause any unreasonable harm or risk of harm.

Duty of care The obligation we all owe to each other not to cause any unreasonable harm or risk of harm.

Examples Each person owes a duty to drive his or her car carefully, not to push or shove on escalators, not to leave skateboards on the sidewalk, and the like. Businesses owe a duty to make safe products, not to cause accidents, and so on.

The courts decide whether a duty of care is owed in specific cases by applying a **reasonable person standard.** Under this test, the courts attempt to determine how an *objective, careful, and conscientious person would have acted in the same circumstances*, and then measure the defendant's conduct against this standard. The defendant's subjective intent ("I didn't mean to do it") is immaterial in asserting liability. Certain impairments do not affect the reasonable person standard.

Example There is no reasonable alcoholic standard.

Defendants with specific expertise or competence are measured against a **reasonable professional standard.** This standard is applied in much the same way as the reasonable person standard.

Examples A brain surgeon is measured against a reasonable brain surgeon standard rather than against the lower, reasonable doctor standard. Children are generally required to act as a *reasonable child* of similar age and experience would act.

Breach of Duty

Once a court finds that the defendant actually owed the plaintiff a duty of care, it must determine whether the defendant breached that duty. A **breach of the duty of care** is the failure to exercise care. In other words, it is the failure to act as a reasonable person would act. A breach of this duty may consist of an action.

Breach of the duty of care Failure to exercise care or to act as a reasonable person would act.

Examples Throwing a lit match on the ground in a forest and causing a fire is a breach of a duty of care. A breach of duty may also consist of a failure to act when there is a duty to act. A firefighter who refuses to put out a fire when her safety is not at stake is a breach of a duty of care. Generally, passersby are not expected to rescue others gratuitously to save them from harm.

Injury to Plaintiff

Even though a defendant's act might have breached a duty of care owed to the plaintiff, this breach is not actionable unless the plaintiff suffers **injury.**

Injury A plaintiff's personal injury or damage to his or her property that enables him or her to recover monetary damages for the defendant's negligence.

Example A business's negligence causes an explosion and fire at its factory at night, but no one is injured and there is no damage to the neighbors' property. The negligence is not actionable.

The damages recoverable depend on the injury's effect on the plaintiff's life or profession.

Example Suppose two men injure their hands when a train door malfunctions. The first man is a professional basketball player. The second is a college professor. The first man can recover greater damages.

Causation

A person who commits a negligent act is not liable unless this act was the *cause* of the plaintiff's injuries. Courts have divided **causation** into two categories—causation in fact and proximate cause—and require each to be shown before the plaintiff may recover damages.

Causation The two types of causation that must be proven are (1) causation in fact (actual cause) and (2) proximate cause (legal cause).

1. ***Causation in fact.*** The defendant's negligent act must be the **causation in fact** (or **actual cause**) of the plaintiff's injuries.

   Examples Suppose a corporation negligently pollutes the plaintiff's drinking water. The plaintiff dies of a heart attack unrelated to the polluted

Actual cause The actual cause of negligence. A person who commits a negligent act is not liable unless actual cause can be proven. Also called *causation in fact*.

water. Although the corporation has acted negligently, it is not liable for the plaintiff's death. There was a negligent act and an injury, but there was no *cause-and-effect* relationship between them. If, instead, the plaintiff had died from the polluted water, there would have been causation in fact and the polluting corporation would have been liable.

2. ***Proximate cause.*** Under the law, a negligent party is not necessarily liable for all damages set in motion by his or her negligent act. Based on public policy, the law establishes a point along the damage chain after which the negligent party is no longer responsible for the consequences of his or her actions. This limitation on liability is referred to as **proximate cause,** or **legal cause.** The general test of proximate cause is *foreseeability*. A negligent party who is found to be the actual cause—but not the proximate cause—of the plaintiff's injuries is not liable to the plaintiff. Situations are examined on a case-by-case basis.

Proximate cause A point along a chain of events caused by a negligent party after which that party is no longer legally responsible for the consequences of his or her actions. Also called *legal cause.*

Example The landmark case establishing the doctrine of proximate cause is *Palsgraf v. Long Island Railroad Company.* See 248 N.Y. 339, 162 N.E. 99, 1928 N.Y. Lexis 1269 (1928). Helen Palsgraf was standing on a platform waiting for a passenger train. The Long Island Railroad Company owned and operated the trains and employed the station guards. As a man carrying a package wrapped in a newspaper tried to board the moving train, railroad guards tried to help him. As they did so, the package, which contained fireworks, was dislodged from the man's arm, fell to the railroad tracks, and exploded. The explosion shook the railroad platform, causing a scale on the platform to fall on Palsgraf and injure her. She sued the railroad for negligence. Justice Cardozo denied her recovery, finding that the railroad was not the proximate cause of her injuries.

A complaint alleging negligence appears as Exhibit 13.1.

Learning Objective 5
List and describe special negligence doctrines.

Special Negligence Doctrines

The courts have developed many *special negligence doctrines*. The most important of these are discussed in the paragraphs that follow.

Professional Malpractice

Professionals, including doctors, lawyers, architects, and accountants, owe a duty of ordinary care in providing their services. This duty is known as the *reasonable professional standard*. A professional who breaches this duty of care is liable for the injury that his or her negligence causes. This liability is commonly referred to as **professional malpractice.**

Professional malpractice The liability of a professional who breaches his or her duty of ordinary care.

Examples A doctor who amputates the wrong leg is liable for *medical malpractice*. A lawyer who fails to file a document with the court on time, resulting in the client's case being dismissed, is liable for *legal malpractice*. An accountant who fails to use reasonable care, knowledge, skill, and judgment when providing auditing and other accounting services to a client is liable for *accounting malpractice*.

Negligent Infliction of Emotional Distress

Some jurisdictions have extended the tort of emotional distress to include the **negligent infliction of emotional distress.** The most common example of this tort involves bystanders who witness the injury or death of a loved one caused by another's negligent conduct. Under this tort, the bystander, even though not personally physically injured, can sue the negligent party for his or her own mental suffering.

Negligent infliction of emotional distress A tort that permits a person to recover for emotional distress caused by the defendant's negligent conduct.

Generally, to be successful in this type of case, the plaintiff must prove that (1) a relative was killed or injured by the defendant, (2) the plaintiff suffered severe emotional distress, and (3) the plaintiff's mental distress resulted from a sensory and contemporaneous observance of the accident. Some states require that the plaintiff's

Exhibit 13.1 Complaint for negligence

Percival R. Cheeseman
Clarence K. Fields
Cheeseman & Fields, LLP
100 Main Street
Los Angeles, CA 90089
213-750-1234

Attorney for Plaintiff

SUPERIOR COURT OF THE STATE OF CALIFORNIA
COUNTY OF LOS ANGELES

Edith A. Rhodes, Plaintiff v. Retail Corporation Defendant	)	CASE NO: 62-2009-0009428 COMPLAINT FOR NEGLIGENCE

Plaintiff complains and for causes of action alleges as follows:

1. Plaintiff, Edith A. Rhodes, is an individual and is now, and at all times mentioned in this complaint was, a resident of Los Angeles County, California.
2. Defendant Retail Corporation is now, and at all times mentioned in this complaint was, a corporation organized and existing under the laws of the State of California, with its place of business in Los Angeles County, California.
3. At all times mentioned in this complaint, defendant Retail Corporation operated a clothing store known as On the Edge Clothing Store located at 500 Exposition Boulevard, Los Angeles, County of Los Angeles, California.
4. Defendant Retail Corporation invited the general public, including plaintiff, to enter the premises of defendant's clothing store and purchase various clothing and other items from the defendant.
5. On February 1, 2011, at approximately 4:30 p.m. plaintiff was on the premises of defendants' clothing store for the purpose of shopping and possibly to purchase clothing. Upon entering the defendant's store, plaintiff proceeded to a location in the store when plaintiff suddenly and without warning slipped on a clothes hanger on the floor and fell to the floor, causing plaintiff to sustain the serious injuries and damages described below.
6. Defendant, as owner and operator of the clothing store negligently:
   a. Failed to maintain the floor of the clothing store in a reasonably safe condition;
   b. Allowed a clothes hanger to come into contact with and remain on the floor of the clothing store when defendant knew, or in the exercise of reasonable care should have known, that the clothes hanger created an unreasonable risk of harm to customers in the store;
   c. Failed to warn plaintiff of the danger presented by the presence of the clothes hanger on the floor;
   d. Failed to otherwise exercise due care with respect to the matters alleged in this complaint.
7. As a direct and proximate result of the negligence of defendant as set forth above plaintiff slipped and fell while in the clothing store.
8. As a further direct and proximate result of the negligence of the defendant, plaintiff sustained the following serious injuries and damages: cost of a hip replacement operation and other medical expenses, lost wages, physical injuries, and pain and suffering.

(continued)

Exhibit 13.1 Complaint for negligence *(continued)*

WHEREFORE, plaintiff demands judgment against the defendant for the following:

1. General damages according to proof;
2. Damages for medical expenses according to proof;
3. Damages for loss of earnings according to proof;
4. Pain and suffering according to proof;
5. Interest according to law;
6. Costs of this action;
7. Expert fees; and
8. Any other and further relief that the court considers proper.

DEMAND FOR JURY TRIAL: Plaintiff hereby demands trial by jury for each and every claim for which the plaintiff has a right to jury trial.

DATED: February 28, 2011
By: Percival R. Cheeseman

Attorney for Plaintiff
Cheeseman & Fields, LLP
Percival R. Cheeseman
Clarence K. Fields

VERIFICATION

I, Edith A. Rhodes, am the plaintiff in the above-entitled action. I have read the foregoing *Complaint for Negligence* and know the contents thereof. The same is true of my own knowledge, except as to those matters which are therein alleged on information and belief, and as to those matters, I believe it to be true.

I declare under penalty of perjury that the foregoing is true and correct and that this declaration was executed at Los Angeles, Los Angeles County, California.

DATED: February 28, 2011.

Edith A. Rhodes

(Signature)

---

mental distress be manifested by some physical injury; other states have eliminated this requirement.

Example A father is driving his young daughter to school in his automobile when another driver negligently runs a red light and hits their automobile. Suppose that the daughter dies from her injuries, and the father is uninjured. If the father suffers severe emotional distress by seeing his daughter die (and if he manifests this by a physical injury if required by state law), the father can recover damages for negligent infliction of emotional distress.

Learning Objective 6
Explain a paralegal's duty not to commit professional malpractice.

The ethical duty of a paralegal professional not to commit professional malpractice is discussed in the following feature.

ETHICAL PERSPECTIVE

Paralegal's Duty Not to Commit Professional Malpractice

Paralegals work in a profession that requires them to carefully and reasonably perform their assignments. As professionals, they are subject to malpractice lawsuits if they are negligent in the performance of their work. In determining whether a paralegal has been negligent, the court will examine what a reasonable paralegal would have done in similar circumstances.

Therefore, while performing the tasks assigned to them by supervising attorneys, a paralegal must be constantly vigilant to perform at the highest level of care and competence. Paralegal professionals are therefore required to be conscientious when conducting legal research to make sure that they have explored all avenues of research. When drafting documents, paralegals must draft the documents carefully, and spend time proofreading the documents so that there are no errors.

If a paralegal does not meet the reasonable professional standards of the paralegal profession, he or she can be found to be negligent. Such negligence could result in a loss to a client, a loss to the law firm that employs the paralegal, and a loss to the insurance company that provides liability insurance to the law firm. As the tortfeasor, a paralegal who has committed professional malpractice could also be held personally liable for the damages caused by his or her negligence.

It is a paralegal's ethical duty to perform the tasks assigned to him or her with competence, diligence, and reasonable care. If a paralegal's violation of this ethical duty causes malpractice, the result could be a negligent lawsuit brought against the paralegal, the law firm he or she works for, and possibly a client whom the law firm represents.

Negligence *Per Se*

Statutes often establish duties that one person owes to another. Violating a statute that proximately causes an injury is **negligence *per se*.** The plaintiff in such an action must prove that (1) a statute exists, (2) the statute was enacted to prevent the type of injury suffered, and (3) the plaintiff was within a class of persons the statute is meant to protect.

Negligence *per se* Tort where the violation of a statute or ordinance constitutes the breach of the duty of care.

Example Most cities have an ordinance that places the responsibility for fixing public sidewalks in residential areas on the homeowners whose homes front the sidewalk. A homeowner is liable if he or she fails to repair a damaged sidewalk in front of his or her home and a pedestrian falls and is injured because of the damage. The injured party does not have to prove that the homeowner owed the duty because the statute establishes the homeowner's duty.

Res Ipsa Loquitur

If a defendant is in control of a situation in which a plaintiff has been injured and has superior knowledge of the circumstances surrounding the injury, the plaintiff might have difficulty proving the defendant's negligence. In such a situation, the law applies the doctrine of ***res ipsa loquitur*** (Latin for "the thing speaks for itself"). This doctrine raises a presumption of negligence and switches the burden to the defendant to prove that he or she was *not* negligent. *Res ipsa loquitur* applies in cases where the following elements are met:

1. The defendant had exclusive control of the instrumentality or situation that caused the plaintiff's injury.
2. The injury ordinarily would not have occurred "but for" someone's negligence.

Res ipsa loquitur Tort where the presumption of negligence arises because (1) the defendant was in exclusive control of the situation, and (2) the plaintiff would not have suffered injury except for the defendant's negligence. The burden switches to the defendant(s) to prove they were not negligent.

Example Haeran goes in for major surgery and is given anesthesia to put her to sleep during the operation. Sometime after the operation, it is discovered that a surgical instrument had been left inside Haeran during the operation. She suffers severe injury because of the left-in instrument. Although Haeran would be hard-pressed to identify which doctor or nurse had been careless and left the instrument in her body, she could bring a negligence lawsuit and name the doctor, the nurse, any other medical personnel who assisted in the operation, and the hospital as defendants. In this case, the court can apply the doctrine of *res ipsa loquitur* and place the presumption of negligence on the defendants. Any defendant who can prove that he or she did not leave the instrument in Haeran escapes liability, whereas any defendant who cannot disprove his or her negligence is liable. Other typical *res ipsa loquitur* cases involve commercial airplane crashes, falling elevators, and the like.

Good Samaritan Law

Good Samaritan law A state statute that relieves medical professionals from liability for ordinary negligence when they stop and render aid to victims in emergency situations.

In the past, exposure to liability made many doctors, nurses, and other medical professionals reluctant to stop and render aid to victims in emergency situations such as highway accidents. Today, almost all states have enacted a **Good Samaritan law** that relieves medical professionals from liability for injury caused by their ordinary negligence in such circumstances.

Good Samaritan laws protect medical professionals from liability only for their *ordinary negligence*, not for injuries caused by their gross negligence or reckless or intentional conduct. Most Good Samaritan laws protect licensed doctors and nurses and laypersons who have been certified in CPR. However, Good Samaritan statutes generally do not protect laypersons who are not trained in CPR—that is, they are liable for injuries caused by their ordinary negligence in rendering aid.

Example A driver is injured in an automobile accident and is unconscious in his car. A medical doctor who is driving by the scene of the accident stops, pulls the injured driver from the car, and administers first aid. In doing so, the doctor negligently breaks the person's shoulder. If the doctor's negligence is ordinary negligence, she is not liable to the injured party because the Good Samaritan law protects her. If, however, the doctor was grossly negligent or reckless in administering aid, she is liable for the injuries she caused.

Dram Shop Act

Negligence is the omission to do something which a reasonable man would do, or doing something which a prudent and reasonable man would not do.

B. Alderson
Blyth v. Birmingham Waterworks Co. (1856)

Many states have enacted a **Dram Shop Act** that makes a tavern and a bartender civilly liable for injuries caused to or by patrons who are served too much alcohol. The alcohol must either be served in sufficient quantity to make the patron intoxicated or be served to an already intoxicated person. Both the tavern and the bartender are liable to third persons injured by the patron and for injuries the patron suffered. They are also liable for injuries caused by or to minors served by the tavern, regardless of whether the minor is intoxicated.

Liability of Landowners

Owners and renters of real property owe certain duties to protect visitors from injury while on the property. A landowner's and tenant's liability generally depends on the visitor's status. Visitors fall into the following two categories:

1. ***Invitees and licensees.*** An **invitee** is a person who has been expressly or impliedly invited onto the owner's premises for the *mutual benefit* of both parties (such as guests invited for dinner, the mail carrier, and customers of a business). A **licensee** is a person who, *for his or her own benefit*, enters the premises with the express or implied consent of the owner (such as an Avon representative, an encyclopedia salesperson,

and Jehovah's Witnesses). An owner owes a **duty of ordinary care** to invitees and licensees and is liable if he or she negligently causes injury to an invitee or licensee.

Duty of ordinary care The duty an owner or renter of real property owes an invitee or a licensee to prevent injury or harm when the invitee or licensee steps onto the owner's premises.

Example A homeowner is liable if she leaves across the walkway a garden hose on which an invitee or a licensee trips and is injured.

2. **Trespassers.** A **trespasser** is a person who has no invitation, permission, or right to be on another's property. Burglars are a common type of trespasser. Generally, an owner does not owe a duty of ordinary care to a trespasser.

   Example If a trespasser trips and injures himself on a bicycle the owner negligently left out, the owner is not liable. An owner does, however, owe a **duty not to willfully or wantonly injure** a trespasser. Thus, an owner cannot set traps to injure trespassers.

Duty not to willfully or wantonly injure The duty an owner or renter of real property owes a trespasser to prevent intentional injury or harm to the trespasser when the trespasser is on the owner's premises.

A few states have eliminated the invitee–licensee–trespasser distinction. These states hold that owners and renters owe a duty of ordinary care to all persons who enter the property.

Liability of Common Carriers and Innkeepers

The common law holds common carriers and innkeepers to a higher standard of care than that of most other businesses. **Common carriers** and **innkeepers** owe a **duty of utmost care**—rather than a duty of ordinary care—to their passengers and guests.

Example Innkeepers must provide security for their guests. If a large hotel does not provide security measures and a third party posing as a "waiter" delivering room service injures a guest, the hotel could be held liable to the injured guest. Obviously, a large hotel must provide greater security to guests than a "mom-and-pop" motel needs to provide. Some states and cities have adopted specific statutes and ordinances relating to this duty.

Defenses to Negligence

A defendant in a negligence lawsuit may raise several defenses to the imposition of liability. These defenses are discussed in the following paragraphs.

Superseding or Intervening Event

Under negligence, a person is liable only for foreseeable events. Therefore, an original negligent party can raise a **superseding (or intervening) event** as a defense to liability.

Example Assume that an avid golfer negligently hits a spectator with a golf ball, knocking the spectator unconscious. While lying on the ground waiting for an ambulance to arrive, the spectator is struck by a bolt of lightning and killed. The golfer is liable for the injuries caused by the golf ball. He is not liable for the death of the spectator, however, because the lightning bolt was an unforeseen intervening event.

Assumption of the Risk

If a plaintiff knows of and voluntarily enters into or participates in a risky activity that results in injury, the law recognizes that the plaintiff assumed, or took on, the risk involved. Thus, the defendant can raise the defense of **assumption of the risk** against the plaintiff. This defense assumes that the plaintiff (1) had knowledge of the specific risk, and (2) voluntarily assumed that risk.

Assumption of the risk A defense that a defendant can use against a plaintiff who knowingly and voluntarily enters into or participates in a risky activity that results in injury.

Example Under this theory, a race car driver assumes the risk of being injured or killed in a crash.

Learning Objective 7
Describe and apply the doctrine of strict liability to product liability cases.

Contributory Negligence

Under the common law doctrine of **contributory negligence,** a plaintiff who is partially at fault for his or her own injury cannot recover against the negligent defendant.

Example A driver who is driving faster than the speed limit negligently hits and injures a pedestrian who is jaywalking. The jury finds that the driver is 80 percent responsible for the accident and that the jaywalker is 20 percent responsible. The pedestrian suffered $100,000 in injuries, but under the doctrine of contributory negligence, the pedestrian cannot recover any damages from the driver.

The doctrine of contributory negligence has one major exception: The defendant has a duty under the law to avoid the accident if at all possible. This rule is known as the *last clear chance rule*.

Example A driver who sees a pedestrian walking across the street against a "Don't Walk" sign must avoid hitting the pedestrian if possible. When deciding cases involving this rule, the courts consider the attentiveness of the parties and the amount of time each had to respond to the situation.

Comparative Negligence

As you have seen, application of the doctrine of contributory negligence could have an unfair result in which a party only slightly at fault for his or her injuries cannot recover from an otherwise negligent defendant. Many states have replaced the doctrine of contributory negligence with the doctrine of **comparative negligence.** Under this doctrine, damages are apportioned according to fault.

Comparative negligence A doctrine under which damages are apportioned according to fault.

Example When the comparative negligence rule is applied to the previous example, the result is much fairer. The plaintiff–pedestrian can recover 80 percent of his or her damages (or $80,000) from the defendant–driver. This is an example of *pure comparative negligence*. Several states have adopted *partial comparative negligence*, which provides that a plaintiff must be less than 50 percent responsible for causing his or her own injuries to recover under comparative negligence; otherwise, contributory negligence applies.

In the following feature, a paralegal professional discusses her specialty in the field of personal injury and product liability litigation.

Product Liability and Strict Liability

Where a product causes injury or death to a person, a lawsuit may be brought by the injured person or the heirs of the deceased person against the manufacturer or seller of the product for negligence. In order to prove negligence, the elements of negligence must be proven.

In the landmark case *Greenmun v. Yuba Power Products, Inc.*, 59 Cal.2d 57, 27 Cal.Rptr. 697, 377 P.2d 897, 1963 Cal. Lexis 140 (1963), the California Supreme Court adopted the **doctrine of strict liability in tort** as a basis for **product liability** actions. Most states now have adopted this doctrine as a basis for product liability actions. The doctrine of strict liability removes many of the difficulties for the plaintiff that are associated with proving a case based on negligence. In this section of the chapter, we will examine the scope of the strict liability doctrine.

Product liability The liability of manufacturers, sellers, and others in the chain of distribution for the injuries caused by defective products.

Liability without Fault

Unlike negligence, strict liability does not require the injured person to prove that the defendant breached a duty of care. **Strict liability** *is imposed irrespective of fault.* A seller can be found strictly liable even though he or she has exercised all possible care in the preparation and sale of his or her product.

Strict liability A tort doctrine that makes manufacturers, distributors, wholesalers, retailers, and others in the chain of distribution of a defective product liable for the damages caused by the defect *irrespective of fault.*

Paralegals *in* Practice

PARALEGAL PROFILE
Ruth S. Conley

Ruth S. Conley's legal specialty is personal injury and product liability litigation. A paralegal for over 20 years, she is currently employed by the law firm of Andrews Kurth LLP in Houston, Texas. Ruth has a Bachelor of Science degree in Communications, and obtained the Certified Paralegal designation from the National Association of Legal Assistants (NALA). Previously elected as the first president of the Houston Paralegal Association, Ruth currently serves on NALA's Continuing Education Council. She also serves on the Paralegal Advisory Committee at San Jacinto College's North Campus in Houston.

I feel that the ability to manage time well is the most important skill a litigation paralegal must master. You may have the ability to prepare an excellent trial notebook, and to color-code and cross-reference trial exhibits with fact and expert witness testimony. But, if you cannot prepare these items in a timely manner, then your work product serves no benefit to your attorney, your client, or the progression of your case.

Personal injury and product liability litigation is a "trendy" area of law. Many subjects in news headlines eventually end up in a courtroom, such as Firestone tires, Phen-Fen, and Vioxx. These products were, and continue to be, the source of massive personal injury and product liability litigation across the country. Therefore, as a litigation paralegal, it is important to daily read your newspaper and watch national news television shows. In addition, join a paralegal association and attend its continuing legal education events. Knowledge gained from these resources will help keep you informed.

With the growth of technology and the acceptability of paperless files, many law firms are becoming open to the idea of flexible working hours and work-at-home options for paralegals. As little as ten years ago, this practice would never have been extended to non-attorney staff. However, these options are generally offered only to trusted and experienced paralegals. As a novice paralegal, you must first prove your reliability, work ethic, and profitability to your employer.

The doctrine of strict liability applies to sellers and lessors of products who are engaged in the business of selling and leasing products. Casual sales and transactions by nonmerchants are not covered. Thus, a person who sells a defective product to a neighbor in a casual sale is not strictly liable if the product causes injury.

Strict liability applies only to products, not services. In hybrid transactions involving both services and products, the dominant element of the transaction dictates whether strict liability applies.

Example In a medical operation that requires a blood transfusion, the operation would be the dominant element and strict liability would not apply. Strict liability may not be disclaimed.

All in the Chain of Distribution Are Liable

All parties in the **chain of distribution** of a defective product are strictly liable for the injuries caused by that product. Thus, all manufacturers, distributors, wholesalers, retailers, lessors, and subcomponent manufacturers may be sued under this doctrine. This view is based on public policy. Lawmakers presume that sellers and lessors will insure against the risk of a strict liability lawsuit and spread the cost to their consumers by raising the price of products.

Chain of distribution All manufacturers, distributors, wholesalers, retailers, lessors, and subcomponent manufacturers involved in a transaction.

Example Suppose a subcomponent manufacturer produces a defective tire and sells it to a truck manufacturer. The truck manufacturer places the defective tire on one of its new-model trucks. The truck is distributed by a distributor to a retail dealer. Ultimately, the retail dealer sells the truck to a buyer. The defective tire causes an accident in which the buyer is injured. All of the parties in the tire's chain of distribution can be sued by the injured party. In this case, the liable parties are the subcomponent manufacturer, the truck manufacturer, the distributor, and the retailer.

Exhibit 13.2 Doctrines of negligence and strict liability compared

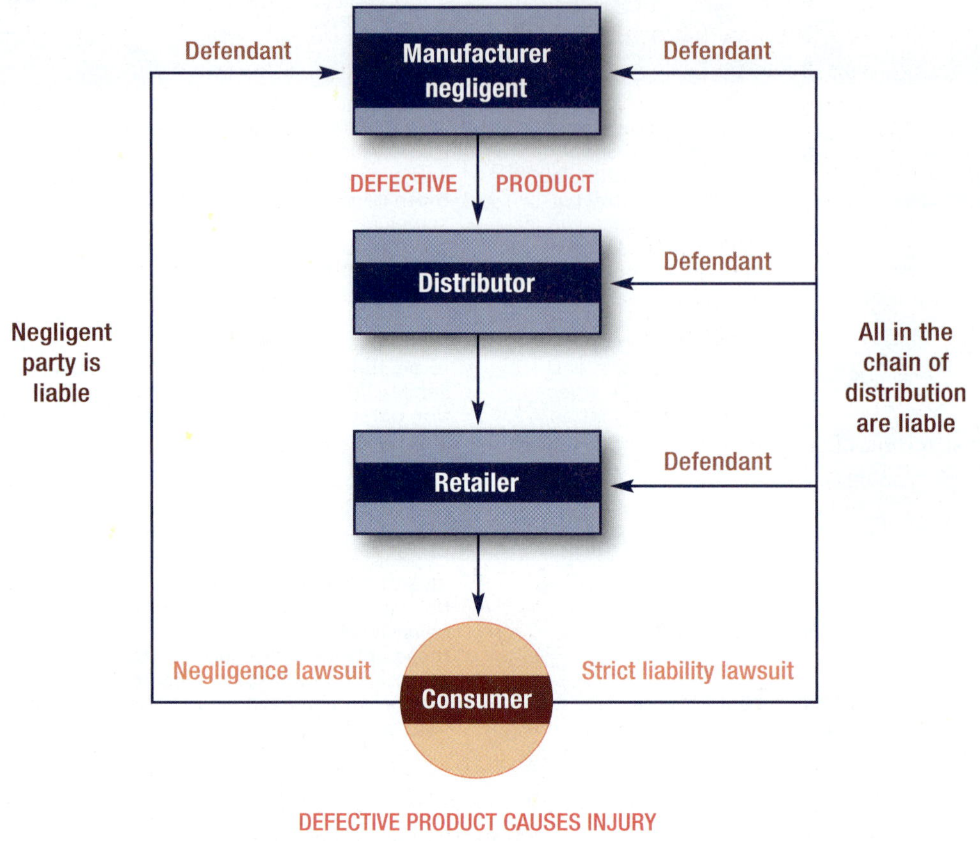

A manufacturer is strictly liable in tort when an article he places on the market, knowing that it is to be used without inspection for defects, proves to have a defect that causes injury to a human being.

Traynor, Justice

A defendant who has not been negligent but who is made to pay a strict liability judgment can bring a separate action against the negligent party in the chain of distribution to recover its losses. In the preceding example, the retailer could sue the manufacturer to recover the strict liability judgment assessed against it. Exhibit 13.2 compares the doctrines of negligence and strict liability.

Parties Who Can Recover for Strict Liability

Because strict liability is a tort doctrine, privity of contract between the plaintiff and the defendant is not required. The doctrine applies even if the injured party had no contractual relations with the defendant. Under strict liability, sellers and lessors are liable to the ultimate user or consumer. Users include the purchaser or lessee, family members, guests, employees, customers, and persons who passively enjoy the benefits of the product (such as passengers in automobiles).

Most jurisdictions have judicially or statutorily extended the protection of strict liability to bystanders. The courts have stated that bystanders should be entitled to even greater protection than a consumer or user because the latter has the chance to inspect for defects and to limit his or her purchases to articles manufactured by reputable manufacturers and sold by reputable retailers, whereas bystanders do not have the same opportunities.

Web Exploration

Go to **http://www.productliability-lawblog.com/2008/03/general_motors_settles_defecti.html** and read the article about General Motors settling a product liability lawsuit.

Example Fred purchases an automobile manufactured by Motors Corporation. The automobile has a defect in it that causes Fred to get into an automobile accident with an automobile driven by Sarah. Both Fred and Sarah are severely injured. Motors Corporation is liable to Fred, the owner and user of the automobile, and to Sarah, a bystander.

Damages Recoverable for Strict Liability

The damages recoverable in a strict liability action vary by jurisdiction. Damages for personal injuries are recoverable in all jurisdictions that have adopted the doctrine of strict liability, although some jurisdictions limit the dollar amount of the award. Property damage is recoverable in most jurisdictions, but economic loss (such as lost income) is recoverable in only a few jurisdictions. **Punitive damages** are generally allowed if the plaintiff can prove that the defendant either intentionally injured him or her or acted with reckless disregard for his or her safety.

A court can award punitive damages against a defendant in a product liability lawsuit if it finds that the defendant's conduct was committed with intent or reckless disregard for human life. Punitive damages are meant to punish the defendant and to send a message to the defendant that such behavior will not be tolerated. Large punitive damage awards usually make the headlines.

Learning Objective 8
Describe punitive damages and explain when they are awarded.

Punitive damages Monetary damages that are awarded to punish a defendant who either intentionally or recklessly injured the plaintiff.

Concept of Defect

To recover for strict liability, the injured party must show that the product that caused the injury had a **defect.** (Remember that the injured party does not have to prove who caused the product to become defective.) A product can be found to be defective in many ways. The most common types of defects are *defects in manufacture*, *failure to warn*, *defects in design*, and *defects in packaging*. These defects are discussed in the following paragraphs.

Learning Objective 9
Describe the type of defects to which the doctrine of strict liability applies.

Defect Something wrong, inadequate, or improper in the manufacture, design, packaging, warning, or safety measures of a product.

Defect in Manufacture

A **defect in manufacture** occurs when the manufacturer fails to (1) properly assemble a product, (2) properly test a product, or (3) adequately check the quality of the product.

> **Example** If a manufacturer of ladders fails to bolt one step to the ladder side and the step breaks off while being used and the user is injured, the manufacturer would be strictly liable for a defect in manufacture.

Defect in manufacture A defect that occurs when a manufacturer fails to (1) properly assemble a product, (2) properly test a product, or (3) adequately check the quality of the product.

Failure to Warn

Certain products are inherently dangerous and cannot be made any safer and still accomplish the task for which they are designed. Manufacturers and sellers of such products are under a *duty to warn* users about the product's dangerous propensities. A proper and conspicuous warning placed on the product insulates the manufacturer and others in the chain of distribution from strict liability. **Failure to warn** of these dangerous propensities is a defect that will support a strict liability action.

> **Example** Certain prescription drugs cause side effects, allergies, and other injuries to some users. If a manufacturer or seller of prescription drugs fails to warn about these side effects and dangers, it can be held liable to anyone injured because of the failure to warn.

Failure to warn A defect that occurs when a manufacturer does not place a warning on the packaging of products that could cause injury if the danger is unknown.

Defect in Design

A **defect in design** can support a strict liability action. A design defect is where an entire product line is defectively designed. In evaluating the adequacy of a product's design, the courts apply a risk–utility analysis and consider the gravity of the danger posed by the design, the likelihood that injury will occur, the availability and cost of producing a safer alternative design, the social utility of the product, and similar factors.

> **Examples** Design defects that have supported strict liability awards include toys that are designed with removable parts that could be swallowed by children, machines and appliances designed without proper safeguards, and trucks and other vehicles designed without warning devices to let people know that the vehicle is backing up.

Defect in design A flaw that occurs when a product is improperly designed.

Defect in Packaging

Web Exploration

Go to **http://www.core77.com/blog/object_culture/antitamper_bottle_cap_5086.asp** to see a version of a tamperproof cap for beverage bottles.

Manufacturers owe a duty to design and provide safe packages for their products. A manufacturer's failure to meet this duty subjects that manufacturer and others in the chain of distribution of the product to strict liability for **defect in packaging.**

Examples This duty requires manufacturers to provide packages and containers that are tamperproof or that clearly indicate when they have been tampered with. Certain manufacturers, such as drug manufacturers, owe a duty to place their products in containers that cannot be opened by children.

Other Product Defects

Other product defects can prove the basis for a strict liability action.

Example **Failure to provide adequate instructions** for either the safe assembly or the safe use of a product is a defect that subjects the manufacturer and others in the chain of distribution to strict liability. Other defects include inadequate testing of products, inadequate selection of component parts of materials, and improper certification of the safety of a product. The concept of defect is an expanding area of the law.

A complaint alleging product liability appears as Exhibit 13.3.

Defenses to Product Liability

Defendant manufacturers and sellers in strict liability or negligence actions may raise the following defenses to the imposition of liability:

1. ***Generally known danger.*** Certain products are inherently dangerous and are known to the general population to be so. Manufacturers and sellers are not strictly liable for failing to warn of generally known dangers.

   Example Because it is a known fact that guns shoot bullets, manufacturers and sellers of guns do not have to place a label on the barrel of a gun warning of this generally known danger.

2. ***Government contractor defense.*** Defense and other contractors that manufacture products to government specifications are not usually liable if the product causes injury.

   Example A manufacturer that produces a weapon to U.S. Army specifications is not liable if the weapon is defective and causes injury.

3. ***Misuse of the product.*** A manufacturer or seller is relieved of product liability if the plaintiff has *abnormally misused* the product.

   Example A manufacturer or seller of a power lawn mower is not liable if a consumer lifts a power lawn mower on its side to cut the hedge, which causes the lawn mower to fall, cutting the consumer.

4. ***Supervening event.*** A manufacturer or seller is not liable if the product is materially altered or modified after it leaves the seller's possession and the alteration or modification causes an injury.

   Example A seller is not liable if a consumer purchases a truck and then replaces the tires with large off-road tires that cause the truck to roll over, injuring the driver or passenger.

Some states have enacted **statutes of repose** that limit a manufacturer's and seller's liability to a certain number of years from the date when the product was first sold. The period of repose varies from state to state.

Exhibit 13.3 Complaint for product liability

UNITED STATES DISTRICT COURT
WESTERN DISTRICT OF KENTUCKY
LOUISVILLE DIVISION

CASE NO. 3:08-CV-349

---X
ALISON COX PREGLIASCO, mother and natural guardian of A.P., an infant, and ALISON COX PREGLIASCO, Individually,

Plaintiffs,

-against-

AMENDED COMPLAINT

Plaintiff Demands Trial by Jury

CROCS, INC.,
A Colorado Corporation

Defendant.
---X

Plaintiffs, ALISON COX PREGLIASCO, mother and natural guardian of A.P., an infant, and ALSION COX PREGLIASCO, Individually, by their attorneys, WATERS LAW GROUP, PLLC and ROBINSON & YABLON, P.C., complaining of the defendant, sets forth as follows:

1. This is an action pursuant to Kentucky products liability law. Jurisdiction of the Court is predicated upon diversity of citizenship pursuant to 28 U.S.C. §1332 (a) (1) because the dispute involves the plaintiffs, who are citizens of Kentucky, and defendant, a Colorado corporation, and because the amount in controversy is greater than $100,000.00.

<u>FIRST CAUSE OF ACTION</u>

PRODUCT LIABILITY

(continued)

Exhibit 13.3 Complaint for product liability *(continued)*

2. At all times hereinafter mentioned, Plaintiff A.P., an infant under the age of fourteen, and her mother and natural guardian, ALISON COX PREGLIASCO, were residents of Kentucky, residing in the City of Louisville. At all times hereinafter mentioned, defendant, CROCS, INC. ("CROCS") was and still is a foreign corporation transacting business in the state of New York.

3. At all times hereinafter mentioned, CROCS was and is a foreign corporation, duly authorized to do business in the state of Kentucky.

4. At all times hereinafter mentioned, CROCS was a Colorado corporation.

5. At all times hereinafter mentioned, CROCS had its principal place of business in Niwot, Colorado.

6. At all times hereinafter mentioned, CROCS contracted to supply goods in the state of Kentucky.

7. At all times hereinafter mentioned, CROCS regularly did and solicited business and/or engaged in other persistent courses of conduct and/or derived financial revenue from the goods supplied in the state of Kentucky.

8. At all times hereinafter mentioned, CROCS expected, or reasonably should have expected acts done by it to have consequences in the state of Kentucky.

Exhibit 13.3 Complaint for product liability *(continued)*

9. At all times hereinafter mentioned, CROCS was engaged in the business of manufacturing, selling and/or distributing footwear, and, in particular, colored footwear comprised of closed-cell resin.

10. In or about 2002, CROCS began to manufacture, sell and distribute a line of closed-cell resin footwear.

11. In or about 2002, CROCS promoted, advertised and marketed its footwear as a slip-resistant outdoor shoe for boating and other outdoor use.

12. In or about 2005, CROCS did commence promotion, marketing and advertising its footwear as an all-purpose shoe for children in small sizes for children.

13. In furtherance of the promotion, marketing, and advertising geared toward the child marketplace, CROCS did commence the selling of footwear in small sizes for children, in child-friendly colors, made use of Disney characters, and promotion of Jibbitz, all in an effort to generate revenue from the sale of CROCS to parents of small children.

14. CROCS did engage in this course of promotion, marketing and sales, directly and through its distributors in the state of Kentucky.

15. In 2005, CROCS did become aware of reports of children being injured while wearing CROCS' shoes when said shoes were sucked into moving escalators.

(continued)

Exhibit 13.3 Complaint for product liability *(continued)*

16. In 2005, the issue of CROCS' shoes being sucked into escalators causing injuries to children was featured on ABC's *Good Morning America.*

17. In 2005, in response to reports of CROCS' shoes being sucked into escalators causing injuries to children, CROCS did issue statements to media that its shoes were safe and that the reported escalator incidents were the fault not of CROCS but rather the parents of the injured children and/or those responsible for maintenance and repair of escalators. CROCS further stated that it was looking into the happening of such incidents and that it was concerned about escalator safety.

18. The statements issued by CROCS and its employees and/or agents, as referenced in ¶17, *supra*, were patently false.

19. CROCS recklessly and knowingly issued the aforementioned false statements in an effort to deflect blame and so as to maximize its corporate profits.

20. In 2006, CROCS did become aware of multiple further reports of children being injured while wearing CROCS' shoes when said shoes were sucked into moving escalators.

21. In 2006, in response to reports of CROCS' shoes being sucked into escalators causing injuries to children, CROCS did issue statements to media that its shoes were safe and that the reported escalator incidents were the fault not of CROCS but rather the parents of the injured children and/or those responsible for maintenance and repair of escalators. CROCS further stated that it was looking into the happening of such incidents and that it was concerned about escalator safety.

Exhibit 13.3 Complaint for product liability *(continued)*

22. The statements issued by CROCS and its employees and/or agents, as referenced in 21, *supra*, were patently false.

23. CROCS knowingly issued the aforementioned false statements in an effort to deflect blame and so as to maximize its corporate profits.

24. On or about March 21, 2008, Plaintiff, ALISON COX PREGLIASCO did purchase a pair of children's CROCS for her daughter, the infant plaintiff, in the state of Kentucky.

25. At the time of the manufacture, distribution, and sale of said pair of CROCS footwear, the footwear contained no safety design features, safety guards and/or warnings of any kind.

26. At the time of the manufacture, distribution and sale of said pair of CROCS, defendant knew, or had reason to know that, despite its promotion, marketing and advertising, CROCS were not suitable and were unsafe as "all purpose shoes for comfort and fashion."

27. At the time of the manufacture, distribution and sale of said pair of CROCS, defendant knew, or had reason to know, of multiple prior reported incidents where young children wearing CROCS were injured when their CROCS were caught in escalators. Defendant further knew that said prior reported incidents all involved claims of similar serious foot injuries to young children.

(continued)

Exhibit 13.3 Complaint for product liability *(continued)*

28. On or about June 4, 2008, infant plaintiff A.P., while wearing CROCS, was severely and permanently injured when one of her CROC shoes was caught in an escalator at Hartsfield Airport in Atlanta, Georgia, causing her right foot to be seriously injured as depicted in the two (2) color photographs annexed as Exhibit "1."

29. The aforesaid occurrence and the injuries resulting therefrom and suffered by the plaintiffs were caused solely by reason of the recklessness, negligence and carelessness of the defendant in its design, manufacturing, testing, inspection, production, assembly, distribution, and sale of its CROCS footwear including the aforesaid pair of CROCS footwear worn by infant plaintiff.

30. By reason of the foregoing, plaintiffs have been damaged and are entitled to compensatory damages in the amount of ONE MILLION DOLLARS ($1,000,000.00).

SECOND CAUSE OF ACTION

BREACH OF EXPRESS & IMPLIED WARRANTY

31. Plaintiffs, repeat, restate and reallege each and every allegation contained in paragraphs "1" through "30" with the same force and effect as if fully set forth herein.

32. CROCS in connection with its business activities aforementioned herein, made both express and implied warranties with regard to the aforesaid product; warranting that it was fit, safe, capable and suitable for the use and purpose intended, and that it was not unsafe or defective.

Exhibit 13.3 Complaint for product liability *(continued)*

33. The aforesaid warranties and representations were false, misleading and inaccurate in that the aforesaid CROCS footwear was unsafe, dangerous and defective.

34. Both express and implied warranties were breached by CROCS.

35. Solely as a result of the aforesaid breaches of warranty, plaintiffs suffered severe injuries and damages while using CROCS footwear for their warranted use and purpose.

36. By reason of the foregoing, plaintiffs have been damaged in a sum in the amount of ONE MILLION DOLLARS ($1,000,000.00).

THIRD CAUSE OF ACTION

FAILURE TO WARN OF KNOWN DEFECT

37. Plaintiffs, repeat, restate and reallege each and every allegation contained in paragraphs "1" through "36" with the same force and effect as if fully set forth herein.

38. At all times herein mentioned, defendant CROCS was aware of problems with regard to the safety and suitability of its footwear as manufactured, sold and marketed.

39. Defendant, notwithstanding said knowledge, failed to design its footwear with adequate safety features and failed to notify and warn purchasers and users of its dangerous product, including plaintiffs herein.

(continued)

Exhibit 13.3 Complaint for product liability *(continued)*

40. As a result of said failure to warn, CROCS is liable to plaintiffs for the injuries and damages they suffered.

41. By reason of the foregoing, plaintiffs have been damaged in the sum of ONE MILLION DOLLARS ($1,000,000.00).

FOURTH CAUSE OF ACTION

LOSS OF SERVICES

42. Plaintiffs, repeat, restate and reallege each and every allegation contained in paragraphs "1" through "41" with the same force and effect as if fully set forth herein.

43. That the Plaintiff, ALISON COX PREGLIASCO, individually, is the mother and natural guardian of the infant-plaintiff, A.P.

44. That by reason of the foregoing incident, Plaintiff, ALSION COX PREGLIASCO was caused to sustain pecuniary losses due to the injuries suffered by her daughter, infant plaintiff, A.P.

45. That by reason of the foregoing incident, Plaintiff, ALSION COX PREGLIASCO was deprived her daughter's services stemming from the serious nature and severity of infant plaintiff, A.P.'s injuries, incurred substantial expenses and was forced to provide services on her behalf.

Exhibit 13.3 Complaint for product liability *(continued)*

46. By reason of the foregoing, plaintiffs have been damaged in the sum of ONE MILLION DOLLARS ($1,000,000.00).

FIFTH CAUSE OF ACTION

PUNITIVE DAMAGES

47. Plaintiffs, repeat, restate and reallege each and every allegation contained in paragraphs "1" through "46" with the same force and effect as if fully set forth herein.

48. The acts and omissions of CROCS, demonstrate a reckless and willful pattern of wanton and depraved indifference to the likelihood of harm to children as a result of product defects in CROCS' footwear.

49. At every crucial juncture, when the onus was upon CROCS to modify its footwear and its marketing so as to warn consumers of dangers known to CROCS, CROCS instead recklessly and knowingly made misleading statements in an effort to maximize its corporate profits at the expense of injuries to young and innocent children.

50. When confronted with incident upon incident of children being injured due to product defects in its footwear, rather than act to protect children and inform their parents and consumers of known dangers, CROCS, instead issued false statements, baselessly attempting to blame persons and entities who were wholly free from fault.

(continued)

Exhibit 13.3 Complaint for product liability *(continued)*

51. The acts and omissions of CROCS, as detailed, *supra*, demonstrate a high degree of moral turpitude warranting the imposition of punitive and/or exemplary damages in the amount of ONE MILLION DOLLARS ($1,000,000.00)

WHEREFORE, Plaintiffs, ALISON COX PREGLIASCO, mother and natural guardian of A.P., an infant and ALISON COX PREGLIASCO, individually demand judgment against the defendant along with such other and further relief as may be granted by the Court, including but not limited to the costs and disbursements of this action.

Dated: July 1, 2008

Respectfully submitted,

s/ Benjamin S. Shively
WATERS LAW GROUP, PLLC
Robert R. Waters, Esq.
rrwaters@waterslawoffice.com
Benjamin S. Shively, Esq.
bsshively@waterslawoffice.com
Enrico A. Mazzoli, Esq.
eamazzoli@waterslawoffice.com
714 Lyndon Lane, Suite 6
Louisville, KY 40222
T: 502-425-2424
F: 502-425-9724

\- and –

ROBINSON & YABLON, P.C.
Andrew M. Laskin, Esq. (AL9379)
ALaskin@robyablaw.com
232 Madison Avenue, Suite 1200
New York, New York 10016
(212) 725-8566

Attorneys for Plaintiffs

Exhibit 13.3 Complaint for product liability *(continued)*

CERTIFICATE OF SERVICE

I hereby declare that on this 1st day of July, 2008, I electronically filed a true and accurate copy of the foregoing document through the ECF system, which will send a notice of electronic filing to Andrew Laskin of Robinson & Yablon, P.C., and on this 1st day of July, 2008, I mailed a true and accurate copy of the foregoing document, postage prepaid, via United States Certified Mail, return receipt requested, to the following:

CROCS, INC.
6328 Monarch Park Place
Niwot, CO 80503

Certified Mail #: 7004 2890 0001 7826 8480

(Principal Office / Street Address for Defendant)

- and -

The Corporation Company
1675 Broadway, Suite 1200
Denver, CO 80202

Certified Mail #: 7004 2890 0001 7826 8473

(Registered Agent for Defendant)

s/ Benjamin S. Shively, Esq

Example Assume that a state statute of repose is seven years. If a consumer purchases a product on May 1, 2011, the statute of repose expires on May 1, 2018. If the product is defective but does not cause injury until after that date, the manufacturer and seller are not liable.

The ethical duty of a paralegal professional to disclose information that could result in bodily harm is discussed in the following feature.

Learning Objective 10

Explain a paralegal's duty to disclose information that could cause bodily harm.

ETHICAL PERSPECTIVE

Duty to Disclose Information That Could Result in Bodily Harm

Ms. Phan is a paralegal who works for a large law firm that represents major corporate clients. One of the clients that the law firm represents is the Wheels Corporation, which manufactures and sells automobile tires. Wheels Corporation is a major supplier of automobile tires to automobile manufacturers who then install the tires on their automobiles, SUVs, trucks, and other vehicles that they sell to the public.

Wheels Corporation designed and manufactured a new automobile tire it calls SafeTrack, which it advertises as having new technology that makes the vehicles' ride safer as well as being longer-lasting than tires made by other tire manufacturers. Millions of SafeTrack tires have been purchased by vehicle manufacturers and placed on new and used vehicles that are sold around the world.

After one year, Wheels Corporation has received thousands of complaints from vehicle owners who allege that their SafeTrack tires easily shred and explode, causing accidents in which drivers and passengers have been injured or killed. Many lawsuits alleging product defects in the SafeTrack tires have been filed against Wheels Corporation.

Wheels Corporation determines, after a secret internal investigation, that the SafeTrack tires most likely shred and explode when the temperature rises above 85 degrees Fahrenheit. Therefore, most of the accidents involving SafeTrack tires have occurred in areas of the United States and other parts of the world that have warmer climates. Wheels Corporation does not make this information available to the public.

Ms. Phan is assigned by her defense law firm to work on many of the product liability lawsuits that Wheels Corporation now faces concerning the defects in its SafeTrack tires. At one of the meetings with the lawyers of the law firm and the executives of Wheels Corporation that Ms. Phan attends, the executives of the Wheels Corporation disclose a cost-benefit analysis they have prepared showing that it will be cheaper for the corporation to let the existing SafeTrack tires remain on vehicles without a recall and pay monetary damages to injured victims and the heirs of deceased victims than to recall and replace the defective tires. The lawyers and the executives agree to this strategy and decide not to recall any of the defective tires and not to inform government authorities of the cost-benefit analysis.

Does Ms. Phan have an ethical duty to disclose this confidential information to government authorities?

A paralegal professional is ordinarily under a duty not to voluntarily disclose information about a client to a government regulatory authority. However, model and state paralegal codes of conduct and social responsibility provide that a paralegal is under an ethical duty to disclose information about a client or the client's conduct that could cause serious bodily harm or death to consumers or others.

PARALEGAL'S ETHICAL DECISION

In this case, although the information revealed at the meeting is normally confidential, Ms. Phan owes an ethical duty to disclose this information to the appropriate government authority because it is necessary to prevent the client, Wheels Corporation, from committing an act that will result in bodily injury and deaths to consumers driving vehicles equipped with the SafeTrack tires, to passengers, to drivers of other vehicles, to pedestrians, and to others. Ms. Phan must disclose these confidential facts to the appropriate government authorities.

Concept Review *and* Reinforcement

LEGAL TERMINOLOGY

Assault 475
Assumption of the risk 487
Battery 475
Breach of the duty of care 481
Causation 481
Causation in fact (actual cause) 481
Chain of distribution 489
Civil fraud 479
Common carrier 487
Comparative negligence 488
Contributory negligence 488
Conversion of personal property 480
Defamation of character 476
Defect 491
Defect in design 491
Defect in manufacture 491
Defect in packaging 492
Disparagement 477
Doctrine of strict liability in tort 488
Doctrine of transferred intent 476
Dram Shop Act 486
Duty not to willfully or wantonly injure 487
Duty of care 480
Duty of ordinary care 487
Duty of utmost care 487
Failure to provide adequate instructions 492
Failure to warn 491
False imprisonment 476
Fraud 478
Good Samaritan law 486
Injury 481
Innkeeper 487
Intentional infliction of emotional distress 478
Intentional torts 474
Invasion of the right to privacy 477
Invitee 486
Libel 476
Licensee 486
Malicious prosecution 478
Merchant protection statute 476
Misappropriation of the right to publicity 477
Negligence 480
Negligence *per se* 485
Negligent infliction of emotional distress 482
Product liability 488
Professional malpractice 482
Proximate cause (legal cause) 482
Punitive damages 491
Reasonable person standard 481
Reasonable professional standard 481
Res ipsa loquitur 485
Scienter 479
Shopkeeper's privilege 476
Slander 476
Statutes of repose 492
Strict liability 488
Superseding (or intervening) event 487
Tort 474
Tort damages 474
Trespass to land 479
Trespass to personal property 479
Trespasser 487
Unintentional tort 480
Wrongful death action 474

SUMMARY OF KEY CONCEPTS

Intentional Torts Against Persons

Assault	Assault is the threat of immediate harm or offensive contact, or any action that arouses reasonable apprehension of imminent harm.
Battery	Battery is the unauthorized and harmful or offensive physical contact with another person. *Transferred intent doctrine:* If a person intends to injure a certain person but actually injures another person, the law transfers the perpetrator's intent from the target to the actual victim.
False Imprisonment	False imprisonment is the intentional confinement or restraint of another person without authority or justification and without that person's consent

Merchant Protection	Merchant protection statutes permit businesses to stop, detain, and investigate suspected shoplifters (and not be held liable for false imprisonment) if the following requirements are met. 1. There are reasonable grounds for the suspicion. 2. Suspects are detained for only a reasonable time. 3. Investigations are conducted in a reasonable manner.
Defamation of Character	Defamation of character occurs when the defendant makes an untrue statement of fact about the plaintiff that is published to a third party. Truth is an absolute defense. Types of defamation: 1. *Slander:* Oral defamation 2. *Libel:* Written defamation Public figure plaintiffs must prove the additional element of *malice*. *Disparagement* is an untrue statement made by a person or business about the products, services, property, or reputation of another business.
Misappropriation of the Right to Publicity	Also called *tort of appropriation,* this tort means appropriating another person's name or identity for commercial purposes without that person's consent.
Invasion of the Right to Privacy	Invasion of the right to privacy is the unwarranted and undesired publicity of a private fact about a person. The fact does not have to be untrue. Truth is not a defense.
Intentional Infliction of Emotional Distress	Intentional infliction of emotional distress, also known as *tort of outrage,* is extreme and outrageous conduct intentionally or recklessly done that causes severe emotional distress. Some states require that the mental distress be manifested by physical injury.
Malicious Prosecution	In malicious prosecution, a successful defendant in a prior lawsuit can sue the plaintiff if the first lawsuit was frivolous.
Civil Fraud	Civil fraud occurs when one party fraudulently deceives another party and steals his or her money or property. To prove fraud, the following elements must be shown: 1. The wrongdoer made a false representation of material fact. 2. The wrongdoer intended to deceive the innocent party. 3. The innocent party justifiably relied on the misrepresentation. 4. The innocent party was injured.
Intentional Torts Against Property	
Trespass to Land	In this form of trespass, a person interferes with an owner's right to exclusive possession of land.
Trespass to Personal Property	In this form of trespass, a person injures another person's personal property or interferes with that person's enjoyment of his or her property.
Conversion of Personal Property	Conversion of personal property means taking over another person's personal property and depriving him or her of the use and enjoyment of the property.
Unintentional Torts—Negligence	
Definition	Negligence is defined as the omission to do something that a reasonable person would do, or doing something that a prudent and reasonable person would not do.
Elements of Negligence	To establish negligence, the plaintiff must prove: 1. The defendant owed *a duty of care* to the plaintiff. 2. The defendant *breached this duty*. 3. The plaintiff suffered *injury*. 4. The defendant's negligent act *caused* the plaintiff's injury. Two types of causation must be shown: a. Causation in fact (or actual cause): The defendant's negligent act was the actual cause of the plaintiff's injury. b. Proximate cause (or legal cause): The defendant is liable only for the foreseeable consequences of his or her negligent act.

Special Negligence Doctrines	
Professional Malpractice	Doctors, lawyers, architects, accountants, and other professionals owe a duty of ordinary care in providing their services and are judged by a *reasonable professional standard*. Professionals who breach this duty are liable to clients and some third parties for *professional malpractice*.
Negligent Infliction of Emotional Distress	A person who witnesses a close relative's injury or death may sue the negligent party who caused the accident to recover damages for any emotional distress the bystander suffered. To recover for *negligent infliction of emotional distress*, the plaintiff must prove: 1. A relative was killed or injured by the defendant. 2. The plaintiff suffered severe emotional distress. 3. The plaintiff's mental distress resulted from a sensory and contemporaneous observance of the accident. Some states require that the mental distress be manifested by physical injury.
Negligence *Per Se*	A statute or ordinance establishes the duty of care. A violation of the statute or ordinance constitutes a breach of this duty of care, or negligence *per se*.
Res Ipsa Loquitur	*Res ipsa loquitur* is a presumption of negligence that is established if the defendant had exclusive control of the instrumentality or situation that caused the plaintiff's injury and if the injury would not have occurred without the defendant's negligence. The defendants may rebut this presumption.
Good Samaritan Law	Good Samaritan laws relieve doctors and other medical professionals from liability for ordinary negligence when they render medical aid in emergency situations.
Dram Shop Act	A Dram Shop Act is a state statute that makes taverns and bartenders liable for injuries caused to or by patrons who are served too much alcohol and cause injury to themselves or others.
Liability of Landowners	Landowners (and tenants) owe the following duties to persons who come upon their property: 1. *Invitees:* Duty of ordinary care 2. *Licensees:* Duty of ordinary care 3. *Trespassers:* Duty not to willfully and wantonly injure trespassers
Liability of Common Carriers and Innkeepers	Common carriers and innkeepers owe a *duty of utmost care*, rather than the duty of ordinary care, to protect their passengers and patrons from injury.
Defenses to Negligence	
Superseding or Intervening Event	A superseding or intervening event is an unforeseeable intervening event that relieves the defendant from liability for causing the plaintiff's injuries.
Assumption of the Risk	Assumption of the risk means that a defendant is not liable for the plaintiff's injuries if the plaintiff had knowledge of a specific risk and voluntarily assumed that risk.
Contributory and Comparative Negligence	States have adopted one of the following two rules that affect a defendant's liability if the plaintiff had been partially at fault for causing his or her own injuries: 1. *Contributory negligence:* A plaintiff cannot recover anything from the defendant. 2. *Comparative negligence:* Damages are apportioned according to the parties' fault. Also called *comparative fault*.
Product Liability and Strict Liability	
Product Liability	Product liability is the liability of manufacturers, sellers, and others in the chain of distribution for the injuries caused by defective products.

Strict Liability	In strict liability, a manufacturer or seller who sells a defective product is liable to the ultimate user who is injured by the product. All in the chain of distribution are liable irrespective of fault.
Defect	To recover for strict liability, the injured party must show that the product that caused the injury was defective. The most common types of defects are: 1. Defect in manufacture 2. Failure to warn 3. Defect in design 4. Defect in packaging 5. Failure to provide adequate instructions

WORKING THE WEB

1. Visit the website http://www.atra.org.html. Click on "State and Federal Reform," and then click on your state. Write a one-page report describing recent tort reforms in your state.
2. Go to the website http://www.google.com/html or a similar Internet search engine and find your state's Good Samaritan law. Print out this law or write a half-page brief of this law.
3. Go to the website http://stellaawards.com/html, and subscribe to receive True Stella Awards case write-ups for free. Many of these case write-ups are about tort cases. For the next tort case that you receive from this site, write a half-page report describing this case.

CRITICAL THINKING & WRITING QUESTIONS

1. What is an *intentional* tort?
2. Define and differentiate assault and battery.
3. Define false imprisonment. What do merchant protection statutes provide? What requirements must be met for a merchant to be protected by these statutes?
4. Describe the following intentional torts: (a) defamation of character, (b) misappropriation of the right to publicity, (c) invasion of the right to privacy, and (d) intentional infliction of emotional distress.
5. What is negligence? What elements must be proven to find negligence? Describe duty of care and breach of duty of care.
6. What is the difference between causation in fact (actual cause) and proximate cause (legal cause)?
7. Describe the following special negligence doctrines: (a) professional malpractice, (b) negligence *per se*, (c) *res ipsa loquitur*, and (d) negligent infliction of emotional distress.
8. Describe the following two defenses to negligence: (a) superseding event and (b) assumption of the risk.
9. Describe the difference between contributory negligence and comparative negligence. Give an example of each.
10. Describe the doctrine of strict liability. To what type of lawsuit does this doctrine apply? Describe how strict liability differs from negligence.
11. Describe the following types of product defects and give an example of each: (a) defect in manufacture, (b) failure to warn, (c) defect in design, and (d) defect in packaging.

Building Paralegal Skills

VIDEO CASE STUDIES

A Salesman's Courtroom Testimony: Fact or Misrepresentation?

The salesman for a company that sells truck brake parts admits in trial testimony that the parts sold may not have been appropriate for the required use.

After viewing the video case study in MyLegalStudiesLab, answer the following:

1. What are the elements necessary to make a case for fraudulent misrepresentation?
2. Is the salesman's employer bound by the conduct in making the sale and therefore liable for any harm caused by the sale of the inappropriate products?
3. If a product is shipped in a defective condition that makes it inherently dangerous, do the representations of the salesman matter?

Solicitation in the ER: Ethical Duties of the Profession

The parents of a child injured in a school bus accident are approached in the emergency room by a law clerk who offers them the opportunity of hiring a lawyer to handle their case and shares their information with a paralegal who is in the emergency room.

After viewing the video case study in MyLegalStudiesLab, answer the following:

1. Are the clerk and the paralegal guilty of solicitation?
2. Has the parents' and the child's information been improperly divulged?
3. Is the claim that the bus driver appeared woozy and was drunk actionable defamation?

The Judge Instructs the Jury before Deliberation

The trial judge gives a jury instructions on how the trial will proceed and then at the end of the trial, charges the jury with specific instructions that relate to questions of law upon which they must deliberate.

After viewing the video case study in MyLegalStudiesLab, answer the following:

1. What is the purpose of giving the jury preliminary instructions at the beginning of the trial?
2. What is the purpose of the jury charge on a specific point of law?
3. Is the jury bound by the instructions given to them by the judge?

ETHICS ANALYSIS & DISCUSSION QUESTIONS

1. What ethical obligation does the legal team have to inform clients, even when the clients do not ask for advice, of actions they should take to avoid liability?
2. What is the "reasonable professional standard" for a paralegal?
3. As a recent paralegal program graduate with school loans to pay, you also work at a local food market at night. You are working on a slow Tuesday evening and instead of walking the aisles of the store, you take a coffee break in the back. While you are doing so, a customer slips on a small bunch of grapes that are in one of the aisles, breaking a bone in his leg. The injured customer is also a long-time client of the law firm where you work. Is there any conflict of interest? How can the conflict be resolved?

DEVELOPING YOUR COLLABORATION SKILLS

With a group of other students selected by you or assigned by your instructor, review the facts of the following case. As a group, discuss the following questions.

1. Who is the plaintiff in this case? Who is the defendant in this case?
2. What is negligence? What elements must be established to prove negligence?
3. Do you believe that the elements of negligence were proved in this case?
4. What damages, if any, should be awarded?
5. Is an award of punitive damages warranted?

Liebeck v. McDonald's Restaurants, P.T.S., Inc.

Stella Liebeck, a 79-year-old resident of Albuquerque, New Mexico, visited a drive-through window of a McDonald's restaurant with her grandson Chris. Her grandson, the driver of the vehicle, placed the order for breakfast. When breakfast came at the drive-through window, Chris handed a hot cup of coffee to Stella. Chris pulled over so that Stella could put cream and sugar in her coffee. Stella took the lid off the coffee cup she held in her lap, and the hot coffee spilled in her lap. As a result of the spell, Stella suffered third-degree burns on her legs, thighs, groin, and buttocks. Stella was driven to the emergency room and was hospitalized for seven days. She required medical treatment and later returned to the hospital to have skin grafts. She suffered permanent scars from the incident.

Stella's medical costs were $11,000. Stella asked McDonald's to pay her $20,000 to settle the case, but McDonald's offered only $800. Stella refused this settlement and sued McDonald's in court for negligence for selling coffee that was too hot and for failing to warn her of the danger of the hot coffee it served. At trial, McDonald's denied that it had been negligent and asserted that Stella's own negligence—opening a hot coffee cup on her lap—had caused her injuries. The jury heard the following evidence:

- McDonald's enforces a quality-control rule that requires its restaurants and franchises to serve coffee at 180 to 190 degrees Fahrenheit.
- Third-degree burns occur on skin in just two to five seconds when coffee is served at 185 degrees.
- McDonald's coffee temperature was 20 degrees hotter than coffee served by competing restaurant chains.
- The temperature of McDonald's coffee was approximately 40 to 50 degrees hotter than normal house-brewed coffee.
- McDonald's had received more than 700 prior complaints of people who had been scalded by McDonald's coffee.
- McDonald's did not place a warning on its coffee cups to alert patrons that the coffee it served was exceptionally hot.

Based on this evidence, the jury concluded that McDonald's had acted recklessly and awarded Stella $200,000 in compensatory damages, which was then reduced by $40,000 because of her own negligence, and $2.7 million in punitive damages. The trial court judge reduced the amount of punitive damages to $480,000, which was three times the amount of compensatory damages.

Source: Liebeck v. McDonald's Restaurants, P.T.S., Inc. (New Mexico District Court, Bernalillo County, New Mexico)

PARALEGAL PORTFOLIO EXERCISE

Prepare a memorandum, no longer than three pages, that discusses the doctrine of strict liability as used in product liability cases, the different types of defects that can be asserted in a strict liability case, and the types of damages that can be awarded in strict liability cases.

LEGAL ANALYSIS & WRITING CASES

Domingue v. Cameco Industries, Inc.

936 So.2d 282, Web 2006 La. App. Lexis 1593
Court of Appeal of Louisiana

Russel Domingue, Charles Judice, and Brent Gonsoulin, who were employed by M. Matt Durand, Inc. (MMD), were stockpiling barite ore at a mine site. Judice and Gonsoulin were operating Cameco 405-B articulating dump trucks (ADTs) that were manufactured by Cameco Industries, Inc. Each of the trucks weighed over 25 tons and could carry a load of more than 20 metric tons. Judice and Gonsoulin were offloading ore from a barge and transporting and dumping it at a site where Domingue was using a bulldozer to push the barite onto a growing pile of ore. The two ADTs would make trips, passing each other on the way to and from the barge.

Gonsoulin, who was new to the job, had trouble dumping a large load of barite. Domingue, who was an experienced ADT operator, got off the bulldozer and walked to Gonsoulin's ADT to give his co-worker advice on how to dump a heavy load. Meanwhile, Judice made another trip to dump ore and turned his ADT around to return to the barge. At the same time, Domingue was walking back to his bulldozer. Judice testified that he then saw "a pair of sunglasses and cigarettes fly." Judice immediately stopped his ADT and discovered Domingue's body, which he had run over. Domingue's widow, on behalf of herself and her children, filed suit against Cameco, alleging that there was [a] design defect in the ADT that caused a forward "blind spot" for anyone operating an ADT. The trial court found a design defect and held Cameco 30 percent responsible for causing Domingue's death. Damages were set at $1,101,050. Cameco appealed.

Question

1. Is Cameco Industries liable?

Lilya v. The Greater Gulf State Fair, Inc.

855 So.2d 1049, Web 2003 Ala. Lexis 57
Supreme Court of Alabama

The Greater Gulf State Fair, Inc. operated the Gulf State Fair in Mobile County, Alabama. One of the events at the fair was a mechanical bull ride for which participants paid money to ride the mechanical bull. A mechanical bull is a ride where the rider sits on a motorized device shaped like a real bull, and the ride simulates a real bull ride as the mechanical bull turns, twists, and bucks. The challenge is to stay on the bull and not be thrown off. A large banner above the ride read "Rolling Thunder."

John Lilya and a friend watched as a rider was thrown from the mechanical bull. Lilya also watched as his friend paid and rode the bull and also was thrown off. Lilya then paid the $5 admission charge and signed a release agreement that stated:

> I acknowledge that riding a mechanical bull entails known and unanticipated risks which could result in physical or emotional injury, paralysis, death, or damage to myself, to property, or to third parties. I expressly agree and promise to accept and assume all of the risks existing in this activity. My participation in this activity is purely voluntary, and I elect to participate in spite of the risks.

Lilya boarded the mechanical bull and was immediately thrown off onto a soft pad underneath the bull. Lilya reboarded the bull for a second ride. The bull ride began again and became progressively faster, spinning and bucking to the left and right until Lilya fell off the bull. On the fall, Lilya landed on his head and shoulders, and he suffered a fractured neck. Lilya sued Gulf State Fair to recover damages for his severe injuries. The trial court granted summary judgment to Gulf State Fair, finding that Lilya had voluntarily assumed an open and obvious danger. Lilya appealed.

Question

1. Is Gulf State Fair liable?

WORKING WITH THE LANGUAGE OF THE COURT CASE

Wal-Mart Stores, Inc. v. Cockrell 61 S.W.3d 774, 2001 Tex. App. Lexis 7992

Court of Appeals of Texas

Read the following case, excerpted from the Court of Appeals opinion. Review and brief the case. In your brief answer the following questions:

1. Who is the plaintiff? Who is the defendant?
2. What laws does the plaintiff claim have been violated?
3. What is the merchant protection statute? What elements must be proven to successfully assert this doctrine?
4. Were the damages awarded to the plaintiff by the jury appropriate based on the facts of the case?

Dorsey, Justice

Wal-Mart Stores, Inc., appeals from a judgment, following a jury verdict, finding that it had assaulted and falsely imprisoned a suspected shoplifter, Karl Cockrell. Based upon these findings the jury awarded Cockrell $300,000 for past mental anguish. The question raised on appeal is whether the evidence is legally and factually sufficient to support the verdict. We affirm.

Karl Cockrell and his parents went to the layaway department at a Wal-Mart store. Cockrell stayed for about five minutes and decided to leave. As he was going out the front door Raymond Navarro, a loss-prevention officer, stopped him and requested that Cockrell follow him to the manager's office. Once in the office Navarro told him to pull his pants down. Cockrell put his hands between his shorts and underwear, pulled them out, and shook them. Nothing fell out. Next Navarro told him to take off his shirt. Cockrell raised his shirt, revealing a large bandage which covered a surgical wound on the right side of his abdomen. Cockrell had recently had a liver transplant. Navarro asked him to take off the bandage, despite Cockrell's explanation that the bandage maintained a sterile environment around his

(continued)

surgical wound. On Navarro's insistence Cockrell took down the bandage, revealing the wound. Jay Garrison and Nancy Suchomel, both Wal-Mart employees, were in the office when Cockrell lifted his shirt. Afterwards Navarro apologized and let Cockrell go.

By issues one and two Wal-Mart attacks the legal and factual sufficiency of the evidence to support the jury's findings that it had assaulted and falsely imprisoned Cockrell.

The elements of false imprisonment are: (1) a willful detention; (2) performed without consent; and (3) without the authority of law. A person may falsely imprison another by acts alone or by words alone, or by both, operating on the person's will.

Here Ray Navarro, the loss-prevention officer, testified that Cockrell was in his custody at the point when he escorted him to the office. When Cockrell's counsel asked Navarro, "Was it your decision as to when he [Cockrell] could leave?" he replied, "I guess." Navarro testified that he probably would have let Cockrell leave after seeing that he did not have anything under his shirt.

Cockrell testified that he was not free to leave when Navarro stopped him and that Navarro was not going to let him go. He also testified that Navarro and two other Wal-Mart employees accompanied him to the office. When counsel asked Cockrell why he did not leave the office, he replied, "Because the impression I was getting from him, I wasn't going no place." We conclude that these facts are sufficient to support the jury's finding that Cockrell was willfully detained without his consent.

Question One asked the jury whether Wal-Mart falsely imprisoned Karl Cockrell. "Falsely imprison" was defined to mean "willfully detaining another without legal justification…." The court instructed the jury on the "shopkeeper's privilege." This instruction stated: "when a person reasonably believes that another has stolen or is attempting to steal property, that person has legal justification to detain the other in a reasonable manner and for a reasonable time to investigate ownership of the property." Thus the jury could only find false imprisonment if it found no justification for Wal-Mart's actions.

Neither Raymond Navarro nor any other store employee saw Cockrell steal merchandise. However Navarro claimed he had two reasons to suspect Cockrell of shoplifting. First he said that Cockrell was acting suspiciously, because he saw him in the women's department standing very close to a rack of clothes and looking around. Later he saw Cockrell looking around and walking slowly by the cigarette aisle and then "pass out of the store." Second he saw a little "bulge" under Cockrell's shirt.

Cockrell testified that he had done "nothing" and that there was "no way" a person could see anything under his shirt. We conclude that a rational jury could have found that Navarro did not "reasonably believe" a theft had occurred and therefore lacked authority to detain Cockrell.

The extent to which Wal-Mart searched Cockrell compels us to address the reasonable manner of the detention. The "shopkeeper's privilege" expressly grants an employee the authority of law to detain a customer to investigate the ownership of property in a *reasonable manner*.

At least one appellate court has stated that when a store employee has probable cause to arrest a person for shoplifting, the employee may do so and make a "contemporaneous search" of the person and the objects within that person's control. *See Raiford v. The May Dep't Stores Co.*, 2 S.W.3d 527, 531 (Tex.App.-Houston [14th Dist.] 1999, no pet.).

We therefore hold that when a store employee has probable cause to arrest a person for shoplifting, the employee may do so and make a contemporaneous search of the person and objects within that person's immediate control. The contemporaneous search is limited to instances in which a search of the body is reasonably necessary to investigate ownership of property believed stolen. Accordingly Navarro's contemporaneous search was unreasonable in scope, because he had no probable cause to believe that Cockrell had hidden any merchandise under the bandage. Removal of the bandage compromised the sterile environment surrounding the wound. Having found the evidence sufficient with respect to each of the essential elements of false imprisonment we overrule issue one.

Question Two asked whether Wal-Mart assaulted Cockrell. The jury answered affirmatively. The trial court instructed the jury that a person commits an assault "if he intentionally or knowingly causes physical contact with another, when he knows or should reasonably believe that the other will regard the contact as offensive or provocative." Cockrell's testimony was that as he was going out the outer set of front doors Navarro put his hands on his back and shoulder and "twisted" him around. He thought that Navarro was going to rob him. Navarro did not believe that he had touched Cockrell. We conclude that a rational jury could find that Navarro knew or should have reasonably believed that Cockrell would regard the contact as offensive or provocative. We hold that the evidence is legally and factually sufficient to support the jury's finding that Wal-Mart assaulted Cockrell. We overrule issue two.

By issue three Wal-Mart asserts that there is no evidence to support the $300,000 award for past mental anguish. Alternatively Wal-Mart argues that the award is against the great weight and preponderance of the evidence. We conclude that there is evidence to support the award.

To recover for mental anguish a plaintiff must offer direct evidence of the nature, duration, and severity of their mental anguish, thus establishing a substantial disruption in the plaintiffs' daily routine, or other evidence of a high degree of mental pain and distress that is more than mere worry, anxiety, vexation, embarrassment, or anger. Courts should "closely scrutinize" awards of mental anguish damages. There must also be evidence that the amount of mental anguish damages awarded is fair and reasonable, and the appellate court must perform a "meaningful evidentiary review" of the amount found.

Evidence of Cockrell's mental anguish comes largely from the following testimony: Counsel asked Cockrell to describe his demeanor when he took down his bandage in the manager's office. He stated that Navarro:

> made me feel like I was scum, like...I was no part of society, that I had no say-so in the matter, that—just made me feel like a little kid on the block, like the bully beating the kid up and saying, "Well, I didn't catch you with nothing; but I'm going to humiliate him, twist a knife a little bit more into them."

When counsel asked Cockrell how he felt when people looked at the scar he said, "Humiliated.... Your dignity has been stripped, been raped. All your rights have been—might as well have been taken away at that time because I had no rights back there.... [E]ven after it was over with, I felt like I had no rights."

Cockrell testified that after Navarro let him go he was shaking, crying, nervous, scared, and looking around to make sure no one else was trying to stop him. When he got home his demeanor was about the same.

Cockrell's parents saw him in the Wal-Mart store immediately after he was let go. They said he was upset, nervous, had tears in his eyes, and looked scared, pale, and badly shaken up. When he arrived at home he was crying, nervous, and still "pretty well shook up." His mother said that he stayed upset for a "long time" and would not go out of the house or go anywhere with his parents. She explained that

> he won't go out hardly. And if he does, he just goes with us. And he's always looking around if we go in a store, like he's looking over his shoulder to see if anybody's following him. And he's self-conscious of his stomach, and he feels like everybody knows it....

This is direct evidence of the nature, duration, and severity of Cockrell's mental anguish, thus establishing a substantial disruption in his daily routine. His mental pain and distress was more than mere worry, anxiety, vexation, embarrassment, or anger.

We hold that the evidence is legally and factually sufficient to support the award of mental anguish damages. We overrule issue three.

During oral argument Wal-Mart waived its complaint under issue four, which concerned the calculation of prejudgment interest.

We AFFIRM the trial court's judgment.

MYLEGALSTUDIESLAB

MyLegalStudiesLab Virtual Law Office Experience Assignments

Complete the pre-test, study plan, and post-test for this chapter and answer the Legal Applications questions as assigned. These will help you confirm your mastery of the concepts and their application to legal scenarios. Then complete the Virtual Law Office assignments as assigned by your instructor. These assignments are designed to develop your workplace skills. Completing the assignments for this chapter will result in producing the following documents for inclusion in your portfolio:

VLOE 13.1	Electronic copies of documents to proceed with the case using the American Arbitration Association procedures
VLOE 13.2	Office memo summary of the law on product liability and strict liability in your state

CHAPTER

14

Contracts and E-Commerce

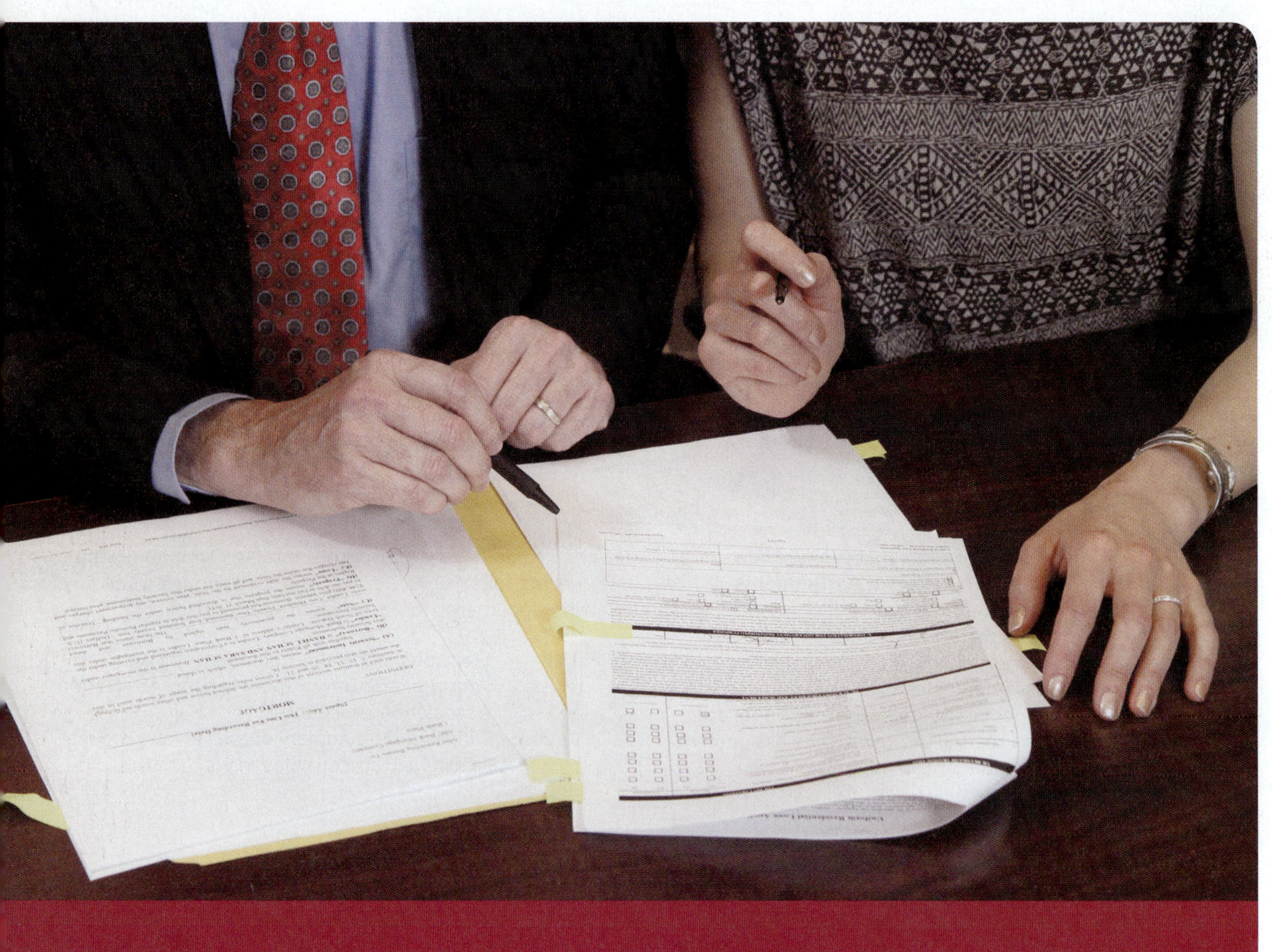

LEARNING OBJECTIVES

After studying this chapter, you should be able to:

1. Recognize the professional opportunities for paralegals in contract and e-commerce law.
2. List the elements necessary to form a valid contract.
3. Define an offer and an acceptance.
4. Define consideration and analyze whether contracts are lacking in consideration.
5. Identify illegal contracts that are contrary to statutes and that violate public policy.
6. List and describe the contracts that must be in writing under the Statute of Frauds.
7. Describe compensatory, consequential, and liquidated damages.
8. Define sales contracts governed by Article 2 of the UCC and lease contracts governed by Article 2A of the UCC.
9. Define *e-contract* and describe the formation and enforcement of e-contracts.
10. Describe the main features of the federal E-SIGN Act.

Paralegals at Work

You are a paralegal who works for Mr. Andrew Copan, a lawyer who represents small businesses. A significant part of Mr. Copan's practice is the drafting of contracts for the business clients when they are dealing with individuals and other businesses. Mr. Copan also engages in civil litigation and represents his clients bringing or defending contract-related cases in court.

One of Mr. Copan's clients is Jewelry Associates Corporation (JAC), a small corporation that is in the retail jewelry business. The business has three owners. The business buys jewels in overseas markets and sells the jewels in a retail store serving customers.

One day, the three owners of Jewelry Associates Corporation make an appointment to see Mr. Copan to discuss several business matters. Because you are his paralegal, Mr. Copan asks you to sit in on the meeting, which you do. At the meeting, the three owners explain that they have found a new source of jewels, Overseas Mines Inc., which is a foreign company located in Sri Lanka. The owners ask Mr. Copan to draft a contract between JAC and Overseas Mines. JAC will be the buyer, and the foreign company will be the seller of jewels. The owners ask Mr. Copan to research the law applicable to the situation and prepare a contract for this transaction.

The owners further explain that they have obtained the web address jewelryjewelry.com and that they want to begin selling jewelry through e-commerce. They are having a website designed, and they need an online contract drafted for the sale of jewelry online. They ask Mr. Copan to draft the necessary online contract that will be placed on the website.

In addition, the owners of Jewelry Associates Corporation inform Mr. Copan that the business currently leases its retail store space from the owner of a large building, but that their lease will end in nine months. The owners disclose that their corporation entered into a contract with Real Estate Developers Inc. to purchase a building

> "The movement of the progressive societies has hitherto been a movement from status to contract."
>
> Sir Henry Maine, *Ancient Law*

and land to which they will move their retail business. However, Real Estate Developers Inc. now refuses to go through with the contract and sell JAC the building and land. The owners ask Mr. Copan what course of action to take to obtain the building.

After the clients have left, Mr. Copan asks you to assist him in conducting the legal research necessary for these matters, and to prepare first drafts of the contracts discussed at the meeting.

Consider the issues involved in this scenario as you read this chapter.

Learning Objective 1
Recognize the professional opportunities for paralegals in contract and e-commerce law.

INTRODUCTION FOR THE PARALEGAL

Many paralegal professionals work in the field of contract law. This field of law makes up a substantial portion of many lawyers' practices. Lawyers rely heavily on the help of paralegals in drafting and reviewing contracts. Paralegals are called upon to assist lawyers in preparing and reviewing all sorts of contracts, including those for the sale of personal property and real property, those for commercial sales and lease contracts, those for licenses, and other types of contracts.

"When I use a word," Humpty Dumpty said, in rather a scornful tone, "it means just what I choose it to mean—neither more nor less." "The question is," said Alice, "whether you can make words mean so many different things." "The question is," said Humpty Dumpty, "which is to be master—that's all."
Lewis Carroll
Alice's Adventures in Wonderland (1865)

Contracts are the basis of many of our daily activities. They provide the means for individuals and businesses to sell and otherwise transfer property, services, and other rights. The purchase of goods is based on sales contracts; the hiring of employees is based on service contracts; and the lease of apartments is based on rental contracts. In addition, electronic contracts—e-contracts—are formed using email and the Internet. The list of contracts is almost endless. Without enforceable contracts, commerce would collapse.

Contracts are voluntarily entered into by parties. The terms of the contract become *private law* between the parties. The courts are obliged to give legal effect to such contracts according to the true interests of the parties.

This chapter covers the study of traditional contract law, e-contracts, and e-commerce.

The following feature discusses the career opportunities for paralegal professionals in contract law.

Sources of Contract Law

There are several sources of contract law. These include the common law of contracts, the Uniform Commercial Code (UCC), and electronic commerce law. Each of these is described in the following paragraphs.

The Common Law of Contracts

Common law of contracts Contract law developed primarily by state courts.

A major source of contract law is the **common law of contracts.** The common law of contracts developed from early court decisions that became precedent for later decisions. A limited federal common law of contracts applies to contracts made by the federal government. The larger and more prevalent body of common law has been developed from state court decisions. Thus, although the general principles remain the same throughout the country, there is some variation from state to state.

Uniform Commercial Code (UCC)

Uniform Commercial Code (UCC) A comprehensive statutory scheme that includes laws covering aspects of commercial transactions.

Another major source of contract law is the **Uniform Commercial Code (UCC).** The UCC, which was first drafted by the National Conference of Commissioners on Uniform State Laws in 1952, has been amended several times. Its goal is to create

CAREER OPPORTUNITIES FOR PARALEGALS IN CONTRACT LAW

There is probably no area of substantive law in which paralegals are more involved than contract law. Contracts make the world go 'round. The number of contracts in an individual's life and those of businesses is staggering.

Contracts are used to support most commercial transactions. Business contracts include those for the sale and lease of goods and the provision of services. Lawyers who practice in the area of business law are constantly called upon to draft contracts for their clients. And business contracts may range from those for smaller businesses, such as sole proprietorships and general partnerships, to those between Fortune 500 companies, such as Microsoft Corporation and Intel Corporation.

Contracts are also needed for the sale, transfer, and lease of real property. Lawyers involved in real estate law must draft contracts for these transfers of interests in real estate. These include short contracts for simple matters such as an apartment lease to long, detailed contracts for the construction of shopping malls, the building of skyscrapers, and other real estate matters.

Other contracts are needed to sell, lease, or transfer ownership of any property. For example, contracts are required for the settlement of divorce cases, the agreements between owners of businesses, the creation of franchises, the licensing of intellectual property (such as patents and copyrights), the mergers of large corporations, and so on. In addition, the provision of services, such as those of architects, lawyers, doctors, consultants, and other professionals, requires a contract between the client and the professional.

Paralegals are indispensable in assisting lawyers in drafting and reviewing contracts for individuals and businesses that are the lawyers' clients. A paralegal must be familiar with general contract law principles and also must become familiar with the specific types of contracts that the lawyer he or she works for practices in. Thus, a paralegal who works for a lawyer practicing in the real estate field must be familiar with real estate contracts. A paralegal who works for a lawyer practicing family law must be familiar with the specifics of divorce settlement agreements. And so on.

Many lawsuits are brought concerning contracts. For example, a client of the law firm may have reason to bring a lawsuit against the other contracting party for breach of contract. On the other hand, a client of the law firm may find itself being sued for an alleged breach of a contract. This is where a paralegal's skill in conducting interviews, uncovering evidence, preparing the file for trial, and conducting contract law research is needed.

Paralegals familiar with contract law, drafting contracts, and researching contract law are in substantial demand. This demand will continue as the number and complexity of contracts increase in importance to individuals and businesses.

a uniform system of commercial law among the 50 states. Provisions of the UCC normally take precedence over the common law of contracts.

The UCC is divided into nine main articles, and every state has adopted at least part of the UCC. In the area of contract law, two of the major provisions of the UCC are:

1. ***Article 2 (Sales).*** This article prescribes a set of uniform rules for the creation and enforcement of contracts for the sale of goods. These contracts are often referred to as **sales contracts.** For example, the sale of equipment is a sales contract subject to Article 2 of the UCC.
2. ***Article 2A (Leases).*** This article prescribes a set of uniform rules for the creation and enforcement of contracts for the lease of goods. These contracts are referred to as **lease contracts.** For example, the lease of an automobile is a lease subject to Article 2A of the UCC.

Sales contracts A contract for the sale of goods.

Lease contract A contract for the lease of goods.

E-Contract Law

As we entered the twenty-first century, a new economic shift brought the United States and the rest of the world into the Information Age, as computer technology and the use of the Internet increased dramatically. A new form of commerce—**electronic commerce,** or **e-commerce**—is now flourishing, and all sorts of goods and services are sold by **e-contract** over the Internet. You can

Electronic commerce (e-commerce) The sale of goods and services by computer over the Internet.

E-contract A contract that is entered into by email and over the World Wide Web.

purchase automobiles and children's toys, participate in auctions, purchase airline tickets, make hotel reservations, and purchase many other goods and services over the Internet.

Much of the new cyberspace economy is based on electronic contracts and the licensing of computer information. Because e-commerce created problems for forming contracts over the Internet, enforcing e-commerce contracts, and providing consumer protection, the National Conference of Commissioners on Uniform State Laws (a group of lawyers, judges, and legal scholars) drafted the **Uniform Computer Information Transactions Act (UCITA).**

Uniform Computer Information Transactions Act (UCITA) A model state law that creates contract law for the licensing of information technology rights.

The UCITA established uniform legal rules for the formation and enforcement of electronic contracts and licenses and addresses most of the legal issues that are encountered while conducting e-commerce over the Internet. However, the UCITA is a model act that does not become law until a state legislature adopts it as a statute for the state. Since its promulgation in July 1999, many states have adopted the UCITA in whole or in part. Because of the need for uniformity of e-commerce rules, the UCITA is becoming the basis for the creation and enforcement of cyberspace contracts and licenses.

Learning Objective 2
List the elements necessary to form a valid contract.

Formation of a Contract

A **contract** is an agreement that is enforceable by a court of law or equity. A simple and widely recognized definition is:

> A contract is a promise or a set of promises for the breach of which the law gives a remedy or the performance of which the law in some way recognizes a duty. [Restatement (Second) of Contracts, Section 1].

Most contracts are performed without the aid of the court system, usually because the parties feel a moral duty to perform as promised. Although some contracts, such as illegal contracts, are not enforceable, most are **legally enforceable.** This means that if a party fails to perform the duties stated in a contract, the other party may call upon the courts to enforce the contract.

Legally enforceable A contract in which if one party fails to perform as promised, the other party can use the court system to enforce the contract and recover damages or other remedy.

Elements of a Contract

For a contract to be enforceable, the following four basic requirements must be met:

1. ***Agreement.*** There must be an agreement between the parties.
2. ***Consideration.*** The promise must be supported by a bargained-for consideration that is legally sufficient.
3. ***Contractual capacity.*** The parties to a contract must have the capacity to contract.
4. ***Lawful object.*** The object of the contract must be lawful, or legal.

The text of this chapter discusses these requirements in greater detail.

Every contract involves at least two parties. The **offeror** is the party who makes an offer to enter into a contract. The **offeree** is the party to whom the offer is made (see Exhibit 14.1). In making an offer, the offeror promises to do—or to refrain from doing something. The offeree then has the power to create a contract by accepting the offeror's offer. A contract is created if the offer is accepted. No contract is created if the offer is not accepted.

Offeror The party who makes an offer to enter into a contract.

Offeree The party to whom an offer to enter into a contract is made.

Learning Objective 3
Define an offer and an acceptance.

Agreement

Agreement is the manifestation by two or more persons of the substance of a contract. It requires an *offer* and an *acceptance*. The process of reaching an agreement usually proceeds as follows: Prior to entering into a contract, the parties

Agreement The manifestation by two or more persons of the substance of a contract.

Exhibit 14.1 Parties to a contract

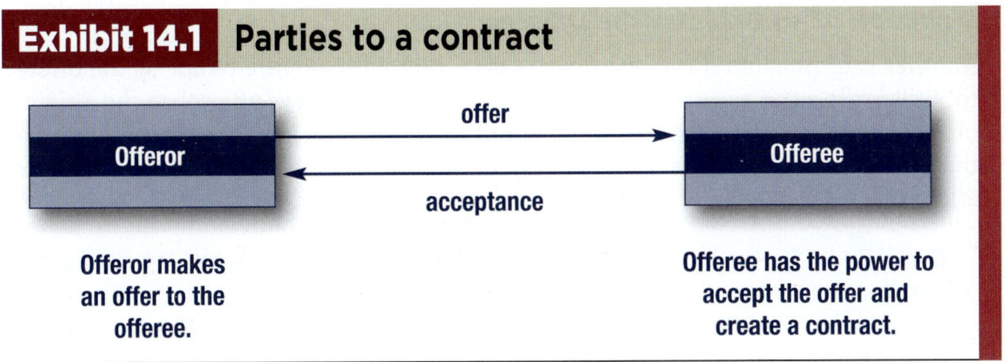
offer
Offeror
Offeree
acceptance
Offeror makes an offer to the offeree.
Offeree has the power to accept the offer and create a contract.

may engage in preliminary negotiations about price, time of performance, and other issues. At some point during these negotiations, one party makes an **offer.** The offer sets forth the terms under which the offeror is willing to enter into the contract.

Offer The manifestation of willingness to enter into a bargain, so made as to justify another person in understanding that his or her assent to that bargain is invited and will conclude it.

Offer

Section 24 of the Restatement (Second) of Contracts defines an offer as:

> The manifestation of willingness to enter into a bargain, so made as to justify another person in understanding that his assent to that bargain is invited and will conclude it.

To be effective, (1) the offeror must *objectively intend* to be bound by the offer; (2) the terms of the offer must be definite or reasonably *certain*; and (3) the offer must be *communicated* to the offeree. Also, the offer must be unequivocal.

An honest man's word is as good as his bond.

Don Quixote

Example A question such as "Are you interested in selling your building for $2 million?" is not an offer. It is an invitation to make an offer or an invitation to negotiate. But the statement "I will buy your building for $2 million" is a valid offer because it indicates the offeror's present intent to contract.

An offer may be terminated by several means. The termination of an offer is discussed in the following paragraphs.

Revocation of an Offer by the Offeror

Under the common law, an offeror may revoke (that is, withdraw) an offer any time prior to its acceptance by the offeree. Generally, an offer can be so revoked even if the offeror had promised to keep the offer open for a longer time. The **revocation** may be communicated to the offeree by the offeror or by a third party and made by (1) the offeror's express statement (such as, "I hereby withdraw my offer") or (2) an act of the offeror that is inconsistent with the offer (such as by selling the goods to another party). Most states provide that a revocation is not effective until it is actually received by the offeree or the offeree's agent.

Revocation Withdrawal of an offer by the offeror, which terminates the offer.

Offers made to the public may be revoked by communicating the revocation by the same means used to make the offer.

Example If a reward offer for a lost watch was published in two local newspapers each week for four weeks, notice of revocation must be published in the same newspapers for the same length of time. The revocation is effective against all offerees, even those who saw the reward offer but not the notice of revocation.

Rejection of an Offer by the Offeree

Rejection Express words or conduct by the offeree that rejects an offer. Rejection terminates the offer.

An offer is terminated if the offeree rejects it. Any subsequent attempt by the offeree to accept the offer is ineffective and is construed as a new offer that the original offeror (now the offeree) is free to accept or reject. A **rejection** may be evidenced by the offeree's express words (oral or written) or conduct. Generally, a rejection is not effective until it is actually received by the offeror.

> **Example** Harriet Jackson, sales manager of IBM Corporation, offers to sell 1,000 computers to Ted Green, purchasing manager of General Motors Corporation, for $250,000. The offer is made on August 1. Green telephones Jackson to say that he is not interested. This rejection terminates the offer. If Green later decides that he wants to purchase the computers, an entirely new contract must be formed.

Counteroffer by the Offeree

Counteroffer A response by an offeree that contains terms and conditions different from or in addition to those of the offer. A counteroffer terminates an offer.

A **counteroffer** by the offeree simultaneously terminates the offeror's offer and creates a new offer.

> **Example** Suppose that Fei Jia says to Harold Brown, "I will sell you my house for $700,000." Brown says, "I think $700,000 is too high; I will pay you $600,000." Brown has made a counteroffer. The original offer is terminated, and the counteroffer is a new offer that Jia is free to accept or reject.

SIDEBAR

TERMINATION OF AN OFFER

Action	Description
Revocation	The offeror *revokes* (withdraws) the offer any time prior to its acceptance by the offeree.
Rejection	The offeree rejects the offer by his or her words or conduct.
Counter-offer	A counteroffer by the offeree creates a new offer and terminates the offeror's offer.

Option contracts

An offeree can prevent the offeror from revoking his or her offer by paying the offeror compensation to keep the offer open for an agreed-upon period of time. This is called an **option contract,** in which the offeror agrees not to sell the property to anyone but the offeree during the option period. The death or incompetency of either party does not terminate an option contract unless it is for the performance of a personal service.

> **Example** Anne Mason offers to sell a piece of real estate to Harold Greenberg for $1 million. Mr. Greenberg wants time to make a decision, so he pays Ms. Mason $20,000 to keep her offer open to him for 6 months. At any time during the option period, Mr. Greenberg may exercise his option and pay Ms. Mason the $1 million purchase price. If he lets the option expire, however, Ms. Mason may keep the $20,000 and sell the property to someone else.

Acceptance

Acceptance A manifestation of assent by the offeree to the terms of the offer in a manner invited or required by the offer as measured by the objective theory of contracts.

Acceptance is a manifestation of assent by the offeree to the terms of the offer in a manner invited or required by the offer as measured by the objective theory of contracts. Recall that generally (1) unilateral contracts can be accepted only by the offeree's performance of the required act, and (2) a bilateral contract can be accepted by an offeree who promises to perform (or, where permitted, by performance of) the requested act.

Only the offeree has the legal power to accept an offer and create a contract. Third persons usually do not have the power to accept an offer. If an offer is made individually to two or more persons, each has the power to accept the offer. Once an offeree accepts the offer, though, it terminates as to the other offerees. An offer that is made to two or more persons jointly must be accepted jointly.

Mirror image rule A rule that states that for an acceptance to exist, the offeree must accept the terms as stated in the offer.

The offeree's acceptance must be unequivocal. For an acceptance to exist, the offeree must accept the terms as stated in the offer. This is called the **mirror image rule.** Generally, a "grumbling acceptance" is a legal acceptance.

Examples A response such as "Okay, I'll take the car, but I sure wish you would make me a better deal" creates an enforceable contract. An acceptance is equivocal if certain conditions are added to the acceptance. If the offeree responds, "I accept, but only if you repaint the car red," there is no acceptance in this case.

Express and Implied Contracts

An actual contract (as distinguished from a quasi-contract, discussed later in this chapter) may be either *express* or *implied-in-fact.*

1. **Express contracts** are stated in oral or written words. Examples of such contracts include an oral agreement to purchase a neighbor's bicycle and a written agreement to buy an automobile from a dealership.
2. **Implied-in-fact contracts** are implied from the conduct of the parties and leave more room for questions. The following elements must be established to create an implied-in-fact contract:
   a. The plaintiff provided property or services to the defendant.
   b. The plaintiff expected to be paid by the defendant for the property or services and did not provide the property or services gratuitously.
   c. The defendant was given an opportunity to reject the property or services provided by the plaintiff but failed to do so.

Express contract An agreement that is expressed in written or oral words.

Implied-in-fact contract A contract in which agreement between the parties has been inferred from their conduct.

Consideration

Learning Objective 4

Define consideration and analyze whether contracts are lacking in consideration.

Consideration is a necessary element for a contract to exist. Consideration is defined as something of legal value given in exchange for a promise and can come in many forms.

Examples The most common types consist of either a tangible payment (such as money or property) or the performance of an act (such as providing legal services). Less usual forms of consideration include the forbearance of a legal right (such as accepting an out-of-court settlement in exchange for dropping a lawsuit) and noneconomic forms (such as refraining from using alcohol).

Written contracts are presumed to be supported by consideration, although this is a rebuttable presumption that may be overcome by sufficient evidence. A few states provide that contracts made under seal cannot be challenged for lack of consideration.

Consideration Something of legal value given in exchange for a promise.

Gift Promise

Gift promises, also called **gratuitous promises,** are unenforceable because they lack consideration. To change a gift promise into an enforceable promise, the promisee must offer to do something in exchange—that is, consideration—for the promise.

Gift promise (gratuitous promise) A promise that is unenforceable because it lacks consideration.

Examples Suppose Mrs. Colby promised to give her son $10,000 and then rescinded the promise. Her son would have no recourse to recover the $10,000 because it was a gift promise that lacked consideration. If, however, Mrs. Colby promised her son $10,000 for getting an "A" in his Introduction to Paralegal course and he performed as required, the contract would be enforceable. A completed gift promise cannot be rescinded for lack of consideration.

Capacity to Contract

Generally, the law presumes that the parties to a contract have the requisite **capacity to contract** to enter into the contract. Certain persons, however, do not have this capacity, including minors, mentally incompetent persons, and intoxicated persons. The common law of contracts and many state statutes protect persons who lack

contractual capacity from having contracts enforced against them. The party asserting incapacity or his or her guardian, conservator, or other legal representative bears the burden of proof.

Minors

Minors do not always have the maturity, experience, or sophistication needed to enter into contracts with adults. States have thus enacted statutes that specify the *age of majority*. The most prevalent age of majority is 18 years for males and females alike. Any age below the statutory age of majority is called the *period of minority*.

Infancy doctrine A doctrine that allows minors to disaffirm (cancel) most contracts they have entered into with adults.

To protect minors, the law recognizes the **infancy doctrine,** which allows minors to **disaffirm** (or cancel) most contracts they have entered into with adults. This right to disaffirm a contract is based on public policy, with the reasoning that minors should be protected from unscrupulous adult behavior.

Under the infancy doctrine, a minor has the option of choosing whether or not to enforce the contract (meaning that the contract is *voidable* by the minor). The adult party is bound to the minor's decision. If both parties to the contract are minors, both parties have the right to disaffirm the contract.

A minor can expressly disaffirm a contract orally, in writing, or by the minor's conduct; no special formalities are required. The minor may disaffirm the contract at any time prior to reaching the age of majority plus a "reasonable time." The designation of a reasonable time is determined on a case-by-case basis.

Minors are, however, obligated to pay for the **necessaries of life** that they contract for. Otherwise, many adults would refuse to sell these items to minors. There is no standard definition of a *necessary of life*, but items such as food, clothing, shelter, medical services, and the like are generally understood to fit this category. Goods and services such as automobiles, tools of trade, education, and vocational training also have been found to be necessaries of life in some situations. Basically, the minor's age, lifestyle, and status in life influence what is considered necessary.

Mentally Incompetent Persons

Freedom of contract begins where equality of bargaining power begins.
Oliver Wendell Holmes, Jr.
June 4, 1928

Mental incapacity may arise because of mental illness, brain damage, mental retardation, senility, and similar medical conditions. The law protects **mentally incompetent persons** from enforcement of contracts against them because these persons may not understand the consequences of their actions in entering into a contract.

Intoxicated Persons

Most states provide that contracts entered into by certain **intoxicated persons** are voidable by that person. The intoxication may result from alcohol or drug use. The contract is not voidable by the other party if that party had contractual capacity. Under the majority rule, the contract is voidable only if the person was so intoxicated when the contract was entered into that he or she was incapable of comprehending the nature of the transaction. In most states, this rule holds even if the intoxication was self-induced. A contract disaffirmed based on intoxication generally must be returned to the status quo.

Learning Objective 5
Identify illegal contracts that are contrary to statutes and that violate public policy.

Lawful Object

Illegal contract A contract to perform an illegal act; cannot be enforced by either party to the contract.

An essential element for the formation of a contract is that the object of the contract must be *lawful*. This is referred to as a **lawful object**. A contract to perform an illegal act is called an **illegal contract.** Illegal contracts are void; they cannot be enforced by either party to the contract. Because illegal contracts are void, the parties cannot sue for nonperformance. Further, if an illegal contract is executed, the court will generally leave the parties where it finds them. Because most contracts are presumed to be lawful, the burden of proving that a contract is unlawful rests on the party who asserts its illegality.

Illegality—Contracts Contrary to Statutes

Federal and state legislatures alike have enacted statutes prohibiting certain **contracts contrary to statutes.** Contracts to perform an activity that is prohibited by statute are illegal contracts. These include gambling contracts, contracts that provide for usurious rates of interest, and contracts that violate Sabbath laws and licensing statutes.

Example An agreement between two companies to engage in price fixing in violation of federal antitrust statutes is illegal and therefore void. Thus, neither company to this illegal contract can enforce the contract against the other company.

Illegality—Contracts Contrary to Public Policy

Certain contracts are illegal because they are **contracts contrary to public policy.** Although *public policy* eludes a precise definition, the courts have held contracts to be contrary to public policy if they have a negative impact on society or interfere with the public's safety and welfare.

Example Assume a husband purchases a life insurance policy on his wife and names himself beneficiary of this policy. If the husband then kills his wife, he cannot recover on the life insurance policy because it would violate public policy to allow him to recover for his murderous deed.

Unconscionable Contract

The general rule of freedom of contract holds that if (1) the object of a contract is lawful and (2) the other elements for the formation of a contract are met, the courts will enforce the contract according to its terms. Although it is generally presumed that parties are capable of protecting their own interests when contracting, it is a fact of life that dominant parties sometimes take advantage of weaker parties. As a result, some lawful contracts are so oppressive or manifestly unfair that they are unjust.

An unconscionable contract is one which no man in his senses, not under delusion, would make, on the one hand, and which no fair and honest man would accept on the other.

Fuller, Chief Justice
Hume v. United States (1889)

To prevent the enforcement of such contracts, the courts developed the equitable doctrine of unconscionability, which is based on public policy. A contract found to be unconscionable under this doctrine is called an **unconscionable contract,** or a *contract of adhesion*.

Unconscionable contract
A contract that courts refuse to enforce in part or at all because it is so oppressive or manifestly unfair as to be unjust.

The courts are given substantial discretion in determining whether a contract or contract clause is unconscionable; there is no single definition of *unconscionability*. However, the doctrine may not be used merely to save a contracting party from a bad bargain.

The following elements must be shown in order to prove that a contract or clause in a contract is unconscionable:

- The parties possessed severely unequal bargaining power.
- The dominant party unreasonably used its unequal bargaining power to obtain oppressive or manifestly unfair contract terms.
- The adhering party had no reasonable alternative.

If the court finds that a contract or contract clause is unconscionable, it may (1) refuse to enforce the contract, (2) refuse to enforce the unconscionable clause but enforce the remainder of the contract, or (3) limit the applicability of any unconscionable clause so as to avoid any unconscionable result. The appropriate remedy depends on the facts and circumstances of each case. Note that because unconscionability is a matter of law, the judge may opt to decide the case without a jury trial.

Example Suppose a door-to-door salesperson sells a poor family a freezer full of meat and other foods for $3,000, with monthly payments for 60 months at 20 percent interest. If the actual cost of the freezer and the food is $1,000, this contract could be found to be unconscionable. The court could either find the entire contract unenforceable or rewrite the contract to have reasonable terms.

Learning Objective 6
List and describe the contracts that must be in writing under the Statute of Frauds.

Statute of Frauds—Writing Requirement

All states have enacted a **Statute of Frauds** that requires certain types of contracts to be in *writing*. This statute is intended to ensure that the terms of important contracts are not forgotten, misunderstood, or fabricated.

Statute of Frauds A state statute that requires certain types of contracts to be in writing.

Generally, an **executory contract** that is not in writing even though the Statute of Frauds requires it to be is unenforceable by either party. (If the contract is valid in all other respects, however, it may be voluntarily performed by the parties.) The Statute of Frauds is usually raised by one party as a defense to enforcement of the contract by the other party.

However, if an oral contract that should have been in writing under the Statute of Frauds is already executed (fully performed), neither party can seek to rescind the contract on the ground of noncompliance with the Statute of Frauds. Contracts that are required to be in writing under the Statute of Frauds are discussed in the following paragraphs.

Contracts Involving Interests in Real Property

A verbal contract isn't worth the paper it's written on.
Samuel Goldwyn

Any contract that transfers an ownership interest in real property must be in writing to be enforceable under the Statute of Frauds. Real property includes the land itself, buildings, trees, soil, minerals, timber, plants, crops, fixtures, and things permanently affixed to the land or buildings. Certain personal property that is permanently affixed to the real property—for example, built-in cabinets in a house—is a *fixture* that becomes part of the real property.

Other contracts that transfer an ownership interest in land must be in writing under the Statute of Frauds.

> **Example** Borrowers often give a lender an interest in real property as security for the repayment of a loan. This must be done through a written *mortgage* or *deed of trust*. A *lease* is the transfer of the right to use real property for a specified period of time. Most Statutes of Frauds require leases for a term of more than one year to be in writing.

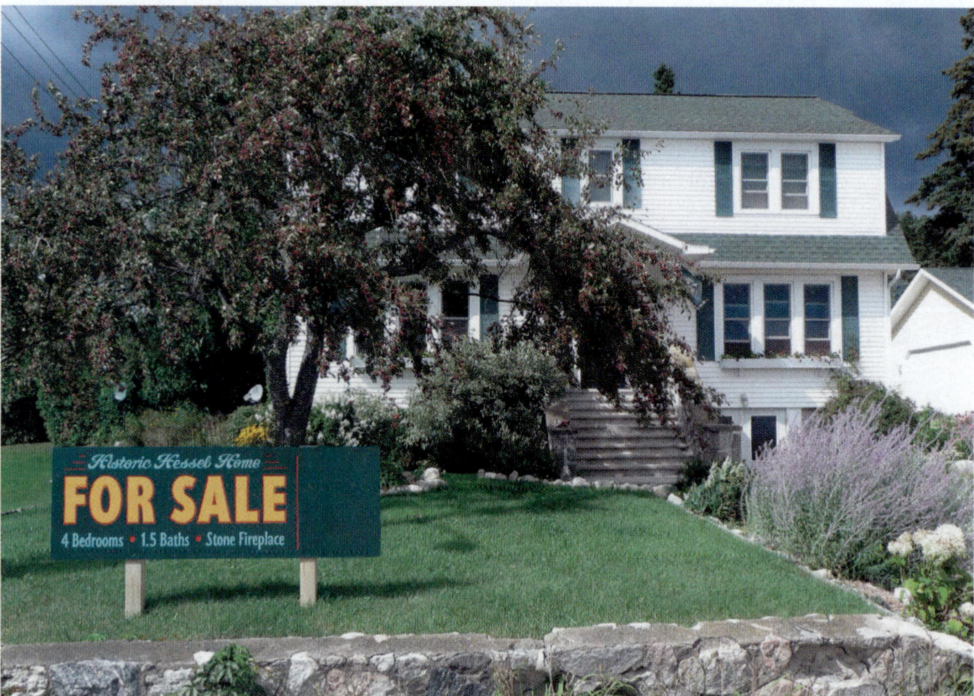

Real Estate Under the Statute of Frauds, any contract that transfers an ownership interest in real property must be in writing to be enforceable.

One-Year Rule

Don't get it right, just get it written.
James Thurber

According to the Statute of Frauds, an executory contract that cannot be performed by its own terms within one year of its formation must be in writing. This **one-year rule** is intended to prevent disputes about contract terms that otherwise may occur toward the end of a long-term contract. If performance of the contract is possible within the one-year period, the contract may be oral.

Examples An employer hires a person as an employee for 6 months. This contract may be oral. If the employment contract was for 13 months, it would have to be in writing to be enforceable.

Formality of the Writing

Many written commercial contracts are long, detailed documents that have been negotiated by the parties and drafted and reviewed by their lawyers. Other written contracts are preprinted forms that are prepared in advance to be used in recurring situations.

To be legally binding, a written contract does not have to be either drafted by a lawyer or formally typed. Regarding the **formality of the writing,** the law generally requires only a writing containing the essential terms of the parties' agreement. Under this rule, any writing—letters, telegrams, invoices, sales receipts, handwritten agreements written on scraps of paper, and such—can be an enforceable contract.

Required Signature

Most of the disputes in the world arise from words.
Lord Mansfield, C. J.
Morgan v. Jones (1773)

The Statute of Frauds and the UCC require the written contract, whatever its form, to be signed *by the party against whom the enforcement is sought.* The signature of the person who is enforcing the contract is not necessary. Thus, a written contract may be enforceable against one party but not the other party.

Generally, the signature may appear anywhere on the writing. In addition, it does not have to be a person's full legal name. The person's last name, first name, nickname, initials, seal, stamp, engraving, or other symbol or mark (such as an X) that indicates the person's intent can be binding. The signature may also be affixed by an authorized agent.

The following feature discusses a Statute of Frauds case involving a paralegal professional.

ETHICAL PERSPECTIVE

Paralegal Loses $900,000 for Failing to Get a Contract in Writing

Barbara Lucinda Sawyer worked as a paralegal for Melbourne Mills, Jr., an attorney at a law firm. Ms. Sawyer proposed that Mr. Mills and the law firm become engaged in class-action lawsuits. Mr. Mills agreed to pay Ms. Sawyer an unspecified bonus when "the ship comes in." After Ms. Sawyer's assistance and persistence, the law firm became involved in class-action litigation—primarily the Fen-Phen class-action litigation. After the law firm received millions of dollars in fees from the Fen-Phen class-action lawsuits, Ms. Sawyer and her husband, Steve, met with Mills to discuss Ms. Sawyer's bonus. Mr. Mills orally agreed to pay Ms. Sawyer $1,065,000 as a bonus to be paid in monthly installments over 167 months. Ms. Sawyer secretly tape-recorded the conversation. Mr. Mills later refused to sign a written contract conveying the terms of the oral agreement.

(continued)

After Mr. Mills had paid $165,000, he quit making further payments. Ms. Sawyer sued Mr. Mills to collect the remaining $900,000. Mr. Mills defended, arguing that the oral contract exceeded one year and was therefore unenforceable because it was not in writing as required by the Statute of Frauds. The jury ruled in favor of Ms. Sawyer. Mr. Mills made a motion to the trial court judge to refuse to enforce the oral contract against him. The trial court heard and decided the motion. The trial court ruled in favor of Mr. Mills, finding that the oral contract was for over one year and was not in writing as required by the Statute of Frauds. The court stated:

Sawyer produced no writing signed by Mills consistent with the oral discussions of the parties. Sawyer argues that the "writing" requirement of the Statute of Frauds has been satisfied in this case because of the cassette tape which was played to the jury and which [was] surreptitiously recorded....[T]he cassette tape recording is not a "writing signed by the party to be charged" as required by the Statute of Frauds. The Court is aware of the apparent harshness of this ruling. The trial jury found, and the Court heard Mills state on the tape recording, that he agreed to make monthly payments to Sawyer which would eventually total over one million dollars. Honoring that oral agreement would be the "moral" and "right" thing for Mills to do. However, this Court is obligated by Oath of Office and Kentucky law, to consider cases based on the facts presented and the applicable law. The end result may not seem "fair" to Sawyer. The Statute of Frauds, by its own terms, can be considered "harsh" in that it will bar oral agreements between parties under certain conditions. This is simply the nature of the beast.

The Court of Appeals of Kentucky affirmed the trial court's decision.

In this case, the lawyer acted unethically. The Statute of Frauds protected the attorney from legally having to perform an oral contract to pay his paralegal the remaining $900,000 due on their oral contract. Ms. Sawyer should have gotten the contract in writing with Mr. Mills and therefore have avoided the unfair result reached by the application of the Statute of Frauds.

Source: *Sawyer v. Mills*, Web 2007 Ky. App. Lexis (Court of Appeals of Kentucky, 2007).

SIDEBAR

TYPES OF PERFORMANCE

Type of Performance	Legal Consequence
Complete performance	The contract is discharged.
Substantial performance (minor breach)	The nonbreaching party may recover damages caused by the breach.
Inferior performance (material breach)	The non-breaching party may either (1) rescind the contract and recover restitution or (2) affirm the contract and recover damages.

Performance and Breach

Paralegal professionals who work in the area of contract law must know the legal rules regarding the performance and breach of contracts. They must also know the remedies that may be awarded where a breach of contract has been found.

In contracts, parties make certain promises to each other. These promises may be classified as *covenants* or *conditions*. Performance may be classified as complete performance, substantial performance (minor breach), or inferior performance (material breach). A **breach of contract** occurs when a contracting party fails to perform an absolute duty owed under the contract. These topics are covered in the following paragraphs.

Breach of contract A contracting party's failure to perform an absolute duty owed under a contract.

Covenant

A **covenant** is an unconditional promise to perform. Nonperformance of a covenant is a breach of contract that gives the other party the right to sue.

Covenant An unconditional promise to perform.

Example If Medcliff Corporation borrows $100,000 from a bank and signs a promissory note to repay this amount plus 10 percent interest in one year, this promise is a covenant. It is an unconditional promise to perform.

Condition Precedent

Condition precedent A condition that requires the occurrence of an event before a party is obligated to perform a duty under a contract.

If the contract requires the occurrence (or nonoccurrence) of an event before a party is obligated to perform a contractual duty, there is a **condition precedent.** The happening (or nonhappening) of the event triggers the contract or duty of performance. If the event does not occur, no duty to perform arises, because there is a failure of condition.

Example Suppose X Company offers Joan Andrews a job as an industrial engineer upon her graduation from college. If Ms. Andrews graduates, the condition has been met. If the employer refuses to hire Ms. Andrews at that time, she can sue the employer for breach of contract. But if Ms. Andrews does not graduate, X company is not obligated to hire her because there has been a failure of condition.

Complete Performance

Most contracts are discharged by the **complete performance** of the contracting parties. Complete performance occurs when a party to a contract renders performance exactly as required by the contract. A fully performed contract is called an **executed contract.**

Tender of performance also discharges a party's contractual obligations. Tender is an unconditional and absolute offer by a contracting party to perform his or her obligations under the contract.

Complete performance A situation in which a party to a contract renders performance exactly as required by the contract. Complete performance discharges that party's obligations under the contract.

Example Suppose Ashley's Dress Shops, Inc., contracts to purchase dresses from a dress manufacturer for $25,000. Ashley's has performed its obligation under the contract once it tenders the $25,000 to the manufacturer. If the manufacturer fails to deliver the dresses, Ashley's can sue it for breach of contract.

Substantial Performance (Minor Breach)

Substantial performance occurs when there has been a **minor breach** of contract, such as when a party to a contract renders performance that deviates only slightly from complete performance. The nonbreaching party may (1) convince the breaching party to elevate his or her performance to complete performance, (2) deduct the cost to repair the defect from the contract price and remit the balance to the breaching party, or (3) sue the breaching party to recover the cost to repair the defect if the breaching party has already been paid.

Example Suppose Donald Trump contracts with Big Apple Construction Co. to have Big Apple construct an office building for $50 million. The architectural plans call for installation of three-ply windows in the building. Big Apple constructs the building exactly to plan except that it installs two-ply windows. There has been substantial performance. It would cost $300,000 to install the correct windows. If Big Apple agrees to replace the windows, its performance is elevated to complete performance and Trump must remit the entire contract price. But if Trump has to hire someone else to replace the windows, he may deduct this cost of repair from the contract price and remit the difference to Big Apple.

Substantial performance Performance by a contracting party that deviates only slightly from complete performance.

Minor breach A breach that occurs when a party renders substantial performance of his or her contractual duties.

Inferior Performance (Material Breach)

Inferior performance occurs when there has been a **material breach** of a contract, such as when a party's failure to perform certain express or implied obligations impairs or destroys the essence of the contract. Because there is no clear line between a minor breach and a material breach, determination is made on a case-by-case basis. Where there has been a material breach of a contract, the nonbreaching party has two choices:

1. The nonbreaching party may *rescind* the contract, seek restitution of any compensation paid under the contract to the breaching party, and be discharged from any further performance under the contract.
2. The nonbreaching party may treat the contract as being in effect and sue the breaching party to recover *damages*.

Inferior performance A situation in which a party fails to perform express or implied contractual obligations and impairs or destroys the essence of the contract.

Material breach A breach that occurs when a party renders inferior performance of his or her contractual duties.

Learning Objective 7
Describe compensatory, consequential, and liquidated damages.

TYPES OF MONETARY DAMAGES

SIDEBAR

Type of Damage	Description
Compensatory	Damages that compensate a nonbreaching party for the loss of a bargain. It places the nonbreaching party in the same position as if the contract had been fully performed.
Consequential	Damages that compensate a nonbreaching party for foreseeable special damages. The breaching party must have known or should have known that these damages would result from the breach.
Liquidated	An agreement by the parties in advance that sets the amount of damages recoverable in case of breach. These damages are lawful if they do not cause a penalty.

Monetary damages An award of money.

Compensatory damages An award of money intended to compensate a nonbreaching party for loss of the bargain. Compensatory damages place the nonbreaching party in the same position as if the contract had been fully performed by restoring the "benefit of the bargain."

Consequential damages Foreseeable damages that arise from circumstances outside the contract. To be liable for these damages, the breaching party must know or have reason to know that the breach will cause special damages to the other party.

Liquidated damages Damages to which parties to a contract agree in advance should be paid if the contract is breached.

Example Suppose a university contracts with a general contractor to build a new three-story building with classroom space for 1,000 students. But the completed building can support the weight of only 500 students because the contractor used inferior materials. The defect cannot be repaired without rebuilding the entire structure. Because this is a material breach, the university may rescind the contract and require removal of the building. If the university did so, it would then be discharged of any obligations under the contract and free to employ another contractor to rebuild the building. Alternatively, the university could accept the building and deduct from the contract price the damages resulting from the inferior materials.

Monetary Damages

If a breach of contract has been found, the nonbreaching party is awarded a **remedy** for the breach. The most common remedy for a breach of contract is an award of **monetary damages.** This is often called the "law remedy." Monetary damages are discussed in the following paragraphs.

Compensatory Damages

Compensatory damages are intended to compensate a nonbreaching party for the loss of the bargain. They place the nonbreaching party in the same position as if the contract had been fully performed by restoring the "benefit of the bargain."

Examples Suppose Lederle Laboratories enters into a written contract to employ a manager for three years at a salary of $6,000 per month. Before work is to start, the manager is informed that he will not be needed. This is a material breach of contract. Now assume that the manager finds another job, but it pays only $5,000 a month. The manager may recover $1,000 per month for 36 months (total $36,000) from Lederle Laboratories as compensatory damages. These damages place the manager in the same situation as if the contract with Lederle had been performed.

Consequential Damages

A nonbreaching party sometimes can recover *special* or **consequential damages** from the breaching party. Consequential damages are *foreseeable* damages that arise from circumstances outside the contract. To be liable for consequential damages, the breaching party must know or have reason to know that the breach will cause special damages to the other party.

Example Suppose Soan-Allen Co., a wholesaler, enters into a contract to purchase 1,000 men's suits for $150 each from the Fabric Manufacturing Co., a manufacturer. Prior to contracting, the wholesaler tells the manufacturer that the suits will be resold to retailers for $225. The manufacturer breaches the contract by failing to manufacture the suits. The wholesaler cannot get the suits manufactured by anyone else in time to meet its contracts. It can, however, recover $75,000 of lost profits on the resale contracts (1,000 suits × $75 profit) as consequential damages from the manufacturer because the manufacturer knew of this special damage to Soan-Allen Co. if it were to breach the contract.

Liquidated Damages

Under certain circumstances, the parties to a contract may agree in advance to the amount of damages payable upon a breach of contract. These are called **liquidated damages.** To be lawful, the actual damages must be difficult or impracticable to determine, and the liquidated amount must be reasonable in the circumstances. An enforceable liquidated damage clause is an exclusive remedy even if actual damages are later determined to be different.

Example A buyer enters into a contract to purchase a condominium for $5 million in a high-rise cooperative building to be built in New York City by a real estate developer. The contract requires the buyer to pay a nonrefundable deposit of 10 percent of the purchase price at the time of contracting that may be retained by the real estate developer if the buyer refuses to complete the purchase once the building is completed. This is a reasonable liquidated damage clause.

A liquidated damage clause is considered a *penalty* if actual damages are clearly determinable in advance or if the liquidated damages are excessive or unconscionable. If a liquidated damage clause is found to be a penalty, it is unenforceable. The nonbreaching party then may recover actual damages.

Mitigation of Damages

If a contract has been breached, the law places a duty on the innocent, nonbreaching party to take reasonable efforts to mitigate (that is, avoid and reduce) the resulting damages. The extent of **mitigation of damages** required depends on the type of contract involved.

Mitigation of damages A nonbreaching party's legal duty to avoid or reduce damages caused by a breach of contract.

Example If an employer breaches an employment contract, the employee owes a duty to mitigate damages by trying to find substitute employment. The employee is required only to accept comparable employment. In determining the comparability of jobs, the courts consider factors such as compensation, rank, status, job description, and geographical location.

Equitable Remedies

If a monetary award does not provide adequate relief, the court may order any one of several nonmonetary remedies—**equitable remedies**—including specific performance, injunction, reformation, and quasi-contract. Equitable remedies are based on the concept of fairness. These remedies are discussed in the following paragraphs.

Specific Performance

An award of **specific performance** orders the breaching party to *perform* the acts promised in the contract. The courts have the discretion to award this remedy if the subject matter of the contract is unique. Works of art, antiques, items of sentimental value, rare coins, stamps, heirlooms, and such also fit the requirement for uniqueness. Most other personal property does not.

This remedy is also available to enforce land contracts because every piece of real property is considered unique.

Example If a buyer has entered into a contract to purchase a house from a seller but the seller refuses to sell the house when the time for sale arrives, the buyer can bring an action of specific performance and obtain a judgment that orders the seller to sell the house to the buyer.

Specific performance of personal-service contracts is not granted because the courts would find it difficult or impracticable to supervise or monitor performance of the contract.

Example If a professional basketball player has a three-year contract to play for a professional team but quits before his contract is completed, the professional team cannot obtain an order of specific performance that would make the athlete play for the team. In this case, the team's remedy is to sue the athlete for damages caused by his breach.

SIDEBAR

TYPES OF EQUITABLE REMEDIES

Type of Equitable Remedy	Description
Specific Performance	A court orders the breaching party to perform the acts promised in the contract. The subject matter of the contract must be unique.
Reformation	A court rewrites a contract to express the parties' true intentions. It is usually used to correct clerical errors.
Injunction	A court prohibits a party from doing a certain act. Injunctions are available in contract actions only in limited circumstances.
Quasi-Contract	A court awards monetary damages to a plaintiff for providing work or services to the defendant even though no actual contract existed in order to prevent unjust enrichment to the defendant.

Injunction

An **injunction** is a court order that prohibits a person from doing a certain act. To obtain an injunction, the requesting party must show that he or she will suffer irreparable injury unless the injunction is issued.

Example Suppose a professional football team enters into a five-year employment contract with a star quarterback. The quarterback breaches the contract and enters into a contract to play for a competing team. Here, the first team can seek an injunction to prevent the quarterback from playing for the other team.

Reformation

Reformation is an equitable doctrine that permits the court to *rewrite* a contract to express the parties' true intentions.

Example Suppose a clerical error is made during the typing of the contract and both parties sign the contract without discovering the error. If a dispute later arises, the court can reform the contract to correct the clerical error to read what the parties originally intended.

Web Exploration

Go to **http://www.oscn.net/applications/oscn/DeliverDocument.asp?CiteID=74212** to read a jury instruction on the issue of quasi-contract.

Quasi-Contract

A **quasi-contract** (also called an ***implied-in-law contract***) is an equitable doctrine that permits the recovery of compensation even though no enforceable contract exists between the parties because of lack of consideration, the Statute of Frauds has run out, or the like. Such contracts are imposed by law to prevent unjust enrichment. Under quasi-contract, a party can recover the reasonable value of the services or materials provided.

Example A physician who stops to render aid to an unconscious victim of an automobile accident may recover the reasonable value of his services from that person.

Equity

Equity A doctrine that permits judges to make decisions based on fairness, equality, moral rights, and natural law.

Although the courts usually interpret a valid contract as a solemn promise to perform, this view of the sanctity of a contract may cause an unjust result. Therefore, a judge may apply the doctrine of **equity** and save a contracting party from the strict enforcement of a contract or contract terms. Equity is based on the concepts of fairness, equality, and moral rights.

In the following feature, a paralegal professional discusses her experience in the field of contract law.

Learning Objective 8

Define sales contracts governed by Article 2 of the UCC and lease contracts governed by Article 2A of the UCC.

Uniform Commercial Code (UCC)

Paralegal professionals who work in the contract law field often must know how UCC rules differ from traditional contract law. This difference arose because one of the major frustrations of businesspersons conducting interstate business was that they were subject to the laws of each of the states in which they operated. To address this problem, in 1949 the National Conference of Commissioners on Uniform State Laws promulgated the **Uniform Commercial Code (UCC).**

The UCC is a model act that contains uniform rules that govern commercial transactions. To create this uniformity, individual states had to enact the UCC as their commercial law statute. In fact, every state (except Louisiana, which has adopted only parts of the UCC) enacted the UCC as a commercial statute. The UCC is being revised continually to reflect changes in modern commercial practices and technology.

Paralegals *in* Practice

PARALEGAL PROFILE

Annette R. Brown

Annette R. Brown, ACP, has been employed by the Rocky Mountain Elk Foundation, Inc. virtually since the creation of its in-house legal department in 1995. The Elk Foundation is a charitable nonprofit corporation in Missoula, Montana, with a mission to protect habitat for elk and other wildlife. In addition to her paralegal degree, Annette also has Advanced Paralegal Certifications in Real Estate, Trademarks, and Contracts Administration/ Contracts Management from the National Association of Legal Assistants (NALA). She is currently serving as NALA's Region VIII Director, which includes the states of Alaska, Idaho, Montana, Oregon, and Washington.

My practice is mainly centered on real estate and other transactions. This includes drafting and reviewing purchase and sale contracts, deeds and closing documents, title review, water rights, and other due diligence elements. I also work with other types of contracts such as independent contractor, convention center, fundraising, entertainment, trademark licensing, sponsorship, and many more.

Our corporation owns a 100,000-acre working ranch in New Mexico that is managed for habitat conservation, and land managers work alongside educators, biologists, and government agencies to test new land-management practices. I've handled employment contracts, water rights, hunting contracts, easements, and state grazing applications for this project.

When working in a busy corporate legal department, you need the ability to move from one project to another without losing track of your priorities. In addition to legal knowledge, my position requires proficiency in contract drafting, research skills, organizational skills, proofreading, and editing.

Technology advancements have streamlined many processes. When negotiating and drafting contracts, we work across the country with landowners, government agencies, title companies, appraisers, and attorneys. The word processing tracking feature allows for documents' data to be edited by various sources while maintaining an information "trail." Some of our contracts allow the parties to digitally scan and e-mail the signed document to confirm execution. We can also scan and save incoming documents relevant to our projects for easier data retrieval.

The UCC is divided into articles, with each article establishing uniform rules for a specific facet of commerce in the United States. The articles of the UCC are:

Article 1	General provisions
Article 2	Sales
Article 2A Revised	Leases
Article 3	Negotiable instruments
Article 4	Bank deposits and collections
Article 4A	Wire transfers
Article 5	Letters of credit
Article 6	Bulk transfers
Article 7	Documents of title
Article 8	Investment securities
Article 9	Secured transactions

Paralegal professionals who work in the area of contract law should be familiar with the major provisions of the Uniform Commercial Code.

Article 2 (Sales) of the UCC

Article 2 (Sales) of the UCC applies to *transactions in goods*—that is, the sale of goods [UCC 2-102]. All states except Louisiana have adopted some version of Article 2 of the UCC. A sale consists of the passing of title from a seller to a buyer for a price [UCC 2-106(1)].

Article 2 (Sales) of the UCC An article of the UCC that governs the sale of goods.

Example The purchase of a plasma television is a sale subject to Article 2. This is so whether the television was paid for by cash, check, credit card, or another form of consideration.

Article 2 establishes a uniform law covering the formation, performance, and default of sales contracts.

Goods are defined as tangible things that are movable at the time of their identification to the contract [UCC 2-105(1)]. Examples of goods are specially manufactured goods and the unborn young of animals. Money and intangible items, such as stocks, bonds, and patents, are not tangible goods, and, therefore, are not subject to Article 2.

Real estate is not subject to Article 2, either, because it is not movable [UCC 2-105(1)]. Minerals, structures, growing crops, and other things that are severable from real estate may be classified as goods subject to Article 2, however.

> **Examples** The sale and removal of a chandelier in a house is a sale of goods subject to Article 2 because its removal would not materially harm the realty. But the sale and removal of the furnace would be a sale of real property because its removal would cause material harm [UCC 2-107(2)].

Article 2A (Leases) of the UCC An article of the UCC that governs the lease of goods.

Contracts for the provision of services—including legal services, medical services, dental services, and such—are not covered by Article 2. Sometimes, however, a sale involves the provision of both a service and a good in the same transaction. This is referred to as a *mixed sale*. Article 2 applies to mixed sales only if the goods are the predominant part of the transaction. However, the UCC provides no guidance for deciding cases based on mixed sales. Therefore, the courts decide these issues on a case-by-case basis.

CONVENTION ON CONTRACTS FOR THE INTERNATIONAL SALE OF GOODS (CISG)

SIDEBAR

Businesspersons who engage in international commerce face the daunting task of trying to comply with the laws of many nations. To ease this burden, more than 60 countries are signatories to the **United Nations Convention on Contracts for the International Sale of Goods (CISG).** This treaty took more than 50 years to negotiate and incorporates rules from all the major legal systems of the world.

The CISG establishes uniform rules for the formation and enforcement of contracts involving the international sale of goods. Many of its provisions are remarkably similar to the provisions of the American UCC. The CISG applies if the buyer and seller have their places of business in different countries and both nations are parties to the convention.

The contracting parties may agree to exclude (that is, opt out of) the CISG and let other laws apply. The parties to any international contract can agree that the CISG controls, even if one or both of their countries are not signatories to the convention.

Article 2A (Leases) of the UCC

Personal property leases are a billion-dollar industry. Consumer rentals of automobiles and equipment, and commercial leases of such items as aircraft and industrial machinery, fall into this category.

Article 2A (Leases) of the UCC was promulgated in 1987. This article, cited as the Uniform Commercial Code–Leases, directly addresses personal property leases [UCC 2A-101]. It establishes a comprehensive, uniform law covering the formation, performance, and default of leases in goods [UCC 2A-102, 2A-103(h)].

Article 2A is similar to Article 2. In fact, many Article 2 provisions were changed to reflect leasing terminology and practices and carried over to Article 2A. Many states have adopted Article 2A, and many more are expected to do so in the future.

A lease is a transfer of the right to the possession and use of the named goods for a set term in return for certain consideration [UCC 2A-103(1)(i)(x)]. The leased goods can be anything from a hand tool leased to an individual for a few hours to a complex line of industrial equipment leased to a multinational corporation for a number of years.

In an ordinary lease, the **lessor** is the person who transfers the right of possession and use of goods under the lease [UCC 2A-103(1)(p)]. The **lessee** is the person who acquires the right to possession and use of goods under a lease [UCC 2A-103(1)(n)].

UCC Firm Offer Rule

Recall that the common law of contracts allows the offeror to revoke an offer any time prior to its acceptance. The only exception allowed by the common law is an *option contract* (that is, where the offeree pays the offeror consideration to keep the offer open).

The UCC recognizes another exception, which is called the **firm offer rule.** This rule states that a merchant who (1) offers to buy, sell, or lease goods and (2) gives a written and signed assurance on a separate form that the offer will be held open cannot revoke the offer for the time stated or, if no time is stated, for a reasonable time. The maximum amount of time permitted under this rule is three months [UCC 2-205, 2A-205].

> **Example** On June 1, a merchant–seller offers to sell a Mercedes-Benz to a buyer for $50,000. The merchant–seller signs a written assurance to keep that offer open until August 30. On July 1, the merchant–seller sells the car to another buyer. On August 21, the original offeree tenders $50,000 for the car. The merchant–seller is liable to the original offeree for breach of contract.

UCC Statute of Frauds

The UCC includes Statute of Frauds provisions that apply to all sales and lease contracts. The **UCC Statute of Frauds** provides that all contracts for the sale of goods costing $500 or more (Revised Article 2 raises this amount to $5,000 or more) and lease contracts involving payments of $1,000 or more (Revised Article 2A raises this amount to $20,000) must be in writing [UCC 2-201(1), 2A-201(1)]. The writing must be sufficient to indicate that a contract has been made between the parties. The writing must also be signed by the party against whom enforcement is sought or by his or her authorized agent or broker. If a contract falling within these parameters is not written, it is unenforceable.

> Example A seller orally agrees to sell her computer to a buyer for $550. When the buyer tenders the purchase price, the seller asserts the Statute of Frauds and refuses to sell the computer to him. The seller is correct. The contract must be in writing to be enforceable because the contract price for the computer exceeds $499.99.

E-Commerce and E-Contracts

Learning Objective 9
Define *e-contract* and describe the formation and enforcement of e-contracts.

Use of the Internet and the World Wide Web to sell goods and services through e-commerce is commonplace today. **Electronic commerce** (also **e-commerce**) is also referred to as **online commerce.** Businesses and individuals sell goods and services over the Internet through websites and registered domain names. Consumers and businesses can purchase or sell almost any good or service they want over the Internet, using their own sites or sites such as Amazon, eBay, and others. In addition, software and information may be licensed either by physically purchasing the software or information and installing it on a computer or by merely downloading the software or information directly into the computer.

E-Contracts

Email and the web have exploded as a means of personal and business communication. In the business environment, email and the web are sometimes the methods used to negotiate and agree on contract terms and to send and agree to a final contract. Are

Cars for Sale All contracts for the sale of goods costing $500 or more (Revised Article 2 raises this amount to $5,000 or more) and lease contracts involving payments of $1,000 or more (Revised Article 2A raises this amount to $20,000) must be in writing [UCC 2-201(1), 2A-201(1)].

CAREER OPPORTUNITIES FOR PARALEGALS IN E-COMMERCE

As a paralegal, you have witnessed the explosive growth of electronic commerce, or e-commerce, around the world. You can find almost anything being sold over the Internet through web pages. Large and small companies alike, as well as individuals, are selling and buying over the Internet.

When someone sells or purchases something over the Internet, he or she usually enters into an electronic contract (e-contract), also called a web contract or online contract. Originally, state contract law solely regulated the formation and performance of e-contracts. This led to an often nonuniform application of law to e-contracts.

Some of the common law of contracts and provisions of the Uniform Commercial Code (UCC) did not directly apply to e-contracts. To alleviate this problem, the UCC has been updated to apply to sales and leases made over the Internet. Modern changes to the UCC have helped considerably in bringing uniform contract rules to electronic commerce. A uniform law for e-contracts has also been promulgated and is being adopted in whole or in part by state legislatures.

A special kind of contracting that is especially suited for online commerce is licensing. Many companies transfer software, data, information technology, and other forms of intellectual property over the Internet through the use of licenses. Special rules of licensing apply to these **e-licenses**. A model act, called the Uniform Computer Information Transactions Act (UCITA), has been promulgated to apply to e-licenses. Many states have adopted this act or provisions similar to this act that create more uniform contract law for e-licenses.

In addition, the federal government has stepped in and enacted federal statutes to bring uniformity to e-commerce transactions. The major law in this area is the Electronic Signature in Global and National Commerce Act. This federal act establishes special rules that recognize e-contracts and signatures. The federal government is expected to continue to adopt laws as is necessary to bring more uniform law to the area of e-commerce.

Paralegals have a unique opportunity to become experts in this relatively new area of the law. E-contracts and e-licenses face special rules in their formation, performance, and enforcement. In addition, many lawsuits involving e-contracts and e-licenses will be litigated in the courts. Paralegals will be needed to assist lawyers in drafting e-contracts and e-licenses, as well as assisting in the litigation of disputes involving e-commerce.

email and web contracts enforceable? Assuming that all the elements to establish a contract are present, an email or **web contract** is valid and enforceable. These are typically called e-contracts. The main problem in a lawsuit seeking to enforce an e-contract is evidence; but this problem, which exists in almost all lawsuits, can be overcome by printing out the e-contract and its prior email or web negotiations, if necessary.

The feature above discusses the career opportunities for paralegal professionals in e-commerce.

Learning Objective 10

Describe the main features of the federal E-SIGN Act.

E-Writing

In 2000, the federal government enacted the **Electronic Signature in Global and National Commerce Act (E-SIGN Act).** This is a federal statute enacted by the U.S. Congress and, therefore, it has a national reach. The act is designed to place the world of electronic commerce on par with the world of paper contracts in the United States.

Electronic Signature in Global and National Commerce Act (E-SIGN Act) A federal statute that recognizes that electronic contracts, or e-contracts, meet the writing requirement of the Statute of Frauds and gives electronic signatures, or e-signatures, the same force and effect as pen-inscribed signatures on paper.

One of the main features of the E-SIGN Act is that it recognizes electronic contracts as meeting the *writing requirement* of the Statute of Frauds for most contracts. As you'll recall from earlier in this chapter, Statutes of Frauds are state laws that require certain types of contracts to be in writing. The E-SIGN Act provides that electronically signed contracts cannot be denied effect because they are in electronic form or delivered electronically. The act also provides that record retention requirements are satisfied if the records are stored electronically.

The federal law was passed with several provisions to protect consumers:

1. Consumers must consent to receive electronic records and contracts.
2. To receive electronic records, consumers must be able to demonstrate that they have access to the electronic records.
3. Businesses must tell consumers that they have the right to receive hard-copy documents of their transactions.

In the past, signatures were hand-applied by the person signing the document. No more. In the electronic commerce world, it is now, "What is your mother's maiden name?", "Slide your smart card into the sensor," or "Look into the iris scanner."

E-Signature

Another main feature of the E-SIGN Act is that it recognizes an *electronic signature* or **e-signature.** The act gives an e-signature the same force and effect as a pen-inscribed signature on paper. The act is technology neutral, however, in that the law does not define or decide which technologies should be used to create a legally binding signature in cyberspace.

Loosely defined, a **digital signature** is an electronic method for identifying an individual. The challenge is to make sure that someone who uses a digital signature is the person he or she claims to be. Thus the act provides that a digital signature basically can be verified in one of three ways:

1. By something the signatory knows, such as a secret password, pet's name, and so forth
2. By something a person has, such as a "smart card," which looks like a credit card and stores personal information
3. By biometrics, which uses a device that digitally recognizes fingerprints or the retina or iris of the eye

The verification of electronic signatures is creating a need for scanners and methods to verify personal information.

E-License

Intellectual property and information rights are extremely important assets of many individuals and companies. Software programs, data, copyrights, and such constitute valuable intellectual property and information rights.

The owners of intellectual property and information rights often wish to transfer limited rights in the property or information to parties for specified purposes and limited duration. The agreement that is used to transfer such limited rights is called a **license.** The parties to a license are the licensor and the licensee. The **licensor** is the party who owns the intellectual property or information rights and obligates himself or herself to transfer rights in the property or information to the licensee. The **licensee** is the party who is granted limited rights in or access to the intellectual property or information rights. An electronic license is called **e-license.** A licensing arrangement is illustrated in Exhibit 14.2.

Licensee A party who is granted limited rights in or access to intellectual property or informational rights owned by a licensor.

Licensor An owner of intellectual property or informational rights who transfers rights in the property or information to the licensee.

E-license A contract that transfers limited rights in intellectual property and informational rights.

Uniform Computer Information Transactions Act (UCITA)

In 1999 the National Conference of Commissioners on Uniform State Laws (a group of lawyers, judges, and legal scholars) drafted the **Uniform Computer Information Transactions Act (UCITA).** This model act establishes a uniform and

Exhibit 14.2 Parties to a license

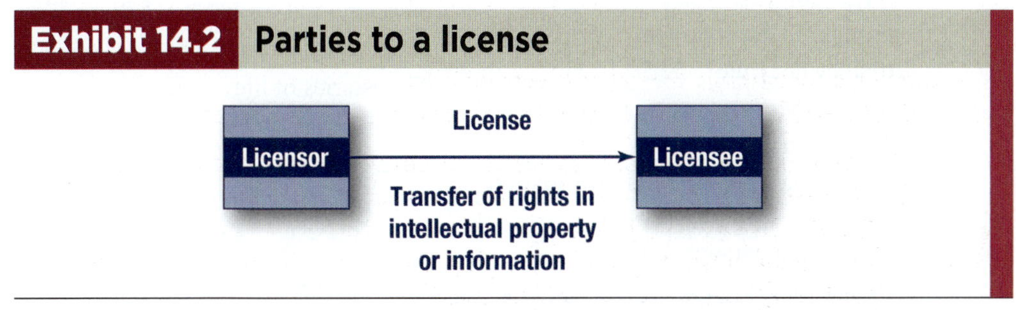

comprehensive set of rules that govern the creation, performance, and enforcement of computer information transactions. A computer information transaction is an agreement to create, transfer, or license computer information or information rights [UCITA Section 102(a)(11)].

The UCITA does not become law until a state's legislature enacts it as a state statute. Many states have adopted the UCITA or laws similar to the UCITA as their law for computer transactions and the licensing of informational rights.

Licensing agreement A detailed and comprehensive written agreement between a licensor and a licensee that sets forth the express terms of their agreement.

Licensing Agreement

A licensor and a licensee usually enter into a written **licensing agreement** that expressly states the terms of their agreement. Licensing agreements tend to be very detailed and comprehensive contracts. This is primarily because of the nature of the subject matter and the limited uses granted in the intellectual property or informational rights.

Web Exploration

Go to http://www.microsoft.com/about/legal/useterms. Find the licensing agreement for a Microsoft software product. Do you have any ability to negotiate the terms of this licensing agreement?

The parties to a contract for the licensing of information owe a duty to perform the obligations stated in the contract. If a party fails to perform as required, there is a breach of the contract. Breach of contract by one party to a licensing agreement gives the nonbreaching party the right to recover damages or other remedies.

Concept Review *and* Reinforcement

LEGAL TERMINOLOGY

Acceptance 520
Agreement 518
Article 2 (Sales) of the UCC 531
Article 2A (Leases) of the UCC 532
Breach of contract 526
Capacity to contract 521
Common law of contracts 516
Compensatory damages 528
Complete performance 527
Condition precedent 526
Consequential damages 528
Consideration 521
Contract 518
Contracts contrary to public policy 523
Contracts contrary to statutes 523
Contractual capacity 522
Counteroffer 520
Covenant 526
Digital signature 535
Disaffirm 522
E-contract 517
E-licenses 534
E-signature 535
Electronic commerce (e-commerce) 517
Electronic Signature in Global and National Commerce Act (E-SIGN Act) 534
Equitable remedies 529
Equity 530
Executed contract 527
Executory contract 524
Express contract 521
Firm offer rule 532
Formality of the writing 525
Gift promise (gratuitous promise) 521
Goods 532
Illegal contract 522
Implied-in-fact contract 521
Infancy doctrine 522
Inferior performance 527
Injunction 530
Intellectual property and information rights 535
Intoxicated persons 522
Lawful object 522
Lease 517
Legally enforceable 518
Lessee 532
Lessor 532
License 535
Licensee 535
Licensing agreement 536
Licensor 535
Liquidated damages 528
Material breach 527
Mental incapacity 522
Mentally incompetent persons 522
Minor breach 527
Minors 522
Mirror image rule 520
Mitigation of damages 529
Monetary damages 528
Necessaries of life 522
Offer 519
Offeree 518
Offeror 518
One-year rule 525
Online commerce 533

SUMMARY OF KEY CONCEPTS

Sources of Contract Law

1. Common law of contracts (law)
2. Uniform Commercial Code (law)
3. Restatement (Second) of Contracts (advisory only, not law)

Formation of a Contract

	A contract is a promise or set of promises for the breach of which the law gives a remedy or the performance of which the law in some way recognizes as a duty.
Parties to a Contract	1. *Offeror:* Party who makes an offer to enter into a contract. 2. *Offeree:* Party to whom the offer is made.
Elements of a Contract	1. Agreement 2. Consideration 3. Contractual capacity 4. Lawful object

Agreement

	An agreement is the manifestation by two or more persons of the substance of a contract. It requires an *offer* and an *acceptance*.
Offer	1. *Offer:* Manifestation by one party of a willingness to enter into a contract. 2. *Offeror:* Party who makes an offer. 3. *Offeree:* Party to whom an offer is made. This party has the power to create an agreement by accepting the terms of the offer.
Termination of an Offer by Action of the Parties	1. *Revocation:* The offeror may *revoke* (withdraw) an offer any time prior to its acceptance by the offeree. 2. *Rejection:* An offer is terminated if the offeree rejects the offer by his or her words or conduct. 3. *Counteroffer:* An offer by the offeree that terminates the offeror's offer and creates a new offer.
Option Contract	An option contract is a contract that is created if an offeree pays the offeror compensation to keep an offer open for an agreed-upon period of time. The offeror cannot sell the property to anyone else during the *option period.*
Acceptance	An acceptance is a manifestation of assent by the offeree to the terms of the offer. Acceptance of the offer by the offeree creates a contract.
Express and Implied Contracts	1. *Express contract:* A contract expressed in oral or written words. 2. *Implied-in-fact contract:* A contract implied from the conduct of the parties.

Consideration

Consideration is a thing of value given in exchange for a promise. It may be tangible or intangible property, performance of a service, forbearance of a legal right, or another thing of value.

Gift Promise	A gift promise is a promise to make gifts that are unenforceable because they lack consideration. Also called a *gratuitous promise*.
Capacity to Contract	
	1. *Minors:* Under the *infancy doctrine*, minors under the age of majority may *disaffirm* (cancel) most contracts they have entered into with adults. The contract is *voidable* by the minor but not by the adult. 2. *Mental incompetence:* Contracts made by persons who are insane are *voidable* by the insane person but not by the competent party to the contract. 3. *Intoxicated persons:* Contracts made by *intoxicated* persons are *voidable* by the intoxicated person but not by the competent party to the contract.
Lawful Object	
	The object of the contract must be *lawful* for the contract to be enforceable.
Illegal Contract	An illegal contract is *void*. Therefore, the parties cannot sue for nonperformance. If the contract has been executed, the court will *leave the parties where it finds them*. 1. Contracts that violate statutes are illegal, void, and unenforceable. 2. Contracts that violate public policy are illegal, void, and unenforceable.
Unconscionable Contract	
	Unconscionable contracts are oppressively unfair or unjust. They are also called *contracts of adhesion*. *Elements:* The elements of an unconscionable contract are: 1. The parties possessed severely unequal bargaining power. 2. The dominant party unreasonably used its power to obtain oppressive or manifestly unfair contract terms. 3. The adhering party had no reasonable alternative. *Remedies:* Where a contract or contract clause is found to be unconscionable, the court may do one of the following: 1. Refuse to enforce the contract. 2. Refuse to enforce the unconscionable clause but enforce the remainder of the contract. 3. Limit the applicability of any unconscionable clause so as to avoid any unconscionable result.
Statute of Frauds—Writing Requirement	
	A state statute requires the following contracts to be in writing: 1. *Contracts involving the transfer of interests in real property:* Includes contracts for the sale of land, buildings, items attached to land, mortgages, leases for a term of more than one year, and express easements. 2. *Contracts that cannot be performed within one year of their formation* (one-year rule). 3. *Contracts for the sale of goods costing $500 or more* (UCC 201). (The 2003 amendments to the UCC changed this amount to $5,000 or more.)
Sufficiency of the Writing	1. *Formality of the writing:* A written contract does not have to be formal or drafted by a lawyer to be enforceable. Informal contracts, such as handwritten notes, letters, invoices, and the like, are enforceable contracts. 2. *Required signature:* The party against whom enforcement of the contract is sought must have signed the contract. The signature may be the person's full legal name, last name, first name, nickname, initials, or other symbol.
Performance and Breach	
Covenant	A covenant is an unconditional promise to perform. Nonperformance of a covenant is a breach of contract that gives the other party the right to sue.
Condition Precedent	A condition precedent requires the occurrence or nonoccurrence of an event before a party is obligated to perform.

Levels of Performance	1. *Complete performance:* A party renders performance exactly as the contract requires. That party's contractual duties are discharged. 2. *Substantial performance:* A party renders performance that deviates only slightly from complete performance. There is a *minor breach*. The nonbreaching party may recover damages caused by the breach. 3. *Inferior performance:* A party's failure to perform express or implied contractual duties that impairs or destroys the essence of the contract. There is a *material breach*. The nonbreaching party may either (1) rescind the contract and recover restitution or (2) affirm the contract and recover damages.
Monetary Damages	
Types of Monetary Damages	1. *Compensatory damages:* Damages that compensate a nonbreaching party for loss of the contract and restore the "benefit of the bargain" to the nonbreaching party as if the contract had been fully performed. 2. *Consequential damages:* Foreseeable damages that arise from circumstances outside the contract and of which the breaching party either knew or had reason to know. Also called *special damages*. 3. *Liquidated damages:* Damages payable upon breach of contract that are agreed on in advance by the contracting parties. Liquidated damages substitute for actual damages.
Mitigation of Damages	The mitigation of damages is the duty the law places on a nonbreaching party to take reasonable efforts to avoid or reduce the resulting damages from a breach of contract. To mitigate a breach of an employment contract, the nonbreaching party must accept only "comparable" employment.
Equitable Remedies	
Specific Performance	Specific performance is a court order that requires the breaching party to perform his or her contractual duties. It is available only if the subject matter of the contract is *unique*.
Injunction	An injunction is a court order that prohibits a person from doing a certain act. The requesting party must show that he or she will suffer irreparable injury if the injunction is not granted.
Reformation	Reformation permits the court to rewrite a contract to express the parties' true intentions. It is available to correct clerical and mathematical errors.
Quasi-Contract	A quasi-contract permits the court to order recovery of compensation even though no enforceable contract exists between the parties. It is used to prevent unjust enrichment. Also called an *implied-in-law contract* or *quantum meruit*.
Equity	Equity is a doctrine that permits judges to make decisions based on fairness, equality, moral rights, and natural law.
Uniform Commercial Code (UCC)	
	The UCC is a comprehensive statutory scheme that includes laws covering most aspects of sales and lease contracts of goods.
Article 2 (Sales)	Article 2 of the UCC applies to sales transactions in goods.
Article 2A (Leases)	Article 2A of the UCC applies to personal property leases of goods.
UCC Firm Offer Rule	The UCC firm offer rule says that a merchant who (1) makes an offer to buy, sell, or lease goods and (2) assures the other party in a separate writing that the offer will be held open cannot revoke the offer for the time stated, or if no time is stated, for a reasonable time.
UCC Statute of Frauds	The UCC Statute of Frauds requires contracts for the sale of goods costing $500 or more and lease contracts involving payments of $1,000 or more to be in writing.
Convention on Contracts for the International Sale of Goods (CISG)	The CISG establishes uniform rules for the formation and enforcement of contracts involving the international sale of goods. The parties to any international contract can agree that the CISG controls their contract.

E-Commerce and E-Contracts

	Electronic commerce, or e-commerce, is the use of the Internet and the World Wide Web to sell goods and services. Also called *online commerce*.
E-Contract	An electronic contract is entered into by email or over the Internet for the sale or lease of goods, other property, or services.
Electronic Signature in Global and National Commerce Act (E-SIGN Act)	This federal act applies to e-commerce and does the following: 1. *E-writing:* The federal act recognizes that e-contracts meet the writing requirements of the Statutes of Fraud. 2. *E-signature:* The federal act gives electronic signatures the same force and effect as pen-inscribed signatures on paper.

E-License

	The electronic license is a contract that is entered into by email or over the Internet and that transfers limited rights in intellectual property and information rights. 1. *Licensor:* An owner of intellectual property or information rights who transfers rights in the property or information to the licensee. 2. *Licensee:* A party who is granted limited rights in or access to intellectual property or information rights owned by a licensor.
Uniform Computer Information Transactions Act (UCITA)	The UCITA is a model act issued by the National Conference of Commissioners on Uniform State Laws that establishes a uniform and comprehensive set of rules that govern the creation, performance, and enforcement of computer information transactions.
Licensing Agreement	A licensing agreement is a detailed and comprehensive written agreement between a licensor and a licensee that sets forth the express terms of their agreement.

WORKING THE WEB

1. Visit the website http://www.lectlaw.com/formb/html and click on the words "Contract, Sale of Goods." Print out and review this form.
2. Using the website http://www.google.com/html or another Internet search engine, locate an article about a Facebook software-licensing agreement. Write a one-page report on the specifics of the licensing agreement.
3. Visit the website http://lectlaw.com/forma/html and click on the words "Fee Agreement—Contingent." Read this form in its entirety. What type of form contract is this?
4. Using the website http://www.google.com/html or another Internet search engine, locate an article about a recent contract dispute. Write a one-page report on the specifics of this contract dispute.

CRITICAL THINKING & WRITING QUESTIONS

1. Define an offer. Who is the offeror? Who is the offeree?
2. What are the four elements necessary for an enforceable contract?
3. What is an acceptance? Explain the mirror image rule.
4. Describe the following: (a) express contract, (b) implied-in-fact contract, and (c) quasi-contract. Give an example of each.
5. What is consideration? Give an example.
6. Define "capacity to contract." Explain the enforceability of contracts made by (a) minors (the infancy doctrine), (b) mentally incompetent persons, and (c) intoxicated persons.
7. Define "lawful object." What is an illegal contract? What is the effect of an illegal contract?
8. What is the Statute of Frauds? What types of contracts does the Statute of Frauds cover? Give examples. What is the effect if the Statute of Frauds is not met?
9. Describe substantial performance. Is there a breach of the contract? Give an example. Describe inferior performance. Is this a breach of contract? Give an example.
10. Explain the following types of monetary damages: (a) compensatory damages, (b) consequential damages, and (c) liquidated damages. Give an example of each.
11. Describe the following types of equitable remedies: (a) specific performance, (b) injunction, and (c) reformation. Give an example of each.
12. What is Article 2 (Sales) of the Uniform Commercial Code? What type of contracts does it cover? Give an example.

13. What is Article 2A (Leases) of the Uniform Commercial Code? What type of contracts does it cover? Give an example.
14. What is e-commerce? Explain (a) e-contract and (b) e-license.
15. What is the Electronic Signature in Global and National Commerce Act? Explain how this statute (a) affects the Statute of Frauds for e-contracts and (b) gives effect to e-signatures.

Building Paralegal Skills

VIDEO CASE STUDIES

Parents and Child Consult the Legal Team: Confidentiality Issues

A family is meeting with the attorney provided for them by their insurance company. Issues of what is and what is not covered by the insurance contract are discussed and a question arises as to who the client really is.

After viewing the video case study in MyLegalStudiesLab, answer the following:

1. How are the rights of the parties determined by the insurance contract?
2. If the attorney is being paid by the insurance company, who is the client to whom the lawyer has a loyalty and duty?
3. Is there a conflict of interest between representing the parents and representing the child?

ETHICS ANALYSIS & DISCUSSION QUESTIONS

1. Is it ethical to copy into your word processor, and use as your own, a standard-form real estate contract that contains a copyright notice from the state association of realtors?
2. You have been asked by a lawyer at your firm to state that you witnessed a client of the firm sign a document although you were not present when the client signed the document. Are there any ethical issues?
3. You are a paralegal not otherwise licensed to practice law. Because of your substantial expertise, you are requested to prepare a complex set of legal documents for a former client. You enter into a fee agreement and are paid upon completion of the work. The "client" then seeks return of the funds paid, claiming he did not understand the significance of the UPL law in the state. See *Vista Designs v. Silverman*, 774 So.2d 884 (Fla.App. 4 Dist. 2001). Can you be compelled to return the fee paid? Has the client breached his contract?

DEVELOPING YOUR COLLABORATION SKILLS

With a group of other students selected by you or assigned by your instructor, review the facts of the following case. As a group, discuss the following questions:

1. What type of contract was involved in this case?
2. Who is the plaintiff? Who is the defendant?
3. Was there a valid offer and acceptance?
4. Is the contract enforceable? If so, what remedy should be awarded?

Alba v. Kaufmann

Jean-Claude Kaufmann owned approximately 37 acres of real property located in the town of Stephentown, Rensselaer County, New York. The property is located in a wooded area and is improved with a 19th-century farmhouse. Kaufmann and his spouse, Christine Cacace, resided in New York City and used the property as a weekend or vacation home. After Kaufmann and Cacace lost their jobs, their financial situation prompted Kaufmann to list the property for sale for $350,000.

Richard Alba and his spouse (Albas) looked at the property and offered Kaufmann the full asking price. The parties executed a contract for sale, and the Albas paid a deposit, obtained a mortgage commitment, and procured a satisfactory home inspection and title insurance. A date for closing the transaction was set. Prior to closing, Cacace sent the Albas an e-mail, indicating that she and Kaufmann had "a change of heart" and no longer wished to go forward with the sale. [The] Albas sent a reply e-mail, stating their intent to go forward with the scheduled closing. Cacace responded with another e-mail, informing the Albas that she had multiple sclerosis and alleging that the "remorse and dread" over the impending sale was making her ill. When Kaufmann refused to close, the Albas sued, seeking specific performance, and moved for summary judgment.

Source: Alba v. Kaufman, 810 N.Y.S.2d 539, Web 2006 N.Y. App. Div. Lexis 2321 (Supreme Court of New York, Appellate)

PARALEGAL PORTFOLIO EXERCISE

Find a sample buy–sell agreement between owners of a business where the owners agree that if one of them leaves the business or dies, the remaining owners will purchase his or her shares, either by paying the leaving partner or by paying the beneficiaries or heirs of a deceased owner. Using this sample agreement, draft the buy–sell agreement for the three owners of Jewelry Associates Corporation (JAC) referred to in the opening scenario. The owners are Maxine Armstrong, ViVi Wei, and Jose Ramirez.

LEGAL ANALYSIS & WRITING CASES

Montgomery v. English 902 So.2d 836, Web 2005 Fla. App. Lexis 4704

Court of Appeal of Florida

Norma English made an offer to purchase a house owned by Michael and Laurie Montgomery (Montgomery) for $272,000. In her offer, English also proposed to purchase certain personal property—paving stones and a fireplace screen worth a total of $100—from Montgomery. When Montgomery received English's offer, Montgomery made many changes to English's offer, including deleting the paving stones and fireplace screen from the personal property that English wanted. When English received the Montgomery counteroffer, English accepted and initialed all of Montgomery's changes[,] except that English did not initial the change that deleted the paving stones and fireplace screen from the deal.

Subsequently, Montgomery notified English that because English had not completely accepted the terms of Montgomery's counteroffer, Montgomery was therefore withdrawing from the deal. That same day, Montgomery signed a contract to sell the house to another buyer for $285,000. English sued Montgomery for specific performance of the contract. Montgomery defended, arguing that the mirror image rule was not satisfied because English had not initialed the provision that deleted the paving stones and fireplace screen.

Question

1. Is there an enforceable contract between English and Montgomery?

Dees, d/b/a David Dees Illustration v. Saban Entertainment, Inc.

131 F.3d 146, Web 1997 U.S. App. Lexis 39173

United States Court of Appeals for the Ninth Circuit

Mighty Morphin' Power Rangers was a phenomenal success as a television series. The Power Rangers battled to save the universe from all sorts of diabolical plots and bad guys. They were also featured in a profitable line of toys and garments bearing the Power Rangers logo. The name and logo of the Power Rangers are known to millions of children and their parents worldwide. The claim of ownership of the logo for the Power Rangers ended up in a battle in a courtroom.

David Dees is a designer who works as d.b.a. David Dees Illustration. Saban Entertainment, Inc. (Saban), which owns the copyright and trademark to Power Rangers figures and the name "Power Ranger," hired Dees as an independent contractor to design a logo for the Power Rangers. The contract signed by the parties was titled "Work-for-Hire/Independent Contractor Agreement." The contract was drafted by Saban with the help of its attorneys; Dees signed the agreement without the representation of legal counsel.

Dees designed the logo currently used for the Power Rangers and was paid $250 to transfer his copyright ownership in the logo. Subsequently, Dees sued Saban to recover damages for copyright and trademark infringement. Saban defended, arguing that Dees was bound by the agreement he had signed.

Question

1. Is Dees bound by the contract?

WORKING WITH THE LANGUAGE OF THE COURT CASE

Facebook, Inc. v. Pacific Northwest Software

640 F.3d 1034, Web 2011 U.S. App. Lexis 1034
United States Court of Appeals for the Ninth Circuit

Read and then brief the following case, excerpted from the Court of Appeals opinion. In your brief, answer the following questions.

1. Who were the parties to the lawsuit?
2. What did the settlement agreement provide?
3. What was the Winklevosses' claim on appeal?
4. What did the Court of Appeals mean when it stated, "At some point, litigation must come to an end. That point has now been reached"?

Kozinski, Chief Judge

Cameron Winklevoss, Tyler Winklevoss and Divya Narendra (the Winklevosses) claim that Mark Zuckerberg stole the idea for Facebook (the social networking site) from them. They sued Facebook and Zuckerberg (Facebook) in Massachusetts. Facebook countersued them and their competing social networking site, ConnectU, in California, alleging that the Winklevosses and ConnectU hacked into Facebook to purloin user data, and tried to steal users by spamming them. The ensuing litigation involved several other parties and gave bread to many lawyers, but the details are not particularly relevant here.

The district court in California eventually dismissed the Winklevosses from that case for lack of personal jurisdiction. It then ordered the parties to mediate their dispute. The mediation session included ConnectU, Facebook and the Winklevosses so that the parties could reach a global settlement. Before mediation began, the participants signed a Confidentiality Agreement stipulating that all statements made during mediation were privileged, non-discoverable and inadmissible "in any arbitral, judicial, or other proceeding."

After a day of negotiations, ConnectU, Facebook and the Winklevosses signed a handwritten, one-and-a-third page "Term Sheet & Settlement Agreement" (the Settlement Agreement). The Winklevosses agreed to give up ConnectU in exchange for cash and a piece of Facebook. The parties stipulated that the Settlement Agreement was "confidential," "binding" and "may be submitted into evidence to enforce [it]." The Settlement Agreement also purported to end all disputes between the parties.

The settlement fell apart during negotiations over the form of the final deal documents, and Facebook filed a motion with the district court seeking to enforce it. ConnectU argued that the Settlement Agreement was unenforceable because it lacked material terms and had been procured by fraud. The district court found the Settlement Agreement enforceable and ordered the Winklevosses to transfer all ConnectU shares to Facebook. This had the effect of moving ConnectU from the Winklevosses' to Facebook's side of the case.

The Winklevosses appeal.

The Settlement Agreement envisioned that Facebook would acquire all of ConnectU's shares in exchange for cash and a percentage of Facebook's common stock. The parties also agreed to grant each other "mutual releases as broad as possible," and the Winklevosses represented and warranted that "[t]hey have no further right to assert against Facebook" and "no further claims against Facebook & its related parties."

Facebook moved to enforce the Settlement Agreement, and also asked the district court to order ConnectU and the Winklevosses to sign more than 130 pages of documents, including a Stock Purchase Agreement, a ConnectU Stockholders Agreement and a Confidential Mutual Release Agreement. Facebook's deal lawyers claimed that the terms in these documents were "required to finalize" the Settlement Agreement, and its expert dutifully opined that they were "typical of acquisition documents."

The parties agreed that Facebook would swallow up ConnectU, the Winklevosses would get cash and a small piece of Facebook, and both sides would stop fighting and get on with their lives.

(continued)

The Settlement Agreement even specifies how to fill in the "material" terms that the Winklevosses claim are missing from the deal:

> Facebook will determine the form & documentation of the acquisition of ConnectU's shares consistent with a stock and cash for stock acquisition.

California allows parties to delegate choices over terms, so long as the delegation is constrained by the rest of the contract and subject to the implied covenant of good faith and fair dealing. Delegation isn't necessary for a contract like the Settlement Agreement to be enforceable, as the court may fill in missing terms by reference to the rest of the contract, extrinsic evidence and industry practice. But the clause quoted above leaves no doubt that the Winklevosses and Facebook meant to bind themselves and each other, even though everyone understood that some material aspects of the deal would be papered later.

The Winklevosses' contractual delegation is valid because the Settlement Agreement obligates Facebook to draw up documents "consistent with a stock and cash for stock acquisition." And, if Facebook should draft terms that are unfair or oppressive, or that deprive the Winklevosses of the benefit of their bargain, the district court could reject them as a breach of the implied covenant of good faith and fair dealing. The district court got it exactly right when it found the Settlement Agreement enforceable but refused to add the stack of documents drafted by Facebook's deal lawyers.

After signing the Settlement Agreement, Facebook notified the Winklevosses that an internal valuation prepared to comply with Section 409A of the tax code put the value of its common stock at $8.88 per share. The Winklevosses argue that Facebook misled them into believing its shares were worth four times as much. Had they known about this valuation during the mediation, they claim, they would never have signed the Settlement Agreement.

The Winklevosses are sophisticated parties who were locked in a contentious struggle over ownership rights in one of the world's fastest-growing companies. They engaged in discovery, which gave them access to a good deal of information about their opponents. They brought half-a-dozen lawyers to the mediation. Howard Winklevoss—father of Cameron and Tyler, former accounting professor at Wharton School of Business and an expert in valuation—also participated.

The Settlement Agreement grants "all parties" "mutual releases as broad as possible"; the Winklevosses "represent and warrant" that "[t]hey have no further right to assert against Facebook" and "no further claims against Facebook & its related parties." The Winklevosses maintain that they didn't discover the facts giving rise to their [fraud] claims until after they signed these releases.

An agreement meant to end a dispute between sophisticated parties cannot reasonably be interpreted as leaving open the door to litigation about the settlement negotiation process.

The district court correctly concluded that the Settlement Agreement meant to release claims arising out of the settlement negotiations, and that the release was valid.

The Winklevosses make two related claims: that Facebook led them to believe during the settlement negotiations that its shares were worth $35.90, even though Facebook knew that its shares were, in fact, worth only $8.88; and that Facebook failed to disclose material information, namely the $8.88 tax valuation, during the negotiations.

Nevertheless, the district court was right to exclude the proffered evidence. The Confidentiality Agreement, which everyone signed before commencing the mediation, provides that:

> All statements made during the course of the mediation or in mediator follow-up thereafter at any time prior to complete settlement of this matter are privileged settlement discussions... and are nondiscoverable and inadmissible for any purpose including in any legal proceeding.... *No aspect of the mediation shall be relied upon or introduced as evidence in any arbitral, judicial, or other proceeding.* (emphasis added).

This agreement precludes the Winklevosses from introducing in support of... [fraud] claims any evidence of what Facebook said, or did not say, during the mediation.

The Winklevosses are not the first parties bested by a competitor who then seek to gain through litigation what they were unable to achieve in the marketplace. And the courts might have obliged, had the Winklevosses not settled their dispute and signed a release of all claims against Facebook. With the help of a team of lawyers and a financial advisor, they made a deal that appears quite favorable in light of recent market activity. For whatever reason, they now want to back out. Like the district court, we see no basis for allowing them to do so. At some point, litigation must come to an end. That point has now been reached.

MYLEGALSTUDIESLAB

MyLegalStudiesLab Virtual Law Office Experience Assignments
Complete the pre-test, study plan, and post-test for this chapter and answer the Legal Applications questions as assigned. These will help you confirm your mastery of the concepts and their application to legal scenarios. Then complete the Virtual Law Office assignments as assigned by your instructor. These assignments are designed to develop your workplace skills. Completing the assignments for this chapter will result in producing the following documents for inclusion in your portfolio:

VLOE 14.1 Memo on applicability of Carnival Cruise Line holding to the facts of the client's case

CHAPTER

15

Property Law

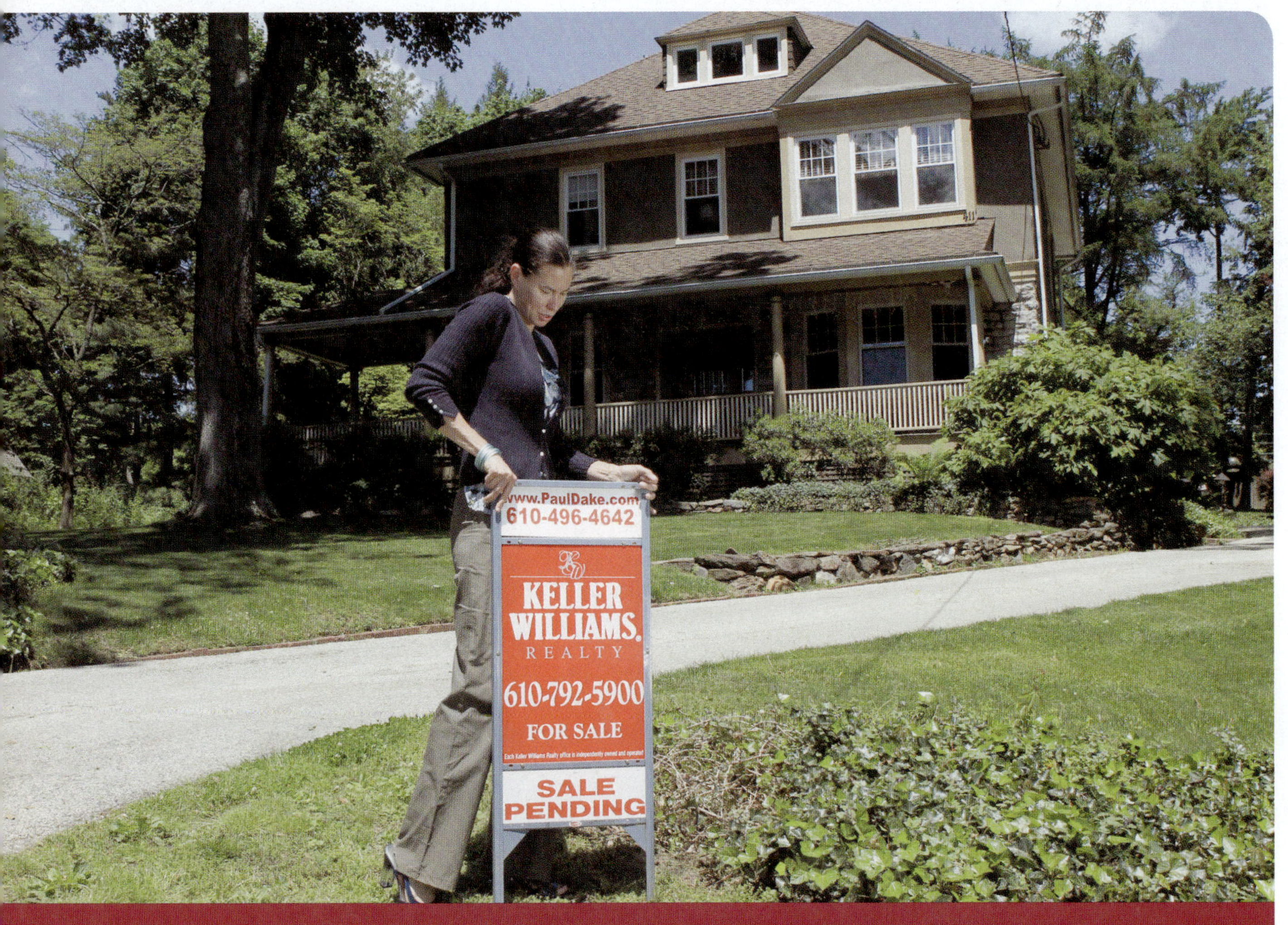

LEARNING OBJECTIVES

After studying this chapter, you should be able to:

1. Recognize the professional opportunities for paralegals in the property law area.
2. Define *personal property* and describe the methods for acquiring ownership.
3. Explain bailments and the parties to a bailment.
4. List and describe the types of real property.
5. Name and describe the types of freehold estates.
6. Identify the types of co-ownership.
7. Name and describe the methods of transferring ownership of real property.
8. Identify and describe the various types of leaseholds and explain the landlord–tenant relationship.
9. Explain features of land-use control, such as zoning laws.
10. Explain a paralegal's duty not to engage in conduct that would exceed the paralegal professional's authority under the law.

Paralegals at Work

You work for Mr. Nicholas Klapova, a lawyer who specializes in real estate law. As a paralegal working in real estate law, you are often assigned to conduct legal research on real estate law issues, and to draft documents and contracts that Mr. Klapova reviews. You also attend conferences with Mr. Klapova and his clients concerning property law issues.

One day, Ms. Eve Trump, an existing client of the law firm, arrives at the law office for a meeting with Mr. Klapova. Mr. Klapova invites you to sit in on the initial meeting. At the meeting, Ms. Trump discloses the following information: She owns a 200-acre parcel of land that is beachfront property, with 3,000 feet of beach at the property. Ms. Trump purchased the property 25 years ago for $250,000 when the property and the entire surrounding area were all vacant land. Ms. Trump has been approached by a real estate developer who wants to buy the property from her for $7,000,000. The developer wants to develop the property and build a resort hotel.

Ms. Trump states that she would like to sell the property and then adds the following facts: Her property currently is zoned for single-family residences. Many of the large vacant properties in the area have been sold and developed as individual housing tracts over the past 10 years. Ms. Trump says that when she purchased the property 25 years ago, an old fence line separated her property and the 100-acre beachfront property owned by Mrs. Lorraine Gasper on the west side of Ms. Trump's property. Upon conducting a recent survey, it was determined that the fence line encroaches upon Ms. Trump's property by 120 feet. The proposed purchaser wants the 120 feet to be included in the purchase.

Ms. Trump also says that about 10 years ago, when the 150-acre parcel of beachfront property to the east of her property was purchased by Clive Jones, he asked whether he could continue to reach his property using the existing dirt road that runs through Ms. Trump's property as the prior owner of his property had done for 20 years. The dirt road runs from the highway that is north of Ms. Trump's, Mrs. Gasper's, and Mr. Jones's properties. The south side of each of the three

> "Property and law are born and must die together."
>
> Jeremy Bentham, *Principles of the Civil Code*

properties is the lake and beach. The dirt road runs from the highway beginning about one-third of the way from the east lot line of Mr. Jones's property, traverses across Ms. Trump's property, and arrives at the front of Mr. Jones's property at the beach, about 20 feet across the lot line with Ms. Trump's property. Mr. Jones and Ms. Trump have no formal written agreement, however.

Ms. Trump asks Mr. Klapova to look into these matters for her and to advise her whether she has any legal problems concerning the proposed sale of her property. Consider the issues involved in this scenario as you read the chapter.

Learning Objective 1
Recognize the professional opportunities for paralegals in the property law area.

INTRODUCTION FOR THE PARALEGAL

Private ownership of property forms the foundation of our economic system. As such, a comprehensive body of law has been developed to protect property rights. The law protects the rights of property owners to use, sell, dispose of, control, and prevent others from trespassing on their property.

This chapter discusses the different kinds of personal property, the methods of acquiring ownership in personal property, and the property rights in mislaid, lost, and abandoned property. Sometimes persons entrust their property to others for transport or safekeeping, a situation that could create a bailment, which is also covered in this chapter.

Property and ownership rights in real property play an important part in U.S. society and the U.S. economy. Individuals and families own houses, farmers and ranchers own farmland and ranches, and businesses own commercial and office buildings. The concept of real property is concerned with the legal rights to the property rather than with the physical attributes of the tangible land. Other rights in real property, such as mineral and air rights, are also covered in this chapter.

Although the United States has the most advanced private property system in the world, the ownership and possession of real estate are not free from government regulation. Pursuant to constitutional authority, federal, state, and local governments have enacted myriad laws that regulate the ownership, possession, lease, and use of real property. These laws include zoning and other laws.

Only a ghost can exist without material property.
Ayn Rand
Atlas Shrugged (1957)

Individuals and families rent houses and apartments, professionals and businesses lease office space, small businesses rent stores, and other businesses lease commercial and manufacturing facilities. In these situations, a landlord–tenant relationship is created. The party who owns or controls the leased space is called the lessor and the party who is renting the space is called the lessee. The contract between them is called a lease. The parties to a landlord–tenant relationship have certain legal rights and duties that are governed by a mixture of real estate and contract law.

Although the ownership and possession of real estate in the United States is commonly a private affair, the ownership and leasing of real property is not free from government regulation. For example, the government may also take private property for public use under its power of eminent domain, assuming that certain requirements are met and just compensation is paid to the owner.

Many lawyers practice in the area of real estate law. A paralegal working for one of these lawyers is often called upon to assist in preparing the necessary documents for the sale of real property and for the recording of transfers of real property.

This chapter covers the topics of personal property, real property, landlord–tenant relationships, and land-use regulation.

The following feature discusses the career opportunities for paralegal professionals in property law.

CAREER OPPORTUNITIES FOR PARALEGALS IN PROPERTY LAW

Many paralegal professionals work for lawyers who practice in the area of real estate law. Most real estate law is state law and, therefore, is state-specific. In addition to having general knowledge of real estate law, then, these paralegals must have significant knowledge of the intricacies of the real estate law of the state in which they work.

A paralegal is often involved in drafting and completing documents for real estate transactions, including the purchase and sale of single-family houses, condominiums, cooperatives, and other housing units. Although the buyer and the seller usually use real estate brokers to represent them, lawyers often are involved in representing clients in these transactions. Thus the paralegal must know the specific documents required in these transactions.

Lawyers, and therefore their paralegals, are often also involved in the purchase, sale, or transfer of vacant real property. This might involve a single buyer or multiple buyers. In these transactions, paralegals usually are called upon to prepare documents and otherwise assist the lawyers on both the seller's and the buyer's side in completing the transaction.

Paralegals frequently are called upon to use their expertise in complex real estate transactions. These include transactions where a developer is going to develop an entire housing tract, shopping mall, office building, or commercial building. Each of these types of development requires substantial work by lawyers, and thus their paralegals, representing clients on both sides of the transaction.

Another facet of real estate law in which paralegals assist lawyers is the area of leasing. Some leases are simple—for example, the lease of an apartment, in which the lawyer for the owner of the property usually drafts the lease for the landowner. Other leases are extremely complex—for example, leases on large office building space and commercial properties are negotiated individually by both sides, usually using their lawyers. The lawyers then draft the leases and other documents necessary to complete an agreed-upon lease transaction. Paralegals often assist lawyers in representing clients in these complicated lease transactions.

Paralegals who work in the real estate area often acquire expertise in specific types of real estate transactions. Many paralegals learn the intricate procedures, documents, and law that are necessary to complete the real estate transactions handled by the lawyers for whom they work.

Personal Property

Learning Objective 2

Define *personal property* and describe the methods for acquiring ownership.

The two kinds of property are real property and personal property.

1. Real property includes land and the property that is permanently attached to that land.

   Examples Minerals, crops, timber, and buildings that are attached to land are generally considered real property.

2. **Personal property** (sometimes referred to as *goods* or *chattels*) consists of everything that is not real property.

Personal property Tangible property such as automobiles, furniture, and equipment, and intangible property such as securities, patents, and copyrights.

Personal property can be either tangible or intangible. **Tangible property** includes physically defined property, such as goods, animals, and minerals. **Intangible property** represents rights that cannot be reduced to physical form, such as stock certificates, certificates of deposit, bonds, and copyrights.

Personal property that is permanently affixed to land or buildings is called a *fixture*. Such property, which includes things such as heating systems and storm windows, is categorized as real property. Unless otherwise agreed, fixtures remain with a building when it is sold. Personal property (such as furniture, pictures, and other easily portable household items) may be removed by the seller prior to sale. Real property can become personal property if it is removed from the land.

Example A tree that is part of a forest is real property; a tree that is cut down is personal property.

Purchase or Production

The most common method of acquiring title to personal property is by *purchasing* the property from its owner.

> **Example** Urban Concrete Corporation owns a large piece of equipment. City Builders, Inc. purchases the equipment from Urban Concrete for $50,000. Urban Concrete signs the title to the equipment to City Builders. City Builders is now the owner of the equipment.

Production is another common method of acquiring ownership in personal property. Thus, a manufacturer that purchases raw materials and produces a finished product owns that product.

Gift

Gift A voluntary transfer of title to property without payment of consideration by the donee. To be a valid gift, three elements must be shown: (1) *donative intent,* (2) *delivery,* and (3) *acceptance.*

Donor A person who gives a gift.

Donee A person who receives a gift.

A **gift** is a voluntary transfer of property without consideration. The lack of consideration is what distinguishes a gift from a purchase. The person making a gift is called the **donor.** The person who receives the gift is called the **donee.** The three elements of a valid gift are:

1. ***Donative Intent.*** For a gift to be effective, the donor must have intended to make a gift. Donative intent can be inferred from the circumstances or language used by the donor. The courts also consider factors such as relationship of the parties, size of the gift, and mental capacity of the donor.
2. ***Delivery.*** Delivery must occur for there to be a valid gift. Although *physical delivery* is the usual method of transferring personal property, it is sometimes impracticable. In such circumstances, *constructive delivery* (or *symbolic delivery*) is sufficient.

   > **Example** If the property being gifted is kept in a safe-deposit box, physically giving the key to the donee is enough to signal the gift. Most intangible property is transferred by written conveyance (for example, conveying a stock certificate represents a transfer of ownership in a corporation).

3. ***Acceptance.*** Acceptance usually is not a problem because most donees readily accept gifts. In fact, the courts presume acceptance unless there is proof that the gift was refused. Nevertheless, a person cannot be forced to accept an unwanted gift.

A gift made during a person's lifetime that is an irrevocable present transfer of ownership is a **gift *inter vivos.*** A **gift *causa mortis*** is a gift made in contemplation of death. A gift *causa mortis* is established when (1) the donor makes a gift in anticipation of approaching death from an existing sickness or peril and (2) the donor dies from such sickness or peril without having revoked the gift. A gift *causa mortis* can be revoked by the donor up until the time he or she dies, and takes precedence over a prior, conflicting will.

> **Example** Suppose Sandy is to have a major operation from which she may not recover. Prior to going into surgery, Sandy removes her diamond ring and gives it to her friend Pamela, stating, "In the event of my death, I want you to have this." This is a gift *causa mortis.* If Sandy dies from the operation, the gift is effective and Pamela owns the ring. If Sandy lives, the requisite condition for the gift (her death) has not occurred; therefore, the gift is not effective, and Sandy can recover the ring from Pamela.

Uniform Gift to Minors Act

Uniform Gift to Minors Act or Revised Uniform Gift to Minors Act Acts that establish procedures for adults to make gifts of money and securities to minors.

All states have adopted in whole or in part the **Uniform Gift to Minors Act** or the **Revised Uniform Gift to Minors Act.** These laws establish procedures for adults to make irrevocable gifts of money and securities to minors. Gifts of money can be made by depositing the money in an account in a financial institution with the donor or another trustee (such as another adult or bank) as custodian for the minor. Gifts of securities can be made by registering the securities in the name of a trustee as custodian for the minor. The laws give custodians broad discretionary powers to invest the money or securities for the benefit of the minor.

Will or Inheritance

Title to personal property is frequently acquired by **will** or **inheritance.** If the person who dies had a valid will, the property is distributed to the **beneficiaries** pursuant to the provisions of that will. Otherwise the property is distributed to the **heirs,** as provided in the relevant state's inheritance statute.

Mislaid Property

Property is called **mislaid property** when its owner voluntarily places the property somewhere and then inadvertently forgets it. It is likely that the owner will return for the property upon realizing that it was misplaced.

Mislaid property Property that an owner voluntarily places somewhere and then inadvertently forgets about.

The owner of the premises where the property is mislaid is entitled to take possession of the property against all except the rightful owner. This right is superior to the rights of the person who finds it. Such possession does not involve a change of title. Instead, the owner of the premises becomes an involuntary bailee of the property (bailments are discussed later in this chapter) and owes a duty to take reasonable care of the property until it is reclaimed by the owner.

Example Suppose Felicity is on a business trip and stays in a hotel during her trip. Felicity accidentally leaves her diamond engagement ring in the hotel room she has stayed in and checks out of the hotel. The engagement ring is mislaid property, and the hotel has a duty to return it to Felicity, its rightful owner.

Lost Property

Property is considered **lost property** when its owner negligently, carelessly, or inadvertently leaves it somewhere. The finder obtains title to such property against the whole world except the true owner. The lost property must be returned to its rightful owner, whether the finder discovers the loser's identity or the loser finds the person who found the property. A finder who refuses to return the property is liable for the tort of conversion and the crime of larceny. Many states require the finder to conduct a reasonable search (such as by placing advertisements in newspapers) to find the rightful owner.

Lost property Property that an owner leaves somewhere because of negligence, carelessness, or inadvertence.

Example If a commuter finds a laptop computer on the floor of a subway station in New York City, the computer is considered lost property. The finder can claim title to the computer against the whole world except the true owner. If the true owner discovers that the finder has her computer, she may recover it from the finder. If there is identification of the owner on the computer (such as name, address, and telephone number), the finder owes a duty to contact the rightful owner and give back the computer.

Estray Statutes

Most states have enacted **estray statutes** that permit a finder of *mislaid* or *lost* property to clear title to the property if:

1. The finder reports the found property to the appropriate government agency and then turns over possession of the property to this agency,

Web Exploration

Use **www.google.com** to find the estray statute or other law in your state that applies to the finding of personal property. If there is an estray statute, what requirements must be met and what is the waiting period?

2. Either the finder or the government agency posts notices and publishes advertisements describing the lost property, and
3. A specified time (usually a year or a number of years) has passed without the rightful owner's reclaiming the property.

Many state estray statutes require that the government receive a portion of the value of the property. Some statutes provide that title cannot be acquired in found property that is the result of illegal activity.

Example Title has been denied to finders of property and money deemed to have been used for illegal drug purchases.

Learning Objective 3
Explain bailments and the parties to a bailment.

Abandoned Property

Property is classified as **abandoned property** if (1) an owner discards the property with the intent to relinquish his or her rights in it or (2) an owner of mislaid or lost property gives up any further attempts to locate it. Anyone who finds abandoned property acquires title to it. The title is good against the whole world, including the original owner.

Example Property left at a garbage dump is abandoned property. It belongs to the first person who claims it.

SIDEBAR

MISLAID, LOST, AND ABANDONED PROPERTY

Type of Property	Ownership Rights
Mislaid property	The owner of the premises where property is mislaid is entitled to possession but does not acquire title. He or she holds the property as an involuntary bailor until the owner reclaims it.
Lost property	The finder acquires title to the property against the whole world except the true owner; the owner may reclaim his or her property from the finder.
Abandoned property	The finder acquires title to the property, even against its original owner.

Bailment

A **bailment** occurs when the owner of personal property delivers his or her property to another person to be held, stored, or delivered, or for some other purpose. In a bailment, the owner of the property is the **bailor,** and the party to whom the property is delivered for safekeeping, storage, or delivery (such as a warehouse or common carrier) is the **bailee** (see Exhibit 15.1).

A bailment is different from a sale or a gift because title to the goods does not transfer to the bailee. Instead, the bailee must follow the bailor's directions concerning the goods.

Example Suppose Hudson Corp. is relocating its offices and hires American Van Lines to move its office furniture and equipment to the new location. American Van Lines (the bailee) must follow Hudson's (the bailor) instructions regarding delivery. The law of bailments establishes the rights, duties, and liabilities of parties to a bailment.

Mutual Benefit Bailment

A **mutual benefit bailment** is a bailment that *benefits both parties*. The bailee owes a **duty of reasonable care,** or **ordinary care,** to protect the bailed goods. This means that the bailee is liable for any goods that are lost, damaged, or destroyed because of his or her negligence.

Bailment A transaction in which an owner transfers his or her personal property to another to be held, stored, delivered, or for some other purpose. Title to the property does not transfer.

Bailor The owner of property in a bailment.

Bailee A holder of goods who is not a seller or a buyer (such as a warehouse or common carrier).

Exhibit 15.1 Parties to a bailment

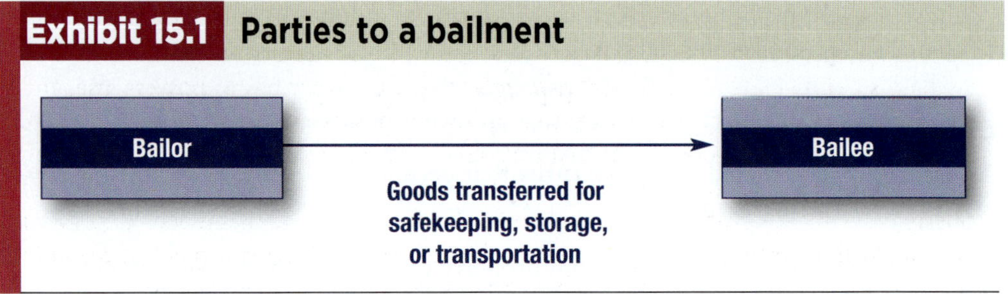

Example Suppose ABC Garment Co. delivers goods to Lowell, Inc., a commercial warehouse, for storage. A fee is charged for this service. ABC Garment Co. receives the benefit of having its goods stored, and Lowell, Inc. receives the benefit of being paid compensation for storing the goods. In this example, Lowell, Inc. (the bailee) owes a duty of ordinary care to protect the goods.

Learning Objective 4
List and describe the types of real property.

Real Property

Property and ownership rights in real property play an important part in this country's society and economy. Individuals and families own or rent houses, farmers and ranchers own farmland and ranches, and businesses own or lease commercial and office buildings. **Real property** includes the following:

Real property The land itself as well as buildings, trees, soil, minerals, timber, plants, and other things permanently affixed to the land.

1. ***Land and buildings.*** **Land** is the most common form of real property. A landowner usually purchases the **surface rights** to the land—that is, the right to occupy the land. The owner may use, enjoy, and develop the property as he or she sees fit, subject to any applicable government regulations.

   Examples **Buildings** constructed on land—such as houses, apartment buildings, manufacturing plants, and office buildings—are real property. Things such as radio towers, bridges, and the like are considered real property as well.

2. ***Subsurface rights.*** The owner of land possesses **subsurface rights** (or **mineral rights**), to the earth located beneath the surface of the land. These rights can be valuable.

   Examples Gold, uranium, oil, or natural gas may lie beneath the surface of land. Theoretically, mineral rights extend to the center of the earth. In reality, mines and oil wells usually extend only several miles into the earth. Subsurface rights may be sold separately from surface rights.

3. ***Plant life and vegetation.*** **Plant life and vegetation** growing on the surface of land are considered real property. This includes natural plant life (such as trees) and cultivated plant life (such as crops). When land is sold, any plant life growing on the land is included unless the parties agree otherwise. Plant life that is severed from the land is considered personal property.

4. ***Fixtures.*** Certain personal property is associated so closely with real property that it becomes part of the realty. These items are called **fixtures.**

   Examples Kitchen cabinets, carpeting, and doorknobs are fixtures, but throw rugs and furniture are personal property. Unless otherwise provided, if a building is sold, the fixtures are included in the sale. If the sale agreement is silent as to whether an item is a fixture, the courts make their determinations on the basis of whether the item can be removed without causing substantial damage to the realty.

Fixtures Goods that are affixed to real estate so as to become part thereof.

Estate (estate in land) Ownership rights in real property; the bundle of legal rights of the owner to possess, use, and enjoy the property.

Freehold estate An estate in which the owner has a present possessory interest in the real property.

AIR RIGHTS

SIDEBAR

Common law provided that the owners of real property owned that property from the center of the earth to the heavens. This rule has been eroded by modern legal restrictions such as land-use control laws, environmental protection laws, and air navigation requirements. Even today, however, the owners of land may sell or lease air-space parcels above their land.

An **air-space parcel** is a three-dimensional cube of air above the surface of the earth. Air-space parcels are valuable property rights, particularly in densely populated metropolitan areas where building property is scarce.

Example Many developments have been built in air-space parcels in New York City. The most notable are Madison Square Garden and Two Penn Plaza, which were built in air-space parcels above Penn Station.

Freehold Estates in Land

A person's ownership rights in real property are called an **estate in land,** or **estate.** An estate is defined as the bundle of *legal rights* that the owner has to possess, use, and enjoy the property. The type of estate that an owner possesses is determined from the deed, will, lease, or other document that transferred the ownership rights to him or her.

A **freehold estate** is one in which the owner has a *present possessory interest* in the real property; that is, the owner may use and enjoy the property as he or she sees fit, subject to any applicable government regulation or private restraint. The two types of freehold estates are *estates in fee* and *life estates*, which are discussed in the following paragraphs.

Fee simple absolute (fee simple) A type of ownership of real property that grants the owner the fullest bundle of legal rights that a person can hold in real property.

Fee simple defeasible (qualified fee) A type of ownership of real property that grants the owner all the incidents of a fee simple absolute, except that it may be taken away if a specified condition occurs or does not occur.

Life estate An interest in land for a person's lifetime; upon that person's death, the interest will be transferred to another party.

Cottage, Mackinac Island, Michigan. A person's house is often his or her most valuable asset.

Learning Objective 5

Name and describe the types of freehold estates.

SIDEBAR

FREEHOLD ESTATES

Estate	Description
Fee simple absolute	Is the highest form of ownership of real property. Ownership (1) is infinite in duration, (2) has no limitation on inheritability, and (3) does not end upon the occurrence or nonoccurrence of an event.
Fee simple defeasible	Grants the owner all the incidents of a fee simple absolute, except that it may be taken away if a specified condition occurs or does not occur.
Life estate	Is an interest in property that lasts for the life of a specified person. A life estate terminates upon the death of the named person and reverts back to the grantor or his or her estate or other designated person.

Estates in Fee

A **fee simple absolute** (or **fee simple**) is the highest form of ownership of real property because it grants the owner the fullest bundle of legal rights that a person can hold in real property. This **estate in fee** is the type of ownership that most people connect with "owning" real property. A fee simple owner has the right to exclusively possess and use his or her property to the extent that the owner has not transferred any interest in the property (such as by lease).

A **fee simple defeasible,** or **qualified fee,** grants the owner all the incidents of a fee simple absolute except that it may be taken away if a specified *condition* occurs or does not occur.

Example A conveyance of property to a church "as long as the land is used as a church or for church purposes" creates a qualified fee. The church has all of the rights of an owner of a fee simple absolute except that its ownership rights are terminated if the property is no longer used for church purposes.

Life Estate

A **life estate** is an interest in real property that lasts for the life of a specified person, usually the grantee.

Examples A conveyance of real property "to Anna for her life" creates a life estate. A life estate may also be measured by the life of a third party (for example, "to Anna for the life of Benjamin"). This is called an **estate *pur autre vie.*** A life estate may be defeasible (for example, "to John for his life, but only if he continues to occupy this residence"). Upon the death of the named person, the life estate terminates and the property reverts to the grantor or the grantor's estate or other designated person.

A life tenant is treated as the owner of the property during the duration of the life estate. He or she has the right to possess and use the property except to the extent that it would cause permanent *waste* of the property. A life tenant may

Exhibit 15.2 Future interests

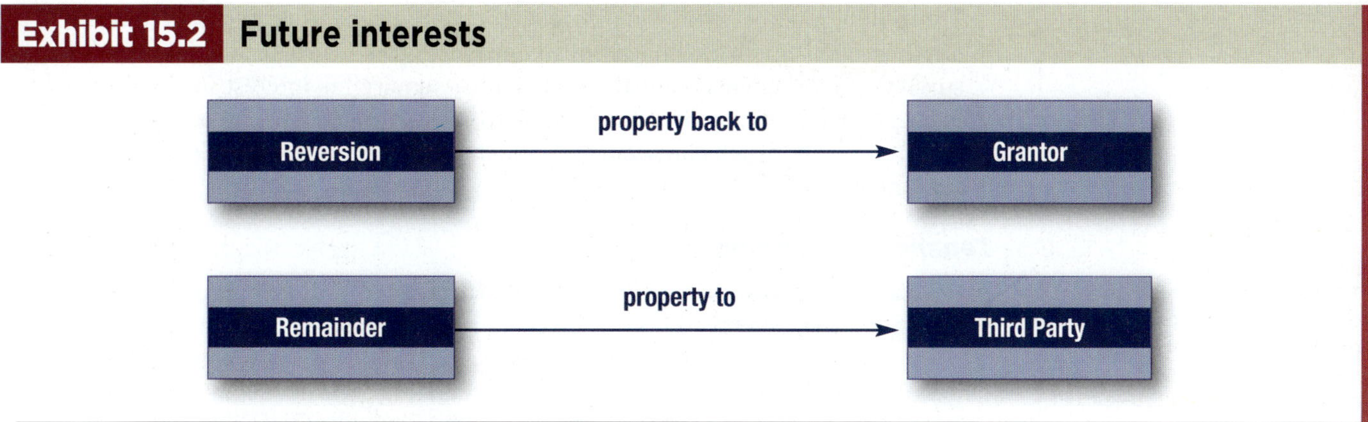

sell, transfer, or mortgage his or her estate in the land. The mortgage, however, cannot exceed the duration of the life estate. A life tenant is obligated to keep the property in repair and to pay property taxes.

Future Interests

A person may be given the right to possess property in the *future* rather than in the present. This right is called a **future interest.** The two forms of future interests are *reversion* and *remainder* (see Exhibit 15.2).

1. ***Reversion.*** A **reversion** is a right of possession that returns to the *grantor* after the expiration of a limited or contingent estate. Reversions do not have to be stated expressly because they arise automatically by law.

   Example If a grantor conveys property "to M. R. Harrington for life," the grantor has retained a reversion in the property. That is, when Harrington dies, the property reverts to the grantor or, if he or she is not living, then to his or her estate.

2. ***Remainder.*** If the right of possession returns to a *third party* upon the expiration of a limited or contingent estate, it is called a **remainder.** The person who is entitled to the future interest is called a **remainder person.**

   Example A conveyance of property "to Joe for life, remainder to Meredith" is a vested remainder—the only contingency to Meredith's possessory interest is Joe's death.

Concurrent Ownership

When two or more persons own a piece of real property, it is called **co-ownership** or **concurrent ownership.** The following forms of co-ownership are recognized: *joint tenancy*, *tenancy in common*, *tenancy by the entirety*, *community property*. These are discussed in the following paragraphs.

Joint Tenancy

To create a **joint tenancy,** words that clearly show a person's intent to create a joint tenancy must be used. Language such as "Marsha Leest and James Leest, as joint tenants" is usually sufficient. The most distinguishing feature of a joint tenancy is the co-owners' **right of survivorship.** This means that upon the death of one of the co-owners or **joint tenants,** the deceased person's interest in the property passes automatically to the surviving joint tenants. Any contrary provision in the deceased's will is ineffective.

Future interest The interest that the grantor retains for him- or herself or a third party.

Learning Objective 6
Identify the types of co-ownership.

Reversion A right of possession that returns to the grantor after the expiration of a limited or contingent estate.

Remainder (remainder person) A right of possession that returns to a third party upon the expiration of a limited or contingent estate.

Co-ownership (concurrent ownership) A situation in which two or more persons own a piece of real property.

Joint tenancy A form of co-ownership that includes the right of survivorship.

SIDEBAR

FUTURE INTERESTS

Future Interest	Description
Reversion	Right to possession of real property returns to the grantor after the expiration of a limited or contingent estate.
Remainder	Right to possession of real property goes to a third person upon the expiration of a limited or contingent estate.

Example Jones, one of four people who own a piece of property in joint tenancy, executes a will leaving all of his property to a university. Jones dies. The surviving joint tenants—not the university—acquire his interest in the piece of property. Each joint tenant has a right to sell or transfer his or her interest in the property, but such conveyance terminates the joint tenancy. The parties then become tenants in common.

Tenancy in Common

Tenancy in common A form of co-ownership in which the interest of a surviving tenant in common passes to the deceased tenant's estate and not to the co-tenants.

In a **tenancy in common,** the interests of a surviving **tenant in common** pass to the deceased tenant's estate and not to the co-tenants. A tenancy in common may be created by express words, such as "Iran Cespedes and Joy Park, as tenants in common." Unless otherwise agreed, a tenant in common can sell, give, devise, or otherwise transfer his or her interest in the property without the consent of the other co-owners.

Example Lopez, one of four tenants in common who own a piece of property, has a will that leaves all of his property to his granddaughter. When Lopez dies, the granddaughter receives his interest in the tenancy in common, and the granddaughter becomes a tenant in common with the three other owners.

A co-tenancy is presumed to be a tenancy in common if it is not clear that the co-tenancy is a joint tenancy.

Tenancy by the Entirety

Tenancy by the entirety A form of co-ownership of real property that can be used only by married couples.

Tenancy by the entirety is a form of co-ownership of real property that can be used only by married couples. This type of tenancy must be created by express words such as "Harold Jones and Maude Jones, husband and wife, as tenants by the entireties." A surviving spouse has the right of survivorship.

Tenancy by the entirety is distinguished from a joint tenancy in that neither spouse may sell or transfer his or her interest in the property without the other spouse's consent. Only about half of the states recognize a tenancy by the entirety.

ETHICAL PERSPECTIVE

Paralegal's Duty to Act Carefully When Preparing Legal Documents

Ms. Webster is a paralegal professional who works for Mr. Anderson, an attorney who practices law in a small, rural town. Ms. Susan White and Mr. Mark Smith, who were recently married, come to Mr. Anderson's office to see him about having a new deed drawn up for a piece of real estate owned by Ms. White prior to marriage. They explain that Ms. White inherited the property prior to their marriage and that the real estate deed to the property is currently in her name only. Ms. White wants to place the name of Mr. Smith, her new husband, on the deed so as to make them joint tenant owners of the property with the right to survivorship. Mr. Anderson agrees to do so.

Mr. Anderson explains the situation to Ms. Webster and assigns her the task of preparing a new deed that accomplishes the intended result. Ms. Webster prepares the deed but when Mr. Anderson reviews it, he sees that the deed states, "Ms. Susan White and Mr. Mark Smith, co-tenants." Because this language is unclear that there is a joint tenancy, if it were signed by Ms. White, it would create a tenancy in common with Mr. Smith instead of a joint tenancy. Mr. Anderson has Ms. Webster prepare a new deed that correctly states, "Ms. Susan White and Mr. Mark Smith, joint tenants."

A paralegal owes an ethical duty to be careful when he or she is preparing legal documents to make sure that they are completed properly. This example shows how important it is for a paralegal to carefully prepare documents and to proofread the documents to make sure that they are correct before giving them to the supervising attorney for review.

The ethical duty of a paralegal professional to act carefully when preparing legal documents is discussed in the above feature.

Community Property

Nine states—Arizona, California, Idaho, Louisiana, Nevada, New Mexico, Texas, Washington, and Wisconsin—recognize a form of co-ownership known as **community property.** This method of co-ownership applies only to married couples and is based on the notion that a husband and wife should share equally in the fruits of the marital partnership.

Under these laws, each spouse owns an equal, one-half share of the income of both spouses and the assets acquired during the marriage regardless of who earns the income. Property that is acquired through gift or inheritance either before or during marriage remains separate property.

When a spouse dies, the surviving spouse automatically receives one-half of the community property. The other half passes to the heirs of the deceased spouse as directed by will or by state intestate statute if there is no will.

During the marriage, neither spouse can sell, transfer, or gift community property without the consent of the other spouse. Upon a divorce, each spouse has a right to one-half of the community property.

The location of the real property determines whether community property law applies. For example, if a married couple who lives in a non-community property state purchases real property located in a community property state, community property laws apply to that property.

Community property A form of ownership in which each spouse owns an equal, one-half share of the income of both spouses and the assets acquired during the marriage.

Condominium A common form of ownership in a multiple-dwelling building in which the purchaser has title to the individual unit and owns the common areas as a tenant in common with the other condominium owners.

Cooperative A form of co-ownership of a multiple-dwelling building in which a corporation owns the building and the residents own shares in the corporation.

Example A husband and wife have community property assets of $1.5 million and the wife dies with a will. The husband automatically has a right to receive $750,000 of the community property. The remaining $750,000 passes as directed by the wife's will. Any separate property owned by the wife, such as jewelry she inherited, also passes in accordance with her will. Her husband has no vested interest in that property.

Other Forms of Ownership

Condominium

The **condominium** is a common form of ownership in multiple-dwelling buildings. Purchasers of a condominium (1) have title to their individual units and (2) own the common areas (for example, hallways, elevators, parking areas, and recreational facilities) as tenants in common with the other owners. Owners may sell or mortgage their units without the permission of the other owners. Owners are assessed monthly fees for maintenance of common areas. In addition to dwelling units, the condominium form of ownership is offered for office buildings, boat docks, and such.

Cooperative

A **cooperative** is a form of co-ownership of a multiple-dwelling building in which a corporation owns the building and the residents own shares in the corporation. Each cooperative owner then leases a unit in the building from the corporation under a renewable, long-term, proprietary lease. Individual residents may not secure loans with the units they occupy.

SIDEBAR

CONCURRENT OWNERSHIP

Form of Ownership	Right of Survivorship	Tenant May Unilaterally Transfer His or Her Interest
Joint tenancy	Yes, deceased tenant's interest automatically passes to co-tenants.	Yes, tenant may transfer his or her interest without the consent of co-tenants. Transfer severs joint tenancy.
Tenancy in common	No, deceased tenant's interest passes to his or her estate.	Yes, tenant may transfer his or her interest without the consent of co-tenants. Transfer does not sever tenancy in common.
Tenancy by the entirety	Yes, deceased tenant's interest passes to his or her estate.	No, neither spouse may transfer his or her interest without the other spouse's consent.
Community property	Yes, when a spouse dies, the surviving spouse automatically receives one-half of the community property. The other half passes to the heirs of the deceased spouse, as directed by a valid will or by state intestate statute if there is no will.	No, neither spouse may transfer his or her interest without the other spouse's consent.

The corporation may borrow money on a blanket mortgage, and each shareholder is jointly and severally liable on the loan. Usually, cooperative owners may not sell their shares or sublease their units without the approval of the other owners.

Learning Objective 7
Name and describe the methods of transferring ownership of real property.

Transfer of Ownership of Real Property

Deed A writing that describes a person's ownership interest in a piece of real property.

Grantor The party who transfers an ownership interest in real property.

Grantee The party to whom an interest in real property is transferred.

Ownership of real property may be transferred from one person to another. Title to real property may be transferred by sale, tax sale, gift, will, or inheritance. A **deed** is used to convey real property by sale or gift. The seller or donor is called the **grantor.** The buyer or recipient is called the **grantee.** A deed may be used to transfer a fee simple absolute interest in real property or any lesser estate (such as life estate).

State laws recognize different types of deeds that provide differing degrees of protection to grantees. A **warranty deed** contains the greatest number of warranties and provides the most protection to grantees. A **quitclaim deed** provides the least amount of protection because the grantor conveys only whatever interest he or she has in the property.

Sale of Real Estate

Sale The passing of title from a seller to a buyer for a price. Also called a *conveyance*.

A **sale** or conveyance is the most common method for transferring ownership rights in real property. An agreement for the sale of real property under the state Statute of Frauds must be in writing to be enforceable. Exhibit 15.3 shows the parties to a real estate sale. The seller delivers a deed to the buyer and the buyer pays the purchase price at the closing or settlement.

A copy of an agreement form for the sale of real estate is set forth in Exhibit 15.4. A **settlement statement** is shown in Exhibit 15.5.

Recording Statutes

Recording statute A state statute that requires a mortgage or deed of trust to be recorded in the county recorder's office of the county in which the real property is located.

Every state has a **recording statute** that provides that copies of deeds and other documents concerning interests in real property (such as mortgages, liens, and easements) may be filed in a government office, where they become public records open to viewing by the public. Recording statutes are intended to prevent fraud and to establish certainty in the ownership and transfer of property. Instruments usually are

Exhibit 15.3 Parties and documents in a real estate transaction

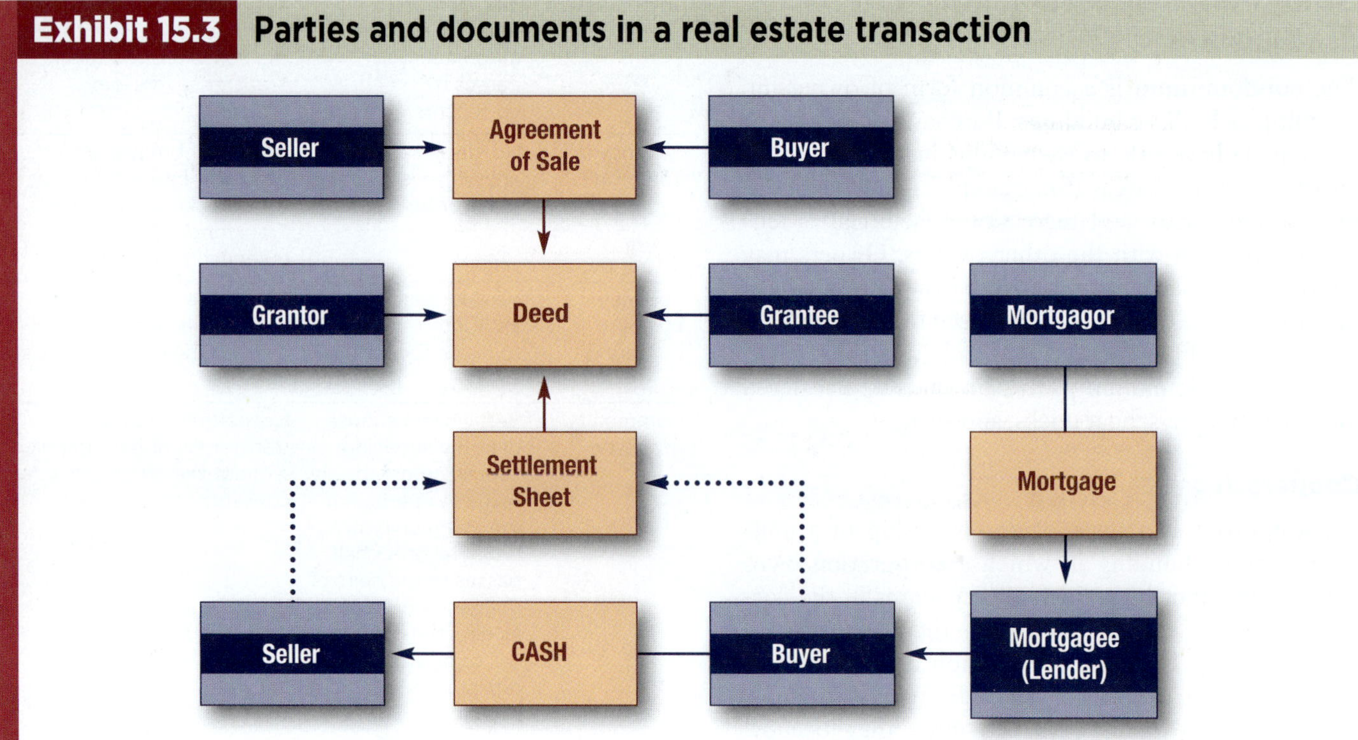

Exhibit 15.4 Agreement for the sale of real property

STANDARD AGREEMENT FOR THE SALE OF REAL ESTATE A/S-R

This form recommended and approved for, but not restricted to use by, the members of the Pennsylvania Association of REALTORS® (PAR).

SELLER'S BUSINESS RELATIONSHIP WITH PA LICENSED BROKER

BROKER (Company) ________________________ **PHONE** ____________
ADDRESS ________________________ **FAX** ____________
LICENSEE(S) ________________________ **Designated Agent?** ☐ **Yes** ☐ **No**
BROKER IS THE AGENT FOR SELLER. OR (if checked below):
Broker is NOT the Agent for Seller and is a/an: ☐ **AGENT FOR BUYER** ☐ **TRANSACTION LICENSEE**

BUYER'S BUSINESS RELATIONSHIP WITH PA LICENSED BROKER

BROKER (Company) ________________________ **PHONE** ____________
ADDRESS ________________________ **FAX** ____________
LICENSEE(S) ________________________ **Designated Agent?** ☐ **Yes** ☐ **No**
BROKER IS THE AGENT FOR BUYER. OR (if checked below):
Broker is NOT the Agent for Buyer and is a/an: ☐ **AGENT FOR SELLER** ☐ **SUBAGENT FOR SELLER** ☐ **TRANSACTION LICENSEE**

When the same Broker is Agent for Seller and Agent for Buyer, Broker is a Dual Agent. All of Broker's licensees are also Dual Agents UNLESS there are separate Designated Agents for Buyer and Seller. If the same Licensee is designated for Seller and Buyer, the Licensee is a Dual Agent.

1. **This Agreement, dated** ________________________, **is between**

SELLER(S): ________________________
____
________________________, **called "Seller," and**

BUYER(S): ________________________
____
________________________, **called "Buyer."**

2. **PROPERTY (9-05) Seller hereby agrees to sell and convey to Buyer, who hereby agrees to purchase:**
ALL THAT CERTAIN lot or piece of ground with buildings and improvements thereon erected, if any, known as:
____
____________ **in the** ____________ **of** ____________
County of ____________ **in the Commonwealth of Pennsylvania. Identification (e.g., Tax ID #; Parcel #; Lot, Block; Deed Book, Page, Recording Date):** ____________

3. **TERMS (9-05)**
(A) **Purchase Price** ________________________
________________________ **U.S. Dollars,**
which will be paid to Seller by Buyer as follows:
1. Cash or check at signing this Agreement: ____________ $ ________
2. Cash or check within _____ days of the execution of this Agreement: ____________ $ ________
3. ____________ $ ________
4. Cash or cashier's check at time of settlement: ____________ $ ________

TOTAL $ ________

(B) Deposits paid by Buyer within __30__ DAYS of settlement will be by cash or cashier's check. Deposits, regardless of the form of payment and the person designated as payee, will be paid in U.S. Dollars to Broker for Seller (unless otherwise stated here), ________________________, who will retain deposits in an escrow account until consummation or termination of this Agreement in conformity with all applicable laws and regulations. Any check tendered as deposit monies may be held uncashed pending the acceptance of this Agreement.
(C) Seller's written approval to be on or before: ________________________
(D) Settlement to be on ________________________, or before if Buyer and Seller agree.
(E) Settlement will occur in the county where the Property is located or in an adjacent county, during normal business hours, unless Buyer and Seller agree otherwise.
(F) Conveyance from Seller will be by fee simple deed of special warranty unless otherwise stated here: ________________________
(G) Payment of transfer taxes will be divided equally between Buyer and Seller unless otherwise stated here: ________________________
(H) At time of settlement, the following will be adjusted pro-rata on a daily basis between Buyer and Seller, reimbursing where applicable: current taxes (see Information Regarding Real Estate Taxes); rents; interest on mortgage assumptions; condominium fees and homeowner association fees; water and/or sewer fees, together with any other lienable municipal service. All charges will be pro-rated for the period(s) covered. Seller will pay up to and including the date of settlement and Buyer will pay for all days following settlement, unless otherwise stated here: ________________________

(continued)

Exhibit 15.4 Agreement for the sale of real property *(continued)*

4. FIXTURES & PERSONAL PROPERTY (9-05)

(A) INCLUDED in this sale are all existing items permanently installed in the Property, free of liens, including plumbing; heating; lighting fixtures (including chandeliers and ceiling fans); water treatment systems; pool and spa equipment; garage door openers and transmitters; television antennas; unpotted shrubbery, plantings and trees; any remaining heating and cooking fuels stored on the Property at the time of settlement; sump pumps; storage sheds; mailboxes; wall to wall carpeting; existing window screens, storm windows and screen/storm doors; window covering hardware, shades and blinds; awnings; built-in air conditioners; built-in appliances; and the range/oven unless otherwise stated. Also included: ____

____

(B) LEASED items (not owned by Seller): ____

____

(C) EXCLUDED fixtures and items: ____

____

5. DATES/TIME IS OF THE ESSENCE (9-05)

(A) The settlement date and all other dates and times referred to for the performance of any of the obligations of this Agreement are of the essence and are binding.

(B) For purposes of this Agreement, the number of days will be counted from the date of execution, excluding the day this Agreement was executed and including the last day of the time period. The Execution Date of this Agreement is the date when Buyer and Seller have indicated full acceptance of this Agreement by signing and/or initialing it. All changes to this Agreement should be initialed and dated.

(C) The settlement date is not extended by any other provision of this Agreement and may only be extended by mutual written agreement of the parties.

(D) Certain time periods are pre-printed in this Agreement as a convenience to the Buyer and Seller. All pre-printed time periods are negotiable and may be changed by striking out the pre-printed text and inserting a different time period acceptable to all parties.

6. MORTGAGE CONTINGENCY (9-05)

☐ WAIVED. This sale is NOT contingent on mortgage financing, although Buyer may still obtain mortgage financing.

☐ ELECTED.

(A) This sale is contingent upon Buyer obtaining mortgage financing as follows:

First Mortgage on the Property	**Second Mortgage on the Property**
Loan Amount $______________	Loan Amount $______________
Minimum Term __________ years	Minimum Term __________ years
Type of mortgage ______________	Type of mortgage ______________
______________	______________
Mortgage lender ______________	Mortgage lender ______________
______________	______________
Interest rate __________%; however, **Buyer agrees to accept the interest rate as may be committed by the mortgage lender,** not to exceed a maximum interest rate of __________%.	Interest rate __________%; however, **Buyer agrees to accept the interest rate as may be committed by the mortgage lender,** not to exceed a maximum interest rate of __________%.
Discount points, loan origination, loan placement and other fees charged by the lender as a percentage of the mortgage loan (excluding any mortgage insurance premiums or VA funding fee) not to exceed __________% (0% if not specified) of the mortgage loan.	Discount points, loan origination, loan placement and other fees charged by the lender as a percentage of the mortgage loan (excluding any mortgage insurance premiums or VA funding fee) not to exceed __________% (0% if not specified) of the mortgage loan.

The interest rate(s) and fee(s) provisions in paragraph 6(A) are satisfied if the mortgage lender(s) gives Buyer the right to guarantee the interest rate(s) and fee(s) at or below the maximum levels stated. Buyer gives Seller the right, at Seller's sole option and as permitted by law and the mortgage lender(s), to contribute financially, without promise of reimbursement, to the Buyer and/or the mortgage lender(s) to make the above mortgage terms available to Buyer.

(B) Within ______ days (10 if not specified) from the Execution Date of this Agreement, Buyer will make a completed, written mortgage application for the mortgage terms stated above to the mortgage lender(s) identified in paragraph 6 (A), if any, otherwise to a responsible mortgage lender(s) of Buyer's choice. **Broker for Buyer, if any, otherwise Broker for Seller, is authorized to communicate with the mortgage lender(s) to assist in the mortgage loan process.**

(C) **Should Buyer furnish false or incomplete information to Seller, Broker(s), or the mortgage lender(s) concerning Buyer's legal or financial status, or fail to cooperate in good faith in processing the mortgage loan application, which results in the mortgage lender(s) refusing to approve a mortgage loan commitment, Buyer will be in default of this Agreement.**

(D) 1. **Mortgage commitment date:** ______________________. If Seller does not receive a copy of Buyer's mortgage commitment(s) by this date, **Buyer and Seller agree to extend the mortgage commitment date until Seller terminates this Agreement by written notice to Buyer.**

2. Upon receiving a mortgage commitment, Buyer will promptly deliver a copy of the commitment to Seller.

3. Seller may terminate this Agreement in writing after the mortgage commitment date, if the mortgage commitment(s):

   a. Is not valid until the date of settlement, OR

   b. Is conditioned upon the **sale and settlement of any other property,** OR

   c. Does not satisfy all the mortgage terms as stated in paragraph 6 (A), OR

   d. Contains any other condition not specified in this Agreement that is not satisfied and/or removed in writing by the mortgage lender(s) within __7__ DAYS after the **mortgage commitment date in paragraph 6 (D) (1),** other than those conditions that are customarily satisfied at or near settlement, such as obtaining insurance and confirming employment status.

4. If this Agreement is terminated pursuant to paragraphs 6 (D) (1) or (3), or the mortgage loan(s) is not obtained for settlement, all deposit monies will be returned to Buyer according to the terms of paragraph 30 and this Agreement will be VOID. Buyer will be responsible for any costs incurred by Buyer for any inspections or certifications obtained according to the terms of this Agreement, and any costs incurred by Buyer for: (1) Title search, title insurance and/or mechanics' lien insurance, or any fee for cancellation; (2) Flood insurance and/or fire insurance with extended coverage, mine subsidence insurance, or any fee for cancellation; (3) Appraisal fees and charges paid in advance to mortgage lender(s).

Buyer Initials: ______________ **A/S-R Page 2 of 10** **Revised 9/05** **Seller Initials:** ______________

Source: Pennsylvania Association of Realtors. Used with permission.

Exhibit 15.5 Settlement Agreement

A. Settlement Statement — **U.S. Department of Housing and Urban Development** — OMB Approval No. 2502-0265

B. Type of Loan

1. ☐ FHA 2. ☐ FmHA 3. ☐ Conv. Unins. 4. ☐ VA 5. ☐ Conv. Ins.	6. File Number:	7. Loan Number:	8. Mortgage Insurance Case Number:

C. Note: This form is furnished to give you a statement of actual settlement costs. Amounts paid to and by the settlement agent are shown. Items marked "(p.o.c.)" were paid outside the closing; they are shown here for informational purposes and are not included in the totals.

D. Name & Address of Borrower:	E. Name & Address of Seller:	F. Name & Address of Lender:
Ethan & Ariel Marshall 52 Moritz Way Anyplace, PA 55555	Sara and Natasha Elliot 138 Weisser Place Anyplace, PA 55555	4th National Bank OneSouth Main St. Newcity, PA 44444

G. Property Location:	H. Settlement Agent:	
1 Zollinger Way	Roberts	
	Place of Settlement: Newcity	I. Settlement Date: 08-19-2002

J. Summary of Borrower's Transaction		K. Summary of Seller's Transaction	
100. Gross Amount Due From Borrower		**400. Gross Amount Due To Seller**	
101. Contract sales price	150000	401. Contract sales price	150000
102. Personal property		402. Personal property	
103. Settlement charges to borrower (line 1400)	21000	403.	
104.		404.	
105.		405.	
Adjustments for items paid by seller in advance		**Adjustments for items paid by seller in advance**	
106. City/town taxes 08-19-2002 to 12-31-2002	650	406. City/town taxes 08-19-2002 to 12-31-2002	650
107. County taxes to		407. County taxes to	
108. Assessments to		408. Assessments to	
109.		409.	
110.		410.	
111.		411.	
112.		412.	
120. Gross Amount Due From Borrower	152750	**420. Gross Amount Due To Seller**	150650
200. Amounts Paid By Or In Behalf Of Borrower		**500. Reductions In Amount Due To Seller**	
201. Deposit or earnest money		501. Excess deposit (see instructions)	
202. Principal amount of new loan(s)		502. Settlement charges to seller (line 1400)	9000
203. Existing loan(s) taken subject to		503. Existing loan(s) taken subject to	
204.		504. Payoff of first mortgage loan	75000
205.		505. Payoff of second mortgage loan	
206.		506.	
207.		507.	
208.		508.	
209.		509.	
Adjustments for items unpaid by seller		**Adjustments for items unpaid by seller**	
210. City/town taxes to		510. City/town taxes to	
211. County taxes to		511. County taxes to	
212. Assessments to		512. Assessments to	
213.		513.	
214.		514.	
215.		515.	
216.		516.	
217.		517.	
218.		518.	
219.		519.	
220. Total Paid By/For Borrower	135000	**520. Total Reduction Amount Due Seller**	84000
300. Cash At Settlement From/To Borrower		**600. Cash At Settlement To/From Seller**	
301. Gross Amount due from borrower (line 120)	152750	601. Gross amount due to seller (line 420)	150650
302. Less amounts paid by/for borrower (line 220)	(135000)	602. Less reductions in amt. due seller (line 520)	(84000)
303. Cash ☑ **From** ☐ **To Borrower**	17750	**603. Cash** ☑ **To** ☐ **From Seller**	

Section 5 of the Real Estate Settlement Procedures Act (RESPA) requires the following: • HUD must develop a Special Information Booklet to help persons borrowing money to finance the purchase of residential real estate to better understand the nature and costs of real estate settlement services; • Each lender must provide the booklet to all applicants from whom it receives or for whom it prepares a written application to borrow money to finance the purchase of residential real estate; • Lenders must prepare and distribute with the Booklet a Good Faith Estimate of the settlement costs that the borrower is likely to incur in connection with the settlement. These disclosures are manadatory.

Section 4(a) of RESPA mandates that HUD develop and prescribe this standard form to be used at the time of loan settlement to provide full disclosure of all charges imposed upon the borrower and seller. These are third party disclosures that are designed to provide the borrower with pertinent information during the settlement process in order to be a better shopper.

The Public Reporting Burden for this collection of information is estimated to average one hour per response, including the time for reviewing instructions, searching existing data sources, gathering and maintaining the data needed, and completing and reviewing the collection of information.

This agency may not collect this information, and you are not required to complete this form, unless it displays a currently valid OMB control number.

The information requested does not lend itself to confidentiality.

Previous editions are obsolete — Page 1 of 2 — form **HUD-1** (3/86) ref Handbook 4305.2

Exhibit 15.6 Title insurance policy

1889

Form No. PA 13
(10-17-92)
ALTA Owner's Policy

POLICY OF TITLE INSURANCE

FIRST AMERICAN

ISSUED BY

First American Title Insurance Company

SUBJECT TO THE EXCLUSIONS FROM COVERAGE, THE EXCEPTIONS FROM COVERAGE CONTAINED IN SCHEDULE B AND THE CONDITIONS AND STIPULATIONS, FIRST AMERICAN TITLE INSURANCE COMPANY, a California corporation, herein called the Company, insures, as of Date of Policy shown in Schedule A, against loss or damage, not exceeding the Amount of Insurance stated in Schedule A, sustained or incurred by the insured by reason of:

1. Title to the estate or interest described in Schedule A being vested other than as stated therein;
2. Any defect in or lien or encumbrance on the title;
3. Unmarketability of the title;
4. Lack of a right of access to and from the land.

The Company will also pay the costs, attorneys' fees and expenses incurred in defense of the title, as insured, but only to the extent provided in the Conditions and Stipulations.

First American Title Insurance Company

BY Parker S. Kennedy PRESIDENT

ATTEST Mark R. Arnesen SECRETARY

BY COUNTERSIGNED

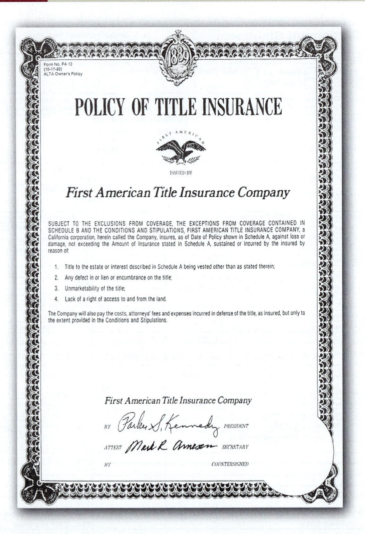

filed in the *county recorder's office* of the county in which the property is located. A fee is charged to record an instrument.

Persons interested in purchasing the property or lending on the property check these records to determine whether the grantor or borrower actually owns the property and whether any other parties (such as lienholders, mortgages, and easement holders) have an interest in the property. The recordation of a deed is not required to pass the title from the grantor to the grantee. Recording the deed gives *constructive notice* to the world of the owner's interest in the property.

Quiet title action An action brought by a party seeking an order of the court declaring who has title to disputed property. By its decision, the court "quiets title."

A party who is concerned about his or her ownership rights in a parcel of real property can bring a **quiet title action** to have a court determine the extent of those rights. Public notice of the hearing must be given so that anyone claiming an interest in the property may appear and be heard. After the hearing, the judge declares who has title to the property—that is, the court "quiets title" by its decision.

Registrar of Deeds

Records of all transfers of real estate, claims against real estate, and the forms of mortgages and means are generally maintained in a separate office under the direction of the Registrar, or Recorder, of Deeds. The **Registrar of Deeds** may be an elected or appointed official and is responsible for recording documents related to the transfer of real estate, and documents related to claims against property in the form of mortgages and liens. These records may be hard copy or electronic copies, or a combination.

Exhibit 15.6 Title insurance policy *(continued)*

FIRST AMERICAN TITLE INSURANCE COMPANY

OWNERS FORM

SCHEDULE A

Policy Number	Date of Policy	Amount of Insurance
00000000000	**January 1, 2002**	**$200,500.00**

File Number **ABC 12345**

1. Name of Insured on the Owner's Policy:

   Mary Jane Smith

2. The estate or interest in the land described in this Schedule and which is encumbered by the insured mortgage is Fee Simple.

3. The estate or interest referred to herein is at Date of Policy vested in the insured:

   The Insured by virtue of a Deed from Thomas Jones dated 12/31/2001 and recorded 1/1/2002 in Bucks County in Land Record Book 1111 page 111.

4. The land herein described is encumbered by the following mortgage or trust deed, and assignments:

   $150,500.00 Mary Jane Smith to Country Bank dated 12/31/2001 and recorded 1/1/2002 in Bucks County in land Record Book 1111 page 222.
   and the mortgage or trust deeds, if any, shown in Schedule B hereof.

5. The land referred to in this policy is situated in the State of Pennsylvania, County of Bucks and is described as follows:

   See attached Exhibit "A"
   Commonly known as:

   County Parcel Number 12-12-12-12-12
   123 Main Street
   Main Township
   Bucks County, Pennsylvania

PA-3

The Registrar of Deeds office is concerned with the authenticity of the deeds filed and proper authentication by way of notarization. In filing documents, it is necessary to determine the standards of the individual office with regard to the form of the notarization and any additional paperwork required before the office will accept the document for recording.

This office may also collect the taxes as an agent for the taxing authority, whether local or state, and additional paperwork is required in this regard. The Registrar also generally charges a fee for filing documents, which may include additional charges when the pages exceed a certain number. It is always best to check with the office to determine the number and amounts of the checks, drafts, or other forms of payment required.

Marketable Title

Marketable title means that the title is free from any encumbrances, defects in title, or other defects that are not disclosed but would affect the value of the property. A buyer of real property can purchase **title insurance** from a title insurance company, and the **title insurance policy** lists defects in the title of the property, if any, and insures against unlisted defects in title.

Marketable title Title to real property that is free from any encumbrances or other defects that are not disclosed but would affect the value of the property. Also called *good title*.

The title insurer must reimburse the insured for any losses caused by undiscovered defects in the title. Each time a property is transferred, a new title insurance policy must be obtained. Exhibit 15.6 shows the opening two pages of a title insurance policy.

Adverse possession A situation in which a person who wrongfully possesses someone else's real property obtains title to that property if certain statutory requirements are met.

Web Exploration

Use www.google.com to find the time for adverse possession in your state.

Adverse Possession

In most states, a person who wrongfully possesses someone else's real property obtains title to that property if certain statutory requirements are met. This is called **adverse possession.** Property owned by federal and state governments is not subject to adverse possession.

Under this doctrine, the transfer of the property is involuntary and does not require delivery of a deed. For a person to obtain title under adverse possession, the wrongful possession must be:

- **for a statutorily prescribed period of time.** In most states, this period is between 10 and 20 years.
- **open, visible, and notorious.** The adverse possessor must occupy the property so as to put the owner on notice of the possession.
- **actual and exclusive.** The adverse possessor must physically occupy the premises. The planting of crops, grazing of animals, or building of a structure on the land constitutes physical occupancy.
- **continuous and peaceful.** The occupancy must be uninterrupted for the required statutory period. Any break in normal occupancy terminates the adverse possession. This means that the adverse possessor may leave the property to go to work, to the store, on a vacation, and such. Also, the adverse possessor cannot take the property by force from its owner.
- **hostile and adverse.** The possessor must occupy the property without the express or implied permission of the owner. Thus, a lessee cannot claim title to property under adverse possession.

If the elements of adverse possession are met, the adverse possessor acquires clear title to the land. But title is acquired only as to the property actually possessed and occupied during the statutory period, and not the entire tract.

Example An adverse possessor who occupies one acre of a 200,000-acre ranch for the statutory period of time acquires title to only the one acre.

Easements

Easement A given or required right to make limited use of someone else's land without owning or leasing it.

An **easement** is an interest in land that gives the holder the right to make limited use of another's property without taking anything from it. Typical easements include common driveways, party walls, right-of-ways, and such.

Easements may be *expressly* created by (1) grant, in which an owner gives another party an easement across his or her property, called **easement by grant,** or (2) **easement by reservation,** where an owner sells land he or she owns but reserves an easement on the land.

There may also be (3) **easements by implication** in which an owner subdivides a piece of property with a well, path, road, or other beneficial appurtenant that serves the entire parcel, or (4) **easements by necessity**—for example, "landlocked" property has an implied easement across surrounding property to enter and exit the landlocked property.

Easements can also be created by adverse possession.

Exhibit 15.7 shows a dominant and servient easement with a common driveway. Exhibit 15.8 shows landlocked real property and easement by necessity.

Web Exploration

Go to http://www.nature.org/aboutus/howwework/conservationmethods/privatelands/conservationeasements/ and read about "Conservation Easements."

Learning Objective 8

Identify and describe the various types of leaseholds and explain the landlord-tenant relationship.

Landlord–Tenant Relationship

Landlord–tenant relationships are common in the United States because (1) more than half of the population rent their homes and (2) many businesses lease office space, stores, manufacturing facilities, and other commercial property. The parties

Exhibit 15.7 Dominant and servient easement

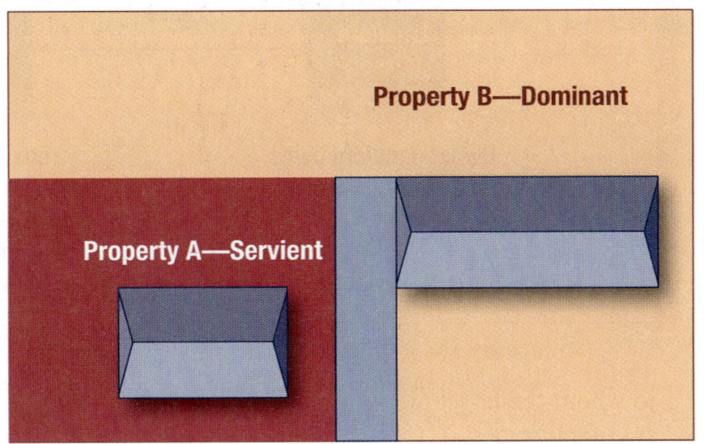

to the relationship have certain legal rights and duties governed by a mixture of real estate and contract law.

A landlord–tenant relationship is created when the owner of a freehold estate (that is, an estate in fee or a life estate) transfers a right to exclusively and temporarily possess the owner's property. The tenant receives a **nonfreehold estate** in the property—that is, the tenant has a right to possession of the property but not the title to the property.

Exhibit 15.9 shows the parties to a lease.

Types of Tenancy

The tenant's interest in the property is called a **leasehold estate,** or **leasehold.** The owner who transfers the leasehold estate is called the **landlord,** or **lessor.** The party

Leasehold (leasehold estate) A tenant's interest in property.

Landlord (lessor) An owner who transfers a leasehold.

Exhibit 15.8 Easement by necessity

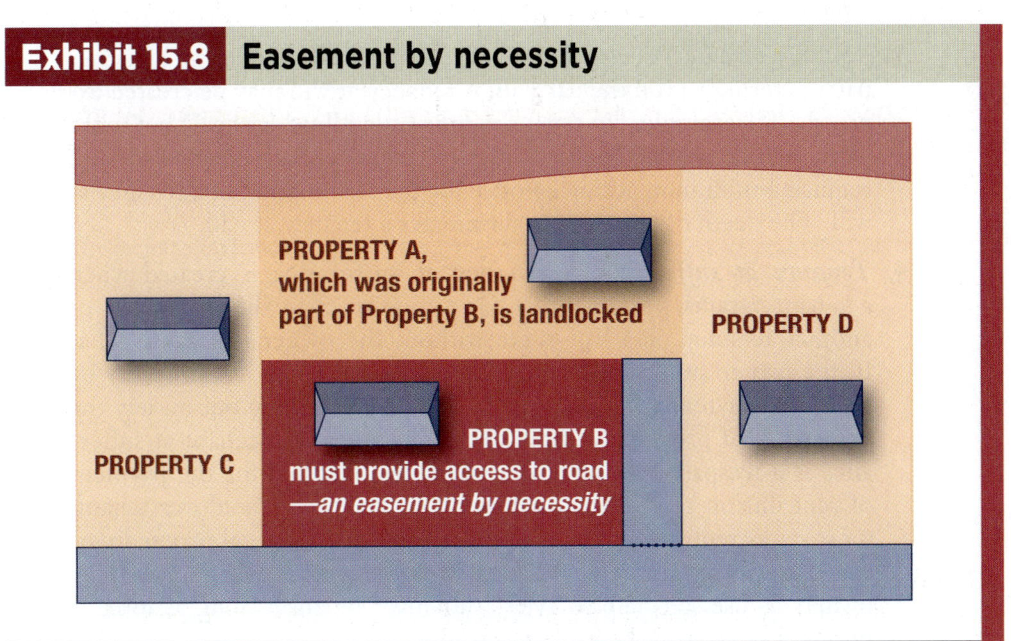

Exhibit 15.9 Parties to a lease

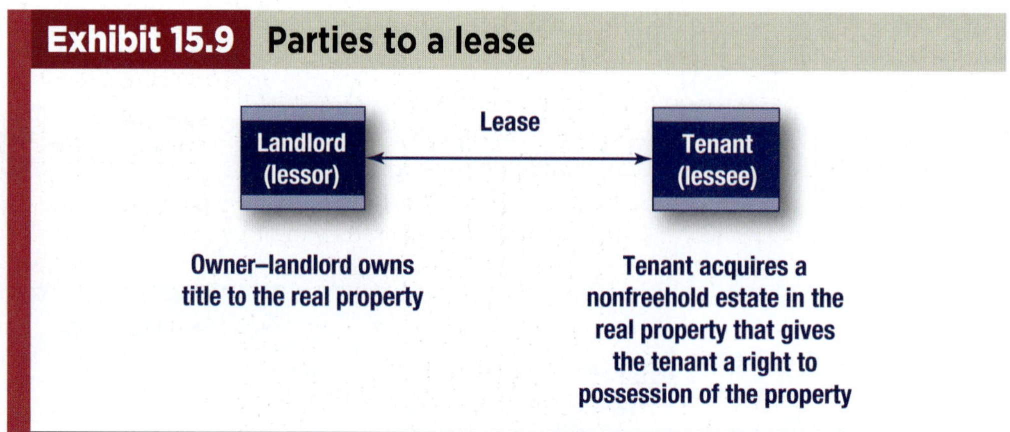
Lease
Landlord (lessor)
Tenant (lessee)
Owner–landlord owns title to the real property
Tenant acquires a nonfreehold estate in the real property that gives the tenant a right to possession of the property

to whom the leasehold estate is transferred is called the **tenant,** or **lessee.** *Tenancies* are of four types:

Tenant (lessee) The party to whom a leasehold is transferred.

Tenancy for years A tenancy created when the landlord and the tenant agree on a specific duration for a lease.

Periodic tenancy A tenancy created when a lease specifies intervals at which payments are due but does not specify the length of the lease.

Tenancy at will A tenancy created by a lease that may be terminated at any time by either party.

Tenancy at sufferance A tenancy created when a tenant retains possession of property after the expiration of another tenancy or a life estate without the owner's consent.

1. ***Tenancy for years.*** A **tenancy for years** is created when the landlord and the tenant agree on a specific duration for the lease. Any lease for a stated period—no matter how long or short—is called a tenancy for years.

   Examples These arrangements range from office space leased in a high-rise office building on a 30-year lease to a cabin leased for the summer. A tenancy for years terminates automatically, without notice, upon expiration of the stated term.

2. ***Periodic tenancy.*** A **periodic tenancy** is created when a lease specifies intervals at which payments are due but does not specify the duration of the lease.

   Example A lease that states, "Rent is due on the first day of the month" establishes a periodic tenancy. Many such leases are created by implication. A periodic tenancy may be terminated by either party at the end of any payment interval, but adequate notice of the termination must be given. At common law, the notice period equaled the length of the payment period. Therefore, a month-to-month tenancy requires a one-month notice of termination.

3. ***Tenancy at will.*** A lease that may be terminated at any time by either party is termed a **tenancy at will.** A tenancy at will may be created expressly (for example, "to tenant as long as landlord wishes") but more likely is to be created by implication. Most states have enacted statutes requiring minimum advance notice for the termination of a tenancy at will. The death of either party terminates a tenancy at will.

4. ***Tenancy at sufferance.*** A **tenancy at sufferance** is created when a tenant retains possession of the property after the expiration of another tenancy or a life estate without the owner's consent. That is, the owner suffers the *wrongful possession* of his or her property by the holdover tenant. This is not really a true tenancy but merely the possession of property without right. Technically, a tenant at sufferance is a trespasser. A tenant at sufferance is liable for the payment of rent during the period of sufferance. To evict a holdover tenant, most states require an owner to go through certain legal proceedings, called *eviction proceedings* or *unlawful detainer actions.* A few states allow owners to use self-help to evict a holdover tenant as long as force is not used.

The Lease

The rental agreement between the landlord and the tenant is called the **lease.** Leases generally can be either oral or written, except that most statutes of frauds require written leases for periods of time longer than one year. The lease must contain the essential terms of the parties' agreement. The lease frequently is a form contract prepared by the landlord and presented to the tenant. This is particularly true of residential leases. Other leases are negotiated between the parties.

> **Example** A bank's lease of a branch office would be negotiated with the owner of the building. Lease forms typically are considerably longer than two pages.

TYPES OF TENANCIES

SIDEBAR

Types of Tenancy	Description
Tenancy for years	Continues for the duration of the lease and then terminates automatically without requiring notice. It does not terminate upon the death of either party.
Periodic tenancy	Continues from payment interval to payment interval. It may be terminated by either party with adequate notice. It does not terminate upon the death of either party.
Tenancy at will	Continues at the will of the parties and may be terminated by either party at any time with adequate notice. It terminates upon the death of either party.
Tenancy at sufferance	Arises when a tenant wrongfully occupies real property after the expiration of another tenancy or life estate. It continues until the owner either evicts the tenant or holds him or her over for another term. It terminates upon the death of the tenant.

Implied Warranty of Habitability

The courts of many jurisdictions hold that an **implied warranty of habitability** applies to residential leases for their duration. This warranty provides that the leased premises must be fit, safe, and suitable for ordinary residential use. On the one hand, unchecked rodent infestation, leaking roofs, and unworkable bathroom facilities have been held to breach the implied warranty of habitability. On the other hand, a small crack in the wall or some paint peeling from a door does not breach this warranty.

If the landlord's failure to maintain or repair the leased premises affects the tenant's use or enjoyment of the premises, state statutes and judicial decisions provide various remedies. Generally, the tenant may (1) withhold from his or her rent the amount by which the defect reduced the value of the premises to him or her, (2) repair the defect and deduct the cost of repairs from the rent due for the leased premises, (3) cancel the lease if the failure to repair constitutes constructive eviction, or (4) sue for damages for the amount the landlord's failure to repair the defect reduced the value of the leasehold.

In the following feature, a paralegal professional discusses his experience in the field of property law.

Lease A transfer of the right to the possession and use of real property for a set term in return for certain consideration; the rental agreement between a landlord and a tenant.

Implied warranty of habitability A warranty that provides that leased premises must be fit, safe, and suitable for ordinary residential use.

Land-Use Control

Generally, the ownership of property entitles the owner to use his or her property as he or she wishes. Such use, however, is subject to limitations imposed by government regulation. These limitations are collectively referred to as **land-use control,** or **land-use regulation.** Several forms of land-use regulation are discussed in the following paragraphs.

Learning Objective 9
Explain features of land-use control, such as zoning laws.

Land-use control or land-use regulation The collective term for the laws that regulate the possession, ownership, and use of real property.

Zoning

Most counties and municipalities have enacted **zoning ordinances** to regulate land use. Zoning ordinances generally (1) establish use districts within the municipality (that is, areas are generally designated residential, commercial, or industrial); (2) restrict the height, size, and location of buildings on a building site; and (3) establish aesthetic requirements or limitations for the exterior of buildings.

A **zoning commission** usually formulates zoning ordinances, conducts public hearings, and makes recommendations to the city council, which must vote to enact an ordinance. Once a zoning ordinance is enacted, the zoning ordinance commission enforces it. If landowners believe that a zoning ordinance is illegal or that it has been applied unlawfully to them or to their property, they may institute a court proceeding seeking judicial review of the ordinance or its application.

Zoning ordinances Local laws that are adopted by municipalities and local governments to regulate land use within their boundaries.

Paralegals *in* Practice

PARALEGAL PROFILE
John M. Rizzini

John M. Rizzini is a Senior Real Estate Paralegal with over 22 years of paralegal experience. He is currently employed by the law firm of Edwards Angell Palmer & Dodge LLP in Providence, Rhode Island. John has a Bachelor of Arts Degree in Political Science and a Paralegal Studies Certificate from Roger Williams University. He is also a member of the Rhode Island Paralegal Association and the National Federation of Paralegal Associations.

Some of my daily duties include drafting and reviewing real estate documents such as deeds, promissory notes, mortgages, title affidavits, release documents, leases, and more. On some days, I may focus on a simple residential sale of real estate. On other days, I only work on matters related to zoning and subdivisions. I also address litigation and trust/estate issues that involve real estate.

One of the biggest trends in property law is the ability to search real estate titles online. For some states, you can search titles by city, town, or county on a registry Web site, as far back as the early 1950s. Another trend is the ability to electronically file real estate documents. We cannot do this in Rhode Island yet, so paralegals must go in person to the city or town hall to record original documents.

There is a lot of discussion within the legal community about regulating paralegals. I would not say that regulation would expand my paralegal role, but I do think that it would create a pool of paralegals who have met certain judicial or legislative requirements. In other words, regulation would eliminate the so-called "fly-by-night" paralegal programs.

My advice to new paralegals is: never "burn bridges." Working relationships developed at the beginning of your career are as important as contacts made in coming years. Also, find an experienced paralegal willing to give you career guidance and learn as much as possible from him or her. Having a mentor in this profession is priceless.

An owner who wishes to use his or her property for a use different from that permitted under a current zoning ordinance may seek relief from the ordinance by obtaining a **variance.** To obtain a variance, the landowner must prove that the ordinance causes an undue hardship by preventing him or her from making a reasonable return on the land as zoned. Variances usually are difficult to obtain.

Web Exploration

Go to **http://www.housingnyc.com/html/about/about.html** and read the Mission Statement of the New York City Rent Guidelines Board.

Rent Control

Many local communities across the country have enacted **rent control ordinances** that set an amount of rent a landlord can charge for residential housing. Most of these ordinances fix the rent at a specific amount and provide for minor annual increases. Although many communities have adopted rent control ordinances, New York City is the most famous one.

Landlords, of course, oppose **rent control**, arguing that rent control ordinances are merely a "regulatory tax" that transfers wealth from landowners to tenants. Tenants and proponents of rent control say that it is necessary to create affordable housing, particularly in high-rent urban areas.

Eminent domain The government's power to take private property for public use, provided that just compensation is paid to the private property holder.

Just Compensation Clause A clause of the U.S. Constitution that requires the government to compensate the property owner, and possibly others, when the government takes property under its power of eminent domain.

Eminent Domain

The government may use its power of **eminent domain** to acquire private property for public purposes. However, the **Due Process Clause** of the Fifth Amendment to the U.S. Constitution (and state constitutions, where applicable) requires that the government take property only for "public use." The government must allow the owner of the property to make a case for keeping the property.

The **Just Compensation Clause** of the Fifth Amendment to the U.S. Constitution requires the government to compensate the property owner (and possibly others, such as lessees) when it exercises the power of eminent domain. Anyone who is not satisfied with the compensation offered by the government can bring an action to have the court determine the compensation to be paid.

Example Assume that Henry owns a large piece of vacant beachfront property with the intention of building his retirement house on the property at some future time. Now suppose the city government wants to build a new public boat dock on the property. The city government can use its power of eminent domain to acquire the needed property for this public use. There has been a "taking," so the government must pay Henry just compensation.

Civil Rights Acts

Federal and state laws guarantee **civil rights** in the purchase, sale, lease, and use of real property. Several major federal statutes that regulate real estate are:

1. ***Civil Rights Act.*** A federal statute that prohibits racial discrimination in the transfer of real property, including housing, commercial, and industrial property. The act prohibits private and public discrimination and permits lawsuits to recover damages and obtain injunctions against offending conduct [42 U.S.C. Section 1971 *et seq.*].
2. ***Fair Housing Act.*** A federal statute that makes it unlawful for a party to refuse to rent or sell a dwelling to any person because of his or her race, color, national origin, sex, or religion. The act also prohibits discrimination by real estate brokers, mortgage lenders, and advertisers concerning the sale or rental of real property [42 U.S.C. Section 360 *et seq.*].
3. ***Title III of the Americans with Disabilities Act (ADA).*** Title III of the ADA is a part of a federal statute that prohibits discrimination on the basis of disability in places of public accommodation operated by private entities. Title III applies to public accommodations and commercial facilities such as motels, hotels, restaurants, theaters, recreation facilities, colleges and universities, department stores, retail stores, and office buildings. It does not generally apply to residential facilities (single- and multifamily housing). The ADA provides for both private right of action and enforcement by the attorney general. Individuals may seek injunctive relief and monetary damages, while the attorney general may seek equitable relief and civil fines for any violation [42 UCC Section 1201 *et seq.*].

Civil Rights Act A federal statute that prohibits racial discrimination in the transfer of real property.

Fair Housing Act A federal statute that makes it unlawful for a party to refuse to rent or sell a dwelling to any person because of his or her race, color, national origin, sex, or religion.

Title III of the Americans with Disabilities Act (ADA) A federal statute that prohibits discrimination on the basis of disability in places of public accommodation operated by private entities.

The ethical duty not to engage in conduct that would exceed a paralegal professional's authority under the law is discussed in the following feature.

Laws are always useful to persons of property, and hurtful to those who have none.
Jean-Jacques Rousseau
Du Contrat Social (1761)

Learning Objective 10

Explain a paralegal's duty not to engage in conduct that would exceed the paralegal professional's authority under the law.

ETHICAL PERSPECTIVE

Duty Not to Engage in Conduct That Would Exceed a Paralegal Professional's Authority Under the Law

Mr. Fields is an attorney who practices law in the credit and bankruptcy areas. Mr. Fields' clients are mainly individuals who file for bankruptcy. Ms. Harrington, an experienced paralegal in the bankruptcy law area, is hired by Mr. Fields.

Several months after Ms. Harrington's employment, Mr. Fields opens a second law office in another part of the city to attract additional clients. Mr. Fields spends Mondays, Wednesdays, and Fridays at his first office, and Tuesdays and Thursdays at the new, second office. Both offices are successful in attracting clients.

(continued)

Mr. Fields assigns Ms. Harrington to work at the office that he is not working at—that is, when he is working at the first office, Ms. Harrington is assigned to work at the second office. Mr. Fields directs Ms. Harrington to sign up as many clients who come into the office she is covering as she can.

Mr. Fields instructs Ms. Harrington to answer any questions that clients or potential clients may have regarding how unsecured credit, credit card debt, secured credit, and assets are handled under bankruptcy law, and to answer any other questions that they may have. Mr. Fields tell Ms. Harrington that because she is an expert in credit and bankruptcy law, she should give whatever advice she thinks is pertinent to a client's case.

The issue is whether Ms. Harrington would be engaged in the unauthorized practice of law.

Model and state paralegal professional codes of ethics and responsibility require that a paralegal professional comply with the applicable law that governs the unauthorized practice of law by a paralegal. Bankruptcy law permits a paralegal to complete the forms necessary for a bankruptcy filing. The law does not allow a paralegal to give legal advice, however.

PARALEGAL'S ETHICAL DECISION

Mr. Fields' instruction to Ms. Harrington to give legal advice to potential and actual clients violates his ethical duties as an attorney. In addition, model and state ethics codes prohibit professional paralegals from engaging in the unauthorized practice of law. Therefore, Ms. Harrington may perform the functions allowed by bankruptcy law, but must refuse to engage in the unauthorized practice of law.

Concept Review *and* Reinforcement

LEGAL TERMINOLOGY

Abandoned property 552
Adverse possession 564
Air-space parcel 553
Bailee 552
Bailment 552
Bailor 552
Beneficiaries 551
Buildings 553
Civil Rights Act 569
Community property 557
Concurrent ownership (co-ownership) 555
Condominium 557
Cooperative 557
Deed 558
Donee 550
Donor 550
Due Process Clause 568
Duty of reasonable care or ordinary care 552
Easement 564
Easement by grant 564
Easement by implication 564
Easement by necessity 564
Easement by reservation 564
Eminent domain 568
Estate (estate in land) 553
Estate in fee 554
Estate *pur autre vie* 554
Estray statute 551
Fair Housing Act 569
Fee simple absolute (fee simple) 554
Fee simple defeasible (qualified fee) 554
Fixtures 553
Freehold estate 553
Future interest 555
Gift 550
Gift *causa mortis* 550
Gift *inter vivos* 550
Grantee 558
Grantor 558
Heirs 551
Implied warranty of habitability 567
Inheritance 551
Intangible property 549
Joint tenancy 555
Joint tenants 555
Just Compensation Clause 568
Land 553
Landlord (lessor) 565
Landlord–tenant relationship 564
Land-use control or land-use regulation 567
Lease 567
Leasehold estate (leasehold) 565
Life estate 554
Lost property 551
Marketable title 563
Mineral rights 553
Mislaid property 551
Mutual benefit bailment 552
Nonfreehold estate 565
Periodic tenancy 566

Personal property 549
Plant life and vegetation 553
Quiet title action 562
Quitclaim deed 558
Real property 553
Recording statute 558
Registrar of Deeds 562
Remainder 555
Remainder person 555
Rent control ordinances 568
Reversion 555
Right of survivorship 555
Sale 558
Settlement statement 558
Subsurface rights (mineral rights) 553
Surface rights 553
Tangible property 549
Tenancy at sufferance 566
Tenancy at will 566
Tenancy by the entirety 556
Tenancy for years 566
Tenancy in common 556
Tenant (lessee) 566
Tenant in common 556
Title III of the Americans with Disabilities Act (ADA) 569
Title insurance 563
Title insurance policy 563
Uniform Gift to Minors Act or Revised Uniform Gift to Minors Act 550
Variance 568
Warranty deed 558
Will 551
Zoning commission 567
Zoning ordinances 567

SUMMARY OF KEY CONCEPTS

Personal Property

	Personal property is everything that is not real property; it is sometimes referred to as *goods* or *chattels*.
Types of Personal Property	1. *Tangible property:* Physically defined property such as goods, animals, and minerals. 2. *Intangible property:* Rights that cannot be reduced to physical form, such as stock certificates, bonds, and copyrights.
Acquiring Ownership of Personal Property	Ownership to personal property may be acquired by the following means: 1. *Purchase:* A person can purchase property from its rightful owner. 2. *Production:* A person can produce a finished product from raw materials and supplies. 3. *Gift:* A gift is a voluntary transfer of property by its owner to a donee without consideration. The three elements necessary to create a valid gift are: a. Donative intent b. Delivery c. Acceptance 4. *Will or inheritance:* Gifts made to beneficiaries of a will, and inheritances stipulated in an inheritance statute.
Types of Gifts	1. *Gift* inter vivos: These gifts are made during a donor's lifetime. 2. *Gift* causa mortis: These gifts are made in anticipation of death.
Mislaid and Lost Personal Property	1. *Mislaid property:* Mislaid property is personal property that an owner voluntarily places somewhere and then inadvertently forgets about. The owner of the premises where the property is mislaid does not acquire title to the property but has the right of possession against all except the rightful owner. The rightful owner can reclaim the property. 2. *Lost property:* Lost property is personal property that an owner leaves somewhere because of negligence or carelessness. The finder obtains title to the property against the whole world except the true owner. The true owner can reclaim the property. 3. *Abandoned property:* Abandoned property is property that an owner discards with the intent to relinquish his or her rights in it, or property that an owner has mislaid or lost and has given up any further attempts to locate it. Anyone who finds abandoned property acquires title to it. 4. *Estray statutes:* These state statutes permit a finder of mislaid or lost property to obtain title to the property. To obtain clear title, the finder must: a. Report the find to the appropriate government agency and turn over possession of the property to the agency. b. Post and publish required notices. c. Wait the statutorily required time (for example, one year) without the rightful owner claiming the property.

Bailment	
	Bailments occur when the owner of personal property delivers the property to another person to be held, stored, or delivered, or for some other purpose.
Parties	1. *Bailor:* Owner of the property 2. *Bailee:* Party to whom the property is delivered
Mutual Benefit Bailment	A mutual benefit bailment arises when both parties benefit from the bailment. This includes commercial bailments. The bailee owes a duty of *reasonable care* (or *ordinary care*) and is liable for *ordinary negligence*.
Real Property	
Nature of Real Property	Real property is immovable; it includes land, buildings, subsurface rights, air rights, plant life, and fixtures.
Freehold Estates in Land	Freehold estates in land are estates where the owner has a present possessory interest in the real property.
Types of Fees	Estates in Fee: 1. *Fee simple absolute* (or *fee simple*): Highest form of ownership 2. *Fee simple defeasible* (or *qualified fee*): Estate that ends if a specified condition occurs
Life Estate	A life estate is an interest in real property that lasts for the life of a specified person; called an estate *pur autre vie* if the time is measured by the life of the third person.
Future Interests	Future interest means the right to possess real property in the future rather than currently. Two types are the following: 1. *Reversion:* A right to possession that returns to the grantor after the expiration of a limited or contingent estate. 2. *Remainder:* A right to possession that goes to a third person after the expiration of a limited or contingent estate; the third person is called a *remainder person*.
Concurrent Ownership	Concurrent ownership is a situation in which two or more persons jointly own real property. Types of concurrent ownership are: 1. *Joint tenancy:* Owners may transfer their interests without the consent of co-owners; transfer severs the joint tenancy. Under the *right of survivorship*, the interest of a deceased owner passes to his or her co-owners. 2. *Tenancy in common:* Owners may transfer their interests without the consent of co-owners; transfer does not sever the tenancy in common. Interest of a deceased owner passes to his or her estate. 3. *Tenancy by the entirety:* A form of co-ownership that can be used only by a married couple; neither spouse may transfer his or her interest without the other spouse's consent. A surviving spouse has the right of survivorship. 4. *Community property:* A form of co-ownership in certain states that applies only to a married couple; neither spouse may transfer his or her interest without the other spouse's consent. When a spouse dies, the surviving spouse automatically receives one-half of the community property.
Other Forms of Ownership	1. *Condominium:* Owners have title to their individual units and own the common areas as tenants in common; owners may transfer their interests without the consent of other owners. 2. *Cooperative:* A corporation owns the building, and the residents own shares of the corporation. Usually, owners may not transfer their shares without the approval of the other owners.
Transfer of Ownership of Real Property	
Sale of Real Estate	In a sale of real estate, an owner sells his or her property to another for consideration.
Recording Statutes	Recording statutes permit copies of deeds and other documents concerning interests in real property (such as mortgages and liens) to be filed in a government office, where they become public record. This puts third parties on notice of recorded interests.

Deed	A deed is an instrument used to convey real property by sale or gift. 1. *Warranty deed:* Provides the most protection to the grantee because the grantor makes warranties against defect in title. 2. *Quitclaim deed:* Provides the least amount of protection to the grantee because the grantor transfers only the interest he or she has in the property.
Quiet Title Action	A quiet title action is a lawsuit in which a court determines ownership rights to real property.
Marketable Title	A marketable title is a title free of encumbrances, defects in title, and other defects.
Adverse Possession	In adverse possession, a person who occupies another's property acquires title to the property if the occupation has been: 1. for a statutory period of time (in many states, 10 to 20 years). 2. open, visible, and notorious. 3. actual and exclusive. 4. continuous and peaceful. 5. hostile and adverse.
Easement	An easement is an interest in land that gives the holder the right to make limited use of another's property without taking anything from it (such as driveways and party walls).
Landlord–Tenant Relationship	
	A landlord–tenant relationship is created when an owner of a freehold estate transfers a right to another to exclusively and temporarily possess the owner's property.
Types of Tenancy	1. *Tenancy for years:* Tenancy for a specified period of time 2. *Periodic tenancy:* Tenancy for a period of time determined by the payment interval 3. *Tenancy at will:* Tenancy that may be terminated at any time by either party 4. *Tenancy at sufferance:* Tenancy created by the wrongful possession of property
The Lease	A lease is a rental agreement between the landlord and the tenant that contains the essential terms of the parties' agreement.
Implied Warranty of Habitability	An implied warranty of habitability provides that leased premises must be fit, safe, and suitable for ordinary residential use.
Land-Use Control	
Zoning	*Zoning ordinances* are laws adopted by local governments that restrict the use of property, set building standards, and establish architectural requirements. *Variance* permits an owner to make a nonzoned use of his or her property; it requires permission from a zoning board.
Rent Control	Rent control is a law that fixes the amount of rent a landlord can charge for residential housing. Most rent control laws provide for minor annual increases.
Eminent Domain	*Eminent domain:* Grants power to the government to acquire private property for public purposes.
	Just Compensation Clause: A clause of the U.S. Constitution that mandates that the government provide the property owner and possibly others (such as renters) with just compensation when the government exercises its power of eminent domain.
Civil Rights Acts	
	Federal and state laws guarantee civil rights in the purchase, sale, lease, and use of real property. 1. *Civil Rights Act:* A federal statute that prohibits racial discrimination in the transfer of real property, including housing, commercial, and industrial property. 2. *Fair Housing Act:* A federal statute that makes it unlawful for a party to refuse to rent or sell a dwelling to any person because of his or her race, color, national origin, sex, or religion. 3. *Title III of the Americans with Disabilities Act (ADA):* The part of the ADA that prohibits discrimination on the basis of disability in places of public accommodation operated by private entities.

WORKING THE WEB

1. Using the website http://www.google.com/html, a similar Internet search engine, or the Internet legal search services Westlaw or LexisNexis, find the estray statute for your state. What requirements must be met for a finder to obtain title to mislaid or lost property that he or she finds?
2. Using the website http://www.google.com/html or a similar Internet search engine, find a listing of houses or property that is for sale in your area. Compare home prices. Are the prices higher or lower than you thought they would be?
3. Visit the website http://nationalatlas.gov/printable/image/pdf/fedlands/id.pdf. The map will show the lands owned by the federal government in the state of Idaho. Substitute your state's two-letter code (for example, "al" for Alabama, "ny" for New York) where the "id" appears in the website address, and find the map showing the lands that are owned by the federal government in your state. Does the federal government own land where you live? If so, what department or bureau of the federal government owns the land?

CRITICAL THINKING & WRITING QUESTIONS

1. Define "personal property." What is the difference between tangible and intangible personal property? Give an example of each.
2. Describe an estray statute. What is the purpose of an estray statute? Explain how an estray statute works.
3. Define a bailment. Who is the bailor? Who is the bailee?
4. Define "real property." Describe each of the following: (a) land, (b) building, (c) surface rights, (d) subsurface rights, and (e) fixtures.
5. What is an estate in land (estate)? Define a freehold estate.
6. Define a fee simple absolute (or fee simple). Define a fee simple defeasible (or qualified fee).
7. What is a future interest? What is the difference between a reversion and a remainder? Give an example of each.
8. Describe each the following: (a) joint tenancy, (b) tenancy in common, (c) tenancy by the entirety, and (d) community property.
9. What is the difference between a condominium and a cooperative?
10. Define the following: (a) deed, (b) warranty deed, and (c) quitclaim deed. In each case, who is the grantor and who is the grantee?
11. Describe a recording statute. Explain what the Registrar of Deeds does.
12. What does the legal doctrine of adverse possession provide? What elements have to be met for adverse possession to occur? Give an example.
13. What is an easement? Describe the difference between the following types of easements: (a) easement by grant, (b) easement by reservation, (c) easement by implication, and (d) easement by necessity.
14. Describe the following types of tenancies: (a) tenancy for years, (b) periodic tenancy, (c) tenancy at will, and (d) tenancy at sufferance.
15. Define "zoning." What does a zoning ordinance do? Give an example of zoning. What is a variance?
16. Define "eminent domain." What is a "taking"? What does the Just Compensation Clause of the U.S. Constitution require?

Building Paralegal Skills

VIDEO CASE STUDIES

UPL Issue: Traditional Exceptions

Sara has inherited a large sum of money and asks her friend Barbara, an investment counselor with a bank, for advice. Barbara gives her tax advice and some recommendations.

After viewing the video case study in MyLegalStudiesLab, answer the following:

1. What are the incidental activities that a paralegal may perform or about which he or she may give advice without violating the UPL laws in your state?
2. Does a real estate salesperson give what would be considered legal advice to buyers and sellers? Would it be UPL if a paralegal working in a law firm that specializes in real estate gave legal advice?
3. Is it UPL when someone working in an accounting firm gives tax advice? Would it be UPL if a paralegal working in a law firm that specializes in taxation gave tax advice?

ETHICS ANALYSIS & DISCUSSION QUESTIONS

1. Does preparing a report for a client that shows the history of the ownership of a property, as shown in public records, and claims against the property, as shown in public records, constitute the practice of law?
2. In your jurisdiction, is priority given to real estate based upon the time of filing of deeds? Is the failure to promptly file a deed considered malpractice?
3. As an experienced paralegal, you have investigated many complex cases and developed a reputation for discovering little-known facts and obtaining information not normally obtained by investigators. A law firm proposes to have its client hire you to conduct the investigation of a complex and troublesome environmental case involving a major corporation that appears to be hiding information. See *Ethics Opinion 510, Texas Professional Ethics Committee Opinions*. Can you accept the case and have your compensation based on a contingent fee if paid directly from the client from his or her award, if any? From the firm? Can you accept a "substantial" bonus from the law firm?

DEVELOPING YOUR COLLABORATION SKILLS

With a group of other students selected by you or your instructor, review the facts of the following case. As a group, discuss the following questions.

1. Who is the plaintiff in this case? Who is the defendant?
2. What is adverse possession?
3. What requirements must be established to find adverse possession?
4. Do you believe that the requirements of adverse possession were proved in this case?

Witt v. Miller

Edward and Mary Shaughnessey purchased a 16-acre tract in St. Louis County, Missouri. Subsequently, they subdivided 12 acres into 18 lots offered for sale and retained possession of the remaining four-acre tract. Thirteen years later, Charles and Elaine Witt purchased lot 12, which is adjacent to the four-acre tract. The Witts constructed and moved into a house on their lot. The next year, they cleared an area of land that ran the length of their property and extended 40 feet onto the four-acre tract. The Witts constructed a pool and a deck, planted a garden, made a playground for their children, set up a dog run, and built a fence along the edge of the property line, which included the now-disputed property. Neither the Witts nor the Shaughnesseys realized that the Witts had encroached on the Shaughnesseys' property. Twenty years later, the Shaughnesseys sold their four-acre tract to Thomas and Rosanne Miller. When a survey showed the Witts' encroachment, the Millers demanded that the Witts remove the pool and cease using the property. When the Witts refused to do so, the lawsuit ensued.

Source: Witt v. Miller, 845 S.W.2d 665, Web 1993 Mo. App. Lexis 20 (Court of Appeals of Missouri)

PARALEGAL PORTFOLIO EXERCISE

Prepare a memorandum, no longer than three pages, that does the following two things: (1) describes the requirements for title to property to be obtained by the doctrine of adverse possession in your state; (2) finds two cases in your state where the doctrine of adverse possession has been asserted to try to obtain title to property, and discuss the results of the cases.

LEGAL ANALYSIS & WRITING CASES

Willsmore v. Township of Oceola, Michigan

308 N.W.2d 796, Web 1981 Mich. App. Lexis 2993
Court of Appeals of Michigan

While hunting on unposted and unoccupied property in Oceola Township, Michigan, Duane Willsmore noticed an area with branches arranged in a crisscross pattern. When he kicked aside the branches and sod, he found a watertight suitcase in a freshly dug hole. Willsmore informed the Michigan State Police of his find. A state trooper and Willsmore together pried open the suitcase and discovered $383,840 in cash. The state police took custody of the money, which was deposited in an interest-bearing account. Michigan's Lost Goods Act provides that the finder and the township in which the property was found must share the value of the property if the finder publishes required notices and the true owner does not claim the property within one year.

Willsmore published the required notices and brought a declaratory judgment action, seeking a determination of the ownership of the money. Thomas Powell, the owner of the land on which the suitcase was found, claimed he was the owner of the suitcase. After Powell incorrectly named the amount of money in the suitcase, he asserted his Fifth Amendment right not to testify at his deposition and at trial.

Question

1. Who is entitled to the briefcase and its contents?

Solow v. Wellner

150 Misc.2d 642, 569 N.Y.S.2d 882, Web 1991 N.Y. Misc. Lexis 169 Civil Court of the City of New York

The defendants are approximately 80 tenants of a 300-unit luxury apartment building on the upper east side of Manhattan. The monthly rents in the all-glass-enclosed building, which won several architectural awards, were very high. The landlord brought a summary proceeding against the tenants to recover rent when they engaged in a rent strike in protest against what they viewed as deteriorating conditions and services. Among other things, the evidence showed that during the period in question, the elevator system made tenants and their guests wait interminable lengths of time, the elevators skipped floors and opened on the wrong floors, a stench emanated from garbage stored near the garage and mice appeared in that area, fixtures were missing in public areas, water seeped into mailboxes, the air conditioning in the lobby was inoperative, and air conditioners in individual units leaked. The defendant-tenants sought abatement of rent for breach of the implied warranty of habitability.

Question

1. Does the landlord breach the implied warranty of habitability?

WORKING WITH THE LANGUAGE OF THE COURT CASE

Kelo v. City of New London, Connecticut

545 U.S. 469, 125 S.Ct. 2655, 162 L.Ed.2d 439, Web 2005 U.S. Lexis 5011
Supreme Court of the United States of America

Read and then brief the following case, excerpted from the U.S. Supreme Court's opinion. In your brief, answer the following questions:

1. Who were the plaintiffs (appellees)? Who was the defendant (appellant)?
2. For government to take private property, what must be shown?
3. What was the issue in this case? How did the U.S. Supreme Court decide this issue?
4. How close was the vote?

Stevens, Justice (joined by Kennedy, Souter, Ginsburg, and Breyer)

The city of New London (hereinafter City) sits at the junction of the Thames River and the Long Island Sound in southeastern Connecticut. Decades of economic decline led a state agency in 1990 to designate the City a "distressed municipality." In 1998, the City's unemployment rate was nearly double that of the State, and its population of just under 24,000 residents was at its lowest since 1920.

These conditions prompted state and local officials to target New London, and particularly its Fort Trumbull area, for economic revitalization. To this end, respondent New London Development Corporation (NLDC), a private non-profit entity established some years earlier to assist the City in planning economic development, was reactivated. Upon obtaining state-level approval, the NLDC finalized an integrated development plan focused on 90 acres of the Fort Trumbull area. The Fort Trumbull area is situated on a peninsula that juts into the Thames River. The area comprises approximately 115 privately owned properties, as well as the 32 acres of land formerly occupied by the naval facility.

In addition to creating jobs, generating tax revenue, and helping to "build momentum for the revitalization of downtown New London," the plan was also designed to make the City more attractive and to create leisure and recreational opportunities on the waterfront and in the park.

The city council approved the plan in January 2000, and designated the NLDC as its development agent in charge of implementation. The city council also authorized the NLDC to purchase property or to acquire property by exercising eminent domain in the City's name. The NLDC successfully negotiated the purchase of most of the real estate in the 90-acre area, but its negotiations with petitioners failed. As a consequence, in November 2000, the NLDC initiated the condemnation proceedings that gave rise to this case.

Petitioner Susette Kelo has lived in the Fort Trumbull area since 1997. She has made extensive improvements to her house, which she prizes for its water view. Petitioner Wilhelmina Dery was born in her Fort Trumbull house in 1918 and has lived there her entire life. Her husband Charles (also a petitioner) has lived in the house since they married some 60 years ago. In all, the nine petitioners own 15 properties in Fort Trumbull. Ten of the parcels are occupied by the owner or a family member; the other five are held as investment properties. There is no allegation that any of these properties is blighted or otherwise in poor condition; rather, they were condemned only because they happen to be located in the development area.

In December 2000, petitioners brought this action in the New London Superior Court. They claimed, among other things, that the taking of their properties would violate the "public use" restriction in the Fifth Amendment. After a 7-day bench trial, the Superior Court granted a permanent restraining order prohibiting the taking of the properties....

After the Superior Court ruled, both sides took appeals to the Supreme Court of Connecticut. That court held, over a dissent, that all of the City's proposed takings were valid. [T]he court held that such economic development qualified as a valid public use under both the Federal and State Constitutions.

We granted certiorari to determine whether a city's decision to take property for the purpose of economic development satisfies the "public use" requirement of the Fifth Amendment.

The disposition of this case therefore turns on the question whether the City's development plan serves a "public purpose." Without exception, our cases have defined that concept broadly, reflecting our longstanding policy of deference to legislative judgments in this field. For more than a century, our public use jurisprudence has wisely eschewed rigid formulas and intrusive scrutiny in favor of affording legislatures broad latitude in determining what public needs justify the use of the takings power.

Those who govern the City were not confronted with the need to remove blight in the Fort Trumbull area, but their determination that the area was sufficiently distressed to justify a program of economic rejuvenation is entitled to our deference. The City has carefully formulated an economic development plan that it believes will provide appreciable benefits to the community, including—but by no means limited to—new jobs and increased tax revenue. As with other exercises in urban planning and development, the City is endeavoring to coordinate a variety of commercial, residential, and recreational uses of land, with the hope that they will form a whole greater than the sum of its parts. To effectuate this plan, the City has invoked a state statute that specifically authorizes the use of eminent domain to promote economic development. Because that plan unquestionably serves a public purpose, the takings challenged here satisfy the public use requirement of the Fifth Amendment.

To avoid this result, petitioners urge us to adopt a new bright-line rule that economic development does not qualify as a public use. Clearly, there is no basis for exempting economic development from our traditionally broad understanding of public purpose. Petitioners contend that using eminent domain for economic development impermissibly blurs the boundary between public and private takings. Again, our cases foreclose this objection. Quite simply, the government's pursuit of a public purpose will often benefit individual private parties.

Just as we decline to second-guess the City's considered judgments about the efficacy of its development plan, we also decline to second-guess the City's determinations as to what lands it needs to acquire in order to effectuate the project.

The judgment of the Supreme Court of Connecticut is affirmed.

MYLEGALSTUDIESLAB

MyLegalStudiesLab Virtual Law Office Experience Assignments

Complete the pre-test, study plan, and post-test for this chapter and answer the Legal Applications questions as assigned. These will help you confirm your mastery of the concepts and their application to legal scenarios. Then complete the Virtual Law Office assignments as assigned by your instructor. These assignments are designed to develop your workplace skills. Completing the assignments for this chapter will result in producing the following documents for inclusion in your portfolio:

VLOE 15.1 Letter to client explaining the different forms of property ownership for real estate and the advantages and disadvantages, if any, of each form.

CHAPTER

16

Estates and Elder Law

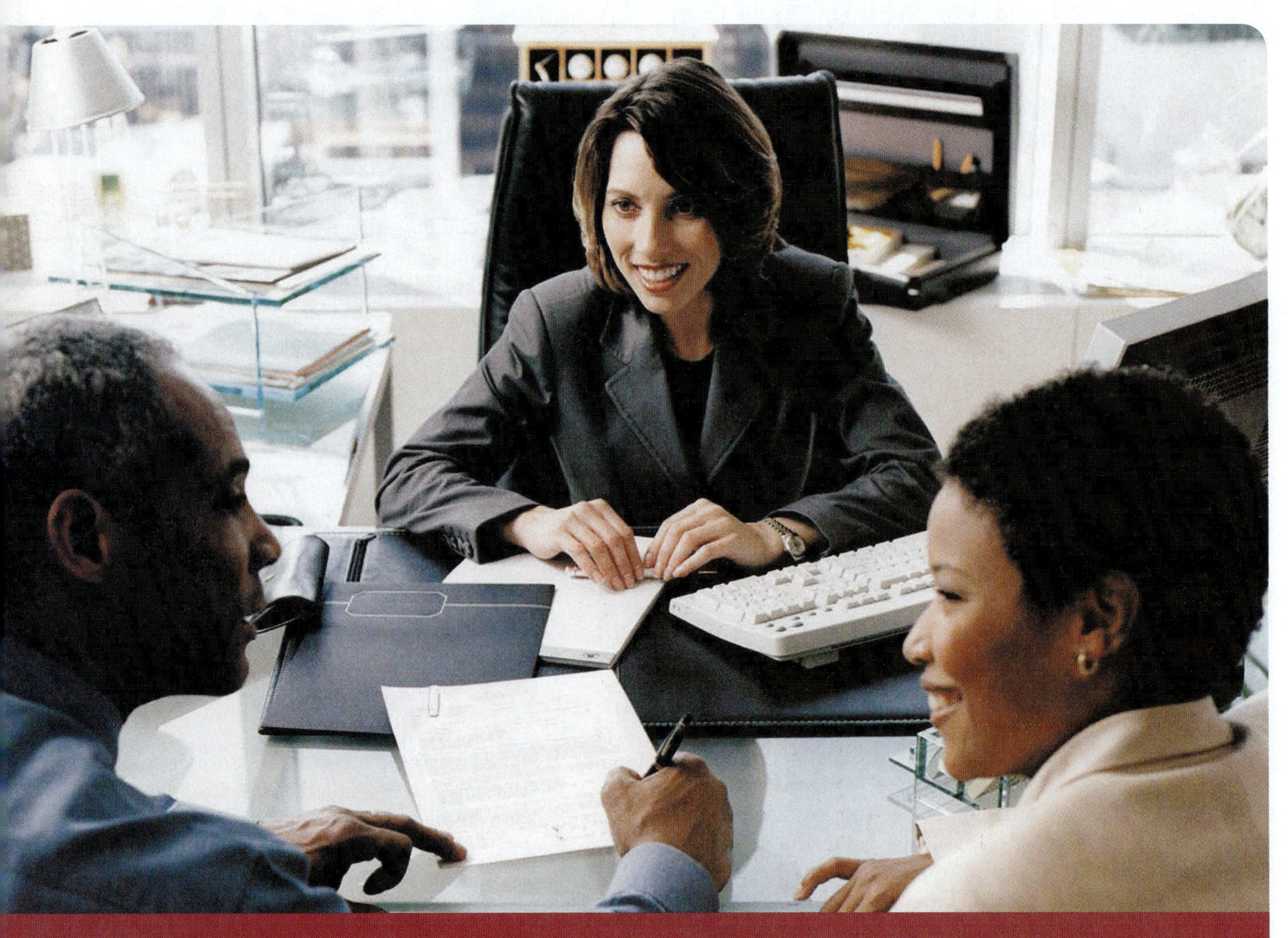

LEARNING OBJECTIVES

After studying this chapter, you should be able to:

1. Recognize the professional opportunities for paralegals in the area of wills, trusts, estates, and elder law.
2. List and describe the requirements for making a valid will.
3. Distinguish between different forms of testamentary gifts.
4. Describe the process of probate.
5. Define an *intestacy statute* and identify how property is distributed if a person dies without a will or living trust.
6. Explain what a living will and a health care directive are.
7. Define trust and identify the parties to a trust.
8. Describe a living trust and the benefits of a living trust.
9. Describe elder law.
10. Explain a paralegal's duty to report dishonest or fraudulent acts pertaining to the handling of funds.

Paralegals at Work

You are a paralegal for Mr. Patrick O'Rourke, an expert in estate planning law. As his paralegal, you conduct research, attend client conferences, and prepare estate planning documents for Mr. O'Rourke's review.

One day, Mr. O'Rourke asks you to sit in on a client conference with Ms. Harriet Huntington and Mr. Theodore Huntington. At the meeting, the Huntingtons relate the following information: Ms. Huntington is 45 years old, and Mr. Huntington is 50 years old. They have been married 15 years. Mr. Huntington owns his own business, a successful retail store. Ms. Huntington is a manager at a large software company. Mr. Huntington earns about $150,000 per year, and Ms. Huntington earns about $250,000 per year. They have three children, ages 13, 10, and 7.

During the course of their marriage, the Huntingtons have accumulated the following assets: a home that is worth $1,000,000, with a $300,000 mortgage; securities of $500,000; and cash savings in bank accounts totaling $100,000. Ms. Huntington and Mr. Huntington each have a pension at work, and each has a life insurance policy for $1,000,000. Together they have accumulated two automobiles, furniture, and jewelry worth $50,000.

The Huntingtons explain that because they currently do not have any wills or trusts, they would like Mr. O'Rourke to advise them on matters of estate planning and prepare the necessary documents to effectuate the plans they agree to. They each want the other to receive all of their property if one of them should die. Further, they want to have control over their assets during their lifetimes and receive all of the income from their property during their lives; however, they would like to avoid probate.

Both Mr. and Ms. Huntington also say that they do not want certain life-saving measures to be taken should they become severely ill or injured. In addition, each wants the other to make health care decisions for him or her if he or she is unable to do so.

> "When you have told someone you have left him a legacy, the only decent thing to do is to die at once."
>
> *Samuel Butler*

The Huntingtons ask Mr. O'Rourke to develop an estate plan for them. As Mr. O'Rourke's paralegal, you will assist him in developing the estate plan for the Huntingtons and help him prepare the necessary documents to implement the estate plan.

Consider the issues involved in this scenario as you read this chapter.

Learning Objective 1

Recognize the professional opportunities for paralegals in the area of wills, trusts, estates, and elder law.

INTRODUCTION FOR THE PARALEGAL

Many paralegals work for lawyers who represent clients in estate planning. Paralegals often assist lawyers in drafting wills, trusts, and other estate planning documents. Paralegals who work in this field also assist lawyers in the transfers of assets pursuant to trust and living trust arrangements, and in handling matters of probate. Clients often want living trusts and health care proxies completed while they are living.

Disinherit: The prankish action of the ghosts in cutting the pockets out of trousers.
Frank McKinney Hubbard
The Roycroft Dictionary (1923)

Wills transfer property upon a person's death. When that person dies, his or her property is distributed as provided in the will. If a person dies without a will, state law provides how the deceased person's property is distributed. A person may transfer property to a trust while he or she is living. Some trusts are living trusts—the trust is created for the benefit of the beneficiaries while they are living. Other trusts are established to go into effect when a person dies. In addition, many people sign a living will, which states their wishes should an accident or illness disable them to the point they can no longer make decisions themselves, and a health care *proxy*, which appoints someone else to make any necessary decisions for them.

A paralegal working in the estate planning field must be knowledgeable about wills, trusts, living trusts, living wills, health care proxies, probate, and other matters related to estate planning. This chapter covers all of the legal issues and documents associated with estate planning.

A growing specialty in law is the area of elder law. Many attorneys now represent older individuals in obtaining benefits that are due them, protecting elders against unscrupulous and fraudulent conduct, and otherwise enforcing the rights of elders. Paralegal professionals are now also specializing in this area of law.

The following feature discusses the career opportunities available to paralegal professionals in the area of wills, trusts, estates, and elder law.

Will A declaration of how a person wants his or her property to be distributed upon death.

Testator or testatrix The person who makes a will.

Wills

A **will** is a declaration of how a person wants his or her property to be distributed upon his or her death. It is a *testamentary* deposition of property. The person who makes the will is called the **testator** (or **testatrix**). The persons designated in the will to receive the testator's property are called **beneficiaries.** Exhibit 16.1 shows the parties to a will.

Web Exploration

Go to **http://www.abanet.org/soloseznet/threads/0511/storewills.html** and read the article "Where is the Best Place to Store a Will."

Learning Objective 2

List and describe the requirements for making a valid will.

Requirements for Making a Will

Every state has a **Statute of Wills** that establishes the requirements for making a valid will in that state. These requirements are:

Statute of Wills A state statute that establishes the requirements for making a valid will.

- **Testamentary capacity.** The testator must have been of legal age and "sound mind" when the will was made. The courts determine **testamentary capacity** on a case-by-case basis. The legal age for executing a will is set by state statute.
- **Writing.** Wills must be in writing to be valid (except for dying declarations, discussed later in this chapter). The writing may be formal or

CAREER OPPORTUNITIES FOR PARALEGALS IN THE AREA OF WILLS, TRUSTS, ESTATES, AND ELDER LAW

An important area of law that paralegals can work in is that of wills, trusts, and estates. Many lawyers and their paralegals specialize in this area.

"Estate law" is a composite of many areas of law, including providing estate planning; giving tax advice; drafting wills and trusts; preparing living wills and health care proxies; representing clients in Medicaid, Social Security, and disability matters; and other areas of the law that affect the elderly.

Many lawyers specialize in estate planning—that is, planning how a client's estate will be distributed when the client dies. Estate planning requires detailed knowledge of state and federal inheritance laws and tax laws. Attorneys working in this field advise clients as to the best means of accomplishing their goals.

Paralegals assist lawyers in estate planning by attending meetings, obtaining information from clients, and conducting legal research. Paralegals also assist lawyers in drafting wills, trust agreements, and other documents required to effectuate a client's estate plan.

Today, many individuals want to direct how their medical care will be handled if they are not able to make such decisions. Persons who do not want their life prolonged indefinitely by artificial means can sign a living will setting forth their wishes in advance. In addition, people can sign a health care proxy naming individuals to make medical decisions for them if they are unable to do so. Paralegals assist lawyers in drafting living wills, health care proxies, and other related documents in this field of law.

A relatively new area of the law involves living trusts, which persons establish while they are alive. A living trust is a method of holding property during one's lifetime and distributing that property upon his or her death. Living trusts have become a major form of estate planning. Paralegals assist lawyers in this area of the law by preparing the documents necessary to create the living trusts.

Elder law involves advising clients about their rights under government programs such as Social Security, Medicaid, and other government-sponsored programs for the elderly. Paralegals often are called upon to assist lawyers in obtaining such benefits for elderly clients.

The specialized and complex area of elder law provides substantial employment opportunities for paralegals. Paralegals who work in this field must have detailed knowledge of state and federal laws, regulations, procedures, forms, applications, and other documents necessary to carry forth the estate planning wishes and other goals of clients who are represented by the lawyer the paralegal works for.

Exhibit 16.1 Parties to a will

Testator
or
Testatrix
Will
A written document that names a beneficiary or beneficiaries to receive the testator's or testatrix's property upon the death of the testator or testatrix.
Beneficiary
or
Beneficiaries

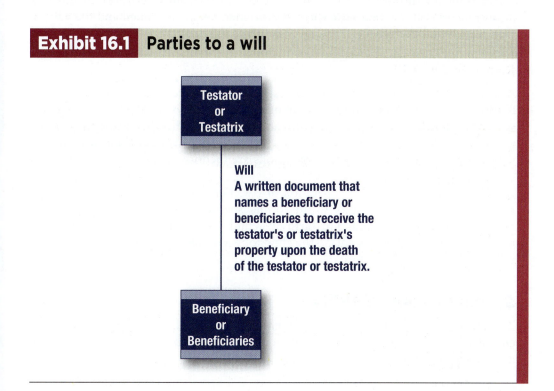

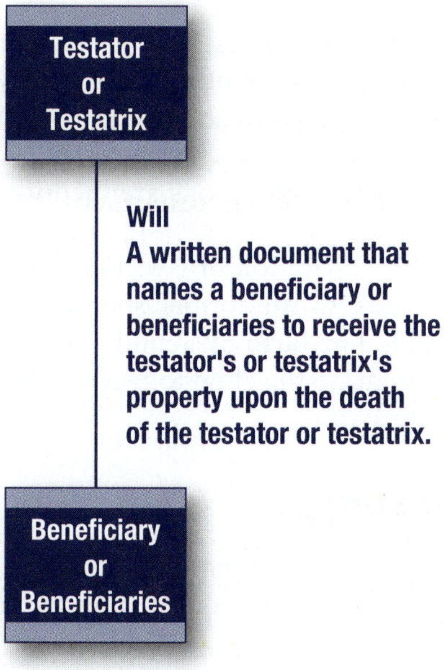

informal. Although most wills are typewritten, they can be handwritten (see the discussion of holographic wills). The writing may be on legal paper, scratch paper, envelopes, napkins, or other paper. A will may incorporate additional documents by reference.

- **Testator's signature.** Wills must be signed.

Most jurisdictions require the testator's signature to appear at the end of the will. This is to prevent the fraud that could occur if someone were to add provisions to the will below the testator's signature. Generally, courts have held that initials ("R. K. H."), a nickname ("Buffy"), a title ("mother"), or even an "X" is a valid signature on a will if it can be proven that the testator intended it to be his or her signature.

Attestation by Witnesses

Attestation The action of a will being witnessed by the required number of competent people.

Wills must be attested to by mentally competent witnesses. Although state law varies, most states require two or three witnesses to provide **attestation.** The witnesses do not have to reside in the jurisdiction in which the testator is domiciled. Most jurisdictions stipulate that interested parties (such as a beneficiary under the will or the testator's attorney) cannot be witnesses. If an interested party has attested to a will, state law either voids any clauses that benefit this party or voids the entire will.

Witnesses usually sign the will following the signature of the testator. This is called the **attestation clause.** Most jurisdictions require that each witness attest to the will in the presence of the other witnesses.

A will that meets the requirements of the Statute of Wills is called a *formal will.* A sample will is shown as Exhibit 16.2.

Changing a Will

Codicil A separate document that must be executed to amend a will. It must be executed with the same formalities as a will.

A will cannot be amended by merely striking out existing provisions and adding new ones. Rather, **codicils** are the legal way to change an existing will. A codicil is a separate document that must be executed with the same formalities as a will. In addition, it must incorporate by reference the will it is amending. The codicil and the will are then read as one instrument. A codicil is shown as Exhibit 16.3.

Revoking a Will

A will may be revoked by acts of the testator. A will is revoked if the testator intentionally burns, tears, obliterates, or otherwise destroys it. A properly executed **subsequent will** revokes a prior will if it specifically states that it is the testator's intention to do so. If the second will does not expressly revoke the prior will, the wills are read together. If any will provisions are inconsistent, the provisions in the second will control.

Wills can be revoked by operation of law. For example, divorce or annulment revokes disposition of property to the former spouse under the will. However, the remainder of the will is valid. The birth of a child after a will has been executed does not revoke the will but does entitle the child to receive his or her share of the parents' estate as determined by state statute.

Special Types of Wills

The law recognizes some types of wills that do not meet all of the requirements discussed above. Two special types of wills admitted by the courts are holographic wills and nuncupative wills.

Exhibit 16.2 Sample will

Last Will and Testament of Florence Winthorpe Blueblood

I, FLORENCE WINTHORPE BLUEBLOOD, presently residing at Boston, County of Suffolk, Massachusetts, being of sound and disposing mind and memory, hereby make, publish, and declare this to be my Last Will and Testament.

FIRST. I hereby revoke any and all Wills and Codicils previously made by me.

SECOND. I direct that my just debts and funeral expenses be paid out of my Estate as soon as practicable after my death.

THIRD. I am presently married to Theodore Hannah Blueblood III.

FOURTH. I hereby nominate and appoint my husband as the Personal Representative of this my Last Will and Testament. If he is unable to serve as Personal Representative, then I nominate and appoint Mildred Yardly Winthorpe as Personal Representative of this my Last Will and Testament. I direct that no bond or other security be required to be posted by my Personal Representative.

FIFTH. I hereby nominate and appoint my husband as Guardian of the person and property of my minor children. In the event that he is unable to serve as Guardian, then I nominate and appoint Mildred Yardly Winthorpe Guardian of the person and property of my minor children. I direct that no bond or other security be required to be posted by any Guardian herein.

SIXTH. I give my Personal Representative authority to exercise all the powers, rights, duties, and immunities conferred upon fiduciaries under law with full power to sell, mortgage, lease, invest, or reinvest all or any part of my Estate on such terms as he or she deems best.

SEVENTH. I hereby give, devise, and bequeath my entire estate to my husband, except for the following specific bequests:

I give my wedding ring to my daughter, Hillary Smythe Blueblood.

I give my baseball card collection to my son, Theodore Hannah Blueblood IV.

In the event that either my above-named daughter or son predeceases me, then and in that event, I give, devise, and bequeath my deceased daughter's or son's bequest to my husband.

EIGHTH. In the event that my husband shall predecease me, then and in that event, I give, devise and bequeath my entire estate, with the exception of the bequests in paragraph SEVENTH, to my beloved children or grandchildren surviving me, per stirpes.

NINTH. In the event I am not survived by my husband or any children or grandchildren, then and in that event, I give, devise, and bequeath my entire estate to Harvard University.

IN WITNESS WHEREOF, I Florence Winthorpe Blueblood, the Testatrix, sign my name to this Last Will and Testament this 3rd day of January, 2007.

____
(Signature)

Signed, sealed, published and declared by the above-named Testatrix, as and for her Last Will and Testament, in the presence of us, who at her request, in her presence and in the presence of one another, have hereunto subscribed our names as attesting witnesses, the day and year last written above.

Witness	*Address*

Exhibit 16.3 Sample codicil

SECOND CODICIL TO
THE LAST WILL AND TESTAMENT OF
SARA ELLIOTT

I, SARA ELLIOTT, of Scottsdale, Maricopa County, Arizona, declare this to be a Second Codicil to my Last Will and Testament dated March 13, 2000, and the Codicil to my Last Will and Testament dated June 22, 2002.

ARTICLE FIRST: I hereby revoke Article Third of my Will dated March 13, 2000, as amended by the Codicil of June 22, 2002, and substitute the following:

(a) I devise and bequeath all my jewelry to my daughter, Kaylee E. Sam, presently of Mesa, Arizona.

(b) I devise and bequeath the house and real property located at 1840 Norwood Place, Clearwater, Florida, to my daughter, Kaylee E. Sam, presently of Mesa, Arizona.

ARTICLE SECOND: I do hereby reaffirm all other provisions of my Last Will and Testament dated March 13, 2000, as amended by my First Codicil to my Last Will and Testament dated June 22, 2002.

IN WITNESS WHEREOF, I have hereunto set my hand this ____ day of ______________ 2007.

____
SARA ELLIOTT

The preceding instrument consisting of two typewritten pages, identified by the signature of the testatrix, was on the date thereof, signed, published and declared by SARA ELLIOTT in the presence of us who, in her presence and at her request and in the presence of each other, have subscribed our names as witnesses hereto.

____
(Name) *(Address)*

____
(Name) *(Address)*

____
(Name) *(Address)*

Holographic Wills

Holographic will A will that is entirely handwritten and signed by the testator.

Holographic wills are entirely handwritten and signed by the testator. The writing may be in ink, pencil, crayon, or some other writing instrument. Many states recognize the validity of such wills even though they are not witnessed.

Memorial Day The National Holiday Act, enacted by the U.S. Congress in 1971, made the last Monday in May Memorial Day. Memorial Day is a national holiday for remembrance of the veterans of the nation's military services.

Noncupative Wills

Nuncupative wills are oral wills made before witnesses. These wills are usually valid only if they are made during the testator's last illness. They sometimes are called **deathbed wills or dying declarations.**

Learning Objective 3
Distinguish between different forms of testamentary gifts.

Deathbed will (nuncupative will or dying declaration) An oral will that is made before a witness during the testator's last illness.

Testamentary Gifts

In a will, a gift of real estate by will is called a **devise.** A gift of personal property by will is called a **bequest** or **legacy.** Gifts in wills can be specific, general, or residuary.

- **Specific gifts** are specifically named pieces of property, such as a ring, a boat, or a piece of real estate.
- **General gifts** are gifts that do not identify the specific property from which the gift is to be made, such as a cash amount that can come from any source in the decedent's estate.
- **Residuary gifts** are established by a **residuary clause** in the will. The clause might state, for example, "I give my daughter the rest, remainder, and residual of my estate." This means that any portion of the estate left after the debts, taxes, and specific and general gifts have been paid belongs to the decedent's daughter.

Specific gift A gift of a specifically named piece of property.

General gift A gift that does not identify the specific property from which the gift is to be made.

Residuary gift A gift of the estate left after the debts, taxes, and specific and general gifts have been paid.

A person who inherits property under a will or an intestacy statute takes the property subject to all of the outstanding claims against it (such as liens or mortgages). A person can **renounce an inheritance**—and often does—when the liens or mortgages against the property exceed the value of the property.

Videotaped Wills

Many will contests involve written wills. The contesters allege things such as mental incapacity of the testator at the time the will was made, undue influence, fraud, or duress. Although the written will speaks for itself, the mental capacity of the testator and the voluntariness of his or her actions cannot be determined from the writing alone.

To prevent unwarranted will contests, a testator can use a **videotaped will** to supplement a written will. However, videotaping a will that can withstand challenges by disgruntled relatives and alleged heirs involves a certain amount of planning.

Web Exploration

Go to **http://www.cnn.com/WORLD/9803/04/diana.will/index.html** to read the will of Princess Diana of England.

The following procedure should be followed: A written will should be prepared to comply with the state's Statute of Wills. The video session should not begin until after the testator has become familiar with the document. The video should begin with the testator reciting the will verbatim. Next, the lawyer should ask the testator questions to demonstrate the testator's sound mind and understanding of the implications of his or her actions. The execution ceremony—the signing of the will by the testator and the attestation by the witnesses—should be the last segment on the film. The videotape then should be stored in a safe place.

With the testator's actions crystallized on videotape, a judge or jury will be able to determine the testator's mental capacity at the time the will was made and the voluntariness of his or her testamentary gifts. In addition, fraudulent competing wills will fall in the face of such proof.

Web Exploration

Go to **http://www.ibiblio.org/elvis/elvwill.html** to read the will of Elvis Presley, "The King."

Simultaneous Deaths

Sometimes people who would inherit property from each other die simultaneously. If it is impossible to determine who died first, the question becomes one of inheritance. The **Uniform Simultaneous Death Act** provides that each deceased person's property is distributed as if he or she survived.

Example Suppose a husband and wife make wills that leave their entire estate to each other. Assume that the husband and wife are killed simultaneously in an airplane crash. Here, the husband's property would go to his relatives and the wife's property would go to her relatives.

Joint and Mutual Wills

If two or more testators execute the same instrument as their will, the document is called a **joint will.** A joint will may be held invalid as to one testator but not to the other(s).

Mutual or **reciprocal wills** are developed when two or more testators execute separate wills that make testamentary dispositions of their property to each other on the condition that the survivor leave the remaining property on his or her death as agreed by the testators. The wills usually are separate instruments with reciprocal terms. Because of their contractual nature, mutual wills cannot be revoked unilaterally after one of the parties has died.

In the following feature, a paralegal professional discusses her specialty in the field of probate, trust administration, and estate planning.

Undue Influence

Undue influence Occurs where one person takes advantage of another person's mental, emotional, or physical weakness and unduly persuades that person to make a will; the persuasion by the wrongdoer must overcome the free will of the testator.

A will may be found to be invalid if it was made as a result of **undue influence** on the testator. Undue influence can be inferred from the facts and circumstances surrounding the making of the will. For example, if an 85-year-old woman leaves all of her property to the lawyer who drafted her will and ignores her blood relatives, the court is likely to presume undue influence.

Undue influence is difficult to prove by direct evidence, but it may be proved by circumstantial evidence. The elements that courts examine to detect the presence of undue influence include the following:

- The benefactor and beneficiary are involved in a relationship of confidence and trust.
- The will contains substantial benefit to the beneficiary.
- The beneficiary caused or assisted in effecting execution of the will.
- There was an opportunity to exert influence.
- The will contains an unnatural disposition of the testator's property.
- The bequests constitute a change from a former will.
- The testator was highly susceptible to the undue influence.

Paralegals *in* Practice

PARALEGAL PROFILE

Victoria M. Newman

Victoria M. Newman specializes in the legal areas of probate, trust administration, and estate planning. After working 28 years for Livingston, Stone & McGowan in San Francisco, California, she decided to become a contract paralegal. Vickie not only obtained the PACE™ Registered Paralegal® designation from the National Federation of Paralegal Associations (NFPA), but she also helps promote the PACE (Paralegal Advanced Competency Exam). As the current PACE Coordinator—Ambassadors, she develops guidelines and goals for the Ambassador Program, and assists PACE Ambassadors from NFPA member associations.

As a contract paralegal, I work mostly for solo legal practitioners and small law firms with less than ten attorneys. In addition to ethics, organizational skills, and efficient time management, some of the aptitudes most needed by someone in my position are:

- **People Skills.** In probate and trust administration, you work with people who are grieving and/or emotional. Thus, do not take behaviors personally, and gently remind clients of deadlines. In estate planning, you must frequently deal with procrastinators. Many clients avoid filling out the initial questionnaire, making it necessary to send out multiple reminders and/or call them.
- **Attentiveness to Details.** The probate process is very detail oriented. Not all probate, trust administrations, or estate plans are alike, even though procedures are much the same. Preparing and regularly updating checklists will help you monitor case progress, avoid missing deadlines, and quickly locate information.
- **Strong Mathematical and Analytical Skills.** Numbers are an integral part of probate and trust administration. For example, you will need to prepare court accountings, calculate distributions, allocate assets between trusts, determine if taxes are owed, and sometimes pro-rate taxes among beneficiaries.

My advice to new paralegals is to always keep current. Forms, laws, and codes change often. Simply using an outdated form might get your paperwork rejected by the court. Also, build relationships with people who can help you in unfamiliar situations. For example, in some courts, the probate examiners are available to answer procedural questions.

Probate

Learning Objective 4

Describe the process of probate.

When a person dies, his or her property must be collected, debts and taxes paid, and the remainder of the estate distributed to the beneficiaries of the will or the heirs under the state intestacy statute. This process is called **settlement of the estate** or **probate.** The process and procedures for settling an estate are governed by state statute. A specialized state court, called the probate court, usually supervises the administration and settlement of an estate.

Settlement of the estate (probate) The process of a deceased's property being collected, debts and taxes being paid, and the remainder of the estate being distributed.

A *personal representative* must be appointed to administer the estate during its settlement phase. If the testator's will names a personal representative, that person is called an **executor** or **executrix.** If a will does not name a personal representative, an **administrator** or an **administratrix** will be appointed by the probate court.

Initiation of the proceedings involving wills and the administration of estates may be delegated to the **Registrar of Wills,** who may be an elected official or one appointed to oversee the authentication of wills. The process, usually referred to as probate, starts with the filing of the will and any codicils to the will with the court. Typically this involves presenting the will, together with a death certificate, to the court-designated officers.

The named executor or executrix—or appointed administrator or administratrix—usually must appear at the same time and acknowledge his or her willingness to act as the executor or administrator. Depending upon the requirements of the local jurisdiction, the subscribing witnesses to the will also may be required to appear to authenticate their signatures and the will and the signature of the deceased.

Filing fees are part of the process, and appropriate checks for payment are generally required. Fees may vary depending upon the size of the probate estate. Additional forms may be required with regard to the assets and their values. In some jurisdictions, the Registrar of Wills or his or her agents may come to the attorney's office or to other locations as a convenience to the parties or when the parties, by virtue of age or disability, are unable to go to the courthouse.

The **Uniform Probate Code (UPC)** was promulgated to establish uniform rules for creating wills, administering estates, and resolving conflicts in estate settlements. These rules provide a speedy, efficient, and less expensive method than many existing state laws for settling estates. However, only about one-third of the states have adopted all or part of the UPC.

Lineal Descendants

Lineal descendants The testator's children, grandchildren, great-grandchildren, and so on.

***Per stirpes* distribution** A distribution of the estate that makes grandchildren and great-grandchildren of the deceased inherit by representation of their parent.

***Per capita* distribution** A distribution of the estate that makes each grandchild and great-grandchild of the deceased inherit equally with the children of the deceased.

A testator's will may state that property is to be left to his or her **lineal descendants** (children, grandchildren, great-grandchildren, or other relatives) either per stirpes or per capita. The difference between these two methods is discussed in the following paragraphs.

Per Stirpes Distribution

Pursuant to ***per stirpes* distribution,** the lineal descendants *inherit by representation of their parent*; that is, they split what their deceased parent would have received. If their parent is not deceased, they receive nothing.

Example Suppose Anne dies without a surviving spouse and she had three children, Bart, Beth, and Bruce. Bart, who survives his mother, has no children. Beth has one child, Carla, and they both survive Anne. Bruce, who predeceased his mother, had two children, Clayton and Cathy; and Cathy, who predeceased Anne, had two children, Deborah and Dominic, both of whom survive Anne.

If Anne leaves her estate to her lineal descendants *per stirpes*, Bart and Beth each get one-third, Carla receives nothing because Beth is alive, Clayton gets one-sixth, and Deborah and Dominic each get one-twelfth. Exhibit 16.4 illustrates this example.

Per Capita Distribution

Pursuant to ***per capita* distribution,** the lineal descendants equally share the property of the estate. That is, children of the testator share equally with grandchildren, great-grandchildren, and so forth.

Example Suppose the facts are the same as in the previous example, except that Anne leaves her estate to her lineal descendants *per capita*. In this case, all of the surviving lineal descendants—Bart, Beth, Carla, Clayton, Deborah, and Dominic—share equally in the estate. That is, they each get one-sixth of Anne's estate. See Exhibit 16.5.

Ademption and Abatement

Ademption A principle that says if a testator leaves a specific devise of property to a beneficiary, but the property is no longer in the estate when the testator dies, the beneficiary receives nothing.

Abatement If the property the testator leaves is not sufficient to satisfy all the beneficiaries named in a will and there are both general and residuary bequests, the residuary bequest is abated first (that is, paid last).

If a testator leaves a specific gift of property to a beneficiary, but the property is no longer in the estate of the testator when he or she dies, the beneficiary receives nothing. This doctrine is called the doctrine of **ademption.**

If the testator's estate is not large enough to pay all the devises and bequests, the doctrine of **abatement** applies. The doctrine works as follows:

- If a will provides for both general and residuary gifts, the residuary gifts are abated first.

  Example Suppose that when a testator owns $500,000 of property, he executes a will that leaves (1) $100,000 to the Red Cross, (2) $100,000 to a university, and (3) the residue to his niece. Suppose that when the testator dies, his estate is worth only $225,000. Here, the Red Cross and the university each receive $100,000 and the niece receives $25,000.

- If a will provides only for general gifts, the reductions are proportionate.

  Example Suppose a testator's will leaves $75,000 to two beneficiaries, but the estate is only $100,000. Each beneficiary would receive $50,000.

Exhibit 16.4 Example of *per stirpes* distribution

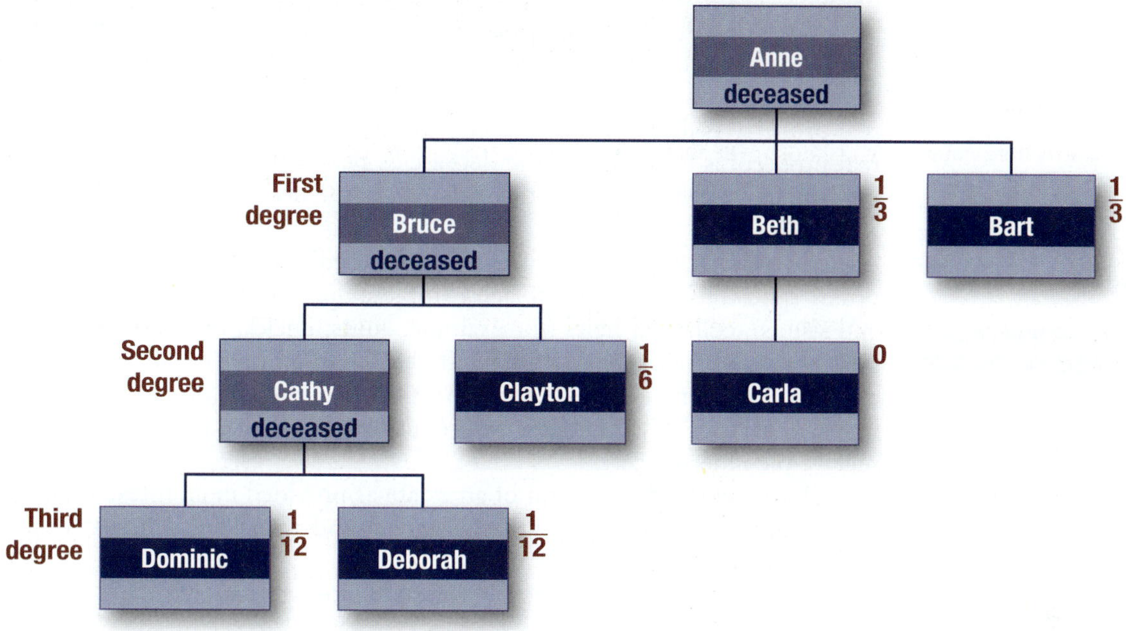

Anne
deceased

First degree
Bruce
deceased
Beth $\frac{1}{3}$
Bart $\frac{1}{3}$

Second degree
Cathy
deceased
Clayton $\frac{1}{6}$
Carla 0

Third degree
Dominic $\frac{1}{12}$
Deborah $\frac{1}{12}$

Exhibit 16.5 Example of *per capita* distribution

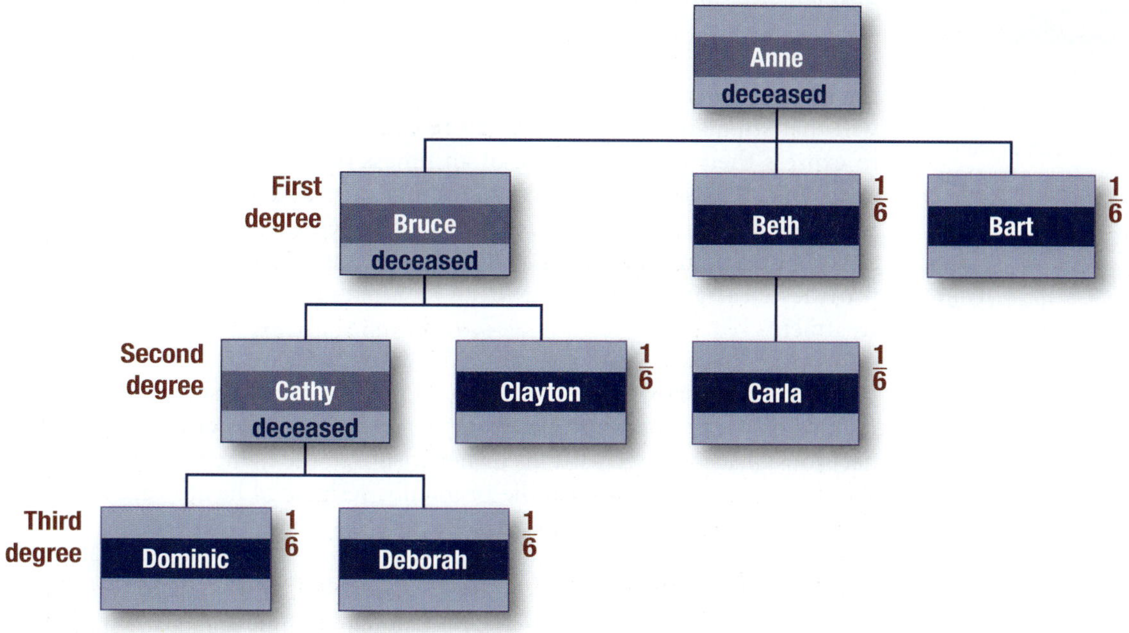

Anne
deceased

First degree
Bruce
deceased
Beth $\frac{1}{6}$
Bart $\frac{1}{6}$

Second degree
Cathy
deceased
Clayton $\frac{1}{6}$
Carla $\frac{1}{6}$

Third degree
Dominic $\frac{1}{6}$
Deborah $\frac{1}{6}$

Learning Objective 5

Define an *intestacy statute* and identify how property is distributed if a person dies without a will or living trust.

Intestate The state of having died without leaving a will.

Intestacy statute A state statute that specifies how a deceased's property will be distributed if he or she dies without a will or if the last will is declared void and there is no prior valid will.

SIDEBAR

COMPARISON OF DYING WITH AND WITHOUT A VALID WILL

Situation	Parties Who Receive Deceased's Property
Deceased dies with a valid will	Beneficiaries named in the will.
Deceased dies without a valid will	Heirs set forth in the applicable state intestacy statute. If no heirs, the deceased's property escheats to the state.

Learning Objective 6

Explain what a living will and a health care directive are.

Web Exploration

Go to **http://livingtrustnetwork.com/index.php?option=com_content&task=view&id=64&Itemid=44**. On the map that appears, click on your state and read the intestacy law of your state.

Living will A document that states which life-saving measures the signer does and does not want, and can specify that he or she wants such treatments withdrawn if doctors determine that there is no hope of a meaningful recovery.

Health care directive (health care proxy) A document in which the maker names someone to be his or her health care agent to make all health care decisions in accordance with his or her wishes in the living will.

Intestate Succession

If a person dies without a will or living trust, or his or her will or living trust fails for some legal reason, that person dies **intestate.** In this case, the deceased person's property is distributed to his or her relatives pursuant to the state's **intestacy statute.**

Relatives who receive property under these statutes are called **heirs.** Although intestacy statutes differ from state to state, the general rule is that the deceased's real property is distributed according to the intestacy statute of the state where the real property is located, and the deceased's personal property is distributed according to the intestacy statute of the state where the deceased had his or her permanent residence.

Intestacy statutes usually leave the deceased's property to his or her heirs in this order: spouse, children, lineal heirs (for example, grandchildren, parents, brothers and sisters), collateral heirs (for example, aunts, uncles, nieces, nephews), and other next of kin (for example, cousins). If the deceased had no surviving relatives, the deceased's property **escheats** (goes) to the state. In-laws do not inherit under most intestacy statutes. If a child dies before his or her parents, the child's spouse does not receive the inheritance.

To avoid the distribution of an estate as provided in an intestacy statute, a person should have a properly written, signed, and witnessed will that distributes the estate property as the testator wishes.

Exhibit 16.6 sets forth the Florida state intestacy statute.

Living Will and Health Care Directive

Technological breakthroughs have greatly increased the life span of human beings. This same technology, however, permits life to be sustained long after a person is "brain dead." Some people say they have a right to refuse such treatment. Others argue that human life must be preserved at all costs. In 1990, the U.S. Supreme Court was called upon to decide the **right to die** issue. See *Cruzan v. Director, Missouri Department of Health*, 497 U.S. 261, 110 S.Ct. 2841, 111 L.Ed.2d 224, 1990 U.S. Lexis 3301 (1990).

In the *Cruzan* case, the U.S. Supreme Court acknowledged that the right to refuse medical treatment is a personal liberty protected by the Due Process Clause of the U.S. Constitution. The Court also stated that this interest must be expressed through clear and convincing proof that the patient did not want to be sustained by artificial means.

The clear message of the Supreme Court's opinion is that people who do not want their lives prolonged indefinitely by artificial means should sign a **living will** that stipulates their wishes before catastrophe strikes and they become unable to express their wishes because of an illness or an accident. The living will should state which life-saving measures the signer does and does not want. In addition, the signer can specify that he or she wants to have any such treatments withdrawn if doctors determine that there is no hope of a meaningful recovery. The living will provides clear and convincing proof of a patient's wishes with respect to medical treatment.

In a living will, or in a separate document usually called a **health care directive** or **health care proxy**, the maker should name someone, such as a spouse or another relative or trusted party, to be his or her **health care agent** to make all health care decisions in accordance with his or her wishes in the living will. An alternative person should also be named in case the originally designated health care agent is unable or chooses not to serve in that capacity.

A well-known example in which a person didn't have a living will and health care proxy was the Terri Schiavo case. In February 1990, Terri collapsed and was placed on life support systems. For 15 years, Terri remained in a vegetative state. Her husband wanted Terri to be taken off the life support systems, but her parents did not. After

Exhibit 16.6 Florida intestacy statute

Intestate Estate

(1) Any part of the estate of a decedent not effectively disposed of by will passes to the decedent's heirs as prescribed in the following section of this code.
(2) The decedent's death is the event that vests the heirs' right to the decedent's intestate property. Florida Statutes, 732.101

Spouse's Share of Intestate Estate

The intestate share of the surviving spouse is:

(1) If there is no surviving descendant of the decedent, the entire intestate estate.
(2) If there are surviving descendants of the decedent, all of whom are also lineal descendants of the surviving spouse, the first $60,000 of the intestate estate, plus one-half of the balance of the intestate estate. Property allocated to the surviving spouse to satisfy the $60,000 shall be valued at the market value on the date of distribution.
(3) If there are surviving descendants, one or more of whom are not lineal descendants of the surviving spouse, one-half of the intestate estate. Florida Statutes, 732.102

Share of Other Heirs

The part of the intestate estate not passing to the surviving spouse under s. 732.102, or the entire intestate estate if there is no surviving spouse, descends as follows:

(1) To the descendants of the decedent.
(2) If there is no descendant, to the decedent's father and mother equally, or to the survivor of them.
(3) If there is none of the foregoing, to the decedent's brothers and sisters and the descendants of deceased brothers and sisters.
(4) If there is none of the foregoing, the estate shall be divided, one-half of which shall go to the decedent's paternal, and the other half to the decedent's maternal, kindred in the following order:
    (a) To the grandfather and grandmother equally, or to the survivor of them.
    (b) If there is no grandfather or grandmother, to uncles and aunts and descendants of deceased uncles and aunts of the decedent.
    (c) If there is either no paternal kindred or no maternal kindred, the estate shall go to the other kindred who survive, in the order stated above.
(5) If there is no kindred of either part, the whole of the property shall go to the kindred of the last deceased spouse of the decedent as if the deceased spouse had survived the decedent and then died intestate entitled to the estate.
(6) If none of the foregoing, and if any of the descendants of the decedent's great-grandparents were Holocaust victims as defined in s. 626.9543(3)(a), including such victims in countries cooperating with the discriminatory policies of Nazi Germany, then to the descendants of the great-grandparents. The court shall allow any such descendant to meet a reasonable, not unduly restrictive, standard of proof to substantiate his or her lineage. This subsection only applies to escheated property and shall cease to be effective for proceedings filed after December 31, 2004. Florida Statutes, 732.103

Inheritance Per Stirpes

Descent shall be per stirpes, whether to descendants or to collateral heirs. Florida Statutes, 732.104

Half Blood

When property descends to the collateral kindred of the intestate and part of the collateral kindred are of the whole blood to the intestate and the other part of the half blood, those of the half blood shall inherit only half as much as those of the whole blood; but if all are of the half blood they shall have whole parts. Florida Statutes. 732.105

Afterborn Heirs

Heirs of the decedent conceived before his or her death, but born thereafter, inherit intestate property as if they had been born in the decedent's lifetime. Florida Statutes, 732.106

(continued)

Exhibit 16.6 Florida intestacy statute (*continued*)

Escheat

(1) When a person dies leaving an estate without being survived by any person entitled to a part of it, that part shall escheat to the state.
(2) Property that escheats shall be sold as provided in the Florida Probate Rules and the proceeds paid to the Chief Financial Officer of the state and deposited in the State School Fund.
(3) At any time within 10 years after the payment to the Chief Financial Officer, a person claiming to be entitled to the proceeds may reopen the administration to assert entitlement to the proceeds. If no claim is timely asserted, the state's rights to the proceeds shall become absolute.
(4) The Department of Legal Affairs shall represent the state in all proceedings concerning escheated estates. Florida Statutes, 732.107

Adopted Persons and Persons Born out of Wedlock

(1) For the purpose of intestate succession by or from an adopted person, the adopted person is a descendant of the adopting parent and is one of the natural kindred of all members of the adopting parent's family, and is not a descendant of his of her natural parents, nor is he or she one of the kindred of any member of the natural parent's family or any prior adoptive parent's family, except that:
   (a) Adoption of a child by the spouse of a natural parent has no effect on the relationship between the child and the natural parent or the natural parent's family.
   (b) Adoption of a child by a natural parent's spouse who married the natural parent after the death of the other natural parent has no effect on the relationship between the child and the family of the deceased natural parent.
   (c) Adoption of a child by a close relative, as defined in s. 63.172(2), has no effect on the relationship between the child and the families of the deceased natural parents.
(2) For the purpose of intestate succession in cases not covered by subsection (1), a person bore out of wedlock is a descendant of his or her mother and is one of the natural kindred of all members of the mother's family. The person is also a descendant of his or her father and is one of the natural kindred of all members of the father's family, if:
   (a) The natural parents participated in a marriage ceremony before or after the birth of the person born out of wedlock, even though the attempted marriage is void.
   (b) The paternity of the father is established by an adjudication before or after the death of the father.
   (c) The paternity of the father is acknowledged in writing by the father. Florida Statutes, 732.108

Aliens

Aliens shall have the same rights of inheritance as citizens. Florida Statutes. 32.1101.

Trust A legal arrangement established when one person transfers title to property to another person to be held and used for the benefit of a third person.

Learning Objective 7
Define *trust* and identify the parties to a trust.

Settlor, trustor, or transferor A person who creates a trust.

Trustee A person or entity that holds legal title to the trust *corpus* and manages the trust for the benefit of the beneficiary or beneficiaries.

years of legal battles that included more than fifty trial and appellate court hearings, in April 2005 the Florida Supreme Court ordered Terri to be taken off life support systems. Days later she died.

Much of the legal battle concerned what Terri's intention would have been about staying on, or being removed from, life support systems. If Terri had had a living will and health care proxy, her intentions would have been clear. A living will and health care proxy is set forth in Exhibit 16.7.

Trusts

A **trust** is a legal arrangement under which one person—the **settlor, trustor,** or **transferor**—delivers and transfers legal title to property to another person, bank, or other entity, called the **trustee,** to be held and used for the benefit of a third person or entity (the **beneficiary of a trust**). The property and assets held in trust are called the **trust *corpus* or trust *res*.** The trust has legal title to the trust *corpus*, and the beneficiary has equitable title. Unlike wills, trusts are not public documents, so property can be transferred in privacy.

Exhibit 16.7 Sample living will and health care proxy

Living Will and Health Care Proxy

I. Living Will Including Statement Concerning Right to Die

Death is as much a reality as birth, growth, maturity and old age—it is the one certainty of life. If the time comes when I, John Doe, can no longer take part in decisions for my own future, let this statement stand as an expression of my wishes and directions to my Health Care Agent and others while I am still of sound mind. I intend, without otherwise limiting the absolute authority granted to my Health Care Agent in this instrument, that this instrument be binding upon my Health Care Agent.

If the situation should arise in which there is no reasonable expectation of my recovery from extreme physical or mental disability, including, but not limited to, a circumstance where there is no reasonable expectation that I will recover consciousness, commonly referred to as "brain dead," I direct that I be allowed to die and not be kept alive by medications, artificial means, including but not limited to artificial nutrition and hydration, or "heroic measures." Without limiting the generality of the foregoing, I hereby consent in such situation to an order not to attempt cardiopulmonary resuscitation. I do, however, ask that medication be mercifully administered to me to alleviate suffering even though this may shorten my remaining life and retard my consciousness.

II. Health Care Proxy

I hereby appoint my spouse, Jane Doe, to be my health care agent to make any and all health care decisions in accordance with my wishes and instructions as stated above and as otherwise known to her. In the event the person I appoint above is unable, unwilling or unavailable to act as my Health Care Agent, I hereby appoint my twin brother, Jack Doe, as my Health Care Agent.

This health care proxy shall take effect in the event that I become unable to make my own health care decisions. I hereby revoke any prior health care proxy given by me to the extent it purports to confer the authority herein granted. I understand that, unless I revoke it, this health care proxy will remain in effect indefinitely.

Although I do not know today the exact circumstances that will exist when my Health Care Agent is called upon to make a decision or decisions on my behalf, I have selected my Health Care Agent with the confidence that such person understands my feelings in these matters and will make the decision I will want made considering the circumstances as they exist at the time. It is my intention, therefore, that the decision of my Health Care Agent be taken as a final and binding decision of mine, and will be the conclusive interpretation of the wishes I have made known in this document.

III. Waiver and Indemnity

To the extent permitted by law, I, for myself and for my heirs, executors, legal representatives and assigns, hereby release and discharge and agree to indemnify and hold harmless my Health Care Agent from and against any claim or liability whatsoever resulting from or arising out of my Health Care Agent's reliance on my wishes and directions as expressed herein. To induce any third party to act hereunder, I hereby agree that any third party receiving a duly executed copy or facsimile of this instrument may act hereunder, and that revocation or termination by me hereof shall be ineffective as to such third party unless and until actual notice or knowledge of such revocation shall have been received by such third party, and, to the extent permitted by law, I, for myself and for my heirs, executors, legal representatives and assigns, hereby release and discharge and agree to indemnify and hold harmless any such third party from and against any claims or liability whatsoever that may arise against such third party by reason of such third party having relied on the provisions of this instrument.

I understand the full import of this directive and I am emotionally and mentally competent to make this directive.

Signed ______________________________

The declarant has been personally known to me and I believe him or her to be of sound mind.

Witness ______________________________

Witness ______________________________

A trust can be created and become effective during a trustor's lifetime, or it can be created during a trustor's lifetime to become effective upon the trustor's death.

During the existence of the trust, the trustee collects money owed to the trust, pays taxes and necessary expenses of the trust, makes investment decisions, pays the income to the income beneficiary, and keeps necessary records of transactions.

Trusts often provide that any trust income is to be paid to a person or entity called the **income beneficiary.** The person or entity to receive the trust *corpus* upon the termination of the trust is called the **remainder beneficiary.** The income

Trust *corpus* or trust *res* The property and assets held in trust.

Income beneficiary A person or entity to be paid income from the trust.

Remainder beneficiary A person or entity to receive the trust *corpus* upon termination of the trust.

beneficiary and the remainder beneficiary can be the same person or different persons. The designated beneficiary can be any identifiable person, animal (such as a pet), charitable organization, or other institution or cause that the settlor chooses. There can be multiple income and remainder beneficiaries. An entire class of persons—for example, "my grandchildren"—can be named.

A trust can allow the trustee to invade (use) the trust *corpus* for certain purposes. These purposes can be named (such as, "for the beneficiary's college education"). The trust agreement usually specifies how the receipts and expenses of the trust are to be divided between the income beneficiary and the remainder beneficiary.

Generally, the trustee has broad management powers over the trust property. Thus, the trustee can invest the trust property to preserve its capital and make it productive. The trustee must follow any restrictions on investments contained in the trust agreement or state statute.

Exhibit 16.8 shows the parties to a trust.

Exhibit 16.8 Parties to a trust

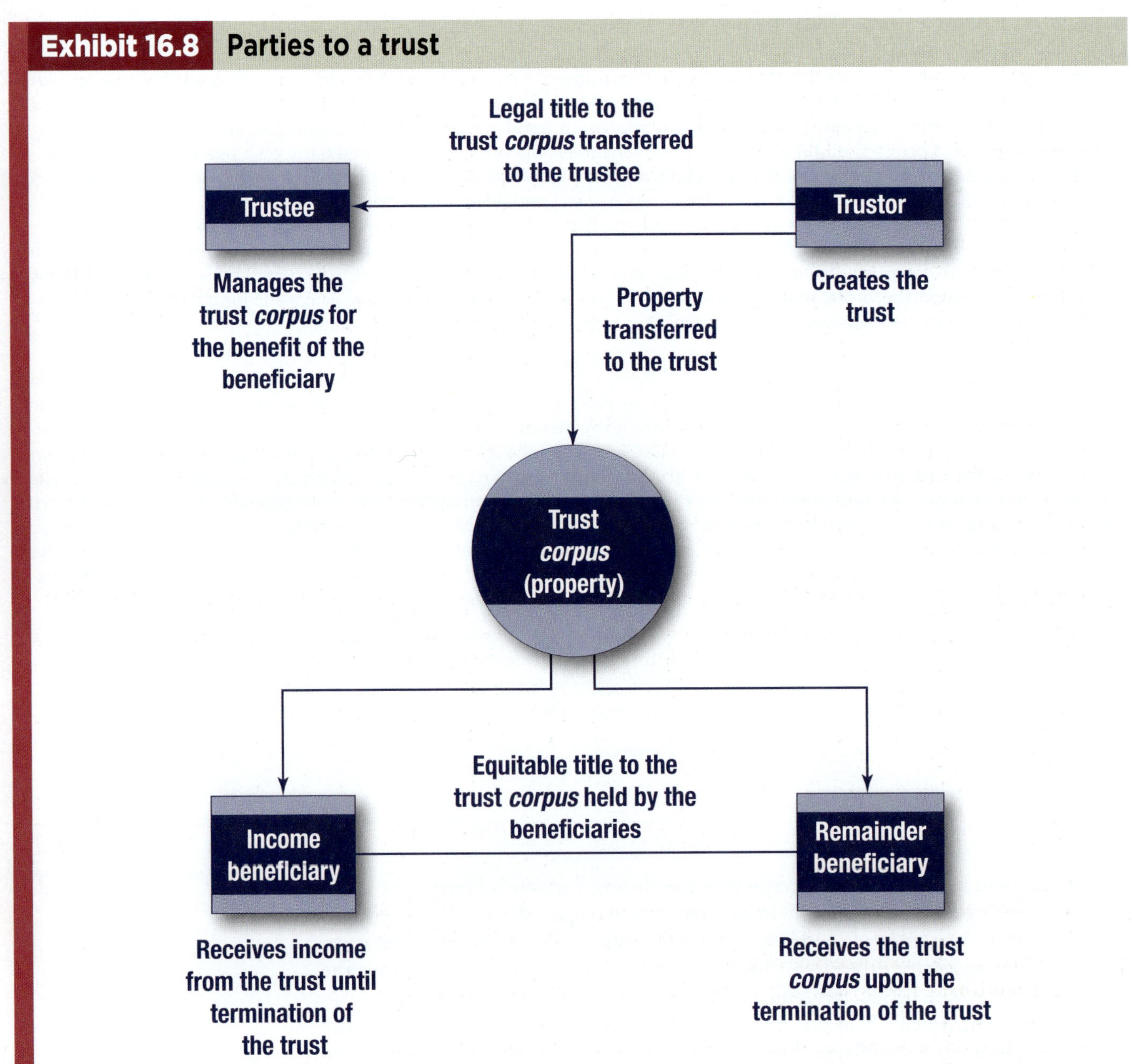

Express Trust

An **express trust** is created voluntarily by the settlor. It usually is written. The agreement is called a *trust instrument* or *trust agreement*. Express trusts fall into two categories:

Express trust A trust created voluntarily by the settlor.

1. ***Inter vivos* trust,** created while the settlor is alive. The settlor transfers legal title of property to a named trustee to hold, administer, and manage for the benefit of named beneficiaries.
2. **Testamentary trust,** created by will. The trust comes into existence when the settlor dies. If the will that establishes the trust is found to be invalid, the trust is also invalid.

***Inter vivos* trust** A trust that is created while the settlor is alive.

Testamentary trust A trust created by will; thus the trust comes into existence when the settlor dies.

Example Suppose a grandmother creates a testamentary trust and places assets in the trust that consist of stocks, bonds, bank accounts, and an apartment building. In the trust document, the grandmother designates her daughter to receive the income from the trust (such as dividends, interest, and rental income) until the daughter dies, and upon the daughter's death, the trust *corpus* is to be divided equally among the grandmother's three granddaughters. The grandmother names Country Bank the trustee. Thus the grandmother is the trustor, Country Bank is the trustee, the daughter is the income beneficiary, and the three granddaughters are the remainder beneficiaries.

Constructive Trust

A **constructive trust** is an equitable trust that is implied by law to avoid fraud, unjust enrichment, and injustice. In constructive trust arrangements, the holder of the actual title to property (that is, the trustee) holds the property in trust for its rightful owner.

Constructive trust An equitable trust that is implied by law to avoid fraud, unjust enrichment, and injustice.

Example Suppose Thad and Kaye are partners. Assume Kaye embezzles partnership funds and uses the stolen funds to purchase a piece of real estate. In this case, the court can impose a constructive trust under which Kaye (who holds actual title to the land) is considered a trustee who is holding the property in trust for Thad, its rightful owner.

Resulting Trust

A **resulting trust** is implied from the conduct of the parties.

Resulting trust A trust that is implied by the conduct of the parties.

Example Suppose Henry is purchasing a piece of real estate but cannot attend the closing. He asks his brother, Gregory, to attend the closing and take title to the property until he, Henry, can return. In this case, Gregory holds the title to the property as trustee for Henry until he returns.

Special Types of Trusts

Trusts may be created for special purposes. Three types of special trusts that are fairly common are:

1. **Charitable trusts,** created for the benefit of a segment of society or society in general. An example is a trust that is created for the construction and maintenance of a public park.
2. **Spendthrift trusts,** designed to prevent a beneficiary's personal creditors from reaching his or her trust interest. All control over the trust is removed from the beneficiary. Personal creditors can still go after trust income that is paid to the beneficiary, however.

3. **Totten trusts,** created when a person deposits money in a bank account in his or her own name and holds it as a trustee for the benefit of another person. A totten trust is a tentative trust because (a) the trustee can add or withdraw funds from the account, and (b) the trust can be revoked at any time prior to the trustee's death or prior to completing delivery of the funds to the beneficiary.

Termination of a Trust

A trust is irrevocable unless the settlor reserves the right to revoke it. Most trusts fall into the first category. Usually, a trust either contains a specific termination date or provides that it will terminate upon the happening of an event (such as when the remainder beneficiary reaches a certain age). Upon termination, the trust *corpus* is distributed as provided in the trust agreement.

The ethical duty of a paralegal professional to act honestly and not misappropriate client funds is discussed in the following feature.

Learning Objective 8

Describe a living trust and the benefits of a living trust.

Living Trusts

Living trust A method for holding property during a person's lifetime and distributing the property upon that person's death. Also called a *grantor's trust* and a *revocable trust.*

Grantor (trustor) The person who creates a living trust.

Living trusts have become a popular method for holding property during a person's lifetime and for distributing that property upon the person's death. A living trust works as follows: During his or her life, a person establishes a living trust, which is a legal entity used for estate planning. A living trust is also referred to as a **grantor's trust** or a **revocable trust.** The person who creates the trust is called the **grantor,** or the **trustor.**

ETHICAL PERSPECTIVE

Paralegal's Duty Not to Misappropriate Trust Funds

Ms. Nottingham, a paralegal, works for attorney Mr. Zachery, who is a partner in a law firm. Mr. Zachery is an estate attorney. A client who is the executor of a will employs Mr. Zachery's law firm to handle the probate of the will. The assets of the estate consist of several pieces of real property, securities, bank accounts, and bearer bonds. The total value of the estate is $4 million. The beneficiaries of the will are the deceased's three children, who are to split the estate equally. Mr. Zachery assigns Ms. Nottingham to assist him in handling the estate.

Bearer bonds are bonds that are payable to the bearer—that is, to the person in possession of the bonds. The bearer bonds, totaling $300,000, are placed in the trust account of the law firm of which Mr. Zachery is a partner.

Ms. Nottingham, as the paralegal on the estate, has access to the bearer bonds. She is also in financial difficulty because of the accumulation of too much credit card and other debt, and faces the possibility of losing her house to foreclosure because of nonpayment of her mortgage. Ms. Nottingham sees no way to avoid losing her home and having to declare bankruptcy.

However, she soon realizes the significance of the bearer bonds: Whoever possesses them may cash them in and obtain payment from the issuer of the bonds. Ms. Nottingham steals the bearer bonds, delivers them to the issuer, and receives the $300,000 in cash. She then pays off her mortgage and other debts.

Soon after, the law firm discovers Ms. Nottingham's action. In this case, she has violated model and state codes of ethical conduct for paralegal professionals. As such, the state board that licenses paralegals could rescind her license to practice as a paralegal. In addition, the lawyers are under an ethical duty to report the defalcation to the client and to the law firm's insurance carrier. If there were no insurance carrier or the insurance did not cover such a loss, the law firm would be responsible for paying the loss. Ms. Nottingham has also violated the law by her action. She could face criminal charges by the state, and, if convicted, could be sentenced to jail.

Benefits of a Living Trust

The primary purpose of a living trust is being able to avoid the probate associated with using a will. If a person dies with a will, the will must be probated so that the deceased's assets can be properly distributed according to the will. A probate judge is named to oversee the probate process, and all documents, including the will, are public record. By contrast, a living trust is private.

When the grantor dies, the assets are owned by the living trust and therefore are not subject to probate proceedings. In addition, if real property is owned in more than one state and a will is used, ancillary probate must be conducted in the other state, whereas if a living trust is used, ancillary probate is avoided.

Living trusts are often promoted as having benefits that they do not actually have. The truth is that a living trust:

- does not reduce estate taxes any more than a will does.
- does not reduce the grantor's income taxes. All the income earned by the trust is attributed to the grantor, who must pay income taxes on the earnings just as if the trust did not exist.
- does not avoid creditors. Thus, creditors can obtain liens against property in the trust.
- is subject to property division upon divorce.
- is usually not cheaper than a will. Both require payments to lawyers and usually to accountants and other professionals who draft and probate a will or draft and manage a living trust.
- does not avoid controversies upon the grantor's death. Like wills, living trusts can be challenged for lack of capacity, undue influence, duress, and other legal grounds.

Another good thing about being poor is that when you are seventy your children will not have you declared legally insane in order to gain control of your estate.

Woody Allen

Funding and Operation of a Living Trust

To fund a living trust, the grantor transfers to the trust the title to his or her property. This property is called the trust *corpus*. Bank accounts, stock certificates, real estate, personal property, intangible property, and other property owned by the grantor must be retitled to the trust's name.

For example, the grantor must execute deeds transferring title to real estate to the trust. Once property is transferred to the trust, the trust is considered funded. A living trust is revocable during the grantor's lifetime. Thus, a grantor can later change his or her mind and undo the trust and retake title of the property in his or her own name.

A living trust names a trustee who is responsible for maintaining, investing, buying, or selling trust assets. The trustee is usually the grantor. Thus, the grantor who establishes the trust does not lose control of the property placed in the trust and may manage and invest trust assets during his or her lifetime. The trust should also name a *successor trustee* to replace the grantor–trustee if the grantor becomes incapacitated or too ill to manage the trust.

Beneficiaries

A living trust names a beneficiary or beneficiaries who is/are entitled to receive income from the living trust while it is in existence and to receive the property of the trust when the grantor dies. Usually the grantor is the income beneficiary, who receives the income from the trust during his or her lifetime. Upon the death of the grantor, assets of the trust are distributed to the remainder beneficiary or beneficiaries named in the trust. The designated trustee has the fiduciary duties of identifying assets, paying creditors, paying income and estate taxes, transferring assets to named beneficiaries, and rendering an accounting.

A sample living trust is shown as Exhibit 16.9.

Exhibit 16.9 Sample living trust

Revocable Living Trust

Article 1 Name of Trust

The name of this revocable living trust is the Vivienne Lorraine Anderson Trust (trust).

Article 2 Declaration of Trust

Vivienne Lorraine Anderson, called the grantor, declares that she has transferred and delivered to the trustee all of her interest in the property described in Schedule A attached to this Declaration of Trust (trust property).

Article 3 Additions to the Trust

The grantor may add property to the trust.

Article 4 Amendment

The grantor may amend this trust at any time. An amendment must be made in writing and signed by the grantor.

Article 5 Revocation

The grantor may revoke this trust at any time. Revocation may be in writing or any manner allowed by law.

Article 6 Trustee

The trustee of the trust shall be Vivienne Lorraine Anderson. The trustee acknowledges receipt of the trust property. The trustee agrees to hold the property in trust according to the provisions of the Declaration of Trust.

Article 7 Successor Trustee

In the event of the death or incapacity of the grantor, the trustee of this trust shall be Harold Robert Anderson. In the event of the death, incapacity, refusal, or removal of Harold Robert Anderson as trustee, the trustee of the trust shall be Julia Kay Simpson. In the event of the death, incapacity, refusal, or removal of Julia Kay Simpson as trustee, the trustee of the trust shall be Edgar Neil Anderson.

Article 8 Removal of Trustee

The grantor may remove any trustee or successor trustee.

Article 9 Resignation of Trustee

A trustee or successor trustee may resign at any time. If a successor trustee named in this Declaration of Trust is unable or unwilling to serve as trustee, the last acting trustee may appoint a successor trustee.

Exhibit 16.9 Sample living trust *(continued)*

Article 10 Compensation of Trustee
A trustee shall not be paid compensation for acting as a trustee of this trust.

Article 11 Bond
A trustee or successor trustee is not required to post a bond.

Article 12 Annual Statements by Successor Trustee
A successor trustee shall furnish annual statements to the beneficiaries of the trust showing the disbursements, receipts, and assets of the trust.

Article 13 Liability of Trustee
A trustee shall not be liable for exercising or not exercising discretionary powers granted by the trust if such actions were taken in good faith.

Article 14 Withdrawal of Assets
The grantor may withdraw all or any part of the assets of the trust.

Article 15 Powers of Trustee
The trustee shall have the powers permitted by law, which include, but are not limited to:

1. To manage trust property as if the trustee were the owner of the trust property.
2. To sell trust property.
3. To borrow money, to encumber trust property, including trust real estate, and to execute promissory notes, mortgages, deeds of trust, or other obligations on behalf of the trust.
4. To lease trust property.
5. To grant options to sell or lease trust property.
6. To invest trust property in every kind of investment, including but not limited to real property, personal property, stocks, bonds, debentures, notes, mortgages, stock options, mutual funds, commodities, options, futures, and to purchase investments on margin.
7. To deposit and hold funds in bank accounts, money market accounts, or other accounts, whether interest bearing or noninterest bearing, and whether FDIC insured or not, and to enter into electronic funds transfers with financial institutions.
8. To receive property and add it to the trust.
9. To operate and continue any business owned or operated by the grantor.
10. To defend or institute legal actions concerning the trust or grantor's affairs.
11. To enter into contracts and execute any documents necessary to administer the trust.
12. To employ and pay reasonable fees to accountants, lawyers, investment advisors, and experts for the administration of the trust.

Article 16 Death of Grantor
This trust becomes irrevocable when the grantor dies. The trustee may pay out of trust property amounts necessary to pay grantor's debts, expenses, and estate taxes.

Article 17 Homestead Rights
The grantor has the right to possess and occupy her principal residence for life, without charge except payment of taxes, insurance, maintenance, and costs. This right gives the grantor beneficial interest in the property and ensures that the grantor qualifies for the state homestead exemption.

(continued)

Exhibit 16.9 Sample living trust *(continued)*

Article 18 Beneficiaries

The trustee, at the death of the grantor, shall distribute the trust property as follows:

Edgar Neil Anderson, grantor's son, shall be given the real property located on Graham Avenue, Petoskey, Michigan; If Edgar Neil Anderson does not survive the grantor, that property shall be given to Addison Carol Anderson and Liam Perry Anderson, equally.

Julia Kay Simpson, grantor's daughter, shall be given the real property located on Bay Lane, Boca Raton, Florida; If Julia Kay Simpson does not survive the grantor, that property shall be given to Sally Anderson Simpson.

Addison Carol Anderson, grantor's granddaughter, shall be given the shares of the United States Mutual Fund.

Liam Perry Anderson, grantor's grandson, shall be given the shares of the International Mutual fund.

Sally Anderson Simpson, grantor's granddaughter, shall be given the real property located on Pine Shores Drive, Mackinac Island, Michigan.

Clifford Albert Anderson, grantor's brother, shall be given the shares of First National Bank; If Clifford Albert Anderson does not survive the grantor, that property shall be given to Cathleen Kay Anderson.

The University of Chicago shall be given $100,000.

Harold Robert Anderson, grantor's spouse, shall be given grantor's interest in trust property not otherwise specifically and validly disposed of by this Article. If Harold Robert Anderson does not survive the grantor, that property shall be given to Edgar Neil Anderson and Julia Kay Simpson equally.

Article 19 Survivorship of Beneficiaries

A beneficiary must survive the grantor by 168 hours to receive property under the trust.

Article 20 Uniform Transfers to Minors Act

All distributions are subject to the provisions of the state's Uniform Transfers to Minors Act.

Article 21 Custodianship

If property is given by the trust to a beneficiary named in this trust that is under the age of 21, Julia Kay Simpson shall be custodian for that beneficiary until that beneficiary reaches the age of 21. If Julia Kay Simpson is unable or ceases to serve as custodian, Edgar Neil Anderson shall serve as custodian.

Article 22 Encumbrances and Liens

All real and personal property left by this trust shall pass subject to any encumbrances or liens placed on the property as security for the repayment of a loan or debt.

Article 23 Severability of Clauses

If any provision of this Declaration of Trust is ruled unenforceable, the remaining provisions shall stay in effect.

Certification of Grantor

I certify that I have read this Declaration of Trust and that it correctly states the terms and conditions under which the trust property is to be held, managed, and disposed of by the trustee, and I approve the Declaration of Trust.

Vivienne Lorraine Anderson April 2, 2013

Vivienne Lorraine Anderson Date

Pour-Over Will

A **pour-over will,** which is usually created at the same time that the living trust is established, is necessary to distribute any property acquired in the name of the grantor after the living trust is established or any property that was not transferred to the trust in the first place. The pour-over will transfers this property to the trust upon the grantor's death, and it is then distributed to the named beneficiaries of the trust. A pour-over will is subject to probate and is therefore public.

Pour-over will A will that, upon the grantor's death, distributes the grantor's property that is not in the living will.

A living trust is a legitimate planning tool for many people. A person should seek professional advice from and have an attorney draft the living trust, pour-over will, and other necessary documents.

The ethical duty of a paralegal professional to report dishonest or fraudulent acts pertaining to the handling of funds is discussed in the following feature.

Elder Law

Learning Objective 9
Describe elder law.

Paralegals should be aware of a growing area of the law called **elder law.** This is a specialized area that involves many subjects other than estates. Elders often employ lawyers who specialize in elder law to assist them in pursuing their rights and

Learning Objective 10
Explain a paralegal's duty to report dishonest or fraudulent acts pertaining to the handling of funds.

ETHICAL PERSPECTIVE

Paralegal's Duty to Report Dishonest or Fraudulent Acts Pertaining to the Handling of Funds

Ms. Vivian Zhong works as a paralegal for a law firm that specializes in the area of wills, trusts, and estates. The lawyers of the firm engage in estate planning for clients, draft wills and trusts, and represent clients in other areas of elder law. As required by law, the law firm has established trust funds at banks where clients' funds are kept on deposit during the period that a will or trust is being administered by the law firm.

Mr. Richard Hawthorne, a partner of the law firm, is currently going through a divorce and has several children in college whom he helps support. Because Mr. Hawthorne needs money to support himself and his family, he falsifies records at the law firm and misappropriates $200,000 from a trust fund being administered by the law firm.

Ms. Zhong, the paralegal assigned to assist in administering this particular trust fund, discovers Mr. Hawthorne's misappropriation of the funds from the trust. She then faces the dilemma of whether to report Mr. Hawthorne's misappropriation of the funds, and if so, to whom.

Does Ms. Zhong have a duty to report the dishonest and fraudulent act of Mr. Hawthorne? If so, to whom?

Model and state paralegal codes of ethics and professional responsibility provide that a paralegal is under a duty to report knowledge of any dishonest or fraudulent acts by any person pertaining to the handling of the funds or assets of a client. Depending on the nature and circumstances of the misconduct, a paralegal owes a duty to report knowledge of a dishonest or fraudulent act to partners of the law firm, local prosecutors, bar associations, or another appropriate party. A paralegal's failure to report such knowledge violates model and state paralegal ethics codes.

PARALEGAL'S ETHICAL DECISION

Thus, Ms. Zhong owes a duty to report Mr. Hawthorne's dishonest and fraudulent conduct of stealing funds from a client's trust fund. At minimum, Ms. Zhong owes a duty to report Mr. Hawthorne's conduct to the ethics committee of the law firm, and if there is no such committee, then to the managing partners of the law firm. Under the circumstances of this case, Ms. Zhong would probably owe a duty to report Mr. Hawthorne's conduct to the appropriate government agency, such as the state attorney general's office, as well as to the state bar association.

protecting them from unscrupulous and fraudulent behavior by others. Paralegals often assist elder law attorneys in these matters.

Some of the areas in which elderly people may need legal assistance are the following:

- Obtaining Social Security benefits and representing elders who have been defrauded out of their Social Security benefits.
- Obtaining and protecting rights to Medicare and Medicaid and other government health care–related programs.
- Protecting elders from undue influence in executing wills, trusts, and contracts, and suing to have contracts and documents that were signed under undue influence rescinded.
- Obtaining and enforcing contracts for the provision of long-term care insurance if an insurance carrier denies benefits for which elders have paid premiums.
- Protecting elders from elder abuse and pursuing charges against those who have abused them.
- Protecting elders from age discrimination and bringing lawsuits to enforce the antidiscrimination laws that protect elders.
- Helping elders defend against charges of incompetency that may be unfairly brought against them by relatives or others.
- Protecting elders from unscrupulous parties, including some relatives, who might take advantage of elders who suffer from diminished mental capacity and prevent them from making informed decisions.
- Helping elders have their wishes, which they have clearly delineated in living wills, enforced.
- Enforcing the wishes of elders to receive medical treatment in their homes rather than be forced to move to nursing homes.

The legal issues that elders may be involved in are numerous, and lawyers are often employed to help elders address many of these issues. Paralegals who work in the field of elder law must become familiar with the many government programs, contract issues, and other legal issues that are involved in representing elders and protecting them from fraud, undue influence, and others' misconduct toward them.

Exhibit 16.10 sets forth excerpts of the standards that attorneys should follow when engaging in the practice of elder law.

Exhibit 16.10 Aspirational standards for the practice of elder law

Excerpts from National Academy of Law Attorneys

Preamble

In the past 20 years, Elder Law has developed as a separate specialty area because of the unique and complex issues faced by older persons. Elder Law includes helping such persons and their families with planning for incapacity and long-term care, Medicaid and Medicare, including coverage of nursing home and home care, health and long-term care insurance, and health care decision making. It also includes the drafting of special needs and other trusts, the selection of long-term care providers, home care and nursing home problem solving, retiree health and income benefits, retirement housing, and fiduciary services or representation.

In these and other areas, the Elder Law Attorney is often asked to advocate for clients with diminished capacity. Family members and persons with fiduciary responsibilities become involved. The traditional client–attorney relationship is not always clear. Issues such as substituted judgment, best interests, and "who is the client?" present problems not regularly faced by other lawyers.

In recognizing Elder Law as a specialty practice area to meet the legal needs of older persons and persons with disabilities and their families, the National Academy of Elder Law Attorneys (NAELA) was founded in 1987. The following Guidelines set out Aspirational Standards of professionalism and ethical behavior for Elder Law Attorneys. They are the product of study and deliberation by NAELA members and, specifically, NAELA's Professionalism and Ethics Committee.

Competent Legal Representation

The Elder Law Attorney:

(1) Recognizes the special range of client needs and professional skills unique to the practice of Elder Law and holds himself or herself out as an Elder Law Attorney only after ensuring his or her professional competence in handling elder law and disability related matters.

(2) Approaches client matters in a holistic manner, recognizing that legal representation of clients often is enhanced by the involvement of other professionals, support groups, and aging network resources.

(3) Regularly pursues continuing professional education and peer collaboration in Elder Law. Continuing education should include a broad range of Elder Law related subjects as well as an understanding of the physical, cognitive, and psycho-social challenges of aging and disability, and the skills needed to serve persons who are physically or mentally challenged.

(4) Ensures adequate training and supervision of legal and non-legal staff with a corresponding emphasis on the knowledge and skills needed to best serve persons facing the challenges of aging and disability.

Source: Copyright © The National Academy of Elder Law Attorneys (NAELA). Reprinted with permission.

Concept Review *and* Reinforcement

LEGAL TERMINOLOGY

Abatement 588
Ademption 588
Administrator/administratrix 587
Attestation 582
Attestation clause 582
Beneficiaries 580
Beneficiary of a trust 592
Bequest (legacy) 585
Charitable trust 595
Codicil 582
Constructive trust 595
Devise 585
Elder law 601
Escheats 590
Executor/executrix 587
Express trust 595
General gift 585
Grantor (trustor) 596
Grantor's trust 596
Health care agent 590
Health care directive (health care proxy) 590
Heirs 590
Holographic will 584
Income beneficiary 593
Inter vivos trust 595
Intestacy statute 590
Intestate 590
Joint will 586
Lineal descendants 588
Living trust 596
Living will 590
Mutual (reciprocal) will 586
Nuncupative will (deathbed will or dying declaration) 585
Per capita distribution 588
Per stirpes distribution 588
Pour-over will 601
Probate (settlement of an estate) 587
Remainder beneficiary 593
Renounce an inheritance 585
Registrar of Wills 587
Residuary clause 585
Residuary gift 585
Resulting trust 595

SUMMARY OF KEY CONCEPTS

Wills

	A will is a declaration of how a person wants his or her property to be distributed upon his or her death.
Parties to a Will	1. *Testator or testatrix*: The person who makes a will. 2. *Beneficiary:* The person designated in the will to receive the testator's property. There may be multiple beneficiaries. 3. *Executor or executrix:* The person named in the will to administer the testator's estate during settlement of the estate.
Requirements for Making a Will	1. *Statute of Wills:* A state statute that establishes the requirements for making a valid will. 2. The normal requirements for making a will are: a. *Testamentary capacity* (legal age and "sound mind") b. *In writing* c. *Testator's signature* d. *Attestation by witnesses* (mentally competent and uninterested)
Changing a Will	1. *Codicil:* a legal way to change an existing will 2. Must be executed with the same formalities as a will

Special Types of Wills

Holographic Will	A holographic will is entirely handwritten and is signed by the testator. Most states recognize the validity of these wills even though they are not witnessed.
Nuncupative Will	A nuncupative will is an oral will made by a dying person before witnesses. Many states recognize these oral wills. Also called a *deathbed will* or a *dying declaration*.

Testamentary Gifts

Types of Gifts	1. *Specific gift:* A gift of a specifically mentioned piece of property (such as a ring) 2. *General gift:* A gift that does not identify the specific property from which the gift is to be made (such as a gift of cash) 3. *Residuary gift:* A gift of the remainder of the testator's estate after the debts, taxes, and specific and general gifts have been paid
Simultaneous Deaths	The Uniform Simultaneous Death Act provides that if people who would inherit property from each other die simultaneously, each deceased person's property is distributed as if he or she had survived.
Mutual or Reciprocal Will	In the case of a mutual or reciprocal will, two or more testators execute separate wills that leave property in favor of the other on condition that the survivor leave the remaining property upon his or her death as agreed by the testators.

Undue Influence	A will may be found to be invalid if it was made under undue influence, in which one person takes advantage of another person's mental, emotional, or physical weakness and unduly persuades that person to make a will.
Probate	
	Probate is the legal process of settling a deceased person's estate.
Administrator or Administratrix	An administrator or administratrix is a person named to administer the estate of a deceased person who dies intestate. An administrator is also named if an executor is not named in a will or the executor cannot or does not serve.
Lineal Descendants	1. In *per stirpes* distribution, lineal descendants inherit by representation of their parent; they split what their deceased parent would have received. 2. In *per capita* distribution, lineal descendants equally share the property of the estate without regard to degree.
Ademption	Ademption occurs when a testator leaves a specific gift but the property is no longer in the estate when the testator dies; thus the beneficiary of that gift receives nothing.
Abatement	Abatement occurs when the testator's estate is insufficient to pay the stated gifts, and the gifts are abated (reduced) in the following order: (1) residuary gifts, and then (2) general gifts proportionately.
Intestate Succession	
	1. *Intestacy statute:* A state statute that stipulates how a deceased's property will be distributed if he or she dies without leaving a will or if the will fails for some legal reason. 2. *Heirs:* Relatives who receive property under an intestacy statute. 3. *Escheat:* If there are no heirs, the deceased's property goes to the state, under intestacy statutes.
Living Will and Health Care Directive	
Right to Die	The right to die is a personal liberty protected by the U.S. Constitution.
Living Will	A living will is a document signed by a person that stipulates his or her wishes not to have his or her life prolonged by artificial means.
Health Care Directive	A health care directive is a document that names a person as a health care agent who has the authority to make health care decisions for the maker of the health care directive in accordance with the maker's wishes. Also called a *health care proxy*.
Trusts	
	A trust is a legal arrangement whereby one person delivers and transfers legal title to property to another person to be held and used for the benefit of a third person.
Trust *Corpus*	Trust *corpus* is the property that is held in trust; also called "trust *res*."
Parties	1. *Settlor:* A person who establishes a trust; also called a *trustor* or *transferor*. 2. *Trustee:* The person to whom *legal title* of the trust assets is transferred; this person is also responsible for managing the trust assets as established by the trust and law. 3. *Beneficiary:* The person for whose benefit a trust is created and who holds *equitable title* to the trust assets. There can be multiple beneficiaries, including: a. *Income beneficiary:* A person to whom trust income is to be paid b. *Remainder beneficiary:* A person who is entitled to receive the trust *corpus* upon termination of the trust

Express Trusts	Express trusts are voluntarily created by the settlor. Two types are: 1. Inter vivos *trust:* A trust created while the settlor is alive; also called a *living trust.* 2. *Testamentary trust:* A trust created by will and comes into existence when the settlor dies.
Constructive Trust	Constructive trusts are equitable trusts imposed by law to avoid fraud, unjust enrichment, and injustice.
Resulting Trust	Resulting trusts are created from the conduct of the parties.
Special Types of Trusts	1. *Charitable trust:* A trust created for the benefit of a segment of society or society in general. 2. *Spendthrift trust:* A trust whereby the creditors of the beneficiary cannot recover the trust's assets to satisfy debts owed to them by the beneficiary. 3. *Totten trust:* A trust created when a person deposits money in a bank account in his or her own name and holds it as a trust for the benefit of another person.
Living Trusts	
	A living trust is a legal entity used for estate planning. Also called a *grantor's trust, revocable trust,* or inter vivos *trust.*
Trust *Corpus*	The trust *corpus* is the property that is placed in a living trust to fund the trust.
Parties	1. *Grantor:* A person who establishes a living trust. 2. *Trustee:* A person who is responsible for maintaining, investing, buying, and selling trust assets. 3. *Income beneficiary:* A person who is entitled to receive income from a living trust. 4. *Remainder beneficiary:* A person who is entitled to receive the assets of a trust upon the death of the grantor.
Pour-Over Will	A pour-over will is necessary to distribute to the trust, upon the grantor's death, any of the grantor's property not in the living trust at the time of the grantor's death.
Elder Law	
	Elder law involves protecting the rights of elders, obtaining benefits due to elders, and otherwise representing elders in legal issues and cases that they are involved in.

WORKING THE WEB

1. Using Internet search engines such as www.google.com or Internet legal search services such as Westlaw or LexisNexis, find your state's will statute. What are the requirements for completing a valid will in your state? What are the attestation requirements? Write a one-page report on your findings. If you can, print out a sample will and attach it to your report.
2. Using Internet legal search services such as Westlaw or LexisNexis or Internet search engines such as www.google.com, find your state's intestacy statute. Make a list, in descending order of heirs, of how the property of a deceased person will be distributed if he or she dies without a will. When does the property escheat to the state?
3. Using Internet search engines such as www.google.com or Internet legal search services such as Westlaw or LexisNexis, find your state's living trust statute. What are the requirements for completing a valid living trust in your state? Write a one-page report on your findings. If you can, print out a sample living trust and attach it to your report.
4. Using Internet legal search services such as Westlaw or LexisNexis or Internet search engines such as www.google.com, find your state's living will statute. What are the requirements for completing a valid living will in your state? Also find your state's health care directive (health care proxy) statute. What are the requirements for completing a valid health care directive in your state? Write a one-page report on your findings. If you can, print out a sample living will and a sample health care directive and attach these to your report.

CRITICAL THINKING & WRITING QUESTIONS

1. What is a will? What are the requirements for making a will?
2. Define a beneficiary of a will.
3. What is a codicil? What is a subsequent will?
4. Define "holographic will" and "nuncupative will."
5. What is a devise (or legacy)? Describe the following types of devises: (a) specific gift, (b) general gift, and (c) residuary gift.
6. Define a lineal descendant. Explain the difference between *per capita* and *per stirpes* distribution of property to lineal descendants.
7. What is the difference between abatement and ademption?
8. What is a joint (or mutual) will?
9. Explain the doctrine of undue influence. Give an example.
10. What does it mean for a person to die intestate? Describe what an intestacy statute does. Who is an heir? What is escheat?
11. What is a trust? Define settlor (trustor or transferor). What is trust *corpus* (trust *res*)? Define an income beneficiary and a remainder beneficiary.
12. Define the following types of trusts: (a) express trust, (b) constructive trust, (c) resulting trust, (d) charitable trust, (e) spendthrift trust, and (f) totten trust.
13. Describe a living will and what it accomplishes. Describe a health care directive (health care proxy) and what it accomplishes.
14. What is a living (grantor's or revocable) trust? Define the following parties: grantor (trustor), trustee, and beneficiary. What are the benefits of establishing a living trust?

Building Paralegal Skills

VIDEO CASE STUDY

A Senior Citizen Consults a New Lawyer: Conflict of Interest

A client is meeting with his attorney to seek advice about actions that he can take to protect himself from actions that he took based on the advice of another attorney.

After viewing the video case study in MyLegalStudiesLab, answer the following:

1. What are the standards and the elements that must be proven to make a case of malpractice against a lawyer?
2. What is the obligation of the lawyer to determine the legal competency of his or her clients?
3. Would the manner in which the property was titled have changed the need for legal action after the death of the wife?

ETHICS ANALYSIS & DISCUSSION QUESTIONS

1. As a paralegal, what duty of honesty do you owe regarding the handling of funds held in trust by the law firm you work for in probate, estate, and trust administration matters?
2. What duty does a paralegal owe if he knows that a will he has been assigned to draft for a client of his supervising attorney has been obtained through undue influence? What if the supervising attorney has knowledge of the situation?
3. A client of the law firm you work for dies intestate. No immediate relatives can be located. Your supervising attorney assigns you the task of locating persons who could take over the state's intestate statute. How hard must you look for distant relatives?

DEVELOPING YOUR COLLABORATION SKILLS

With a group of other students selected by you or your instructor, review the facts of the following case. As a group, discuss the following questions.

1. What is the doctrine of undue influence?
2. What wills have been filed for probate?
3. Who has the burden of proof in this case? Why?
4. Has Jerald rebutted the presumption of undue influence?

Medlock v. Mitchell

Richard Mitchell executed a will leaving his estate equally to two of his children, Mark and Michelle. Four months later, Richard married Glenda Kay. On the same day, Richard created a revocable living trust. The trust was to terminate 10 years after Richard's death. Upon termination of the trust, the trust *corpus* was to be distributed to Mark and Michelle. Five years later, Richard was diagnosed with terminal lung cancer. Three months later, he executed another will, leaving his entire $3.5 million estate to Kay. Richard died two months later.

Michelle filed her father's earlier will for probate. Kay filed Richard's most recent will for probate, arguing that Richard's earlier will had been revoked by the most recent will. Michelle responded that her father's most recent will was invalid because of Richard's incompetence at the time it was executed and was a product of undue influence by Kay. Kay died pending trial, and her son Jerald pursued the lawsuit. The trial court found that there was a confidential relationship between Richard and Kay, and therefore the burden shifted to Jerald to prove that there was no undue influence in the making of Richard's last will.

Source: Medlock v. Mitchell, Web 2006 Ark. App. Lexis 320 (Court of Appeals of Arkansas)

PARALEGAL PORTFOLIO EXERCISE

Review this chapter's opening scenario. Prepare a joint will for Mr. and Ms. Huntington that meets your state's will requirements. Have another person and you sign the will as if you were Mr. and Ms. Huntington, and have the proper attestation of the will as required in your state.

LEGAL ANALYSIS & WRITING CASES

Succession of Talbot

530 So.2d 1132, Web 1988 La. Lexis 1597 Supreme Court of Louisiana

During his first marriage to Miriam Talbot, Robert Mirkil Talbot executed a will in multiple originals that bequeathed his entire estate to Miriam, or if she should predecease him, to his friend J. Barker Killgore. After his first wife's death, Robert married Lois McClen Mills. After consulting a Louisiana intestacy chart, the Talbots determined that if Robert died, Lois would receive Robert's entire estate because he had no descendants, surviving parents, or siblings. However, Lois did have descendants. Lois wanted to leave Robert a portion of her estate. Robert and his new wife went to an attorney to execute the new wife's will. While there, the attorney took Robert aside and showed him his prior will that made Killgore the contingent beneficiary. The attorney asked Robert if he wanted to leave his estate to his new wife, and Robert answered "yes." Robert then tore the old will in half in the attorney's presence. After leaving the attorney's office, Robert and Lois went shopping for furnishings for their new house. That night, Robert became short of breath and was taken to a hospital, where he died. Killgore retrieved a multiple original of Robert's 1981 will and petitioned to have it probated. Lois opposed the petition.

Question

1. Who wins and why?

In re Estate of Campbell

56 Ore.App. 222, 641 P.2d 610, Web 1982 Ore.App. Lexis 2448
Court of Appeals of Oregon

Mr. and Mrs. Campbell were out in a small boat on Hyatt Lake near Ashland, Oregon. The boat capsized near the middle of the lake sometime in the afternoon. No one saw the capsizing or either of the Campbells in the water. The deputy sheriff was called to the lake about 5 o'clock, after the Campbells' boat was found. Numerous people searched the shoreline and lake, but the Campbells were not located by nightfall. The body of Mrs. Campbell was found the next morning. The body of Mr. Campbell was found four days later. The pathologists who conducted the autopsies testified that both Mr. and Mrs. Campbell died of drowning but could not determine the exact time of death. Both parties died intestate. Mr. Campbell was survived by three sisters and a brother, and Mrs. Campbell was survived by a daughter and son from a prior marriage.

Question

1. Who inherits the Campbells' property?

WORKING WITH THE LANGUAGE OF THE COURT CASE

Gonzales, Attorney General of the United States v. Oregon

546 U.S. 243, 126 S.Ct. 904, 163 L.Ed.2d 748, Web 2006 U.S. Lexis 767
Supreme Court of the United States

Read and then brief the following case, excerpted from the U.S. Supreme Court opinion. In your brief, answer the following questions.

1. What does the Oregon Death With Dignity Act (ODWDA) provide?
2. What is the Controlled Substances Act (CSA)? What is the main purpose of the CSA?
3. What does the U.S. Attorney do?
4. Who are the plaintiffs in this case? Who is the defendant?
5. What is the issue in this case?
6. What decision did the U.S. Supreme Court reach?

Kennedy, Justice (joined by Stevens, O'Connor, Souter, Ginsburg, and Breyer)

The question before us is whether the Controlled Substances Act allows the United States Attorney General to prohibit doctors from prescribing regulated drugs for use in physician-assisted suicide, notwithstanding a state law permitting the procedure. As the Court has observed, "Americans are engaged in an earnest and profound debate about the morality, legality, and practicality of physician-assisted suicide."

In 1994, Oregon became the first State to legalize assisted suicide when voters approved a ballot measure enacting the Oregon Death With Dignity Act (ODWDA). Ore. Rev. Stat. § 127.800 *e[t] seq.* (2003). ODWDA … exempts from civil or criminal liability state-licensed physicians who, in compliance with the specific safeguards in ODWDA, dispense or prescribe a lethal dose of drugs upon the request of a terminally ill patient.

The drugs Oregon physicians prescribe under ODWDA are regulated under a federal statute, the Controlled Substances Act (CSA or Act). 84 Stat. 1242, as amended, 21 U. S. C. § 801 *et seq.* The CSA allows these particular drugs to be available only by a written prescription from a registered physician.

A November 9, 2001, Interpretive Rule issued by the Attorney General addresses the implementation and enforcement of the CSA with respect to ODWDA. It determines that using controlled substances to assist suicide is not a legitimate medical practice and that dispensing or prescribing them for this purpose is unlawful under the CSA. The Interpretive Rule's validity under the CSA is the issue before us.

Oregon voters enacted ODWDA in 1994. For Oregon residents to be eligible to request a prescription under ODWDA, they must receive a diagnosis from their attending physician that they have an incurable and irreversible disease that, within reasonable medical judgment, will cause death within six months. Attending physicians must also determine whether a patient has made a voluntary request, ensure a patient's choice is informed, and refer patients to counseling if they might

(continued)

be suffering from a psychological disorder or depression causing impaired judgment. A second "consulting" physician must examine the patient and the medical record and confirm the attending physician's conclusions. Oregon physicians may dispense or issue a prescription for the requested drug, but may not administer it.

In 2001, John Ashcroft was appointed Attorney General. On November 9, 2001, without consulting Oregon or apparently anyone outside his Department, the Attorney General issued an Interpretive Rule announcing his intent to restrict the use of controlled substances for physician-assisted suicide.

There is little dispute that the Interpretive Rule would substantially disrupt the ODWDA regime. In response the State of Oregon, joined by a physician, a pharmacist, and some terminally ill patients, all from Oregon, challenged the Interpretive Rule in federal court. The United States District Court for the District of Oregon entered a permanent injunction against the Interpretive Rule's enforcement.

A divided panel of the Court of Appeals for the Ninth Circuit granted the petitions for review and held the Interpretive Rule invalid. We granted the Government's petition for certiorari.

The Attorney General has rulemaking power to fulfill his duties under the CSA. The specific respects in which he is authorized to make rules, however, instruct us that he is not authorized to make a rule declaring illegitimate a medical standard for care and treatment of patients that is specifically authorized under state law.

The Government contends the Attorney General's decision here is a legal, not a medical, one. This generality, however, does not suffice. The Attorney General's Interpretive Rule, and the Office of Legal Counsel memo it incorporates, place extensive reliance on medical judgments and the views of the medical community in concluding that assisted suicide is not a "legitimate medical purpose." This confirms that the authority claimed by the Attorney General is both beyond his expertise and incongruous with the statutory purposes and design.

The idea that Congress gave the Attorney General such broad and unusual authority through an implicit delegation in the CSA's registration provision is not sustainable. "Congress, we have held, does not alter the fundamental details of a regulatory scheme in vague terms or ancillary provisions—it does not, one might say, hide elephants in mouseholes." The importance of the issue of physician-assisted suicide, which has been the subject of an "earnest and profound debate" across the country, makes the oblique form of the claimed delegation all the more suspect. Under the Government's theory, moreover, the medical judgments the Attorney General could make are not limited to physician-assisted suicide. Were this argument accepted, he could decide whether any particular drug may be used for any particular purpose, or indeed whether a physician who administers any controversial treatment could be deregistered.

In deciding whether the CSA can be read as prohibiting physician-assisted suicide, we look to the statute's text and design. The statute and our case law amply support the conclusion that Congress regulates medical practice insofar as it bars doctors from using their prescription-writing powers as a means to engage in illicit drug dealing and trafficking as conventionally understood. Beyond this, however, the statute manifests no intent to regulate the practice of medicine generally. The silence is understandable given the structure and limitations of federalism, which allow the States "'great latitude under their police powers to legislate as to the protection of the lives, limbs, health, comfort, and quiet of all persons.'"

The structure and operation of the CSA presume and rely upon a functioning medical profession regulated under the States' police powers.

In the face of the CSA's silence on the practice of medicine generally and its recognition of state regulation of the medical profession[,] it is difficult to defend the Attorney General's declaration that the statute impliedly criminalizes physician-assisted suicide.

The judgment of the Court of Appeals is *Affirmed.*

MYLEGALSTUDIESLAB

MyLegalStudiesLab Virtual Law Office Experience Assignments Complete the pre-test, study plan, and post-test for this chapter and answer the Legal Applications questions as assigned. These will help you confirm your mastery of the concepts and their application to legal scenarios. Then complete the Virtual Law Office assignments as assigned by your instructor. These assignments are designed to develop your workplace skills. Completing the assignments for this chapter will result in producing the following documents for inclusion in your portfolio:

VLOE 16.1	Office memo on how a decedent's property is divided when there is no will and there is a surviving spouse, and a legitimate and an illegitimate child

CHAPTER

17

Family Law

Paralegals at Work

You are the paralegal who works for Ms. Sara Khan, a lawyer who specializes in family law and domestic relations issues. With this specialty in family law, you are often assigned to investigate and discover information pertinent to clients' cases, conduct legal research on family law issues, and draft documents for review by Ms. Khan before they are submitted to the family law court. You also attend Ms. Khan's meetings wherein the clients are interviewed to obtain relevant information about their family law matter.

One day, Ms. Jennifer Aston, a new client, arrives at the law office. Ms. Khan invites you to sit in on the initial meeting with Ms. Aston. At the meeting, Ms. Aston discloses that she wants to obtain a divorce from her spouse, Mr. Breton, and relates the following facts about her marriage: Ms. Aston and Mr. Breton met after she graduated from medical school. They have been married 15 years. Ms. Aston is now 45 years old, and Mr. Breton is 42 years old. They have two children: Kayla, their 10-year-old daughter born to the spouses, and Jason, an adopted son who is 6 years old.

Ms. Aston then relates the following facts about her and her spouse's financial situation: Ms. Aston is a medical doctor who earns $500,000 per year. Mr. Breton is an actor/waiter who earns $50,000 per year. They have a joint bank account into which both of their earnings are deposited. During the course of their marriage, they have accumulated the following assets: (1) their house, valued at $1,000,000 and with a $300,000 mortgage (loan) against it; (2) $800,000 of securities in the stock market; (3) a $200,000 savings account at a bank; (4) two automobiles, each valued at $25,000; and (5) personal property, including furniture, valued at $150,000.

Ms. Aston adds that during the course of the marriage, she inherited $1,000,000 of securities from her

LEARNING OBJECTIVES

After studying this chapter, you should be able to:

1. Recognize the professional opportunities for paralegals in the family law area.
2. Define *marriage* and enumerate the legal requirements of marriage.
3. Define *adoption* and describe how adoption proceedings work.
4. List and describe the issues covered in a prenuptial agreement.
5. Explain a paralegal's duty to keep information confidential.
6. Define *annulment* and describe its consequences.
7. Define *divorce* and *no-fault divorce*, and describe divorce proceedings.
8. Describe how assets are distributed upon the termination of marriage.
9. Explain the requirements for awarding spousal support.
10. Explain child custody, visitation rights, joint custody of children, and child support.

"The happiest moments of my life have been the few which I have passed at home in the bosom of my family."

Thomas Jefferson, *Letter to Francis Willis, Jr.*, 1790

grandmother, which Ms. Aston has kept in her own name. The securities have increased to $1,600,000 in value. Mr. Breton has no separate property.

Ms. Khan asks Ms. Aston if there is a prenuptial agreement, and Ms. Aston states that there is no such agreement. However, Ms. Aston nevertheless wants to keep the house and retain custody of the two children.

Consider the issues involved in this scenario as you read the chapter.

INTRODUCTION FOR THE PARALEGAL

Family law and domestic relations is a broad area of the law, involving premarital issues, prenuptial agreements, marriage, dissolution of marriage, division of property upon dissolution of marriage, spousal and child support payments, child custody, and other family law issues.

A successful marriage requires falling in love many times, always with the same person.
Mignon McLaughlin

Paralegals who work in the area of family law and domestic relations are called upon to interview clients, investigate and obtain relevant information, draft letters and documents to be sent to clients, and prepare legal forms that will be submitted to the family law or domestic relations court. The paralegal must report to and submit letters, documents, and forms to the supervising attorney for approval and often signature.

This chapter provides the paralegal with an introduction to the issues most commonly encountered in a family law legal practice.

Career opportunities for paralegal professionals in the family law area are discussed in the next feature.

Premarriage Issues

Prior to marriage, several legal issues may arise. These include promises to marry, engagement, and prenuptial agreements.

Learning Objective 1
Recognize the professional opportunities for paralegals in the family law area.

Promise to Marry

In the nineteenth century, many courts recognized an action for breach of a **promise to marry.** This breach would usually occur when a man proposed marriage, the woman accepted, and then the man backed out before the marriage took place. The lawsuit was based on a breach-of-contract theory.

Today, most courts do not recognize a breach of a promise-to-marry lawsuit. The denial of such lawsuits is based on current social norms. If, however, the potential groom backs out after many of the items for the pending marriage (such as flowers and the rental of the reception hall) had been purchased or contracted for, he may be responsible for paying these costs.

Engagement

As a prelude to getting married, many couples go through a period of time known as **engagement.** The engagement usually begins when the male proposes marriage to the female, and if the female accepts, he gives her an engagement ring (usually a diamond ring). Today, a female might propose marriage to a male. During an engagement, the female is called the **fiancée** and the male is called the **fiancé.** The engagement period runs until the wedding is held or the engagement is broken off. If a couple gets married, they often exchange wedding bands during the marriage ceremony.

Web Exploration

Using **www.google.com**, find out whether your state uses the fault rule or the objective rule in determining which party gets the engagement ring if an engagement is terminated.

CAREER OPPORTUNITIES FOR PARALEGALS IN FAMILY LAW

With the divorce rate in this country around 50 percent, a substantial number of lawyers and paralegals work in the family law area. A paralegal in the family law area is usually involved in a broad spectrum of legal issues.

A divorce case is a lawsuit. Therefore, the legal rules and procedures involving the court system apply. Paralegals must know these procedures for the state in which they work. For example, a divorce case usually involves investigating finances and other issues concerning the divorce, preparing notices for discovery of evidence, drafting interrogatories, and preparing other documents needed in the divorce case.

Most divorces are settled before they go to trial. Reaching an acceptable settlement agreement often requires negotiation between the parties and their lawyers. The paralegal frequently sits in on many of the meetings and negotiation sessions between the parties and their attorneys.

If a settlement is reached, the paralegal is often called upon to prepare a draft of the settlement agreement. This will require substantial knowledge of the law of the state as well as of the facts of the individual divorce case. In addition, the paralegal may be assigned to prepare the necessary documents associated with the settlement, such as deeds and documents to transfer real property, securities, bank accounts, and other property, in order to complete the divorce.

In many divorce cases, custody battles over children arise. The lawyers will represent the parties in these custody disputes, and their paralegals will assist the lawyers in preparing for these disputes. Other issues in divorce cases may include visitation rights, child support payments, and alimony. Again, the paralegal must be familiar with these legal issues and the associated procedures and documents.

In many instances, the parties sign a prenuptial agreement prior to marriage. These agreements establish the rights of parties should they separate. The paralegal is often responsible for preparing drafts of prenuptial agreements and other documents necessary to support the prenuptial agreement.

Other issues in the family law area concern the adoption of children; contracts for surrogate mothers; proceedings to determine the capacity of parents, spouses, and other loved ones; the appointment of conservators; and other family law matters. These areas usually require the expertise of family law lawyers and their paralegals.

Another area of family law pertains to the rights and duties of same-sex partners. These couples require legal representation in the drafting of legal documents, the adoption of children, the separation of the partners, the division of assets upon the separation of the partners, and other issues. In addition, lawyers are called upon to represent same-sex partners in cases to establish legal rights and duties, and to eliminate laws that treat same-sex partners differently from heterosexual partners.

The family law area provides a wealth of opportunities for well-trained and knowledgeable paralegals.

When the engagement is broken off prior to the wedding, the issue becomes: Who gets the engagement ring? Some states follow a **fault rule,** which works as follows:

- If the prospective groom breaks off the engagement, the prospective bride gets to keep the engagement ring.
- If the prospective bride breaks off the engagement, she must return the engagement ring to the prospective groom.

However, the fault rule is sometimes difficult to apply. Questions often arise as to who broke off the engagement, which then requires a trial to decide the issue.

The modern trend is to abandon the fault rule and adopt an **objective rule:** If the engagement is broken off, the prospective bride must return the engagement ring regardless of who broke off the engagement. This rule is unambiguous and avoids litigation, unless the female refuses to return the ring.

Objective rule A rule stating that if an engagement is broken off, the prospective bride must return the engagement ring, regardless of which party broke off the engagement.

Learning Objective 2
Define *marriage* and enumerate the legal requirements of marriage.

Marriage

Marriage A legal union between spouses that confers certain legal rights and duties upon the spouses and upon the children born of the marriage.

Each state has marriage laws that recognize a legal union between a man and a woman. **Marriage** confers certain legal rights and duties upon the spouses as well as upon the children born of the marriage. A couple wishing to marry must meet the legal requirements established by the state in which they are to be married. The following paragraphs discuss these legal rights and duties.

Marriage Requirements

State law establishes certain **marriage requirements** that must be met before two people can be married. Most states require that the parties be a man and a woman. The parties must also be of a certain age (usually at least 18 years old). States will permit younger persons to be married if they have the consent of their parents or are emancipated from their parents. **Emancipation** means that a person is not supported by his or her parents and provides for himself or herself.

Web Exploration

Using **www.google.com**, find out the marriage requirements in your state.

All states provide that persons under a certain age, such as 14 or 15 years old, cannot be married. States also prohibit marriages between persons who are closely related, usually by blood. For example, a brother could not marry his sister or half-sister. Cousins may marry in some states. Another requirement of marriage is that neither party is currently married to someone else.

Marriage License

To be legally married, certain legal procedures must be followed. State law requires that the parties obtain a **marriage license** issued by the state. Marriage licenses are usually obtained at the county clerk's office. Some states require the parties to take a blood test prior to obtaining a license to determine whether the parties have certain diseases, particularly sexually transmitted diseases.

Marriage license A legal document issued by a state certifying that two people are married.

In addition to a marriage license, some states require that there be some sort of **marriage ceremony.** This ceremony is usually held in front of a justice of the peace or similar government officer, or at a church, temple, or synagogue in front of a minister, priest, or rabbi. At the ceremony, the parties exchange wedding vows in which they make a public statement that they will take each other as wife and husband.

After the wedding ceremony, the marriage license is recorded. Some states require a waiting period between the time the marriage license is obtained and when the wedding ceremony takes place.

Financial Support

Most states require a spouse to provide **financial support** to the other spouse and their children during their marriage. This includes providing for necessities such as food, shelter, clothing, and medical care. However, a spouse is obligated only up to the level he or she is able to provide. In some states this duty exists even if the spouses are living apart. The spouses are free to agree on additional duties in separate contracts. Contracts to provide sex violate public policy and therefore are illegal.

Common-Law Marriage

Several states recognize a form of marriage called a **common-law marriage.** A common-law marriage is one in which the parties have not obtained a valid marriage license or participated in a legal marriage ceremony. Instead, a common-law marriage is recognized if the following requirements are met: (1) The parties are eligible to marry; (2) the parties voluntarily intend to be husband and wife; (3) the parties live together; and (4) the parties hold themselves out as husband and wife.

Common-law marriage A type of marriage recognized in some states where a marriage license has not been issued but certain requirements are met.

Two facts about common-law marriages are: (1) cohabitation is not sufficient in and of itself to establish a common-law marriage, and (2) the length of time the parties live together is not sufficient alone to establish a common-law marriage. For example, couples who immediately live together and intend a common-law marriage have one, whereas couples who live together a long time but do not intend a common-law marriage do not have one.

Web Exploration

Using **www.google.com**, find out whether your state recognizes common-law marriages. If so, what requirements must be met for there to be a common-law marriage?

When a state recognizes a common-law marriage and the necessary requirements are met to establish one, the couple has a legal and formal marriage, and all the rights and duties of a normal licensed marriage apply. As such, a court decree of divorce must be obtained to end a common-law marriage.

Same-Sex Marriage

Same-sex partners have been fighting for years to obtain the same right to marry that heterosexual couples have. In most states, same-sex couples do not have this same right to marry. This is because most state marriage statutes are expressly drafted to permit only couples of different sexes to marry.

Same-sex partners have been lobbying their state legislatures and bringing lawsuits in the courts to change marriage statutes to permit **same-sex marriage.** In these lawsuits, same-sex partners allege that the state statutes that permit heterosexual but not same-sex partners to marry cause discrimination that violates equal protection clauses of state constitutions and the U.S. Constitution.

Same-sex marriage A marriage between two people of the same sex.

Web Exploration

Using **www.google.com**, find out whether your state recognizes same-sex marriages or civil unions of same-sex partners.

In 2004, the state of Massachusetts became the first state to grant equal rights to same-sex couples to get married. Connecticut, Iowa, New Hampshire, New York, Vermont, and Washington, D.C., also permit same-sex marriage. Some states that do not permit gay partners to marry provide that they can enter into a **civil union.** Civil unions usually provide gay partners with rights, benefits, and responsibilities similar to those of opposite-sex marriage. Approximately half of the states have enacted constitutional amendments to their state constitutions that ban same-sex marriages.

Many employers provide the same health, pension, and other employment benefits to same-sex partners as they do to heterosexual married couples. The granting of same-sex partners such employment rights will continue to increase in the future.

In 1996, the federal government enacted the **Defense of Marriage Act (DOMA)** (see 28 U.S.C. Section 1738C), which bars same-sex couples from enjoying federal benefits (such as Social Security benefits, veterans' benefits, and such) that are otherwise accorded to heterosexual married couples. Same-sex partners argue that this part of DOMA violates the Equal Protection Clause of the U.S. Constitution because it treats same-sex partners differently from heterosexual married couples.

DOMA also provides that states cannot be forced to recognize same-sex marriages performed in other states. For example, if a same-sex couple gets lawfully married in Massachusetts and moves to another state that does not recognize same-sex marriages, this new state does not have to recognize the partners' same-sex marriage from Massachusetts.

The battle for the recognition of same-sex marriages and the granting of rights to same-sex partners equal to those of heterosexual couples will continue to be waged in state and federal legislatures, as well as in state and federal courts.

SIDEBAR

FAMILY LAW JUDGES

Many states have specialized courts that handle family law matters. These courts most often are called Family Law Courts. Other states provide that family law matters be heard and decided by their courts of general jurisdiction. In these cases, the courts that hear family law matters typically are a separate division of the general court system.

Judges that hear family law matters are usually referred to as Family Law Judges. These judges are experts in family law issues. In the course of their work, these judges hear and decide matters of paternity, annulments, divorce, division of property upon divorce, child custody, child visitation rights, child support, conservatorship, and other family law issues.

Because of the number of family law issues that arise in society, family law judges hear and decide a significant number of cases. Family law judges will continue to be an integral part of each state's judicial system.

Parents and Children

In many instances, a major purpose of marriage is to have children. Couples who have children have certain legal rights and duties that develop from their parental status.

Parents' Rights and Duties

Parents have the obligation to provide food, shelter, clothing, medical care, and other necessities to their children until each child reaches the age of 18 or until emancipation. The law imposes certain **parents' duties** as well. For example, a parent must see to it that the child attends school until 16 or 18 years of age, depending on the state, unless the child is home-schooled. Parents may be legally responsible for a child beyond the age of majority if the child has a disability.

Also, **parents' right** to control the behavior of a child is legally mandated. In addition, parents have the right to select the schools their children will attend and the religion they will practice and the right to use corporal punishment (physical punishment) as long as it does not rise to the level of child abuse. For example, mild slapping or spanking is legally permitted.

Child neglect A parent's failure to provide a child with the necessities of life or other basic needs.

Child neglect occurs when a parent fails to provide a child with the necessities of life or other basic needs. The state may remove a child, either temporarily or permanently, from situations of child neglect. A parent's refusal to obtain medical care for a child can be punished as a crime.

Paternity Actions

If there is any question as to who the father of a child is, called **paternity,** a **paternity action** may be filed in court to determine the true identity of the father. Most of these actions are filed by a mother against a man whom the mother claims to be the father of her child. This often is done to seek financial assistance from the father for the child's upbringing.

Paternity action A legal proceeding that determines the identity of the father of a child.

Paternity lawsuits are sometimes brought by the government if the mother is receiving welfare payments. In these cases, the government seeks to recover the financial assistance payments due to the mother and to establish the father's financial responsibility in the future. Sometimes a paternity action is brought by a male to prove that he is not the father of a child.

At other times, a father will bring a paternity action to establish that he is the biological father of a child. This is usually done when the father seeks to obtain legal rights, such as custody or visitation rights, concerning the child. Most states have a **father's registry** in which a male may register as the father of a child. This registration ensures that the father will be notified of a planned adoption of the child and will be able to appear and oppose the adoption.

In most states, the law presumes that the husband of a wife who bears a child is the legal father of that child. In about half of the states, a husband who believes that he is not the father can bring a lawsuit to prove that he is not the father. The other half of the states do not permit such actions.

A male can be proven to be or not to be the father of a child through DNA testing. Also, a male may prove that he is not the father of a child if he had no access to the mother at the time of pregnancy or if he is impotent or had a vasectomy prior to the pregnancy.

Parents' Liability for a Child's Wrongful Act

Generally, parents are not liable for their children's negligent acts. For example, if a child negligently injures another child while they are playing, the parents of the child who caused the injury are not liable. Parents are, however, liable if their negligence caused their child's act. For example, if a parent lets a child who does not have a driver's license drive an automobile and the child-driver injures someone, the parents are liable.

About half of the states have enacted **child liability statutes** that make the parents financially liable for the intentional torts of their children. This liability is usually limited to a specified dollar amount, such as $5,000.

Learning Objective 3

Define *adoption* and describe how adoption proceedings work.

Adoption

Adoption A situation in which a person becomes the legal parent of a child who is not his or her biological child.

Adoption occurs when a person becomes the legal parent of a child who is not his or her biological child. Thus, a married couple can adopt a child together, a single parent can adopt a child, and a spouse can adopt the child of his or her new spouse.

The process for adoption is complicated and is regulated by state law. Basically, the procedure for adoption consists of the following requirements:

- All procedures of the state law for adoption are met.
- The biological parents' legal rights as parents are terminated by legal decree or death.
- A court formally approves the adoption.

The two main ways by which persons can become adoptive parents are *agency adoptions* and *independent adoptions.*

Agency Adoption

An **agency adoption** occurs when a person adopts a child from a social service organization of a state. The state often obtains jurisdiction over children who are born out of wedlock and whose biological parents gave them up for adoption by terminating their parental rights. The state may also obtain jurisdiction over a child if the child has been permanently removed from parents who are judged unsuitable to be parents, or where parents are deceased and no relative wants or qualifies to become the child's parents.

Agency adoption An adoption that occurs when a person adopts a child from a social service organization of a state.

In the past, the identity of the biological parents of adopted children was kept confidential in an agency adoption. Currently, many states allow for disclosure of the identity of the biological parents in certain circumstances. Usually, the court will notify the other side—either the child or the biological parent—that the other wishes to meet with him or her. If both sides consent, the meeting will be arranged.

Open Adoption

In many cases today, **open adoption** procedures are being used. In these cases, the biological and **adoptive parents** are introduced prior to the adoption. The **biological parents** may screen the prospective adoptive parents to ensure that they are suitable for the child. In many instances, the adoptive and biological parents remain in contact with each other, and the biological parents are given visitation rights to see the child.

Independent Adoption

An **independent adoption** occurs when there is a private arrangement between the biological and adoptive parents. Often an intermediary, such as a lawyer, doctor, or private adoption agency, introduces the two parties. The biological parents and the adoptive parents then enter into a private arrangement for adoption of the child. Adoptive parents usually pay intermediaries a fee for their services and also pay the costs of the adoption.

Independent adoption An adoption in which there is a private arrangement between the biological parents and the adoptive parents.

Many divorced people who have children remarry. Often, a new stepparent formally adopts the child or children of his or her new spouse. To do so, the child's other biological parent must relinquish his or her legal rights concerning the child. This can be done voluntarily or by order of the court if it is deemed to be in the best interests of the child.

Court Approval of Adoption

In both agency adoptions and independent adoptions, the court must approve the adoption before it is legal. The court will consider the home environment, financial resources, and family stability of the adoptive parents, as well as their religious beliefs, ages, and other factors. The decision of the court will be based on the best interests of the child. Although preference is usually given to couples, single parents may adopt children. States vary as to whether they permit homosexual couples to adopt children.

Once the court approves an adoption, the adoptive couple is subject to a probation period that is usually six months or one year. During this time, government social workers investigate whether the adoptive parents are caring for the adopted child properly. If they are not, the court can remove the child from the adoptive parents.

Foster Care

A child may become the responsibility of the state under several circumstances. The first is when a child's parents or parent dies and there are no relatives to take the child or no other arrangements have been made for the care of the child. Another situation is when the state institutes a proceeding to remove a child from the parents' or parent's custody based upon the parent being unfit to care for the child or because the child is in danger (such as from child abuse).

Foster care An arrangement in which a child is placed temporarily with a foster family. The state government pays the foster family for caring for the foster child.

Today, the primary means of caring for children under the state's jurisdiction is to place such children in **foster care.** This is usually a temporary arrangement. The state pays the **foster family** for the care given to the **foster child.** This temporary arrangement will be terminated if the child is returned to his or her biological parents or if the child is legally adopted. Sometimes the **foster parents** will legally adopt a child who has been placed in their care.

Learning Objective 4

List and describe the issues covered in a prenuptial agreement.

Prenuptial Agreement

Prenuptial agreement (premarital agreement) A contract entered into prior to marriage that specifies how property will be distributed upon the termination of the marriage or death of a spouse.

In today's society, many spouses sign prenuptial agreements in advance of their marriage. **Prenuptial agreements**—also called **premarital agreements**—are contracts that specify how property will be distributed upon termination of the marriage or death of a spouse. To be enforced, a prenuptial agreement must be in writing.

Prenuptial agreements are often used when both parties to a marriage have their own careers and have accumulated assets prior to the marriage, or when one of the spouses acquired significant assets prior to the marriage. Prenuptial agreements are also often used when there are children from a prior marriage because the agreement guarantees that these children will receive a certain share of the assets of the remarrying spouse if he or she dies or the marriage is terminated.

Issues Covered in a Prenuptial Agreement

Prenuptial agreements often include the following issues:

- **Separate Property.** A prenuptial agreement can list the property that each party is bringing to the marriage and include the statement that the listed property shall remain separate property unless changed by writing during the course of the marriage.

  Example Miles and Nikki are getting married. Nikki has the following separate property: securities worth $1 million, a pension worth $1 million, real estate worth $1 million, and bank accounts of $1 million. Miles has $50,000 in the bank. The prenuptial agreement could state that Nikki's separate property is her separate property and will remain so during the course of the marriage unless Nikki transfers ownership to any of her separate property in writing to Miles. The prenuptial agreement could treat Miles's $50,000 separate property similarly.

- **Income.** The prenuptial agreement can include an agreement as to how income will be treated during the marriage. For example, a high-income earner may be awarded a certain percentage or dollar amount of his or her income as separate property.

  Example Miles and Nikki are getting married. Nikki is a brain surgeon who makes $1 million per year in income. Miles makes $80,000 per year in income. The prenuptial agreement can state that a certain percent (such as 50 percent) or a certain amount ($500,000) of Nikki's income is her separate property each year, and the remainder is joint property.

- **Marital Property.** The prenuptial agreement can handle the division of marital property upon divorce by addressing the division of marital property that has been acquired during the marriage.

  Example If one party is a high-income earner during the marriage, a prenuptial agreement can be structured to award a larger share of the property acquired during the marriage to the high-earning partner upon divorce.

- **Specific Property.** A prenuptial agreement can set forth which party is to receive designated property upon divorce.

Example The agreement may state that a designated party will receive the parties' primary residence upon divorce. The award of other property, such a second home, rental property, a farm, investment property, and securities, may also be agreed upon.

- **Valuation of a Business.** If one partner owns a business prior to the marriage, the agreement can value the business upon the date of marriage, declare that value to be separate property, provide for the distribution of the business upon termination of the marriage, and stipulate a formula (such as by percentage) for the division of the increase in value of the business that occurred during the marriage.
- **Profession and License.** If one party is a professional, the prenuptial agreement can set forth the value or a formula for determining the value of the professional practice and license, and it can also stipulate how much the professional will pay the other party upon divorce.
- **Pension.** If one or both parties have contributed to a pension prior to marriage, this amount can be recognized as separate property, and any contributions made during the marriage can be either designated as separate property or divided upon divorce using some agreed-upon formula.
- **Intellectual Property and Royalties.** If one party owns intellectual property such as patents, copyrights, and such, the value of the intellectual property and its income stream may be agreed upon, and the parties can also provide how this property and its income stream may be divided upon divorce.
- **Personal Items.** The agreement may allocate specifically identified personal items to designated parties.

Examples Furniture, jewelry, works of art, collectibles, china, and household items may be awarded to specifically named parties.

- **Alimony.** The prenuptial agreement can set forth the alimony that will be paid if the parties divorce.

Example The prenuptial agreement could set forth that Nikki, the high-income earner, will pay Miles, the low-income earner, a specified amount of alimony each month (such as $3,000) for a specified period of time (such as five years) if the parties divorce.

- **Child Custody.** The prenuptial agreement can provide for child custody and visitation rights .

Example Child custody may be awarded to one parent, with agreed-upon visitation rights granted to the other parent (such as every other weekend and two weeks in the summer).

- **Child Support.** The prenuptial agreement can provide for the payment of child support, often by the noncustodial parent.

Example Child support may be set at a certain dollar amount for each child. The agreement may also provide for the payment of college and other expenses.

- **Other Issues.** The prenuptial agreement can also handle the treatment of other issues that arise in a marriage and subsequent divorce.

Sometimes the parties enter into an agreement during the marriage that sets forth the distribution of property upon the termination of the marriage or death of a spouse and settles other issues usually addressed in a prenuptial agreement. This is called a **postnuptial agreement.** With these agreements, the courts apply the same standards for enforceability that they do to prenuptial agreements.

Web Exploration

Go to **http://www.people.com/people/archive/article/0,20186762,00.html** and read the article about the divorce judgment in the Paul McCartney-Heather Mills divorce proceeding.

Enforceable Prenuptial Agreement

For a prenuptial agreement to be enforceable, each party must make full disclosure of all his or her assets and liabilities, and each party should be represented by his or her own attorney. Prenuptial agreements must be entered into voluntarily, without threats or undue pressure, and they must provide for the fair distribution of assets and not be unconscionable. Generally, courts will enforce a properly negotiated prenuptial agreement even if the agreement provides for an unequal distribution of assets and eliminates financial support of a spouse if the marriage is terminated.

Courts will not enforce a prenuptial agreement in the following circumstances:

- One of the parties was not represented by an attorney.
- One of the parties failed to make full disclosure of his or her assets and liabilities.
- The agreement was entered into at the "last moment"—that is, immediately prior to the marriage.
- The terms of the agreement are unfair or unconscionable.
- The agreement violates public policy (for example, by having the result that a party will be forced to live on government assistance if the agreement is enforced).

The following feature discusses a paralegal's duty not to discuss confidential information learned while employed as a paralegal professional.

Termination of Marriage

Once a state has recognized the marital status of a couple, only the state can terminate this marital status. This is so even if the couple separates and lives apart from one another. As long as they are married, they continue to have certain legal rights and duties to one another. The law recognizes two methods for **marriage termination:** *annulment* and *divorce.*

Learning Objective 5

Explain a paralegal's duty to keep information confidential.

ETHICAL PERSPECTIVE

Paralegal's Duty to Keep Information Confidential

Ms. White, a paralegal professional, works for attorney Mr. Polk, who is a family law specialist. Mr. Polk is also a renowned lawyer who represents celebrity and wealthy clients in their divorce proceedings. One day a new client comes to the law office to see Mr. Polk. Ms. White recognizes this person as a celebrity.

After Mr. Polk and the client spend approximately one hour in a private meeting, Mr. Polk asks Ms. White to come into the meeting room, where he introduces her to the celebrity client. Mr. Polk then tells the client that Ms. White will be assisting him in the preparation of the forms, documents, and information necessary for the filing and pursuing of the divorce proceedings on behalf of the client.

That night, Ms. White and her husband go out to dinner with several friends, all of whom know that Ms. White works in the divorce area and that the lawyer she works for represents important clients. At dinner, Ms. White's friends ask her if she is working on any important cases involving celebrities or wealthy persons. Can Ms. White divulge that she is working on a divorce case involving a celebrity client? No, Ms. White cannot divulge this information.

Ms. White politely tells her friends that she is not at liberty to discuss any information about her professional involvement with clients. By telling her friends this, and by not divulging confidential information, Ms. White has met her ethical duty as a paralegal professional not to discuss confidential information learned on the job with persons other than her supervising attorney and the persons she is authorized to contact and discuss the case with in her capacity as a professional paralegal.

Annulment

An **annulment** is an order of the court declaring that a marriage did not exist, thus invalidating the marriage. Annulments are granted rarely today, now that most states recognize no-fault divorces.

Certain grounds must be asserted to obtain a legal annulment. One ground is that the parties lacked capacity to consent. Examples are:

1. One of the parties was a minor and had not obtained his or her parents' consent to marry.
2. One of the parties was mentally incapacitated at the time of the marriage.
3. One party was intoxicated at the time of the marriage.
4. The marriage was never consummated.

A marriage can also be annulled if the parties are too closely related to one another, if there was bigamy (one of the parties was already married), or if there was duress or fraud leading to the marriage (for example, one of the parties declared that he or she could conceive children even though the person knew for a fact that he or she could not).

Many annulments are sought because of a person's religion. For example, a Roman Catholic cannot be remarried in the church if he or she is divorced, but an annulment would allow for a subsequent marriage in the church. A person may also be required to go through a procedure to seek an annulment from the church. Thus a legal annulment and a religious annulment are two separate and distinct procedures.

The law considers children born of a marriage that is annulled to be legitimate. When a marriage is annulled, issues of child support, child custody, spousal support, and property settlement must be agreed upon by the couple or decided by the court.

Learning Objective 6
Define *annulment* and describe its consequences.

Annulment An order of the court declaring that a marriage did not exist.

Divorce

The most common option used by married partners to terminate their marriage is divorce. **Divorce** is a legal proceeding whereby the court issues a decree that legally orders a marriage terminated.

Traditionally, a married person who sought a divorce had to prove that the other person was *at fault* for causing a major problem in the marriage. An **at-fault divorce** requires the petitioning party to allege grounds for seeking the divorce such as adultery, physical or emotional abuse, abandonment, substance or alcohol abuse, or insanity.

Beginning in the 1960s, states began to recognize **no-fault divorce,** in which a spouse wishing to obtain a divorce merely has to assert **irreconcilable differences** with his or her spouse. Basically, in a no-fault divorce, neither party is blamed for the divorce. Today, every state recognizes no-fault divorce. However, a spouse may still decide to assert that the other party was at fault for causing the divorce in those states that consider fault when deciding how to divide **marital assets** and award spousal support.

Learning Objective 7
Define *divorce* and *no-fault divorce,* and describe divorce proceedings.

Divorce An order of the court that terminates a marriage.

No-fault divorce A divorce recognized by the law of a state whereby neither party is blamed for the divorce.

Divorce Proceedings

A divorce proceeding is commenced by a spouse filing a **petition for divorce** with the proper state court. The petition must contain required information such as the names of the spouses, the date and place of marriage, the names of minor children, and the reason for the divorce. The petition must be served on the other spouse, who then has a certain period of time (usually 20 to 30 days) to file an answer to the petition.

If the spouses do not reach a settlement of the issues involved in the divorce—such as property division, custody of the children, and spousal and child support—the case will go to trial. The parties are permitted to conduct discovery, which includes taking depositions and obtaining the production of documents. If the case goes to trial, each side is permitted to call witnesses, including expert witnesses (such as

Petition for divorce A document filed with the proper state court that commences a divorce proceeding.

financial experts), to testify on his or her behalf. Both parties are also allowed to introduce evidence that will support their claims.

Many states require a certain waiting period from the date a divorce petition is filed to the date the court grants a divorce. A typical waiting period is six months. The public policy reason for this waiting period is to give the parties time for reconciliation. After the waiting period has passed, a court will enter a **decree of divorce,** which is a court order terminating the marriage. The parties are then free to marry again. The decree of divorce may be granted even if the other issues concerning the divorce, such as division of property or support payments, have not yet been settled or tried.

Decree of divorce A court order that terminates a marriage.

If there is a showing that one partner is likely to injure the other partner, a court may issue a **restraining order.** This places limitations on the ability of the dangerous partner to go near the innocent partner.

Exhibit 17.1 shows a petition for a divorce.

Pro Se Divorce

***Pro se* divorce** A divorce proceeding in which the parties represent themselves in the divorce action.

In a ***pro se* divorce,** the parties do not have to hire lawyers to represent them and may represent themselves in the divorce proceeding. Most states permit *pro se*—commonly called "do-it-yourself"—divorces. If substantial assets are at stake in the divorce, or if there are complicated issues involving child custody, child support, or spousal support, the parties usually hire lawyers to represent them in the divorce proceeding.

Divorce Settlement

Approximately 90 percent of divorce cases are settled between the parties prior to trial. The parties often engage in negotiations to try to settle a divorce lawsuit in order to save the time and expense of a trial and to reach a **divorce settlement** that is acceptable to each side. These negotiations are usually conducted between the parties with the assistance of their attorneys.

Some divorcing parties use mediation to try to reach a settlement of the issues involved in terminating their marriage, and some states have mandatory mediation before divorcing couples can use the court to try the case. In **mediation,** a neutral third party—an attorney, a retired judge, or another party—acts as a **mediator** between the parties. A mediator is not empowered to make a decision but instead acts as a go-between and facilitator to try to help the parties reach an acceptable settlement of the issues. Mediation tends to be successful because it forces the parties to consider all facets of the case, including the opposing side's position.

Settlement agreement A written document signed by divorcing parties that evidences their agreement settling property rights and other issues of their divorce.

If a settlement is reached, a **settlement agreement** is drafted, usually by the attorneys. After being signed by the parties, the settlement agreement is presented to the court, which will accept the terms of the settlement agreement if the judge believes the settlement is fair and the rights of the parties and minor children are properly taken care of. If a case is not settled, it goes to trial.

Learning Objective 8

Describe how assets are distributed upon the termination of marriage.

Division of Assets and Spousal Support

Upon termination of a marriage, the parties may own certain assets, including property owned prior to the marriage, gifts and inheritances received during the marriage, and assets purchased with income earned during the marriage. In most cases, the parties reach a settlement as to how these assets are to be divided. If no settlement agreement is reached, the court will order the **division of assets.**

Separate Property

Separate property Property owned by a spouse prior to marriage, as well as inheritances and gifts received by a spouse during the marriage.

In most states, each spouse's separate property is awarded to the spouse who owns the separate property. **Separate property** includes property owned by a spouse prior to the marriage as well as inheritances and gifts received during the marriage. In most states, upon the termination of a marriage, each spouse is awarded his or her separate property.

Exhibit 17.1 Petition for divorce

IN THE CIRCUIT COURT OF THE ____________________ JUDICIAL CIRCUIT,
IN AND FOR ____________________ COUNTY, FLORIDA

Case No.: ______________________
Division: ______________________

______________________,
Petitioner, and
Respondent ______________________,

PETITION FOR DISSOLUTION OF MARRIAGE
WITH DEPENDENT OR MINOR CHILD(REN)

I, {**full legal name** ____, the [**one** only]
( ) Husband ( ) Wife, being sworn, certify that the following statements are true:

1. JURISDICTION/RESIDENCE
( ) Husband ( ) Wife ( ) Both has (have) lived in Florida for at least 6 months before the filing of this Petition for Dissolution of Marriage.

2. The husband [one only] ( ) is ( ) is not a member of the military service.
The wife [one only] ( ) is ( ) is not a member of the military service.

3. MARRIAGE HISTORY
Date of marriage: *{month, day, year}*______________________________
Place of marriage: *{city, state, country}* ______________________________
Date of separation: *{month, day, year}* ____________________ (ffl if approximate)

4. DEPENDENT OR MINOR CHILD(REN)
[all that apply]

a. [___] The wife is pregnant. Baby is due on: *{date}* ______________________

b. [___]The minor (under 18) child(ren) common to both parties are:

Name	Place of Birth	Birth date	Sex

c. [___]The minor child(ren) born or conceived during the marriage who are not common to both parties are:

Name	Place of Birth	Birth date	Sex

The birth father(s) of the above minor child(ren) is (are) *{name and address}* ____________
____

d. [___]The child(ren) common to both parties who are 18 or older but who are dependent upon the parties due to a mental or physical disability are:

Name	Place of Birth	Birth date	Sex

(continued)

Exhibit 17.1 Petition for divorce *(continued)*

5. A completed Uniform Child Custody Jurisdiction and Enforcement Act (UCCJEA) Affidavit, Florida Supreme Court Approved Family Law Form 12.902(d), is filed with this petition. (You must complete and attach this form in a dissolution of marriage with minor child(ren)).
6. A completed Notice of Social Security Number, Florida Supreme Court Approved Family Law Form 12.902(j), is filed with this petition.
7. This petition for dissolution of marriage should be granted because:
   [**one** only]
   a. [__] The marriage is irretrievably broken.
   b. [__] One of the parties has been adjudged mentally incapacitated for a period of 3 years prior to the filing of this petition. A copy of the Judgment of Incapacity is attached.

SECTION I. MARITAL ASSETS AND LIABILITIES

[**one** only]

1. [___] There are no marital assets or liabilities.
2. [___] There are marital assets or liabilities. All marital and nonmarital assets and liabilities are (or will be) listed in the financial affidavits, Florida Family Law Rules of Procedure Form 12.902(b) or (c), to be filed in this case.
   [ffl all that apply]
   a. [___] All marital assets and liabilities have been divided by a written agreement between the parties, which is attached, to be incorporated into the final judgment of dissolution of marriage. (The parties may use Marital Settlement Agreement for Dissolution of Marriage with Dependent or Minor Child(ren), Florida Supreme Court Approved Family Law Form 12.902(f)(1).
   b. [___] The Court should determine how the assets and liabilities of this marriage are to be distributed, under section 61.075, Florida Statutes.
   c. [___] Petitioner should be awarded an interest in Respondent's property because:

____

____

____

____

SECTION II. SPOUSAL SUPPORT (ALIMONY)

[one only]

1. [___] Petitioner forever gives up his/her right to spousal support (alimony) from Respondent.
2. [___] Petitioner requests that the Court order Respondent to pay the following spousal support (alimony) and claims that he or she has a need for the support that he or she is requesting **and Respondent has the ability to pay that support.** Spousal support (alimony) is requested in the amount of $________________ every ( ) week ( ) other week ( ) month, beginning *{date}* ________________________ and continuing until *{date or event}* ____________________________________.
   Explain why the Court should order Respondent to pay and any specific request(s) for type of alimony (temporary, permanent, rehabilitative, and/or lump sum):

____

____

____

____

____

[**if** applies] ( ) Petitioner requests life insurance on Respondent's life, provided by Respondent, to secure such support.

Exhibit 17.1 Petition for divorce *(continued)*

SECTION III. PARENTING PLAN ESTABLISHING PARENTAL RESPONSIBILITY AND TIME-SHARING

1. The minor child(ren) currently reside(s) with ( ) Mother ( ) Father ( ) Other: *{explain}*

____

2. **Parental Responsibility.** It is in the child(ren)'s best interests that parental responsibility be: [one only]
   a. [___] shared by both Father and Mother.
   b. [___] awarded solely to ( ) Father ( ) Mother. Shared parental responsibility would be detrimental to the child(ren) because: ____

   ____

   ____

   ____

3. **Parenting Plan and Time-Sharing.** It is in the best interests of the child(ren) that the family be ordered to comply with a Parenting Plan that ( ) includes ( ) does not include parental time-sharing with the child(ren). The Petitioner states that it is in the best interests of the child(ren) that: (Choose only one)
   a. [___] The attached proposed Parenting Plan should be adopted by the court. The parties ( ) have ( ) have not agreed to the Parenting Plan.
   b. [___]The court should establish a Parenting Plan with the following provisions:
      [___]No time-sharing for the [___] Husband [___] Wife.
      [___] Limited time-sharing with the [___] Husband [___] Wife.
      [___] Supervised Time-Sharing for the [___] Husband [___] Wife.
      [___] Supervised or third-party exchange of the child(ren).
      [___]Time-Sharing Schedule as follows:

   ____

   ____

4. Explain why this request is in the best interests of the child(ren):

____

____

____

____

SECTION IV. CHILD SUPPORT

[**all** that apply]

1. [___] Petitioner requests that the Court award child support as determined by Florida's child support guide lines, section 61.30, Florida Statutes. A completed Child Support Guidelines Worksheet, Florida Family Law Rules of Procedure Form 12.902(e), is, or will be filed. Such support should be ordered retroactive to:
   a. [___]the date of separation *{date}* _________ .
   b. [___] the date of the filing of this petition.
   c. [___] other *{date}* _________ *{explain}* ____.
2. [___] Petitioner requests that the Court award child support to be paid beyond the age of 18 years because:
   a. [___] the following child(ren) *{name(s)}* ____ is (are) dependent because of a mental or physical incapacity which began before the age of 18. *{explain}*

   ____

   ____

(continued)

Exhibit 17.1 Petition for divorce (*continued*)

b. [___] the following child(ren) *{name(s)}* ________________________________ is (are) dependent in fact and is (are) in high school while he/she (they) are between the ages of 18 and 19; said child(ren) is (are) performing in good faith with reasonable expectation of graduation before the age of 19.

3. [___] Petitioner requests that the Court award a child support amount that is more than or less than Florida's child support guidelines. Petitioner understands that Motion to Deviate from Child Support Guidelines, Florida Supreme Court Approved Family Law Form 12.943, **must** be filed before the court will consider this request.
4. [___] Petitioner requests that medical/dental insurance coverage for the minor child(ren) be provided by: [one only]
   a. [___] Father.
   b. [___] Mother.
5. [___] Petitioner requests that uninsured medical/dental expenses for the child(ren) be paid: [**one** only]
   a. [___] by Father.
   b. [___] by Mother.
   c. [___] by Father and Mother [each pay one-half].
   d. [___] according to the percentages in the Child Support Guidelines Worksheet, Florida Family Law Rules of Procedure Form 12.902(e).
   e. [___] Other *{explain}*:

   ____

   ____

6. Petitioner requests that life insurance to secure child support be provided by:
   a. [___] Father.
   b. [___] Mother.
   c. [___] Both.

SECTION V. OTHER

1. [If Petitioner is also the Wife, please indicate by either ( ) yes ( ) or no whether Petitioner/Wife wants to be known by her former name, which was *{full legal name}*

   ____

2. Other relief {specify}:

   ____

   ____

   ____

   ____

   ____

SECTION VI. PETITIONER'S REQUEST (This section summarizes what you are asking the Court to include in the final judgment of dissolution of marriage.)

Petitioner requests that the Court enter an order dissolving the marriage **and:**

[all that apply]

1. [___] distributing marital assets and liabilities as requested in Section I of this petition;
2. [___] awarding spousal support (alimony) as requested in Section II of this petition;
3. [___] adopt or establish a Parenting Plan containing provisions for parental responsibility and time sharing for the dependent or minor child(ren) common to both parties, as requested in Section III of this petition;
4. [___] establishing child support for the dependent or minor child(ren) common to both parties, as requested in Section IV of this petition;
5. [___] restoring Wife's former name as requested in Section V of this petition;
6. [___] awarding other relief as requested in Section V of this petition; and any other terms the Court deems necessary.

Exhibit 17.1 Petition for divorce (*continued*)

I understand that I am swearing or affirming under oath to the truthfulness of the claims made in this petition and that the punishment for knowingly making a false statement includes fines and/or imprisonment.

Dated: ________________ ______________________________ Signature of Petitioner

Printed Name: ______________________________

Address: ______________________________

City, State, Zip: ______________________________

Telephone Number: ______________________________

Fax Number: ______________________________

STATE OF FLORIDA
COUNTY OF ____________________

Sworn to or affirmed and signed before me on _________ by ____________________.
______________________________ NOTARY PUBLIC or DEPUTY CLERK
______________________________ [Print, type, or stamp commissioned name of notary or deputy clerk.]
[___] Personally known
[___] Produced identification
Type of identification produced ______________________________

IF A NONLAWYER HELPED YOU FILL OUT THIS FORM, HE/SHE MUST FILL IN THE BLANKS BELOW: [fill in **all** blanks]
I, *{full legal name and trade name of nonlawyer}* ______________________________, a nonlawyer, located at *{street}* ______________________________, *{city}* , ______________ ______________ *{state}* ______________, *{phone}* ______________, helped *{name}* ______________________________ who is the petitioner, fill out this form.

Assets In a divorce proceeding, the assets of the parties are distributed as agreed to in a prenuptial agreement, as provided in a settlement agreement, or as awarded by the court.

But if separate property is commingled with marital property during the course of the marriage, or if the owner of the separate property changes the title to the separate property by placing the other spouse's name on the title to the property (such as real estate), the separate property is considered a marital asset.

Marital Property

Marital property Property acquired during the course of marriage using income earned during the marriage, and separate property that has been converted to marital property.

Marital property consists of property acquired during the course of the marriage using income earned by the spouses during the marriage, and separate property that has been converted to marital property.

Different states adhere to two major legal theories when dividing marital assets upon the termination of a marriage. These are the theories of *equitable distribution* and *community property*.

Equitable Distribution

Equitable distribution A law used by many states where the court orders a *fair distribution* of marital property to the divorcing spouses.

In states that follow the rule of **equitable distribution,** the court may order the **fair distribution** of property, which does not necessarily mean the equal distribution of property. In determining the fair distribution of property, the court may consider factors such as:

- Length of the marriage
- Occupation of each spouse
- Standard of living during the marriage
- Wealth and income-earning ability of each spouse
- Which party is awarded custody of the children
- Health of the individuals
- Other factors relevant to the case

In most states, the house is most often awarded to the parent who is granted custody of the children. A court may also order the house to be sold and the proceeds divided fairly between the individuals.

Community Property

Community property A law used by some states in which the court orders an *equal division* of marital property to the divorcing spouses.

Under the doctrine of **community property,** all property acquired during the marriage using income earned during the marriage is considered marital property. It does not matter whose income was used to purchase the property or which spouse earned the higher income. Pension funds, stock options, the value of businesses, the value of professional licenses, and such are also considered community property.

In community-property states, marital property is divided *equally* between the individuals. An **equal division** of property does not necessarily mean that each piece of property is sold and the proceeds divided equally between the individuals. Typically, each asset of the marital property is valued by appraisers and expert witnesses. The court then awards the property to the spouses. For example, if one spouse is awarded the house, the other spouse is awarded other property of equal value.

Web Exploration

Using **www.google.com**, find out whether your state is an equitable distribution or community-property state.

SIDEBAR: DIVISION OF MARITAL PROPERTY

Law	Description
Equitable distribution	The marital property is distributed fairly. This does not necessarily mean the equal distribution of the property.
Community property	The marital property is divided *equally* between the parties.

Division of Debts

Upon termination of the marriage, individuals often have debts that must be divided. How these debts are divided depends on the type of debt and on state law. In most states, each spouse is personally liable for his or her own premarital debts and is not liable for the other spouse's debts. This is because the debt was incurred prior to the marriage. Student loans are a good example of this type of debt.

However, if a debt is not paid by the spouse to whom the court has distributed the debt, the third-party creditor may recover payment of the debt from the other spouse. This individual's only recourse is to recover the amount paid from his or her prior spouse.

Debts that are incurred during the marriage for necessities and other joint needs, including but not limited to shelter, clothing, automobiles, medical expenses, and such, are **joint marital debts** and are the joint responsibility of both spouses. The court may distribute these debts equally upon termination of the marriage. Spouses are also jointly liable for taxes incurred during their marriage.

Upon the termination of their marriage, it is wise for the individuals to notify prior creditors that they will no longer be responsible for the other's debts. This is particularly true if the individuals have joint credit cards.

Spousal Support

Learning Objective 9
Explain the requirements for awarding spousal support.

In some cases where a marriage is terminated, a court may award **spousal support**—also called **alimony**—to one of the divorced spouses. The other divorced spouse typically is ordered to pay the alimony in monthly payments. The parties may agree to the amount of alimony to be paid. If they do not reach an agreement, the court will determine whether the payment of alimony is warranted and, if so, the amount of alimony to be paid. In the past, alimony was usually awarded to the female, but today, with the female often earning more than the male, the male has been awarded alimony in some cases.

Spousal support Payments made by one divorced spouse to the other divorced spouse. Also called *alimony*.

Alimony is usually awarded for a specific period of time. This alimony is called **temporary alimony** or **rehabilitation alimony** and is designed to provide the receiving individual with payment for a limited time during which the individual can obtain the education or job skills necessary to enter the job force. Alimony is also awarded in cases where a parent, usually the female, needs to care for a child with a disability and must remain home to provide this care. Basically, the amount of alimony is based on the needs of the individual who will receive the alimony and on the income and ability of the other individual to pay.

Temporary alimony Alimony that is ordered by the court to be paid by one divorcing spouse to the other divorcing spouse for a limited period of time. Also called *rehabilitation alimony*.

Spousal support payments terminate if the former spouse dies, remarries, or otherwise becomes self-sufficient. Spousal support awards may also be modified by the court if circumstances change, such as if the paying individual loses his or her

Paralegals *in* Practice

PARALEGAL PROFILE
Adam M. Johnston

Adam M. Johnston has been a paralegal for four years. He specializes in family law at the firm of Murphy, Murphy & Nugent in New Haven, Connecticut. Adam graduated from the University of Rhode Island and obtained his Paralegal Certificate from Branford Hall Career Institute.

I work most frequently on child custody cases. My supervising attorney is often appointed by the court as a guardian ad litem to represent the best interests of a child or children. The attorney meets with the parents and the child or children, and also speaks with collateral sources such as teachers, school psychologists, therapists, and healthcare workers. My job involves coordinating the communications between the attorney and all the individuals directly or indirectly involved in the dispute. This includes frequent contact with both parents as they present their respective positions and concerns throughout the case. Strict confidentiality must always be maintained by the paralegal.

The most challenging cases are the ones that involve a parent who has alienated the child or children from the other parent. In these situations, mental health professionals often play a significant role. Since these cases are typically complicated and emotionally charged, agreements can be difficult to reach. Thus, as a family law paralegal, it is important not to take anything personal[ly], but instead to remember you are helping people through a very stressful and life-altering time in their lives.

Every divorce case I've worked on has settled prior to trial. Connecticut is a "no-fault" state and follows the equitable distribution doctrine for dividing marital property. However, many factors can influence the division of marital property, such as prenuptial agreements, the earning capacity of the parties, the length of the marriage, and custody issues. The recent downturn in the economy has resulted in more *pro se* divorce filings. Interacting with *pro se* parties can be difficult because they may be unaware of court proceedings, appropriate interaction between opposing sides, and the sequencing of events throughout the course of litigation.

job or his or her income decreases, if the receiving individual's income increases, or similar circumstances. A party wishing to have a spousal support award changed must petition the court to *modify* the award.

Permanent alimony Alimony that is ordered by the court to be paid by one divorcing spouse to the other divorcing spouse until the receiving spouse dies or remarries. Also called *lifetime alimony*.

The award of **permanent alimony**—sometimes called **lifetime alimony**—is usually awarded only if the individual to receive the alimony is of an older age or has been a homemaker and has had little opportunity to obtain job skills to enter the workplace. Permanent alimony must be paid until the individual receiving it dies or remarries.

In the feature above, a paralegal professional discusses his specialty in the field of family law.

Child Custody and Child Support

When a marriage is terminated, the custody of a child or children must be decided. In addition, child support may be awarded. These issues are discussed next.

Learning Objective 10

Explain child custody, visitation rights, joint custody of children, and child support.

Child Custody

Child custody The awarding of legal custody of a child to a parent based on the best interests of the child. The parent awarded custody is called the *custodial parent*.

When a couple terminates their marriage and they have children, the issue of who is legally and physically responsible for raising the children must be decided, either by settlement or by the court. The legal term **custody** is used to describe who has the legal responsibility for raising a child. **Child custody** is one of the most litigated issues between divorcing couples.

Traditionally, the court almost always granted custody of a child to the mother. Today, with fathers taking a more active role in childrearing, and with many mothers working, the courts sometimes grant custody to the father.

In **child custody disputes,** where both parents want custody of their child, the courts will determine what is in the **best interests of the child** in awarding custody. Some of the factors that a court considers are:

- The ability of each parent to provide for the needs of the child, such as education.
- The ability of each parent to provide for the emotional needs of the child.
- The ability of each parent to provide a stable environment for the child.
- The ability of each parent to provide for the special needs of a child who has a disability or requires special care.
- The desire of each parent to provide for the needs of the child.
- The wishes of the child. This factor is given more weight the older the child is.
- The religion of each parent.
- Other factors the court deems relevant.

The awarding of custody to a **custodial parent** is not permanent but may be altered by the court if circumstances change. The parent who is awarded custody has **legal custody** of the child. This usually includes physical custody of the child. The custodial parent has the right to make day-to-day and major decisions concerning the child's education, religion, and other such matters.

The court will not award custody to a certain parent, and sometimes not to either parent, if it is in the child's best interest for the custody not to be awarded to that parent or to either parent, such as if there has been **child abuse,** or because of other, extenuating circumstances. In such cases, the court may award custody to other relatives, such as grandparents, or place the child in a foster home.

Joint Custody

Joint custody A custody arrangement that gives both parents responsibility for making major decisions concerning their child.

Most states now permit joint custody of a child. **Joint custody** means that both parents are responsible for making major decisions concerning the child, such as his or her education, religion, and other major matters.

Parents are sometimes awarded **joint physical custody** of the child as well. This means that the child will spend a certain portion of time being raised by each parent. For example, the child may spend every other week with each parent, or the weekdays with one parent and the weekends with the other parent. These arrangements are awarded only if the child's best interests are served—for example, the child remaining in the same school while in the physical custody of each parent.

Joint physical custody A custody arrangement whereby the child of divorcing parents spends a certain amount of time being raised by each parent.

Visitation Rights

If the parents do not have joint custody of their child, the noncustodial parent typically is awarded **visitation rights.** This means that the noncustodial parent is given the right to visit the child for limited periods of time, as determined by a settlement agreement or by the court.

Visitation rights Rights of a noncustodial parent to visit his or her child for limited periods of time.

If the court is concerned about the safety of the child, the court may grant only supervised visitation rights to the noncustodial parent. This means that a court-appointed person must be present during the noncustodial parent's visitation with the child. This is usually done if there has been a history of child abuse or if there is a strong possibility that the noncustodial parent may kidnap the child.

Child Support

The noncustodial parent is obligated to contribute to the financial support of his or her natural and adopted children. This includes the costs for the child's food, shelter, clothing, medical expenses, and other necessities of life. This payment is called **child support.** The custodial and noncustodial parents may agree to the amount of child support. If they do not, the court will determine the amount of child support to be paid.

Child support Payments made by the noncustodial parent to help pay for the financial support of his or her children.

In awarding child support, the court considers several factors, including the number of children, the needs of the children, the net income of the parents, the standard of living of the children prior to the termination of their parents' marriage, any special medical or other needs of the children, and other factors that the court deems relevant. The duty to pay child support usually continues until a child reaches the age of majority, graduates from high school, or emancipates himself or herself by voluntarily choosing to live on his or her own.

Web Exploration

Go to www.google.com and find a Legal Aid Society serving your area for which you would like to volunteer to do pro bono work.

To help in the determination of child support, about half of the states have adopted a formula for computing the amount of child support that is based on a percentage of the noncustodial parent's income. A court is permitted to deviate from the formula if a child has special needs, such as if the child has a disability or requires special educational assistance.

An award of child support may be *modified* if conditions change. For example, an award of child support may be decreased if the noncustodial parent loses his or her job. Or the amount of child support may be modified if the child's needs change, such as if the child needs special care because of a disability. The parent wishing to obtain modification of child support must petition the court to change the award of child support.

Family Support Act

In the past, many noncustodial parents failed to pay child support when due. This often required long and expensive legal procedures by the custodial parent to obtain child support payments. To prevent noncustodial parents from failing to make required support payments, the federal government enacted the **Family Support Act.** This federal law, effective in 1994, provides that all original or modified child support orders require automatic wage withholding from a noncustodial parent's income.

Family Support Act A federal statute that provides for the automatic wage withholding of child support payments from a noncustodial parent's income.

Assume that a court order requires a noncustodial parent to pay 25 percent of his or her gross monthly income for child support. In this case, the court will order that noncustodial parent's employer to deduct this amount from the parent's income and send a check in this amount to the custodial parent. The noncustodial parent then receives a check for the remainder of his or her income.

Concept Review *and* Reinforcement

LEGAL TERMINOLOGY

Adoption 618
Adoptive parents 619
Agency adoption 619
Alimony 621
Annulment 623
At-fault divorce 623
Best interests of the child 632
Biological parents 619
Child abuse 632
Child custody 632
Child custody disputes 632
Child liability statutes 618
Child neglect 618
Child support 633
Civil union 617
Common-law marriage 616
Community property 630
Custodial parent 632
Custody 632
Decree of divorce 624
Defense of Marriage Act (DOMA) 617
Division of assets 624
Divorce 623
Divorce settlement 624
Emancipation 616
Engagement 614
Equal division 630
Equitable distribution 630
Fair distribution 630
Family Support Act 633
Father's registry 618
Fault rule 615
Fiancé 614
Fiancée 614
Financial support 616
Foster care 620
Foster child 620
Foster family 620
Foster parents 620
Independent adoption 619
Irreconcilable differences 623
Joint custody 632
Joint marital debts 631
Joint physical custody 633
Legal custody 632
Lifetime alimony 632
Marital assets 623
Marital property 630
Marriage 615
Marriage ceremony 616
Marriage license 616
Marriage requirements 616
Marriage termination 622
Mediation 624
Mediator 624
No-fault divorce 623
Objective rule 615
Open adoption 619
Parents 617
Parents' duties 617
Parents' right 617
Paternity 618
Paternity action 618
Permanent alimony 632
Petition for divorce 623
Postnuptial agreement 621
Premarital agreement 620
Prenuptial agreement 620
Pro se divorce 624
Promise to marry 614
Rehabilitation alimony 631
Restraining order 624
Same-sex marriage 617
Separate property 624
Settlement agreement 624
Spousal support 631
Temporary alimony 631
Visitation rights 633

SUMMARY OF KEY CONCEPTS

Premarriage Issues

Promise to Marry	A promise to marry takes place when a promise by one person to marry is made to another person. The courts usually do not enforce such promises as contracts.
Engagement	The engagement is a period of time that begins when one person asks another person to marry him or her, and ends when the parties get married or terminate their engagement.
	The prospective bride is called the *fiancée*, and the prospective groom is called the *fiancé*. Most often, the male is the one who gives the female an engagement ring to signify their engagement. Females may also give males engagement rings.

Termination of an Engagement	If a party ends the engagement, states apply one of the following rules regarding the return of the engagement ring. a. *Fault rule:* If the prospective groom breaks off the engagement, the prospective bride may keep the ring. If the prospective bride breaks off the engagement, the ring must be returned to the prospective groom. b. *Objective rule:* If the engagement is broken off, the prospective bride must return the ring to the prospective groom irrespective of which party broke off the engagement.
Marriage	
	Marriage has been defined as a legal union between a male and a female that confers certain duties and rights upon the spouses. Some states permit the marriage of people of the same sex.
Marriage License	A marriage license is a legal document issued by the state certifying that two people are married.
Marriage Ceremony	A marriage ceremony is held before a designated government official or at a church, temple, synagogue, mosque, or other place of worship before a minister, priest, rabbi, or mullah. At the ceremony, the parties exchange wedding vows.
Common-Law Marriage	A common-law marriage is a type of marriage recognized by several states wherein two people who have not been officially married are considered married if certain requirements are met, such as living together for a specified period of time.
Same-Sex Marriage	Same-sex marriage is a marriage between two people of the same sex. Several states permit same-sex marriages. Some other states permit *civil unions* between persons of the same sex.
Parents and Children	
Emancipation	Emancipation occurs when a child leaves his or her parents and voluntarily lives on his or her own. The child is then responsible for providing his or her own livelihood.
Paternity Action	A paternity action is a legal proceeding in which the court identifies the true identity of the father of a child.
Adoption	Adoption occurs when a person becomes the legal parent of a child who is not his or her biological child. 1. *Agency adoption:* A person adopts a child from a social organization of a state. 2. *Open adoption:* The biological mother is introduced to the adoptive parent or parents prior to the adoption. 3. *Independent adoption:* The biological mother or parents enter into a private arrangement with the adoptive parent or parents for the adoption of the child.
Foster Care	Foster care is an arrangement in which a child is placed temporarily with a foster family. The state government pays the foster family a fee for caring for the foster child.
Prenuptial Agreement	
	A prenuptial agreement is a contract entered into by prospective spouses prior to marriage that specifies how property will be distributed upon termination of the marriage or death of a spouse. Prenuptial agreements often include agreements regarding the following financial and family issues: 1. Separate property 2. Marital or community property 3. Income and debt of the spouses 4. Alimony 5. Child custody 6. Child support 7. Other financial and family issues

Postnuptial Agreement	A postnuptial agreement is a contract entered into by spouses during marriage that specifies how property will be distributed upon termination of the marriage or death of a spouse.
Termination of Marriage	
Annulment	An annulment is an order of the court declaring that a marriage did not exist.
Divorce	A divorce is an order of the court that terminates a marriage. A *decree of divorce* is issued by the court that terminates the divorce. 1. *At-fault divorce:* A divorce recognized by the law of a state that requires the petitioning party to allege and prove grounds for obtaining a divorce. 2. *No-fault divorce:* A divorce recognized by the law of a state where neither party is blamed for the divorce; the petitioning party merely has to assert irreconcilable differences.
Pro Se Divorce	*Pro se* denotes a divorce proceeding in which the parties do not hire an attorney but instead represent themselves in the divorce action.
Divorce Settlement	In a divorce settlement, the parties settle their divorce voluntarily and prior to going to court. The *settlement agreement* is the written document signed by the divorcing parties that evidences their agreement to settle property rights and other issues of their divorce.
Division of Assets and Spousal Support	
Separate Property	Separate property is the property owned by a spouse prior to marriage, as well as inheritances and gifts received by the spouse during the marriage.
Marital Property	Marital property is the property acquired during the course of the marriage using income earned during the marriage, plus property that has been converted into marital property. Two methods of dividing this property are: 1. A method used by some states where the court orders *equitable* (fair) *distribution* of marital property to the divorcing spouses. This does not necessarily mean the equal distribution of marital property. 2. A method used by some states where the court orders an *equal distribution* of marital property to the divorcing spouses.
Division of Debts	In the division of debts, *joint marital debts* incurred during the marriage are the joint responsibility of the divorcing spouses. The court may distribute these debts to individual divorcing spouses, but if one divorced spouse does not pay the debt, the creditor can seek payment from the other divorced spouse.
Spousal Support	Spousal support is an amount of money ordered by a court to be paid by one divorcing spouse to another divorcing spouse for a period of time during and after the divorce is final. Also called *alimony*, of which there are two types: 1. *Temporary alimony:* An amount ordered by the court to be paid from one divorcing spouse to the other divorcing spouse for a limited period of time. Also called *rehabilitation alimony*. 2. *Permanent alimony:* An amount ordered by the court to be paid from one divorcing spouse to the other divorcing spouse until the receiving spouse dies or remarries. Sometimes called *lifetime alimony*.
Child Custody and Child Support	
Child Custody	The awarding of child custody to a parent is based on the best interests of the child. The parent awarded custody is called the *custodial parent*. The other parent is called the *noncustodial parent*.

Joint Custody	Joint custody means that both divorced parents are responsible for making major decisions concerning their child.
Joint Physical Custody	Joint physical custody means that the child of divorced parents spends a certain amount of time being raised by each parent.
Visitation Rights	Visitation rights confer to the noncustodial parent the right to visit his or her child for limited periods of time.
Child Support	Child support consists of payments made by the noncustodial parent to help pay for the financial support of his or her children.
Family Support Act	The Family Support Act is a federal statute that provides for the automatic withholding of child support payments from a noncustodial parent's income.

WORKING THE WEB

1. Using http://google.com or a similar Internet search engine, find the marriage requirements in your state. Write a one-page report describing these requirements.
2. Go to the website http://en.wikipedia.org/wiki/cohabitation_agreement. What is a cohabitation agreement? When would such an agreement be used? Write a one-page report describing a cohabitation agreement, and the advantages and disadvantages of using one.
3. Using http://google.com or a similar Internet search engine, find the law about dividing marital property upon divorce in your state. Does your state follow the equitable distribution rule or the community-property rule for dividing marital property?

CRITICAL THINKING & WRITING QUESTIONS

1. What is a promise to marry? Is such a promise enforceable?
2. What is an engagement? Who gets the engagement ring if the engagement is broken off under (a) the fault rule and (b) the objective rule?
3. Describe a prenuptial agreement. What are some of the issues addressed in a prenuptial agreement?
4. Define "marriage." What are the legal requirements to be able to be married? What is a common-law marriage?
5. What is same-sex marriage? In which states are same-sex marriages recognized?
6. Describe the following: (a) agency adoption, (b) open adoption, and (c) independent adoption.
7. What is an annulment? What are the requirements for obtaining an annulment?
8. Define "divorce." Describe the difference between (a) at-fault divorce and (b) no-fault divorce.
9. Describe the following: (a) petition for divorce, (b) decree of divorce, and (c) *pro se* divorce.
10. Describe a divorce settlement. What is a settlement agreement?
11. Describe the difference between (a) separate property and (b) marital property.
12. Describe the rule of equitable distribution. Describe the doctrine of community property.
13. What is spousal support? Explain the difference between (a) temporary alimony or rehabilitation alimony and (b) permanent alimony or lifetime alimony.
14. Describe (a) child custody, (b) joint custody, (c) joint physical custody, and (d) visitation rights.
15. What is child support? What does the Family Support Act provide?

Building Paralegal Skills

VIDEO CASE STUDIES

Lillian Harris, Small Family Law Practice

Interview with Lillian Harris, Esq., a sole practitioner with a family law practice.

After viewing the video case study in MyLegalStudiesLab, answer the following:

1. What are the soft skills necessary for working in a small office? How do these differ from the skills needed when working in a large firm?
2. How important are the functions performed by a paralegal in a small office?
3. What are the advantages of working in a small firm?

UPL Issue: Helping the Client without Practicing Law

Paralegal Michael Reed is asked questions by a client in an interview discussing custody issues and what the client should do.

After viewing the video case study in MyLegalStudiesLab, answer the following:

1. Did the paralegal commit UPL by answering the client's questions?
2. Are clients in domestic cases different from those in other areas of practice?
3. What additional skills does the paralegal need in working in a family law practice?

ETHICS ANALYSIS & DISCUSSION QUESTIONS

1. What are the ethical obligations of a paralegal regarding discussing facts about a client's divorce with others? Explain.
2. As a paralegal, can you give any advice to clients of your law firm regarding the procedures for obtaining a divorce in your state? What are the limits on the types of information that you can tell a client about such procedures?
3. The attorney you work for has requested that you research how to adopt a child from another country, which you do. When the client calls to see if you have found this information, are you, as a paralegal, at liberty to share this information with the client? Explain.

DEVELOPING YOUR COLLABORATION SKILLS

With a group of other students selected by you or your instructor, review the facts of the following case. As a group, discuss the following questions.

1. Who are the parties to this case?
2. What is the test that is applied by a court in determining the custody of a child?
3. Should Michael's motion to be the designated residential parent of J.E. be granted?
4. Should Michael's motion to be permitted unsupervised parenting time with J.E. be granted?
5. Should Judith's motion to permit Michael only supervised parenting time with J.E. be granted?

Eitutis v. Eitutis

Michael and Judith Eitutis were married on May 20, 2000. On January 23, 2004, they had a daughter, J.E. On February 1, 2006, the trial court issued a judgment of divorce, terminating the parties' marriage on grounds of incompatibility. The judgment granted Judith legal custody and appointed her residential parent of J.E. The court awarded Michael unsupervised parenting time with J.E., allowing Michael visits during the middle of the week and alternating weekends. Judith remarried. Michael remarried a woman who had a male child.

In 2007, Judith did not permit Michael to see J.E. because he had been abusing prescription drugs that led to his hospitalization. On September 28, 2007, Judith filed an emergency ex parte motion alleging that Michael had overdosed on prescription drugs and asked the court to only permit Michael supervised visitation rights with J.E. The order was issued. Michael admitted to being addicted to prescription drugs. He went to a detox program and later started attending a weekly 12-step program for addicts. Michael failed to attend some of the 12-step program meetings. Michael was ordered to take drug tests every two weeks, but missed several appointments and was caught modifying a drug test. On October 1, 2007, Michael was charged with criminally damaging Judith's car. Michael subsequently pleaded guilty to the charge.

In 2008, Judith testified that J.E. informed her that Michael's stepson, an eleven-year[-]old boy at the time, had touched J.E. inappropriately by putting his hands down J.E.'s underwear. On June 9, 2009, Michael sent a threatening e-mail to Judith. A temporary restraining order was issued against Michael, protecting Judith, J.E., and Judith's husband.

On August 21, 2008, Michael filed two motions with the court. The first motion was to be designated the residential parent of J.E. In the alternative, Michael's second motion was for unsupervised parenting time with J.E. Judith made a motion to only permit Michael supervised parenting time with J.E. Testimony of expert witnesses stated that Michael has an ongoing problem with drug use.

Source: Eitutis v. Eitutis, 2011 Ohio 2838 (Court of Appeals of Ohio, 2011)

PARALEGAL PORTFOLIO EXERCISE

Refer to the Paralegals at Work scenario at the beginning of the chapter. Prepare a memorandum, no longer than three pages, that describes how the property of Ms. Aston and Mr. Breton would be distributed under (1) the rule of equitable distribution and (2) the rule of community property. Make any assumptions you think are necessary, but be sure to list those assumptions in your memorandum.

LEGAL ANALYSIS & WRITING CASES

Sides v. Sides 717 S.E.2d 472 (2011)

Supreme Court of Georgia

Richard Sides and Barbara Sides began dating in 1989. Barbara became pregnant, and Richard agreed to marry her on the condition that the parties enter into a prenuptial agreement. Each side was represented by their own attorney in negotiating the prenuptial agreement. Richard made full disclosure of his assets and financial interests. Richard owned his own telecommunications company and had a net worth of $4.2 million. Barbara was a flight attendant with few financial assets. The attorneys fully discussed the terms of the prenuptial agreement with their clients before the parties signed the agreement. The prenuptial agreement provided for the division of property and alimony to be paid Barbara upon divorce. Barbara would be entitled to substantially more resources if the parties divorced after their twenty-year anniversary.

Over the course of their marriage Richard's estate grew to a value of $8 million. Prior to their twentieth anniversary Richard filed for divorce. The trial court enforced the prenuptial agreement and Barbara was awarded her car and $250,000 (payable in installments of $25,000 per year for ten years). The divorce was finalized 62 days prior to their twenty-year anniversary. Barbara appealed the trial court's decision, alleging that that the prenuptial agreement should not be enforced because it would be unfair, unreasonable, and unconscionable to do so.

Question

1. Is the prenuptial agreement enforceable?

Campbell v. Thomas 897 N.Y.S.2d 460 (2010)

Appellate Division of the Supreme Court of New York

In early 2000, Howard Nolan Thomas was diagnosed with terminal prostate cancer and severe dementia attributed to Alzheimer's disease. During the last years of Howard's life, his dementia caused him to become extremely forgetful, [and he] experienced great confusion, paranoia, and was prone to temper outbursts. He would w[a]nder off and not know where he was. Howard was heavily sedated and was taking substantial amounts of prescription medicine for his conditions.

Howard lived with his daughter, Nancy Thomas. Howard required constant care. In 2001, when Nancy went away on a one-week vacation, she left Howard, who was then 72 years old, in the care of Nidia Colon, who was 58 years old. During Nancy's vacation, Nidia married Howard and had Howard transfer his assets into her name.

Specifically, Nidia caused the ownership of Howard's account at Citibank of $150,000 to be changed from Howard individually to Nidia and Howard jointly, and caused her to be named the sole beneficiary of Howard's pension account with the New York City Teachers' Retirement System, valued at $147,000. Nidia kept this marriage and the property transfers secret. Subsequently Nancy and two of Howard's other children, Christopher Campbell and Keith Thomas, learned of [the] marriage and property transfers. When Nancy confronted Howard about the marriage[,] he had no knowledge of the marriage and adamantly denied that it occurred, stating: "What are you talking about? . . . I'm not married. . . . Are you crazy?"

Howard died in August 2001. Christopher filed Howard's will, dated March 24, 1976, for probate, which left his estate equally among his children. Nancy, Christopher, and Keith commenced this action against Nidia, seeking a judgment declaring Nidia's marriage to Howard, as well as the changes to the bank account ownership and the retirement account beneficiary, to be null and void. They asserted that Howard lacked the legal capacity to enter into the marriage or execute the changes to his accounts.

Question

1. Are the marriage and the property transfers to Nidia null and void?

WORKING WITH THE LANGUAGE OF THE COURT CASE

In the Matter of the Marriage of Joyner

196 S.W.3d 883, Web 2006 Tex. App. Lexis 5691
Court of Appeals of Texas

Read and brief the following case, excerpted from the court of appeals opinion. In your brief, answer the following questions.

1. Who are the parties to the lawsuit?
2. What asset are the parties disputing ownership of?
3. What is community property?
4. When was the date of the final judgment in the divorce action?
5. As a question of fact, do you think that the court ruled correctly?

Carter, Justice

The trial court announced, "Your divorce is granted." The question presented is whether that pronouncement was the rendition of a final judgment in a divorce and child conservatorship case when the parties had previously entered a mediated settlement agreement complying with statutory provisions which made the agreement immediately binding and irrevocable on the parties and entitled them to a judgment on the agreement. We find the trial court rendered judgment by its oral pronouncement.

On May 29, 2001, Belinda Joyner filed for divorce from Thomas Joyner. At the end of their third mediation April 7, 2003, the parties signed a mediated settlement agreement that delineated and partitioned most of their property and conservatorship and support of their minor son. The parties met for their "final hearing" on July 2, 2003, to argue the few personal property issues they had been unable to resolve in mediation.

On July 3, 2003, the day after the final hearing, Thomas purchased a winning lottery ticket worth $2,080,000.00. Almost a year later, on May 7, 2004, Belinda filed a motion for final trial setting, claiming the divorce had never been finalized, she was still married to Thomas, and the $2,080,000.00 should be divided as community property. On June 28, 2004, the court signed a "Final Decree of Divorce," which stated the divorce had been judicially pronounced and rendered on July 2, 2003. Belinda appeal[ed], claiming the divorce was not final until June 28, 2004.

The issue in this case is whether the trial court's actions on July 2, 2003, constituted an oral rendition of judgment on the Joyners' divorce. A decision on this issue directly affects the categorization of the lottery winnings as Thomas' separate or the Joyners' community property. Belinda . . . contends she and Thomas were still married when he won the lottery, and therefore she is entitled to a just and right division of those winnings.

A judgment is rendered when the court makes an official announcement, either in writing or orally in open court, of its decision on the matter submitted for adjudication. In order to be an official judgment, the trial court's oral pronouncement must indicate intent to render a full, final, and complete judgment at that point in time. Whether a particular action constitutes a rendition of judgment is a question of fact.

In this case, the words granting a divorce are undeniably there. The statement by the trial court was made in open court while officiating as the presiding judge after all evidence had been presented and in the presence of all parties and attorneys. During the process of ruling on some rings and other personal property items, the court recognized that Thomas acknowledged a gift of a diamond ring to his son because he knew that was his (Thomas') mother's wish; however, he did not recognize a similar gift of a ring to his daughter because he did not hear his mother make such a statement. The court then stated,

> There is evidence, and, you know, probably credible evidence that your mother made a similar statement in regard to this lady's ring, broach, and broach guard, in regard to your daughter, but since you didn't hear it yourself, you've elected not to make yourself a gift of these items to your daughter. And that's your prerogative. You have every legal right to do so. And it may be that—*your divorce is granted*—so I'll now say—your former wife has made all this up.

We interpret that as a clear statement granting the divorce. The trial court then referred to Belinda as "your former wife." The present intent to grant a divorce by oral pronouncement is clear to us. In light of the tone of the court throughout the day, the language "your divorce is granted" expressed present intent to render judgment.

Once a couple is divorced, they can no longer accumulate community property, for there is no longer a community. By looking at the record of the hearing in its entirety, we conclude the trial court rendered an oral pronouncement granting a judgment of divorce which necessarily incorporated the terms of the binding mediated settlement agreement. The judgment of the trial court is affirmed.

MYLEGALSTUDIESLAB

MyLegalStudiesLab Virtual Law Office Experience Assignments Complete the pre-test, study plan, and post-test for this chapter and answer the Legal Applications questions as assigned. These will help you confirm your mastery of the concepts and their application to legal scenarios. Then complete the Virtual Law Office assignments as assigned by your instructor. These assignments are designed to develop your workplace skills. Completing the assignments for this chapter will result in producing the following documents for inclusion in your portfolio:

VLOE 17.1	Office memo describing the procedures in your state for changing visitation or support obligations

CHAPTER

18

Agency, Employment, and Immigration Law

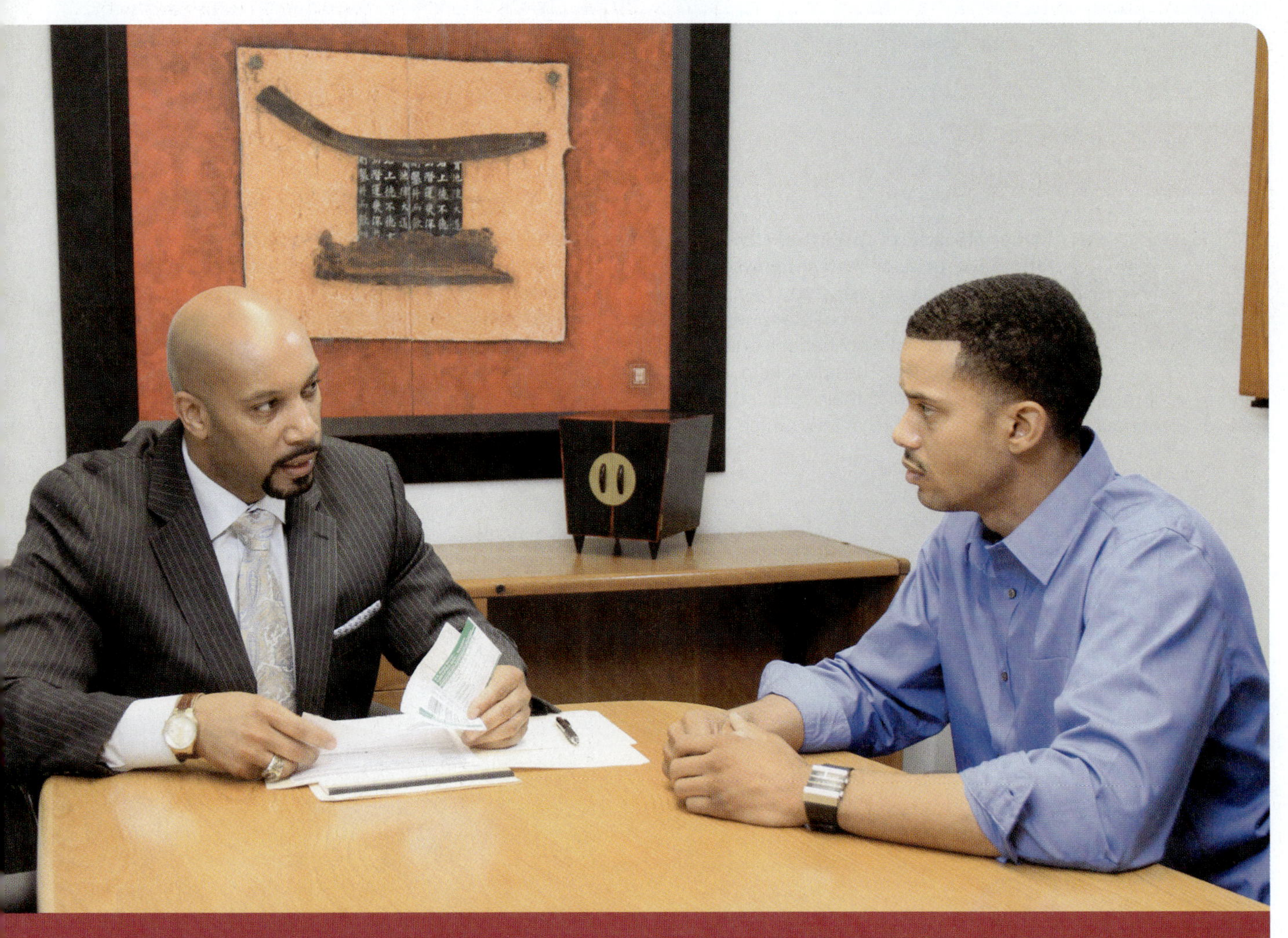

Paralegals at Work

You are a paralegal for Ms. Francis Brown, a renowned attorney in the area of employment law. You have been Ms. Brown's paralegal for more than ten years. One day, Ms. Brown calls you into her office so that you can sit in on a conference with a new client, Ms. Maria Rodriquez. Ms. Rodriquez has hired Ms. Brown to determine whether she has an employment law case against her employer, Retro Bank, N.A., a private bank that has hundreds of branch offices across the United States. During the conference, Ms. Rodriquez explains her situation.

Ms. Rodriquez has worked for Retro Bank for fifteen years. She started as an assistant branch manager and was promoted to branch manager and assistant vice president seven years ago. Ms. Rodriquez is still an assistant vice president and branch manager in a branch office located in the Hispanic community. She had earned a bachelor's degree in business administration from the Wharton School, University of Pennsylvania, just before starting with the bank.

Several months ago, Ms. Rodriquez applied for a promotion to district manager of a region of the bank. The only other candidate to apply for this position was Mr. Rich Huntington, a white male who graduated with a Master in Business Administration (MBA) degree from a university and has worked as a branch manager for three years.

The candidate to be promoted to the new district manager position would be in charge of at least ten branch offices, and the promotion would include the title "Vice

LEARNING OBJECTIVES

After studying this chapter, you should be able to:

1. Recognize the professional opportunities for paralegals in the employment law area.
2. Describe how express, implied, and apparent agencies are created.
3. Identify and describe the principal's liability for the tortious conduct of an agent.
4. Explain how state workers' compensation programs work and describe the benefits available.
5. Describe the scope of coverage of Title VII of the Civil Rights Act of 1964.
6. Describe the scope of coverage of the Age Discrimination in Employment Act.
7. Describe the protections afforded by the Americans with Disabilities Act.
8. Describe how a labor union is organized and employees' rights to strike and picket.
9. Understand immigration laws that apply to employment law.
10. Explain a paralegal's duty to disclose his or her paralegal status.

> "It is difficult to imagine any grounds, other than our own personal economic predilections, for saying that the contract of employment is any the less an appropriate subject of legislation than are scores of others, in dealing with which this Court has held that legislatures may curtail individual freedom in the public interest."
>
> Justice Stone *Dissenting Opinion, Morehead v. New York 298 U.S. 587, 56 S.Ct. 918* (1936)

President" and a salary increase of $50,000 per year. The requirements for the new position were a bachelor's degree, experience as a bank branch manager for three or more years, the passing of a financial analysis test, and an interview with the president and the board of directors of the bank. Ms. Rodriquez and Mr. Huntington both passed the financial test.

At the interview, the president and board members asked Ms. Rodriquez questions about her job experience and management style, and she found several questions somewhat troubling, particularly the questions about the ages of her two children (4 and 6), whether she would be willing to attend charity events on some evenings to promote the bank, and whether traveling on bank business would cause any problems with her family. Later, Ms. Rodriquez was told that she had not received the promotion but that Mr. Huntington had.

Ms. Rodriquez wants to know if she has any cause to sue Retro Bank. She had once heard that the bank promoted majority-race males over minority-race females in the past, particularly for positions as district managers, including for oversight of bank branches in primarily white areas. Currently the bank has forty district managers, only four of whom are female. None of them are minorities.

Consider the issues involved in this scenario as you read this chapter.

INTRODUCTION FOR THE PARALEGAL

Paralegals often work for lawyers who specialize in employment law matters. Lawyers in this area of practice negotiate and draft employment contracts, advise businesses on compliance with federal and state worker protection and antidiscrimination laws, and represent businesses and employees in the litigation of employment law disputes. Paralegals who work in this area must have an understanding of agency law, federal and state employment statutes, and administrative law that affects the employment relationship.

It isn't the people you fire who make your life miserable, it's the people you don't.

Harvey MacKay

If individuals and businesses had to conduct all of their business personally, the scope of their activities would be severely curtailed. The use of agents (or agency), which allows one person to act on behalf of another, solves this problem. Among the many examples of agency relationships are a salesperson who sells goods for a store, an executive who works for a corporation, a partner who acts on behalf of a partnership, an attorney who is hired to represent a client, and a real estate broker who is employed to sell a house. Agency is governed by a large body of common law known as *agency law*.

The United States Congress has enacted many federal statutes that provide protections and benefits for employees. For example, Congress has enacted federal statutes establishing worker safety rules, providing for the payment of minimum wages, and prohibiting discrimination based on race, sex, religion, age, disability, and other protected classes. States have enacted similar laws.

Learning Objective 1

Recognize the professional opportunities for paralegals in the employment law area.

Another area of the law that is becoming more important is that of immigration law. Immigration law includes the issues involved in becoming a citizen of the United States. In the employment law area, immigration law includes advising employers as to how to comply with immigration laws. It also includes assisting employers in obtaining foreign worker visas for their prospective employees.

CAREER OPPORTUNITIES FOR PARALEGALS IN EMPLOYMENT AND IMMIGRATION LAW

The paralegal who works in the employment law area may be involved in many different areas, as employment law consists of an array of state and federal laws. A paralegal who works in this field must have good knowledge of the state and federal laws that apply to employers and employees in the state in which he or she works.

The law of agency applies to employers and employees as well as to other employment relationships. Principals generally are liable for the torts of their agents, and usually are liable for the contracts entered into by agents on behalf of the principal while the agent is acting within the scope of his or her employment.

Employers are often sued by third parties, either to recover for the negligence and other torts committed by employees or to enforce contracts that their employees have entered. Agency law is an area of the law in which paralegals are needed to support attorneys, particularly when an attorney is representing the employer, employee, or third party in lawsuits involving agency and employment law matters.

In the employment law area, attorneys are called upon to negotiate and draft employment contracts. Attorneys are sometimes hired by corporations and other businesses to draft form employment contracts that the employer requires employees to sign. In other cases, attorneys represent either the executive or the employer in negotiating complex employment law agreements—bonuses, stock option plans, and the like. Paralegals usually prepare drafts of these employment contracts for the attorneys.

Paralegals often work for attorneys who represent clients who must comply with complex federal and state worker safety and protection statutes. These include workers' compensation laws, the federal Occupational Safety and Health Act, the federal Fair Labor Standards Act, and other state and federal laws. Attorneys represent employers and employees in administrative proceedings and lawsuits involving these safety laws. Paralegals must understand these laws and regulatory procedures because they often draft documents required to comply with these laws, conduct research, and perform other tasks for lawyers involved in this area of employment law.

One exciting area for paralegals in this field is the compliance and enforcement of equal opportunity in employment laws. A major federal statute in this area is Title VII of the Civil Rights Act of 1964, which prohibits employment discrimination based on race, national origin, color, religion, and sex. Other federal antidiscrimination statutes include the Equal Pay Act, the Age Discrimination in Employment Act, and the Americans with Disabilities Act, among others. States also have statutes that prohibit job discrimination.

In the area of equal opportunity in employment laws, paralegals may be engaged in researching statutes, regulations, or case law; preparing documents to be submitted to the government administrative agencies that enforce these laws; or preparing for lawsuits involving equal opportunity in employment laws. If there is an administrative hearing or a lawsuit, a paralegal will be called upon by his or her attorney to help prepare the case for the hearing or lawsuit.

Another growing area of employment opportunities for paralegal professionals is in immigration law. Many paralegals do a substantial amount of the work in preparing documents and assisting attorneys in representing clients who have immigration law issues.

The area of employment law covers a vast array of employment opportunities for paralegals. As a growing area of the law, there will be even more need in the future for paralegals qualified for positions in employment law.

Employment law is a burgeoning area of the law. Paralegals will be called on to conduct research, assist lawyers in the preparation and review of employment contracts, and prepare for litigation in this exciting area of the law.

The feature above discusses the career opportunities for paralegal professionals in employment and immigration law.

Agency Law

Learning Objective 2

Describe how express, implied, and apparent agencies are created.

Agency relationships are formed by the mutual consent of a principal and an agent. Section 1(1) of the Restatement (Second) of Agency defines *agency* as a *fiduciary relationship* "which results from the manifestation of consent by one person to another that the other shall act in his behalf and subject to his control, and consent by the other so to act." The Restatement (Second) of Agency is the reference source of the rules of agency. A party who employs another person to act on his or her behalf is called a **principal.** A party who agrees to act on behalf of another

Principal A party who employs another person to act on his or her behalf.

Exhibit 18.1 The principal-agent relationship

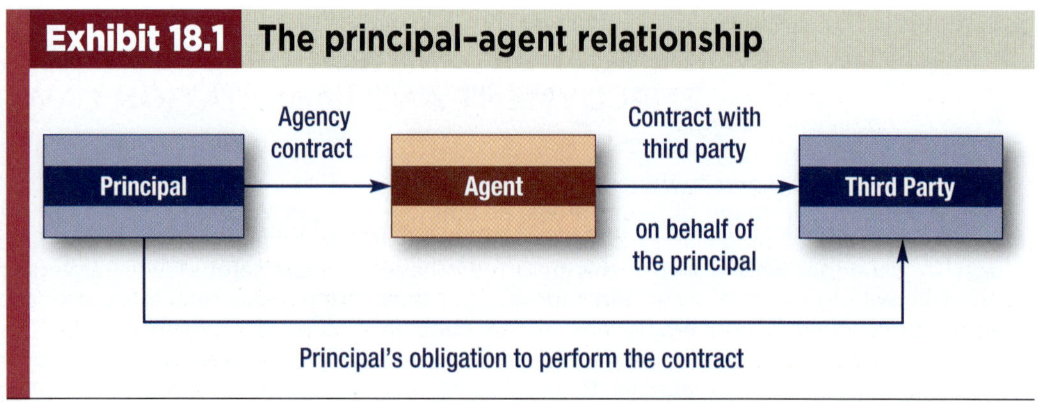

Agent A party who agrees to act on behalf of another.

Agency A principal-agent relationship; the fiduciary relationship "which results from the manifestation of consent by one person to another that the other shall act in his behalf and subject to his control, and consent by the other so to act."

is called an **agent.** The principal–agent relationship is commonly referred to as an **agency.** This relationship is depicted in Exhibit 18.1.

Any person who has the capacity to contract can appoint an agent to act on his or her behalf. Generally, persons who lack contractual capacity, such as insane persons and minors, cannot appoint an agent. But the court can appoint a legal guardian or other representative to handle the affairs of insane persons, minors, and others who lack this capacity. With court approval, these representatives can enter into enforceable contracts on behalf of the persons they represent.

An agency can be created only to accomplish a lawful purpose. Agency contracts that are created for illegal purposes or are against public policy are void and unenforceable.

> Examples A principal cannot hire an agent to kill another person. Some agency relationships are prohibited by law. Unlicensed agents cannot be hired to perform the duties of certain licensed professionals (such as doctors and lawyers).

Kinds of Employment Relationships

Businesses usually have three kinds of employment relationships: (1) employer–employee relationships; (2) principal–agent relationships; and (3) principal–independent contractor relationships.

Employer-Employee Relationship

Employer-employee relationship A relationship that results when an employer hires an employee to perform some form of physical service.

An **employer–employee relationship** exists when an employer hires an employee to perform some form of physical service.

> Example A welder on General Motors Corporation's assembly line is employed in an employer–employee relationship because she performs a task.

An employee is not an agent unless he or she is specifically empowered to enter into contracts on the principal employer's behalf. Employees may enter only into the contracts that are within the scope of their employment.

> Example The welder in the prior example is not an agent because she cannot enter into contracts on behalf of General Motors Corporation. If the company empowers her to enter into contracts, she becomes an agent.

Principal-Agent Relationship

Principal-agent relationship A relationship in which an employer hires an employee and gives that employee authority to act and enter into contracts on the employer's behalf.

A **principal–agent relationship** is formed when an employer hires an employee and gives that employee authority to act and enter into contracts on the employer's behalf. The extent of this authority is governed by any express agreement between the parties and is implied from the circumstances of the agency.

Example The president of a corporation usually has the authority to enter into major contracts on the corporation's behalf, but a supervisor on the corporation's assembly line may have the authority only to purchase the supplies necessary to keep the line running.

Principal–Independent Contractor Relationship

A **principal–independent contractor relationship** exists when principals employ outsiders—persons and businesses who are not employees—to perform certain tasks on their behalf. These persons and businesses are called **independent contractors.** Professionals and tradespeople who typically act as independent contractors include doctors, dentists, stockbrokers, architects, certified public accountants, real estate brokers, and plumbers.

A principal can authorize an independent contractor to enter into contracts. Principals are bound by the authorized contracts of their independent contractors.

Example If a client authorizes an attorney to settle a case within a certain dollar amount and the attorney does so, the settlement agreement is binding.

SIDEBAR

SUMMARY OF EMPLOYMENT RELATIONSHIPS

Type of Relationship	Description
Employer-employee	The employer has the right to control the physical conduct of the employee.
Principal-agent	The agent has the authority to act on behalf of the principal as authorized by the principal and implied from the agency. An employee is often the agent of his or her employer.
Principal-independent contractor	The principal has no control over the details of the independent contractor's conduct. An independent contractor usually is not an agent of the principal.

Formation of the Agency Relationship

An agency and the resulting authority of an agent can arise in any of four ways: (1) express agency, (2) implied agency, (3) apparent agency, and (4) agency by ratification. Each of these types of agencies is discussed in the following pages.

Express Agency

The most common form of agency is **express agency.** In an express agency, the agent has the authority to contract or otherwise act on the principal's behalf as expressly stated in the agency agreement. In addition, the agent may possess certain implied or apparent authority to act on the principal's behalf (as discussed a little later in this chapter).

Express agency occurs when a principal and an agent expressly agree to enter into an agency agreement with each other. Express agency contracts can be either oral or written, unless the Statute of Frauds stipulates that they must be written.

Independent contractor A person or business that is not an employee and is employed by a principal to perform a certain task on the principal's behalf.

Example In most states a real estate broker's contract to sell real estate must be in writing.

If the principal and the agent enter into an **exclusive agency contract,** the principal cannot employ any agent other than the exclusive agent. If the principal does so, the exclusive agent can recover damages from the principal. If an agency is not an exclusive agency, the principal can employ more than one agent to try to accomplish a stated purpose. When multiple agents are employed, the agencies with all of the agents terminate when any one of the agents accomplishes the stated purpose.

Express agency An agency that occurs when a principal and an agent expressly agree to enter into an agency agreement with each other.

Power of Attorney. A **power of attorney** is one of the most formal types of express agency agreements. It is often used to give an agent the power to sign legal documents, such as deeds to real estate, on behalf of the principal. The two kinds of powers of attorney are (1) **general power of attorney,** which confers broad powers on the agent to act in any matters on the principal's behalf; and (2) **special power of attorney,** which limits the agent to acts specifically enumerated in an agreement. The agent is called an **attorney-in-fact** even though he or she does not have to be a lawyer. Powers of attorney must be written, and usually they must be notarized. A general power of attorney is shown in Exhibit 18.2.

Power of attorney An express agency agreement that is often used to give an agent the power to sign legal documents on behalf of the principal.

Implied Agency

In many situations, a principal and an agent do not expressly create an agency. Instead, the agency is implied from the conduct of the parties. This type of agency

Exhibit 18.2 Sample general power of attorney

POWER OF ATTORNEY

Know All Men by These Presents: That ______________________ the undersigned (jointly and severally, if more than one) hereby make, constitute and appoint ______________________ My true and lawful Attorney for me and in my name, place and stead and for my use and benefit:

(a) To ask, demand, sue for, recover, collect and receive each and every sum of money, debt, account, legacy, bequest, interest, dividend, annuity and demand (which now is or hereafter shall become due, owing or payable) belonging to or claimed by me, and to use and take any lawful means for the recovery thereof by legal process or otherwise, and to execute and deliver a satisfaction or release therefor, together with the right and powers to compromise or compound any claim or demand;

(b) To exercise any or all of the following powers as to real property, any interest therein and/or any building thereon: To contract for, purchase, receive and take possession thereof and of evidence of title thereto; to lease the same for any term or purpose, including leases for business, residence, and oil and/or mineral development; to sell, exchange, grant or convey the same with or without warranty; and to mortgage, transfer in trust, or otherwise encumber or hypothecate the same to secure payment of a negotiable or non-negotiable note or performance of any obligation or agreement;

(c) To exercise any or all of the following powers as to all kinds of personal property and goods, wares and merchandise, chosen in action and other property in possession or in action: To contract for, buy, sell, exchange, transfer and in any legal manner deal in and with the same and to mortgage, transfer in trust, or otherwise encumber or hypothecate the same to secure payment of a negotiable or non-negotiable note or performance of any obligation or agreement;

(d) To borrow money and to execute and deliver negotiable or non-negotiable notes therefor with or without security, and to loan money and receive negotiable or non-negotiable notes therefor with such security as said Attorney shall deem proper;

(e) To create, amend, supplement and terminate any trust and to instruct and advise the trustee of any trust wherein I am or may be trustor or beneficiary; to represent and vote stock, exercise stock rights, accept and deal with any dividend, distribution or bonus, join in any corporate financing reorganization, merger, liquidation, consolidation or other action and the extension, compromise, conversion, adjustment, enforcement or foreclosure, singly or in conjunction with others of any corporate stock, bond, note, debenture or other security; to compound, compromise, adjust, settle and satisfy any obligation secured or unsecured, owing by or to me and to give or accept any property and/or money whether or not equal to or less in value than the amount owing in payment, settlement or satisfaction thereof;

(f) To transact business of any kind or class and as my act and deed to sign, execute, acknowledge and deliver any deed, lease, assignment of lease covenant, indenture, indemnity, agreement, mortgage, deed of trust, assignment of mortgage or of the beneficial interest under deed of trust, extension or renewal of any obligation, subordination or waiver or priority, hypothecation, bottomry, charter-party, bill of lading, bill of sale, bill, bond, note, whether negotiable or non-negotiable, receipt, evidence of debt, full or partial release or satisfaction of mortgage, judgment and other debt, request for partial or full reconveyance of deed of trust and such other instruments in writing of any kind or class as may be necessary or proper in the premises.

Giving and Granting unto my said Attorney full power and authority to do and perform all and every act and thing whatsoever, requisite, necessary or appropriate to be done in and about the premises as fully to all intents, and purposes as I might or could do it personally present, hereby ratifying all that my said Attorney shall lawfully do or cause to be done by virtue of these presents. The powers and authority hereby conferred upon my said Attorney shall be applicable to all real and personal property or interests therein now owned or hereafter required by me and whenever situate.

My said Attorney is empowered hereby to determine in said Attorney's sole discretion the time when, purpose for and manner in which any power herein conferred upon said Attorney shall be exercised, and the conditions, provisions and covenants of any instrument or document which may be executed by said Attorney pursuant hereto and in the acquisition or disposition of real or personal property, my said Attorney shall have exclusive power to fix the terms thereof for cash, credit and/or property, and if on credit with or without security.

The undersigned, if a married person, hereby further authorizes and empowers my said Attorney, as my duly authorized agent, to join in my behalf, in the execution of any instrument by which any community real property or any interest therein, now owned or hereafter acquired by my spouse and myself, or either of us, is sold, leased, encumbered, or conveyed.

When the context so? requires, the masculine gender includes the feminine and/or neuter, and the singular number includes the plural.

Witness my hand this ______________ day of ______________________ 20__________

STATE OF CALIFORNIA, COUNTY OF ______________________ SS.
On ______________________ before me, the undersigned, a Notary Public
in and for said State personally appeared ______________________

______________________ ______________________

personally known to me (or proved to me on the basis of satisfactory evidence) to be the person
______________ whose name ______________ subscribed
to the within instrument and acknowledge that ______________ executed
the same.

WITNESS my hand and official seal.

Signature ______________________

Name *(Typed or Printed)* ______________________

(This area for official seal)

is referred to as **implied agency.** The extent of the agent's authority is determined from the facts and circumstances of the particular situation. Implied authority can be conferred by

1. industry custom,
2. prior dealing between the parties,
3. the agent's position, and
4. the acts deemed necessary to carry out the agent's duties.

The court may deem other factors relevant as well. Implied authority cannot conflict with express authority or with stated limitations on express authority. Often, even an express agency agreement does not provide enough detail to cover all contingencies that may arise in the future regarding the performance of the agency. In this case, the agent possesses certain implied authority to act. This implied authority sometimes is referred to as *incidental authority*. Certain emergency situations may arise in the course of an agency; if the agent cannot contact the principal for instructions, the agent has implied emergency powers to take all actions reasonably necessary to protect the principal's property and rights.

SIDEBAR

FORMATION OF AGENCY RELATIONSHIPS

Type of Agency	Definition	Enforcement of the Contract
Express	Authority is expressly given to the agent by the principal.	Principal and third party are bound to the contract.
Implied	Authority is implied from the conduct of the parties, custom and usage of trade, or act incidental to carrying out the agent's duties.	Principal and third-party acts are bound to the contract.
Apparent	Authority created when the principal leads a third party to believe that the agent has authority.	Principal and third party are bound to the contract.
By ratification	Acts of the agent committed outside the scope of his or her authority.	Principal and third party are not bound to the contract unless the principal ratifies the contract.

Apparent Agency

Apparent agency, or **agency by estoppel,** arises when a principal creates the appearance of an agency that in actuality does not exist. Where an apparent agency is established, the principal is estopped from denying the agency relationship and is bound to contracts entered into by the apparent agent while acting within the scope of the apparent agency. Note that the principal's action—not the agent's action—is what creates an apparent agency.

Apparent agency (agency by estoppel) Agency that arises when a principal creates the appearance of an agency that in actuality does not exist.

Example Suppose Georgia Pacific, Inc., interviews Albert Iorio for a sales representative position. Mr. Iorio, accompanied by Jane Franklin, the national sales manager, visits retail stores located in the open sales territory. While visiting one store, Jane tells the store manager, "I wish I had more sales reps like Albert." Nevertheless, Albert is not hired. If Albert later enters into contracts with the store on behalf of Georgia Pacific and Jane has not controverted the impression of Albert she left with the store manager, the company will be bound to the contracts.

Agency by Ratification

Agency by ratification occurs when (1) a person misrepresents himself or herself as another's agent when in fact he or she is not, and (2) the purported principal ratifies (accepts) the unauthorized act. In such cases, the principal is bound to perform and the agent is relieved of any liability for misrepresentation.

Agency by ratification An agency that occurs when (1) a person misrepresents himself or herself as another's agent when in fact he or she is not and (2) the purported principal ratifies the unauthorized act.

Example Bill Levine sees a house for sale and thinks his friend Sherry Maxwell would want it. Bill enters into a contract to purchase the house from the seller and signs the contract "Bill Levine, agent for Sherry Maxwell." Because Bill is not Sherry Maxwell's agent, she is not bound to the contract. If, however, Sherry agrees to purchase the house, there is an agency by ratification. The ratification "relates back" to the moment Bill Levine entered into the contract. Upon ratification of the contract, Sherry Maxwell is obligated to purchase the house.

EMPLOYMENT-AT-WILL

Employees who are offered express employment contracts for a definite term cannot be discharged in violation of the contract. Most employees, however, do not have employment contracts; their status is termed **employment-at-will**.

Under common law, an at-will employee could be discharged by an employer at any time and for any reason. This laissez-faire doctrine gave the employer great flexibility in responding to its changing needs. It also caused unfair results for some employees. Today, there are many statutory, contract, public policy, and tort exceptions to the at-will doctrine. These exceptions are:

- **Statutory exception.** Some federal and state statutes restrict the employment-at-will doctrine.

  Examples Federal labor laws prohibit employers from discharging employees who are members of labor unions in violation of labor laws or collective bargaining agreements. Title VII and other federal and state antidiscrimination laws that prohibit employers from engaging in race, sex, religious, age, disability, or other forms of discrimination are additional examples of such laws.

- **Contract exception.** The courts have held that an implied-in-fact contract can be created between an employer and an employee. Implied-in-fact contracts develop from the conduct of the parties.

  Example A company bulletin, handbook, or personnel policy might mention that employees who do their jobs properly will not be discharged. This can be construed as an implied promise that an employee can be discharged only for good cause. Thus, the employer's ability to discharge an employee at will is removed. An employee who is discharged in violation of an implied-in-fact contract can sue the employer for breach of contract.

- **Public policy exception.** The most used common law exception to the employment-at-will doctrine is the public policy exception. This rule states that an employee cannot be discharged if such discharge violates the public policy of the jurisdiction.

  Examples Violations of public policy include discharging an employee for serving as a juror, for refusing to act in violation of the law (such as dumping toxic wastes in violation of environmental protection laws), for refusing to engage in illegal research (such as research that violates patent laws or animal protection laws), and for refusing to distribute defective products.

An employee who has been wrongfully discharged can sue his or her employer for damages and other remedies (reinstatement, back pay, and such). Punitive damages may be recovered if the employer has engaged in fraud or other intentional conduct.

Learning Objective 3

Identify and describe the principal's liability for the tortious conduct of an agent.

The crowning fortune of a man is to be born to some pursuit which finds him employment and happiness, whether it be to make baskets, or broad swords, or canals, or statues, or songs.

Ralph Waldo Emerson

Tort Liability of Principals and Agents to Third Parties

The principal and the agent are each personally liable for his or her own tortious conduct. The principal is liable for the tortious conduct of an agent who is acting within the scope of the principal's authority. The agent, however, is liable only for the tortious conduct of the principal if he or she directly or indirectly participates in or aids and abets the principal's conduct.

The courts have applied a broad and flexible standard in interpreting scope of authority in the context of employment. Although other factors may also be considered, the courts rely on the following factors to determine whether an agent's conduct occurred within the scope of his or her employment:

- Was the act specifically requested or authorized by the principal?
- Was it the kind of act that the agent was employed to perform?
- Did the act occur substantially within the time period of employment authorized by the principal?
- Did the act occur substantially within the location of employment authorized by the employer?
- Was the agent advancing the principal's purpose when the act occurred?

Where liability is found, tort remedies are available to the injured party. These include recovery for medical expenses, lost wages, pain and suffering, emotional distress, and, in some cases, punitive damages.

Intentional Torts

Intentional torts include acts such as assault, battery, false imprisonment, and other intentional conduct that causes injury to another person. Most jurisdictions apply the **work-related test,** which holds that if an agent commits an intentional tort within a work-related time or space, the principal is liable for any injuries caused by the agent's intentional tort.

Work-related test A test that says if an agent commits an intentional tort within a work-related time or space, the principal is liable for any injury caused by the agent's intentional tort.

> **Example** If an employee commits battery on another employee during working hours or on the principal's premises, under the work-related test the employer would be held liable.

If a state follows the **motivation test** instead of the work-related test, the court must determine the motivation of the perpetrator for committing the intentional tort.

> **Example** If an employee commits the tort of battery on a customer because of a personal dispute with the customer, then the employer would not be liable under the motivation test.

A principal is also not liable for the intentional torts of agents and employees that are committed outside the principal's scope of business.

> **Example** If an employee attends a sporting event after working hours and gets into a fight with another spectator at the event, the employer is not liable.

Negligence

Principals are liable for the negligent conduct of agents acting within the scope of their employment. This liability for **negligence** is based on the common law doctrine of ***respondeat superior*** ("let the master answer"), which, in turn, is based on the legal theory of **vicarious liability** (liability without fault). The principal is liable because of his or her employment contract with the negligent agent, not because the principal was personally at fault.

Respondeat superior A rule that says an employer is liable for the tortious conduct of its employees or agents while they are acting within the scope of its authority.

This doctrine rests on the principle that if someone (such as the principal) expects to derive certain benefits from acting through others (such as an agent), that person should also bear the liability for injuries caused to third persons by the negligent conduct of an agent who was acting within the scope of his or her employment.

Frolic and Detour

Agents sometimes do things during the course of their employment to further their own interests rather than the principal's interests.

> **Example** An agent takes a detour to run a personal errand while on assignment for the principal.

This is commonly referred to as a **frolic and detour.** Agents always are personally liable for their tortious conduct in such situations. Principals are generally relieved of liability if the agent's frolic and detour is substantial. If the deviation is minor, however, the principal is liable for the injuries caused by the agent's tortious conduct.

Frolic and detour A situation in which an agent does something during the course of his or her employment to further his or her own interests rather than the principal's interests.

> **Example** A salesperson stops home for lunch while on an assignment for his principal. While leaving his home, the agent hits and injures a pedestrian with his automobile.

The principal is liable if the agent's home was not too far out of the way from the agent's assignment. But the principal would not be liable if an agent who is supposed to be on assignment to Los Angeles, California, drives to Irvine,

California (50 miles away), to meet a friend and is involved in an accident. Negligence actions stemming from frolic and detour are examined on a case-by-case basis.

The "Coming and Going" Rule

"Coming and going" rule A rule that says a principal is generally not liable for injuries caused by its agents and employees while they are on their way to and from work.

Under the common law, a principal generally is not liable for injuries caused by its agents and employees while they are on their way to or from work. This so-called **"coming and going" rule** applies even if the principal supplies the agent's automobile or other transportation or pays for gasoline, repairs, and other automobile operating expenses. This rule is quite logical. Because principals do not control where their agents and employees live, they should not be held liable for tortious conduct of agents on their way to and from work.

Dual-Purpose Mission

Dual-purpose mission An errand or another act that a principal requests of an agent while the agent is on his or her own personal business.

Sometimes principals request that agents run errands or conduct other acts on their behalf while the agent or employee is on personal business. In this case, the agent is on a **dual-purpose mission.** That is, he or she is acting partly for himself or herself and partly for the principal. Most jurisdictions hold both the principal and the agent liable if the agent injures someone while on such a mission.

Example Suppose a principal asks an employee to drop off a package at a client's office on the employee's way home. If the employee negligently injures a pedestrian while on this dual-purpose mission, the principal is liable to the pedestrian.

SIDEBAR

TORT LIABILITY OF PRINCIPALS AND AGENTS TO THIRD PARTIES

Agent's Conduct	Agent Liable	Principal Liable
Intentional tort	Yes	Motivation test: The principal is liable if the agent's motivation in committing the intentional tort was to promote the principal's business.
Intentional tort	Yes	Work-related test: The principal is liable if the agent committed the intentional tort within work-related time and space.
Negligence	Yes	The principal is liable under the doctrine of *respondeat superior* if the agent's negligent act was committed within his or her scope of employment.

Independent Contractor

Section 2 of the Restatement (Second) of Agency defines an independent contractor as "a person who contracts with another to do something for him [or her] who is not controlled by the other nor subject to the other's right to control with respect to his [or her] physical conduct in the performance of the undertaking." Independent contractors usually work for a number of clients, have their own offices, hire employees, and control the performance of their work.

Merely labeling someone an "independent contractor" is not enough. The crucial factor in determining whether someone is an employee or an independent contractor is the *degree of control* the employer has over the agent. Critical factors in determining independent contractor status include:

- Whether the agent is engaged in a distinct occupation or an independently established business
- The length of time the agent has been employed by the principal
- The amount of time the agent works for the principal
- Whether the principal supplies the tools and equipment used in the work
- The method of payment, whether by time or by the job
- The degree of skill necessary to complete the task
- Whether the worker hires employees to assist him or her
- Whether the employer has the right to control the manner and means of the agent's accomplishing the desired result

If an examination of these factors shows that the principal asserts little control, the person is an independent contractor. Substantial control indicates an employer–employee relationship.

Torts of Independent Contractors

Generally, a principal is not liable for the torts of its independent contractors, but independent contractors are personally liable for their own torts. The rationale behind this rule is that principals do not control the means by which the results are accomplished.

> **Example** A client employs an attorney who is an independent contractor to represent him in a lawsuit. While driving to the courthouse in her automobile, the attorney negligently causes an automobile accident that causes severe injury to another person. Here, the attorney, but not the client, is liable to the injured person.

The way to wealth is as plain as the way to market. It depends chiefly on two words, industry and frugality: that is, waste neither time nor money, but make the best use of both. Without industry and frugality nothing will do, and with them everything.

Benjamin Franklin

Nevertheless, this rule has several exceptions where a principal is held liable for the torts of an independent contractor it has employed. These are:

- **Nondelegable duties.** Certain duties, called **nondelegable duties,** may not be delegated.

  Example Railroads owe a duty to maintain safe railroad crossings. They cannot escape this liability by assigning the task to an independent contractor.

- **Special risks.** Principals cannot avoid strict liability for dangerous activities assigned to independent contractors.

  Example The use of explosives, clearing land by fire, crop dusting, and such involve special risks that are shared by the principal.

- **Negligence in the selection of an independent contractor.** A principal who knowingly hires an unqualified or dangerous person as an independent contractor is liable if that person injures someone while on the job.

Web Exploration

Go to **http://en.wikipedia.org/wiki/Walt_Disney_World**. Read the information about how the Walt Disney Company used dummy corporations to acquire much of the land in central Florida for its Walt Disney World Resort.

Termination of an Agency

An agency contract is similar to other contracts in that it can be terminated either by an act of the parties or by operation of law. These different methods of termination are discussed next. Note that once an agency relationship is terminated, the agent can no longer represent the principal or bind the principal to contracts.

Termination by Acts of the Parties

The parties to an agency contract can terminate the contract by agreement or by their actions. The four methods of termination of an agency relationship by acts of the parties are:

1. ***Mutual agreement.*** As with any contract, the parties to an agency contract can mutually agree to terminate their agreement. By doing so, the parties relieve each other of any further rights, duties, obligations, or powers provided for in the agency contract. Either party can propose the termination of an agency contract.
2. ***Lapse of time.*** Agency contracts are often written for a specific period of time. The agency terminates when the specified time period elapses.

   Example Suppose that a principal and an agent enter into an agency contract "beginning January 1, 2012, and ending December 31, 2015." The agency automatically terminates on December 31, 2015. If the agency contract does not set forth a specific termination date, the agency terminates after a

What people have always sought is equality of rights before the law. For rights that were not open to all equally would not be rights.

Cicero De Officilis, Book II, Chapter XII

reasonable time has elapsed. The courts often look to the custom of an industry in determining the reasonable time for termination of the agency.

3. ***Purpose achieved.*** A principal can employ an agent for the time it takes to accomplish a certain task, purpose, or result. Such agencies automatically terminate once they are completed.

   Example Suppose a principal employs a licensed real estate broker to sell his house. The agency terminates when the house is sold and the principal pays the broker the agreed-upon compensation.

4. ***Occurrence of a specified event.*** An agency contract can specify that the agency exists until a specified event occurs. The agency terminates when the specified event happens.

   Example If a principal employs an agent to take care of her dog until she returns from a trip, the agency terminates when the principal returns from the trip.

Wrongful Termination of an Agency or Employment Contract

Generally, agency and employment contracts that do not specify a definite time for their termination can be terminated at will by either the principal or the agent without liability to the other party. When a principal terminates an agency contract, it is called a *revocation of authority*. When an agent terminates an agency contract, it is called a *renunciation of authority*.

Unless an agency is irrevocable, both the principal and the agent have an individual power to unilaterally terminate any agency contract. Note that having the power to terminate an agency agreement is not the same as having the right to terminate it. The unilateral termination of an agency contract may be wrongful. If the principal's or agent's termination of an agency contract breaches the contract, the other party can sue for damages for **wrongful termination of an agency.**

Wrongful termination of an agency The termination of an agency contract in violation of the terms of the agency contract. In this situation, the nonbreaching party may recover damages from the breaching party.

Example A principal employs a licensed real estate agent to sell his house. The agency contract gives the agent an exclusive listing for three months. After one month, the principal unilaterally terminates the agency. The principal has the power to do so, and the agent can no longer act on behalf of the principal. Because the principal did not have the right to terminate the contract, however, the agent can sue him and recover damages (such as lost commission) for wrongful termination.

Workers' Compensation

Learning Objective 4

Explain how state workers' compensation programs work and describe the benefits available.

Many types of employment are dangerous, and each year many workers are injured on the job. At common law, employees who were injured on the job could sue their employer for negligence. This time-consuming process placed the employee at odds with his or her employer. In addition, there was no guarantee that the employee would win the case. Ultimately, many injured workers—or the heirs of deceased workers—were left uncompensated.

Workers' compensation acts were enacted in response to the unfairness of that result. These acts create an administrative procedure for workers to receive compensation for injuries that occur on the job—**workers' compensation.** First, the injured worker files a claim with the appropriate state government agency (often called the workers' compensation board or commission). Next, that entity determines the legitimacy of the claim. If the worker disagrees with the agency's findings, he or she may appeal the decision through the state court system. Workers' compensation benefits are paid according to preset limits established by statute or regulation. The amounts that are recoverable vary from state to state.

Workers' compensation acts Laws that compensate workers and their families if workers are injured in connection with their jobs.

Exhibit 18.3 shows a state complaint form that must be filed to claim workers' compensation benefits.

Exhibit 18.3 Workers' compensation complaint form

PRINT CLEAR

State of California
Department of Industrial Relations
DIVISION OF WORKERS' COMPENSATION

Estado de California
Departamento de Relaciones Industriales
DIVISION DE COMPENSACIÓN AL TRABAJADOR

WORKERS' COMPENSATION CLAIM FORM (DWC 1)

PETITION DEL EMPLEADO PARA DE COMPENSACIÓN DEL TRABAJADOR (DWC 1)

Employee: Complete the **"Employee"** section and give the form to your employer. Keep a copy and mark it **"Employee's Temporary Receipt"** until you receive the signed and dated copy from your employer. You may call the Division of Workers' Compensation and hear recorded information at **(800) 736-7401**. An explanation of workers' compensation benefits is included as the cover sheet of this form.

You should also have received a pamphlet from your employer describing workers' compensation benefits and the procedures to obtain them.

Any person who makes or causes to be made any knowingly false or fraudulent material statement or material representation for the purpose of obtaining or denying workers' compensation benefits or payments is guilty of a felony.

Empleado: *Complete la sección **"Empleado"** y entregue la forma a su empleador. Quédese con la copia designada **"Recibo Temporal del Empleado"** hasta que Ud. reciba la copia firmada y fechada de su empleador. Ud. puede llamar a la Division de Compensación al Trabajador al **(800) 736-7401** para oir información gravada. En la hoja cubierta de esta forma esta la explicatión de los beneficios de compensación al trabjador.*

Ud. también debería haber recibido de su empleador un folleto describiendo los benficios de compensación al trabajador lesionado y los procedimientos para obtenerlos.

Toda aquella persona que a propósito haga o cause que se produzca cualquier declaración o representación material falsa o fraudulenta con el fin de obtener o negar beneficios o pagos de compensación a trabajadores lesionados es culpable de un crimen mayor "felonia".

Employee—complete this section and see note above ***Empleado—complete esta sección y note la notación arriba.***

1. Name. *Nombre.* ____________ Today's Date. *Fecha de Hoy.* ____________
2. Home Address. *Dirección Residencial.* ____________
3. City. *Ciudad.* ____________ State. *Estado.* ____________ Zip. *Código Postal.* ____________
4. Date of Injury. *Fecha de la lesión (accidente).* ____________ Time of Injury. *Hora en que ocurrió.* ________a.m. ________p.m.
5. Address and description of where injury happened. *Dirección/lugar dónde occurió el accidente.* ____________
6. Describe injury and part of body affected. *Describa la lesión y parte del cuerpo afectada.* ____________
7. Social Security Number. *Número de Seguro Social del Empleado.* ____________
8. Signature of employee. *Firma del empleado.* ____________

Employer—complete this section and see note below. ***Empleador—complete esta sección y note la notación abajo.***

9. Name of employer. *Nombre del empleador.* ____________
10. Address. *Dirección.* ____________
11. Date employer first knew of injury. *Fecha en que el empleador supo por primera vez de la lesión o accidente.* ____________
12. Date claim form was provided to employee. *Fecha en que se le entregó al empleado la petición.* ____________
13. Date employer received claim form. *Fecha en que el empleado devolvió la petición al empleador.* ____________
14. Name and address of insurance carrier or adjusting agency. *Nombre y dirección de la compañía de seguros o agencia adminstradora de seguros.* ____________
15. Insurance Policy Number. *El número de la póliza de Seguro.* ____________
16. Signature of employer representative. *Firma del representante del empleador.* ____________
17. Title. *Título.* ____________ 18. Telephone. *Teléfono.* ____________

Employer: You are required to date this form and provide copies to your insurer or claims administrator and to the employee, dependent or representative who filed the claim within <u>**one working day**</u> of receipt of the form from the employee.

SIGNING THIS FORM IS NOT AN ADMISSION OF LIABILITY

Empleador: *Se requiere que Ud. feche esta forma y que provéa copias a su compañía de seguros, administrador de reclamos, o dependiente/representante de reclamos y al empleado que hayan presentado esta petición dentro del plazo de <u>**un día hábil**</u> desde el momento de haber sido recibida la forma del empleado.*

EL FIRMAR ESTA FORMA NO SIGNIFICA ADMISION DE RESPONSABILIDAD

☐ Employer copy/*Copia del Empleador* ☐ Employee copy/ *Copia del Empleado* ☐ Claims Administrator/*Administrador de Reclamos* ☐ Temporary Receipt/*Recibo del Empleado*

7/1/04 Rev.

Workers' Compensation Insurance

States usually require employers to purchase **workers' compensation insurance** from private insurance companies or state funds to cover workers' compensation claims. Some states permit employers to self-insure if they demonstrate that they have the ability to pay workers' compensation claims. Many large companies self-insure. Workers can sue an employer in court to recover damages for employment-related injuries if the employer does not carry workers' compensation insurance or does not self-insure if permitted to do so.

Web Exploration

Go to **http://www.dir.ca.gov/dwc/WCFaqIW.html#1** to learn more about workers' compensation. Read the first four questions and answers.

Web Exploration

Go to **http://www.ohiobwc.com/basics/guidedtour/generalinfo/emp-generalinfo22.asp** and "Fraud Red Flags." Read the section "Spotting injured worker claim fraud."

Employment-Related Injury

For an injury to be compensable under workers' compensation, the claimant must prove that the injury arose out of and in the course of his or her employment—that it was an **employment-related injury.** An accident that occurs while an employee is actively working is clearly within the scope of this rule. Accidents that occur at a company cafeteria or while on a business lunch for an employer are also covered. However, accidents that happen while the employee is at an off-premises restaurant during his or her personal lunch hour are not covered. Many workers' compensation acts include stress as a compensable work-related injury.

Exclusive Remedy

Workers' compensation is an **exclusive remedy.** Thus, workers cannot sue their employers in court for damages. The one exception to this rule is that if an employer intentionally injures a worker, the worker can collect workers' compensation benefits *and* sue the employer. Workers' compensation acts do not bar injured workers from suing responsible third parties to recover damages.

Occupational Safety and Health Act

Occupational Safety and Health Act A federal act enacted in 1970 that promotes safety in the workplace.

In 1970, Congress enacted the **Occupational Safety and Health Act** to promote safety in the workplace. Virtually all private employers are within the scope of the act, but federal, state, and local governments are exempt. Industries regulated by other federal safety legislation are also exempt. The act also established the **Occupational Safety and Health Administration (OSHA),** a federal administrative agency within the Department of Labor that is empowered to enforce the act. The act imposes record-keeping and reporting requirements on employers and requires them to post notices in the workplace informing employees of their rights under the act.

Specific and General Duty Standards

OSHA is empowered to adopt rules and regulations to interpret and enforce the Occupational Safety and Health Act. OSHA has adopted thousands of regulations to enforce the safety standards established by the act. These include the following:

- **Specific duty standards.** Many of the OSHA standards address safety problems of a specific duty nature. These are called **specific duty standards.**

  Example OSHA standards establish safety requirements for equipment (such as safety guards), set maximum exposure levels to hazardous chemicals, regulate the location of machinery, establish safety procedures for employees, and the like.

- **General duty standards.** The act imposes a general duty on an employer to provide a work environment free from recognized hazards that are causing or are likely to cause death or serious physical harm to employees. This duty applies even if no specific regulation applies to the situation. These are called **general duty standards.**

Web Exploration

Go to **http://www.osha.gov** and find the address of the office of the federal Occupational Safety and Health Administration (OSHA) that serves your area.

Web Exploration

Go to the website **www.dol.gov/esa/minwage/america.htm**. What is the minimum wage for your state?

OSHA is empowered to inspect places of employment for health hazards and safety violations. If a violation is found, OSHA can issue a *written citation* that requires the employer to abate or correct the situation. Contested citations are reviewed by the Occupational Safety and Health Review Commission. Its decision is appealable to the Federal Circuit Court of Appeals. Employers who violate the act, OSHA rules and regulations, or OSHA citations are subject to both civil and criminal penalties. Exhibit 18.4 shows a safety and health poster that must be posted in workplaces in the state of Arizona. Exhibit 18.5 shows a federal OSHA poster in Spanish that must be posted in workplaces.

Fair Labor Standards Act

In 1938, Congress enacted the **Fair Labor Standards Act (FLSA)** to protect workers. The FLSA applies to private employers and employees engaged in the production of goods for interstate commerce.

Fair Labor Standards Act (FLSA) A federal act enacted in 1938 to protect workers by prohibiting child labor and establishing minimum wage and overtime pay requirements.

Child Labor

The FLSA forbids the use of oppressive **child labor** and makes it unlawful to ship goods produced by businesses that use oppressive child labor. The Department of Labor has adopted the following regulations that define lawful child labor:

1. Children under the age of 14 cannot work except as newspaper deliverers.
2. Children ages 14 and 15 may work limited hours in nonhazardous jobs approved by the Department of Labor (such as restaurants and gasoline stations).
3. Children ages 16 and 17 may work unlimited hours in nonhazardous jobs.

The Department of Labor determines which occupations are hazardous (such as mining, roofing, working with explosives). Children who work in agricultural employment and child actors and performers are exempt from these restrictions. Persons age 18 and older may work at any job, whether it is hazardous or not.

Minimum Wage and Overtime Pay Requirements

The FLSA establishes minimum wage and overtime pay requirements for workers. Managerial, administrative, and professional employees are exempt from the act's wage and hour provisions. As outlined in the following paragraphs, the FLSA requires employers to pay covered workers at least the minimum wage for their regular work hours and to provide overtime pay:

Web Exploration

Go to **http://www.eeoc.gov/offices/html** and click on your state on the map to find the address of the federal Equal Employment Opportunity Commission (EEOC) that serves your area.

- **Minimum wage.** The **minimum wage** is set by Congress and can be changed. As of 2012, it was set at $7.25 per hour. The Department of Labor permits employers to pay less than the minimum wage to students and apprentices. An employer may reduce minimum wages by an amount equal to the reasonable cost of food and lodging provided to employees.
- **Overtime pay.** Under the FLSA, an employer cannot require nonexempt employees to work more than 40 hours per week unless they are paid one-and-a-half times their regular pay for each hour worked in excess of 40 hours. Each week is treated separately.

  Example If an employee works 50 hours one week and 30 hours the next, the employer owes the employee 10 hours of **overtime pay** for the first week.

Exhibit 18.4 OSHA English poster

EMPLOYEE SAFETY AND HEALTH PROTECTION

The Arizona Occupational Safety and Health Act of 1972 (Act), provides safety and health protection for employees in Arizona. The Act requires each employer to furnish his employees with a place of employment free from recognized hazards that might cause serious injury or death. The Act further requires that employers and employees comply with all workplace safety and health standards, rules and regulations promulgated by the Industrial Commission. The Arizona Division of Occupational Safety and Health (ADOSH), a division of the Industrial Commission of Arizona, administers and enforces the requirements of the Act.

As an employee, you have the following rights:

You have the right to notify your employer or ADOSH about workplace hazards. You may ask ADOSH to keep your name confidential.

You have the right to request that ADOSH conduct an inspection if you believe there are unsafe and/or unhealthful conditions in your workplace. You or your representative may participate in the inspection.

If you believe you have been discriminated against for making safety and health complaints, or for exercising your rights under the Act, you have a right to file a complaint with ADOSH within 30 days of the discriminatory action. You are also afforded protection from discrimination under the Federal Occupational Safety and Health Act and may file a complaint with the U.S. Secretary of Labor within 30 days of the discriminatory action.

You have the right to see any citations that have been issued to your employer. Your employer must post the citations at or near the location of the alleged violation.

You have the right to protest the time frame given for correction of any violation.

You have the right to obtain copies of your medical records or records of your exposure to toxic and harmful substances or conditions.

Your employer must post this notice in your workplace.

The Industrial Commission and ADOSH do not cover employers of household domestic labor, those in maritime activities (covered by OSHA), those in atomic energy activities (covered by the Atomic Energy Commission) and those in mining activities (covered by the Arizona Mine Inspector's office). To file a complaint, report an emergency or seek advice and assistance from ADOSH, contact the nearest ADOSH office:

Phoenix:
800 West Washington
Phoenix AZ. 85007
602-542-5795

Tucson:
2675 East Broadway
Tucson, AZ. 85716
520-628-5478

Industrial Commission web site: www.ica.state.az.us

Note: Persons wishing to register a complaint alleging inadequacy in the administration of the Arizona Occupational Safety and Health plan may do so at the following address:

U.S. Department of Labor – OSHA
3221 N. 16th St., Suite 100
Phoenix, AZ 85016
Telephone: 1-800-475-4020

Revised 11/01

Exhibit 18.5 OSHA Spanish poster

Seguridad y Salud en el Trabajo

¡Es la Ley!

EMPLEADOS:

- Usted tiene el derecho de notificar a su empleador o a la OSHA sobre peligros en el lugar de trabajo. Usted también puede pedir que la OSHA no revele su nombre.
- Usted tiene el derecho de pedir a la OSHA que realize una inspección si usted piensa que en su trabajo existen condiciones peligrosas o poco saludables. Usted o su representante pueden participar en esa inspección.
- Usted tiene 30 días para presentar una queja ante la OSHA si su empleador llega a tomar represalias o discriminar en su contra por haber denunciado la condición de seguridad o salud o por ejercer los derechos consagrados bajo la Ley OSH.
- Usted tiene el derecho de ver las citaciones enviadas por la OSHA a su empleador. Su empleador debe colocar las citaciones en el lugar donde se encontraron las supuestas infracciones o cerca del mismo.
- Su empleador debe corregir los peligros en el lugar de trabajo para la fecha indicada en la citación y debe certificar que dichos peligros se hayan reducido o desaparecido.
- Usted tiene derecho de recibir copias de su historial o registro médico y el registro de su exposición a sustancias o condiciones tóxicas o dañinas.
- Su empleador debe colocar este aviso en su lugar de trabajo.
- Usted debe cumplir con todas las normas de seguridad y salud ocupacionales expedidas conforme a la Ley OSH que sean aplicables a sus propias acciones y conducta en el trabajo.

EMPLEADORES:

- Usted debe proporcionar a sus empleados un lugar de empleo libre de peligros conocidos.
- Usted debe cumplir con las normas de seguridad y salud ocupacionales expedidas conforme a la Ley OSH.

OSHA

Administración de Seguridad y Salud Ocupacional

Departamento del Trabajo de los Estados Unidos

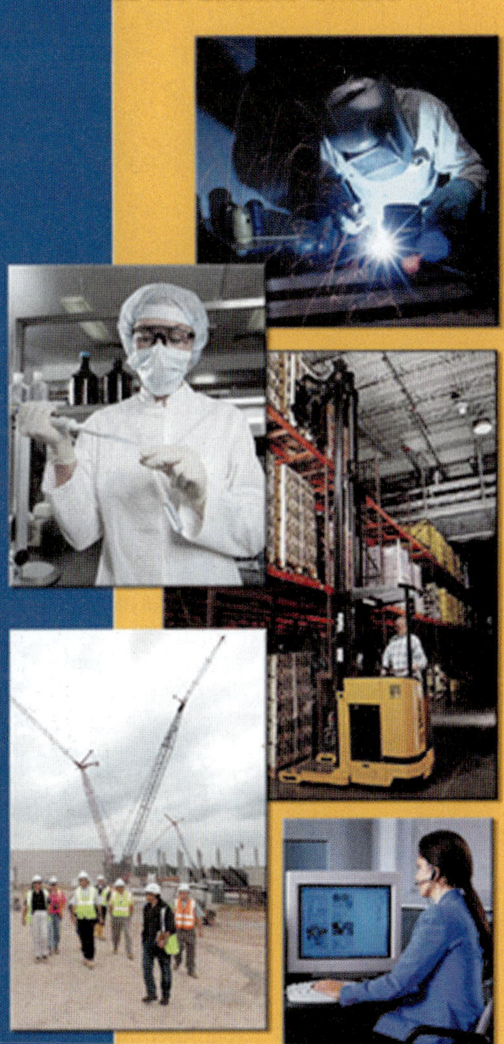

Los empleadores pueden obtener ayuda gratis para identificar y corregir las fuentes de peligro y para cumplir con las normas, sin citación ni multa, por medio de programas de consulta respaldados por la OSHA en cada estado del país.

1-800-321-OSHA

www.osha.gov

OSHA 3167-01-07R

Civil Rights Act of 1964
This is a photograph of President Lyndon Baines Johnson signing the Civil Rights Act of 1964 on July 2, 1964. Dr. Martin Luther King, Jr. is standing directly behind the president. Dr. King was an influential civil rights leader who worked to end racial segregation and discrimination.

Learning Objective 5
Describe the scope of coverage of Title VII of the Civil Rights Act of 1964.

Title VII of the Civil Rights Act of 1964

Title VII of the Civil Rights Act of 1964 A title of a federal statute enacted to eliminate job discrimination based on five protected classes: *race, color, religion, sex,* and *national origin.*

After substantial debate, Congress enacted the **Civil Rights Act of 1964. Title VII** of that act (entitled the Fair Employment Practices Act) was intended to eliminate job discrimination based on the following **protected classes:** (1) *race,* (2) *color,* (3) *national origin,* (4) *religion,* and (5) *sex.* Title VII provides in a pertinent part that:

> It shall be an unlawful employment practice for an employer
>
> 1. To fail or refuse to hire or to discharge any individual, or otherwise to discriminate against any individual with respect to his [or her] compensation, terms, conditions, or privileges of employment, because of such individual's race, color, religion, sex, or national origin; or
> 2. To limit, segregate, or classify his [or her] employees or applicants for employment in any way which would deprive or tend to deprive any individual of employment opportunities or otherwise adversely affect his [or her] status as an employee, because of such individual's race, color, religion, sex, or national origin.

Equal Employment Opportunity Commission (EEOC)

Equal Employment Opportunity Commission (EEOC) A federal administrative agency responsible for enforcing most federal antidiscrimination laws.

The **Equal Employment Opportunity Commission (EEOC)** is a federal agency responsible for enforcing most federal antidiscrimination laws. Members of the EEOC are appointed by the U.S. president. The EEOC is empowered to conduct investigations, interpret the statutes, encourage conciliation between employees and employers, and bring suit to enforce the law. The EEOC also can seek injunctive relief. Exhibit 18.6 shows a map of the fifteen districts of the EEOC.

Scope of Coverage of Title VII

Title VII prohibits discrimination in hiring, decisions regarding promotion or demotion, payment of compensation and fringe benefits, availability of job training and apprenticeship opportunities, referral systems for employment, decisions regarding dismissal, work rules, and any other "term, condition, or privilege" of employment. Any employee of covered employers, including undocumented aliens, may bring actions for employment discrimination under Title VII.

Exhibit 18.6 **Fifteen districts of the Equal Employment Opportunity Commission (EEOC)**

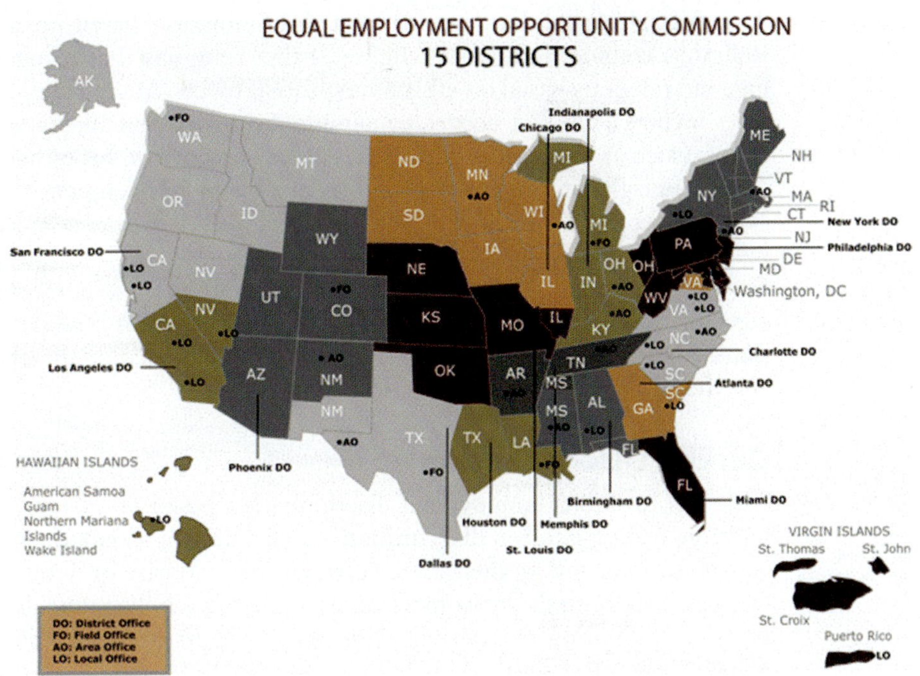

District Offices

Atlantic District Office
Birmingham District Office
Charlotte District Office
Chicago District Office
Dallas District Office
Houston District Office
Indianapolis District Office
Los Angeles District Office
Memphis District Office
Miami District Office
New York District Office
Philadelphia District Office
Phoenix District Office
San Francisco District Office
St. Louis District Office

Source: Equal Employment Opportunity Commission (EEOC)

Race, Color, and National Origin Discrimination

Title VII of the Civil Rights Act of 1964 was enacted primarily to prohibit **race discrimination, color discrimination,** and **national origin discrimination** in employment.

Race refers to broad categories such as African American, Caucasian, Asian, Native American, and Pacific Islander.

Example An employer's refusing to hire someone because he or she is a member of a minority race constitutes illegal race discrimination in violation of Title VII.

Color refers to the color of a person's skin.

Example Light-skinned members of a race refusing to hire dark-skinned members of the same race is color discrimination in violation of Title VII.

National origin refers to the country of a person's ancestors or cultural characteristics.

Race discrimination
Employment discrimination against a person because of his or her race.

National origin discrimination
Employment discrimination against a person because of his or her heritage, cultural characteristics, or the country of his or her ancestors.

Example An employer's refusing to hire Hispanics or persons of Irish descent is national origin discrimination in violation of Title VII.

Religious Discrimination

Title VII also prohibits employment discrimination based on a person's religion. Religions include traditional religions, other religions that recognize a supreme being, and religions based on ethical or spiritual tenets. Many **religious discrimination** cases involve a conflict between an employer's work rule and an employee's religious beliefs (such as when an employee is required to work on his or her religious holiday).

The right of an employee to practice his or her religion is not absolute, however. Under Title VII, an employer is under a duty to *reasonably accommodate* the religious observances, practices, or beliefs of its employees if it does not cause an *undue hardship* on the employer. The courts must apply these general standards to specific fact situations. In making their decisions, the courts must consider factors such as the number of employees of the employer, the importance of the employee's position, and the availability of alternative workers.

Gender Discrimination

Gender discrimination Employment discrimination against a person because of his or her gender. Also known as *sex discrimination*.

Title VII prohibits employment discrimination based on gender. Although the prohibition against **gender discrimination,** also known as **sex discrimination,** applies equally to men and women, the overwhelming majority of Title VII sex discrimination cases are brought by women. An example of such discrimination is the old airline practice of ignoring the marital status of male flight attendants but hiring only single female flight attendants.

In 1978, the **Pregnancy Discrimination Act** was enacted as an amendment to Title VII. This amendment forbids employment discrimination because of "pregnancy, childbirth, or related medical conditions." Thus, a work rule that prohibits the hiring of pregnant women violates Title VII.

Sexual Harassment

In today's work environment, coworkers sometimes become sexually interested or involved with each other voluntarily. On other occasions, though, a coworker's sexual advances are not welcome.

Sexual harassment Lewd remarks, touching, intimidation, posting of pinups, and other verbal or physical conduct of a sexual nature that occur on the job.

Refusing to hire or promote someone unless he or she has sex with the manager or supervisor is sex discrimination that violates Title VII. Other forms of conduct, such as lewd remarks, touching, intimidation, posting pinups, and other verbal or physical conduct of a sexual nature, constitute **sexual harassment** and violate Title VII. To determine what conduct creates a hostile work environment, the U.S. Supreme Court stated, in *Harris v. Forklift Systems, Inc.*, 510 U.S. 17, 114 S. Ct. 367, 126 L.Ed.2d 295, 1999 U.S. Lexis 7155 (1993):

> We can say that whether an environment is "hostile" or "abusive" can be determined only by looking at all the circumstances. These may include the frequency of the discriminatory conduct; its severity; whether it is physically threatening or humiliating, or a mere offensive utterance; and whether it unreasonably interferes with an employee's work performance.

Exhibit 18.7 sets forth the EEOC's description of sexual harassment. Exhibit 18.8 sets forth a company's policy against sexual harassment.

Bona Fide Occupational Qualification (BFOQ)

Bona fide occupational qualification (BFOQ) Lawful employment discrimination that is based on a protected class (other than race or color) and is *job-related* and a *business necessity*. This exception is narrowly interpreted by the courts.

Discrimination based on protected classes (other than race or color) is permitted if it is shown to be a **bona fide occupational qualification (BFOQ).** To be legal, a BFOQ must be both *job-related* and a *business necessity*.

Exhibit 18.7 EEOC's description of sexual harassment

Sexual harassment is a form of sex discrimination that violates Title VII of the Civil Rights Act of 1964.

Unwelcome sexual advances, requests for sexual favors, and other verbal or physical conduct of a sexual nature constitutes sexual harassment when submission to or rejection of this conduct explicitly or implicitly affects an individual's employment, unreasonably interferes with an individual's work performance, or creates an intimidating, hostile, or offensive work environment.

Sexual harassment can occur in a variety of circumstances, including but not limited to the following:

- The victim as well as the harasser may be a woman or a man. The victim does not have to be of the opposite sex.
- The harasser can be the victim's supervisor, an agent of the employer, a supervisor in another area, a coworker, or a non-employee.
- The victim does not have to be the person harassed but could be anyone affected by the offensive conduct.
- Unlawful sexual harassment may occur without economic injury to or discharge of the victim.
- The harasser's conduct must be unwelcome.

It is helpful for the victim to directly inform the harasser that the conduct is unwelcome and must stop. The victim should use any employer complaint mechanism or grievance system available.

When investigating allegations of sexual harassment, EEOC looks at the whole record: the circumstances, such as the nature of the sexual advances, and the context in which the alleged incidents occurred. A determination on the allegations is made from the facts on a case-by-case basis.

Prevention is the best tool to eliminate sexual harassment in the workplace. Employers are encouraged to take steps necessary to prevent sexual harassment from occurring. They should clearly communicate to employees that sexual harassment will not be tolerated. They can do so by establishing an effective complaint or grievance process and taking immediate and appropriate action when an employee complains.

Source: Equal Employment Opportunity Commission (EEOC)

Example Allowing only women to be locker-room attendants in a women's gym is a valid BFOQ, but prohibiting males from being managers or instructors at the same gym would not be a BFOQ.

The ethical duty of a paralegal professional to report sexual harassment conduct is discussed in the following feature.

Equal Pay Act

Discrimination often takes the form of different pay scales for men and women who perform the same job. The **Equal Pay Act of 1963** protects both sexes from pay discrimination based on sex. This act covers all levels of private-sector employees and state and local government employees. Federal workers are not covered, however.

Equal Pay Act of 1963 A federal statute that protects both sexes from pay discrimination based on sex. It extends to jobs that require equal skill, equal effort, equal responsibility, and similar working conditions.

The act prohibits disparity in pay for jobs that require *equal skill* (that is, equal experience), *equal effort* (that is, mental and physical exertion), *equal responsibility* (that is, supervision and accountability), or *similar working conditions* (such as dangers of injury, exposure to the elements). To make this determination, the courts examine the actual requirements of jobs to determine whether they are equal and similar. If two jobs are determined to be equal and similar, an employer cannot pay disparate wages to members of different sexes.

Legislation to apply the principle of equal pay for equal work without discrimination because of sex is a matter of simple justice.
Dwight D. Eisenhower

Employees can bring a private cause of action against an employer for violating the act, and back pay and liquidated damages are recoverable. In addition, the employer must increase the wages of the discriminated-against employee to eliminate the unlawful disparity of wages, and cannot not do so by lowering the wages of other employees.

Exhibit 18.8 Company's policy against sexual harassment

Many businesses have taken steps to prevent sexual harassment in the workplace. For example, some businesses have explicitly adopted policies (see below) forbidding sexual harassment, implemented procedures for reporting incidents of sexual harassment, and conducted training programs to sensitize managers and employees about the issue.

Statement of Prohibited Conduct

The management of Company considers the following conduct to illustrate some of the conduct that violates Company's Sexual Harassment Policy:

A. Physical assaults of a sexual nature, such as

1. Rape, sexual battery, molestation, or attempts to commit these assaults.
2. Intentional physical conduct that is sexual in nature, such as touching, pinching, patting, grabbing, brushing against another employee's body, or poking another employee's body.

B. Unwanted sexual advances, propositions, or other sexual comments, such as

1. Sexually oriented gestures, noises, remarks, jokes, or comments about a person's sexuality or sexual experience directed at or made in the presence of any employee who indicates or has indicated in any way that such conduct is unwelcome in his or her presence.
2. Preferential treatment or promises of preferential treatment to an employee for submitting to sexual conduct, including soliciting or attempting to solicit any employee to engage in sexual activity for compensation or reward.
3. Subjecting, or threats of subjecting, an employee to unwelcome sexual attention or conduct or intentionally making performance of the employee's job more difficult because of the employee's sex.

C. Sexual or discriminatory displays or publications anywhere in Company's workplace by Company employees, such as

1. Displaying pictures, posters, calendars, graffiti, objects, promotional materials, reading materials, or other materials that are sexually suggestive, sexually demeaning, or pornographic, or bringing into Company's work environment or possessing any such material to read, display, or view at work.

   A picture will be presumed to be sexually suggestive if it depicts a person of either sex who is not fully clothed or in clothes that are not suited to or ordinarily accepted for the accomplishment of routine work in and around the workplace and who is posed for the obvious purpose of displaying or drawing attention to private portions of his or her body.
2. Reading or otherwise publicizing in the work environment materials that are in any way sexually revealing, sexually suggestive, sexually demeaning, or pornographic.
3. Displaying signs or other materials purporting to segregate an employee by sex in any area of the workplace (other than restrooms and similar semi-private lockers/changing rooms).

The Equal Pay Act expressly provides four criteria that justify a differential in wages. These defenses include payment systems that are based on

1. Seniority
2. Merit (as long as there is some identifiable measurement standard)
3. Quantity or quality of product (commission, piecework, or quality-control–based payment systems are permitted)
4. "Any factor other than sex" (including shift differentials, such as night versus day shifts)

The employer bears the burden of proving these defenses.

ETHICAL PERSPECTIVE

Paralegal's Duty to Report Sexual Harassment Conduct

Ms. Heath is hired as a paralegal for the large law firm of White, Cassel, and Smith, and is assigned to assist Mr. White. During the first couple of weeks on the job, on numerous occasions when Ms. Heath was in Mr. White's office on legal and paralegal matters, Mr. White made rude comments such as talking about people having sex, bragging how good he is in bed, making obscene gestures, and touching Ms. Heath on the shoulder. After several weeks of being subjected to such conduct, Ms. Heath is distressed about going to work because she may face continuing similar conduct by Mr. White.

What should Ms. Heath do?

In this case there is a clear pattern of sexual harassment by Mr. White that is creating a hostile work environment for Ms. Heath and is violating Title VII of the Civil Rights Act of 1964. Ms. Heath should go to the Human Resource Department of the law firm, if it has one, or to the managing partner or partners of the law firm, and disclose Mr. White's conduct and how it is affecting her at work. She should also file a written complaint so that there is evidence of her disclosure of the problem.

The law firm is under the duty to correct the situation by reprimanding Mr. White and notifying him that his conduct violates the law firm's policy against sexual harassment, reassigning Ms. Heath to a partner of the firm that has equal status as Mr. White if necessary, or dismissing Mr. White if his conduct rises to a level that would warrant such dismissal.

Ms. Heath could also report this matter to the local office of the state equal opportunity commission or to the office of the Equal Employment Opportunity Commission (EEOC). If the law firm retaliates against Ms. Heath for reporting this matter, the firm is engaging in conduct that further violates Title VII, for which Ms. Heath could seek redress. If the EEOC gives Ms. Heath a right-to-sue letter, she can bring a civil lawsuit under Title VII to recover damages for the sexual harassment and retaliation.

If a paralegal is being sexually harassed on the job, she or he should immediately report such conduct, and if the law firm does not immediately correct the situation, the paralegal should notify the proper government authorities, state and federal, to obtain redress. The paralegal may also hire an attorney to represent her or him in a civil lawsuit against the law firm.

Family and Medical Leave Act

In February 1993, Congress enacted the **Family and Medical Leave Act.** This law guarantees workers unpaid time off from work for medical emergencies. The act, which applies to companies with 50 or more workers as well as federal, state, and local governments, covers about half of the nation's workforce. To be covered by the act, an employee must have worked for the employer for at least one year and have performed more than 1,250 hours of service during the previous 12-month period.

Family and Medical Leave Act (FMLA) A federal act that guarantees workers up to 12 weeks of unpaid leave in a 12-month period to attend to family and medical emergencies and other specified situations.

Covered employers are required to provide up to 12 weeks of unpaid leave during any 12-month period as a result of the

1. birth of, and care for, a son or daughter.
2. placement of a child for adoption or in foster care.
3. serious health condition that makes the employee unable to perform his or her duties.
4. care for a spouse, child, or parent with a serious health problem.

Leave because of the birth of a child or the placement of a child for adoption or foster care cannot be taken intermittently unless the employer agrees. Other leaves may be taken on an intermittent basis. The employer may require medical proof of claimed serious health conditions.

Paralegals *in* Practice

PARALEGAL PROFILE

Jaxine L. Wintjen

Jaxine L. Wintjen is a board-certified paralegal (CP) with 30 years of experience. She specializes in employee benefits, an area that combines employment law and tax law. Jaxine is a member and past chair of the Paralegal/Legal Assistants Section of the State Bar of Michigan. She is also a member of the Employee Benefits Committee of the Michigan State Bar Taxation Section. Jaxine currently works in the Labor, Employment and Benefits Practice Group of Foster, Swift, Collins & Smith in Lansing, Michigan.

Technology plays a major role in my everyday work. For example, I use the Internet extensively for legal research and e-discovery. Online services, such as Accurint® and KnowX®, help me find current addresses of pension plan participants who no longer work for a client. Other frequently-used online materials include Internal Revenue Service (IRS) code/regulations and Department of Labor (DOL) regulations/rulings. During a recent litigation case, I gathered online data to compare retirement plans offered by both the plaintiff's former employer and current employer. This information was used to prove that the plaintiff was not disadvantaged by the loss of his 401(k) benefit when he was discharged from his former employer.

Pension plans are normally long, complex documents that involve a series of supplemental resource files. Working with our in-house programmer, I helped design a document preparation system that uses macros in Microsoft® Word. The system can draw from nearly 3,000 different provisions, and assemble the various paragraphs into an individualized plan for a client. This plan is then merged with the client's employee database to quickly produce a large number of customized documents. I also use Microsoft Excel spreadsheets to perform annual mathematical tests on pension plans.

Finally, all IRS forms for obtaining benefit plan approvals and filing annual returns are computer generated using Relius Government Forms software. Beginning in 2010, we [have been] required to electronically file all Form 5500 returns. This process...includes electronically obtaining author, signer, and transmitter credentials from the IRS and DOL.

An eligible employee who takes leave must, upon returning to work, be restored to either the same or an equivalent position with equivalent employment benefits and pay. The restored employee is not entitled to the accrual of seniority during the leave period, however. A covered employer may deny restoration to a salaried employee who is among the highest-paid 10 percent of that employer's employees if the denial is necessary to prevent "substantial and grievous economic injury" to the employer's operations.

In the feature above, a paralegal professional discusses her experience in the field of employment benefits.

Learning Objective 6

Describe the scope of coverage of the Age Discrimination in Employment Act.

Age Discrimination in Employment Act

Age Discrimination in Employment Act (ADEA) A federal statute that prohibits age discrimination practices against employees who are age 40 and older.

In the past, some employers discriminated against employees and prospective employees based on their age. For example, employers often refused to hire older workers. The **Age Discrimination in Employment Act (ADEA),** which prohibits certain age discrimination practices, was enacted in 1967.

ADEA prohibits age discrimination in all employment decisions, including hiring, promotions, payment of compensation, and other terms and conditions of employment. Originally, ADEA prohibited employment discrimination against persons between 40 and 65 years of age. In 1978, its coverage was extended to persons up to 70 years of age. Further amendments complctcly eliminated an age ceiling, so ADEA now applies to employees who are age 40 and older.

Learning Objective 7

Describe the protections afforded by the Americans with Disabilities Act.

Americans with Disabilities Act

The **Americans with Disabilities Act (ADA),** signed into law on July 26, 1990, is the most comprehensive piece of civil rights legislation since the Civil Rights Act of 1964. The ADA imposes obligations on employers and providers of public transportation, telecommunications, and public accommodations to accommodate individuals with disabilities. Congress passed the **Americans with Disabilities Act Amendments Act (ADAAA)** of 2008, which amends the ADA by expanding the definition of disability.

Title I of ADA prohibits employment discrimination against qualified individuals with disabilities in regard to job application procedures, hiring, compensation, training, promotion, and termination. It requires an employer to make *reasonable accommodations* to individuals with disabilities that do not cause undue hardship to the employer. Reasonable accommodations may include making facilities readily accessible to individuals with disabilities, providing part-time or modified work schedules, acquiring equipment or devices, modifying examination and training materials, and providing qualified readers or interpreters.

Americans with Disabilities Act (ADA) A federal statute that imposes obligations on employers and providers of public transportation, telecommunications, and public accommodations to accommodate individuals with disabilities.

Employers are not obligated to provide accommodations that would impose an *undue burden*, or actions that would require significant difficulty or expense. The courts consider factors such as the nature and cost of accommodation, the employer's overall financial resources, and the employer's type of operation. Obviously, what may be a significant difficulty or expense for a small employer may not be an undue hardship for a large employer.

Civil Rights Act of 1866

The **Civil Rights Act of 1866** was enacted after the Civil War. **Section 1981** of this act states that all persons "have the same right...to make and enforce contracts...as is enjoyed by white persons." This law was enacted to give African Americans, just freed from slavery, the same right to contract as Caucasians. Section 1981 expressly prohibits racial discrimination; it has also been held to forbid discrimination based on national origin.

Civil Rights Act of 1866 A federal statute enacted after the Civil War that says all persons "have the same right...to make and enforce contracts...as is enjoyed by white persons." It prohibits racial and national origin employment discrimination.

Employment decisions are covered by Section 1981 because the employment relationship is contractual. Although most racial and national origin employment discrimination cases are brought under Title VII, there are two reasons that a complainant would bring the action under Section 1981:

1. A private plaintiff can bring an action without going through the procedural requirements of Title VII.
2. There is no cap on the recovery of compensatory or punitive damages.

Labor Union Law

Learning Objective 8
Describe how a labor union is organized and employees' rights to strike and picket.

Prior to the Industrial Revolution, employees and employers had somewhat equal bargaining power. Once the country became industrialized in the late 1800s, however, large corporate employers had much more bargaining power than their employees. In the early 1900s, members of the labor movement lobbied Congress to pass laws to protect their rights to organize and bargain with management. During the Great Depression of the 1930s, several statutes were enacted to give workers certain rights and protections. Other statutes have been added since then. The major federal statutes in this area are:

- **Norris-LaGuardia Act.** Enacted in 1932, this act stipulates that it is legal for employees to organize and form labor unions.
- **National Labor Relations Act (NLRA).** This act, also known as the Wagner Act, was enacted in 1935. The NLRA establishes the right for employees to form, join, and assist labor organizations; to bargain collectively with employers; and to engage in concerted activity to promote these rights.
- **Labor Management Relations Act.** In 1947, Congress enacted the Labor Management Relations Act (the Taft-Hartley Act). This act (1) expands the activities that labor unions can engage in, (2) gives

National Labor Relations Board (NLRB) A federal administrative agency that oversees union elections, prevents employers and unions from engaging in illegal and unfair labor practices, and enforces and interprets certain federal labor laws.

Strong responsible unions are essential to industrial fair play. Without them the labor bargain is wholly one-sided.
Louis D. Brandeis (1935) United States Supreme Court Justice

employers the right to engage in free speech efforts against unions prior to a union election, and (3) gives the president of the United States the right to seek an injunction (for up to 80 days) against a strike that would create a national emergency.

- **Labor Management Reporting and Disclosure Act.** Congress enacted the Labor Management Reporting and Disclosure Act of 1959 (the Landrum-Griffin Act). This act regulates internal union affairs and establishes the rights of union members.
- **Railway Labor Act.** The Railway Labor Act of 1926, as amended in 1934, covers employees of railroad and airline carriers.

Today, approximately 10 percent of private-sector wage and salary workers belong to labor unions: Many government employees also belong to unions.

National Labor Relations Board (NLRB)

The NLRA created the **National Labor Relations Board (NLRB).** The NLRB is an administrative body composed of five members appointed by the president and approved by the Senate. The NLRB oversees union elections, prevents employers and unions from engaging in illegal and unfair labor practices, and enforces and interprets certain federal labor laws. The decisions of the NLRB are enforceable in court.

Organizing a Union

Section 7 of the National Labor Relations Act A law that gives employees the right to join together and form a union.

Web Exploration

Go to **http://www.nlrb.gov/html** to find the office of the Federal National Labor Relations Board (NLRB) that serves your area.

Section 7 of the National Labor Relations Act gives employees the right to join together and form a union. Section 7 provides that employees have the right to self-organization; to form, join, or assist labor organizations; to bargain collectively through representatives of their own choosing; and to engage in other concerted activities for the purpose of collective bargaining or other mutual aid protection.

Section 8(a) of the National Labor Relations Act makes it an **unfair labor practice** for an employer to interfere with, coerce, or restrain employees from exercising their statutory right to form and join unions.

> **Examples** Threats of a loss of benefits for joining the union, statements such as "I'll close this plant if a union comes in here," and the like are unfair labor practices. Also, an employer may not form a company union. Section 8(b) of the NLRA prohibits unions from engaging in unfair labor practices, such as coercion and physical threats, that interfere with a union election.

Collective bargaining The act of negotiating contract terms between an employer and the members of a union.

Once a union has been elected, the employer and the union discuss the terms of employment of union members and try to negotiate a contract that embodies these terms. The act of negotiating is called **collective bargaining,** and the resulting contract is called a **collective bargaining agreement.** The employer and the union must negotiate with each other in good faith.

Strikes and Picketing

Strike Cessation of work by union members to obtain economic benefits or correct an unfair labor practice.

Picketing The action of strikers walking in front of the employer's premises carrying signs announcing the reason for their strike.

The NLRA gives union management the right to recommend that the union call a **strike** if a collective bargaining agreement cannot be reached. Before there can be a strike, though, a majority vote of the union's members must agree to the action.

Striking union members often engage in **picketing** in support of their strike. Picketing usually takes the form of the striking employees and union representatives walking in front of the employer's premises carrying signs announcing their strike. Picketing is used to put pressure on an employer to settle a strike. The right to picket is implied from the NLRA.

Picketing is lawful unless it

1. is accompanied by violence,
2. obstructs customers from entering the employer's place of business,

3. prevents nonstriking employees from entering the employer's premises, or
4. prevents pickups and deliveries at the employer's place of business.

An employer may seek an injunction against unlawful picketing.

Illegal Strikes

Several types of strikes have been held to be illegal and are not protected by federal labor laws. **Illegal strikes** take the form of:

- **Violent strikes.** In **violent strikes,** striking employees cause substantial damage to the property of the employer or a third party. Courts usually tolerate a certain amount of isolated violence before finding that the entire strike is illegal.
- **Sit-down strikes.** In **sit-down strikes,** striking employees continue to occupy the employer's premises. Such strikes are illegal because they deny the employer's statutory right to continue its operations during the strike.
- **Partial or intermittent strikes.** In **partial or intermittent strikes,** employees strike part of the day or workweek and work the other part. This type of strike is illegal because it interferes with the employer's right to operate its facilities at full operation.

Management and union may be likened to that serpent of the fables who on one body had two heads that fighting with poisoned fangs, killed themselves.

Peter Drucker
The New Society (1951)

A union is required to give an employer a 60-day notice before commencing a strike. This is called a **cooling-off period.** This mandatory cooling-off period is designed to give the employer and the union time to negotiate a settlement of the union grievances and avoid a strike. Any strike without a proper 60-day notice is illegal, and illegal strikers may be discharged by the employer with no rights to reinstatement.

Crossover and Replacement Workers

Individual members of a union do not have to honor a strike. They may (1) choose not to strike, or (2) return to work after joining the strikers for a time. Employees who choose either of these two options are known as **crossover workers.**

Once a strike begins, the employer may continue operations by using management personnel or hiring **replacement workers** to take the place of the striking employees. Replacement workers can be hired on either a temporary or a permanent basis. If replacement workers are given permanent status, they do not have to be dismissed when the strike is over.

Immigration Law

Many immigrants arrive in the United States daily. Most of these immigrants have come here legally and can obtain employment. Other immigrants are here illegally and cannot legally work. The **Immigration Reform and Control Act of 1986 (IRCA)** and the **Immigration Act of 1990,** both federal statutes, regulate immigration and the employment of immigrants in the United States.

For many people like myself, it can be called the Ellis Island of the 20th century.

Theodore H. M. Prudon
Describing Kennedy Airport

Learning Objective 9
Understand immigration laws that apply to employment law.

In 1921, the United States enacted its first immigration quota law, which set a limit on the number of immigrants that could be admitted to the United States from each foreign country each year. During different times, the quotas for each foreign country have been raised or lowered, depending on the world situation. A quota system is in effect today.

Currently, the immigration laws of this country are administered by the **U.S. Citizenship and Immigration Services (USCIS),** which is part of the U.S. Department of Homeland Security. The USCIS processes immigrant visa and naturalization petitions.

U.S. Citizenship and Immigration Services (USCIS) A federal agency empowered to enforce U.S. immigration laws.

Foreign nationals who qualify and have met the requirements to do so may become citizens of the United States. During their swearing-in ceremony, they must swear an **Oath of Citizenship.** This oath is presented in Exhibit 18.9.

Exhibit 18.9 Oath of Citizenship

I hereby declare, on oath, that I absolutely and entirely renounce and adjure all allegiance and fidelity to any foreign prince, potentate, state, or sovereignty of whom or which I have heretofore been a subject or citizen; that I will support and defend the Constitution and laws of the United States of America against all enemies, foreign and domestic; that I will bear true faith and allegiance to the same; that I will bear arms on behalf of the United States when required by law; that I will perform noncombatant service in the Armed Forces of the United States when required by law; that I will perform work of national importance under civilian direction when required by law; and that I take this obligation freely without any mental reservation or purpose of evasion; so help me God. In acknowledgment whereof I have hereunto affixed my signature.

Employment Eligibility Verification

Form I-9, Employment Eligibility Verification A form that must be completed by prospective employees.

Employers have an affirmative duty to verify that the employees they hire are authorized to work in the United States. Employers are required to have prospective employees complete **Form I-9, Employment Eligibility Verification,** and must obtain a completed Form I-9 for every employee, regardless of citizenship or national origin. Employers must examine evidence of prospective employees' identity and employment eligibility. A state-issued driver's license is not sufficient. Rather, employers must review other documents to establish eligibility, such as Social Security cards and birth certificates.

Employers must maintain records and post in the workplace notices of the contents of the law. The IRCA imposes criminal and financial penalties on employers who knowingly hire undocumented workers.

Exhibit 18.10 shows Form I-9, Employment Eligibility Verification.

H-1B Foreign Guest Worker Visa

H-1B Foreign Guest Worker Visa (H1-B visa) A nonimmigrant visa that allows U.S. employers to employ foreign nationals in the United States who are skilled in specialty occupations. They are called *foreign guest workers.*

An **H-1B Foreign Guest Worker Visa,** or **H-1B visa,** is a nonimmigrant visa that allows U.S. employers to employ foreign nationals in the United States who are skilled in specialty occupations. A foreign guest worker under an H-1B visa must have a bachelor's degree or higher and a "specialty occupation," such as engineering, mathematics, computer science, physical sciences, or medicine. A **foreign guest worker** must be sponsored by a U.S. employer. Employers, and not individual applicants, apply for H-1B visas for proposed foreign guest workers. The USCIS judges H1-B eligibility.

The number of H-1B visas is limited, usually to fewer than 100,000 per year, so the competition is fierce to obtain such visas. H-1B visa holders are allowed to bring their immediate family members (that is, spouse and children under age 21) to the United States under the **H4 visa** category as dependents. An H4 visa holder may remain in the United States as long as he or she remains in legal status. An H4 visa holder is not eligible to work in the United States.

The duration of stay for a worker on an H-1B visa is three years, which can be extended another three years. During this time, an employer may sponsor an H-1B holder for a green card, which if issued, permits the foreign national to eventually obtain U.S. citizenship. If the employer does not apply for a green card for the foreign national or the foreign national is denied a green card, he or she must leave the country after six years from the time of employment.

EB-1 Extraordinary Ability Visa

EB-1 Extraordinary Ability Visa (EB-1 visa) A nonimmigrant visa that allows U.S. employers to employ foreign nationals in the United States who possess exceptional qualifications for certain types of employment.

An **EB-1 Extraordinary Ability Visa,** or **EB-1 visa,** is a nonimmigrant visa that allows U.S. employers to employ foreign nationals in the United States who possess extraordinary ability for certain types of employment. The three categories of workers who can qualify for an EB-1 visa are (1) persons who can demonstrate extraordinary

Exhibit 18.10 Form I-9, Employment Eligibility Verification

OMB No. 1615-0047; Expires 06/30/09

Department of Homeland Security
U.S. Citizenship and Immigration Services

Form I-9, Employment Eligibility Verification

Please read instructions carefully before completing this form. The instructions must be available during completion of this form.

ANTI-DISCRIMINATION NOTICE: It is illegal to discriminate against work eligible individuals. Employers CANNOT specify which document(s) they will accept from an employee. The refusal to hire an individual because the documents have a future expiration date may also constitute illegal discrimination.

Section 1. Employee Information and Verification. To be completed and signed by employee at the time employment begins.

Print Name: Last	First	Middle Initial	Maiden Name
Address *(Street Name and Number)*		Apt. #	Date of Birth *(month/day/year)*
City	State	Zip Code	Social Security #

I am aware that federal law provides for imprisonment and/or fines for false statements or use of false documents in connection with the completion of this form.

I attest, under penalty of perjury, that I am (check one of the following):

☐ A citizen or national of the United States
☐ A lawful permanent resident (Alien #) A ____________
☐ An alien authorized to work until ____________
(Alien # or Admission #) ____________

Employee's Signature	Date *(month/day/year)*

Preparer and/or Translator Certification. *(To be completed and signed if Section 1 is prepared by a person other than the employee.) I attest, under penalty of perjury, that I have assisted in the completion of this form and that to the best of my knowledge the information is true and correct.*

Preparer's/Translator's Signature	Print Name
Address *(Street Name and Number, City, State, Zip Code)*	Date *(month/day/year)*

Section 2. Employer Review and Verification. To be completed and signed by employer. Examine one document from List A OR examine one document from List B and one from List C, as listed on the reverse of this form, and record the title, number and expiration date, if any, of the document(s).

	List A	OR	List B	AND	List C
Document title:	____________		____________		____________
Issuing authority:	____________		____________		____________
Document #:	____________		____________		____________
Expiration Date *(if any)*:	____________		____________		____________
Document #:	____________				
Expiration Date *(if any)*:	____________				

CERTIFICATION - I attest, under penalty of perjury, that I have examined the document(s) presented by the above-named employee, that the above-listed document(s) appear to be genuine and to relate to the employee named, that the employee began employment on *(month/day/year)* ____________ **and that to the best of my knowledge the employee is eligible to work in the United States. (State employment agencies may omit the date the employee began employment.)**

Signature of Employer or Authorized Representative	Print Name	Title
Business or Organization Name and Address *(Street Name and Number, City, State, Zip Code)*		Date *(month/day/year)*

Section 3. Updating and Reverification. To be completed and signed by employer.

A. New Name *(if applicable)*	B. Date of Rehire *(month/day/year) (if applicable)*

C. If employee's previous grant of work authorization has expired, provide the information below for the document that establishes current employment eligibility.

Document Title: ____________ Document #: ____________ Expiration Date (if any): ____________

I attest, under penalty of perjury, that to the best of my knowledge, this employee is eligible to work in the United States, and if the employee presented document(s), the document(s) I have examined appear to be genuine and to relate to the individual.

Signature of Employer or Authorized Representative	Date *(month/day/year)*

Form I-9 (Rev. 06/16/08) N

(continued)

Exhibit 18.10 Form I-9, Employment Eligibility Verification *(continued)*

LISTS OF ACCEPTABLE DOCUMENTS

LIST A Documents that Establish Both Identity and Employment Eligibility	OR — LIST B Documents that Establish Identity	AND — LIST C Documents that Establish Employment Eligibility
1. U.S. Passport (unexpired or expired)	**1.** Driver's license or ID card issued by a state or outlying possession of the United States provided it contains a photograph or information such as name, date of birth, gender, height, eye color and address	**1.** U.S. Social Security card issued by the Social Security Administration *(other than a card stating it is not valid for employment)*
2. Permanent Resident Card or Alien Registration Receipt Card (Form I-551)	**2.** ID card issued by federal, state or local government agencies or entities, provided it contains a photograph or information such as name, date of birth, gender, height, eye color and address	**2.** Certification of Birth Abroad issued by the Department of State *(Form FS-545 or Form DS-1350)*
3. An unexpired foreign passport with a temporary I-551 stamp	**3.** School ID card with a photograph	**3.** Original or certified copy of a birth certificate issued by a state, county, municipal authority or outlying possession of the United States bearing an official seal
4. An unexpired Employment Authorization Document that contains a photograph (Form I-766, I-688, I-688A, I-688B)	**4.** Voter's registration card	**4.** Native American tribal document
	5. U.S. Military card or draft record	**5.** U.S. Citizen ID Card *(Form I-197)*
5. An unexpired foreign passport with an unexpired Arrival-Departure Record, Form I-94, bearing the same name as the passport and containing an endorsement of the alien's nonimmigrant status, if that status authorizes the alien to work for the employer	**6.** Military dependent's ID card	**6.** ID Card for use of Resident Citizen in the United States *(Form I-179)*
	7. U.S. Coast Guard Merchant Mariner Card	
	8. Native American tribal document	**7.** Unexpired employment authorization document issued by DHS *(other than those listed under List A)*
	9. Driver's license issued by a Canadian government authority	
	For persons under age 18 who are unable to present a document listed above:	
	10. School record or report card	
	11. Clinic, doctor or hospital record	
	12. Day-care or nursery school record	

Illustrations of many of these documents appear in Part 8 of the Handbook for Employers (M-274)

Form I-9 (Rev. 06/16/08) N Page 2

Learning Objective 10
Explain a paralegal's duty to disclose his or her paralegal status.

ETHICAL PERSPECTIVE

Duty to Disclose Paralegal Status

Ms. Abigail Knight works as a paralegal for a small law firm, where she works directly for Mr. Abdul Farid, one of the two partners in the law firm. In her capacity as a paralegal, Ms. Knight conducts legal research and prepares drafts of agreements and documents for review by Mr. Farid. Because the law firm is small, Ms. Knight is also the firm's business manager. In this capacity, she is responsible for bookkeeping and ordering supplies for the law firm.

Recently, the law firm hired a consultant to redesign the law firm's name and create a marketing strategy for the firm. Soon after, the new design for the name of the law firm was completed and approved by the two lawyers of the firm. Now Ms. Knight is to order business cards with the new design for the two attorneys and herself. On the business cards of the two attorneys, she places their names and the words "Attorney at Law." Ms. Knight is also to have a business card with her name and the law firm's name and address on it.

Does Ms. Knight owe a duty to disclose her status as a paralegal on the business cards she orders for herself?

Many model and state paralegal professional codes of ethics and responsibility require a paralegal to identify himself or herself as a paralegal on business cards, letterhead, brochures, and such. In addition, failing to include this title violates paralegal ethical standards and could possibly subject the paralegal to disciplinary actions of the licensing agency of the state.

PARALEGAL'S ETHICAL DECISION

Thus, Ms. Knight owes an ethical duty to disclose her position as a paralegal professional on the business cards she is ordering for herself. This ethical duty is designed to prevent a paralegal from holding himself or herself out as an attorney. Therefore, Ms. Knight must include the word "Paralegal" on her business cards so that she properly identifies her position in the law firm.

ability in the sciences, arts, education, business, or athletics through sustained national or international acclaim; (2) outstanding professors and researchers who can demonstrate international recognition for outstanding achievements in a particular academic field; and (3) multinational managers or executives employed by a firm outside the United States and who seek to continue working for that firm in the United States. Employers must file for the visa for workers in categories (2) and (3), whereas applicants in category (1) can file for the visa themselves. Fewer than 50,000 EB-1 visas are granted each year. The USCIS judges EB-1 eligibility.

The ethical duty of a paralegal professional to disclose his or her paralegal status is discussed in the feature above.

Concept Review *and* Reinforcement

LEGAL TERMINOLOGY

Age Discrimination in Employment Act (ADEA) 666
Agency 646
Agency by ratification 649
Agent 646
Americans with Disabilities Act (ADA) 666
Americans with Disabilities Act Amendments Act (ADAAA) 667
Apparent agency (agency by estoppel) 649
Attorney-in-fact 647
Bona fide occupational qualification (BFOQ) 662

SUMMARY OF KEY CONCEPTS

Agency Law

	Agency is a fiduciary relationship that results from the manifestation of consent by one person to act on behalf of another person with that person's consent.
Parties	1. *Principal:* The party who employs another person to act on his or her behalf. 2. *Agent:* The party who agrees to act on behalf of another person.
Kinds of Employment Relationships	*Employer–employee relationship:* An employer hires an employee to perform some form of physical service. An employee is not an agent unless the principal authorizes him or her to enter into contracts on the principal's behalf.

	Principal–agent relationship: An employer hires an employee and authorizes the employee to enter into contracts on the employer's behalf. *Principal–independent contractor relationship:* A principal employs a person who is not an employee of the principal. The independent contractor has authority to enter into only those contracts authorized by the principal.
Formation of the Agency Relationship	1. *Express agency:* The principal and the agent expressly agree in words to enter into an agency agreement. The agency contract may be oral or written, unless the Statute of Frauds requires it to be in writing. 2. *Implied agency:* An agency is inferred from the conduct of the parties. 3. *Apparent agency:* A principal creates an appearance of an agency that in actuality does not exist. Also called *agency by estoppel* or *ostensible agency.* 4. *Agency by ratification:* A person misrepresents himself or herself as another's agent even though he or she is not, and the purported principal ratifies (accepts) the unauthorized act.
Tort Liability of Principals and Agents to Third Parties	
	Principals are liable for the *tortious conduct* of an agent who is acting within the *scope of the principal's authority*. Liability is imposed for misrepresentation, negligence, and intentional torts.
Intentional Torts	States apply one of the following rules: 1. *Motivation test:* The principal is liable if the agent's intentional tort was committed to promote the principal's business. 2. *Work-related test:* The principal is liable if the agent's intentional tort was committed within a work-related time or space.
	Agents are personally liable for their own tortious conduct.
Negligence	Principals are liable for the negligent conduct of agents acting within the scope of the principals' employment. Special negligence doctrines include: 1. *Frolic and detour:* Principals are generally relieved of liability if the agent's negligent act occurred on a substantial frolic and detour from the scope of employment. 2. *"Coming and going" rule:* Principals are not liable if the agent's tortious conduct occurred while the agent was on the way to or from work. 3. *Dual-purpose mission:* If the agent is acting on his or her own behalf and on behalf of the principal, the principal is generally liable for the agent's tortious conduct.
Independent Contractor	
	Generally, principals are not liable for the tortious conduct of independent contractors. Exceptions to the rule are for: 1. *Nondelegable duties.* 2. *Special risks.* 3. *Negligence in selecting an independent contractor.* 4. Independent contractors are personally liable for their own torts.
Termination of an Agency	
Termination by Acts of the Parties	The following *acts of the parties* terminate agency contracts: 1. *Mutual agreement* 2. *Lapse of time* 3. *Purpose achieved* 4. *Occurrence of a specified event*
Wrongful Termination of an Agency of Employment Contract	If an agency is for an agreed-upon term or purpose, the *unilateral termination* of the agency contract by either the principal or the agent constitutes the *wrongful termination* of the agency. The breaching party is liable to the other party for damages caused by the breach.

Workers' Compensation

Workers' Compensation Acts	Workers' compensation acts are state statutes that create an administrative procedure for workers to receive payments for job-related injuries.
Workers' Compensation Insurance	Most states require employers to carry private or government-sponsored *workers' compensation insurance*. Some states permit employers to self-insure.
Employment-Related Injury	For an employment-related injury to be compensable under workers' compensation, the claimant must prove that the injury arose out of and in the course of his or her employment.
Exclusive Remedy	Workers' compensation is an exclusive remedy. Thus, workers cannot sue their employers to recover damages for job-related injuries.

Occupational Safety and Health Act

	1. *Occupational Safety and Health Act:* A federal statute that requires employers to provide safe working conditions. 2. *Occupational Safety and Health Administration (OSHA):* A federal administrative agency that administers and enforces the Occupational Safety and Health Act.
Duty Standards	OSHA enforces the following duty standards on employers: 1. *Specific duty standards:* OSHA safety standards established for specific equipment (such as a chain saw) or a specific industry (such as mining). 2. *General duty standards:* OSHA standards that impose a general duty on employers to provide safe working conditions.

Fair Labor Standards Act

	Fair Labor Standards Act (FLSA): A federal statute that protects workers. 1. *Child labor:* The FLSA forbids the use of illegal child labor. The U.S. Department of Labor defines what illegal child labor is. 2. *Minimum wage:* Workers must be paid a minimum wage. The federal minimum wage as of 2012 was $7.25 per hour. The minimum wage can be changed by Congress. 3. *Overtime pay:* An employer cannot require employees to work more than 40 hours per week unless they are paid 1.5 times their regular pay for each hour worked in excess of 40 hours.

Title VII of the Civil Rights Act of 1964

	Title VII of the Civil Rights Act of 1964 is a federal statute that prohibits job discrimination based on the (1) race, (2) color, (3) religion, (4) sex, or (5) national origin of the job applicant.
Scope of Coverage of Title VII	*Employment decisions subject to Title VII:* Decisions regarding hiring; promotion; demotion; payment of salaries, wages, and fringe benefits; job training and apprenticeships; work rules; or any other "term, condition, or privilege of employment."
Protected Classes	Title VII prohibits employment discrimination based on the following protected classes: 1. *Race:* A broad class based on common physical characteristics 2. *Color:* Skin color 3. *National origin:* A person's national heritage 4. *Sex:* Male or female 5. *Religion:* Discrimination solely because of a person's religious beliefs or practices. An employer has a duty to *reasonably accommodate* an employee's religious beliefs if it does not cause an *undue hardship* on the employer.
Sexual Harassment	Sexual harassment consists of lewd remarks, touching, intimidation, posting pinups, and other verbal or physical conduct of a sexual nature that occurs on the job. Sexual harassment that creates a *hostile work environment* violates Title VII; see *Meritor Savings Bank v. Vinson*, 477 U.S. 57 (1986).

Equal Pay Act

	The Equal Pay Act is a federal statute that forbids pay discrimination for the same job based on the sex of the employee performing the job, where the job requires equal skill, effort, responsibility, and working conditions.
Criteria That Justify a Differential in Wages	The Equal Pay Act expressly provides the following four criteria that justify a differential in wages for the same job: 1. Seniority 2. Merit (based on a measurable standard) 3. Quantity or quality of product (such as commission, piecework) 4. "Any factor other than sex" (such as night shift)

Family and Medical Leave Act

	The Family and Medical Leave Act is a federal statute that guarantees covered workers unpaid time off from work for the birth or adoption of a child, serious health problems of the worker, and serious health problems of a spouse, child, or parent.

Age Discrimination in Employment Act (ADEA)

	ADEA is a federal statute that prohibits employment discrimination against applicants and employees who are 40 years of age and older.

Americans with Disabilities Act (ADA)

	The ADA is a federal law that imposes obligations on employers and providers of public transportation, telecommunications, and public accommodations to accommodate individuals with disabilities.
Title I of ADA	Title I of the ADA is a federal law that prohibits employment discrimination against qualified individuals with disabilities. It requires employers to make *reasonable accommodations* for employees with disabilities that do not cause *undue hardship* to the employer.

Civil Rights Act of 1866

Section 1981	Section 1981 of the Civil Rights Act of 1866, enacted after the Civil War, states that all persons "have the same right... to make and enforce contracts... as enjoyed by white persons."
Protected Class	Section 1981 prohibits discrimination because of *race* or *national origin* concerning employment contracts.
Remedies	A successful plaintiff can recover compensatory and punitive damages. There is no monetary cap on compensatory and punitive damages.

Labor Union Law

National Labor Relations Act (NLRA)	The NLRA is a federal statute that established the right of employees to form, join, and assist labor unions.
National Labor Relations Board (NLRB)	The NLRB is a federal administrative agency empowered to administer federal labor law, oversee union elections, and decide labor disputes.
Unfair Labor Practice	1. *Employer:* Section 8(a) of the NLRA makes it an *unfair labor practice* for an employer to interfere with, coerce, or restrain employees from exercising their right to form and join unions. 2. *Labor union:* Section 8(b) makes it an *unfair labor practice* for a union to interfere with a union election.

Collective Bargaining	1. *Collective bargaining:* A process whereby a union and an employer negotiate the terms and conditions of employment for the covered employee union members. 2. *Collective bargaining agreement:* A contract between an employer and a labor union that results from collective bargaining.
Strikes and Picketing	1. *Strike:* A strike is cessation of work by union members in order to obtain economic benefits, correct for the purpose of an unfair labor practice, or preserve their work. The NLRA gives employees the right to strike. 2. *Cooling-off period:* The requirement that a labor union give an employer at least 60 days' prior notice of a strike. 3. *Picketing:* Striking employees and union organizers may picket—walk around the employer's premises, usually carrying signs notifying the public of their grievance against the employer. 4. *Illegal strikes and picketing:* The following types of picketing and strikes are illegal: a. *Illegal picketing:* Picketing that is accompanied by violence or obstructs customers, nonstriking workers, or suppliers from entering the employer's premises. b. *Violent strike:* A strike in which striking employees cause substantial damage to the employer's or a third party's property. c. *Sit-down strike:* A strike in which the striking employees occupy and refuse to leave the employer's premises. d. *Partial or intermittent strike:* A strike in which the striking employees strike for only parts of each day or week.
Immigration Law	
Federal Immigration Law	1. *Federal statutes:* The Immigration Reform and Control Act of 1986 (IRCA) and the Immigration Act of 1990 are federal statutes that make it unlawful for employers to hire illegal immigrants. 2. *U.S. Citizenship and Immigration Services (USCIS):* The federal administrative agency that enforces federal immigration laws. 3. *Form I-9, Employment Eligibility Verification:* A form that must be completed by prospective employees. Employers must also examine evidence of prospective employees' identity and employment eligibility. 4. *H-1B Foreign Guest Worker Visa (H-1B visa):* A nonimmigrant visa that allows U.S. employers to employ foreign nationals in the United States who are skilled in specialty occupations. 5. *EB-1 Extraordinary Ability Visa (EB-1 visa):* A nonimmigrant visa that allows U.S. employers to employ foreign nationals in the United States who possess exceptional qualifications for certain types of employment.

WORKING THE WEB

1. Visit the website of the federal Equal Employment Opportunity Commission (EEOC), http://www.eeoc.gov; Under the category "Discrimination by Types," find the description of "Pregnancy Discrimination." Write a one-page report on pregnancy discrimination.
2. Visit the website of the federal Occupational Safety and Health Administration (OSHA), http://www.osha.gov; Find an OSHA workplace safety rule that interests you. Write a one-page report that describes the rule.
3. Visit the website of the federal Equal Employment Opportunity Commission (EEOC), http://www.eeoc.gov; Under the category "News," find a current case or news event that interests you and write a one-page report on the case or news item.
4. Visit the website of the U.S. Department of Labor (DOL), http://www.dol.gov; Click on "Wages." On the next page click on "minimum wage." On the next page click on "states." On the next page click on "Current State Minimum Wage Rates." On the map that is shown, click on your state. Based on federal and state law, what is the minimum wage for your state?

CRITICAL THINKING & WRITING QUESTIONS

1. Define an agency, a principal, and an agent.
2. Define an independent contractor. What elements are examined to determine whether a person or party is an independent contractor?
3. Describe the differences among the following: (1) express agency, (2) implied agency, (3) agency by ratification, and (4) apparent agency.
4. What is the principal's liability for an agent's negligence? What does "scope of authority" mean?
5. Describe a principal's liability for the torts of an agent under the following special doctrines: (1) frolic and detour, (2) "coming and going" rule, and (3) dual-purpose mission.
6. What is workers' compensation? Describe the following: (1) work-related injury and (2) exclusive remedy.
7. What does the Occupational Safety and Health Act require? Describe the difference between specific duty standards and general duty standards.
8. What are the Fair Labor Standards Act (FLSA) requirements concerning (1) child labor, (2) minimum wage, and (3) overtime pay?
9. What does Title VII of the Civil Rights Act of 1964 provide? What are the protected classes under Title VII?
10. What is a bona fide occupational qualification (BFOQ)? Give an example.
11. Define "sexual harassment." Give an example.
12. What is age discrimination? What age group is protected by the Age Discrimination in Employment Act?
13. What does the Americans with Disabilities Act (ADA) provide? What is the duty of an employer concerning protecting employees under this ADA? Give an example.
14. What benefits does the Family Medical Leave Act provide? Explain.
15. Define a labor union. What benefit does the National Labor Relations Act (NLRA) provide to workers?

Building Paralegal Skills

VIDEO CASE STUDIES

Mechanic's Deposition: Duties of the Agent and Liability of the Principal

The mechanic who worked on the brake system of the truck involved in an accident reveals during his deposition/trial testimony that he bought cheaper replacement parts and disposed of the original parts when he fixed the truck after the accident.

After viewing the video case study in MyLegalStudiesLab, answer the following:

1. When does a mechanic have the authority to purchase repair parts?
2. Is it reasonable for a salesperson to believe that a mechanic working in a trucking company would have the authority to act on behalf of the trucking company?
3. What are the potential consequences of the mechanic throwing out the original brake parts?

Truck Driver's Deposition: Agent on a Detour and Liability of the Principal

A truck driver during his deposition admits that he left his assigned route to attend to personal business before going on his lunch break, during which he was involved in the accident in which his brakes failed.

After viewing the video case study in MyLegalStudiesLab, answer the following:

1. Is an employer liable for the actions of the employee when the employee deviates from an assigned route?
2. If an employee deviates from his assigned route when he is deemed to be on business for the employer, is the employee liable for his behavior?
3. Is the employer liable for everything the employee does during the working day?

ETHICS ANALYSIS & DISCUSSION QUESTIONS

1. What ethical issues may be involved when a paralegal acts under a power of attorney for a client of the firm?
2. Is a paralegal who is investigating the facts of a case acting as an agent for the client or for the law firm? Does the answer change the ethical obligations of the paralegal?
3. A corporate client is concerned about testimony that an employee may give in a pending civil action even though the corporation has not been named as a defendant (see Colorado Bar Association Ethics Opinion 79). May a paralegal attend depositions for the sole purpose of taking notes on testimony given or taken in the action?

DEVELOPING YOUR COLLABORATION SKILLS

With a group of other students selected by you or your instructor, review the facts of the following case. As a group, discuss the following questions.

1. Who is the plaintiff in this case?
2. Who is the defendant in this case?
3. What is the doctrine of *respondeat superior*?
4. Was Hall acting within the scope of her employment at the time of the incident?
5. Who wins?

Matthews v. Food Lion, LLC

Brigitte Hall was a part-time cashier at a grocery store owned and operated by Food Lion, LLC. When Hall's shift was over, she clock[ed] out of work and headed toward the bathroom before leaving the premises. Hall entered the bathroom at a brisk pace, and upon opening the door discovered that she had knocked Diamond Matthews to the floor. Employees at Food Lion called 911. Rescue assistants accompanied Matthews to the hospital. Matthews sued Hall and Food Lion to recover damages for negligence and *respondeat superior*. Food Lion filed a motion for summary judgment, alleging that Hall was not acting within the scope of her employment at the time of the incident.

Source: Matthews v. Food Lion, LLC, 695 S.E.2d 828, Web 2010 N.C. App. Lexis 1151 (North Carolina Court of Appeals)

PARALEGAL & PORTFOLIO EXERCISE

Using the website http://google.com a similar Internet website, the Internet legal services Westlaw or LexisNexis, or law books, find a sample general power of attorney for your state. Complete this form as if you were the principal and someone you choose is the attorney-in-fact, and make sure the form meets all of your state's requirements for creating a valid general power of attorney.

LEGAL ANALYSIS & WRITING CASES

Kelley v. Coca-Cola Enterprises, Inc. Web 2010 Ohio App. Lexis 1269

Court of Appeals of Ohio

Chad Kelley, an account manager with Coca-Cola Enterprises, Inc., attended a mandatory corporate kick-off event celebrating the release of a new Coca-Cola product. As part of a team building event, all of the employees in attendance, including Kelley, were encouraged to canoe down a three-mile stretch of a river. Kelley, along with a co-worker, paddled on the river without incident. Thereafter, Kelley walked up an embankment to the parking lot, and waited for a bus to arrive to take him back to his vehicle. However, while Kelley waited for the bus, a number of employees, including Whitaker, who was in charge of the entire event, were seen splashing, tipping canoes, and getting everyone wet. A short time later, Whitaker, who was soaking wet, and Hall, a Coca-Cola distribution manager, grabbed Kelley and tried to pull him down the embankment and into the river. When their efforts failed, Hall grabbed Kelley and slammed him to the ground, causing Kelley to injure his neck. As a result of the incident, Kelley was treated for a herniated disc and a cervical dorsal strain. Kelley filed a claim for workers' compensation. Coca-Cola opposed the claim, asserting that because Kelley was involved in employee horseplay he was not entitled to workers' compensation benefits.

Question

1. Is Kelley entitled to workers' compensation benefits?

Pennsylvania State Police v. Suders, 542 U.S. 129, 124 S.Ct. 2342, 159 L.Ed.2d 204, Web 2004 U.S. Lexis 4176

Supreme Court of the United States

The Pennsylvania State Police (PSP) hired Nancy Drew Suders as a police communications operator for the McConnellsburg barracks. Suders's supervisors were Sergeant Eric D. Easton, station commander at the McConnellsburg barracks, Patrol Corporal William D. Baker, and Corporal Eric B. Prendergast. Those three supervisors subjected Suders to a continuous barrage of sexual harassment that ceased only when she resigned from the force. Easton would bring up the subject of people having sex with animals each time Suders entered his office. He told Prendergast, in front of Suders, that young girls should be given instruction in how to gratify men with oral sex. Easton also would sit down near Suders, wearing Spandex shorts, and spread his legs apart. Baker repeatedly made obscene gestures in Suders's presence and shouted out vulgar comments inviting sex. Baker made these gestures as many as five to ten times per night throughout Suders's employment at the barracks. Further, Baker would rub his rear end in front of her and remark, "I have a nice ass, don't I?"

Five months after being hired, Suders contacted Virginia Smith-Elliot, PSP's equal opportunity officer, and stated that she was being harassed at work and was afraid. Smith-Elliot's response appeared to Suders to be insensitive and unhelpful. Two days later, Suders resigned from the force. Suders sued PSP, alleging that she had been subject to sexual harassment and constructively discharged and forced to resign.

Question

1. Can an employer be held liable when the sexual harassment conduct of its employees is so severe that the victim of the harassment resigns?

WORKING WITH THE LANGUAGE OF THE COURT CASE

Thompson v. North American Stainless, LP

131 S.Ct. 863, 178 L.Ed.2d 694, Web 2011 U.S. Lexis 913
Supreme Court of the United States

Read and then brief the following case, excerpted from the U.S. Supreme Court opinion. In your brief, answer the following questions:

1. Who filed the original charge of discrimination against their employer with the Equal Employment Opportunity Commission (EEOC)?
2. Who did the employer fire? Was there any relationship between the person who filed the original complaint with the EEOC and the person who was fired?
3. Does Title VII prohibit retaliation by an employer against an employee?
4. Does Title VII permit third-party retaliation claims against an employer?
5. Who wins?

Scalia, Justice, Opinion of the Court

Until 2003, both petitioner Eric Thompson and his fiancée, Miriam Regalado, were employees of respondent North American Stainless (NAS). In February 2003, the Equal Employment Opportunity Commission (EEOC) notified NAS that Regalado had filed a charge alleging sex discrimination. Three weeks later, NAS fired Thompson.

Thompson then filed a charge with the EEOC. After conciliation efforts proved unsuccessful, he sued NAS in the United States District Court for the Eastern District of Kentucky under Title VII of the Civil Rights Act of 1964, claiming that NAS had fired him in order to retaliate against Regalado for filing her charge with the EEOC. The District Court granted summary judgment to NAS, concluding that Title VII "does not permit third party retaliation claims." After a panel of the Sixth Circuit reversed the District Court, the Sixth Circuit granted rehearing en banc and affirmed by a 10-to-6 vote. The court reasoned that because Thompson did not "engag[e] in any statutorily protected activity, either on his own behalf or on behalf of Miriam Regalado," he "is not included in the class of persons for whom Congress created a retaliation cause of action." We granted certiorari.

Title VII provides that "[i]t shall be an unlawful employment practice for an employer to discriminate against any of his employees... because he has made a charge" under Title VII. It is undisputed that Regalado's filing of a charge with the EEOC was protected conduct under Title VII. This case therefore presents two questions: First, did NAS's firing of Thompson constitute unlawful retaliation? And second, if it did, does Title VII grant Thompson a cause of action?

With regard to the first question, we have little difficulty concluding that if the facts alleged by Thompson are true, then NAS's firing of Thompson violated Title VII. In *Burlington N. & S. F. R. Co. v. White*, 548 U. S. 53 (2006), we held that Title VII's antiretaliation provision must be construed to cover a broad range of employer conduct. Title VII's antiretaliation provision prohibits any employer action that "well might have dissuaded a reasonable worker from making or supporting a charge of discrimination."

We think it obvious that a reasonable worker might be dissuaded from engaging in protected activity if she knew that her fiancé would be fired. NAS raises the concern, however, that prohibiting reprisals against third parties will lead to difficult line-drawing problems concerning the types of relationships entitled to protection. Although we acknowledge the force of this point, we do not think it justifies a categorical rule that third-party reprisals do not violate Title VII.

We must also decline to identify a fixed class of relationships for which third-party reprisals are unlawful. Given the broad statutory text and the variety of workplace contexts in which retaliation may occur, Title VII's antiretaliation provision is simply not reducible to a comprehensive set of clear rules.

We conclude that Thompson falls within the zone of interests protected by Title VII. Thompson was an employee of NAS, and the purpose of Title VII is to protect employees from their employers' unlawful actions. Moreover, accepting the facts as alleged, Thompson is not an accidental victim of the retaliation—collateral damage, so to speak, of the employer's unlawful act. To the contrary, injuring him was the employer's intended means of harming Regalado. Hurting him was the unlawful act by which the employer punished her. In those circumstances, we think Thompson well within the zone of interests sought to be protected by Title VII. He is a person aggrieved with standing to sue.

The judgment of the Sixth Circuit is reversed, and the case is remanded for further proceedings consistent with this opinion.

It is so ordered.

MYLEGALSTUDIESLAB

MyLegalStudiesLab Virtual Law Office Experience Assignments
Complete the pre-test, study plan, and post-test for this chapter and answer the Legal Applications questions as assigned. These will help you confirm your mastery of the concepts and their application to legal scenarios. Then complete the Virtual Law Office assignments as assigned by your instructor. These assignments are designed to develop your workplace skills. Completing the assignments for this chapter will result in producing the following documents for inclusion in your portfolio:

VLOE 18.1

1. Standard form fee agreement template for new clients
2. Power of attorney template for use in our jurisdiction
3. Living will for use in our jurisdiction
4. Cover letter template to clients explaining the differences between a power of attorney and a living will, and explaining the conflict of interest.

VLOE 18.2

1. Standard form fee agreement
2. Power of attorney template for use in our jurisdiction
3. Living will for use in our jurisdiction
4. Cover letter to clients explaining the differences between a power of attorney and a living will, and explaining the conflict of interest.

CHAPTER

19

Business Organizations and Bankruptcy Law

Paralegals at Work

You are a paralegal who works for Mr. Abraham Weinstein, a well-known business attorney. One day Mr. Weinstein asks you to come into the conference room for a meeting with him, during which he informs you that he has been retained by new clients, Ms. Sophia Lopez and four other persons, who want to form a new business venture.

Mr. Weinstein tells you that the five prospective owners each will invest $300,000 in the new business, which will open and operate a new men's clothing store called Victor's Secret. The store will sell upscale casual clothes, formal clothes, undergarments, cologne, and other accessories for men. The owners plan to open the first store six months from now, and then expand and open one additional store each year for the next five years.

Mr. Weinstein then tells you that the owners would like to form a type of business organization in which they will have limited liability—that is, they will have no personal liability beyond their capital in the business. They also want to have flow-through taxation—that is, the entity will pay no taxes and all of the gains and losses of the business will flow through to their individual tax returns. In addition, the five owners want two of the owners, Ms. Lopez and Ms. Genevieve Cross, to manage the business; the other three owners want only to remain owners and investors.

Mr. Weinstein asks you to compare the different forms of business organizations available and determine which type or types of organizations best meet the owners' requirements.

Consider the issues involved in this scenario as you read the chapter.

LEARNING OBJECTIVES

After studying this chapter, you should be able to:

1. Recognize the professional opportunities for paralegals in the business organizations and corporation law area.
2. Define a "sole proprietorship" and explain the liability of a sole proprietor.
3. Define "general partnership" and describe how general partnerships are formed.
4. Define "limited partnership" and distinguish between limited and general partners.
5. Define "limited liability company (LLC)" and "limited liability partnership (LLP)" and describe the limited liability of owners of an LLC and an LLP.
6. Define "corporation" and describe the process of forming a corporation.
7. Explain the functions of shareholders, directors, and officers in managing the affairs of a corporation.
8. Recognize the professional opportunities for paralegals in the bankruptcy law area.
9. Identify the major forms of bankruptcy permitted under federal bankruptcy law.
10. Explain a paralegal's duty not to use confidential information.

> "The biggest corporation, like the humblest private citizen, must be held to strict compliance with the will of the people."
>
> *Theodore Roosevelt*

Learning Objective 1

Recognize the professional opportunities for paralegals in the business organizations and corporation law area.

INTRODUCTION FOR THE PARALEGAL

Many paralegals work for lawyers who represent various forms of businesses, such as entrepreneurs and other small business owners, as well as the largest multinational corporations in the world. Corporations and other forms of business employ lawyers to represent the business in all sorts of matters ranging from starting the entity, to advising the business as to compliance with the law, to representing the business and its owners or managers in bringing or defending lawsuits.

Morality cannot be legislated, but behavior can be regulated. Judicial decrees may not change the heart, but they can restrain the heartless.
Martin Luther King, Jr.
Strength to Love (1963)

Among the many different types of business organizations are *sole proprietorships, general partnerships, limited partnerships, limited liability partnerships (LLPs), limited liability companies (LLCs),* and *corporations*. These are collectively referred to as *business organizations*. An entrepreneur must make a choice as to which type of business to form and operate. Once formed, these business organizations employ lawyers to represent them in their ongoing business transactions.

Paralegals often assist lawyers in representing corporations and other business organizations. This assistance ranges from drafting the original documents to form a business to helping the lawyer represent businesses and their management in many other ways. Therefore, a paralegal working in this field must have knowledge of the law of business organizations.

The U.S. economy is a credit economy. Consumers borrow money to make major purchases (such as homes, automobiles, and appliances) and use credit cards to purchase goods and services. Businesses use credit to purchase equipment, supplies, and other goods and services. On occasion, borrowers become overextended and are unable to meet their debt obligations. Congress has enacted federal bankruptcy laws that provide methods for debtors to be relieved of some debt or enter into arrangements to pay debts off in the future.

This chapter covers the law regarding the formation and operation of corporations and other forms of business, as well as credit and bankruptcy law.

The following feature discusses the career opportunities for paralegal professionals in small business law.

Learning Objective 2

Define a "sole proprietorship" and explain the liability of a sole proprietor.

Sole Proprietorship

The **sole proprietorship** is the simplest form of **business organization.** The owner, called a **sole proprietor,** is the business; there is no separate legal entity. Sole proprietorships are the most common form of business organization in the United States, and many small businesses—and a few large ones—operate this way.

Sole proprietorship A form of business in which the owner is actually the business; the business is not a separate legal entity.

Sole proprietor The owner of a sole proprietorship.

Operating a business as a sole proprietorship has these advantages:

1. Ease and low cost of formation.
2. The owner's right to make all management decisions concerning the business, including those involving hiring and firing employees.
3. The right to receive all of the ownership of the business's profits.
4. Ease of transfer or sale if and when the owner desires to do so; no other approval (such as from partners or shareholders) is necessary.

This business form has disadvantages, too, among them:

1. The sole proprietor's access to capital is limited to personal funds plus any loans he or she can obtain.
2. The sole proprietor is legally responsible for the business's contracts and the torts he or she or any of his or her employees commit in the course of employment.

CAREER OPPORTUNITIES FOR PARALEGALS IN SMALL BUSINESS LAW

Many paralegals work for lawyers who represent small businesses and their owners. Small businesses are everywhere in this country. For example, most businesses in small towns and cities are operated by local businesspersons. These businesses include the local department store, restaurants, insurance agencies, automobile repair shops, the local bank, plumbers, and so forth. The small businesses in local communities comprise a substantial amount of work for lawyers.

In addition, thousands of small businesses operate in large cities. These include small businesses serving specific areas of the larger metropolitan area in which they are located. In large cities, many of the small businesses serve ethnic communities. Thousands of small businesses located in large cities require the services of lawyers.

In smaller communities, small businesses are more likely to rely on local attorneys to handle their legal needs. These attorneys tend to be sole practitioners or work for smaller law firms. The attorneys are members of the local community and are well known, often friends or acquaintances of their clients. Small businesses in large cities tend to rely on smaller law firms to handle their legal affairs, although some use larger law firms.

Small businesses often require the services of lawyers. For instance, to get started, entrepreneurs need advice as to the type of legal form under which their business should operate. Some of these businesses are sole proprietorships, general partnerships, limited partnerships, limited liability companies, limited liability partnerships, or small corporations. The lawyer representing such clients must advise them as to the form of organization that would best suit their needs, and the paralegal must also have knowledge of these different forms of organizations.

Paralegals working for small law firms that represent small businesses are often called upon to draft the necessary legal documents to start the business. If it is to be a small corporation or a limited liability company, the paralegal will draft the initial articles of incorporation or articles of organization, as well as other documents such as bylaws, minutes of the first meeting of the owners, and such. If a type of partnership is chosen, the paralegal will draft the articles of partnership.

Once established, small businesses often rely on their lawyer to represent them in other transactions. For example, if contracts are required for the operation of the business, the business will employ the attorney to draft these contracts. Here, the paralegal is often the first person to complete a draft of the contract. If the business requires a sale or purchase of real estate, the attorney will represent the small business and will complete or review the necessary documents. Again, the paralegal for these attorneys is often called upon to prepare drafts of these documents.

In addition, small businesses sometimes sue or are sued, and the lawyer will represent the small business in these lawsuits. Most of these lawsuits are in state court, although some are tried in federal court. Because these lawyers are sole practitioners or work for small law firms, they often need the assistance of a paralegal to prepare the law case.

Thus, paralegals often work in smaller law firms representing local businesses and individuals. These paralegals are usually involved in all aspects of the legal services provided to small business clients. Work in small law firms will continue to be a substantial source of jobs for paralegals, particularly those who live in small communities across the country, as well as those who work for smaller law firms in metropolitan areas that derive a substantial amount of their work from representing small businesses and their owners.

Creation of a Sole Proprietorship

It is easy to create a sole proprietorship. There are no formalities, and no federal or state government approval is required. Some local governments require all businesses, including sole proprietorships, to obtain a license to do business within the city. If no other form of business organization is chosen, the business is a sole proprietorship by default.

d.b.a. ("Doing Business As")

A sole proprietorship can operate under the name of the sole proprietor or under a *trade name*. For example, the author of this book can operate a sole proprietorship under the name "Henry R. Cheeseman" or under a trade name such as "The Big Cheese." Operating under a trade name is commonly designated as a **d.b.a. (doing business as)** (such as Henry R. Cheeseman, doing business as "The Big Cheese").

d.b.a. (doing business as) A designation for a business that is operating under a trade name.

Fictitious business name statement A document that is filed with the state that designates a trade name of a business, the name and address of the applicant, and the address of the business.

Most states require all businesses that operate under a trade name to file a **fictitious business name statement** (or a *certificate of trade name*) with the appropriate government agency. The statement must contain the name and address of the applicant, the trade name, and the address of the business. Most states also require that

Web Exploration

Go to **http://www.business.gov/guides/business_law/dba.html.** Scroll down to the name of your state and read the requirements for obtaining a d.b.a. in your state. If there is an online link for your state, go to that link for further information.

notice of the trade name be published in a newspaper of general circulation serving the area in which the applicant does business.

These requirements are intended to disclose the real owner's name to the public. Noncompliance can result in a fine, and some states prohibit violators from maintaining lawsuits in the state's courts. A sample fictitious business name statement is shown in Exhibit 19.1.

Personal Liability of Sole Proprietors

The sole proprietor bears the entire risk of loss of the business; thus the owner will lose his or her entire capital contribution if the business fails. In addition, the sole proprietor has unlimited **personal liability** (see Exhibit 19.2). Therefore, creditors

Exhibit 19.1 Sample fictitious business name statement

Return To:

Name: Kerry Fields, Esq.
Address: 115 S. Chaparral Court
City: Anaheim, CA 92808
Telephone # (714) 283-0140
Cust. Ref. # 53247

☒ First Filing ☐ Renewal Filing
Current Registration No.

PUBLISH IN:

COUNTY CLERK'S FILING STAMP

FICTITIOUS BUSINESS NAME STATEMENT

THE FOLLOWING PERSON(S) IS (ARE) DOING BUSINESS AS:

1	Fictitious Business Name(s) The Big Cheese			
2	Street address & Principal place of Business in California 1000 Exposition Boulevard	Los Angeles	California	Zip Code 90089
3	Full name of Registrant Henry R. Cheeseman		(if corporation - incorporated in what state)	
	Residence Address 575 Barrington Ave.	City Los Angeles	State California	Zip Code 90049
	Full Name of Registrant		(if corporation - incorporated in what state)	
	Residence Address	City	State	Zip Code
	Full name of Registrant		(if corporation - incorporated in what state)	
	Residence Address	City	State	Zip Code
	Full name of Registrant		(if corporation - incorporated in what state)	
	Residence Address	City	State	Zip Code

4 This Business is conducted by: (check one only) (X) an Individual ( ) co-partners ( ) a general partnership ( ) husband and wife ( ) joint venture ( ) a corporation ( ) a business trust ( ) a limited partnership ( ) an unincorporated association other than a partnership ( ) other—(*please specify*) ____

5 The registrant commenced to transact business under the fictitious business name or names listed above on ____

6 **a.** Signed: Henry R. Cheeseman (SIGNATURE) Henry R. Cheeseman (TYPE OR PRINT NAME)
SIGNATURE ____ TYPE OR PRINT NAME ____
SIGNATURE ____ TYPE OR PRINT NAME ____

b. If Registrant a corporation sign below:
CORPORATION NAME ____
SIGNATURE & TITLE ____
TYPE OR PRINT NAME ____

This statement was filed with the County Clerk of Los Angeles County on date indicated by file stamp above.

NOTICE THIS FICTITIOUS NAME STATEMENT EXPIRES FIVE YEARS FROM THE DATE IT WAS FILED IN THE OFFICE OF THE COUNTY CLERK. A NEW FICTITIOUS BUSINESS NAME STATEMENT MUST BE FILED BEFORE THAT TIME. THE FILING OF THIS STATEMENT DOES NOT OF ITSELF AUTHORIZE THE USE IN THIS STATE OF A FICTITIOUS BUSINESS NAME IN VIOLATION OF THE RIGHTS OF ANOTHER UNDER FEDERAL, STATE, OR COMMON LAW (SEE SECTION 14400 ET SEQ., BUSINESS AND PROFESSIONS CODE).

I HEREBY CERTIFY THAT THIS COPY IS A CORRECT COPY OF THE ORIGINAL STATEMENT ON FILE IN MY OFFICE.

Helen Pitts
COUNTY CLERK

BY Deborah Cantrell DEPUTY

FILE NO. 081646

Exhibit 19.2 Sole proprietorship

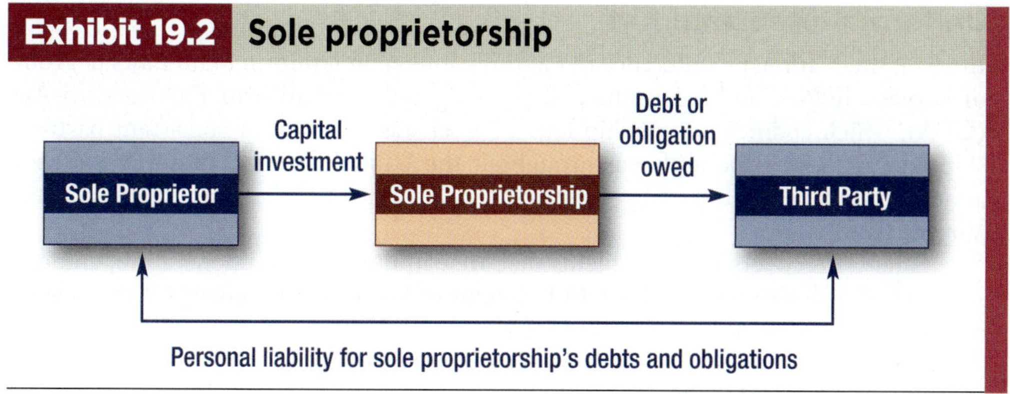

may recover claims against the business from the sole proprietor's personal assets (such as home, automobile, and bank accounts).

Example Suppose Ken Smith opens a clothing store called The Rap Shop and operates it as a sole proprietorship. Smith files the proper statement and publishes the necessary notice of the use of the trade name. He contributes $25,000 of his personal funds to the business and borrows $100,000 in the name of the business from a bank. Assume that after several months, Smith closes the business because it was unsuccessful. At the time it is closed, the business has no assets, owes the bank $100,000, and owes rent, trade credit, and other debts of $25,000. Here, Smith is personally liable to pay the bank and all of the debts from his personal assets.

Learning Objective 3
Define "general partnership" and describe how general partnerships are formed.

General partnership A voluntary association of two or more persons for carrying on a business as co-owners for profit. Also called a *partnership*.

General partnership agreement A written agreement that partners sign to form a general partnership. Also called *articles of general partnership*.

General partner A partner of a general partnership who is liable for the debts and obligations of the general partnership. Also called a *partner*.

General Partnership

General, or ordinary, partnerships have been recognized since ancient times. The English common law of partnerships governed early U.S. partnerships. The individual states then expanded the body of partnership law.

A **general partnership,** or **partnership,** is a voluntary association of two or more persons for carrying on a business as co-owners for profit. The formation of a partnership creates certain rights and duties among partners and with third parties. These rights and duties are established in the **partnership agreement** and by law. **General partners,** or **partners,** are personally liable for the debts and obligations of the partnership (see Exhibit 19.3).

Exhibit 19.3 General partnership

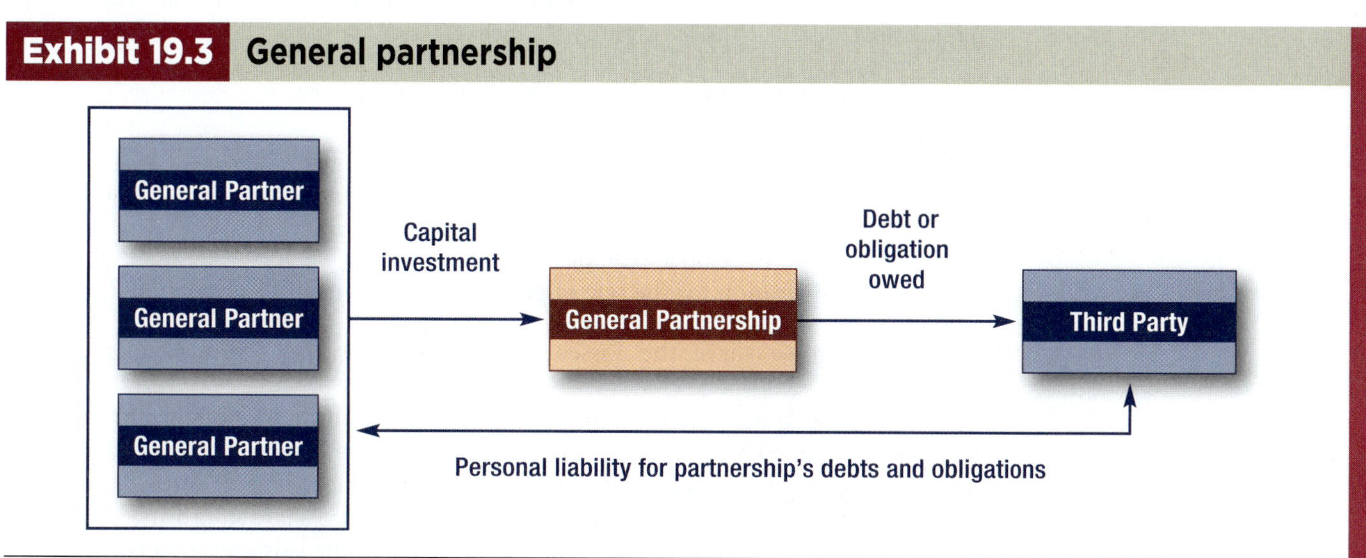

Uniform Partnership Act

Uniform Partnership Act (UPA) A model act that codifies partnership law. Most states have adopted the UPA in whole or in part.

In 1914, the National Conference of Commissioners on Uniform State Laws (a group of lawyers, judges, and legal scholars) promulgated the **Uniform Partnership Act (UPA),** which codifies partnership law. Its goal was to establish consistent partnership law that would be uniform throughout the United States. The UPA has been adopted in whole or in part by 48 states, the District of Columbia, Guam, and the Virgin Islands.

The UPA covers most problems that arise in the formation, operation, and dissolution of ordinary partnerships. Other rules of law or equity govern if there is no applicable provision of the UPA [UPA § 5].

The UPA adopted the **entity theory** of partnership, which considers partnerships as separate legal entities. As such, partnerships can hold title to personal and real property, transact business in the partnership name, and the like.

Formation of a Partnership

A business must meet four criteria to qualify as a partnership under the Uniform Partnership Act [UPA Section 6(1)]. It must be

1. an association of two or more persons
2. carrying on a business
3. as co-owners
4. for profit.

One of the most fruitful sources of ruin to a man of the world is the recklessness or want of principle of partners, and it is one of the perils to which every man exposes himself who enters into a partnership.
Vice Chancellor Malins, *Mackay v. Douglas, 14 Eq. 106 at 118* (1872)

In other words: Partnerships are voluntary associations of two or more persons. All partners must agree to the participation of each co-partner. A person cannot be forced to be a partner or to accept another person as a partner. The UPA definition of "person" includes natural persons, partnerships (including limited partnerships), corporations, and other associations. A business—trade, occupation, or profession—must be carried on. Finally, to qualify as a partnership, the organization or venture must have a profit motive, even though the business does not actually have to make a profit.

A general partnership may be formed with little or no formality. Co-ownership of a business is essential to creating a partnership. The most important factor in determining co-ownership is whether the parties share the business's profits and management responsibility.

Receipt of a share of business profits is *prima facie* evidence of a partnership because nonpartners are usually not given the right to share in the business's profits. No inference of the existence of a partnership is drawn if profits are received in payment of

1. a debt owed to a creditor in installments or otherwise,
2. wages owed to an employee,
3. rent owed to a landlord,
4. an annuity owed to a widow, widower, or representative of a deceased partner,
5. interest owed on a loan, or
6. consideration for the sale of goodwill of a business [UPA Section 7].

An agreement to share the losses of a business is also strong evidence of a partnership.

The right to participate in the management of a business is important evidence for determining the existence of a partnership, but it is not conclusive evidence because the right to participate in management is sometimes given to employees, creditors, and others. If, however, a person is given the right to share in profits, losses, and management of a business, it is compelling evidence of the existence of a partnership.

The Partnership Agreement

The agreement to form a partnership may be oral, written, or implied from the conduct of the parties. It may even be created inadvertently. No formalities are necessary, although a few states require general partnerships to file certificates of partnership with the appropriate government agency. Partnerships that exist for more than one year or are authorized to deal in real estate must be in writing under the Statute of Frauds. It is good practice for partners to put their partnership agreement in writing because a written document is important evidence of the terms of the agreement, particularly if a dispute arises among the partners.

A written partnership agreement is called a partnership agreement or **articles of partnership.** The partners can agree to any terms in their partnership agreement except those that are illegal. The articles of partnership can be short and simple or long and complex. If the agreement fails to provide for an essential term or contingency, the provisions of the UPA control. Thus, the UPA acts as a gap-filling device to the partners' agreement.

SIDEBAR

PARTNERSHIP AGREEMENT

The partnership agreement should contain the following information:

- the firm name
- the names and addresses of the partners
- the principal office of the partnership
- the nature and scope of the partnership business
- the duration of the partnership
- the capital contributions of each partner
- the division of profits and losses among the partners
- the salaries, if any, to be paid to the partners
- the duties of the partners regarding management of the partnership
- the limitations, if any, on the authority of partners to bind the partnership
- the provisions for the admission and withdrawal of partners from the firm and the terms, conditions, and notices required for withdrawal
- the provisions for continuing the partnership upon withdrawal of a partner, death of a partner, or other dissolution of the partnership
- any other provisions deemed relevant by the partners

Contract Liability

As a legal entity, a partnership must act through its agents—that is, its partners. Contracts entered into with suppliers, customers, lenders, or others on the partnership's behalf are binding on the partnership.

Under the UPA, partners have **joint liability** for the contracts and debts of the partnership [UPA Section 15(b)]. This means that a third party who sues to recover on a partnership contract or debt must name all of the partners in the lawsuit. If the lawsuit is successful, the plaintiff can collect the entire amount of the judgment against any or all of the partners. However, if the third party's suit does not name all of the partners, the judgment cannot be collected against any of the partners or the partnership assets. Similarly, releasing any partner from the lawsuit releases all partners. A partner who is made to pay more than his or her proportionate share of contract liability may seek *indemnification* from the partnership and from those partners who have not paid their share of the loss.

Tort Liability

While acting on partnership business, a partner or an employee of the partnership may commit a tort that causes injury to a third person. This tort could be caused by a negligent act, a breach of trust (such as embezzlement from a customer's account), a breach of fiduciary duty, defamation, fraud, or another intentional tort. The partnership is liable if the act is committed while the person is acting within the ordinary course of partnership business or with the authority of his or her co-partners.

Under the UPA, partners have **joint and several liability** for torts and breaches of trust [UPA Section 15(a)]. This is so even if a partner did not participate in commission of the act. This type of liability permits a third party to sue one or more of the partners separately. Judgment can be collected only against the partners who are sued. The partnership and partners who are made to pay tort liability may seek indemnification from the partner who committed the wrongful act. A release of one partner does not discharge the liability of the other partners.

Joint and several liability Tort liability where general partners are liable as a group or separately. This means that the plaintiff can sue one or more of the partners separately. If successful, the plaintiff can recover the entire amount of the judgment from any or all of the defendant-partners.

> **Example** Suppose Nicole, Jim, and Maureen form a partnership. Jim, while on partnership business, causes an automobile accident that injures Kurt, a pedestrian. Kurt suffers $100,000 in injuries. At his option, Kurt can sue Nicole, Jim, or Maureen separately, or any two of them, or all three of them.

Dissolution of Partnerships

The duration of a partnership can be for a fixed term (such as five years), until a specific undertaking is accomplished (for example, until a real estate development is completed), or for an unspecified term. A partnership with a fixed duration is

Paralegals *in* Practice

PARALEGAL PROFILE

Kelly A. LaGrave

Kelly A. LaGrave specializes in business/corporate law. Her credentials include a Bachelor of Arts degree in International Relations from Michigan State University, and the Certified Legal Assistant Specialty designation from the National Association of Legal Assistants (NALA) in both Intellectual Property and Real Estate. She also earned the Advanced Paralegal Certification (ACP) from NALA in Contract Management/Contract Administration. During her 25-year paralegal career, Kelly has served on various professional boards including the Advisory Committee for Lansing Community College's Paralegal Program. She is currently employed by the law firm of Foster, Swift, Collins & Smith in Lansing, Michigan.

In my area of practice, it is vital that a paralegal understands the various types of business entities allowed under the state's statutes. Some specific tasks that I do on a regular basis include drafting all documentation necessary to form, dissolve, or merge business entities; performing due diligence such as obtaining and reviewing Uniform Commercial Code documents (affidavits, notices, financing statements, etc.), litigation dockets, and government agency certified documents; completing copyright applications; and preparing documentation for the purchase/sale of businesses.

One of my most interesting experiences in corporate law occurred when I was asked to set up and maintain an electronic data room. This "room" is actually a dedicated Web site that allows approved users to search hundreds of due diligence documents. Technology has definitely changed the way we handle transactions!

What I find most rewarding about my job is the variety of work, and the opportunity to take a project from start to completion. I have also been given the chance to learn new areas of the law. A new paralegal entering my practice area needs to have a willingness to learn, an extreme attention to detail, the ability to organize and track many tasks at once, and fearlessness when it comes to using technology in the workplace.

called a **partnership for a term.** A partnership with no fixed duration is called a **partnership at will.**

Although a partner has the *power* to withdraw and dissolve the partnership at any time, he or she may not have the *right* to do so. For example, a partner who withdraws from a partnership before expiration of the term stated in the partnership agreement does not have the right to do so. The partner's action causes a **wrongful dissolution** of the partnership, and the partner is liable for damages caused by this wrongful dissolution.

In the feature above a paralegal professional discusses her experience in the field of business entities.

Learning Objective 4

Define "limited partnership" and distinguish between limited and general partners.

Limited Partnership

Limited partnership A special form of partnership that is formed only if certain formalities are followed. A limited partnership has both general and limited partners.

Limited partnerships are statutory creations that have been used since the Middle Ages. They include both general (manager) and limited (investor) partnerships. Today, all states have enacted statutes that provide for the creation of limited partnerships. In most states these partnerships are called **limited partnerships** or *special partnerships*. Limited partnerships are used for business ventures such as investing in real estate, drilling oil and gas wells, investing in movie productions, and the like.

Revised Uniform Limited Partnership Act

Revised Uniform Limited Partnership Act (RULPA) A 1976 revision of the ULPA that provides a more modern, comprehensive law for the formation, operation, and dissolution of limited partnerships.

In 1916 the National Conference of Commissioners on Uniform State Laws, a group composed of lawyers, judges, and legal scholars, promulgated the **Uniform Limited Partnership Act (ULPA).** The ULPA contains a set of provisions for the formation, operation, and dissolution of limited partnerships. Most states originally enacted this law.

In 1976, the National Conference on Uniform State Laws promulgated the **Revised Uniform Limited Partnership Act (RULPA),** which provides a more modern, comprehensive law for the formation, operation, and dissolution of limited partnerships. This law supersedes the ULPA in the states that have adopted it. The RULPA provides the basic foundation for our discussion of limited partnership law.

General and Limited Partners

Limited partnerships have two types of partners:

1. General partners, who invest capital, manage the business, and are personally liable for partnership debts.
2. **Limited partners,** who invest capital but do not participate in management and are not personally liable for partnership debts beyond their capital contributions.

Limited partners Partners in a limited partnership who invest capital but do not participate in management and are not personally liable for partnership debts beyond their capital contribution.

Exhibit 19.4 illustrates a limited partnership. A limited partnership must have at least one or more general partners and one or more limited partners [RULPA Section 101 (7)]. There are no restrictions on the number of general or limited partners allowed in a limited partnership. Any person may be a general or limited partner, including natural persons, partnerships, limited partnerships, trusts, estates, associations, and corporations. A person may be both a general and a limited partner in the same limited partnership.

Formation of Limited Partnerships

The creation of a limited partnership is formal and requires public disclosure. The entity must comply with the statutory requirements of the Revised Uniform Limited Partnership Act or other state statutes.

Under the RULPA, two or more persons must execute and sign a **certificate of limited partnership** [RULPA Sections 201 and 206]. The certificate must contain the following information:

1. the name of the limited partnership
2. the general character of the business
3. the address of the principal place of business, and name and address of the agent to receive service of legal process

Exhibit 19.4 Limited partnership

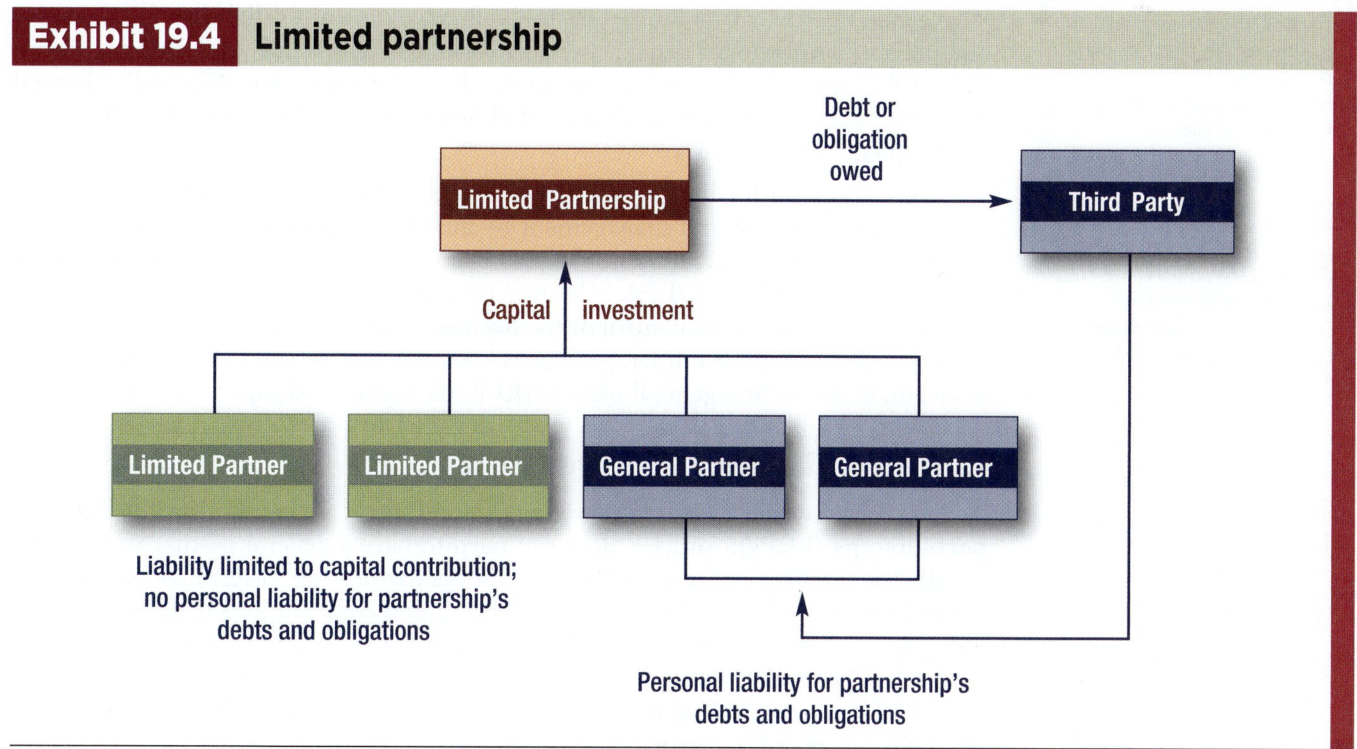

4. the name and business address of each general and limited partner
5. the latest date upon which the limited partnership is to dissolve
6. the amount of cash, property, or services (and description of property or services) contributed by each partner, and any contributions of cash, property, or services promised to be made in the future
7. any other matters that the general partners determine to include

The certificate of limited partnership must be filed with the secretary of state of the appropriate state and, if required by state law, with the county recorder in the county or counties in which the limited partnership carries on business. The limited partnership is formed when the certificate of limited partnership is filed.

Limited Partnership Agreement

Limited partnership agreement A document that sets forth the rights and duties of the general and limited partners; the terms and conditions regarding the operation, termination, and dissolution of the partnership; and so on. Also called *articles of limited partnership.*

Articles of limited liability partnership A public document that must be filed with the secretary of state to form a limited liability partnership.

Although not required by law, the partners of a limited partnership often draft and execute a **limited partnership agreement** (also called the **articles of limited partnership**) that sets forth the rights and duties of the general and limited partner(s); the terms and conditions regarding the operation, termination, and dissolution of the partnership; and so on. Where there is no such agreement, the certificate of limited partnership serves as the articles of limited partnership.

The limited partnership agreement may specify how profits and losses from the limited partnership are to be allocated among the general and limited partners. If there is no such agreement, the RULPA provides that profits and losses from a limited partnership are shared on the basis of the value of the partner's capital contribution [RULPA Section 503]. A limited partner is not liable for losses beyond his or her capital contribution.

In addition, it is good practice to establish voting rights in the limited partnership agreement or certificate of limited partnership. The limited partnership agreement can also provide which transactions must be approved by which partners (that is, general, limited, or both). General and limited partners may be given unequal voting rights. A sample limited partnership agreement is set forth in Exhibit 19.5.

Web Exploration

Using **http://google.com** or another Internet search engine, locate the website for your state's limited liability partnership (LLP) law and make note of this website.

Liability of General and Limited Partners

The general partners of a limited partnership have **unlimited liability** for the debts and obligations of the limited partnership. This liability extends to debts that cannot be satisfied with the existing capital of the limited partnership. Generally, limited partners are liable only for the debts and obligations of the limited partnership up to their capital contributions.

As a trade-off for **limited liability,** limited partners give up their right to participate in the control and management of the limited partnership. This means, in part, that limited partners have no right to bind the partnership to contracts or other obligations. Under the RULPA, a limited partner is liable as a general partner if his or her participation in the control of the business is substantially the same as that of a general partner, but the limited partner is liable only to persons who reasonably believe him or her to be a general partner [RULPA Section 303(a)].

Learning Objective 5

Define "limited liability company (LLC)" and "limited liability partnership (LLP)" and describe the limited liability of owners of an LLC and an LLP.

Limited Liability Partnership (LLP)

Limited liability partnership (LLP) A form of partnership in which all partners are limited partners and there are no general partners.

Many states have enacted legislation to permit the creation of **limited liability partnerships (LLPs).** An LLP does not need to have a general partner who is personally liable for the debts and obligations of the partnership. Instead, *all* partners are limited partners who stand to lose only their capital contributions if the partnership fails. None of the partners is personally liable for the debts and obligations of the partnership beyond his or her capital contribution (see Exhibit 19.6).

LLPs enjoy the "flow-through" tax benefit of other types of partnerships; that is, no tax is paid at the partnership level and all profits and losses are reported on the

Exhibit 19.5 Sample limited partnership agreement

LIMITED PARTNERSHIP AGREEMENT

1. Introduction. This agreement of Limited Partnership dated January 2, 2007 by and between John Weston, Wai Chan, and Susan Martinez (General Partners) and Shari Berkowitz, Raymond Wong, and Harold Johnson (Limited Partners).

The General Partners and Limited Partners agree to form a Limited Partnership (Partnership) pursuant to the provisions of the California Revised Limited Partnership Act on the terms and conditions hereinafter set forth.

2. Name of Partnership. The name of the Partnership shall be "The Wilshire Investment Company, a California Limited Partnership." The business of the Partnership shall be conducted in that name.

3. Principal Place of Business. The principal office of the Partnership shall be at 4000 Wilshire Boulevard, Los Angeles, California 90010 or at such other place within California as may be determined from time to time by the General Partners.

4. Purpose of the Partnership. The Partnership shall be engaged in the business of buying, selling, and developing commercial and industrial real estate and such activities as are related or incidental thereto.

5. Agent for Service of Process. The name of the agent for service of process is Frederick Friendly, whose address is 2500 Century Park East, Suite 600, Los Angeles, California 90067.

6. Term of Partnership. The term of the Partnership shall commence on the date on which the Partnership's Certificate of Limited Partnership is filed by the Secretary of State of California and shall continue until it terminates in accordance with the provisions of this Agreement.

7. Certificate of Limited Partnership. The General Partners shall immediately execute a Certificate of Limited Partnership and cause that Certificate to be filed in the office of the secretary of state of California. The General Partners shall also record a certified copy of the Certificate in the office of the county recorder of every county in which the Partnership owns real property.

8. Members of the Partnership.

(a) The names and addresses of each original General Partner are as follows:

NAME		ADDRESS	
	John Weston		500 Ocean Boulevard, Los Angeles, California
	Wai Chan		700 Apple Road, Seattle, Washington
	Susan Martinez		800 Palm Drive, Miami, Florida

(b) The names and addresses of each original Limited Partner are as follows:

NAME		ADDRESS	
	Shari Berkowitz		700 Apple Street, New York, New York
	Raymond Wong		900 Flower Avenue, San Francisco, California
	Harold Johnson		300 Oil Field Road, Houston, Texas

9. General Partners' Capital Contributions. The General Partners shall make the following contributions to the Partnership's capital no later than January 2, 2007.

CASH	John Weston	$60,000
PROPERTY	Wai Chan	$30,000
	Susan Martinez	$30,000

No interest will be paid on any balances in the General Partners' capital accounts.

10. Limited Partners' Capital Contributions. The Limited Partners shall make the following contributions to the Partnership's capital no later than January 2, 2007.

CASH	Shari Berkowitz	$100,000
	Raymond Wong	$ 50,000
	Harold Johnson	$ 50,000

No interest will be paid on any balances in the Limited Partners' capital accounts.

11. Additional Capital Contributions from Limited Partners. The General Partners may call for additional cash contributions to the Partnership's capital from the Limited Partners. The aggregate of all additional capital contributions made by the Limited Partners pursuant to this Paragraph shall not exceed 100 percent of the original capital contributions made by them pursuant to Paragraph 10 of this Agreement. Notice of the call shall be made by registered mail, return receipt requested, and shall be deemed made when posted. The Limited Partners' additional capital contribution must be made no later than 60 days following the call.

12. Division of Profits. Each Partner shall receive the following share of the net profits of the Partnership:

	PARTNER	PERCENT
General Partners:	John Weston	30%
	Wai Chan	15%
	Susan Martinez	15%
Limited Partners:	Shari Berkowitz	20%
	Raymond Wong	10%
	Harold Johnson	10%

(continued)

Exhibit 19.5 Sample limited partnership agreement *(continued)*

13. Sharing of Losses. Each Partner shall bear a share of the losses of the Partnership equal to the share of the profits to which he or she is entitled. The share of the losses of each Partner shall be charged against his contribution to the capital of the Partnership.

The Limited Partners will not be liable for any Partnership debts or losses beyond the amounts to be contributed to them pursuant to Paragraphs 10 and 11 of this Agreement.

After giving effect to the share of losses chargeable against the capital contributions of Limited Partners, the remaining Partnership losses shall be borne by the General Partners in the same proportions in which, between themselves, they are to share profits.

14. Management of Partnership. The General Partners shall have the sole and exclusive control of the Limited Partnership.

The General Partners shall have an equal voice in the management of the Partnership, and each shall devote his or her full time to the conduct of the Partnership's business.

The General Partners shall have the power and authority to take such action from time to time as they may deem to be necessary, appropriate, or convenient in connection with the management and conduct of the business and affairs of the Partnership, including, without limitation, the power to

(a) Acquire property, including real and personal property.
(b) Dispose of Partnership property.
(c) Borrow or lend money.
(d) Make, deliver, or accept commercial paper.
(e) Pledge, mortgage, encumber, or grant a security interest in the Partnership properties as security for repayment of loans.
(f) Take any and all other action permitted by law that is customary in or reasonably related to the conduct of the Partnership business or affairs.

15. Limited Partners Not to Manage Business. The Limited Partners will not manage the business of the Partnership or assist in its management.

16. Partnership Books and Records. The Partnership books of account will be kept in accordance with generally accepted accounting principles. The books and supporting records will be maintained at the Partnership's principal office and will be examined by the Partnership's certified public accountants at least annually. The Partnership's fiscal year shall start on January 1 and close on December 31.

17. General Partners' Salaries. The General Partners shall each receive a salary of $60,000 per annum, payable in monthly installments, as compensation for managing the Partnership. No increases shall be made in the General Partners' salaries without the written consent of a majority of the Limited Partners.

18. Admission of New General Partners. No new General Partners will be admitted to the Partnership without the written consent of all the General Partners and Limited Partners as to both his or her admission and the terms on which the new General Partner is admitted.

19. Admission of New Limited Partners. No new Limited Partners will be admitted to the Partnership without the written consent of all the General Partners and Limited Partners as to both his or her admission and the terms on which the new Limited Partner is admitted.

20. No Sale or Assignment of or Granting Lien on Partnership Interest by General Partner. Without the written consent of all the General Partners and Limited Partners, no General Partner shall assign, mortgage, or give a security interest in his or her Partnership interest.

21. Right of Limited Partner to Assign Partnership Interest or Substitute New Limited Partner. Upon 30 days' written notice to the General Partners, a Limited Partner can assign his or her interest in the Partnership's profits to a third party. Such assignment shall not constitute a substitution of the third party as a new Limited Partner in the place of the assignor. A Limited Partner may substitute a third party in his or her place as a new Limited Partner only with the consent in writing of all the General Partners and Limited Partners.

22. Effect of Death, Disability, or Retirement of a General Partner. The death, retirement, or permanent disability of a General Partner (the withdrawing General Partner) that makes it impossible for him or her to carry out his or her duties under this Agreement shall terminate the Partnership.

If a General Partner survives, the remaining General Partners may continue the Partnership business and may purchase the interest of the withdrawing General Partner in the assets and goodwill of the Partnership. The remaining General Partners have the option, exercisable by them at any time within 30 days after the date on which the withdrawing General Partner ceases to be a General Partner, to purchase the withdrawing General Partner's interest by paying to the person legally entitled thereto the value of that interest as shown on the last regular accounting of the Partnership preceding the date on which the General Partner ceased to be a General Partner, together with the full unwithdrawn portion of the withdrawing General Partner's distributive share of any net profits earned by the Partnership between the date of that accounting and the date on which the withdrawing General Partner ceased to be a General Partner of the Partnership.

Exhibit 19.5 Sample limited partnership agreement *(continued)*

23. Duties of Remaining Purchasing General Partners. Upon the purchase of a withdrawing General Partner's interest, the remaining General Partners shall assume all obligations of the Partnership and shall hold the withdrawing General Partner, the personal representative and estate of the withdrawing General Partner, and the property of the withdrawing General Partner free and harmless from all liability for those obligations.

The remaining General Partners shall immediately amend the Certificate of Limited Partnership and shall file such amendment with the office of the Secretary of State, and shall cause to be prepared, filed, served, and published all other notices required by law to protect the withdrawing General Partner or the personal representative and estate of the withdrawing General Partner from all liability for the future obligations of the Partnership business.

24. Effect of Death of Limited Partner or Substitution of Limited Partner. The death of a Limited Partner or the substitution of a new Limited Partner for a Limited Partner shall not affect the continuity of the Partnership or the conduct of its business.

25. Voluntary Dissolution. A General Partner may terminate the Partnership at any time upon 120 days written notice to each Limited Partner. Upon termination of the Partnership, it shall be liquidated in accordance with Paragraph 26 of this Agreement.

26. Liquidation of Partnership. If the Partnership is liquidated, its assets, including its goodwill and name, shall be sold in the manner designed to produce the greatest return. The proceeds of the liquidation shall be distributed in the following order:

(a) To creditors of the Partnership including Partners who are creditors to the extent permitted by law, in satisfaction of liabilities of the Partnership

(b) To Partners in payment of the balances in their income accounts

(c) To Partners in payment of the balances in their capital accounts

(d) To Partners in payment of the remainder of the proceeds

27. Certificate of Dissolution. Upon dissolution of the Partnership, the General Partners shall execute and file in the office of the Secretary of State a Certificate of Dissolution. If dissolution occurs after a sole General Partner ceases to be a General Partner, the Limited Partners conducting the winding up of the Partnership's affairs shall file the Certificate of Dissolution.

28. Entire Agreement. This Agreement contains the entire understanding among the Partners and supersedes any prior written or oral agreements between them respecting the subject matter contained herein. There are no representations, agreements, arrangements, or understandings, oral or written, between and among the Partners relating to the subject matter of this Agreement that are not fully expressed herein.

29. Controlling Law. This Agreement shall be interpreted under the law of the State of California. Further, each Partner consents to the jurisdiction of the courts of the State of California.

30. Service of Notices. Service of notice upon the Partnership will be made by registered or certified mail, return receipt requested, addressed to the Partnership's principal place of business.

Service of notice upon any or all Partners will be made by certified mail, return receipt requested, addressed to the addresses given in this Agreement or such other addresses as a Partner may from time to time give to the Partnership.

31. Severability. If any provisions of this Agreement shall be declared by a court of competent jurisdiction to be invalid, void, or unenforceable, the remaining provisions shall continue in full force and effect.

32. Arbitration of Disputes. Any controversy concerning this Agreement will be settled by arbitration according to the rules of the American Arbitration Association, and judgment upon the award may be entered and enforced in any court.

GENERAL PARTNER ______________________ LIMITED PARTNER ______________________

GENERAL PARTNER ______________________ LIMITED PARTNER ______________________

individual partners' income tax returns. LLPs must be created formally by filing **articles of limited liability partnership** with the secretary of state of the state in which the LLP is organized. This is a public document.

The LLP is a domestic LLP in the state in which it is organized. The **Uniform Limited Liability Partnership Act (ULLPA)** is a model act that codifies the law governing LLPs. Many states have adopted all or part of the ULLPA to govern LLPs. The limited liability partnership law of the state governs the operation of the LLP. An LLP may do business in other states, however. To do so, the LLP must register as a foreign LLP in any state in which it wants to conduct business.

Exhibit 19.6 Limited liability partnership (LLP)

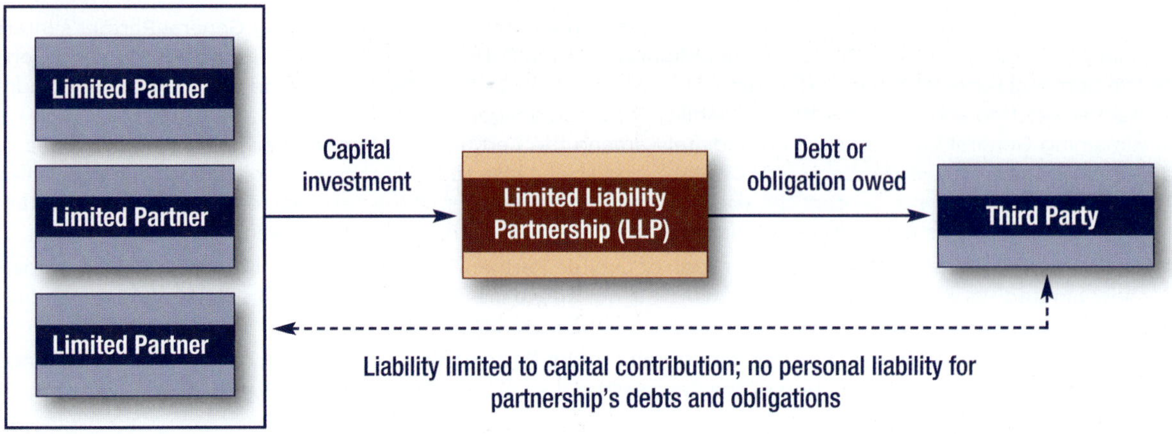

Example An accounting firm has 20 partners and other employees, and organizes itself as a limited liability company (LLP). When one of the partners is managing an audit of a client corporation, the auditors fail to discover a large fraud being perpetrated by the owners and executives of the corporation in which a "cooked" set of fraudulent financial reports is provided to the auditors. Subsequently, the corporation fails, ruining the shareholders of the corporation and leaving many of the creditors of the corporation unpaid. The shareholders and creditors sue the accounting firm, alleging that it is liable because of the negligence of one of its partners. Here, the negligent partner is personally liable because he was the tortfeasor. The injured plaintiffs can recover against the accounting firm itself. However, because the accounting firm was formed as an LLP, the other partners of the accounting firm are not personally liable.

Limited Liability Company (LLC)

A majority of states have approved a new form of business entity called a **limited liability company (LLC).** An LLC is an unincorporated business entity that combines the most favorable attributes of general partnerships, limited partnerships, and corporations. For example, an LLC may elect to be taxed as a partnership. The owners, usually called **members,** can manage the business and have limited liability. Many entrepreneurs who begin new businesses choose the LLC as their legal form for conducting business.

Limited liability company (LLC) An unincorporated business entity that combines the most favorable attributes of general partnerships, limited partnerships, and corporations.

Member An owner of an LLC.

Uniform Limited Liability Company Act (ULLCA) A model act that provides comprehensive and uniform laws for the formation, operation, and dissolution of LLCs.

Web Exploration

Using **http://google.com** or other Internet search engine, locate the website for your state's limited liability company (LLC) law and make a note of this website.

Uniform Limited Liability Company Act

In 1995, the National Conference of Commissioners on Uniform State Laws (a group of lawyers, judges, and legal scholars) issued the **Uniform Limited Liability Company Act (ULLCA).** The ULLCA codifies limited liability company law. Its goal is to establish comprehensive LLC law that is uniform throughout the United States.

The ULLCA covers most problems that arise in the formation, operation, and termination of LLCs. The ULLCA is not law unless a state adopts it as its LLC statute. Many states have adopted all or part of the ULLCA as their limited liability company law.

Limited liability companies are creatures of state law, not federal law. Thus limited liability companies can be created only pursuant to the laws of the state in which the LLC is being organized. These statutes, commonly referred to as limited liability company codes, regulate the formation, operation, and dissolution of LLCs. The state legislature may amend its LLC statute at any time. The courts then interpret state LLC statutes to decide LLC and member disputes.

Members' Limited Liability

The general rule is that members are not personally liable to third parties for the debts, obligations, and liabilities of an LLC beyond their capital contribution. Members are said to have limited liability (see Exhibit 19.7). The debts, obligations, and liabilities of an LLC, whether arising from contracts, torts, or otherwise, are solely those of the LLC [ULLCA Section 303(a)].

Example Jasmin, Shan-Yi, and Vanessa form an LLC and each contributes $25,000 in capital. The LLC operates for a period of time during which it borrows money from banks and purchases goods on credit from suppliers. After some time, the LLC experiences financial difficulty and goes out of business. If the LLC fails with $500,000 in debts, each of the members will lose her capital contribution of $25,000 but will not be personally liable for the rest of the unpaid debts of the LLC.

Formation of an LLC

Forming an LLC is similar to organizing a corporation. Two or more persons (which include individuals, partnerships, corporations, and associations) may form an LLC for any lawful purpose. To form an LLC, **articles of organization** must be filed with the appropriate state office, usually the secretary of state's office (see Exhibit 19.8). The articles of organization must state the LLC's name, duration, and other information required by statute or that the organizers deem important to include. The name of an LLC must contain the words Limited Liability Company or the abbreviation *L.L.C.* or *L.C.*

Articles of organization The formal document that must be filed with the secretary of state to form an LLC.

The owners of an LLC are usually called members, although in some states they are referred to as shareholders. Members of an LLC may enter into an **operating agreement** that regulates the affairs of the company and the conduct of its business, and governs relations among the members, managers, and company [ULLCA Section 103(a)]. The operating agreement may be amended by the approval of all members unless otherwise provided in the agreement. The operating agreement and amendments may be oral but are usually written.

Operating agreement An agreement entered into by members that governs the affairs and business of the LLC and the relations among members, managers, and the LLC.

Partnership Taxation for LLCs

A federal tax default rule provides that LLCs are treated as partnerships with flow-through taxation unless an election is made to be taxed as a corporation. This election to be taxed as a corporation is made by filing Form 8832 with the IRS and must be signed by all owners or by a manager who is given the authority to sign such an election. Most states automatically apply the federal classification rules for state income tax purposes, although a few do not.

Exhibit 19.7 Limited liability company (LLC)

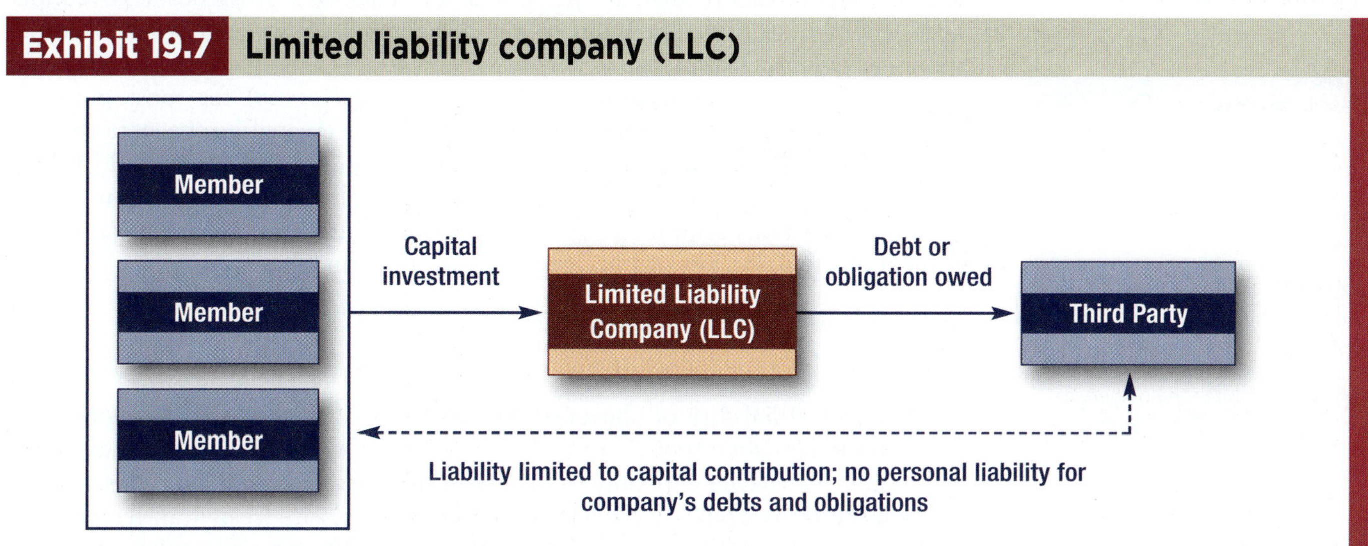

Exhibit 19.8 Sample LLC articles of organization

ARTICLES OF ORGANIZATION
FOR FLORIDA LIMITED LIABILITY COMPANY

ARTICLE I - NAME

The name of the Limited Liability Company is
iCitrusSystems.com

ARTICLE II - ADDRESS

The mailing address and street address of the principal office of the Limited Liability Company is
3000 Dade Boulevard
Suite 200
Miami Beach, Florida 33139

ARTICLE III - DURATION

The period of duration for the Limited Liability Company shall be
50 years

ARTICLE IV - MANAGEMENT

The Limited Liability Company is to be managed by a manager and the name and address of such manager is
Susan Escobar
1000 Collins Avenue
Miami Beach, Florida 33141

Thomas Blandford

Pam Rosales

Learning Objective 6

Define "corporation" and describe the process of forming a corporation.

Web Exploration

Using **http://google.com** or another Internet search engine, locate the website for your state's corporation law and make a note of this website.

Corporation A fictitious legal entity that is created according to statutory requirements.

Shareholders The owners of corporations whose ownership interests are evidenced by stock certificates.

Corporation

Corporations are the dominant form of business organization in the United States, generating more than 85 percent of the country's gross business receipts. Corporations range in size from one owner to thousands of owners. Owners of corporations are called **shareholders.**

A corporation is a separate *legal entity* (or *legal person*) for most purposes. Corporations are treated, in effect, as artificial persons created by the state that can sue or be sued in their own names, enter into and enforce contracts, hold title to and transfer property, and be found civilly and criminally liable for violations of law. Because corporations cannot be put in prison, the normal criminal penalty is the assessment of a fine, the loss of a license, or some other sanction.

Characteristics of Corporations

Corporations have the following unique characteristics:

- **Limited liability of shareholders.** As separate legal entities, corporations are liable for their own contracts and debts. Generally, the shareholders have liability only to the extent of their capital contributions.
- **Free transferability of shares.** Corporate shares are freely transferable by the shareholder—by sale, assignment, pledge, or gift—unless they

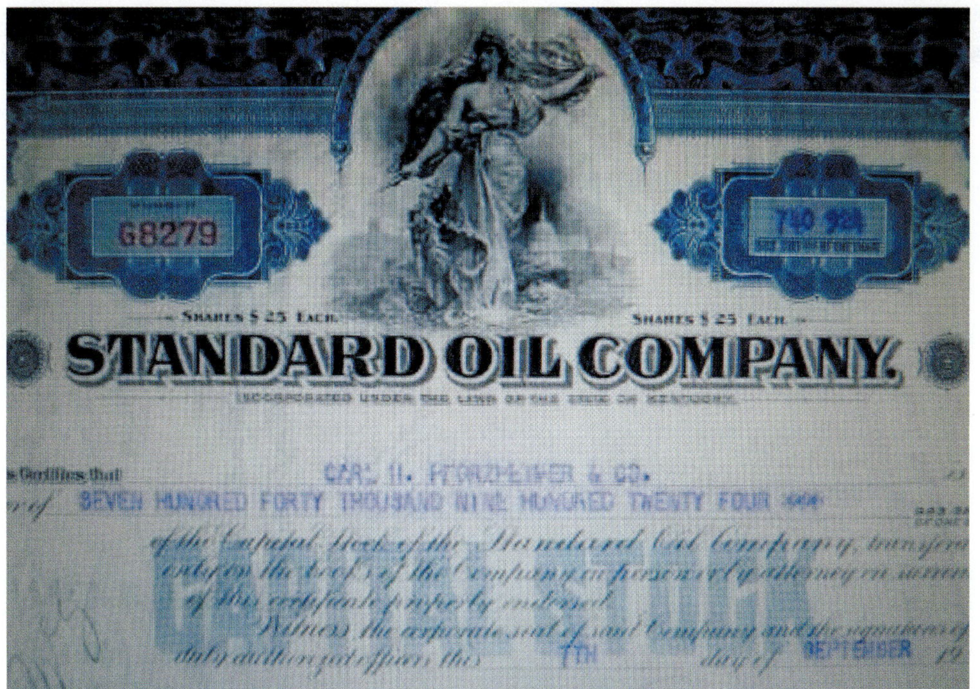

Stock Certificate
A corporation is owned by its shareholders, who elect board of director members to make policy decisions and employ corporate officers to run the day-to-day operation of the corporation.

are issued pursuant to certain exemptions from securities registration. Shareholders may agree among themselves on restrictions on the transfer of shares. National securities markets, such as the New York Stock Exchange, the American Stock Exchange, and NASDAQ, have been developed for the organized sale of securities.

- **Perpetual existence.** Corporations exist in perpetuity unless a specific duration is stated in the corporation's articles of incorporation. The existence of a corporation can be terminated voluntarily by the shareholders. Corporations may also be terminated involuntarily by the corporation's creditors if an involuntary petition for bankruptcy against the corporation is granted. The death, insanity, or bankruptcy of a shareholder, a director, or an officer of the corporation does not affect its existence.
- **Centralized management.** The board of directors makes policy decisions concerning the operation of the corporation. Members of the board of directors are elected by the shareholders. The directors, in turn, appoint **corporate officers** to run the corporation's day-to-day operations. Together, the directors and the officers form the corporate "management."

Exhibit 19.9 depicts a corporation and shows the limited liability of shareholders.

Revised Model Business Corporation Act

The Committee on Corporate Laws of the American Bar Association drafted the Model Business Corporation Act (MBCA) in 1950. The model act was intended to provide a uniform law regulating the formation, operation, and termination of corporations.

In 1984, the committee completely revised the MBCA and issued the **Revised Model Business Corporation Act (RMBCA).** Certain provisions of the RMBCA have been amended since 1984. The RMBCA arranged the provisions of the MBCA more logically, revised the language of the act to be more consistent, and made substantial changes in the provisions of the act. Many states have adopted all or part of the RMBCA as their corporation codes. The RMBCA serves as the basis for our discussion of corporation law in this book.

Revised Model Business Corporation Act (RMBCA) A 1984 revision of the MBCA that arranged the provisions of the original act more logically, revised the language to be more consistent, and made substantial changes in the provisions.

The following feature discusses the career opportunities for paralegal professionals in corporation law.

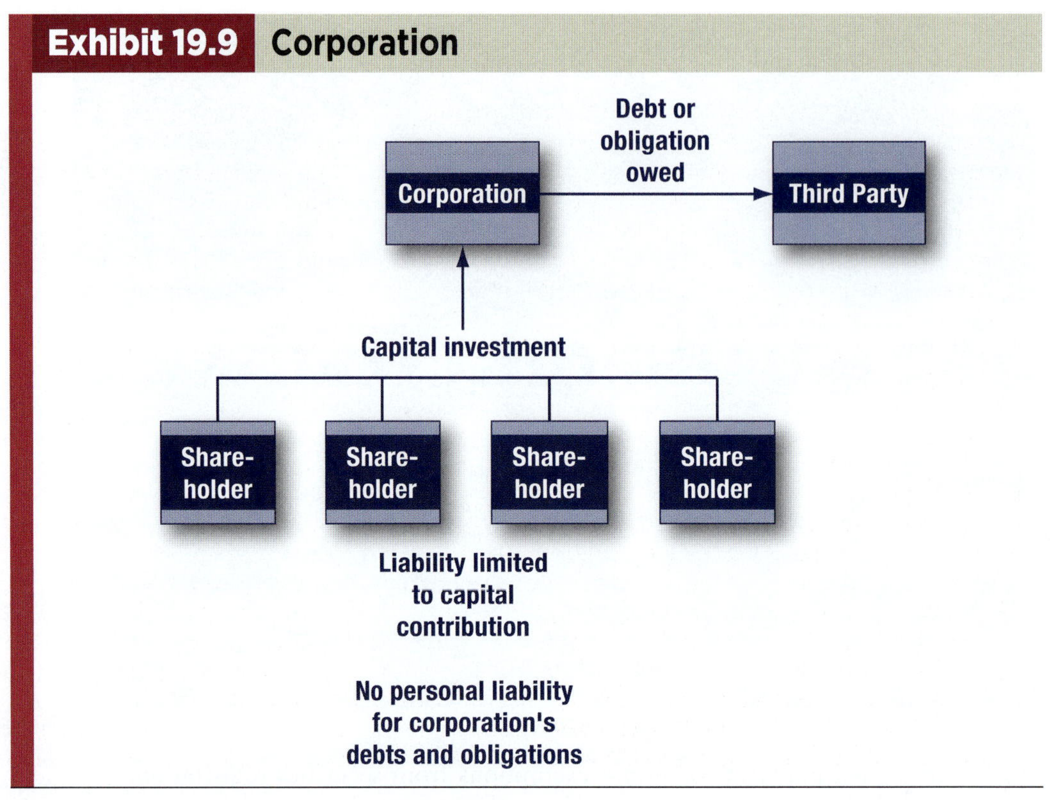

Classifications of Corporations

Domestic corporation A corporation in the state in which it was formed.

A private, for-profit corporation is a **domestic corporation** in the state in which it is incorporated. It is a **foreign corporation** in all other states and jurisdictions. Suppose a corporation is incorporated in Texas and does business in Montana. The corporation is a domestic corporation in Texas and a foreign corporation in Montana. An **alien corporation** is incorporated in another country.

Web Exploration

Go to the website of the Department of State of Delaware, Division of Corporations, at **http://corp.delaware.gov/faqs.shtml**. Read information about incorporating a corporation in Delaware.

Incorporation Procedure

Corporations are creatures of statute. Thus, the organizers of the corporation must comply with the state's incorporation statute to form a corporation. Although relatively similar, the procedure for **incorporation** varies somewhat from state to state.

Although a corporation can be incorporated in only one state, it may do business in all other states in which it qualifies to do business. In choosing a **state of incorporation,** the incorporators, directors, and/or shareholders must consider the corporation law of the states under consideration.

For the sake of convenience, most corporations (particularly small ones) choose as the state for incorporation the state in which the corporation will be doing most of its business. Large corporations generally opt to incorporate in the state with the laws that are most favorable to the corporation's internal operations.

Articles of incorporation The basic governing document of the corporation. This document must be filed with the secretary of state of the state of incorporation. Also called *corporate charter.*

Articles of Incorporation

Web Exploration

Go to **www.microsoft.com/about/companyinformation/corporategovernance/articlesincorp.mspx** to view the articles of incorporation of Microsoft Corporation.

The **articles of incorporation,** or **corporate charter,** are the basic governing document of the corporation. They must be drafted and filed with, and approved by, the state before the corporation can be officially incorporated. Under the RMBCA [§ 2.02(a)], the articles of incorporation must include:

(1) the name of the corporation
(2) the number of shares the corporation is authorized to issue

CAREER OPPORTUNITIES FOR PARALEGALS IN CORPORATION LAW

Many paralegals work for large law firms that represent corporate America. Major corporations operate across America, and transnational corporations operate throughout the world. These corporations are huge, and they control an enormous proportion of the economy. Large corporations usually hire large law firms to represent them in all types of legal work. Sometimes large corporations hire boutique law firms to represent them in specialized areas of the law—for instance, patent law.

The largest law firms in America have hundreds of lawyers. The law firm itself typically is divided into different practice groups, including transactional work, real estate, securities regulation, environmental law, employment law, mergers and acquisitions, and so forth. Therefore, corporations can find most of the law talent they need in large law firms that serve corporate clients.

Paralegals who work for large law firms typically are assigned to one of the areas practiced by the law firm. Therefore, the paralegals who work for these large law firms often become experts in one area of law—the type of law practiced by the attorney or attorneys to whom they have been assigned.

Transactional work makes up most of large firms' legal services provided to clients. This may consist of drafting the complex contracts the client needs. These contracts generally are negotiated with the help of the lawyers and drafted by the lawyers. The contracts may be sales contracts, purchase contracts, service contracts, licenses, leases, and other contracts and agreements.

Major corporations need securities lawyers to represent them in issuing securities to the public and in negotiating collective bargaining agreements with labor unions, to draft the agreements for stock option and pension plans, to consummate mergers with other corporations, and the like. Paralegals who work for these lawyers acquire expertise in these areas of practice.

Corporations also require lawyers to represent them in proceedings at administrative agencies, such as the federal Environmental Protection Agency (EPA), the federal Food and Drug Administration (FDA), the Securities and Exchange Commission (SEC), the Equal Employment Opportunity Commission (EEOC), and other federal and state administrative agencies. Paralegals who work in these areas must acquire knowledge of the administrative law that is practiced before these administrative agencies.

Many corporations operate in foreign markets. These corporations have lawyers who are experts in import law and export law, as well as specialists representing multinational corporations in their dealings in individual countries. Large law firms have international groups in America and have also opened offices in other countries to provide these services. Therefore, large law firms that represent multinational corporations offer an opportunity for paralegals in the international law area.

For paralegals, then, these large law firms offer tremendous employment opportunities. Although these firms seem to pay the highest salaries, they also tend to demand the most hours of work from paralegals. Because large law firms are located almost solely in urban areas, these employment opportunities can be expected to be found in large cities.

Corporations themselves usually have their own legal departments consisting of lawyers who are employees of the corporation. These in-house attorneys provide all sorts of legal services to the large corporation.

In-house legal departments of corporations offer another employment opportunity for paralegals: Paralegals who work in legal departments of large corporations are employees of the corporation and, therefore, often enjoy special employee benefits such as stock option plans. Corporate legal departments will continue to offer excellent employment opportunities for paralegals. Again, though, many corporate legal offices are located at the head office of the corporation in urban areas.

Corporate America will continue to employ substantial numbers of lawyers and their paralegals. These paralegals may work for the large law firms that represent corporate America or for the large national and multinational corporations themselves.

(3) the address of the corporation's initial registered office and the name of the initial registered agent
(4) the name and address of each incorporator

The articles of incorporation may also include provisions concerning

1. the period of duration, which may be perpetual
2. the purpose or purposes for which the corporation is organized
3. limitation or regulation of the powers of the corporation
4. regulation of the affairs of the corporation
5. any provision that otherwise would be contained in the corporation's bylaws.

The RMBCA provides that corporate existence begins when the articles of incorporation are filed. The secretary of state's filing of the articles of incorporation is *conclusive proof* that the incorporators satisfied all conditions of incorporation. The corollary to this rule is that failure to file articles of incorporation is conclusive proof of the nonexistence of the corporation.

The articles of incorporation can be amended to contain any provision that could have been lawfully included in the original document. After the amendment is approved by the shareholders, the corporation must file articles of amendment with the secretary of state [RMBCA Section 10.06]. Exhibit 19.10 shows sample articles of incorporation.

Exhibit 19.10 Sample articles of incorporation

ARTICLES OF INCORPORATION
OF
THE BIG CHEESE CORPORATION

ONE: The name of this corporation is:

THE BIG CHEESE CORPORATION

TWO: The purpose of this corporation is to engage in any lawful act or activity for which a corporation may be organized under the General Corporation Law of California other than the banking business, the trust company business, or the practice of a profession permitted to be incorporated by the California Corporations Code.

THREE: The name and address in this state of the corporation's initial agent for service of process is:

Nikki Nguyen, Esq. 1000 Main Street, Suite 800
Los Angeles, California 90010

FOUR: This corporation is authorized to issue only one class of shares which shall be designated common stock. The total number of shares it is authorized to issue is 1,000,000 shares.

FIVE: The names and addresses of the persons who are appointed to act as the initial directors of this corporation are:

Shou-Yi Kang	100 Maple Street	Los Angeles, California 90005
Frederick Richards	200 Spruce Road	Los Angeles, California 90006
Jessie Quian	300 Palm Drive	Los Angeles, California 90007
Richard Eastin	400 Willow Lane	Los Angeles, California 90008

SIX: The liability of the directors of the corporation from monetary damages shall be eliminated to the fullest extent possible under California law.

SEVEN: The corporation is authorized to provide indemnification of agents (as defined in Section 317 of the Corporations Code) for breach of duty to the corporation and its stockholders through bylaw provisions or through agreements with the agents, or both, in excess of the indemnification otherwise permitted by Section 317 of the Corporations Code, subject to the limits on such excess indemnification set forth in Section 204 of the Corporations Code.

IN WITNESS WHEREOF, the undersigned, being all the persons named above as the initial directors, have executed these Articles of Incorporation.

____

____

____

Dated: January 2, 2007

Corporate Bylaws

In addition to the articles of incorporation, corporations are governed by their **corporate bylaws.** Either the incorporators or the initial directors can adopt the bylaws of the corporation. The **bylaws** are much more detailed than the articles of incorporation and may contain any provision for managing the business and affairs of the corporation that is not inconsistent with law or the articles of incorporation [RMBCA Section 2.06]. They do not have to be filed with any government official. The bylaws are binding on the directors, officers, and shareholders of the corporation.

Corporate bylaws A detailed set of rules that are adopted by the board of directors after the corporation is incorporated, containing provisions for managing the business and the affairs of the corporation.

The bylaws govern the internal management structure of the corporation. Typically, they specify the time and place of the annual shareholders' meeting, how special meetings of shareholders are called, the time and place of annual and monthly board of directors' meetings, how special meetings of the board of directors are called, the notice required for meetings, the quorum necessary to hold a shareholders' or board of directors' meeting, the required vote necessary to enact a corporate matter, the corporate officers and their duties, the committees of the board of directors and their duties, where the records of the corporation are to be kept, directors' and shareholders' inspection rights of corporate records, the procedure for transferring shares of the corporation, and such.

Web Exploration

Go to **www.microsoft.com/about/companyinformation/corporategovernance/bylaws.mspx** to view the bylaws of Microsoft Corporation.

The board of directors has the authority to amend the bylaws unless the articles of incorporation reserve that right for the shareholders. The shareholders of the corporation have the absolute right to amend the bylaws even though the bylaws may also be amended by the board of directors. Sample provisions of corporate bylaws are set forth in Exhibit 19.11.

Organizational Meeting

An **organizational meeting** of the initial directors of the corporation must be held after the articles of incorporation are filed. At this meeting the directors must adopt the bylaws, elect corporate officers, and transact other business that may come before the meeting [RMBCA Section 2.05]. The latter category includes matters such as accepting share subscriptions, approving the form of the stock certificate, authorizing issuance of the shares, ratifying or adopting promoters' contracts, selecting a bank, choosing an auditor, forming committees of the board of directors, fixing the salaries of officers, hiring employees, authorizing the filing of applications for government licenses to transact the business of the corporation, and empowering corporate officers to enter into contracts on behalf of the corporation. Exhibit 19.12 contains sample **corporate resolutions** from an organizational meeting of the board of directors of a corporation.

Organizational meeting A meeting that must be held by the initial directors of the corporation after the articles of incorporation are filed.

S Corporations

In 1982, Congress enacted the Subchapter S Revision Act. The act divides all corporations into two groups: **S corporations,** which are those that elect to be taxed under Subchapter S, and **C corporations,** which are all other corporations [26 U.S.C. Sections 6242 et seq.].

S corporation A corporation that has elected S corporation status. An S corporation pays no federal income tax at the corporate level. The gains or losses of an S corporation flow through to the shareholders.

If a corporation elects to be taxed as an S Corporation, it pays no federal income tax at the corporate level. As in a partnership, the corporation's income or loss flows to the shareholders' individual income tax returns. Thus, this election is particularly advantageous if (1) the corporation is expected to have losses that can be offset against other income of the shareholders, or (2) the corporation is expected to make profits and the shareholders' income tax brackets are lower than the corporation's. Profits are taxed to the shareholders even if the income is not distributed. The shares retain other attributes of the corporate form, including limited liability.

Web Exploration

Go to **www.irs.gov/pub/irs-pdf/f2553.pdf** to view IRS Form 2553, which must be filed by a corporation selecting Subchapter S status.

Exhibit 19.11 Sample provisions of corporate bylaws

BYLAWS OF

THE BIG CHEESE CORPORATION

ARTICLE I Offices

Section 1. Principal Executive Office. The corporation's principal executive office shall be fixed and located at such place as the Board of Directors (herein called the "Board") shall determine. The Board is granted full power and authority to change said principal executive office from one location to another.

Section 2. Other Offices. Branch or subordinate offices may be established at any time by the Board at any place or places.

ARTICLE II Shareholders

Section 1. Annual Meetings. The annual meetings of shareholders shall be held on such date and at such time as may be fixed by the Board. At such meetings, directors shall be elected and any other proper business may be transacted.

Section 2. Special Meetings. Special meetings of the shareholders may be called at any time by the Board, the Chairman of the Board, the President, or by the holders of shares entitled to cast not less than ten percent of the votes at such meeting. Upon request in writing to the Chairman of the Board, the President, any Vice President or the Secretary by any person (other than the Board) entitled to call a special meeting of shareholders, the officer forthwith shall cause notice to be given to the shareholders entitled to vote that a meeting will be held at a time requested by the person or persons calling the meeting, not less than thirty-five nor more than sixty days after the receipt of the request. If the notice is not given within twenty days after receipt of the request, the persons entitled to call the meeting may give the notice.

Section 3. Quorum. A majority of the shares entitled to vote, represented in person or by proxy, shall constitute a quorum at any meeting of shareholders. If a quorum is present, the affirmative vote of a majority of the shares represented and voting at the meeting (which shares voting affirmatively also constitute at least a majority of the required quorum) shall be the act of the shareholders, unless the vote of a greater number or voting by classes is required by law or by the Articles, except as provided in the following sentence. The shareholders present at a duly called or held meeting at which a quorum is present may continue to do business until adjournment, notwithstanding the withdrawal of enough shareholders to leave less than a quorum, if any action taken (other than adjournment) is approved by at least a majority of the shares required to constitute a quorum.

ARTICLE III Directors

Section 1. Election and Term of Office. The directors shall be elected at each annual meeting of the shareholders, but if any such annual meeting is not held or the directors are not elected thereat, the directors may be elected at any special meeting of shareholders held for that purpose. Each director shall hold office until the next annual meeting and until a successor has been elected and qualified.

Section 2. Quorum. A majority of the authorized number of directors constitutes a quorum of the Board for the transaction of business. Every act or decision done or made by a majority of the directors present at a meeting duly held at which a quorum is present shall be regarded as the act of the Board, unless a greater number be required by law or by the Articles. A meeting at which a quorum is initially present may continue to transact business notwithstanding the withdrawal of directors, if any action taken is approved by at least a majority of the required quorum for such meeting.

Section 3. Participation in Meetings by Conference Telephone. Members of the Board may participate in a meeting through use of conference telephone or similar communications equipment, so long as all members participating in such meeting can hear one another.

Section 4. Action Without Meeting. Any action required or permitted to be taken by the Board may be taken without a meeting if all members of the Board shall individually or collectively consent in writing to such action. Such consent or consents shall have the same effect as a unanimous vote of the Board and shall be filed with the minutes of the proceedings of the Board.

Exhibit 19.12 Sample corporate resolutions from an organizational meeting

MINUTES OF FIRST MEETING
OF
BOARD OF DIRECTORS
OF
THE BIG CHEESE CORPORATION
January 2, 2007
10:00 A.M.

The Directors of said corporation held their first meeting on the above date and at the above time pursuant to required notice.

The following Directors, constituting a quorum of the Board of Directors, were present at such meeting:

Shou-Yi Kang
Frederick Richards
Jessie Quian
Richard Eastin

Upon motion duly made and seconded, Shou-Yi was unanimously elected Chairman of the meeting and Frederick Richards was unanimously elected Secretary of the meeting.

1. Articles of Incorporation and Agent for Service of Process

The Chairman stated that the Articles of Incorporation of the Corporation were filed in the office of the California Secretary of State. The Chairman presented to the meeting a certified copy of the Articles of Incorporation. The Secretary was directed to insert the copy in the Minute Book. Upon motion duly made and seconded, the following resolution was unanimously adopted.

RESOLVED, that the agent named as the initial agent for service of process in the Articles of Incorporation of this corporation is hereby confirmed as this corporation's agent for the purpose of service of process.

2. Bylaws

The matter of adopting Bylaws for the regulation of the affairs of the corporation was next considered. The Secretary presented to the meeting a form of Bylaws, which was considered and discussed. Upon motion duly made and seconded, the following recitals and resolutions were unanimously adopted:

WHEREAS, there has been presented to the directors a form of Bylaws for the regulation of the affairs of this corporation; and

WHEREAS, it is deemed to be in the best interests of this corporation that said Bylaws be adopted by this Board of Directors as the Bylaws of this corporation;

NOW, THEREFORE, BE IT RESOLVED, that Bylaws in the form presented to this meeting are adopted and approved as the Bylaws of this corporation until amended or repealed in accordance with applicable law.

RESOLVED FURTHER, that the Secretary of this corporation is authorized and directed to execute a certificate of the adoption of said Bylaws and to enter said Bylaws as so certified in the Minute Book of this corporation, and to see that a copy of said Bylaws is kept at the principal executive or business office of this corporation in California.

3. Corporate Seal

The secretary presented for approval a proposed seal of the corporation. Upon motion duly made and seconded, the following resolution was unanimously adopted:

RESOLVED, that a corporate seal is adopted as the seal of this corporation in the form of two concentric circles, with the name of this corporation between the two circles and the state and date of incorporation within the inner circle.

4. Stock Certificate

The Secretary presented a proposed form of stock certificate for use by the corporation. Upon motion duly made and seconded, the following resolution was unanimously adopted:

RESOLVED, that the form of stock certificate presented to this meeting is approved and adopted as the stock certificate of this corporation. The secretary was instructed to insert a sample copy of the stock certificate in the Minute Book immediately following these minutes.

5. Election of Officers

The Chairman announced that it would be in order to elect officers of the corporation. After discussion and upon motion duly made and seconded, the following resolution was unanimously adopted:

RESOLVED, that the following persons are unanimously elected to the offices indicated opposite their names

Title	Name
Chief Executive Officer	Shou-Yi Kang
President	Frederick Richards
Secretary and Vice President	Jessie Quian
Treasurer	Richard Eastin

There being no further business to come before the meeting, on motion duly made, seconded and unanimously carried, the meeting was adjourned.

Corporations that meet the following criteria can elect to be taxed as S corporations:

1. The corporation must be a domestic corporation.
2. The corporation cannot be a member of an affiliated group of corporations.
3. The corporation can have no more than 100 shareholders.
4. Shareholders must be individuals, estates, or certain trusts. Corporations and partnerships cannot be shareholders.
5. Shareholders must be citizens or residents of the United States. Nonresident aliens cannot be shareholders.
6. The corporation cannot have more than one class of stock. Shareholders do not need to have equal voting rights.

An S corporation election is made by filing a **Form 2553** with the Internal Revenue Service (IRS). The election can be rescinded by shareholders who collectively own at least a majority of the shares of the corporation. If the election is rescinded, however, another S Corporation election cannot be made for five years.

The ethical duty of a paralegal professional to file corporate documents on time is discussed in the following feature.

Learning Objective 7

Explain the functions of shareholders, directors, and officers in managing the affairs of a corporation.

Shareholders

Common stock A type of equity security that represents the residual value of the corporation.

Common shareholder A person who owns common stock.

Common stock is an equity security that represents the residual value of the corporation. Common stock has no preferences—that is, creditors and preferred shareholders must receive their required interest and dividend payments before **common shareholders** receive anything. Common stock also does not have a fixed maturity date. If the corporation is liquidated, the creditors and preferred shareholders are paid the value of their interests first, and the common shareholders are paid the value of their interest (if any) last. Corporations may issue different classes of common stock [RMBCA Section 6.01 (a) and (b)].

Rights and Duties of Common Shareholders

Persons who own common stock are called common shareholders. A common stockholder's investment in the corporation is represented by a common stock certificate. Common shareholders have the right to elect directors and to vote on mergers and other important matters, and in return for their investment, common shareholders receive dividends declared by the board of directors.

A corporation's shareholders *own* the corporation. Nevertheless, they are not agents of the corporation (that is, they cannot bind the corporation to any contracts), and the only management duty they have is the right to vote on matters such as the election of directors and the approval of fundamental changes in the corporation.

Disregard of the Corporate Entity

Piercing the corporate veil A doctrine that says that if a shareholder dominates a corporation and misuses it for improper purposes, a court of equity can disregard the corporate entity and hold the shareholder personally liable for the corporation's debts and obligations. Also called *alter-ego doctrine.*

Shareholders of a corporation generally have limited liability (that is, they are liable for the debts and obligations of the corporation only to the extent of their capital contributions). But if a shareholder or shareholders dominate a corporation and misuse it for improper purposes, a court of equity can **disregard the corporate entity** and hold the shareholders personally liable for the corporation's debts and obligations. This doctrine, commonly referred to as **piercing the corporate veil,** is often resorted to by unpaid creditors who are trying to collect from shareholders a debt owed by the corporation. The piercing the corporate veil doctrine is also called the **alter-ego doctrine** because the corporation has become the alter ego of the shareholder.

Courts will pierce the corporate veil if (1) the corporation has been formed without sufficient capital—called *thin capitalization*—or (2) the corporation and its shareholders have not maintained separateness (such as by commingling personal

ETHICAL PERSPECTIVE

Paralegal's Duty to File Corporate Documents on Time

Ms. Nguyen is a paralegal for a law firm, and her supervising attorney is Mr. Arnold. Several persons come into the law office to talk with Mr. Arnold about having him represent them in incorporating a new corporation. Mr. Arnold asks Ms. Nguyen to be present at the meeting. After explaining their plan, the organizers employ Mr. Arnold to form the corporation for them and to draft and file the necessary documents. During the meeting, Mr. Arnold obtains the necessary information to prepare the articles of incorporation, bylaws, and other documents for the corporation.

After the clients have left, Mr. Arnold instructs Ms. Nguyen to prepare the articles of incorporation for the new corporation, which she does. After Mr. Arnold reviews the articles and approves them, he instructs Ms. Nguyen to send the articles to the incorporators for their signatures. Ms. Nguyen does so and the articles are returned to the law office signed by the incorporators. Mr. Arnold then instructs Ms. Nguyen to immediately file the articles of incorporation electronically with the state's division of corporations' office. Ms. Nguyen agrees to file the articles of incorporation electronically but fails to do so.

One week later, Ms. Nguyen discovers a note that she had made to herself about filing the articles of incorporation. After realizing that she had failed to do so, she electronically files the articles of incorporation with the state's division of corporations.

Ms. Nguyen's failure to file the articles of incorporation on time could easily cause serious problems for the organizers. For example, if the incorporators had entered into contracts on behalf of the corporation during this one-week period, they would be personally bound by those contracts if the corporation did not later ratify those contracts as its own or if the corporation does ratify these contracts but fails to pay them.

Also, if one of the organizers had injured someone during this one-week period while on company business, for example, by negligently causing an automobile accident that injured another person, the organizers would be personally liable for the damages. This is because the corporation was not yet in existence and therefore the organizers were not yet shareholders who would have been sheltered from personal liability, but instead general partners of a general partnership who would have been held personally liable.

Thus, a paralegal's failure to file articles of incorporation on time could cause serious financial consequences to the organizers of the corporation. Also, such negligence could lead to a lawsuit against the law firm to recover damages resulting from such negligence.

and corporate assets, failing to hold required shareholders' meetings, and failing to maintain corporate records and books). The courts examine this doctrine on a case-by-case basis.

Board of Directors

The **board of directors** of a corporation is responsible for formulating the policy decisions affecting the management, supervision, and control of the operation of the corporation [RMBCA Section 8.01]. Such policy decisions include deciding the business or businesses in which the corporation should be engaged, selecting and removing the top officers of the corporation, determining the capital structure of the corporation, declaring dividends, and the like.

Typically, boards of directors are composed of inside directors and outside directors. An **inside director** is a person who is also an officer of the corporation. For example, the president of a corporation often sits as a director of the corporation. An

Web Exploration

Go to **www.microsoft.com/investor/CorporateGovernance/BoardOfDirectors/Contacts/MSFinanceCode.aspx** and read the Microsoft Finance Code of Professional Conduct adopted pursuant to the Sarbanes-Oxley Act.

Board of directors A panel of decision makers, the members of which are elected by a corporation's shareholders.

DELAWARE CORPORATION LAW

The state of Delaware is the corporate haven of the United States. More than 50 percent of the publicly traded corporations in America, including 60 percent of the Fortune 500 companies, are incorporated in Delaware. In total, over 500,000 business corporations are incorporated in Delaware. But why?

Remember, it is the corporation code of the state where a corporation is incorporated that applies to such things as election of directors, voting and other requirements for a merger to occur, laws for fending off corporate raiders, and such. So, even if a corporation does no business in Delaware, it can obtain the benefits of Delaware incorporation law by incorporating in Delaware.

On the legislative side, Delaware has enacted the **Delaware General Corporation Law.** This law is the most advanced corporation law in the country, and the statute is particularly written to be of benefit to large corporations. For example, the Delaware corporation code provides for the ability of corporations incorporated in Delaware to adopt "poison pills" that make it virtually impossible for another company to take over a Delaware corporation unless the board of directors of the target corporation agrees and removes such poison pills. In addition, the legislature keeps amending the corporation code as the demands of big business warrant or need such changes. For instance, the legislature has enacted a state antitakeover statute that makes it almost legally impossible to take over a Delaware corporation unless the corporation's directors wave the state's antitakeover law and agree to be taken over.

On the judicial side, Delaware has a special court—the **Court of Chancery**—that hears and decides business cases. This court has been around for over 200 years, and in that time it has interpreted Delaware corporation law favorably to large corporations in such matters as electing corporate boards of directors, eliminating negligence liability of outside directors, and upholding the antitakeover provisions of the Delaware corporation code. And there are no emotional juries for a corporation to worry about. The decisions of the Chancery Court are made by judges who are experts at deciding corporate law disputes. The court is known for issuing decisions favorable to large corporations as the court applies Delaware corporation law to decide disputes. Appeals from the Court of Chancery are brought directly to the Supreme Court of Delaware. Thus, Delaware courts have created a body of precedent of legal decisions that provides more assurance to Delaware corporations when trying to decide whether they will be sued and what the outcome might be if they do get sued.

The state of Delaware makes a substantial sum of money each year on fees charged to corporations incorporated within the state. The state of Delaware is the "business state," providing advanced corporate laws and an expert judiciary for deciding corporate disputes.

outside director is a person who sits on the board of directors but is not an officer of that corporation. Outside directors are often officers and directors of other corporations, or bankers, lawyers, professors, and other professionals. Outside directors are usually selected for their business knowledge and expertise.

The director is really a watch-dog, and the watch-dog has no right, without the knowledge of his master, to take a sop from a possible wolf.

Lord Justice Bowen, *Re The North Australian Territory Co. Ltd.* (1891)

The directors can act only as a board. They cannot act individually on the corporation's behalf. Every director has the right to participate in any meeting of the board of directors. Each director has one vote, and directors cannot vote by proxy.

Regular meetings of the board of directors are held at the times and places established in the bylaws. Such meetings can be held without notice. The board can call special meetings as provided in the bylaws [RMBCA Section 8.20(a)]. They typically are convened for reasons such as issuing new shares, considering proposals to merge with other corporations, adopting maneuvers to defend against hostile takeover attempts, and the like.

The board of directors may act without a meeting if all of the directors sign written consents that set forth the actions taken. Such consent has the effect of a unanimous vote. The RMBCA also permits meetings of the board to be held via conference calls.

Corporate Officers

Officers of the corporation
Employees of a corporation who are appointed by the board of directors to manage the day-to-day operations of the corporation.

The board of directors has the authority to appoint the **officers of the corporation.** The officers are elected by the board of directors at such time and by such manner as prescribed in the corporation's bylaws. The directors can also delegate certain management authority to the officers of the corporation.

At minimum, most corporations have the following officers: (1) a president, (2) one or more vice presidents, (3) a secretary, and (4) a treasurer. The bylaws or the board of directors can authorize duly appointed officers to have the power to appoint assistant officers. The same individual may simultaneously hold more than one office in the corporation [RMBCA Section 8.40]. The duties of each officer are specified in the bylaws of the corporation. Officers of the corporation have such authority as may be provided in the bylaws or as determined by resolution of the board of directors.

The hierarchy of the ownership and control of a corporation is set forth in Exhibit 19.13.

Directors' and Officers' Duty of Loyalty

The **duty of loyalty** requires directors and officers to subordinate their personal interests to those of the corporation and its shareholders. Justice Benjamin Cardozo defined this duty of loyalty as follows:

Duty of loyalty A responsibility of directors and officers not to act adversely to the interests of the corporation and to subordinate their personal interests to those of the corporation and its shareholders.

> A corporate director or officer owes loyalty and allegiance to the corporation—a loyalty that is undivided and an allegiance that is influenced by no consideration other than the welfare of the corporation. Any adverse interest of a director or officer will be subjected to scrutiny rigid and uncompromising. He may not profit at the expense of his corporation and in conflict with its rights; he may not for personal gain divert unto himself the opportunities that in equity and fairness belong to the corporation.
>
> Many forms of conduct permissible in a workaday world for those acting at arm's length are forbidden to those bound by fiduciary ties. Not honesty alone, but the punctilio of an honor the most sensitive, is then the standard of behavior. As to this there has developed a tradition that is unbending and inveterate. *Source: Meinhard v. Salmon*, 164 N.E. 545, 546 (N.Y. App. 1928)

One of the common breaches of the duty of loyalty is a corporate director or officer competing with the corporation without board of directors' approval, secretly dealing with the corporation, secretly usurping a corporate opportunity, or making secret profits from bribes. If a director or officer breaches his or her duty of loyalty and makes a secret profit on a transaction, the corporation can sue the director or officer to recover the secret profit.

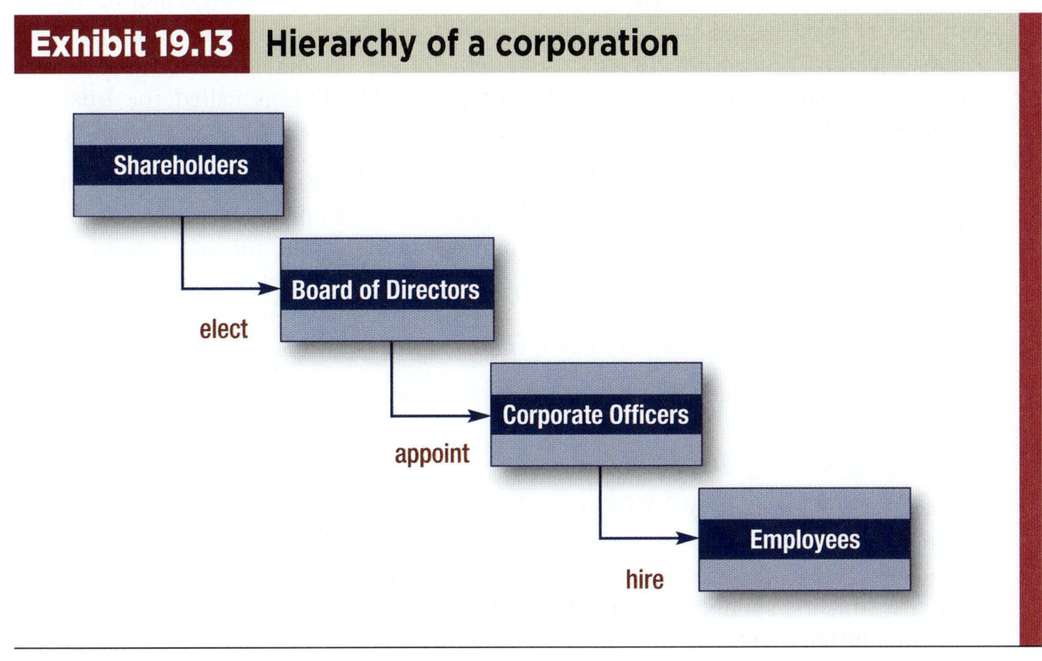

E-CORPORATION

Most states have amended their corporation codes to permit the use of electronic communications to shareholders and among directors. For example, the Delaware General Corporation law recognizes the following uses of electronic technology:

- Delivery of notices to stockholders may be made electronically if the stockholder consents to the delivery of notices in this form.
- Proxy solicitation for shareholder votes may be made by electronic transmission.
- The shareholder list of a corporation that must be made available during the 10 days prior to a stockholder meeting may be made available either at the principal place of business of the corporation or by posting the list on an electronic network.
- Stockholders who are not physically present at a meeting may be deemed present, participate in, and vote at the meeting by electronic communication; a meeting may be held solely by electronic communication, without a physical location.
- The election of directors of the corporation may be held by electronic transmission.
- Directors' actions by unanimous consent may be taken by electronic transmission.

The use of electronic transmissions, electronic networks, and communications by e-mail will make the operation and administration of corporate affairs more efficient.

Directors' and Officers' Duty of Care

Duty of care A responsibility of corporate directors and officers to use care and diligence when acting on behalf of the corporation.

The **duty of care** requires corporate directors and officers to use *care and diligence* when acting on behalf of the corporation. To meet this duty, the directors and officers must discharge their duties (1) in good faith, (2) with the care that an *ordinary prudent person* in a like position would use under similar circumstances, and (3) in a manner that he or she reasonably believes to be in the best interests of the corporation [RMBCA Sections 8.30 (a) and 8.42(a)].

Negligence Failure of a corporate director or officer to exercise the duty of care while conducting the corporation's business.

A director or officer who breaches this duty of care is personally liable to the corporation and its shareholders for any damages caused by the breach. Such breaches, which are normally caused by **negligence,** often involve a director's or officer's failure to (1) make a reasonable investigation of a corporate matter, (2) attend board meetings on a regular basis, (3) properly supervise any subordinate who causes a loss to the corporation through embezzlement and such, or (4) stay adequately informed about corporate affairs. Breaches are examined by the courts on a case-by-case basis.

Business judgment rule A rule stating that directors and officers are not liable to the corporation or its shareholders for honest mistakes of judgment.

The determination of whether a corporate director or officer has met his or her duty of care is measured as of the time the decision is made. The benefit of hindsight is not a factor. Therefore, directors and officers are not liable to the corporation or its shareholders for honest mistakes of judgment. This is called the **business judgment rule.**

> **Example** Suppose, after conducting considerable research and investigation, the directors of a major automobile company decide to produce a large, expensive automobile. When the car is introduced to the public for sale, few of the automobiles are sold because the public is interested in buying smaller, less expensive automobiles. Because this was an honest mistake of judgment on the part of corporate management personnel, their judgment is shielded by the business judgment rule.

Sarbanes-Oxley Act

In the late 1990s and early 2000s, many large corporations in the United States were found to have engaged in massive financial frauds. Many of these frauds were perpetrated by the chief executive officers and other senior officers of the companies. Financial officers, such as chief financial officers and controllers, were also found to have been instrumental in committing these frauds.

One Hundred Seventh Congress
of the
United States of America

AT THE SECOND SESSION

Begun and held at the City of Washington on Wednesday, the twenty-third day of January, two thousand and two

An Act

To protect investors by improving the accuracy and reliability of corporate disclosures made pursuant to the securities laws, and for other purposes.

Be it enacted by the Senate and House of Representatives of the United States of America in Congress assembled,

SECTION 1. SHORT TITLE; TABLE OF CONTENTS.

(a) SHORT TITLE.—This Act may be cited as the "Sarbanes-Oxley Act of 2002".

(b) TABLE OF CONTENTS.—The table of contents for this Act is as follows:

Sarbanes-Oxley Act
The Sarbanes-Oxley Act, a federal statute, improves corporate transparency, imposes rules for the governance of public corporations, and promotes corporate ethics.

In response, Congress enacted the **Sarbanes-Oxley Act of 2002 (SOX),** which makes certain conduct by public companies and their directors and officers illegal and establishes criminal penalties for violations. The act prompts public companies to adopt a **code of ethics.** Section 406 of the Sarbanes-Oxley Act requires a public company to disclose whether it has adopted a code of ethics for senior financial officers, including its principal financial officer and its principal accounting officer. In response, public companies have adopted codes of ethics for their senior financial officers. Many public companies have included all officers and employees in the coverage of their codes of ethics.

A typical code of ethics is illustrated in Exhibit 19.14.

Sarbanes-Oxley Act of 2002 (SOX) A federal statute enacted by Congress to improve corporate governance.

Bankruptcy

Learning Objective 8

Recognize the professional opportunities for paralegals in the bankruptcy law area.

The extension of credit from creditors to debtors in commercial and personal transactions is important to the viability of the U.S. and world economies. On occasion, however, borrowers become overextended and are unable to meet their debt obligations. Federal bankruptcy law provides methods for debtors to be relieved of some debt in order to obtain a "fresh start."

Prior to 2005, the most recent overhaul of federal bankruptcy law occurred in 1978. The 1978 law was structured to make it easier for debtors to be relieved of much of their debt by declaring bankruptcy. The 1978 act was deemed "debtor friendly" because it allowed many debtors to escape from their unsecured debts.

After a decade of lobbying by credit card companies and banks, Congress enacted the **Bankruptcy Abuse Prevention and Consumer Protection Act of 2005.** The act makes it much more difficult for debtors to escape from their debts under federal bankruptcy law. The 2005 act, which has been criticized by consumer groups for being too "creditor friendly," has been praised by many businesses, banks, and credit card issuers.

Bankruptcy Abuse Prevention and Consumer Protection Act of 2005 A federal act that substantially amended federal bankruptcy law. It makes it more difficult for debtors to file for bankruptcy and have their unpaid debts discharged.

Exhibit 19.14 Code of ethics

Big Cheese Corporation
Code of Ethics

Big Cheese Corporation's mission includes the promotion of professional conduct in the practice of general management worldwide. Big Cheese's Chief Executive Officer (CEO), Chief Financial Officer (CFO), corporate Controller, and other employees of the finance organization and other employees of the corporation hold an important and elevated role in the corporate governance of the corporation. They are empowered and uniquely capable to ensure that all constituents' interests are appropriately balanced, protected, and preserved.

This Code of Ethics embodies principles to which we are expected to adhere and advocate. The CEO, CFO, finance organization employees, and other employees of the corporation are expected to abide by this Code of Ethics and all business conduct standards of the corporation relating to areas covered by this Code of Ethics. Any violation of the Code of Ethics may result in disciplinary action, up to and including termination of employment. All employees will:

- Act with honesty and integrity, avoiding actual or apparent conflicts of interest in their personal and professional relations.
- Provide stakeholders with information that is accurate, fair, complete, timely, objective, relevant, and understandable, including in our filings with and other submissions to the U.S. Securities and Exchange Commission.
- Comply with rules and regulations of federal, state, provincial, and local governments and other appropriate private and public regulatory agencies.
- Act in good faith, responsibly, with due care, competence, and diligence, without misrepresenting material facts or allowing one's independent judgment to be subordinated.
- Respect the confidentiality of information acquired in the course of one's work, except when authorized or otherwise legally obligated to disclose. Confidential information acquired in the course of one's work will not be used for personal advantage.
- Share knowledge and maintain professional skills important and relevant to stakeholders' needs.
- Proactively promote and be an example of ethical behavior as a responsible partner among peers, in the work environment and the community.
- Achieve responsible use, control, and stewardship over all Big Cheese's assets and resources that are employed or entrusted to us.
- Not unduly or fraudulently influence, coerce, manipulate, or mislead any authorized audit or interfere with any auditor engaged in the performance of an internal or independent audit of Big Cheese's financial statements or accounting books and records.

If you are aware of any suspected or known violations of this Code of Ethics or other Big Cheese policies or guidelines, you have a duty to promptly report such concerns either to your manager, another responsible member of management, a Human Resources representative, or the Director of Compliance or the 24-hour Business Conduct Line.

If you have a concern about a questionable accounting or auditing matter and wish to submit the concern confidentially or anonymously, you may do so by sending an e-mail to (bc.codeofethics@bigcheese.cc) or calling the Business Conduct Line 24-hour number at 1-888-666-BIGC (2442).

Big Cheese will handle all inquiries discreetly and make every effort to maintain, within the limits allowed by law, the confidentiality of anyone requesting guidance or reporting questionable behavior and/or a compliance concern.

It is Big Cheese's intention that this Code of Ethics be its written code of ethics under Section 406 of the Sarbanes-Oxley Act of 2002 complying with the standards set forth in Securities and Exchange Commission Regulation S-K Item 406.

Learning Objective 9

Identify the major forms of bankruptcy permitted under federal bankruptcy law.

Types of Bankruptcy

Four special chapters of the Bankruptcy Code provide different types of bankruptcy under which individual and business debtors may be granted remedy. These four types of bankruptcies established by the 2005 act are:

Chapter	Type of Bankruptcy
Chapter 7	Liquidation
Chapter 11	Reorganization
Chapter 12	Adjustment of debts of a family farmer or fisherman with regular income
Chapter 13	Adjustment of debts of an individual with regular income

Bankruptcy courts Special federal courts that hear and decide bankruptcy cases.

Congress also created a system of federal **bankruptcy courts.** These special courts are necessary because the number of bankruptcies would overwhelm the federal district courts. The bankruptcy courts are part of the federal court system, and one bankruptcy court is attached to each of the 96 U.S. district courts located across the country.

The following feature discusses career opportunities for paralegal professionals in bankruptcy law.

Web Exploration

There are three major credit reporting agencies from whom you can obtain a copy of your credit report. Go to each of the following websites to see how to order a free credit report. If you want, order your credit report.

1. Equifax at **www.equifax.com/home**
2. Experian at **www.experian.com**
3. TransUnion at **www.transunion.com**

Bankruptcy Procedure

The Bankruptcy Code provides procedures and requirements for filing petitions for bankruptcy, defines the bankruptcy estate, provides certain protections to debtors during the course of bankruptcy, and establishes the rights of creditors.

The 2005 act added a new provision that requires an individual filing for bankruptcy to receive prepetition and postpetition credit and financial counseling. The debtor must receive prepetition credit counseling within 180 days prior to filing his or her petition for bankruptcy. In addition, the 2005 act requires that before an individual debtor receives a discharge in a Chapter 7 or Chapter 13 bankruptcy, the debtor must attend a personal financial management course.

A bankruptcy case is commenced when a **petition** is filed with the bankruptcy court. A debtor can file a **voluntary petition** in Chapter 7 (liquidation), Chapter 11 (reorganization), Chapter 12 (family farmer or fisherman), and Chapter 13 (adjustment of debts) bankruptcy cases.

Petition A document filed with the bankruptcy court that starts a bankruptcy proceeding.

A creditor or creditors can file an **involuntary petition** and place a debtor into bankruptcy in Chapter 7 (liquidation) and Chapter 11 (reorganization) cases if certain requirements are met. An involuntary petition cannot be filed in Chapter 12 (family farmer or fisherman) or Chapter 13 (adjustment of debts).

CAREER OPPORTUNITIES FOR PARALEGALS IN BANKRUPTCY LAW

For years, many paralegals have worked in the area of federal bankruptcy law. In the past, the majority of bankruptcy filings were for Chapter 7 liquidation bankruptcy. This type of bankruptcy was easy to file, and debtors were usually able to walk away from most of their unsecured credit such as credit card debt. This type of bankruptcy was "debtor friendly." Chapter 7 bankruptcy required the completion of forms, and was procedurally oriented. Paralegals were important in completing these forms and assisting in the completion of the bankruptcy proceeding.

However, the Bankruptcy Abuse Prevention and Consumer Protection Act of 2005 was enacted to make it more difficult for debtors to obtain Chapter 7 liquidation bankruptcy. The new act establishes detailed income and means tests that must be met before a debtor qualifies for Chapter 7 bankruptcy and is designed to force many debtors into Chapter 13 bankruptcy, a form of rehabilitation bankruptcy that requires debtors to use part of their future income to pay off some of their preexisting debts. The 2005 act also establishes certain requirements that must be met by a debtor before qualifying for Chapter 13 bankruptcy. Thus the 2005 act is said to be "creditor friendly."

The 2005 act provides for Chapter 12 bankruptcy, a special type of rehabilitation bankruptcy designed for family farmers and family fishermen. In addition, the 2005 act made some changes to Chapter 11 bankruptcy, a form of bankruptcy usually used by large corporations to reorganize their financial structure. Chapter 11 is a very complicated form of bankruptcy, and requires a special knowledge of debtor and creditor rights. The 2005 act also made some procedural changes to federal bankruptcy law.

What does all this mean for paralegals either working in or interested in working in the bankruptcy field? The area of federal bankruptcy law is more complex than before. This will require that the paralegal learn substantive knowledge of the different forms of bankruptcy and how to determine who qualifies for each form of bankruptcy. Second, the procedures for filing and maintaining a bankruptcy are also more detailed. Therefore, paralegals who work in the bankruptcy field will be required to have a greater knowledge of bankruptcy procedures than before.

In the future, many paralegals will find opportunities to work in the field of bankruptcy law. Lawyers and paralegals will be called upon to assist debtors as well as creditors in bankruptcy proceedings. The bankruptcy field will continue to offer jobs for the well-educated and well-trained paralegal professional.

The 2005 act places a new burden on attorneys who represent debtors in bankruptcy because the act requires the attorney to certify the accuracy of the information contained in the bankruptcy petition and the schedules, under penalty of perjury. If there are any factual discrepancies, the attorney is subject to monetary fines and sanctions. Many attorneys may no longer be willing to represent debtors in bankruptcy because of this rule.

A creditor must file a **proof of claim** stating the amount of his or her claim against the debtor. The proof of claim must be filed in a timely manner, which generally means within six months of the first meeting of the creditors. A secured creditor whose claim exceeds the value of the collateral may submit a proof of claim and become an unsecured claimant as to the difference. An equity security holder (such as a shareholder of a corporation) must file a **proof of interest.**

Trustee A legal representative of a debtor's estate.

A **trustee** must be appointed in the following types of bankruptcy cases: Chapter 7 (liquidation), Chapter 12 (family farmer or family fisherman), and Chapter 13 (adjustment of debts). A trustee may be appointed in a Chapter 11 (reorganization) case upon a showing of fraud, dishonesty, incompetence, or gross mismanagement of the affairs of the debtor by current management. Once appointed, a trustee becomes a legal representative of the debtor's estate.

Exhibit 19.15 sets forth a voluntary petition for bankruptcy that would be filed by a debtor. Exhibit 19.16 sets forth a proof of claim form that would be filed by a creditor.

The Bankruptcy Estate

Bankruptcy estate A debtor's property and earnings that comprise the estate of a bankruptcy proceeding.

The **bankruptcy estate** is created upon the commencement of a bankruptcy case. It includes all the debtor's legal and equitable interests in real, personal, tangible, and intangible property, wherever located, that exist when the petition is filed, and all interests of the debtor and the debtor's spouse in community property. Gifts, inheritances, life insurance proceeds, and property from divorce settlements that the debtor is entitled to receive within 180 days after the petition is filed become part of the bankruptcy estate.

Earnings from services performed by an individual debtor are not part of the bankruptcy estate in a Chapter 7 (liquidation) bankruptcy. However, the 2005 act provides that a certain amount of postpetition earnings from services performed by the debtor may be required to be paid as part of the completion of Chapter 12 (family farmer or family fisherman), Chapter 11 (reorganization), and Chapter 13 (adjustment of debts) cases.

Exempt property Property that may be retained by a debtor pursuant to federal or state law and that does not become part of the bankruptcy estate.

Homestead exemption Equity in a debtor's home that the debtor is permitted to retain.

Because the Bankruptcy Code is not designed to make the debtor a pauper, certain property is exempt from the bankruptcy estate. The debtor may retain **exempt property,** which is property of the debtor that he or she can keep and that does not become part of the bankruptcy estate. Thus the creditors cannot claim this property. Federal bankruptcy law establishes federal exemptions, but permits states to enact their own exemptions.

The federal Bankruptcy Code permits homeowners to claim a **homestead exemption** in their principal residence. However, the 2005 act limits abusive homestead exemptions and provides that a debtor may not exempt an amount greater than $125,000 if the property was acquired by the debtor within 1,215 days (approximately three years and four months) before the filing of the petition for bankruptcy.

The 2005 act gives the bankruptcy court the power to void certain **fraudulent transfers** of the debtor's property and obligations incurred by the debtor within two years of the filing of the petition for bankruptcy.

Chapter 7: Liquidation

Chapter 7 liquidation bankruptcy A form of bankruptcy in which the debtor's nonexempt property is sold for cash, the cash is distributed to the creditors, and any unpaid debts are discharged. Also known as *straight bankruptcy.*

Chapter 7 liquidation bankruptcy (also called **straight bankruptcy**) is a familiar form of bankruptcy. In this type of bankruptcy proceeding, the debtor is permitted to keep a substantial portion of his or her assets (*exempt assets*), the debtor's nonexempt property is sold for cash and the cash is distributed to the creditors, and any of the

B 1 (Official Form 1) (1/08) AZB

United States Bankruptcy Court	Voluntary Petition
Name of Debtor (if individual, enter Last, First, Middle):	Name of Joint Debtor (Spouse) (Last, First, Middle):
All Other Names used by the Debtor in the last 8 years (include married, maiden, and trade names):	All Other Names used by the Joint Debtor in the last 8 years (include married, maiden, and trade names):
Last four digits of Soc. Sec. or Indvidual-Taxpayer I.D. (ITIN) No./Complete EIN (if more than one, state all):	Last four digits of Soc. Sec. or Indvidual-Taxpayer I.D. (ITIN) No./Complete EIN (if more than one, state all):
Street Address of Debtor (No. and Street, City, and State): ZIP CODE	Street Address of Joint Debtor (No. and Street, City, and State): ZIP CODE
County of Residence or of the Principal Place of Business:	County of Residence or of the Principal Place of Business:
Mailing Address of Debtor (if different from street address): ZIP CODE	Mailing Address of Joint Debtor (if different from street address): ZIP CODE
Location of Principal Assets of Business Debtor (if different from street address above):	ZIP CODE

Type of Debtor
(Form of Organization)
(Check **one** box.)

☐ Individual (includes Joint Debtors)
See Exhibit D on page 2 of this form.
☐ Corporation (includes LLC and LLP)
☐ Partnership
☐ Other (If debtor is not one of the above entities, check this box and state type of entity below.)

____

Nature of Business
(Check **one** box.)

☐ Health Care Business
☐ Single Asset Real Estate as defined in 11 U.S.C. § 101(51B)
☐ Railroad
☐ Stockbroker
☐ Commodity Broker
☐ Clearing Bank
☐ Other

Tax-Exempt Entity
(Check box, if applicable.)

☐ Debtor is a tax-exempt organization under Title 26 of the United States Code (the Internal Revenue Code).

Chapter of Bankruptcy Code Under Which the Petition is Filed (Check **one** box.)

☐ Chapter 7
☐ Chapter 9
☐ Chapter 11
☐ Chapter 12
☐ Chapter 13
☐ Chapter 15 Petition for Recognition of a Foreign Main Proceeding
☐ Chapter 15 Petition for Recognition of a Foreign Nonmain Proceeding

Nature of Debts
(Check one box.)

☐ Debts are primarily consumer debts, defined in 11 U.S.C. § 101(8) as "incurred by an individual primarily for a personal, family, or household purpose."
☐ Debts are primarily business debts.

Filing Fee (Check one box.)

☐ Full Filing Fee attached.

☐ Filing Fee to be paid in installments (applicable to individuals only). Must attach signed application for the court's consideration certifying that the debtor is unable to pay fee except in installments. Rule 1006(b). See Official Form 3A.

☐ Filing Fee waiver requested (applicableto chapter 7 individuals only). Must attach signed application for the court's consideration. See Official Form 3B.

Chapter 11 Debtors

Check one box:
☐ Debtor is a small business debtor as defined in 11 U.S.C. § 101(51D).

☐ Debtor is not a small business debtor as defined in 11 U.S.C. § 101(51D).

Check if:
☐ Debtor's aggregate noncontingent liquidated debts (excluding debts owed to insiders or affiliates) are less than $2,190,000.

- -

Check all applicable boxes:
☐ A plan is being filed with this petition.
☐ Acceptances of the plan were solicited prepetition from one or more classes of creditors, in accordance with 11 U.S.C. § 1126(b).

Statistical/Administrative Information

THIS SPACE IS FOR COURT USE ONLY

☐ Debtor estimates that funds will be available for distribution to unsecured creditors.
☐ Debtor estimates that, after any exempt property is excluded and administrative expenses paid, there will be no funds available for distribution to unsecured creditors.

Estimated Number of Creditors

☐	☐	☐	☐	☐	☐	☐	☐	☐	☐
1-49	50-99	100-199	200-999	1,000-5,000	5,001-10,000	10,001-25,000	25,001-50,000	50,001-100,000	Over 100,000

Estimated Assets

☐	☐	☐	☐	☐	☐	☐	☐	☐	☐
$0 to $50,000	$50,001 to $100,000	$100,001 to $500,000	$500,001 to $1 million	$1,000,001 to $10 million	$10,000,001 to $50 million	$50,000,001 to $100 million	$100,000,001 to $500 million	$500,000,001 to $1 billion	More than $1 billion

Estimated Liabilities

☐	☐	☐	☐	☐	☐	☐	☐	☐	☐
$0 to $50,000	$50,001 to $100,000	$100,001 to $500,000	$500,001 to $1 million	$1,000,001 to $10 million	$10,000,001 to $50 million	$50,000,001 to $100 million	$100,000,001 to $500 million	$500,000,001 to $1 billion	More than $1 billion

(continued)

AZB

B 1 (Official Form 1) (1/08) **Page 2**

Voluntary Petition *(This page must be completed and filed in every case.)*	Name of Debtor(s):	
All Prior Bankruptcy Cases Filed Within Last 8 Years (If more than two, attach additional sheet.)		
Location Where Filed:	Case Number:	Date Filed:
Location Where Filed:	Case Number:	Date Filed:
Pending Bankruptcy Case Filed by any Spouse, Partner, or Affiliate of this Debtor (If more than one, attach additional sheet.)		
Name of Debtor:	Case Number:	Date Filed:
District:	Relationship:	Judge:

Exhibit A

(To be completed if debtor is required to file periodic reports (e.g., forms 10K and 10Q) with the Securities and Exchange Commission pursuant to Section 13 or 15(d) of the Securities Exchange Act of 1934 and is requesting relief under chapter 11.)

☐ Exhibit A is attached and made a part of this petition.

Exhibit B

(To be completed if debtor is an individual whose debts are primarily consumer debts.)

I, the attorney for the petitioner named in the foregoing petition, declare that I have informed the petitioner that [he or she] may proceed under chapter 7, 11, 12, or 13 of title 11, United States Code, and have explained the relief available under each such chapter. I further certify that I have delivered to the debtor the notice required by 11 U.S.C. § 342(b).

X ______________________________
Signature of Attorney for Debtor(s) (Date)

Exhibit C

Does the debtor own or have possession of any property that poses or is alleged to pose a threat of imminent and identifiable harm to public health or safety?

☐ Yes, and Exhibit C is attached and made a part of this petition.

☐ No.

Exhibit D

(To be completed by every individual debtor. If a joint petition is filed, each spouse must complete and attach a separate Exhibit D.)

☐ Exhibit D completed and signed by the debtor is attached and made a part of this petition.

If this is a joint petition:

☐ Exhibit D also completed and signed by the joint debtor is attached and made a part of this petition.

Information Regarding the Debtor - Venue
(Check any applicable box.)

☐ Debtor has been domiciled or has had a residence, principal place of business, or principal assets in this District for 180 days immediately preceding the date of this petition or for a longer part of such 180 days than in any other District.

☐ There is a bankruptcy case concerning debtor's affiliate, general partner, or partnership pending in this District.

☐ Debtor is a debtor in a foreign proceeding and has its principal place of business or principal assets in the United States in this District, or has no principal place of business or assets in the United States but is a defendant in an action or proceeding [in a federal or state court] in this District, or the interests of the parties will be served in regard to the relief sought in this District.

Certification by a Debtor Who Resides as a Tenant of Residential Property
(Check all applicable boxes.)

☐ Landlord has a judgment against the debtor for possession of debtor's residence. (If box checked, complete the following.)

____
(Name of landlord that obtained judgment)

____
(Address of landlord)

☐ Debtor claims that under applicable nonbankruptcy law, there are circumstances under which the debtor would be permitted to cure the entire monetary default that gave rise to the judgment for possession, after the judgment for possession was entered, and

☐ Debtor has included with this petition the deposit with the court of any rent that would become due during the 30-day period after the filing of the petition.

☐ Debtor certifies that he/she has served the Landlord with this certification. (11 U.S.C. § 362(l)).

Exhibit 19.15 Voluntary petition for bankruptcy *(continued)*

AZB

B 1 (Official Form) 1 (1/08) **Page 3**

Voluntary Petition *(This page must be completed and filed in every case.)*	Name of Debtor(s):

Signatures

Signature(s) of Debtor(s) (Individual/Joint)

I declare under penalty of perjury that the information provided in this petition is true and correct.
[If petitioner is an individual whose debts are primarily consumer debts and has chosen to file under chapter 7] I am aware that I may proceed under chapter 7, 11, 12 or 13 of title 11, United States Code, understand the relief available under each such chapter, and choose to proceed under chapter 7.
[If no attorney represents me and no bankruptcy petition preparer signs the petition] I have obtained and read the notice required by 11 U.S.C. § 342(b).

I request relief in accordance with the chapter of title 11, United States Code, specified in this petition.

X ______________________________
Signature of Debtor

X ______________________________
Signature of Joint Debtor

____
Telephone Number (if not represented by attorney)

____
Date

Signature of a Foreign Representative

I declare under penalty of perjury that the information provided in this petition is true and correct, that I am the foreign representative of a debtor in a foreign proceeding, and that I am authorized to file this petition.

(Check only **one** box.)

☐ I request relief in accordance with chapter 15 of title 11, United States Code. Certified copies of the documents required by 11 U.S.C. § 1515 are attached.

☐ Pursuant to 11 U.S.C. § 1511, I request relief in accordance with the chapter of title 11 specified in this petition. A certified copy of the order granting recognition of the foreign main proceeding is attached.

X ______________________________
(Signature of Foreign Representative)

____
(Printed Name of Foreign Representative)

____
Date

Signature of Attorney*

X ______________________________
Signature of Attorney for Debtor(s)

____
Printed Name of Attorney for Debtor(s)

____
Firm Name

____
Address

____

____

____
Telephone Number

____
Date

*In a case in which § 707(b)(4)(D) applies, this signature also constitutes a certification that the attorney has no knowledge after an inquiry that the information in the schedules is incorrect.

Signature of Non-Attorney Bankruptcy Petition Preparer

I declare under penalty of perjury that: (1) I am a bankruptcy petition preparer as defined in 11 U.S.C. § 110; (2) I prepared this document for compensation and have provided the debtor with a copy of this document and the notices and information required under 11 U.S.C. §§ 110(b), 110(h), and 342(b); and, (3) if rules or guidelines have been promulgated pursuant to 11 U.S.C. § 110(h) setting a maximum fee for services chargeable by bankruptcy petition preparers, I have given the debtor notice of the maximum amount before preparing any document for filing for a debtor or accepting any fee from the debtor, as required in that section. Official Form 19 is attached.

____
Printed Name and title, if any, of Bankruptcy Petition Preparer

____
Social-Security number (If the bankruptcy petition preparer is not an individual, state the Social-Security number of the officer, principal, responsible person or partner of the bankruptcy petition preparer.) (Required by 11 U.S.C. § 110.)

____
Address

____

X ______________________________

____
Date

Signature of bankruptcy petition preparer or officer, principal, responsible person, or partner whose Social-Security number is provided above.

Names and Social-Security numbers of all other individuals who prepared or assisted in preparing this document unless the bankruptcy petition preparer is not an individual.

If more than one person prepared this document, attach additional sheets conforming to the appropriate official form for each person.

A bankruptcy petition preparer's failure to comply with the provisions of title 11 and the Federal Rules of Bankruptcy Procedure may result in fines or imprisonment or both. 11 U.S.C. § 110; 18 U.S.C. § 156.

Signature of Debtor (Corporation/Partnership)

I declare under penalty of perjury that the information provided in this petition is true and correct, and that I have been authorized to file this petition on behalf of the debtor.

The debtor requests the relief in accordance with the chapter of title 11, United States Code, specified in this petition.

X ______________________________
Signature of Authorized Individual

____
Printed Name of Authorized Individual

____
Title of Authorized Individual

____
Date

Exhibit 19.16 Proof of claim

B 10 (Official Form 10) (12/08)

UNITED STATES BANKRUPTCY COURT __________ DISTRICT OF __________ | **PROOF OF CLAIM**

Name of Debtor: | Case Number:

NOTE: *This form should not be used to make a claim for an administrative expense arising after the commencement of the case. A request for payment of an administrative expense may be filed pursuant to 11 U.S.C. § 503.*

Name of Creditor (the person or other entity to whom the debtor owes money or property):

Name and address where notices should be sent:

Telephone number:

☐ Check this box to indicate that this claim amends a previously filed claim.

Court Claim Number:_____________
(*If known*)

Filed on:___________________

Name and address where payment should be sent (if different from above):

Telephone number:

☐ Check this box if you are aware that anyone else has filed a proof of claim relating to your claim. Attach copy of statement giving particulars.

☐ Check this box if you are the debtor or trustee in this case.

1. Amount of Claim as of Date Case Filed: $_______________________

If all or part of your claim is secured, complete item 4 below; however, if all of your claim is unsecured, do not complete item 4.

If all or part of your claim is entitled to priority, complete item 5.

☐ Check this box if claim includes interest or other charges in addition to the principal amount of claim. Attach itemized statement of interest or charges.

2. Basis for Claim: ______________________
(See instruction #2 on reverse side.)

3. Last four digits of any number by which creditor identifies debtor: ________________

3a. Debtor may have scheduled account as: ________________
(See instruction #3a on reverse side.)

4. Secured Claim (See instruction #4 on reverse side.)
Check the appropriate box if your claim is secured by a lien on property or a right of setoff and provide the requested information.

Nature of property or right of setoff: ☐ Real Estate ☐ Motor Vehicle ☐ Other
Describe:

Value of Property:$______________ **Annual Interest Rate**___%

Amount of arrearage and other charges as of time case filed included in secured claim,

if any: $______________ **Basis for perfection:** ______________

Amount of Secured Claim: $______________ **Amount Unsecured: $**______________

5. Amount of Claim Entitled to Priority under 11 U.S.C. §507(a). If any portion of your claim falls in one of the following categories, check the box and state the amount.

Specify the priority of the claim.

☐ Domestic support obligations under 11 U.S.C. §507(a)(1)(A) or (a)(1)(B).

☐ Wages, salaries, or commissions (up to $10,950*) earned within 180 days before filing of the bankruptcy petition or cessation of the debtor's business, whichever is earlier – 11 U.S.C. §507 (a)(4).

☐ Contributions to an employee benefit plan – 11 U.S.C. §507 (a)(5).

☐ Up to $2,425* of deposits toward purchase, lease, or rental of property or services for personal, family, or household use – 11 U.S.C. §507 (a)(7).

☐ Taxes or penalties owed to governmental units – 11 U.S.C. §507 (a)(8).

☐ Other – Specify applicable paragraph of 11 U.S.C. §507 (a)(__).

Amount entitled to priority:

$______________

**Amounts are subject to adjustment on 4/1/10 and every 3 years thereafter with respect to cases commenced on or after the date of adjustment.*

6. Credits: The amount of all payments on this claim has been credited for the purpose of making this proof of claim.

7. Documents: Attach redacted copies of any documents that support the claim, such as promissory notes, purchase orders, invoices, itemized statements of running accounts, contracts, judgments, mortgages, and security agreements. You may also attach a summary. Attach redacted copies of documents providing evidence of perfection of a security interest. You may also attach a summary. (*See instruction 7 and definition of "redacted" on reverse side.*)

DO NOT SEND ORIGINAL DOCUMENTS. ATTACHED DOCUMENTS MAY BE DESTROYED AFTER SCANNING.

If the documents are not available, please explain:

Date:

Signature: The person filing this claim must sign it. Sign and print name and title, if any, of the creditor or other person authorized to file this claim and state address and telephone number if different from the notice address above. Attach copy of power of attorney, if any.

FOR COURT USE ONLY

Penalty for presenting fraudulent claim: Fine of up to $500,000 or imprisonment for up to 5 years, or both. 18 U.S.C. §§ 152 and 3571.

debtor's unpaid debts are discharged. The debtor's future income cannot be reached to pay the discharged debt. Thus, a debtor would be left to start life anew without the burden of his or her prepetition debts.

The 2005 act substantially restricts the ability of many debtors to obtain a Chapter 7 liquidation bankruptcy because it adds certain *median income* and dollar-based *means* tests that must be met before a debtor is permitted to obtain a discharge of debts under Chapter 7. If these tests are not met, the 2005 act provides that the debtor's Chapter 7 proceeding may, with the debtor's consent, be dismissed or be converted to a Chapter 13 or Chapter 11 bankruptcy proceeding.

In a Chapter 7 bankruptcy, the property of the estate is sold and the proceeds are distributed to satisfy allowed claims. The remaining unpaid debts that the debtor incurred prior to the date of the order for relief are discharged. **Chapter 7 discharge** means that the debtor is no longer legally responsible for paying those claims. Only individual debtors may be granted discharge. Unsecured claims are to be satisfied out of the bankruptcy estate in order of their statutory priority, as established by the Bankruptcy Code.

Chapter 7 discharge The termination of the legal duty of a debtor to pay unsecured debts that remain unpaid upon the completion of a Chapter 7 proceeding.

Example Annabelle finds herself overburdened with debt, particularly credit card debt. At the time she files for Chapter 7 bankruptcy, her unsecured credit is $100,000. Annabelle has few assets, and most of those are exempt property (such as her clothes and some furniture). Her nonexempt property is $10,000, which will be sold to raise cash. The $10,000 in cash will be distributed to her debtors on a pro rata basis; that is, each creditor will receive ten cents for every dollar of debt owed. The other $90,000 is *discharged*, that is, the creditors have to absorb this loss. Annabelle is free from this debt forever. Annabelle is given a "fresh start" and her future earnings are hers.

Chapter 13 adjustment of debts of an individual with regular income A rehabilitation form of bankruptcy that permits bankruptcy courts to supervise the debtor's plan for the payment of unpaid debts in installments over the plan period.

Chapter 13 discharge A discharge in a Chapter 13 case that is granted to the debtor after the debtor's plan of payment is completed (which could be up to three or up to five years).

Chapter 13: Adjustment of Debts of an Individual with Regular Income

Chapter 13, which is called **adjustment of debts of an individual with regular income,** is a rehabilitation form of bankruptcy for individuals. Chapter 13 permits a qualified debtor to propose a plan to pay all or a portion of the debts that he or she owes in installments over a specified period of time, pursuant to the requirements of Chapter 13. The bankruptcy court supervises the debtor's plan for the payment. A Chapter 13 proceeding can be initiated only by the voluntary filing of a petition by an individual debtor with regular income. The 2005 act establishes dollar limits on the secured and unsecured debt that a debtor may have in order to qualify to file for Chapter 13 bankruptcy.

The debtor must file a plan of payment and information about his or her finances, including a budget of estimated income and expenses during the period of the plan. The Chapter 13 plan may be either up to three years or up to five years, depending on requirements established by the 2005 act. A Chapter 13 plan of payment may modify the rights of unsecured creditors and some secured creditors.

The court will grant an order discharging the debtor from all unpaid unsecured debts covered by the plan after all the payments required under the plan are completed (which could be up to three years or up to five years). This is called a **Chapter 13 discharge.**

DISCHARGE OF STUDENT LOANS

SIDEBAR

While they attend college and other professional schools, many students borrow money for their tuition and living expenses. Upon graduation, when a student might have large student loans and very few assets, the student might be inclined to file for bankruptcy in an attempt to have his or her student loans discharged.

To prevent such abuse of bankruptcy law, Congress amended the Bankruptcy Code to make it more difficult for students to have their student loans discharged in bankruptcy. Student loans are defined by the Bankruptcy Code to include loans made by or guaranteed by governmental units. The 2005 act added to this definition student loans made by nongovernmental commercial institutions, such as banks, as well as funds for scholarships, benefits, or stipends granted by educational institutions.

The Bankruptcy Code now states that student loans can be discharged in bankruptcy only if the nondischarge would cause an "undue hardship" to the debtor and his or her dependants. Undue hardship is construed strictly and would be difficult for a debtor to prove unless he or she could show severe physical or mental disability or the inability to pay for the basic necessities of food or shelter for himself or herself and any dependents.

Cosigners (such as parents who guarantee their child's student loan) must also meet the heightened undue hardship test to discharge their obligation.

Example Annabelle owes unsecured credit of $100,000. Annabelle earns too high an income to qualify for Chapter 7 bankruptcy, so she files for Chapter 13 bankruptcy. Her plan of payment, whereby she will pay $700 disposable income each month for five years toward her prepetition debts, is accepted by the court. During the five-year period, Annabelle's lifestyle will be reduced considerably because she will be using her disposable income to pay off her prepetition debt. At the end of five years, she will have paid $42,000 (60 months × $700) toward her debt; at that time her unpaid prepetition debt of $58,000 ($100,000 – $42,000) will be discharged.

Chapter 11: Reorganization

Chapter 11 of the Bankruptcy Code provides a method for reorganizing a debtor's financial affairs under the supervision of the bankruptcy court. The goal of Chapter 11 is to reorganize the debtor with a new capital structure so that it will emerge from bankruptcy as a viable concern. This option is referred to as **reorganization bankruptcy.** The majority of Chapter 11 proceedings are filed by corporations that want to reorganize their capital structures by receiving discharge of a portion of their debts, obtain relief from burdensome contracts, and emerge from bankruptcy as going concerns.

Chapter 11 reorganization bankruptcy A bankruptcy method that allows the reorganization of the debtor's financial affairs under the supervision of the bankruptcy court.

In a Chapter 11 proceeding, the court will appoint a **creditors' committee** composed of representatives of the class of unsecured claims. The court may also appoint a committee of secured creditors and a committee of equity holders. Committees may appear at bankruptcy court hearings, participate in the negotiation of a plan of reorganization, assert objections to proposed plans of reorganization, and the like.

The debtor has the exclusive right to file a **plan of reorganization** with the bankruptcy court within the first 120 days after the date of the order for relief. Under the 2005 act, this period may be extended up to 18 months. If the debtor fails to do so, any party of interest (such as a trustee, a creditor, an equity holder) may propose a plan.

Plan of reorganization A plan that sets forth a proposed new capital structure for the debtor to have when it emerges from Chapter 11 reorganization bankruptcy.

A debtor in a Chapter 11 bankruptcy has the following benefits:

1. ***Automatic stay.*** The filing of a Chapter 11 petition stays (that is, suspends) actions by creditors to recover the debtor's property. This **automatic stay** suspends legal actions against the debtor or the debtor's property, including the ability of creditors to foreclose on assets given as collateral for their loans to the debtor. An automatic stay is extremely important to a business trying to reorganize under Chapter 11 because the debtor needs to keep its assets to stay in business.

   Example Big Oil Company owns a manufacturing plant and has borrowed $50 million from a bank and used the plant as collateral for the loan. If Big Oil Company files for Chapter 11 bankruptcy, the automatic stay prevents the bank from foreclosing and taking the property. Once out of bankruptcy, Big Oil Company must pay the bank any unpaid arrearages and begin making the required loan payments again.

2. ***Executory contract or unexpired lease.*** Another major benefit of Chapter 11 bankruptcy is that the debtor is given the opportunity to accept or reject certain executory contracts and unexpired leases. An **executory contract** or **unexpired lease** is a contract or lease that has not been fully performed.

   Example Big Oil Company enters into a three-year contract to sell oil to another company, and there are two years to go on the contract when the oil

Executory contract or unexpired lease A contract or lease that has not been fully performed. With the bankruptcy court's approval, executor contracts and unexpired leases may be rejected by a debtor in bankruptcy.

company files for Chapter 11 bankruptcy. This is an *executory contract*. Big Oil Company has leased an office building for 20 years from a landlord to use as its headquarters, and there are 15 years left on the lease when the oil company declares bankruptcy. This is an *unexpired lease*. In the Chapter 11 reorganization proceeding, Big Oil Company can reject (get out of) either the executory contract or the unexpired lease without any liability; it can also keep either one if doing so is in its best interests.

3. ***Discharge.*** In its plan of reorganization, the debtor will propose reducing its unsecured debt so that it can come out of bankruptcy with fewer debts to pay than when it filed for bankruptcy. If the plan is approved by the creditors and the court, the court will confirm the plan of reorganization. Any unsecured debt that is not carried forward with the reorganized firm is **discharged;** that is, the creditors have to absorb the loss.

   Example Big Oil Company has $100 million secured debts (such as real estate mortgages and personal property–secured transactions) and $100 million unsecured credit when it files for Chapter 11 bankruptcy. In its plan of reorganization, Big Oil Company proposes to eliminate 60 percent—$60 million—of unsecured credit. If the unsecured creditors agree and the court approves, then Big Oil will emerge from bankruptcy owing only $40 million of prepetition unsecured debt. The other $60 million is discharged and the creditors can never recover these debts in the future.

There must be **confirmation** of the plan of reorganization by the bankruptcy court for the debtor to be reorganized under Chapter 11. The bankruptcy court will confirm a plan of reorganization under the acceptance method if the plan is feasible (that is, the new, reorganized company is likely to succeed if other necessary requirements are met). If a class of creditors does not accept the plan, the plan can still be confirmed by the court, using the Bankruptcy Code's **cram-down provision.** In order for the court to confirm a plan over the objection of a class of creditors, certain requirements as established by bankruptcy law must be met.

Confirmation The bankruptcy court's approval of a plan of reorganization.

Chapter 12: Family Farmer and Family Fisherman Bankruptcy

The 2005 act establishes special definitions and rules that allow family farmers and family fishermen to file for bankruptcy reorganization under **Chapter 12—adjustment of debts of a family farmer or fisherman with regular income.** *Family farmer* and *family fisherman* are defined by the 2005 act.

Chapter 12—adjustment of debts of a family farmer or fisherman with regular income A form of bankruptcy reorganization permitted to be used by family farmers and family fishermen.

The family farmer or family fisherman debtor must file a plan of reorganization. Generally, the plan may provide for payments to creditors over a period no longer than three years, but the court can increase the period up to five years based on a showing of cause. The plan of reorganization, which must be confirmed by the court before it becomes operable, can modify the rights of secured creditors and unsecured creditors.

Once the family farmer or family fisherman debtor has made all payments required by the plan (which is usually for three years but could be up to five years), the bankruptcy court will grant the debtor discharge of all debts provided for by the plan. This is called a **Chapter 12 discharge.**

Chapter 12 discharge A discharge in a Chapter 12 case that is granted to a family farmer or family fisherman debtor after the debtor's plan of payment is completed (which is usually three years but could be up to five years).

Example If a Chapter 12 plan calls for the debtor to pay 55 percent of the outstanding unsecured debt to the unsecured creditors and this amount has been paid by the debtor during the plan period, the court will grant discharge of the unpaid 45 percent of this unsecured debt.

The ethical duty of a paralegal professional not to use confidential information is discussed in the following feature.

Learning Objective 10
Explain a paralegal's duty not to use confidential information.

ETHICAL PERSPECTIVE

Duty Not to Use Confidential Information

Mr. Drovski is a paralegal who works at a very large law firm that represents major corporate clients. He works directly for Ms. Ross, a senior partner of the law firm and an expert in mergers and acquisitions law.

One day Ms. Ross asks Mr. Drovski to accompany her to a meeting at the corporate offices of MicroHard Corporation, a client of the law firm. The corporation is one of the largest multinational corporations in the United States. Ms. Wong, the chief executive officer (CEO) of MicroHard Corporation, and other top corporate officers of the corporation, attend the meeting.

At the meeting, Ms. Wong and the other executives disclose that they want MicroHard Corporation to make a secret tender offer to purchase the stock of Quail Technology Inc. from the shareholders of Quail Technology Inc. Ms. Wong explains that Quail Technology Inc. holds many patents that would be beneficial to MicroHard Corporation and says that her corporation wants Ms. Ross and her law firm to draft the documents necessary to make this secret tender offer. The drafting of these documents will take three weeks. Ms. Ross agrees, on behalf of her law firm, to represent MicroHard Corporation and draft the legal documents necessary for MicroHard Corporation's acquisition of Quail Technology Inc.

Ms. Wong also says that the purchase price that MicroHard Corporation will offer for each share of Quail Technology Inc. stock in the tender offer will be $50 per share. Quail Technology Inc.'s stock is currently priced at $30 per share on the New York Stock Exchange.

Ms. Wong stresses that the preparation of the legal documents for the tender offer must remain an utmost secret while Ms. Ross and her law firm prepare the necessary documents for the tender offer. Ms. Ross assures Ms. Wong that she and the personnel of her law firm will keep the tender offer secret while they draft the necessary legal documents.

Later that day, Mr. Drovski, who sat through the entire meeting and heard everything that was said, is tempted to call a securities broker and purchase 4,000 shares of Quail Technology Inc. stock.

Does Mr. Drovski owe a duty not to use this confidential information to benefit himself?

Many model and state paralegal professional codes of ethics and responsibility provide that a paralegal should not use confidential information obtained while he or she is working as a paralegal. A violation of these codes could lead to the paralegal's being censored or facing other disciplinary actions from paralegal licensing agencies, cause pecuniary loss to the law firm's clients, cause a loss to the law firm such as that of a client's trust and possibly the client's business, and result in the paralegal's being sued for violating the law, in this case both state and federal securities laws.

PARALEGAL'S ETHICAL DECISION

Thus, Mr. Drovski owes an ethical duty not to use the confidential information that he heard regarding MicroHard Corporation's proposed tender offer for shares of Quail Technology Inc. stock. To do so would violate paralegal ethical and social responsibility codes, the law firm's rules, and the law. Mr. Drovski must refrain from using the confidential information for his own benefit or that of others.

Concept Review *and* Reinforcement

LEGAL TERMINOLOGY

Alien corporation 702
Alter-ego doctrine 708
Articles of incorporation 702
Articles of limited liability partnership 697
Articles of limited partnership 694
Articles of organization 699
Articles of partnership 691
Automatic stay 722
Bankruptcy Abuse Prevention and Consumer Protection Act of 2005 713
Bankruptcy courts 714
Bankruptcy estate 716
Board of directors 709
Business judgment rule 712
Business organization 686
Bylaws 705
Certificate of limited partnership 693
Chapter 7 discharge 721
Chapter 7 liquidation bankruptcy (straight bankruptcy) 716
Chapter 11 reorganization bankruptcy 722
Chapter 12—adjustment of debts of a family farmer or fisherman with regular income 723
Chapter 12 discharge 723
Chapter 13 adjustment of debts of an individual with regular income 721
Chapter 13 discharge 721
Code of ethics 713
Common shareholders 708
Common stock 708
Confirmation 723
Corporate bylaws 705
Corporate charter 702
Corporate officers 701
Corporate resolutions 705
Corporation 700
Court of Chancery 710
Cram-down provision 723
Creditors' committee 722
d.b.a. (doing business as) 687
Delaware General Corporation Law 710
Discharged 723
Disregard the corporate entity 708
Domestic corporation 702
Duty of care 712
Duty of loyalty 711
Entity theory 690
Executory contract or unexpired lease 722
Exempt property 716
Fictitious business name statement 687
Foreign corporation 702
Form 2553 708
Fraudulent transfers 716
General partner (partner) 689
General partnership (partnership) 689
Homestead exemption 716
Incorporation 702
Inside director 709
Involuntary petition 715
Joint and several liability 691
Joint liability 691
Limited liability 694
Limited liability company (LLC) 698
Limited liability partnership (LLP) 694
Limited partners 693
Limited partnership 692
Limited partnership agreement 694
Member 698
Negligence 712
Operating agreement 699
Organizational meeting 705
Outside director 710
Partnership agreement 689
Partnership at will 692
Partnership for a term 692
Personal liability 688
Petition 715
Piercing the corporate veil 708
Plan of reorganization 722
Proof of claim 716
Proof of interest 716
Reorganization bankruptcy 722
Revised Model Business Corporation Act (RMBCA) 701
Revised Uniform Limited Partnership Act (RULPA) 692
S corporation 705
Sarbanes-Oxley Act of 2002 (SOX) 713
Shareholders 700
Sole proprietor 686
Sole proprietorship 686
State of incorporation 702
Trustee 716
Uniform Limited Liability Company Act (ULLCA) 698
Uniform Limited Liability Partnership Act (ULLPA) 697
Uniform Limited Partnership Act (ULPA) 692
Uniform Partnership Act (UPA) 690
Unlimited liability 694
Voluntary petition 715
Wrongful dissolution 692

SUMMARY OF KEY CONCEPTS

Sole Proprietorship

	A sole proprietorship is a form of business in which the owner and the business are one; the business is not a separate legal entity.
Business Name	A sole proprietorship can operate under the name of the sole proprietor, or under a *trade name*. Operating under a trade name is commonly designated as *d.b.a. (doing business as)*. If a trade name is used, a *fictitious business name statement* must be filed with the appropriate state government office.
Liability	The sole proprietor is personally liable for the debts and obligations of the sole proprietorship.

General Partnership

	A general partnership is an association of two or more persons to carry on as co-owners of a business for profit [UPA Section 6(1)].
Uniform Partnership Act (UPA)	The UPA is a model act that codifies partnership law. Most states have adopted all or part of the UPA.
Entity Theory of Partnerships	The entity theory holds that partnerships are *separate legal entities* that can hold title to personal and real property, transact business in the partnership name, and the like.
Taxation of Partnerships	Partnerships do not pay federal income taxes; the income and losses of partnerships flow onto individual partners' federal income tax returns.
Partnership Agreement	The partnership agreement establishes a general partnership and sets forth terms of the partnership. It is good practice to have a written partnership agreement that the partners sign.
Partners' Contract Authority	A contract entered into by a partner with a third party on behalf of a partnership is binding on the partnership.
Tort Liability	1. *Tort:* A partner causes injury to a third party by his or her negligent act, breach of trust, breach of fiduciary duty, or intentional tort. 2. *Partnership liability:* The partnership is liable to third persons who are injured by torts committed by a partner while he or she is acting within the ordinary course of partnership business. 3. *Joint and several liability of partners:* Partners are personally liable for torts committed by partners acting on partnership business. This liability is *joint and several*, which means that the plaintiff can sue one or more of the partners separately. If successful, the plaintiff can recover the entire amount of the judgment from any or all of the defendant–partners.
Dissolution of Partnerships	Dissolution is a change in the relation of the partners caused by any partner ceasing to be associated in carrying on the business [UPA Section 29]. Wrongful dissolution occurs when a partner withdraws from a partnership without having the *right* to do so at the time. The partner is then liable for damages caused by wrongful dissolution of the partnership.

Limited Partnership

Uniform Limited Partnership Act (ULPA)	The ULPA is a 1916 model act that contains a uniform set of provisions for the formation, operation, and dissolution of limited partnerships.

Revised Uniform Limited Partnership Act (RULPA)	The RULPA is a 1976 revision of the ULPA that provides a more modern, comprehensive law for the formation, operation, and dissolution of limited partnerships.
General and Limited Partnerships	1. *General partners:* Partners in a limited partnership who invest capital, manage the business, and are personally liable for partnership debts. 2. *Limited partners:* Partners in a limited partnership who invest capital but do not participate in management and are not personally liable for partnership debts beyond their capital contributions.
Formation of Limited Partnerships	1. *Certificate of limited partnership:* A document that two or more persons must execute and sign that establishes a limited partnership. The certificate of limited partnership must be filed with the secretary of state of the appropriate state. 2. *Limited partnership agreement:* A document that sets forth the rights and duties of general and limited partners; the terms and conditions regarding the operation, termination, and dissolution of the partnership; and so on.
Liability of General and Limited Partners	1. *General partners:* General partners of a limited partnership have *unlimited personal liability* for the debts and obligations of the limited partnership. 2. *Limited partners:* Limited partners of a limited partnership are liable only for the debts and obligations of the limited partnership up to their capital contributions. 3. *Limited partners and management:* Limited partners have no right to participate in the management of the partnership. A limited partner is *liable as a general partner* if his or her participation in the control of the business is substantially the same as that of a general partner, but the limited partner is liable only to persons who reasonably believe him or her to be a general partner.

Limited Liability Partnership (LLP)

	The LLP is a form of business in which there does not have to be a general partner who is personally liable for debts and obligations of the partnership. All partners are limited partners and stand to lose only their capital contribution should the partnership fail. LLPs are formed by accountants and other professionals as allowed by LLP law.
Partners	The partners are owners of an LLP.
Articles of Partnership	Articles of partnership constitute a document that the partners of an LLP must execute, sign, and file with the secretary of state of the appropriate state to form an LLP.
Taxation	An LLP does not pay federal income taxes unless it elects to do so. If an LLP is taxed as a partnership, the income and losses of the LLP flow onto individual partners' federal income tax returns.

Limited Liability Company (LLC)

	The LLC is a special form of unincorporated business entity that combines the tax benefits of a partnership with the limited personal liability attribute of a corporation.
Members	Members are owners of an LLC.
Articles of Organization	Articles of organization constitute a document that owners of an LLC must execute, sign, and file with the secretary of state of the appropriate state to form an LLC.

Operating Agreement	An operating agreement is entered into by members that govern the affairs and business of the LLC and the relations among partners, managers, and the LLC.
Taxation	An LLC does not pay federal income taxes unless it elects to do so. If an LLC is taxed as a partnership, the income and losses of the LLP flow onto individual members' federal income tax returns.
Corporation	
	A corporation is a legal entity created pursuant to the laws of the state of incorporation. A corporation is a separate legal entity—an *artificial person*—that can own property, sue and be sued, enter into contracts, and such.
Characteristics of Corporations	1. *Limited liability of shareholders:* Shareholders are liable for the debts and obligations of the corporation only to the extent of their capital contributions. 2. *Free transferability of shares:* Shares of a corporation are freely transferable by the shareholders unless they are expressly restricted. 3. *Perpetual existence:* Corporations exist in perpetuity unless a specific duration is stated in the corporation's articles of incorporation. 4. *Centralized management:* The *board of directors* of the corporation makes policy decisions of the corporation. Corporate *officers* appointed by the board of directors run the corporation's day-to-day operations. Together, the directors and officers form the corporation's management.
Business Corporation Acts	1. *Model Business Corporation Act (MBCA):* A model act drafted in 1950 that was intended to provide a uniform law for the regulation of corporations. 2. *Revised Model Business Corporation Act (RMBCA):* A revision of the MBCA promulgated in 1984 that arranged the provisions of the model to act more logically, revised the language to be more consistent, and made substantial changes that modernized the provisions of the act.
Classifications of Corporations	1. *Domestic corporation:* A corporation in the state in which it is incorporated. 2. *Foreign corporation:* A corporation in any state other than the one in which it is incorporated. A domestic corporation often transacts business in states other than its state of incorporation; hence, it is a foreign corporation in these other states. A foreign corporation must obtain a *certificate of authority* from these other states to be able to transact intrastate business in those states. 3. *Alien corporation:* A corporation that is incorporated in another country. Alien corporations are treated as foreign corporations for most purposes.
Incorporation Procedure	Incorporation is the process of incorporating (forming) a new corporation. Although a corporation may be incorporated in only one state, it may conduct business in other states.
Articles of Incorporation	1. The articles of incorporation are the basic governing document of a corporation; it must be filed with the secretary of state of the state of incorporation. This is a public document and is also called the *corporate charter.* 2. The corporation code of each state sets out the information that must be included in the articles of incorporation. Additional information may be included in the articles of incorporation as deemed necessary or desirable by the incorporators.
Corporate Bylaws	Corporate bylaws are a detailed set of rules adopted by the board of directors after the corporation is formed; they contain provisions for managing the business and affairs of the corporation. This document does not have to be filed with the secretary of state.

Organizational Meeting	An organizational meeting must be held by the initial directors of the corporation after the articles of incorporation are filed. At this meeting the directors adopt the bylaws, elect corporate officers, ratify promoters' contracts, adopt a corporate seal, and transact such other business as may come before the meeting.
Common Stock	Common stock is a type of equity security that represents the *residual value* of the corporation. Common stock has no preferences, and its shareholders are paid dividends and assets upon liquidation only after creditors and preferred shareholders have been paid. 1. *Common shareholder:* A person who owns common stock. 2. *Common stock certificate:* A document that represents the common shareholders' investment in the corporation.
Liability of Shareholders	1. Shareholders of corporations typically have *limited liability;* that is, they are liable for the debts and obligations of the corporation only to the extent of their capital contributions to the corporation. 2. Shareholders may be found *personally liable* for the debts and obligations of the corporation under the doctrine called *piercing the corporate veil.* Courts can disregard the corporate entity and hold shareholders personally liable for the debts and obligations of the corporation if (a) the corporation has been formed without sufficient capital (*thin capitalization*), or (b) separateness has not been maintained between the corporation and its shareholders (such as the commingling of personal and corporate assets, failure to hold required shareholders' meetings, and such). Also called the *alter-ego doctrine.*
Board of Directors	The board of directors is a panel of decision makers for the corporation, the members of which are elected by the shareholders. The directors of a corporation are responsible for formulating the policy decisions affecting the corporation, such as deciding what businesses to engage in, determining the capital structure of the corporation, selecting and removing top officers of the corporation, and the like. 1. *Inside director:* A member of the board of directors who is also an officer of the corporation. 2. *Outside director:* A member of the board of directors who is not an officer of the corporation.
Meetings of the Board of Directors	1. *Regular meeting:* A meeting of the board of directors held at the time and place scheduled in the bylaws. 2. *Special meeting:* A meeting of the board of directors convened to discuss an important or emergency matter, such as a proposed merger, a hostile takeover attempt, and such. 3. *Written consents:* The board of directors acting without a meeting if all of the directors sign written consents that set forth the action taken.
Corporate Officers	*Officers:* Employees of the corporation who are appointed by the board of directors to manage the *day-to-day operations* of the corporation. 1. *Duty of loyalty:* A duty that directors and officers have not to act adversely to the interests of the corporation and to subordinate their personal interests to those of the corporation and its shareholders. 2. *Duty of care:* A duty that corporate directors and officers have to use care and diligence when acting on behalf of the corporation. This duty is discharged if they perform their duties (a) in good faith, (b) with the care that an *ordinary prudent person* in a like position would use under similar circumstances, and (c) in a manner they reasonably believe to be in the best interests of the corporation. a. *Negligence:* Failure of a corporate director or officer to exercise this duty of care when conducting the corporation's business. b. *Business judgment rule:* A rule that says directors and officers are not liable to the corporation or its shareholders for honest mistakes of judgment.

Sarbanes-Oxley Act (SOX)	A federal statute that makes certain conduct by public companies and their officers and directors illegal and establishes criminal penalties for violations. The act also prompts public companies to adopt a code of ethics.
Bankruptcy	
Bankruptcy Law	1. *Bankruptcy Reform Act of 1978, as amended:* This federal statute establishes the requirements and procedures for filing for bankruptcy. 2. *Bankruptcy Abuse Prevention and Consumer Protection Act of 2005:* This federal act substantially amends federal bankruptcy law. The 2005 act makes it more difficult for debtors to file for bankruptcy and have their unpaid debts discharged. 3. *Bankruptcy courts:* Bankruptcy courts have exclusive jurisdiction to hear bankruptcy cases. A bankruptcy court is attached to each federal district court. Bankruptcy judges are appointed for 14-year terms.
Bankruptcy Procedure	1. *Filing of a petition:* The filing of a petition commences a bankruptcy case. a. *Voluntary petition:* A voluntary petition is filed by a debtor. b. *Involuntary petition:* An involuntary petition is filed by a creditor or creditors. 2. *Proof of claims:* Each unsecured creditor must file proof of claim, stating the amount of its claim against the debtors.
The Bankruptcy Estate	The *bankruptcy estate* includes: 1. All the debtor's legal and equitable interests in real, personal, tangible, and intangible property at the time the petition is filed. 2. Gifts, inheritances, life insurance proceeds, and property from divorce settlements that the debtor is entitled to receive within 180 days after the petition is filed.
Exempt Property	The Bankruptcy Code permits the debtor to retain certain property that does not become part of the bankruptcy estate. Exemptions are stipulated in federal and state law.
Types of Bankruptcy	1. *Chapter 7—Liquidation bankruptcy:* A form of bankruptcy where the debtor's nonexempt property is sold for cash, the cash is distributed to the creditors, and unpaid debts are discharged. a. *Median income and means tests:* The 2005 act establishes certain median income and means tests that a debtor must meet in order to qualify for Chapter 7 liquidation relief. b. *Discharge of student loans:* A student loan may be discharged after it is due only if nondischarge would cause an *undue hardship* on the debtor or his or her family. 2. *Chapter 13—Adjustment of debts of an individual with regular income:* A rehabilitation form of bankruptcy that permits bankruptcy courts to supervise the debtor's plan for the repayment of unpaid debts by installment. Called *consumer debt adjustment*. The court will grant an order discharging the debtor from all unpaid debts covered by the plan only after all the payments required under the plan are completed. 3. *Chapter 11—Reorganization bankruptcy:* A form of bankruptcy for reorganizing the debtor's financial affairs under the supervision of the bankruptcy court. The debtor files a plan of reorganization that sets forth the debtor's proposed new capital structure. A plan of reorganization must be confirmed by the bankruptcy court before it becomes effective. Upon confirmation of a plan of reorganization, the debtor is granted a discharge of all claims not included in the plan. The debtor's legal obligation to pay the discharged debts is terminated. 4. *Chapter 12—Family farmer and family fisherman bankruptcy:* A rehabilitation form of bankruptcy that provides a method for reorganizing the family farmer or family fisherman debtor's financial affairs under the supervision of the bankruptcy court.

WORKING THE WEB

1. Use the website http://google.com or a similar Internet search engine to find an Internet business that provides services to incorporate a corporation. Look over the website and write a one-half-page report on what you found, answering questions such as how fast a corporation can be formed and how much it costs to do so.
2. Visit the website http://www.business.gov Where the words "Access Additional Information by" appear on the screen, click on "Region." On the map that appears, click on your state, and then click on "Starting a Business." Find out how to reserve a business or corporate name in your state. Write a one-page report about this process.
3. Visit the website http://www.sba.gov/regions/states. Whose website is this? Click on your state on the map. Read "About Us." Write a one-half-page report on what this organization does.

CRITICAL THINKING & WRITING QUESTIONS

1. Define "sole proprietorship." Describe the liability of a sole proprietor.
2. What does the term *d.b.a. (doing business as)* mean? How is it obtained?
3. Define "general partnership." Describe the liability of general partners.
4. Explain the difference between *joint liability* and *joint and several liability*.
5. Define "limited partnership." What is the liability exposure of (a) a general partner and (b) a limited partner? Explain.
6. Define "limited liability partnership (LLP)." Describe the liability of its partners.
7. Define "limited liability company (LLC)." Describe the liability of its members.
8. Define "corporation." Describe the liability of shareholders.
9. Describe the difference among (a) a domestic corporation, (b) a foreign corporation, and (c) an alien corporation.
10. Describe the following: (a) articles of incorporation, (b) bylaws, and (c) organizational meeting.
11. Explain the difference between a C corporation and an S corporation. How is S corporation status obtained?
12. Describe the function of the board of directors of a corporation. What is the difference between an *inside director* and an *outside director*?
13. Define a corporate officer's and a director's duty of loyalty. Give examples of breaches of this duty.
14. Define a corporate officer's and a director's duty of care. When is this duty breached?

Building Paralegal Skills

VIDEO CASE STUDIES

A Corporate Officer Seeks Legal Counsel: Conflict of Interest

The owner of a trucking company that is experiencing financial difficulty is meeting with his attorney to investigate potential alternatives for continuing with the business. The owner is concerned because he has been told that the court may try to pierce the corporate veil and hold him personally responsible for a judgment for which there is not enough insurance.

After viewing the video case study in MyLegalStudiesLab, answer the following:

1. Are the stockholders or officers of a corporation liable for the debts of the corporation?
2. What are the different kinds of legal entities that may be used to offer some protection from personal liability?
3. Is it ethical or legal to transfer a potential asset of the corporation to a new company owned by an officer or stockholder of the original corporation?

ETHICS ANALYSIS & DISCUSSION QUESTIONS

1. May a paralegal be a partner in a law firm?
2. May a paralegal be a partner with a client of the law firm?
3. Because of the volume of work and an impending deadline, you are hired as a temporary paralegal in a large Wall Street law firm to work on a case involving a major corporate client. One of the lawyers tells you that the client will soon announce a major breakthrough that will lead to a highly profitable business opportunity. May a paralegal take advantage of inside information learned about a public corporate client to trade in stock of the client?

DEVELOPING YOUR COLLABORATION SKILLS

With a group of other students selected by you or your instructor, review the facts of the following case. As a group, discuss the following questions.

1. What is a limited liability company (LLC)?
2. What is the liability of member–owners of an LLC?
3. What was the name of the LLC in this case? Who were the owners of the LLC?
4. What entities entered into the contract at issue in this case?
5. Is Richard Hess personally liable for the debt owed by the LLC?

Siva v. 1138 LLC

Five members—Richard Hess, Robert Haines, Lisa Hess, Nathan Hess, and Zack Shahin—formed a limited liability company called 1138 LLC. Ruthiran Siva owned a commercial building located at 1138 Bethel Road, Franklin County, Ohio. Siva entered into a written lease agreement with 1138 LLC whereby 1138 LLC leased premises in Siva's commercial building for a term of five years, at a monthly rental of $4,000. 1138 LLC began operating a bar on the premises. Six months later, 1138 LLC was in default and in breach of the lease agreement. Siva sued 1138 LLC and Richard Hess to recover damages. Siva received a default judgment against 1138 LLC, but there was no money in 1138 LLC to pay the judgment. Hess, who had been sued personally, defended, arguing that as a member–owner of the LLC, he was not personally liable for the debts of the LLC. The trial court found in favor of Hess and dismissed Siva's complaint against Hess. Siva appealed.

Source: Siva v. 1138 LLC, 2007 Ohio 4667, Web 2007 Ohio App. Lexis 4202 (Court of Appeals of Ohio)

PARALEGAL PORTFOLIO EXERCISE

Locate on the Internet or in the library a source that explains the requirements for preparing the articles of incorporation for a new corporation to be formed in your state, and prepare those articles. Select a corporate name, and make up other information that you need to complete the articles of incorporation.

LEGAL ANALYSIS & WRITING CASES

Bank of America, N.A. v. Barr, 9 A.3d 816 (2010)

Supreme Judicial Court of Maine

Constance Barr was the sole owner of The Stone Scone, a business operated as a sole proprietorship. Based on documents signed by Barr on behalf of The Stone Scone, Fleet Bank approved a $100,000 unsecured small business line of credit for The Stone Scone. Fleet Bank sent a letter addressed to Barr and The Stone Scone, which stated, "Dear Constance H Barr: Congratulations! Your company has been approved for a $100,000 Small Business Credit Express Line of Credit." The bank sent account statements addressed to both The Stone Scone and Barr. For four years, Fleet Bank provided funds to The Stone Scone. After that time, however, The Stone Scone did not make any further payments on the loan, leaving $91,444 unpaid principal. Pursuant to the loan agreement, interest on the unpaid principal balance continued to accrue at a rate of 6.5 percent per year. Bank of America, N.A., which had acquired Fleet Bank, sued The Stone Scone and Barr to recover the unpaid principal and interest. Barr stipulated to a judgment against The Stone Scone, which she had converted to [a] limited liability company, but denied personal responsibility for the unpaid debt.

Question

1. Is Barr, the sole owner of The Stone Scone, personally liable for the unpaid debt to the bank?

In re Lebovitz, 344 B.R. 556, Web 2006 Bankr. Lexis 1044

United States Bankruptcy Court for the Western District of Tennessee

Dr. Morris Lebovitz and Kerrye Hill Lebovitz, husband and wife, were residents of the state of Tennessee. Dr. Lebovitz filed for bankruptcy protection as a result of illness. Mrs. Lebovitz (Debtor) filed for bankruptcy because she had cosigned on a large loan with Dr. Lebovitz. Debtor is the owner of the following pieces of jewelry: a Tiffany 5-carat diamond engagement ring (purchase price $40,000–$50,000), a pair of diamond stud earrings of approximately 1 carat each, a diamond drop necklace of approximately 1 carat, and a Cartier watch. All these items were gifts from Dr. Lebovitz.

Tennessee opted out of the federal bankruptcy exemption provisions and adopted its own bankruptcy exemption provisions. Tennessee does not provide for an exemption for jewelry. Tennessee does provide for an exemption for "necessary and proper wearing apparel." Debtor claimed that her jewelry was necessary and proper wearing apparel and was therefore exempt property from the bankruptcy estate. The bankruptcy trustee filed an objection to the claim of exemption, arguing that Debtor's jewelry does not qualify for an exemption and should be part of the bankruptcy estate.

Question

1. Does Debtor's jewelry qualify as necessary and proper wearing apparel and therefore is exempt property from the bankruptcy estate?

WORKING WITH THE LANGUAGE OF THE COURT CASE

Menendez v. O'Niell

986 So.2d 255
United States Court of Appeals, Sixth Circuit

Read and then brief the following case, excerpted from the Court of Appeals opinion. In your brief, answer the following questions.

1. Who is the plaintiff? Who is the plaintiff suing on behalf of?
2. Who are the defendants?
3. What is the *alter-ego doctrine*?
4. Is Marc Fraioli liable? Why or why not?

Welch, Justice

In this appeal, plaintiff, Lissette Savoy Menendez, challenges a summary judgment entered by the trial court dismissing defendant, Marc Fraioli, from this tort litigation. We affirm.

On February 22, 2004, a vehicle driven by Michael O'Niell crashed while travelling on Louisiana Highway 30 in East Baton Rouge Parish. Vanessa Savoy, a 19-year[-]old guest passenger in the vehicle, sustained severe injuries as a result of the collision. On April 20, 2004, Vanessa's tutrix, Lissette Savoy Menendez, filed this lawsuit seeking to recover damages arising from the collision on behalf of her daughter. Named as defendants were Michael O'Niell and Progressive Security Insurance Company, the alleged insurer of O'Niell. In the petition, plaintiff alleged that O'Niell was intoxicated at the time of the accident and that his intoxication caused the collision.

In a supplemental and amending petition, plaintiff added additional defendants to the litigation, including Triumvirate of Baton Rouge, Inc., d/b/a Fred's Bar and Grill and its owner, Marc Fraioli. In the petition, plaintiff alleged that O'Niell, who was under the legal drinking age, consumed alcohol at Fred's...on the evening of the accident. She asserted that O'Niell became intoxicated as a result of the negligent supervision of the bar employees, premising liability against Triumvirate on the theory of *respondeat superior*. She also alleged that Triumvirate...violated Louisiana law prohibiting the sale of alcohol to under-age patrons and thus breached a statutory duty. Plaintiff further alleged that Mr. Fraioli, as the owner of Triumvirate...[, was] liable under the *alter ego doctrine*.

Mr. Fraioli filed a motion for summary judgment, asserting Triumvirate's corporate shield as a defense to his personal liability. He charged that plaintiff had no evidence to support her allegation that he is the alter ego of Triumvirate and that plaintiff could not carry her heavy burden of proof placed by law on plaintiffs seeking to pierce the corporate veil. In support of the motion, Mr. Fraioli attached an affidavit in which he attested that Triumvirate owns and operates Fred's Bar and Grill and that he is the corporation's sole shareholder. He also introduced a certificate issued by the Secretary of State on July 6, 2006, in which the Secretary certified that Triumvirate filed its charter and qualified to do business in this state on January 18, 1982, and that Triumvirate is currently in good standing and is authorized to do business in this state. Additionally, Mr. Fraioli introduced Triumvirate's 1982 articles of incorporation, the corporation's initial report, along with various annual reports filed by the corporation from 1983 through January 18, 2006.

In opposition to the motion, plaintiff urged that there were genuine issues of material fact as to whether Triumvirate is the alter ego of Mr. Fraioli, thus preventing Mr. Fraioli from hiding behind its corporate veil and making him personally liable for the actions of Fred's. She also introduced the corporate deposition of Triumvirate, which was represented by Mr. Fraioli. In the deposition, Mr. Fraioli attested that Triumvirate owned Fred's and that he was the president and sole owner of Triumvirate, and as such, had sole control over Fred's operation. Mr. Fraioli...was not present at Fred's on the night in question.

The issue presented by the motion for summary judgment was thus whether Mr. Fraioli could be held personally liable for the debt of Triumvirate, a corporation of which he is the sole shareholder.

The law on shareholder liability for the debts of a corporation is well-settled. As a general rule, a corporation is a distinct legal entity, separate from the individuals who comprise them, and individual shareholders are not liable for the debts of the corporation. Where a shareholder asserts the corporate shield as a defense from liability, the shareholder has the initial burden of proving the existence of the corporation, and may carry this burden by the use of corporate charter or other documents. The burden then shifts to the plaintiff to show the exceptional circumstances which merit piercing the corporate veil and holding the individual shareholder liable.

Mr. Fraioli met his burden of proving Triumvirate's corporate existence. To survive the motion for summary judgment, the burden of proof shifted to plaintiff, requiring her to produce evidence in support of her alter ego theory of liability. Plaintiff failed to offer any evidence identified by law as indicia that Mr. Fraioli and Triumvirate are not actually separate entities. Plaintiff instead relies on the fact that Triumvirate is solely owned, operated, and controlled by Mr. Fraioli. However, the involvement of a sole or majority shareholder in a corporation is not sufficient alone, as a matter of law, to establish a basis for disregarding the corporate entity. It is clear that plaintiff failed to offer evidence to create a material issue of fact as to Mr. Fraioli's liability on an alter ego theory.

For the foregoing reasons, the judgment appealed from is affirmed. All costs of this appeal are assessed to appellant, Lissette Savoy Menendez.

MYLEGALSTUDIESLAB

MyLegalStudiesLab Virtual Law Office Experience Assignments

Complete the pre-test, study plan, and post-test for this chapter and answer the Legal Applications questions as assigned. These will help you confirm your mastery of the concepts and their application to legal scenarios. Then complete the Virtual Law Office assignments as assigned by your instructor. These assignments are designed to develop your workplace skills. Completing the assignments for this chapter will result in producing the following documents for inclusion in your portfolio:

VLOE 19.1

1. Letter to client advising of the types of bankruptcy that may be filed
2. Completed paperwork needed to form a new corporation
3. Checklist of the procedure and costs to set up a corporation
4. Information on the availability of the names "Apex Trucking" and "Ace Trucking Company"

CHAPTER

20

Intellectual Property and Digital Law

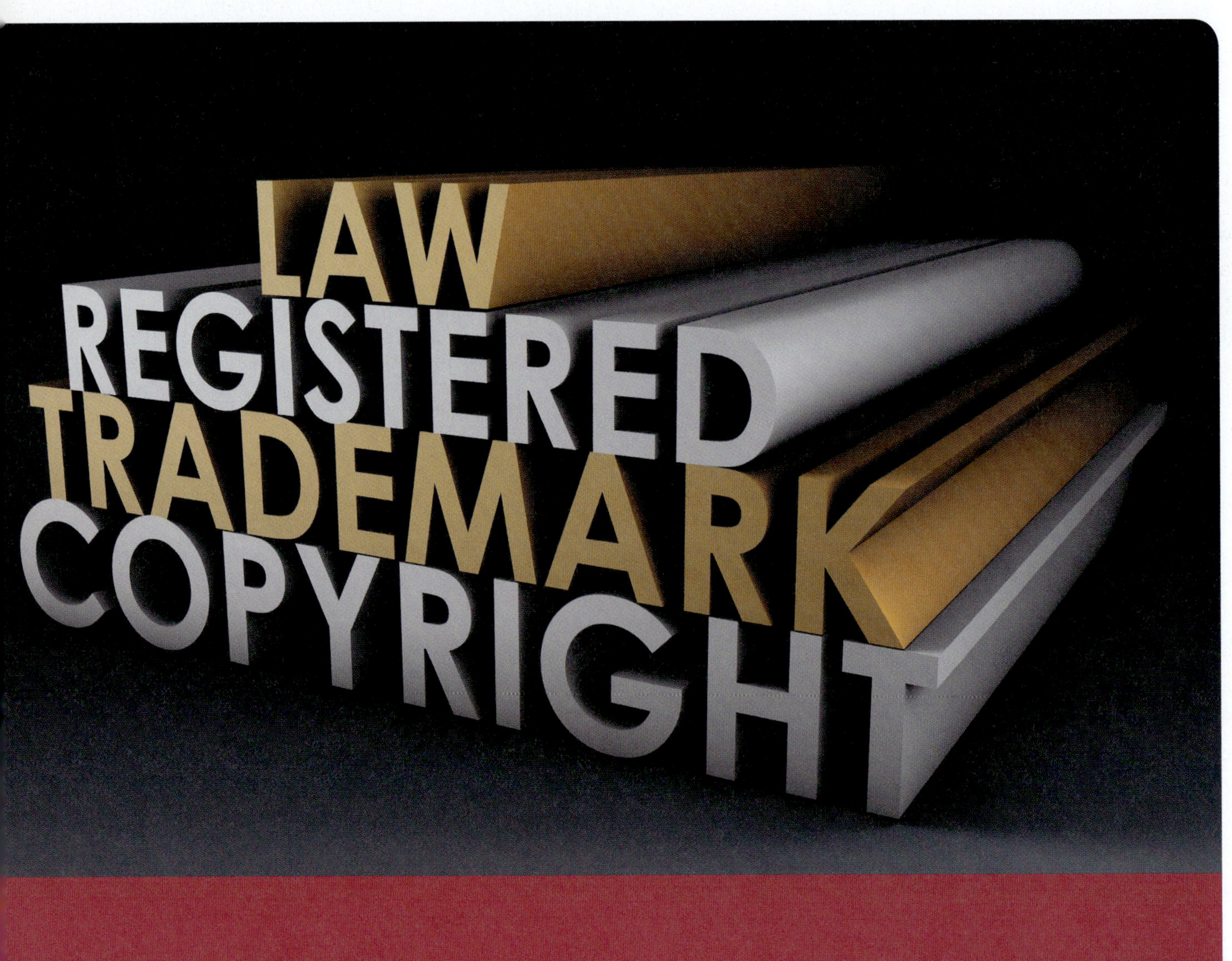

Paralegals at Work

You are a paralegal for a boutique law firm that specializes in intellectual property and Internet law. The lawyers of the firm are known for their expertise in this area. You often work for different partners of the law firm, depending upon the needs of the firm.

One day, Ms. Maria Rodriquez, an intellectual property lawyer and partner at the firm, calls you into her office. Waiting in the office is a client, Mr. Geek Einstein. Ms. Rodriquez introduces you to Mr. Einstein and asks you to sit in on a meeting between them. Ms. Rodriquez also cautions you that everything said is highly confidential.

Mr. Einstein explains that he has invented a new, digital basketball shoe that will allow wearers of the shoe to jump at least 8 inches higher in the air than if they were wearing nondigital basketball shoes. Mr. Einstein then describes the digital technology that allows a wearer to jump so high. He also says that he believes no such digital technology existed prior to his invention.

Further, Mr. Einstein tells you that he would like to call the basketball shoe "Einstein+2" and shows you a design that he wants to be used as the logo for the shoe, which is an "E" with a superimposed "2" in script writing. He also has a slogan—"Plus 2"—for the advertising campaign for the shoe.

Mr. Einstein then shows you a ten-page User's Manual he has written that is to be inserted into each shoebox explaining how to use his digital basketball shoe. He also says that he would like to sell the shoe not only in stores but also over the Internet, using the website name "Einstein+2."

Consider the issues involved in this scenario as you read the chapter.

LEARNING OBJECTIVES

After studying this chapter, you should be able to:

1. Recognize the professional opportunities for paralegals in digital and intellectual property law.
2. Describe the business tort of misappropriating a trade secret.
3. Describe how an invention can be patented under patent laws and the penalties for patent infringement.
4. List the writings and other works that can be copyrighted, and describe the penalties for copyright infringement.
5. Describe the protections provided by the federal Digital Millennium Copyright Act.
6. Define "trademarks" and "service marks," and describe the penalties for trademark infringement.
7. Explain the process for obtaining Internet domain names.
8. Describe the protections provided by the federal Anticybersquatting Consumer Protection Act.
9. Describe important digital laws.
10. Explain a paralegal's duty to disclose conflict of interest.

> "The Congress shall have the power...to promote the Progress of Science and useful Arts, by securing for limited Times to Authors and Inventors the exclusive Right to their respective Writings and Discoveries."
>
> *Article 1, Section 8, Clause 8, U.S. Constitution*

Learning Objective 1
Recognize the professional opportunities for paralegals in digital and intellectual property law.

INTRODUCTION FOR THE PARALEGAL

Often, a paralegal will work in an area of the law that requires a unique and special expertise of statutory law. One of these areas is cyber law and intellectual property. Many boutique law firms or departments of large law firms specialize in **intellectual property** such as patents, copyrights, trademarks, trade secrets, and domain names. Other lawyers specialize in e-commerce and Internet law. A paralegal who works for lawyers in these areas must be knowledgeable about the major statutes, cases, and issues of these law subjects.

Intellectual property Patents, copyrights, trademarks, trade secrets, trade names, domain names, and other valuable business assets. Federal and state laws protect intellectual property rights from misappropriation and infringement.

The American economy is based on the freedom of ownership of property. In addition to real estate and personal property, intellectual property rights have value to both businesses and individuals. This is particularly true in today's Information Age.

Trade secrets, the basis of many successful businesses, are protected from misappropriation. Federal law also provides protections for intellectual property rights such as patents, copyrights, and trademarks. In addition, businesses and individuals may register domain names to use on the Internet. Anyone who infringes on these rights may be lawfully stopped from doing so and is liable for damages. Computers and computer software are also accorded special protections from infringement.

And he that invents a machine augments the power of a man and the well-being of mankind.
Henry Ward Beecher
Proverbs from Plymouth Pulpit—Business

The use of the Internet and the World Wide Web, along with the sale of goods and services through e-commerce, has exploded. Large and small businesses sell goods and services over the Internet through websites and registered domain names. Consumers and businesses can purchase almost any good or service they want over the Internet. Businesses and individuals may register domain names to use on the Internet. Anyone who infringes on these rights may be lawfully stopped from doing so and is liable for damages.

Intellectual property rights and digital law are important, developing areas of the law. Therefore, a paralegal has to acquire knowledge of these important areas of the law to search government websites, conduct research in the areas of intellectual property rights and digital law, and help prepare documents for the creation and transfer of intellectual property rights. This chapter covers trade secrets, patents, copyrights, trademarks, digital law, and domain names.

The following feature discusses the career opportunities for paralegal professionals in intellectual property and digital law.

Trade Secret

Many businesses are successful because their **trade secrets** set them apart from their competitors. Trade secrets may be product formulas, patterns, designs, compilations of data, customer lists, or other business secrets. However, many trade secrets do not qualify to be—or simply are not—patented, copyrighted, or trademarked. Many states have thus adopted the Uniform Trade Secrets Act to give statutory protection to trade secrets.

Trade secret A product formula, pattern, design, compilation of data, customer list, or other business secret.

Web Exploration

Use **www.google.com** to see whether you can find the purported secret recipe for original Coca-Cola posted on someone's website.

Example The most famous trade secret is the formula for Coca-Cola. This secret recipe, which is referred to by the code name "Merchandise 7X," is kept in a bank vault in Atlanta, Georgia. The formula is supposedly known by only two executives, who have signed nondisclosure agreements.

Web Exploration

Go to **http://www.usatoday.com/money/industries/food/2005-07-22-kfc-secret-recipe_x.htm** and read how KFC protects its secret recipe.

Misappropriation of a Trade Secret

State unfair competition laws allow the owner of a trade secret to bring a civil lawsuit for **misappropriation** against anyone who steals it. To be actionable, the defendant (often an employee of the owner, or a competitor) must have obtained the trade secret

CAREER OPPORTUNITIES FOR PARALEGALS IN INTELLECTUAL PROPERTY AND DIGITAL LAW

Paralegals may work in one of the most explosive areas of the law today: intellectual property rights. Both lawyers and paralegals have been able to find excellent positions in this dynamic area of the law provided that they have significant knowledge of intellectual property laws and procedures.

Who does not recognize the business names "McDonald's Corporation" and "Microsoft Corporation"? And who does not know the famous phrases "Diamonds are Forever" and "Just Do It"? These are examples of famous trademarks. Paralegals who work for lawyers that practice in the trademark field must know how to search for available names at the U.S. Patent and Trademark Office as well as how to complete the necessary documents for obtaining or renewing trademarks.

The copyright area is similar in that it requires paralegals who know how to work with copyright lawyers. Copyrights are an extremely important intellectual property right. Movies, books, screenplays, paintings, sculptures, and software can be copyrighted. Therefore, a paralegal must know how the U.S. Copyright Office works, how to check on the availability of proposed names and phrases, and how to complete the documentation for obtaining a copyright.

Of all the intellectual property rights areas, the area of patent law is the most complex for lawyers and paralegals alike. Lawyers who practice in this area must pass a separate patent law examination. The determination of whether an invention, drug, biomedicine, or other innovation is patentable, or whether a patent already exists, requires significant skill and knowledge. Drafting the patent application to be filed with the U.S. Patent and Trademark Office is extremely complicated, and paralegals with science, biology, chemistry, engineering, or related education are indispensable in assisting patent lawyers.

A new form of intellectual property has developed with the advent of the Internet and the World Wide Web. Businesses and individuals can now sell and purchase goods and services using the Internet, and cyber law provides that businesses and individuals can operate using web addresses and domain names. Domain names are sometimes valuable property rights. Many federal and state laws protect business and privacy rights involving the Internet. This area of the law offers paralegals a new avenue in which to apply their skills.

In addition, paralegals support lawyers who are engaged in lawsuits and arbitration proceedings that allege infringement of trademarks, copyrights, patents, or domain names. Paralegals support lawyers involved on both sides of these infringement cases. Therefore, paralegals who provide support in litigation and arbitration of intellectual property rights must know the area of the law involved as well as the procedures, pleadings, documents, discovery, and other issues involved in the dispute.

Intellectual property and digital law is a growing area for lawyers and paralegals. Paralegals have a great opportunity to join this complex and dynamic area of the law.

through unlawful means such as theft, bribery, or industrial espionage. No tort has occurred if there is no misappropriation.

Learning Objective 2
Describe the business tort of misappropriating a trade secret.

Example A competitor can lawfully discover a trade secret by performing *reverse engineering* (that is, by taking apart and examining a rival's product).

The owner of a trade secret is obliged to take all reasonable precautions to prevent others from discovering that secret. These precautions include fencing in buildings, placing locks on doors, hiring security guards, and the like. If the owner fails to take such actions, the secret is no longer subject to protection under state unfair-competition laws.

Generally, a successful plaintiff in a trade secret action can:

1. recover the profits made by the offender from the use of the trade secret,
2. recover for damages, and
3. obtain an injunction prohibiting the offender from divulging or using the trade secret.

Economic Espionage Act

Until recently, even though stealing trade secrets exposes the offender to a civil lawsuit by the injured party to recover economic damages, the offender seldom faced criminal charges except under a few state laws. All of that changed with the enactment

Economic Espionage Act A federal statute that makes it a crime for any person to steal a trade secret for his or her or another's benefit, knowing or intending to cause injury to the owners of the trade secret.

of the federal **Economic Espionage Act** of 1996 [18 U.S.C. Sections 1831–1839], which makes it a federal crime to steal another's trade secrets.

Under the Espionage Act, the definition of *trade secret* is broad and covers any economic, business, financial, technical, scientific, or engineering information, including processes, software programs, and codes. Under this act, it is a federal crime for any person to convert a trade secret to his or her benefit or for the benefit of others, knowing or intending that the act will cause injury to the owner of the trade secret.

One of the major reasons for passing the Espionage Act was to address the ease of stealing trade secrets through espionage and using the Internet. For example, hundreds of pages of confidential information can be downloaded onto a small computer disk, placed into someone's pocket, and taken from the legal owner.

Learning Objective 3

Describe how an invention can be patented under patent laws and the penalties for patent infringement.

Patent

Federal Patent Statute A federal statute that establishes the requirements for obtaining a patent and protects patented inventions from infringement.

Pursuant to the express authority granted in the U.S. Constitution [Article I, Section 8, clause 8], Congress enacted the **Federal Patent Statute** of 1952 [35 U.S.C. Sections 10 et seq.]. This law is intended to provide an incentive for inventors to invent and make their inventions public, and to protect patented inventions from infringement. Federal patent law is exclusive; there are no state patent laws. The **United States Court of Appeals for the Federal Circuit** in Washington, D.C., was created in 1982 to hear patent appeals and to promote uniformity in patent law.

Patenting an Invention

Patent A grant by the federal government upon the inventor of an invention for the exclusive right to use, sell, or license the invention for a limited amount of time.

To obtain a **patent**, a **patent application** must be filed with the **United States Patent and Trademark Office (PTO)** in Washington, D.C. The PTO also provides for the online submission of patent applications and supporting documents through its **EFS-Web system.** Because patent applications are complicated, an inventor should hire a patent attorney to assist in obtaining a patent for an invention.

Patentable subject matter includes (1) machines; (2) processes; (3) compositions of matter; (4) improvements to existing machines, processes, or compositions of matter; (5) designs for an article of manufacture; (6) asexually reproduced plants; and (7) living material invented by a person. Abstractions and scientific principles cannot be patented unless they are part of the tangible environment.

Example Einstein's theory of relativity ($E = MC^2$) cannot be patented.

If a patent is granted, the invention is assigned a patent number. Patent holders usually affix the word *Patent* or *Pat.* and the patent number to the patented article. If a patent application has been filed but a patent has not yet been issued, the applicant usually places the words **patent pending** on the article. Any party can challenge either the issuance of a patent or the validity of an existing patent.

Requirements for Obtaining a Patent

Web Exploration

Go to the website of the U.S. Patent and Trademark Office (PTO) at **www.uspto.gov**. Read the basic facts about patents. What is the approximate cost for filing a patent application with the PTO?

To be patented, an **invention** must be (1) *novel*, (2) *useful*, and (3) *nonobvious:*

1. ***Novel.*** An invention is **novel** if it is new and has not been invented and used in the past. If the invention has been used in "prior art," it is not novel and cannot be patented.

   Example College and professional football games are often televised on television and cable stations. Inventors received a patent for a system whereby a yellow line is digitally drawn across the football field on television at the distance that a team has to go to obtain a first down. This "yellow line" invention is novel.

2. ***Useful.*** An invention is **useful** if it has some practical purpose. If an invention has only theoretical benefit and no useful purpose, it cannot be patented.

   Example An inventor received a patent for "forkchops," which are a set of chopsticks where one chopstick has a spoon at the handle end and the other chopstick has a fork on the handle end. This invention is novel.

3. ***Nonobvious.*** If the invention is **nonobvious,** it qualifies for a patent; if the invention is obvious, then it does not qualify for a patent.

   Example Inventors received a patent for a cardboard or heavy paper sleeve that can be placed over the outside of a paper coffee cup so that the cup will not be as hot as if there were no sleeve. This invention serves a useful purpose.

Web Exploration

Go to **www.uspto.gov**. Click on "5 Search Patents" and then "Database Contents" and then "Pat Num." Look up the following two patents by entering their seven-digit patent numbers in the box. Click on "Search." Patent numbers 5205473 and 6863644.

To be patented, an invention must meet all three of these requirements. If an invention is found to meet these requirements, a patent will be granted. Such a patent is called a **utility patent.** If an invention is found not to meet any of these requirements, it cannot be patented.

Exhibit 20.1 shows the patent for Thomas Edison's electric light bulb.

Utility patent A patent that protects the functionality of an invention.

Patent Period

In 1995, in order to bring the U.S. patent system into harmony with the systems of the majority of other developed nations, Congress made the following important changes in U.S. patent law:

The patent system added the fuel of interest to the fire of genius.
Abraham Lincoln

1. Patents for inventions are valid for *20 years* (instead of the previous term of 17 years). Design patents are valid for 14 years.
2. The patent term begins to run from the date the patent application is *filed* (instead of when the patent is issued, as was previously the case).

First-to-Invent Rule

The United States still follows the **first-to-invent rule** rather than the first-to-file rule followed by some other countries. Thus, in the United States, the first person to invent an item or a process is given patent protection over another party who was first to file a patent application.

Example On January 3, 2010, Nerdette, a straight-A student in college, invents "smork," a chemical formula that can be released into the air and eliminates air pollution. Smork causes no harmful effects to humans, any other living being, or the environment. She keeps her discovery secret, however. Two years later, Nerd, who is a straight-C student in college, invents "dork," which is the same chemical formula as previously invented by Nerdette. The next day Nerd rushes out and files a patent application with the U.S. Patent and Trademark Office. Subsequently, Nerd is issued a patent for Dork. Nerdette later discovers this fact and challenges Nerd's patent since she wishes to patent Smork. Nerdette will win her patent challenge against Nerd because she was the first to invent the invention. Nerd, although he was the first to file for a patent, loses his patent.

Web Exploration

Go to **www.uspto.gov**. Click on "5 Search Patents" and then "Database Contents" and then "Pat Num." Type the patent number 3741662 in the open box. Click on "Search." Read the information about this patent.

Public-Use Doctrine

Under the **public-use doctrine,** a patent may not be granted if the invention was used by the public for more than one year prior to the filing of the patent application. This doctrine forces inventors to file their patent applications as soon as possible.

Example Suppose Cindy Parsons invents a new product on January 1. She allows the public to use this product and does not file a patent application until February of the following year. She has lost the right to patent her invention.

Exhibit 20.1 Thomas Edison's patent for the electric light bulb

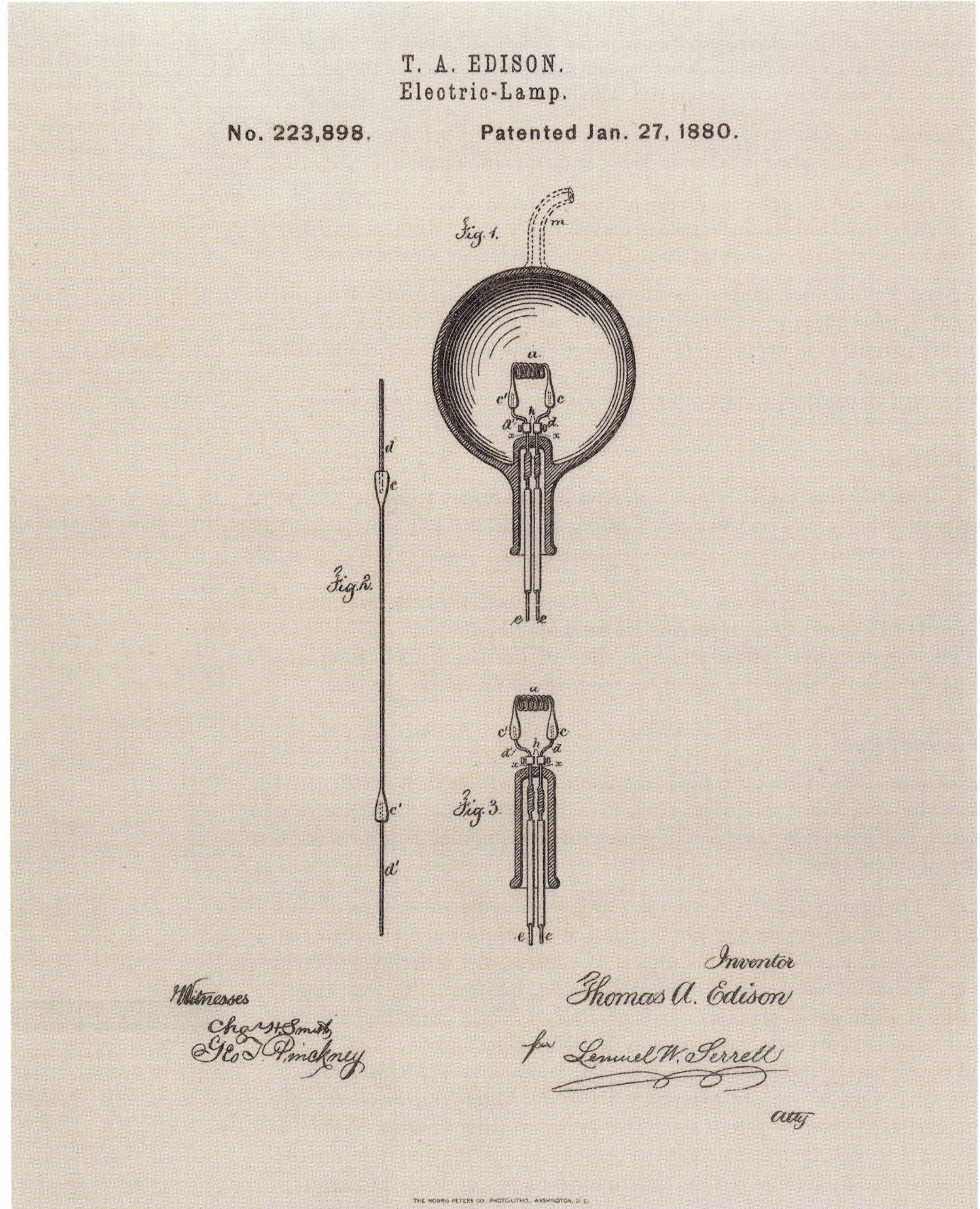

Patent Expiration and Public Domain

After the patent period runs out, the invention or design enters the **public domain,** which means that anyone can produce and sell the invention without paying the prior patent holder.

Example A patent application for a prescription drug is filed on June 1, 2000, and the invention is subsequently granted a patent. When the 20-year patent period expires on June 1, 2020, any other manufacturer can make this prescription drug. *Note:* The new manufacturer cannot use the trademark name of the patent holder.

The American Inventors Protection Act

In 1999, Congress enacted the **American Inventors Protection Act.** This statute does the following:

American Inventors Protection Act A federal statute that permits an inventor to file a *provisional application* with the U.S. Patent and Trademark Office (PTO) three months before the filing of a final patent application, among other provisions.

1. Permits an inventor to file a **provisional application** with the PTO, pending the preparation and filing of a final and complete patent application. This part of the law grants "provisional rights" to an inventor for three months, pending the filing of a final application.
2. Requires the PTO to issue a patent within three years after the filing of a patent application unless the applicant engages in dilatory activities.
3. Provides that nonpatent holders may challenge a patent as being overly broad by requesting a contested reexamination of the patent application by the PTO. This provides that the reexamination will be within the confines of the PTO; the decision of the PTO can be appealed to the U.S. Court of Appeals for the Federal Circuit in Washington, D.C.

Patent Infringement

Patent holders own exclusive rights to use and exploit their patents. **Patent infringement** occurs when someone makes unauthorized use of another's patent. In a suit for patent infringement, a successful plaintiff can recover:

Patent infringement The unauthorized use of another's patent. A patent holder may recover damages and other remedies against a patent infringer.

1. money damages equal to a reasonable royalty rate on the sale of the infringed articles,
2. other damages caused by the infringement (such as loss of customers),
3. an order requiring the destruction of the infringing article, and
4. an injunction preventing the infringer from such action in the future.

The court has the discretion to award up to triple the amount of damages if the infringement was intentional.

Exhibit 20.2 shows Google Inc.'s international patent application filed with the World Intellectual Property Organization (WIPO) for "Recognizing Text in Images."

Design Patent

Design patent A patent that may be obtained for the ornamental, nonfunctional design of an item.

In addition to utility patents, a party can obtain a design patent. A **design patent** is a patent that may be obtained for the ornamental, nonfunctional design of an item. A design patent is valid for fourteen years.

Examples The design of a chair, a door knob, a perfume bottle, and the outside of a computer are design patents.

Copyright A legal right that gives the author of qualifying subject matter, and who meets other requirements established by copyright law, the exclusive right to publish, produce, sell, license, and distribute the work.

Copyright

Learning Objective 4

List the writings and other works that can be copyrighted, and describe the penalties for copyright infringement.

A **copyright** is the exclusive legal right to reproduce, publish, and sell a literary, musical, or artistic work. Congress enacted a federal copyright law pursuant to an express grant of authority in the U.S. Constitution [Article I, Section 8, clause 8]. This law protects the work of authors and other creative persons from the unauthorized use

Exhibit 20.2 Google Inc.'s patent application filed with the World Intellectual Property Organization (WIPO)

(12) INTERNATIONAL APPLICATION PUBLISHED UNDER THE PATENT COOPERATION TREATY (PCT)

(19) World Intellectual Property Organization
International Bureau

(43) International Publication Date
3 January 2008 (03.01.2008)

PCT

(10) International Publication Number
WO 2008/003095 A3

(51) International Patent Classification:
G06F 17/30 (2006.01)

(21) International Application Number:
PCT/US2007/072578

(22) International Filing Date: 29 June 2007 (29.06.2007)

(25) Filing Language: English

(26) Publication Language: English

(30) Priority Data:

11/479,957	29 June 2006 (29.06.2006)	US
11/479,155	29 June 2006 (29.06.2006)	US
11/479,115	29 June 2006 (29.06.2006)	US

(71) Applicant *(for all designated States except US)*: **GOOGLE INC.** [US/US]; 1600 Amphitheatre Parkway, Mountain View, California 94043 (US).

(72) Inventors; and

(75) Inventors/Applicants *(for US only)*: **VINCENT, Luc** [US/US]; 4237 Manuela Avenue, Palo Alto, California 94306 (US). **ULGES, Adrian** [DE/DE]; Ehrlichsweg 15, 56130 Bad Ems (DE).

(74) Agent: **GUSTAFSON, Brian, J.**; Fish & Richardson P.C., P.O. Box 1022, Minneapolis, Minnesota 55440-1022 (US).

(81) Designated States *(unless otherwise indicated, for every kind of national protection available)*: AE, AG, AL, AM, AT, AU, AZ, BA, BB, BG, BH, BR, BW, BY, BZ, CA, CH, CN, CO, CR, CU, CZ, DE, DK, DM, DO, DZ, EC, EE, EG, ES, FI, GB, GD, GE, GH, GM, GT, HN, HR, HU, ID, IL, IN, IS, JP, KE, KG, KM, KN, KP, KR, KZ, LA, LC, LK, LR, LS, LT, LU, LY, MA, MD, ME, MG, MK, MN, MW, MX, MY, MZ, NA, NG, NI, NO, NZ, OM, PG, PH, PL, PT, RO, RS, RU, SC, SD, SE, SG, SK, SL, SM, SV, SY, TJ, TM, TN, TR, TT, TZ, UA, UG, US, UZ, VC, VN, ZA, ZM, ZW.

(84) Designated States *(unless otherwise indicated, for every kind of regional protection available)*: ARIPO (BW, GH, GM, KE, LS, MW, MZ, NA, SD, SL, SZ, TZ, UG, ZM, ZW), Eurasian (AM, AZ, BY, KG, KZ, MD, RU, TJ, TM), European (AT, BE, BG, CH, CY, CZ, DE, DK, EE, ES, FI, FR, GB, GR, HU, IE, IS, IT, LT, LU, LV, MC, MT, NL, PL,

[Continued on next page]

(54) Title: RECOGNIZING TEXT IN IMAGES

(57) Abstract: Methods, systems, and apparatus including computer program products for using extracted image text are provided. In one implementation, a computer-implemented method is provided. The method includes receiving an input of one or more image search terms and identifying keywords from the received one or more image search terms. The method also includes searching a collection of keywords including keywords extracted from image text, retrieving an image associated with extracted image text corresponding to one or more of the image search terms, and presenting the image.

WO 2008/003095 A3

Statue of Liberty
The Statue of Liberty is one of the most famous design patents. It was patented in the United States by Auguste Bartholdi on February 18, 1879. Patent No. 11,023.

of their copyrighted materials and provides a financial incentive for authors to write, thereby increasing the number of creative works available in society. The **Copyright Revision Act** of 1976 governs copyright law [17 U.S.C. Sections 101 et seq.]. Federal copyright law is exclusive; there are no state copyright laws.

Copyright Revision Act A federal statute that (1) establishes the requirements for obtaining a copyright and (2) protects copyrighted works from infringement.

Only **tangible writings**—those that can be physically seen—are subject to copyright registration and protection. The term *writing* has been defined broadly to include books, periodicals, and newspapers; lectures, sermons, and addresses; musical compositions; plays, motion pictures, radio and television productions; maps; works of art, including paintings, drawings, sculpture, jewelry, glassware, tapestry, and lithographs; architectural drawings and models; photographs, including prints, slides, and filmstrips; greeting cards and picture postcards; photoplays, including feature films, cartoons, newsreels, travelogues, and training films; and sound recordings published in the form of cassettes, compact discs, and phonograph albums. Software can also be copyrighted.

To be protected under federal copyright law, a work must be the original work of the author. Note that a copyright is created as soon as an author produces his or her work.

Example When a student writes a term paper for her class, she owns a copyright to that term paper.

Published and unpublished works may be registered with the **United States Copyright Office** in Washington, D.C. *Registration* is permissive and voluntary and can be affected at any time during the term of the copyright.

Copyright Term and Notice

In 1989, the United States signed the **Berne Convention,** an international copyright treaty. This law eliminated the need to place the symbol © or the word "copyright" or "copr." on a copyrighted work. Although notice is now permissive, it is recommended that notice be placed on copyrighted works to defeat a defendant's claim of innocent infringement.

The law in respect to literature ought to remain upon the same footing as that which regards the profits of mechanical inventions and chemical discoveries.
William Wordsworth
Letter (1838)

Example The author of this book would place the following on all his manuscripts written in the year 2014:

"Henry Richard Cheeseman © 2014"

Under the **Copyright Term Extension Act of 1998,** copyright protection is provided for the following time periods:

1. An individual is granted copyright protection for his or her life plus 70 years.
2. Copyrights owned by businesses are protected for the shorter of either
   a. 95 years from the year of first publication
   b. 120 years from the year of creation

Example At age 30, Ernst writes the great novel *To Save a Hummingbird*. Ernst lives until he is 70. The copyright period of Ernst's great novel is 110 years, which includes the 40 years of his life and the 70 years after he is deceased. Thus, Ernst's heirs will receive royalties or other payments due for the publication of the novel for 70 years after Ernst's death.

Copyright Expiration and Public Domain

After the copyright period runs out, the work enters the public domain, which means that anyone can publish the work without paying the prior copyright holder.

Example Continuing with the previous example, 70 years after Ernst's death, his copyrighted work enters the public domain. This means that anyone can publish Ernst's book and compete with his heirs in selling the book to the public. After that date, you might find several versions of Ernst's book for sale in a bookstore, and you would be able to buy whoever's book you think you'd like the best.

Copyright Infringement

Copyright infringement An act in which a party copies a substantial and material part of the plaintiff's copyrighted work without permission. A copyright holder may recover damages and other remedies against the infringer.

Copyright infringement occurs when a party copies a substantial and material part of the plaintiff's copyrighted work without permission. The copying does not have to be either word-for-word or the entire work. A successful plaintiff can recover:

1. the profit made by the infringer from the copyright infringement,
2. damages suffered by the plaintiff,
3. an order requiring the impoundment and destruction of the infringing works, and
4. an injunction preventing the infringer from doing so in the future.

The court, at its discretion, can award statutory damages for willful infringement in lieu of actual damages.

NET Act: Criminal Copyright Infringement

No Electronic Theft Act (NET Act) A federal statute that makes it a crime to willfully infringe on a copyrighted work that exceeds $1,000 in retail value.

A copyright holder owns a valuable right and may sue an infringer in a civil lawsuit to recover damages and to obtain injunctions and other remedies for the copyright infringement. In 1997, Congress enacted the **No Electronic Theft Act (NET Act),** which criminalizes certain copyright infringement.

Congress passed the NET Act to directly criminalize copyright infringement. The NET Act prohibits any person from willfully infringing a copyright for the purpose of commercial advantage or financial gain, or the purpose of reproducing or distributing the work even without commercial advantage or financial gain, including by electronic means. The act provides for criminal penalties including fines and imprisonment.

Fair-use Doctrine

The copyright holder's rights in the work are not absolute. The law permits certain limited unauthorized use of copyrighted materials under the **fair-use doctrine.** Protected under this doctrine are:

Fair-use doctrine A doctrine that permits certain limited use of a copyrighted work by someone other than the copyright holder without the permission of the copyright holder.

1. quotation of the copyrighted work for review or criticism or in a scholarly or technical work,
2. use in a parody or satire,
3. brief quotation in a news report,
4. reproduction by a teacher or student of a small part of the work to illustrate a lesson,
5. incidental reproduction of a work in a newsreel or broadcast of an event being reported, and
6. reproduction of a work in a legislative or judicial proceeding.

Examples A college student is assigned to write a paper on the history of the Statue of Liberty. The student finds many sources on the Internet about the history of the Statue of Liberty. If the student uses two paragraphs from a copyrighted Internet article in her paper and places the materials in quotation marks and cites the source and author in a footnote, this is fair use for academic purposes. If, however, she copies and uses three pages from the article, this would not be fair use but would constitute copyright infringement, whether she cites the author or not.

Digital Millennium Copyright Act

Learning Objective 5
Describe the protections provided by the federal Digital Millennium Copyright Act.

The Internet makes it easy for people to illegally copy and distribute copyrighted works. To combat this, software and entertainment companies developed "wrappers" and encryption technology to protect their copyrighted works from unauthorized access. Not to be outdone, software pirates and other Internet users devised ways to crack these wrappers and protection devices.

Seeing that they were losing the battle, software companies and the entertainment industry lobbied Congress to enact legislation that would make it illegal to crack their wrappers and sell the technology to do so. In 1998, Congress responded by enacting the **Digital Millennium Copyright Act (DMCA)** [17 U.S.C. Section 1201], which does the following:

Digital Millennium Copyright Act (DMCA) A federal statute that prohibits unauthorized access to copyrighted digital works by circumventing encryption technology or manufacturing and distributing technologies designed to circumvent the encryption protection of digital works.

- Prohibits the unauthorized access of copyrighted digital works by circumventing the wrapper or encryption technology that protects the intellectual property.
- Prohibits the manufacture and distribution of technologies, products, or services designed primarily to circumvent wrappers or encryption protection.

The DMCA imposes civil and criminal penalties. A successful plaintiff in a civil action can recover actual damages from first-time offenders and triple the amount of damages from repeat offenders, costs and attorney's fees, an order for the destruction of illegal products and devices, and an injunction against future violations by the offender. Criminal penalties include fines and imprisonment.

In the following feature, a paralegal professional discusses her work in the field of intellectual property.

Paralegals *in* Practice

PARALEGAL PROFILE

Kathleen D. Kasiorek

Kathleen D. Kasiorek, a Certified Paralegal, is a graduate of Ferris State University with a bachelor's degree in Business Administration and an associate's degree in Legal Assisting. She is currently employed as a Senior Paralegal at the law firm of Warner Norcross & Judd in Grand Rapids, Michigan. Kathleen is also an active participant in several professional associations including the Council of the State Bar of Michigan's Paralegal/Legal Assistant Section.

Most of my 13-year paralegal career has been spent working in intellectual property. In my position, tasks include performing trademark and patent research, filing documents with the U.S. Patent and Trademark Office, maintaining a docketing system and electronic database, communicating with clients and their attorneys, registering and maintaining domain names, tracking time and billing clients, and preparing various reports.

Additional responsibilities include assisting with trademark oppositions and cancellation proceedings, which are administered by the U.S. Patent and Trademark Office, Trademark Trial and Appeal Board, and similar agencies in other countries. I also assist in cases in which counterfeit goods are intercepted by customs officials here and abroad. It is very interesting work and always rewarding when we can successfully stop the "bad guys" from stealing our clients' intellectual property.

My advice to new paralegals is: make an effort to continue learning throughout your career. Things are constantly changing in this field, so it is imperative to stay current on the latest changes and issues. For example, to help keep myself up to date, I regularly read journals and periodicals. I also attend seminars and conferences related to the intellectual property practice area. A large part of my work involves collaborating with attorneys from all over the world. In order to communicate more effectively with them, I try to learn as much as I can about other countries and their cultures.

Learning Objective 6

Define "trademarks" and "service marks," and describe the penalties for trademark infringement.

Lanham Trademark Act A federal statute that (1) establishes the requirements for obtaining a federal mark and (2) protects marks from infringement.

Trademark Law Revision Act of 1988 ® A symbol that is used to designate marks that have been registered with the U.S. Patent and Trademark Office.

Web Exploration

Go to **http://www.coca-cola.com/template1/index.jsp** to see the trademarks of the Coca-Cola Corporation.

Trademark

Trademark law is intended to (1) protect the owner's investment and goodwill in a mark, and (2) prevent consumers from being confused as to the origin of goods and services. In 1946, Congress enacted the **Lanham Trademark Act** to provide federal protection to trademarks, service marks, and other marks [15 U.S.C. Sections 1114 et seq.]. Four decades later, Congress passed the **Trademark Law Revision Act of 1988,** which amended trademark law in several respects. The amendments make it easier to register a trademark but harder to maintain it. States also may enact trademark laws.

Registration of Trademarks

Trademarks are registered with the United States Patent and Trademark Office (PTO) in Washington, D.C. The PTO provides for the paper filing of the application or the electronic filing of the application through its **Trademark Electronic Application System (TEAS).** The original *registration* of a mark is valid for 10 years and can be renewed for an unlimited number of 10-year periods. The registration of a trademark, which is given nationwide effect, serves as constructive notice that the mark is the registrant's personal property. The registrant is then entitled to use the registered trademark symbol ® in connection with a registered trademark or service mark. Use of the symbol is not mandatory; however, during the application period, a registrant can use the symbol **TM** for goods or **SM** for services to alert the public to his or her claim. The notations "TM" and "SM" have no legal significance, however.

Example McDonald's Corporation owns the trademark "I'm lovin' it." McDonald's received an initial trademark period of 10 years, and must renew "I'm lovin' it" every 10 years to keep the trademark.

An applicant can register a mark if (1) it was in use in commerce (that is, it was actually used in the sale of goods or services) or (2) the applicant verifies a *bona fide* intention to use the mark in commerce and actually does so within six months of the mark's registration. Failure to use the mark during this period results in the registrant losing the mark. A party other than the registrant can submit an opposition to a proposed registration of a mark or to the cancellation of a previously registered mark.

Distinctiveness of a Mark

To qualify for federal protection, a mark must either (1) be **distinctive** or (2) have acquired a **secondary meaning.**

Web Exploration

Go to **http://www.microsoft.com/library/toolbar/3.0/trademarks/en-us.mspx** to view a list of the trademarks of Microsoft Corporation.

- **Distinctive.** A distinctive mark is a word or design that is unique. The words of the mark cannot be ordinary words or symbols.

  Examples Words such as *Xerox* (Xerox Corporation), *Acura* (Honda Motor Corporation), *Google* (Google Inc.), *Exxon* (Exxon Mobil Corporation), and *Pinkberry* (Pinkberry, Inc.) are distinctive words and therefore qualify as marks.

- **Secondary meaning.** Ordinary words or symbols that have taken on a secondary meaning can qualify as marks. These are words or symbols that already have an established meaning but have acquired a secondary meaning that is attached to a product or service.

  Examples *Just Do It* (Nike Corporation), *I'm lovin' it* (McDonald's Corporation), *Windows* (Microsoft Corporation), and *Ben & Jerry's Ice Cream* (Unilever) are ordinary words that have taken on a secondary meaning when used to designate the products or services of the owners of the marks.

Words that are descriptive but have no secondary meaning cannot be trademarked.

Types of Marks

The word **mark** collectively refers to *trademarks*, *service marks*, *certification marks*, and *collective membership marks:*

Mark Any trade name, symbol, word, logo, design, or device used to identify and distinguish the goods of a manufacturer or seller and the services of a provider from those of other manufacturers, sellers, or providers.

- **Trademark.** A **trademark** is a distinctive mark, symbol, name, word, motto, or device that identifies the *goods* of a particular business.

  Examples *Coca-Cola* (The Coca-Cola Company), *Big Mac* (McDonald's Corporation), *Mac* (Apple Computer), *Intel Inside* (Intel Corporation), *Better Ingredients. Better Pizza.* (Papa John's Pizza), and *Harley* (Harley-Davidson Motor Company) are trademarks.

Trademark A distinctive mark, symbol, name, word, motto, or device that identifies the goods of a particular business.

- **Service mark.** A **service mark** is used to distinguish the *services* of the holder from those of its competitors.

  Examples *Andersen Consulting* (Andersen Consulting Group), *FedEx* (FedEx Corporation), *The Friendly Skies* (United Airlines, Inc.), *Big Brown* (UPS Corporation), *Weight Watchers* (Weight Watchers International, Inc.), and *Citi* (Citigroup, Inc.) are service marks.

Service mark A mark that distinguishes the services of the holder from those of its competitors.

- **Certification mark.** A **certification mark** is a mark usually owned by a nonprofit cooperative or association. The owner of the mark establishes certain geographical location requirements, quality standards, material standards, or mode of manufacturing standards that must be met by a seller of products or services in order for the seller to be able to use the certification mark. If a seller meets these requirements, the seller applies to the cooperative or association to use the mark on its products or in connection with the sale of services. The owner of the certification mark usually licenses sellers who meet the requirements to use the mark. A party does not have to be a member of the organization to use the mark.

  Examples A *UL* mark certifies products that meet the safety standards set by Underwriters Laboratories, Inc. The *Good Housekeeping Seal of Approval*

Certification mark A mark that certifies that a seller of a product or service has met certain geographical location requirements, quality standards, material standards, or mode of manufacturing standards established by the owner of the mark.

certifies products that meet certain quality specifications set by *Good Housekeeping* magazine (Good Housekeeping Research Institute). Other certification marks are *Certified Maine Lobster*, which indicates lobster or lobster products originating in the coastal waters of the state of Maine (Maine Lobster Promotion Council); *100% Napa Valley*, which is associated with grape wine from the Napa Valley of California (Napa Valley Vintners Association); and *Grown in Idaho*, which indicates potatoes grown in the state of Idaho (State of Idaho Potato Commission).

Collective membership mark A mark that indicates that a person has met the standards set by an organization and is a member of that organization.

- **Collective membership mark.** A **collective membership mark** is owned by an organization (such as an association) whose *members* use it to identify themselves with a level of quality, accuracy, or other characteristics set by the organization. Only members of the association or organization can use the mark. A collective membership mark does not identify goods or services.

  Examples *CPA* is used to indicate that someone is a member of the Society of Certified Public Accountants, *Teamster* is used to indicate that a person is a member of The International Brotherhood of Teamsters (IBT) labor union, and *Realtor* is used to indicate that a person is a member of the National Association of Realtors. Other collective marks are *Boy Scouts of America*, *League of Women Voters*, and *National Honor Society*.

Certain marks cannot be registered. They include (1) the flag or coat of arms of the United States, any state, a municipality, or a foreign nation; (2) marks that are immoral or scandalous; (3) geographical names standing alone such as "South"; (4) surnames standing alone such as "Smith" (note, however, that a surname can be registered if it is accompanied by a picture or fanciful name, such as *Smith Brothers cough drops*); and (5) any mark that resembles a mark already registered with the federal PTO.

Trademark Infringement

Trademark infringement The unauthorized use of another's mark. The holder may recover damages and other remedies from the infringer.

The owner of a mark can sue a third party for the unauthorized use of that mark. To succeed in a **trademark infringement** case, the owner must prove that (1) the defendant infringed the plaintiff's mark by using it in an unauthorized manner, and that (2) such use is likely to confuse or deceive the public as to the origin of the goods or services. A successful plaintiff can recover:

1. the profits made by the infringer through the unauthorized use of the mark,
2. damages caused to the plaintiff's business and reputation,
3. an order requiring the defendant to destroy all goods containing the unauthorized mark, and
4. an injunction preventing the defendant from engaging in such infringement in the future.

Web Exploration

Go to **www.videojug.com/film/how-to-spot-a-fake-louis-vuitton-bag** and watch the video "How to Spot a Fake Louis Vuitton Bag."

The court has discretion to award up to three times the amount of damages where intentional infringement is found.

Generic Names

If a word, name, or slogan is too generic, it cannot be registered as a trademark. If a word is not generic, it can be trademarked.

Examples The word "apple" cannot be trademarked because it is a generic name. However, the brand name "Apple Computer" is permitted to be trademarked because it is not a generic name. The word "secret" cannot be trademarked because it is a generic name. However, the brand name "Victoria's Secret" is permitted to be trademarked because it is not a generic name.

Once a company has been granted a trademark or service mark, the company usually uses the mark as a brand name to promote its goods or services. However, sometimes a company is *too* successful in promoting a mark, and at some point in time, the public begins to use the brand name as a common name to denote the type of product or service being sold, rather than as the trademark or service mark of the individual seller. A trademark that becomes a common term for a product line or type of service is called a **generic name.** Once a trademark becomes a generic name, it loses its protection under federal trademark law.

Example Sailboards are surfboards that have sails mounted on them and are used by one person to glide on oceans and lakes. Although there were many manufacturers and sellers of sailboards, the most successful brand was "Windsurfer." However, the word "windsurfing" was used so often by the public for all brands of sailboards that the trademarked name "Windsurfer" was found to be a generic name and its trademark was canceled.

Diluting, Blurring, or Tarnishing Trademarks

The government enacted the **Federal Trademark Dilution Act (FTDA)** of 1995 to protect famous marks from **dilution.** *Dilution* is broadly defined as the lessening of the capability of a famous mark to identify and distinguish its holder's goods and services.

Congress revised the FTDA when it enacted the **Trademark Dilution Revision Act** of 2006. The FTDA, as amended, has three fundamental requirements that the holder of the senior mark must show to prove dilution: (1) its mark is famous, (2) the mark's use by the other party is commercial, and (3) the mark's use by the other party causes a likelihood of dilution of the distinctive quality of the mark.

The two most common forms of dilution are:

- **Blurring.** This occurs when a party uses another party's famous mark to designate a product or service in another market, thus weakening the unique significance of the famous mark.

  Examples Instances of blurring include "Rolex skateboards" or "eBay toiletries."

- **Tarnishment.** This occurs when a famous mark is linked to products of inferior quality or is portrayed in an unflattering, immoral, or reprehensible context likely to evoke negative feelings about the mark's owner.

  Example An example of tarnishment would be using the mark "Microsoft" on a deck of unsavory playing cards.

The ethical duty of a paralegal professional to keep a client's intellectual property information confidential is discussed in the following feature.

SIDEBAR: GENERIC NAMES

The following once-trademarked names have been so overused to designate an entire class of products that they have been found to be generic and have lost their trademark status.

Aspirin	Nylon
Butterscotch	Raisin bran
Cornflakes	Thermos
Escalator	Tollhouse cookies
Formica	Trampoline
Frisbee	Windsurfer
Kerosene	Yo-yo
Laser	Zipper
Linoleum	

Several trademark names have come close to becoming generic, but have not yet been held to be generic. These include the marks *Band-Aid, Kleenex, Plexiglas,* and *Xerox.*

Generic name A term for a mark that has become a common term for a product line or type of service and therefore has lost its trademark protection.

Federal Trademark Dilution Act (FTDA) A federal statute that protects famous marks from dilution, blurring, or tarnishing.

ETHICAL PERSPECTIVE

Paralegal's Duty to Keep a Client's Intellectual Property Information Confidential

Mr. Edwards is hired as a paralegal for the law firm of Berkowitz, Brown, and McGregor, which specializes in intellectual property law, and is assigned to assist Mr. Berkowitz. One day a new client, Ms. Newton, comes into the office to see Mr. Berkowitz about representing her in obtaining trademarks for her company's name, a new product, and a slogan that will be used in selling the product.

Mr. Berkowitz invites Mr. Edwards to attend the meeting with Ms. Newton. At the meeting, Ms. Newton tells them specifically what she would like to have trademarked and agrees to employ the law firm to obtain the trademarks.

(continued)

Realizing that the proposed name for the product is unique and would have a large commercial value, Mr. Edwards considers telling a friend about the name and suggesting that he and his friend share any monetary gain from obtaining a trademark on the name. If his friend obtained the trademark before Ms. Newton, then Ms. Newton would have to buy the name from the friend if she wanted it, or forgo using the name.

What should Mr. Edwards do?

PARALEGAL'S ETHICAL DECISION

In this case, it is clear that Mr. Edwards cannot act upon his thoughts about this matter. A paralegal professional owes an ethical duty not to misuse confidential information obtained in his or her employment and cannot make a monetary gain by misusing the confidential information. Therefore, even though he is tempted to disclose the name to his friend and share in the possible profits from doing so, Mr. Edwards must make the ethical decision to keep the information confidential.

Internet

Internet (Net) A collection of millions of computers and electronic devices that provides a network of connections among the computers and electronic devices.

The **Internet,** or **Net,** is a collection of hundreds of millions of computers and other electronic devices that comprises a network of electronic connections. The Internet's evolution helped usher in the Information Age of today in which individuals and businesses use the Internet to communicate information and data.

Through the use of chat rooms, any person with a phone line can become a town crier with a voice that resonates farther than it could from any soapbox. Through the use of Web pages, mail exploders, and newsgroups, the same individual can become a pamphleteer.

Stevens, Justice
Reno v. American Civil Liberties Union, 521 U.S. 844 (1997)

The **World Wide Web,** or **web,** which is a small part of the Internet, consists of millions of computers that support a standard set of rules for the exchange of information. Web-based documents are formatted using common coding languages such as hypertext transfer protocol (HTTP). Individuals and businesses can have their own websites, which are composed of electronic documents known as web pages. Websites and pages in turn are stored on servers throughout the world that are operated by **Internet service providers (ISPs).** Each website, which has its own unique online address, can be viewed by using web-browsing software such as Microsoft Internet Explorer.

The web has made it extremely profitable to conduct commercial activities online. Companies such as Amazon.com and eBay sell all sorts of goods and services online. Existing brick-and-mortar companies, such as Wal-Mart, Merrill Lynch, and Dell Computers, also sell their goods and services online. E-commerce over the web will continue to grow dramatically each year.

Electronic Mail

Electronic mail, or **email,** is one of the most widely used applications for communicating via the Internet. Using email, individuals around the world can instantaneously communicate in electronic writing with one another. Each person can have an email address that uniquely identifies him or her. Email's use will continue to grow as it replaces some telephone and paper correspondence and increases communication between persons.

Learning Objective 7
Explain the process for obtaining Internet domain names.

Domain Name

Most businesses conduct e-commerce by using websites, each of which is identified by a unique **domain name.**

Domain name A unique name that identifies an individual's or a company's website.

Examples The domain name for the publisher of this book—Pearson Education, Inc.—is www.pearson.com. Other domain names are www.microsoft.com for Microsoft Corporation, www.mcdonalds.com for McDonald's Corporation, www.naacp.org for the National Association for the Advancement of Colored People, and www.uchicago.edu for the University of Chicago.

Domain names can be registered. The first step in registering a domain name is to determine whether any other party already owns the name. For this purpose, InterNIC maintains a "Whois" database that contains the domain names that have been registered. The InterNIC website is located at www.internic.net.

Domain names can then be registered at Network Solutions, Inc.'s website, which is located at www.networksolutions.com. An applicant must complete a registration form, which may be done online. It usually costs less than $30–$100 to register a domain name for one year, and the fee may be paid by credit card online. The most commonly used **domain name extensions** for **top-level domain names (TLDs)** are set forth in Exhibit 20.3.

Exhibit 20.3 Commonly used top-level domain names (TLDs)

.com	This extension represents the word *commercial* and is the most widely used extension in the world. Most businesses prefer a .com domain name because it is a highly recognized business symbol.
.net	This extension represents the word *network*, and it is most commonly used by ISPs, Web-hosting companies, and other businesses that are directly involved in the infrastructure of the Internet. Some businesses also choose domain names with a .net extension.
.org	This extension represents the word *organization* and is primarily used by nonprofit groups and trade associations.
.info	This extension signifies a resource website. It is an unrestricted global name that may be used by businesses, individuals, and organizations.
.biz	This extension is used for small-business websites.
.us	This extension is for U.S. websites. Many businesses choose this extension, which is a relatively new extension.
.mobi	This extension is reserved for websites that are viewable on mobile devices.
.bz	This extension was originally the country code for Belize, but it is now unrestricted and may be registered by anyone from any country. It is commonly used by small businesses.
.name	This extension is for individuals, who can use it to register personalized domain names.
.museum	This extension enables museums, museum associations, and museum professionals to register websites.
.coop	This extension represents the word *cooperative* and may be used by cooperative associations around the world.
.aero	This extension is exclusively reserved for the aviation community. It enables organizations and individuals in that community to reserve websites.
.pro	This extension is available to professionals, such as doctors, lawyers, and consultants.
.edu	This extension is for educational institutions.

There are other domain name extensions available. Countries have country-specific extensions assigned to the country. Many countries make these domain name extensions available for private purchase for commercial use.

Specific domain name extensions are assigned to each country. Some countries make these domain name extensions available for public purchase.

Examples .af for Afghanistan, .br for Brazil, .bt for Bhutan, .ca for Canada, .cn for mainland China, .fr for France, .in for India, .ir for Iran, .jp for Japan, .ml for Mali, .mx for Mexico, .sa for Saudi Arabia, .tv for Tuvalu, .uk for the United Kingdom, .us for the United States, .ve for Venezuela, and .zm for Zambia.

In 2011, the **Internet Corporation for Assigned Names and Numbers (ICANN),** the organization that oversees the registration and regulation of domain names, issued new rules that permit a party to register a domain name with new TLD suffixes that are personalized. Thus the new rules permit companies to have their own company name TLD, such as .canon, .google, .cocacola, and such. In addition, companies can obtain TLDs for specific products such as .ipad or .prius. Such TLDs will help companies with the branding of their company names and products. New TLDs can also be registered for industries and professions, such as .bank, .food, .basketball, and .dentist.

Under the new rules, cities and other governmental agencies can register their names, such as .nyc (New York City), .paris (Paris, France), and .quebec (Quebec, Canada). Even persons sharing a cultural identity could have their own TLD, such as .kurd (for Kurds living in Iraq and elsewhere) or .ven (for the Venetian community in Italy). Another important change is that TLDs can be registered in languages other than English, including Arabic, Chinese, French, Russian, and Spanish.

Learning Objective 8

Describe the protections provided by the federal Anticybersquatting Consumer Protection Act.

Anticybersquatting Consumer Protection Act

Anticybersquatting Consumer Protection Act (ACPA) A federal statute that permits trademark owners and famous persons to recover domain names using their names when the domain name has been registered by another person or business in bad faith.

In November 1999, the U.S. Congress enacted, and the president signed, the **Anticybersquatting Consumer Protection Act (ACPA)** [15 U.S.C. Section 1125(d)]. The act is specifically aimed at cybersquatters, who register Internet domain names of famous companies and people and hold those domain names hostage by demanding ransom payments from the famous company or person.

In the past, trademark law was of little help in this area, either because the famous person's name was not trademarked or because, even if the name was trademarked, trademark laws required distribution of goods or services to find infringement, and most cybersquatters did not distribute goods or services but merely sat on the Internet domain name.

The 1999 act has two fundamental requirements: (1) The name must be famous and (2) the domain name must have been registered in bad faith. Thus, the law prohibits the act of **cybersquatting** itself if it is done in *bad faith*.

The first issue in applying the statute is whether the domain name is that of someone famous. Trademarked names qualify; nontrademarked names—such as those of famous actors, actresses, singers, sports stars, politicians, and such—are also protected. In determining bad faith, the law provides that courts may consider the extent to which the domain name resembles the holder's name or the famous person's name, whether goods or services are sold under the name, the amount of the holder's offer to sell or transfer the name, and whether the holder has acquired multiple Internet domain names of famous companies and persons.

The act provides that the court can issue cease-and-desist orders and injunctions. In addition, the law adds monetary penalties: A plaintiff has the option of seeking statutory damages in lieu of proving damages. The Anticybersquatting Consumer Protection Act thus gives owners of trademarks and persons with famous names a new weapon to attack the kidnapping of Internet domain names by cyberpirates.

Digital Law

Learning Objective 9
Describe important digital laws.

With the advent of the Information Age, the government has had to develop laws that apply to and regulate the use of computers, the Internet, and other electronic media. These laws are sometimes collectively referred to as **digital law.** The following paragraphs discuss some of the major digital laws that have been enacted.

Electronic Communications Privacy Act (ECPA)

Electronic Communications Privacy Act (ECPA) A federal statute that makes it a crime to intercept an electronic communication at the point of transmission, while in transit, when stored by a router or server, or after receipt by the intended recipient.

Email, computer data, and other electronic communications are sent daily by millions of people using computers and the Internet. Recognizing that the use of computer and electronic communications raises special issues of privacy, the federal government enacted the **Electronic Communications Privacy Act (ECPA)** [18 U.S.C. Section 2510].

An electronic communication includes the transfer of signals, writings, images, sounds, data, and intelligence of any nature. The ECPA makes it a crime to intercept an electronic communication at the point of transmission, while in transit, when stored by a router or server, or after receipt by the intended recipient. The ECPA also makes it illegal to access stored email and email in transmission.

Example Henry owns a computer on which he sends and receives email. Harriet learns Henry's access code to his email account and then opens and reads his emails. In doing so, Harriet has violated the ECPA.

The ECPA provides that stored electronic communications may be accessed without violating the law by the following:

1. The party or entity providing the electronic communication service. The primary example would be an employer, who can access the stored email communications of employees who use the employer's service.
2. Government and law enforcement entities that are investigating suspected illegal activity. Disclosure of this access would be required only pursuant to a validly issued warrant.

The ECPA provides for criminal penalties and also for the injured party to bring a civil lawsuit to recover monetary damages from the violator.

SIDEBAR

DOMAIN NAMES SOLD FOR MILLIONS

Most domain names are originally registered for less than $100. What are some other domain names worth? The domain name www.business.com sold for $7.5 million, www.wine.com sold for $3 million, www.bingo.com for $1.1 million, www.drugs.com for $800,000, www.pizza.com for $2.6 million, www.vip.com for $1.4 million, www.insure.com for $16 million, www.casino.com for $5.5 million, www.fund.com for $10 million, www.beer.com for $7 million, and www.sex.com for $14 million. Toys "R" Us paid $5.1 million for the domain name www.toys.com.

Information Infrastructure Protection Act (IIP Act)

Web Exploration

Go to **www.networksolutions.com** and see if your name is available in the .com and .name extensions. Then think up a name that you would like to use for a business. Check to see if this business name is available in the .com extension.

The Internet and Information Age ushered in a whole new world for education, business, and consumer transactions. But what followed was a rash of cybercrimes. Prosecutors and courts wrestled over how to apply existing laws written in a nondigital age to new, Internet-related abuses.

In 1996, Congress responded by enacting the **Information Infrastructure Protection Act (IIP Act)** [18 U.S.C. Section 1030]. In this federal law, Congress addressed computer-related crimes as distinct offenses. The IIP Act provides protection for any computer attached to the Internet.

Information Infrastructure Protection Act (IIP Act) A federal statute that makes it a federal crime for anyone to intentionally access and acquire information from a protected computer without authorization.

The IIP Act makes it a federal crime for anyone to intentionally access and acquire information from a protected computer without authorization; the IIP Act does not require that the defendant accessed the protected computer for commercial benefit. Thus, persons who transmit a computer virus over the Internet or hackers who trespass into Internet-connected computers may be criminally prosecuted under the IIP Act. Even merely observing data on a protected computer without authorization meets the requirement that the defendant has accessed a protected computer. Criminal penalties for violating the IIP Act include imprisonment and fines.

Learning Objective 10
Explain a paralegal's duty to disclose conflict of interest.

ETHICAL PERSPECTIVE

Duty to Disclose Conflict of Interest

Mr. Frederick Aston, a paralegal, leaves his employment at the law firm at which he had worked for years to take a paralegal position at a different law firm. Upon joining the new law firm, Mr. Aston is provided with a list of clients that the firm represents and a list of the lawsuits and other matters in which the law firm represents clients, including the names of the adversarial parties and the opposing law firms that represent these clients.

As Mr. Aston reviews the list, he sees a pending lawsuit in which his prior law firm is representing a client in a case against the client being represented by his new law firm. In fact, Mr. Aston worked on that case during his previous employment.

Does Mr. Aston owe a duty to disclose this conflict of interest to the new law firm? Does he owe a duty not to work on the case if it would involve a conflict of interest for him?

Model and state paralegal professional codes of ethics and responsibility require that a paralegal disclose any conflict of interest that he or she has identified, refrain from working on matters where he or she has identified a conflict of interest, and refrain from disclosing any information from his or her previous employment from which the conflict of interest arises.

PARALEGAL'S ETHICAL DECISION

Mr. Aston, as a paralegal professional, owes an ethical duty to disclose to his new employer the fact that when he was employed by a prior law firm, he worked on one of the cases that the firm is currently involved in. In addition, Mr. Aston cannot work on this case if it would cause a conflict of interest for him to do so. He also must not disclose to his new employer any information about the case that he learned at his prior employment.

The IIP Act gives the federal government a much-needed weapon for directly prosecuting cybercrooks, hackers, and others who enter, steal, destroy, or look at others' computer data without authorization.

The ethical duty of a paralegal professional to disclose any conflict of interest is discussed in the feature above.

Concept Review *and* Reinforcement

LEGAL TERMINOLOGY

American Inventors Protection Act 743
Anticybersquatting Consumer Protection Act (ACPA) 754
Berne Convention 745
Blurring 751
Certification mark 749
Collective membership mark 750
Copyright 743
Copyright infringement 746
Copyright Revision Act 745
Copyright Term Extension Act of 1998 746
Cybersquatting 754
Design patent 743
Digital law 755
Digital Millennium Copyright Act (DMCA) 747
Dilution 751
Distinctive 757
Domain name 752
Domain name extensions 753
Economic Espionage Act 740
EFS-Web system 740
Electronic Communications Privacy Act (ECPA) 755
Electronic mail (email) 752
Fair-use doctrine 747
Federal Patent Statute 740
Federal Trademark Dilution Act (FTDA) 751
First-to-invent rule 741
Generic name 751

Information Infrastructure Protection Act (IIP Act) 755
Intellectual property 738
Internet (Net) 752
Internet Corporation for Assigned Names and Numbers (ICANN) 754
Internet service provider (ISP) 752
Invention 736
Lanham Trademark Act 748
Mark 749
Misappropriation 738
No Electronic Theft Act (NET Act) 746
Nonobvious 741
Novel 740
Patent 740
Patent application 740
Patent infringement 743
Patent pending 740
Provisional application 743
Public domain 742
Public-use doctrine 741
Secondary meaning 749
Service mark 749
SM 748
Tangible writings 745
Tarnishment 751
TM 748
Top-level domain name (TLD) 753
Trade secret 738
Trademark 749
Trademark Dilution Revision Act 751
Trademark Electronic Application System (TEAS) 748
Trademark infringement 750
Trademark Law Revision Act of 1988 748
United States Copyright Office 745
United States Court of Appeals for the Federal Circuit 740
United States Patent and Trademark Office (PTO) 740
Useful 741
Utility patent 741
World Wide Web (web) 752

SUMMARY OF KEY CONCEPTS

Trade Secret

	A *trade secret* is a product formula, pattern, design, compilation of data, customer list, or other business secret that makes a business successful. The owner of a trade secret must take reasonable precautions to prevent the trade secret from being discovered by others.
Misappropriation	Misappropriation is a tort in which another's trade secret is obtained through unlawful means such as theft, bribery, or espionage. A successful plaintiff can recover profits, damages, and an injunction against the offender.
Economic Espionage Act	The federal Economic Espionage Act makes it a crime for any person to convert a trade secret for his or her or another's benefit, knowing or intending to cause injury to the owner of the trade secret.

Patent

Federal Patent Statute	Patent law is exclusively federal law; there are no state patent laws.
Scope	Patentable subject matter includes machines; processes; compositions of matter; improvements to existing machines, processes, or compositions of matter; designs for articles of manufacture; asexually reproduced plants; and living matter invented by humans.
Criteria	To be patented, an invention must be: 1. Novel 2. Useful 3. Nonobvious
Patent Application	An application containing a written description of the invention must be filed with the United States Patent and Trademark Office in Washington, D.C.
Term	Patents are valid for 20 years.

Public-Use Doctrine	A patent may not be granted if the invention was used by the public for more than one year prior to the inventor's filing the patent application.
The American Inventors Protection Act	The American Inventors Protection Act: 1. Permits an inventor to file a *provisional application* with the U.S. Patent and Trademark Office, which grants the inventor three months of "provisional rights," pending the filing of a final patent application. 2. Requires the PTO to issue a patent within three years after the filing of a patent application.
Patent Infringement	The patent holder may recover damages and other remedies against a person who makes unauthorized use of the holder's patent.
Patent Appeal	The United States Court of Appeals for the Federal Circuit in Washington, D.C., hears patent appeals.
Copyright	
Scope	Copyright law is exclusively federal law; there are no state copyright laws. Only tangible writings can be copyrighted. These include books, newspapers, addresses, musical compositions, motion pictures, works of art, architectural plans, greeting cards, photographs, sound recordings, computer programs, and mask works fixed in semiconductor chips.
Requirements for Copyright	The only requirement to obtain a copyright is that the writing is the original work of the author.
Copyright Registration	Copyright registration is permissive and voluntary. Published and unpublished works may be registered with the United States Copyright Office in Washington, D.C. However, registration itself does not create the copyright.
Term	Copyrights are for the following terms: 1. *Individual holder:* Life of the author plus 70 years. 2. *Corporate holder:* Either (a) 95 years from the date of publication or (b) 120 years from the date of creation, whichever is shorter.
Copyright Infringement	When copyright infringement has occurred, the copyright holder may recover damages and other remedies against the person who copied a substantial and material part of the copyrighted work without the holder's permission.
No Electronic Theft Act (NET Act)	The federal NET Act makes it a crime for a person to willfully infringe a copyright work, even if that person does so without commercial advantages or financial gain.
Fair-Use Doctrine	The fair-use doctrine permits the use of copyrighted material without the consent of the copyright holder for limited uses (such as in a scholarly work, parody, or satire, and brief quotation in news reports).
Digital Millennium Copyright Act (DMCA)	The federal DMCA, enacted in 1998, provides civil and criminal penalties that 1. Prohibit the manufacture and distribution of technologies, products, and services designed primarily to circumvent wrappers or encryption protection. 2. Prohibit unauthorized access to copyrighted digital works by circumventing the wrapper or encryption technology that protects the intellectual property.

Trademark	
Mark	Marks are collectively referred to as trademarks and consist of the trade name, symbol, word, logo, design, or device that distinguishes the owner's good or services.
Registration of Trademarks	Marks are registered with the United States Patent and Trademark Office in Washington, D.C.
Types of Marks	1. *Trademark:* Identifies the goods of a particular business 2. *Service mark:* Identifies the services of a particular business 3. *Certification mark:* Certifies that goods or services are of a certain quality or origin 4. *Collective membership mark:* Used by cooperatives, associations, and fraternal organizations to identity themselves as members of an organization
Requirements for a Trademark	A trademark is required to either (1) be *distinctive* or (2) have acquired a *secondary meaning*. The mark must be used in commerce, or the holder must intend to use the mark in commerce and actually do so within six months after registering the mark.
Term	The term of the original registration of a mark is 10 years and can be renewed for an unlimited number of 10-year periods.
Trademark Infringement	When trademark infringement has occurred, the mark holder may recover damages and other remedies from the person who made unauthorized use of the holder's registered mark.
Generic Name	A generic name is a mark that has become a common term for a product line or type of service and loses its protection under federal trademark law.
Internet	
	The Internet is a collection of millions of computers that provides a network of electronic connections among computers.
World Wide Web	The World Wide Web is an electronic connection of computers that supports a standard set of rules for the exchange of information called hypertext transfer protocol (HTTP).
Electronic Mail (Email)	Email is electronic written communication between individuals using computers connected to the Internet.
Domain Name	
	The domain name is a unique name that identifies an individual's or a company's website.
Anticybersquatting Consumer Protection Act	The Anticybersquatting Consumer Protection Act (ACPA) is a federal statute that permits a court to issue cease-and-desist orders and injunctions and to award monetary damages against anyone who has registered a domain name (1) of a famous name (2) in bad faith.
Digital Law	
Electronic Communications Privacy Act (ECPA)	The Electronic Communications Privacy Act is a federal statute that makes it a crime to intercept an electronic communication at the point of transmission, while in transit, when stored by a router or server, or after receipt by the intended recipient.
Information Infrastructure Protection Act (IIP Act)	The Information Infrastructure Protection Act is a federal statute that makes it a federal crime for anyone to intentionally access and acquire information from a protected computer without authorization.

WORKING THE WEB

1. Go to the website http://networksolutions.com Pick an Internet domain name you would be interested in registering, and check to see if this name is available. What is the cost of registering an Internet domain name?
2. Visit the website http://www.uspto Select "Trademarks" and click on "search." Select a name for which you are interested in determining whether a trademark or service mark is available. Then select "New User Form Search" and search to see if this name is available. What are the results of your search?
3. Visit the website http://coca-cola.com Search this website for the history of the "Coca-Cola" trademark. Write a half-page history of the trademark. Find and list five other trademarks that the Coca-Cola Company owns.

CRITICAL THINKING & WRITING QUESTIONS

1. What is intellectual property?
2. What is a trade secret? How is a trade secret protected? For how long is protection available? Explain.
3. What does the Digital Millennium Copyright Act (DMCA) provide?
4. What is a patent? What can be patented? What are the statutory requirements for a patent? How is a patent obtained?
5. Explain patent infringement. What types of remedies are available for patent infringement?
6. What is a copyright? What can be copyrighted? How is a copyright obtained?
7. Explain copyright infringement. What types of remedies are available for copyright infringement?
8. Explain and give an example of the fair-use doctrine.
9. What is a mark? What are the requirements for obtaining a mark?
10. Describe the differences among: (1) trademark, (2) service mark, (3) certification mark, and (4) collective membership mark.
11. Describe and give an example of a generic name.
12. What is a domain name? How is a domain name registered? What are some of the top-level domain name (TLD) extensions?

Building Paralegal Skills

VIDEO CASE STUDIES

Confidentiality Issue: Need-to-Know Circle

Two paralegals working in the same law firm meet in the coffee room. They begin to discuss a case that one of the paralegals is working on.

After viewing the video case study in MyLegalStudiesLab, answer the following:

1. Can every matter being handled within the firm be discussed with everyone else in the law firm? Why or why not?
2. Will disclosure of information about intellectual property jeopardize the client's rights?
3. How should a paralegal find out with whom he or she may discuss a case?

ETHICS ANALYSIS & DISCUSSION QUESTIONS

1. Does a paralegal working in the area of intellectual property law have any ethical obligation to obtain specialized training or education?
2. Are memoranda of law and other reports prepared by a paralegal protected by copyright law? If so, to whom do the rights belong—the paralegal, the client, or the firm?
3. You are not a lawyer, but under regulations issued by the Commissioner of Patents with the approval of the Secretary of Commerce pursuant to 35 U.S.C. Section 31, you are authorized to practice before the United States Patent Office [*Sperry v. Florida ex rel. Florida Bar*, 373 U.S. 379, 83 S.Ct. 1322, 10 L.Ed.2d 428, 1963 U.S. Lexis 2486 (1963)]. May you represent patent applicants, prepare and prosecute their applications, and advise applicants in connection with their applications in Florida?

DEVELOPING YOUR COLLABORATION SKILLS

With a group of other students selected by you or your instructor, review the facts of the following case. As a group, discuss the following questions.

1. What trademarks are owned by the plaintiff?
2. What trademark is owned by the defendant?
3. Whose trademark is the senior mark?
4. Has the defendant infringed on the plaintiff's marks?

Intel Corporation v. Intelsys Software, LLC

Intel Corporation is a large company that distributes its entire line of products and services under the registered trademark and service mark "INTEL." The company also owns numerous marks that incorporate its INTEL marks as a permanent component, such as the marks "INTEL INSIDE," INTEL SPEEDSTEP," and "INTEL NETMERGE." Intelsys Software, LLC, which is owned by another party, develops software applications for network utilities and wireless applications. Intelsys uses the mark "Intelsys Software" and maintains a website at www.intelsys.com. Intel Corporation brought an action in U.S. District Court against Intelsys Software, LLC, alleging that Intelsys infringed on Intel's trademarks and service marks in violation of the Lanham Act. Intel filed a motion for judgment and a permanent injunction against Intelsys's use of the mark "INTEL" in any of its company, product, or service names.

Source: Intel Corporation v. Intelsys Software, LLC, Web 2009 U.S. Dist. Lexis 14761

PARALEGAL PORTFOLIO EXERCISE

Go to the website http://www.loc.gov Find and print out the proper form and instructions to obtain a copyright for a nondramatic literary work. Read the instructions for completing this form, and then complete the form as if you were the writer of a nondramatic literary work to be registered. Make up whatever information is necessary to complete the form. Search the website and determine where to submit the form and the fee that must be paid to submit the form.

LEGAL ANALYSIS & WRITING CASES

Titlecraft, Inc. v. National Football League

Web 2010 U.S. Dist. Lexis 134367 (2010) United States *District Court for the District of Minnesota*

The National Football League (NFL), an association of 32 member teams, is a professional football league that plays games in stadiums in different cities of the country and televises these games on television and cable networks. The league's winner each year is determined by one of the most watched events on television, the Super Bowl, after which the victor is presented with the Vince Lombardi Trophy. The trophy, which was designed and manufactured for the NFL by the well-known jeweler Tiffany & Co., is made of sterling silver and consists of a replica football sitting, at a downward angle, at the top of a three-sided base with concave sides, which taper as they rise. The NFL holds a valid registered copyright for the trophy.

Fantasy football allows persons to act as owners and general managers of a pseudo-football team wherein they manage football players of the NFL. In an interactive, virtual Internet world they join a fantasy football league and each person's team compete[s] with other players. A person's "roster" might consist of a quarterback from one NFL team and a running back from another NFL team. Points are awarded based on how the real players on a person's team perform each week in actual NFL games. As in the real league, fantasy football owners can draft, add, drop, and trade players. And as with the NFL, fantasy football leagues crown a winner.

Titlecraft, Inc. manufactures fantasy football league trophies that it sells through its website to fantasy football leagues to be given to league winners. Its trophies are similar in appearance to the Vince Lombardi Trophy in that they consist of a football sitting, at a downward angle, atop a base with three tapered sides. Titlecraft trophies are made of wood rather than silver. In a lawsuit filed in U.S. District Court, the NFL sued Titlecraft for copyright infringement.

Question

1. Has Titlecraft infringed on the NFL's copyright of the Vince Lombardi Trophy?

New York Yankees Partnership d/b/a The New York Yankees Baseball Club

Claim Number FA0609000803277 (2006)
National Arbitration Forum

The New York Yankees Partnership d/b/a/ The New York Yankees Baseball Club (Yankees) is among the world's most recognized and followed sports teams, having won more than twenty World Series Championships and more than thirty American League pennants. The Yankees own the trademark for the NEW YORK YANKEES (Reg. No. 1,073,346), which was issued to the Yankees by the U. S. Patent and Trademark Office (USPTO) on September 13, 1977. Moniker Online Services, Inc. (Moniker), registered the domain name www.nyyankees.com. Moniker operated a commercial website under this domain name, where it offered links to third-party commercial websites that sold tickets to Yankees baseball games and where it sold merchandise bearing the NEW YORK YANKEES trademark without the permission of the Yankees. The Yankees filed a complaint with the National Arbitration Forum alleging that Moniker had registered the domain in bad faith in violation of Internet law, and seeking to obtain the domain name from Moniker.

Question

1. Who wins?

WORKING WITH THE LANGUAGE OF THE COURT CASE

V Secret Catalogue, Inc. and Victoria's Secret Stores, Inc. v. Moseley, dba Victor's Little Secret and Victor's Secret

605 F.3d 382, Web 2010 U.S. App. Lexis 10150
United States Court of Appeals for the Sixth Circuit

Read and then brief the following case, excerpted from the court of appeals opinion. In your brief, answer the following questions.

1. Who is the plaintiff? What products does the plaintiff sell? Under what trademarked name does the plaintiff sell its products?
2. Who is the defendant? What products does the defendant sell? Under what name does the defendant sell his products?
3. What federal statute is at issue in this case?
4. Did the court find that there was a likelihood of dilution by tarnishment?

Merritt, Circuit Judge

In this trademark "dilution by tarnishment" case, brought under the Trademark Dilution Revision Act of 2006, the question is whether the plaintiff, an international lingerie company that uses the trade name designation "Victoria's Secret" has a valid suit for injunctive relief against the use of the name "Victor's Little Secret" or "Victor's Secret" by the defendants, a small retail store in a mall in Elizabethtown, Kentucky, that sells assorted merchandise, including "sex toys" and other sexually oriented products. The District Court issued the injunction. The District Court concluded that even though the two parties do not compete in the same market, the "Victor's Little Secret" mark—because it is sex related—disparages and tends to reduce the positive associations and the "selling power" of the "Victoria's Secret" mark.

The question is whether the plaintiff's case meets the definitions and standards for "dilution by tarnishment" set out in the new Act which amended the old Act, *i.e.*, the Federal Trademark Dilution Act of 1995. The House Judiciary Committee Report states the purpose of the new 2006 legislation as follows: "The new language in the legislation [provides]...specifically that the standard for proving a dilution claim is 'likelihood of dilution' and that both dilution by blurring and dilution by tarnishment are actionable." The question for us then is whether "Victor's Little Secret" with its association with lewd sexual toys creates a "likelihood of dilution by tarnishment" of [the] Victoria's Secret mark.

There have been at least eight federal cases in six jurisdictions that conclude that a famous mark is tarnished when its mark is semantically associated with a new mark that is used to sell sex-related products.

We find no exceptions in the case law that allow such a new mark associated with sex to stand. *See Pfizer Inc. v. Sachs*, (defendants' display at an adult entertainment exhibition of two models riding a VIAGRA-branded missile and distributing condoms would likely harm the reputation of Pfizer's trademark); *Williams-Sonoma, Inc. v. Friendfinder, Inc.*, (defendants' use of POTTERY BARN mark on their sexually-oriented websites likely to tarnish "by associating those marks for children and teenager furnishings"); *Kraft Foods Holdings, Inc. v. Helm*, (pornographic website's use of "VelVeeda" tarnishes VELVEETA trademark); *Victoria's Cyber Secret Ltd. P'ship v. V Secret Catalogue, Inc.*, (defendants' internet trade names likely to tarnish famous mark when websites "will be used for entertainment of a lascivious nature suitable only for adults"); *Mattel, Inc. v. Internet Dimensions Inc.*, (linking BARBIE with pornography will adversely color the public's impressions of BARBIE); *Polo Ralph Lauren L.P. v. Schuman*, (defendants' use of "The Polo Club" or "Polo Executive Retreat" as an adult entertainment club tarnished POLO trademark); *Pillsbury Co. v. Milky Way Prods., Inc.*, (defendant's sexually-oriented variation of the PILLSBURY DOUGHBOY tarnished plaintiff's mark); *Dallas Cowboys Cheerleaders, Inc. v. Pussycat Cinema, Ltd.*, (pornographic depiction of a Dallas Cowboys Cheerleader-style cheerleader in an adult film tarnished the professional mark of the Dallas Cowboys).

The burden-of-proof problem... should now be interpreted, we think, to create a kind of rebuttable presumption, or at least a very strong inference, that a new mark used to sell sex-related products is likely to tarnish a famous mark if there is a clear semantic association between the two. This... places on the owner of the new mark the burden of coming forward with evidence that there is no likelihood or probability of tarnishment. The evidence could be in the form of expert testimony or surveys or polls or customer testimony. In the present case, the Moseleys have had two opportunities in the District Court to offer evidence that there is no real probability of tarnishment and have not done so.

The new law seems designed to protect trademarks from any unfavorable sexual associations. Thus, any new mark with a lewd or offensive-to-some sexual association raises a strong inference of tarnishment. The inference must be overcome by evidence that rebuts the probability that some consumers will find the new mark both offensive and harmful to the reputation and the favorable symbolism of the famous mark.

We have now fully considered the case on the merits... and conclude that the District Court did not err in its decision in favor of the plaintiff, Victoria's Secret.

Accordingly, the judgment of the District Court is AFFIRMED.

MYLEGALSTUDIESLAB

MyLegalStudiesLab Virtual Law Office Experience Assignments

Complete the pre-test, study plan, and post-test for this chapter and answer the Legal Applications questions as assigned. These will help you confirm your mastery of the concepts and their application to legal scenarios. Then complete the Virtual Law Office assignments as assigned by your instructor. These assignments are designed to develop your workplace skills. Completing the assignments for this chapter will result in producing the following documents for inclusion in your portfolio:

VLOE 20.1	Completed forms to copyright the images and the book itself
VLOE 20.2	Separate billing summary for each matter worked on during internship and cumulative total hours

APPENDIX A

How to Brief a Case

CRITICAL LEGAL THINKING

Judges apply legal reasoning in reaching a decision in a case. In doing so, the judge must specify the issue presented by the case, identify the key facts in the case and the applicable law, and then apply the law to the facts to come to a conclusion that answers the issue presented. This process is called **critical legal thinking.** Skills of analysis and interpretation are important in deciding legal cases.

Key Terms

Before embarking upon the study of law, the student should be familiar with the following key legal terms:

Plaintiff The party who originally brought the lawsuit.

Defendant The party against whom the lawsuit has been brought.

Petitioner or Appellant The party who has appealed the decision of the trial court or lower court. The petitioner may be either the plaintiff or the defendant, depending on who lost the case at the trial court or lower court level.

Respondent or Appellee The party who must answer the petitioner's appeal. The respondent may be either the plaintiff or the defendant, depending upon which party is the petitioner. In some cases, both the plaintiff *and* the defendant may disagree with the trial court's or lower court's decision and both parties may appeal the decision.

Briefing a Case

"Briefing" a case is important to clarify the legal issues involved and to gain a better understanding of the case.

The student must summarize (brief) the court's decision in no more than 400 words (some professors may shorten or lengthen this limit). The format is highly structured, consisting of five parts, each of which is numbered and labeled:

Part	Maximum Words
1. Case name and citation	25
2. Summary of key facts in the case	125
3. Issue presented by the case, stated as a one-sentence question answerable only by *yes* or *no*	25
4. Holding—the court's resolution of the issue	25
5. A summary of the court's reasoning justifying the holding	200
Total words	400

1. Case Name and Citation

The name of the case is placed at the beginning of each briefed case. The case name usually contains the names of the parties to the lawsuit. If there are multiple plaintiffs or defendants, however, some of the names of the parties may be omitted from the case name. Abbreviations often are used in case names.

The case citation—which consists of a number plus the year in which the case was decided, such as "126 L.Ed.2d 295 (1993)"—is set forth below the case name. The case citation identifies the book in the law library in which the case may be found. For example, the case in the above citation may be found in volume 126 of the *Supreme Court Reporter Lawyer's Edition (Second)*, page 295. The name of the court that decided the case appears below the case name.

2. Summary of Key Facts in the Case

The important facts of a case are stated briefly. Extraneous facts and facts of minor importance are omitted from the brief. The facts of the case usually can be found at the beginning of the case, but not necessarily. Important facts may be found throughout the case.

3. Issue Presented by the Case

It is crucial in briefing a case to identify the issue presented to the court to decide. The issue on appeal is most often a legal question, although questions of fact sometimes are the subject of an appeal. The issue presented in each case usually is quite specific and should be asked in a one-sentence question that is answerable only by a *yes* or *no*. For example, the issue statement, "Is Mary liable?" is too broad. A more proper statement of the issue would be, "Is Mary liable to Joe for breach of the contract made between them based on her refusal to make the payment due on September 30?"

4. Holding

The holding is the decision reached by the present court. It should be *yes* or *no*. The holding also states which party won.

5. Summary of the Court's Reasoning

When an appellate court or supreme court issues a decision—which often is called an *opinion*—the court normally states the reasoning it used in reaching its decision. The rationale for the decision may be based on the specific facts of the case, public policy, prior law, or other matters. In stating the reasoning of the court, the student should reword the court's language into the student's own language. This summary of the court's reasoning should pick out the meat of the opinions and weed out the nonessentials.

Following are two U.S. Supreme Court opinions for briefing. The case is presented in the language of the U.S. Supreme Court. A "Brief of the Case" follows each of the two cases. A third case, from the New York State Court of Appeals, also is included for briefing.

CASE 1

For Briefing

Harris v. Forklift Systems, Inc.	**CASE NAME**	
510 U.S. 17, 114 S.Ct. 367, 126 L.Ed.2d 295	**CITATION**	***1993 U.S. LEXIS 7155 (1993)***
	COURT	***Supreme Court of the United States***

OPINION OF THE COURT. O'CONNOR, JUSTICE

FACTS. Teresa Harris worked as a manager at Forklift Systems, Inc., an equipment rental company, from April 1985 until October 1987. Charles Hardy was Forklift's president. Throughout Harris's time at Forklift, Hardy often insulted her because of her gender and often made her the target of unwanted sexual innuendos. Hardy told Harris on several occasions, in the presence of other employees, "You're a woman, what do you know" and "We need a man as the rental manager"; at least once, he told her she was "a dumb-ass woman." Again in front of others, he suggested that the two of them "go to the Holiday Inn to negotiate Harris' raise." Hardy occasionally asked Harris and other female employees to get coins from his front pants pocket. He threw objects on the ground in front of Harris and other women, and asked them to pick the objects up. He made sexual innuendos about Harris' and other women's clothing.

In mid-August 1987, Harris complained to Hardy about his conduct. Hardy said he was surprised that Harris was offended, claimed he was only joking, and apologized. He also promised he would stop and based on his assurance Harris stayed on the job. But in early September, Hardy began anew: While Harris was arranging a deal with one of Forklift's customers, he asked her, again in front of other employees, "What did you do, promise the guy some sex Saturday night?" On October 1, Harris collected her paycheck and quit.

LOWER COURTS' OPINIONS. Harris then sued Forklift, claiming that Hardy's conduct had created an abusive work environment for her because of her gender. The United States District Court for the Middle District of Tennessee found this to be "a close case," but held that Hardy's conduct did not create an abusive environment. The court found that some of Hardy's comments offended Harris, and would offend the "reasonable woman," but that they were not "so severe as to be expected to seriously affect Harris' psychological well-being." A reasonable woman manager under like circumstances would have been offended by Hardy, but his conduct would not have risen to the level of interfering with that person's work performance. The United States Court of Appeals for the Sixth Circuit affirmed in a brief unpublished decision.

ISSUE. We granted certiorari to resolve a conflict among the Circuits on whether conduct, to be actionable as "abusive work environment" harassment, must "seriously affect an employee's psychological well-being" or lead the plaintiff to "suffer injury."

STATUTE BEING INTERPRETED. Title VII of the Civil Rights Act of 1964 makes it "an unlawful employment practice for an employer…to discriminate against any individual with respect to his compensation, terms, conditions, or privileges of employment, because of such individual's race, color, religion, sex, or national origin." 42 U.S.C. §2000e-2(a)(1).

U.S. SUPREME COURT'S REASONING. When the workplace is permeated with discriminatory intimidation, ridicule, and insult that is sufficiently severe or pervasive to alter the conditions of the victim's employment and create an abusive working environment, Title VII is violated. This standard takes a middle path between making actionable any conduct that is merely offensive and requiring the conduct to cause a tangible psychological injury. Mere utterance of an epithet which engenders offensive feelings in an employee does not sufficiently affect the conditions of employment to implicate Title VII. Conduct that is not severe or pervasive enough to create an objectively hostile or abusive work environment—an environment that a reasonable person would find hostile or abusive—is beyond Title VII's purview. Likewise, if the victim does not subjectively perceive the environment to be abusive, the conduct has not actually altered the conditions of the victim's employment, and there is no Title VII violation.

But Title VII comes into play before the harassing conduct leads to a nervous breakdown. A discriminatorily abusive work environment, even one that does not seriously affect employees' psychological well-being, can and often will detract from employees' job performance, discourage employees from remaining on the job, or keep them from advancing in their careers. Moreover, even without regard to these tangible effects, the very fact that the discriminatory conduct was so severe or pervasive that it created a work environment abusive to employees because of their race, gender, religion, or national origin offends Title VII's broad rule of workplace equality.

HOLDING. We therefore believe the district court erred in relying on whether the conduct "seriously affected plaintiff's psychological well-being" or led her to "suffer injury." Such an inquiry may needlessly focus the factfinder's attention on concrete psychological harm, an element Title VII does not require. So long as the environment would reasonably be perceived, and is perceived, as hostile or abusive, there is no need for it also to be psychologically injurious. This is not, and by its nature cannot be, a mathematically precise test. But we can say that whether an environment is "hostile" or "abusive" can be determined only by looking at all the circumstances.

We therefore reverse the judgment of the Court of Appeals, and remand the case for further proceedings consistent with this opinion.

CONCURRING OPINION. GINSBURG, JUSTICE
The critical issue, Title VII's text indicates, is whether members of one sex are exposed to disadvantageous terms or conditions of employment to which members of the other sex are not exposed. The adjudicator's inquiry should center, dominantly, on whether the discriminatory conduct has reasonably interfered with the plaintiff's work performance. To show such interference, the plaintiff need not prove that his or her tangible productivity has declined as a result of the harassment.

Brief of the Case: *Harris v. Forklift Systems, Inc.*

1. Case Name, Citation, and Court

Harris v. Forklift Systems, Inc.
126 L.Ed.2d. 295 (1993)
United States Supreme Court

2. Summary of the Key Facts

A. While Harris worked at Forklift, Hardy continually insulted her because of her gender and made her the target of unwanted sexual innuendos.
B. This conduct created an abusive and hostile work environment, causing Harris to terminate her employment.
C. Harris sued Forklift, alleging sexual harassment in violation of Title VII of the Civil Rights Act of 1964, which makes it an unlawful employment practice for an employer to discriminate in employment because of an individual's sex.

3. The Issue

Must an employee prove that she suffered psychological injury before she can prove a Title VII claim for sexual harassment against her employer?

4. The Holding

No. The Supreme Court remanded the case for further proceedings consistent with its opinion.

5. Summary of the Court's Reasoning

The Supreme Court held that a workplace that is permeated with discriminatory intimidation, ridicule, and insult so severe that it alters the conditions of the victim's employment creates an abusive and hostile work environment that violates Title VII. The Court held that the victim is not required to prove that she suffered tangible psychological injury to prove her Title VII claim. The Court noted that Title VII comes into play before the harassing conduct leads the victim to have a nervous breakdown.

CASE 2

For Briefing

PGA Tour, Inc. v. Martin	**CASE NAME**	
121 S.Ct. 1879, 149 L.Ed.2d 904 (2001)	**CITATION**	***2001 U.S. LEXIS 4115***
	COURT	***Supreme Court of the United States***

OPINION OF THE COURT. STEVEN, JUSTICE

ISSUE. This case raises two questions concerning the application of the Americans with Disabilities Act of 1990 [42 U.S.C. § 12101 *et seq.*] to a gifted athlete: first, whether the Act protects access to professional golf tournaments by a qualified entrant with a disability; and second, whether a disabled contestant may be denied the use of a golf cart because it would "fundamentally alter the nature" of the tournaments to allow him to ride when all other contestants must walk.

FACTS. Petitioner PGA TOUR, Inc., a nonprofit entity formed in 1968, sponsors and cosponsors professional golf tournaments conducted on three annual tours. About 200 golfers participate in the PGA TOUR; about 170 in the NIKE TOUR; and about 100 in the SENIOR PGA TOUR. PGA TOUR and NIKE TOUR tournaments typically are 4-day events, played on courses leased and operated by petitioner. The revenues generated by television, admissions, concessions, and contributions from cosponsors amount to about $300 million a year, much of which is distributed in prize money. The "Conditions of Competition and Local Rules," often described as the "hard card," apply specifically to petitioner's professional tours. The hard cards for the PGA TOUR and NIKE TOUR require players to walk the golf course during tournaments, but not during open qualifying rounds. On the SENIOR PGA TOUR, which is limited to golfers age 50 and older, the contestants may use golf carts. Most seniors, however, prefer to walk.

RESPONDENT. Casey Martin is a talented golfer. As an amateur, he won 17 Oregon Golf Association junior events before he was 15, and won the state championship as a high school senior. He played on the Stanford University golf team that won the 1994 National Collegiate Athletic Association (NCAA) championship. As a professional, Martin qualified for the NIKE TOUR in 1998 and 1999, and based on his 1999 performance, qualified for the PGA TOUR in 2000. In the 1999 season, he entered 24 events, made the cut 13 times, and had 6 top-10 finishes, coming in second twice and third once.

Martin is also an individual with a disability as defined in the Americans with Disabilities Act of 1990 (ADA or Act). Since birth he has been afflicted with Klippel-Trenaunay-Weber Syndrome, a degenerative circulatory disorder that obstructs the flow of blood from his right leg back to his heart. The disease is progressive; it causes severe pain and has atrophied his right leg. During the latter part of his college career, because of the progress of the disease, Martin could no longer walk an 18-hole golf course. Walking not only caused him pain, fatigue, and anxiety, but also created a significant risk of hemorrhaging, developing blood clots, and fracturing his tibia so badly that an amputation might be required.

When Martin turned pro and entered the petitioner's Qualifying-School, the hard card permitted him to use a cart during his successful progress through the first two stages. He made a request, supported by detailed medical records, for permission to use a golf cart during the third stage. Petitioner refused to review those records, or to waive its walking rule for the third stage. Martin therefore filed this action.

DISTRICT COURT'S DECISION 994 F.SUPP. 1242 [DISTRICT: OREGON (1998)]. At trial, petitioner PGA TOUR did not contest the conclusion that Martin has a disability covered by the ADA, or the fact that his disability prevents him from walking the course during a round of golf. Rather, petitioner asserted that the condition of walking is a substantive rule of competition, and that waiving it as to any individual for any reason would fundamentally alter the nature of the competition. Petitioner's evidence included the testimony of a number of experts, among them some of the greatest golfers in history. Arnold Palmer, Jack Nicklaus, and Ken Venturi explained that fatigue can be a critical factor in a tournament, particularly on the last day when psychological pressure is at a maximum. Their testimony makes it clear that, in their view, permission to use a cart might well give some players a competitive advantage over other players who must walk.

The judge found that the purpose of the rule was to inject fatigue into the skill of shot-making, but that the fatigue injected "by walking the course cannot be deemed significant under normal circumstances." Furthermore, Martin presented evidence, and the judge found, that even with the use of a cart, Martin must walk over a mile during an 18-hole round, and that the fatigue he suffers from coping with his disability is "undeniably greater" than the fatigue his able-bodied competitors endure from walking the course. As a result, the judge concluded that it would "not fundamentally alter the nature of the PGA Tour's game to accommodate him with a cart." The judge accordingly entered a permanent injunction requiring petitioner to permit Martin to use a cart in tour and qualifying events.

COURT OF APPEALS DECISION 204 F.3D 994 [9TH CIRCUIT (2000)]. The Court of Appeals concluded that golf courses remain places of public accommodation during PGA tournaments. On the merits, because there was no serious dispute about the fact that permitting Martin to use a golf cart was both a reasonable and a necessary solution to the problem of providing him access to the tournaments, the Court of Appeals regarded the central dispute as whether such permission would "fundamentally alter" the nature of the PGA TOUR or NIKE

TOUR. Like the District Court, the Court of Appeals viewed the issue not as "whether use of carts generally would fundamentally alter the competition, but whether the use of a cart by Martin would do so." That issue turned on "an intensively fact-based inquiry," and, the court concluded, had been correctly resolved by the trial judge. In its words, "all that the cart does is permit Martin access to a type of competition in which he otherwise could not engage because of his disability."

FEDERAL STATUTE BEING INTERPRETED. Congress enacted the ADA in 1990 to remedy widespread discrimination against disabled individuals. To effectuate its sweeping purpose, the ADA forbids discrimination against disabled individuals in major areas of public life, among them employment (Title I of the Act), public services (Title II), and public accommodations (Title III). At issue now is the applicability of Title III to petitioner's golf tours and qualifying rounds, in particular to petitioner's treatment of a qualified disabled golfer wishing to compete in those events.

U.S. SUPREME COURT'S REASONING. It seems apparent, from both the general rule and the comprehensive definition of "public accommodation," that petitioner's golf tours and their qualifying rounds fit comfortably within the coverage of Title III, and Martin within its protection. The events occur on "golf courses," a type of place specifically identified by the Act as a public accommodation. Section 12181(7)(L). In this case, the narrow dispute is whether allowing Martin to use a golf cart, despite the walking requirement that applies to the PGA TOUR, the NIKE TOUR, and the third stage of the Qualifying-School, is a modification that would "fundamentally alter the nature" of those events.

As an initial matter, we observe that the use of carts is not itself inconsistent with the fundamental character of the game of golf. From early on, the essence of the game has been shot-making—using clubs to cause a ball to progress from the teeing ground to a hole some distance away with as few strokes as possible. Golf carts started appearing with increasing regularity on American golf courses in the 1950's. Today they are everywhere. And they are encouraged. For one thing, they often speed up play, and for another, they are great revenue producers. There is nothing in the Rules of Golf that either forbids the use of carts, or penalizes a player for using a cart.

Petitioner, however, distinguishes the game of golf as it is generally played from the game that it sponsors in the PGA TOUR, NIKE TOUR, and the last stage of the Qualifying-School—golf at the "highest level." According to petitioner, "the goal of the highest-level competitive athletics is to assess and compare the performance of different competitors, a task that is meaningful only if the competitors are subject to identical substantive rules." The waiver of any possibly "outcome-affecting" rule for a contestant would violate this principle and therefore, in petitioner's view, fundamentally alter the nature of the highest level athletic event. The walking rule is one such rule, petitioner submits, because its purpose is "to inject the element of fatigue into the skill of shot-making," and thus its effect may be the critical loss of a stroke. As a consequence, the reasonable modification Martin seeks would fundamentally alter the nature of petitioner's highest level tournaments.

The force of petitioner's argument is, first of all, mitigated by the fact that golf is a game in which it is impossible to guarantee that all competitors will play under exactly the same conditions or that an individual's ability will be the sole determinant of the outcome. For example, changes in the weather may produce harder greens and more head winds for the tournament leader than for his closest pursuers. A lucky bounce may save a shot or two. Whether such happenstance events are more or less probable than the likelihood that a golfer afflicted with Klippel-Trenaunay-Weber Syndrome would one day qualify for the NIKE TOUR and PGA TOUR, they at least demonstrate that pure chance may have a greater impact on the outcome of elite golf tournaments than the fatigue resulting from the enforcement of the walking rule.

Further, the factual basis of petitioner's argument is undermined by the District Court's finding that the fatigue from walking during one of petitioner's 4-day tournaments cannot be deemed significant. The District Court credited the testimony of a professor in physiology and expert on fatigue, who calculated the calories expended in walking a golf course (about five miles) to be approximately 500 calories—"nutritionally less than a Big Mac." What is more, that energy is expended over a 5-hour period, during which golfers have numerous intervals for rest and refreshment. In fact, the expert concluded, because golf is a low intensity activity, fatigue from the game is primarily a psychological phenomenon in which stress and motivation are the key ingredients. And even under conditions of severe heat and humidity, the critical factor in fatigue is fluid loss rather than exercise from walking. Moreover, when given the option of using a cart, the majority of golfers in petitioner's tournaments have chosen to walk, often to relieve stress or for other strategic reasons. As NIKE TOUR member Eric Johnson testified, walking allows him to keep in rhythm, stay warmer when it is chilly, and develop a better sense of the elements and the course than riding in a cart. As we have demonstrated, the walking rule is at best peripheral to the nature of petitioner's athletic events, and thus it might be waived in individual cases without working a fundamental alteration.

HOLDING AND REMEDY. Under the ADA's basic requirement that the need of a disabled person be evaluated on an individual basis, we have no doubt that allowing Martin to use a golf cart would not fundamentally alter the nature of petitioner's tournaments. As we have discussed, the purpose of the walking rule is to subject players to fatigue, which in turn may influence the outcome of tournaments. Even if the rule does serve that purpose, it is an uncontested finding of the District Court that Martin "easily endures greater fatigue even with a cart than his able-bodied competitors do by walking." The purpose of the walking rule is therefore not compromised in the slightest by allowing Martin to use a cart. A modification that provides an exception to a peripheral tournament rule without impairing its purpose cannot be said to "fundamentally alter" the tournament. What it can be said to do, on the other hand, is to allow Martin the chance to qualify for and compete in the athletic events petitioner offers to those members of the public who have the skill and desire to enter. That is exactly what the ADA requires. As a result, Martin's request for a waiver of the walking rule should have been granted.

The judgment of the Court of Appeals is affirmed. It is so ordered.

DISSENTING OPINION. SCALIA, JUSTICE

In my view, today's opinion exercises a benevolent compassion that the law does not place it within our power to impose. The judgment distorts the text of Title III, the structure of the ADA, and common sense. I respectfully dissent.

The Court, for its part, assumes that conclusion for the sake of argument, but pronounces respondent to be a "customer" of the PGA TOUR or of the golf courses on which it is played. That seems to me quite incredible. The PGA TOUR is a professional sporting event, staged for the entertainment of a live and TV audience. The professional golfers on the tour are no more "enjoying" (the statutory term) the entertainment that the tour provides, or the facilities of the golf courses on which it is held, than professional baseball players "enjoy" the baseball games in which they play or the facilities of Yankee Stadium. To be sure, professional baseball players *participate* in the games, and *use* the ballfields, but no one in his right mind would think that they are *customers* of the American League or of Yankee Stadium. They are themselves the entertainment that the customers pay to watch. And professional golfers are no different. A professional golfer's practicing his profession is not comparable to John Q. Public's frequenting "a 232-acre amusement area with swimming, boating, sun bathing, picnicking, miniature golf, dancing facilities, and a snack bar."

Having erroneously held that Title III applies to the "customers" of professional golf who consist of its practitioners, the Court then erroneously answers—or to be accurate simply ignores—a second question. The ADA requires covered businesses to make such reasonable modifications of "policies, practices, or procedures" as are necessary to "afford" goods, services, and privileges to individuals with disabilities; but it explicitly does not require "modifications that would fundamentally alter the nature" of the goods, services, and privileges. Section 12182(b)(2)(A)(ii). In other words, disabled individuals must be given *access* to the same goods, services, and privileges that others enjoy.

A camera store may not refuse to sell cameras to a disabled person, but it is not required to stock cameras specially designed for such persons. It is hardly a feasible judicial function to decide whether shoe stores should sell single shoes to one-legged persons and if so at what price, or how many Braille books the Borders or Barnes and Noble bookstore chains should stock in each of their stores. Eighteen-hole golf courses, 10-foot-high basketball hoops, 90-foot baselines, 100-yard football fields—all are arbitrary and none is essential. The only support for any of them is tradition and (in more modern times) insistence by what has come to be regarded as the ruling body of the sport—both of which factors support the PGA TOUR's position in the present case. One can envision the parents of a Little League player with attention deficit disorder trying to convince a judge that their son's disability makes it at least 25% more difficult to hit a pitched ball. (If they are successful, the only thing that could prevent a court order giving a kid four strikes would be a judicial determination that, in baseball, three strikes are metaphysically necessary, which is quite absurd.)

Agility, strength, speed, balance, quickness of mind, steadiness of nerves, intensity of concentration—these talents are not evenly distributed. No wild-eyed dreamer has ever suggested that the managing bodies of the competitive sports that test precisely these qualities should try to take account of the uneven distribution of God-given gifts when writing and enforcing the rules of competition. And I have no doubt Congress did not authorize misty-eyed judicial supervision of such revolution. The year was 2001, and "everybody was finally equal." K. Vonnegut, Harrison Bergeron, in *Animal Farm and Related Readings* 129 (1997).

Brief of the Case: *PGA TOUR, Inc. v. Martin*

1. Case Name, Citation, and Court

PGA TOUR, Inc. v. Martin

121 S.Ct. 1879, 2001 LEXIS 415 (2001)

Supreme Court of the United States

2. Summary of the Key Facts

A. PGA TOUR, Inc. is a nonprofit organization that sponsors professional golf tournaments.

B. The PGA establishes rules for its golf tournaments. A PGA rule requires golfers to walk the golf course, and not use golf carts.

C. Casey Martin is a professional golfer who suffers from Klippel-Trenaunay-Weber Syndrome, a degenerative circulatory disorder that atrophied Martin's right leg and causes him pain, fatigue, and anxiety when walking.

D. When Martin petitioned the PGA to use a golf cart during golf tournaments, the PGA refused.

E. Martin sued the PGA, alleging discrimination against a disabled individual in violation of the American with Disabilities Act of 1990, a federal statute.

3. Issue

Does the Americans with Disabilities Act require the PGA to accommodate Martin by permitting him to use a golf cart while playing in PGA golf tournaments?

4. Holding

Yes. The Supreme Court held that the PGA must allow Martin to use a golf cart when competing in PGA golf tournaments. Affirmed.

5. Court's Reasoning

The Supreme Court held that:

A. Martin was disabled and covered by the Act.
B. Golf courses are "public accommodations" covered by the Act.
C. The use of golf carts is not a fundamental characteristic of the game of golf.
D. Other than the PGA rule, no Rule of Golf forbids the use of golf carts.
E. It is impossible to guarantee all players in golf will play under the exact same conditions, so allowing Martin to use a golf cart gives him no advantage over other golfers.
F. Martin, because of his disease, will probably suffer more fatigue playing golf using a golf cart than other golfers will suffer without using a cart.
G. The PGA's "walking rule" is only peripheral to the game of golf and not a fundamental part of golf.
H. Allowing Martin to use a golf cart will not fundamentally alter the PGA's highest-level professional golf tournaments.

CASE 3

For Briefing

Palsgraf v. Long Island R.R. Co. **CASE NAME**
248 N.Y. 339 (1928) **CITATION** ***162 N.E. 99***
COURT ***Court of Appeals of the State of New York***

OPINION OF THE COURT. CARDOZO, Ch. J.

FACTS. Plaintiff was standing on a platform of defendant's railroad after buying a ticket to go to Rockaway Beach. A train stopped at the station, bound for another place. Two men ran forward to catch it. One of the men reached the platform of the car without mishap, though the train was already moving. The other man, carrying a package, jumped aboard the car, but seemed unsteady as if about to fall. A guard on the car, who had held the door open, reached forward to help him in, and another guard on the platform pushed him from behind. In this act, the package was dislodged, and fell upon the rails. It was a package of small size, about fifteen inches long, and was covered by a newspaper. In fact it contained fireworks, but there was nothing in its appearance to give notice of its contents. The fireworks when they fell exploded. The shock of the explosion threw down some scales at the other end of the platform, many feet away. The scales struck the plaintiff, causing injuries for which she sues.

The conduct of the defendant's guard, if a wrong in its relation to the holder of the package, was not a wrong in its relation to the plaintiff, standing far away. Relatively to her it was not negligence at all. Nothing in the situation gave notice that the falling package had in it the potency of peril to persons thus removed. Negligence is not actionable unless it involves the invasion of a legally protected interest, the violation of a right. "Proof of negligence in the air, so to speak, will not do" (Pollock, *Torts* [11th ed.], p. 455; *Martin v. Herzog*, 228 N.Y. 164, 170; cf. Salmond, Torts [6th ed.], p.24). "Negligence is the absence of care, according to the circumstances" (WILLES, J., in *Vaughan v. Taff Vale Ry. Co.*, 5 H. & N. 679, 688; 1 Beven, Negligence [4th ed.], 7; *Paul v. Consol. Fireworks Co.*, 212 N.Y. 117; *Adams v. Bullock*, 227 N.Y. 208, 211; *Parrott v. Wells-Fargo Co.*, 15 Wall. [U.S.] 524). The plaintiff as she stood upon the platform of the station might claim to be protected against intentional invasion of her bodily security. Such invasion is not charged. She might claim to be protected against unintentional invasion by conduct involving in the thought of reasonable men an unreasonable hazard that such invasion would ensue. These, from the point of view of the law, were the bounds of her immunity, with perhaps some rare exceptions, survivals for the most part of ancient forms of liability, where conduct is held to be at the peril of the actor (*Sullivan v. Dunham*, 161 N.Y. 290 Page 342). If no hazard was apparent to the eye of ordinary vigilance, an act innocent and harmless, at least to outward seeming, with reference to her, did not take to itself the quality of a tort because it happened to be a wrong, though apparently not one involving the risk of bodily insecurity, with reference to some one else. "In every instance, before negligence can be predicated of a given act, back of the act must be sought and found a duty to the individual complaining, the observance of which would have averted or avoided the injury" (McSHERRY, C.J., in *W. Va. Central R. Co. v. State*, 96 Md. 652, 666; cf. *Norfolk & Western Ry. Co. v. Wood*, 99 Va. 156, 158, 159; *Hughes v. Boston & Maine R.R. Co.*, 71 N.H. 279, 284; *U.S. Express Co. v. Everest*, 72 Kan. 517; *Emry v. Roanoke Nav. Co.*, 111 N.C. 94, 95; *Vaughan v. Transit Dev. Co.*, 222 N.Y. 79; *Losee v. Clute*, 51 N.Y. 494; *DiCaprio v. N.Y.C.R.R. Co.*, 231 N.Y. 94; 1 Shearman & Redfield on Negligence, § 8, and cases cited; Cooley on Torts [3d ed.], p. 1411; Jaggard on Torts, vol. 2, p. 826; Wharton, *Negligence*, § 24; Bohlen, *Studies in the Law of Torts*, p. 601). "The ideas of negligence and duty are strictly correlative" (BOWEN, L.J., in *Thomas v. Quartermaine*, 18 Q.B.D. 685, 694). The plaintiff sues in her own right for a wrong personal to her, and not as the vicarious beneficiary of a breach of duty to another.

A different conclusion will involve us, and swiftly too, in a maze of contradictions. A guard stumbles over a package which has been left upon a platform. It seems to be a bundle of newspapers. It turns out to be a can of dynamite. To the eye of ordinary vigilance, the bundle is abandoned waste, which may be kicked or trod on with impunity. Is a passenger at the other end of the platform protected by the law against the unsuspected hazard concealed beneath the waste? If not, is the result to be any different, so far as the distant passenger is concerned, when the guard stumbles over a valise which a truckman or a porter has left upon the walk? The passenger far away, if the victim of a wrong at all, has a cause of action, not derivative, but original and primary. His claim to be protected against invasion of his bodily security is neither greater nor less because the act resulting in the invasion is a wrong to another far removed. In this case, the rights that are said to have been violated, the interests said to have been invaded, are not even of the same order. The man was not injured in his person nor even put in danger. The purpose of the act, as well as its effect, was to make his person safe. If there was a wrong to him at all, which may very well be doubted, it was a wrong to a property interest only, the safety of his package. Out of this wrong to property, which threatened injury to nothing else, there has passed, we are told, to the plaintiff by derivation or succession a right of action for the invasion of an interest of another order, the right to bodily security. The diversity of interests emphasizes the futility of the effort to build the plaintiff's right upon the basis of a wrong to some one else. The gain is one of emphasis, for a like result would follow if the interests were the same. Even then, the orbit of the danger as disclosed to the eye of reasonable vigilance would be the orbit of the duty. One who jostles one's neighbor in a crowd does not invade the rights of others standing at the outer fringe when the unintended contact casts a bomb upon the ground. The wrongdoer as to them is the man who carries the bomb, not the one who explodes it without suspicion of the danger. Life will have to be made over, and human nature transformed, before prevision so extravagant can be accepted as the norm of conduct, the customary standard to which behavior must conform. The argument for the plaintiff is built upon the shifting meanings of such words as "wrong" and "wrongful," and shares their instability. What the plaintiff must show is "a wrong" to herself, i.e., a violation of her own right, and not merely a wrong to some one else, nor conduct "wrongful" because unsocial, but not "a wrong" to any one. We are told that one who drives at reckless speed through a crowded city street is guilty of a negligent act and, therefore, of a wrongful one irrespective of the consequences. Negligent the act is, and wrongful in the sense that it is unsocial, but wrongful and unsocial in relation to other travelers, only because the eye of vigilance perceives the risk of damage. If the same act were to be committed on a speedway or a race course, it would lose its wrongful quality. The risk reasonably to be perceived defines the duty to be obeyed, and risk imports relation; it is risk to another or to others within the range of apprehension (Seavey, Negligence, Subjective or Objective, 41 H.L. Rv. 6; *Boronkay v. Robinson & Carpenter*, 247 N.Y. 365). This does not mean, of course, that one who launches a destructive force is always relieved of liability if the force, though known to be destructive, pursues an unexpected path. "It was not necessary that the defendant should have had notice of the particular method in which an accident would occur, if the possibility of an accident was clear to the ordinarily prudent eye" (*Munsey v. Webb*, 231 U.S. 150, 156; *Condran v. Park & Tilford*, 213 N.Y. 341, 345; *Robert v. U.S.E.F. Corp.*, 240 N.Y. 474, 477). Some acts, such as shooting, are so imminently dangerous to any one who may come within reach of the missile, however unexpectedly, as to impose a duty of prevision not far from that of an insurer. Even today, and much oftener in earlier stages of the law, one acts sometimes at one's peril (Jeremiah Smith, Tort and Absolute Liability, 30 H.L. Rv. 328; Street, *Foundations of Legal Liability*, vol. 1, pp. 77, 78). Under this head, it may be, fall certain cases of what is known as transferred intent, an act willfully dangerous to A resulting by misadventure in injury to B (*Talmage v. Smith*, 101 Mich. 370, 374) These cases aside, wrong is defined in terms of the natural or probable, at least when unintentional (*Parrot v. Wells-Fargo Co.* [The Nitro-Glycerine Case], 15 Wall. [U.S.] 524). The range of reasonable apprehension is at times a question for the court, and at times, if varying inferences are possible, a question for the jury. Here, by concession, there was nothing in the situation to suggest to the most cautious mind that the parcel wrapped in newspaper would spread wreckage through the station. If the guard had thrown it down knowingly and willfully, he would not have threatened the plaintiff's safety, so far as appearances could warn him. His conduct would not have involved, even then, an unreasonable probability of invasion of her bodily security. Liability can be no greater where the act is inadvertent.

Negligence, like risk, is thus a term of relation. Negligence in the abstract, apart from things related, is surely not a tort, if indeed it is understandable at all (BOWEN, L.J., in *Thomas v. Quartermaine*, 18 Q.B.D. 685, 694). Negligence is not a tort unless it results in the commission of a wrong, and the commission of a wrong imports the violation of a right, in this case, we are told, the right to be protected against interference with one's bodily security. But bodily security is protected, not against all forms of interference or aggression, but only against some. One who seeks redress at law does not make out a cause of action by showing without more that there has been damage to his person. If the harm was not willful, he must show that the act as to him had possibilities of danger so many and apparent as to entitle him to be protected against the doing of it though the harm was unintended. Affront to personality is still the keynote of the wrong. Confirmation of this view will be found in the history and development of the action on the case. Negligence as a basis of civil liability was unknown to mediaeval law (8 Holdsworth, *History of English Law*, p. 449; Street, *Foundations of Legal Liability*, vol. 1, pp. 189, 190). For damage to the person, the sole remedy was trespass, and trespass did not lie in the absence of aggression, and that direct and personal (Holdsworth, op. cit. p. 453; Street, op. cit. vol. 3, pp. 258, 260, vol. 1, pp. 71, 74.) Liability for other damage, as where a servant without orders from the master does or omits something to the damage of another, is a plant of later growth (Holdsworth, op. cit. 450, 457;Wigmore, *Responsibility or Tortious Acts*, vol. 3, *Essays in Anglo- American Legal History*, 520, 523, 526, 533). When it emerged out of the legal soil, it was thought of as a variant of trespass, an offshoot of the parent stock. This appears in the form of action, which was known as trespass on the case (Holdsworth, op. cit. p. 449; cf. *Scott v. Shepard*, 2 Wm. Black. 892; Green, *Rationale of Proximate Cause*, p. 19). The victim does not sue derivatively, or by right of subrogation, to vindicate an interest invaded in the person of another. Thus to view his cause of action is to ignore the fundamental difference between tort and crime (Holland, *Jurisprudence* [12th ed.], p. 328). He sues for breach of a duty owing to himself.

The law of causation, remote or proximate, is thus foreign to the case before us. The question of liability is always anterior to the question of the measure of the consequences that go with liability. If there is no tort to be redressed, there is no occasion to consider what damage might be recovered if there were a finding of a tort. We may assume, without deciding, that negligence, not at large or in the abstract, but in relation to the plaintiff, would entail liability for any and all consequences, however novel or extraordinary (*Bird v. St. Paul F. & M. Ins. Co.*, 224 N.Y. 47, 54; *Ehrgott v. Mayor, etc., of N.Y.*, 96 N.Y. 264; *Smith v. London & S.W. Ry. Co.*, L.R. 6 C.P. 14; 1 Beven, Negligence, 106; Street, op. cit. vol. 1, p. 90; Green, *Rationale of Proximate Cause*, pp. 88, 118; cf. *Matter of Polemis*, L.R. 1921, 3 K.B. 560; 44 *Law Quarterly Review*, 142). There is room for argument that a distinction is to be drawn according to the diversity of interests invaded by the act, as where conduct negligent in that it threatens an insignificant invasion of an interest in property results in an unforeseeable invasion of an interest of another order, as, e.g., one of bodily security. Perhaps other distinctions may be necessary. We do not go into the question now. The consequences to be followed must first be rooted in a wrong.

HOLDING. The judgment of the Appellate Division and that of the Trial Term should be reversed, and the complaint dismissed, with costs in all courts.

DISSENTING OPINION. ANDREWS, J.

Assisting a passenger to board a train, the defendant's servant negligently knocked a package from his arms. It fell between the platform and the cars. Of its contents the servant knew and could know nothing. A violent explosion followed. The concussion broke some scales standing a considerable distance away. In falling they injured the plaintiff, an intending passenger.

Upon these facts may she recover the damages she has suffered in an action brought against the master? The result we shall reach depends upon our theory as to the nature of negligence. Is it a relative concept—the breach of some duty owing to a particular person or to particular persons? Or where there is an act which unreasonably threatens the safety of others, is the doer liable for all its proximate consequences, even where they result in injury to one who would generally be thought to be outside the radius of danger? This is not a mere dispute as to words. We might not believe that to the average mind the dropping of the bundle would seem to involve the probability of harm to the plaintiff standing many feet away whatever might be the case as to the owner or to one so near as to be likely to be struck by its fall. If, however, we adopt the second hypothesis we have to inquire only as to the relation between cause and effect. We deal in terms of proximate cause, not of negligence.

Negligence may be defined roughly as an act or omission which unreasonably does or may affect the rights of others, or which unreasonably fails to protect oneself from the dangers resulting from such acts. Here I confine myself to the first branch of the definition. Nor do I comment on the word "unreasonable." For present purposes it sufficiently describes that average of conduct that society requires of its members.

There must be both the act or the omission, and the right. It is the act itself, not the intent of the actor, that is important. (*Hover v. Barkhoof*, 44 N.Y. 113; *Mertz v. Connecticut Co.*, 217 N.Y. 475.) In criminal law both the intent and the result are to be considered. Intent again is material in tort actions, where punitive damages are sought, dependent on actual malice—not on merely reckless conduct. But here neither insanity nor infancy lessens responsibility. (*Williams v. Hays*, 143 N.Y. 442.)

As has been said, except in cases of contributory negligence, there must be rights which are or may be affected. Often though injury has occurred, no rights of him who suffers have been touched. A licensee or trespasser upon my land has no claim to affirmative care on my part that the land be made safe. (*Meiers v. Koch Brewery*, 229 N.Y. 10.) Where a railroad is required to fence its tracks against cattle, no man's rights are injured should he wander upon the road because such fence is absent. (*DiCaprio v. N.Y.C.R.R.*, 231 N.Y. 94.) An unborn child may not demand immunity from personal harm. (Drobner v. Peters, 232 N.Y. 220.)

But we are told that "there is no negligence unless there is in the particular case a legal duty to take care, and this duty must be one which is owed to the plaintiff himself and not merely to others." (Salmond Torts [6th ed.], 24.) This, I think too narrow a conception. Where there is the unreasonable act, and some right that may be affected there is negligence whether damage does or does not result. That is immaterial. Should we drive down Broadway at a reckless speed, we are negligent whether we strike an approaching car or miss it by an inch. The act itself is wrongful. It is a wrong not only to those who happen to be within the radius of danger but to all who might have been there—a wrong to the public at large. Such is the language of the street. Such the language of the courts when speaking of contributory negligence. Such again and again their language in speaking of the duty of some defendant and discussing proximate cause in cases where such a discussion is wholly irrelevant on any other theory. (*Perry v. Rochester Line Co.*, 219 N.Y. 60.) As was said by Mr. Justice HOLMES many years ago, "the measure of the defendant's duty in determining whether a wrong has been committed is one thing, the measure of liability when a wrong has been committed is another." (*Spade v. Lynn & Boston R.R. Co.*, 172 Mass. 488.) Due care is a duty imposed on each one of us to protect society from unnecessary danger, not to protect A, B or C alone.

It may well be that there is no such thing as negligence in the abstract. "Proof of negligence in the air, so to speak, will not do." In an empty world negligence would not exist. It does involve a relationship between man and his fellows. But not merely a relationship between man and those whom he might reasonably expect his act would injure. Rather, a relationship between him and those whom he does in fact injure. If his act has a tendency to harm some one, it harms him a mile away as surely as it does those on the scene. We now permit children to recover for the negligent killing of the father. It was never prevented on the theory that no duty was owing to them. A husband may be compensated for the loss of his wife's services. To say that the wrongdoer was negligent as to the husband as well as to the wife is merely an attempt to fit facts to theory. An insurance company paying a fire loss recovers its payment of the negligent incendiary. We speak of subrogation—of suing in the right of the insured. Behind the cloud of words is the fact they hide, that the act, wrongful as to the insured, has also injured the company. Even if it be true that the fault of father, wife or insured will prevent recovery, it is because we consider the original negligence not the proximate cause of the injury. (Pollock, *Torts* [12th ed.], 463.)

In the well-known *Polemis* case (1921, 3 K.B. 560), SCRUTTON, L.J., said that the dropping of a plank was negligent for it might injure "workman or cargo or ship." Because of either possibility the owner of the vessel was to be made good for his loss. The act being wrongful the doer was liable for its proximate results. Criticized and explained as this statement may have been, I think it states the law as it should be and as it is. (*Smith v. London & Southwestern Ry. Co.*, [1870-71] 6 C.P. 14; *Anthony v. Slaid*, 52 Mass. 290; *Wood v. Penn. R.R.Co.*, 177 Penn. St. 306; *Trashansky v. Hershkovitz*, 239 N.Y. 452.)

The proposition is this. Every one owes to the world at large the duty of refraining from those acts that may unreasonably threaten the safety of others. Such an act occurs. Not only is he wronged to whom harm might reasonably be expected to result, but he also who is in fact injured, even if he be outside what would generally be thought the danger zone. There needs be duty due the one complaining but this is not a duty to a particular individual because as to him harm might be expected. Harm to some one being the natural result of the act, not only that one alone, but all those in fact injured may complain. We have never, I think, held otherwise. Indeed in the Di Caprio case we said that a breach of a general ordinance defining the degree of care to be exercised in one's calling is evidence of negligence as to every one. We did not limit this statement to those who might be expected to be exposed to danger. Unreasonable risk being taken, its consequences are not confined to those who might probably be hurt.

If this be so, we do not have a plaintiff suing by "derivation or succession." Her action is original and primary. Her claim is for a breach of duty to herself—not that she is subrogated to any right of action of the owner of the parcel or of a passenger standing at the scene of the explosion.

The right to recover damages rests on additional considerations. The plaintiff's rights must be injured, and this injury must be caused by the negligence. We build a dam, but are negligent as to its foundations. Breaking, it injures property down stream. We are not liable if all this happened because of some reason other than the insecure foundation. But when injuries do result from our unlawful act we are liable for the consequences. It does not matter that they are unusual, unexpected, unforeseen and unforeseeable. But there is one limitation. The damages must be so connected with the negligence that the latter may be said to be the proximate cause of the former.

These two words have never been given an inclusive definition. What is a cause in a legal sense, still more what is a proximate cause, depend in each case upon many considerations, as does the existence of negligence itself. Any philosophical doctrine of causation does not help us. A boy throws a stone into a pond. The ripples spread. The water level rises. The history of that pond is altered to all eternity. It will be altered by other causes also. Yet it will be forever the resultant of all causes combined. Each one will have an influence. How great only omniscience can say. You may speak of a chain, or if you please, a net. An analogy is of little aid. Each cause brings about future events. Without each the future would not be the same. Each is proximate in the sense it is essential. But that is not what we mean by the word. Nor on the other hand do we mean sole cause. There is no such thing.

Should analogy be thought helpful, however, I prefer that of a stream. The spring, starting on its journey, is joined by tributary after tributary. The river, reaching the ocean, comes from a hundred sources. No man may say whence any drop of water is derived. Yet for a time distinction may be possible. Into the clear creek, brown swamp water flows from the left. Later, from the right comes water stained by its clay bed. The three may remain for a space, sharply divided. But at last, inevitably no trace of separation remains. They are so commingled that all distinction is lost.

As we have said, we cannot trace the effect of an act to the end, if end there is. Again, however, we may trace it part of the way. A murder at Sarajevo may be the necessary antecedent to an assassination in London twenty years hence. An overturned lantern may burn all Chicago. We may follow the fire from the shed to the last building. We rightly say the fire started by the lantern caused its destruction.

A cause, but not the proximate cause. What we do mean by the word "proximate" is, that because of convenience, of public policy, of a rough sense of justice, the law arbitrarily declines to trace a series of events beyond a certain point. This is not logic. It is practical politics. Take our rule as to fires. Sparks from my burning haystack set on fire my house and my neighbor's. I may recover from a negligent railroad. He may not. Yet the wrongful act as directly harmed the one as the other. We may regret that the line was drawn just where it was, but drawn somewhere it had to be. We said the act of the railroad was not the proximate cause of our neighbor's fire. Cause it surely was. The words we used were simply indicative of our notions of public policy. Other courts think differently. But somewhere they reach the point where they cannot say the stream comes from any one source.

Take the illustration given in an unpublished manuscript by a distinguished and helpful writer on the law of torts. A chauffeur negligently collides with another car which is filled with dynamite, although he could not know it. An explosion follows. A, walking on the sidewalk nearby, is killed. B, sitting in a window of a building opposite, is cut by flying glass. C, likewise sitting in a window a block away, is similarly injured. And a further illustration. A nursemaid, ten blocks away, startled by the noise, involuntarily drops a baby from her arms to the walk. We are told that C may not recover while A may. As to B it is a question for court or jury. We will all agree that the baby might not. Because, we are again told, the chauffeur had no reason to believe his conduct involved any risk of injuring either C or the baby. As to them he was not negligent.

But the chauffeur, being negligent in risking the collision, his belief that the scope of the harm he might do would be limited is immaterial. His act unreasonably jeopardized the safety of any one who might be affected by it. C's injury and that of the baby were directly traceable to the collision. Without that, the injury would not have happened. C had the right to sit in his office, secure from such dangers. The baby was entitled to use the sidewalk with reasonable safety.

The true theory is, it seems to me, that the injury to C, if in truth he is to be denied recovery, and the injury to the baby is that their several injuries were not the proximate result of the negligence. And here not what the chauffeur had reason to believe would be the result of his conduct, but what the prudent would foresee, may have a bearing. May have some bearing, for the problem of proximate cause is not to be solved by any one consideration.

It is all a question of expediency. There are no fixed rules to govern our judgment. There are simply matters of which we may take account. We have in a somewhat different connection spoken of "the stream of events." We have asked whether that stream was deflected—whether it was forced into new and unexpected channels. (*Donnelly v. Piercy Contracting Co.*, 222 N.Y. 210.) This is rather rhetoric than law. There is in truth little to guide us other than common sense.

There are some hints that may help us. The proximate cause, involved as it may be with many other causes, must be, at the least, something without which the event would not happen. The court must ask itself whether there was a natural and continuous sequence between cause and effect. Was the one a substantial factor in producing the other? Was there a direct connection between them, without too many intervening causes? Is the effect of cause on result not too attenuated? Is the cause likely, in the usual judgment of mankind, to produce the result? Or by the exercise of prudent foresight could the result be foreseen? Is the result too remote from the cause, and here we consider remoteness in time and space. (*Bird v. St. Paul F. & M. Ins. Co.*, 224 N.Y. 47, where we passed upon the construction of a contract—but something was also said on this subject.) Clearly we must so consider, for the greater the distance either in time or space, the more surely do other causes intervene to affect the result. When a lantern is overturned the firing of a shed is a fairly direct consequence. Many things contribute to the spread of the conflagration—the force of the wind, the direction and width of streets, the character of intervening structures, other factors. We draw an uncertain and wavering line, but draw it we must as best we can.

Once again, it is all a question of fair judgment, always keeping in mind the fact that we endeavor to make a rule in each case that will be practical and in keeping with the general understanding of mankind.

Here another question must be answered. In the case supposed it is said, and said correctly, that the chauffeur is liable for the direct effect of the explosion although he had no reason to suppose it would follow a collision. "The fact that the injury occurred in a different manner than that which might have been expected does not prevent the chauffeur's negligence from being in law the cause of the injury." But the natural results of a negligent act—the results which a prudent man would or should foresee—do have a bearing upon the decision as to proximate cause. We have said so repeatedly. What should be foreseen? No human foresight would suggest that a collision itself might injure one a block away. On the contrary, given an explosion, such a possibility might be reasonably expected. I think the direct connection, the foresight of which the courts peak, assumes prevision of the explosion, for the immediate results of which, at least, the chauffeur is responsible.

It may be said this is unjust. Why? In fairness he should make good every injury flowing from his negligence. Not because of tenderness toward him we say he need not answer for all that follows his wrong. We look back to the catastrophe, the fire kindled by the spark, or the explosion. We trace the consequences—not indefinitely, but to a certain point. And to aid us in fixing that point we ask what might ordinarily be expected to follow the fire or the explosion.

This last suggestion is the factor which must determine the case before us. The act upon which defendant's liability rests is knocking an apparently harmless package onto the platform. The act was negligent. For its proximate consequences the defendant is liable. If its contents were broken, to the owner; if it fell upon and crushed a passenger's foot, then to him. If it exploded and injured one in the immediate vicinity, to him also as to A in the illustration. Mrs. Palsgraf was standing some distance away. How far cannot be told from the record—apparently twenty-five or thirty feet. Perhaps less. Except for the explosion, she would not have been injured. We are told by the appellant in his brief "it cannot be denied that the explosion was the direct cause of the plaintiff's injuries." So it was a substantial factor in producing the result—there was here a natural and continuous sequence—direct connection. The only intervening cause was that instead of blowing her to the ground the concussion smashed the weighing machine which in turn fell upon her. There was no remoteness in time, little in space. And surely, given such an explosion as here it needed no great foresight to predict that the natural result would be to injure one on the platform at no greater distance from its scene than was the plaintiff. Just how no one might be able to predict. Whether by flying fragments, by broken glass, by wreckage of machines or structures no one could say. But injury in some form was most probable.

Under these circumstances I cannot say as a matter of law that the plaintiff's injuries were not the proximate result of the negligence. That is all we have before us. The court refused to so charge. No request was made to submit the matter to the jury as a question of fact, even would that have been proper upon the record before us.

The judgment appealed from should be affirmed, with costs.

National Federation of Paralegal Associations, Inc.

Model Code of Ethics and Professional Responsibility and Guidelines for Enforcement

PREAMBLE

The National Federation of Paralegal Associations, Inc.("NFPA") is a professional organization comprised of paralegal associations and individual paralegals throughout the United States and Canada. Members of NFPA have varying backgrounds, experiences, education, and job responsibilities that reflect the diversity of the paralegal profession. NFPA promotes the growth, development, and recognition of the paralegal profession as an integral partner in the delivery of legal services.

In May 1993 NFPA adopted its Model Code of Ethics and Professional Responsibility ("Model Code") to delineate the principles for ethics and conduct to which every paralegal should aspire.

Many paralegal associations throughout the United States have endorsed the concept and content of NFPA's Model Code through the adoption of their own ethical codes. In doing so, paralegals have confirmed the profession's commitment to increase the quality and efficiency of legal services, as well as recognized its responsibilities to the public, the legal community, and colleagues.

Paralegals have recognized, and will continue to recognize, that the profession must continue to evolve to enhance their roles in the delivery of legal services. With increased levels of responsibility comes the need to define and enforce mandatory rules of professional conduct. Enforcement of codes of paralegal conduct is a logical and necessary step to enhance and ensure the confidence of the legal community and the public in the integrity and professional responsibility of paralegals.

In April 1997 NFPA adopted the Model Disciplinary Rules ("Model Rules") to make possible the enforcement of the Canons and Ethical Considerations contained in the NFPA Model Code. A concurrent determination was made that the Model Code of Ethics and Professional Responsibility, formerly aspirational in nature, should be recognized as setting forth the enforceable obligations of all paralegals.

The Model Code and Model Rules offer a framework for professional discipline, either voluntarily or through formal regulatory programs.

§1 NFPA Model Disciplinary Rules and Ethical Considerations

1.1. A Paralegal Shall Achieve and Maintain a High Level of Competence.

Ethical Considerations

EC-1.1 (a) A paralegal shall achieve competency through education, training, and work experience.

EC-1.1 (b) A paralegal shall aspire to participate in a minimum of twelve (12) hours of continuing legal education, to include at least one (1) hour of ethics education, every two (2) years in order to remain current on developments in the law.

EC-1.1 (c) A paralegal shall perform all assignments promptly and efficiently.

1.2. A Paralegal Shall Maintain a High Level of Personal and Professional Integrity.

Ethical Considerations

EC-1.2 (a) A paralegal shall not engage in any ex parte communications involving the courts or any other adjudicatory body in an attempt to exert undue influence or to obtain advantage or the benefit of only one party.

EC-1.2 (b) A paralegal shall not communicate, or cause another to communicate, with a party the paralegal knows to be represented by a lawyer in a pending matter without the prior consent of the lawyer representing such other party.

EC-1.2 (c) A paralegal shall ensure that all timekeeping and billing records prepared by the paralegal are thorough, accurate, honest, and complete.

EC-1.2 (d) A paralegal shall not knowingly engage in fraudulent billing practices. Such practices may include, but are not limited to: inflation of hours billed to a client or employer; misrepresentation of the nature of tasks performed; and/or submission of fraudulent expense and disbursement documentation.

EC-1.2 (e) A paralegal shall be scrupulous, thorough, and honest in the identification and maintenance of all funds, securities, and other assets of a client and shall provide accurate accounting as appropriate.

EC-1.2 (f) A paralegal shall advise the proper authority of non-confidential knowledge of any dishonest or fraudulent acts by any person pertaining to the handling of the funds, securities or other assets of a client. The authority to whom the report is made shall depend on the nature and circumstances of the possible misconduct, (e.g., ethics committees of law firms, corporations and/or paralegal associations, local or state bar associations, local prosecutors, administrative agencies, etc.). Failure to report such knowledge is in itself misconduct and shall be treated as such under these rules.

1.3. A Paralegal Shall Maintain a High Standard of Professional Conduct.

Ethical Considerations

EC-1.3 (a) A paralegal shall refrain from engaging in any conduct that offends the dignity and decorum of proceedings before a court or other adjudicatory body and shall be respectful of all rules and procedures.

EC-1.3 (b) A paralegal shall avoid impropriety and the appearance of impropriety and shall not engage in any conduct that would adversely affect his/her fitness to practice. Such conduct may include, but is not limited to: violence, dishonesty, interference with the administration of justice, and/or abuse of a professional position or public office.

EC-1.3 (c) Should a paralegal's fitness to practice be compromised by physical or mental illness, causing that paralegal to commit an act that is in direct violation of the Model Code/Model Rules and/or the rules and/or laws governing the jurisdiction in which the paralegal practices, that paralegal may be protected from sanction upon review of the nature and circumstances of that illness.

EC-1.3 (d) A paralegal shall advise the proper authority of non-confidential knowledge of any action of another legal professional that clearly demonstrates fraud, deceit, dishonesty, or misrepresentation. The authority to whom the report is made shall depend on the nature and circumstances of the possible misconduct (e.g., ethics committees of law firms, corporations and/or paralegal associations, local or state bar associations, local prosecutors, administrative agencies, etc.). Failure to report such knowledge is in itself misconduct and shall be treated as such under these rules.

EC-1.3 (e) A paralegal shall not knowingly assist any individual with the commission of an act that is in direct violation of the Model Code/Model Rules and/or the rules and/or laws governing the jurisdiction in which the paralegal practices.

EC-1.3 (f) If a paralegal possesses knowledge of future criminal activity, that knowledge must be reported to the appropriate authority immediately.

1.4. A Paralegal Shall Serve the Public Interest by Contributing to the Improvement of the Legal System and Delivery of Quality Legal Services, Including Pro Bono Publico Services.

Ethical Considerations

EC-1.4 (a) A paralegal shall be sensitive to the legal needs of the public and shall promote the development and implementation of programs that address those needs.

EC-1.4 (b) A paralegal shall support efforts to improve the legal system and access thereto and shall assist in making changes.

EC-1.4 (c) A paralegal shall support and participate in the delivery of Pro Bono Publico services directed toward implementing and improving access to justice, the law, the legal system or the paralegal and legal professions.

EC-1.4 (d) A paralegal should aspire annually to contribute twenty-four (24) hours of Pro Bono Publico services under the supervision of an attorney or as authorized by administrative, statutory or court authority to:

1. persons of limited means; or
2. charitable, religious, civic, community, governmental and educational organizations in matters that are designed primarily to address the legal needs of persons with limited means; or
3. individuals, groups or organizations seeking to secure or protect civil rights, civil liberties or public rights.

The twenty-four (24) hours of Pro Bono Publico services contributed annually by a paralegal may consist of such services as detailed in this EC-1.4(d), and/or administrative matters designed to develop and implement the attainment of this aspiration as detailed above in EC-1.4(a) or (c), or any combination of the two.

1.5. A Paralegal Shall Preserve all Confidential Information Provided by the Client or Acquired from Other Sources Before, During, and After the Course of the Professional Relationship.

Ethical Considerations

EC-1.5 (a) A paralegal shall be aware of and abide by all legal authority governing confidential information in the jurisdiction in which the paralegal practices.

EC-1.5 (b) A paralegal shall not use confidential information to the disadvantage of the client.

EC-1.5 (c) A paralegal shall not use confidential information to the advantage of the paralegal or of a third person.

EC-1.5 (d) A paralegal may reveal confidential information only after full disclosure and with the client's written consent; or, when required by law or court order; or, when necessary to prevent the client from committing an act that could result in death or serious bodily harm.

EC-1.5 (e) A paralegal shall keep those individuals responsible for the legal representation of a client fully informed of any confidential information the paralegal may have pertaining to that client.

EC-1.5 (f) A paralegal shall not engage in any indiscreet communications concerning clients.

1.6. A Paralegal Shall Avoid Conflicts of Interest and Shall Disclose any Possible Conflict to the Employer or Client, as Well as to the Prospective Employers or Clients.

Ethical Considerations

EC-1.6 (a) A paralegal shall act within the bounds of the law, solely for the benefit of the client, and shall be free of compromising influences and loyalties. Neither the paralegal's personal or business interest, nor those of other clients or third persons, should compromise the paralegal's professional judgment and loyalty to the client.

EC-1.6 (b) A paralegal shall avoid conflicts of interest that may arise from previous assignments, whether for a present or past employer or client.

EC-1.6 (c) A paralegal shall avoid conflicts of interest that may arise from family relationships and from personal and business interests.

EC-1.6 (d) In order to be able to determine whether an actual or potential conflict of interest exists, a paralegal shall create and maintain an effective recordkeeping system that identifies clients, matters, and parties with which the paralegal has worked.

EC-1.6 (e) A paralegal shall reveal sufficient non-confidential information about a client or former client to reasonably ascertain if an actual or potential conflict of interest exists.

EC-1.6 (f) A paralegal shall not participate in or conduct work on any matter where a conflict of interest has been identified.

EC-1.6 (g) In matters where a conflict of interest has been identified and the client consents to continued representation, a paralegal shall comply fully with the implementation and maintenance of an Ethical Wall.

1.7. A Paralegal's Title Shall be Fully Disclosed.

Ethical Considerations

EC-1.7 (a) A paralegal's title shall clearly indicate the individual's status and shall be disclosed in all business and professional communications to avoid misunderstandings and misconceptions about the paralegal's role and responsibilities.

EC-1.7 (b) A paralegal's title shall be included if the paralegal's name appears on business cards, letterhead, brochures, directories, and advertisements.

EC-1.7 (c) A paralegal shall not use letterhead, business cards or other promotional materials to create a fraudulent impression of his/her status or ability to practice in the jurisdiction in which the paralegal practices.

EC-1.7 (d) A paralegal shall not practice under color of any record, diploma, or certificate that has been illegally or fraudulently obtained or issued or which is misrepresentative in any way.

EC1.7 (e) A paralegal shall not participate in the creation, issuance, or dissemination of fraudulent records, diplomas, or certificates.

1.8. A Paralegal Shall Not Engage in the Unauthorized Practice of Law.

Ethical Considerations

EC-1.8 (a) A paralegal shall comply with the applicable legal authority governing the unauthorized practice of law in the jurisdiction in which the paralegal practices.

§2 NFPA Guidelines for the Enforcement of the Model Code of Ethics and Professional Responsibility

2.1. Basis for Discipline

2.1(a) Disciplinary investigations and proceedings brought under authority of the Rules shall be conducted in accord with obligations imposed on the paralegal professional by the Model Code of Ethics and Professional Responsibility.

2.2. Structure of Disciplinary Committee

2.2(a) The Disciplinary Committee ("Committee") shall be made up of nine (9) members including the Chair.

2.2(b) Each member of the Committee, including any temporary replacement members, shall have demonstrated working knowledge of ethics/professional responsibility-related issues and activities.

2.2(c) The Committee shall represent a cross-section of practice areas and work experience. The following recommendations are made regarding the members of the Committee.

1. At least one paralegal with one to three years of law-related work experience.
2. At least one paralegal with five to seven years of law related work experience.
3. At least one paralegal with over ten years of law related work experience.
4. One paralegal educator with five to seven years of work experience; preferably in the area of ethics/professional responsibility.
5. One paralegal manager.
6. One lawyer with five to seven years of law-related work experience.
7. One lay member.

2.2(d) The Chair of the Committee shall be appointed within thirty (30) days of its members' induction. The Chair shall have no fewer than ten (10) years of law-related work experience.

2.2(e) The terms of all members of the Committee shall be staggered. Of those members initially appointed, a simple majority plus one shall be appointed to a term of one year, and the remaining members shall be appointed to a term of two years. Thereafter, all members of the Committee shall be appointed to terms of two years.

2.2(f) If for any reason the terms of a majority of the Committee will expire at the same time, members may be appointed to terms of one year to maintain continuity of the Committee.

2.2(g) The Committee shall organize from its members a three-tiered structure to investigate, prosecute, and/or adjudicate charges of misconduct. The members shall be rotated among the tiers.

2.3. Operation of Committee

2.3(a) The Committee shall meet on an as-needed basis to discuss, investigate, and/or adjudicate alleged violations of the Model Code/Model Rules.

2.3(b) A majority of the members of the Committee present at a meeting shall constitute a quorum.

2.3(c) A Recording Secretary shall be designated to maintain complete and accurate minutes of all Committee meetings. All such minutes shall be kept confidential until a decision has been made that the matter will be set for hearing as set forth in Section 6.1 below.

2.3(d) If any member of the Committee has a conflict of interest with the Charging Party, the Responding Party, or the allegations of misconduct, that member shall not take part in any hearing or deliberations concerning those allegations. If the absence of that member creates a lack of a quorum for the Committee, then a temporary replacement for the member shall be appointed.

2.3(e) Either the Charging Party or the Responding Party may request that, for good cause shown, any member of the Committee not participate in a hearing or deliberation. All such requests shall be honored. If the absence of a Committee member under those circumstances creates a lack of a quorum for the Committee, then a temporary replacement for that member shall be appointed.

2.3(f) All discussions and correspondence of the Committee shall be kept confidential until a decision has been made that the matter will be set for hearing as set forth in Section 6.1 below.

2.3(g) All correspondence from the Committee to the Responding Party regarding any charge of misconduct and any decisions made regarding the charge shall be mailed certified mail, return receipt requested, to the Responding Party's last known address and shall be clearly marked with a "Confidential" designation.

2.4. Procedure for the Reporting of Alleged Violations of the Model Code/Disciplinary Rules

2.4(a) An individual or entity in possession of non-confidential knowledge or information concerning possible instances of misconduct shall make a confidential written report to the Committee within thirty (30) days of obtaining same. This report shall include all details of the alleged misconduct.

2.4(b) The Committee so notified shall inform the Responding Party of the allegation(s) of misconduct no later than ten (10) business days after receiving the confidential written report from the Charging Party.

2.4(c) Notification to the Responding Party shall include the identity of the Charging Party, unless, for good cause shown, the Charging Party requests anonymity.

2.4(d) The Responding Party shall reply to the allegations within ten (10) business days of notification.

2.5. Procedure for the Investigation of a Charge of Misconduct

2.5(a) Upon receipt of a Charge of Misconduct ("Charge"), or on its own initiative, the Committee shall initiate an investigation.

2.5(b) If, upon initial or preliminary review, the Committee makes a determination that the charges are either without basis in fact or, if proven, would not constitute professional misconduct, the Committee shall dismiss the allegations of misconduct. If such determination of dismissal cannot be made, a formal investigation shall be initiated.

2.5(c) Upon the decision to conduct a formal investigation, the Committee shall:

1. mail to the Charging and Responding Parties within three (3) business days of that decision notice of the commencement of a formal investigation. That notification shall be in writing and shall contain a complete explanation of all Charge(s), as well as the reasons for a formal investigation and shall cite the applicable codes and rules;
2. allow the Responding Party thirty (30) days to prepare and submit a confidential response to the Committee, which response shall address each charge specifically and shall be in writing; and
3. upon receipt of the response to the notification, have thirty (30) days to investigate the Charge(s). If an extension of time is deemed necessary, that extension shall not exceed ninety (90) days.

2.5(d) Upon conclusion of the investigation, the Committee may:

1. dismiss the Charge upon the finding that it has no basis in fact;
2. dismiss the Charge upon the finding that, if proven, the Charge would not constitute Misconduct;
3. refer the matter for hearing by the Tribunal; or
4. in the case of criminal activity, refer the Charge(s) and all investigation results to the appropriate authority.

2.6. Procedure for a Misconduct Hearing Before a Tribunal

2.6(a) Upon the decision by the Committee that a matter should be heard, all parties shall be notified and a hearing date shall be set. The hearing shall take place no more than thirty (30) days from the conclusion of the formal investigation.

2.6(b) The Responding Party shall have the right to counsel. The parties and the Tribunal shall have the right to call any witnesses and introduce any documentation that they believe will lead to the fair and reasonable resolution of the matter.

2.6(c) Upon completion of the hearing, the Tribunal shall deliberate and present a written decision to the parties in accordance with procedures as set forth by the Tribunal.

2.6(d) Notice of the decision of the Tribunal shall be appropriately published.

2.7. Sanctions

2.7(a) Upon a finding of the Tribunal that misconduct has occurred, any of the following sanctions, or others as may be deemed appropriate, may be imposed upon the Responding Party, either singularly or in combination:

1. letter of reprimand to the Responding Party; counseling;
2. attendance at an ethics course approved by the Tribunal; probation;
3. suspension of license/authority to practice; revocation of license/authority to practice;
4. imposition of a fine; assessment of costs; or
5. in the instance of criminal activity, referral to the appropriate authority.

2.7(b) Upon the expiration of any period of probation, suspension, or revocation, the Responding Party may make application for reinstatement. With the application for reinstatement, the Responding Party must show proof of having complied with all aspects of the sanctions imposed by the Tribunal.

2.8. Appellate Procedures

2.8(a) The parties shall have the right to appeal the decision of the Tribunal in accordance with the procedure as set forth by the Tribunal.

DEFINITIONS

"Appellate Body" means a body established to adjudicate an appeal to any decision made by a Tribunal or other decision-making body with respect to formally-heard Charges of Misconduct.

"Charge of Misconduct" means a written submission by any individual or entity to an ethics committee, paralegal association, bar association, law enforcement agency, judicial body, government agency, or other appropriate body or entity, that sets forth non-confidential information regarding any instance of alleged misconduct by an individual paralegal or paralegal entity.

"Charging Party" means any individual or entity who submits a Charge of Misconduct against an individual paralegal or paralegal entity.

"Competency" means the demonstration of: diligence, education, skill, and mental, emotional, and physical fitness reasonably necessary for the performance of paralegal services.

"Confidential Information" means information relating to a client, whatever its source, that is not public knowledge nor available to the public.("Non-Confidential Information" would generally include the name of the client and the identity of the matter for which the paralegal provided services.)

"Disciplinary Hearing" means the confidential proceeding conducted by a committee or other designated body or entity concerning any instance of alleged misconduct by an individual paralegal or paralegal entity.

"Disciplinary Committee" means any committee that has been established by an entity such as a paralegal association, bar association, judicial body, or government agency to: (a) identify, define, and investigate general ethical considerations and concerns with respect to paralegal practice; (b) administer and enforce the Model Code and Model Rules and; (c) discipline any individual paralegal or paralegal entity found to be in violation of same.

"Disclose" means communication of information reasonably sufficient to permit identification of the significance of the matter in question.

"Ethical Wall" means the screening method implemented in order to protect a client from a conflict of interest. An Ethical Wall generally includes, but is not limited to, the following elements: (1) prohibit the paralegal from having any connection with the matter; (2) ban discussions with or the transfer of documents to or from the paralegal; (3) restrict access to files; and (4) educate all members of the firm, corporation, or entity as to the separation of the paralegal (both organizationally and physically) from the pending matter. For more information regarding the Ethical Wall, see the NFPA publication entitled "The Ethical Wall—Its Application to Paralegals."

"Ex parte" means actions or communications conducted at the instance and for the benefit of one party only, and without notice to, or contestation by, any person adversely interested.

"Investigation" means the investigation of any charge(s) of misconduct filed against an individual paralegal or paralegal entity by a Committee.

"Letter of Reprimand" means a written notice of formal censure or severe reproof administered to an individual paralegal or paralegal entity for unethical or improper conduct.

"Misconduct" means the knowing or unknowing commission of an act that is in direct violation of those Canons and Ethical Considerations of any and all applicable codes and/or rules of conduct.

"Paralegal" is synonymous with "Legal Assistant" and is defined as a person qualified through education, training, or work experience to perform substantive legal work that requires knowledge of legal concepts and is customarily, but not exclusively, performed by a lawyer. This person may be retained or employed by a lawyer, law office, governmental agency, or other entity or may be authorized by administrative, statutory, or court authority to perform this work.

"Pro Bono Publico" means providing or assisting to provide quality legal services in order to enhance access to justice for persons of limited means; charitable, religious, civic, community, governmental, and educational organizations in matters that are designed primarily to address the legal needs of persons with limited means; or individuals, groups or organizations seeking to secure or protect civil rights, civil liberties or public rights.

"Proper Authority" means the local paralegal association, the local or state bar association, Committee(s) of the local paralegal or bar association(s), local prosecutor, administrative agency, or other tribunal empowered to investigate or act upon an instance of alleged misconduct.

"Responding Party" means an individual paralegal or paralegal entity against whom a Charge of Misconduct has been submitted.

"Revocation" means the recision of the license, certificate or other authority to practice of an individual paralegal or paralegal entity found in violation of those Canons and Ethical Considerations of any and all applicable codes and/or rules of conduct.

"Suspension" means the suspension of the license, certificate or other authority to practice of an individual paralegal or paralegal entity found in violation of those Canons and Ethical Considerations of any and all applicable codes and/or rules of conduct.

"Tribunal" means the body designated to adjudicate allegations of misconduct.

Model Standards and Guidelines for Utilization of Legal Assistants—Paralegals

Table of Contents:

INTRODUCTION

The purpose of this annotated version of the National Association of Legal Assistants, Inc. Model Standards and Guidelines for the Utilization of Legal Assistants (the "Model," "Standards" and/or the "Guidelines") is to provide references to the existing case law and other authorities where the underlying issues have been considered. The authorities cited will serve as a basis upon which conduct of a legal assistant may be analyzed as proper or improper.

The Guidelines represent a statement of how the legal assistant may function. The Guidelines are not intended to be a comprehensive or exhaustive list of the proper duties of a legal assistant. Rather, they are designed as guides to what may or may not be proper conduct for the legal assistant. In formulating the Guidelines, the reasoning and rules of law in many reported decisions of disciplinary cases and unauthorized practice of law cases have been analyzed and considered. In addition, the provisions of the American Bar Association's Model Rules of Professional Conduct, as well as the ethical promulgations of various state courts and bar associations, have been considered in the development of the Guidelines.

These Guidelines form a sound basis for the legal assistant and the supervising attorney to follow. This Model will serve as a comprehensive resource document and as a definitive, well-reasoned guide to those considering voluntary standards and guidelines for legal assistants.

I
PREAMBLE

Proper utilization of the services of legal assistants contributes to the delivery of cost-effective, high-quality legal services. Legal assistants and the legal profession should be assured that measures exist for identifying legal assistants and their role in assisting attorneys in the delivery of legal services. Therefore, the National Association of Legal Assistants, Inc., hereby adopts these Standards and Guidelines as an educational document for the benefit of legal assistants and the legal profession.

Comment

The three most frequently raised questions concerning legal assistants are (1) How do you define a legal assistant; (2) Who is qualified to be identified as a legal assistant; and (3) What duties may a legal assistant perform? The definition adopted in 1984 by the National Association of Legal Assistants answers the first question. The Model sets forth minimum education, training, and experience through standards which will assure that an individual utilizing the title "legal assistant" or "paralegal" has the qualifications to be held out to the legal community and the public in that capacity. The Guidelines identify those acts which the reported cases hold to be proscribed and give examples of services which the legal assistant may perform under the supervision of a licensed attorney.

These Guidelines constitute a statement relating to services performed by legal assistants, as defined herein, as approved by court decisions and other sources of authority. The purpose of the Guidelines is not to place limitations or restrictions on the legal assistant profession. Rather, the Guidelines are intended to outline for the legal profession an acceptable course of conduct. Voluntary recognition and utilization of the Standards and Guidelines will benefit the entire legal profession and the public it serves.

II
DEFINITION

The National Association of Legal Assistants adopted the following definition in 1984:

> Legal assistants, also known as paralegals, are a distinguishable group of persons who assist attorneys in the delivery of legal services. Through formal education, training, and experience, legal assistants have knowledge and expertise regarding the legal system and substantive and procedural law which qualify them to do work of a legal nature under the supervision of an attorney.

In recognition of the similarity of the definitions and the need for one clear definition, in July 2001, the NALA membership approved a resolution to adopt the definition of the American Bar Association as well. The ABA definition reads as follows:

> A legal assistant or paralegal is a person qualified by education, training or work experience who is employed or retained by a lawyer, law office, corporation, governmental agency or other entity who performs specifically delegated substantive legal work for which a lawyer is responsible. (Adopted by the ABA in 1997)

Comment

These definitions emphasize the knowledge and expertise of legal assistants in substantive and procedural law obtained through education and work experience. They further define the legal assistant or paralegal as a professional working under the supervision of an attorney as distinguished from a non-lawyer who delivers services directly to the public without any intervention or review of work product by an attorney. Such unsupervised services, unless authorized by court or agency rules, constitute the unauthorized practice of law.

Statutes, court rules, case law, and bar association documents are additional sources for legal assistant or paralegal definitions. In applying the Standards and Guidelines, it is important to remember that they were developed to apply to the legal assistant as defined herein. Lawyers should refrain from labeling those as paralegals or legal assistants who do not meet the criteria set forth in these definitions and/or the definitions set forth by state rules, guidelines or bar associations. Labeling secretaries and other administrative staff as legal assistants/paralegals is inaccurate.

For billing purposes, the services of a legal secretary are considered part of overhead costs and are not recoverable in fee awards. However, the courts have held that fees for paralegal services are recoverable as long as they are not clerical functions, such as organizing files, copying documents, checking docket, updating files, checking court dates, and delivering papers. As established in *Missouri v. Jenkins*, 491 U.S.274, 109 S.Ct. 2463, 2471, n.10 (1989) tasks performed by legal assistants must be substantive in nature which, absent the legal assistant, the attorney would perform.

There are also case law and Supreme Court Rules addressing the issue of a disbarred attorney serving in the capacity of a legal assistant.

III
STANDARDS

A legal assistant should meet certain minimum qualifications. The following standards may be used to determine an individual's qualifications as a legal assistant:

1. Successful completion of the Certified Legal Assistant (CLA)/Certified Paralegal (CP) certifying examination of the National Association of Legal Assistants, Inc.;
2. Graduation from an ABA approved program of study for legal assistants;
3. Graduation from a course of study for legal assistants which is institutionally accredited but not ABA approved, and which requires not less than the equivalent of 60 semester hours of classroom study;
4. Graduation from a course of study for legal assistants, other than those set forth in (2) and (3) above, plus not less than six months of in-house training as a legal assistant;
5. A baccalaureate degree in any field, plus not less than six months in-house training as a legal assistant;
6. A minimum of three years of law-related experience under the supervision of an attorney, including at least six months of in-house training as a legal assistant; or
7. Two years of in-house training as a legal assistant.

For purposes of these Standards, "in-house training as a legal assistant" means attorney education of the employee concerning legal assistant duties and these Guidelines. In addition to review and analysis of assignments, the legal assistant should receive a reasonable amount of instruction directly related to the duties and obligations of the legal assistant.

Comment

The Standards set forth suggest minimum qualifications for a legal assistant. These minimum qualifications, as adopted, recognize legal related work backgrounds and formal education backgrounds, both of which provide the legal assistant with a broad base in exposure to and knowledge of the legal profession. This background is necessary to assure the public and the legal profession that the employee identified as a legal assistant is qualified.

The Certified Legal Assistant (CLA) /Certified Paralegal (CP) examination established by NALA in 1976 is a voluntary nationwide certification program for legal assistants. (*CLA and CP are federally registered certification marks owned by NALA.*) The CLA/CP designation is a statement to the legal profession and the public that the legal assistant has met the high levels of knowledge and professionalism required by NALA's certification program. Continuing education requirements, which all certified legal assistants must meet, assure that high standards are maintained. The CLA/CP designation has been recognized as a means of establishing the qualifications of a legal assistant in supreme court rules, state court and bar association standards, and utilization guidelines.

Certification through NALA is available to all legal assistants meeting the educational and experience requirements. Certified Legal Assistants may also pursue advanced certification in specialty practice areas through the APC, Advanced Paralegal Certification, credentialing program. Legal assistants/paralegals may also pursue certification based on state laws and procedures in California, Florida, Louisiana, and Texas.

IV
GUIDELINES

These Guidelines relating to standards of performance and professional responsibility are intended to aid legal assistants and attorneys. The ultimate responsibility rests with an attorney who employs legal assistants to educate them with respect to the duties they are assigned and to supervise the manner in which such duties are accomplished.

Comment

In general, a legal assistant is allowed to perform any task which is properly delegated and supervised by an attorney, as long as the attorney is ultimately responsible to the client and assumes complete professional responsibility for the work product.

ABA Model Rules of Professional Conduct, Rule 5.3 provides:

With respect to a non-lawyer employed or retained by or associated with a lawyer:

a. a partner in a law firm shall make reasonable efforts to ensure that the firm has in effect measures giving reasonable assurance that the person's conduct is compatible with the professional obligations of the lawyer;
b. a lawyer having direct supervisory authority over the non-lawyer shall make reasonable efforts to ensure that the person's conduct is compatible with the professional obligations of the lawyer; and
c. a lawyer shall be responsible for conduct of such a person that would be a violation of the rules of professional conduct if engaged in by a lawyer if:
    1. the lawyer orders or, with the knowledge of the specific conduct ratifies the conduct involved; or
    2. the lawyer is a partner in the law firm in which the person is employed, or has direct supervisory authority over the person, and knows of the conduct at a time when its consequences can be avoided or mitigated but fails to take remedial action.

There are many interesting and complex issues involving the use of legal assistants. In any discussion of the proper role of a legal assistant, attention must be directed to what constitutes the practice of law. Proper delegation to legal assistants is further complicated and confused by the lack of an adequate definition of the practice of law.

Kentucky became the first state to adopt a Paralegal Code by Supreme Court Rule. This Code sets forth certain exclusions to the unauthorized practice of law:

> For purposes of this rule, the unauthorized practice of law shall not include any service rendered involving legal knowledge or advice, whether representation, counsel or advocacy, in or out of court, rendered in respect to the acts, duties, obligations, liabilities or business relations of the one requiring services where:
> a. The client understands that the paralegal is not a lawyer;
> b. The lawyer supervises the paralegal in the performance of his or her duties; and
> c. The lawyer remains fully responsible for such representation including all actions taken or not taken in connection therewith by the paralegal to the same extent as if such representation had been furnished entirely by the lawyer and all such actions had been taken or not taken directly by the attorney. Paralegal Code, Ky.S.Ct. R3.700, Sub-Rule 2.

South Dakota Supreme Court Rule 97-25 Utilization Rule a(4) states:

> The attorney remains responsible for the services performed by the legal assistant to the same extent as though such services had been furnished entirely by the attorney and such actions were those of the attorney.

GUIDELINE 1

Legal assistants should:

1. Disclose their status as legal assistants at the outset of any professional relationship with a client, other attorneys, a court or administrative agency or personnel thereof, or members of the general public;
2. Preserve the confidences and secrets of all clients; and
3. Understand the attorney's Rules of Professional Responsibility and these Guidelines in order to avoid any action which would involve the attorney in a violation of the Rules, or give the appearance of professional impropriety.

Comment

Routine early disclosure of the paralegal's status when dealing with persons outside the attorney's office is necessary to assure that there will be no misunderstanding as to the responsibilities and role of the legal assistant. Disclosure may be made in any way that avoids confusion. If the person dealing with the legal assistant already knows of his/her status, further disclosure is unnecessary. If at any time in written or oral communication the legal assistant becomes aware that the other person may believe the legal assistant is an attorney, immediate disclosure should be made as to the legal assistant's status.

The attorney should exercise care that the legal assistant preserves and refrains from using any confidence or secrets of a client, and should instruct the legal assistant not to disclose or use any such confidences or secrets.

The legal assistant must take any and all steps necessary to prevent conflicts of interest and fully disclose such conflicts to the supervising attorney. Failure to do so may jeopardize both the attorney's representation of the client and the case itself.

Guidelines for the Utilization of Legal Assistant Services adopted December 3, 1994 by the Washington State Bar Association Board of Governors states:

> Guideline 7: A lawyer shall take reasonable measures to prevent conflicts of interest resulting from a legal assistant's other employment or interest insofar as such other employment or interests would present a conflict of interest if it were that of the lawyer.

In Re Complex Asbestos Litigation, 232 Cal. App. 3d 572 (Cal. 1991), addresses the issue wherein a law firm was disqualified due to possession of attorney-client confidences by a legal assistant employee resulting from previous employment by opposing counsel.

In Oklahoma, in an order issued July 12, 2001, in the matter of *Mark A. Hayes, M.D. v. Central States Orthopedic Specialists, Inc.*, a Tulsa County District Court Judge disqualified a law firm from representation of a client on the basis that an ethical screen was an impermissible device to protect from disclosure confidences gained by a nonlawyer employee while employed by another law firm. In applying the same rules that govern attorneys, the court found that the Rules of Professional Conduct pertaining to confidentiality apply to nonlawyers who leave firms with actual knowledge of material, confidential information, and a screening device is not an appropriate alternative to the imputed disqualification of an incoming legal assistant who has moved from one firm to another during ongoing litigation and has actual knowledge of material, confidential information. The decision was appealed and the Oklahoma Supreme Court determined that, under certain circumstances, screening is an appropriate management tool for non-lawyer staff.

In 2004 the Nevada Supreme Court also addressed this issue at the urging of the state's paralegals. The Nevada Supreme Court granted a petition to rescind the Court's 1997 ruling in *Ciaffone v. District Court*. In this case, the court clarified the original ruling, stating "mere opportunity to access confidential information does not merit disqualification." The opinion stated instances in which screening may be appropriate, and listed minimum screening requirements. The opinion also set forth guidelines that a district court may use to determine if screening has been or may be effective. These considerations are:

1. substantiality of the relationship between the former and current matters
2. the time elapsed between the matters
3. size of the firm
4. number of individuals presumed to have confidential information
5. nature of their involvement in the former matter
6. timing and features of any measures taken to reduce the danger of disclosure
7. whether the old firm and the new firm represent adverse parties in the same proceeding rather than in different proceedings.

The ultimate responsibility for compliance with approved standards of professional conduct rests with the supervising attorney. The burden rests upon the attorney who employs a legal assistant to educate the latter with respect to the duties which may be assigned and then to supervise the manner in which the legal assistant carries out such duties. However, this does not relieve the legal assistant from an independent obligation to refrain from illegal conduct. Additionally, and notwithstanding that the Rules are not binding upon non-lawyers, the very nature of a legal assistant's employment imposes an obligation not to engage in conduct which would involve the supervising attorney in a violation of the Rules.

The attorney must make sufficient background investigation of the prior activities and character and integrity of his or her legal assistants.

Further, the attorney must take all measures necessary to avoid and fully disclose conflicts of interest due to other employment or interests. Failure to do so may jeopardize both the attorney's representation of the client and the case itself.

Legal assistant associations strive to maintain the high level of integrity and competence expected of the legal profession and, further, strive to uphold the high standards of ethics.

NALA's Code of Ethics and Professional Responsibility states "A legal assistant's conduct is guided by bar associations' codes of professional responsibility and rules of professional conduct."

GUIDELINE 2

Legal assistants should not:

1. Establish attorney-client relationships; set legal fees; give legal opinions or advice; or represent a client before a court, unless authorized to do so by said court; nor
2. Engage in, encourage, or contribute to any act which could constitute the unauthorized practice of law.

Comment

Case law, court rules, codes of ethics and professional responsibilities, as well as bar ethics opinions now hold which acts can and cannot be performed by a legal assistant. Generally, the determination of what acts constitute the unauthorized practice of law is made by state supreme courts.

Numerous cases exist relating to the unauthorized practice of law. Courts have gone so far as to prohibit the legal assistant from preparation of divorce kits and assisting in preparation of bankruptcy forms and, more specifically, from providing basic information about procedures and requirements, deciding where information should be placed on forms, and responding to questions from debtors regarding the interpretation or definition of terms.

Cases have identified certain areas in which an attorney has a duty to act, but it is interesting to note that none of these cases state that it is improper for an attorney to have the initial work performed by the legal assistant. This again points out the importance of adequate supervision by the employing attorney.

An attorney can be found to have aided in the unauthorized practice of law when delegating acts which cannot be performed by a legal assistant.

GUIDELINE 3

Legal assistants may perform services for an attorney in the representation of a client, provided:

1. The services performed by the legal assistant do not require the exercise of independent professional legal judgment;
2. The attorney maintains a direct relationship with the client and maintains control of all client matters;
3. The attorney supervises the legal assistant;
4. The attorney remains professionally responsible for all work on behalf of the client, including any actions taken or not taken by the legal assistant in connection therewith; and
5. The services performed supplement, merge with, and become the attorney's work product.

Comment

Paralegals, whether employees or independent contractors, perform services for the attorney in the representation of a client. Attorneys should delegate work to legal assistants commensurate with their knowledge and experience and provide appropriate instruction and supervision concerning the delegated work, as well as ethical acts of their employment. Ultimate responsibility for the work product of a legal assistant rests with the attorney. However, a legal assistant must use discretion and professional judgment and must not render independent legal judgment in place of an attorney.

The work product of a legal assistant is subject to civil rules governing discovery of materials prepared in anticipation of litigation, whether the legal assistant is viewed as an extension of the attorney or as another representative of the party itself. Fed.R.Civ.P. 26 (b) (3) and (5).

GUIDELINE 4

In the supervision of a legal assistant, consideration should be given to

1. Designating work assignments that correspond to the legal assistant's abilities, knowledge, training, and experience;
2. Educating and training the legal assistant with respect to professional responsibility, local rules and practices, and firm policies;
3. Monitoring the work and professional conduct of the legal assistant to ensure that the work is substantively correct and timely performed;
4. Providing continuing education for the legal assistant in substantive matters through courses, institutes, workshops, seminars and in-house training; and
5. Encouraging and supporting membership and active participation in professional organizations.

Comment

Attorneys are responsible for the actions of their employees in both malpractice and disciplinary proceedings. In the vast majority of cases, the courts have not censured attorneys for a particular act delegated to the legal assistant, but rather, have been critical of and imposed sanctions against attorneys for failure to adequately supervise the legal assistant. The attorney's responsibility for supervision of his or her legal assistant must be more than a willingness to accept responsibility and liability for the legal assistant's work. Supervision of a legal assistant must be offered in both the procedural and substantive legal areas. The attorney must delegate work based upon the education, knowledge, and abilities of the legal assistant and must monitor the work product and conduct of the legal assistant to insure that the work performed is substantively correct and competently performed in a professional manner.

Michigan State Board of Commissioners has adopted Guidelines for the Utilization of Legal Assistants (April 23, 1993). These guidelines, in part, encourage employers to support legal assistant participation in continuing education programs to ensure that the legal assistant remains competent in the fields of practice in which the legal assistant is assigned.

The working relationship between the lawyer and the legal assistant should extend to cooperative efforts on public service activities wherever possible. Participation in pro bono activities is encouraged in ABA Guideline 10.

GUIDELINE 5

Except as otherwise provided by statute, court rule or decision, administrative rule or regulation, or the attorney's rules of professional responsibility, and within the preceding parameters and proscriptions, a legal assistant may perform any function delegated by an attorney, including, but not limited to the following:

1. Conduct client interviews and maintain general contact with the client after the establishment of the attorney-client relationship, so long as the client is aware of

the status and function of the legal assistant, and the client contact is under the supervision of the attorney.

2. Locate and interview witnesses, so long as the witnesses are aware of the status and function of the legal assistant.
3. Conduct investigations and statistical and documentary research for review by the attorney.
4. Conduct legal research for review by the attorney.
5. Draft legal documents for review by the attorney.
6. Draft correspondence and pleadings for review by and signature of the attorney.
7. Summarize depositions, interrogatories and testimony for review by the attorney.
8. Attend executions of wills, real estate closings, depositions, court or administrative hearings and trials with the attorney.
9. Author and sign letters providing the legal assistant's status is clearly indicated and the correspondence does not contain independent legal opinions or legal advice.

Comment

The United States Supreme Court has recognized the variety of tasks being performed by legal assistants and has noted that use of legal assistants encourages cost-effective delivery of legal services, *Missouri v. Jenkins*, 491 U.S.274, 109 S.Ct. 2463, 2471, n.10 (1989). In *Jenkins*, the court further held that legal assistant time should be included in compensation for attorney fee awards at the market rate of the relevant community to bill legal assistant time.

Courts have held that legal assistant fees are not a part of the overall overhead of a law firm. Legal assistant services are billed separately by attorneys, and decrease litigation expenses. Tasks performed by legal assistants must contain substantive legal work under the direction or supervision of an attorney, such that if the legal assistant were not present, the work would be performed by the attorney.

In *Taylor v. Chubb*, 874 P.2d 806 (Okla. 1994), the Court ruled that attorney fees awarded should include fees for services performed by legal assistants and, further, defined tasks which may be performed by the legal assistant under the supervision of an attorney including, among others: interview clients; draft pleadings and other documents; carry on legal research, both conventional and computer aided; research public records; prepare discovery requests and responses; schedule depositions and prepare notices and subpoenas; summarize depositions and other discovery responses; coordinate and manage document production; locate and interview witnesses; organize pleadings, trial exhibits and other documents; prepare witness and exhibit lists; prepare trial notebooks; prepare for the attendance of witnesses at trial; and assist lawyers at trials.

Except for the specific proscription contained in Guideline 1, the reported cases do not limit the duties which may be performed by a legal assistant under the supervision of the attorney.

An attorney may not split legal fees with a legal assistant, nor pay a legal assistant for the referral of legal business. An attorney may compensate a legal assistant based on the quantity and quality of the legal assistant's work and value of that work to a law practice.

CONCLUSION

These Standards and Guidelines were developed from generally accepted practices. Each supervising attorney must be aware of the specific rules, decisions, and statutes applicable to legal assistants within his/her jurisdiction.

ADDENDUM

For further information, the following cases may be helpful to you:

Duties

Taylor v. Chubb, 874 P.2d 806 (Okla. 1994)

McMackin v. McMackin, 651 A.2d 778 (Del.Fam Ct 1993)

Work Product

Fine v. Facet Aerospace Products Co., 133 F.R.D. 439 (S.D.N.Y. 1990)

Unauthorized Practice of Law

Akron Bar Assn. v. Green, 673 N.E.2d 1307 (Ohio 1997)

In Re Hessinger & Associates, 192 B.R. 211 (N.D. Calif. 1996)

In the Matter of Bright, 171 B.R. 799 (Bkrtcy. E.D. Mich)

Louisiana State Bar Assn v. Edwins, 540 So.2d 294 (La. 1989)

Attorney/Client Privilege

In Re Complex Asbestos Litigation, 232 Cal. App. 3d 572 (Calif. 1991)

Makita Corp. v. U.S., 819 F.Supp. 1099 (CIT 1993)

Conflicts

In Re Complex Asbestos Litigation, 232 Cal. App. 3d 572 (Calif. 1991)

Makita Corp. v. U.S., 819 F.Supp. 1099 (CIT 1993)

Phoenix Founders, Inc., v. Marshall, 887 S.W.2d 831 (Tex. 1994)

Smart Industries v. Superior Court, 876 P.2d 1176 (Ariz. App. Div.1 1994)

Supervision

Matter of Martinez, 754 P.2d 842 (N.M. 1988)

State v. Barrett, 483 P.2d 1106 (Kan. 1971)

Hayes v. Central States Orthopedic Specialists, Inc., 2002 OK 30, 51 P.3d 562

Liebowitz v. Eighth Judicial District Court of Nevada Nev Sup Ct., No 39683, November 3, 2003 clarified in part and overrules in part *Ciaffone v. District Court*, 113 Nev 1165, 945. P2d 950 (1997)

Fee Awards

In Re Bicoastal Corp., 121 B.R. 653 (Bktrcy.M.D.Fla. 1990)

In Re Carter, 101 B.R. 170 (Bkrtcy.D.S.D. 1989)

Taylor v. Chubb, 874 P.2d 806 (Okla.1994)

Missouri v. Jenkins, 491 U.S. 274, 109 S.Ct. 2463, 105 L.Ed.2d 229 (1989) 11 U.S.C.A.§ 330

McMackin v. McMackin, Del.Fam.Ct. 651 A.2d 778 (1993)

Miller v. Alamo, 983 F.2d 856 (8th Cir. 1993)

Stewart v. Sullivan, 810 F.Supp. 1102 (D.Hawaii 1993)

In Re Yankton College, 101 B.R. 151 (Bkrtcy. D.S.D. 1989)

Stacey v. Stroud, 845 F.Supp. 1135 (S.D.W.Va. 1993)

Court Appearances

Louisiana State Bar Assn v. Edwins, 540 So.2d 294 (La. 1989)

In addition to the above referenced cases, you may contact your state bar association for information regarding guidelines for the utilization of legal assistants that may have been adopted by the bar, or ethical opinions concerning the utilization of legal assistants. The following states have adopted a definition of "legal assistant" or "paralegal" either through bar association guidelines, ethical opinions, legislation or case law:

Legislation

California
Florida
Illinois
Indiana
Maine
Pennsylvania

Supreme Court Cases or Rules

Kentucky
New Hampshire
New Mexico
North Dakota
Rhode Island
South Dakota
Virginia

Cases

Arizona
New Jersey
Oklahoma

Cases (Cont.)

South Carolina
Washington

Guidelines

Colorado
Connecticut
Georgia
Idaho
New York
Oregon
Utah
Wisconsin

Bar Association Activity

Alaska
Arizona
Colorado
Connecticut
Florida
Illinois

Bar Association Activity (Cont.)

Iowa
Kansas
Kentucky
Massachusetts
Michigan
Minnesota
Missouri
Nevada
New Mexico
New Hampshire
North Carolina
North Dakota
Ohio
Oregon
Rhode Island
South Carolina
South Dakota
Tennessee
Texas
Virginia
Wisconsin

APPENDIX D

Federal Court Name Abbreviations

Court	Abbrev.
United States Supreme Court	U.S.
UNITED STATES COURTS OF APPEALS	
First Circuit	1st Cir.
Second Circuit	2d Cir.
Third Circuit	3d Cir.
Fourth Circuit	4th Cir.
Fifth Circuit	5th Cir.
Sixth Circuit	6th Cir.
Seventh Circuit	7th Cir.
Eighth Circuit	8th Cir.
Ninth Circuit	9th Cir.
Tenth Circuit	10th Cir.
Eleventh Circuit	11th Cir.
D.C. Circuit	D.C. Cir.
Federal Circuit	Fed. Cir.
UNITED STATES DISTRICT COURTS	
Middle District of Alabama	**M.D. Ala.**
Northern District of Alabama	**N.D. Ala.**
Southern District of Alabama	**S.D. Ala.**
District of Alaska	**D. Alaska**
District of Arizona	**D. Ariz.**
Eastern District of Arkansas	**E.D. Ark.**
Western District of Arkansas	**W.D. Ark.**
Central District of California	**C.D. Cal.**
Eastern District of California	**E.D. Cal.**

(Note: The D.C.Z. ceased to exist on March 31, 1982.)

Reprinted with permission of Aspen Publishers, from ALWD Citation Manual: A Professional System of Citation.

Court	Abbrev.
Northern District of California	**N.D. Cal.**
Southern District of California	**S.D. Cal.**
District of the Canal Zone	**D.C.Z.**
District of Colorado	**D. Colo.**
District of Connecticut	**D. Conn.**
District of Delaware	**D. Del.**
District of D.C.	**D.D.C.**
Middle District of Florida	**M.D. Fla.**
Northern District of Florida	**N.D. Fla.**
Southern District of Florida	**S.D. Fla.**
Middle District of Georgia	**M.D. Ga.**
Northern District of Georgia	**N.D. Ga.**
Southern District of Georgia	**S.D. Ga.**
District of Guam	**D. Guam**
District of Hawaii	**D. Haw.**
District of Idaho	**D. Idaho**
Central District of Illinois	**C.D. Ill.**
Northern District of Illinois	**N.D. Ill.**
Southern District of Illinois	**S.D. Ill.**
Northern District of Indiana	**N.D. Ind.**
Southern District of Indiana	**S.D. Ind.**
Northern District of Iowa	**N.D. Iowa**
Southern District of Iowa	**S.D. Iowa**
District of Kansas	**D. Kan.**
Eastern District of Kentucky	**E.D. Ky.**
Western District of Kentucky	**W.D. Ky.**
Eastern District of Louisiana	**E.D. La.**
Middle District of Louisiana	**M.D. La.**
Western District of Louisiana	**W.D. La.**
District of Maine	**D. Me.**
District of Maryland	**D. Md.**
District of Massachusetts	**D. Mass.**
Eastern District of Michigan	**E.D. Mich.**
Western District of Michigan	**W.D. Mich.**
District of Minnesota	**D. Minn.**
Northern District of Mississippi	**N.D. Miss.**
Southern District of Mississippi	**S.D. Miss.**
Eastern District of Missouri	**E.D. Mo.**
Western District of Missouri	**W.D. Mo.**
District of Montana	**D. Mont.**
District of Nebraska	**D. Neb.**

Court	Abbrev.
District of Nevada	**D. Nev.**
District of New Hampshire	**D.N.H.**
District of New Jersey	**D.N.J.**
District of New Mexico	**D.N.M.**
Eastern District of New York	**E.D.N.Y.**
Northern District of New York	**N.D.N.Y.**
Southern District of New York	**S.D.N.Y.**
Western District of New York	**W.D.N.Y.**
Eastern District of North Carolina	**E.D.N.C.**
Middle District of North Carolina	**M.D.N.C.**
Western District of North Carolina	**W.D.N.C.**
District of North Dakota	**D.N.D.**
District of the Northern Mariana Islands	**D.N. Mar. I.**
Northern District of Ohio	**N.D. Ohio**
Southern District of Ohio	**S.D. Ohio**
Eastern District of Oklahoma	**E.D. Okla.**
Northern District of Oklahoma	**N.D. Okla.**
Western District of Oklahoma	**W.D. Okla.**
District of Oregon	**D. Or.**
Eastern District of Pennsylvania	**E.D. Pa.**
Middle District of Pennsylvania	**M.D. Pa.**
Western District of Pennsylvania	**W.D. Pa.**
District of Puerto Rico	**D.P.R.**
District of Rhode Island	**D.R.I.**
District of South Carolina	**D.S.C.**
District of South Dakota	**D.S.D.**
Eastern District of Tennessee	**E.D. Tenn.**
Middle District of Tennessee	**M.D. Tenn.**
Western District of Tennessee	**W.D. Tenn.**
Eastern District of Texas	**E.D. Tex.**
Northern District of Texas	**N.D. Tex.**
Southern District of Texas	**S.D. Tex.**
Western District of Texas	**W.D. Tex.**
District of Utah	**D. Utah**
District of Vermont	**D. Vt.**
Eastern District of Virginia	**E.D. Va.**
Western District of Virginia	**W.D. Va.**
District of the Virgin Islands	**D.V.I.**
Eastern District of Washington	**E.D. Wash.**
Western District of Washington	**W.D. Wash.**
Northern District of West Virginia	**N.D.W. Va.**

Court	Abbrev.
Southern District of West Virginia	**S.D.W. Va.**
Eastern District of Wisconsin	**E.D. Wis.**
Western District of Wisconsin	**W.D. Wis.**
District of Wyoming	**D. Wyo.**
MILITARY COURTS	
United States Court of Appeals for the Armed Forces	**Armed Forces App.**
United States Court of Veterans Appeals	**Vet. App.**
United States Air Force Court of Criminal Appeals	**A.F. Crim. App.**
United States Army Court of Criminal Appeals	**Army Crim. App.**
United States Coast Guard Court of Criminal Appeals	**Coast Guard Crim. App.**
United States Navy-Marine Corps Court of Criminal Appeals	**Navy-Marine Crim. App.**

BANKRUPTCY COURTS

Each United States District Court has a corresponding bankruptcy court. To cite a bankruptcy court, add Bankr. to the district court abbreviation.

Examples:

Bankr. N.D. Ala.

Bankr. D. Mass.

OTHER FEDERAL COURTS

Court	Abbrev.
Court of Federal Claims	**Fed. Cl.**
Court of Customs and Patent Appeals	**Cust. & Pat. App.**
Court of Claims	**Ct. Cl.**
Claims Court	**Cl. Ct.**
Court of International Trade	**Ct. Intl. Trade**
Tax Court	**Tax**

APPENDIX E

Effective Learning

How to Study

Everyone learns differently. Some people seem to absorb information like a sponge while others must work hard to soak up any information. Although some people truly do have photographic memories, they are few and far between. Most likely, the people who seem to absorb information "like a sponge" have learned how to maximize their learning experiences. Most of us do not take the time to figure out how we learn best and, as a result, probably spend more time than necessary to achieve the same results as more proficient learners.

Have you ever wondered how some people who are just average students seem to always get As? If you were to ask them, they probably would tell you that they spend more time than most people studying and preparing, or that they have learned how to study more effectively and efficiently in the time they have available. A good starting point is to determine how you learn best and work out methods to maximize the time and effort you have available.

LEARNING STYLES

A learning style is the way you learn most effectively. Everyone has his or her own learning style, and there are no "better" or "correct" ways to learn. Somewhere in your school career you may have been given tests—such as the Hogan/Champagne Personal Style Indicator or the Kolb Learning Style Inventory—to determine your personal learning styles. These and similar assessments are available through most school advisors and guidance counselors. If you want help in determining your learning styles, take the initiative for your own success and make an appointment with someone who can administer an assessment.

Learning styles fall into these categories:

- independent (competitive) versus collaborative
- structured versus unstructured
- auditory versus visual
- spatial versus verbal
- practical versus creative
- applied versus conceptual
- factual versus analytical
- emotional versus logical

This sounds like a lot to consider, but taking a few minutes to determine which learning style best suits you can save you countless hours of frustration—hours that could be better devoted to studying or other activities.

Independent Versus Collaborative

Do you prefer to work with a group or independently? Some people like to avoid all distractions by working alone. Others prefer to work in a study group and share information.

If you prefer to work independently, you may want to obtain additional course information from study guides and computer-assisted instruction. You may prefer lecture-format classes to small discussion courses. If you prefer to work collaboratively, you may wish to form study groups early in the semester or find a tutor to work with, and you should choose courses that include small discussion groups or group projects.

Structured Versus Unstructured

Structured learners feel more comfortable when they formalize their study habits—for example, by selecting a definite time and place in which to study every day. If you are a structured learner, you may find it useful to create "to-do" lists and keep a written schedule of classes, study times, and activities.

Unstructured learners tend to resist formalizing their study plan and try to avoid feeling "locked-in." They tend to procrastinate. Procrastinators need to find ways to give more structure to their learning activities. One method is to join a study group of students who are more organized.

Auditory Versus Visual

Auditory learners learn best by listening. Visual learners learn best from what they see. Visual learners cannot always learn everything by listening to lectures or by reading and watching video presentations. Auditory learners may find it more efficient to listen to lectures and then read related material. Visual learners may do better reading the book first, and then attending lectures. Auditory learners may also find group discussion and study group activities beneficial.

Spatial Versus Verbal

Spatial learners are better then verbal learners at reading and interpreting maps, charts, and other graphics. Verbal learners prefer to read words than to interpret graphics. Spatial learners need to create and incorporate their own diagrams, maps, timelines, and other graphics into their notes.

Verbal learners need to translate or obtain translations of graphics into words. A useful technique for verbal learners is to take notes that describe the material, including the graphics, in such a way that a visually impaired student could understand the graphic representation from the verbal description. Teaming up with a visually impaired student may be mutually beneficial.

Practical Versus Creative

Practical learners tend to be methodical and systematic. They prefer specific instruction that is directed and focused. Creative learners prefer experimentation and creative activities. Practical learners may benefit from creating an organized study plan for each course, including detailed "to-do" lists and a calendar. For creative learners, courses that allow writing and other creative approaches may be more satisfying.

Applied Versus Conceptual

Applied learners want to know how information can be transferred to given situations. Conceptual learners are not so much concerned with the application as with the underlying concepts. Applied learners need to focus on ways in which the ideas presented in courses and lectures can be applied. Taking notes that include examples for applying the concepts helps them recall the concepts later. Conceptual learners may find it useful to consider the concepts in a broader context than that of the narrow lecture presentation.

Factual Versus Analytical

Factual learners are good with details and enjoy learning interesting and unusual facts. They prefer objective tests. Analytical learners like to break down a topic into its component parts to understand how the parts relate to each other. Analytical learners prefer essay exams that allow them to demonstrate how their knowledge relates to the question. Factual learners may want to make lists of facts, which they can associate with prior knowledge. Analytical learners may want to analyze the organization as they read a textbook, looking for trends and patterns.

Emotional Versus Logical

Emotional learners tend to prefer human-interest stories to material that presents just facts and logic. Logical learners want to understand the factual basis, including statistics, of an argument. Emotional learners may find that reading biographical sketches helps them understand factual subjects.

PUTTING IT ALL TOGETHER

1. ***Understand yourself.*** From the previous list of types of learners, select the descriptions in each category that best fit your style of learning. Look back at courses and classes you have taken in which you have done well or that you enjoyed the most. You may see a pattern that will help you understand your learning style.

2. ***Set goals.*** Determine your personal and occupational goals. Do you want a career working with people or with things? Do you want a professional career working directly with people or behind the scenes supporting others? What courses will help you acquire the skills and knowledge you need to achieve these goals?

3. ***Make a plan.*** Your educational path should lead to a goal. It may be a personal goal to be an outstanding parent or partner, or it may be a goal to be a generalist or a specialist in an occupation or profession. To achieve these goals, you will have to focus on courses that give you the necessary skills and knowledge. Within the courses may be options that accommodate your learning style, such as large lecture classes versus small-group discussion classes, face-to-face courses versus distance-learning courses, and so on.

   Create a personal plan that allows for flexibility as your goals or interests change. A good foundation will allow you more flexibility in courses and curriculum. Don't be afraid to admit that you did not enjoy some courses you expected to enjoy or that you enjoyed some classes you didn't think would give you pleasure. These insights may help you fine-tune your personal and professional goals.

4. ***Check your progress.*** Periodically assess how well you are doing in individual classes, as well as in your overall program of study. Use the opportunity to assess why you are doing better than you expected in some classes and not as well in others. You may have to adjust your overall plan or merely your learning methods. Or outside influences such as work, family, or personal issues may be interfering with your learning. Periodic self-assessment is the first step in modifying your goals.

5. ***Make adjustments.*** As your goals change, so will your plan. Don't be afraid to make the adjustments necessary to achieve your goals or to change your goals as your interests change. Life rarely follows a straight path. Be adaptable and make adjustments when necessary.

SCHEDULING TIME

Most people use a calendar to keep track of information such as birthdays, appointments, or upcoming events. Calendars may include vacations, concerts, and other special events or activities. Depending on your personal style, you might include "to-do" lists or an hour-by-hour schedule of classes and other activities. Scheduling school and study time is helpful to most students.

Whichever method works best for you, use it to track the amount of time you spend in all of your activities so you can budget your time more accurately. When scheduling, keep in mind that the power of concentration has a limitation for everyone. Don't schedule so many activities that they exceed your mental or physical abilities.

SUPPLEMENTAL LEARNING AIDS

1. ***Study guides.*** Many textbooks have a study guide that will give you additional information, including sample tests and quizzes. Your instructor may or may not require the use of a study guide. If you need additional reinforcement, you may want to purchase a study guide even if it is not a required part of the course.

2. ***Flash cards.*** Flash cards are available in college bookstores for many courses. But you will learn more by preparing your own and customizing them to the course you are taking. On the front side of an index card, write a word, phrase, or concept, and write the definition or explanation on the reverse side. With a properly prepared set of flash cards, you may not have to refer to the text or your notes when studying for a test.

3. ***Companion websites.*** Many publishers offer companion websites for their textbooks. These websites frequently are available on the publisher's website without cost or for a nominal fee. Often these websites are the equivalent of an online study guide. Others offer self-tests. The publisher may post information that has become available since the publication of the textbook.

4. ***Outlining.*** Few people have a photographic memory or the ability to absorb material on one reading. The following approach can help you use your textbook effectively.

   a. ***How long is the chapter?*** Before you start, check the length of the chapter and your reading assignment. Most textbooks are filled with graphics and illustrations that reduce the amount of actual reading time to a manageable level.
   b. ***Scan the chapter.*** Look over the material quickly to get a sense of what will be covered.
   c. ***Chapter objectives.*** At the beginnings of each chapter, most textbooks list what you should learn from reading the chapter. These chapter objectives help you focus on important topics, information, and themes.
   d. ***Read the chapter.*** Quickly read through the chapter to get an overall sense of the material and how the sections relate to each other.
   e. ***Underline the important items.*** After you have done this go back over the material and underline in pencil the items you believe are important.
   f. ***Go to class.*** From the instructor's lecture and class discussion, you may find that what you think is important changes.
   g. ***Highlight the important material.*** After class, use a highlighter to highlight what you now believe to be the important information in the text. You probably will find that it is substantially less than what you underlined in pencil.
   h. ***Make your flash cards.*** From the highlighted information, create a set of flash cards for each chapter.

5. ***Tutors.*** Not everyone can afford the luxury of a personal tutor, but most colleges and universities have a tutoring center or offer some form of tutoring assistance. If you are having difficulty, don't be afraid to ask for help before it is too late. At the beginning of the semester determine what personalized help is available for each course. You may not need to use this information, but having it available will reduce your anxiety and panic if you realize that you need some help.

Don't be afraid to ask your instructor for help. Your instructor wants you to succeed. If you are doing everything you can to be successful in a class, the instructor should be more than happy to help you or direct you for help.

6. ***Study groups.*** If you are the type of learner who benefits from working with others, form a study group at the beginning of each semester in each course. After the first class, ask if others wish to form a study group, or post a notice on the course bulletin board website.

One advantage of study groups is the opportunity to share class notes as well as ideas. Verbal learners can benefit from having visual learners in the study group to interpret and explain charts, graphs, and maps. Study groups can motivate procrastinators to complete tasks on time.

7. ***Tests.*** Most students suffer from some form of test anxiety. At the beginning of each course, ask the instructor for the exam schedule and the type of tests he or she will be giving. Some schools maintain copies of all tests that students can use for practice. If your school does not maintain these, ask your instructors if they will make available sample tests and quizzes. Practice tests may be available in the study guide for the text or on a companion website. If you are in a study group, members can prepare practice tests as part of test preparation.

For more detailed information about study skills, see *Effective Study Skills: Maximizing Your Academic Potential,* by Judy M. Roberts (Prentice Hall, 1998).

The Constitution of the United States of America

PREAMBLE

We the People of the United States, in Order to form a more perfect Union, establish Justice, insure domestic Tranquility, provide for the common defense, promote the general Welfare, and secure the Blessings of Liberty to ourselves and our Posterity, do ordain and establish this Constitution for the United States of America.

ARTICLE I

Section 1. All legislative Powers herein granted shall be vested in a Congress of the United States, which shall consist of a Senate and House of Representatives.

Section 2. The House of Representatives shall be composed of Members chosen every second Year by the People of the several States, and the Electors in each State shall have the Qualifications requisite for Electors of the most numerous Branch of the State Legislature.

No Person shall be a Representative who shall not have attained to the Age of twenty five Years, and been seven Years a Citizen of the United States, and who shall not, when elected, be an Inhabitant of that State in which he shall be chosen.

Representatives and direct Taxes shall be apportioned among the several States which may be included within this Union, according to their respective Numbers, which shall be determined by adding to the whole Number of free Persons, including those bound to Service for a Term of Years, and excluding Indians not taxed, three fifths of all other Persons. The actual Enumeration shall be made within three Years after the first Meeting of the Congress of the United States, and within every subsequent Term of ten Years, in such Manner as they shall by Law direct. The Number of Representatives shall not exceed one for every thirty Thousand, but each State shall have at Least one Representative; and until such enumeration shall be made, the State of New Hampshire shall be entitled to chuse three, Massachusetts eight, Rhode Island and Providence Plantations one, Connecticut five, New York six, New Jersey four, Pennsylvania eight, Delaware one, Maryland six, Virginia ten, North Carolina five, South Carolina five, and Georgia three.

When vacancies happen in the Representation from any State, the Executive Authority thereof shall issue Writs of Election to fill such Vacancies.

The House of Representatives shall chuse their Speaker and other Officers; and shall have the sole Power of Impeachment.

Section 3. The Senate of the United States shall be composed of two Senators from each State, chosen by the Legislature thereof for six Years; and each Senator shall have one Vote.

Immediately after they shall be assembled in Consequence of the first Election, they shall be divided as equally as may be into three Classes. The Seats of the Senators of the first Class shall be vacated at the Expiration of the second Year, of the second Class at the Expiration of the fourth Year, and of the third Class at the Expiration of the sixth Year, so that one third may be chosen every second Year; and if Vacancies happen by Resignation, or otherwise, during the Recess of the Legislature of any State, the Executive thereof may make temporary Appointments until the next Meeting of the Legislature, which shall then fill such Vacancies.

No Person shall be a Senator who shall not have attained to the Age of thirty Years, and been nine Years a Citizen of the United States, and who shall not, when elected, be an Inhabitant of that State for which he shall be chosen.

The Vice President of the United States shall be President of the Senate, but shall have no Vote, unless they be equally divided.

The Senate shall chuse their other Officers, and also a President pro tempore, in the Absence of the Vice President, or when he shall exercise the Office of President of the United States.

The Senate shall have the sole Power to try all Impeachments. When sitting for that Purpose, they shall be on Oath or Affirmation. When the President of the United States is tried, the Chief Justice shall preside: And no Person shall be convicted without the Concurrence of two thirds of the Members present.

Judgment in Cases of Impeachment shall not extend further than to removal from Office, and disqualification to hold and enjoy any Office of honor, Trust or Profit under the United States: but the Party convicted shall nevertheless be liable and subject to Indictment, Trial, Judgment and Punishment, according to Law.

Section 4. The Times, Places and Manner of holding Elections for Senators and Representatives, shall be prescribed in each State by the Legislature thereof; but the Congress may at any time by Law make or alter such Regulations, except as to the Places of chusing Senators.

The Congress shall assemble at least once in every Year, and such Meeting shall be on the first Monday in December, unless they shall by Law appoint a different Day.

Section 5. Each House shall be the Judge of the Elections, Returns and Qualifications of its own Members, and a Majority of each shall constitute a Quorum to do Business; but a smaller Number may adjourn from day to day, and may be authorized to compel the Attendance of absent Members, in such Manner, and under such Penalties as each House may provide.

Each House may determine the Rules of its Proceedings, punish its Members for disorderly Behaviour, and, with the Concurrence of two thirds, expel a Member.

Each House shall keep a Journal of its Proceedings, and from time to time publish the same, excepting such Parts as may in their Judgment require Secrecy; and the Yeas and Nays of the Members of either House on any question shall, at the Desire of one fifth of those Present, be entered on the Journal.

Neither House, during the Session of Congress, shall, without the Consent of the other, adjourn for more than three days, nor to any other Place than that in which the two Houses shall be sitting.

Section 6. The Senators and Representatives shall receive a Compensation for their Services, to be ascertained by Law, and paid out of the Treasury of the United States. They shall in all Cases, except Treason, Felony and Breach of the Peace, be privileged from Arrest during their Attendance at the Session of their respective Houses, and in going to and returning from the same; and for any Speech or Debate in either House, they shall not be questioned in any other Place.

No Senator or Representative shall, during the Time for which he was elected, be appointed to any civil Office under the Authority of the United States, which shall have been created, or the Emoluments whereof shall have been encreased during such time; and no Person holding any Office under the United States, shall be a Member of either House during his Continuance in Office.

Section 7. All Bills for raising Revenue shall originate in the House of Representatives; but the Senate may propose or concur with Amendments as on other Bills.

Every Bill which shall have passed the House of Representatives and the Senate, shall, before it become a Law, be presented to the President of the United States: If he approve he shall sign it, but if not he shall return it, with his Objections to that House in which it shall have originated, who shall enter the Objections at large on their Journal, and proceed to reconsider it. If after such Reconsideration two thirds of that House shall agree to pass the Bill, it shall be sent, together with the Objections, to the other House, by which it shall likewise be reconsidered, and if approved by two thirds of that House, it shall become a Law. But in all such Cases the Votes of both Houses shall be determined by yeas and Nays, and the Names of the Persons voting for and against the Bill shall be entered on the Journal of each House respectively. If any Bill shall not be returned by the President within ten Days (Sundays excepted) after it shall have been presented to him, the Same shall be a Law, in like Manner as if he had signed it, unless the Congress by their Adjournment prevent its Return, in which Case it shall not be a Law.

Every Order, Resolution, or Vote to which the Concurrence of the Senate and House of Representatives may be necessary (except on a question of Adjournment) shall be presented to the President of the United States; and before the Same shall take Effect, shall be approved by him, or being disapproved by him, shall be repassed by two thirds of the Senate and House of Representatives, according to the Rules and Limitations prescribed in the Case of a Bill.

Section 8. The Congress shall have Power To lay and collect Taxes, Duties, Imposts and Excises, to pay the Debts and provide for the common Defence and general Welfare of the United States; but all Duties, Imposts and Excises shall be uniform throughout the United States;

To borrow Money on the credit of the United States;

To regulate Commerce with foreign Nations, and among the several States, and with the Indian Tribes;

To establish an uniform Rule of Naturalization, and uniform Laws on the subject of Bankruptcies throughout the United States;

To coin Money, regulate the Value thereof, and of foreign Coin, and fix the Standard of Weights and Measures;

To provide for the Punishment of counterfeiting the Securities and current Coin of the United States;

To establish Post Offices and post Roads;

To promote the Progress of Science and useful Arts, by securing for limited Times to Authors and Inventors the exclusive Right to their respective Writings and Discoveries;

To constitute Tribunals inferior to the supreme Court;

To define and punish Piracies and Felonies committed on the high Seas, and Offences against the Law of Nations;

To declare War, grant Letters of Marque and Reprisal, and make Rules concerning Captures on Land and Water;

To raise and support Armies, but no Appropriation of Money to that Use shall be for a longer Term than two Years; To provide and maintain a Navy;

To make Rules for the Government and Regulation of the land and naval Forces;

To provide for calling forth the Militia to execute the Laws of the Union, suppress Insurrections and repel Invasions;

To provide for organizing, arming, and disciplining, the Militia, and for governing such Part of them as may be employed in the Service of the United States, reserving to the States respectively, the Appointment of the Officers, and the Authority of training the Militia according to the discipline prescribed by Congress;

To exercise exclusive Legislation in all Cases whatsoever, over such District (not exceeding ten Miles square) as may, by Cession of particular States, and the Acceptance of Congress, become the Seat of the Government of the United States, and to exercise like Authority over all Places purchased by the Consent of the Legislature of the State in which the Same shall be, for the Erection of Forts, Magazines, Arsenals, dockYards, and other needful Buildings;—And

To make all Laws which shall be necessary and proper for carrying into Execution the foregoing Powers, and all other Powers vested by this Constitution in the Government of the United States, or in any Department or Officer thereof.

Section 9. The Migration or Importation of such Persons as any of the States now existing shall think proper to admit, shall not be prohibited by the Congress prior to the Year one thousand eight hundred and eight, but a Tax or duty may be imposed on such Importation, not exceeding ten dollars for each Person.

The Privilege of the Writ of Habeas Corpus shall not be suspended, unless when in Cases of Rebellion or Invasion the public Safety may require it.

No Bill of Attainder or ex post facto Law shall be passed.

No Capitation, or other direct, Tax shall be laid, unless in Proportion to the Census or enumeration herein before directed to be taken.

No Tax or Duty shall be laid on Articles exported from any State.

No Preference shall be given by any Regulation of Commerce or Revenue to the Ports of one State over those of another; nor shall Vessels bound to, or from, one State, be obliged to enter, clear, or pay Duties in another.

No Money shall be drawn from the Treasury, but in Consequence of Appropriations made by Law; and a regular Statement and Account of the Receipts and Expenditures of all public Money shall be published from time to time.

No Title of Nobility shall be granted by the United States: And no Person holding any Office of Profit or Trust under them, shall, without the Consent of the Congress, accept of any present, Emolument, Office, or Title, of any kind whatever, from any King, Prince, or foreign State.

Section 10. No State shall enter into any Treaty, Alliance, or Confederation; grant Letters of Marque and Reprisal; coin Money; emit Bills of Credit; make any Thing but gold and silver Coin a Tender in Payment of Debts; pass any Bill of Attainder, ex post facto Law, or Law impairing the Obligation of Contracts, or grant any Title of Nobility.

No State shall, without the Consent of the Congress, lay any Imposts or Duties on Imports or Exports, except what may be absolutely necessary for executing it's inspection Laws: and the net Produce of all Duties and Imposts, laid by any State on Imports or Exports, shall be for the Use of the Treasury of the United States; and all such Laws shall be subject to the Revision and Controul of the Congress.

No State shall, without the Consent of Congress, lay any Duty of Tonnage, keep Troops, or Ships of War in time of Peace, enter into any Agreement or Compact with another State, or with a foreign Power, or engage in War, unless actually invaded, or in such imminent Danger as will not admit of delay.

ARTICLE II

Section 1. The executive Power shall be vested in a President of the United States of America. He shall hold his Office during the Term of four Years, and, together with the Vice President, chosen for the same Term, be elected, as follows:

Each State shall appoint, in such Manner as the Legislature thereof may direct, a Number of Electors, equal to the whole Number of Senators and Representatives to which the State may be entitled in the Congress: but no Senator or Representative, or Person holding an Office of Trust or Profit under the United States, shall be appointed an Elector.

The Electors shall meet in their respective States, and vote by Ballot for two Persons, of whom one at least shall not be an Inhabitant of the same State with themselves. And they shall make a List of all the Persons voted for, and of the Number of Votes for each; which List they shall sign and certify, and transmit sealed to the Seat of the Government of the United States, directed to the President of the Senate. The President of the Senate shall, in the Presence of the Senate and House of Representatives, open all the Certificates, and the Votes shall then be counted. The Person having the greatest Number of Votes shall be the President, if such Number be a Majority of the whole Number of Electors appointed; and if there be more than one who have such Majority, and have an equal Number of Votes, then the House of Representatives shall immediately chuse by Ballot one of them for President; and if no Person have a Majority, then from the five highest on the List the said House shall in like Manner chuse the President. But in chusing the President, the Votes shall be taken by States, the Representation from each State having one Vote; A quorum for this purpose shall consist of a Member or Members from two thirds of the States, and a Majority of all the States shall be necessary to a Choice. In every Case, after the Choice of the President, the Person having the greatest Number of Votes of the Electors shall be the Vice President. But if there should remain two or more who have equal Votes, the Senate shall chuse from them by Ballot the Vice President.

The Congress may determine the Time of chusing the Electors, and the Day on which they shall give their Votes; which Day shall be the same throughout the United States.

No Person except a natural born Citizen, or a Citizen of the United States, at the time of the Adoption of this Constitution, shall be eligible to the Office of President; neither shall any Person be eligible to that Office who shall not have attained to the Age of thirty five Years, and been fourteen Years a Resident within the United States.

In Case of the Removal of the President from Office, or of his Death, Resignation, or Inability to discharge the Powers and Duties of the said Office, the Same shall devolve on the Vice President, and the Congress may by Law provide for the Case of Removal, Death, Resignation or Inability, both of the President and Vice President, declaring what Officer shall then act as President, and such Officer shall act accordingly, until the Disability be removed, or a President shall be elected.

The President shall, at stated Times, receive for his Services, a Compensation, which shall neither be increased nor diminished during the Period for which he shall have been elected, and he shall not receive within that Period any other Emolument from the United States, or any of them.

Before he enter on the Execution of his Office, he shall take the following Oath or Affirmation:—"I do solemnly swear (or affirm) that I will faithfully execute the Office of President of the United States, and will to the best of my Ability, preserve, protect and defend the Constitution of the United States."

Section 2. The President shall be Commander in Chief of the Army and Navy of the United States, and of the Militia of the several States, when called into the actual Service of the United States; he may require the Opinion, in writing, of the principal

Officer in each of the executive Departments, upon any Subject relating to the Duties of their respective Offices, and he shall have Power to grant Reprieves and Pardons for Offences against the United States, except in Cases of Impeachment.

He shall have Power, by and with the Advice and Consent of the Senate, to make Treaties, provided two thirds of the Senators present concur; and he shall nominate, and by and with the Advice and Consent of the Senate, shall appoint Ambassadors, other public Ministers and Consuls, Judges of the supreme Court, and all other Officers of the United States, whose Appointments are not herein otherwise provided for, and which shall be established by Law: but the Congress may by Law vest the Appointment of such inferior Officers, as they think proper, in the President alone, in the Courts of Law, or in the Heads of Departments.

The President shall have Power to fill up all Vacancies that may happen during the Recess of the Senate, by granting Commissions which shall expire at the End of their next Session.

Section 3. He shall from time to time give to the Congress Information of the State of the Union, and recommend to their Consideration such Measures as he shall judge necessary and expedient; he may, on extraordinary Occasions, convene both Houses, or either of them, and in Case of Disagreement between them, with Respect to the Time of Adjournment, he may adjourn them to such Time as he shall think proper; he shall receive Ambassadors and other public Ministers; he shall take Care that the Laws be faithfully executed, and shall Commission all the Officers of the United States.

Section 4. The President, Vice President and all civil Officers of the United States, shall be removed from Office on Impeachment for, and Conviction of, Treason, Bribery, or other high Crimes and Misdemeanors.

ARTICLE III

Section 1. The judicial Power of the United States shall be vested in one supreme Court, and in such inferior Courts as the Congress may from time to time ordain and establish. The Judges, both of the supreme and inferior Courts, shall hold their Offices during good Behaviour, and shall, at stated Times, receive for their Services a Compensation, which shall not be diminished during their Continuance in Office.

Section 2. The judicial Power shall extend to all Cases, in Law and Equity, arising under this Constitution, the Laws of the United States, and Treaties made, or which shall be made, under their Authority;—to all Cases affecting Ambassadors, other public Ministers and Consuls;—to all Cases of admiralty and maritime Jurisdiction;—to Controversies to which the United States shall be a Party;—to Controversies between two or more States;—between a State and Citizens of another State;—between Citizens of different States;—between Citizens of the same State claiming Lands under Grants of different States, and between a State, or the Citizens thereof, and foreign States, Citizens or Subjects.

In all Cases affecting Ambassadors, other public Ministers and Consuls, and those in which a State shall be Party, the supreme Court shall have original Jurisdiction. In all the other Cases before mentioned, the supreme Court shall have appellate Jurisdiction, both as to Law and Fact, with such Exceptions, and under such Regulations as the Congress shall make.

The Trial of all Crimes, except in Cases of Impeachment, shall be by Jury; and such Trial shall be held in the State where the said Crimes shall have been committed; but when not committed within any State, the Trial shall be at such Place or Places as the Congress may by Law have directed.

Section 3. Treason against the United States, shall consist only in levying War against them, or in adhering to their Enemies, giving them Aid and Comfort. No Person shall be convicted of Treason unless on the Testimony of two Witnesses to the same overt Act, or on Confession in open Court.

The Congress shall have Power to declare the Punishment of Treason, but no Attainder of Treason shall work Corruption of Blood, or Forfeiture except during the Life of the Person attainted.

ARTICLE IV

Section 1. Full Faith and Credit shall be given in each State to the public Acts, Records, and judicial Proceedings of every other State. And the Congress may by general Laws prescribe the Manner in which such Acts, Records and Proceedings shall be proved, and the Effect thereof.

Section 2. The Citizens of each State shall be entitled to all Privileges and Immunities of Citizens in the several States.

A Person charged in any State with Treason, Felony, or other Crime, who shall flee from Justice, and be found in another State, shall on Demand of the executive Authority of the State from which he fled, be delivered up, to be removed to the State having Jurisdiction of the Crime.

No Person held to Service or Labour in one State, under the Laws thereof, escaping into another, shall, in Consequence of any Law or Regulation therein, be discharged from such Service or Labour, but shall be delivered up on Claim of the Party to whom such Service or Labour may be due.

Section 3. New States may be admitted by the Congress into this Union; but no new State shall be formed or erected within the Jurisdiction of any other State; nor any State be formed by the Junction of two or more States, or Parts of States, without the Consent of the Legislatures of the States concerned as well as of the Congress.

The Congress shall have Power to dispose of and make all needful Rules and Regulations respecting the Territory or other Property belonging to the United States; and nothing in this Constitution shall be so construed as to Prejudice any Claims of the United States, or of any particular State.

Section 4. The United States shall guarantee to every State in this Union a Republican Form of Government, and shall protect each of them against Invasion; and on Application of the Legislature, or of the Executive (when the Legislature cannot be convened), against domestic Violence.

ARTICLE V

The Congress, whenever two thirds of both Houses shall deem it necessary, shall propose Amendments to this Constitution, or, on the Application of the Legislatures of two thirds of the several States, shall call a Convention for proposing Amendments, which, in either Case, shall be valid to all Intents and Purposes, as Part of this Constitution, when ratified by the Legislatures of three fourths of the several States, or by Conventions in three fourths thereof, as the one or the other Mode of Ratification may be proposed by the Congress; Provided that no Amendment which may be made prior to the Year One thousand eight hundred and eight shall in any Manner affect the first and fourth Clauses in the Ninth Section of the first Article; and that no State, without its Consent, shall be deprived of its equal Suffrage in the Senate.

ARTICLE VI

All Debts contracted and Engagements entered into, before the Adoption of this Constitution, shall be as valid against the United States under this Constitution, as under the Confederation.

This Constitution, and the Laws of the United States which shall be made in Pursuance thereof; and all Treaties made, or which shall be made, under the Authority of the United States, shall be the supreme Law of the Land; and the Judges in every State shall be bound thereby, any Thing in the Constitution or Laws of any State to the Contrary notwithstanding.

The Senators and Representatives before mentioned, and the Members of the several State Legislatures, and all executive and judicial Officers, both of the United States and of the several States, shall be bound by Oath or Affirmation, to support this Constitution; but no religious Test shall ever be required as a Qualification to any Office or public Trust under the United States.

ARTICLE VII

The Ratification of the Conventions of nine States, shall be sufficient for the Establishment of this Constitution between the States so ratifying the Same.

AMENDMENTS TO THE CONSTITUTION OF THE UNITED STATES

[Amendments I–X make up the Bill of Rights]

AMENDMENT I

Congress shall make no law respecting an establishment of religion, or prohibiting the free exercise thereof; or abridging the freedom of speech, or of the press; or the right of the people peaceably to assemble, and to petition the Government for a redress of grievances.

AMENDMENT II

A well regulated Militia, being necessary to the security of a free State, the right of the people to keep and bear Arms, shall not be infringed.

AMENDMENT III

No Soldier shall, in time of peace be quartered in any house, without the consent of the Owner, nor in time of war, but in a manner to be prescribed by law.

AMENDMENT IV

The right of the people to be secure in their persons, houses, papers, and effects, against unreasonable searches and seizures, shall not be violated, and no Warrants shall issue, but upon probable cause, supported by Oath or affirmation, and particularly describing the place to be searched, and the persons or things to be seized.

AMENDMENT V

No person shall be held to answer for a capital, or otherwise infamous crime, unless on a presentment or indictment of a Grand Jury, except in cases arising in the land or naval forces, or in the Militia, when in actual service in time of War or public danger; nor shall any person be subject for the same offence to be twice put in jeopardy of life or limb; nor shall be compelled in any criminal case to be a witness against himself, nor be deprived of life, liberty, or property, without due process of law; nor shall private property be taken for public use, without just compensation.

AMENDMENT VI

In all criminal prosecutions, the accused shall enjoy the right to a speedy and public trial, by an impartial jury of the State and district wherein the crime shall have been committed, which district shall have been previously ascertained by law, and to be informed of the nature and cause of the accusation; to be confronted with the witnesses against him; to have compulsory process for obtaining witnesses in his favor, and to have the Assistance of Counsel for his defence.

AMENDMENT VII

In suits at common law, where the value in controversy shall exceed twenty dollars, the right of trial by jury shall be preserved, and no fact tried by a jury, shall be otherwise reexamined in any Court of the United States, than according to the rules of the common law.

AMENDMENT VIII

Excessive bail shall not be required, nor excessive fines imposed, nor cruel and unusual punishments inflicted.

AMENDMENT IX

The enumeration in the Constitution, of certain rights, shall not be construed to deny or disparage others retained by the people.

AMENDMENT X

The powers not delegated to the United States by the Constitution, nor prohibited by it to the States, are reserved to the States respectively, or to the people.

AMENDMENT XI

The Judicial power of the United States shall not be construed to extend to any suit in law or equity, commenced or prosecuted against one of the United States by Citizens of another State, or by Citizens or Subjects of any Foreign State.

AMENDMENT XII

The Electors shall meet in their respective states and vote by ballot for President and Vice-President, one of whom, at least, shall not be an inhabitant of the same state with themselves; they shall name in their ballots the person voted for as President, and in distinct ballots the person voted for as Vice-President, and they shall make distinct lists of all persons voted for as President, and of all persons voted for as Vice-President, and of the number of votes for each, which lists they shall sign and certify, and transmit sealed to the seat of the government of the United States, directed to the President of the Senate;—the President of the Senate shall, in the presence of the Senate and House of Representatives, open all the certificates and the votes shall then be counted;—The person having the greatest number of votes for President, shall be the President, if such number be a majority of the whole number of Electors appointed; and if no person have such majority, then from the persons having the highest numbers not exceeding three on the list of those voted for as President, the House of Representatives shall choose immediately, by ballot, the President. But in choosing the President, the votes shall be taken by states, the representation from each state having one vote; a quorum for this purpose shall consist of a member or members from two-thirds of the states, and a majority of all the states shall be necessary to a choice. [And if the House of Representatives shall not choose a President whenever the right of choice shall devolve upon them, before the fourth day of March next following, then the Vice-President shall act as President, as in case of the death or other constitutional disability of the President.—]* The person having the greatest number of votes as Vice-President, shall be the Vice-President, if such number be a majority of the whole number of Electors appointed, and if no person have a majority, then from the two highest numbers on the list, the Senate shall choose the Vice-President; a quorum for the purpose shall consist of two-thirds of the whole number of Senators, and a majority of the whole number shall be necessary to a choice. But no person constitutionally ineligible to the office of President shall be eligible to that of Vice-President of the United States.

AMENDMENT XIII

Section 1. Neither slavery nor involuntary servitude, except as a punishment for crime whereof the party shall have been duly convicted, shall exist within the United States, or any place subject to their jurisdiction.

Section 2. Congress shall have power to enforce this article by appropriate legislation.

AMENDMENT XIV

Section 1. All persons born or naturalized in the United States, and subject to the jurisdiction thereof, are citizens of the United States and of the State wherein they reside. No State shall make or enforce any law which shall abridge the privileges or immunities of citizens of the United States; nor shall any State deprive any person of life, liberty, or property, without due process of law; nor deny to any person within its jurisdiction the equal protection of the laws.

Section 2. Representatives shall be apportioned among the several States according to their respective numbers, counting the whole number of persons in each State, excluding Indians not taxed. But when the right to vote at any election for the choice of electors for President and Vice-President of the United States, Representatives in Congress, the

Executive and Judicial officers of a State, or the members of the Legislature thereof, is denied to any of the male inhabitants of such State, being twenty-one years of age,* and citizens of the United States, or in any way abridged, except for participation in rebellion, or other crime, the basis of representation therein shall be reduced in the proportion which the number of such male citizens shall bear to the whole number of male citizens twenty-one years of age in such State.

Section 3. No person shall be a Senator or Representative in Congress, or elector of President and Vice-President, or hold any office, civil or military, under the United States, or under any State, who, having previously taken an oath, as a member of Congress, or as an officer of the United States, or as a member of any State legislature, or as an executive or judicial officer of any State, to support the Constitution of the United States, shall have engaged in insurrection or rebellion against the same, or given aid or comfort to the enemies thereof. But Congress may by a vote of two-thirds of each House, remove such disability.

Section 4. The validity of the public debt of the United States, authorized by law, including debts incurred for payment of pensions and bounties for services in suppressing insurrection or rebellion, shall not be questioned. But neither the United States nor any State shall assume or pay any debt or obligation incurred in aid of insurrection or rebellion against the United States, or any claim for the loss or emancipation of any slave; but all such debts, obligations and claims shall be held illegal and void.

Section 5. The Congress shall have the power to enforce, by appropriate legislation, the provisions of this article.

AMENDMENT XV

Section 1. The right of citizens of the United States to vote shall not be denied or abridged by the United States or by any State on account of race, color, or previous condition of servitude—

Section 2. The Congress shall have the power to enforce this article by appropriate legislation.

AMENDMENT XVI

The Congress shall have power to lay and collect taxes on incomes, from whatever source derived, without apportionment among the several States, and without regard to any census or enumeration.

AMENDMENT XVII

The Senate of the United States shall be composed of two Senators from each State, elected by the people thereof, for six years; and each Senator shall have one vote. The electors in each State shall have the qualifications requisite for electors of the most numerous branch of the State legislatures.

When vacancies happen in the representation of any State in the Senate, the executive authority of such State shall issue writs of election to fill such vacancies:

Provided, That the legislature of any State may empower the executive thereof to make temporary appointments until the people fill the vacancies by election as the legislature may direct.

This amendment shall not be so construed as to affect the election or term of any Senator chosen before it becomes valid as part of the Constitution.

AMENDMENT XVIII

Section 1. After one year from the ratification of this article the manufacture, sale, or transportation of intoxicating liquors within, the importation thereof into, or the exportation thereof from the United States and all territory subject to the jurisdiction thereof for beverage purposes is hereby prohibited.

Section 2. The Congress and the several States shall have concurrent power to enforce this article by appropriate legislation.

Section 3. This article shall be inoperative unless it shall have been ratified as an amendment to the Constitution by the legislatures of the several States, as provided in the Constitution, within seven years from the date of the submission hereof to the States by the Congress.

AMENDMENT XIX

The right of citizens of the United States to vote shall not be denied or abridged by the United States or by any State on account of sex.

Congress shall have power to enforce this article by appropriate legislation.

AMENDMENT XX

Section 1. The terms of the President and the Vice President shall end at noon on the 20th day of January, and the terms of Senators and Representatives at noon on the 3d day of January, of the years in which such terms would have ended if this article had not been ratified; and the terms of their successors shall then begin.

Section 2. The Congress shall assemble at least once in every year, and such meeting shall begin at noon on the 3d day of January, unless they shall by law appoint a different day.

Section 3. If, at the time fixed for the beginning of the term of the President, the President elect shall have died, the Vice President elect shall become President. If a President shall not have been chosen before the time fixed for the beginning of his term, or if the President elect shall have failed to qualify, then the Vice President elect shall act as President until a President shall have qualified; and the Congress may by law provide for the case wherein neither a President elect nor a Vice President shall have qualified, declaring who shall then act as President, or the manner in which one who is to act shall be selected, and such person shall act accordingly until a President or Vice President shall have qualified.

Section 4. The Congress may by law provide for the case of the death of any of the persons from whom the House of Representatives may choose a President whenever the right of choice shall have devolved upon them, and for the case of the death of any of the persons from whom the Senate may choose a Vice President whenever the right of choice shall have devolved upon them.

Section 5. Sections 1 and 2 shall take effect on the 15th day of October following the ratification of this article.

Section 6. This article shall be inoperative unless it shall have been ratified as an amendment to the Constitution by the legislatures of three-fourths of the several States within seven years from the date of its submission.

AMENDMENT XXI

Section 1. The eighteenth article of amendment to the Constitution of the United States is hereby repealed.

Section 2. The transportation or importation into any State, Territory, or Possession of the United States for delivery or use therein of intoxicating liquors, in violation of the laws thereof, is hereby prohibited.

Section 3. This article shall be inoperative unless it shall have been ratified as an amendment to the Constitution by conventions in the several States, as provided in the Constitution, within seven years from the date of the submission hereof to the States by the Congress.

AMENDMENT XXII

Section 1. No person shall be elected to the office of the President more than twice, and no person who has held the office of President, or acted as President, for more than two years of a term to which some other person was elected President shall be elected to the office of President more than once. But this Article shall not apply to any person holding the office of President when this Article was proposed by Congress, and shall not prevent any person who may be holding the office of President, or acting as President, during the term within which this Article becomes operative from holding the office of President or acting as President during the remainder of such term.

Section 2. This article shall be inoperative unless it shall have been ratified as an amendment to the Constitution by the legislatures of three-fourths of the several States within seven years from the date of its submission to the States by the Congress.

AMENDMENT XXIII

Section 1. The District constituting the seat of Government of the United States shall appoint in such manner as Congress may direct:

A number of electors of President and Vice President equal to the whole number of Senators and Representatives in Congress to which the District would be entitled if it were a State, but in no event more than the least populous State; they shall be in addition to those appointed by the States, but they shall be considered, for the purposes of the election of President and Vice President, to be electors appointed by a State; and they shall meet in the District and perform such duties as provided by the twelfth article of amendment.

Section 2. The Congress shall have power to enforce this article by appropriate legislation.

AMENDMENT XXIV

Section 1. The right of citizens of the United States to vote in any primary or other election for President or Vice President, for electors for President or Vice President, or for Senator or Representative in Congress, shall not be denied or abridged by the United States or any State by reason of failure to pay poll tax or other tax.

Section 2. The Congress shall have power to enforce this article by appropriate legislation.

AMENDMENT XXV

Section 1. In case of the removal of the President from office or of his death or resignation, the Vice President shall become President.

Section 2. Whenever there is a vacancy in the office of the Vice President, the President shall nominate a Vice President who shall take office upon confirmation by a majority vote of both Houses of Congress.

Section 3. Whenever the President transmits to the President pro tempore of the Senate and the Speaker of the House of Representatives his written declaration that he is unable to discharge the powers and duties of his office, and until he transmits to them a written declaration to the contrary, such powers and duties shall be discharged by the Vice President as Acting President.

Section 4. Whenever the Vice President and a majority of either the principal officers of the executive departments or of such other body as Congress may by law provide, transmit to the President pro tempore of the Senate and the Speaker of the House of Representatives their written declaration that the President is unable to discharge the powers and duties of his office, the Vice President shall immediately assume the powers and duties of the office as Acting President.

Thereafter, when the President transmits to the President pro tempore of the Senate and the Speaker of the House of Representatives his written declaration that no inability exists, he shall resume the powers and duties of his office unless the Vice President and a majority of either the principal officers of the executive department or of such other body as Congress may by law provide, transmit within four days to the President pro tempore of the Senate and the Speaker of the House of Representatives their written declaration that the President is unable to discharge the powers and duties of his office. Thereupon Congress shall decide the issue, assembling within forty-eight hours for that purpose if not in session. If the Congress, within twenty-one days after receipt of the latter written declaration, or, if Congress is not in session, within twenty-one days after Congress is required to assemble, determines by two-thirds vote of both Houses that the President is unable to discharge the powers and duties of his office, the Vice President shall continue to discharge the same as Acting President; otherwise, the President shall resume the powers and duties of his office.

AMENDMENT XXVI

Section 1. The right of citizens of the United States, who are eighteen years of age or older, to vote shall not be denied or abridged by the United States or by any State on account of age.

Section 2. The Congress shall have power to enforce this article by appropriate legislation.

AMENDMENT XXVII

No law, varying the compensation for the services of the Senators and Representatives, shall take effect, until an election of representatives shall have intervened.

Internet Resources

Courts—Alternative Dispute Resolution—Government

U.S. Courts	www.uscourts.gov
U.S. Tax Court	www.ustaxcourt.gov/ustcweb.htm
U.S. Court of Federal Claims	www.uscfc.uscourts.gov/
U.S. Court of International Trade	www.uscit.gov/
U.S Court for the Federal Circuit	www.fedcir.gov/
U.S. Supreme Court	www.supremecourtus.gov
National Mediation Board	www.nmb.gov
American Arbitration Association	www.adr.org
Pacer System	http://pacer.psc.uscourts.gov/
U.S. Court of Appeals	www.uscourts.gov/courtsofappeals.html
Internal Revenue Service	www.irs.gov
Government Printing Office	www.gpo.gov/
Code of Federal Regulations	www.access.gpo.gov/nara/cfr/index.html

Legal Research

VersusLaw	www.versuslaw.com/
Lexis	www.lexisnexis.com/
Westlaw	www.westlaw.com/
Library of Congress	www.loc.gov
Loislaw	www.loislaw.com
Cornell University LII	www.law.cornell.edu/citation
ALWD Manual	www.alwd.org

Legal Organizations

American Bar Association	www.abanet.org
National Federation of Paralegal Associations, Inc.	www.paralegals.org
National Association of Legal Assistants	www.nala.org
American Association of Legal Administrators	www.alanet.org/home.html
American Association for Paralegal Education	www.aafpe.org
ABA Standing Committee on Legal Assistants	www.abanet.org/legalassts
Legal Nurse Consultants	www.aalnc.org

State Bar Associations

Alabama	www.alabar.org
Alaska	www.alaskabar.org
Arizona	www.azbar.org.org
Arkansas	www.arkbar.org
California	www.calbar.org
Colorado	www.cobar.org
Connecticut	www.ctbar.org
Delaware	www.dsba.org
District of Columbia	www.dcbar.org
Florida	www.flabar.org
Georgia	www.gabar.org
Hawaii	www.hsba.org
Idaho	www2.state.id.us/isb/
Illinois	www.isba.org
Indiana	www.inbar.org
Iowa	www.iowabar.org
Kansas	www.ksbar.org
Kentucky	www.kybar.org
Louisiana	www.lsba.org
Maine	www.maine.org
Maryland	www.msba.org
Massachusetts	www.massbar.org
Michigan	www.michbar.org
Minnesota	www.mnbar.org
Mississippi	www.msbar.org
Missouri	www.mobar.org
Montana	www.montanabar.org
Nebraska	www.nebar.org
Nevada	www.nvbar.org
New Hampshire	www.nhbar.org
New Jersey	www.njsba.com
New Mexico	www.nmbar.org
New York	www.nysba.org
North Carolina	www.ncbar.com
North Dakota	www.sband.org
Ohio	www.ohiobar.org
Oklahoma	www.okbar.org
Oregon	www.osbar.org
Pennsylvania	www.pa-bar.org
Rhode Island	www.ribar.com
South Carolina	www.scbar.org

South Dakota	www.sdbar.org
Tennessee	www.tba.org
Texas	www.texasbar.com
Utah	www.utahbar.org
Vermont	www.vtbar.org
Virginia	www.vsb.org
Washington	www.wsba.org
West Virginia	www.wvbar.org
Wisconsin	www.wisbar.org
Wyoming	www.wyomingbar.org

Other

Religious calendar	www.interfaithcalendar.org/
AOL	www.aol.com
Compuserve	www.compuserve.com
The Affiliate	www.futurelawoffice.com/practice.html
Adobe Systems	www.adobe.com
Mapquest	www.mapquest.com

Internet Search Engines

AltaVista	www.altavista.com
Ask Jeeves	www.askjeeves.com
Dogpile	www.dogpile.com
Excite	www.excite.com
Google	www.google.com
Metacrawler	www.metacrawler.com
Netscape	www.netscape.com
Yahoo!	www.yahoo.com
Findlaw	www.findlaw.com

APPENDIX H

Glossary of Spanish Equivalents for Important Legal Terms

A

a priori Desde antes, del pasado.

AAA Siglas para **American Arbitration Association** Asociación de Arbitraje.

ABA Siglas para **American Bar Association** Colegio de Abogados Estadounidenses.

accept Aceptar, admitir, aprobar, recibir reconocer.

accession Accesión, admisión, aumento, incremento.

accord Acuerdo, convenio, arreglo, acordar, conceder.

acquittal Absolución, descargo, veredicto de no culpable.

act Acto, estatuto, decreto, actuar, funcionar.

actionable Justiciable, punible, procesable.

adjourn Levantar, posponer, suspender la sesión.

adjudicate Adjudicar, decidir, dar fallo a favor de, sentenciar, declarar.

administrative Administrativo, ejecutivo.

administrative agency Agencia administrativa.

administrative hearing Juicio administrativo.

administrative law Derecho administrativo.

administrative law judge Juez de derecho, Administrativo.

administrator Administrador.

admit Admitir, conceder, reconocer, permitir entrada, confesar, asentir.

adverse Adverso, contrario, opuesto.

adverse possession Posesión adversa.

advice Consejo, asesoramiento, notificación.

affected class Clase afectada, grupo iscriminado.

affidavit Declaración voluntaria, escrita y bajo uramento, afidávit, atestiguación, testificata.

affirmative action Acción positiva.

affirmative defense Defensa justificativa.

after acquired property Propiedad adquirida con garantía adicional.

against En contra.

agency Agencia, oficina, intervención.

agent Agente, representante autorizado.

aggrieved party Parte dañada, agraviada, perjudicada.

agreement Acuerdo, arreglo, contrato, convenio, pacto.

alibi Coartada.

alien Extranjero, extraño, foráneo.

annul Anular, cancelar, invalidar, revocar, dejar sin efecto.

answer Contestación, réplica, respuesta, alegato.

antecedent Antecedente, previo, preexistente.

appeal Apelar, apelación.

appear Aparecer, comparecer.

appellate court Tribunal de apelaciones.

appellate jurisdiction Competencia de apelación.

applicable Aplicable, apropiado, pertinente a, lo que puede ser aplicado.

arraign Denunciar, acusar, procesar, instruir de cargos hechos.

arrears Retrasos, pagos atrasados, decursas.

arrest Arresto, arrestar, aprehensión, aprehender, detener.

arson Incendio intencional.

articles of incorporation Carta de organización corporativa.

assault Agresión, asalto, ataque, violencia carnal, agredir, atacar, acometer.

assault and battery Amenazas y agresión, asalto.

assign Asignar, ceder, designar, hacer cesión, traspasar, persona asignada un derecho.

attachment Secuestro judicial.

attorney Abogado, consejero, apoderado.

award Fallo, juicio, laudo, premio.

B

bail Caución, fianza.

bail bondsman Fiador, fiador judicial.

bailee Depositario de bienes.

bailment Depósito, encargo, depósito mercantil, depósito comercial.

bailment For hire, depósito oneroso.

bailor Fiador.

bankruptcy Bancarrota, quiebra, insolvencia.

battery Agravio, agresión.

bearer bond Título mobiliario.

bearer instrument Título al portador.

bench Tribunal, los jueces, la magistratura.

beneficiary Beneficiario, legatario.

bequeath Legar.

bilateral contract Contrato bilateral.

bill of lading Póliza de embarque, boleto de carga, documento de tránsito.

bill of rights Las primeras diez enmiendas a la Constitución de los Estados Unidos de América.

binder Resguardo provisional, recibo para garantizar el precio de un bien inmueble.

birth certificate Acta de nacimiento, partida de nacimiento, certificado de nacimiento.

blue sky laws Estatutos para prevenir el fraude en la compraventa de valores.

bond Bono, título, obligación, deuda inversionista, fianza.

booking Término dado en el cuartel de policía al registro de arresto y los cargos hechos al arrestado.

breach of contract Violación, rotura, incumplimiento de contrato.

brief Alegato, escrito memorial.

burglary Escalamiento, allanamiento de morada.

buyer Comprador.

bylaws Estatutos sociales, reglamentos internos.

C

capacity to contract Capacidad contractual.

case Causa, caso, acción legal, proceso, proceso civil, asunto, expediente.

case law Jurisprudencia.

cashier's check Cheque bancario.

cease and desist order Orden judicial de cese.

censure Censura.

certificate of deposit Certificado de depósito.

certified check Cheque certificado.

certify Certificar, atestiguar.

charge Cobrar, acusar, imputar.

charitable trust Fideicomiso caritativo.

chattel Bienes muebles, bártulos.

cheat Fraude, engaño, defraudador, trampa, tramposo, estafar.

check Cheque, talón, comprobación.

cite Citación, citar, referir, emplazar.

citizenship Ciudadanía.

civil action Acción, enjuiciamiento civil, demanda.

civil law Derecho civil.

Claims Court Tribunal federal de reclamaciones.

client Cliente.

closing arguments Alegatos de clausura.

closing costs Gastos ocasionados en la venta de bienes raíces.

clue Pista, indicio.

codicil Codicilo.

coercion Coerción, coacción.

collateral Colateral, auxiliar, subsidiario, seguridad colateral, garantía prendaria.

collect Cobrar, recobrar, recaudar.

collision Choque, colisión.

common law Derecho consuetudinario.

comparative negligence Negligencia comparativa.

compensatory damages Indemnización compensatoria por daños y perjuicios, daños compensatorios.

competency Competencia, capacidad legal.

concurrent conditions Condiciones concurrentes.

concurrent jurisdiction Jurisdicción simultanea, conocimiento acumulativo.

concurrent sentences Sentencias que se cumplen simultáneamente.

concurring opinion Opinión coincidente.

condemn Condenar, confiscar, expropiar.

condition precedent Condición precedente.

condition subsequent Condición subsecuente.

confession Confesión, admisión.

confidential Confidencial, íntimo, secreto.

confiscation Confiscación, comiso, decomiso.

consent decree Decreto por acuerdo mutuo.

consequential damages Daños especiales.

consideration Contraprestación.

consolidation Consolidación, unión, concentración.

constructive delivery Presunta entrega.

contempt of court Desacato, contumacia o menosprecio a la corte.

contract Contrato, convenio, acuerdo, pacto.

contributory negligence Negligencia contribuyente.

conversion Conversión, canje.

conviction Convicción, fallo de culpabilidad, convencimiento, sentencia condenatoria, condena.

copyright Derecho de autor, propiedad literaria, propiedad intelectual, derecho de impresión.

corroborate Corroborar, confirmar.

counterclaim Contrademanda, excepción de compensación.

counteroffer Contra oferta.

courts Cortes o tribunales establecidas por la constitución.

covenant for quiet enjoyment Convenio de disfrute y posesión pacífica.

creditor Acreedor.

crime Crimen, delito.

criminal act Acto criminal.

criminal law Derecho penal.

cross examination Contrainterrogatorio, repregunta.

cure Curar, corregir.

D

damages Daños y perjuicios, indemnización pecuniaria.

DBA Sigla para **doing business as** En negociación comercial.

deadly force Fuerza mortífera.

debt Deuda, débito.

debtor Deudor.

decision Decisión judicial, fallo, determinación auto, sentencia.

deed Escritura, título de propiedad, escritura de traspaso.

defamation Difamación, infamación.

default Incumplir, faltar, no comparecer, incumplimiento.

defendant Demandado, reo, procesado, acusado.

delinquent Delincuente, atrasado en pagos, delictuoso.

denial Denegación, negación, denegatoria.

deponent Deponente, declarante.

deportation Deportación, destierro.

deposition Deposición, declaración bajo juramento.

detain Detener, retardar, retrasar.

devise Legado de bienes raíces.

direct examination Interrogatorio directo, interrogatorio a testigo propio.

directed verdict Veredicto expedido por el juez, veredicto por falta de pruebas.

disaffirm Negar, rechazar, repudiar, anular.

discharge Descargo, cumplimiento, liberación.

disclose Revelar.

discovery Revelación de prueba, exposición reveladora.

discriminate Discriminar.

dismiss Despedir, desechar, desestimar.

dissenting opinion Opinión en desacuerdo.

dissolution Disolución, liquidación.

diversity of citizenship Diversidad de ciudadanías, ciudadanías diferentes.

dividend Acción librada, dividendo.

divorce Divorcio, divorciar.

docket Orden del día, lista de casos en la corte.

double jeopardy Non bis in idem.

driving under the influence Manejar bajo los efectos de bebidas alcohólicas o drogas.

duress Coacción.

E

earnest money Arras, señal.

easement Servidumbre.

edict Edicto, decreto, auto.

embezzlement Malversación de fondos.

eminent domain Dominio eminente.

encroachment Intrusión, usurpación, invasión, uso indebido.

encumbrance Gravamen, afectación, cargo.

enforce Hacer cumplir, dar valor, poner en efecto.

entitlement Derecho, título.

equal protection clause Cláusula de protección de igualdad ante la ley.

equal protection of the law Igualdad ante la ley.

equity Equidad. Derecho equitativo.

escheat Reversión al estado al no haber herederos.

estate Bienes, propiedad, caudal hereditario, cuerpo de la herencia, caudal, derecho, título, interés sobre propiedad.

estop Impedir, detener, prevenir.

ethics Sistema ético.

eviction Evicción, desalojo, desalojamiento, desahucio, lanzamiento.

evidence Testimonio, prueba, pruebas documentales, pieza de prueba.

examination Examen, reconocimiento, interrogatorio.

executed contract Contrato firmado, contrato ejecutado.

execution Ejecución, desempeño, cumplimiento.

executory contract Contrato por cumplirse.

executory interests Intereses futuros.

exempt Franquear, exentar, exencionar, eximir, libre, franco, exento, inmune.

exoneration Exoneración, descargo, liberación.

expert witness Testigo perito.

express contract Contrato explícito.

expropriation Expropiación, confiscación.

eyewitness Testigo ocular o presencial.

F

fact Hecho falsificado.

failure to appear Incomparecencia.

fault Falta, defecto, culpa, negligencia.

fee Honorarios, retribución, cuota, cargo, derecho, dominio, asesoría, propiedad, bienes raíces.

fee simple estate Propiedad en dominio pleno.

felon Felón, autor de un delito.

felony Delito mayor o grave.

fiduciary Fiduciario.

find against Fallar o decidir en contra.

find for Fallar o decidir a favor.

finding Determinación de los hechos.

fine Multa, castigo.

fixture Accesorio fijo.

foreclose Entablar juicio hipotecario, embargar bienes hipotecados.

forgery Falsificación.

franchise Franquicia, privilegio, patente, concesión social, derecho de votar.

fraud Fraude, engaño, estafa, trampa, embuste, defraudación.

full disclosure Revelación completa.

G

garnishment Embargo de bienes.

gift Regalo, dádiva, donación.

gift causa mortis Donación de propiedad en expectativa de muerte.

gift inter vivos Donación entre vivos.

gift tax Impuesto sobre donaciones.

good and valid consideration Causa contractual válida.

good faith Buena fe.

goods Mercaderías, bienes, productos.

grace period Período de espera.

grantee Concesionario, cesionario.

grantor Otorgante, cesionista.

grievance Agravio, injuria, ofensa, queja formal.

gross negligence Negligencia temeraria, negligencia grave.

H

habitation Habitación, lugar donde se vive.

harassment Hostigamiento.

hearing Audiencia, vista, juicio.

hearsay Testimonio de oídas.

holder Tenedor, poseedor.

holding Decisión, opinión, tenencia posesión, asociación, grupo industrial.

holographic will Testamento hológrafo.

homeowner Propietario, dueño de casa.

homestead Casa, solariega, hogar, heredad, excepción de embargo, bien de familia.

hung jury Jurado sin veredicto.

I

identify Identificar, verificar, autenticar.

illegal Ilegal, ilícito, ilegítimo.

illegal entry Entrada ilegal.

illegal search Registro domiciliario, allanamiento ilegal, cacheo ilegal.

immunity Inmunidad, exención.

implied warranty Garantía implícita.

impossibility of performance Imposibilidad de cumplimiento.

impound Embargar, incautar, confiscar, secuestrar.

inadmissible Inadmisible, inaceptable.

income Ingreso, ganancia, entrada, renta, rédito.

incriminate Incriminar, acriminar.

indictment Procesamiento, acusación por jurado acusatorio, inculpatoria.

indorsement Endose, endoso, respaldo, garantía.

informant Informador, denunciante, delator.

information Información, informe, acusación por el fiscal, denuncia.

informed consent Conformidad por información.

inherit Heredar, recibir por herencia.

injunction Mandato judicial, amparo, prohibición judicial, interdicto.

innocent Inocente, no culpable.

inquiry Indagatoria judicial, pesquisa.

insufficient evidence Prueba insuficiente.

interrogation Interrogación.

interstate commerce Comercio interestatal.

intestate Intestado, intestar, sin testamento.

intestate succession Sucesión hereditaria.

investigation Investigación, indagación, encuesta.

issue Emisión, cuestión, punto, edición, número, tirada, sucesión, descendencia, resultado, decisión.

J

jail Cárcel, calabozo, encarcelar.

joint tenancy Condominio.

judge Magistrado, juez, juzgar, adjudicar, enjuiciar, fallar.

judgment Sentencia, fallo, juicio, decisión, dictamen, criterio.

judicial proceeding Proceso o diligencia judicial.

judicial review Revisión judicial.

jump bail Fugarse bajo fianza.

jurisdiction Jurisdicción, fuero competencia.

jury Jurado

L

landlord Arrendatario, propietario.

larceny Hurto, latrocinio, ladronicio.

law Ley, derecho.

lease Contrato de arrendamiento, arrendamiento, arriendo, contrato de locación, arrendar, alquilar.

leasehold estate Bienes forales.

legatee Legatario, asignatario.

lender Prestamista.

lessee Arrendatario, locatario, inquilino.

lessor Arrendatario, arrendador, arrendante, locador.

letter of credit Letra de crédito.

liability Responsiva, responsabilidad.

libel Libelo por difamación por escrito.

license Licencia, permiso, privilegio, matrícula, patente, título, licenciar, permitir.

lien Gravamen, derecho prendario o de retención, embargo preventivo.

life estate Hipoteca legal, dominio vitalicio.

limited liability company Sociedad de responsabilidad limitada.

limited partnership Sociedad en comandita, sociedad comanditaria.

litigated Pleiteado, litigado, sujeto a litigación.

M

majority opinion Opinión que refleja la mayoría de los miembros de la corte de apelaciones.

maker Otorgante, girador.

malice Malicia, malignidad, maldad.

malpractice Incompetencia profesional.

manslaughter Homicidio sin premeditación.

material witness Testigo esencial.

mechanics lien Gravamen de construcción.

mediation Mediación, tercería, intervención, interposición.

medical examiner Médico examinador.

merger Fusión, incorporación, unión, consolidación.

minor Menor, insignificante, pequeño, trivial.

misdemeanor Delito menor, fechoría.

mitigation of damages Mitigación de daños, minoración, atenuación.

monetary damages Daños pecuniarios.

mortgage Hipoteca, gravamen, hipotecar, gravar.

motion to dismiss Petición para declaración sin lugar.

motion to suppress Moción para suprimir, reprimir o suspender.

motive Motivo.

murder Asesinato, asesinar, homicidio culposo.

N

naturalization Naturalización.

negligence Negligencia, descuido, imprudencia.

negotiable Negociable.

negotiate Negociar, agenciar, hacer efectivo, traspasar, tratar.

net assets Haberes netos.

notice Aviso, notificación, advertencia, conocimiento.

novation Novación, delegación de crédito.

nuisance Daño, molestia, perjuicio.

nuncupative will Testamento abierto.

O

oath Juramento.

objection Objeción, oposición, disconformidad, recusación, impugnación, excepción, réplica, reclamación.

obstruction of justice Encubrimiento activo.

offer Oferta, ofrecimiento, propuesta, ofrecer, proponer.

omission Omisión, falla, falta.

opinion Opinión, dictamen, decisión de la corte.

oral argument Alegato oral.

order instrument Instrumento de pago a la orden.

owe Deber, estar en deuda, adeudo.

owner Dueño, propietario, poseedor.

P

pain and suffering Angustia mental y dolor físico.

pardon Perdón, indulto, absolución, indultar, perdonar.

parol evidence rule Principio que prohíbe la modificación de un contrato por prueba verbal.

parole Libertad vigilada.

partnership Sociedad, compañía colectiva, aparcería, consorcio, sociedad personal.

patent Patente, obvio, evidente, aparente, privilegio de invención, patentar.

penalty Pena, multa, castigo, penalidad, condena.

pending Pendiente, en trámite, pendiente de, hasta que.

per capita Por cabeza.

performance Cumplimiento, desempeño, ejecución, rendimiento.

perjury Perjurio, testimonio falso, juramento falso.

personal property Bienes personales, bienes mobiliarios.

plea bargain Declaración de culpabilidad concertada.

plea of guilty Alegación de culpabilidad.

pleadings Alegatos, alegaciones, escritos.

pledge Prenda, caución, empeño, empeñar, dar en prenda, pignorar.

police power Poder policial.

policy Póliza, escritura, práctica política.

possession Posesión, tenencia, goce, disfrute.

possibility of reverter Posibilidad de reversión.

power of attorney Poder de representación, poder notarial, procura.

precedent Precedente, decisión previa por el mismo tribunal.

preemptive right Derecho de prioridad.

prejudicial Dañoso, perjudicial.

preliminary hearing Audiencia preliminar.

premeditation Premeditación.

presume Presumir, asumir como hecho basado en la experiencia, suponer.

prevail Prevalecer, persuadir, predominar, ganar, triunfar.

price discrimination Discriminación en el precio.

principal Principal, jefe, de mayor importancia, valor actual.

privileged communication Comunicación privilegiada.

privity Coparticipación, intereses comunes.

procedural Procesal.

proceeds Ganancias.

profit Ganancia, utilidad, lucro, beneficio.

prohibited Prohibido.

promise Promesa.

promissory estoppel Impedimento promisorio.

promissory note Pagaré, vale, nota de pago.

proof Prueba, comprobación, demostración.

prosecutor Fiscal, abogado público acusador.

proximate cause Causa relacionada.

proxy Poder, delegación, apoderado, mandatario.

punishment Pena, castigo.

punitive damages Indemnización punitiva por daños y perjuicios, daños ejemplares.

Q

qualification Capacidad, calidad, preparación.

qualified indorsement Endoso limitado endoso con reservas.

quasi contract Cuasicontrato.

query Pregunta, interrogación.

question of fact Cuestión de hecho.

question of law Cuestión de derecho.

quiet enjoyment Uso y disfrute.

quitclaim deed Escritura de traspaso de finiquito.

R

race discrimination Discriminación racial.

rape Estupro, violación, ultraje, rapto, violar.

ratification Ratificación, aprobación, confirmación.

ratify Aprobar, confirmar, ratificar, convalidar, adoptar.

real property Bienes raíces, bienes inmuebles, arraigo.

reasonable doubt Duda razonable.

rebut Rebatir, refutar, negar, contradecir.

recognizance Obligación impuesta judicialmente.

recordation Inscripción oficial, grabación.

recover Recobrar, recuperar, obtener como resultado de decreto.

redress Reparación, compensación, desagravio, compensar, reparar, satisfacer, remediar.

regulatory agency Agencia reguladora.

reimburse Reembolsar, repagar, compensar, reintegrar.

rejoinder Respuesta, réplica, contrarréplica.

release Descargo, liberación, librar, relevar, descargar, libertar.

relevance Relevancia.

remainder Resto, restante, residuo, derecho expectativo a un bien raíz.

remedy Remedio, recurso.

remuneration Remuneración, compensación.

reply Réplica, contestación, contestar, responder.

reprieve Suspensión de la sentencia, suspensión, indulto, indultar, suspender.

reprimand Reprender, regañar, reprimenda, reprensión.

repudiate Repudiar, renunciar, rechazar.

rescission Rescisión, abrogación, cancelación de un contrato.

respondeat superior Responsabilidad civil al supervisor.

respondent Apelado, demandado.

restitution Restitución, devolución.

restraining order Inhibitoria, interdicto, orden de amparo.

retain Retener, emplear, guardar.

reversion Reversión, derecho de sucesión.

revocation Revocación, derogación, anulación.

reward Premio.

right of first refusal Retracto arrendaticio.

right of subrogation Derecho de sustituir.

right of survivorship Derecho de supervivencia entre dueños de propiedad mancomunada.

right to work laws Leyes que prohíben la filiación sindical como requisito para poder desempeñar un puesto, derecho de trabajo.

rights Derechos.

robbery Robo, atraco.

ruling Determinación oficial, auto judicial.

S

sale Venta.

sale on approval Venta por aprobación.

satisfaction Satisfacción, liquidación, cumplimiento, pago, finiquito.

scope of authority Autoridad explícitamente otorgada o implícitamente concedida.

search and seizure Allanamiento, registro e incautación.

search warrant Orden de registro o de allanamiento.

secured party Persona con interés asegurado.

secured transaction Transacción con un interés asegurado.

securities Valores, títulos, obligaciones.

security agreement Acuerdo que crea la garantía de un interés.

security deposit Deposito de seguridad.

seize Arrestar, confiscar, secuestrar, incautar.

settlement Arreglo, composición, ajuste, liquidación, componenda, acomodo.

sex discrimination Discriminación sexual.

sexual harassment Acoso sexual.

shoplifting Ratería en tiendas.

signature Firma.

slander Calumnia, difamación oral, calumniar.

source of income Fuente de ingresos.

specific performance Prestación específica contractual.

split decision Decisión con opiniones mixtas.

spousal abuse Abuso conyugal.

stare decisis Vinculación con decisiones judiciales anteriores.

state of mind Estado de ánimo, estado mental.

statement Alegación, declaración, relato, estado de cuentas.

statutory foreclosure Ejecución hipotecaria estatutaria.

statutory law Derecho estatutario.

statutory rape Estupro, violación de un menor de edad.

steal Robar, hurtar, robo, hurto.

stock Acciones, capital, existencias, semental.

stock option Opción de comprar o vender acciones.

stop payment order Suspensión de pago.

strict liability Responsabilidad rigurosa.

sublease Subarriendo, sublocación, subarrendar.

subpoena Citación, citatorio, comparendo, cédula de citación, citación judicial, subpoena.

sue Demandar, procesar.

summary judgment Sentencia sumaria.

summon Convocar, llamar, citar.

suppress Suprimir, excluir pruebas ilegalmente obtenidas, reprimir, suspender.

surrender Rendir, entregar, entrega, rendirse, entregarse.

surviving spouse Cónyuge sobreviviente.

suspect Sospecha, sospechar, sospechoso.

T

tangible evidence Prueba real.

tangible property Propiedad tangible, bienes tangibles.

tenancy at sufferance Tenencia o posesión por tolerancia.

tenancy at will Tenencia o inquilinato sin plazo fijo.

tenancy by the entirety Tenencia conyugal.

tenancy for life Tenencia vitalicia.

tenancy for years Inquilinato por tiempo fijo.

tender Propuesta, oferta, presentar.

testator Testador.

testify Atestar, atestiguar, dar testimonio.

theft Hurto.

title Título, derecho de posesión, rango, denominación.

tort Agravio, torticero, entuerto, daño legal, perjuicio, acto ilícito civil.

Totten trust Fideicomiso bancario Totten.

trade name Nombre comercial, marca de fábrica, marca comercial.

trademark Marca registrada, marca industrial.

transgression Ofensa, delito, transgresión.

trespass Transgresión, violación de propiedad ajena, translimitación, traspasar, violar, infringir, transgredir.

trial court Tribunal de primera instancia.

trust Fideicomiso, confianza, confidencia, confianza, crédito, combinación, consorcio, grupo industrial.

truth Verdad, verdadero, veracidad.

try Probar, juzgar.

U

ultra vires Mas allá de la facultad de actuar.

unanimous verdict Veredicto unánime.

unbiased Imparcial, neutral.

unconditional pardon Perdón, amnistía, indulto incondicional.

unconscionable Reprochable, repugnante, desmedido.

under arrest Arrestado, bajo arresto.

underwrite Subscribir, asegurar, firmar.

undisclosed Escondido, no revelado.

undue influence Influencia indebida, coacción, abuso de poder.

unenforceable Inejecutable.

unilateral contract Contrato unilateral.

unlawful Ilegal, ilícito, ilegítimo.

unsound mind Privado de razón, de mente inestable.

usury Usura, agiotaje, logrería.

V

vagrancy Vagancia, vagabundeo.

validity Validez, vigencia.

valuable consideration Causa contractual con cierto valor, causa contractual onerosa.

venue Partido judicial.

verbal contract Contrato verbal.

verbatim Al pié de la letra.

verdict Veredicto, fallo, sentencia, decisión.

victim Víctima.

voidable Anulable, cancelable.

W

wage Salario, jornal, sueldo.

waive Renunciar, ceder, suspender, abdicar.

waiver Renunciar, desistir, ceder, suspender, abdicar, renuncia.

warrant Autorización, resguardo, comprobante, certificado, justificación, decisión judicial.

warranty Garantía, seguridad.

warranty of habitability Garantía de habitabilidad.

welfare Asistencia pública.

will Testamento, voluntad.

willful misconduct Mala conducta intencional.

withhold Retener, detener.

witness Testigo, declarante, atestar, testificar, atestiguar.

writ of attachment Mandamiento de embargo.

writ of certiorari Pedimento de avocación.

writ of execution Auto de ejecución, ejecutoria.

Glossary

ABA Model Rules of Professional Conduct A recommended set of ethics and professional conduct guidelines for lawyers, prepared by American Bar Association, originally released in 1983; prior release was Model Code of Professional Conduct.

Abandoned property Property that an owner has discarded with the intent to relinquish his or her rights in it; mislaid or lost property that the owner has given up any further attempts to locate.

Abatement If the property the testator leaves is not sufficient to satisfy all the beneficiaries named in a will and there are both general and residuary bequests, the residuary bequest is abated first (i.e., paid last).

Acceptance A manifestation of assent by the offeree to the terms of the offer in a manner invited or required by the offer as measured by the objective theory of contracts.

Actus reus "Guilty act"—the actual performance of the criminal act.

Ademption A principle that says if a testator leaves a specific devise of property to a beneficiary, but the property is no longer in the estate when the testator dies, the beneficiary receives nothing.

Administrative agencies Agencies that the legislative and executive branches of federal and state governments establish.

Administrative law Substantive and procedural law that governs the operation of administrative agencies.

Administrative law judge (ALJ) A judge who presides over an administrative proceeding and who decides the questions of law and fact that arise in the proceeding.

Administrative Procedure Act (APA) An act that establishes certain administrative procedures that federal administrative agencies must follow in conducting their affairs.

Admitted A possible response of the defendant to the complaint which accepts the facts of the averment are true.

Adoption A situation in which a person becomes the legal parent of a child who is not his or her biological child.

Adverse possession A situation in which a person who wrongfully possesses someone else's real property obtains title to that property if certain statutory requirements are met.

Affirm The appellate court agrees with the outcome of trial and can find no reversible error and the decision of the trial court stands.

Age Discrimination in Employment Act (ADEA) A federal statute that prohibits age discrimination practices against employees who are age 40 and older.

Agency A principal–agent relationship; the fiduciary relationship "which results from the manifestation of consent by one person to another that the other shall act in his behalf and subject to his control, and consent by the other so to act."

Agency adoption An adoption that occurs when a person adopts a child from a social service organization of a state.

Agency by ratification An agency that occurs when (1) a person misrepresents himself or herself as another's agent when in fact he or she is not and (2) the purported principal ratifies the unauthorized act.

Agent A party who agrees to act on behalf of another.

Agreement The manifestation by two or more persons of the substance of a contract.

Aiding and abetting the commission of a crime Rendering support, assistance, or encouragement to the commission of a crime; harboring a criminal after he or she has committed a crime.

Alien corporation A corporation that is encorporated in another country.

ALS (Acredited Legal Secretary) The basic certification for legal professionals from NALS.

Alternative dispute resolution (ADR) Methods of resolving disputes other than litigation.

American Arbitration Association (AAA) A private nonprofit organization providing lists of potential arbitrators for the parties to select from and a set of rules for conducting the private arbitration.

American Association for Paralegal Education (AAfPE) National organization of paralegal educators and institutions offering paralegal education programs.

American Bar Association (ABA) Largest professional legal organization in the United States.

American Inventors Protection Act A federal statute that permits an inventor to file a *provisional application* with the U.S. Patent and Trademark Office (PTO) three months before the filing of a final patent application, among other provisions.

Americans with Disabilities Act (ADA) A federal statute that imposes obligations on employers and providers of public transportation, telecommunications, and public accommodations to accommodate individuals with disabilities.

Amicus curia Briefs submitted by interested parties who do not have standing in the action as a "friend of the court."

Annulment An order of the court declaring that a marriage did not exist.

Answer Document by which the defendant responds to the allegations contained in the plaintiff's complaint.

Antenuptial agreement A contract entered into after marriage to specify how property will be distributed upon termination of the marriage.

Apparent agency Agency that arises when a principal creates the appearance of an agency that in actuality does not exist.

Appeal The act of asking an appellate court to overturn a decision after the trial court's final judgment has been entered.

Appellant The appealing party in an appeal. Also known as *petitioner*.

Appellate courts Courts which review the record from the trial court to determine if the trial judge made an error in applying the procedural or substantive law.

Appellee The responding party in an appeal. Also known as *respondent*.

Applications software Applications programs are software that perform generic tasks such as word processing.

Arbitration A form of ADR in which the parties choose an impartial third party to hear and decide the dispute.

Arbitration clause A clause in contracts that requires disputes arising out of the contract to be submitted to arbitration. A clause contained in many international contracts that stipulates that any dispute between the parties concerning the performance of the contract will be submitted to an arbitrator or arbitration panel for resolution.

Arraignment A hearing during which the accused is brought before a court and is (1) informed of the charges against him or her and (2) asked to enter a plea.

Arrest warrant A document for a person's detainment based upon a showing of probable cause that the person committed the crime.

Arson Willfully or maliciously burning another's building.

Article 2 (Sales) of the Uniform Commercial Code (UCC) An article of the UCC that governs the sale of goods.

Article 2A (Leases) of the Uniform Commercial Code (UCC) An article of the UCC that governs the lease of goods.

Articles of incorporation The basic governing document of the corporation. This document must be filed with the secretary of state of the state of incorporation.

Articles of limited liability partnership A public document that must be filed with the secretary of state to form a limited liability partnership.

Articles of organization The formal document that must be filed with the secretary of state to form an LLC.

Assault The threat of immediate harm or offensive contact or (2) any action that arouses reasonable apprehension of imminent harm. Actual physical contact is unnecessary.

Associate's degree A college degree in science (AS) arts (AA), or applied arts (AAS), generally requiring two years of full-time study.

Association of Legal Writing Directors (ALWD) A society for professors who coordinate legal writing instruction.

Assumption of the risk A defense a defendant can use against a plaintiff who knowingly and voluntarily enters into or participates in a risky activity that results in injury.

Attachment A popular method of transmitting text files and graphic images by attaching the file to an email.

Attempt to commit a crime When a crime is attempted but not completed.

Attestation The action of a will being witnessed by the required number of competent people.

Attestation clause Section of a will where witnesses sign to acknowledge testation of the will.

Attorney-client privilege A client's right to have anything told to a lawyer while seeking legal advice, kept confidential in most instances.

Automatic stay The result of the filing of a voluntary or involuntary petition; the suspension of certain actions by creditors against the debtor or the debtor's property.

Bachelor's degree A college degree generally requiring four years of full-time study.

Backup of data Making a copy of critical files and programs in case of a loss of the original computer files.

Bailee A holder of goods who is not a seller or a buyer (e.g., a warehouse or common carrier).

Bailment A transaction in which an owner transfers his or her personal property to another to be held, stored, delivered, or for some other purpose. Title to the property does not transfer.

Bailor The owner of property in a bailment.

Bankruptcy Abuse Prevention and Consumer Protection Act of 2005 A federal act that substantially amended federal bankruptcy law. It makes it more difficult for debtors to file for bankruptcy and have their unpaid debts discharged.

Bankruptcy courts Special federal courts that hear and decide bankruptcy cases.

Bankruptcy estate A debtor's property and earnings that comprise the estate of a bankruptcy proceeding.

Battery Unauthorized and harmful or offensive physical contact with another person. Direct physical contact is not necessary.

Bench opinions The initial version of a decision issued from the bench of the court.

Beneficiary A person or organization designated in the will that receives all or a portion of the testator's property at the time of the testator's death.

Bequest A gift of personal property by will. Also known as a legacy.

Best interests of the child A legal doctrine used by the court to decide what is best for the child.

Bicameral In the American system a legislature of a house of representatives and a senate.

Bill of Rights The first 10 amendments to the Constitution. They were added to the U.S. Constitution in 1791.

Board of directors A panel of decision makers, the members of which are elected by a corporation's shareholders.

Bona fide occupational qualification (BFOQ) Lawful employment discrimination that is based on a protected class (other than race or color) and is *job-related* and a *business necessity*. This exception is narrowly interpreted by the courts.

Breach of contract A contracting party's failure to perform an absolute duty owed under a contract.

Breach of duty of care Failure to exercise care or to act as a reasonable person would act.

Bribery A crime in which one person gives another person money, property, favors, or anything else of value for a favor in return. Often referred to as a payoff or *kickback*.

Briefs Documents submitted by the parties' attorneys to the judge that contain legal support for their side of the case.

Building A structure constructed on land.

Burden of proof The level of proof required to establish an entitlement to recovery.

Burglary The taking of personal property from another's home, office, or commercial or other type of building.

Business judgment rule A rule stating that directors and officers are not liable to the corporation or its shareholders for honest mistakes of judgment.

Bylaws A detailed set of rules adopted by the board of directors after the corporation is incorporated that contains provisions for managing the business and the affairs of the corporation.

Candor A duty of honesty to the court.

Case and litigation management software Case and litigation management programs are used to manage documents and the facts and issues of cases.

Case syllabus In a court opinion a headnote for the convenience of the reader.

Causation The two types of causation that must be proven are (1) causation in fact (actual cause) and (2) proximate cause (legal cause)

Causation in fact or **actual cause** The actual cause of negligence. A person who commits a negligent act is not liable unless causation in fact can be proven.

Central processing unit (CPU) The computer chip and memory module that perform the basic computer functions.

Certificate A recognition of the completion of a program of study that requires less than that needed for a degree.

Certificate of limited partnership A document that two or more persons must execute and sign that makes the limited partnership legal and binding.

Certified Legal Assistant (CLA) Designation by National Association of Legal Assistants for those who take and pass NALA certification program two-day comprehensive examination.

Chain of distribution All manufacturers, distributors, wholesalers, retailers, lessors, and subcomponent manufacturers involved in a transaction.

Chapter 7 discharge The termination of the legal duty of a debtor to pay unsecured debts that remain unpaid upon the completion of a Chapter 7 proceeding.

Chapter 7 liquidation A form of bankruptcy in which the debtor's nonexempt property is sold for cash, the cash is distributed to the creditors, and any unpaid debts are discharged.

Chapter 11 reorganization A bankruptcy method that allows the reorganization of the debtor's financial affairs under the supervision of the bankruptcy court.

Chapter 12 adjustment of debts of a family farmer or family fisherman with regular income A form of bankruptcy reorganization permitted to be used by family farmers and family fishermen.

Chapter 12 discharge A discharge in a Chapter 12 case that is granted to a family farmer or family fisherman debtor after the debtor's plan of payment is completed (which is usually three years but could be up to five years).

Chapter 13 adjustment of debts of an individual with regular income A rehabilitation form of bankruptcy that permits bankruptcy courts to supervise the debtor's plan for the payment of unpaid debts in installments over the plan period.

Chapter 13 discharge A discharge in a Chapter 13 case that is granted to the debtor after the debtor's plan of payment is completed (which could be up to three or up to five years).

Charitable trust A trust for the benefit of a charity.

Child custody The awarding of legal custody of a child to a parent based on the best interests of the child. The parent awarded custody is called the *custodial parent*.

Child neglect Failure to provide necessities to a child for whom one is legally responsible.

Child support Payments made by the noncustodial parent to help pay for the financial support of his or her children.

Choice-of-law clause Clause in an international contract that designates which nation's laws will be applied in deciding a dispute.

Chronological resume format Presents education and job history in chronological order with the most recent experience listed first.

Citation A reference to the source of the information.

Citator An index of cases.

Cite checking The process of verifying proper citation format in a document.

Civil litigation Resolution of legal disputes between parties seeking a remedy for a civil wrong or to enforce a contract.

Civil Rights Act A federal statute that prohibits racial discrimination in the transfer of real property.

Civil Rights Act of 1866 A federal statute enacted after the Civil War that says all persons "have the same right . . . to make and enforce contracts . . . as is enjoyed by white persons." It prohibits racial and national origin employment discrimination.

Closing arguments The last opportunity for the attorneys to address the jury, summing up the client's case and persuading the jury to decide in his client's favor.

Codicil A separate document that must be executed to amend a will. It must be executed with the same formalities as a will.

Collective bargaining The act of negotiating contract terms between an employer and the members of a union.

Collective bargaining agreement The resulting contract from a collective bargaining procedure.

"Coming and going" rule A rule that says a principal is generally not liable for injuries caused by its agents and employees while they are on their way to and from work.

Commerce Clause A clause of the U.S. Constitution that grants Congress the power "to regulate commerce with foreign nations, and among the several states, and with Indian tribes."

Commercial speech Speech used by businesses, such as advertising. It is subject to time, place, and manner restrictions.

Common carrier A firm that offers transportation services to the general public. The bailee. Owes a duty of strict liability to the bailor.

Common interest privilege To permit a client to share confidential information with the attorney for another who shares a common legal interest.

Common law Developed by judges who issue their opinions when deciding cases. The principles announced in these cases became precedent for later judges deciding similar cases.

Common law of contracts Contract law developed primarily by state courts.

Common stock A type of equity security that represents the residual value of the corporation.

Common stockholder (common shareholders) A person who owns common stock.

Common-law marriage A type of marriage recognized in some states where a marriage license has not been issued but certain requirements are met.

Community property A form of ownership in which each spouse owns an equal one-half share of the income of both spouses and the assets acquired during the marriage.

Comparative negligence A doctrine under which damages are apportioned according to fault.

Compensatory damages An award of money intended to compensate a nonbreaching party for loss of the bargain. Compensatory damages place the nonbreaching party in the same position as if the contract had been fully performed by restoring the "benefit of the bargain."

Competence/competent The minimum level of knowledge and skill required of a professional.

Complaint The document the plaintiff files with the court and serves on the defendant to initiate a lawsuit.

Complete performance A situation in which a party to a contract renders performance exactly as required by the contract. Complete performance discharges that party's obligations under the contract.

Complex litigation Cases involving many parties as in a class action or multiple or complex legal issues.

Computer addresses and locations The modern equivalent of a person's telephone number is the email address. Pages on the Internet also have addresses known as the Uniform Resource Locator (URL), made up of three parts: protocol, computer, and path.

Computer hardware Hardware is the term that encompasses all of the tangible or physical items including computers, monitors, printers, fax machines, duplicators, and similar items that usually have either an electrical connection or use batteries as a power source.

Computer network A set of workstations connected together.

Computer system A combination of an input device, a processor, and an output device.

Computer viruses Viruses are programs that attack and destroy computer programs, internal computer operating systems, and occasionally the hard disk drives of computers.

Conciliation A form of dispute resolution in which a conciliator transmits offers and counteroffers between the disputing parties in helping to reach a settlement of their dispute.

Conciliator A third party in a conciliation proceeding who assists the disputing parties in reaching a settlement of their dispute. The conciliator cannot make a decision or an award.

Concurrent jurisdiction Jurisdiction shared by two or more courts.

Concurrent ownership (co-ownership) When two or more persons own a piece of real property.

Condition precedent A condition that requires the occurrence of an event before a party is obligated to perform a duty under a contract.

Condominium A common form of ownership in a multiple-dwelling building in which the purchaser has title to the individual unit and owns the common areas as a tenant in common with the other condominium owners.

Confidentiality A duty imposed on the attorney to enable clients to obtain legal advice by allowing the client to freely and openly give the attorney all the relevant facts.

Confirmation The bankruptcy court's approval of a plan of reorganization.

Conflict checking Verifying that the attorneys in the firm do not have a personal conflict and have not previously represented and are not currently representing any party with an adverse interest or conflict with the potential client.

Conflict of interest The representation of one client being directly adverse to the interest of another client.

Connectors Instructions in a search query on how to treat the words in the query.

Consequential damages Foreseeable damages that arise from circumstances outside the contract. To be liable for these damages, the breaching party must know or have reason to know that the breach will cause special damages to the other party.

Consideration Something of legal value given in exchange for a promise.

Consolidation The act of a court to combine two or more separate lawsuits into one lawsuit. Occurs when two or more corporations combine to form an entirely new corporation.

Constitution of the United States of America The supreme law of the United States. The Constitution of the United States of America establishes the structure of the federal government, delegates powers to the federal government, and guarantees certain fundamental rights.

Constructive trust An equitable trust that is implied by law to avoid fraud, unjust enrichment, and injustice.

Contract An agreement entered by two parties for valid consideration.

Contracts contrary to public policy Contracts that have a negative impact on society or that interfere with the public's safety and welfare.

Contributory negligence An affirmative defense which states there is no recovery where the plaintiff's negligence contributed to his injuries.

Controlling the Assault of Non-Solicited Pornography and Marketing Act (CAN-SPAM Act) A federal statute that prohibits certain deceptive and misleading email. The act is administered by the Federal Trade Commission (FTC).

Conversion of personal property A tort that deprives a true owner of the use and enjoyment of his or her personal property by taking over such property and exercising ownership rights over it.

Cooling-off period Requires a union to give an employer at least 60 days' notice before a strike can commence.

Cooperative A form of coownership of a multiple-dwelling building in which a corporation owns the building and the residents own shares in the corporation.

Co-ownership (concurrent ownership) A situation in which two or more persons own a piece of real property. Also called *concurrent ownership*.

Copyright infringement An act in which a party copies a substantial and material part of the plaintiff's copyrighted work without permission. A copyright holder may recover damages and other remedies against the infringer.

Copyright Revision Act A federal statute that (1) establishes the requirements for obtaining a copyright and (2) protects copyrighted works from infringement.

Corporate bylaws A detailed set of rules that are adopted by the board of directors after the corporation is incorporated, containing provisions for managing the business and the affairs of the corporation.

Corporation A fictitious legal entity that is created according to statutory requirements.

Cost-benefit analysis Process by which a litigant determines the costs of pursuing litigation and compares that to what is likely to be gained.

Counterfeit Access Device and Computer Fraud and Abuse Act (CFAA) A federal statute that makes it a federal crime to access a computer knowingly to obtain (1) restricted federal government information, (2) financial records of financial institutions, and (3) consumer reports of consumer reporting agencies.

Counteroffer A response by an offeree that contains terms and conditions different from or in addition to those of the offer. A counteroffer terminates an offer.

Court accounting An accounting with the local court that administers or supervises trust and estate matters. These reports are designed to show that the fiduciary has properly administered the estate or trust.

Court of Appeals for the Federal Circuit A court of appeals in Washington, DC, that has special appellate jurisdiction to review the decisions of the Claims Court, the Patent and Trademark Office, and the Court of International Trade.

Court of Chancery Court that granted relief based on fairness. Also called *equity court*.

Courts of record Those courts in which the testimony and evidence presented are recorded and preserved.

Covenant An unconditional promise to perform.

Cover letter A brief letter sent with a document identifying the intended recipient and the purpose of the attachment.

Creditors' committee The creditors holding the seven largest unsecured claims are usually appointed to the creditors' committee. Representatives of the committee appear at Bankruptcy Court hearings, participate in the negotiation of a plan of reorganization, assert objections to proposed plans and so on.

Crime An act done by an individual in violation of those duties that he or she owes to society and for the breach of which the law provides that the wrongdoer shall make amends to the public.

Criminal conspiracy A crime in which two or more persons enter into an agreement to commit a crime and an overt act is taken to further the crime.

Criminal fraud (false pretenses or deceit) Obtaining title to property through deception or trickery. Also known as false pretenses or deceit.

Criminal laws A violation of a statute for which the government imposes a punishment.

Criminal trial A trial to determine if a person has violated a statue for which the government imposes a penalty.

Critical legal thinking The process of identifying the issue, the material facts, and the applicable law and applying the law to come to a conclusion.

Cross-complaint Filed by the defendant against the plaintiff to seek damages or some other remedy.

Cross-examination Opportunity of defense (opposing) counsel to question a witness after the direct examination of the witness.

Crossover worker A person who does not honor a strike who either (1) chooses not to strike or (2) returns to work after joining the strikers for a time.

Cruel and unusual punishment A clause of the Eighth Amendment that protects criminal defendants from torture or other abusive punishment.

Custodial parent The parent to whom physical custody of the child is legally given.

Damages Compensation for loss suffered.

Database program A database program is an electronic repository of information of all types that can be sorted and presented in a meaningful manner.

Deathbed will Oral will that is made dying declaration before a witness during the testator's last illness.

Decree of divorce A court order that terminates a marriage.

Deed A writing that describes a person's ownership interest in a piece of real property.

Defamation of character False statement(s) made by one person about another. In court, the plaintiff must prove that (1) the defendant made an untrue statement of fact about the plaintiff and (2) the statement was intentionally or accidentally published to a third party.

Default judgment Judgment obtained by the plaintiff against the defendant where the defendant has failed to respond in a timely fashion to the complaint.

Defect Something wrong, inadequate, or improper in manufacture, design, packaging, warning, or safety measures of a product.

Defect in design A flaw that occurs when a product is improperly designed.

Defect in manufacture A defect that occurs when the manufacturer fails to (1) properly assemble a product, (2) properly test a product, or (3) adequately check the quality of the product.

Defect in packaging A defect that occurs when a product has been placed in packaging that is insufficiently tamperproof.

Defendant The party who files the answer.

Defendant's case Process by which the defendant calls witnesses and introduces evidence to (1) rebut the plaintiff's evidence, (2) prove affirmative defenses, and (3) prove allegations made in a cross-complaint.

Defense of Marriage Act (DOMA) A federal statute banning same sex couples from federal benefits given heterosexual couples.

Delegation doctrine A doctrine that says when an administrative agency is created, it is delegated certain powers; the agency can only use those legislative, judicial, and executive powers that are delegated to it.

Denied A possible response of the defendant to the complaint which asserts the facts of the averment are not true.

Deponent Party who gives his or her deposition.

Deposition Oral testimony given by a party or witness prior to trial. The testimony is given under oath and is transcribed.

Devise A gift of real estate by will.

Dicta Court comments on issues not directly related to the holding and therefore not having precedential effect.

Digital format A computerized format utilizing a series of 0's and 1's.

Digital Millennium Copyright Act (DMCA) A federal statute that prohibits unauthorized access to copyrighted digital works by circumventing encryption technology or the manufacture and distribution of technologies designed for the purpose of circumventing encryption protection of digital works.

Digital (or electronic) signature Some electronic method that identifies an individual.

Direct examination Questions addressed to a witness by the attorney who has called that witness to testify on behalf of his client.

Disaffirm The act of a minor to rescind a contract under the infancy doctrine. Disaffirmance may be done orally, in writing, or by the minor's conduct.

Discharge Actions or events that relieve certain parties from liability on negotiable instruments. There are three methods of discharge: (1) payment of the instrument; (2) cancellation; and (3) impairment of the right of recourse. The termination of the legal duty of a debtor to pay debts that remain unpaid upon the completion of a bankruptcy proceeding. Creditors' claims that are not included in a Chapter 11 reorganization are discharged. A discharge is granted to a debtor in a Chapter 13 consumer debt adjustment bankruptcy only after all the payments under the plan are completed by the debtor.

Discovery A legal process during which both parties engage in various activities to elicit facts of the case from the other party and witnesses prior to trial.

Diversity of citizenship A case between (1) citizens of different states, (2) a citizen of a state and a citizen or subject of a foreign country, and (3) a citizen of a state and a foreign country where a foreign country is the plaintiff.

Divorce An order of the court that terminates a marriage.

Doctrine of Equity A doctrine that permits judges to make decisions based on fairness, equality, moral rights, and natural law.

Doctrine of strict liability A tort doctrine that makes manufacturers, distributors, wholesalers, retailers, and others in the chain of distribution of a defective product liable for the damages caused by the defect irrespective of fault.

Doctrine of transferred intent An offender may be held responsible for an intent crime or intentional tort when someone other than the intended victim is injured.

Domain name A unique name that identifies an individual's or a company's Web site.

Domestic corporation A corporation in the state in which it was formed.

Dominant easement The land that benefits from the easement.

Donee A person who receives a gift.

Donor A person who gives a gift.

Double Jeopardy Clause A clause of the Fifth Amendment that protects persons from being tried twice for the same crime.

Dram Shop Act Statute that makes taverns and bartenders liable for injuries caused to or by patrons who are served too much alcohol.

Dual-purpose mission An errand or another act that a principal requests of an agent while the agent is on his or her own personal business.

Due Process Clause A clause that provides that no person shall be deprived of "life, liberty, or property" without due process of the law.

Duty not to willfully or wantonly injure The duty an owner or renter of real property owes a trespasser to prevent intentional injury or harm to the trespasser when the trespasser is on his or her premises.

Duty of candor Honesty to the court.

Duty of care The obligation we all owe each other not to cause any unreasonable harm or risk of harm. A responsibility of corporate directors and officers to use care and diligence when acting on behalf of the corporation.

Duty of loyalty A responsibility of directors and officers not to act adversely to the interests of the corporation and to subordinate their personal interests to those of the corporation and its shareholders.

Duty of ordinary care The duty an owner or renter of real property owes an invitee or a licensee to prevent injury or harm when the invitee or licensee steps on the owner's premises.

Duty of reasonable care The duty that a reasonable bailee in like circumstances would owe to protect the bailed property.

Duty of utmost care A duty of care that goes beyond ordinary care that says common carriers and innkeepers.

Easement A given or required right to make limited use of someone else's land without owning or leasing it.

Easement by grant One party gives another party an easement across his or her property.

Easement by implication A right erected on division of land to allow each owner use.

Easement by necessity Right to access another's property in order to reach one's landlocked property.

Easement by reservation A retained right to use land after a transfer.

E-commerce The sale of goods and services by computer over the Internet.

Economic Espionage Act A federal statute that makes it a crime for any person to convert a trade secret for his or another's benefit, knowing or intending to cause injury to the owners of the trade secret.

E-contract A contract that is entered into by email and over the World Wide Web.

E-discovery The discovery of emails, electronically stored data, e-contracts, and other electronically stored records.

E-filing The electronic filing of pleadings, briefs, and other documents related to a lawsuit with the court.

Elder law Advocacy for the elderly.

Electronic Communications Privacy Act (ECPA) A federal statute that makes it a crime to intercept an electronic communication at the point of transmission, while in transit, when stored by a router or server, or after receipt by the intended recipient.

Electronic Mail (email) Electronic written communication between individuals using computers connected to the Internet.

Electronic repository A secure protected file server to which everyone authorized has access over the internet.

Electronic Signature in Global and National Commerce Act (E-SIGN Act) A federal statute that recognizes that electronic contracts, or e-contracts, meet the writing requirement of the Statute of Frauds and gives electronic signatures, or e-signatures, the same force and effect as peninscribed signatures on paper.

E-license A contract that transfers limited rights in intellectual property and informational rights.

Emancipation When a minor voluntarily leaves home and lives apart from his or her parents.

Embezzlement The fraudulent conversion of property by a person to whom that property was entrusted.

Eminent domain The government's power to take private property for public use, provided that just compensation is paid to the private property holder.

Employer–employee relationship A relationship that results when an employer hires an employee to perform some form of physical service.

Encryption Encryption is technology that allows computer users to put a "lock" around information to prevent discovery by others.

Engagement (1) A formal entrance into a contract between a client and an accountant; (2) the period between acceptance of offer to marry and the marriage.

Entity theory A theory that holds that partnerships are separate legal entities that can hold title to personal and real property, transact business in the partnership name, sue in the partnership name, and the like.

Enumerated powers Certain powers delegated to the federal government by the states.

Environmental law An area of the law dealing with the protection of the environment.

Equal Access to Justice Act An act that was enacted to protect persons from harassment by federal administrative agencies.

Equal Employment Opportunity Commission (EEOC) A federal administrative agency responsible for enforcing most federal antidiscrimination laws.

Equal Pay Act of 1963 A federal statute that protects both sexes from pay discrimination based on sex. It extends to jobs that require equal skill, equal effort, equal responsibility, and similar working conditions.

Equal Protection Clause A clause that provides that state, local, and federal governments cannot deny to any person the "equal protection of the laws."

Equitable distribution A law used by many states where the court orders a *fair distribution* of marital property to the divorcing spouses.

Equitable remedies Used where no amount of monetary damages can make the injured party whole.

Escheat When property goes to the state in the absence of claim by heir.

Establishment Clause A clause to the First Amendment that prohibits the government from either establishing a state religion or promoting one religion over another.

Estate (estate in land) Ownership rights in real property; the bundle of legal rights of the owner to possess, use, and enjoy the property.

Ethical wall An environment in which an attorney or a paralegal is isolated from a particular case or client to avoid a conflict of interest or to protect a client's confidences and secrets.

Exclusionary rule A rule that says evidence obtained from an unreasonable search and seizure can generally be prohibited from introduction at a trial or administrative proceeding against the person searched.

Exclusive agency contract A contract a principal and agent enter into that says the principal cannot employ any agent other than the exclusive agent.

Exculpatory evidence Evidence which tends to prove the innocence of the accused or prove the facts of the defendant's case.

Executed contract A contract that has been fully performed on both sides; a completed contract.

Executive branch One of the three co-equal branches of government represented by the president and administrative agencies.

Executor/executrix (male/female) A person representative named in a will.

Executory contract or unexpired lease A contract or lease that has not been fully performed. With the bankruptcy court's approval, executor contracts and unexpired leases may be rejected by a debtor in bankruptcy.

Exempt property Property that may be retained by a debtor pursuant to federal or state law that does not become part of the bankruptcy estate.

Expert witness A person qualified by education or experience to render an opinion based on a set of facts.

Express agency An agency that occurs when a principal and an agent expressly agree to enter into an agency agreement with each other.

Express contract An agreement that is expressed in written or oral words.

Express trust A trust created voluntarily by the settlor.

Extension of time to respond Request by the defendant to enlarge the time to respond to the complaint beyond that which is permitted under the rules.

Extortion Threat to expose something about another person unless that other person gives money or property. Often referred to as "blackmail."

Fact pleading Pleadings required to include all relevant facts in support of all claims asserted.

Facts Information or details.

Failure to provide adequate instructions A defect that occurs when a manufacturer does not provide detailed directions for safe assembly and use of a product.

Failure to warn A defect that occurs when a manufacturer does not place a warning on the packaging of products that could cause injury if the danger is unknown.

Fair Housing Act A federal statute that makes it unlawful for a party to refuse to rent or sell a dwelling to any person because of his or her race, color, national origin, sex, or religion.

Fair Labor Standards Act (FLSA) A federal act enacted in 1938 to protect workers that prohibits child labor and establishes minimum wage and overtime pay requirements.

Fair-use doctrine A doctrine that permits certain limited use of a copyright by someone other than the copyright holder without the permission of the copyright holder.

False imprisonment The intentional confinement or restraint of another person without authority or justification and without that person's consent.

Father's registry Where a male may register as the father of a child.

Federal administrative agencies Agencies established by legislative and executive branches of federal and state governments.

Federal Arbitration Act (FAA) A federak statute that provides that arbitration agreements in commercial contracts are valid, irrevocable, and enforceable unless some legal or equitable (fraud, duress) grounds exist to invalidate them.

Federal Patent Statute A federal statute that establishes the requirements for obtaining a patent and protects patented inventions from infringement.

Federal question A casc arising undcr the U.S. Constitution, treaties, or federal statutes and regulations.

Federal Trade Commission (FTC) Federal government agency empowered to enforce federal franchising rules. Federal administrative agency empowered to enforce the Federal Trade Commission Act and other federal consumer protection statutes.

Federalism The U.S. form of government; the federal government and the 50 state governments share powers.

Fee simple absolute (fee simple) A type of ownership of real property that grants the owner the fullest bundle of legal rights that a person can hold in real property.

Fee simple defeasible (qualified fee) A type of ownership of real property that grants the owner all the incidents of a fee simple absolute except that it may be taken away if a specified condition occurs or does not occur.

Felony The most serious type of crime; inherently evil crime. Most crimes against the person and some business-related crimes are felonies.

Fiduciary relationship A relationship under which one party has a duty to act for the interest and benefit of another while acting within the scope of the relationship.

File attachment The attachment is a popular method for transmitting text files, and occasionally graphic images, by attaching the file to an email.

File extension When a file is saved, a file extension (a period followed by three characters) is added to the end of the filename to identify the program or format in which the file has been saved.

Finding tools Publications used to find primary and secondary sources.

Firewalls Programs designed to limit access to authorized users and applications.

Fixtures Goods that are affixed to real estate so as to become part thereof.

Foreign corporation A corporation in any state or jurisdiction other than the one in which it was formed.

Foreign Corrupt Practices Act (FCPA) A federal statute that makes it illegal for U.S. companies, or their officers, directors, agents, or employees, to bribe a foreign official or foreign political party official to influence the awarding of new business or the retention of continuous business activity.

Forgery The fraudulent making or alteration of a written document that affects the legal liability of another person.

Form I-9 "Employment Eligibility Verification" A form that must be completed by prospective employees.

Formal will A will that meets all the requirements of the state will statute.

Forum-selection clause Contract provision that designates a certain court to hear any dispute concerning nonperformance of the contract.

Foster care Parent care, sponsored by the state, by those not the adoptive or biological parents.

Fraud A knowing misrepresentation or concealment of a material fact to induce another to act to their detriment.

Fraudulent transfer Occurs when (1) a debtor transfers property to a third person within one year before the filing of a petition in bankruptcy and (2) the transfer was made by the debtor with an intent to hinder, delay, or defraud creditors.

Free Exercise Clause A clause to the First Amendment that prohibits the government from interfering with the free exercise of religion in the United States.

Freedom of Information Act A law that was enacted to give the public access to most documents in the possession of federal administrative agencies.

Freedom of speech The right to engage in oral, written, and symbolic speech protected by the First Amendment.

Freehold estate An estate in which the owner has a present possessory interest in the real property.

Frolic and detour A situation in which an agent does something during the course of his or her employment to further his or her own interests rather than the principal's interests.

Functional resume format Lists a summary of the individual's qualifications with current experience and education without any emphasis on dates of employment.

Future interest The interest that the grantor retains for him- or herself or a third party.

General denial In some jurisdictions, the word "Denied" alone is insufficient and the averment of the complaint is treated as if it were "Admitted."

General gift A gift that does not identify the specific property from which the gift is to be made.

General government regulation Government regulation that applies to many industries collectively.

General law practice A general law practice is one that handles all types of cases.

General partner A partner of a general partnership who is liable for the debts and obligations of the general partnership. Also, Partners in a limited partnership who invest capital, manage the business, and are personally liable for partnership debts.

General partnership A voluntary association of two or more persons for carrying on a business as co-owners for profit. Also called a *partnership*.

General-jurisdiction trial court (courts of record) A court that hears cases of a general nature that are not within the jurisdiction of limited-jurisdiction trial courts.

Generally known dangers A defense that acknowledges that certain products are inherently dangerous and are known to the general population to be so.

Generic name A term for a mark that has become a common term for a product line or type of service and therefore has lost its trademark protection.

Gift A voluntary transfer of title to property without payment of consideration by the donee. To be a valid gift, three elements must be shown: (1) *donative intent*, (2) *delivery*, and (3) *acceptance*.

Gift *causa mortis* A gift that is made in contemplation of death.

Gift *inter vivos* A gift made during a person's lifetime that is an irrevocable present transfer of ownership.

Gift promise A promise that is unenforceable because it lacks consideration.

GlobalCite Loislaw's tool for searching cases containing references to another case.

Good Samaritan law A state statute that relieves medical professionals from liability for ordinary negligence when they stop and render aid to victims in emergency situations.

Goods Tangible things that are movable at the time of their identification to the contract.

Government employment Working for federal, state, and local government agencies and authorities.

Government in the Sunshine Act An act that was enacted to open certain federal administrative agency meetings to the public.

Grantee The party to whom an interest in real property is transferred.

Grantor The party who transfers an ownership interest in real property.

Grantor (trustor) The person who creates a living trust. Also called the *trustor*.

Graphic user interface (GUI) A set of screen presentations and metaphors that utilize graphic elements such as icons in an attempt to make an operating system easier to operate.

H-1B visa A nonimmigrant visa that allows U.S. employers to employ foreign nationals in the United States that are skilled in specialty occupations.

Hacking Unauthorized access to a computer or computer network.

Hardcopy Paper copies of documents.

Headnotes The syllabus or summary of the points of law prepared by the editorial staff of a publisher.

Health care agent One designated by a person in a health care directive to act for a person in making health care decisions.

Health care directive (health care proxy) A document in which the maker should name someone to be his or her health care agent to make all health care decisions in accordance with his or her wishes in the living will.

Heir One who receives property from a deceased relative under intestacy statute.

Highest state court The top court in a state court system; it hears appeals from intermediate state courts and certain trial courts.

Holding The actual decision on the specific point of law the court was asked to decide.

Holographic will Will that is entirely handwritten and signed by the testator.

Homestead exemption Equity in a debtor's home that the debtor is permitted to retain.

Hot spot A wireless access point, generally in a public area.

Hung jury A jury that does not come to a unanimous decision about the defendant's guilt. The government may choose to retry the case.

Identity theft (ID theft) A crime where one person steals information about another person and poses as that person and takes the innocent person's money or property or purchases goods and services using the victim's credit information.

Identity Theft and Assumption Deterrence Act A federal statute that makes identity theft a felony that is punishable by a prison sentence.

Illegal contract A contract to perform an illegal act. Cannot be enforced by either party to the contract.

Immaterial facts A fact not essential to the matter or issue at hand.

Immigration Reform and Control Act of 1986 (IRCA) A federal statute that makes it unlawful for employers to hire illegal immigrants.

Immunity from prosecution The government agrees not to use any evidence given by a person granted immunity against that person.

Implied agency An agency that occurs when a principal and an agent do not expressly create an agency, but it is inferred from the conduct of the parties.

Implied attorney–client relationship Implied attorney–client relationship may result when a prospective client divulges confdential information during a consultation with an attorney for the purpose of retaining the attorney, even if actual employment does not result.

Implied warranty of habitability A warranty that provides that leased premises must be fit, safe, and suitable for ordinary residential use.

Implied-in-fact contract A contract in which agreement between parties has been inferred from their conduct.

***In personam* (personal) jurisdiction** Jurisdiction over the parties to a lawsuit.

***In rem* jurisdiction** Jurisdiction to hear a case because of jurisdiction over the property of the lawsuit.

Income beneficiary Person or entity to be paid income from the trust.

Indemnification Right of a partner to be reimbursed for expenditures incurred on behalf of the partnership.

Independent adoption An adoption in which there is a private arrangement between the biological parents and adoptive parents.

Independent contractor A person or business that is not an employee and is employed by a principal to perform a certain task on his or her behalf.

Independent Medical Examination (IME) Term formerly used to describe a defense medical evaluation.

Indictment The charge of having committed a crime (usually a felony), based on the judgment of a grand jury.

Infancy doctrine A doctrine that allows minors to disaffirm (cancel) most contracts they have entered into with adults.

Inferior performance A situation in which a party fails to perform express or implied contractual obligations and impairs or destroys the essence of the contract.

Information The charge of having committed a crime (usually a misdemeanor), based on the judgment of a judge (magistrate).

Information Infrastructure Protection Act (IIP Act) A federal statute that makes it a federal crime for anyone to intentionally access and acquire information from a protected computer without authorization.

Injunction A court order that prohibits a person from doing a certain act.

Injury The plaintiff must suffer personal injury or damage to his or her property to recover monetary damages for the defendant's negligence.

Innkeeper The owner of a facility that provides lodging to the public for compensation.

Inside director A member of the board of directors who is also an officer of the corporation.

Intangible property Rights that cannot be reduced to physical form such as stock certificates, certificates of deposit, bonds, and copyrights.

Intellectual property and information rights Patents, copyrights, trademarks, trade secrets, trade names, domain names, and other valuable business assets. Federal and state laws protect intellectual property rights from misappropriation and infringement.

Intentional infliction of emotional distress A tort that occurs when a person's extreme and outrageous conduct intentionally or recklessly causes severe emotional distress to another person. Also known as the *tort of outrage*.

Intentional torts A category of torts that requires that the defendant possessed the intent to do the act that caused the plaintiff's injuries.

***Inter vivos* trust** A trust that is created while the settlor is alive.

Intermediate appellate court An intermediate court that hears appeals from trial courts.

Intermediate scrutiny test Test that is applied to classifications based on protected classes other than race (e.g., sex or age).

International Paralegal Management Association (IPMA) A North American association for legal assistant managers.

Internet A collection of millions of computers that provide a network of electronic connections between the computers.

Internet (Web) browsers An Internet or Web browser is a software program that allows a person to use a computer to access the Internet. The two most popular Web browsers are Microsoft Internet Explorer and AOL.

Internet search engine An Internet search engine is a program designed to take a word or set of words and locate websites on the Internet.

Internet service provider (ISP) The company providing the connection between the user and the Internet.

Interpretive rules Rules issued by administrative agencies that interpret existing statutory language.

Interrogatories Written questions submitted by one party to another party. The questions must be answered in writing within a stipulated time.

Interstate commerce Commerce that moves between states or that affects commerce between states.

Intervention The act of others to join as parties to an existing lawsuit.

Intestacy statute A state statute that specifies how a deceased's property will be distributed if he or she dies without a will or if the last will is declared void and there is no prior valid will.

Intestate The state of having died without leaving a will.

Intoxicated person A person who is under contractual incapacity because of ingestion of alcohol or drugs to the point of incompetence.

Invasion of the right to privacy A tort that constitutes the violation of a person's right to live his or her life without being subjected to unwarranted and undesired publicity.

Invitee One expressly or by implication invited onto the premises of the owner for mutual benefit.

Involuntary petition A petition filed by creditors of the debtor; alleges that the debtor is not paying his or her debts as they become due.

IOLTA account Where the amount is too small to earn interest, court rules require the funds be deposited into a special interest-bearing account, and the interest generally paid to support legal aid projects (Interest on Lawyers Trust Accounts).

Irreconcilable differences The legal matter in dispute.

Joint and several liability Tort liability where general partners are liable as a group or separately. This means that the plaintiff can sue one or more of the partners separately. If successful, the plaintiff can recover the entire amount of the judgment from any or all of the defendant–partners.

Joint custody Custody given to both parents with each having a period of physical custody and shared decision making power.

Joint liability Partners are jointly liable for contracts and debts of the partnership. This means that a plaintiff must name the partnership and all of the partners as defendants in a lawsuit.

Joint tenancy A form of co-ownership that includes the right of survivorship.

Joint will A will that is executed by two or more testators.

Judgment The official decision of the court.

Judicial branch The court system.

Judicial decision A ruling about an individual lawsuit issued by federal and state courts.

Jurisdiction The authority of the court to hear disputes and impose resolution of the dispute upon the litigants.

Jurisprudence The philosophy or science of law.

Jury deliberation The process where the jury meets to discuss and resolve the dispute.

Jury instructions (charges) Instructions given by the judge to the jury that informs them of the law to be applied in the case.

Jury selection Process by which a group of six or more people is chosen to serve on the jury.

Just Compensation Clause A clause of the U.S. Constitution that requires the government to compensate the property owner, and possibly others, when the government takes property under its power of eminent domain.

KeyCite Westlaw's tool for searching cases containing references to another case.

Land The most common form of real property; includes the land and buildings and other structures permanently attached to the land.

Landlord/lessor An owner who transfers a leasehold.

Landlord-tenant relationship A relationship created when the owner of a freehold estate (landlord) transfers a right to exclusively and temporarily possess the owner's property to another (tenant).

Land-use control or **land-use regulation** The collective term for the laws that regulate the possession, ownership, and use of real property.

Lanham Trademark Act A federal statute that (1) establishes the requirements for obtaining a federal mark, and (2) protects marks from infringement.

Larceny The taking of another's personal property other than from his or her person or building.

Large law offices Large law offices are an outgrowth of traditional law offices that have expanded over the years, adding partners and associates along the way.

Law That which must be obeyed and followed by citizens subject to sanctions or legal consequences; a body of rules of action or conduct prescribed by controlling authority, and having binding legal force.

Law court A court that developed and administered a uniform set of laws decreed by the kings and queens after William the Conqueror; legal procedure was emphasized over merits at this time.

Leading question A question which suggests the answer.

Lease A transfer of the right to the possession and use of real property for a set term in return for certain consideration; the rental agreement between a landlord and a tenant.

Leasehold estate/leasehold A tenant's interest in property.

Legal assistant See *Paralegal.*

Legal research The process for finding the answer to a legal question.

Legally enforceable A contract in which if one party fails to perform as promised, the other party can use the court system to enforce the contract and recover damages or other remedy.

Legislative branch The part of the government that consists of Congress (the Senate and the House of Representatives).

Lessee The person who acquires the right to possession and use of goods under the lease.

Lessor The person who transfers the right of possession and use of goods under the lease.

Libel A false statement that appears in a letter, newspaper, magazine, book, photograph, movie, video, or other media.

License A contract that transfers limited rights in intellectual property and information rights. Grants a person the right to enter upon another person's property for a specified and usually short period of time.

Licensee A party who is granted limited rights in or access to intellectual property or informational rights owned by a licensor.

Licensing agreement A detailed and comprehensive written agreement between a licensor and a licensee that sets forth the express terms of their agreement.

Licensor An owner of intellectual property or informational rights who transfers rights in the property or information to the licensee.

Life estate An interest in land for a person's lifetime; upon that person's death, the interest will be transferred to another party.

Limited liability Members are liable for the LLC's debts, obligations, and liabilities only to the extent of their capital contributions. Liability that shareholders have only to the extent of their capital contribution. Shareholders are generally not personally liable for debts and obligations of the corporation.

Limited liability company (LLC) An unincorporated business entity that combines the most favorable attributes of general partnerships, limited partnerships, and corporations.

Limited liability partnership (LLP) A form of partnership in which all partners are limited partners and there are no general partners.

Limited partners Partners in a limited partnership who invest capital but do not participate in management and are not personally liable for partnership debts beyond their capital contribution.

Limited partnership A special form of partnership that is formed only if certain formalities are followed. A limited partnership has both general and limited partners.

Limited partnership agreement A document that sets forth the rights and duties of the general and limited partners, the terms and conditions regarding the operation, termination, and dissolution of the partnership, and so on.

Limited-jurisdiction trial courts Courtsauthorized to hear certain types of disputes such as divorce or bankruptcy.

Lineal descendants The testator's children, grandchildren, great-grandchildren, and so on.

Liquidated damages Damages to which parties to a contract agree in advance should be paid if the contract is breached.

Litigation The process of bringing, maintaining, and defending a lawsuit.

Living trust A method for holding property during a person's lifetime and distributing the property upon that person's death. Also called a *grantor's trust* and a *revocable trust.*

Living will A document that states which life-saving measures the signor does and does not want, and can specify that he or she wants such treatments withdrawn if doctors determine that there is no hope of a meaningful recovery.

Local area network (LAN) A network of computers at one location.

Long-arm statute A statute that extends a state's jurisdiction to nonresidents who were not served a summons within the state.

Lost property Property that the owner leaves somewhere because of negligence, carelessness, or inadvertence.

Mainframe A large computer system used primarily for bulk processing of data and financial information.

Malicious prosecution A lawsuit in which the original defendant sues the original plaintiff for bringing a lawsuit without probable cause and with malice.

Mandatory authority Court decisions that are binding on all lower courts.

Marital property Property acquired during the course of marriage using income earned during the marriage, and separate property that has been converted to marital property.

Mark The collective name for trademarks, service marks, certification marks, and collective marks.

Marketable title Title to real property that is free from any encumbrances or other defects that are not disclosed but would affect the value of the property. Also called *good title*.

Marriage A legal union between two people that confers certain legal rights and duties upon the parties and upon the children born of the marriage.

Marriage ceremony A mutual exchange of intent to be married.

Marriage license A legal document issued by a state certifying that two people are married.

Marriage requirements Minimum standards for marriage under state law.

Material breach A breach that occurs when a party renders inferior performance of his or her contractual duties.

Material facts A fact significant or essential to the issue.

Mediation A form of negotiation in which a neutral third party assists the disputing parties in reaching a settlement of their dispute.

Mediator A neutral third party who assists the disputing parties in reaching a settlement of their dispute. The mediator cannot make a decision or an award.

Member An owner of an LLC.

Memorandum A working legal document for the legal team for use in preparation and presentation of a case.

Mens rea "Evil intent"—the possession of the requisite state of mind to commit a prohibited act.

Merchant protection statute A state statute that allows merchants to stop, detain, and investigate suspected shoplifters without being held liable for false imprisonment if (1) there are reasonable grounds for the suspicion, (2) suspects are detained for only a reasonable time, and (3) investigations are conducted in a reasonable manner.

Mineral rights (subsurface rights) Rights to the earth located beneath the surface of the land.

Minitrial A voluntary private proceeding in which the lawyers for each side present a shortened version of their case to representatives of the other side, and usually to a neutral third party, in an attempt to reach a settlement of the dispute.

Minor A person who has not reached the age of majority.

Minor breach A breach that occurs when a party renders substantial performance of his or her contractual duties.

***Miranda* rights** Rights that a suspect must be informed of before being interrogated, so that the suspect will not unwittingly give up his or her Fifth Amendment right.

Mirror image rule A rule that states that for an acceptance to exist, the offeree must accept the terms as stated in the offer.

Misappropriation of the right to publicity A tort in which one party appropriates a person's name or identity for commercial purposes.

Misdemeanor A less serious crime; not inherently evil but prohibited by society. Many crimes against property are misdemeanors.

Mislaid property Property that an owner voluntarily places somewhere and then inadvertently forgets.

Mitigation of damages A nonbreaching party's legal duty to avoid or reduce damages caused by a breach of contract.

Model Guidelines for the Utilization of Legal Assistant Services A set of guidelines by ABA policymaking body, the House of Delegates, intended to govern conduct of lawyers when utilizing paralegals or legal assistants.

Modem A device to translate electrical signals to allow computers to communicate with each other.

Monetary damages An award of money.

Money Laundering Control Act A federal statute that makes it a crime to (1) knowingly engage in a *money transaction* through a financial institution involving property worth more than $10,000 and (2) knowingly engage in a *financial transaction* involving the proceeds of an illegal activity.

Moral obligation An obligation based on one's own conscience.

Motion for judgment on the pleadings A motion that alleges that if all the facts presented in the pleadings are taken as true, the party making the motion would win the lawsuit when the proper law is applied to these asserted facts.

Motion for summary judgment A motion that asserts that there are no factual disputes to be decided by the jury and that the judge can apply the proper law to the undisputed facts and decide the case without a jury. These motions are supported by affidavits, documents, and deposition testimony.

Motion to dismiss A motion that alleges that the plaintiff's complaint fails to state a claim for which relief can be granted. Also called a *demurrer*.

Motivation test A test to determine the liability of the principal; if the agent's motivation in committing the intentional tort is to promote the principal's business, then the principal is liable for any injury caused by the tort.

Murder The unlawful killing of a human being by another with intent.

Mutual benefit bailment A bailment for the mutual benefit of the bailor and bailee. The bailee owes a duty of ordinary care to protect the bailed property.

Mutual (reciprocal) will Occurs where two or more testators execute separate wills that leave their property to each other on the condition that the survivor leave the remaining property on his or her death as agreed by the testators.

Narrative opportunity A question that allows the giving of a full explanation.

National Association of Legal Assistants (NALA) Professional organization for legal assistants that provides continuing education and professional certification for paralegals, incorporated in 1975.

National Association of Legal Secretaries (NALS) Since 1999, an association for legal professionals, originally formed in 1949 as an association for legal secretaries.

National Federation of Paralegal Associations (NFPA) Professional organization of state and local paralegal associations founded in 1974.

National Labor Relations Board (NLRB) A federal administrative agency that oversees union elections, prevents employers and unions from engaging in illegal and unfair labor practices, and enforces and interprets certain federal labor laws.

Necessaries of life A minor must pay the reasonable value of food, clothing, shelter, medical care, and other items considered necessary to the maintenance of life.

Negligence Failure of a corporate director or officer to exercise the duty of care while conducting the corporation's business.

Negligence *per se* Tort where the violation of a statute or ordinance constitutes the breach of the duty of care.

Negligent infliction of emotional distress A tort that permits a person to recover for emotional distress caused by the defendant's negligent conduct.

Negotiation A procedure in which the parties to a dispute engage in negotiations to try to reach a voluntary settlement of their dispute.

Network administrator The network administrator usually is the person with the highest-level access to the network file server.

Network file server A separate computer in a network that acts as the traffic cop of the system controlling the flow of data.

Network rights and privileges Rights or privileges determine who has access to the server, the data stored on the server, and the flow of information between connections.

Networking The establishment of contact with others with whom questions and information are shared.

No Electronic Theft Act (NET Act) A federal statute that makes it a crime for a person to willfully infringe on a copyright work that exceeds $1,000 in retail value.

No-fault divorce A divorce recognized by the law of a state whereby neither party is blamed for the divorce.

Noncupative will Oral will that is made before a witness during the testator's last illness.

Nonfreehold estate An estate in which the tenant has a right to possession of the property but not title to the property.

Non-intent crime A crime that imposes criminal liability without a finding of *mens rea* (intent).

Notice pleading Pleadings required to include sufficient facts to put the parties on notice of the claims asserted against them.

Nurse paralegals Nurses who have gained medical work experience and combine it with paralegal skills. Also referred to as *legal nurse consultants*.

Objective rule A rule stating that if an engagement is broken off, the prospective bride must return the engagement ring, regardless of which party broke off the engagement.

Obscene speech Speech that (1) appeals to the prurient interest, (2) depicts sexual conduct in a patently offensive way, and (3) lacks serious literary, artistic, political, or scientific value.

Occupational Safety and Health Act A federal act enacted in 1970 that promotes safety in the workplace.

Offensive speech Speech that is offensive to many members of society. It is subject to time, place, and manner restrictions.

Offer The manifestation of willingness to enter into a bargain, so made as to justify another person in understanding that his assent to that bargain is invited and will conclude it.

Offeree The party to whom an offer to enter into a contract is made.

Offeror The party who makes an offer to enter into a contract.

Office software suites This software consists of commonly used office software programs that manage data and database programs; manipulate financial or numeric information, spreadsheet programs; or display images and presentation graphics programs.

Officers of the corporation Employees of a corporation who are appointed by the board of directors to manage the day-to-day operations of the corporation.

One-year rule An executory contract that cannot be performed by its own terms within one year of its formation must be in writing.

Online collaboration Using the internet to conduct meetings and share documents.

Open adoption Where biological and adoptive parents are known to each other.

Open-ended question A question that usually does not have a yes or no answer.

Opening brief The first opportunity for the attorneys to address the jury and describe the nature of the lawsuit.

Operating agreement An agreement entered into by members that governs the affairs and business of the LLC and the relations among members, managers, and the LLC.

Operating system The operating system is a basic set of instructions to the computer on how to handle basic functions—how to process input from "input devices" such as the keyboard and mouse, the order in which to process information, and what to show on the computer monitor.

Opinion letter A formal statement of advice based on the lawyers expert knowledge.

Order Decision issued by an administrative law judge.

Ordinances Laws enacted by local government bodies such as cities and municipalities, countries, school districts, and water districts.

Organizational meeting A meeting that must be held by the initial directors of the corporation after the articles of incorporation are filed.

Outside director A member of the board of directors who is not an officer of the corporation.

Outsourcing Use of persons or services outside of the immediate office staff.

Paperless office The paperless office is one in which documents are created and stored electronically.

Paralegal A person qualified by education, training, or work experience who is employed or retained by a lawyer, law office, corporation, governmental agency, or other entity who performs specifically delegated substantive legal work for which a lawyer is responsible. Also referred to as *legal assistant*.

Paralegal Advanced Competency Exam (PACE) National Association of Paralegal Association's certification program that requires the paralegal to have two years of experience and a bachelor's degree and have completed a paralegal course at an accredited school.

Paralegal manager Someone who hires, supervises, trains, and evaluates paralegals.

Parallel citation The citation to the same case in a different publication.

Parent A person who by adoption or as the biological parent is legally responsible for a child.

Partnership Two or more natural (human) or artificial (corporation) persons who have joined together to share ownership and profit or loss.

Partnership agreement A written partnership agreement that the partners sign. Also called articles of partnership.

Partnership at will A partnership with no fixed duration.

Partnership for a term A partnership with a fixed duration.

Patent infringement Unauthorized use of another's patent. A patent holder may recover damages and other remedies against a patent infringer.

Paternity action A legal proceeding that determines the identity of the father of a child.

Penal codes Statutes that define crimes.

***Per capita* distribution** A distribution of the estate that makes each grandchild and greatgrandchild of the deceased inherit equally with the children of the deceased.

***Per stirpes* distribution** A distribution of the estate that makes grandchildren and greatgrandchildren of the deceased inherit by representation of their parent.

Periodic tenancy A tenancy created when a lease specifies intervals at which payments are due but does not specify the length of the lease.

Permanent (lifetime) alimony Payments of spousal support paid until remarriage or death of recipient.

Personal jurisdiction Requires the court to have authority over the persons as well as the subject matter of the lawsuit.

Personal property Tangible property such as automobiles, furniture, and equipment, and intangible property such as securities, patents, and copyrights.

Personal representative The person(s) appointed by the court to administer an estate.

Persuasive authority Court decisions the court is not required to follow but are well reasoned and from a respected court.

Petition for bankruptcy A document filed with the bankruptcy court that starts a bankruptcy proceeding.

Petition for *certiorari* A petition asking the Supreme Court to hear one's case.

Petition for divorce A document filed with the proper state court that commences a divorce proceeding.

Petitioner The party appealing the decision of an administrative agency.

Physical and mental examination A form of discovery that permits the physical or mental examination of a party by a qualified expert of the opposing party's choosing where the physical or mental condition of the party is at issue in the lawsuit.

Picketing The action of strikers walking in front of the employer's premises carrying signs announcing their strike.

Piercing the corporate veil A doctrine that says that if a shareholder dominates a corporation and misuses it for improper purposes, a court of equity can disregard the corporate entity and hold the shareholder personally liable for the corporation's debts and obligations.

Plaintiff The party who files the complaint.

Plaintiff's case Process by which the plaintiff calls witnesses and introduces evidence to prove the allegations contained in his or her complaint.

Plan of reorganization A plan that sets forth a proposed new capital structure for the debtor to have when it emerges from Chapter 11 reorganization bankruptcy.

Plant life and vegetation Real property that is growing in or on the surface of the land.

Plea bargain agreement An agreement in which the accused admits to a lesser crime than charged. In return, the government agrees to impose a lesser sentence than might have been obtained had the case gone to trial.

Pleadings The paperwork that is filed with the court to initiate and respond to a lawsuit.

Pocket parts An update to a book that is a separate document that slips into a pocket in the back of the main volume.

Police power The power of states to regulate private and business activity within their borders.

Pour-over will A will that, upon the grantor's death, distributes the grantor's property that is not in the living will.

Power of attorney An express agency agreement that is often used to give an agent the power to sign legal documents on behalf of the principal.

Precedent Prior case law that is controlling.

Preemption doctrine The concept that federal law takes precedence over state or local law.

Pregnancy Discrimination Act Amendment to Title VII that forbids employment discrimination because of "pregnancy, childbirth, or related medical conditions."

Prenuptial agreement A contract entered into prior to marriage that specifies how property will be distributed upon the termination of the marriage or death of a spouse. Also referred to as a *premarital agreement.*

Pretrial hearing A hearing before the trial in order to facilitate the settlement of a case. Also called a settlement conference.

Pretrial motion A motion a party can make to try to dispose of all or part of a lawsuit prior to trial.

Primary authority The actual law itself.

Primary source of law The actual law itself.

Principal A party who employs another person to act on his or her behalf.

Principal-agent relationship A relationship in which an employer hires an employee and gives that employee authority to act and enter into contracts on his or her behalf.

Privacy Act An act stipulating that federal administrative agencies can maintain only information about an individual that is relevant and necessary to accomplish a legitimate agency purpose.

Privilege A special legal right.

Privileged communication A communication that the person has a right to be kept confidential based on the relationship with the other part such as attorney and client.

Pro bono Working without compensation on behalf of individuals and organizations that otherwise could not afford legal assistance.

Pro se Parties represent themselves.

Probate (settlement of estate) The process of a deceased's property being collected, debts and taxes being paid, and the remainder of the estate being distributed.

Procedural due process Due process that requires the respondent to be given (1) proper and timely notice of the allegations or charges against him or her and (2) an opportunity to present evidence on the matter.

Procedural law Law which realtes to how the trial is conducted and is usually based upon Rules of Court and Rules of Evidence.

Production of documents Request by one party to another party to produce all documents relevant to the case prior to the trial.

Products liability The liability of manufacturers, sellers, and others for the injuries caused by defective products.

Professional Legal Secretary (PLS) The advanced certification for legal professionals from NALS.

Professional malpractice The liability of a professional who breaches his or her duty of ordinary care.

Professional Paralegal (PP) Certification from NALS for those performing paralegal duties.

Promise to marry An offer to marry that is accepted.

Proof of claim A document required to be filed by unsecured creditors that states the amount of their claim against the debtor.

Proprietary school Private, as opposed to public, institution, generally for profit, offering training and education.

Protocol In a URL the required format of the Web address.

Proximate cause A point along a chain of events caused by a negligent party after which this party is no longer legally responsible for the consequences of his or her actions. Also referred to as *legal cause*.

Published opinion A court's written explanation of its decision on a case intended to be relied upon as a statement of the law based on the facts of the case.

Punitive damages Damages that are awarded to punish the defendant, to deter the defendant from similar conduct in the future, and to set an example for others.

***Quasi in rem* (attachment) jurisdiction** Jurisdiction allowed a plaintiff who obtains a judgment in one state to try to collect the judgment by attaching property of the defendant located in another state.

Quasi-contract (implied-in-law contract) An equitable doctrine whereby a court may award monetary damages to a plaintiff for providing work or services to a defendant even though no actual contract existed.

Quiet title An action brought by a party seeking an order of the court declaring who has title to disputed property. By its decision, the court "quiets title."

Racketeer Influenced Corrupt Organizations Act (RICO) A federal statute that defines the crime of racketeering and provides for both criminal and civil penalties for racketeering.

Random access memory (RAM) Temporary computer memory that stores work in processs.

Rational basis test Test that is applied to classifications not involving a suspect or protected class.

Real property The land itself as well as buildings, trees, soil, minerals, timber, plants, and other things permanently affixed to the land.

Reasonable person standard Acting as a responsible, prudent person would act under the same or similar circumstances.

Reasonable professional standard Acting as a responsible, prudent professional would act as measured by other similar professionals.

Rebuttal Phase of the trial that gives the plaintiff the chance to address or respond to information contained in the defendant's case-in-chief.

Receiving stolen property A person (1) knowingly receives stolen property and (2) intends to deprive the rightful owner of that property.

Recording statute A state statute that requires a mortgage or deed of trust to be recorded in the county recorder's office of the county in which the real property is located.

Recross examination Permits opposing counsel to again challenge the credibility of the witness but only as to matters questioned on redirect examination.

Redirect examination After cross-examination, counsel who originally called the witness on direct examination may ask the witness additional questions.

Reformation An equitable doctrine that permits the court to rewrite a contract to express the parties' true intentions.

Registrar of Deeds A public official with whom property deeds are filed and maintained.

Regulatory statutes Statutes, such as environmental laws, securities laws, and antitrust laws that provide for criminal violations and penalties.

Rejection Express words or conduct by the offeree that rejects an offer. Rejection terminates the offer.

Relevant facts Facts crucial to the case and having legal significance.

Religious discrimination Discrimination against a person solely because of his or her religion or religious practices.

Remainder (remainderman) A right of possession that returns to a third party upon the expiration of a limited or contingent estate.

Remainder beneficiary Person or entity to receive the trust *corpus* upon termination of the trust.

Remand When the basis of federal jurisdiction is resolved and only state claims remain to be litigated, the federal court must send the matter back to the state trial court. Also, when the appellate court disagrees with the outcome of the trial court but sends the matter back to the trial court for further proceeding in accordance with its opinion, which may include additional proceedings or a new trial to correct the error, in accordance with the appellate court's decision.

Remote collaboration Working on a common document utilizing remote access by two or more parties.

Renounce an inheritance A beneficiary rejection of a bequest or right to take property.

Replacement workers Workers who are hired to take the place of striking workers. They can be hired on either a temporary or permanent basis.

Reply Filed by the original plaintiff to answer the defendant's cross-complaint.

Request for admission A form of discovery in which written requests are made to the opposing party asking him to admit the truth of certain facts or liability.

Res ipsa loquitur Tort where the presumption of negligence arises because (1) the defendant was in exclusive control of the situation, and (2) the plaintiff would not have suffered injury but for someone's negligence. The burden switches to the defendant(s) to prove they were not negligent.

Residuary gift A gift of the estate left after the debts, taxes, and specific and general gifts have been paid.

Respondeat superior A rule that says an employer is liable for the tortious conduct of its employees or agents while they are acting within the scope of its authority.

Respondent The party who must respond to the appeal, usually the verdict winner at trial.

Restatement of the Law Third, Torts A legal treatise with suggested rules of laws relating to torts.

Restraining order A court order directing one party to avoid contact with another.

Resulting trust A trust that is implied from the conduct of the parties.

Resume A short description of a person's education, a summary of work experience, and other related and supporting information that potential employers use in evaluating a person's qualifications for a position in a firm or an organization.

Retainer A payment at the beginning of the handling of a new matter for a client. This amount may be used to offset the fees for services rendered or costs advanced on behalf of the client.

Reverse The appellate court disagrees with the outcome of the trial and finds reversible error was made and judgment should be overturned and entered in favor of the appellant.

Reversion A right of possession that returns to the grantor after the expiration of a limited or contingent estate.

Revised Model Business Corporation Act (RMBCA) A 1984 revision of the MBCA that arranged the provisions of the original act more logically, revised the language to be more consistent, and made substantial changes in the provisions.

Revised Uniform Limited Partnership Act (RULPA) A 1976 revision of the ULPA that provides a more modern, comprehensive law for the formation, operation, and dissolution of limited partnerships.

Revocation Withdrawal of an offer by the offeror which terminates the offer.

Robbery The taking of personal property from another person by the use of fear or force.

Rules of court A court's rules for the processing and presentation of cases.

S corporation A corporation that has elected S corporation status. An S corporation pays no federal income tax at the corporate level. The gains or losses of an S corporation flow-through to the shareholders.

Sale The passing of title from a seller to a buyer for a price. Also called a *conveyance*.

Sales contract under UCC A passage of the title to goods for a price.

Scienter Means international conduct. Scienter is required for there to be a violation of Section 10(b) and Rule 10b-5.

Screening interview Limited first contact with a prospective new client.

Search query Specific words used in a computerized search.

Search warrant A warrant issued by a court that authorizes the police to search a designated place for specified contraband, articles, items, or documents. The search warrant must be based on probable cause.

Secondary authority Writings that explain the law.

Secondary meaning When an ordinary term has become a brand name.

Secondary source of law Writings about the law.

Section 7 of the NLRA A law that gives employees the right to join together and form a union.

Section 8(a) of the NLRA A law that makes it an unfair labor practice for an employer to interfere with, coerce, or restrain employees from exercising their statutory right to form and join unions.

Self-employment Working independently either as a freelance paralegal for different lawyers or, when authorized by state or federal law, performing services for the public.

Self-incrimination The Fifth Amendment states that no person shall be compelled in any criminal case to be a witness against himor herself.

Separate property Property owned by a spouse prior to marriage, as well as inheritances and gifts received by a spouse during the marriage.

Service mark A mark that distinguishes the services of the holder from those of its competitors.

Service of process settlement agreement A summons is served on the defendant to obtain personal jurisdiction over him or her.

Servient easement The land that is used by dominant easement.

Settlement agreement An agreement voluntarily entered into by the parties to a dispute that settles the dispute. In a divorce, a written document signed by divorcing parties that evidences their agreement settling property rights and other issues of their divorce.

Settlor, trustor, or **transferor** Person who creates a trust. Also referred to as *trustor* or *transferor*.

Sex discrimination Discrimination against a person solely because of his or her sex.

Sexual harassment Lewd remarks, touching, intimidation, posting of pinups, and other verbal or physical conduct of a sexual nature that occur on the job.

Shareholders The owners of corporations, whose ownership interests are evidenced by stock certificates.

Slander Oral defamation of character.

Slip opinion A copy of the opinion sent to the printer.

Small offices Small-office arrangements range from individual practitioners sharing space to partnerships.

Small-claims court A court that hears civil cases involving small dollar amounts.

Software Refers to programs containing sets of instructions that tell the computer and the other computer-based electronic devices what to do and how to do it.

Sole proprietorship A form of business in which the owner is actually the business; the business is not a separate legal entity.

Solo practice One lawyer practicing alone without the assistance of other attorneys.

Special federal courts Federal courts that hear matters of specialized or limited jurisdiction.

Specialty application programs Specialty programs combine many of the basic functions found in software suites, word processing, database management, spreadsheets, and graphic presentations to perform law office, case, and litigation management.

Specialty practice A specialty practice is involved in practice in one area of law.

Specific duty An OSHA standard that addresses a safety problem of a specific duty nature (e.g., requirement for a safety guard on a particular type of equipment.)

Specific gift A gift of a specifically named piece of property.

Specific government regulation Government regulation that applies to individual industries.

Specific performance A remedy that orders the breaching party to perform the acts promised in the contract. Specific performance usually is awarded in cases where the subject matter is unique, such as in contracts involving land, heirlooms, and paintings.

Spendthrift trust A trust for a beneficiary with limits on the use of the funds to prevent claims of the beneficiary's creditors.

Spoliation of evidence Destruction of evidence.

Spousal support Payments made by one divorced spouse to the other divorced spouse. Also called *alimony*.

Spreadsheet programs Programs that permit the calculation and presentation of financial information in a grid format of rows and columns.

Standing to sue The plaintiff must have some stake in the outcome of the lawsuit.

Stare decisis Latin: "to stand by the decision." Adherence to precedent. The legal principle that prior case law should apply unless there is a substantial change in society necessitating a change in the case law.

State administrative agencies Administrative agencies that states create to enforce and interpret state law.

Statement of policy A statement issued by administrative agencies announcing a proposed course of action that an agency intends to follow in the future.

Statute Written law enacted by the legislative branch of the federal and state governments that establishes certain courses of conduct that the covered parties must adhere to.

Statute of Frauds A state statute that requires certain types of contracts to be in writing.

Statute of limitations A time limit within which a case must be brought or lose the right to seek redress in court.

Statute of repose A statute that limits the seller's liability to a certain number of years from the date when the product was first sold.

Statute of Wills A state statute that establishes the requirements for making a valid will.

Strict liability A tort doctrine that makes manufacturers, distributors, wholesalers, retailers, and others in the chain of distribution of a defective product liable for the damages caused by the defect *irrespective of fault*. Also, liability without fault.

Strict scrutiny test Test that is applied to classifications based on race.

Strike Cessation of work by union members to obtain economic benefits or correct an unfair labor practice.

Subject-matter jurisdiction Jurisdiction over the subject matter of a lawsuit.

Subpoena A court order compelling a witness to attend and testify, must accompany a Notice of deposition served on a non-party witness.

Substantial performance Performance by a contracting party that deviates only slightly from complete performance.

Substantive due process Due process that requires that the statute or rule that the respondent is charged with violating be clearly stated.

Substantive law Law which relates to the law of the case, such as the law of negligence or contract.

Substantive rule A rule issued by an administrative agency that has much the same power as a statute: It has the force of law and must be adhered to by covered persons and businesses.

Subsurface rights (mineral rights) Rights to the earth located beneath the surface of the land.

Summons A court order directing the defendant to appear in court and answer the complaint.

Superseding (or intervening) event A defendant is not liable for injuries caused by a superseding or intervening event for which he or she is not responsible.

Supervising attorney The member of the legal team to whom all others on the team report and who has the ultimate responsibility for the actions of the legal team.

Supremacy Clause A clause of the U.S. Constitution that establishes that the federal Constitution, treaties, federal laws, and federal regulations are the supreme law of the land.

Tangible property All real property and physically defined personal property such as buildings, goods, animals, and minerals.

Teleworker People who work from remote locations, typically home.

Temporary (rehabilitation) alimony Spousal support paid for a limited period of time.

Tenancy at sufferance A tenancy created when a tenant retains possession of property after the expiration of another tenancy or a life estate without the owner's consent.

Tenancy at will A tenancy created by a lease that may be terminated at any time by either party.

Tenancy by the entirety A form of co-ownership of real property that can be used only by married couples.

Tenancy for years A tenancy created when the landlord and the tenant agree on a specific duration for a lease.

Tenancy in common A form of co-ownership in which the interest of a surviving tenant in common passes to the deceased tenant's estate and not to the co-tenants.

Tenant The party to whom a leasehold is transferred.

Tender of performance Tender is an unconditional and absolute offer by a contracting party to perform his or her obligations under the contract. Occurs when a party who has the ability and willingness to perform offers to complete the performance of his or her duties under the contract.

Testamentary trust A trust created by will: the trust comes into existence when the settlor dies.

Testator or **testatrix** The person who makes a will.

Thin client A computer system where programs and files are maintained on a centralized server.

Third-party documents Documents prepared by a third party in the ordinary course of business that would have been prepared in similar form if there was no litigation.

Title III of the Americans with Disabilities Act A federal statute that prohibits discrimination on the basis of disability in places of public accommodation by private entities.

Title VII of the Civil Rights Act of 1964 A title of a federal statute enacted to eliminate job discrimination based on five protected classes: *race, color, religion, sex, and national origin.*

Title insurance Insurance that owners of real property purchase to insure that they have clear title to the property.

Tort A wrong. There are three categories of torts: (1) intentional torts, (2) unintentional torts (negligence), and (3) strict liability.

Totten trust Typically a bank account payable to a benefactor only on death of the person opening the account.

Track Changes Track Changes, as found in MS Word, shows the original text, the deleted text, and the new text as well as a strike through for deleted text, underlining or highlighting of new text, as well as margin notes on the document.

Trade secret A product formula, pattern, design, compilation of data, customer list, or other business secret.

Trademark A distinctive mark, symbol, name, word, motto, or device that identifies the goods of a particular business.

Trademark infringement Unauthorized use of another's mark. The holder may recover damages and other remedies from the infringer.

Treaty A compact made between two or more nations.

Trespass to land A tort that interferes with an owner's right to exclusive possession of land.

Trespass to personal property A tort that occurs whenever one person injures another person's personal property or interferes with that person's enjoyment of his or her personal property.

Trial brief Document presented to the court setting forth a legal argument to persuade the court to rule in a particular way on a procedural or substantive legal issue.

Trial notebook A summary of the case tabbed for each major activity, witness, or element of proof.

Trier of facts The trier of facts decides what facts are to be accepted and used in making the decision. It is usually a jury, but may be a judge who hears a case without a jury and decides the facts and applies the law.

Trust A legal arrangement established when one person transfers title to property to another person to be held and used for the benefit of a third person.

Trust account The funds of the client.

Trust *corpus* or **trust *res*** The property and assets held in trust.

Trustee Person or entity that holds legal title to the trust *corpus* and manages the trust for the benefit of the beneficiary or beneficiaries.

Trustee in bankruptcy A legal representative of a debtor's estate.

UCC Statute of Frauds A rule that requires all contracts for the sale of goods costing $500 or more and lease contracts involving payments of $1,000 or more to be in writing.

U.S. Courts of Appeals The federal court system's intermediate appellate courts.

U.S. District Courts The federal court system's trial courts of general jurisdiction.

U.S. Immigration and Customs Enforcement (ICE) The federal administrative agency that enforces federal immigration laws.

U.S. Supreme Court The Supreme Court was created by Article III of the U.S. Constitution. The Supreme Court is the highest court in the land. It is located in Washington, DC.

Unauthorized Practice of Law (UPL) Giving legal advice, if legal rights may be affected, by anyone not licensed to practice law.

Undue influence Occurs where one person takes advantage of another person's mental, emotional, or physical weakness and unduly persuades that person to make a will; the persuasion by the wrongdoer must overcome the free will of the testator.

Uniform Arbitration Act A uniform act adopted by more than half of the states, similar to the Federal Arbitration Act it describes procedures that must be followed for arbitration to be initiated, how the panel of arbitrators is to be selected, and the procedures for conducting arbitration hearings.

Uniform Commercial Code (UCC) A comprehensive statutory scheme that includes laws covering aspects of commercial transactions.

Uniform Computer Information Transactions Act (UCITA) A model state law that creates contract law for the licensing of information technology rights.

Uniform Gift to Minors Act or Revised Uniform Gift to Minors Act Acts that establish procedures for adults to make gifts of money and securities to minors.

Uniform Limited Liability Company Act (ULLCA) A model act that provides comprehensive and uniform laws for the formation, operation, and dissolution of LLCs.

Uniform Partnership Act (UPA) A model act that codifies partnership law. Most states have adopted the UPA in whole or in part.

Uniform Probate Code (UPC) A model law promulgated to establish uniform rules for the creation of wills, the administration of estates, and the resolution of conflicts in settling estates.

Uniform resource locator (URL) The address of a site on the Internet.

Uniform Simultaneous Death Act An act that provides that if people who would inherit property from each other die simultaneously, each person's property is distributed as though he or she survived.

Unintentional tort/negligence The omission to do something which a reasonable person would do or doing something a reasonable person would refrain from doing.

Uninterruptable power supply (UPS) A battery system that can supply power to a computer or computer peripheral for a short period of time.

Universal Citation Format A system for citation relying on the courts to number the paragraphs in their opinions.

Unprotected speech Speech that is not protected by the First Amendment and may be forbidden by the government.

Unpublished opinions Cases which the court does not feel have precedential effect and are limited to a specific set of facts.

Unreasonable search and seizure Any search and seizure by the government that violates the Fourth Amendment.

V. Cite VersusLaw's tool for searching cases containing references to another case.

Variance An exception that permits a type of building or use in an area that would not otherwise be allowed by a zoning ordinance.

Vendor-specific citation format Citation format of a legal publisher adopted by a court.

Venue A concept that requires lawsuits to be heard by the court with jurisdiction that is nearest the location in which the incident occurred or where the parties reside.

Verdict Decision reached by the jury.

Videoconferencing Conferencing from multiple locations using high speed Internet connections to transmit sound and images.

Violation A crime that is neither a felony nor a misdemeanor that is usually punishable by a fine.

Visitation rights A time period for visitation by non-custodial parent with the child.

Voice recognition Computer programs for converting speech into text or commands without the use of other inout devices such as keyboards.

VoIP Voice over internet protocol is a computer internet replacement for traditional telephone connections.

Voir dire Process whereby prospective jurors are asked questions by the judge and attorneys to determine if they would be biased in their decision.

Voluntary petition A petition filed by the debtor; states that the debtor has debts.

White-collar crimes Crimes usually involving cunning and deceit rather than physical force.

Wide area network A wide area network is a network of networks. Each network is treated as if it were a connection on the network.

Will A declaration of how a person wants his or her property to be distributed upon death.

Wire fraud The use of telephone or telegraph to defraud another person.

Wireless computer networks A wireless network uses wireless technology in place of wires for connecting to the network.

Wireless network A wireless network uses wireless technology instead of wires for connecting to the network.

Workers' compensation acts Laws that compensate workers and their families if workers are injured in connection with their jobs.

Work-product doctrine A qualified immunity from discovery for "work product of the lawyer" except on a substantial showing of "necessity or justification" of certain written statements and memoranda prepared by counsel in representation of a client, generally in preparation for trial.

Work-related test A test that says if an agent commits an intentional tort within a work-related time or space, the principal is liable for any injury caused by the agent's intentional tort.

Workstation A computer connected to a network that is used for access consisting of a monitor, input device, and computer.

World Wide Web An electronic connection of millions of computers that support a standard set of rules for the exchange of information.

Writ of certiorari An official notice that the Supreme Court will review one's case.

Wrongful death action Lawsuit seeking compensation for damage caused by death of a relative.

Wrongful dissolution When a partner withdraws from a partnership without have the right to do so at that time.

Wrongful termination of an agency The termination of an agency contract in violation of the terms of the agency contract. In this situation, the nonbreaching party may recover damages from the breaching party.

Zoning commission A local administrative body that formulates zoning ordinances, conducts public hearings, and makes recommendations to the city council.

Zoning ordinances Local laws that are adopted by municipalities and local governments to regulate land use within their boundaries.

Case Index

A

B

C

D

E

F

G

H

I

J

K

L

M

N

P

Q

R

S

T

U

V

W

Z

Subject Index

A

B

D

E

F

G

H

M